Exploring the Humanities

CREATIVITY AND CULTURE IN THE WEST

Exploring the Humanities

CREATIVITY AND CULTURE IN THE WEST

Laurie Schneider Adams

John Jay College, City University of New York

Upper Saddle River, N.J. 07458

Library of Congress Cataloging-in-Publication Data

Adams, Laurie.
Exploring the humanities : creativity and culture in the West / Laurie Schneider Adams.
p. cm.
Includes bibliographical references and index.
ISBN 0–13–049095–4 (vol. 1)—ISBN 0–13–049087–3 (vol. 2)—ISBN 0–13–049091–1 (combined vol.)
1. Civilization, Western—History—Textbooks. I. Title.

CB245.A324 2006
909'.09821—dc22

2005043156

Editor in Chief: Sarah Touborg
Acquisitions Editor: Amber Mackey
Editorial Assistant: Keri Molinari
Director of Marketing: Heather Shelstad
Manufacturing Buyer: Ben Smith
Creative Design Director: Leslie Osher
Interior Designer: Wanda Espana

Credits and acknowledgments of material borrowed from other sources and reproduced, with permission, in this textbook appear on pages 729–734.

Published 2006 by Pearson Education, Inc., Upper Saddle River, New Jersey, 07458. Pearson Prentice Hall.

Pearson Education Ltd.
Pearson Education Australia PTY, Ltd.
Pearson Education Singapore, Pte. Ltd.
Pearson Education North Asia Ltd.
Pearson Education, Canada, Ltd.
Pearson Educación de Mexico, S.A. de C.V
Pearson Education–Japan
Pearson Education Malaysia, Pte. Ltd.

This book was designed and produced by Laurence King Publishing Ltd., London

Commissioning Editor: Melanie White
Editor: Ursula Payne
Copy Editor: Lydia Darbyshire
Picture Researcher: Fiona Kinnear
Layout and Cover Design: Newton Harris Design Partnership, Suffolk
Map Editor: Ailsa Heritage
Maps: Advanced Illustration, Cheshire
Literary Permissions: Nick Wetton
Keyboarding: Marie Doherty

Front Cover: Michelangelo, *Libyan Sibyl*, Sistine Chapel, Vatican, Rome, 1509. Fresco. Photo © Vatican Museums, Rome. Photo: A. Bracchetti/P. Zigrossi, 1993.

Frontispiece: North rose window, Notre Dame, Paris, *c.* 1255. 43 ft. (13.1 m) diameter. Photo © Sonia Halliday and Laura Lushington.

10 9 8 7 6 5 4 3 2 1
ISBN 0–13–049091–1

Contents

Preface xxi
Acknowledgments xxii
Starter Kit xxv

Chapter 1: Prehistory

Key Topics 1
Timeline 2

Society and Culture: The Dating System Used in this Text 3

Human Origins: From Myth to Science 3
Creation Stories 3
Darwin and the Theory of Evolution 3
The Nature of Prehistory 4
Society and Culture: The Study of Human Prehistory 4
Society and Culture: Dating Prehistory 5
Society and Culture: Major Periods of Human Evolution 5
Defining Moment: Bipedalism 6
Society and Culture: Important Developmental Steps in Early Human History 7

What Makes Us Human 7
Symbolic Thinking 7
Creative Arts 7
Shamanism 10

The Upper (Late) Paleolithic Era in Western Europe: *c.* 45,000–*c.* 10,000/8000 B.C. 10

Mesolithic to Neolithic in Western Europe: *c.* 10,000/8000–6000/4000 B.C. 11

The Neolithic Era: *c.* 6000/4000–c. 1500 B.C. 11
Stonehenge 12

Thematic Parallels: Shamanism in Non-Western Imagery 13
Australian Dreaming 13
Shamanistic Imagery in Africa 13
The Anishnabe Drum 13

Key Terms 14
Key Questions 14
Suggested Reading 14
Suggested Films 15

Chapter 2: The Ancient Near East

Key Topics 17
Timeline 18

The Fertile Crescent 19
Urbanization and Architecture 19
Society and Culture: The Mesopotamian Cosmos 20
Society and Culture: Abikhil, a Temple Superintendent 21

The Development of Writing 21
Defining Moment: Urbanization in Mesopotamia 22
Pictographs, Cuneiform, and the Cylinder Seal 22
The First Epic Poem 23
Society and Culture: Language Groups 23
Society and Culture: Dreams and Medicine in the Ancient Near East 24

Mesopotamian Kingship and the Arts 26
Music and Ritual at the Mesopotamian Courts 26
Naram-Sin and the Imagery of Conquest 27
Gudea of Lagash: Piety and Temple-building 28
Hammurabi of Babylon: The Lawgiver 28
Cross-cultural Influences: Indus Valley Civilization 30
Assurbanipal: Assyrian Might 30
The Achaemenids and the Royal Palace at Persepolis 32
Zoroastrianism: A New Religion 34

Thematic Parallels: Kingship and "Heads" of State 35
The Colossal Heads of the Olmec: 1200–400 B.C. 35
The Cambodian Devaraja: Twelfth to Thirteenth Century A.D. 36
Henry VIII: Sixteenth-Century England 37
Africa—the Head and the Crown: Nineteenth to Twentieth Century 37

Mesopotamia and the Hebrews 38
Early History 38

Key Terms 38
Key Questions 39
Suggested Reading 39
Suggested Films 39

Chapter 3: Ancient Egypt

Key Topics 41
Timeline 42

The Nile 43
Defining Moment: Egypt and the Solar Calendar 43

The Pharaohs 44
Society and Culture: Principal Deities of Ancient Egypt 45
The Pharaoh and the Egyptian Concept of Time 45

Religion 45
The Osiris Myth 45
Hymns to the Nile 46
Hymns to the Sun 46
The Egyptian View of Death 47
Society and Culture: Hieroglyphs and Egyptian Literature 49

Old Kingdom Egypt: *c.* 2649–2100 B.C. 50
The Pyramid Complex at Giza 50
The Seated Statue of Khafre and the Egyptian Proportional System 52
The Menkaure Triad 52
The Egyptian Scribe 53

Music in Ancient Egypt 54

Egyptian Society 55
Society and Culture: Egyptian Medicine and Dream Books 56
Female Pharaohs 56
Society and Culture: Egyptian Jewelry 57

Middle Kingdom Egypt: *c.* 1991–1700 B.C. 57
Sculpture and Architecture 57

New Kingdom Egypt: *c.* 1550–1070 B.C. 58
Temples 59
The Amarna Revolution: *c.* 1349–1336 B.C. 61
The Tomb of Tutankhamon 61

Key Terms 62
Key Questions 63
Suggested Reading 63
Suggested Films 63

Chapter 4: The Aegean World

Key Topics 65
Timeline 66

Who Were the Minoans? 67
Society and Culture: The Labyrinth in Myth 68
Minoan Religion 68
The Hagia Triada Sarcophagus 70
Music and Ritual 71

Thera 72
Defining Moment: The Eruption of Thera and Plato's Lost Atlantis 72

Mycenae and the Homeric Heroes 73
Homer's *Iliad* 74
Homeric Literary Devices 74
Mycenaean Art and Architecture 75
Agamemnon and the *Oresteia* of Aeschylus 76
Homer's *Odyssey* 77
Society and Culture: Women, Family, and the Rules of Marriage in the Homeric Age 78
Society and Culture: The Cyclopes and Cyclopaean Masonry 79

The "Dark" Age: *c.* 1150–900 B.C. 80

Key Terms 80
Key Questions 81
Suggested Reading 81
Suggested Films 81

Chapter 5: The Emergence of Historical Greece

Key Topics 83
Timeline 84

The Greek *Polis* 85

Ancient Greek Religion 85
Hesiod's *Theogony* 86
Society and Culture: The Greek Gods and the Nine Muses 87
Greek Goddesses and Gods 87
Pandora's "Box" and Hesiod on Women 87
The Oracle 88

The Geometric Period: *c.* 1000–700 B.C. 88
Pottery, Painting, and Sculpture 88
The Olympic Games 89

The Orientalizing Period: *c.* 700–600 B.C. 90
Pottery and Painting 90
War, Music, and the Chigi Vase 90
Defining Moment: The Greek Phalanx 91

The Archaic Period: *c.* 600–490 B.C. 92
Athens and Sparta 92
Athenian Lawgivers: Draco and Solon 92
Women in Athens 93

Sparta 93
Art and Architecture in the Archaic Period 93
Vase Painting 93
Society and Culture: The Gorgon 94
Sculpture 95
Society and Culture: Archaic Greek Dress 97
Architecture 98
The Temple of Aphaia at Aegina 99
Philosophy: Pre-Socratics of the Archaic Period 101
Pythagoras 102
Lyric Poetry 102
Anacreon 102
Society and Culture: The Greek Symposium 103
Sappho 104
Society and Culture: Homosexuality in Ancient Greece 104

Thematic Parallels: Sun Tzu and *The Art of War* 105

Key Terms 106
Key Questions 106
Suggested Reading 106
Suggested Films 107

Chapter 6: Ancient Greece: Classical to Hellenistic

Key Topics 109
Timeline 110

Herodotus: The "Father of History" 111

Athens from the Late Archaic to the Early Classical Period: *c.* 500–450 B.C. 111

The Early Classical Period: *c.* 480–450 B.C. 111
Sculpture 111
Philosophers on the Real and the Ideal: Parmenides and Zeno 113
Poetry: Pindar on Athletes 114

The High Classical Period: 450–400 B.C. 114
The Parthenon 116
The Sculptural Program of the Parthenon 117
The Temple of Athena Nike 120
The Erechtheum 120
Classical Painting and Sculpture Unrelated to the Acropolis 121
Classical Philosophy 123
Protagoras 123
Empedocles 123
Democritus 123
Socrates and Plato 123
The *Republic* 124
Medicine 124
Hippocrates 124
Society and Culture: A Greek Dinner Party: The Menu 125
Music 126

Greek Theater 126
The Tragic Playwrights 127
Aeschylus 127
Sophocles 128
Euripides 129
Comedy 130
Aristophanes 130

The Peloponnesian War: 431–404 B.C. 130
Defining Moment: The Classical Ideal and Its Decline: The Peloponnesian War 131

The Late Classical Period: *c.* 400–323 B.C. 132
Society and Culture: The Myth of Alexander's Birth 132
Society and Culture: Warfare Technology and Science 132
Cross-cultural Influences: Hellenism and the Far East 134
Siddhartha and the Origin of Buddhism 134
Gandharan and Mathuran Sculpture 134
Aristotle 135
Painting and Sculpture 136

The Hellenistic World: 323 to First Century B.C. 137
Mystery Cults 137
Philosophy in the Hellenistic Period 137
Hellenistic Poetry 138
Developments in Artistic Style 138

Key Terms 140
Key Questions 141
Suggested Reading 141
Suggested Films 141

Chapter 7: Ancient Rome

Key Topics 143
Timeline 144

Myths of the Founding of Rome 145
Virgil's *Aeneid* 145
Romulus and Remus 146
Society and Culture: The Seven Hills of Rome 146

The Etruscans: Ninth Century to 509 B.C. 147
Greece and the Etruscans 147
Etruscan Women: The Envy of Athenian Women 149
Etruscan Funerary Art 149
The End of Etruscan Rule 150

The Roman Republic: 509–27 B.C. 151
Chronology and History 152
The Punic Wars 154
Julius Caesar 155
Society and Culture: Cleopatra, Queen of Egypt 155
Religion and Art 156
Society and Culture: The Roman Gods 156
Art and Architecture of Everyday Life 157
Defining Moment: Rome Builds in Concrete 158
Society and Culture: A Roman Bakery 158
Wall-paintings 159
A Musical Mosaic 160
Philosophy: Lucretius 161
Theater: Roman Comedy 161
Rhetoric: Cicero 162
The Poets 162
The End of the Republic 163

The Roman Empire: 27 B.C.–A.D. 476 163
Society and Culture: Greek and Roman Coinage 164
Imperial Augustan Imagery 164
Augustus as a Patron of Literature 166
Painting in the Age of Augustus 167
Art and Architecture after Augustus 167
The Julio-Claudians 167
Society and Culture: Reign Dates of the Major Roman Emperors 169
The Flavians 169
Society and Culture: The Flavian Coiffure 170
Trajan: *Optimus Princeps* 171
Hadrian: The Pantheon 172
Marcus Aurelius: Emperor and Stoic Philosopher 173
Roman Authors after Augustus 174
History: Tacitus 174
Biography: Suetonius 174
Stoic Philosophy: Seneca 175
Satire: Juvenal and Petronius 176
The Decline and Fall of the Roman Empire 176

Thematic Parallels: Deadly Games: Gladiators and Mesoamerican Ball-players 178

Key Terms 180
Key Questions 180
Suggested Reading 180
Suggested Films 181

Chapter 8: Pagan Cults, Judaism, and the Rise of Christianity

Key Topics 183
Timeline 184

Pagan Cults 185
Mysteries 185
Mithraism 185

Neoplatonism 186

The Israelites and Judaism 186
History, Chronology, and Tradition 186
Society and Culture: The Hebrew Bible and the Dead Sea Scrolls 186
Moses 187
Society and Culture: The Ten Commandments 187
Monarchy and Conflict 188
The Second Temple Destroyed 189
The Hebrew Bible as Literature 190

Christianity: The Birth of Jesus through the Fourth Century 191
Society and Culture: The New Testament 192
Society and Culture: The Typological Reading of History 193
Death and Resurrection 193
Baptism and the Eucharist 193
Society and Culture: Principal Events in the Life of Jesus 194
The Mission of St. Paul 194
Early Christianity in Rome 195
Society and Culture: Women in the Bible 196
The Role of Constantine 196
Early Christian Art and Architecture 196
Painting and Sculpture 197
Architecture 198

The Spread of Christianity 202
The Arian Heresy 202
Manichees, Bogomils, Cathars, and Albigensians 202
Gnosticism 202
The Beginnings of Monasticism 202
Defining Moment: St. Anthony and the Beginnings of Monasticism in the West 203
Christian Authors: The Four Doctors of the Church 204
Music in the Early Church 205

Key Terms 206
Key Questions 206
Suggested Reading 206
Suggested Films 207

Chapter 9: The Byzantine Empire and the Development of Islam

Key Topics 209
Timeline 210

Ravenna under Theodoric 211
Boethius on Theology 211
Boethius on Music 211
Theodoric and the Visual Arts 211

The Byzantine Empire: An Overview—Fourth to Thirteenth Century 212
Society and Culture: Byzantine Scholarship, Ninth to Eleventh Century 213
Justinian I 214
Society and Culture: Theodora and the Court 214
The Barberini Ivory: An Image of Imperial Triumph 214
Society and Culture: Justinian and the Silk Routes 215
Justinian's Law Code 215
Defining Moment: The Code of Justinian 216
The Arts in Ravenna 216
Music in the Western and Eastern Churches 219
Hagia Sophia 219
Icons and the Monastery of St. Catherine 221

The Eastern Orthodox Church 222
The Iconoclastic Controversy 222

The Persistence of Byzantine Style 222

The Rise and Expansion of Islam: Seventh to Seventeenth Century 224
The Life of Muhammad 224
Sunnis and Shi'ites 225
The Five Pillars of Islam 225
The Qur'an (Koran) and the Hadith 226

Islamic Art and Architecture 227
The Dome of the Rock 227
Mosques 228
Tombs 230
Secular Art 231

Islamic Music 232

Islamic Literature 232

Islamic Science, Medicine, and Philosophy 234
Scientists and Physicians 234
Philosophers 235

Key Terms 236
Key Questions 236
Suggested Reading 236
Suggested Films 237

Chapter 10: The Early Middle Ages and the Development of Romanesque: 565–1150

Key Topics 239
Timeline 240

The Early Middle Ages 241
Monasteries 241
Early Medieval Social Structure 241
Feudalism 241
Manorialism 241
Germanic Tribes 241

The Merovingian and Carolingian Dynasties 242

Charlemagne and the Carolingian Renaissance 243
Defining Moment: The Coronation of Charlemagne 244
Literary Epic: *Song of Roland* 245
Charlemagne's Palace 245
The Palace School 245
Carolingian Manuscripts 247
Music in the Carolingian Period 247
Society and Culture: St. Benedict and the Benedictine Rule 248
Monasticism under Charlemagne 248
Cross-cultural Influences: Monasticism 249

From the Carolingian to the Ottonian Period 250

Theater in the Early Middle Ages 250
Liturgy and Drama 251
Non-Liturgical Drama: Hroswitha of Gandersheim 252

Northern Europe: Britain, Ireland, Scandinavia, and Iceland 252
Ireland and the Book of Kells 252
Anglo-Saxon Metalwork and Literature 254
Beowulf 254
The Legend of King Arthur 255
Society and Culture: The Legend of King Arthur through Time 255
Society and Culture: Chivalry and Medieval Paradigms of Women 256
The Vikings: Ninth to Twelfth Century 256
Norse Mythology 256
Dress and Chess 258
Iceland and the Sagas: Ninth to Twelfth Century 259

Romanesque on the European Continent: Eleventh and Twelfth Century 260
Society and Culture: Farming—New Technology and Inventions 260
Romanesque Art and Architecture 260
The Monastery at Cluny 261
Society and Culture: The Pilgrimage Roads 262

Monasticism and Women in the Arts 263
Sainte Marie Madeleine at Vézelay 264
Society and Culture: The Crusades 265

The Bayeux Tapestry: Romanesque Narrative 267

Thematic Parallels: Pilgrimage 269

Key Terms 270
Key Questions 271
Suggested Reading 271
Suggested Films 271

Chapter 11: The Development and Expansion of Gothic: 1150–1300

Key Topics 273
Timeline 274

The Economy, Politics, and Religion 275

Monastic Developments in the Thirteenth Century 275
St. Dominic 275
Defining Moment: The Inquisition 276
St. Francis of Assisi 276
Women Monastics in the Thirteenth Century 277

The Central Role of Paris 278
Abbot Suger and St. Denis 278
The Cathedral of Notre Dame in Paris 280
Building the Cathedral 282
Sainte-Chapelle: The King's Chapel 284
Music at the Cathedral School of Notre Dame 285
The University of Paris 286
Society and Culture: Medicine in the Middle Ages 286
Scholasticism: Peter Abelard and Thomas Aquinas 287
Society and Culture: Abelard and Héloïse 287

The Development of Gothic Style outside Paris 288
The Central Portal of Chartres: A Vision of the End of Time 289
The Cult of the Virgin 289
Late Gothic: Cologne Cathedral 291

Theater and Literature in the Gothic Period 292
Dante and the *Divine Comedy* 292
Dante and Beatrice 292
The Poem 292
The Circles of Hell 293
Purgatory 294
Paradise 294

Thematic Parallels: Views of Paradise 295

Key Terms 296
Key Questions 297
Suggested Reading 297
Suggested Films 297

Chapter 12: The Transition from Gothic to Early Renaissance: 1300–1450

Key Topics 299
Timeline 300

The Late Middle Ages 301
Society and Culture: The Wool Industry in Florence 301
The Hundred Years War 302
Society and Culture: Joan of Arc 302
Conflict in the Church 302
The Great Schism 302
Philosophical Challenges to the Church 303
The Black Death 303
Defining Moment: Plague Devastates Europe 304

Late Gothic Trends in Art 306
The Iconography of Death 306
The Iconography of Wealth 308
Society and Culture: Daily Life in the House of a Prosperous Merchant 309
Society and Culture: A Late Gothic Feast 310

Theater in the Fourteenth Century 311
Music 311
Ars Nova 311
Society and Culture: The Ordinary of the Mass 312

Literature in England and France 312
Geoffrey Chaucer 313
Christine de Pisan 314

Humanism in Italy 314
Literature and Music 316
Petrarch and Boccaccio 316
The Visual Arts 317
Painting: Cimabue and Giotto 318
Petrarch and Boccaccio on Giotto 319
Giotto's Narrative Painting 319
Painting in Siena 322
Dominican Iconography and Scholastic Resistance to Humanism 325

Key Terms 326
Key Questions 326
Suggested Reading 326
Suggested Films 327

Chapter 13: The Early Renaissance in Italy and Northern Europe

Key Topics 329
Timeline 330

The Expansion of Humanism 331
Advances in Technology 331
Defining Moment: The Printing Press 332
Society and Culture: The Humanist Movement 333
Arts and Sciences 333
Exploration 335

Florence in the Fifteenth Century 335
Society and Culture: The Medici Family in the Fifteenth Century 336
Humanism and the State 336
The Platonic Academy 337
Decorating the City 338
The Competition of 1401 339
Brunelleschi's Dome 339
Donatello's *John the Evangelist* 340
Masaccio 340
Society and Culture: Linear Perspective 341
Alberti: A Renaissance Man 342
Alberti's Architecture 343
Medici Patronage 344
Donatello's *David* 344
Fra Angelico in San Marco 345
Inside the Medici Palace 345
Botticelli's *Birth of Venus* 347
Architecture: Giuliano da Sangallo 348
Music in Florence under the Medici 348
Conservative Backlash: Antoninus and Savonarola 349

The Arts Outside Florence 350
Society and Culture: Women and their Education in Early Renaissance Italy 350
The State Portrait 351
The Equestrian Portrait 351
The State Bedroom at Mantua 352
Leonardo in Milan 353

The Early Renaissance in the North 355
Painting 355
Graphic Art 358
Music 358
Guillaume Dufay 358
Josquin Desprez 359

Thematic Parallels: The Classical Tradition: Revival and Opposition 360

Key Terms 362
Key Questions 362
Suggested Reading 362
Suggested Films 363

Chapter 14: The High Renaissance in Italy and Early Mannerism

Key Topics 365
Timeline 366

Political and Economic Developments 367
Cross-cultural Influences: Exploration and Colonialism 369

Florence in the High Renaissance 371
Machiavelli 371
Michelangelo's *David* 371
Leonardo's *Mona Lisa* 372
Society and Culture: Technology and the Inventions of Leonardo da Vinci 373
Leonardo on the Art of Painting versus Sculpture and Poetry 373
Raphael 373

High Renaissance Patronage in Rome 374
A New St. Peter's 374
Raphael's *School of Athens* 376
Michelangelo on Art 377
The Sistine Chapel 377
Defining Moment: The Sistine Chapel Ceiling: Imagery for the Ages 380

Venice in the High Renaissance 382
The Aldine Press 382
Venetian Painting 382
Music in High Renaissance Venice 384
The Gabrielis 385

Literature and Theater 386
Castiglione's *Book of the Courtier* 386
Ariosto's *Orlando Furioso* 387
Theater in High Renaissance Italy: From Latin to the Vernacular 387

Early Mannerism 387
Painting 388
Sculpture: Benvenuto Cellini 390
Society and Culture: Cellini on the Casting of the Perseus 391
Architecture: Giulio Romano and Andrea Palladio 391

Key Terms 392
Key Questions 392
Suggested Reading 393
Suggested Films 393

Chapter 15: Reformation and Reform in Sixteenth-century Europe

Key Topics 395
Timeline 396

The Protestant Reformation 397
Erasmus and Reform 397
Martin Luther 398
John Calvin 399
Defining Moment: Martin Luther and the Ninety-five Theses 400
Henry VIII and Church Reform 401
Society and Culture: The Six Wives of Henry VIII 401

Religious Conflict in France 402
François Rabelais 402
Michel Eyquem de Montaigne 402

The Challenge of Science 403
Society and Culture: Medicine in the Sixteenth Century 404

Painting in the North 404
Albrecht Dürer 404
Matthias Grünewald 406
Hieronymus Bosch 406
Pieter Bruegel the Elder 407

The Counter-Reformation: Catholic Reform 409
The Council of Trent: 1545–1563 409
Monastic Reform 409
The Inquisition 410
Continuing Conflict 410

The Impact of Catholic Reform on the Arts 411
Paolo Veronese 411
Tintoretto 412
Giacomo da Vignola 412
El Greco 413
Music 415

Elizabethan England 415
Elizabeth I 415
Society and Culture: John Knox on Female Rulers 391
Music at the Elizabethan Court 416
William Byrd 416
Thomas Morley 417
Thomas Weelkes 417
Poetry and Theater 417
Philip Sidney and Edmund Spenser 417
Christopher Marlowe 418
William Shakespeare 418
The Globe Playhouse 419
The Plays 420

Key Terms 422
Key Questions 423
Suggested Reading 423
Suggested Films 423

Chapter 16: Absolutism and the Baroque

Key Topics 425
Timeline 426

Politics and Religion 427
The Thirty Years War 428
Eastern Europe: Peter the Great 429
The "New World" 430

Scientists 430
Johannes Kepler 431
Galileo Galilei 431
Bacon, Harvey, Boyle, and Newton 431
Society and Culture: Alchemy 431
Defining Moment: Newton and Leibniz: A Momentous Quarrel 432
Anton van Leeuwenhoek 433

Philosophy 433
Thomas Hobbes and John Locke 433
Hugo Grotius 433
René Descartes and Blaise Pascal 434

Italy: Birthplace of the Baroque 434
Architecture in Rome: Bernini and Borromini 434
Sculpture: Bernini 436
Painting 437
Giovanni Battista Gaulli 437
Caravaggio 438
Society and Culture: Caravaggio: Artist and Criminal 438
Artemisia Gentileschi 438
Music 439
Baroque Style 439
The Rise of Opera 440
Baroque Instrumental Style 440

The Baroque in Spain 441
Literature: Cervantes 441
Painting: Velázquez 442
Spanish Architecture in the New World 443

Absolutism and the French Court 444
The Arts under Louis XIV 445
Versailles 445
Literary Reflections of the French Court: Mme de Sévigné and Mme de Lafayette 446
French Theater 447

Pierre Corneille 447
Jean Racine 447
Molière 448
Painting: Nicolas Poussin and Claude Lorrain 449

Northern Europe 449
Peter Paul Rubens 449
The Marie de' Medici Cycle 450
Painting in Holland 450
Rembrandt van Rijn 451
Judith Leyster 452
Jan Vermeer 453
Cross-cultural Influences: Mughal Art and Western Europe 454
Music 454
Johann Sebastian Bach 455
George Frideric Handel 455

England 456
From Divine Right to Constitutional Monarchy 456
The Arts in England 457
Christopher Wren: St. Paul's Cathedral 458
Literature: Donne and Milton 459

Thematic Parallels: In Search of Outer Space 460

Key Terms 461
Key Questions 462
Suggested Reading 462
Suggested Films 463

Chapter 17: From Enlightenment to Revolution in the Eighteenth Century

Key Topics 465
Timeline 466

Politics and War 467

The Enlightenment 467
Philosophy and the *Philosophes* 467
Denis Diderot 468
Voltaire 469
Charles-Louis de Montesquieu 469
Jean-Jacques Rousseau 470
Philosophy in Germany: Gottfried Leibniz and Immanuel Kant 470
Britain: Philosophy, Economics, and Politics 471

Art in the Eighteenth Century 471
France 472
Jean-Antoine Watteau 472
François Boucher 472
Adélaide Labille-Guiard 472
Rococo in Germany: The Würzburg Residenz 474
Britain: Rococo, Satire, and the Neoclassical Style 475
Robert Adam 475
William Hogarth 476
New Artistic Trends in the Eighteenth Century 477
Chinoiserie 477
Society and Culture: Daily Life: The Chamber Pot 477
Chardin and Bourgeois Style 478
The Vogue for Classicism 478

English Literature in the Eighteenth Century 479
Poetry: Dryden and Pope 479
Prose: Swift and Johnson 479
Drama: Sheridan 480
The Modern Novel 480
Daniel Defoe 480
Samuel Richardson 481
Henry Fielding 481

Music in the Eighteenth Century 481
Classical Style 481
The Musical *Galant* 481
Opera in Transition 482
Musical Instruments of the Classical Period 482
Society and Culture: Great Violin-makers of Italy: The Amati, Stradivari, and Guarneri 483
Classical Instrumental Music 483
Franz Joseph Haydn 484
Wolfgang Amadeus Mozart 484
From Classical to Romantic: Ludwig van Beethoven 485

Revolutions in America and France 485
The American Revolution: 1776–1783 485
"No Taxation without Representation" 485
"The Shot Heard around the World" 486
Society and Culture: Benjamin Franklin and Poor Richard 486
War 486
Toward a New Government: The Constitution and the Bill of Rights 486
Defining Moment: The Declaration of Independence 487
The Federal Style 488
The French Revolution: 1788–1799 489
Phase One: 1789–1792 489
Phase Two: 1792–1795 491
Society and Culture: The Guillotine and the French Executioners 492

Key Terms 492
Key Questions 493
Suggested Reading 493
Suggested Films 493

Chapter 18: The Early Nineteenth Century and the Romantic Movement

Key Topics 495
Timeline 496

France: After the Revolution 497
Napoleon Bonaparte 497
Neoclassical Style under Napoleon 498
Restoration, Republic, and Empire 499
Society and Culture: Revolutions in the New World 500

The Romantic Movement in Western Europe 500
Philosophy 500
Society and Culture: The Industrial Revolution and James Watt's Steam Engine 501
Painting in Spain and France 501
Painting and Architecture in Britain 504
The Romantic Landscape: Turner and Constable 504
Gothic Revival Architecture 506
Painting in Germany: Friedrich 506

Romantic Literature in Europe 507
Germany: Goethe 507
France: de Staël, Chateaubriand, Hugo, and Sand 507
British Romantic Poets 509
William Blake 509
William Wordsworth and Samuel Taylor Coleridge 509
Defining Moment: The Romantic Lyrical Ballads of Wordsworth and Coleridge: 1798 510
Lord Byron, Percy Bysshe Shelley, and John Keats 511
The English Novel in the Early Nineteenth Century 512

The Romantic Movement in America 513
Transcendentalists 513
Ralph Waldo Emerson and Henry David Thoreau 513
Novelists 514
Poets 514
Landscape Painting: Romantic Visions 516

Romantic Music in Europe 518
Romantic Style 518
Genres of Romantic Music 518
Ludwig van Beethoven 518
Art Songs: Schubert and Schumann 520
Symphonies: Mendelssohn, Brahms, and Berlioz 521
Pianist-composers: Liszt and Chopin 522
German Opera: Richard Wagner 523
Italian Opera: Giuseppe Verdi 524
Nationalism in Music 525
Bohemia: Dvořák 525
Russia: Tchaikovsky and Mussorgsky 525
Scandinavia: Grieg and Sibelius 526

Key Terms 526
Key Questions 527
Suggested Reading 527
Suggested Films 527

Chapter 19: Nineteenth-century Realism: Industry and Social Change

Key Topics 529
Timeline 530

Political Developments 531

The Industrial Revolution: Technology and Invention 532

Science 534
Defining Moment: Louis Pasteur and the Germ Theory of Disease 535

Economic and Social Philosophy 536
Bentham, Mill, and the Utopians 536
Marxism 536
Philosophy and Malaise 537

Literature in Europe 537
France 537
Honoré de Balzac 537
Gustave Flaubert 538
Emile Zola 538
Society and Culture: The Dreyfus Affair 539
Guy de Maupassant 539
Britain 539
Charles Dickens 539
George Eliot 540
Samuel Butler 541
Russia 541
Leo Tolstoy 541
Fyodor Dostoyevsky 541

Realist Theater 542
Henrik Ibsen 542
August Strindberg 542
Anton Chekhov 542

Realism in Music 543

Realism in the Visual Arts 543
Gustave Courbet 544
Rosa Bonheur 544
Honoré Daumier 545
Edouard Manet 546
Britain: The Pre-Raphaelite Brotherhood 547
Photography 548

Developments in the United States 549
Manifest Destiny 549
Conflict Between Settlers and Native Americans 549
Civil War: 1861–1865 551
Abolitionists 552
War Breaks Out 553
Society and Culture: Abraham Lincoln, Thinker, Writer, Orator 553
Realism in Art and Architecture 554
Literature 556

Thematic Parallels: News 557

Key Terms 558
Key Questions 558
Suggested Reading 559
Suggested Films 559

Chapter 20: "Modern Life": The Late Nineteenth Century

Key Topics 561
Timeline 562

The Emergence of "Modern Life" 563

Imperialism and the International Economy 563
The British Empire 565

Impressionism 565
Claude Monet 565
Cross-cultural Influences: The Appeal of Japonisme *and the Japanese Woodblock Print* 566
Edouard Manet 568
Edgar Degas 568
Pierre-Auguste Renoir 568
Mary Cassatt 569
James McNeill Whistler 570
Auguste Rodin 571

The Symbolist Movement 571
Society and Culture: The Interpretation of Dreams *and the Oedipus Complex* 572
Symbolist Poetry 573
Charles Baudelaire 573
Stéphane Mallarmé 573
Paul Verlaine 573
Arthur Rimbaud 574
Symbolist Theater: Maeterlinck 574
Society and Culture: Alfred Nobel and the Nobel Prize 574

Music: Debussy 574
Society and Culture: The Indonesian Gamelan 575

Post-Impressionism 576
Henri de Toulouse-Lautrec 576
Georges Seurat 576
Paul Cézanne 576
Paul Gauguin 578
Vincent van Gogh 578
Edvard Munch 580

The Birth of Film 580
Thomas Edison 580
The Lumière Brothers 581
Georges Méliès 581
Defining Moment: The Invention of the Motion Picture Camera 582

Key Terms 583
Key Questions 583
Suggested Reading 583
Suggested Films 583

Chapter 21: Turn of the Century to World War I

Key Topics 585
Timeline 586

Society and Politics in the Early Twentieth Century 587

World War I 588
The Path to War 588
The Archduke Assassinated 588
Defining Moment: The Assassination of Archduke Francis Ferdinand: The Beginning of the End of an Era 589
A New Type of War 589
The End of the War and its Aftermath 590

Developments in Russia 590
Revolution 590

Technology, Science, and Psychology 591
Radioactivity and Atomic Research 591
The Universe of the Unconscious 591

***Fin de Siècle* and the Arts 593**
Art Nouveau 594
Oscar Wilde and Aubrey Beardsley 594
Society and Culture: Gilbert and Sullivan, The "Savoy Operas" 595

European Literature 596
Children's Literature 596
Lewis Carroll 596

Robert Louis Stevenson 596
Society and Culture: Nonsense and the Portmanteau Word 596
J. M. Barrie 597
Britain and Ireland 597
Thomas Hardy and James Joyce 597
Detective Fiction 598
Theater 598
France 599
Theater 599

Modernism and the Avant Garde 600
Futurism: 1909–1915 600
Expressionism in Art and Literature: The Avant Garde in Germany and Russia, 1904–1915 600
Wassily Kandinsky 600
Kazimir Malevich 601
Sergei Diaghilev 601
Franz Kafka 601
Rainer Maria Rilke 602
The Avant Garde in Paris 602
Matisse and the Fauves 602
Pablo Picasso 603
Dada 605

Music and the Avant Garde in Europe 605
Maurice Ravel 605
Gustav Mahler 606
Richard Strauss 606
Arnold Schoenberg 606
Igor Stravinsky 607

Turn-of-the-century America 608
Poetry: Frost, Pound, and H.D. 608
The Visual Arts 608
The Armory Show: 1913 610
Film: D. W. Griffith 610

Music in the United States 611

Key Terms 612
Key Questions 613
Suggested Reading 613
Suggested Films 613

Chapter 22: World War I through World War II

Key Topics 615
Timeline 616

The Political and Economic Aftermath of World War I 617
The Great Depression in the United States 617
Communism in Russia 618
The Rise of Fascism and National Socialism 618
Italy 618
Germany 619
Spain: Civil War 619

World War II 621
Defining Moment: The Holocaust 622
The United States Declares War: 1941–1945 623

Technology and Expanding Horizons 623

Philosophy 624
Logical Positivism 624
Existentialism 625

Art and Architecture Between the Wars 625
The Expansion of the Dada Movement after World War I 625
Surrealism 627
The International Style: *De Stijl* 629
The Prairie Style: Frank Lloyd Wright 630
American Regionalism: Thomas Hart Benton 630

The Jazz Age 631
Blues 631
Hot Jazz: Chicago-based Jazz of the 1920s 631
Swing 632
Society and Culture: The Cotton Club of Harlem 632
Bop 633
The Jazz Age in Paris 633

The Harlem Renaissance 634
James Weldon Johnson 634
Langston Hughes 635
Countee Cullen 635
Zora Neale Hurston 635
William Grant Still 635

Literature Between the Wars 635
American Poets and Novelists 635
Effects of War: Hemingway and Cather 636
American Society and Landscape: Dreiser, Lewis, Dos Passos, Fitzgerald, and Steinbeck 636
Modernist Authors: Cummings, Eliot, and Faulkner 637
Major European Novelists 638
Russia: Mikhail Sholokhov 638
British Modernists: Woolf and Joyce 638
Social Commentary in Britain: Lawrence and Huxley 640
Germany: Hesse and Remarque 640
Scandinavia: Hamsun, Laxness, and Lagerkvist 640

Theater Between the Wars 641
Italy: Luigi Pirandello 641
Germany: Bertolt Brecht 641

Spain: García Lorca 642
France: Giraudoux and Anouilh 642
Ireland: Sean O'Casey 642
The United States: Eugene O'Neill 642

Music and Dance in America 643
Dance: Martha Graham 643
The American Musical 643
George Gershwin 644
Charles Ives 644
Aaron Copland 644

Film 645
Germany: Leni Riefenstahl 645
The Soviet Union: Sergei Eisenstein 646
The United States 647
The Western: James Cruze 647
Social Commentary: Chaplin and Welles 647
Musicals: Vidor and Berkeley 649
Animation: Walt Disney 650
Romance: *Gone with the Wind* 650
Cross-cultural Influences: Films in Japan: Akira Kurosawa 651

Key Terms 652
Key Questions 652
Suggested Reading 652
Suggested Films 653

Chapter 23: 1945 to 1989: The Cold War to Détente

Key Topics 655
Timeline 656

The Cold War 657
Society and Culture: Churchill's "Iron Curtain Speech" 657
The Soviet Union and Eastern Europe 658
The United States 659
The Korean War 659
Latin America 659
The Vietnam War 659
Détente 660
Domestic Turmoil in the United States 661
The Civil Rights Movement 661
Defining Moment: Rosa Parks Keeps her Seat on the Bus 662
The Feminist Movement 662
Society and Culture: Martin Luther King's "I Have a Dream" Speech 663
Israel and Conflict in the Middle East 663
The Emerging Developing World 664
South Africa 664
India and Pakistan 664
The French Colonies 665
China 665

Science and Technology 666

Philosophy 667
Structuralism 667
Post-Structuralism and Deconstruction 668

Art and Architecture 668
The American Scene: Edward Hopper 668
Abstract Expressionism 669
Pop Art 671
Performance 672
Minimalism 672
Conceptual Art: Sol LeWitt 673
Super Realism 674
Earth Art 674
Feminist Iconography: Judy Chicago 675
Gender: Robert Mapplethorpe 676
African-American Appropriation: Robert Colescott 676
Graffiti Art: Jean-Michel Basquiat 677
Video Art: Nam June Paik 677
Postmodern Architecture 678

Literature 679
France: Albert Camus 679
Literature of the Holocaust 680
The Soviet Union: Pasternak and Solzhenitsyn 680
Britain: Orwell and Thomas 680
The United States 681
W. H. Auden 681
John Hersey 682
Joseph Heller 682
J. D. Salinger 682
Sylvia Plath 682
The Beat Writers 682
African-American Themes 683
Africa: Colonial Themes 683
Latin America: Magic Realism 684
Japan: Yasunari Kawabata 684

Theater 685
France 685
The United States 686

Music 687
Dmitry Shostakovich: Symphonies 687
The Emergence of an International Avant Garde 687
Electro-acoustic Music 688
Aleatory Music and Chance 688
Opera 688
Dance 689
Musicals 690

Popular Music 690
Rhythm and Blues 690
Rock Music 691

Film 692
Italy: Federico Fellini 692
Sweden: Ingmar Bergman 692
India: Satyajit Ray 693
France: The New Wave 693
The United States 694

Thematic Parallels: Heartthrobs of Western History 695

Key Terms 696
Key Questions 696
Suggested Reading 697
Suggested Films 697

Chapter 24: After 1989

Key Topics 699
Timeline 700

Europe and the Collapse of Communism 701
Yugoslavia 701
Europe after the Cold War 702

The United States and the Global Struggle with Terrorism 702
Defining Moment: September 11, 2001 704

Asia and the Developing World 705

Science and Technology 706

Art and Architecture 707
Digital Installation 708
Altering the Environment 709
Iconography of Genetic Mutation: Matthew Barney 710
Cross-cultural Art in America 710
Modernism in China 711
Postmodern Architecture after 1989 711

Music at the Turn of the Twenty-first Century 713

Literature 713
Günter Grass: Reflections of the Twentieth Century 714
South Africa: J. M. Coetzee 714
Canada: Margaret Atwood—Futuristic Feminism 714
Japan: Kenzaburo Oe and Kazuo Ishiguro 715
India: Arundhati Roy 716
China: Ha Jin 716

Theater 716
The United States: Wilson, Mamet, and Kushner 716
Britain: Stoppard and Churchill 717

Film 717
Social Commentary Films 717
Film in China: Zhang Yimou 717
Trainspotting: The Drug Culture 718
Osama 718
Special Effects and Animation 718
The Lord of the Rings 718
Finding Nemo 719

Epilogue: The Spirit of the Humanities 719

Key Terms 721
Key Questions 721
Suggested Reading 721
Suggested Films 721

Glossary 722
Literary Credits 729
Picture Credits 731
Index 735

Maps

1.1 Prehistoric art in Europe 8
2.1 Trade in the Ancient Near and Middle East 19
2.2 The Persian (Achaemenid) Empire, *c.* 480 B.C. 32
2.3 Olmec civilization in ancient Mesoamerica, *c.* 1200–400 B.C.; African kingdoms, 1000–1500; major Buddhist sites in southeast Asia, *c.* 1200 35
3.1 Ancient Egypt 50
4.1 The Aegean world, 2000–1200 B.C. 72
5.1 Ancient Greece, *c.* 1000–490 B.C. 92
6.1 Alexander's Empire, 323 B.C. 133
7.1 Ancient Rome 146
7.2 Etruscan Italy, *c.* 500 B.C. 148
7.3 Roman trade routes, *c.* A.D. 200 151
7.4 The expansion of the Roman Empire, 133 B.C.–*c.* A.D. 180 163
7.5 Classic cultures of Mesoamerica, *c.* 400 B.C.–A.D. 1170 178
8.1 Ancient Israel 189
8.2 Paul's missionary journeys, A.D. 46–62 195
9.1 The Byzantine Empire, 565 213
9.2 Intercontinental trade to c. 1000 215
9.3 The Byzantine Empire and the expansion of Islam, 622–750 224
10.1 Movements of Germanic tribes, 370–568 242
10.2 Europe on the death of Charlemagne, 814 243
10.3 The Viking world, *c.* 1000 257
12.1 The Black Death in fourteenth-century Europe 305
12.2 Fourteenth-century Italy 315
13.1 European trade in the fifteenth century 331
14.1 The Holy Roman Empire under Charles V, 1526 369
13.1 European trade in the fifteenth century 331
14.1 The Holy Roman Empire under Charles V, 1526 369
16.1 The division of Europe according to the Treaty of Westphalia, 1648 429
16.2 Early European settlement of North America 430
18.1 Europe at the height of Napoleon's power, 1812 499
19.1 Europe, 1848–1849 531
19.2 Westward expansion of the United States from 1783 550
20.1 World colonization at the end of the nineteenth century 564
21.1 Europe on the eve of World War I 588
22.1 Europe between the world wars 620
23.1 Europe after World War II, showing Soviet satellites 658
23.2 Colonies worldwide and decolonization, *c.* 1975 664
24.1 The world, showing relative wealth, 2005 705

Music Listening Selections

1. Islamic call to prayer *(Adhan)*. CD track 2 232
2. Hildegard of Bingen, "O viridissima Virga." Oxford Camerata, conductor Jeremy Summerly, CD track 4 264
3. Palestrina, Pope Marcellus Mass, "Kyrie." Oxford Camerata, conductor Jeremy Summerly, CD track 7 415
4. Weelkes, "As Vesta was from Latmos hill descending." Oxford Camerata, conductor Jeremy Summerly, CD track 6 417
5. Bach, Brandenburg Concerto No. 2 in F major, third movement, Allegro assai. Cologne Chamber Orchestra, conductor Helmut Muller-Bruhl, CD track 8 455
6. Handel, *Messiah*, Hallelujah Chorus. Scholars Baroque Ensemble, CD track 9 456
7. Haydn, Symphony No. 94 in G major, the "Surprise," second movement, Andante. Capella Istropolitana, conductor Barry Wordsworth, CD track 11 484
8. Mozart, *The Marriage of Figaro*, Act 1, scene 1, "Cinque . . . dieci." Patrizia Pace, soprano, Natale de Carolis, baritone, Hungarian State Opera Orchestra, conductor Pier Giorgio Morandi, CD track 12 485
9. Beethoven, Symphony No. 5 in C minor, first movement, Allegro con Brio. Nicolaus Esterházy Sinfonia, conductor Belah Drahos, CD track 14 520
10. Schubert, "The Erlking," transcribed by Liszt. Antii Siirala, piano, CD track 17 520
11. Berlioz, *Symphonie fantastique*, fifth movement, "Witches' Sabbath." San Diego Symphony Orchestra, conductor Yoav Talmi, CD track 15 522
12. Chopin, "Revolutionary" Etude in C minor, Opus 10. Idil Biret, piano, CD track 16 523
13. Wagner, *Lohengrin*, Bridal Chorus. Slovak Philharmonic Chorus, Slovak Radio Orchestra, conductor Johannes Wildner, CD track 18 524
14. Debussy, *Suite bergamasque*, "Clair de lune." Slovak Radio Orchestra, conductor Keith Clark, CD track 19 575
15. Schoenberg, *Six Little Piano Pieces*, Etwas rasch. Peter Hill, piano, CD track 20 607
16. Stravinsky, *The Rite of Spring*, "Dance of Youths and Maidens." Belgian Radio and Television Philharmonic Orchestra, conductor Alexander Rabhari, CD track 21 607

17. W. C. Handy, "St. Louis Blues." Louis Armstrong Orchestra, Louis Armstrong, cornet, CD track 25 611
18. Gershwin, *Porgy and Bess*, "Bess, You is My Woman Now." Paul Robeson, bass-baritone, Eva Jessye Choir, Decca Symphony Orchestra, conductor Alexander Smallens, CD track 22 644
19. Glass, *Akhnaten*, dance from Act 2, scene 3. Ulster Orchestra, conductor Takuo Yuasa, CD track 24 689
20. Bernstein, *West Side Story*, "Mambo." Nashville Symphony Orchestra, conductor Kenneth Schermerhorn, CD track 23 690

Preface

What are the humanities? Why are they important? And why do we study them? These are significant questions for students at the beginning of the twenty-first century. The humanities, as the term implies, are about what is uniquely human—our art, literature, science, and civilization. We study the humanities because they teach us about our own history. What we learn from our great successes as well as from our colossal failures helps us to confront the tensions of everyday life and gives us insight into ways of shaping our future. In an age of increasing globalization, it is essential that we understand the history of our own civilization and its creative products. Only with that as a foundation does it become possible to gain meaningful insight into other cultures.

In order to provide the most coherent, straightforward, and accessible approach for students, I have organized *Exploring the Humanities: Creativity and Culture in the West* chronologically from prehistory to the present. In the first chapter I cover cave paintings, sculpture, and architecture of prehistory and discuss ideas that shaped our earliest civilizations. The next chapter, the Ancient Near East, is of particular interest because it is there that the earliest evidence of a writing system has been found. It is also there that a number of other "firsts," including cities, evolved. Since it is also important to understand the immediate past, and the recent impact of globalization, the last four chapters contain extended coverage of the twentieth century and the early twenty-first century. While the focus of the text is the West, I believe it is useful to provide students with snapshots of non-Western developments at appropriate points in the historical narrative. These appear in boxes entitled Thematic Parallels and Cross-cultural Influences. The last several chapters of the book also consider works of art and architecture, literature, and film from around the globe.

Exploring the Humanities covers traditional areas of cultural study—painting, sculpture, architecture, music, drama, literature, and history—as well as less frequently featured disciplines such as philosophy and psychology, religion and myth, science and medicine, photography, film, and dance. In all these areas, I explore the humanities as expressions of their time and place. In my view, it is only by exploring the context of a work of art, a piece of music, an invention or a discovery, that one can understand the dynamic and creative role of the humanities in a civilization. In addition, the humanities are interdisciplinary; they are connected to each other and to society as a whole.

In each chapter of *Exploring the Humanities* I begin with a discussion of historical background and then proceed to discuss key disciplines with particular emphasis on art and literature. Each discipline and each work is presented in the context of its historical period. *Exploring the Humanities* covers significant works by major artists, philosophers, writers, and composers, as well as works by important but lesser-known figures. Later chapters also explore modern media such as photography and film, and genres such as children's literature, detective fiction, and rock music. To appeal to the visual culture of today's students, I have selected over 450 color and 200 black and white illustrations, which are analyzed throughout the text. The illustrations reinforce the narrative and reflect aspects of cultural and artistic development. Descriptive captions accompanying many of the images provide additional information about their style, content, and cultural significance. In the literature sections, I have included short excerpts from key works of poetry, prose, and theater to illustrate the author's style and point of view.

Exploring the Humanities is intended to engage students in the relevance of the humanities in today's world. To this end, the book includes in-text pedagogy—such as timelines, maps, and feature boxes—as well as linking with a range of different resources produced by the publisher. These features, together with diagrams and reproductions of major works of art and architecture, make this a user-friendly survey of the Western humanities and one that, I hope, will remind students of their own participation in the creative aspects of their lives and of their cultural history.

Laurie Schneider Adams
May 2005

Acknowledgments

Author's Acknowledgments

A number of scholars have been extremely helpful in lending their expertise to parts of this text. Oscar Muscarella (at the Metropolitan Museum of Art) reviewed the Ancient Near East chapter and Larissa Bonfante (Professor of Classics at New York University) reviewed and sections on Etruscan and Roman art; Kara Hattersley-Smith checked the Byzantine chapter, Carol Lewine (emerita, Queens College, CUNY) read the medieval chapters. Norman Harrington (emeritus, Brooklyn College, CUNY) reviewed sections on medieval literature. Mary Wiseman (emerita, Brooklyn College, CUNY, and the Graduate Center) and Professor Mark Zucker (Louisiana State University) stood ready to answer queries on philosophy and the Renaissance, respectively. I am grateful to Peter Manuel (Professor of Music, John Jay College, CUNY, and the Graduate Center), Jenny Doctor (University of York), and Ursula Sadie Payne, who devoted a great deal of time to improving the sections on music.

I would like to thank all those at Laurence King Publishing Ltd. who were involved in this project for their creative approach to the text and their tireless work. Lee Greenfield supported the project from its inception; Melanie White's valuable input and patient persistence improved the text at all stages of its development; Ursula Sadie Payne efficiently managed the text from manuscript to completion; Lydia Darbyshire copyedited with great skill; Sue Bolsom and Fiona Kinnear did a wonderful job of picture research; and Nick Newton and Randell Harris did excellent work in laying out the book.

At Prentice Hall, Bud Therien, Sarah Touborg, and Amber Mackey encouraged the project from the beginning, and I am also grateful to the development editors Harriett Prentiss and Margaret Manos, who helped organize the text.

Publishers' Acknowledgments

*** Advisers**

The publishers would like to acknowledge the following academics who advised on the text: Barbara Kramer (Santa Fe Community College) for her extensive reviewing of the manuscript and her significant contribution to the Key Topics, Key Questions, and Defining Moment boxes; Judith Stanford for her valuable input on literature; Peter Manuel (John Jay College, CUNY, and the Graduate Center) for his advice on music; Peter Brand (University of Memphis); Henry E. Chambers (California State University, Sacramento); Jessica A. Coope (University of Nebraska-Lincoln); Paul B. Harvey, Jr. (Pennsylvania State University); Linda Mitchell (Alfred University); Cybelle Shattuck (Kalamazoo College); Larissa Taylor (Colby College).

*** Reviewers**

The publishers would also like to thank all those who reviewed the manuscript:
Michael Berberich (Galveston College)
Arnold Bradford (Northern Virginia Community College)
Sarah Breckenridge (Community College at Aurora)
Daniel J. Brooks (Aquinas College)
Ken Bugajski (Rogers State University)
Charles Carroll (Lake City Community College)
Judith Cortelloni (Lincoln College)
Anthony F. Crisafi (University of Central Florida)
Eugene Crook (Florida State University)
Cynthia Donahue (Brevard Community College)
Frank Felsenstein (Ball State University)
Samuel Garren (North Carolina A. & T. State University)
Sharon Gorman (University of the Ozarks)
J. Keith Green (East Tennessee University)
Blue Greenberg (Meredith College)
Craig Hanson (Muskingum College)
Robin Hardee (South Florida Community College)
Viktoria Hertling (University of Nevada Reno)
Bobby Hom (Santa Fe Community College)
Cheryl Hughes (Tulsa Community College)
Sandi Landis (St. Johns River Community College)
David Linebarger (Northeastern State University)
Debra Ann Maukonen (University of Central Florida)
Merritt Moseley (University of North Carolina, Asheville)
Greg Peterson (Rogers State University)
Joyce Porter (Moraine Valley Community College)
Jason Swedene (Lake Superior State University)
Mary Tripp (University of Central Florida)
Margaret Urie (University of Nevada, Reno)
Joel Zimbelman (California State University, Chico)

To Know the Humanities is to Love the Humanities

Welcome to

EXPLORING THE HUMANITIES:

CREATIVITY AND CULTURE IN THE WEST,
Teaching and Learning Classroom Edition (T. L. C.)

Professors . . .

Do your students come to class having read—and thought about—the text material?

Do they leave the course inspired to love the humanities the way you do?

Now they will.

Prentice Hall proudly presents: *Exploring the Humanities: Creativity and Culture in the West, Teaching and Learning Classroom Edition* (T. L. C.) by Laurie Schneider Adams. This T. L. C. Edition will ignite students' passion to know more and think more about the importance of the humanities. This highly visual T. L. C. Edition begins with a simple premise: students will not learn what they have not read. *Exploring the Humanities* was designed especially to engage students to read the text and help them study smarter and perform better in class.

Pique students' curiosity to *read* the text

This T. L. C. Edition invites students into the text with Laurie Schneider Adams' accessible writing style that is clear and easy-to-read. Important works are explored in depth and in context, rather than presenting students with an overwhelming list of details. The book's stunning visual appeal captures student interest with beautiful, full-color reproductions illustrating the text discussion, full-color maps, and illustrated timelines. In addition, the text includes an array of pedagogical features designed to make the material accessible to students, including four kinds of boxed features that appear throughout the book:

Thematic Parallels help students compare cultures and art from around the world. These boxes consider universal themes, such as kingship, pilgrimage, notions of outer space, methods of spreading news, the persistence of the Classical tradition, and "heartthrobs" throughout history.

Cross-cultural Influences focus on areas of historical contact and artistic influence between cultures of the same time period. We discuss, for example, the impact of Greek Hellenistic style on Gandharan art from the first century B.C. to the first century A.D. Similarly, we consider the influence of Japanese woodblock prints of the Edo period on European and American Impressionists and Post-Impressionists in the nineteenth century.

Society and Culture These boxes, which appear throughout the text, elaborate further on a key person, event, or idea, providing more social and cultural background. Topics are of high interest to students and include daily life, medicine and science, technology, religion and myth, and the impact of certain individuals on history.

Defining Moments highlight an exciting turning point that has significantly influenced Western culture, whether a historical event, a scientific discovery, or an artistic innovation. A Critical Question is included at the end of each box to encourage further discussion.

Engage students to *think* about what they are reading

This T. L. C. edition has more learning tools for students than any other humanities book, aimed at helping students understand, process, and appreciate what they are reading.

- A **Starter Kit** gives students a brief overview of the basic principles and terms they will need to know while beginning their study of the visual arts, music, literature, history, and philosophy.
- **Chapter Openers** Each chapter opens with a two-page spread, which has been carefully designed to draw students' attention and prepare them to engage with the material they are about to read. *Striking images* from the chapter capture the imagination, and a *brief introduction* to the key points of the period gets students oriented. A compelling *quotation* that embodies a main theme appears in the opener and is discussed at the end of the introduction. In addition, *Key Topics* are presented to prepare students to pay attention to the most important concepts of the chapter.
- **Timelines** Following each chapter opener is a full-page illustrated timeline designed to reinforce visually the chronology of the period and highlight key historical events, scientific discoveries, and works of art.
- **Maps** Throughout the book, colorful maps provide readers with a sense of geography. Several of the maps are thematic, indicating migrations of cultural groups, trade routes, and art centers.
- **End-of-chapter Study Tools** A consistent set of study tools is found at the end of every chapter.
  Key Terms, printed in bold type in the main text, are explained on first mention and are defined again in the glossary at the end of the chapter.
  Key Questions are included at the end of each chapter to help students focus on and review issues central to the period under discussion.
  Suggested Reading includes an annotated bibliography relevant to each chapter.
  Suggested Films have been selected to bring an era to life and also to reflect film history. Some films are based on literary works or on the lives of key figures.

Empower Students to *do* more than just read

Teaching and Learning Resources for Students and Faculty

This T. L. C. Edition comes with a state-of-the-art package of multimedia and print resources.

Online Resources for Students and Faculty

OneKey

OneKey is a free, all-inclusive online resource giving you the best teaching and learning resources all in one place. OneKey is all your students need for out-of-class work conveniently organized by chapter to reinforce and apply what they have learned in class and from the text. OneKey is all you need to plan and administer your course. All your instructor resources are in one place to maximize your effectiveness and minimize your time and effort. For details, please visit www.prenhall.com/onekey.

Companion Website at www.prenhall.com/adams

This site features unique study and support tools for every chapter of *Exploring the Humanities* (such as chapter objectives and useful links). Multiple choice and short answer quizzes provide instant scoring and feedback to promote self-study. Students can also e-mail essay responses and graded quizzes directly to their instructor.

Student Resources

- ***Music for the Humanities* CD**
  This music CD is bound into each copy of the text and the Music Listening Selections are cited and discussed in the main text.
- **Anthology of Readings, Volumes I and II**
  Each chapter of *Exploring the Humanities* contains references to primary sources discussed in the text, which have been compiled into a two-volume anthology. Instructors also have the option of customizing their own anthology through the Penguin Custom Editions program. This allows them to select only the readings they need from an archive of more than 1700 readings excerpted primarily from the Penguin Classics™. Visit www.pecustomeditions.com for more information on Penguin Custom Editions: The Western World. Contact your local Prentice Hall sales representative for ordering information.
- **Prentice Hall and Penguin Bundle Program**
  Prentice Hall is pleased to provide adopters of *Exploring the Humanities* with an opportunity to receive significant discounts when copies of the text are bundled with Penguin titles. Contact your local Prentice Hall sales representative for details.
- **Humanities Notes: A Study Guide to Accompany *Exploring the Humanities*, Volumes I and II**
  Humanities Notes provides students with practice tests, map exercises, spaces for taking notes on the Key Topics and a place to answer Key Questions from each chapter. Free when packaged with the text.
- **The Prentice Hall *Atlas of the Humanities***
  Prentice Hall collaborates with Dorling Kindersley, the world's most innovative producer of maps and atlases. This atlas features multi-dimensional maps that include global, thematic, regional, and chronological perspectives showing political, economic, and cultural changes over time. Available at a significant discount when packaged with the text.
- 

  TIME Magazine Special Editions. Available for Art, World Religions, and World Politics
  Prentice Hall and TIME Magazine are pleased to offer a way to examine today's most current and compelling issues in an exciting new way. TIME Special Editions offers the same accessible writing style, bold coverage, and photography for which TIME is known, including a selection of articles on today's most current issues in the fields. Useful for classroom discussion and research assignments. Free when packaged with the text.
- 

  OneSearch with Research Navigator
  In addition to information on citing sources and avoiding plagiarism, this guide gives students easy access to three exclusive research databases: The New York Times Search by Subject Archive, ContentSelect Academic Journal Database, and Link Library. Free when packaged with the text.

Faculty Resources

- **Instructor's Resource Binder**
  This innovative, all-in-one resource organizes the instructor's manual, the test item file, and other resources by each chapter of *Exploring the Humanities*, all in an easy-to-access format designed to facilitate class preparation. Designed for both the novice and the seasoned professor, this invaluable guide includes resources for each chapter, such as an overview, objectives, outline, lecture and discussion ideas, and further resources. The test bank consists of multiple choice, true/false, short answer, and essay questions. Contact your local Prentice Hall sales representative for more information.
- **TestGen**
  This commercial-quality computerized test management program for Windows or Macintosh allows instructors to select test bank questions in designing their own exams. Contact your local Prentice Hall sales representative for more information.
- **Fine Art Slides**
  Slides that accompany the text are available to qualified adopters. Contact your local Prentice Hall sales representative for more information.

Starter Kit

In Latin, the word *humanitas* means "human nature" and refers to the quality that distinguishes humans from animals. Today we use the term "humanities" to encompass many educational disciplines. Even hard sciences such as physics and chemistry, and technical disciplines such as engineering, which are not usually considered "humanities," are creative products of the human mind. For the sake of clarity, however, one might divide humanities into the following broad areas of knowledge:

- **creative and expressive arts:** picture-making, sculpture, architecture, music, dance, theater, film, and literature
- **sports:** in which physical aggression and competitiveness are transformed into cultural activity. Note that for the Olympic Games in ancient Greece, all wars on Greek territory were halted so that the athletes could travel safely to the competition.
- **attempts to explain our origins and know our future:** religion and myth
- **the intellectual search for truth:** philosophy
- **the sciences:** physics, chemistry, psychology, biology, medicine, anthropology, and zoology
- **the physical study of our planet and of the cosmos:** geography and astronomy
- **the record of our past:** history and archaeology

The major disciplinary categories, however, are mainly a convenience for the purpose of discussion. We can also benefit from considering the humanities in an interdisciplinary light: it is worth noting, for example, that archaeology—the study of the past by excavating buried civilizations—is a humanist pursuit that relies on various combinations of art, science, and technology. Moreover, the major disciplines have further subdivisions that continue to evolve as the disciplines themselves evolve, and all, over time, have developed appropriate signs and symbols (see Box), rules and principles, systems of analysis, and methods of appreciation and evaluation.

Before we embark on our chronological exploration of the Western humanities, therefore, this Starter Kit introduces some of the basic principles governing the study of visual art, music, literature, history, and philosophy, and the terms used by their practitioners.

The Visual Arts

The traditional visual arts—also called the monumental arts (as opposed to craft)—are pictures, sculpture, and architecture. All are made of materials that arouse the sense of touch by creating an actual or implied **texture**. The material used in making a work of art is its **medium** (plural **media**).

Two-dimensional Art: Pictures

Pictures are images that exist in two dimensions: height and width. Examples of pictures include drawings, paintings, prints, mosaics, stained glass, photographs, and films.

PICTURE SPACE Since pictures are flat in reality, when they appear to have depth as well as height and width, the artist has created a **three-dimensional illusion**. Consider, for example, Masaccio's *Trinity* (figure **0.1**), which appears three-dimensional even though it is painted on a flat wall. Masaccio has used the system of **linear perspective** to produce the impression that a Crucifixion scene is taking place in an actual space beyond the wall. A figure of God stands on a ledge behind the Cross, making him appear farther than Christ from the viewer. And appearing closer to us than Christ are the two figures kneeling on the illusionistic outer step. This perspective system is diagrammed in figure **0.2** and shows the grid pattern of the imaginary floor plan composed of lines parallel to the surface of the picture (the **picture plane**), the position of the viewer, and the **orthogonals** (lines perpendicular to the picture plane) that meet at the **vanishing point**, which is located on the horizon.

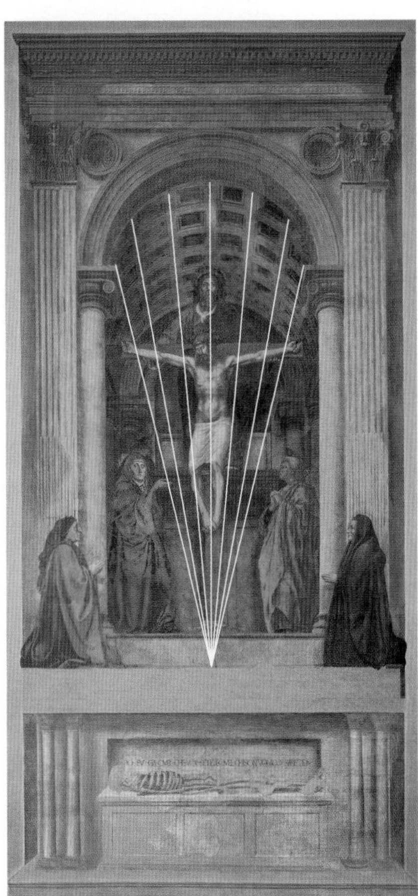

0.1 Masaccio, *Trinity*, 1425–1428, Santa Maria Novella, Florence. Fresco, 21 ft. 10⅝ in. × 10 ft. 4¾ in. (6.67 × 3.17 m).

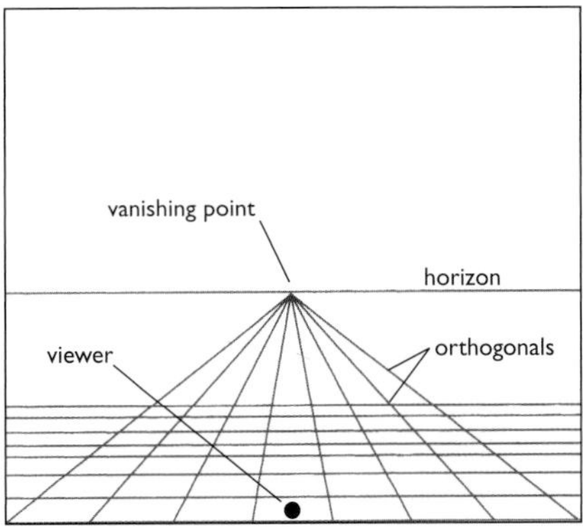

0.2 One-point perspective, according to Alberti.

When artists create pictures, they organize the basic visual elements (units of design) into a **composition**. A good composition generally conveys a sense of coherence, which we read as a unified whole. This may be achieved through balance, patterning, rhythms, contrasts, and so forth.

VISUAL ELEMENTS The main visual units are line, space, shape, color, light, and dark, all of which have expressive character. **Lines** can be horizontal (like the horizon) [——], vertical (like a soldier standing at attention) [|], diagonal (like a falling tree [/], curved (like an arc) [⌒], S-shaped (like a snake) [∿]), wavy (like the ocean) [∿∿], or zigzagged (like a mountain range) [⋀⋀⋀]. When lines enclose a **space**, they create a **shape**. Shapes can be geometric, biomorphic (lifelike), open, or closed. The diagrams in figure **0.3** show regular geometric shapes (square, triangle, circle, rectangle, trapezoid), a biomorphic shape, and shapes having mass (cube, pyramid, sphere). An artist can create the illusion of a three-dimensional shape using **shadows** or **shading**. When a shape such as the cube in figure 0.3 blocks light, it casts a shadow. With the sphere in figure 0.3, we have the impression that light is coming from the right, that it is blocked by the sphere, and thus that it casts a shadow on the surface supporting it. Shading is the gradual change from

0.3 Diagrams of shapes.

flat shapes

square triangle circle

rectangle trapezoid biomorphic shape

3-D shapes

cube pyramid sphere

light to dark, which here creates the impression that the sphere has mass. The edge of the sphere, or of any solid object, is called its **contour**.

Color is a striking element of many pictures, although some pictures, such as black and white photographs, early films, some drawings and prints, and black and white paintings do not have color. The name of a color is its **hue** (red, green, purple, etc.), and the **value** of a color is its relative darkness or lightness. Figure **0.4** illustrates a **color wheel** showing primary, secondary, and tertiary colors. Note that the primary colors are indicated by a 1, the secondaries by a 2, and the tertiaries by a 3. A primary color is one that cannot be made by mixing two different colors. A secondary color is made by mixing two primaries, and a tertiary by mixing the primary and secondary on either side of it. Generally, the most striking contrasts are formed by juxtaposing colors opposite each other on the wheel. So, for example, a blue next to an orange is theoretically more eye-catching than a yellow next to an orange.

Primary colors on this wheel are red, yellow, and blue; they are the colors from which all the other colors of the **visible spectrum** (figure **0.5**) are derived. The spectrum itself is composed of seven colors made visible by passing white light through a prism. White light is the combination of the colors of the spectrum.

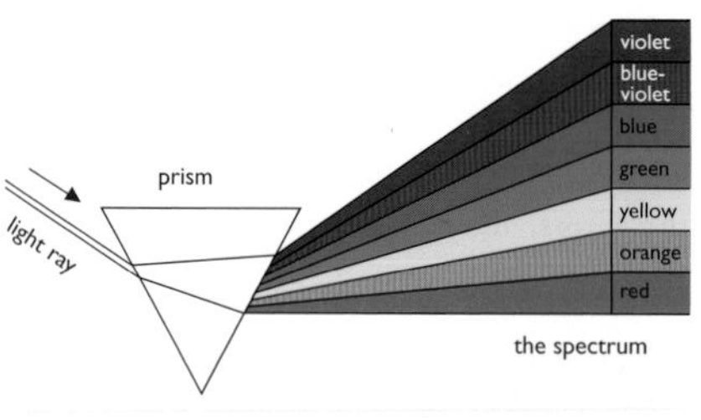

0.5 The visible spectrum.

0.6 Filippo Brunelleschi, *Sacrifice of Isaac*, 1401–1402. Gilt bronze, 21 × 17½ in. (53.3 × 44.4 cm). Museo Nazionale del Bargello, Florence.

THREE-DIMENSIONAL ART: SCULPTURE

In contrast to pictures, sculptures are three-dimensional and can be divided into two broad categories: *relief* and **sculpture-in-the-round** (sometimes called **freestanding**). Relief sculpture, as in Brunelleschi's *Sacrifice of Isaac* (figure **0.6**), has a background plane, just as a picture does, and the image cannot be seen from behind the background. Sculpture-in-the-round, like the *Kritios Boy* (figure **0.7**),

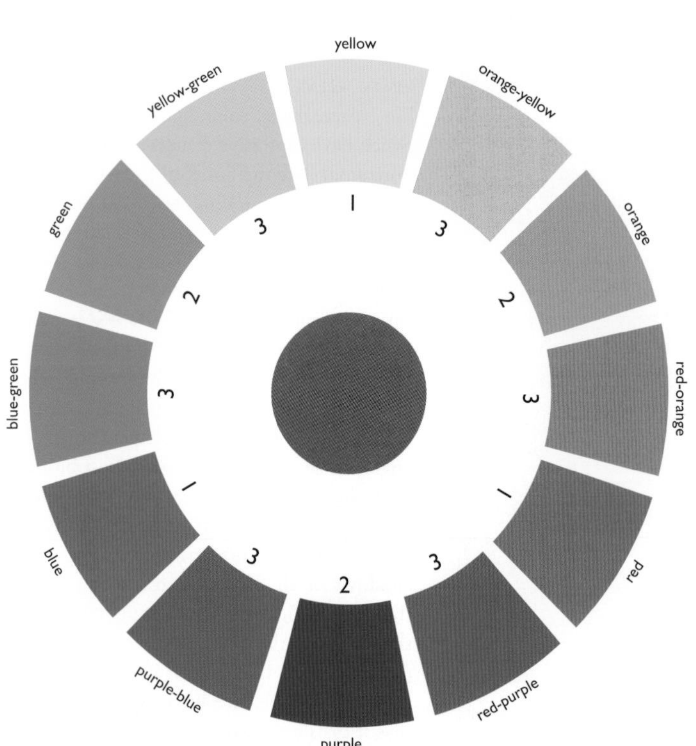

0.4 The color wheel.

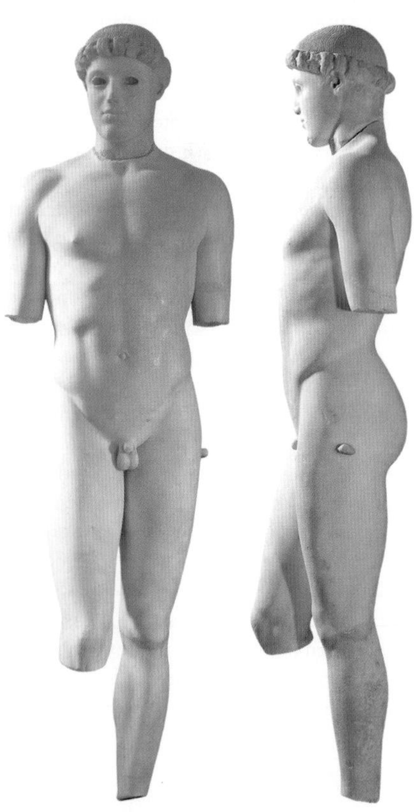

0.7 *Kritios Boy* (front and side), *c.* 480 B.C. Marble, 33⅞ in. (86 cm) high. Acropolis Museum, Athens.

can and should be seen from all sides. The traditional media of sculpture are wood, stone, and bronze, but more recent sculptures have been made of such materials as wire, cloth and stuffing, neon lights, crushed cars, and television monitors.

ARCHITECTURE

The term **architecture** refers to buildings and the practice of architecture is thought of as the most functional of the monumental arts (although paintings and sculptures can also have specific functions). Whereas we look at a picture from one viewpoint and at a sculpture-in-the-round from several viewpoints, we have to enter a building and walk through it in order to experience it fully.

A building is generally constructed with a specific idea about how it will be used and, as a consequence, there are many types of building ranging from private to public, from modest to magnificent, and from traditional to innovative. Domestic architecture can be in the form of apartment blocks or private dwellings such as individual city houses, country villas, and royal palaces; places of worship include synagogues, churches and cathedrals, temples, and mosques; museums are built to display art; bridges are constructed to span spaces; castles and forts are defensive; and in ancient Egypt, monumental pyramids were built to preserve the ruler and his belongings for the afterlife.

Buildings are designed by an **architect**, who first makes a **ground plan** indicating the placement of structural elements at ground level. In this plan of the Parthenon (figure **0.8**), the three outer lines represent the steps, the black circles show where the columns stand on the floor, the solid lines (except for the steps) indicate walls, and the spaces denote open areas—room interiors, spaces between columns, and doorways cut into the walls.

Over the course of time, architects have designed buildings according to a number of structural systems that we will encounter in this text. Figure **0.9** illustrates diagrams of some of the most frequently used systems. **Load-bearing** structures such as the ziggurats of ancient Mesopotamia had supporting walls, no windows, and no interiors. The **post-and-lintel** system consists of vertical supports holding up a horizontal, as in the Neolithic structure of Stonehenge. In ancient Rome, architects used the **round arch** for many purposes, one of which was to construct triumphal arches as passageways for victorious generals and emperors. **Pointed arches** were developed in the twelfth century and became a mainstay of Gothic cathedral architecture, whose soaring verticals are lighter and rise higher than those based on round arches. The ceiling **vaults** made by repeating round and pointed arches (**barrel vaults** and **rib vaults**, respectively) correspond to the effects of the arches themselves: barrel vaults create a sense of heavy mass, and rib vaults create a sense of height and lightness.

0.10 Louis Sullivan, Wainwright Building, St. Louis, Missouri, 1890–1891.

In the nineteenth century, capitalizing on the advances brought about by the Industrial Revolution and with the ability to smelt steel on a large scale, architects began to use **steel-frame** skeletons for skyscrapers. To begin with, stone was used for the outer skin of the buildings, as in Louis Sullivan's Wainwright Building in St. Louis (figure **0.10**), and later, in the twentieth century, glass began to be employed for architectural exteriors.

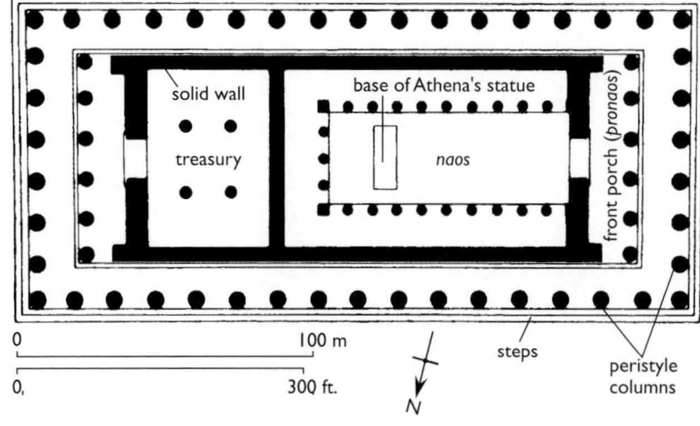

0.8 Plan of the Parthenon, Athens.

0.9 Architectural systems.

load-bearing wall

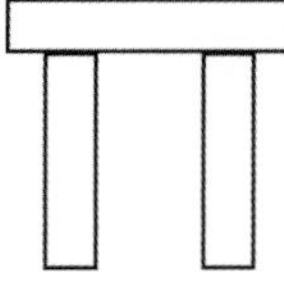

post-and-lintel

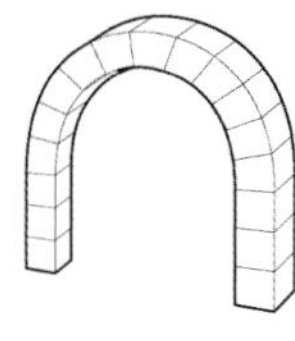

round arch

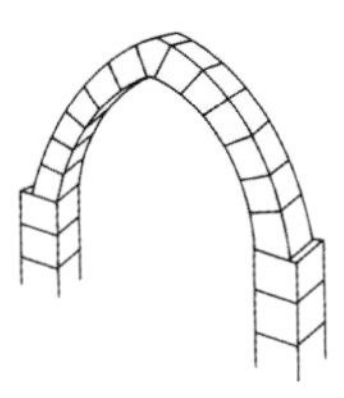

pointed arch

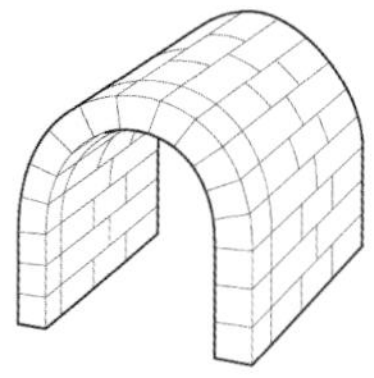

barrel vault

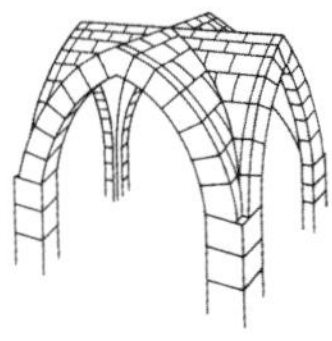

rib vault

Signs and Symbols

Signs and symbols are used in every discipline within the humanities to convey meaning, and we will examine some of the principal ones here. Our ability to think symbolically is a crucial element of being human—fundamental to what differentiates us from animals. The ability to use and read signs and symbols is thus critical to any study of the humanities.

Signs communicate a fact or a direct command and are familiar aspects of everyday life. A red rectangle on a road, for example, is a sign that we are supposed to stop. An arrow signals a one-way street', and a picture of a cigarette with a line through it means no smoking. A **symbol** stands for something besides itself and, in contrast to a sign, usually has more than a single level of meaning. In Christian art, for example, when the Virgin Mary is depicted as unnaturally large, she symbolizes the church building. The circle symbolizes the universal and never-ending character of the Church, and light inside a church symbolizes the presence of God.

In music, we use signs to denote pitch, the length of notes, rests between notes, clefs, key and time signatures, and chords (see figures 0.12 and 0.14). In some musical compositions, the sounds produced convey symbolic meaning. For example, a rising scale can symbolize ascent into heaven and a falling scale can symbolize descent into hell. Sounds can also symbolize moods—hence the Greek musical **modes**, such as the Lydian plaintive and the Mixolydian elegiac.

In literature the elements of **punctuation** are signs that are essential to our ability to read and understand. We use quotation marks (". . .") to indicate that someone is speaking, commas (,) to indicate pauses, and periods (.) to indicate the ends of sentences. There are also literary symbols created by the author's use of words, which generally include an image or comparison of some kind. In a **simile**, we use the word *like* or *as* to make a comparison—if we say that someone is "as fit as a fiddle" we mean that he or she is as taut as a violin string and thus in perfect physical condition. In **metaphor** we create a comparison without using either *like* or *as*—we may say that parks "*are* the lungs of a city." This is not literally true, but it is true in the sense that parks introduce fresh air into an urban landscape. Another device available to an author is **personification**, when something that is not a person is likened to a person. Thus when we say that "Justice is blind," we are portraying the idea of justice as a blind person (usually a woman), who is impartial. That is, she is not swayed by what she sees but, rather, bases her decisions purely on objective facts.

In visual art, especially Christian art, there are an enormous number of signs and symbols and they are essential to an understanding of the meaning of a work. The saints, for example, can be identified by specific elements such as the keys of St. Peter, the knife and flayed skin of St. Bartholomew, and the lamb of John the Baptist. A scallop shell can denote pilgrimage and resurrection, a halo signals the divine nature of a holy person, and a vine can allude to the wine of the Eucharist. In ancient Greek and Roman art, the gods also have attributes that are signs and symbols of their identity. Thus, for example, Zeus and Jupiter wield a thunderbolt as a sign of their power; Aphrodite and Venus are often accompanied by rabbits to show their association with fertility; and Hera and Juno wear a veil as goddesses of marriage.

0.11 Leonardo da Vinci, *Mona Lisa*, c. 1503–1515. Oil on wood, 30¼ × 21 in. (76.7 × 53.3 cm). Louvre, Paris.

As in dreams, the imagery of art can be interpreted in multiple ways and on multiple levels. To take a single, well-known picture, consider Leonardo da Vinci's *Mona Lisa* (figure **0.11**). We know very little about this painting, despite its fame, so it lends itself to many different readings.

One interpretation of the *Mona Lisa* is based on our knowledge of Leonardo's own writing, in which he said that the human body is a metaphor for the earth. He wrote that the soil is flesh, the waterways are blood, and the rocks are bones. Taking this metaphor, we can read Mona Lisa herself as a symbol of the earth, a kind of mythical mother earth-goddess derived from antiquity. Then we might note that her form is indeed an echo of the background mountains, that her transparent veil is similar to the mists enveloping the rocks, that the folds of her sleeves repeat the movement of the spiral road, and that the aqueduct on the right flows into the fold over her left shoulder. Formally and symbolically, therefore, Mona Lisa *is* the world; and she is as imposing and incomprehensible as the world.

In the nineteenth century, the critic Walter Pater described Mona Lisa as timeless, older even than the rocks among which she sits. Pater also found her sinister and menacing, which is a far cry from the analysis of the twentieth-century physician who asserted that she smiles contentedly because she is pregnant. According to Freud—perhaps the most famous interpreter of dreams and their symbols—Mona Lisa's smile is a trace of the smile of the artist's mother, which Leonardo recalled from his childhood and refound in the expression of his sitter.

MUSIC

In societies that have no writing systems, there is no musical notation and music is transmitted orally. In literate societies, however, there are different kinds of musical notation. But there are generally two essential pieces of information communicated by the written notation, namely the note itself (its **pitch**, or highness/lowness) and the length of that note.

Musical notation in the West was rare before the Middle Ages. Today, Western music is written on **staffs** of five parallel horizontal lines (figure **0.12**). Each line and space represents the location of a **note**, which denotes a sung or played sound. The physical appearance of each note indicates its length: a whole note [𝅝], half-note [𝅗𝅥], quarter-note [♩], eighth-note [♪], sixteenth note [𝅘𝅥𝅯], thirty-second note [𝅘𝅥𝅰]. The lengths of silences between notes are indicated by one of several different **rest** signs [𝄻, 𝄼, 𝄽, 𝄾, 𝄿, 𝅀]. There are twelve pitches, or **semitones** (the smallest interval commonly used in Western music): the seven notes **A**, **B**, **C**, **D**, **E**, **F**, and **G**, plus five **sharps** and **flats**. An **octave** is the name given to the interval between two notes of the same name, twelve semitones apart: A to A, B flat to B flat, and so on (figure **0.13**). The sharp sign [♯] indicates that a note is raised by a semitone; the flat sign [♭] indicates that a note is lowered a by semitone.

Many instruments have notation written on a single staff. However, in notation for the piano there are two staffs, one for the left hand and one for the right hand. Figure **0.14** shows a notation of the beginning of "Happy Birthday" for the piano. At the beginning of each staff (at the far left) the **bass clef** sign [𝄢] denotes the pitch played with the left hand. The **treble clef** [𝄞] denotes a higher pitch and is played on the piano with the right hand. The sharps or flats that must be played appear after the clef and are known, collectively, as the **key signature**. Figures on the staff (known as the **time signature**) indicate meter and rhythm.

Together, these written elements make up the **score**, or the music-copy for one or more performers. But there are other elements in music beside these written signs and symbols. A **melody**, for example, is a sequence of notes with a recognizable form, or tune. To create **harmony**, a musician combines tones into **chords** (two or more notes played simultaneously). **Rhythm** refers to meter or pulse, creating a pattern of sounds. The **theme** is the musical idea on which a composition is based—it will often have an identifiable melody. In **monophony**, such as the medieval Gregorian chant, there is a single line of melody with no accompaniment. In **polyphony**, which developed later, two or more lines of melody are combined.

Music can be sung, in which case the voice is the instrument. But many other instruments have been developed since the dawn of human history, and today these tend to be grouped into families: **strings**, either bowed like the violin, viola, cello, and double bass, or plucked like the lyre, harp, and guitar; **keyboards** including the piano and harpsichord; **wind** instruments, which may be further subdivided into **woodwind** (the recorder and flute, and instruments played with a reed, including the oboe, bassoon, clarinet, and saxophone), **brass** instruments (including horn, trumpet, and trombone), and the **organ** (which differs from other wind instruments in that the air required to produce the sound is supplied by an external source rather than by the performer); and **percussion**, or instruments—both tuned and untuned—that are sounded by being struck or shaken (drums, xylophone, cymbals, and bells). In addition to these traditional families, almost any sound can now be reproduced by **electronic** means using a synthesizer. Nevertheless, each instrument makes a distinctive sound and creates its own musical **tone color** (or **timbre**).

Different genres of music use different combinations of instruments or groups of instruments. A **song** (of which there are many different varieties) may be sung by a single voice or by a group of voices (a **choir**). Musical works for **orchestra** can assume a number of forms, but the **symphony**—an extended work played by a large group of instruments for a large audience—is on the grandest scale, involving the largest number of players. Usually symphonies are divided into **movements** (sections of a specific musical character). A **concerto** is a musical performance by one or more solo instruments accompanied by an orchestra, and **chamber music** was originally conceived, as its name suggests, for a small number of players performing in a private room (chamber). **Opera**, which developed in the seventeenth century, is drama set to music. Among the many genres of popular music that have developed since the beginning of the twentieth century are ragtime, blues, jazz, rock (of several varieties), and rap.

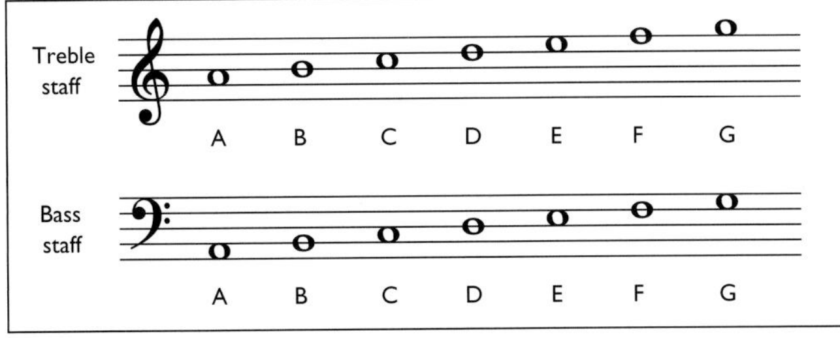

0.12 Music staffs.

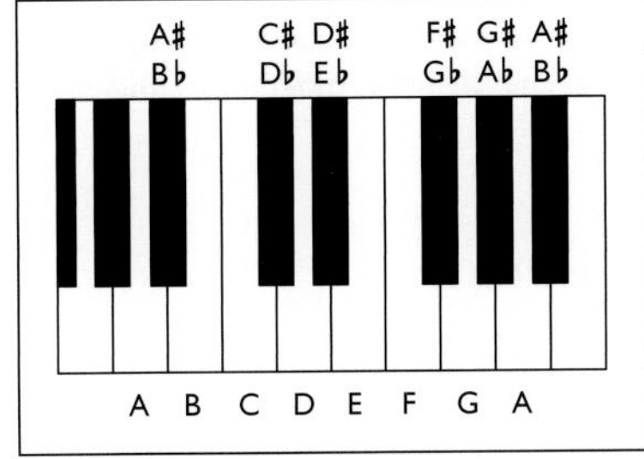

0.13 Octave shown on the piano.

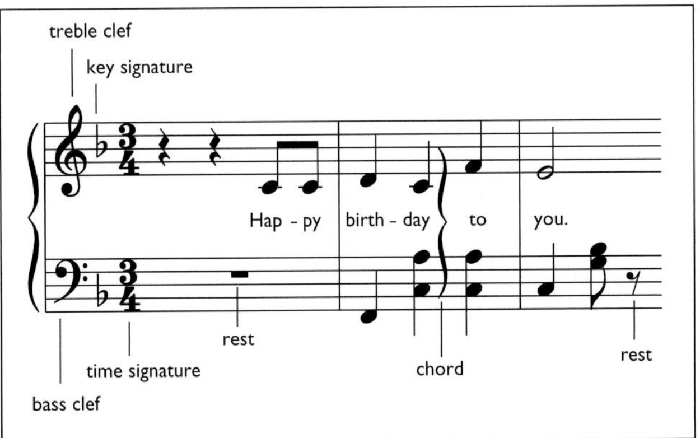

0.14 First bars of "Happy Birthday."

LITERATURE

Literature is a verbal form of expression and its medium is language. The simple building blocks of language are words and sentences. To understand how language works it can be broken down into **parts of speech** (nouns, verbs, adverbs, adjectives, conjunctions, and articles), which are the components of **grammar**, and their arrangement and structure is their **syntax**. Grammar and syntax form the character and structure of sentences and follow certain rules. Literature, however, amounts to far more than mere communication: it is a creative expression of human thought that elevates these building blocks into an art form. Literature can be broadly divided into **prose** and **poetry**. Whereas prose tends to resemble everyday speech and to extend a narrative through time, poets tend to structure their words according to an established rhythm and meter.

POETRY

Poetic lines traditionally **rhyme**, that is, their final sounds (or spellings) are similar—though they do not have to be identical. Consider, for example, the first five lines of Samuel Taylor Coleridge's "Kubla Khan":

In Xanadu did Kubla Khan
A stately pleasure-dome decree:
Where Alph, the sacred river, ran
Through caverns measureless to man
Down to a sunless sea.

"Khan" rhymes with "ran" and "man," and "decree" rhymes with "sea." This rhyme scheme is diagrammed as ABAAB: A (Khan), B (decree), A (ran), A (man), B (sea).

Genres of poetry include **narratives** (which tell a story), **lyric** poems (which are usually brief, melodic, and imbued with emotion and imagination), **epic**, and **nonsense** poems. An epic poem is a long narrative on a grand scale, usually dealing with universal themes, gods, legends, and heroes. The earliest Western epics—the Sumerian *Epic of Gilgamesh* and the Homeric *Iliad* and *Odyssey*—were first transmitted orally and only later written down. On the other hand, Milton wrote down his epic *Paradise Lost* as he was creating it in seventeenth-century England. In nonsense poetry, authors create original word forms and syntactical constructs that do not appear to make rational sense. A famous example of nonsense is Lewis Carroll's "Jabberwocky":

'Twas brillig, and the slithy toves
Did gyre and grimble in the wabe;
All mimsy were the borogoves,
And the mome raths outgrabe.

More recently, poets have written **free verse**, which does not necessarily use regular lines and meter, or rhyme. Nevertheless, even free verse tends to maintain an economy of form and density of meaning that distinguishes it from prose. Derek Walcott's Caribbean epic, *Omeros*, uses structured lines but not rhyme:

Ma Kilman had the oldest bar in the village.
Its gingerbread balcony had mustard gables
with green trim round the eaves, the paint
wrinkled with age.

(II, 1–3)

PROSE

Within the category of prose, a further broad literary distinction can be made between **fiction** and **non-fiction**, the former being an invented narrative and the latter an account of something that actually happened. When we read a **novel** we are reading fiction, and when we read the newspaper we are reading non-fiction. History (see below), biography, and autobiography are also examples of non-fiction, whereas mystery stories and fairytales, like novels, are fiction. The **essay** (from the French word *essayer*, meaning "to try") was invented in sixteenth-century France by Montaigne. It is an author's attempt to consider an issue in depth and from a particular **point of view**, that is, a means of focusing the reader in a particular direction. (The equivalent in a painting would be the use of perspective, which directs the viewer's eye to one or more specific points on the picture plane.)

When a work of literature is written in the **first person**, the point of view is that of a narrator (the *I*). A **third-person** viewpoint is narrated by an individual (*he*, *she*, or *it*); if the story is told by more than one narrator, the viewpoint is composed of *they*. In **epistolary** writing, a story unfolds and character is revealed through letters ("epistle," from the Latin word *epistola*, meaning "a written communication," is another term for a letter). And in **stream of consciousness** a story is told through the inner thoughts of the characters, often with no formal structure or external dialogue.

THEATER

Theater is a branch of literature in which the text is a **play** (either in prose or poetic form) performed on a stage before an audience. Unlike a novel, in which the setting of the action is described in words, a play relies on a **backdrop**—either a natural one if it is outdoors, or a painted and constructed **set**. It is also possible for a play to have no constructed set and a narrator might introduce the story and its characters, thus "setting the stage" verbally rather than visually. The formal structure of a play is **dramatic**—involving conflict and contrast—rather than being an extended narrative like a novel (although novels often have dramatic elements). Both plays and novels revolve around a **plot**, which is the unfolding of events.

Plays, like novels, convey a point of view and are driven by the nature, motivations, and behavior of the characters. Whereas novels are generally divided into chapters, plays are broken down into acts and scenes, with stage directions provided by the playwright. But in a play, the written text is interpreted for the audience through the **actors** and their **director**. The hero, or main character, is called the **protagonist**. In plays, as in other literary forms, there are certain standard genres and techniques. In **tragedy**, a hero falls because of some character flaw, whereas in **comedy** the outcome is usually a happy one, dialogue is generally humorous, and the tone lighthearted.

HISTORY

History writing, like oral history, reflects the need to organize, explain, and justify human decisions. Two great historians of ancient Greece were Herodotus (called the "Father of History") and Thucydides. Herodotus set out to preserve the past by writing about it and also to understand why the Greeks and foreigners (especially Persians) went to war against each other. Thucydides wrote the history of the Peloponnesian War (between Athens and Sparta) in the belief that it would be the greatest conflict yet played out on the world stage.

Historians use **primary sources** and **secondary sources** to construct a narrative of the "**facts**" as they perceive them. Primary sources consist of documentary evidence—actual records that have survived from the past—and also such things as photographs, household objects, and clothing. Secondary sources are accounts written after the event. Historians select their "facts" in order to present a thesis explaining the events they describe. But in any process of selecting "facts" the personal point of view of the historian comes into play. **Historiography** is the study of history and historians. It demonstrates that there is no such thing as "objective" history, since historians are affected by their own cultural context, which colors their interpretation.

History can be subdivided into political history, social history, biography, and even autobiography.

PHILOSOPHY

The Greek philosopher Aristotle said that all human beings by nature desire to know. Philosophy (literally "love of wisdom") deals with people's place in the world, the nature of reality and truth, and the meaning of life.

In contrast to science, philosophy is not primarily driven by a search for factual knowledge. Rather, it tends to examine in a methodical, logical way what is already known and experienced by any ordinary person. Logic is one of its key tools and some philosophical arguments can be expressed in a purely abstract logical form (using "formal logic"). More commonly, however, philosophical arguments are presented discursively.

In the Western tradition, key schools of philosophical thought include scholasticism, rationalism, empiricism, idealism, and materialism. Today, Western philosophy tends to be divided into two distinct, but loosely defined, approaches: Anglo-American or analytical philosophy models itself on mathematics and logic, and demands intellectual rigor. It also focuses on the meaning and use of language and words. Continental philosophy, on the other hand, covers a range of different theories and strives to systematize the world and human experience. Primary examples are phenomenology, existentialism, and structuralism.

Within any of the more broadly defined schools cited above, there are many specialist areas of interest: metaphysics (theories of reality); epistemology (theories of knowledge); ontology (theories of being); ethics (views of morality); aesthetics (the appreciation of beauty); philosophy of religion; and philosophy of science.

INTERDISCIPLINARY ASPECTS OF THE ARTS

All the expressive arts have an interdisciplinary character that is reflected in the similar terminologies denoting their form and content. Opera, for example, combines drama with music. It has a text (the **libretto**) and is performed by singers who act out the parts as they sing the words.

Dance is an art form that combines music, movement, thematic content, lighting, and staging. The notation of dance is called **choreography**, which records the composition and sequence of steps and movements. In dance, the human form moves through space, usually accompanied by music. The main genres of dance are **folk dance**, **ballet**, and **modern dance**. Folk dance, like oral literature and music, develops over time, and has a specific cultural character. Ballet is more formal, notated, and usually tells a story. Modern dance refers to developments from the early twentieth century to the present, and does not adhere to the formal rules of ballet. There is more room for innovative choreography, costumes, sets, and lighting in modern dance than in traditional dance. In all dance genres, however, the formal elements that apply to music and art are also used: lines, shapes, colors, lightness and darkness, patterns, balance, rhythm, and harmony.

Perhaps today's most complex interdisciplinary art form is **film**, which has a technological as well as an aesthetic aspect. As with literature, film can be used to record "reality" in which case it is known as **documentary** and has a primarily historical character. Nevertheless, it must be recognized that, as with history, no documentary can be considered entirely objective because the viewpoint of the creators influences the impression made by such a film. Among major examples of documentary film in the twentieth century are **newsreels**, shown in movie theaters from the 1930s through the 1970s.

In the realm of fiction, film encompasses numerous genres, such as action, adventure, drama, fantasy, animation, science fiction, romance, and crime. Even more so than theater and dance, the production of a film requires the participation of many different people, from lighting and sound technicians to actors, directors, editors, and producers. The text of a film is called a **screenplay** and as in dance and theater, the director tells the actors how to interpret the text and how to move and gesture. The producer (as in dance and theater) raises the money to produce the work. While many screenplays are original (specifically written for the screen), it is often the case—as with the **trilogy** (three-part work) *The Lord of the Rings*—that a well-known novel is turned into a screenplay, and that people from several different countries participate in its production. This kind of participation has contributed to the globalization of the film industry.

The modern world has witnessed increased globalization, and the proliferation of rapid means of communication has expanded the potential for interdisciplinary creativity. We see this, for example, in the sciences, when clinical results are shared via the Internet. Works of art are accessible as museums around the globe digitize their collections and put them on the Web. Films and music are easily downloaded. The easy accessibility of the Web and the speed of globalization have ushered in a new era for the humanities. The Internet itself can be seen as a cross between the written text and oral history. For, on the one hand, computers can store enormous amounts of material and preserve it for future generations. On the other hand, however, computers facilitate the constant updating of material in a way that echoes oral tradition. Whereas oral "texts" change over time, written texts change only in the ways they are interpreted.

1 Prehistory

"In early times,
When Ymir lived,
Was sand, nor sea,
. . . .
One chaos all,
And nowhere grass.
. . . .
Under the armpit grew,
. . . .
A girl and a boy together;
Foot with foot began,
Of that wise Jötun,
A six-headed son.
. . . .
Of Ymir's flesh
Was earth created,
Of his blood the sea,
Of his bones, the hills,
Of his hair trees and plants,
Of his skull the heavens,
And of his brows
The gentle powers
Formed Midgard for the sons of men;
But of his brain
The heavy clouds are
All created."

(NORSE CREATION MYTH)

A humanities text deals with human achievements. These achievements, which are the components of human culture, include the creative arts, inventions that change the course of history, significant world events, scientific discoveries, religious beliefs and myths, and philosophical ideas. In this text, we explore these expressions of human creativity mainly in Western cultures—along with a few comparative glimpses beyond the West—in the context of their time and place in history.

Most of us are curious about where and how we and the universe began. We also wonder about our place in the world and the world's place in the universe. For millennia human cultures have constructed creation myths to answer such questions. These myths vary from culture to culture, but most attribute the idea of making the world to the creative mind of a god. According to many such myths, the world begins like a work of art—with the combination of an idea, a will, and unformed material, which is given shape and life.

The quotation at the beginning of this chapter is from an ancient Norse account of how the world began. The Nordic countries of western Europe (modern Norway, Sweden, Denmark, and, from the ninth century, Iceland) spend much of the year in darkness and snow, and their climate influenced their creation myths. Norse people conceived of an original state of primordial chaos (an abyss) and a universe created through the will of a frozen giant, Ymir, who emerged from blocks of ice.

As soon as he was formed, Ymir noticed that he was hungry. He came upon a cow, who was also made from ice, and drank her milk. The cow then licked salt from an ice block and gave birth to Buri, the Creator. Ymir fell asleep, bearing two children from his armpits and a six-headed giant from his feet. Ymir's body became the source of earth, oceans, and sky, and his children multiplied. They created generations of men and women, giants (the Jötun), and gods. The Jötun wage eternal war against the gods (offspring of Buri) and the battle continues until the final clash—Ragnarök—at the end of time. Meanwhile, the Norse universe is structured according to levels of importance, with humans inhabiting Midgard (Middle Earth).

Key Topics

Human Origins: Myth and Science

- Creation stories and scientific discoveries

Reconstructing Prehistory

- Remains and descent
- Increasing social complexity
- Belief in an afterlife

What Makes Us Human

- Symbolic thinking
- Use of tools
- Story telling
- Body decoration
- Burial practices
- Creative art, music, etc.

TIMELINE	EARLIEST ORIGINS	PALEOLITHIC ERA c. 1,500,000–c. 10,000/8000	MESOLITHIC ERA c. 10,000/8000–c. 6000/4000	NEOLITHIC ERA c. 6000/4000–c. 1500
HISTORY AND CULTURE	Early hominids, 7–1 million *Homo habilis*, c. 2 million: stone tools *Homo erectus*, c. 1.8 million Use of fire, c. 1 million–500,000 Archaic *Homo sapiens*, c. 500,000 Neanderthals and Cro-Magnons, c. 100,000 Food gathering, fishing	Upper Paleolithic from c. 45,000 Hunting and gathering	Transition from hunting and gathering to settled communities	Agricultural communities with wealth-based class divisions Domestication of animals Horse-drawn plows Trade with Near East
RELIGION AND MYTH 	Ritual burial practices, c. 120,000–80,000 Ritual ornaments	Ritual burial practices Gravegoods Ritual dancing Shamanism	Ritual burial practices	Belief systems Ritual practices Ancestor worship Burial mounds
ART 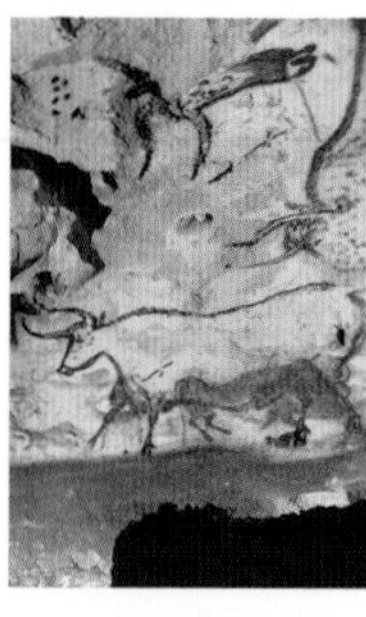	Body decoration: Blombos Cave, c. 90,000	Chauvet cave paintings, c. 30,000–24,000 *Venus of Willendorf*, c. 25,000 Lascaux cave paintings, c. 14,000	Pottery	Pottery Jewelry
ARCHITECTURE 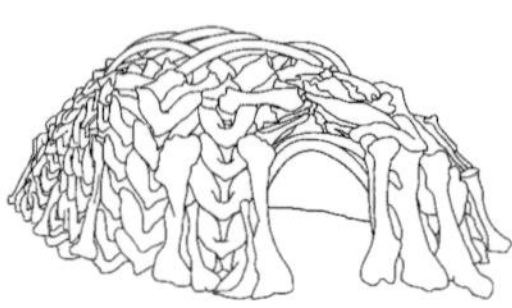		Mammoth-bone house, c. 16,000	Settlements	Villages First cities: Jericho, Çatal Hüyük, Ban Po Monumental stone architecture: Stonehenge, c. 1800–1500 Post-and-lintel construction
MUSIC	Bone whistles and drums			Music in rituals

Although creation myths, such as this one, are devised as a way of explaining the origin of the world, they do not provide scientific information about the birth and evolution of the human race or its cultural developments. The first evidence of the use of language and the creative arts appears during the Upper Paleolithic period (the later Old Stone Age), roughly 45,000 to 10,000/8000 B.C., when people used stone tools. At some point, people told stories that evolved into literature. Music and dance accompanied religious rituals as they often do today. The earliest evidence of painting and sculpture dates to the later Old Stone Age.

Gradually, settled communities formed, with social structures based on rank. As the Paleolithic period evolved into the Middle Stone Age (Mesolithic, c. 8000–6000 B.C.) and New Stone Age (Neolithic, c. 6000–1500 B.C.) people learned to farm and, eventually, to build—first temporary shelters and, later, structures made of permanent material, such as stone. We should note, however, that these ancient dates are flexible and are continually being revised by scholars. Just as biological organisms and the elements of physics are found to be smaller and smaller as research progresses, so human history seems to reach farther and farther back in time with each new discovery. Thus, absolute dates and time periods need to be reconsidered whenever new information becomes available (see Box).

The Dating System Used in this Text

Throughout the world, and even in the West, there are different systems for dating history. This text uses the traditional Western system in which B.C. stands for Before Christ, and A.D. (after the Latin words *anno domini*, meaning "in the year of our Lord") stands for After Christ. Although the exact date of Christ's birth is not certain, the term A.D. 1 is conventionally used to mean the first year after his birth and 1 B.C. to indicate the first year before his birth. There is thus no year 0. The traditional *c.*, meaning *circa* (the Latin word for "about" or "around"), is used here for approximate dates.

Readers of other texts may find that C.E. (for Common Era) or B.C.E. (for Before the Common Era) replace A.D. and B.C., respectively. While such notations may seem to be more religiously neutral, they are also less precise. In this book the more historical flavor of B.C. and A.D. has been chosen over the vaguer and chronologically ambiguous B.C.E. and C.E.

HUMAN ORIGINS: FROM MYTH TO SCIENCE

The actual origin of the human race is a vexing issue, about which there are as many myths as there are cultures, a number of scientific hypotheses, and a considerable amount of hard evidence. But, important as science is, we should not lose sight of the poetic creativity reflected in myth-making. The Norse myth is only one of many attempts to explain the mystery of creation. In our search for origins, whether it assumes a poetic or a scientific form, we differ from other living species. Both poetry and science are uniquely human expressions.

CREATION STORIES

Once the universe is created, most myths consider how people came into existence. The ancient Sumerians of southern Mesopotamia (in modern Iraq), for example, believed that people were created because the gods were aging and needed servants. The Akkadians, who lived in northern Mesopotamia, thought that the first humans were created from the blood of rebel gods. According to the Book of Genesis in the Hebrew Bible, God created the primal couple, Adam and Eve, in his own image. He made Adam from dust in the earth and Eve from one of Adam's ribs.

One Greek myth says that Prometheus formed humanity from clay. In a Native American Mohawk myth the tribe's first man was made of baked clay, hence the red color of his skin. The Hindus of India believe that people originated from the thigh of a giant, and the Maya of Mesoamerica understood the human race to have been created when the gods united their thoughts. In Norse mythology, Odin, the god of wisdom, made the first humans and gave them poetry and the secret of writing. And so on. These and other accounts of the first humans have certain elements in common. In every case, gods precede people; gods are more powerful than people; and gods have the power to create and destroy the human race.

DARWIN AND THE THEORY OF EVOLUTION

Although creation myths are the expression of a creative cultural imagination and a feature of all human societies, they are not scientific. In western Europe, it was not until the eighteenth century that naturalists (scientists and philosophers who study nature) observed similarities between certain species that suggested they were somehow linked. The naturalists then began to question the account of creation given in the Bible, in which God creates each species separately. At first, the naturalists lacked a system that would allow them to organize their knowledge according to the vast timeframe of natural history. They began by compiling encyclopedias and classifying plants and animals, and by the nineteenth century theories of the evolution of species emerged.

Modern evolutionary theory is attributed to the research of two Britons, Charles Darwin (1809–1882) and Alfred Russel Wallace (1823–1913). Both had traveled widely and observed animals in many different habitats—Wallace in the islands of Southeast Asia, and Darwin in the Galapagos Islands, as well as in other parts of the world. In 1858, Wallace published a paper arguing that humans and primates were descended from a common ancestor, and in the same year he co-authored a paper with Darwin explaining the principle of evolution. In 1859, Darwin published his famous *On the Origin of Species by Means of Natural Selection*, which was based on observations made while sailing around the world from 1831 to 1836 aboard the ship *Beagle*.

Darwin argued that each species—including humans—evolved gradually over millennia and survived according to its ability to adapt to the environment. Those that could not adapt died out. This process of **natural selection** is popularly known as the "survival of the fittest," which actually misrepresents Darwin's findings. His view of human evolution contradicted two major aspects of the Bible. One was the notion that life was created with a moral purpose, and the other that species were individually conceived and placed on earth separately rather than evolving from one another.

In 1871, Darwin published *The Descent of Man*, in which he claimed that humans were descended from lower species over a period of millions of years. This led to a new body of research aimed at locating the "missing link"—that is, the species that lies between apes and humans. Today's scientists are continuing that search, which highlights important differences between science and myth. Science continues to build information from around the globe and is open-ended, but myths originate from particular cultures and are specific to those cultures.

THE NATURE OF PREHISTORY

The earliest, and longest, era of history is referred to as **prehistory**, most of which will remain forever dimmed by the mists of time. However, because it is in our nature to search for origins, most intelligent people are curious about their personal past. This curiosity usually extends to the history of one's family, one's culture, and even one's species. Knowing how little we remember about what we did and thought only yesterday, let alone about our early childhood, we realize that information about what took place hundreds of thousands of years ago is likely to be scanty indeed.

In this text, prehistory refers to any time before the invention of writing. But prehistory is not a specific date that can be applied consistently throughout the world. Different cultures develop writing systems at different periods of their history. A civilization such as ancient Egypt in 2500 B.C. (see Chapter 3), for example, was literate long before western Europe, which had no writing until it was conquered by the Romans in the first century B.C. And today, there are regions of the world where oral traditions persist and there are no established writing systems.

Without written records, scholars have to decipher and reconstruct prehistory from physical remains (see Box). The earliest are primarily bones, tools, and weapons. From later prehistoric periods there is evidence of burials, and, as we approach the Upper Paleolithic era, we encounter early examples of the creative arts. There are fragmentary remains of rudimentary musical instruments, decorative ornaments, small-scale statues, wall paintings, and later still, of buildings (see Box, p. 5, top).

Scholars also resort to hypotheses when shaping their theories. These hypotheses often depend on the ability to make connections between the past and modern preliterate cultures, although parallels between prehistoric cultures and contemporary societies must be drawn with caution. Nevertheless, they reflect both the continuum of human development and the fact that people have produced similar forms and ideas in very different times and places.

The term Stone Age may sound ancient, but in fact it followed millions of years during which hominids (near- or proto-humans) evolved into modern humans. This process is generally thought to have begun around 5 million years ago when pre-humans roamed East and north central Africa. Their skulls were the size of an ape's and they lived in small groups, sustaining themselves mainly by gathering edible plants and grains (see Box, p. 5, bottom).

The Study of Human Prehistory

There are many categories of scientists who investigate prehistory by relying on physical, rather than written, evidence. Among these are geologists, who study the minerals of a particular region, which can provide evidence of materials available for tools, weapons, and other objects. Paleontologists analyze fossil remains, anthropologists analyze society and culture, and paleoanthropologists analyze all three. Archaeologists study artifacts such as pots, jewelry, furniture, dwellings, and weapons. Ethnographers deal with contemporary preliterate societies and sometimes make inferences from them about prehistoric cultures that no longer exist. Biologists study skeletons, and forensic scientists attempt to discover causes of death. Geneticists collect the DNA of prehistoric bones, which reinforces some traditional theories and challenges others. Additional evidence comes from the remains of human garbage (garbology), footprints, and even feces (which can offer clues to diet). Art historians study the evolution of style and artistic techniques.

Dating Prehistory

Physical evidence is dated according to a number of systems. Geologists use stratigraphy to measure layers of earth and date objects according to the layer in which they are found. Dendrochronologists determine age from tree rings, which is most useful in regions with large areas of forestation. In seriation, dating is according to stylistic changes, which evolve over time, in similar types of artifacts. Radiocarbon dating, although its accuracy is questioned, is based on the measure of carbon-14 in an organic substance. As organisms decay, the carbon-14 in them begins to decay, making it possible to determine the age of the substance. Thermoluminescence dates objects by measuring radioactive changes as electrons shift their normal positions in relation to the atom. This system is particularly accurate when used on burned materials such as flint, stones, and fired pottery.

In July 2002, in Chad in north central Africa, a skull was discovered with a small brain comparable in size to a chimpanzee brain, and human and ape-like features. Nicknamed Toumai, meaning "Hope of Life" in the local language, this find altered the prevailing view of human development, particularly the point at which the first humans branched off from the line of chimpanzees. Thought to be 6 or 7 million years old, Toumai is considered by some scientists to be the oldest known hominid, although others believe Toumai may not even be a hominid. Toumai has been given the impressive scientific designation *Sahelanthropus tchadensis,* roughly meaning "the man from Chad, in the Sahara."

An early fossil was unearthed in 1974 at Hadar, in Ethiopia. The scientific name of the fossil's genus is *Australopithecus* (which existed around 5 to around 3 million years ago), but the species, *afarensis,* is named for the local Afar culture. Dr. Donald Johanson, whose team discovered the fossil, named it Lucy after the refrain of the Beatles' song "Lucy in the Sky with Diamonds," which he and his co-workers were playing as they celebrated the find. What remains of Lucy are the skull, thighbone, and lower jaw. Although it is not known if Lucy was male or female, the bones belonged to a young adult, who could walk upright (**bipedal**). "Lucy" is only one of hundreds of bipedal *Australopithecus afarensis* fossils that have been found in East and southern Africa. Today Lucy resides in an Arizona laboratory.

Major Periods of Human Evolution

c. 5 million B.C.	evidence of pre-human fossil fragments in Africa
c. 5–3 million B.C.	*Australopithecus*
c. 2 million to c. 1.6 million B.C.	*Homo habilis*
c. 1.8 million to c. 500,000 B.C.	*Homo erectus*
c. 500,000 B.C.	Archaic *Homo sapiens*
c. 130,000–80,000 B.C.	*Homo sapiens*
c. 100,000–33,000 B.C.	Neanderthal Man
c. 40,000 B.C. to the present	*Homo sapiens sapiens*

Homo habilis ("handy man") developed in East and southern Africa some 2 million years ago. *Homo* (meaning "man") is the genus that comprises the human species, and *habilis* designates the species that converted stones into rudimentary weapons and tools for chopping and cutting, which increased its ability to control the environment. At first it was thought that *Homo habilis,* who lived mainly by hunting and gathering, completely supplanted the hominids. But, in 1959, two British researchers, Louis and Mary Leakey, were excavating fossils in Tanzania and found that different stages of hominids could coexist. They discovered many fossils, including one they named Zinj (short for *Zinjanthropus boisei*), whose lifespan overlapped that of *Homo habilis,* but who was not yet a member of the genus *Homo.* All that survived of Zinj, who was around 1,750,000 years old, was a skull, which had to be reconstructed from many small fragments.

Homo erectus ("upright man") evolved in Africa after *Homo habilis* and is thought to have migrated into the Middle East and Asia. Evidence of this migration is suggested by the discovery in Asia in 1891 of a skull, molar, and thighbone, known as "Java Man." In 1929, a Chinese archaeologist discovered the 500,000-year-old skullcap of a *Homo erectus.* Called "Peking Man," this find came from a cave near modern Beijing. Later, more fossils of the same type were discovered around Beijing as well as in Java. In addition, a nearly complete skeleton of *Homo erectus* was found in Kenya, in Africa, in 1984.

Homo erectus, as the term indicates, walked upright, although bipedal motion is actually thought to have started by the time of *Australopithecus afarensis* at least 4.5 million years ago (see Box, p. 6). Upright posture changed the relationship of individuals to the environment, making them seem taller and giving them a wider view of their surroundings. It also freed their hands for more advanced tool-making, especially axes and chisels, and better control of their weapons.

Some time between 1 million and 500,000 years ago, *Homo erectus* had marked another monumental step in human history—the use and control of fire. With fire, people could regulate heat and cook food. Fire reduced the amount of time it took to eat, because cooked food requires less chewing.

Defining Moment

Bipedalism

In the vast time span of human prehistory, there are several landmark steps that advanced the evolution of our species. Among them are the acquisition of language, the making of tools, the control of fire, and the creation of works of art. Preceding these steps, however, was the development of bipedalism—walking on two feet—which evolved over millions of years and became the defining characteristic of *Homo erectus*.

Paleoanthropologists have offered several explanations for why our ancestors adopted the consistently upright gait that differentiates us from other mammals. The prevailing view today is that bipedalism existed even earlier than *Australopithecus afarensis*, but that the pelvis, feet, and knee joints of that group were particularly suited to walking upright. Most scholars today believe that bipedalism evolved in mixed forest and open areas. These are the places where the earliest hominid fossils have been found.

Bipedalism had some important benefits. In open areas, it enabled early hominids to walk around and find food. It also allowed them to carry objects and walk at the same time, a more energy-efficient form of locomotion. Walking upright also provided better visibility and a broader sense of the environment. Bipedalism led our ancestors to use their hands in a number of new ways, including reaching for fruits on trees and carrying food back to other members of the group. Scholars have argued that females could thus leave foraging to the males and lead a more settled existence. This, in turn, allowed mothers to care more effectively for offspring, which improved their chances of survival.

Another development that followed bipedalism was the evolution of the precise opposing thumb, as compared with primates. This facilitated making tools as well as gathering food, constructing shelters, and creating works of art (figure **1.1**). The surviving evidence of art comes late in the Paleolithic period. For whatever reason prehistoric people created art, it surely required a combination of advanced symbolic thinking, an upright stance, and a developed thumb to work opposite the other four fingers.

Critical Question What do you think is the most important result of bipedalism, and why? What are some of its consequences?

1.1 *Scene of the Dead Man*, Shaft of the Dead Man, Lascaux caves, Dordogne, France, *c.* 14,000 B.C. Paint on limestone.

This developmental step, like inventions of modern household appliances, meant people had more free time to perfect other skills.

Somewhat over 500,000 years ago, an archaic form of *Homo sapiens* ("wise man") evolved in Africa and western Asia, seeming to support the view that human development began in Africa. To date, the earliest evidence for modern human behavior also comes from Africa, from preliminary finds in Blombos Cave, which is located to the east of Still Bay in a cliff overlooking the Indian Ocean. As early as around 90,000 years ago, the inhabitants of Blombos Cave, who were *Homo sapiens*, gathered seafood, ranging from shellfish to dolphins, as well as land animals. This is suggested by the oldest known bone tools with points made by a technique called pressure flaking, which was not used in Europe until 70,000 years later. So far, therefore, the Blombos people are the world's earliest known fishing community.

There is also evidence that the Blombos Cave people used ocher pigment, drilled into a fine powder, for body decoration. In addition, their organization of interior space suggests modern human behavior. The cave appears to have had a separate area for a hearth, and another for making stone and bone tools.

Overlapping the Blombos Cave group were the species of *Homo sapiens* known as Neanderthal Man and Cro-Magnon Man. The former, named for the Neander valley (in modern Germany), has so far been found in Europe and western Asia; Cro-Magnon Man was discovered in southern France. Both groups wore animal skins, but Cro-Magnons can be differentiated because they sewed clothing with bone needles and had more advanced tools than Neanderthals.

Scientists used to think that Neanderthal Man died out with the arrival of the Cro-Magnons, but in 1998 this notion was challenged by the discovery of the skeleton of a four-year-old child in the Lapedo valley, in Portugal. The child's anatomical make-up shows evidence of being a "hybrid" between Neanderthals and modern humans. The fact that the child was buried in animal skins painted with red ocher suggests ritual burial practices.

Theorists differ on the origin and lineage of *Homo sapiens*. Most agree that *Homo erectus* originated in Africa, and traveled from there to Asia and Europe. Some argue that *Homo sapiens* supplanted earlier groups in each of these areas. Others believe that the shift from *Homo erectus* to *Homo sapiens* took place in Africa alone and that it was only the latter who migrated.

In 2003, a discovery in Ethiopia provided a new link between Neanderthals and modern humans. Dated to around 160,000 years ago, this find consisted of three fossilized adult skulls and one skull belonging to a child. These skulls are longer than Neanderthal skulls, and the brain area is larger. This marked the earliest fossil evidence of modern humans and reinforced the view that *Homo sapiens* originated in Africa.

Our own species is called by some scholars *Homo sapiens sapiens* ("wise wise man") and *Homo sapiens* by others. This species appeared some 40,000 years ago and had a brain similar to ours. *Homo sapiens sapiens* traveled from Asia, through Europe, to the Americas and Australia. By 15,000 B.C., all of the earth's landmasses, except Antarctica, were inhabited by human groups (see Box).

Society and Culture

Important Developmental Steps in Early Human History

4.5 million years ago	beginning of upright gait (bipedalism)
2 million years ago	erect posture improved; brain development; beginning of stone tools
from 500,000 B.C.	rapid growth of the human brain
from 130,000 B.C.	*Homo sapiens* evolves; early language develops
from 40,000 B.C.	modern humans, with modern brains and speech function; tools assembled from different materials
from 25,000 B.C.	beginning of cave painting and small-scale sculpture
from 10,000 B.C.	bow and arrow invented; reindeer and dog domesticated
from 8000 to 4000 B.C.	sheep and goats domesticated, beginning of pottery production and farming
from 3000 B.C.	writing systems; metallurgy

WHAT MAKES US HUMAN

Certain important features distinguish the human species from other forms of life. Most of these features are aspects of symbolic thinking—the ability to think abstractly and to imagine things that are not physically present. It includes constructing language and theories, inventing new technology, telling stories, creating myths, and making art. All these activities are enriched by the use of **metaphor** (a comparison in which one thing stands for another). When we say, for example, that "the world is our oyster," we don't actually mean that the world is an oyster. We mean that we are ensconced in a comfortable space that we enjoy and can control. As a result, the saying suggests, we are bound for success and happiness. The metaphor thus creates an image that has a greater visual impact than would be conveyed by a literal description of the same idea.

SYMBOLIC THINKING

Beginning with *Homo habilis*, people made simple tools and weapons, whose uses we can usually identify. It is more difficult, however, to know what, if any, symbolic (or metaphorical) meaning may have been attached to such objects. But Stone Age ritual, such as the child burial found in Portugal, indicates symbolic thinking.

Most scholars believe that prehistoric people told stories, transmitting cultural myths orally. Thus they had a sense of **narrative sequence** (in which the events of a story follow chronologically), as well as of memory and time. Human handprints outlined with color on cave walls in different areas of the world—including western Europe, Africa, and South America—almost certainly had a ritual purpose. The prints also form repetitive, patterned images that suggest an awareness of time. Some cave paintings appear to illustrate narratives. In Spain, for example, paintings in Valtorta Gorge show humans moving from left to right and then attacking a herd of animals approaching from the opposite direction.

Another type of symbolic thinking is found in religious practices. One example is the formal burial, in which the body faces east, as if it will be reborn like the sun that rises each day. Food, tools, animal bones, and personal belongings that scholars believe were intended for the afterlife have also been found in burials. Red ocher pigment, such as that used on the child discovered in Portugal, was often sprinkled on corpses and is thought to represent blood. Since blood is a sign of life, the presence of red coloring has been interpreted as evidence of a belief in life after death.

CREATIVE ARTS

Among the most distinctly human achievements are the creative arts. Prehistoric paintings and sculptures such as those found in Europe (map **1.1**, p. 8) are sophisticated enough to

Map 1.1 Prehistoric art in Europe.

suggest that producing imagery was important, requiring both natural talent and training.

For those of us who view prehistory from a distance of thousands of years, works of art offer clues to the concerns and practices of our distant ancestors. Physical evidence of music was limited to rudimentary bone whistles and drums until the discovery of a 40,000-year-old Neanderthal bone flute. Human footprints arranged in circles preserved on cave floors have been read by some scholars as an indication of circle dancing.

The first known sculptures are Upper (Late) Paleolithic and date from around 30,000 B.C. Most represent animals or human females. The latter are usually interpreted as fertility figures, the best known being the so-called *Venus of Willendorf* (figure **1.2**). Discovered in 1908, she was named after the Roman goddess of love and beauty because the exaggeration of the breasts and pelvis suggests that the statue was associated with fertility. Carved from limestone, the *Venus* is small enough to hold in the palm of one's hand. Her small scale is typical of Paleolithic sculptures, making her easily portable and thus practical in a nomadic culture.

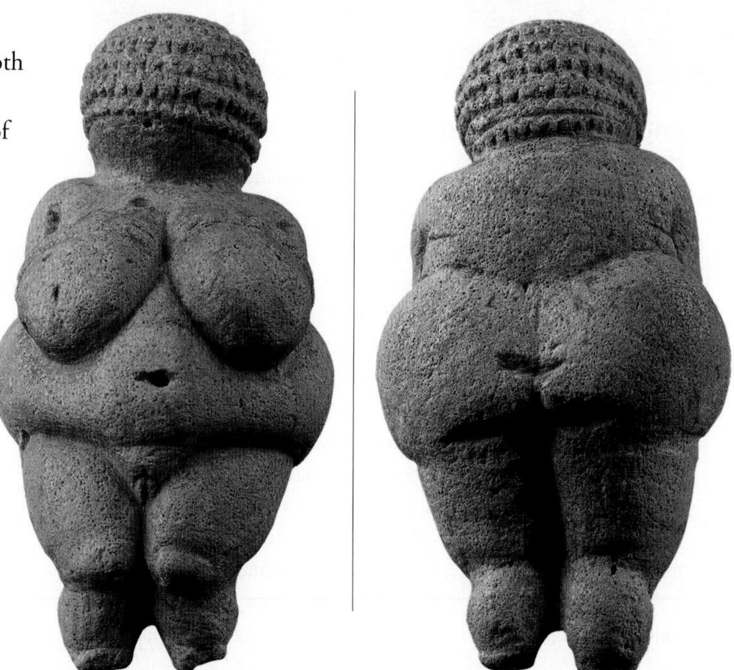

1.2 *Venus of Willendorf* (front and back), *c.* 25,000 B.C. Limestone, 4⅜ in. (11.5 cm) high. Naturhistorisches Museum, Vienna.
By minimizing the arms, eliminating the neck, and covering the face, the artist compresses space and conveys a sense of maternal power. The emphasis on the breasts and pelvis has led some scholars to interpret the figure as a Great Goddess. The elegant rhythms created by the curved contours and bulbous circular forms reveal a high level of artistry.

In 2000, a cave with early Upper Paleolithic incised images of animals and human females was discovered. Located south of the Dordogne region of France, the cave contained mammoths, bison, deer, horses, a rhinoceros, and a couple of geese. Figure **1.3** shows one of the human females, whose outline emphasizes her bulk and clearly delineates her breast.

The later paintings found in the caves at Lascaux, in the Dordogne itself, date to around 14,000 B.C. (figure **1.4**). They depict mainly animals—bison, deer, boar, wolves, horses, and mammoths. Occasional humans at Lascaux are represented as rudimentary stick figures, whereas the animals are **naturalistic**—that is, they resemble the appearance of the actual animals. The paintings are located hundreds of feet inside the caves, where it is thought that they might have been part of a hunting ritual. Since people did not inhabit cave interiors, it is unlikely that the paintings were purely for decoration.

Although cave paintings have been interpreted from many points of view, the most common reading is that they had a ritual, or ceremonial, meaning. The images are believed by some scholars to have been made to help hunters capture animals needed for survival. Likewise, the naturalism of the animals adds to the impression that the actual animal is captured by the image. In some places, one animal is painted over another, suggesting that once the image was fixed to the wall it had served its function. On the other hand, some animals that were hunted are not represented, which undermines the theory that the very act of painting an animal was a symbolic capture.

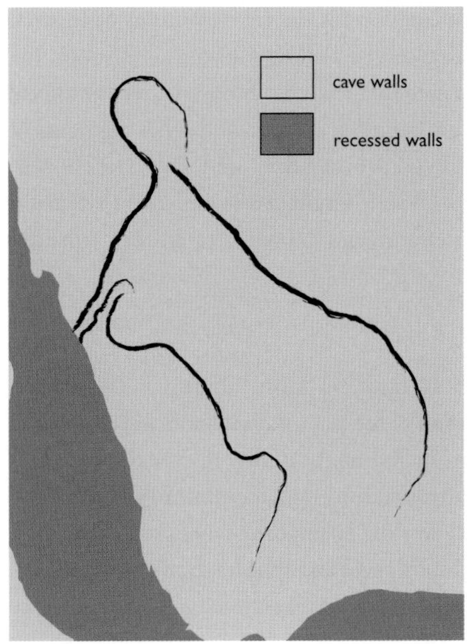

1.3 Diagram of an engraving of a human female, Cussac Cave, France, 28,000–22,000 B.C.

1.4 Hall of Running Bulls, Lascaux caves, *c.* 14,000 B.C. Paint on limestone.

Whatever the explanation for the cave paintings of western Europe, they probably served a ritual purpose. Prehistoric life was not as compartmentalized as modern, technological society. As a result, art, religion, politics, and other segments of culture were more integrated than they are today. The concept of "art for art's sake," which originated in nineteenth-century France, was almost certainly not known in prehistoric cultures.

SHAMANISM

An important religious figure in most hunting and gathering societies is the **shaman**. This is an individual believed to have supernatural powers, including the ability to cure disease, foretell the future, control nature, and communicate with the animal and spiritual worlds. Shamans are associated with fire, which burns natural substances and thus has power over nature. The shaman uses fire in rituals and is believed to have an intense inner heat. This, along with trance-like states and dreams, assists in transporting the shaman to a spiritual plane of existence.

Scholars have noted that although animals and humans do not physically resemble each other, the blood of an animal is virtually indistinguishable from that of a human. For this reason, it is thought that early hunters, who depended on animals for survival, developed a kind of identification with their prey. This was expressed visually in images of the shaman. There are a number of cave paintings with figures that combine human and animal characteristics, and these are interpreted as shamans.

At Chauvet in the south of France, for example, in a recently discovered cave dated by carbon-14 to around 30,000 B.C., explorers found a composite figure with the head and upper body of a bison and the lower body and upright posture of a human (figure **1.5**). In the absence of a Paleolithic writing system, it is difficult to know the exact meaning of such images. They do, however, suggest the transformations of the shaman and the use of animal masks and animal skins in rituals (see Box, p. 13).

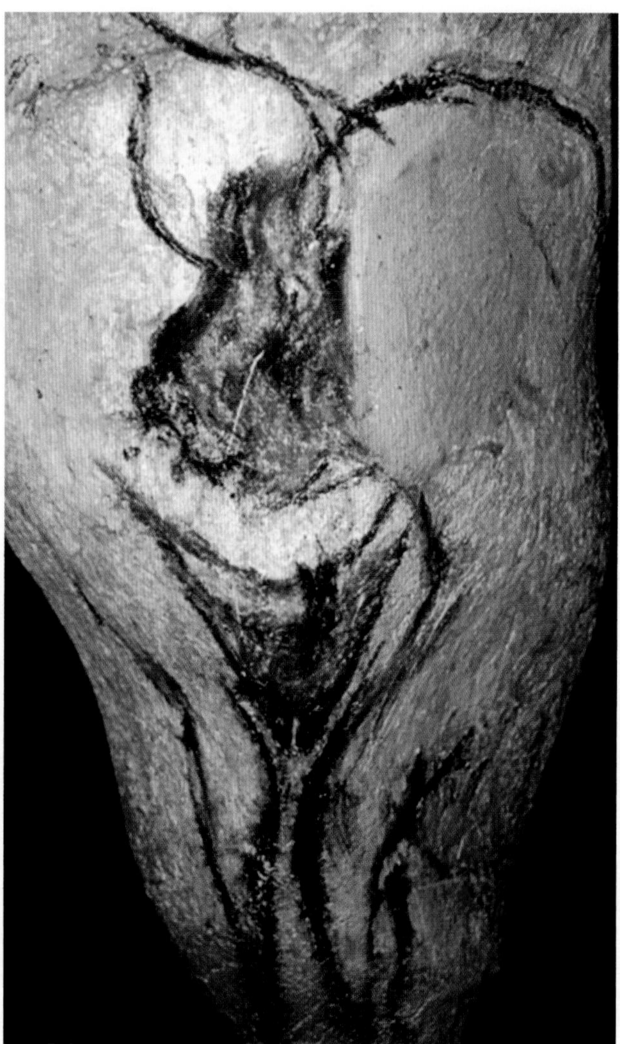

1.5 *Bison-man*, Chauvet cave, Chauvet, France, *c.* 24,000 B.C. Charcoal on a vertical section of rock.
This figure, like the Lascaux animals, is massive and naturalistically portrayed. The merger of human and animal forms reflects the transitional state of the shaman, who changes his shape and navigates between different worlds.

THE UPPER (LATE) PALEOLITHIC ERA IN WESTERN EUROPE: *c.* 45,000–*c.* 10,000/8000 B.C.

We now turn to the three main Stone Age periods in western Europe. By the Upper Paleolithic era, *Homo sapiens sapiens* (also called *Homo sapiens*) had been established on the continent. The economy and survival of this group depended on hunting and gathering. They were constantly on the move, following the seasonal migrations of animals they hunted for food. Among these were bison, deer, horses, and the now-extinct mammoth. There appears to have been a gender-based division of labor; men became hunters, and women gathered grains and plants and were guardians of the home.

The hunters and gatherers built temporary structures, such as tents, using wood, bone, and animal skins, or they found shelter at entrances to caves. In addition, they constructed more elaborate houses made of mammoth bones and skulls. Some structures dating from *c.* 16,000 B.C. have been discovered in eastern Europe and were arranged in groups of as many as ten. The mammoth bones interlocked to form walls and a roof, with large tusks creating an entrance arch. It is likely that animal hides were attached to the structure for warmth and protection. Generally, Upper Paleolithic houses had a hearth in a large central room, or several fires if additional rooms warranted them. Color found on the fragmentary remains of houses suggests that living quarters may have been decorated. The structure diagrammed in figure **1.6**, however, shows no sign of human habitation and probably served a ceremonial rather than a domestic function.

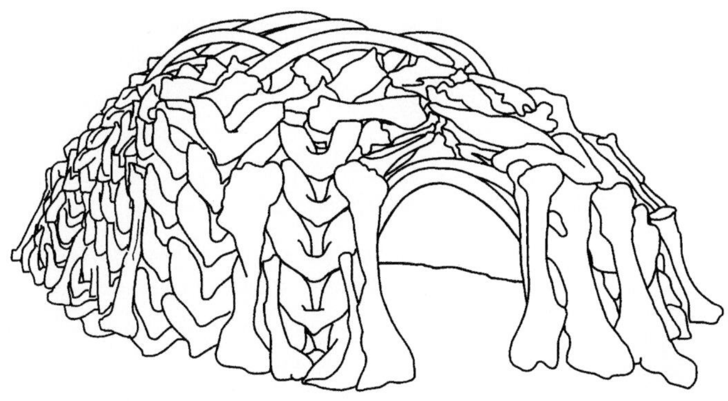

1.6 Diagram of reconstructed mammoth-bone house from Mezhirich, Ukraine, *c.* 16,000 B.C.

MESOLITHIC TO NEOLITHIC IN WESTERN EUROPE: *c.* 10,000/8000–6000/4000 B.C.

The Mesolithic period evolved in western Europe between 10,000 and 8000 B.C. With the rapid warming of the climate, glaciers receded and sea levels rose. The human population increased and migrated into northern Europe. As forests replaced the bleak plains of the Paleolithic landscape, animal populations shifted and hunters found their food supply greatly reduced. They survived by settling in groups and finding new kinds of sustenance. They wove plant fibers for fishing baskets and began to make pottery. There is evidence of early settled societies, especially along the Danube River, and of boatbuilding in the north of Europe.

The first formal human cemeteries date from the latter part of the Mesolithic period. Decorative objects, such as carved animal teeth, were found buried with the dead. This attention to burial reflects increasing social complexity, with class divisions based on wealth, as well as the idea that such objects might be needed in an afterlife. Interesting among Mesolithic developments are elaborate dog cemeteries, which suggest that dogs were valued, possibly because they could be trained to assist hunters and perform other useful tasks. The art of this period, however, is of less interest than Paleolithic and Neolithic works.

THE NEOLITHIC ERA: *c.* 6000/4000–*c.* 1500 B.C.

With the consolidation of farming communities and their expansion into settled villages, the Neolithic period began. People cultivated local staples such as grains and cereals, and used oxen to pull their plows. Other animals—cows, pigs, sheep, and goats—were domesticated and bred for food. In addition, livestock and goods were apparently imported from the Near East. Weaving and pottery became more sophisticated and metal-working developed. The study of Neolithic villages around the world has shown evidence of ancestor worship, a preoccupation with fertility, ritual practices, belief systems, and works of art and architecture.

People who are constantly on the move do not build large-scale stone monuments. But with the evolution of agriculture, settled communities developed in Europe, following a similar pattern of settlement found throughout the world. In Jericho, in the Jordan valley, a Neolithic city dating to around 8000 B.C. was surrounded by massive stone walls and a stone tower 30 feet (9 m) high. Some 2500 years later, at Çatal Hüyük (in modern Turkey), a Neolithic city extended over 30 acres (12 ha) of land. In China, at Ban Po, near modern Xi'an, one of the best-preserved Neolithic settlements dates to around 6000 B.C. It consisted of a large central building with a hearth and smaller buildings, which were surrounded by a moat. The inhabitants of Ban Po produced pottery and burial urns, and cultivated grains.

By around 4500 B.C., copper tools were used in Europe and copper ornaments provided personal objects of decoration. The practice of self-adornment suggests the presence of status- and wealth-based class divisions, as well as the ritual use of ornamentation. A copper pot of around 4000 B.C. from the region of modern Bulgaria (figure **1.7**) is partly polished and marked with sharp incised lines. The eye design

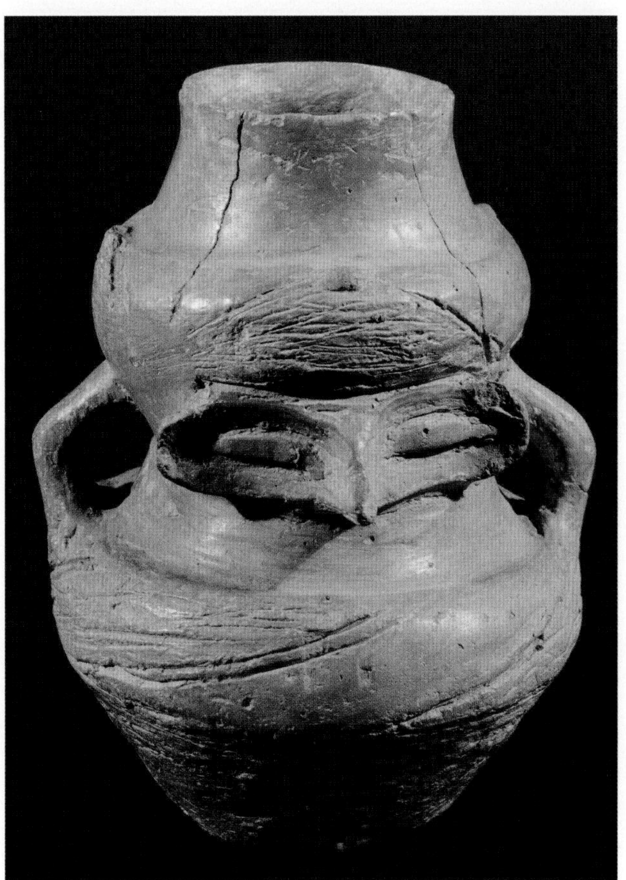

1.7 Vessel from Hotnica, near Veliko Turnovo, Bulgaria, *c.* 4000 B.C.

1.8 Stonehenge, view of the cromlech, Salisbury Plain, Wiltshire, England, *c.* 1800–1500 B.C. Diameter of circle 97 ft. (29.6 m).

suggests that the shape of the vessel was associated with human form.

In western Europe, Neolithic people used stone for burials and various types of ritual structures, which are called **megalithic**, meaning made of large stones. The most famous example of megalithic building in Europe is the **cromlech** (circle of stones) at Stonehenge (figure **1.8**).

STONEHENGE

Located on Salisbury Plain in southwestern England, Stonehenge was first chosen as a sacred site around 3000 B.C. Several stages of construction concluded with the cromlech about 1500 years later.

At first, Stonehenge was simply a circular earth mound used for burials. Later, circles of upright stones (called **menhirs**) and individual **trilithons** (in which two uprights support a horizontal stone) were added. This kind of building system is called **post-and-lintel**, the two verticals being the posts and the horizontal, the lintel. An avenue extends from the earth mound (figure **1.9**) and is marked by the Heel Stone, over

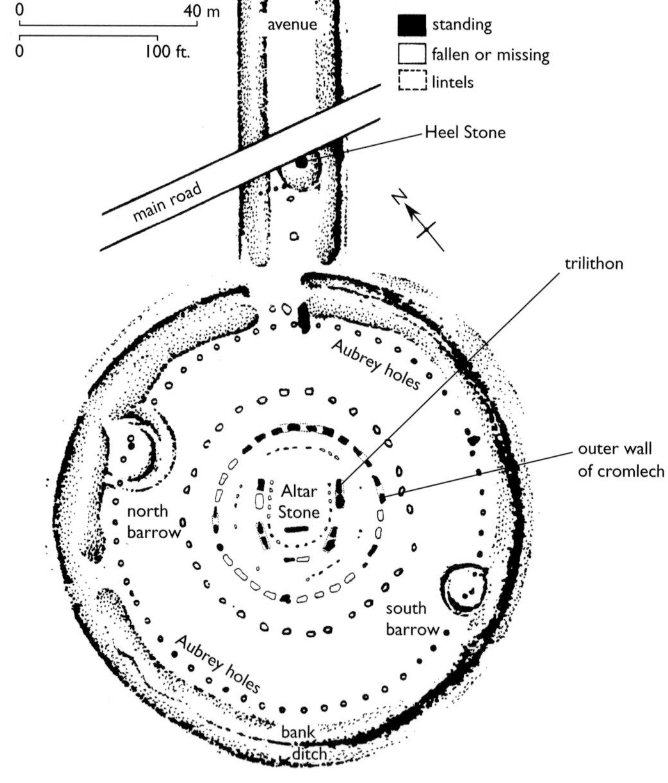

1.9 Plan of Stonehenge.

Thematic Parallels

Shamanism in Non-Western Imagery

Modern hunting and gathering societies share some of the preoccupations of Paleolithic cultures. The persistence of such societies—like the Australian Aboriginals—is a fortunate circumstance for historians, despite the caution with which comparisons must be made.

Australian Dreaming

The Aborigines of Australia have adopted the Western term *Dreaming* to designate a mythological time and place. It includes the present time and place of the Aborigine, and the balance between the human world and a greater universe populated by ancestors. Through imagery and ritual, the Aboriginal shaman contacts the spirit world of ancestors and the store of knowledge built up through time. Dreaming is the main content of rock art in Australia.

Figure **1.10** is an example from around 20,000 B.C. from Australia's Northern Territory. It depicts the Lightning Brothers and other lightning figures believed to be among the malevolent ancestors who created the universe. They stare directly out of the wall, the two Brothers in human form towering over smaller figures with serpentine bodies and human faces. Rays of light radiate from the heads. The repetition of the figures and their frontality create a series of fixed, threatening gazes.

Shamanistic Imagery in Africa

Shamanistic imagery is common among the rock paintings of the South African San, who live mainly in the Kalahari Desert. The eland—a large antelope with twisted horns—is of great importance to San hunters and appears frequently in their art.

1.11 *above* **South African human–eland composite, 19th century.**

Like the bison-man from Chauvet (see figure 1.5), figure **1.11** shows human and animal images that represent the shaman's process of transformation. The figure walks upright with a human torso and legs; but the head is that of an eland. Such works of art express the shaman's identification with the animal as well as the ability of the shaman to straddle the spiritual and the natural world.

The Anishnabe Drum

Shamanism, especially in healing and hunting rituals, plays an important role in certain Native American cultures. Various musical instruments are used by shamans, but the drum is of particular importance. Today, as in earlier cultures, the shaman's drum may be endowed with symbolic meanings related to its organic materials—wood and animal hides—which are associated with the transformations of the shaman.

It is in the nature of music that instruments are silent until taken up and played. The musician thus gives life to the instrument, and musicians, like artists and actors, seem to have magic creative powers. When played by a shaman, the drum's beat elicits ecstatic states and trances. Among the Native American Anishnabe, shaman drums are painted with images of animals, showing their interior anatomical structure. This can be seen in a late eighteenth-century drum (figure **1.12**), on which the heart and other organs are depicted in red ocher inside the outline of the animals. These images reflect the belief that shamans, in contrast to ordinary people, can see their own skeletons and have x-ray vision.

1.10 ***Lightning Brothers and Lightning Figures*, Katherine River, Northern Territory, Australia, *c.* 20,000 B.C.**

1.12 Double-headed Anishnabe drum, late 18th century. Animal hide, wood, red ocher, diameter $18\frac{7}{8}$ in. (48 cm). Städtisches Museum, Braunschweig, Germany.

which the sun rises each year on June 21, the summer solstice. Other stones are aligned according to positions of the moon and stars as well as to eclipses and the path of Halley's Comet. These observations have led scholars to interpret Stonehenge as a monument that was used in agricultural rites to celebrate seasonal changes important in farming.

Hypotheses about the meaning of Stonehenge are numerous, but definitive conclusions remain elusive. Among the mysteries connected with the monument is the question of how the stones were transported, given that the wheel was not yet known in western Europe. The stones were brought to the site from two different quarries, probably rolled on logs. The 40-ton (42,000-kg) bluestones came from Wales, a distance of over 100 miles (160 km), and the 50-ton (50,000-kg) sarsens (made of sandstone) from 20 miles (32 km) away. The construction of Stonehenge was an enormous undertaking in terms of labor, organization, and social commitment.

As Neolithic village communities evolved into the first cities, the process of urbanization began. Early cities marked important social developments, requiring administrative centers and professional differentiation according to such occupations as artisan, merchant, soldier, religious leader, and ruler. Class systems based on rank and status, as well as profession, also evolved. Technological developments in the first cities included an increase in sophisticated tools, the use of the wheel and new modes of land transportation and boats, and the beginning of metallurgy that led from the Stone Age to the Bronze Age. In the next chapter, we consider the development of cities in the Ancient Near East.

KEY TERMS

bipedal able to walk upright on two feet.

cromlech a circle of stones, characteristic of the Neolithic period in western Europe.

megalithic a Neolithic structure made of large stones.

menhir a single upright stone.

metaphor a comparison without using "like" or "as" in which one thing stands for another.

narrative sequence a story that follows chronologically.

natural selection Darwin's theory of the survival of species best adapted to their environment.

naturalistic representing objects as they actually appear in nature.

post-and-lintel an elevation system in which two upright posts support a horizontal lintel; also called a trilithon.

prehistory a period of history before the development of writing systems.

shaman a religious figure believed to have supernatural powers, including the ability of self-transformation from human to animal.

trilithon a single post-and-lintel.

KEY QUESTIONS

1. How would we prove that Upper Paleolithic era (*c.* 45,000–10,000/8000 B.C.) humans were not merely on an endless quest to find the necessities of life? What other activities did they engage in?
2. What does the earliest art show about humanity's first ceremonies or rituals? What elements must be present before we can say an individual can think symbolically?
3. What is an example of one of humanity's earliest "narrative sequences"?
4. What characteristics of cave art make it "naturalistic"?

SUGGESTED READING

Barber, Elizabeth Wayland. *Women's Work: the First 20,000 Years: Women, Cloth, and Society in Early Times*. New York: W. W. Norton, 1994.

▸ A study of the role of women in early society.

Berlo, Janet C., and Ruth B. Phillips. *Native North American Art*. New York: Oxford University Press, 1998.

▸ An introduction to Native Art in North America.

Caruna, Wally. *Aboriginal Art.* London: Thames and Hudson, 1993.
- An introduction to the Aboriginal arts of Australia.

Casteldon, Rodney. *The Making of Stonehenge.* London: Routledge, 1993.
- A study of the origins of Stonehenge.

Clottes, Jean, and David Lewis-Williams. *The Shamans of Prehistory*, trans. Sophie Hawkes. New York: Harry N. Abrams, 1998.
- A study of the role and meaning of prehistoric shamanism.

Corbin, George. *Native Arts of North America, Africa, and the South Pacific.* New York: HarperCollins, 1988.
- A general introduction to the arts and customs of Native North America, Africa, and the South Pacific cultures.

Cunliffe, Barry (ed.). *The Oxford Illustrated Prehistory of Europe.* Oxford and New York: Oxford University Press, 1994.
- A general reference book.

Eliade, Mircea. *Shamanism*, trans. Willard R. Trask. Princeton, NJ: Princeton University Press, 1974.
- A study of shamanism by one of the most original scholars in the field of religious history.

——. *A History of Religious Ideas* (2 vols.). Chicago: University of Chicago Press, 1978.
- A survey of worldwide religious ideas, beginning with prehistory.

——. *The Forge and The Crucible*, trans. Stephen Corrin. New York and Evanston: Harper and Row, 1971.
- A study of the role and meaning of alchemy in different cultures.

Feder, Kenneth L. *The Past in Perspective: Introduction to Human Prehistory.* New York: Houghton Mifflin, 1996.
- A general overview of early human history.

Johanson, Donald, Lenora Johanson, and Blake Edgar. *Ancestors: In Search of Human Origins.* New York: Villard Books, 1994.
- An anthropological study of the search for human origins. Johanson's team discovered Lucy.

Onians, John (ed.). *Atlas of World Art.* London: Laurence King Publishing, and New York: Oxford University Press, 2004.
- A survey of world art showing the impact of geography on the development and spread of art.

Sandars, N. K. *Prehistoric Art in Europe.* New Haven, CT, and London: Yale University Press, 1995.
- An overview of prehistoric art in western and central Europe.

Sayers, Andrew. *Australian Art.* Oxford and New York: Oxford University Press, 2001.
- A survey of the arts of Australia.

Scarre, Chris. *Places in Time: Exploring Prehistoric Europe.* New York and Oxford: Oxford University Press, 1998.
- A study of art and culture in prehistoric Europe.

Smart, Ninian. *The World's Religions.* London: Cambridge University Press, 1998.
- A reference book on the nature and history of world religions.

SUGGESTED FILMS

1968 *Planet of the Apes*, dir. Franklin J. Schaffner

1970 *Beneath the Planet of the Apes*, dir. Ted Post

1973 *Battle for the Planet of the Apes*, dir. J. Lee Thompson

1981 *Quest for Fire*, dir. Jean-Jacques Arnaud

1986 *Clan of the Cave Bear*, dir. Michael Chapman

1993 *Jurassic Park*, dir. Steven Spielberg

1997 *The Lost World: Jurassic Park*, dir. Steven Spielberg

2001 *Jurassic Park III*, dir. Joe Johnston

2 The Ancient Near East

"He ordered built the walls of Uruk of the Sheepfold, the walls of holy Eanna, stainless sanctuary. Observe its walls, whose upper hem is like bronze; behold its inner wall, which no work can equal. Touch the stone threshold, which is ancient; draw near the Eanna, dwelling-place of the goddess Ishtar,a work no king among later kings can match."

(*The Epic of Gilgamesh*, TABLET I, COL. I, LINES 9–15)

The Ancient Near East included many civilizations located in much of what we now call the Middle East and modern Turkey (see map 2.1, p. 20). From the Neolithic period (seventh millennium B.C.), settled communities began to evolve into urban centers. Some monumental architecture has survived, along with distinctive pottery, sculptures, and fragments of painting. There are no surviving musical notations, but texts and works of art indicate that music was an important part of Ancient Near Eastern civilization.

The focus of this chapter will be Mesopotamia, which comprised most of modern Iraq, where many important advances in civilization first occurred. Literally "the land between the rivers," Mesopotamia profited from the Tigris and Euphrates rivers, and early on developed irrigation systems and improved agriculture. At some time in the late fourth millennium B.C. the earliest known writing system emerged, which for the first time in human history made record-keeping and other forms of documentation possible, including the compilation of king lists and accounts of historical events. This led to a rich literature in the Ancient Near East, where the first known epic, The Epic of Gilgamesh, *was recorded.*

"He" in the quotation at the beginning of the chapter is Gilgamesh, the world's earliest literary epic hero. The lines celebrate his incomparable achievement in founding the ancient city of Uruk (modern Warka, in Iraq), which was divided into three parts—the center, an orchard, and the claypits, where bricks and ceramics used in building were located. When the poet says that the "upper hem is like bronze," he is creating a metaphor associating the walls that surround the city with a skirt. He also mentions Ishtar (Inanna), the goddess who ***personified*** *(embodied as a person) war, wisdom, and fertility, and who protected the city. And he uses the* ***epithet*** *(an identifying adjective or phrase) "Uruk of the Sheepfold" to denote the city. All such poetic devices indicate that by the time the epic was written down, a long oral tradition had already established certain literary* ***conventions*** *(accepted practices), which are still used today.*

Key Topics

Cultural Developments

- Urbanization
- Kingship
- The invention of writing
- The first epic poem: *Gilgamesh*
- Hammurabi's law code
- Assurbanipal's library

Geography and War

- The Fertile Crescent
- Military campaigns of Assurbanipal

Humans Seek Their Place in the Cosmos

- Polytheism
- Zoroastrianism

THE ANCIENT NEAR EAST (all dates B.C.)

TIMELINE	URUK PERIOD c. 3500–3000	EARLY DYNASTIC PERIOD c. 3000–2350	AKKADIAN PERIOD c. 2350–2100	NEO-SUMERIAN PERIOD c. 2150–1800	OLD BABYLONIAN PERIOD c. 1900–1600	ASSYRIANS c. 1300–612	NEO-BABYLONIAN PERIOD 625–539
HISTORY AND CULTURE	Development of writing Agricultural economy City-states	Gilgamesh king of Uruk	Sargon I founds Akkadian dynasty, *c.* 2334	Invasions from east destroy Akkadian power Gudea king of Lagash	Arabian Amorite dynasty Hammurabi king of Babylon Law code of Hammurabi, *c.* 1780	Assyrian Empire Assurbanipal king of Assyria Conquests in Egypt and black Africa	Nebuchad-nezzar II king of Babylon
RELIGION AND MYTH	Pantheon of gods	Elaborate temple complexes Priests and temple-workers	Naram-Sin declares himself a god				
ART			Stele of Naram-Sin, *c.* 2254–2210	Statue of Gudea, *c.* 2144–2124		Palace reliefs, 668–627	
ARCHITECTURE	Brick construction City of Uruk founded, *c.* 3500	Ziggurats Uruk's city wall constructed		Temple-building	Babylon built to Hammurabi's plans		Hanging Gardens of Babylon Tower of Babel
LITERATURE				*The Epic of Gilgamesh*, recorded late 3rd millennium		Assurbanipal founds library, 7th century	
MUSIC		Kettledrums, lyres				Stringed instruments	

THE FERTILE CRESCENT

Mesopotamia emerged from the Neolithic era around 4500 B.C., when people began smelting metals and developing metallurgy. Copper and, later, tin were imported, leading to the design of more effective tools, weapons, and vessels.

The two main cultural groups of ancient Mesopotamia roughly correspond to the north–south geographic division of the land. The first period of Sumerian culture in the south lasted from around 3800 to 2250 B.C., when the Akkadians from the north rose to power. They brought the Semitic Akkadian language, which gained primacy in the region, although Sumerian remained the literary language in the entire land for centuries.

The Tigris and Euphrates rivers provided the desert regions of Mesopotamia with an abundant source of water. The invention of the plow and the wheel, as well as irrigation, advanced agriculture and technology. The potter's wheel was used for **ceramics** (pottery), while the wagon wheel made it possible to construct carts (pulled by animals) for travel and transport. This, along with river boats, facilitated Mesopotamian trade with other cultures (map **2.1**).

URBANIZATION AND ARCHITECTURE

According to *The Epic of Gilgamesh*, the foundations of Uruk were "laid down by the seven sages" at some point in the distant past. Archaeologists generally date the founding of the city to around 3500 B.C., and the term "Uruk" also designates an archaeological period beginning at this time. Gilgamesh became Uruk's king hundreds of years later, in the Early Dynastic Period, and he is credited with the construction of the 5¾-mile (9.25-km)-long city wall. Because the poet tells us that Uruk is a sheepfold, we conclude that its economy was originally based on agriculture and farming and that its king was a metaphorical shepherd.

At the center of Uruk, Gilgamesh built the sacred sanctuary of Eanna, which contained the earliest known example of a **ziggurat**, the most characteristic form of Mesopotamian

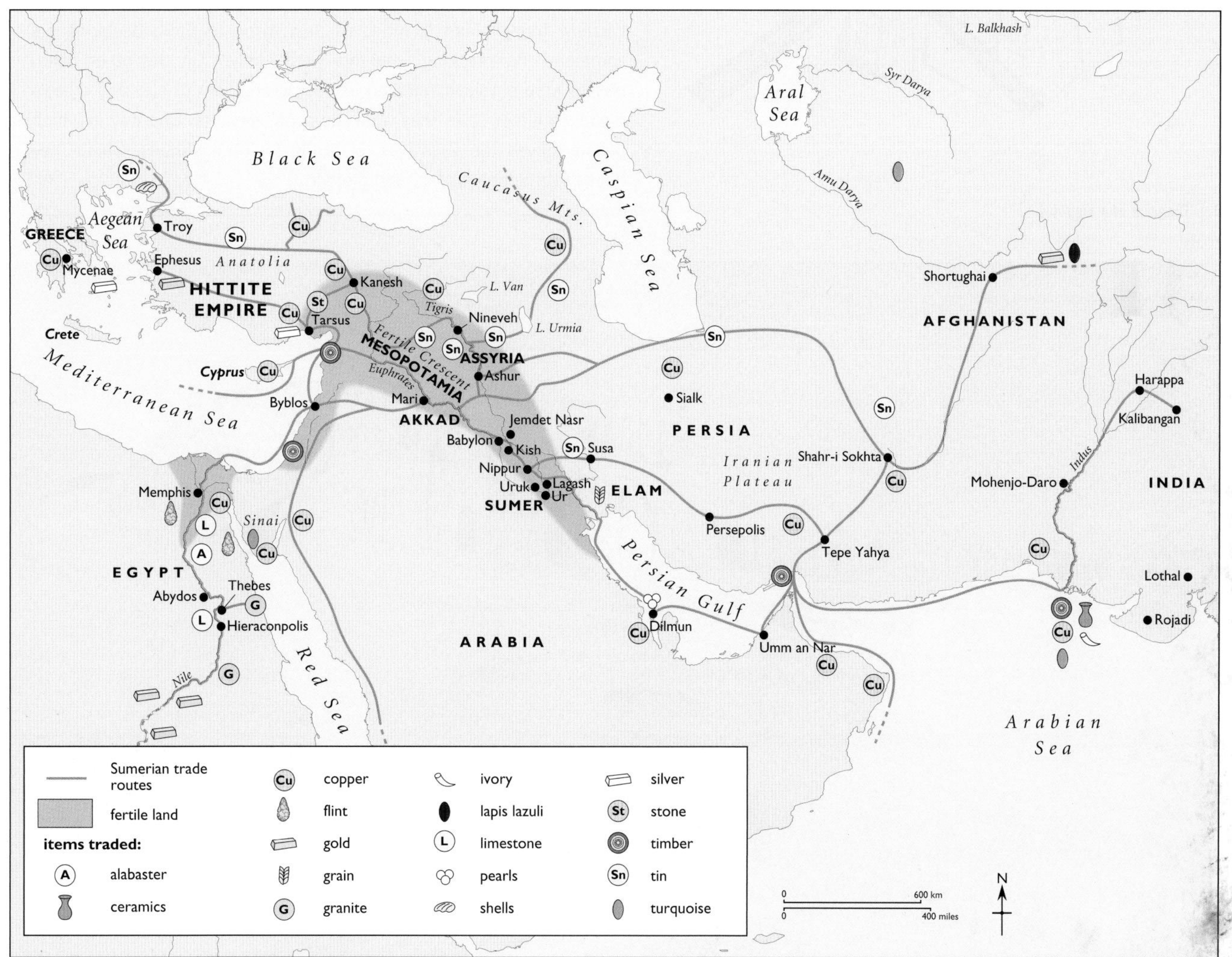

Map 2.1 Trade in the Ancient Near and Middle East.

monumental architecture (figures **2.1** and **2.2**). A ziggurat was usually part of a temple complex and supported a temple on its flat top. On the level terrain of Mesopotamia, these massive, solid structures stood out and were thought of as mountains, where the gods dwelled. By constructing a ziggurat, therefore, the Mesopotamians recognized the gods as inhabitants, patrons, and protectors of their cities (see Box).

The ziggurat at Uruk was made of brick and was over 45 feet (13.7 m) high and 150 feet (45.7 m) wide. Its four corners were oriented to the four points of the compass, reflecting its cosmic significance. At the top stood a shrine called the White Temple, possibly because of the whitewash on its outer surface (figure **2.3**). The precinct

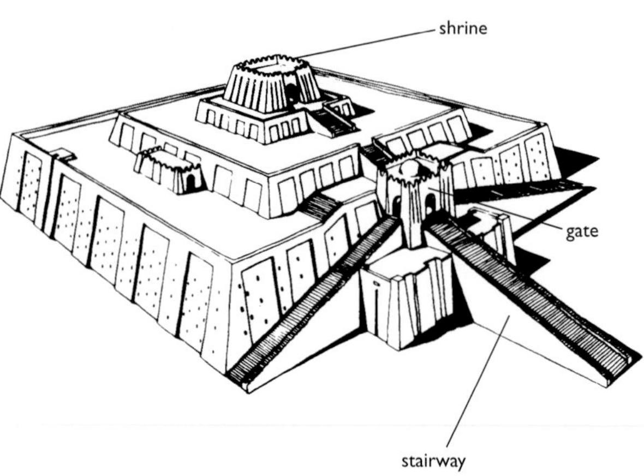

2.1 Diagram of a ziggurat.

The Mesopotamian Cosmos

The Mesopotamians conceived of the earth as a flat disk surmounted by a huge, heavenly vault. In between heaven and earth was the atmosphere, from which the celestial bodies were made. Enclosing the cosmos was an infinite, primeval sea. Death was a dreary and inevitable end to mortal life, and the spirits of the dead dwelled in an underworld. This was a region of darkness, in contrast to the radiant light emitted by gods. Mesopotamian religion was **polytheistic** (consisting of many gods) and the gods were **anthropomorphic** (human in form).

The main sky gods of Sumer were Anu and his consort, Ninhursag. Anu, Enlil (god of the air), and Enki (Akkadian Ea), god of the primeval watery abyss, formed the primary triad of deities. The sun and moon gods were Utu (Akkadian Shamash) and Nanna (Akkadian Sin), respectively; and the powerful and complex Inanna (Akkadian Ishtar) was goddess of love, war, and fertility. The pantheon ("all the gods") was ruled by a king presiding over a divine assembly that controlled fate.

Humans, according to the Mesopotamians, were created in two overlapping ways. On the one hand, they were the product of an utterance, the word of a god. The power of the word has a long history in Western thought and is reflected in a hymn to Enlil, declaring his command "far-reaching" and his word "holy." On the other hand, people were physically created like sculptures, out of clay and a god's blood. In either case, they were the gods' servants. One way in which people served the gods was by caring for their statues, which they housed (in temples), fed, and clothed.

2.2 Northeastern side of the Ziggurat at Uruk, *c.* 2255–2040 B.C. Brick, over 45 ft. (13.7 m) high and 150 ft. (45.7 m) wide.

Society and Culture

Abikhil, a Temple Superintendent

Statues of worshippers have been found in abundance at several early Sumerian temple precincts. An alabaster figure of around 2400 B.C. represents Abikhil, the superintendent of the Ishtar temple at Mari (Tell Hariri, in modern Syria), one of the most prosperous cities in the third millennium B.C. (figure **2.4**). Abikhil is shown in the conventional attitude of prayer, gazing straight ahead, with his hands cupped one around the other in front of his torso. His wide-eyed expression, accentuated by blue inlaid pupils and a sharp, black, stylized eye outline, indicates that he is in a holy sanctuary and in the presence of a god. The slightly upturned lips, as well as the rounded forms characteristic of Sumerian carving, convey an air of well-being and repose.

2.4 Statuette of Abikhil (front and side), Early Dynastic period, *c.* 2400–2300 B.C. Alabaster, 20⅝ in. (52.5 cm) high. Louvre, Paris.

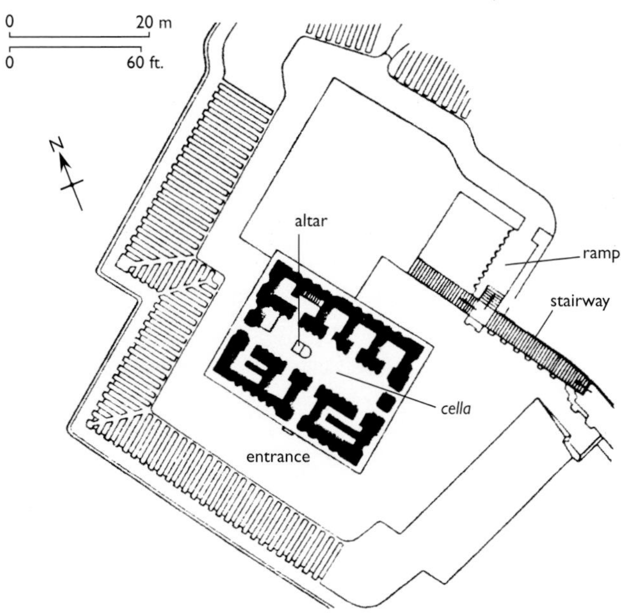

2.3 Plan of the White Temple, Uruk.

also contained two other temples, one red and the other decorated with cones inserted into the wall so that only the round ends were visible. The cones were painted and arranged with the circles forming geometric patterns of color. The layouts of interior rooms and remains found in such temples reflect the elaborate Mesopotamian belief system, sophisticated building techniques, and the presence of a class of priests and other temple-workers of considerable importance (see Box).

THE DEVELOPMENT OF WRITING

The Sumerians began to develop writing sometime before 3000 B.C., during the early Uruk period. At first they devised a system of record-keeping for administrative efficiency and identifying ownership. Soon thereafter, an important body of literature followed.

Defining Moment

Urbanization in Mesopotamia

The city of Uruk today is a vast landscape of ruins in southern Iraq. But in ancient Mesopotamia, Uruk was a city enclosed by protective walls surrounding some 2 square miles (518 ha) of houses, palaces, workshops, and temples. Urbanization started in Mesopotamia in the fourth millennium B.C. and was a defining moment in the so-called cradle of civilization.

Uruk had begun as a village like other villages; its evolution into a major city revolved around its important temple. Temples in Mesopotamia owned estates where peasants cultivated gardens and tended herds of cattle and pigs. Since Mesopotamians believed that people were created to serve and feed the gods, their towns grew up around a god's temple. By around 2500 B.C., however, military lords and kings gained political power that rivaled that of the temple priest.

Urban life offered many benefits, such as security and protection within thick walls, and prosperity through trade with other areas. New technologies, such as metallurgy, the wheeled cart, the oxen-pulled plow, and the sailboat, developed. At the same time, urban life increased the power of religious and political authorities and intensified the differences between social classes. Following urbanization, the benefits of rural life declined, and farmers became little more than slaves. In Mesopotamian cities, women exercised control over children and servants, while men controlled the entire household and participated in urban life. Merchants, as well as temple and palace workers, led a relatively comfortable existence.

2.5 Tablet recording the delivery of bundled reeds, 2028 B.C.

The development of cuneiform writing facilitated urban life through more efficient record-keeping. Because cuneiform was difficult to learn, only the literate elite (mainly priests) could write it. This class also developed sky charts that governed planting times and kept rationing lists documenting payments for agricultural products. An example of cuneiform can be seen in figure **2.5** which was written in month twelve of the first year of the reign of Ibbi-Sin, 2028 B.C. The tablet records the delivery to a central storehouse of bales of bundled reeds, some of which were then set aside for tax payments. A cylinder seal was first rolled over the entire surface of the front and back of the tablet and then cuneiform writing was incised over the seal impressions.

Critical Question What is the function of literacy in a society?

Pictographs, Cuneiform, and the Cylinder Seal

The earliest Sumerian inscriptions are **pictographic** (based on pictures)—that is, they resemble in a rudimentary way what they stand for (figure **2.6**). Pictographs were supplanted by abstract, wedge-shaped characters called **cuneiform** by modern scholars (figure **2.7**). In cuneiform script there is no longer a formal resemblance between the character and what it represents. Characters and words thus replaced the image as units of meaning.

The Sumerians invented the cylinder seal to identify ownership. This was a small stone cylinder decorated with incised images (a process called **intaglio**) that make a relief impression when rolled across a soft surface. Thousands of such seals survive, providing a rich source of Mesopotamian imagery over several millennia. The scene in figure **2.8** depicts two rams eating leaves from branches held by a bearded king or priest. The reed bundles framing the lambs may symbolize Inanna and denote fertility. The male figure wears a cap and a patterned, knee-length skirt,

2.6 Reverse side of pictographic tablet, from Jamdat Nasr, near Kish, Iraq, *c.* 3000 B.C. Clay, 4 3/8 in. (11.1 cm) high. Ashmolean Museum, Oxford.
This illustrates an accounting record of agricultural produce, such as bread and beer, and of farm animals. We can also make out images of storage jars, bowls, stalks of wheat, and ears of grain.

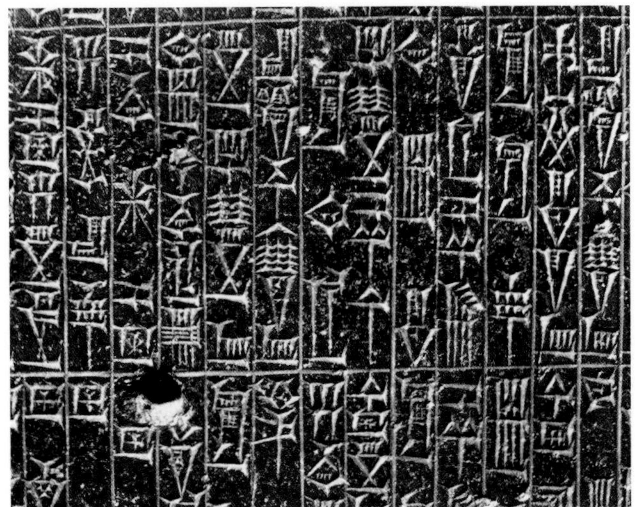

2.7 *above* Stele of Hammurabi, detail, *c.* 1780 B.C. (see figure 2.14).

and his central position reflects not only his importance but also his domination of the animals. Notice that he is **frontal** (facing front) except for his profile head, which has a frontal eye. This is a convention of representation in ancient art, which shows a face from two viewpoints.

THE FIRST EPIC POEM

Ancient Mesopotamia was rich in literature, art, and music, and because so many written records survive, we know quite a lot about its cultures. It is thanks to the invention of writing that *The Epic of Gilgamesh* has been preserved. The epic was initially transmitted orally as a collection of hymns and tales about Gilgamesh shortly after his reign. It was first written down in the late third millennium B.C. in Sumerian, which is unique among all ancient languages. Later it was copied in Akkadian and Babylonian, as well as in Hittite, an Indo-European language and the name of the culture that flourished in ancient Anatolia, modern Turkey (see Box).

2.8 Seal *right* and impression *above*, from southern Iraq, Uruk period, 4th millennium B.C. Marble and copper, 2½ in. (5.4 cm) high, diameter of seal 1¾ in. (4.5 cm). Vorderasiatisches Museum, State Museums, Berlin.

Society and Culture

Language Groups

Today there are 3000 different languages and many dialects in the world. A language that is no longer spoken is called a dead language, and examples include ancient Egyptian (see Chapter 3), Akkadian, Sumerian, Hittite, and Etruscan (see Chapter 7). Scholars who study languages are called linguists. They classify languages into family groups, which apparently developed from a single parent language. When groups of people sharing a common language become separated geographically, their languages continue to evolve. Eventually, the languages diverge to the point where the groups can no longer understand each other, but the languages are still related because they originally came from the same family.

The most widespread language family that exists today is Indo-European, which is spoken by nearly 50 percent of the world's population. It is the dominant language group of Western culture and is also the basis of some major Asian languages. Scholars believe that the parent Indo-European language originated in an area north of the Black Sea, and that as groups of people migrated in different directions their languages changed. Nevertheless, many of these languages share similar words—*mother* in English, *mater* in Latin, *meter* in Greek, *mère* in French, *madre* in Spanish, and *Mutter* in German.

The earliest recorded Indo-European language was Hittite, followed by Greek and Sanskrit. Among the main subgroups of Indo-European are the Balto-Slavic languages, spoken in much of eastern Europe; Celtic (including Gaelic, spoken in Scotland and Ireland, Welsh, spoken in Wales, and Breton, spoken in northern France); Germanic (including Dutch, English, German, and the Scandinavian languages, Danish, Norwegian, Swedish, and Icelandic); Greek; Indo-Iranian, of which Indo-Aryan and Iranian are subgroups (the Indo-Aryan languages are spoken today mainly in India and Pakistan, and the Iranian include Pashto and Persian). The Romance languages, which derive mainly from Latin, include French, Italian, Portuguese, Romanian, and Spanish.

Language groups other than Indo-European are Sino-Tibetan, which includes Chinese with its numerous dialects; Afro-Asian, which is concentrated around North Africa and the Near East and includes Arabic and Hebrew; and the Japanese and Korean group.

Returning again to the quotation at the beginning of the chapter, we can sense the author's cultural pride in Gilgamesh's accomplishments: without peer, now or in the future, the city is "a work no king . . . can match." But, in addition to giving us a view of Mesopotamian culture and mythology, *Gilgamesh* is a literary masterpiece. It is the first epic ever recorded, and it contains themes that have been addressed over the centuries and are relevant today.

The typical epic, like *Gilgamesh,* is a long poem narrating the exploits of a heroic figure on a grand scale. Encompassing mythic, religious, and social themes, epics portray larger-than-life events. The hero is usually a man of high stature, often the founder of a civilization. He suffers, undertakes perilous journeys, and, in evoking the identification of the reader, stands for all of us. Gilgamesh battles the forces of evil and searches for immortality. But in the end, he accepts the reality of death and undergoes a transformation that is both psychological and moral.

When the story opens, the city of Uruk stands as a tribute to its founder and king. Having attained this high position, Gilgamesh undertakes his journey. The first line of the epic introduces Gilgamesh in search of immortality: "The one who saw the abyss, I [the author] will make the land know."

In the course of Gilgamesh's quest, the gods create Enkidu, a double for Gilgamesh and also his opposite. Whereas Gilgamesh is a city-dweller, Enkidu inhabits the wilderness—he is covered with hair and runs with the animals. The taming of Enkidu, turning him from "the man-as-he-was-in-the beginning" (*Gilgamesh,* tablet I, col. iv, line 6) into a human, is one of the most brilliant episodes in Western literature.

Enkidu is transformed by spending six days and seven nights with a temple courtesan. His taming is a metaphor for the civilizing effects of women on men: "She made him know, the man-as-he-was, what a woman is" (tablet I, col. iv, line 19). Enkidu then ceases to "gallop as before. Yet he had knowledge, wider mind" (tablet I, col. iv, lines 28–29). In this episode, Enkidu attains sexual knowledge, which makes him human in the sense of growing up spiritually. He is no longer a carefree child, running wild without responsibility. The courtesan then prepares a meal for Enkidu, which further initiates him into civilized society, and offers to lead him to Uruk, "where Gilgamesh lives, completely powerful, and like a wild bull stands supreme, mounted above his people" (tablet I, col. iv, lines 38–39).

At this point, Gilgamesh has a dream, which he asks his mother, Ninsun, to "untie" (see Box). The dream text reads as follows:

Last night, Mother, I saw a dream.
There was a star in the heavens.
Like a shooting star of Anu it fell on me.
I tried to lift it; it was too much for me.
I tried to move it; I could not move it.

Dreams and Medicine in the Ancient Near East

Dreams played an important role in the ancient world. Fragments of dream books from the Ancient Near East have been preserved, including conventional dream interpretations. These indicate that people believed dreams were sent by the gods and contained secret, enigmatic messages. Dreams thus had to be "untied." Once a dream had been interpreted, its mystery was revealed (untied). Gilgamesh's first dream described here is symbolic and alludes to the future.

The practice of medicine in the Ancient Near East was based on rituals, magic, and natural products. Two medical tablets from the last quarter of the third millennium B.C. contain fifteen prescriptions. They recommend swallowing medicinal potions and applying poultices to diseased parts of the body. Both the potions and the poultices were made by grinding up organic matter, such as herbs, fruits, or seeds, and minerals, such as salt and river bitumen. Animal products were less commonly used than plants; among these were turtle shells, wool, and water snakes. Powdered substances were mixed with liquids, such as water, milk, oil, or beer, to make the potion or poultice.

Uruk, the land, towered over it;
the people swarmed around it;
the people pressed themselves over it;
the men of the city massed above it;
companions kissed its feet.
I myself hugged him like a wife,
and I threw him down at your feet
so that you compared him with me.

(tablet I, col. v, lines 26–38)

The implication of this dream is that Enkidu is Gilgamesh's double. Its manifest text describes the heaven-sent origin of Enkidu, whom the gods made, and his strength. The latent content of the last three lines is the loving but competitive relationship between the men. On the one hand, Gilgamesh hugs Enkidu "like a wife," but on the other hand, he throws him before his mother. By comparing Enkidu with Gilgamesh, Ninsun cements both their sibling rivalry and their sibling bond. Enkidu is Gilgamesh's "other half"—his mirror image.

Ninsun replies:

This means: he is a powerful companion, able to save a friend;
his strength is great in the land.
Like a shooting star of Anu his strength is awesome,
whom you hug like a wife.
He is the one who will take leave of you.
This unties your dream.

(tablet I, col. vi, lines 1–6)

The relationship between Gilgamesh and Enkidu unfolds heroically, as was to become characteristic of later epic literature. They wrestle each other "like bulls," and they embrace like brothers. Encouraged by Shamash (god of the sun and of justice), Gilgamesh and Enkidu set out to slay the evil monster Humbaba, who guards the cedar forest inhabited by the gods. Humbaba, a kind of primordial, fearsome shadow, represents the forces of darkness. In this opposition of Shamash and Humbaba, the poet portrays another theme that became characteristic of the Western epic—the struggle between good and evil exemplified as a conflict between light and dark.

Enkidu warns Gilgamesh against undertaking the task, noting the primeval terror evoked by their quarry:

Humbaba's roar is the deluge,
his mouth is fire,
his breath is death.

(tablet II, col. v)

But for Gilgamesh this quest is a way of permanently establishing his name and his power; Enkidu agrees to accompany him. They find Humbaba near the cedar mountain, and kill him.

Ishtar is so struck by Gilgamesh's physical beauty and strength that she offers to become his lover. But he rebuffs her, noting that she is unfaithful and that her passions blow hot and cold:

You're a cooking fire that goes out in the cold,
a back door that keeps out neither wind nor storm,
. . . .
a well whose lid collapses,
. . . .
a waterskin that soaks the one who lifts it,
. . . .
a shoe that bites the owner's foot!

Which of your lovers have you loved forever?

(tablet VI, col. i)

In addition to Ishtar's inconstancy, Gilgamesh describes the power that a goddess has over a mortal, who can never be her equal. Recognizing that he would live in fear of being destroyed by her, Gilgamesh reminds Ishtar that she transformed one lover (her father's gardener) into a frog, and another (Tammuz) into a wolf, to be devoured by his own dogs.

Incensed by his rejection of her, Ishtar calls on her father, the sky god Anu, to send the great Bull of Heaven to kill Gilgamesh. When the Bull descends to Uruk, his snorting opens up vast crevasses in the earth, causing hundreds of citizens to plummet to their deaths. With Enkidu's assistance, Gilgamesh defeats the Bull, stabbing his neck like a matador. Enkidu further infuriates Ishtar by tossing a piece of the Bull's thigh at her.

The heroes celebrate their victory, but a dream announces the death of Enkidu—one of them is required to die as retribution for killing Humbaba and the Bull of Heaven. Although Enkidu's death had been foretold in the first dream, when Ninsun called Enkidu "the one who will leave you," Gilgamesh did not understand that departure meant death. Gilgamesh mourns Enkidu, as do the elders of Uruk and all of nature (echoing Enkidu's precivilized wild state). "For Enkidu," Gilgamesh cries out,

I weep like a wailing woman,
howling bitterly.
[He was] the axe at my side, the bow at my arm,
the dagger in my belt, the shield in front of me,
my festive garment, my splendid attire . . .
An evil has risen up and robbed me.

(tablet VIII, col. ii, lines 2–5)

In other words, Enkidu is not only Gilgamesh's double, but also his protector (the axe, bow, shield, and dagger) and the source of his happiness (the festive garment and splendid attire). By using the metaphor comparing armor and clothing to Enkidu, Gilgamesh makes explicit the merged identities of the heroes. He then tears off his fine clothes and announces that he will adopt Enkidu's former life in the wild.

To commemorate his deceased companion, Gilgamesh follows the age-old custom of ordering an effigy by which to remember him. Most of the text is lost, but what survives is:

"Artisan!
Metalworker, goldsmith, engraver! Make for my friend . . ."
Then he fashioned an image of his friend, of the friend's own stature.
"Enkidu, of lapis lazuli is your chest, of gold your body."

(tablet I, col. ii, lines 22–23)

It appears from this fragment that the statue replicated Enkidu's actual size and appearance. The use of gold and light blue **lapis lazuli**, considered the two most precious minerals in antiquity, reflects the value that Gilgamesh placed on his poetic double.

At this point, Gilgamesh embarks on the spiritual side of his journey. Fearing death, he sets out to find eternal life and the sage Utnapishtim, the only human ever granted immortality by the gods. Gilgamesh encounters a number of obstacles along the way, including the Scorpion-people, who guard the entrance to Mashu, the mountain of the rising and setting sun. Hearing of Gilgamesh's quest, the Scorpion-man warns that no mortal has ever traveled so far. But after twelve hours of darkness, Gilgamesh reaches daylight and meets the Barmaid, "who dwells at the lip of the sea." She tells him how to find the boatman Urshanabi, who will help him over the waters of death to Utnapishtim.

Having achieved his goal, Gilgamesh tells Utnapishtim of his friendship with Enkidu and his quest for immortality. The sage replies that nothing is forever, that sleep and death are brothers, and that he will tell him "a secret of the gods." This secret turns out to be the story of the Flood, in which humanity was destroyed, and of the great ship built by Utnapishtim at the gods' command. He took on board his family, craftsmen, and every other living thing so that life would regenerate when the waters subsided. (A huge flood that inundated Mesopotamia in 2900 B.C. is thus documented before the account in the Hebrew Bible was written.) Gilgamesh finally accepts his own mortality as the fate of all people and returns to rule Uruk. He recognizes that the city walls, with their "oven-fired brickwork" and foundation laid down by the seven sages, are his legacy and his immortality.

2.9 Plaque with a musician playing a stringed instrument, from Ur III, *c.* 2300 B.C. Fired clay, approx. 4 in. (10 cm) high. Louvre, Paris.

MESOPOTAMIAN KINGSHIP AND THE ARTS

The land of Sumer was divided into city-states. Each was governed by a ruler, who presided over an assembly of important citizens. This mirrored the organization of the Mesopotamian pantheon. The earliest assemblies chose their leaders for particular missions, which were generally of a military nature. Eventually, however, a system of hereditary kingship was put in place as a way of ensuring political stability.

Kingship—its character, chronology, and succession—was the main political institution of ancient Mesopotamia. Kings grew powerful and were supported by ever larger armies. As a result, the palace began to challenge the supremacy of the temple precincts.

Although Gilgamesh is described as two-parts divine and one-part human, the Sumerian kings were not at first conceived of as gods and, as we have seen, even Gilgamesh was denied immortality. But subsequent Akkadian, Babylonian, Assyrian, and Persian rulers had a different view of kingship. Beginning around 2300 B.C., the Akkadian ruler Sargon I (ruled *c.* 2334–2279 B.C.) founded a dynasty that soon conquered Mesopotamia. His grandson, Naram-Sin (*c.* 2254–*c.* 2218), was the first ruler to decree himself a god officially.

2.10 Reconstructed Sumerian lyre, from Ur, 3rd millennium B.C. Wood, inlay, lapis lazuli, and gold leaf. 3 ft. 6 in. (1.06 m) high. British Museum, London.

MUSIC AND RITUAL AT THE MESOPOTAMIAN COURTS

Music was important at the Mesopotamian courts, as well as in religious festivals. This is attested by texts, images, and actual instruments that have survived. In music, as in art, the bull played a symbolic role, standing for the power of the king. Its hide was used for the kettledrum, which was a key instrument in Mesopotamian music.

2.11 Front of a lyre soundbox, from Ur, *c.* 2685 B.C. Shell inlay, approx. 10 in. (25.4 cm) high. University of Pennsylvania Museum, Philadelphia.

In *The Epic of Gilgamesh*, when the temple courtesan persuades Enkidu to accompany her to Uruk, she tells him that "every day there's a festival, and . . . strings and drums are played" (tablet I, col. v, lines 8–9). Her words are backed up by finds such as the **plaque** (a small, decorated slab) in figure **2.9**, which was attached to a temple wall in Ur. It shows a figure playing a hand-held stringed instrument that resembles a lyre. More elaborate Sumerian lyres were also discovered in Ur. The reconstruction in figure **2.10** was almost certainly a royal possession. The head of the bull is of gold and the beard of lapis lazuli, the same materials that Gilgamesh used for Enkidu's statue.

The bull, like the figures on the front of another lyre (figure **2.11**), combines human with animal features. It is not known if these figures represent humans dressed as animals or mythological creatures. But what they are doing is manifest—they are performing various human rituals. At the top, a hero dominates two bulls, showing both his power over the animals and his identification with them. Below, a lion and a dog carry objects associated with sacrifice: jars and animal body parts. The third scene down appears to be a concert, with a donkey playing a lyre exactly like the actual lyre from Ur. And at the bottom a goat carrying two vessels follows a scorpion-man. Although there is no documented connection between these scenes and *The Epic of Gilgamesh*, the scorpion-man resembles the description of the guardian of Mount Mashu.

NARAM-SIN AND THE IMAGERY OF CONQUEST

Whereas Gilgamesh's chief artistic achievement was architectural, Naram-Sin's legacy is a large **stele** (stone marker). In addition to a cuneiform inscription, the stele is decorated with an image in **relief** (a sculpture that is not completely carved away from its original material). Both describe a victory over Naram-Sin's enemies (figure **2.12**). The stele reflects the Akkadian interest in conquest. To this end their armies subjugated the Sumerians and other cultures and imposed the Akkadian language. Akkadian kings were worshipped as gods. Naram-Sin is thus shown as divine in his own right—he is protected by symbols of celestial deities at the top of the stele.

2.12 *right* **Victory Stele of Naram-Sin, from Susa, *c.* 2254–2210 B.C. Pink sandstone, 6 ft. 6 in. (1.98 m) high. Louvre, Paris.**

The horned cap signifies that Naram-Sin is a god. His towering figure and formal prominence are conventions of ancient art, known as **hierarchical proportions**, in which size is equated with status. Another convention is the contrast between Naram-Sin's upward and forward march denoting success, and his defeated enemies, who fall. Similarly, the living are clothed, whereas the dead are nude.

GUDEA OF LAGASH: PIETY AND TEMPLE-BUILDING

After two hundred years of Akkadian rule, the Sumerian city-states reemerged as independent entities. Akkadian power was destroyed by invasions from the east and declined. Around 2150 B.C. a Neo-Sumerian culture gained ascendancy in Mesopotamia. This lasted about three hundred years.

The best-known early Neo-Sumerian king, Gudea (*c.* 2144–*c.* 2124), ruled Lagash (modern Telloh). His royal image depicted him as a pious builder, rather than as a ruthless conqueror, and he commissioned many temple precincts to convey his piety and his power. His relationship to the gods differed from that of the Akkadian rulers, for he was not worshipped as a god, but rather as an intermediary between the gods and his subjects. One way in which the gods communicated with Gudea was through dreams. In contrast to Gilgamesh, whose dreams foretold future events such as Enkidu's death, Gudea dreamed instructions from the gods to build their temples.

2.13 *Gudea of Lagash*, from Telloh, *c.* 2144–2124 B.C. Diorite, 17¾ in. (45 cm) high. Louvre, Paris.
The rounded forms, compact space, and combination of naturalism (the arm muscles) with **stylization** (forms rendered as surface patterns rather than naturalistically)—the eyebrows—are typical of Sumerian style. They recall the figure of Abikhil from the Mari temple (see figure 2.4).

The patron god of Lagash, Ningirsu, appeared in one dream, telling Gudea to build the Eninnu Temple. In Gudea's view, the fact that the temple plan in the dream was drawn on a tablet of lapis lazuli confirmed its divine origin. He then mobilized the city, performed the necessary ceremonies, imported high-quality cedar wood from Lebanon and personally oversaw the construction of the temple. Gudea himself laid the first brick of the foundation. When it was complete, the temple was known as "the House of Fifty Gods." According to a contemporary account, it rose from earth to heaven and illuminated the entire country with its radiance.

Several statues of Gudea, in which he is either seated or standing, have survived, and all show his piety. In figure **2.13** he sits on a modest throne covered with cuneiform inscriptions with his hands clasped in a conventional gesture of prayer. The **curvilinear** (having curved forms) rhythms of the Gudea statue and the sense of controlled dignity convey the king's confidence in himself and in the gods, as well as the highly developed skill of his court artists.

HAMMURABI OF BABYLON: THE LAWGIVER

The Neo-Sumerian rulers were overthrown by foreign invaders, resulting in centuries of political unrest. By around 1900/1800 B.C. a new stability was achieved under the Semitic-speaking Amorites. During this time, known as the Old Babylonian period after the capital city of Babylon, the Amorite dynasty produced King Hammurabi (ruled *c.* 1792–1750 B.C.), who brought about the final eclipse of Sumerian culture. He was a skilled military strategist and an effective administrator, credited with designing the grid plan of Babylon's urban streets. Above all, Hammurabi is famous for his law code (figure **2.14**), which consists of nearly three hundred statutes in fifty-one columns of Akkadian cuneiform text inscribed on a black basalt stele.

Although it was not the oldest law code of the Ancient Near East, Hammurabi's is the best preserved. It provides a clear view of the social order and legal system in second-millennium-B.C. Babylon. It also reflects the previous legal system under the Sumerians, for several of the statutes are similar.

The text opens with the claim that the gods

> named me to promote the welfare of the people, me, Hammurabi, the devout, god-fearing prince, to cause justice to prevail in the land, to destroy the wicked and the evil, that the strong might not oppress the weak, to rise like the sun over the black-headed people [the general population, most of whom had black hair], and to light up the land.

Note the repetition of the pronoun "me," calculated to emphasize the gods' choice of Hammurabi by "naming" him. His identification with Shamash is explicit in that he rises "like the sun" and "lights up the land." This metaphor, equating the ruler with the sun, falls within an age-old tradition that

has become a conventional theme of kingship throughout the world.

Hammurabi's statutes address all aspects of society, including conflicts between neighbors over water rights, marriage, violence, theft, and murder. The laws are aimed at maintaining social order in general and, more specifically, the established class system. Much of the code is based on talion law (*lex talionis*), from the Latin term meaning "like for like punishment"—"an eye for an eye" and "a tooth for a tooth." However, this applies only to people of equal rank. Penalties are harsher if offenses are committed by the lower classes against the upper classes as opposed to vice versa. So if a person knocks out the tooth of someone of equal rank, the offender's tooth is simply knocked out in kind. But if the victims are lower class, upper-class offenders are allowed to keep their teeth, as long as they pay a small fine. The same distinctions apply to the loss of an eye or a broken bone.

The laws of Hammurabi also establish a certain degree of equality in marriage. Both women and men are allowed to own property, and they have the same rights to sue for divorce. Adultery by either party is punished, but not equally: if a woman is unfaithful to her husband she can be drowned, but an unfaithful husband has only to return his wife's dowry.

The death penalty is imposed for a wide range of crimes, including helping slaves to escape, certain types of theft, murder, and failing to lock up an animal that kills someone. Lying and making false accusations are taken so seriously that failure to prove such charges results in the death of the accuser. And in a form of consumer protection legislation, Hammurabi's code condemns to death the perpetrators of poor and dangerous workmanship.

Hammurabi concludes his law code with a summation of his intentions to be, like Shamash, a "king of justice," and also a "father to the people" and a bringer of prosperity for all time. But the Old Babylonian period came to an end around 1600 B.C., when an ethnic group called the Kassites invaded. Mesopotamia became subject to foreign forces until a new stability was achieved with the rise of the Assyrians around 1300 B.C. By 900 B.C. the Assyrians had created a powerful empire. The capital city of Assur, named for its patron god, was located in the north, along the banks of the River Tigris.

2.14 Stele of Hammurabi, *c.* 1780 B.C. Black basalt, 7 ft. (2.13 m) high. Louvre, Paris.

The scene in the relief above Hammurabi's text shows Shamash, the sun god and god of justice, extending the ring and staff of royalty. He is seated on an architectural throne denoting a palace or temple and his feet rest on a stylized mountain (home of the gods). Shamash wears a flared robe and a horned cap of divinity. Light, alluding to his role as sun god, radiates from his shoulders. Standing before him is Hammurabi himself, whose relatively smaller size reflects his lesser importance. Scenes such as this serve a political function—they project the image of a ruler and his policies as sanctioned by the gods.

Cross-cultural Influences

Indus Valley Civilization

One of the ongoing discussions among scholars studying the Ancient Near East concerns the relationship of Mesopotamia to another ancient civilization discovered in the Indus valley, in modern Pakistan. Dating from around 2700 to *c.* 1900 B.C., this Indus valley culture overlaps Mesopotamian history from the Sumerian Early Dynastic to the Old Babylonian period.

Excavations at Mohenjo-Daro, some 140 miles (225 km) to the northeast of Karachi, have revealed a pattern of streets laid out on a grid plan. As in Uruk, Indus valley architects used brick. Some houses were equipped with bathrooms and plumbing, which suggests a highly developed culture.

The Indus valley pictorial script has not yet been deciphered, nor is the religion well understood. There is, however, evidence that the bull was prominent, which may indicate contacts with Mesopotamia. Bull motifs have been found on many Indus valley stamp seals, which differ from Mesopotamian cylinder seals in their square shape and in being made for stamping rather than rolling (figure **2.15**). In addition, unlike the Mesopotamian seals, stamp seals were carved in relief so that the impression was sunken rather than raised.

The *Bearded Man* from Mohenjo-Daro (figure **2.16**) has general parallels with Mesopotamian sculpture. Like the Sumerian statuette of Abikhil (see figure 2.4), the *Bearded Man* is frontal and his gaze is emphasized. He also combines stylization with the organic form that characterizes the statue of Gudea (see figure 2.13).

2.15 *above* **Stamp seal of a bull, from Mohenjo-Daro, *c.* 2300–1750 B.C. White steatite, 1½ in. (3.81 cm) high. National Museum, Delhi, India.**

2.16 *Bearded man from Mohenjo-Daro*, *c.* 2000 B.C. Limestone, 7 in. (17.8 cm) high. National Museum, Karachi, Pakistan.

Assurbanipal: Assyrian Might

The last great Assyrian king, Assurbanipal (ruled *c.* 669–626 B.C.), was known for both his cultural interests and the cruelty of his armies. Tablets dating to his reign contain his description of learning the use of the bow and arrow, how to drive a chariot, and the art of writing. He also mastered "royal decorum and walked in kingly ways." Indeed, Assurbanipal's interest in intellectual achievement inspired him to found a great library containing thousands of tablets. These included letters, literature, scientific and historical documents, and mythological texts. Of his conquests in Egypt and black Africa (see Chapter 3), Assurbanipal writes: "I made Egypt and Nubia feel my weapons bitterly and celebrated my triumph." He describes the determination with which he plundered the Egyptian city of Thebes, killing its inhabitants and looting their valuables.

The walls of Assurbanipal's palaces were lined with reliefs illustrating his ruthless pursuit of conquest. His prowess as a hunter is shown in a segment from the relief called the *Great Lion Hunt* (figure **2.17**). Like other Assyrian rulers, Assurbanipal kept gardens of lions. Because the lion was a royal symbol, the human king demonstrated his supremacy over the king of the beasts by hunting and killing him.

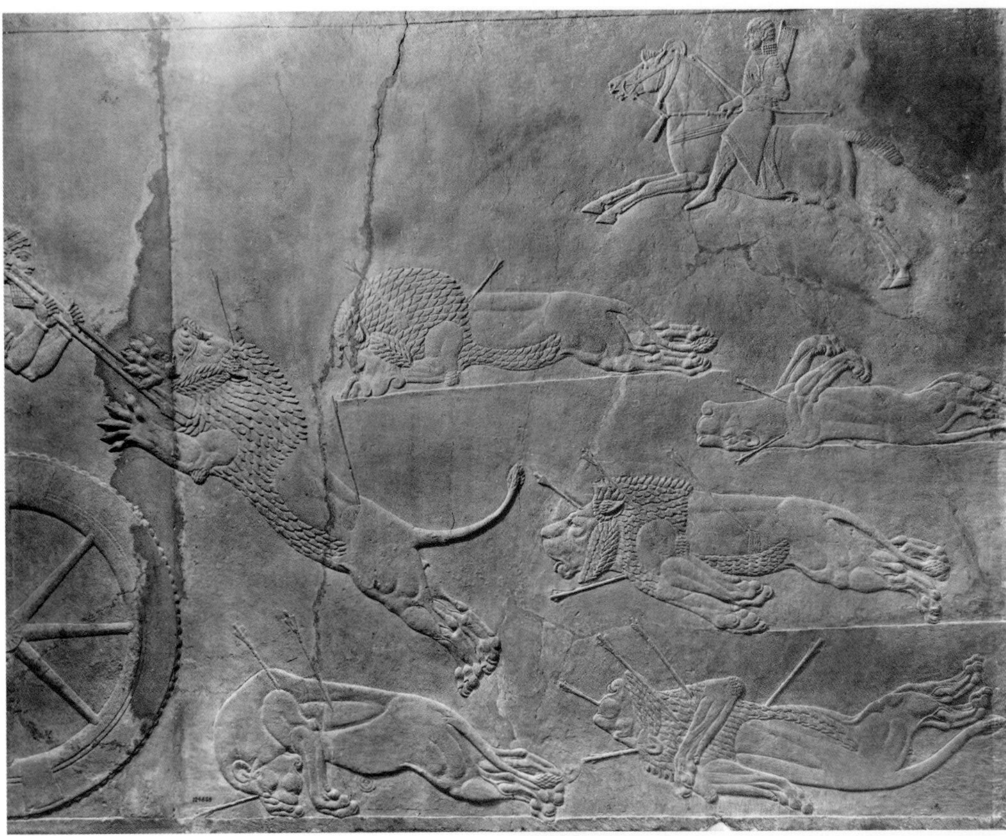

2.17 *Great Lion Hunt*, detail, from Assurbanipal's palace, Nineveh, 668–627 B.C. Alabaster, approx. 5 ft. (1.6 m) high. British Museum, London.
Lions and lionesses are shown dead and dying, shot through with the arrows of the king and his entourage. The naturalism of these reliefs is rendered with great skill and variety. There is both a sense of anatomical structure in the animals and a taste for surface patterning that enlivens the scene.

The skill needed for hunting lions also proved useful in war. Figure **2.18** shows a section of the palace wall relief that represents the Assyrian army storming an Elamite city (located in the southwest of modern Iran). The scene conveys the power of the Assyrians and Assurbanipal's bloodthirsty lust for war. He confirms this lust in the inscription on the upper part of the wall, where he declares that he attacked, captured, destroyed, and plundered the city, and set it on fire.

Having achieved victory, Assurbanipal reports: "With full hands and safely, I returned to Nineveh, the city where I exercise my rule." The relief in figure **2.19** shows the Assyrian conqueror relaxing after a successful military campaign. He reclines on an elaborate couch in a lush, peaceful garden. Servants fan him, and his queen, Ashur-sharrat, is seated by his feet. Both raise a cup as if to drink a toast. They are entertained by musicians at the far left playing a stringed instrument and a drum. All appear indifferent to the severed head of a defeated Elamite king hanging from a tree.

2.18 *Assurbanipal storming an Elamite city*, 668–627 B.C. Alabaster, 3 ft. 7¾ in. (1.11 m) high. British Museum, London.
Climbing a ladder in a steady advance, the Assyrians attack enemy archers positioned on the crenellated city walls. Kneeling Assyrians use their shields for protection against arrows raining down on them. Several wounded Elamites fall from the ramparts and corpses float among the fish in the river below. Here, as in the *Lion Hunt*, there is a continual interplay between arrest and movement, which is characteristic of much ancient art.

2.19 ***Assurbanipal and Queen Ashur-sharrat banqueting after a victory,*** **668–627 B.C. Alabaster, 4 ft. 6¾ in. (1.39 m) wide. British Museum, London.**

The Assyrian Empire declined after the death of Assurbanipal and the fall of Nineveh in 612 B.C. This was followed by the brief but prosperous Neo-Babylonian period (625–539 B.C.). Under Nebuchadnezzar II (ruled 604–562 B.C.), the Hanging Gardens of Babylon (one of the Seven Wonders of the Ancient World) and the ziggurat thought to be the biblical Tower of Babel were built. But by 539 B.C. a new force had risen to power in the Near East—namely, the Persian Empire under the Achaemenid dynasty.

THE ACHAEMENIDS AND THE ROYAL PALACE AT PERSEPOLIS

Persia (modern Iran) lay to the east of Mesopotamia and had a distinctive and distinguished cultural history dating back nearly 5000 years. Cyrus the Great (ruled *c.* 559–529 B.C.) founded the Achaemenid dynasty, forming an alliance between the Persians and Medes, both of whom were Aryan-speaking. In 539 B.C., Cyrus marched into Babylon and overran most of Mesopotamia. Cyrus himself, in an inscription found on a clay cylinder, declares his power in the region: "I am Cyrus, king of

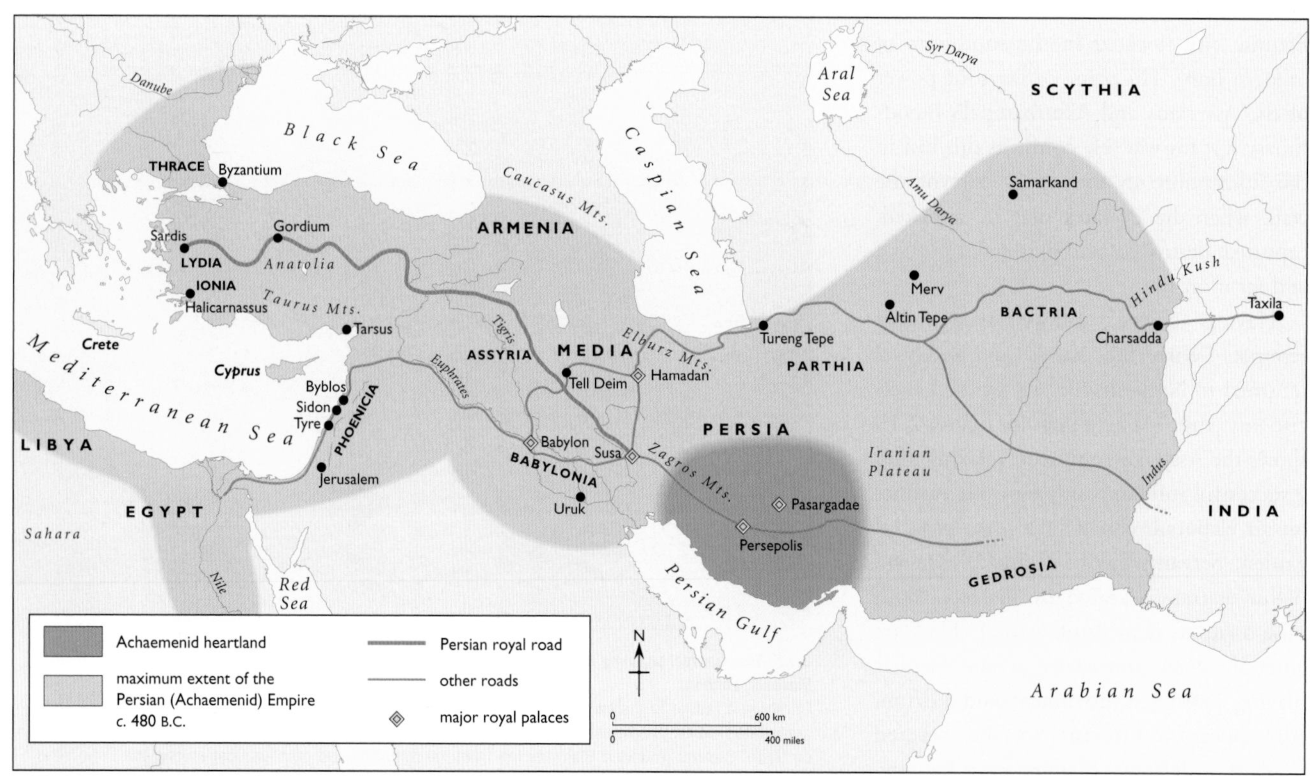

Map 2.2 The Persian (Achaemenid) Empire, *c.* 480 B.C.

2.20 **Apadana and stairway of Darius I, Persepolis, Iran *c.* 500 B.C.**

the world, great king, legitimate king, king of Babylon, king of Sumer and Akkad."

During the next fifty to sixty years Cyrus's successors built up a vast empire (map **2.2**). The Achaemenid rulers constructed a number of palaces; the most important one (now in ruins) is at Persepolis (figure **2.20**). Several kings, including Darius I (ruled 522–486 B.C.), Xerxes I (ruled 486–465 B.C.), and Artaxerxes (ruled 465–424 B.C.), contributed to the building program. The enormous audience hall (the Apadana), visible in the distance, originally had one hundred columns, each 40 feet (12.2 m) high. Figure **2.21** shows a detail of the *Procession of Medes and Persians* carved in relief on the side wall

2.21 ***Procession of Medes and Persians*, detail, stairway leading to the Tripylon, Persepolis, *c.* 500 B.C.**

of one of the staircases; the latter wear fluted hats. The borders of the procession are decorated with stylized plant forms. Compared with the Assyrian reliefs, which are filled with violent scenes of warfare and hunting, those decorating the Persian palaces emphasize the peaceful aftermath of conquest. As a result, there is a general air of orderly calm and a ritual, repetitive quality in the poses and gestures.

ZOROASTRIANISM: A NEW RELIGION The Achaemenid dynasty adopted a religion based on the teachings of the Persian prophet Zoroaster (first millennium B.C.), also called Zarathustra. Zoroastrianism is based on scriptures attributed to Zoroaster himself, which include poems and five *gathas* (celebratory songs). Zoroaster conceived of the universe as being in continual conflict between light and dark, or good and evil. It was up to individuals, who had free will, to decide which path they would follow. At some future time, the two forces would cease their struggle. People who chose the good would become immortal; those who chose evil would suffer. Zorastrianism was essentially a **monotheistic** religion with a single creator god, Ahura Mazda, embodying the force of light, who battled Ahriman, the force of darkness and evil.

Zoroastrians practiced marriage between close relatives, used priests in their rituals, and left their dead to be eaten by animals and birds before burial. In contrast to other Near Eastern religions, Zoroastrians did not worship in or around temples; instead, they worshipped outdoors, using fire altars. In figure **2.22** Darius I, who was a follower of Zoroaster, is enthroned before two such altars. He is elevated and larger than the other figures, which conveys his importance. The flat, open space behind the altars reinforces the impression of the king's distant, aloof character. The overall tranquility of the scene and the formality of the figures create an air of ritual.

Although Zoroastrianism was the main religion of the Achaemenid dynasty, other belief systems later developed in Persia. Among these were Manichaeism (founded by Mani in the early third century A.D.) and Mithraism, which revolved around Mithras, also a god of light. His was a mystery cult involving several stages of initiation. Both Manichaeism and Mithraism, as well as Zoroastrianism, are discussed again later in connection with early Christianity (see Chapter 8).

The dominance of the Achaemenid dynasty lasted until Persia was invaded by the Greek conqueror, Alexander the Great, in 331 B.C. (see map 6.1). The region was then taken over in turn by various cultural groups until the seventh century A.D. At that point, Muslims from Arabia converted Persia to Islam (see map 9.3).

2.22 ***Darius holding an audience before two fire altars*****, detail of a relief from the Persepolis treasury, *c.* 512–494 B.C. Limestone, entire relief 20 ft. (6 m) long. Archaeological Museum, Tehran, Iran.**

Thematic Parallels

Kingship and "Heads" of State

The concept of kingship appears to be a feature of most cultures that become differentiated into a ruling class and a class that is ruled. In this chapter, we have seen that kingship with absolute power was an important aspect of Ancient Near Eastern cultures. Within that structure, however, there are variations in the manner in which kings are represented. Gudea of Lagash, for example, shows himself as a temple builder, whereas the conquering Naram-Sin ascends a mountain to meet the gods, and Assyrian rulers kill lions and destroy cities. In other areas of the world and in different time periods, there are related views of kingship, which are reflected in various cultural and artistic expressions. Many of these use the image of the ruler's head as a metaphor for the head of state.

The Colossal Heads of the Olmec: 1200–400 B.C.

The Olmec of Mesoamerica (map **2.3**) inhabited a region that corresponds to the Gulf Coast of modern Mexico. They developed an agricultural society with a powerful priest class ruled by

2.23 Colossal head from La Venta, Olmec culture, *c.* 900–500 B.C. Basalt, 7 ft. 5 in. (2.26 m) high. La Venta Park, Villahermosa, Tabasco, Mexico.

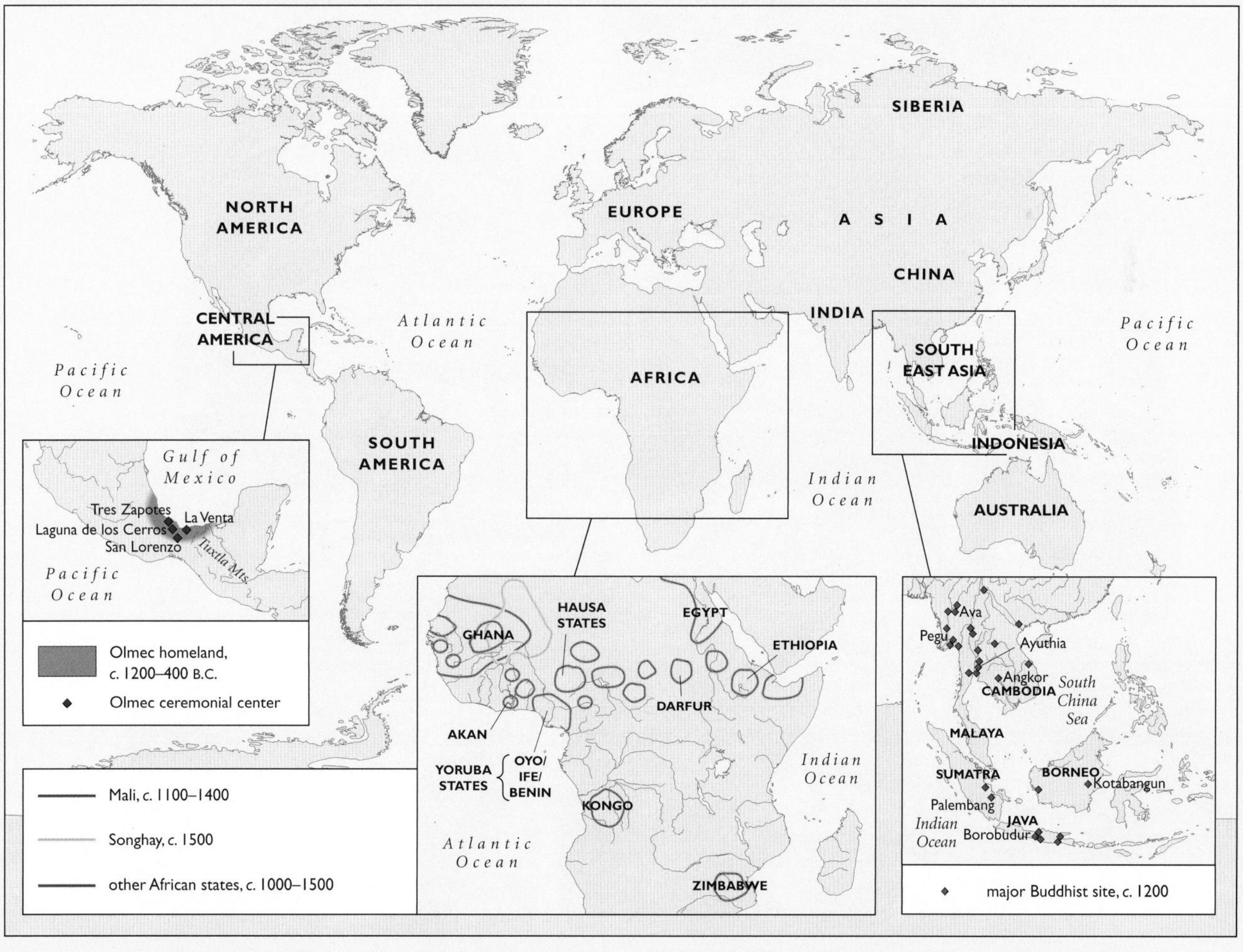

Map 2.3 Olmec civilization in ancient Mesoamerica, *c.* 1200–400 B.C.; African kingdoms, 1000–1500; major Buddhist sites in southeast Asia, *c.* 1200.

kings. The most monumental Olmec sculptures are colossal carved heads from two main ceremonial sites, San Lorenzo and La Venta (figure **2.23**). Each head weighs several tons and, like the huge monoliths at Stonehenge (see Chapter 1), had to be brought to the site from a considerable distance. The basalt quarry that produced the stone was located in the Tuxtla Mountains, 50 miles (80 km) away.

Although the Olmec left no written records, scholars have concluded that the stone heads represented kings. All are similar in style, having a flat nose, thick lips, and a fleshy, organic facial structure. A form-fitting cap, which may be a crown or a helmet, is pulled down over the head to the eyebrows. The imposing quality of the Olmec heads, their colossal size, and their significant locations convey a sense of uncanny power that reflects one ideal of kingship.

The Cambodian Devaraja: Twelfth to Thirteenth Century A.D.

King Jayavarman VII (ruled 1181–1218) reigned during a brief period of Buddhist domination in Cambodia (see map 2.3). To embody his power, he constructed the Bayon, a Buddhist temple in Angkor Thom, near Angkor Wat. Jayavarman conceived of the temple as the mythological Mount Meru, the cosmic center of the Buddhist world, and of himself as a god-king. He had images of his head embedded in the colossal towers (figure **2.24**), which reflected his identification with god and the cosmos and endowed him with absolute power over his subjects.

2.24 Towers of the Bayon Temple, Angkor Thom, Cambodia, 13th century.

Henry VIII: Sixteenth-Century England

In sixteenth-century England, Henry VIII commissioned his court artist, Hans Holbein the Younger (*c.* 1497–1543), to paint his portrait (figure **2.25**). Holbein shows Henry filling the picture space, so that despite the small size of the panel the king appears large. His shoulders expand sideways, creating a square torso surmounted by a frontal head. Henry assumes a regal pose and gazes authoritatively out of the picture. Accentuating his power are not only his relative size and his dominating stance, but also the elaborate costume and formal framing of his head. His head is enclosed by a hat decorated with pearls and feathers and a curved chain across his chest. He is shown both as an individual—the features are unmistakably his own—and as an image of wealth and political power.

2.25 Hans Holbein the Younger, *Henry VIII*, *c.* 1540. Oil on panel, 34¾ × 29½ in. (88.3 × 74.9 cm). Galleria Nazionale d'Arte Antica, Rome.

2.26 Yombe cane finial in the shape of a combined human–leopard, from Kongo kingdom, West Africa. Ivory, 17¾ in. (19.6 cm) high. The Metropolitan Museum of Art, New York.

The **finial** (a decorative feature at the top of an object or building) of this royal cane is made of ivory. The cowrie-shell necklace and carved bracelets are signs of the king's wealth, while his power is conveyed by inlaid eyes, a gaping mouth, and a large head. The prominent teeth are a reminder of the leopard's devouring ferocity and of the king's power over the life and death of his subjects.

Africa—the Head and the Crown: Nineteenth to Twentieth Century

The king's power is embodied in the royal imagery of tribal Africa. In the Kongo kingdom, founded around 1400 on the west coast of Africa (see map 2.3), the king's residence and burial place were located on an elevated mountaintop site. Kongo kings were associated with the leopard, king of the forest and a creature imbued with violence and power (figure **2.26**).

The elaborate beadwork of the Yoruba kingdom in Nigeria (see map 2.3) was an important part of the royal wardrobe. Figure **2.27** illustrates a beaded crown of the Yoruba type, made by artisan families working for the kings. This particular crown is highly decorative, its bright colors endowed with ritual significance. The little enclosure at the top originally contained organic materials with medicinal properties, conveying the king's power to heal. This notion is known in the western European belief in the healing power of the "king's touch."

From even this brief survey of artistic expressions of kingship, it is clear that imagery has been used in very different times and places to convey a king's divine power. Typically, a ruler's palace is elevated above the residences of his subjects. His head must remain over their heads—hence the custom of prostrating oneself, bowing, or curtseying, in the presence of royalty. To reinforce the king's high status, his head is generally large and adorned in some way, usually with a crown or other elegant headdress. In the next chapter, we consider a different type of ruler, namely, the Egyptian pharaoh, who was conceived of as the sun god on earth.

2.27 Yoruba-style crown, from Dahomey, Republic of Benin, 19th century. Beadwork, 17¾ in. (45 cm) high. Musée de l'Homme, Paris.

MESOPOTAMIA AND THE HEBREWS

Another important Near Eastern culture, that of the Hebrews, overlapped with some of the Mesopotamian cultures surveyed in this chapter. At this point we briefly consider their complex early history and draw some parallels with Mesopotamia. The development of Judaism is covered in greater depth in Chapter 8.

EARLY HISTORY

The Hebrews were one of many tribal groups in the Ancient Near East. During the second millennium B.C., they settled in an area that included modern Israel, on the east coast of the Mediterranean Sea, and parts of Jordan (see map 8.1). Their leader was apparently the patriarch Abraham, who is traditionally believed to have come from Ur. According to the Hebrew Bible (Old Testament), a number of Hebrews later moved to Egypt during a period of famine, and after several generations they were enslaved by the pharaohs (see Chapter 3).

Around 1250 B.C., Moses led the Hebrews out of Egypt, through the Sinai Desert, on a forty-year journey called the Exodus (the Greek term for "going out"). During the eleventh to tenth century B.C., a series of powerful kings—Saul, David, and Solomon—reigned in Israel, and under Solomon's rule the Temple was erected in Jerusalem. The Hebrews then split into two kingdoms, Israel and Judah, and fought on and off for generations with other Near Eastern cultures, including the Assyrians.

In the sixth century B.C., King Nebuchadnezzar and the Babylonians overran Israel and destroyed Solomon's Temple. The Hebrews, especially the intellectuals and the rabbis (teachers of God's law), went into exile in 586 B.C., a period known as the Babylonian Captivity. This ended in 539 B.C., when Cyrus II came to power in Persia.

The Hebrews (now referred to as the Jews) were set free to return to Jerusalem and rebuild the Temple. They dedicated the new Temple in 516 B.C. and established a **theocracy** (a government of priests or religious leaders). In the fourth century B.C., the Jews were Hellenized (underwent Greek influence) by the conquests of Alexander the Great (see Chapter 6). In A.D. 70, the Romans destroyed the rebuilt Temple along with the entire city of Jerusalem. The Jewish state thus came to an end and Israel was absorbed into the vast Roman Empire (see Chapter 7).

In the next chapter, we survey the civilization of ancient Egypt, which overlapped the cultures described in this chapter. Not only did Hebrews live in Egypt for several hundred years, but the Egyptians had constant contact with the Near East. Egyptian rulers married foreign wives, traded, and fought wars with Mesopotamia. At the same time, however, whereas the Near East was composed of different civilizations, each with its own social and political organization and distinctive styles of art and architecture, Egypt remained a separate and relatively uniform culture for thousands of years.

KEY TERMS

anthropomorphic human in form.

ceramics pottery made by firing (heating) clay.

convention an accepted practice.

cuneiform a form of writing used in Mesopotamia and consisting of wedge-shaped characters.

curvilinear having curved forms.

epithet an identifying adjective or phrase.

finial a decorative feature at the top of an object or building.

frontal facing front.

hierarchical proportion a convention in ancient art in which size is equated with status.

intaglio a process in which lines or images are incised in a surface.

lapis lazuli a semi-precious, light blue stone.

monotheism a religion whose adherents believe in a single god.

personify embody as a person.

pictographic based on pictures.

plaque a small, decorated slab.

polytheism belief in many gods.

relief a sculpture that is not completely carved away from its original material.

stele a vertical stone marker or pillar.

stylization a technique in art in which forms are rendered as surface patterns rather than naturalistically

theocracy rule by priests or other religious leaders.

ziggurat in Mesopotamia, a monumental stepped building signifying a mountain.

KEY QUESTIONS

1. Why would developing writing aid in urbanization? Which society first developed writing?
2. What characteristics of literary epics are found in *The Epic of Gilgamesh*?
3. What are two goals of the laws of Hammurabi?
4. What are two artistic devices the artist used in figure 2.22 to show Darius's two roles?
5. Which religions discussed in this chapter are monotheistic? What is the explanation given by Zoroastrianism for the presence of evil? Is this explanation used by other Mesopotamian religions?

SUGGESTED READING

Blier, Suzanne Preston. *The Royal Arts of Africa*. London: Laurence King Publishing, 1998.
- A study of royal art in Africa.

Christie, Agatha. *Murder in Mesopotamia*. London: HarperCollins, 2001.

——. *They Came to Baghdad*. London: HarperCollins, 2003.
- Archaeological mysteries set in the Middle East.

Collon, Dominique. *Near Eastern Seals*. London: British Museum Press, 1990.
- A survey of seals from the Ancient Near East with discussions of style and iconography.

Finegan, Jack. *Light from the Ancient Past* (Vol. 1). Princeton, NJ: Princeton University Press, 1974.
- A survey of Ancient Near Eastern culture and history.

Gilgamesh, trans. John Gardner and John Maier (with the assistance of Richard A. Henshaw), from the Sîn-leqi-unninni version. New York: Random House, 1984/Vintage Books, 1985.
- An English translation of the oldest surviving epic poem.

Groenewegen-Frankfort, H. A. *Arrest and Movement*. New York: Hacker Art Books, 1978.
- A study, beginning with the Ancient Near East, of how artists convey motion and stasis in their work.

Kramer, Samuel Noah. *History Begins at Sumer*. New York: Doubleday, 1959.
- A classic work on the Sumerian civilization.

——. *The Sumerians*. Chicago and London: University of Chicago Press, 1966.
- A readable survey of Sumerian arts and culture in context by a noted scholar in the field.

Muscarella, Oscar. *Bronze and Iron*. New York: Metropolitan Museum of Art, 1988.
- Bronze and Iron Age in the Ancient Near East.

——. *The Lie Became Great*. Groningen, The Netherlands: Styx Publications, 1998.
- A study of forgeries from the Ancient Near East and the problems created by the "culture" of forgery.

Oppenheim, A. Leo. *Ancient Mesopotamia*, rev. ed. Chicago and London: University of Chicago Press, 1977.
- An overview of Mesopotamian culture.

Pritchard, James B. (ed.). *The Ancient Near East* (Vol. 1). Princeton, NJ: Princeton University Press, 1973.
- The first of two volumes of a study of all aspects of Ancient Near Eastern history and culture.

SUGGESTED FILMS

1919 *The Fall of Babylon*, dir. D. W. Griffith

2001 *Murder in Mesopotamia* (television movie, based on Christie)

3 Ancient Egypt

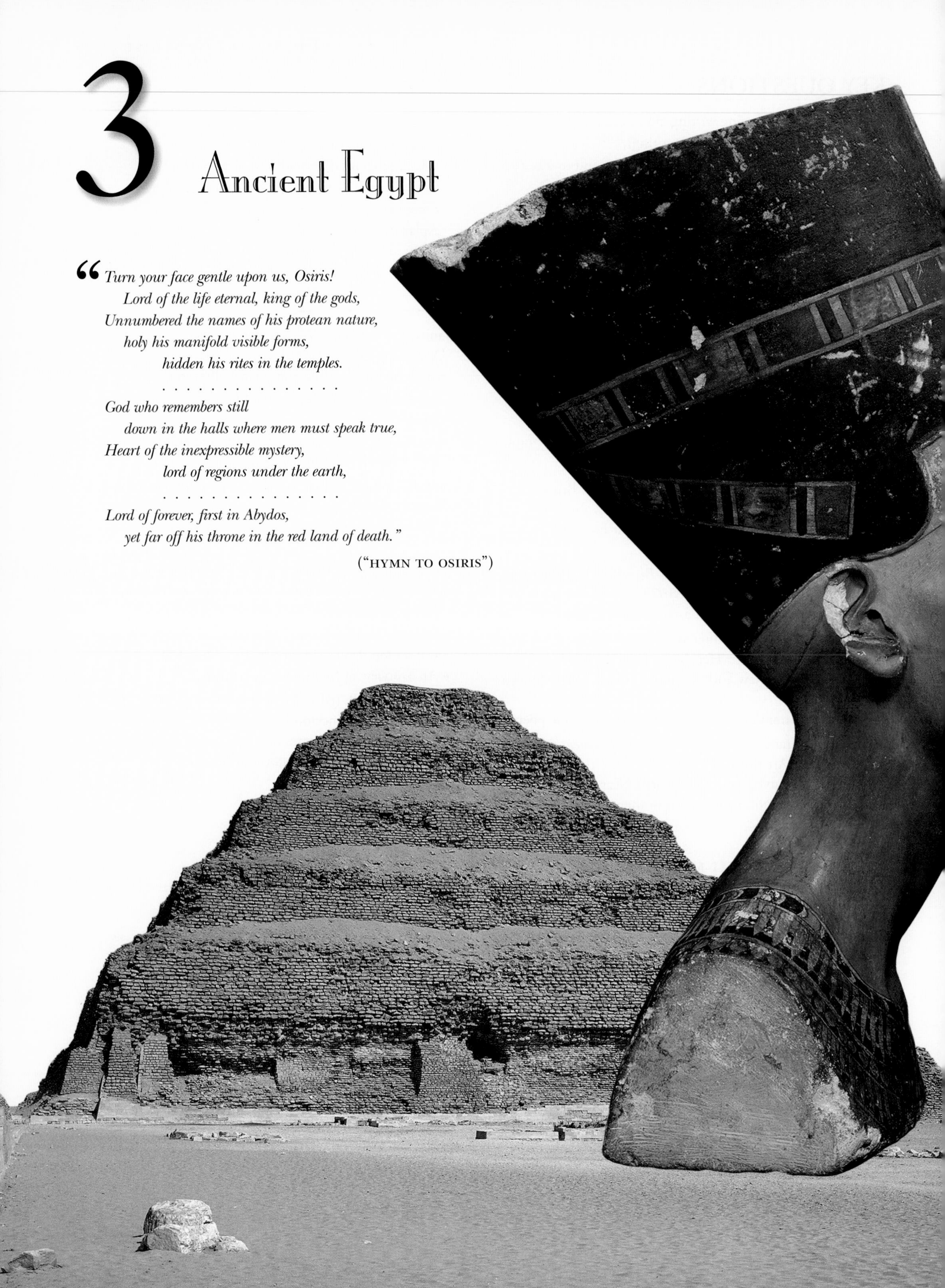

"Turn your face gentle upon us, Osiris!
Lord of the life eternal, king of the gods,
Unnumbered the names of his protean nature,
holy his manifold visible forms,
hidden his rites in the temples.

. . . .

God who remembers still
down in the halls where men must speak true,
Heart of the inexpressible mystery,
lord of regions under the earth,

. . . .

Lord of forever, first in Abydos,
yet far off his throne in the red land of death."

("HYMN TO OSIRIS")

One of the primary differences between ancient Mesopotamia and Egypt was Egypt's political stability. Mesopotamian cultures came and went, some growing into powerful empires while others were relatively short-lived. Egypt, however, maintained its cultural continuity for around 3000 years (roughly from 3100 B.C. until the Roman conquest in 31 B.C.). This was possible in large part because Egypt's social and political structures were more easily controlled than those of Mesopotamia.

Egypt was also more geographically isolated and unified than Mesopotamia. Located in northeast Africa, Egypt was separated from the rest of the Ancient Near East and protected by its geographical borders—the Mediterranean Sea in the north, the first cataract of the Nile in the south, desert and the Sinai Peninsula in the east, and the Sahara in the west—which made Egypt less open to foreign invasions than Mesopotamia. The country itself was united by the Nile, which, at 4160 miles (6695 km) is the longest river in the world, although less than 1000 miles (1610 km) of the Nile is in Egypt.

Egypt also had its own writing system, called "the gods' words" by Egyptians, which differed from Mesopotamian cuneiform. Egyptians used the more pictorial ***hieroglyphs*** *(literally "sacred carvings") for official and religious texts and a simpler cursive script called* ***hieratic***, *derived from hieroglyphs (see Box, p. 49). Because scholars can now read both hieroglyphs and hieratic, a great deal is known about ancient Egyptian culture.*

As in Mesopotamia, most of the Egyptian art that has survived was made for rulers and their courts. But, because of Egypt's long period of cultural continuity, its art styles show less change over time than elsewhere in the Ancient Near East. In addition to highly skilled engineers and architects, Egypt had more local stone available than Mesopotamia, making it possible to build vast works of large-scale architecture. For the ancient Egyptians, especially the rulers, stone symbolized eternity because it lasts. In Egyptian religion, too, eternal life was of paramount importance.

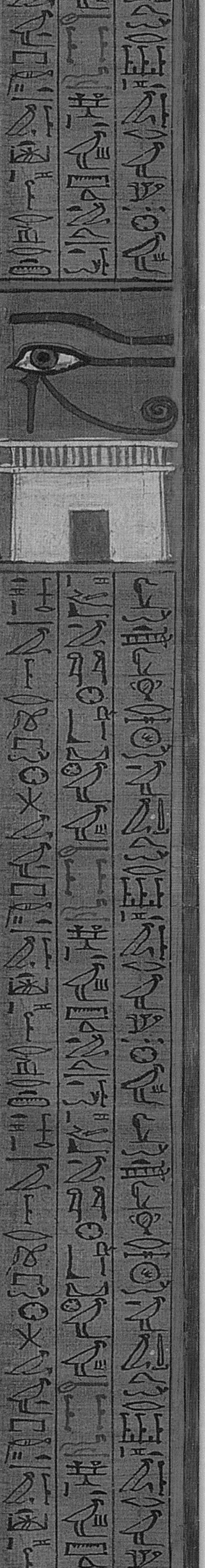

Key Topics

Stability and Eternity

- Myths of the afterlife
- Kings as gods
- Hierarchical society reflected in pyramids

Constructing Monumentality

- Step pyramid at Saqqara
- Pyramid complex at Giza
- Monumental royal sculpture

Religion

- Polytheism: gods, goddesses, demi-gods
- Monotheism: Amenhotep IV becomes Akhenaton

ANCIENT EGYPT (all dates B.C.)

TIMELINE	PHARAONIC RULE 3100–2469	OLD KINGDOM c. 2649–2143	MIDDLE KINGDOM c. 1991–1700	NEW KINGDOM c. 1550–1070
HISTORY AND CULTURE	Dynasties 1–2 Unification of Upper and Lower Egypt by Narmer (Menes)	Dynasties 3–6 Political and social stability Economic prosperity Trade with black Africa Hierarchical society	First Intermediate period, Dynasties 7–11 Middle Kingdom, Dynasties 12–14 Second Intermediate period, Dynasties 15–17 Hyksos introduce chariots Start of Bronze Age Famine and foreign invasion	Dynasties 18–20 Imperial expansion Amarna period, *c.* 1349–1336: capital moved to Amarna
RELIGION AND MYTH	Polytheism Belief in afterlife Soul consisting of *ka*, *akh*, and *ba* Pharaoh as sun god on earth	Elaborate royal burials		Brief period of monotheism under Akhenaton in the Amarna period: worship of the Aton Temples
ART	Palette of Narmer, *c.* 3100	Monumental royal sculpture Hierarchical scale Stylized forms Grids for sculpture and painting Hieroglyphic inscriptions Seated statue of Khafre, *c.* 2520 *Triad of Menkaure*, *c.* 2490–2472 Scribe from Saqqara	More realism in royal sculpture Cubic temple statues Coffin of Senbi, *c.* 2000 Senwosret-senebefny and his wife, *c.* 1878–1840 Head of Amenemhet III, *c.* 1859–1813 Jewelry	Bust of Nefretiti, *c.* 1349–1336 Tutankhamon's throne, *c.* 1336 Tutankhamon's funerary mask, *c.* 1327
ARCHITECTURE	Imhotep, step pyramid of King Zoser, Saqqara, *c.* 2630	Monumental royal architecture Pyramids at Giza, *c.* 2649–2100	Rock-cut tombs	Hatshepsut's building campaign at Deir-el-Bahri, *c.* 1473 Monumental temples Temple of Ramses II, Luxor, begun *c.* 1400
LITERATURE	Prayers for offerings to the dead	"Hymn to Osiris" Hymns to the Nile Hymns to the Sun Secular poetry Wisdom literature	"Tale of Sinuhe" Medical texts	*Book of the Dead*
MUSIC 		Professional musicians, male and female Temple music and music at social gatherings Harp, sistrum (rattle), double-reed pipe		

The quotation at the beginning of this chapter reflects the Egyptian preoccupation with eternity. It is from a **hymn** *(a song praising god) to Osiris, god of the Underworld, where those who had led a moral life were rewarded. As indicated in the hymn, the god's cult center was at Abydos, a town on the bank of the Nile in southern Egypt* *(see map 3.1, p. 50)**, but he reigned as "lord of regions under earth." When Egyptians died, their hearts were weighed against the feather of Maat (goddess of truth, justice, order, and cosmic harmony) in the Underworld: "down in the halls where men must speak true." The deceased who passed the test proceeded to the next life; those who failed were damned, and their hearts were devoured by the monster Amemet. This belief in a last judgment was inspired by the concept of* **maat**, *the ideal order of the universe and society—a fundamental aspect of ancient Egyptian culture.*

THE NILE

Egypt is primarily desert, which makes it dependent on the Nile for water. The source of the Nile is in central Africa, from where it flows north to Memphis, divides into a delta, and empties into the Mediterranean Sea. Along the way, the Nile flows over six large cataracts—outcrops of rock formations that create rapids. The Nile was essential to ancient Egyptians' survival because its annual inundation provided fertile soil for agriculture (see Box and figure 3.1). When the Nile did not flood, vegetation was sparse and the land was beset with famine and death. Dependence on the Nile for agricultural prosperity, which was similar to the crucial role of the Tigris and Euphrates rivers in Mesopotamia, was thus a constant feature of Egyptian culture.

It was along the banks of the Nile that Paleolithic cultures in Egypt established temporary settlements, where people lived by hunting and fishing. From around 7000 to 4000 B.C., remains from more settled Neolithic communities have yielded evidence of farming, pottery, and sculpture—small statues of females might have represented fertility goddesses. Neolithic Egyptians cultivated flax, wheat, and barley, and they domesticated goats, sheep, and cattle. As in Mesopotamia, Egypt had irrigation systems and used metals. Communities became towns, and there is evidence of warfare.

Egypt traded with the Near East, especially the Levant, which had cedar, but its main trading contacts before 1900 B.C. were with Africa. The Land of Punt

Defining Moment

Egypt and the Solar Calendar

Ancient cultures revered star gazers and makers of calendars. Mesopotamians developed star charts to predict the seasons. In Egypt, kingship embodied by the pharaoh was the foundation of life, and the calendar was crucial in supporting royal power. As divine beings, pharaohs were obliged to provide for their people and to maintain *maat* by ruling justly, celebrating daily temple rituals and presiding over major festivals, and defending Egypt against its enemies. Pharaohs had to ensure the annual inundation of the Nile to keep the land fertile, and one means of predicting this was provided by the Egyptian calendar.

The Nile flooded (figure **3.1**) between June and September, a season the Egyptians called *akhet,* the inundation. Heavy summer rains in the Ethiopian highlands swelled the tributaries and other rivers that joined to become the Nile. Ancient Egyptians recognized three seasons revolving around the inundation: one, Emergence (the growing of crops using floodwater caught in man-made canals) from June 21 to October 21; two, from October 21 to February 21; and three, Summer (harvesting crops) from February 21 to June 21.

The original pre-dynastic Egyptian calendar, which divided the year into four lunar months, proved to be inadequate. The later solar calendar, echoing Egyptian cosmology and religion, marked the beginning of the year by the appearance of the star Sirius, in the constellation of Canis Major. This constellation became visible around June 21, and was called "the going up of the goddess Sothis." The calendar had only 360 days, but at the beginning of the year, an additional five days were set aside for feasting, rituals, and celebration.

Critical Question Why do we divide time into years, months, days, hours, and seconds? What is the difference between sequential and cyclical time?

3.1 *Flooding of the Nile*, from the Sanctuary of Fortuna, Praeneste, 1st century B.C. Roman mosaic, 20 × 16 ft. (6 × 4.9 m). Archaeological Museum, Palestrina, Italy.

(somewhere to the southeast, possibly modern Somalia) was famous for its incense, and Nubia (to the south) was a source of gold, ivory, ebony wood, panther skins, ostrich eggs and feathers, and animals, such as monkeys, that were considered exotic. In addition, Nubia controlled trade routes to further south in Africa. From the late third millennium B.C., Nubia was ruled by Egypt and adopted some of its cultural and artistic traditions. At the same time, Egypt itself was influenced by black Africa and from the ninth century B.C. there were periods when Egypt was ruled by Nubia. After 1900 B.C., Egypt increased its trade with the Near East and Sinai, importing turquoise, copper, tin, bronze, and lapis lazuli.

THE PHARAOHS

The supreme Egyptian ruler, the **pharaoh**, was conceived of literally as the sun god on earth. A king list devised in the fourth century B.C. by the Egyptian priest Manetho traces the chronology of the pharaohs from 3100 B.C. to 332 B.C., when the Greek general Alexander the Great conquered Egypt (see Chapter 6). The chronology that is currently used for ancient Egypt marks the beginning of written records, by which time Egypt had formed into a unified culture along the lines of what we think of as a nation-state. The Neolithic era, which precedes this period, is termed "predynastic," because it predates the thirty **dynasties** (families of kings) in the king list. The dynasties comprise the so-called Kingdoms: Old (*c.* 2469–2143 B.C.), Middle (*c.* 1991–1700 B.C.), and New (*c.* 1550–1070 B.C.). Periods in between the Kingdoms, called Intermediate Periods, denote either decline or foreign occupation. The second and most important Intermediate Period included the Hyksos domination. Foreign rulers who spoke a Semitic language, the Hyksos probably introduced horse-drawn chariots and a new and more powerful type of bow into Egypt. Their expulsion was followed by the beginning of the New Kingdom.

Egypt's rule by pharaohs began around 3100 B.C., by which time, after a long period of warfare, Upper (south) and Lower (north) Egypt had been unified. From that time, the Egyptian pharaoh embodied the unification by his two crowns—the white crown of Upper Egypt and the red crown of Lower Egypt. These crowns are shown on the so-called Palette of Narmer (figure **3.2**), a ritual object made of slate, which was a temple dedication.

3.2 Palette of Narmer (front and back), *c.* 3100 B.C. Slate, 25 in. (63.5 cm) high. Egyptian Museum, Cairo.
This palette resembles objects used by women for eye make-up (which was contained in the indented circle), but it is much larger and is assumed to have had a ritual purpose. The images on both sides represent the victory of a pharaoh, identified as Narmer (also called Menes), who was credited in ancient Egypt as the traditional unifier of the country. In the scene at the top, Narmer wears the tall white crown of Upper Egypt; he is about to kill a fallen enemy. The upper register of the scene at the bottom shows Narmer before a group of standard-bearers and ten dead enemies lying on the ground with their heads between their legs. Here, Narmer wears the slightly more elaborate red crown of Lower Egypt. The horned cows at the top of the palette represent Hathor, the goddess who protected the palace of the king.

Society and Culture

Principal Deities of Ancient Egypt

Amon god of Thebes (sometimes a ram), later Amon-Re
Anubis god of the dead and embalmers (depicted as a jackal)
Aten (or **Aton**) the sun-disk (worshipped by Akhenaton in the New Kingdom)
Atum early Old Kingdom creator god and sun god; later, Amon, Re, and Amon-Re
Bes protector of women in childbirth (a leonine dwarf)
Geb the earth, father of Osiris
Hapy god of the Nile and fertility (a man with heavy breasts)
Hathor protector of the palace, goddess of the sky (a horned cow)
Horus sky god and god of kingship (depicted as a falcon), son of Isis and Osiris
Isis mother goddess, guardian of coffins (in human guise), sister and wife of Osiris
Khepre rising sun, a form of Re (depicted as a scarab beetle)
Maat goddess of truth and order (depicted as a feather, or as a woman with a feather-head)
Mut Amon's wife (sometimes a vulture)
Nun the primeval ocean
Nut goddess of the sky, mother of Osiris
Osiris god of the Underworld, identical with the deceased king (depicted as the king's mummy)
Ptah crafts god (depicted as a male mummy)
Re (or **Ra**) sun god and judge, sometimes shown as a falcon, sometimes in combination with Amon as Amon-Re, or Amon-Ra; cult center at Heliopolis (the city of the sun)
Set god of disorder and violence, brother of Osiris
Sobek crocodile god of the Nile
Thoth scribal god and the inventor of writing (depicted as an ibis or a baboon)

The Pharaoh and the Egyptian Concept of Time

Complicating the chronology of Manetho's king list is the fact that every pharaoh began counting time from his personal rule, so that when a new ruler ascended the throne, the date was redesignated as Year One. Each new reign was thought of as a recreation of the world and some kings referred to their first years in power as "the repeating of births." This reflected the Egyptian concept of time as cyclical and the belief that the ruler was omnipotent. Because the pharaoh was all-powerful, he and the royal family had prerogatives denied to the general population, such as making incestuous marriages for political purposes. Pharaohs had a dual human and divine nature; they were both gods and intermediaries between gods and their human subjects.

Pharaohs ruled from Memphis, halfway between the cult centers of the sun god Re at Heliopolis (literally "city of the sun") and of Amon at Thebes. (Amon became combined with Re as Amon-Re.) In addition to being identified with the sun god, whose reappearance each morning conformed to the cyclical idea of time, the pharaoh was seen as the living embodiment of other deities, such as Osiris, god of the dead, and Horus, god of kingship.

RELIGION

Egypt, like much of the ancient world, was polytheistic. Its people worshipped a myriad of gods and goddesses, demi-gods, gods in animal form, in human form, and in combined human and animal form. The gods were everywhere and controlled all aspects of life (see Box). The Egyptians composed hymns through which they prayed to the gods for help while on earth and for eternal life after death. The wish to live forever gave rise in ancient Egypt to some of the most elaborate burial practices the world has ever known.

The Osiris Myth

From around 2400 B.C. Osiris became a major figure in ancient Egyptian myth and religion. The hymn (actually a poem) quoted at the beginning of the chapter is only one of many hymns that are both a means of transmitting religious ideas and works of literature in their own right. Osiris was the son of Geb (dry land) and Nut (the sky as a reflection of the earth's primeval waters, known as Nun). The three siblings of Osiris were Set (the god of disorder) and the goddesses Nephthys and Isis (who was also his wife). Set murdered and dismembered Osiris, but Isis gathered up his bones, flesh, and organs and restored him to life.

Osiris and Isis had a son, Horus, whom Isis defended from evil. She thus evolved into a goddess devoted to mothers and their children. When Horus became an adult, he defeated Set in a battle for their father's throne in the Underworld. Horus's victory led to his role as the god of kingship; typically he is represented in art as a falcon.

There are many illustrations of Osiris as king and judge in the Underworld (figure **3.3**). This example shows Osiris enthroned inside his palace. He wears the tall white crown of Upper Egypt (the location of Abydos) and holds the crook and flail (threshing tool) of kingship. His white linen shroud identifies him with death, and his green skin denotes the rebirth of vegetation with the renewal of spring. Behind him stand his sisters, Isis and Nephthys, and before him on a lotus blossom are the four sons of Horus. Each has an identifying head: a falcon, a jackal, a baboon, and a man. Hovering over the lotus and protecting Osiris is the Horus-falcon.

3.3 ***Papyrus of Hunefer: the god Thoth at the last judgment*****, Thebes, 19th Dynasty, *c.* 1295–1186 B.C. Painted papyrus, 19¼ in. (39 cm) high. British Museum, London.**
At the far left, the jackal-headed god Anubis carries the ankh symbol of life as he leads the dead man toward the scales where his heart is weighed against the feather of Maat. The monstrous Amemet—a composite of several animals—stands poised to devour the heart if the deceased fails the test. Anubis is shown again, adjusting the scales. Tensely awaiting the outcome, Amemet stares at the ibis-headed Thoth, who writes down the final judgment. In this case, the heart weighs the same as the feather, indicating that the man led a moral life. He is then introduced to Osiris by Horus in the guise of his father's avenger. A tribunal of squatting gods lines the top of the weighing scene, and a row of protective cobras fills the space over Osiris's throne.

The Osiris myth was of paramount importance to Egyptian culture in three respects. First, it was an example of death and rebirth and the god's role in the continual cycle of the agricultural year. Second, it reflected the fact that defenseless infants and children need the protection of their mothers. Third, it embodied the notion of Egyptian kingship through the triumph of Horus over the forces of disorder.

HYMNS TO THE NILE

Like the myth of Osiris, the Nile, with its yearly flooding that brought the earth back to life, was a metaphor of rebirth. The importance of the Nile inspired the creation of Hapy, god of the annual inundation, to whom hymns of fertility were addressed:

> Come back to Egypt, bringing your benediction of peace,
> greening the banks of the Nile;
> Save mankind and the creatures, make life likely,
> through the gift of all this your countryside!
> O hidden god, be it well with you! may you flourish, and return!
> Hapy, Lord of Egypt, may you flourish, and return!

Hapy was represented as a man with pendulous, lactating breasts and a pregnant belly. His combined male/female features reflected his role as a fertility god: as a male he had generative power and as a female he provided nourishment.

In contrast to Hapy, the crocodile god, Sobek, was seen as dangerous. Sobek inhabited the Nile, but he required hymns of appeasement. Here the emphasis is not so much on fertility and plenty, but rather on primal fear:

> Hail to you, who arose from the primeval waters,
> lord of the lowlands, ruler of the desert edge,
>
> . . . .
>
> who lives on plunder,
> who goes upstream by his [own] perfection,
> who goes downstream, after hunting a multitude,
> a [great] number.

Note that Sobek is an ever-present menace in voracious pursuit of his prey. He slithers from the desert's edge and disappears into the river. Such vivid characterization of the gods through hymns and other verse forms is typical of ancient Egyptian literature and reflects the view that all aspects of nature are physical embodiments of the gods.

HYMNS TO THE SUN

The Egyptian creator god was the sun, known as Atum in the early Old Kingdom, with his main cult city at Heliopolis, and later he was combined with Re. The journey of the sun across the sky was critical to Egyptian belief, and at night, the sun was thought to descend into the Underworld. This journey, which mirrors the cyclical notion of time, was celebrated in the New Kingdom "Hymn to the Rising Sun":

> Be praised, O Re, in your rising,
> Atum-Horakhty!

Let your perfections be worshipped with my eyes,
and let your sunlight come to be within my breast.
May you proceed in your own peace in the Night Barque,
your heart rejoicing in a following breeze within the Day Barque.
How delightful is the crossing of the skies among the peaceful dead
with all your enemies fallen!
The unwearying stars give praise to you,
the indestructible stars adore you—
You who go to rest in the horizon of the Western Mountains,
beautiful as the Sun each day,
beautiful, enduring, as my Lord.

The setting of the sun and its reemergence at dawn became a model for death and rebirth. The Egyptian view that the pharaoh and the sun were equivalent appears in the following excerpt from "The Greatness of the King." By using the literary device of repetition for emphasis, the poet reinforces the parallel between god and king.

How great is the Lord of his city!
He is exalted a thousand times over; other persons are small.
How great is the Lord of his city!
He is a dyke which holds back the River, restraining its flood of water.
How great is the Lord of his city!
He is a cool room which lets each man sleep until dawn.
How great is the Lord of his city!
He is a rampart with walls of copper from Sinai.
How great is the Lord of his city!
He is a refuge which does not lack his helping hand.

THE EGYPTIAN VIEW OF DEATH

Believing that people continue to exist in the next world, the Egyptians attached paramount importance to the physical preservation of the dead. Figure **3.4** is a photograph of a predynastic burial. The fetal position, as in prehistoric burials (see Chapter 1), suggests that belief in the afterlife began early in human history. Reinforcing this notion are objects of daily life buried with the deceased, presumably for use after death.

From the Old Kingdom, there is evidence of efforts to prevent bodily decay by wrapping the corpse in linen. Eventually, however, the Egyptians realized that decomposition could be avoided only by removing the internal organs. Over the course of Egyptian history, this led to an elaborate, seventy-two-day process of **mummification**. Bodies were dried using natron crystals, embalmed in a covering of plaster and linen, and treated with chemicals. The organs were placed in four individual containers called **canopic jars**.

Figure **3.5** shows the mummy and case of a woman from the Late period (after the New Kingdom) who had been the consort of a priest. Both the mummy (figure **3.5a**) and the case are in the typical form of an embalmed human figure. The mummy netting is decorated with a winged scarab (dung beetle), which was a standard protective device in Egyptian burials. The image of the beetle pushing a sphere of dung symbolized both the sun-disk's daily journey across the sky and spontaneous generation and rebirth. The inside of the mummy case (figure **3.5b**) depicts the goddess of the West (the direction of death) with a falcon on her head. On the lid (figure **3.5c**), below the neck, is a falcon with a ram's head and outstretched protective wings. About halfway down the lid, the mummy itself is shown lying on a bier, and the remaining scenes depict various gods and symbols. Particularly lifelike are the wide open, staring eyes, alluding to the future life of the deceased. This complex iconography was part of an elaborate system of protective magical devices to ensure the safety of the dead person in a dangerous Underworld and his or her ultimate rebirth.

Despite all the effort that went into mummification, it was feared that the bodies still might not reach the afterlife intact. To be on the safe side, the Egyptians placed statues of the dead in their tombs as substitutes for the real person. The Egyptian

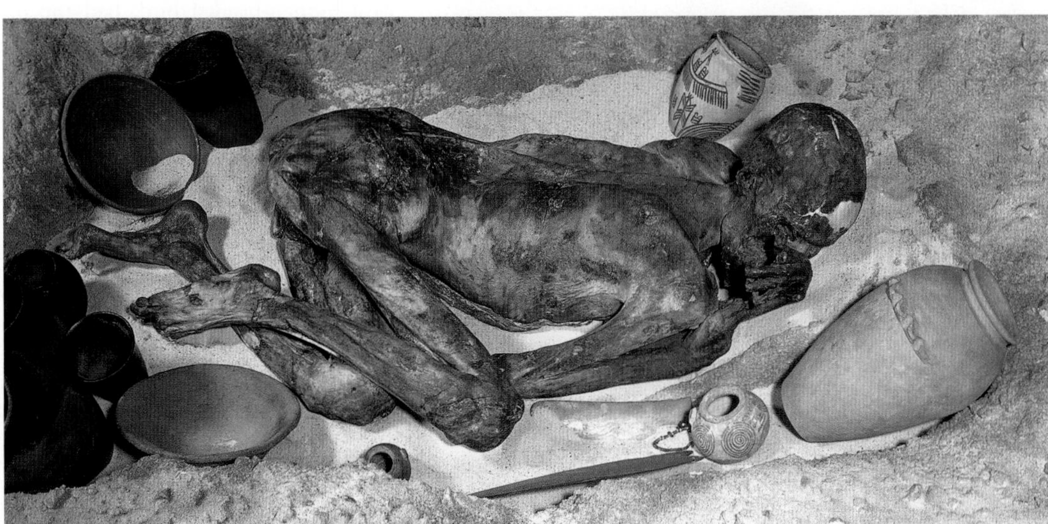

3.4 Predynastic male burial, *c.* 3300 B.C. 5 ft. 4¼ in. (1.63 m) long. British Museum, London.

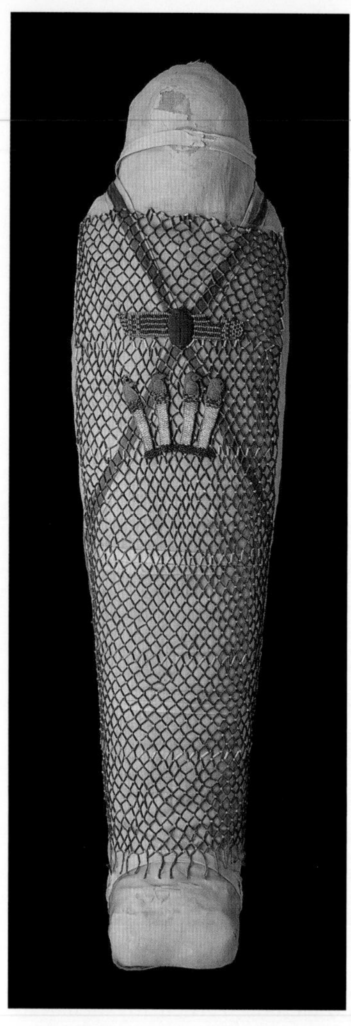

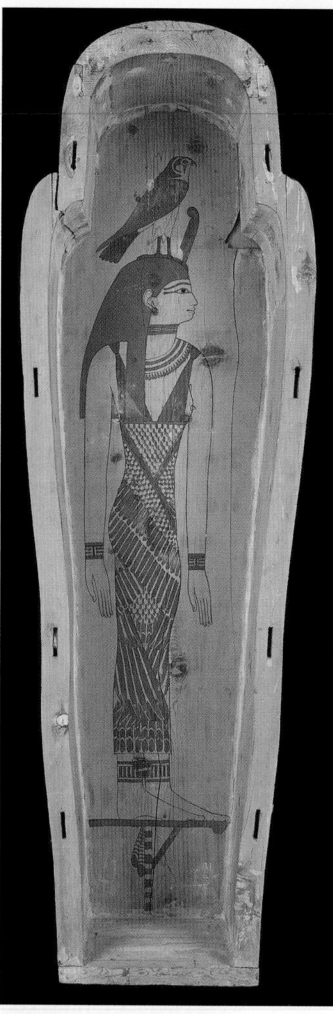

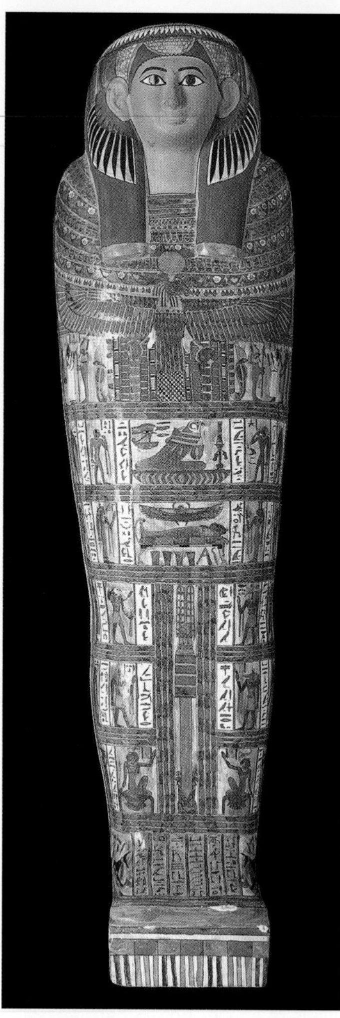

3.5 (a) Mummy, and (b) and (c) Case of Nesmutaatneru, from the Temple of Hatshepsut, Deir-el-Bahri, 25th Dynasty, *c.* 760–660 B.C. Painted wood, linen, mummy net, faience, and polychrome glaze; mummy 4 ft. 11 7/16 in. (1.51 m) long, inner coffin 5 ft. 6 9/16 in. (1.69 m) long, middle coffin 6 ft. 1 3/4 in. (1.86 m) long. Museum of Fine Arts, Boston.

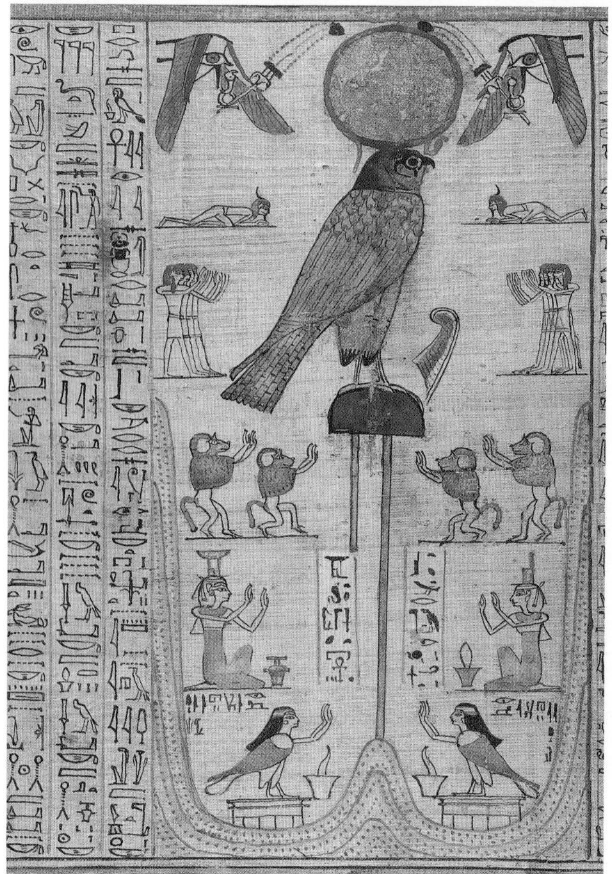

equivalent of the soul—the *ka*, a kind of double containing the life force of the deceased—could then enter the substitute and proceed to the afterlife. Offerings of food and drink were placed in tombs as sustenance for the dead and the *ka*.

The ancient Egyptian soul had two other aspects, the *akh* and the *ba*. The *akh* was overtly spiritual; it was the heavenly transfiguration of the dead into light. The *ba*, often represented as a human-headed bird, had the power of flight and could enter and exit the body at will. This image appears, for example, in a New Kingdom **vignette** (small section of decoration or literary sketch) from the *Book of the Dead*, a series of texts designed to guide the deceased on the journey to the afterlife (figure **3.6**).

3.6 *left* **Funerary papyrus of the chief of the concubines of Osiris, chief of the concubines of Nebtu and Khnum, chantress of Amun, Anhai, *c.* 1300 B.C. British Museum, London.**

Bird imagery appears three times in this vignette. The large falcon surmounted by a sun-disk is the sun god, Aton. He is protected by two winged eyes with ostrich-feather fans and flanked by two rows of gods. Below the falcon, three levels of worshippers include, in descending order, dancing baboons, kneeling figures of Isis and Nephthys, and two human-headed birds. These stand on platforms in the valley of a mountainous terrain and represent the *ba* of the deceased. Note the prevalence of green, denoting rebirth, which is associated with the sun god.

Society and Culture

Hieroglyphs and Egyptian Literature

Writing in Egypt began around 3100 B.C. in the form of hieroglyphs, literally "sacred carvings." These were a mixture of **ideograms** (pictorial representations of ideas) and **phonograms** (images denoting sounds). Hieroglyphs have been found on fragments of stones, pottery, and papyrus (a plant that grows along the Nile). They remained in use until the fourth century A.D.

However, it was not until 1822 that the French scholar Jean-François Champollion (1790–1832) deciphered hieroglyphs, opening up the vast body of ancient Egyptian literature to the world. He was able to translate Egyptian texts after Napoleon's army discovered the Rosetta Stone in 1799 (figure **3.7**). The stone bore three texts, one of which was in Greek and could easily be read and matched to the others: Demotic script (a simplified form of hieroglyphs) and hieroglyphs.

The earliest inscriptions are lists of offerings in tombs. These evolved into prayers for offerings to the dead and for a prosperous afterlife. Since the deceased give an account of themselves and their lives, such prayers can be seen as early examples of autobiography.

Hymns to the gods are an abundant source of Egyptian poetry, with their vivid descriptions of the pantheon and other aspects of religious beliefs in ancient Egypt. Love poems reflect the universal nature of young lovers, their devotion, passion, and even deceit. There is also wisdom literature, in which an older and wiser figure admonishes a younger one and tries to educate him or her in the ways of the world.

Most Egyptian literature is in verse, although prose stories exist as well as combinations of the two genres. The best-known example of Egyptian narrative poetry is the Middle Kingdom "Tale of Sinuhe," about a courtier who leaves Egypt to escape a palace coup. He goes to live in the Near East but at the end of his life returns to Egypt and a warm welcome from the royal family. Sinuhe describes his emotional reconciliation with the pharaoh as follows:

I found his Majesty upon the Throne of Egypt
in the throne room all of silvered gold.
Really there, at last, before him,
I stretched myself full length upon the floor;
But then my foolish brain turned witless in his
presence, just as this god was offering warm welcome.
I was a man seized in the grip of darkness—
my bird-soul flown, my limbs unstrung;
My heart, no longer was it in my body
so that I might distinguish life from death.

The king replies:

Then said his Majesty to an attendant courtier,
"Raise him. Let him speak with me."
And then he said, "Well, well, you have come home,
done wandering the weary world since your departure!
I see the marks of time etched on your body;
you have grown old.
When death must come, your rites shall not be wanting—
your burial shall never be by bedouin tribes.
Now deprecate yourself no longer:
you spoke no treason; your name is honored here."

The king honors his promise, and the tale ends with Sinuhe's description of his tomb and his death. This passage emphasizes Sinuhe's pleasure in having an impressive tomb and a sculpture of himself in gold. He also enjoys the material pleasures of a life that he hopes will continue after death:

There was made for me a pyramid of stone
built in the shadow of the royal tomb.
The god's own masons hewed the blocks for it,
and its walls were portioned out among them;
The draftsman and the painter drew in it,
the master sculptor carved;
The overseer of workmen at the tombs
criss-crossed the length of Egypt on account of it.
Implements and furniture were fitted in its storeroom
and all that would be needful brought within;
Servants for my Spirit were appointed,
a garden was laid out above,
And tended fields ran downward to the village—
just as is ordered for a nearest Friend.
My statue was all brushed with burnished gold,
its kilt set off with silver.

It was his Majesty who did all this for me.
No simple man has ever had so much.
And I enjoyed the sunshine of his royal favor
until my day of mooring dawned.

3.7 Rosetta Stone, 196 B.C. Basalt, 3 ft. 9 in. (1.14 m) high. British Museum, London.

OLD KINGDOM EGYPT: *c.* 2649–2100 B.C.

Old Kingdom Egypt was a period of continuous political and social stability and of the pharaoh's absolute power. It was also a time of relative peace and economic prosperity. The Old Kingdom pharaohs commissioned colossal works of architecture and filled them with stone statues meant to last for eternity.

THE PYRAMID COMPLEX AT GIZA

To express the desire for life after death, the ancient Egyptians evolved monumental burial structures called **pyramids** (map **3.1**). In around 2630 B.C., the first known architect to build huge stone structures, Imhotep, designed the step pyramid of King Zoser (figure **3.8**) as part of a temple complex about 30 miles (48 km) south of Cairo.

Around a hundred years later, the Old Kingdom pyramid complex at Giza was constructed and became one of the Seven Wonders of the Ancient World. Located at the edge of modern Cairo, the Giza pyramids (figure **3.9**) were made of meticulously cut blocks of limestone and capped with gold, symbolizing the sun. Thousands of people from different professions were required to build such monuments, including surveyors, engineers, masons, skilled craftsmen, and paid seasonal workers.

The three pharaohs of the Fourth Dynasty buried at Giza were Khufu (*c.* 2551–2528 B.C.), Khafre (*c.* 2520–2494 B.C.), and Menkaure (*c.* 2490–2472 B.C.). When a pharaoh died, his body was carried by boat to its funerary temple on the opposite side of the Nile. After extensive preparations for

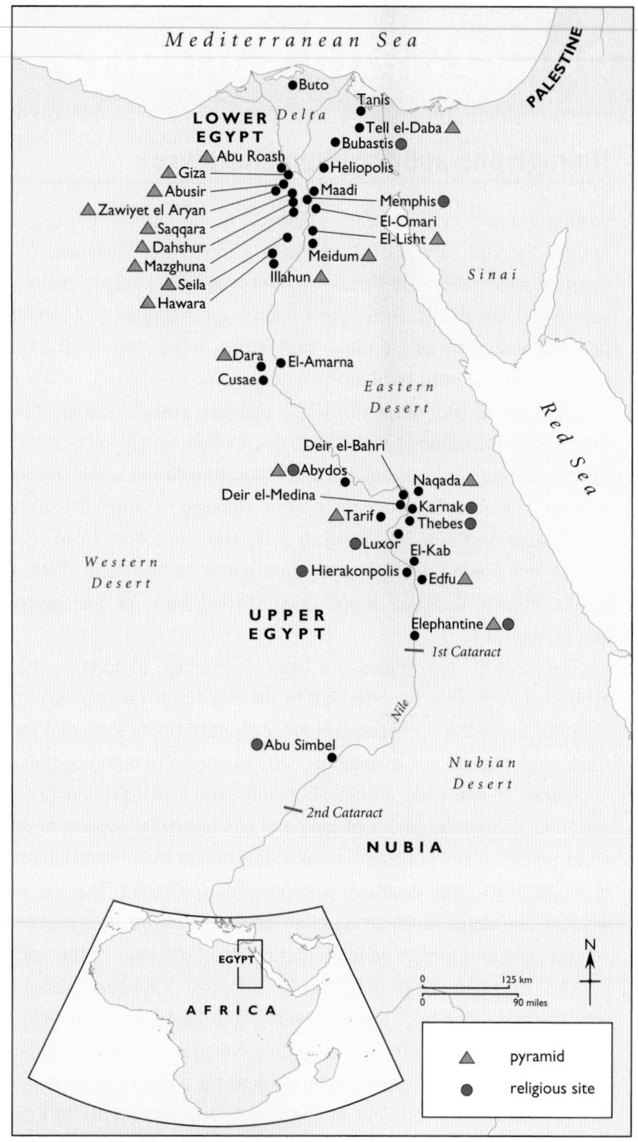

Map 3.1 Ancient Egypt.

3.8 Imhotep, Step pyramid of King Zoser, Saqqara, Egypt, *c.* 2630 B.C. Limestone, 200 ft. (61 m) high.

3.9 Pyramids of Khufu, Khafre, and Menkaure, Giza, Egypt, *c.* 2649–2100 B.C. Limestone, pyramid of Khufu approx. 480 ft. (146 m) high, base of each side 755 ft. (230 m) long.
The plan of the pyramid is a square, with each corner oriented to a cardinal point of the compass. The four triangular walls slant inward, their apexes meeting at the exact center of the square plan. The mathematical precision and architectural skill required for such buildings reflect the high level of artistic and intellectual achievement in ancient Egypt.

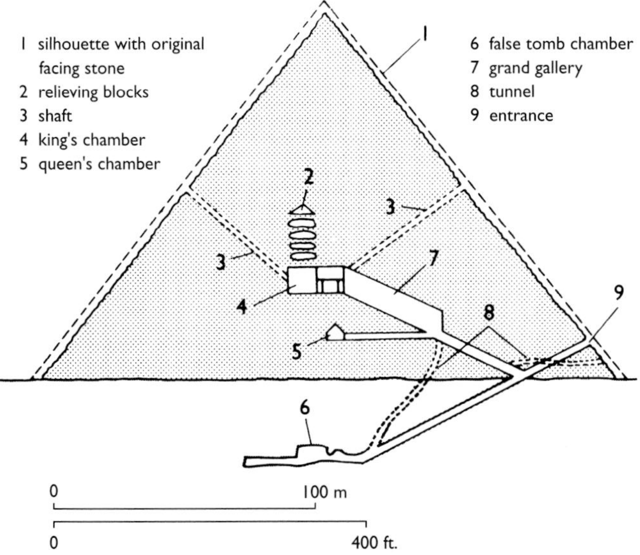

3.10 *left* Diagram of a pyramid showing interior.

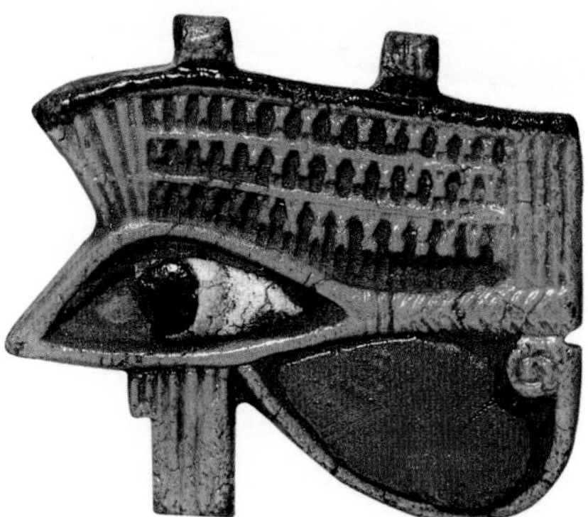

3.12 Eye of Horus. British Museum, London.

3.11 Scarab beetle. British Museum, London.

burial had been completed, the pharaoh's mummy was lowered into its coffin and placed in a chamber within the pyramid (figure **3.10**). In addition to statues and other substitutes for the deceased, offerings, texts, and numerous amulets were placed on the mummy for healing. These included the scarab (figure **3.11**) and the eye of Horus (figure **3.12**), which had been ripped out by Set in the battle for Osiris's throne and was later restored. The eye of Horus was a protection against the pervasive fear of the evil eye and came to symbolize goodness and beneficence.

3.13 Seated statue of Khafre, 4th Dynasty, *c.* 2520 B.C. Diorite, 5 ft. 6¼ in. (1.68 m) high. Egyptian Museum, Cairo.
The trapezoidal *nemes* headcloth with side flaps encloses the space around the pharaoh's head. Perched on the back of the throne is the Horus-falcon. His protective wings, enveloping Khafre's headcloth, reflect the king's literal identification with the god. Both the falcon and Khafre are rendered frontally (facing forward), emphasizing their power and foresight.

3.14 Egyptian grid.
Royal Egyptian artists followed the system of hierarchical scale used in Mesopotamia. The more important figures are thus larger than the less important ones. They are also clothed, for nudity was another sign of lesser importance and could also denote childhood.

THE SEATED STATUE OF KHAFRE AND THE EGYPTIAN PROPORTIONAL SYSTEM

In addition to monumental architecture, the Old Kingdom produced many examples of monumental sculpture. The sense of inherent power conveyed by Egyptian royal sculpture is the result of closed spaces and compact forms. This is evident in the seated statue of Khafre, found in his valley temple (figure **3.13**). Carved from a rectangular block of stone, Khafre and his throne are shown as one harmonious form. Although the feet extend forward, the stone has not been cut away behind the lower legs. Furthermore, individual features, such as the kneecaps and ceremonial beard, are rectangular. Such stylizations convey a sense of eternity, because they appear removed from the natural reality of time and space. Similarly, the use of stone for royal figures denoted the durable, long-lasting power of the kings and their immortality.

The rectangularity of Egyptian royal figures was maintained in part by the use of grids in the planning stage of a sculpture or painting. Grids could be calibrated with a figure of any size, and they changed only slightly in the 3000-year history of ancient Egypt. Figure **3.14** shows one type of grid used by Egyptian artists. A foot is three and a half squares in length, the shoulders are six squares across, and the distance from the shoulders to the bottom of the tunic is ten squares.

Note the pose of the figure and compare it with those in the papyrus paintings described above (see figures 3.3 and 3.6). The head, arms, and legs are in **profile** (side view) whereas the shoulders and eye are frontal. This is a conceptual rather than a natural representation—that is, it depicts a mental image of the human figure rather than the way it is actually seen in three-dimensional space.

THE MENKAURE TRIAD

In the *Triad of Menkaure* (figure **3.15**), Khafre's son Menkaure occupies the conventional standing pose of royal power. Menkaure is frontal, imposing, and rigid. His left leg is extended assertively, his fists are clenched, his shoulders are squared, and his kneecaps and beard are rectangular. The king's importance

3.15 ***Triad of Menkaure*, 4th Dynasty, *c.* 2490–2472 B.C. Schist, 36⅝ in. (93 cm) high. Egyptian Museum, Cairo.**
Hieroglyphs are carved into the base of the statue; the hieroglyph is surrounded by a **cartouche**, the curved oval rectangle that frames the name of the king.

is shown by his greater height compared with the two goddesses flanking and protecting him. Hathor, the sky goddess at the left, carries the sun-disk between her horns. She is the protectress of the king's palace, and she holds Menkaure's hand as a gesture of support. At the right stands a *nome* (province) goddess with the symbol of her province above her head.

The women are less assertive (note the positions of the feet) and more naturalistically depicted than Menkaure. They are also more curvilinear, and their garments reveal the organic character of their bodies. This emphasis on the natural curves of the female is characteristic of royal Egyptian art.

THE EGYPTIAN SCRIBE

In addition to royal figures, Egyptian artists created "professional sculptures." These identify the profession of a figure by its pose. One such type represented the **scribe**, whose job it was to write and to keep records. Literate and highly educated, he was an important member of the royal court. Figure **3.16** shows the conventional seated pose of the scribe, holding a writing instrument (usually made from reeds) in his right hand, and a papyrus roll (the writing surface) in his left. His head is slightly tilted as if he is taking dictation.

The elevated status of the scribe in Egyptian society is apparent from several texts. In one, a father, who is not very different from a modern father, urges his son Pepi to study:

And he said to Pepi:
"I have seen defeated, abject men!—
You must give yourself whole-heartedly to learning,
discover what will save you from the drudgery of underlings.
Nothing is so valuable as education;
it is a bridge over troubled waters."

("The Instruction for Little Pepi on His Way to School: The Satire of Trades")

A scribal student, not very different from modern students, is tired of studying. He escapes to Memphis to indulge in the distractions of city life and seek out female companionship:

Oh, I'm bound downstream on the Memphis ferry,
like a runaway, snapping all ties,
With my bundle of old clothes over my shoulder.

3.16 Scribe, from Saqqara, 5th Dynasty, *c.* 2465–2323 B.C. Painted limestone, 20 in. (51 cm) high. Egyptian Museum, Cairo.
The relative naturalism of the scribe denotes his lesser status as compared with the pharaoh. The scribe has open space between the arms and the torso, the body structure is somewhat flabby, and the features are more lifelike. His expression, enlivened by the surviving paint, adds to the naturalistic impression of the figure.

I'm going down there where the living is,
going down there to that big city,
And there I'll tell Ptah (Lord who loves justice):
"Give me a girl tonight!"

("Oh, I'm bound downstream on the Memphis ferry")

In another poem, a disappointed teacher, echoing the sentiments of many a modern teacher, takes a dissolute scribal student to task for succumbing to the temptations of loose women and drink and for neglecting his work. The teacher describes the emptiness and emasculation of his student's lifestyle and compares his moral decline to a warped oar incapable of steering a boat:

You go about from street to street,
and beer fumes hang wherever you have been.
Don't you know beer kills the man in you?
It stiffens your very soul.

You are like a warped steering-oar
that gives no help to either side!
You are a shrine without its god,
a house with no provisions . . .

You sit there under the hussy's spell,
soaked with perfumes and ointment,
with your wreaths of forget-me-nots round your neck.

("Rebuke Addressed to a Dissipated Scribe")

In the following, more philosophical excerpt from another example of wisdom literature (a genre in which words of wisdom are communicated), the poet extols the immortality of writers:

They [the writers] did not build pyramids in bronze
with gravestones of iron from heaven;
They did not think to leave a patrimony made of children
who would give their names distinction.
Rather, they formed a progeny by means of writings
and in the books of wisdom which they left.
The papyrus roll became their lector-priest,
the writing-board their loving son;
Books of wisdom were their pyramids,
the reed-pen was their child, smoothed
stone their spouse.
In this way great and small became inheritors;
and the writer was the father of them all!

("Epilogue: The Immortality of Writers")

MUSIC IN ANCIENT EGYPT

Although no musical notations have survived from ancient Egypt, it is clear from texts, paintings, and sculptures that music was a significant aspect of Egyptian culture. Most of the hymns and love poems were read to music. Texts describe field workers and slaves singing in the fields, and the visual arts depict musicians and dancers performing at religious rites and social gatherings. Scribes learned music, and women as well as men became professional musicians. Dwarfs were also popular as musicians, especially at court (figure **3.17**).

We can see how musicians performed at temple rituals from the relief block in figure **3.18**. A man at the upper left plays the harp; below are four lively acrobats. At the lower right, three singers are designated "the choir" in the hieroglyphic inscription. At the upper right, three women play the **sistrum** (a kind of rattle), which was sacred to the goddess Hathor and used in her rites (figure **3.19**).

3.17 Dwarf musician, 5th Dynasty, 2465–2323 B.C. Limestone with traces of paint, 4⅞ in. (12.5 cm) high. Oriental Institute, Chicago.

3.18 Musicians and dancers performing at a temple ritual, from the Chapel Rouge of Hatshepsut, block 66, Karnak, Egypt. 1473–1458 B.C.

3.20 Banqueting scene, from the tomb of Nebamun, Thebes, Egypt, 18th Dynasty, 1550–1323 B.C. Painted stucco, 25 in. (63.5 cm) high. British Museum, London.
The frontality of two of the women is a departure from Egyptian pictorial convention. Perhaps this is intended to show that musical exuberance has the power to break through strict, traditional rules.

3.19 *left* **Sistrum handle of Teti, 6th dynasty, 2323–2291 B.C. Alabaster, 10½ in. (26.5 cm) high. The Metropolitan Museum of Art, New York.**
The handle of this elegant alabaster sistrum is in the form of a papyrus stalk. Its blossom supports a building, probably a temple, surmounted by a falcon and a cobra. The inscription on the stalk praises the king and invokes the protection of Hathor.

The banqueting scene in figure **3.20** shows how music enriched life in an aristocratic home. Painted on the wall of a tomb, the scene indicates that Nebamun's comfortable earthly life will be transposed into the afterlife. Banqueters occupy the top register, with dancers and musicians represented below. Reading from left to right, we see three singers clapping, a woman playing a double-reed pipe, and two female dancers. The words of the song are recorded in the hieroglyphs between the dancers and musicians:

> [Flowers of sweet] scents which Ptah sends and Geb makes to grow.
> His beauty is in every body.
> Ptah has done this with his own hands to gladden (?) his heart.
> The pools are filled anew with water.
> The earth is flooded with his love.

EGYPTIAN SOCIETY

Egyptian society was strongly hierarchical and can—very appropriately—be diagrammed as a pyramid. At the top of the universe were the gods and their realms. At the apex of human society was the pharaoh, followed by members of the royal family. Next in descending order came the aristocracy and the scribal class (the bureaucracy), which was entirely male and was administered by the king's vizier. He ran the palace, the army, and irrigation systems across the country, and supervised legal matters. The middle class included business people, builders, artists, and craftsmen. Peasants and agricultural workers were the largest segment of the population. They were assisted by slaves, who could be foreigners captured in war, debtors, or convicts.

Egypt was a male-dominated society, although women had certain important rights, and their status was determined by the same social hierarchy as the rest of the country. As early as the Old Kingdom, women were mummified and prepared for the afterlife along with men. One surviving document identifies a woman who supervised court physicians—most likely those who attended a queen mother (see Box, p. 56).

Until the Eighteenth Dynasty (*c.* sixteenth century B.C.) women could hold the title of priest at a cult site, or be high-ranking dancers and musicians. Literate woman could work in commerce and own land, but fewer women than men learned to read, and they were not permitted to work

Society and Culture

Egyptian Medicine and Dream Books

Three medical texts from the Middle Kingdom are included in the more general category of Egyptian wisdom texts. They are collections of prescriptions, whose effectiveness depended on the magic power of words and incantations. Because disease was believed to be the work of demons, magic spells were considered the best remedy. Spells were used for pregnant women, for headaches, stiffness, and as an aid to surgery, which was mainly practiced to repair injuries. For abdominal ailments, poultices were prescribed. These were made from various combinations of animal fat, blood and feces, herbs and vegetables, wine and beer, honey and ointments. From the first millennium B.C., the Eye of Horus was endowed with healing power against the evil eye.

As in Mesopotamia, dreams were believed to reveal truth. One Egyptian dream book gives the following interpretations: a dream in which a person kills a hippopotamus means that the dreamer will receive a royal meal; diving into a river means purification; looking at an ostrich means the person will suffer harm; having sex with a woman predicts mourning; feeding cattle foretells wandering the earth; and throwing wood into water means bad luck to the house.

Modern dream interpretation recognizes that there can be many layers of hidden meaning in dreams, but in the ancient world each dream image was interpreted as having a single, definitive meaning.

in the administrative bureaucracy. Most Egyptian textiles were produced by women, and in a few cases, women sold surplus textiles as a way of establishing financial independence.

Egyptian families were generally monogamous and having children was a high priority. Divorce law favored men, who could divorce a wife for infidelity or infertility. But, once divorced, both men and women were allowed to remarry. Widows were at a greater disadvantage than widowers, presumably because they were less likely to remarry. Homosexuality was frowned upon, because it interfered with fertility and reproduction.

Children and child-rearing were important features of Egyptian culture, and the high rate of infant mortality was a cause for concern. Most women breast-fed their own children, but wet nurses nourished the children of royal and upper-class families. Representations in art showing children being breast-fed are rare; but a goddess nursing a king was meant to convey the ruler's divine origins.

FEMALE PHARAOHS

Although pharaohs were normally men, when there was no male heir, a woman could become pharaoh. As such, she was accorded the same status and power as a male ruler, but had to be represented in texts and in art as a man. Of ancient Egypt's four female pharaohs, the best known was the ambitious New Kingdom queen, Hatshepsut (ruled *c.* 1473–1458 B.C.). She is famous for having launched a major building campaign at Deir-el-Bahri (see map 3.1, p. 50). In texts, Hatshepsut is described as her father's choice to succeed him, and to legitimize her reign further she had her mother, Queen Ahmose, depicted as the consort of the god Amon-Re in paintings and relief sculpture.

As pharaoh, Hatshepsut ruled as the senior co-ruler with her nephew, who probably led her armies. Under Hatshepsut, trade with the Land of Punt was expanded, and new administrators were appointed. It is not known how her reign ended or how she died, but her stepson, Tutmose III, eventually came to power. In order to eradicate Hatshepsut's memory after her death, Tutmose III erased her name from texts and inscriptions and destroyed her statues. He did not do so for personal reasons, but because kingship was by definition a male office and a female ruler was considered against *maat.*

Figure **3.21** shows Hatshepsut as pharaoh. Although her delicate form and facial features clearly belong to a woman, her pose and costume are those of the male pharaoh. Like him, she wears the

3.21 Hatshepsut enthroned, 18th Dynasty, *c.* 1473–1458 B.C. Crystalline limestone, 6 ft. 5 in. (1.96 m) high. The Metropolitan Museum of Art, New York.

royal *nemes* headcloth with a flap on either side, a necklace, and a short tunic. Her pharaonic pose is frontal, her hands rest on her lap, and there is no space between the arms and the torso or between the legs and the throne. Nevertheless, compared with the seated Khafre (see figure 3.13), which is made of very different stone, there is more open space behind the figure of Hatshepsut. The throne has no back, and the Horus-falcon is not present. This opening up of space probably reflects minor stylistic changes since the Old Kingdom. However, it is likely that it was also done in order to convey a sense of elegance in representing the female pharaoh (see Box).

Society and Culture

Egyptian Jewelry

Egyptian men and women wore elaborate make-up and many types of fine jewelry—rings, necklaces, bracelets, tiaras, and so forth. Most of what has survived belonged to royal or upper-class women and shows both the extraordinary talent of Egyptian craftsmen and the abundance of gold and precious gems. Most were found locally, some were imported or plundered from Nubia, and others, especially lapis lazuli, came by way of trade routes. The pectoral in figure **3.22**, an openwork frame in the shape of a temple, belonged to a Middle Kingdom princess. Spreading out at the top are the protective wings of the Horus-falcon; in the center below are symbols of the tomb chapel in which the pectoral was discovered and the king's cartouches. Symmetrically arranged on either side is the reigning pharaoh, who brandishes a mace to strike the small enemy kneeling before him. Behind each image of the pharaoh, an ankh with arms raises a papyrus stalk. In works such as this the complexity of Egyptian symbolism is combined with intricate workmanship and attention to detail.

3.22 Pectoral of Mereret, 12th Dynasty, *c.* 1820 B.C. Gold, lapis lazuli, carnelian, turquoise, and amethyst, 4½ in. (7.9 cm) high. Egyptian Museum, Cairo.

MIDDLE KINGDOM EGYPT: *c.* 1991–1700 B.C.

The end of the Old Kingdom was followed by the First Intermediate period, which lasted to around 1991 B.C. Civil wars destroyed prosperity and brought economic hardship. Internal unrest grew as priests, aristocrats, and local governors increased their power and threatened the iron-clad control of Old Kingdom pharaohs. The Middle Kingdom followed, beginning with the Twelfth Dynasty, and brought a resurgence of the pharaoh's power. This led to a period of artistic expansion.

Sculpture and Architecture

The problems of the First Intermediate period influenced the political atmosphere of the Middle Kingdom. Rather than projecting an image of abstract permanence as Old Kingdom images of pharaohs had, artists now showed some pharaohs with expressions of concern. This is evident, for example, in a head of Amenemhet III (figure **3.23**).

3.23 Head of Amenemhet III, *c.* 1859–1813 B.C. Obsidian, 4¾ in. (12 cm) high. Museu Calouste Gulbenkian, Lisbon.

The pharaoh wears the traditional *nemes* headcloth, but the facial expression has changed since the Old Kingdom. Amenemhet III has softer features, especially the bulging flesh around the cheeks and upper lip, which convey a more human and humane image than in Old Kingdom royal art. In addition, his eyes and mouth slant slightly downward, imparting an air of gravity, as if he is preoccupied by the weight of his office.

Another Middle Kingdom development in sculpture was a type of cubic statue meant for the interior of a temple (figure **3.24**). This shows a squatting figure with legs and/or feet projecting from the front of the block, which is covered with hieroglyphs. The arms and head emerge from the top, and the small standing figure is Senwosret-senebefny's wife. The discrepancy in their sizes is a striking example of the Egyptian hierarchical system of proportion. The power of these figures lies in their compactness, which entirely eliminates open space, and in the unusual merging of geometric with human form.

Relatively little Middle Kingdom architecture has survived. Tombs were smaller than in the Old Kingdom, and many were made of mud brick rather than stone. The most typical examples of Middle Kingdom burial architecture were rock-cut tombs, with interiors hollowed out of existing cliffs, leaving only the façades visible. Several such tombs dating from the early Twelfth Dynasty are found at Beni Hasan, about 125 miles (200 km) south of Giza (see map 3.1, p. 50).

3.24 Block statue of Senwosret-senebefny and his wife, late 12th Dynasty, *c.* 1878–1840 B.C. Quartzite, 27 × 16½ × 19 in. (68.6 × 41.9 × 48.3 cm). Brooklyn Museum, New York.

3.25 Detail of Senbi's coffin, *c.* 2000 B.C. Painted wood, 24¾ in. (63 cm) high. Egyptian Museum, Cairo.
In its original position, the coffin faced east. Thus, the prominent eyes over the painted door permitted the deceased to look beyond the coffin toward the rising sun.

The Beni Hasan tombs resemble the forms of contemporary houses, reflecting the traditional metaphor equating the tomb with the house of the dead. A particularly impressive expression of this metaphor can be seen on the Twelfth Dynasty coffin of Senbi (figure **3.25**). Its rich decoration is characteristic of the Middle Kingdom and is derived from elements used in actual architecture.

NEW KINGDOM EGYPT: *c.* 1550–1070 B.C.

In the Middle Kingdom, Egyptian pharaohs conquered Nubia and invaded Palestine, Syria, and Phoenicia. Fierce retaliation from the Hittites (in modern Turkey) forced Egypt to a compromise, in which they agreed to share the conquered territory with them and the Assyrians. The Second Intermediate period (*c.* 1640–1550 B.C.) followed, during which Lower Egypt was invaded by the Hyksos. In the sixteenth century B.C., the Hyksos were defeated by the pharaoh Ahmose I of Thebes, and with their expulsion the New Kingdom began and with it a period of stability and architectural activity.

The Hyksos invasion had alarmed Egypt and accentuated its aversion to foreigners. So that Egypt would never again be subjugated, the country went on the offensive in the Near East and Nubia, incursions that ironically increased Egypt's international contacts and made its culture more cosmopolitan. During the New Kingdom, Egypt imported ideas, words, technology, and even gods into its civilization. At the same time, through diplomacy as well as warfare, Egypt reached a peak in its influence on foreign cultures.

TEMPLES

The Egyptians called their temples "houses" or "mansions" of the gods. Temples were not open to the general public, but, as in Mesopotamia, were private residences inhabited by cult statues embodying the deities. Priests, who were called "servants of the god," functioned as household staff, feeding and clothing the statues and caring for their sacred animals.

As in the Middle Kingdom, New Kingdom temple complexes followed the typical house plan (figure **3.26**). A gateway led to an open forecourt at the front—an enclosed front yard—which *was* accessible to the public. At the center of the complex, a **hypostyle** hall containing many columns was the god's "living room" and was usually closed to the public. Beyond the hypostyle were chapels, storage rooms, and the sanctuary that housed the cult statue. Only priests and the pharaoh were allowed inside the sanctuary.

The main New Kingdom temples were either rock-cut or freestanding. The typical freestanding temple had a **pylon** façade consisting of two massive trapezoidal walls (figure **3.27**) on either side of the entrance. Flanking the entrance were two **obelisks** (tall, pointed, square pillars), and colossal statues of the pharaoh. Leading to the entrance, rows of impressive **sphinxes** (human-headed lions) created a spatial avenue. Their repetition represented the power of the pharaoh and the prosperity of Egypt under his rule.

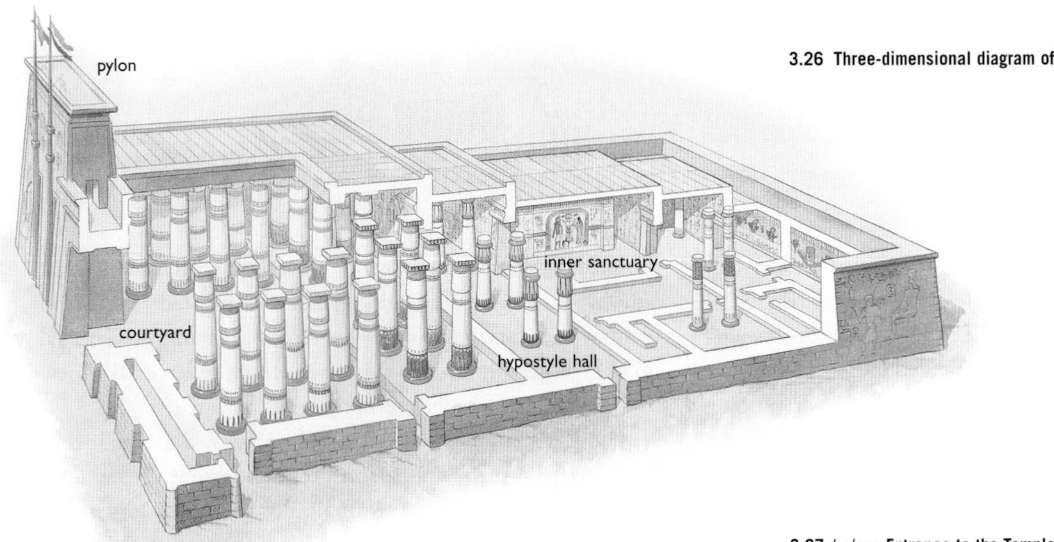

3.26 Three-dimensional diagram of a standard New Kingdom temple.

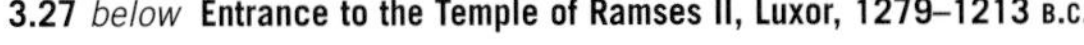

3.27 *below* **Entrance to the Temple of Ramses II, Luxor, 1279–1213 B.C.**

3.28 Festival court of Amenophis III, Temple of Ramses II, 18th Dynasty, *c.* 1390–1352 B.C. Sandstone. Luxor, Egypt.

In the festival court of Amenophis III at the Temple of Ramses II (figure **3.28**), the pharaoh presided over religious festivals. The courtyard was surrounded by a massive open wall of double columns in the form of papyrus bundles. The huge size of such temples and the columns based on vegetation forms denoted both the power of the pharaoh and the fertility produced by the Nile in flood.

The plan in figure **3.29** shows the dramatic progression from the exterior, through the open-air court, into the dimmed light and shadows of the columned hypostyle hall. The hypostyle walls were decorated with painted reliefs, and hieroglyphic carvings covered the colossal columns. Celestial imagery originally on the hypostyle ceiling reflected the view of the temple as a replica of the cosmos on earth.

The Egyptian temple was thus also designed as a model of the universe in time and space. Progressing toward the inner sanctuary, the worshipper symbolically goes back in time to original creation. According to Egyptian myth, the world

3.29 Plan of the Temple of Ramses II, begun *c.* 1400 B.C.

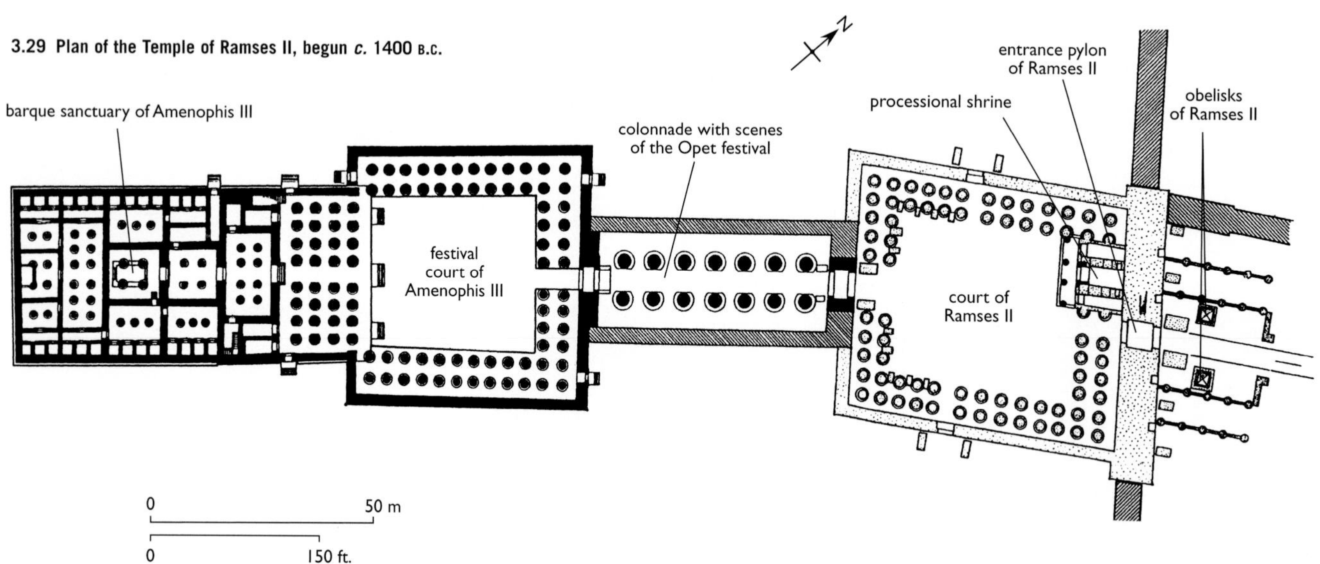

emerged from Nun (the primeval ocean), the waves of which were represented by undulating mudbrick walls surrounding the temple.

THE AMARNA REVOLUTION: *C.* 1349–1336 B.C.

Around 1352 B.C., the pharaoh Amenhotep IV (ruled 1352–1336 B.C.) ascended the throne of Egypt. Within four years, he had introduced religious beliefs that changed artistic conventions, especially in royal imagery. Amenhotep IV has been the subject of extensive, on-going research and controversy. He moved the capital north from Thebes, and south from Memphis, to Amarna (see map 3.1, p. 50), hence the name of the period. Most radical of all, Amenhotep IV challenged the established priesthood, and proclaimed Aton the one living god, which he represented as the sun-disk.

It is not known why this pharaoh changed Egyptian traditions as he did, but his ideas were not generally well received. The departure from polytheism was a short-lived, but intellectually significant, development. It is the earliest known instance of a ruler making monotheism an official religion. In honor of the Aton, Amenhotep IV changed his name to Akhenaton ("servant of the Aton").

In Akhenaton's "Hymn to the Sun," the Aton is called the one and only god and is credited with being the source of all life and the mover of the universe:

> You make Hapy, the Nile, stream through the underworld,
>   and bring him, with whatever fullness you will,
> To preserve and nourish the People
>   in the same skilled way you fashion them.
> You are Lord of each one,
>   who wearies himself in their service,
> Yet Lord of all earth, who shines for them all,
>   Sun-disk of day, Holy Light!

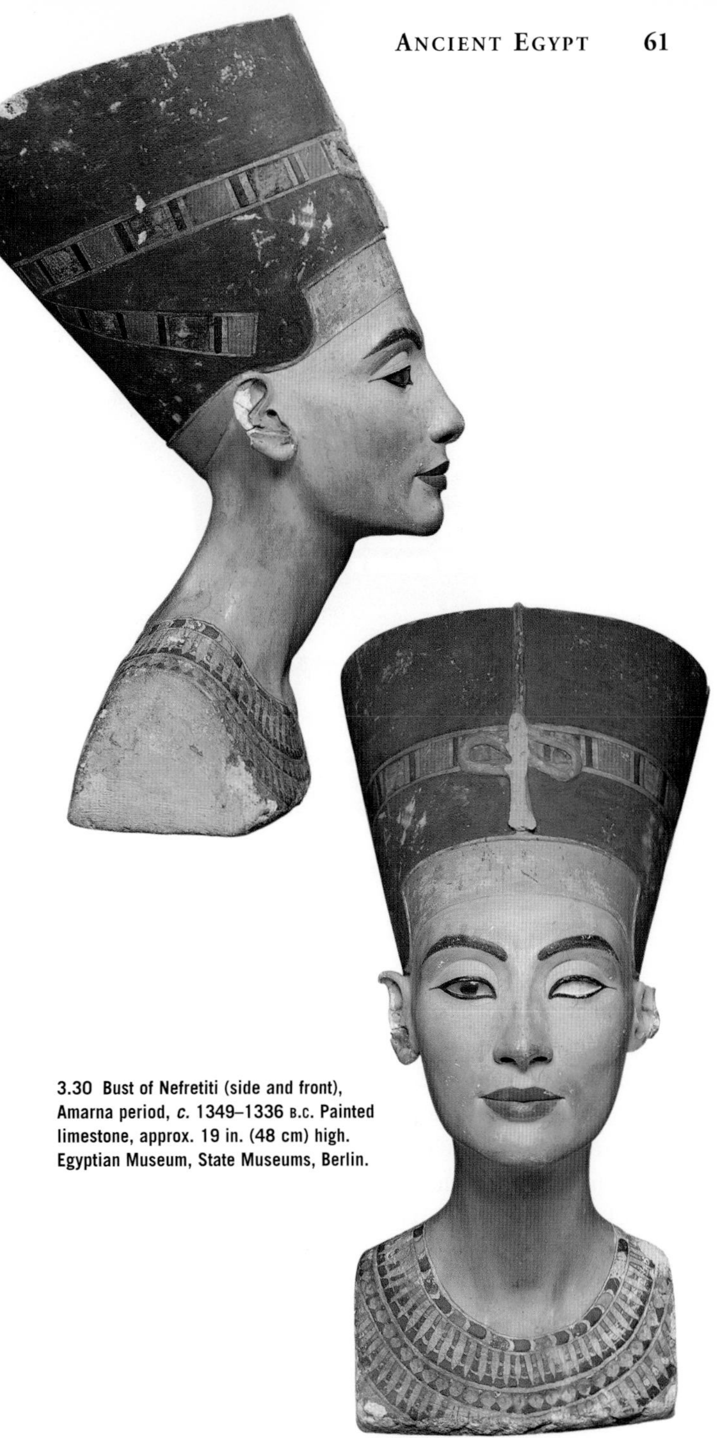

3.30 Bust of Nefretiti (side and front), Amarna period, *c.* 1349–1336 B.C. Painted limestone, approx. 19 in. (48 cm) high. Egyptian Museum, State Museums, Berlin.

The most famous sculpture from the Amarna period is the limestone **bust** (showing a figure from the head to just below the shoulders) of Nefretiti, Akhenaton's principal wife (figure **3.30**). In contrast to more traditional royal sculptures, this has open space, and a long, graceful neck. Instead of the traditional headdress worn by most Egyptian queens, Nefretiti wears a tall crown, which completely covers her hair. The unusual elegance and naturalism of this bust is enhanced by the preservation of the paint. Nevertheless, the artist has also carefully indicated the presence of neck muscles and cheekbones, as well as the organic relation of forms beneath the surface of the skin.

Akhenaton and his religious beliefs were unpopular, and they led to a power struggle between priests and the pharaoh. It is not known how Akhenaton died, and when his tomb was discovered at Amarna in the nineteenth century his mummy was missing. The pharaohs who succeeded Akhenaton reinstated polytheism along with the traditional hierarchy of priests, and destroyed what evidence they could of Akhenaton's reign.

THE TOMB OF TUTANKHAMON

The pharaoh Tutankhamon ruled for only a short time, from about 1336 to 1327 B.C., and his name indicates that he worshipped the older Amon gods. In 1922, his tomb was discovered intact, revealing the vast wealth of the Egyptian pharaohs and their elaborate burials. Thousands of objects made of precious materials were excavated, including chariots, furniture, vases, jewels, amulets, statues, and articles of clothing (right down to the royal underwear).

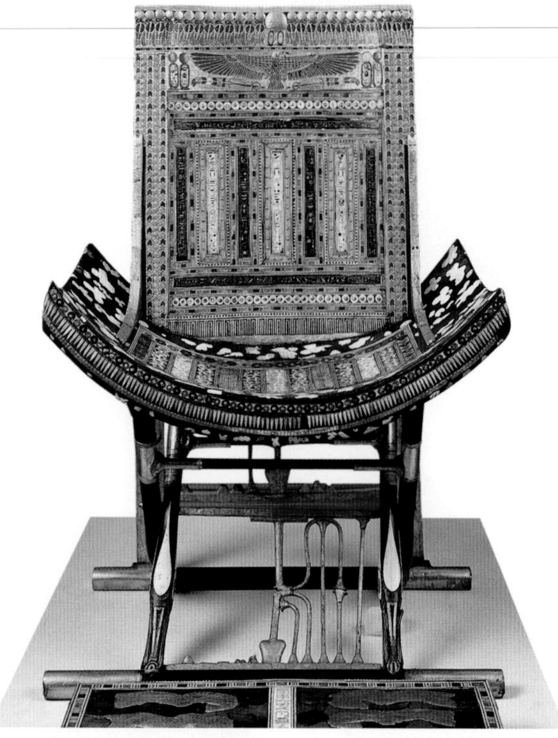

3.31 Tutankhamon's throne, *c.* 1336 B.C. Wood, gold, glass, faience, and gemstones, 3 ft. 4⅛ in. (1.02 m) high. Egyptian Museum, Cairo.

3.32 Funerary mask of Tutankhamon, *c.* 1327 B.C. Gold, lapis lazuli, glass, faience, gemstones, 21¼ in. (54 cm) high. Egyptian Museum, Cairo.

One of Tutankhamon's many thrones is illustrated in figure **3.31**. The elaborate surface decoration culminates in the conventional protective Horus-falcon flanked by cartouches on the back of the throne. Tutankhamon's gold funerary mask (figure **3.32**) retains the traditional *nemes* headcloth with a protective cobra and vulture above the forehead. Compared to representations of Akhenaton, this projects the more traditional image of the pharaoh as the embodiment of eternal royal power. Both works show how royal imagery after Akhenaton reflects a determination to eradicate the ideas and the art of the Amarna revolution.

By the end of the New Kingdom, Egypt's power was on the wane. It succumbed to Assyrian conquest in the seventh century B.C., and to Persian conquest three times (in the sixth, fifth, and fourth centuries B.C.). In 332 B.C., Alexander the Great conquered Egypt and, after his death in 323 B.C., Egypt was ruled by descendants of his Greek general Ptolemy. In 31 B.C., Egypt became part of the Roman Empire and, from the fifth century, was infiltrated by monasteries established by Coptic Christians. Some two hundred years later, as a result of Arab conquests, Egypt converted to Islam, which remains its dominant religion today.

KEY TERMS

bust a sculpture or picture showing a figure from the head to just below the shoulders.

canopic jar a container for organs removed during mummification.

cartouche a rectangle with curved ends framing the name of a king.

dynasty a family of kings.

hieratic a cursive script derived from hieroglyphs.

hieroglyphs a writing system using pictorial representations as characters.

hymn a song praising a god.

hypostyle a hall with a roof supported by rows of columns; the center columns are taller than those at the sides.

ideogram a pictorial representation of an idea.

maat the Egyptian concept of cosmic order, truth, and justice; also (when capitalized) the name of the goddess embodying those qualities.

mummification in ancient Egypt, a process taking seventy-two days in which bodies were embalmed and organs were removed.

obelisk a tall, pointed, square pillar.

pharaoh a king of ancient Egypt.

phonogram an image denoting sounds.

profile the side view of a figure or object.

pylon in ancient Egypt, a massive trapezoidal gateway.

pyramid an Egyptian tomb.

scribe in ancient Egypt, a professional record-keeper, usually a member of the court.

sistrum a type of rattle.

sphinx a human-headed lion.

vignette a small section of decoration or a literary sketch.

KEY QUESTIONS

1. Describe three measures that Egyptians took to ensure an afterlife.
2. What subjects in Egyptian society did artists treat naturalistically? What subjects did artists treat monumentally?
3. Which Egyptian leader did not follow standard religious practices? What innovations in art came about because of his leadership?
4. On what parts of a New Kingdom temple would one find hieroglyphic carvings?

SUGGESTED READING

Arnold, Dorothea. *The Royal Women of Amarna.* New York: Metropolitan Museum of Art, 1996.
- A study of the role of royal women during the Amarna period.

Christie, Agatha. *Death on the Nile.* London: HarperCollins, 2004.
- A murder mystery set in Egypt.

Faulkner, R. O. *The Ancient Egyptian Book of the Dead.* London: British Museum Press, 1989.
- A discussion of the texts and meanings found in the *Book of the Dead.*

Foster, John L. (trans.). *Ancient Egyptian Literature.* Austin, TX: University of Texas Press, 2001.
- A survey of literature in ancient Egypt.

Lichtheim, Miriam. *Ancient Egyptian Literature*, 2 vols. Berkeley and Los Angeles: University of California Press, 1975.
- A study of ancient Egyptian literature, with many excerpts.

Quirke, Stephen, and Jeffrey Spencer (eds.). *The British Museum Book of Ancient Egypt.* London: British Museum Press, 1992.
- A general survey of the arts and culture of ancient Egypt.

Redford, Donald B. *Akhenaton: The Heretic King.* Princeton, NJ: Princeton University Press, 1984.
- A study of Akhenaton and his religious revolution in the context of ancient Egypt.

Robins, Gay. *Women in Ancient Egypt.* Cambridge, MA: Harvard University Press, 1993.
- A discussion of the social role of women in ancient Eygpt and their representation in art.

Taylor, John H. *Egypt and Nubia.* London: British Museum Press, 1991.
- A brief study of the relationship between Egypt and Nubia.

——. *Death and the Afterlife in Ancient Egypt.* London: British Museum Press, 2001.
- A study of Egyptian beliefs about the afterlife and the rituals they engendered.

Waltari, Mika. *The Egyptian.* New York: G. P. Putnam's Sons, 1949, reprinted by Chicago Review Press, 2002.
- A recreation of the "Tale of Sinuhe."

Wilkinson, Richard H. *The Complete Temples of Ancient Egypt.* New York: Thames and Hudson, 2000.
- A discussion of temple architecture and the beliefs it expressed.

SUGGESTED FILMS

1932 *The Mummy*, dir. Karl Freund

1944 *The Mummy's Ghost*, dir. Reginald LeBorg

1945 *The Mummy's Curse*, dir. Leslie Goodwins

1954 *The Egyptian*, dir. Michael Curtiz

1955 *Abbot and Costello Meet the Mummy*, dir. Charles Lamont

1959 *The Mummy*, dir. Terence Fisher

1978 *Death on the Nile* (based on Christie), dir. John Guillermin

1998 *The Prince of Egypt*, dirs. Simon Wells and Steve Hickner, co-director Brenda Chapman

1999 *The Mummy*, dir. Stephen Sommers

2001 *The Mummy Returns*, dir. Stephen Sommers

4 The Aegean World

"Zeus saw Europa the daughter of Phoenix gathering flowers in a meadow with some nymphs and fell in love with her. So he came down and changed himself into a bull and breathed from his mouth a crocus. In this way he deceived Europa, carried her off and crossed the sea to Crete, where he had intercourse with her . . . she conceived and bore three sons, Minos, Sarpedon and Rhadamanthys."

(HESIOD, ATTRIB., *Catalogues of Women and Eoiae* 19)

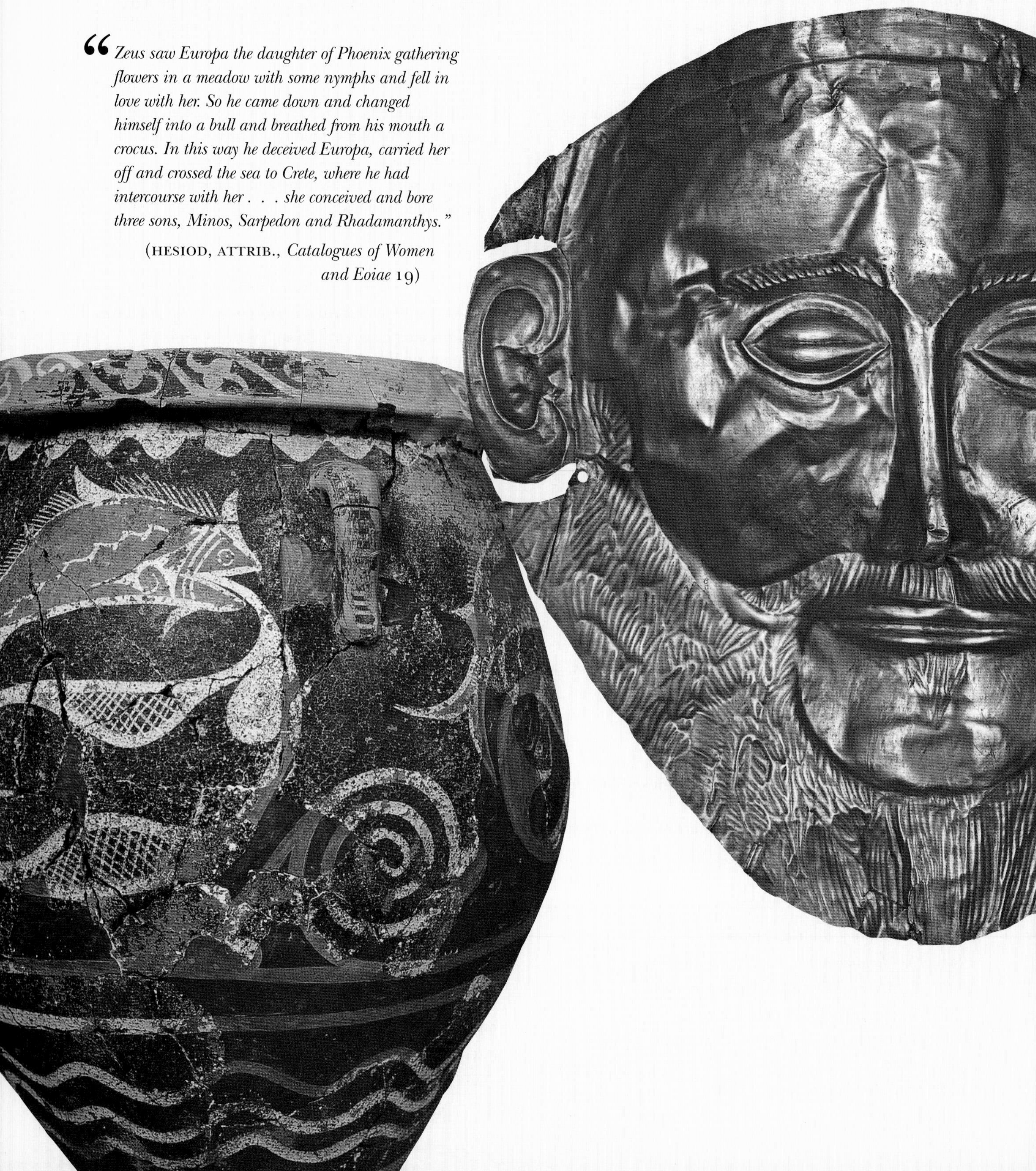

In this chapter we move northwest from Egypt, first to the island of Crete and Minoan culture and then to the Mycenaean culture that developed on the Greek mainland. These civilizations are referred to as Aegean, after the Aegean Sea (see map 4.1, p. 72). In addition, twentieth- and twenty-first-century excavations have unearthed a thriving culture, contemporary with the Minoans, on the volcanic island of Thera, north of Crete. All these Aegean cultures flourished during the Bronze Age, when people used bronze tools and weapons.

Minoan civilization lasted from around 2000 to 1200 B.C., and Crete was a seafaring culture with widespread foreign contacts. The Minoans had a high standard of living, with paved streets, stone houses, and plumbing and drainage systems. Palaces were religious centers with large bureaucratic administrations. Economically, the island was supported by agriculture and piracy, as well as by trade with Egypt, Anatolia (modern Turkey), the Middle East, and the Greek mainland. Minoans also colonized areas throughout the Aegean. Many scholars believe that the Minoans ruled through control of the sea, a system of rule known as ***thalassocracy***.

In the course of its history, Crete suffered several stages of destruction. Around 1600 B.C. an earthquake devastated the island. A century or two later, sometime in the fifteenth century B.C., a volcanic eruption on Thera further damaged northern Crete (see p. 72). Then, around 1400 B.C., the Mycenaeans invaded Crete and conquered the Minoans. From this point, the Greek mainland began its rise to power, expanding westward as far as the Italian peninsula and eastward to the Middle East. The Mycenaeans took over the Minoan colonies, established additional ones of their own, and dominated the Aegean. By about 1150 B.C., Mycenaean civilization entered a period of decline known as the Dark Age.

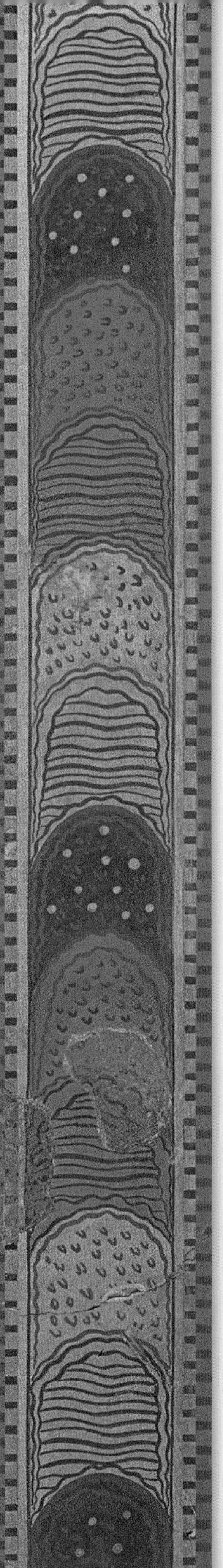

Key Topics

The Mysterious Minoans

- Sacrificial rituals
- Frescoes, pottery, and sculpture
- Palace architecture
- Linear A

The Theran Civilization

- Frescoes
- Plumbing and drains
- The volcanic eruption

Heroic Mycenaean Myths and Legends

- Warrior culture
- Fortified citadels
- The Trojan War
- The Curse on the House of Atreus
- Linear B

THE AEGEAN WORLD (all dates B.C.)

TIMELINE	MINOANS c. 2000–1200	MYCENAEANS c. 1600–1150	THE DARK AGE c. 1150–900
HISTORY AND CULTURE 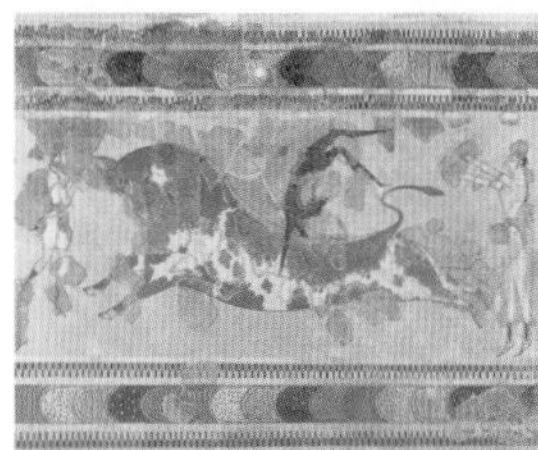	Bronze tools and weapons Earthquake, *c.* 1600 Volcanic eruption, *c.* 1450 Linear A writing system Mycenaean invasion, *c.* 1400 Seafaring economy	Trojan War, *c.* 1180 Aristocratic, warrior culture (subjects of the Homeric epics) Linear B writing system, *c.* 1400	Period of decline Poverty, war, loss of writing Agrarian economy
RELIGION AND MYTH 	Nature goddess Bull sacrifice Outdoor worship Myth of Europa Myth of the Minotaur Theseus and the Labyrinth	Belief in an afterlife Curse on the House of Atreus (subject of Aeschylus's *Oresteia*)	
ART 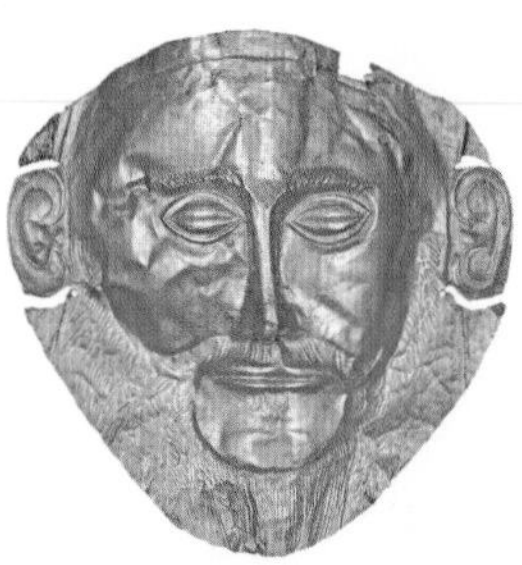	Pithoid jar, 2000–1700 Mistress of the Animals, *c.* 1600 *Harvester Vase*, 1650–1450 *Toreador Fresco*, *c.* 1500 Hagia Triada sarcophagus, *c.* 1400	Gold death masks	*Warrior Vase*, *c.* 1200–1150
ARCHITECTURE 	Palace of Minos, Knossos, *c.* 1600–1400	Citadels Megaron Tholos tombs Lion Gate, Mycenae, 13th century Corbel arch Corbel vault, Tiryns, 13th century Cyclopaean masonry	No large-scale architecture
MUSIC	Instruments: pipes (*auloi*) harp, horn (triton shell), sistrum (rattle)	Same as Minoans	

In addition to myths and legends, much of what we know of Aegean civilization comes from archaeological evidence. But some information is also provided by written scripts. Minoan writing, called ***Linear A****, has not yet been deciphered, though it is known that it was used for record-keeping and religious dedications.* ***Linear B****, which can be read, was the Mycenaean script and an early form of Greek. The Mycenaean use of Linear B for record-keeping has provided information about the vast bureaucratic organization of Mycenaean palaces. The fact that, around 1400* B.C.*, Linear B appeared in Crete and elsewhere in the Aegean world reflects the extent of Mycenaean domination.*

*Oral traditions and later works of Greek literature kept alive the myths and legends about the Minoan–Mycenaean era until the late nineteenth century, when archaeologists began to search for physical evidence of the truth contained in these stories. The quotation that opens this chapter is from a key Greek myth about the origins of Minoan civilization. Attributed to the late eighth-century-*B.C. *Greek author Hesiod, the Europa myth reflects the later Greek tradition that the Minoans came from ancient Phoenicia (roughly equivalent to the modern coastal areas of Israel and Lebanon) and that Europa herself was a Phoenician princess—in Hesiod she is the daughter of Phoenix. According to the myth, Zeus, the king of the Greek gods, disguised himself as a bull and enticed the mortal girl Europa with a sweet-smelling crocus (a sacred flower), swam with her on his back to Crete, and seduced her. Europa's three sons became rulers: Sarpedon ruled Lycia (in modern Turkey), Rhadamanthys ruled the Underworld, and Minos ruled Knossos on Crete.*

4.1 Pithoid jar with fish, from the old palace, Phaistos, 2000–1700 B.C. Kamares ware. Herakleion Museum, Crete.
The jar is decorated with three orange fish (only one is visible in this view) on a dark blue background. Emerging from the fish's mouth is a cross-hatched, white design suggesting a fisherman's net. Curvilinear patterns circling the jar include waves and spirals, which, like the net, convey a sense of lively motion.

WHO WERE THE MINOANS?

Legends notwithstanding, the origins of the Minoans are not known, and there is no evidence of Paleolithic culture on Crete. The island's inhabitants appear to have had links with Anatolia in the Neolithic period (*c.* 6000–3000 B.C.). The Bronze Age followed, until the eight-hundred-year Minoan civilization disappeared and faded into myth and legend. This remained the case until the early twentieth century, when the British archaeologist Sir Arthur Evans (1851–1941) excavated the site of Knossos, located a short distance inland from the north coast of Crete (see map 4.1, p. 72). The discovery of the Minoan civilization, and of others in the Aegean, mirrors the ongoing nature of historical research, which is continually revising perceptions of history.

Evans called the civilization on Crete "Minoan" after its legendary king, Minos. The excavations uncovered a great deal of archaeological evidence, including Linear A script, architecture, paintings, and pottery. Paintings, as well as the myth of Europa, show that the Minoans were seafarers and that the sea was crucial to the Minoan economy. Minoan artists reflected the importance of the sea in their iconography as well as in their fluid pictorial style (figure **4.1**).

The Minoans built elaborate columned palaces, which served as social, religious, and economic centers. They were also the dwelling place of the rulers. Because the sea afforded Crete natural protection from invaders, palaces were not fortified and were typically planned with a large central courtyard where people gathered. Figure **4.2** shows the sprawling, irregular plan of the palace at Knossos (see Box, p. 68). In contrast to the colossal architecture of Egypt, Minoan palaces were

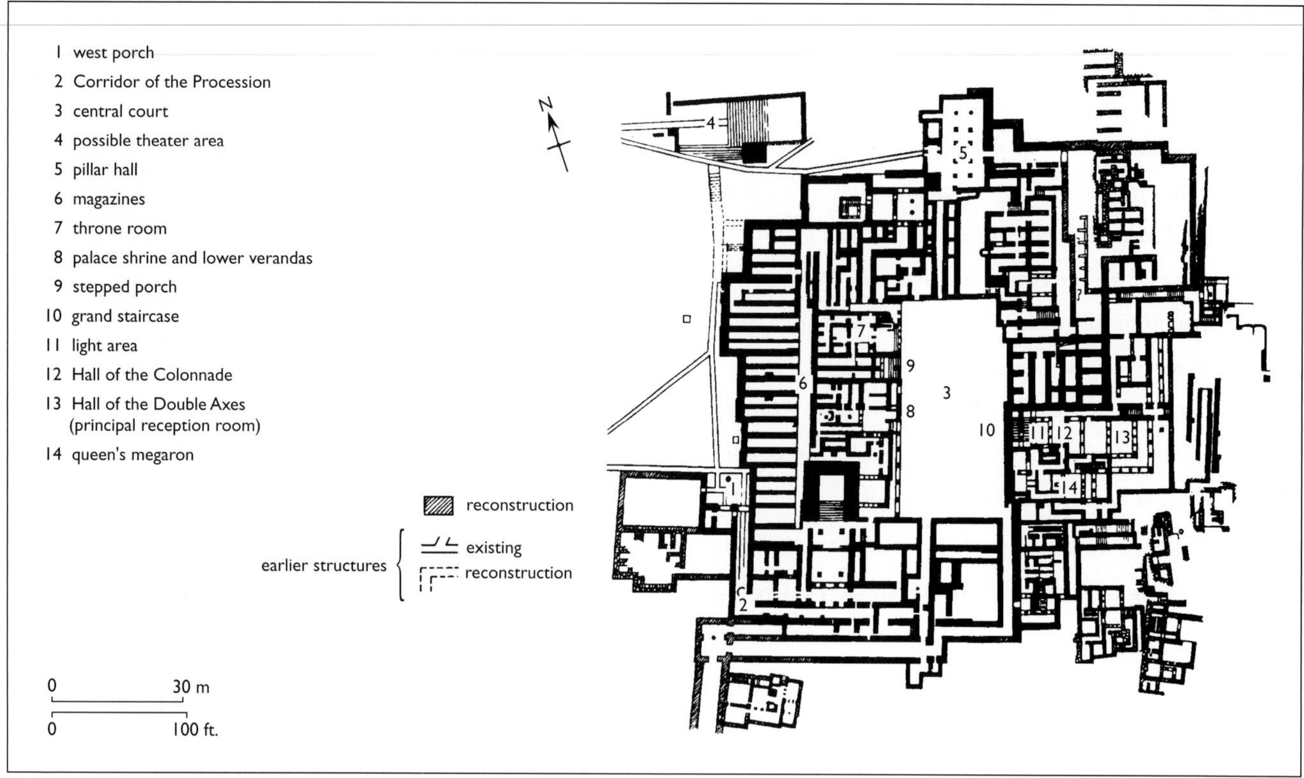

4.2 Plan of the palace of Minos, Knossos, Crete, *c.*1600–1400 B.C.

Society and Culture

The Labyrinth in Myth

The palace at Knossos was called the labyrinth by the Greeks, because of its maze-like plan (see figure 4.2). This structure became a feature of several myths, such as the myth of the Minotaur, the tale of the wife of King Minos who fell in love with a bull. Their union produced the monstrous Minotaur, part-human, part-bull. Minos demanded from Athens an annual tribute of seven boys and seven girls, who were killed and devoured by the Minotaur—an indication that the Greeks viewed the Minoans as a powerful force in the Aegean.

The Athenian hero Theseus decided to journey to Knossos to destroy the Minotaur and end the yearly sacrifice of Athenian youths. But Theseus became lost in the maze, and he escaped only because Ariadne, the daughter of King Minos, fell in love with him. She attached the end of a long thread to the entrance of the palace, and Theseus followed it out of the maze.

human in scale and avoided **symmetry**. They were built of **ashlar** (rectangular blocks) and mud brick, and covered with a thin layer of stone and painted plaster walls. The intricate layout of the plan conforms to the different functions of its parts: long thin rooms for storage at the west, living quarters in the east, and religious rooms facing the courtyard.

The walls of the east wing stairway (figure **4.3**) were decorated with **frescoes** (water-based paint applied to damp plaster surfaces), which are now restored. Small wooden columns are unique in that the shafts taper downward, as humans do, suggesting a relationship to human form and scale. This also creates more open space and allows greater freedom of movement for the inhabitants than do the huge columns and compact spaces of Egyptian architecture, which was designed to emphasize the greatness of the gods and pharaohs.

MINOAN RELIGION

The Minoans had no separate temples, because they worshipped inside palaces, outdoors at small mountain shrines, and in caves. Little is known about Minoan religious practices, although two striking images certainly had religious significance. One of these shows a woman, a priestess or a goddess—known as the Mistress of the Animals (figure **4.4**)—dominating snakes. Her frontal pose and upraised arms convey a sense of power, and her exposed, prominent breasts suggest that she was a fertility figure. As such, she would have been associated with vegetation cults celebrating rebirth every spring. The snakes represent the underground (**chthonic**) forces of the earth. Tree-worship was also a feature of Minoan religion, and trees and their architectural equivalent—columns made of wood—could symbolize a nature goddess.

The bull motif, which is related to the myth of Europa, had a ritual purpose, although the nature and meaning of the ritual are unsure. It appears from certain images that bulls were

4.3 East wing staircase, palace of Minos, Knossos, *c.* 1600–1400 B.C.
Note that whereas the Egyptian columns were in the form of plants, which symbolized fertility and prosperity, the Minoan columns are abstract. They have a small, round base and a short shaft, which is consistent with the lower ceilings compared with Egypt. The Minoan **capital** consists of a round, cushionlike shape surmounted by a square block. Behind the columns, the wall is decorated with shields in the shape of figures-of-eight and the door is framed by a pattern of circles. As on the jar from Phaistos (see figure 4.1), the style is lively and curvilinear.

4.4 Mistress of the Animals, from Knossos, *c.* 1600 B.C. Faience, 13½ in. (34.3 cm) high. Herakleion Museum, Crete.

sacrificed with double axes (axes with two blades). In Minoan art, there are many images of bulls, some of which were associated with the double axe. Actual double axes vary in size, and many small ones have been discovered in Minoan caves and shrines. Images of the double axe were also incised on several **piers** (vertical supports) at Knossos.

A bull ritual is the subject of the most famous painting found at Knossos, the *Toreador Fresco* (figure **4.5**). It shows three slender youths somersaulting over a charging bull, a scene that has been related to the myth of the Minotaur. Notice that two of the young people are white and one is brown, indicating that there are two girls and one boy. As in

4.5 *Toreador Fresco*, from Knossos, *c.* 1500 B.C. 32 in. (81.3 cm) high. Herakleion Museum, Crete.
This fresco had shattered into hundreds of fragments discovered lying on a floor of the palace. Note that it has been heavily restored. The dark fragments are original and the lighter areas are modern.

Egypt, the artistic convention of representing females with light skin and males with dark skin persisted on Crete. Similarly, the Minoans retained the conceptual representation of the profile head and frontal eye prevalent in Mesopotamian and Egyptian paintings and relief sculptures (see Chapters 2 and 3). In contrast to Egyptian style, however, the Minoan figures have natural curves, they turn more freely in space, and their movements are more dynamic. Works such as the *Toreador Fresco* confirm that Minoan artists were influenced by Egypt, but that they also evolved their own distinctive style.

THE HAGIA TRIADA SARCOPHAGUS

The most elaborate image of a Minoan religious ceremony occurs on a sarcophagus found at the site of Hagia Triada (figure **4.6**). This is described here in some detail because it

4.6a Sarcophagus from Hagia Triada (front), *c.* 1400 B.C. Limestone with surface plastered and painted, 4 ft. 5 in. (1.35 m) wide. Herakleion Museum, Crete.

4.6b Back view of 4.6a.

4.7 John Younger, reconstruction of the Hagia Triada harp-player, as seen in figure 4.6a.

is a rare illustration in Minoan art showing figures enacting a ritual; it also reveals something about the kinds of musical instruments used by the Minoans.

The front left depicts a **libation** scene (in which a liquid is poured into a vessel). A woman in a fur skirt, possibly a priestess, pours liquid from one vessel into another (see figure 4.6a). The vessel stands on a platform flanked by vertical posts supporting double axes and birds. Behind the priestess, a second woman carries two jars suspended from a pole, and a man in a long yellow robe plays a type of harp (figure **4.7**). In the offering scene on the right, three men present models of calves and a boat to a figure (possibly the deceased) in front of what may be his tomb or a shrine.

On the other side of the sarcophagus (see figure 4.6b), a flute-player leads a procession of women. At the center, a bull is being sacrificed on a table, and its blood drips into a jar on the ground. Two small goats behind the table await their own sacrifice. To the right, a priestess places her hands over an altar, behind which is a post with double axes surmounted by a bird. At the far right, a second altar is built around an olive tree.

Although the exact meaning of the imagery on the Hagia Triada sarcophagus cannot be identified, it clearly represents a sacrifical ritual. The scenes associate the double axe with killing the bull as well as with the presentation of offerings. They also point to the importance of music during funeral rites, which is confirmed by actual musical instruments found in Minoan burials.

MUSIC AND RITUAL

Surviving Minoan art indicates that ritual music in the Aegean—unlike that in Egypt—was the province of men. No written musical notes or texts of Aegean songs have survived, but several types of instruments have. Stringed instruments included the harp and the lyre, and the wind instruments were single- or double-reed pipes (**auloi**, in Greek); both types are depicted on the Hagia Triada sarcophagus. Horns were made from triton shells, and the sistrum (a type of rattle) was a popular percussion instrument. Singing was also an important part of Minoan religious ritual, which is illustrated in figure **4.8**.

Only the top half of this egg-shaped **rhyton** (drinking cup) is preserved. It is decorated with twenty-seven male figures. The leader wears a long tunic; workers carry farm implements; four are singing, as is indicated by the open mouths and depiction of the ribs, and one man shakes a sistrum. The scene is thought to represent a harvesting ritual, possibly related to gathering ripened olives, which were a staple of the Minoan (and later the Greek) economy.

4.8 *Harvester Vase*, rhyton from Hagia Triada, 1650–1450 B.C. Steatite, $4\frac{1}{2}$ in. (11.3 cm) diameter. Herakleion Museum, Crete.

THERA

On the volcanic island of Thera, north of Crete, archaeologists have discovered the ruins of a thriving civilization contemporary with the Minoans. During the heyday of Minoan power, Therans, like the inhabitants of Crete, had a high standard of living, with an economy based on agriculture and seafaring.

Although civilization on the island came to an end when the volcano erupted in the fifteenth century B.C., under the volcanic ash many elements of the culture were preserved—most notably, frescoes. These indicate a well-developed artistic

Defining Moment

The Eruption of Thera and Plato's Lost Atlantis

The ancient Aegean civilizations on Crete and Thera, which flourished from around 2000 B.C. to around 1200 B.C., were island cultures (map **4.1**). Sometime in the fifteenth century B.C., the area witnessed one of the most devastating volcanic eruptions ever known.

The Aegean island of Thera, now called Santorini, is located in the south of the Cyclades and is the surviving half of an active volcano. Thera's ancient culture was largely unknown until a Greek archaeologist, Spyridon Marinatos, began to excavate in the 1960s. Marinatos discovered building complexes, city streets, and walls up to 24 feet (8 m) high. Evidence was found of textile weaving and objects from many Mediterranean cultures, which indicate a well-established international trade on Thera. Pipes for transporting water, plumbing, and sewage systems attest to a good standard of living and are the earliest examples found so far anywhere in the world. Above all, archaeologists have unearthed a wealth of fresco paintings that reflect Theran life and ties to Minoan Crete. The frescoes illustrate a fleet, which was probably Minoan, dominating the Aegean Sea.

All of this, as well as parts of northern Crete, was destroyed when the volcano erupted. The inhabitants of Thera disappeared, and, as there is no trace of human remains on the island, it seems that they predicted the disaster and left in time. Ash and pumice from the explosion have been found as far away as modern Israel and Egypt, the Black Sea, and Turkey.

The enormity of the eruption on Thera has evoked comparisons with the eruption of Krakatoa, in Indonesia, in the nineteenth century. Most intriguing of all, Thera became associated with Plato's fourth-century-B.C. account of the Lost Atlantis. A mythic island in the Atlantic, Atlantis was said by Plato to have had its story related by Egyptian priests. It was reputed to have been powerful and to have sunk into the sea following a huge volcanic eruption. In reality, the devastation caused by the explosion on Thera completely wiped out Theran culture and contributed to the end of Minoan civilization, allowing the Mycenaeans to conquer Crete.

In 2004, an American researcher announced that he had found the Lost Atlantis off the coast of the island of Cyprus. He claimed that water sonars revealed man-made buildings on a hill sunk deep into the sea. But the main government archaeologist of Cyprus expressed doubts. Whatever the outcome, it is clear that the myth of the Lost Atlantis continues to intrigue researchers and will do so until the mystery has been solved.

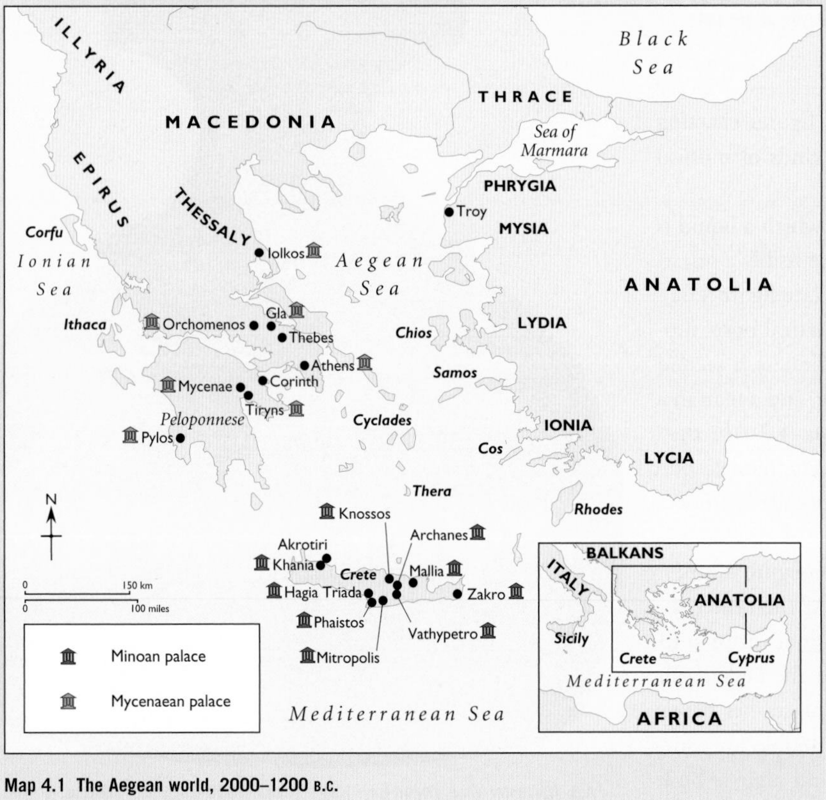

Map 4.1 The Aegean world, 2000–1200 B.C.

READING SELECTION

Plato, *Critias*, the myth of Atlantis, PWC1-128-B

Critical Question Read Plato's account of the Lost Atlantis and decide if you think it is the same as Thera. What could have happened to the Therans when they escaped the eruption?

4.9 *Ship Fresco*, from Akroteri, Thera, *c.* 1650–1500 B.C., 15¾ in. (40 cm) high. National Archaeological Museum, Athens.

tradition; Theran artists were influenced by Minoan painting but developed their own, individual style.

The most important Theran fresco, called the *Ship Fresco* (figure **4.9**), dates to the second millennium B.C. There is disagreement among scholars over the exact meaning of this long painting, which extended across the upper part of three walls, but it has been a source of much information about Theran culture. It shows that ships were propelled by paddles and that dolphins swam in the Aegean. The ships, which are filled with warriors, are just setting out, most likely to engage in acts of piracy as well as to pursue peaceful trade. The *Ship Fresco* also contains examples of architecture and forest animals, such as deer, which provide clues to life on Thera.

Shortly after Thera's eruption, Greeks from the mainland invaded Crete. The invaders were the Mycenaeans, whose civilization lasted from around 1600 to 1150 B.C. It is not known for certain where the Mycenaeans came from, but they are thought to have been Indo-Europeans from the Caucasus who were great horsemen and who migrated to the east and west. From the beginning of the Mycenaean period, works of art and architecture on the mainland reflected Minoan influence.

MYCENAE AND THE HOMERIC HEROES

Mycenaean civilization takes its name from its main archaeological site at Mycenae in the northeast Peloponnese (southern Greece). But there were other important mainland sites, notably at Pylos, Tiryns, Corinth, and Athens. As in the Near East, Mycenaean cities were organized around fortified palaces often located on an elevated **citadel**. At Mycenae, the king and his consort were enthroned in a central room before a hearth where a sacred fire burned. Extending beyond the throne room were administrative offices and storage areas. Outside the palace, monumental city walls enclosed the main part of the citadel, which was inhabited by craftsmen. Beyond the citadel lay open land, which was farmed by peasants.

Above all, Mycenaean culture was a warrior culture. As such, it was celebrated in the two great epics attributed to the blind poet Homer, the *Iliad* and the *Odyssey*, which were not actually written down before the sixth century B.C. No one knows who Homer was, though he is believed to have lived in the eighth century B.C., when writing was revived at the end of the Dark Age. For centuries, professional poets had kept alive the Homeric epics by reciting them and singing them to the music of the harp. In contrast to the Egyptian ideal of eternity in the afterlife, the Homeric epics deal with mortal human heroes. The embodiment of the heroic ideal is Achilles, a warrior who chooses an early, heroic death over a long life.

The *Iliad* recounts the story of the Trojan War; the *Odyssey* tells of Odysseus's ten-year journey home after the war. The heroes of these epics are of two types. In the *Iliad*, Achilles is a great warrior, a kind of superhero, childish at times, unreasonably demanding, but also brave and skilled in fighting. Odysseus, the hero of the *Odyssey*, is crafty and intelligent. Like Achilles, he is a skilled warrior who fights alongside the Greek army at Troy. But when the war is over, Odysseus undertakes an epic quest and, like Gilgamesh (see Chapter 2), undergoes personal transformations as a result of his experiences. These include a series of memorable encounters with danger and temptation, and a visit to the Underworld. Whereas Achilles dies a heroic, youthful death, Odysseus returns home to his faithful wife, Penelope, in Ithaca, where he rules in peace and lives a long life. The *Iliad* and the *Odyssey* were studied in depth by the historical Greeks, and they continue to be an essential part of the Western educational curriculum today.

As with the Minoans, the Mycenaeans were known to the later Greeks, and indeed to the West, only in myth and legend. But in 1870 a successful German businessman, Heinrich Schliemann (1822–1890), set out to prove that the Trojan War actually happened. Inspired by reading Homer, Schliemann believed that there must have been some historical basis in the myths and legends surrounding the Trojan War. Having amassed a fortune, he was able to retire from business and pursue his goal. He first excavated at the site of Troy, a fortified city buried under the Greek and Roman town of Ilium on the northwest coast of Turkey.

HOMER'S *ILIAD*

Rage—Goddess, sing the rage of Peleus' son Achilles,
murderous, doomed, that cost the Achaeans [Greeks]
countless losses,
hurling down to the House of Death so many sturdy souls,
great fighters' souls, but made their bodies carrion,
feasts for the dogs and birds,
and the will of Zeus was moving toward its end.
Begin, Muse, when the two first broke and clashed,
Agamemnon lord of men and brilliant Achilles.

(*Iliad*, lines 1–8)

The first eight lines of Homer's *Iliad* quoted here introduce the basic conflict of the epic. They take us into the middle of the action, rather than to the beginning of the story. The Greeks and their Minoan allies are waging war against the walled city of Troy. In the very first word—"rage"—Homer shows us the attitude of the youthful Achilles and his rash behavior, its consequences in causing the deaths of many warriors, and the violent, destructive character of war itself. Not only are brave soldiers killed, but their corpses are carrion, food for dogs and birds of prey.

Homer's reference to the "will of Zeus" reminds us of the Greek notion that, although humans have free will, their fate is controlled by the gods. This apparent paradox continues into later periods of Greek history and is a frequent theme in Greek literature and myth. It was an attempt to explain events and impulses that people could not control and to resolve inner, psychological conflicts that everyone experiences.

In the last two lines of the quotation, Homer asks his Muse, a goddess who inspires poetry, to begin the tale with the conflict between Achilles and Agamemnon, leader of the Greek army and king of Mycenae. Agamemnon had taken Achilles' war prize, a young Trojan woman, thus mirroring the legendary cause of the war itself. According to Greek legend, Agamemnon's brother, Menelaus, the king of Sparta, had married the beautiful Helen. When the Trojan prince, Paris, visited Menelaus, he was so struck by Helen's beauty that he abducted her and carried her off to Troy. Pledged to defend his brother's honor, Agamemenon led an army against the Trojans and ignited the war that lasted for ten years.

In the *Iliad*, Agamemnon and Achilles continue their feud. Achilles, the greatest of the Greek warriors, defies Agamemnon by refusing to fight and thus places the Greeks at a disadvantage. But when Hector, the bravest of the Trojan warriors, slays Achilles' best friend, Patroclus, Achilles returns to battle. Achilles had given his own armor to Patroclus, but Hector strips the armor and lays claim to Patroclus's naked body. Enraged by Hector's actions and devastated by the death of Patroclus, Achilles asks his mother, who is a goddess, to order him a new set of armor. She, in turn, asks Hephaestus, the blacksmith god, to forge weapons for her son. In a famous passage, Homer describes Achilles' new shield, which is decorated with images of city and country life, festivals and rituals, that mirror contemporary society.

Achilles now ceases to rage at Agamemnon, directing his anger instead at the Trojans. He slays dozens of enemy warriors, forcing them to take refuge inside the city. Finally, Achilles kills Hector in single combat. Achilles then strips Hector of his armor, and drags his nude body around the walls of Troy. Patroclus's spirit appears to Achilles and asks for proper burial rites.

In Greek religion, the soul of a dead person who was not properly buried was condemned to wander forever as a restless shade. Achilles thus arranges an elaborate burial for his friend. He then ransoms Hector's body to the Trojan king Priam. The *Iliad* ends with Hector's splendid funeral—the last line reads: "And so the Trojans buried Hector breaker of horses" (Bk. 24, last line).

HOMERIC LITERARY DEVICES

Homer's language is densely packed with action, which is intensified by colorful epithets (characterizing adjectives or short phrases), **similes** (comparisons using "like" or "as"), and metaphors (comparisons without "like" or "as"). We find, for example, epithets such as "well-greaved Greeks" (greaves being armor on the lower leg), "swift-footed Achilles," "crafty Odysseus," "wide-ruling Agamemnon," "god-like Priam," and "horse-breaking Hector." Achilles' spear is "far-shooting," the dawn is "rosy-fingered," and the sea is "wine-dark." Another device is repetition for the sake of emphasis.

In the following description of Priam's first sight of Achilles, note the use of repetition as well as of similes and metaphors. The Trojan king watches in fear as Achilles races toward the gates of Troy to fight his son, Hector:

And old King Priam was first to see him [Achilles] coming,
surging over the plain, blazing like the star
that rears at harvest, flaming up in its brilliance,—
far outshining the countless stars in the night sky,
that star they call Orion's Dog—brightest of all
but a fatal sign emblazoned on the heavens,
it brings such killing fever down on wretched men.
So the bronze flared on his chest as he raced—
and the old man moaned, flinging both hands high,
beating his head and groaning deep he called,
begging his dear son who stood before the gates,
unshakable, furious to fight Achilles to the death.

(Bk. 22, lines 31–41)

In vain, Priam pleads with Hector not to fight Achilles. Homer compares Hector to a coiled serpent waiting to strike its prey:

As a snake in the hills, guarding his hole, awaits a man—
bloated with poison, deadly hatred seething inside him,
glances flashing fire as he coils round his lair . . .
so Hector, nursing his quenchless fury, gave no ground,
leaning his burnished shield against a jutting wall.

(Bk. 22, lines 112–116)

And when Achilles pursues Hector, he is compared in another simile to a hound chasing a deer:

> And swift Achilles kept on coursing Hector, nonstop
> as a hound in the mountains starts a fawn from its lair,
> hunting him down the gorges, down the narrow glens
> and the fawn goes to ground, hiding deep in brush
> but the hound comes racing fast, nosing him out
> until he lands his kill. So Hector could never throw
> Achilles off his trail, the swift racer Achilles.
>
> (Bk. 22, lines 224–230)

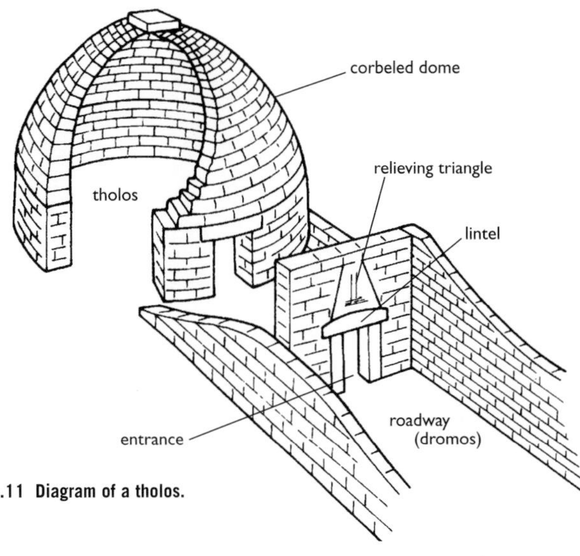

4.11 Diagram of a tholos.

MYCENAEAN ART AND ARCHITECTURE

Echoing the warrior character of the Homeric heroes is the massive, monumental architecture produced by the Mycenaeans. Unlike the Minoans, the Mycenaeans built defensive, fortified citadels as protection against invasion. The interior of the Mycenaean citadel contained a palace, royal tombs, and administrative centers. Most of the citizens were farmers, who lived on the slopes of the hill or in the valley below.

4.10 Lion Gate, Mycenae, Greece, 13th century B.C. Limestone, approx. 9 ft. 6 in. (2.9 m) high.
Note that the gate supports a triangular stone with a relief sculpture. This is composed of two lions guarding a Minoan column, which symbolizes the nature goddess worshipped on Crete, a motif that reflects contacts between the Minoan and Mycenaean cultures. At Mycenae, however, the faces of the lions were turned to the front, facing those who approach the entrance and denoting power.

Figure **4.10** illustrates the Lion Gate entrance to the walled Mycenaean citadel. It is a massive structure set between walls made of huge stone blocks. The large stone **courses** (layers of stone) of the wall increasingly project inward above the lintel to create a **corbel** arch.

A similar type of construction, known as a corbeled dome, was used for the monumental **tholos** tombs in which Mycenaean kings and queens were buried (figures **4.11** and **4.12**). The tholoi and earlier shaft graves at Mycenae contained gold

4.12 Entrance to the so-called Treasury of Atreus, Mycenae, Greece, 13th century B.C. Limestone.
Approached by a roadway, or **dromos**, the tholos was a round structure that tapered toward the top like a beehive. The door, which has not survived, was originally flanked by gypsum columns. Above the door, there is a triangular space, called a **relieving triangle** because it reduces the weight on the lintel; as with the Lion Gate, this space was originally filled in.

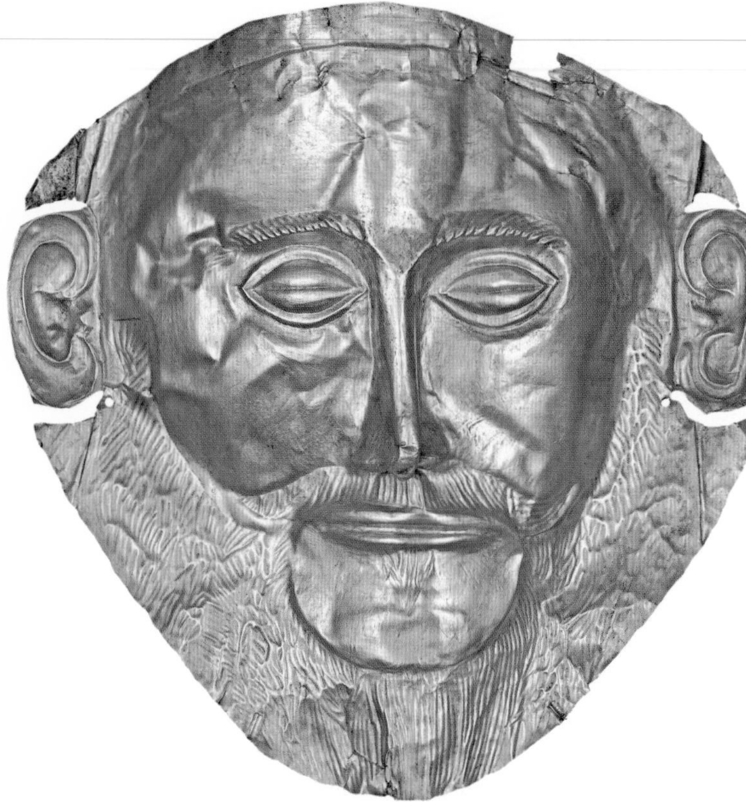

4.13 Mask of a ruler, erroneously called Agamemnon's mask by Schliemann, *c.* 1500 B.C. Gold, 12 in. (30.5 cm) high. National Archaeological Museum, Athens.

objects buried with the dead. Among these were works in the shape of bulls, indicating Minoan influence, and death masks that suggest a belief in the afterlife (figure **4.13**). Although little is known about Mycenaean religion, the Mycenaeans, like the Minoans, worshipped in palace shrines, rather than in separately built temples.

Inside the palace, the **megaron** was the main building within the Mycenaean citadel. The plan (figure **4.14**) shows the front porch with two columns, the **antechamber** (a room before, and leading into, another room), and the large throne room. Inside the throne room, the king sat facing the central hearth, which was surrounded by four columns. The reconstruction in figure **4.15** shows the elaborate painted decoration of the palace. The Minoan-style columns tapering toward the base are another indication of contact between Crete and mainland Greece.

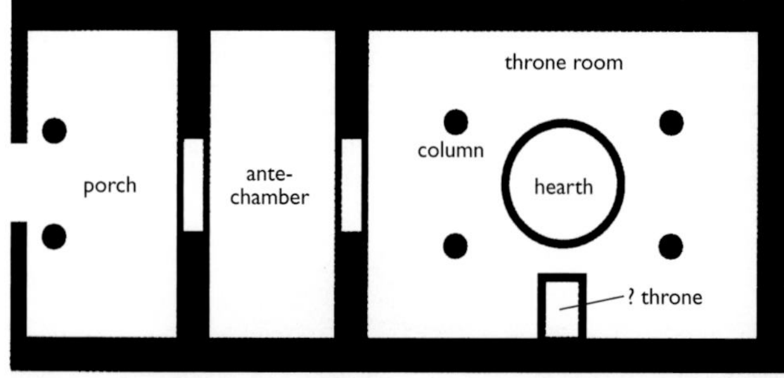

4.14 Plan of a Mycenaean megaron.

AGAMEMNON AND THE *ORESTEIA* OF AESCHYLUS

It was from such a palace that Agamemnon and the other Mycenaean kings mentioned in the *Iliad* would have ruled. As the home of King Agamemnon, Mycenae was the most important Mycenaean city, which Schliemann excavated after Troy. Just as the story of the Trojan War had faded into myth and legend and was known only through the Homeric epics, so the story of Agamemnon and his family was known to the historical Greeks only through literature. The most complete surviving account of Agamemnon's return to Mycenae at the end of the war is a dramatic **trilogy** (set of three related plays), the *Oresteia*, by the fifth-century-B.C. playwright Aeschylus.

4.15 Reconstruction drawing of the Mycenaean megaron.

Although Aeschylus wrote many centuries after the events he described, his narrative is discussed here (fifth-century-B.C. Greek theater is explored further in Chapter 6). As with Homer, the power of Aeschylus's language, with its graphic imagery, emotional intensity, and taste for descriptions of violence, reflects the warrior culture of Mycenae.

The first play of the trilogy, *Agamemnon*, opens with a watchman guarding the palace of Mycenae and awaiting the signal that Agamemnon and his fleet are returning from Troy. When the signal finally comes, after ten years, the watchman's joy is muted by his knowledge of the famous curse on the House of Atreus: Atreus and Thyestes were brothers, but Thyestes seduced his brother's wife. Atreus took revenge by feeding Thyestes his own sons. Thyestes then cursed the descendants of Atreus, whose sons included Agamemnon and Menelaus.

Before setting sail for Troy, Agamemnon had insulted the moon goddess, Artemis, by killing one of her sacred stags. In revenge, Artemis calmed the winds to prevent the Greek ships from sailing. She demanded that Agamemnon atone for his insult by sacrificing his daughter, Iphigenia.

When Agamemnon returned to Mycenae at the end of the Trojan War, he found that his wife, Clytemnestra, had taken as a lover Thyestes' son, Aegisthus. Agamemnon himself had brought home as a war prize the Trojan princess Cassandra. She was cursed with the gift of prophecy but also with the fate that no one would ever believe her. Her warning that Clytemnestra would murder Agamemnon in his bath was thus ignored:

> Keep the bull from his mate! She hath caught him in the
> robe and gores him with the crafty device of her black horn!
> He falls in a vessel of water! It is doom wrought by guile
> in a murderous bath that I am telling thee.
>
> (Aeschylus, *Agamemnon*, lines 1125–1129)

Still angry at Agamemnon for having sacrificed their daughter, Clytemnestra fulfills Cassandra's prophecy. Her description of the murder is graphic indeed:

> Round him [Agamemnon], like as to catch a haul of fish, I
> cast a net impassable—a fatal wealth of robe—so that he
> should neither escape nor ward off doom. Twice I smote him,
> and with two groans his limbs relaxed. Once he had fallen, I
> dealt him yet a third stroke . . . Fallen thus, he gasped
> away his life, and as he breathed forth quick spurts of blood,
> he smote me with dark drops of ensanguined dew; while I
> rejoiced no less than the sown earth is gladdened in
> heaven's refreshing rain at the birthtime of the flower buds.
>
> (lines 1384–1392)

The play closes with Clytemnestra and Aegisthus ruling Mycenae—a reflection of the Mycenaean kingship system. Although kings ruled, they obtained legitimacy by marriage to a queen. On the death of Agamemnon, therefore, Aegisthus was free to marry Clytemnestra and become king of Mycenae.

The curse on the House of Atreus continues into the next generation and is the main theme of the second play of Aeschylus's trilogy, *The Libation Bearers*. Here the leading characters are Agamemnon's children, Electra and Orestes. Orestes has grown up away from the palace after his father's murder. Electra remains but is in perpetual mourning for her lost status as the king's daughter and for her father's death. Because she is female and fatherless, she cannot act. But the sun god, Apollo, orders Orestes to return to Mycenae and avenge Agamemnon's murder. Urged on by Electra as well as by Apollo, Orestes is in the difficult position of having to kill his own mother. Tortured by conflict but steady in his resolve, Orestes kills Clytemnestra and Aegisthus. The play ends with the Furies (goddesses who avenge crime) pursuing Orestes.

The last play of the trilogy, *The Eumenides* ("Kindly Ones"), deals with Orestes' quest for pardon. Pursued by the Furies to the city of Athens, Orestes goes on trial. Apollo himself presents the case to the jury. Reflecting the patriarchal bias of ancient Greece, the sun god argues that Clytemnestra is not really Orestes' blood relative because only a father can be a true parent. The mother, Apollo says, is merely the vessel and caretaker of the father's seed.

The jury fails to reach a verdict by reason of a tied vote. According to the rules of the Athenian court, a tie must be decided by Athena (goddess of war and wisdom), who casts her vote for acquittal. She then transforms the Furies into the Eumenides by promising them permanent sanctuary in Athens. Through the intervention of the gods, the curse on the House of Atreus is finally lifted, and Orestes becomes king of Mycenae.

HOMER'S *ODYSSEY*

Years after Agamemnon's return to Mycenae, the Greek hero Odysseus is still struggling to reach his family and his kingdom. His epic journey over land and sea and his descent into the Underworld are the subjects of Homer's *Odyssey*, which continues to inspire Western authors today. The very term "odyssey" has come to mean a spiritual, psychological, and physical journey that is heroic in character. As in the *Iliad*, Homer invokes the Muse in the opening lines, to sing not of Achilles' rage but of the crafty Odysseus, who wandered for years after the sack of Troy:

> Sing in me, Muse, and through me tell the story
> of that man skilled in all ways of contending,
> the wanderer, harried for years on end,
> after he plundered the stronghold
> on the proud height of Troy.
> He saw the townlands
> and learned the minds of many distant men,
> and weathered many bitter nights and days
> in his deep heart at sea, while he fought only
> to save his life, to bring his shipmates home.
>
> (*Odyssey*, Bk. 1, lines 1–10)

Before departing for the Trojan War, Odysseus had ruled at Ithaca, an island in the Ionian Sea off the west coast of the Greek mainland. He bade farewell to his wife, Penelope, and son, Telemachus, and sailed for Troy.

At the beginning of the *Odyssey*, the war has been over for ten years. For seven of those years Odysseus and his men were imprisoned on an island by the goddess Calypso. In his absence, a number of suitors have tried to marry Penelope in order to rule Ithaca. Telemachus grows ever more afraid that he will lose his status as heir to the throne because, as at Mycenae, marriage to the queen would confer kingship on her new spouse and lower the rank of her children by Odysseus (see Box).

Eventually, Zeus orders Calypso to free Odysseus, who builds a raft and sets sail. But the raft is destroyed by Poseidon (god of the sea), and Odysseus and his men are forced to land on another island. There he meets the king's daughter, Nausicaa, and is well entertained at the palace. A minstrel sings of heroes and gods, and of the wooden horse that made it possible for the Greeks to sack Troy. Unable to penetrate the city gates, the crafty Odysseus devised a plan: the Greeks built a huge wooden horse and offered it to the Trojans as a gift. But Greek soldiers hid inside and when the Trojans pulled it into the city, the Greeks brought:

> slaughter and death upon the men of Troy.
> He [the minstrel] sang, then, of the town sacked by Akhaians
> [Greeks]
> pouring down from the horse's hollow cave,
> this way and that way raping the steep city.
>
> (Bk. VIII, lines 551–554)

Society and Culture

Women, Family, and the Rules of Marriage in the Homeric Age

Aristocratic nuclear families in the age of Homer consisted of the father, who was head of the household, his spouse, and their children. Adult sons, once married, lived at home with *their* wives and children. If a female slave had a son by a legitimate member of the family, that son had some rights, but fewer than the wife's sons. The son of a slave might inherit part of his father's property on his death, but generally property was divided among the wife's sons. If a father died before his son was grown, the son could lose his rights. This was the case with Orestes, providing him with a practical reason for killing Aegisthus and Clytemnestra. It was also a possibility that worried Telemachus.

Daughters were excluded from inheritance, and their fathers arranged their marriages, often for political or social reasons. The daughter had little say in the matter. The family of the bridegroom gave gifts to the bride's family, and the bride received a dowry from her family. Whereas the dowry was an investment in the future, the gifts were a sign of status. They were also a form of competition, in which several suitors might participate. Those who lost forfeited the gifts. Once married, the bride moved in with her husband's family.

In non-aristocratic families, money was the primary motive for marriage. A man might not marry until the age of thirty, but the average age of the bride was fifteen. Furthermore, in order to keep money in the family, marriages were arranged by a small group of close relatives.

According to the picture of Greek society painted by Homer, the Mycenaean period was one of relative social freedom for aristocratic women. Homer depicts wives as joining their husbands in conversation and participating with them in banquets. Women also ran the household economy and could go outdoors without a chaperone. These freedoms would be severely restricted after 800 B.C.

Odysseus describes the ordeals that he and his men have weathered since leaving Troy. A race of cannibal giants destroyed all but one of his twelve ships. The enchantress Circe transformed his men into swine. He journeyed through Hades, where he met the shades of deceased heroes who had fought at Troy. He successfully passed through the straits of Scylla (a monster who killed mariners) and Charybdis (a dangerous whirlpool). He resisted the irresistible Sirens' songs by filling his sailors' ears with wax and having himself tied to the mast of the ship. When he landed on the island of the Cyclopes (cannibal giants with a single eye), Odysseus and his men were captured and imprisoned in a cave. But Odysseus tricked the Cyclops Polyphemus into becoming drunk and then blinded him with a stake (see Box).

When Odysseus finally reaches Ithaca, Athena disguises him as a beggar. This allows him to discover what has been happening during his twenty-year absence. He meets his son Telemachus, reveals his identity, and together they plot to kill Penelope's suitors. In one of the most famous passages in the *Odyssey*, Odysseus is recognized by his old dog, Argos, who sees through his disguise:

> an old hound, lying near, pricked up his ears
> and lifted up his muzzle. This was Argos,
> trained as a puppy by Odysseus,
> but never taken on a hunt before
> his master sailed for Troy. The young men, afterward,
> hunted wild goats with him, and hare, and deer,
> but he had grown old in his master's absence.
> Treated as rubbish now, he lay at last
> upon a mass of dung before the gates—
> manure of mules and cows, piled there until
> fieldhands could spread it on the king's estate.
> Abandoned there, and half destroyed with flies,
> old Argos lay.
> But when he knew he heard
> Odysseus' voice nearby, he did his best
> to wag his tail.
>
> (Bk. XVII, lines 376–391)

Society and Culture

The Cyclopes and Cyclopaean Masonry

The Cyclopes are the source of the term **cyclopaean masonry**, which denotes the huge stone blocks used in Mycenaean citadels. The later Greeks attributed the construction of such walls to giants, believing that no mere mortal was capable of lifting the stones. At Mycenae itself, cyclopaean masonry can be seen in the Lion Gate (see figure 4.10) and the walls of the dromos leading to the tholos tomb in figure 4.12. But in the corbeled enclosure at Tiryns (figure **4.16**), some 10 miles (16 km) from Mycenae, the monumental quality of these rougher stones is even more striking. Such enclosures, used to store weapons and for refuge in times of war, are the origin of the Homeric epithet for the city, "great-walled Tiryns."

4.16 Corbel vault, inside the citadel, Tiryns, Greece, *c.* 1300–1200 B.C.

The condition of the dog, weakened by neglect, is a metaphor for the state of Ithaca. Nevertheless, there is life in the old dog, as there is in the kingdom, and Odysseus quickly takes charge. Penelope, worn down by years of waiting and by the persistence of her suitors, has agreed to marry whoever can string Odysseus's bow and shoot an arrow through twelve axe heads. Still in disguise, Odysseus himself passes the test, kills the suitors and their mistresses, and convinces Penelope of his true identity. He then resumes control of Ithaca, preserves his son's heritage, and rules until his death.

READING SELECTION

Homer: *Iliad*, on the shield of Achilles, PWC1-205; *Odyssey*, in the Underworld, PWC1-211; *Odyssey*, on the Cyclops, PWC1-210; *Odyssey*, on the faithful dog, PWC1-215

Like all great works of literature, the *Iliad* and the *Odyssey* are timeless. Both portray aspects of their context, but also appeal to readers in different times and places. In the Homeric epics, as in Aeschylus's plays, we learn about Greek warrior culture and the structure of Greece's aristocratic and royal families, and we are told how gods and humans interact. But epics are also larger than life. They dramatize universal human themes and externalize internal human conflicts. Their characters are heroic, and their style is the result of poetic genius.

One lesson of the Minoan–Mycenaean civilizations is that myths and legends, like literature and the arts, are human products and therefore have meaning. It is important to take them seriously. Even though they may not be literally true in every respect, they contain grains of truth, as Evans and Schliemann demonstrated when they uncovered two "lost" civilizations and restored them to their place in history.

THE DARK AGE: *c.* 1150–900 B.C.

By around 1150 B.C., the Greek mainland had entered the period known as the Dark Age. This refers to an era of history about which there is very little information. As gaps in historical knowledge are filled in, however, so-called dark ages become less "dark." In the case of the Greek Dark Age, the Mycenaean palaces fell into disuse, widespread poverty resulted in a decline in technology and artistic patronage, and writing disappeared. Communities became mainly agricultural, and houses were flimsily constructed. Warfare was rampant, and it is probable that conflicts such as the Trojan War weakened the Mycenaean kingdoms. Despite the Dark Age, however, there is evidence of cultural continuity between Mycenaean civilization and historical Greece. In addition to the oral transmission of the epics, the Greek language persisted, and certain gods and pottery styles also survived.

4.17 *Warrior Vase*, *c.* 1200–1150 B.C. Terra-cotta, 16 in. (40.6 cm) high. National Archaeological Museum, Athens.
The repeated forms echo the relentless march of an army going to war. Accentuating the forward motion are the long, pointed noses and determined pace. The artist has carefully delineated the Greek armor, including elaborate helmets, shields and spears, and greaves. At the far left, a woman waves to the departing soldiers, reflecting another fact of warrior culture: that women, like Clytemnestra and Penelope, remain at home.

At the close of the Mycenaean period, signs of cultural decline can be seen in the few surviving works of art. The *Warrior Vase* (figure **4.17**) found at Mycenae is flat and crude compared with the Minoan *Toreador Fresco*. Nevertheless, its imagery illustrates Mycenae's warrior culture.

The age of Homeric heroes disappeared with the Minoan–Mycenaean civilizations. Mycenaean citadels were destroyed around 1200 B.C. by severe droughts resulting from changes in climate, by invaders whose identity is still debated, and possibly also by civil wars. Later legends describe invaders from the north called Dorians, who enslaved the native population. It was mainly in Athens that the cultural traditions of the Dark Age were retained and it is with Athens that we begin our exploration of historical Greece in the next chapter.

KEY TERMS

antechamber a room before, and leading into, another room.

ashlar rectangular blocks of stone.

aulos (plural **auloi**) a double-reed pipe.

capital the decorated top of a column.

chthonic relating to underground aspects of the earth.

citadel a fortified elevated area or city.

corbel brick or masonry courses arranged to form an arch or dome.

courses layers of stone.

cyclopaean masonry huge stone blocks used to construct walls, especially in the Mycenaean citadels.

dromos a roadway.

fresco a technique of applying water-based paint to a damp plaster surface, usually a wall or ceiling.

libation the pouring of a drink as an offering to a god.

Linear A undeciphered Minoan writing used for record-keeping and religious dedications.

Linear B readable Mycenaean script; an early form of Greek.

megaron the main building in the Mycenaean citadel.

pier a vertical support, usually rectangular.

relieving triangle in architecture, a space that reduces the weight on the lintel below it.

rhyton a drinking cup.

simile a comparison using "like" or "as."

symmetry a type of balance in which two sides of an object or picture are mirror images of each other.

thalassocracy rule through the control of the sea.

tholos (plural **tholoi**) a circular tomb of beehive shape.

trilogy a set of three related works of literature.

KEY QUESTIONS

1. How do scholars know that artistic works showing musical instruments are factual?
2. What three functions did Minoan palaces fulfill? Were Minoan palaces fortified? Why or why not, according to scholars?
3. How did the Mycenaean warrior culture view death?
4. What was the cause (according to the opening lines of Homer's *Iliad*) of the loss of countless Achaeans?
5. How does the *Iliad* begin? How does it end?
6. Watch the film *Troy* (2004) and read the relevant passages in Homer. Can you identify departures from the original text in the film?
7. Choose a passage from Homer with examples of metaphor, repetition, and epithets and discuss their usage.

SUGGESTED READING

Aeschylus. *Oresteia* (*Agamemnon*, *The Libation Bearers*, and *The Eumenides*), trans. H. Weir Smyth and H. Lloyd-Jones. Loeb Library Edition. Cambridge, MA: Harvard University Press, 1983.
▸ The trilogy of plays dealing with the House of Atreus.

Boardman, John. *Pre-Classical: From Crete to Archaic Greece*. Baltimore: Penguin, 1967.
▸ A standard work on style.

Homer. *Iliad*, trans. Robert Fagles. New York: Viking, 1991.
▸ The epic account of the Trojan War.

——. *Odyssey*, trans. Robert Fitzgerald. New York: Anchor Books, 1989.
▸ The epic journey of Odysseus at the end of the Trojan War.

Immerwahr, Sara A. *Aegean Painting in the Bronze Age*. University Park, PA: Pennsylvania State University Press, 1990.
▸ An illustrated study of Aegean frescoes.

Murray, Oswyn. *Early Greece*. Cambridge, MA: Harvard University Press, 1993.
▸ A study of the Mycenaean period.

Mylonas, George. *Mycenae and the Mycenaean Age*. Princeton, NJ: Princeton University Press, 1966.
▸ Mycenaean studies up to the 1960s by a Greek archaeologist.

Pedley, John Griffiths. *Greek Art and Archaeology*. New York: Harry N. Abrams, 1998.
▸ A general overview of ancient Greek art.

Pomeroy, Sarah B. *Goddesses, Whores, Wives, and Slaves: Women in Classical Antiquity*. New York: Schocken Books, 1995.
▸ An account of the roles and position of women in ancient Greece.

Renault, Mary. *The King Must Die*. New York: Random House, 1958/London: Arrow Books, 2004.
▸ A popular historical novel dealing with the myth of the Minotaur and the story of Theseus and the labyrinth.

——. *The Bull from the Sea*. New York: Longmans, 1962/London: Arrow Books, 2004.
▸ A historical novel based on the Minoan myth of Europa and the bull.

Woodford, Susan. *The Trojan War in Ancient Art*. Ithaca, NY: Cornell University Press, 1993.
▸ An illustrated discussion of the Trojan War as a subject of Greek art.

Younger, John G. *Music in the Aegean Bronze Age*. Philadelphia: Coronet Books Inc., 1998.
▸ A brief account of Aegean music, based mainly on the evidence of the Hagia Triada sarcophagus.

SUGGESTED FILMS

1927 *The Private Life of Helen of Troy*, dir. Alexander Korda
1956 *Helen of Troy*, dir. Robert Wise
1979 *Agamemnon*, dir. Peter Hall
2004 *Troy*, dir. Wolfgang Petersen

5 The Emergence of Historical Greece

"Stand and have pity at the tomb of the dead Kroisos, whom raging Ares slew as he fought in the front line."

(INSCRIPTION ON THE *Anavysos Kouros*)

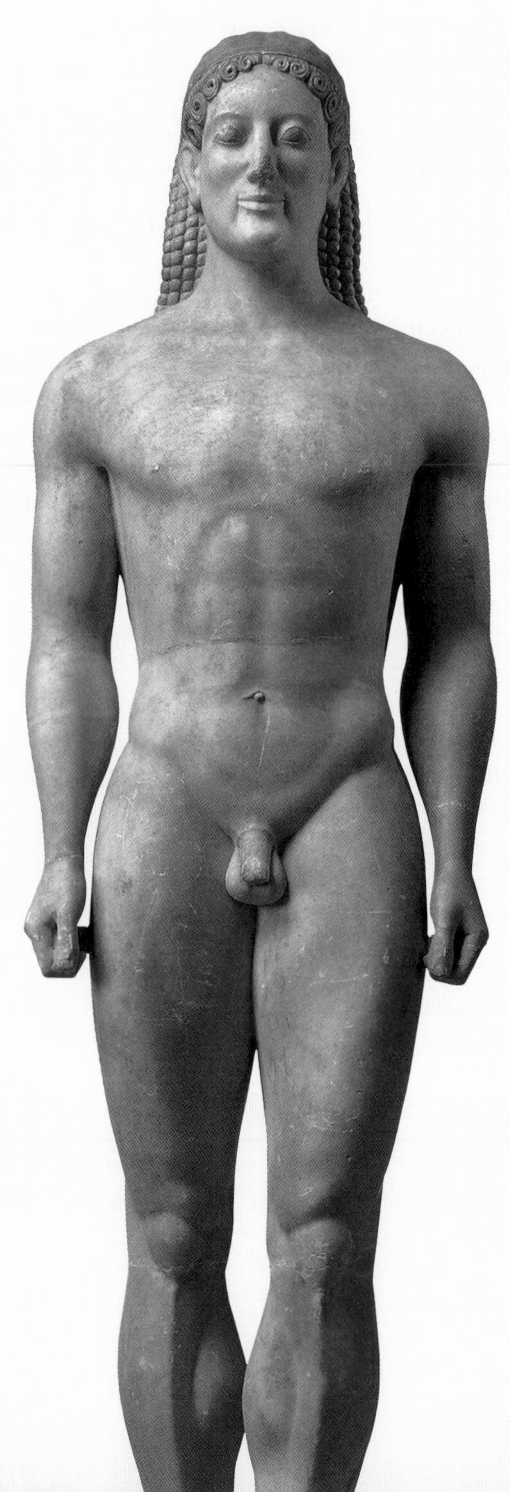

*I*n the eighth century B.C., Greece emerged from the Dark Age into its historical period. This transition coincided with a revival of writing and literacy, improved technology, and vigorous foreign trade, especially in metals. The use of Phoenician letters to stand for Greek sounds indicates contacts with the Near East.*

The mainland Greeks called themselves Hellenes and their country Hellas. By the seventh century B.C., with a growing population and renewed agricultural prosperity, land became scarce. This led many Greeks to leave the mainland and form colonies in search of metals and commercial expansion (see map 5.1, p. 92). Colonies on the eastern Greek islands and on the west coast of Anatolia were known as Ionia. The Greeks also went southeast to Cyprus and Syria, and northeast to the Black Sea. Their colonies in southern Italy and Sicily were called Magna Graecia (meaning "Greater Greece"), but the people of Magna Graecia called the Hellenes Greeks, and Hellas, Greece.

In the early centuries of the historical period, Greeks created a new type of political organization, the **polis** *(city-state). For the first time in the West, the notion of citizenship evolved, and male citizens were required to participate in their own governance. Many Greek city-states remained free of* **tyrants** *and kings. In this they differed from the other ancient civilizations considered so far. In what follows we will explore the major ideologies and events that affected Greek political thought.*

The human focus of Greek religion and the evolving naturalism of Greek art mirrored the emphasis on the role and responsibility of individuals in guiding their own destiny. Similar views are characteristic of early Greek philosophy, which emphasizes the importance of empirical observation, reason, and intellect. These new cultural attitudes, along with a shared language, unified the mainland Greeks with their colonies and reinforced the ideal of the polis*. As the city-state developed, Greece produced large-scale sculpture, painting, and stone architecture, reflecting a new and vital culture.*

Key Topics

Evolving Ideas

- Genealogy of the gods, views of the cosmos
- Tyranny
- Reason and observation
- New types of warfare

Cultural Continuity

- The *polis*
- Oracles
- Olympic Games

Cultural Unrest

- Expansion through colonization
- Economic disparities
- Athens versus Sparta

TIMELINE	GEOMETRIC PERIOD c. 1000–700	ORIENTALIZING PERIOD c. 700–600	ARCHAIC PERIOD c. 600–490
HISTORY AND CULTURE	Greece emerges from Dark Age Revival of literacy Foreign trade, metals Increasing prosperity	Trade with the Near East Colonization begins Improved pottery techniques Influence of Near Eastern forms Warrior culture, hoplites	*Polis* develops Aristocratic warrior culture Idealization of male youth Solon and Lycurgus, lawgivers Athens and Sparta Beginning of philosophy and lyric poetry
RELIGION AND MYTH	Polytheism Anthropomorphic Olympians defeat Titans Afterlife in Hades Burial rites Myth of Pandora's Box Myth of Perseus and Medusa The Nine Muses		Modest grave markers
ART	Dipylon krater, *c.* 750 Geometric bronze horse, *c.* 750	*Chigi Vase*, *c.* 640 Olpe from Corinth, *c.* 600	*Sounion Kouros*, *c.* 580 Exekias, *Suicide of Ajax*, *c.* 540 *Anavysos Kouros*, *c.* 530 *Peplos Kore*, *c.* 530 Aristokles, *Stele of Aristion*, late 6th century Heracles vase, *c.* 520 Brygos painter, red-figure drinking cup, *c.* 500
ARCHITECTURE	Model of a shrine from Perachora, late 8th century		Temple of Aphaia, Aegina, *c.* 500 Doric and Ionic Orders
LITERATURE	Homeric epics (*Iliad* and *Odyssey*) written down Hesiod, *Theogony*, late 8th century		Lyric poets: Sappho (*c.* 640–580) Anacreon (*c.* 582–*c.* 485)
PHILOSOPHY			Pre-Socratics: Thales of Miletus (*c.* 625–*c.* 547) Pythagoras (*c.* 550–*c.* 500) Heraclitus (*c.* 540–*c.* 480)
MUSIC 	No notation Part of rites Epics sung to music	Soldiers march to music	Lyric poetry sung to music

Several new styles of art evolved in the early historical period. In the Geometric period, lasting from around 1000 to 700 B.C., artists produced mainly small-scale sculptures and pottery decorated with geometric figures and designs. During the Orientalizing period (c. 700–600 B.C.) more fluid Eastern forms and subjects influenced painting and sculpture. And in the Archaic period (c. 600–490 B.C.) monumental stone architecture and lifesize sculpture appear.

During the Archaic period, the ideals of the Homeric warrior culture persisted, especially among aristocrats. Archaic artists expressed these ideals in a new type of image—the heroic male youth—which has survived mainly in sculpture. The quotation at the beginning of the chapter, for example, was inscribed on the statue of Kroisos, a young man "slain by Ares" (the war god) in the midst of battle. Just as Homer idealizes young men who choose heroic death over long life, so Archaic art memorializes the image and memory of youths who die bravely. This reflects one way in which the Greeks differed from the Egyptians, who believed in a material afterlife.

THE GREEK *POLIS*

By the end of the Greek Dark Age, disparate farming communities and villages began to gather around religious centers. These were led by rural priests and local landowners whose subsistence was based on agriculture and whose influence was limited by widespread poverty. The wealthiest among them functioned as judges in civil disputes, while criminal cases were decided by individual combat. Eventually, these rural communities evolved into the political center known as the *polis* (from which we get the English word "politics").

The *polis* (plural *poleis*) was composed of an urban area and its surrounding territory. The impetus for the formation of the *polis* came from people gathering together for mutual benefit rather than, as in the Minoan–Mycenaean era, Egypt, or the Middle East, from an imposed administration. As it developed, the central area of the *polis* became the **agora**, an open space for markets and public gatherings, which fostered a sense of social community and cultural identity. In the Geometric period, temples became standard structures in the *polis*, and although worship was held outdoors at sacred sites, mud brick shrines housed statues of the gods (figure **5.1**).

As the *polis* evolved, the rule of kings that had characterized the Minoan–Mycenaean era gave way to rule by heads of powerful families. This led to an **oligarchical** system (rule by a few), in which a class of aristocrats governed the city-state.

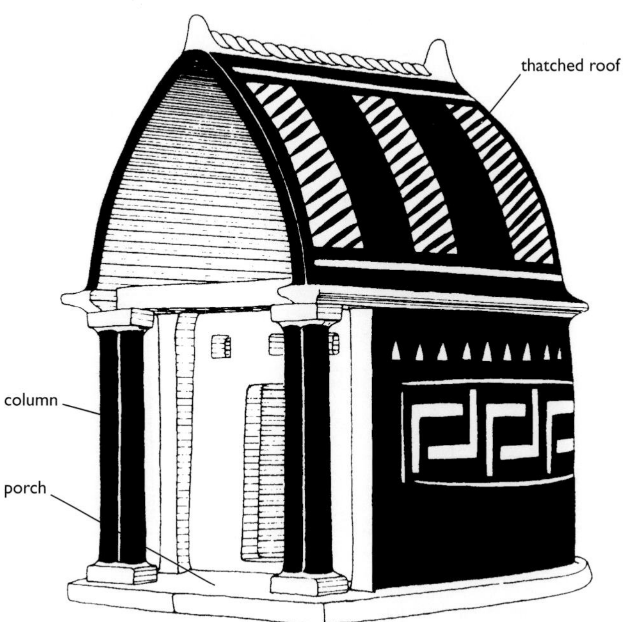

5.1 Model of a shrine from Perachora, late 8th century B.C. Terra-cotta, 13 in. (33 cm) high. National Museum, Athens.
Geometric period shrines consisted of a single room, a narrow front porch with two columns, and a thatched roof. The plan was rectangular on three sides with a curved wall at the back.

They governed through the institution of the assembly and an agreed structure of laws, or constitution. There was a wide variety of Greek *polis* types and forms of government, and many were already in existence by the Archaic period. The general principle of an independently governed city-state, each with its own economy and citizen army, was unique to Greek society.

ANCIENT GREEK RELIGION

Like the Egyptians and Mesopotamians, the Greeks believed in many gods and worshipped them in communal rituals. Rites included sacrifices, processions, music, and dance. Gods were everywhere in nature, and each *polis* had a patron god or goddess, who protected the city and demanded offerings in return. Athens, for example, had Athena as its patron goddess, whereas Olympia had Zeus, and Artemis was the patron goddess of the island of Aegina.

Nonetheless, in Greece there was more emphasis on the individual than in Egypt, where the pharaoh had absolute power and was regarded as a god on earth. Furthermore, the Egyptian gods were distanced from people in being shaped as animals, or as combinations of different species. The Greek gods were human in form (although they could change their shape) and had human personalities; they differed from humans mainly in being immortal.

The Greeks believed that when they died, their souls went to Hades, a dark Underworld populated by shades of the dead. There were no standard punishments for wrongdoing in

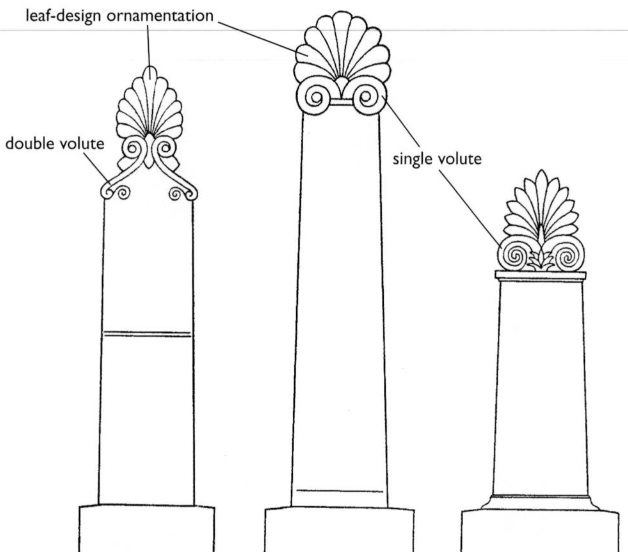

5.2 *above* **Diagram of Attic grave stelae, 6th century B.C.**

5.3 Aristokles, *Stele of Aristion*, late 6th century B.C. Marble, 7 ft. 10 in. (2.4 m) high. National Museum, Athens.
The figure of Aristion is tightly enclosed in the rectangle of the stele and appears to be walking slowly. His head is slightly bowed, as if participating in his own funeral procession. The artist not only memorialized the warrior in this stele, he also preserved his own name, Aristokles, by inscribing it at the base. This reflects the growing sense of individual identity among artists in ancient Greece, and is consistent with the Greek notion of human centrality in the universe.

Hades unless one had offended the gods. In Egypt, on the other hand, Anubis (the jackal-headed god of embalmers) weighed the soul of the deceased to determine its worthiness (see Chapter 3).

As a result of different views of life and death, the burial monuments of Egypt and Greece also differed. Greek burial monuments were far more modest than the colossal Egyptian pyramids. Greeks marked their graves with a modest stele (vertical stone pillar) resting on a base (figure **5.2**).

The stele in figure **5.3** marked the grave of the warrior Aristion. Its style reflects the early Greek interest in showing that the figure, like the hero's memory, is alive. The folds of the clothing are flattened, but the more rounded arms and legs suggest the underlying anatomy. Traces of color indicate that the original was painted, which would have increased the figure's lifelike appearance.

HESIOD'S *THEOGONY*

During the late eighth century B.C., by which time Greek religion was well established, the poet Hesiod wrote the *Theogony*, an account of the genealogy of the gods. This work, like the Homeric epics, reflects the Greek focus on human individuality and shows the commitment of the Greek gods to human creativity. To assist Hesiod in composing his genealogy, the Muses give him a musical voice and a staff of laurel (the plant associated with fame and victory). They instruct him to begin with themselves,

> who gladden the great spirit of their father Zeus in Olympus
> with their songs, telling of things that are and that shall be
> and that were aforetime with consenting voice.
>
> (*Theogony*, lines 36–39)

First, according to Hesiod, the universe was Chaos (the Abyss), then came earth (Gaia), and then love (Eros). Gaia bore the heavens (Uranos), and together they bore six gigantic Titans. The Titans produced a third generation (including the Cyclopes; see Chapter 4). Chronos, a son of Uranos, castrated his father with his sickle, and from the blood emerged the three Furies (who pursued Orestes), a race of giants, and the wood nymphs (female nature deities). When Uranos's genitals were thrown into the sea, the goddess Aphrodite was born.

Chronos married his sister Rhea, who gave birth to five more children. But Chronos feared the prophecy that his offspring would one day destroy him, so he swallowed each infant as it was born. When Zeus was born, Rhea hid him in a cave on Crete and replaced him with a large, swaddled stone, which Chronos swallowed instead of the infant. When Zeus became an adult, he forced his father to cough up the other children and joined with his siblings to declare war on their divine ancestors. After ten years of cataclysmic battle, the younger generation of gods (Olympians) defeated their parents (Titans) and took control of the universe.

Hesiod's vivid description of the battle between the Olympians and the Titans is particularly rich in violent imagery. Note the use of repetition for emphasis in "to see with eyes" and "to hear with ears":

> The hot vapour lapped round the earthborn Titans: flame unspeakable rose to the bright upper air: the flashing glare of the thunder-stone and lightning blinded their [the Titans'] eyes for all that they were strong. Astounding heat seized Chaos: and to see with eyes and to hear the sound with ears it seemed even as if Earth and wide Heaven above came together.
>
> (lines 695–704)

The Olympian victory produced a new world order. No longer giants with cannibalistic tendencies, the gods were anthropomorphic (human in form), had human personalities and particular attributes, and socialized with humans (see Box).

Society and Culture

The Greek Gods and the Nine Muses

Zeus king of the gods (thunderbolt)
Hera goddess of marriage, wife and sister of Zeus (peacock)
Poseidon god of the sea (trident, a large three-pronged fork)
Hades god of the underworld (Cerberus, the triple-headed dog who guards Hades)
Demeter goddess of agriculture, sister of Zeus (grain)
Hestia virgin goddess of the hearth, sister of Zeus
Aphrodite goddess of love, beauty, and fertility
Eros god of love, son of Aphrodite (wings, bow and arrows)
Hephaestos blacksmith and crafts god, son of Hera
Athena virgin goddess of war, wisdom, and weaving, daughter of Zeus (armor, owl, gorgoneion)
Ares god of war (armor)
Apollo god of the sun, music, and prophecy (chariot of the sun, lyre)
Artemis virgin goddess of the moon (huntress, bow and arrow)
Hermes messenger (winged sandals, caduceus—a staff with entwined snakes that later became a symbol of medicine)
Dionysos god of wine and theater (grapes)
Hebe goddess of youth and cup-bearer to the gods

Attributes are shown in parentheses

The Nine Muses (daughters of Zeus)
Calliope epic poetry
Clio history
Erato erotic poetry
Euterpe music and lyric poetry
Melpomene tragedy
Polyhymnia sacred hymns
Terpsichore song and dance
Thalia comedy
Urania astronomy

Zeus frequently took mortal lovers (such as Europa in the Minoan origin myth; see Chapter 4), who gave birth to gods and demi-gods (half-gods).

GREEK GODDESSES AND GODS

Although there were six powerful Greek goddesses, all were subordinate to Zeus and reflected aspects of women as viewed by Greek men. Whereas the historical Greeks idealized men, they accorded women few rights and severely restricted their activities.

Athena, Artemis, and Hestia were virgin goddesses. Athena had the gender of a woman but a masculine character; Artemis preferred the company of women and could be deadly to men; Hestia tended the hearth. Aphrodite personified erotic love but without moral responsibility. Hera, the long-suffering and often vengeful wife of an unfaithful husband (Zeus), was a guardian of marriage. Hebe was essentially a servant.

The three major male gods—Zeus, Poseidon, and Hades—were brothers. Between them they divided up the universe: Zeus ruled the sky, Poseidon the sea, and Hades the Underworld. The war god, Ares, was handsome but not very intelligent. Apollo drove the sun across the sky in a horse-drawn chariot and was also a god of music. Dionysos was the god of wine and theater, and rites in his honor were typically orgiastic. Hephaestos, the lame crafts god, was married to Aphrodite, who was beautiful and unfaithful. She betrayed Hephaestos in a celebrated mythical romance with Ares.

PANDORA'S "BOX" AND HESIOD ON WOMEN

By modern standards, the Greeks were **misogynists** (people who dislike and distrust women). Hesiod, in particular, distrusted women and blamed them for causing men to work and suffer. He recounts the Greek myth of the first woman, Pandora, as the source of the world's evils. According to Hesiod, the Titan Prometheus stole fire from the gods and Zeus took revenge by creating Pandora, whose name literally means "all (*pan*) gifts (*dora*)." She disobeyed her creator by opening a jar, which allowed the evils of the world to escape. Hesiod calls her the source of the:

> deadly race and tribe of women who live amongst mortal men to their great trouble, no helpmeets in hateful poverty, but only in wealth. And as in thatched hives bees feed the drones whose nature is to do mischief—by day and throughout the day until the sun goes down the bees are busy and lay the white combs, while the drones stay at home in the covered skeps [farm baskets] and reap the toil of others into their own bellies—even so Zeus who thunders on high made women to be an evil to mortal men, with a nature to do evil.
>
> (*Theogony*, lines 591–600)

To the Greeks, Pandora was destined to disobey the gods but was also responsible for her actions. The fact that the gods created evil, placed it in the container, and tempted Pandora by telling her not to open it, was seen as a test. In failing the test, as the gods knew she would, Pandora came to represent the failings of all women.

The Oracle

An important feature of ancient Greek religion was the **oracle**, which refers both to the revelations of a god interpreted by a priest or priestess and to the place where the prophecy is spoken. Oracles were established throughout Greece and its colonies and, like the ideal of the *polis*, reinforced the sense of Greek cultural unity and continuity. The most famous oracle was located at the mainland site of Delphi.

After the Dark Age, the god Apollo was believed to preside over the Delphic oracle and answer questions through a priestess. She sat above a crevice in a rock and breathed gaseous fumes that rose from the opening. The fumes caused hallucinations and sent the priestess into a trance, which impressed visitors and created the illusion that she was divinely inspired. She answered questions in verse, which could be difficult to understand and thus seemed mysterious.

The Greeks called the Delphic oracle the *omphalos* (navel), meaning that it was the center of the world. It was located at Apollo's temple in the **precinct** (sacred area) overlooking a spectacular landscape (figure **5.4**). Foreigners as well as Greeks consulted the oracle on a wide variety of topics, including political decisions, the choice of a wife, future crops, and whether to make a career change or embark on a journey. Inscribed in a stone at the site was the famous phrase "know thyself," which advocated insight and self-knowledge. This saying is another instance of the Greek view that people, like Pandora, are responsible for their own lives even though fate is in the hands of the gods.

5.4 Temple of Apollo at Delphi, 4th century B.C.

THE GEOMETRIC PERIOD: *c.* 1000–700 B.C.

Pottery, Painting, and Sculpture

The Geometric period is named for the geometric style of Greek pottery and sculpture that flourished between 1000 and 700 B.C. Beginning around 1000 B.C., toward the end of the Bronze Age, technological advances appear in Greek pottery, which resulted from an increase in prosperity and trade and an artistic revival. The potter's wheel improved, and pots were decorated with geometric designs. By the eighth century B.C., ceramic artists were painting human figures and narrative scenes on their wares (figure **5.5**).

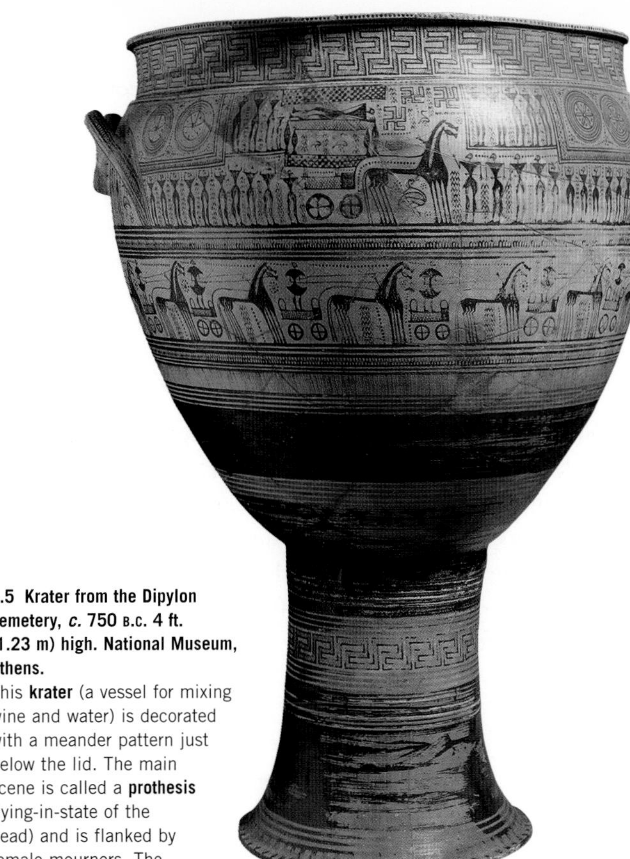

5.5 Krater from the Dipylon cemetery, *c.* 750 B.C. 4 ft. (1.23 m) high. National Museum, Athens.
This **krater** (a vessel for mixing wine and water) is decorated with a meander pattern just below the lid. The main scene is called a **prothesis** (lying-in-state of the dead) and is flanked by female mourners. The figures are flat, their torsos are triangular, and their legs and heads are in profile view. Below the prothesis a row of chariots seems to float in space. All four legs of each horse are visible, indicating that, as with Egyptian art, the artist represents the figure conceptually rather than naturalistically—that is, four legs are shown because we know that a horse has four legs and not because we would actually see them from this angle. The bodies of the charioteers are covered by shields.

The little horse in figure **5.6** is similar to those painted on the krater in its combination of animated stylization and hint of naturalistic form. The horse's head and torso are thin, cylindrical shapes, but the sturdy flanks convey a sense of organic structure. The shoulder merges smoothly into the broad, flattened neck, which continues into the lively curves at the top of the head. Note that the forelegs seem to face backward, which is not natural but which creates a pleasing symmetry with the back legs.

THE OLYMPIC GAMES

Founded toward the end of the Geometric period, the Olympic Games were first held in 776 B.C. in honor of Zeus at the god's precinct in Olympia, on the west coast of the Peloponnese (see map 5.1, p. 92). Greek-speaking men participated in the Games, and wars on Greek soil were halted so that athletes could travel safely to Olympia. Thus the Games provided the Greeks with another means of achieving a sense of cultural unity. The earliest games were devoted exclusively to the foot race. Later, longer races and other sports were added, including jumping, throwing the discus and javelin, wrestling, boxing, and foot races in armor (figure **5.7**).

The Olympic Games were held every four years; each four-year period was an Olympiad, which was the unit by which the Greeks counted time. In A.D. 394 the Christian Roman emperor Theodosius banned the Olympic Games on the grounds that they were pagan, and they were not reinstated until 1896.

5.6 Geometric horse, *c.* 750 B.C. Bronze, 6 15/16 in. (17.6 cm) high. The Metropolitan Museum of Art, New York.

5.7 *right* **Black-figure amphora, from Athens, *c.* 540 B.C. 14 1/8 in. (36 cm) high. Staatliche Antikensammlungen, Munich.**
Male athletes competed in the nude, in keeping with the Greek interest in the ideal male form. Winners were rewarded with honor, with laurel wreaths, and with statues intended to keep their memory alive. Women did not compete at Olympia.

THE ORIENTALIZING PERIOD: *c.* 700–600 B.C.

The term "orientalizing" refers to a style of Greek art influenced by Eastern forms. Orientalizing style resulted from trade with the Near East and Egypt, which increased in the seventh century B.C. after three hundred years of relative isolation during the Dark Age. Greek colonization also encouraged cross-cultural exchange between Greece and the East. The port city of Corinth, north of Mycenae on the mainland, was particularly important in bringing Eastern influence to Greece.

POTTERY AND PAINTING

As in the Geometric period, the best surviving evidence of artistic, technological, and cultural developments in the Orientalizing period is pottery. Corinthian potters and painters absorbed Eastern forms and subjects (figure **5.8**). The animals parading on the beige background of this pitcher are no longer the flat, solid black figures of the Geometric style. The lively stylizations and their patterns are similar to those on the Achaemenid lions of ancient Persia (see Chapter 2).

The frontal eyes and upturned paws showing all five toes indicate that the conceptual imagery characteristic of Near Eastern, Egyptian, and Greek Geometric style continued into the Orientalizing period. Similarly, fantastic animal combinations and elegant designs came from the East. Partly as a result of these Eastern forms, Greek paintings were animated and more freely drawn than in the Geometric period. Orientalizing vases thus reflect both the expansion of Greece through trade and the stylistic trend toward naturalism.

WAR, MUSIC, AND THE *CHIGI VASE*

During the latter part of the Orientalizing period, the Greek mode of warfare underwent important changes. Because there was continual conflict between the Greek city-states, fighting was a way of life. If we compare the image on the Mycenaean *Warrior Vase* (see thumbnail) with the detail of the *Chigi Vase* of the mid-seventh century B.C. (figure **5.9**), we can see that a new type of military formation has developed**.** The soldiers

Warrior Vase
see figure 4.17

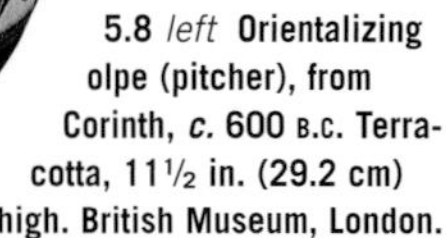

5.8 *left* **Orientalizing olpe (pitcher), from Corinth, *c.* 600 B.C. Terracotta, 11½ in. (29.2 cm) high. British Museum, London.**

5.9 Detail of the *Chigi Vase*, a late proto-Corinthian oinochoe, *c.* 640 B.C. Vessel 10¼ in. (26 cm) high. Villa Giulia Museum, Rome.

As described in the Homeric epics, the soldiers carry shields and wear greaves (shin guards). The artist creates a sense of movement by repeating the advancing figures. At the same time, motion is arrested by the clashing groups. The figures on the left show the insides of the shields, which were carried on the left arm. The group to the right is distinguished by the shield designs. Prominent frontal eyes and opposing profiles emphasize the gaze of the warriors, which accentuates the intensity of conflict and also engages the gaze of the viewer.

Defining Moment

The Greek Phalanx

With the waning of the Dark Age in ancient Greece, a new type of warfare emerged based on the military formation known as the phalanx. Developed in the Spartan warrior culture, the phalanx was adopted by other city-states, including Athens, and was largely responsible for the Greek defeat of Persia in 479 B.C. (see p. 104).

In contrast to the relative disarray of previous formations, the phalanx was organized to protect the Greek fighters and inflict heavy casualties on the enemy. Phalanxes were made up of citizen-soldiers called hoplites after their large round shields. In addition to these shields, which extended from the shoulder to the knee, hoplites' armor consisted of a metal and leather breastplate, a helmet, and greaves. They were more heavily armed than the Homeric fighters: the two main offensive weapons were a long pike with an iron point at one end and a bronze point on the other, and a short sword with a double blade. The armor was heavy, weighing as much as 100 pounds (45.4 kg), so each soldier had to be in excellent physical condition. They waited until just before battle to put it on. At first, hoplites had to provide their own armor, but later in the fifth century B.C. it was supplied by the city-state. Participation in the hoplite ranks, therefore, required a specified economic status from its peasant soldiers. As foot-soldiers, the hoplites did not have as high a social standing as those who fought on horseback or in chariots.

In battle, the typical phalanx could be anywhere from eight to sixteen rows of hoplites arrayed over a quarter of a mile (400 m) across (figure **5.10**). They comprised a wall of armed men advancing at a brisk pace to the music of the double pipe or flute. They fought the enemy head on, fiercely, quickly, and efficiently. Most battles (although not necessarily wars) were short, allowing the hoplites to return to their civilian lives as soon as possible.

Throughout Greek history the power of the phalanx was legendary. Shields were used for protection, and also to carry the dead—hence the famous quotation from a Spartan mother to her hoplite son to return "with your shield or on it." Several centuries later, the Roman biographer Plutarch described the sight of a phalanx as "terrifying when they marched in step with the rhythm of the flute, without any gap in their line of battle, and with no confusion in their souls, but calmly and cheerfully moving with the strains of their hymn to their deadly fight" (*Lycurgus*, 22:2–3).

The hoplites were an integral part of the structure of the *polis* and they fought for the good of the *polis*, rather than for personal glory. According to some scholars, the unity of the phalanx, the sense of mutual cohesion and protection, as well as the effectiveness of the formation, influenced the idea that ordinary peasants, not just an aristocratic elite, could also work together in ruling the *polis*. The phalanx remained the military formation of choice until the rise of Rome and the development of the more flexible Roman legions.

Critical Question Is discipline (as used, for example, for troops) compatible with freedoms necessary for democracies?

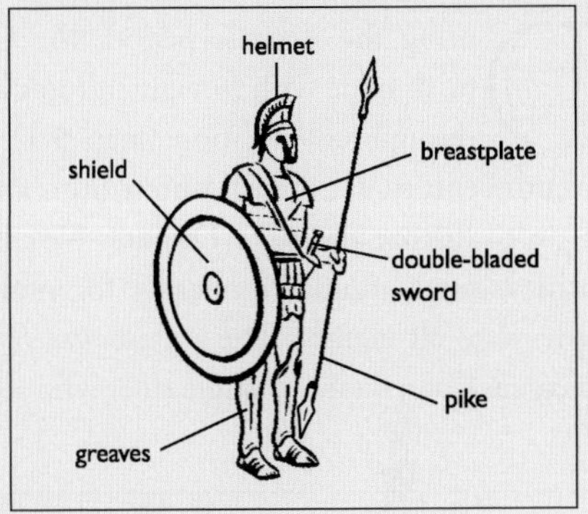

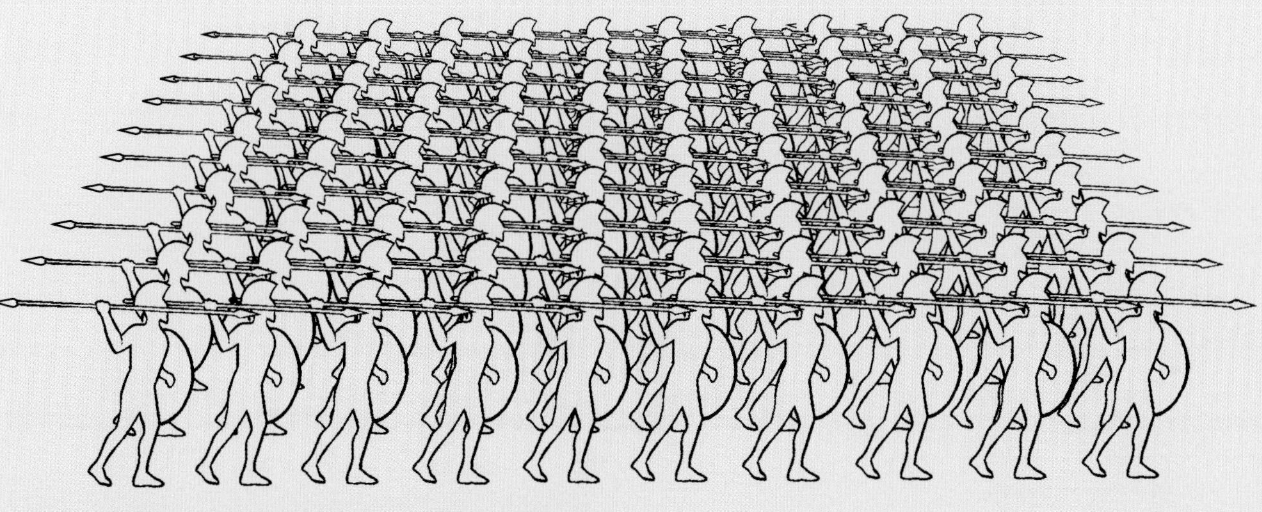

5.10 *above* **Diagram of a phalanx of hoplites, and** *above right* **hoplite armor.**

shown are **hoplites**, named for the *hoplon* (plural, *hopla*), a large wooden shield covered with a protective layer of bronze. Hoplites were foot-soldiers who fought next to each other and one behind the other, creating a **phalanx.** This was a formidable, densely packed military formation, with each soldier trained to step in and take the place of a fallen comrade. The image on the *Chigi Vase* is the earliest surviving representation of a hoplite phalanx, and it illustrates the way in which the *hoplon* shielded both its owner and the soldier next to him. The overlapping of the hoplites emphasizes the solidity of the phalanx and also reflects the painter's interest in the naturalism of three-dimensional space.

Notice that an unarmed boy between two phalanxes plays a double pipe (*aulos*) to signal the charge. This indicates that the hoplite army, like modern troops, marched in time. Music in ancient Greece was used not only in religious ritual and the recitation of epic poetry—it also inspired soldiers. Harmonious music was related to the harmony of the phalanx. In the *Theogony*, Hesiod says that Harmonia is the daughter of Aphrodite and Ares, thus embodying the ideal balance between love and war. She maintains the "harmony" of the phalanx, whereas her sisters, Panic and Fear, create disorder and disharmony, which lead to defeat.

THE ARCHAIC PERIOD: *c.* 600–490 B.C.

During the Archaic period, the Greeks continued a brisk trade with foreign cultures as well as expansion through colonization (map **5.1**). From early in the seventh century B.C., social unrest from a number of quarters began to disrupt the *polis*. Disputes over land, economic disparities, rural groups competing for power, and expanding trade were all factors. The unrest was often quelled by the emergence of a tyrant, a single ruler who seized power without the legal authority to do so. Some tyrants were relatively benevolent, but others were harsh and oppressive. By the end of the sixth century B.C., after a period of rule by tyrants, Athens abolished tyranny.

ATHENS AND SPARTA

Athens and Sparta were two city-states in ancient Greece that embodied extremes of the political spectrum during the Archaic period and would continue to do so. Their principal differences lay in the nature of their government structures and institutions as well as in their views of society and war. They also differed in their attitudes toward women.

ATHENIAN LAWGIVERS: DRACO AND SOLON Athens's first lawgiver by tradition was Draco, who in the seventh century B.C. inscribed a set of laws in stone and made them available to the general population. Few of Draco's laws survive, but they are known for harsh penalties, such as death for trivial theft. Today we speak of a "Draconian" measure to convey unreasonable severity.

The next major lawgiver after Draco was Solon (*c.* 640–558 B.C.), an aristocrat who revised the constitution of the *polis* and laid the foundations of Athenian law for the remainder of its history. His laws were crucial to the Athenian concept of citizenship, and, in contrast to Draco, Solon has gone down in history as an exemplar of wisdom.

In order to avoid the social unrest that had led to tyranny in some *poleis*, Solon established a council of four hundred male citizens from a broad social spectrum and a court of appeals to ensure social justice for all citizens. He wanted to

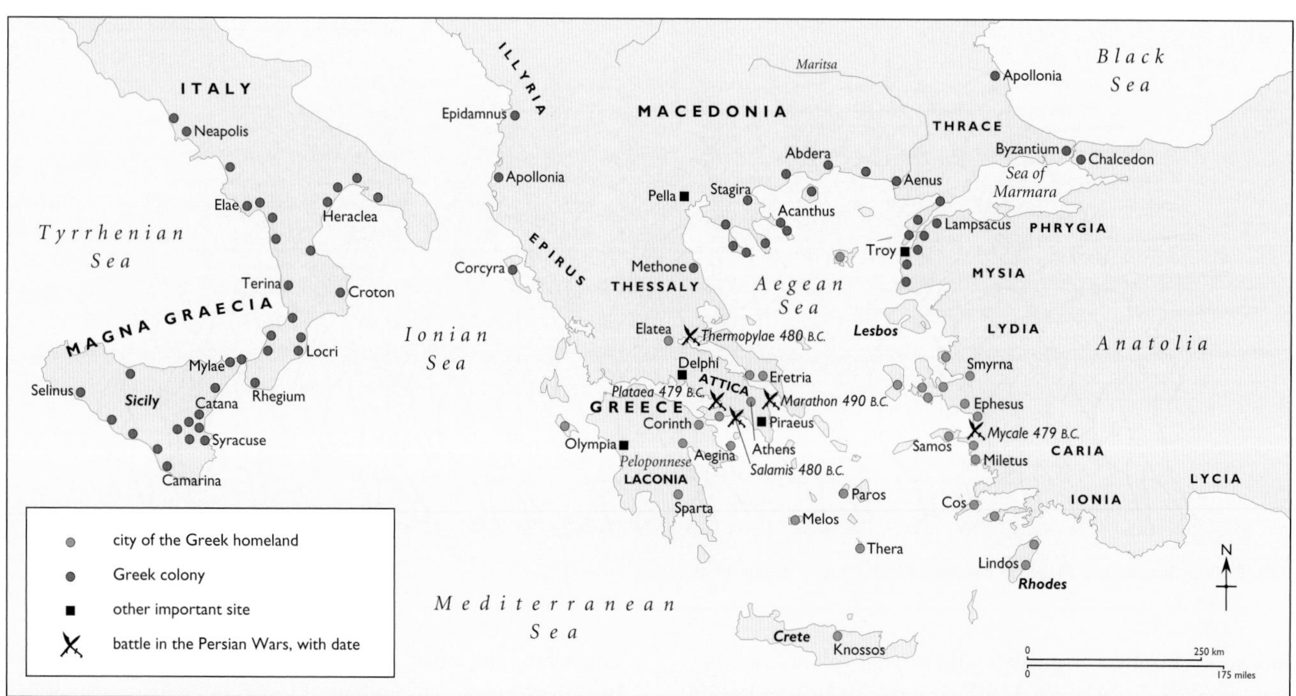

Map 5.1 Ancient Greece, *c.* 1000–490 B.C.

increase their participation in government, but had in mind only the citizens of Athens. Solon also effected the return of former citizens who had been sold into slavery to pay debts and he financed buying back their freedom.

To restart the economy, Solon abolished outstanding debts and revived industry and trade. He encouraged potters and other skilled workers to move to Athens, and he recommended exporting surplus goods, such as oil and wine, while retaining wheat to insure against famine. In addition, he altered the structure of social status in the *polis*, basing it on wealth rather than on inherited rank. So that his programs would continue beyond the present generation, Solon required fathers to educate their sons in a craft or trade. Once his reforms were in place, Solon retired from politics so that he would not be tempted to become a tyrant.

In the course of the next two centuries, coinage and currency reform calculated to favor Athenian trade and commerce were instituted. Laws against public displays of wealth (called sumptuary laws) were instituted. These were designed to reduce further the visibility and influence of the aristocracy.

WOMEN IN ATHENS Athenian men preferred that women be neither seen nor heard. The laws of Athens restricted women to the house, sharply limited their activity, and treated them intellectually and emotionally as children. The woman's primary function was to produce sons who would become Athenian citizens—hence the custom of a bride eating fruit with many seeds. If a family had no sons, the woman inherited the family property and became an attractive marriage prospect. Although all women entered into marriage with a dowry, which remained theirs for life, they were always under the control of a father, uncle, brother, or some other male family member.

The ideal marriage age for an Athenian female was considered to be fourteen, but for a man it was thirty. Both husbands and wives could sue for divorce, although the procedure was easier for the man: he had only to remove his wife from his household, whereas she needed a male relative to bring the issue to court.

SPARTA Sparta, like Athens, had an agrarian economy. But, unlike Athens, Sparta continued to rely exclusively on farming and its powerful hoplite army. It did not produce much literature or encourage the arts in the late Archaic period (although it had done so earlier). Sparta's laws are attributed to Lycurgus, who supposedly lived in the seventh century B.C. According to tradition, he advocated a strict oligarchy, in which a few citizens elected a council of five elders. These maintained tight control over the most intimate details of a person's life, including dress and grooming, diet, and decisions about marriage and childbirth. The term "spartan," referring to an austere way of life, comes from the social organization of Sparta in the late sixth century B.C.

The Spartan system was designed to provide the basics for its citizens, freeing them to concentrate on the welfare of the state. The socio-economic foundation that made this possible was the institution of the **helot**, a member of the native population enslaved by the Spartans. Helots worked the land and had no rights. Because they were engaged in a constant struggle for their freedom, their conquerors exercised rigid control over them. Helots were beaten every year as a sign of their subservience, and were forced to dress in animal skins to acknowledge their sub-human status.

From birth, Spartan boys trained to become warriors and remained such to the age of sixty. Boys left home at seven, and male infants considered unsuitable for war were left to die outside the city. Education was controlled by the state. The curriculum did not include reading, writing, or the arts (except for martial music), focusing instead almost entirely on physical survival skills. Those who failed to live up to the established standards of bravery were ridiculed, humiliated, and considered unmarriageable.

Spartan women also exercised regularly. They were not confined to household activities, as Athenian women were. The ideal marriage age for both men and women was considered to be eighteen, but up to the age of thirty, men lived in army quarters, visiting their wives secretly for purposes of procreation. Monogamy in Sparta was not as strictly enforced as in Athens, in part so that women could produce future Spartan citizens while their husbands were away at war.

ART AND ARCHITECTURE IN THE ARCHAIC PERIOD

While the Spartans were busy producing an ideal warrior state during the Archaic period, Athens and other cities created some of the most impressive works of art, poetry, and philosophy in Western history. The vigorous pottery industry in Corinth spread to Athens in this period. Corinth had invented the black-figure technique of vase decoration, in which artists painted black figures on a red clay background and incised details with a **burin** (a sharp instrument). Large-scale paintings most often depicted mythological and Homeric scenes, but none has survived.

VASE PAINTING One of the most impressive Athenian black-figure paintings shows the Homeric warrior Ajax preparing to commit suicide (figure **5.11**). The artist, Exekias, was the leading Athenian black-figure painter, known for insightful dramatic scenes conveying the psychology of his figures. In figure 5.11 Exekias depicts a well-known event from the end of the Trojan War. Ajax was a brave Greek chieftain who competed with Odysseus for the armor of the slain Achilles. Odysseus won the prize, and Ajax was driven temporarily mad by Athena, the Greek goddess of war, wisdom, and weaving. In his madness, he killed a herd of sheep and cattle, believing them to be men. When Ajax regained his sanity, he was ashamed before his family and friends and committed suicide.

5.11 **Exekias, *Suicide of Ajax*, black-figure amphora, *c.* 540 B.C. Painted scene 9½ in. (24 cm) high. Musée des Beaux Arts, Boulogne, France.**

Exekias's picture shows a solitary Ajax fixing his sword in the ground. Apart from the lone palm tree suggesting Athena's presence (in temples, her statues were erected near palm trees), Ajax is surrounded by empty space, which symbolizes his feeling of emotional emptiness and social isolation. Ironically, reinforcing our gaze as viewers are the frontal Gorgon head on the shield and the blank stare of the sightless helmet (see Box).

Some time around 530 B.C. the red-figure vase painting technique developed in Athens. This reversed the black-figure technique by outlining the figures, leaving them the red color of the vase, and painting the background black. Details were added in black with a brush, rather than being incised with a burin. As a result, red-figure artists painted more freely, and their paintings have greater depth than black-figure ones. Some vases, known as "bilingual," show a red-figure painting on one side and a black-figure painting on the other (figure **5.13**).

Society and Culture

The Gorgon

In Greek myth, *the* Gorgon refers to Medusa, the only mortal of three monstrous Gorgon sisters, all with snakey hair, fangs, and bulging eyes. Medusa, who was originally beautiful, offended Athena, who made her ugly by turning her hair into snakes. The sight of Medusa was so terrifying that any man who looked at her turned to stone. Only by watching her indirectly in the reflection on his shield could the Greek hero Perseus overcome this obstacle and kill her. When he beheaded her, two sons were born from her blood—Chrysaor, the boy with the golden sword, and Pegasus, the winged horse.

The scene on the vase in figure **5.12** shows Perseus killing Medusa. She is in the bent-knee pose, which in Archaic art means that she is trying to run away. From the torso up Medusa is frontal, assertively displaying her monstrous attributes to the viewer. She wears a snakey tunic, snakes emanate from her head, and she glares fiercely at Perseus.

Perseus aims his sword directly at Medusa's neck but turns to avoid looking at her. After Medusa's death, Perseus gives her head, the **gorgoneion**, to Athena, who places it on her armor to terrify her enemies.

5.12 Amasis painter, *Perseus Decapitates Medusa*, black-figure olpe from Vulci. 10¼ in. (26 cm) high. British Museum, London.

5.13 *above* **Two sides of a vase showing Heracles driving a bull, *c.* 520 B.C. 21 in. (53 cm) high. Museum of Fine Arts, Boston.**
Heracles wears a lion skin—a symbol of strength. In Greek myth, Heracles was the son of Zeus and a hero of great intelligence. He was the only mortal admitted to Mount Olympus after his death.

SCULPTURE Beginning in the late seventh century B.C., two main types of marble sculpture—the standing male youth (*kouros*) and the standing young female (*kore*)—were produced on mainland Greece and its eastern islands. At first, Greek artists traveled to Egypt to learn monumental stone carving, and their work shows Egyptian influence. But as with vase painting, Archaic sculpture soon developed in the direction of greater naturalism as a way of emphasizing lifelike qualities.

The Archaic *kouros* (Greek for "boy") represented an aristocratic youth of special achievement and was usually lifesize or larger and carved from a marble block. In the *Sounion Kouros* (figure **5.14**), the influence of Egyptian sculpture is evident in the tense, frontal pose and extended left leg (see thumbnail of the *Menkaure Triad*). Both statues retain the overall shape of the rectangular block of stone from which the artist carved the figures. But the *kouros* is nude and reveals more interest in anatomy. It is distinctively Greek, having scroll-shaped ears, bulging eyes, and hair

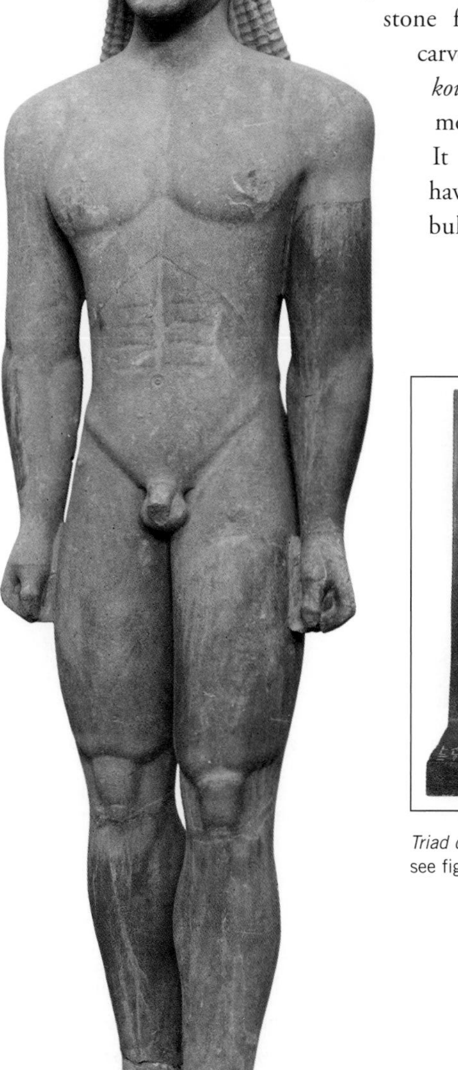

5.14 *left* ***Sounion Kouros*, from the sanctuary of Poseidon, Sounion, *c.* 580 B.C. Marble, 9 ft. 10 in. (3 m) high. National Museum, Athens.**
This figure is named for its discovery in Poseidon's sanctuary at Sounion, a site near Athens.

Triad of Menkaure
see figure 3.15

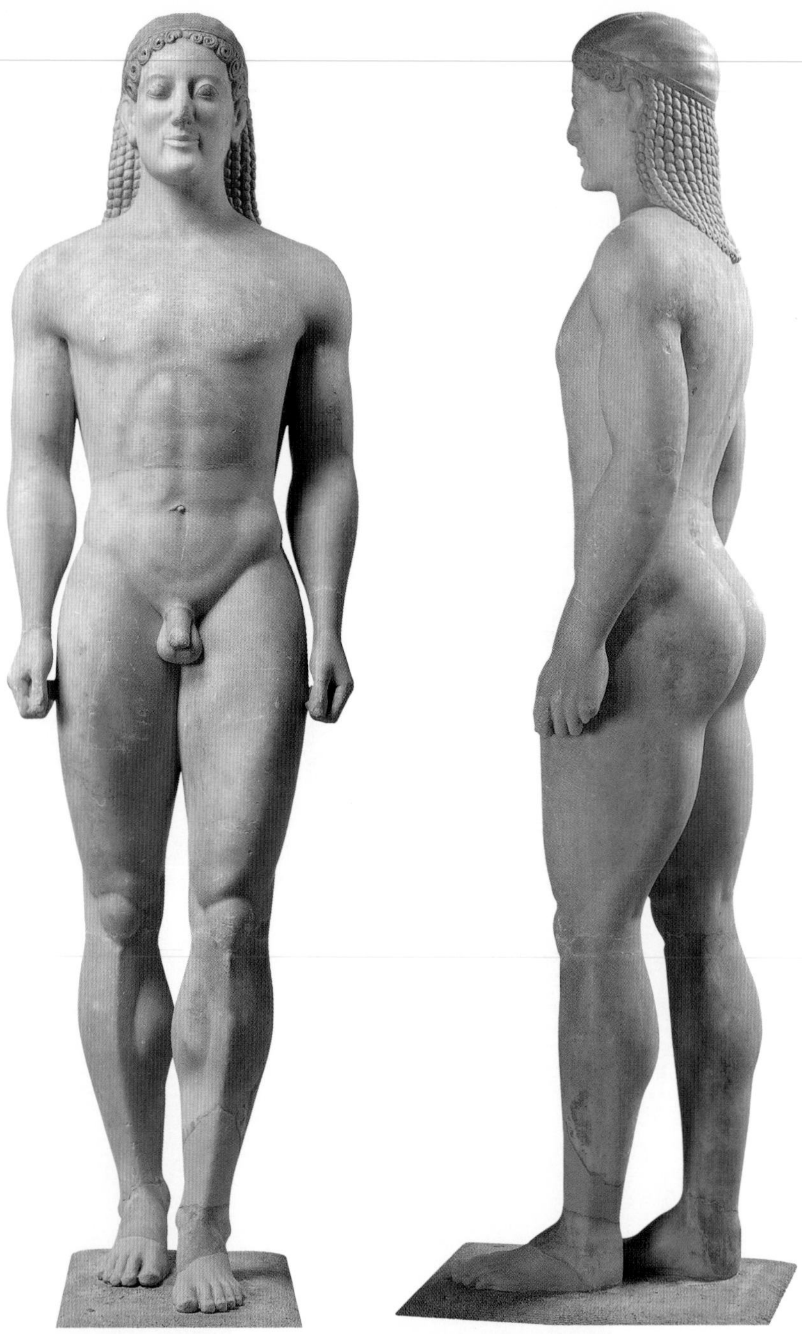

5.16a *Peplos Kore*, *c.* 530 B.C. Marble, 4 ft. (1.21 m) high. Acropolis Museum, Athens.

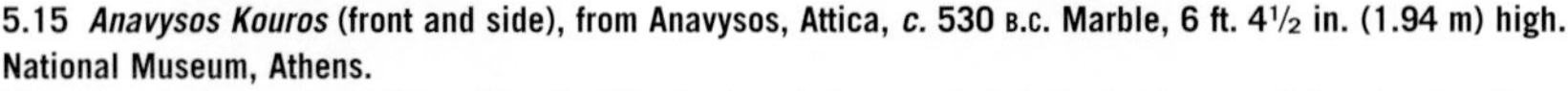

5.15 *Anavysos Kouros* (front and side), from Anavysos, Attica, *c.* 530 B.C. Marble, 6 ft. 4½ in. (1.94 m) high. National Museum, Athens.
This figure represents Kroisos, described in the inscription quoted at the beginning of the chapter. He embodies the ideal of the heroic, aristocratic youth who dies in battle. The artist urges viewers to pause and mourn the dead youth, whose image is preserved in marble.

composed of curls in the front and beads at the back. Horizontal lines define the rib cage as if it is on the surface of the torso, but the kneecaps and sternum emphasize the interior structure of the body. In contrast to the Egyptian figure of the pharaoh in the *Menkaure Triad*, the *Sounion Kouros* has open space between the arms and the body, and between the legs. This reduces the impression of immobility and eternity idealized in Egyptian royal sculpture.

The *Anavysos Kouros* (figure **5.15**) was carved about fifty years after the *Sounion Kouros* and shows the increase in naturalism over that time. It is more rounded than the *Sounion Kouros*, and the muscles and bone structure appear to be beneath the flesh rather than on its surface. The ears are no longer scroll-shaped, but resemble human ears. But both *kouroi* are tense and stand at attention. Both convey the impression of an inherent energy, as if they are ready to spring forth and take command of the three-dimensional space around them.

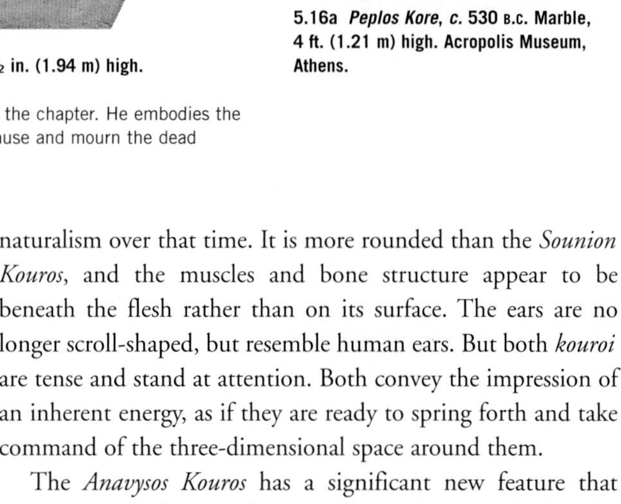

The *Anavysos Kouros* has a significant new feature that appears in Archaic sculpture—the Archaic smile (in the *Sounion Kouros*, the mouth is broken). As the lips curve

5.16b Painted reconstruction of a cast of the *Peplos Kore*. Museum of Classical Archaeology, Cambridge, U.K.

upward, the cheekbones push upward, indicating that Greek artists wanted their sculptures to represent living, breathing people. The smile also shows that naturalism was increasingly the standard guiding artists in their representation of the human figure.

Archaic sculptures of girls (*korai*, singular *kore*) were also depicted with a smile. But *korai* are not nude, and their poses are somewhat less assertive than those of *kouroi*. The *Peplos Kore* (figure **5.16a**), named after the smooth *peplos* (her outer garment; see Box), bends one arm in a gesture of offering. Traces of paint on the lips, eyes, and *peplos* are reminders that the ancient Greeks painted their statues to make them appear lifelike (figure **5.16b**).

Society and Culture

Archaic Greek Dress

The Doric *peplos* was a plain, sleeveless, rectangular wool garment (figure **5.17**). It was pinned at the shoulders and folded at the top. Another type of garment, the linen *chiton*, originated in Ionia and, paralleling the Ionic Order, was elegant and graceful. Like the *peplos*, the *chiton* was rectangular, but it did not fold over across the upper torso. At the shoulders, it was pinned or sewn, and buttoned at the top, leaving openings for the head and arms. Both the *chiton* and the *peplos* were belted when worn by adults, but not for small children.

The *peplos* could be worn over the *chiton*, as in the *Peplos Kore* (see figure 5.16a); it was open on the right side to free the right hand. Spartan women preferred the *peplos* because it was the more traditional, simpler garment, in line with the austerity of the culture. A *himaton* (mantle) was worn over the *chiton* and fell in an array of folds. Because the *chiton* was the least revealing Greek garment, it was generally worn in public.

Light skin was the ideal for Greek women (see the poem by Anacreon, pp. 102–103), because it showed that they were wealthy enough not to have to go outdoors. To enhance the lightness of their skin, many women used powder. Men wore shorter clothing than women, and prostitutes sported translucent materials. The most typical Greek shoe was the sandal, but Greeks who wanted to appear taller wore elevated shoes.

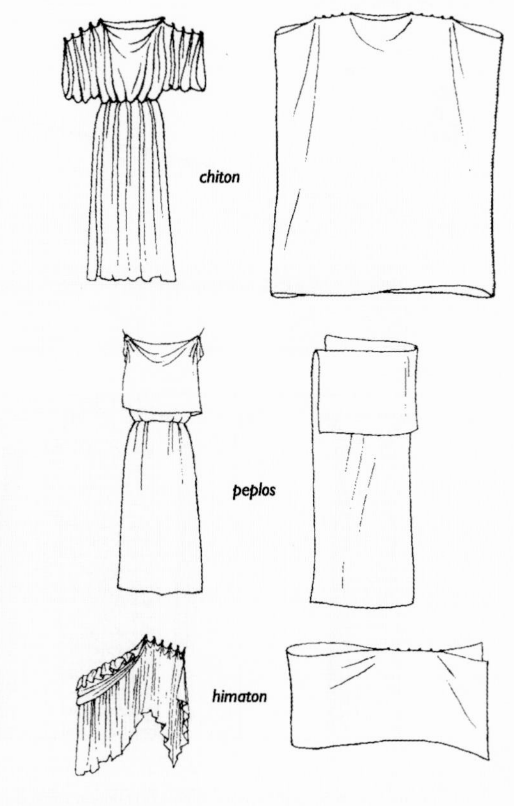

5.17 Greek modes of dress.

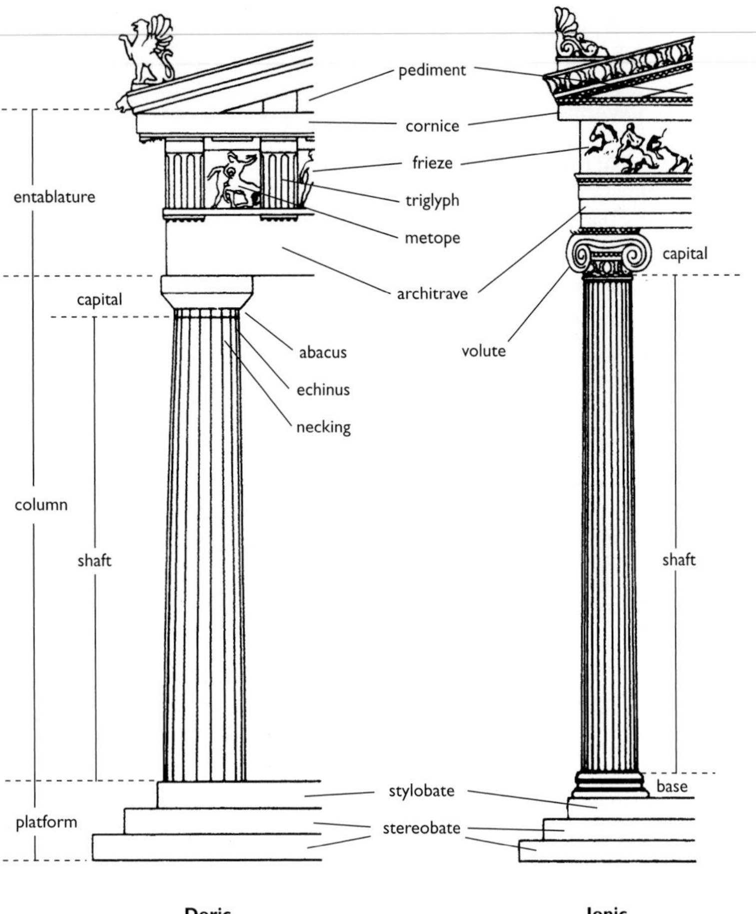

5.18 The Doric and Ionic Orders.

ARCHITECTURE In the Archaic period, the Greeks built monumental stone architecture. To house statues of gods, they constructed temples which were of two main types, called Orders: the Doric Order originated on the mainland, and the Ionic Order originated in eastern Greece. The term "Order" refers to a system in which the parts of a structure are arranged in a particular sequence from the bottom to the top. These Greek Orders are diagrammed in figure **5.18**.

In the Doric Order, the columns rise directly from the top step (the **stylobate**), and their shafts bulge slightly (**entasis**) to give an impression of organic stretching. The Doric capital (consisting of the **necking**, the ovoid **echinus**, and the square **abacus**) was conceived of as the head (*caput* in Latin) of the column, and it provides a visual transition from the vertical shaft to the horizontal sections of the Order. The **entablature**, like the capital, is divided into three parts. A long horizontal **architrave** (meaning "high beam") supports the **frieze**, whose vertical **triglyphs** alternate with square **metopes**, which often contain relief sculptures. The thin **cornice** that completes the Order projects slightly to drain rainwater from the roof.

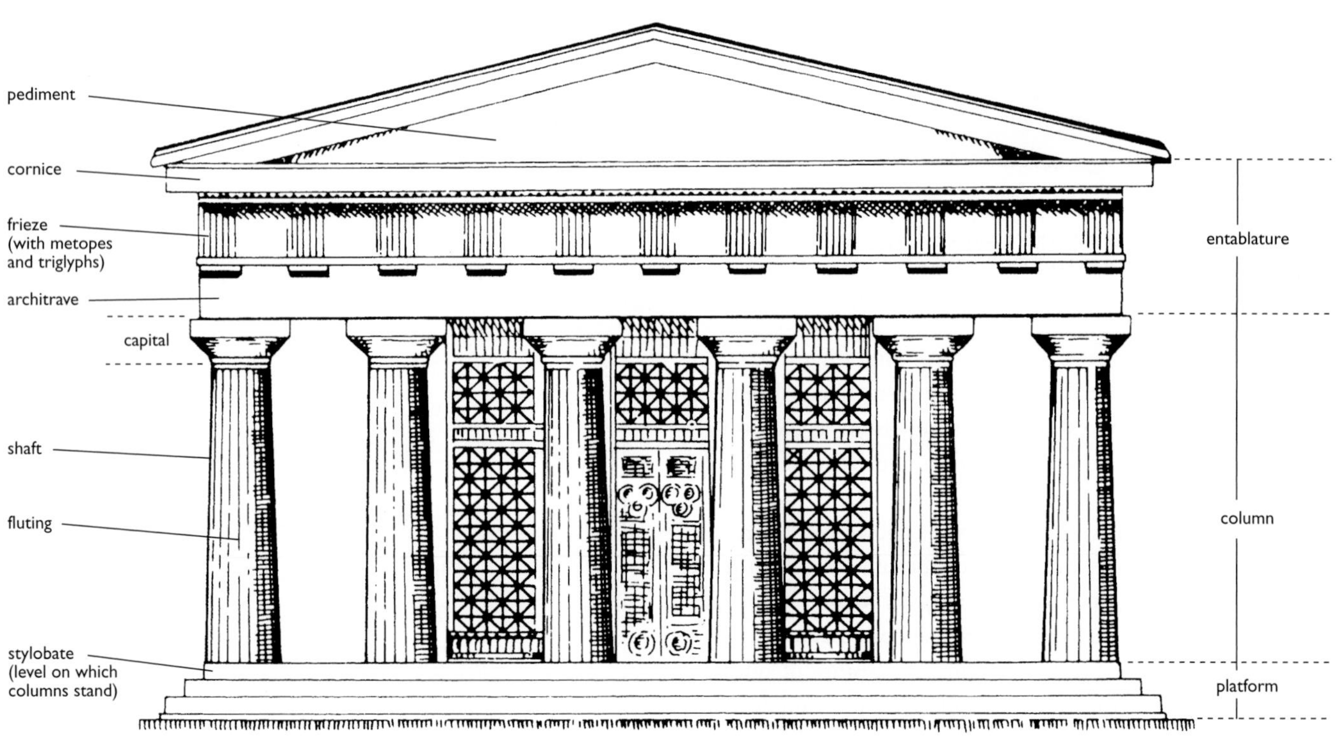

5.19 The basic elements of a Greek Doric temple façade.

Note that the Doric forms are heavier and plainer than their Ionic counterparts. Ionic columns are proportionally taller and slimmer; they have a round base and are decorated with elegant surface patterns.

In keeping with their focus on humanity, the Greeks conceived of the Orders in human terms. They associated the Doric Order with sturdy, masculine qualities, and the more graceful Ionic Order with feminine qualities. Unlike Egyptian columns, which were based on plant forms, the Greek Orders are geometric. Each part is designed to create a harmonious, unified relationship with every other part and to ensure smooth transitions between parts.

Greek temples, conceived on a more human scale than Egyptian ones, were rectangular in shape, with one or two interior rooms, a solid inner wall, and an outer wall of freestanding columns (the **peristyle**). They owed their gleaming white exteriors to the abundance of marble quarries in Greece and the precision of their carving to the well-trained artisans, sculptors, engineers, and architects who built them. Temples were located in precincts sacred to a god, whose statue was placed in the main room (*naos*). Parts of the buildings were decorated with freestanding and relief sculptures, which were painted.

Figure **5.19** shows the basic elements of a Doric temple façade, which was designed to appear orderly, regular, and symmetrical. At the short sides of the Greek temple, a triangular **pediment** contained freestanding sculptures-in-the-round, which, like the metope reliefs, were usually painted. The imposing, sturdy appearance of the façade is characteristic of the Doric Order. Its columns have been compared to the military formation and orderly force of the hoplite phalanx.

THE TEMPLE OF APHAIA AT AEGINA The Doric temple on the island of Aegina in the Saronic Gulf (see map 5.1, p. 92) is a good example of late Archaic architecture (figure **5.20**). Figure **5.21** shows the plan of the temple, which has three steps supporting four outer walls of columns. There is a porch at either end and a long *naos*, the main room that housed the cult statue of Artemis, goddess of the moon.

5.20 The Temple of Aphaia, Aegina, *c.* 500 B.C. Marble.
The temple is dedicated to the mythic nymph Aphaia, who was loved by King Minos of Knossos. She eluded his advances by diving off a cliff into the sea. The moon goddess, Artemis, rescued Aphaia and brought her to Aegina. Artemis then became the island's patron goddess.

Few of the exterior sculptures have survived, but it appears that the pediment figures depicted a war scene, most likely from the Trojan War (figure **5.22**). As with all Greek pediments, the Aphaia artist had to accommodate the sloping sides of a triangular space. The central figure from the west pediment represents Athena in her aspect as the goddess of war. She is frontal, armed, and stands upright, filling the space under the top angle of the triangle (figure **5.23**). Her large size, frontality, and detached air convey her status; she is, literally, "above the fray" of battle.

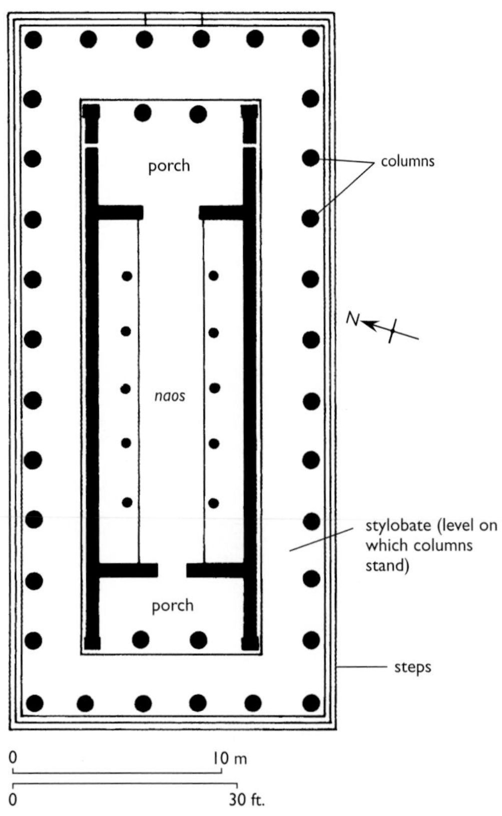

5.21 Plan of the Temple of Aphaia, Aegina, *c.* 500 B.C.

5.23 *Athena*, from the Temple of Aphaia, Aegina, *c.* 500 B.C. Marble, 5 ft. 6 in. (1.68 m) high. Staatliche Antikensammlungen, Munich.

5.22 *below* **Reconstruction diagram of the pediments from the Temple of Aphaia, Aegina.**

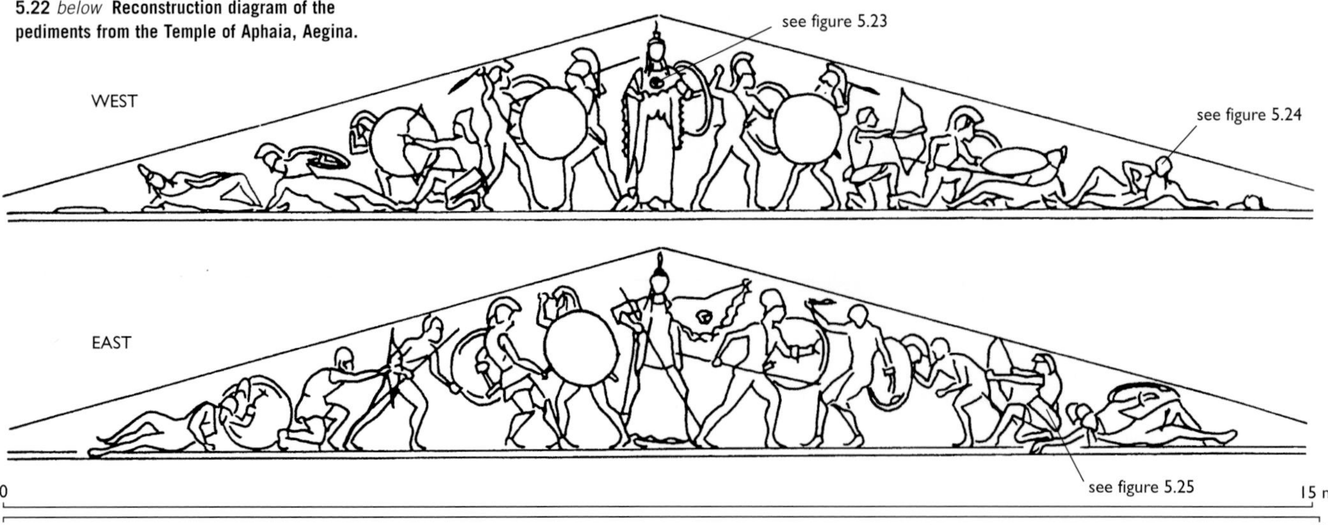

5.24 *above* ***Dying Warrior***, **from the west pediment of the Temple of Aphaia, Aegina, *c.* 500 B.C. Marble, 5 ft. 2¾ in. (1.59 m) long. Staatliche Antikensammlungen, Munich.**

5.25 ***Heracles***, **from the east pediment of the Temple of Aphaia, Aegina, *c.* 490 B.C. Marble, 31 in. (79 cm) high. Staatliche Antikensammlungen, Munich.**

The corners of the pediment are filled with dying warriors: The soldier in figure **5.24** is trying to extract an arrow from his chest. The sculptor has retained the Archaic smile to show that he is alive, rather than portraying him in pain. His stylized hair is also typical of late Archaic sculpture.

The kneeling figure of Heracles (figure **5.25**) from the east pediment would have fit into a space nearer the center than the *Dying Warrior*. Heracles is shown as an archer, tensely aiming his bow and arrow at an enemy. He wears short armor and a lion helmet, denoting his strength. As with the *Dying Warrior*, the *Heracles* has an Archaic smile, but here the muscles and the taut veins in his hands are visible beneath the flesh. Both sculptures thus reflect the transition from the rigid poses and surface patterns of the Archaic period toward naturalism.

PHILOSOPHY: PRE-SOCRATICS OF THE ARCHAIC PERIOD

In the sixth century B.C., different schools of Greek philosophy ("love of wisdom") began to emerge. Greek philosophy was the first in the Mediterranean world to diverge from religious thinking, seeking to explain the world empirically, that is, according to observation and reason, rather than according to a belief system, faith, or emotion. In so doing, Greek philosophers saw man as a rational being, capable of understanding himself in relation to the world. Greek philosophy thus shares with Greek art a kind of idealized naturalism.

The Archaic philosophers are known as pre-Socratic, because they pre-dated Socrates (469–399 B.C.), the great philosopher of fifth-century-B.C. Athens. Pre-Socratics are sometimes called Naturalist philosophers because they sought truth by observing nature, which was consistent with the sixth-century-B.C. artistic trend toward lifelike naturalism. Greek philosophers, like Greek artists, studied nature and tried to define it—the former in words and the latter in images.

Thales of Miletus (*c.* 625–*c.* 547 B.C.), who came from Anatolia, is considered to have been the first philosopher, although none of his writings survives. He founded the Ionian school of philosophy, which drew conclusions based on empirical observations. To this end, Thales studied astronomy and learned to predict eclipses of the sun and determine when the summer and winter solstices (the longest and shortest days of the year) would occur. He thus demonstrated that a rational logic is inherent in nature.

In his effort to reduce the origins of the universe to a single element, Thales concluded that all matter begins with water, which can be transformed into gas and ice. In other words, the three states of water—liquid, gas, and solid—encompass all the conditions of nature and therefore must comprise nature's basic unit of matter. Thales also believed that the earth was flat and that it floated on water.

Two other Naturalist philosophers at Miletus were Anaximander (610–*c.* 547 B.C.) and Anaximenes (active *c.* 545 B.C.), who both based their views of the cosmos on natural phenomena. Anaximander believed in the existence of a single intelligent force behind the universe and argued that the earth stands still because of its symmetrical location in the cosmos. Anaximenes reduced the cosmos to air in varying degrees of density. He used empirical experience to support his theories, whereas Anaximander preferred biological and legal models.

One of the most complex and obscure of the pre-Socratics was Heraclitus (*c.* 540–*c.* 480 B.C.), who lived in Ephesus, a Greek colony in western Anatolia. Because he believed that reality was in constant motion and that growth and unity are achieved from tension between opposites, Heraclitus is considered a Dualist. Some of his best known examples of dualism are: (1) seawater is both pure and polluted—it gives life to fish and is poisonous to humans, (2) a man cannot step in the same stream twice, and (3) the same road goes uphill and downhill.

PYTHAGORAS Pythagoras (*c.* 550–*c.* 500 B.C.), from the Ionian island of Samos, was the most influential pre-Socratic philosopher. His views impressed Plato, the great philosopher taught by Socrates (see Chapter 6), and infiltrated much of later Western philosophy. But Pythagoras is best known to students today as the author of the **Pythagorean theorem**: the square of the hypotenuse of a right-angled triangle equals the sum of the squares of the other two sides.

Pythagoras saw the universe in a more mystical way than the empiricists. He believed that people and animals are reborn after death and that their souls move into a new body where they have a new life (transmigration of souls). As a result he advocated vegetarianism to avoid eating a potential body that might otherwise be available to house a new soul. He established a communal school of philosophy in Crotona, in southern Italy. This and other philosophical, "Pythagorean" communities included women as well as men and were run by strict routines.

Pythagoras was a student of geometry and mathematics, who believed that numbers rather than elements defined the structure of the universe. He also thought that numbers formed the basis of musical harmony. From this he concluded that the earth was a sphere surrounded by stars and planets, which were attached to more distant spheres. The sphere containing the stars turned from east to west, whereas the sphere with the planets turned in the opposite direction. This movement of the spheres, in Pythagoras's view, created inaudible sounds, which formed a musical harmony in the universe.

LYRIC POETRY

Lyric poetry is named for the lyre, a stringed instrument resembling a small harp. One of the great achievements of ancient Greece, lyric poetry was an ancient poetic form originally sung to the music of the lyre (or the flute). But neither the texts nor the music were written down before the eighth century B.C. Lyric poems differ from the Homeric epics in being shorter and more intimate, and in dealing primarily with individual emotions. The modern term "lyrical" connotes the light, lilting pace of lyric poetry. The two most famous lyric poets of the Archaic period are Anacreon and Sappho.

ANACREON Anacreon (*c.* 582–*c.* 485 B.C.) was born in Ionia. His poems, which survive mainly in fragments, celebrate courtly subjects such as love, wine, and banqueting. But he could plumb the depths of emotion as well as be witty and to the point. On the inevitability of death, he writes:

> My temples are already gray and my head is white; graceful youth is no more with me, my teeth are old, and no long span of sweet life remains now. And so I often weep in fear of Tartarus [the Underworld]: for the recess of Hades is grim, and the road down to it is grievous; and it is certain that he who goes down does not come up again.

In another poem, Anacreon's speaker asks a painter to depict his absent mistress. He tells the artist to use **encaustic**, a type of paint in which beeswax is mixed with pigment. Its waxy texture and rich colors produce a lifelike effect, just as Archaic artists strove to make their sculptures seem alive. By the end of the poet's description, we should be able to visualize the image, and the painting ["the wax"] should be so true to life that it would talk:

> Come, best of painters! Paint, best of painters, master of the Rhodian art [painting]! Paint my absent girl according to my

instructions. First paint her soft black hair; and if the wax is able, make it smell of perfume. Paint her whole cheek and then her ivory brow beneath her dark hair. Do not part her eyebrows nor run them together, but let her keep, as in real life, the black rims of her eyes meeting imperceptibly. Now make her eyes as they are, from fire, both flashing like Athena's, and moist, like Cythere's [Aphrodite]. Paint her nose and her cheeks, mingling roses and cream. Paint her lips like Persuasion's, provoking kisses. Under her soft chin let all the Graces fly around her marble-white neck. Dress the rest of her in robes of light purple, but let her skin show through a little to prove the quality of her body. Enough—I can see her! Soon, wax, you will be talking too.

(Anacreonta 16)

And in a short, humorous poem, punctuated with sharp imagery, which matches the subject matter, Anacreon portrays an exchange between Eros and his mother Aphrodite:

Love [Eros] once failed to notice a bee that was sleeping among the roses, and he was wounded: he was struck in the finger, and he howled. He ran and flew to beautiful Cythere [Aphrodite] and said, "I have been killed, mother, killed. I am dying. I was struck by the small winged snake that farmers call 'the bee.'" She replied, "If the bee-sting is painful, what pain, Love, do you suppose all your victims suffer?"

(Anacreonta 35)

A lover of wine, song, and the Greek banquet known as the **symposium** (see Box), Anacreon wrote the following:

When Bacchus [the wine god Dionysos] comes, my worries go to sleep, and I imagine that I have the wealth of Croesus; I want to sing beautifully; I lie garlanded with ivy [an attribute of the wine god] and in my heart I disdain the world. Prepare the wine and let me drink it. Bring me a cup, boy, for it is far better that I should lie drunk than lie dead.

(Anacreonta 48)

Society and Culture

The Greek Symposium

In the Homeric age, Greek warriors feasted to songs and poems of battle. Under the influence of the Near East, these feasts became more elaborate and pleasure-oriented (as described by Anacreon). Libations and prayers were offered to the gods at the opening and closing of each gathering. In the Archaic period, the *symposion* (literally, a "drinking together" reserved for aristocratic men) preceded the feast. Figure **5.26** illustrates a wine cup of the type used at a symposium.

As in the image on the outside of the cup, Greeks drank (and dined) while reclining on a couch and leaning on the left elbow, a practice taken up later by the Romans (see Chapter 7). Women did not participate in the symposium, but female slaves, or *hetairai* (courtesans), might be hired to entertain. In the vase painting, we can see one woman offering a cup and two female musicians—one with a lyre and one with a double flute. The music accompanied lyric poetry.

The Greeks diluted their wine with water to achieve the alcohol content of today's beer, which meant they could drink for a long time. Because there was no plumbing, chamber pots were a standard feature of the symposium, and waste was thrown into the street.

5.26 Brygos painter, red-figure drinking cup, *c.* 500 B.C. 12½ in. (32 cm) diameter. British Museum, London.

SAPPHO Sappho (*c.* 640–580 B.C.) is the only woman known to have achieved literary fame in the Archaic period. Unfortunately, only one of her poems has survived intact; the rest are fragmentary. Sappho was born on the island of Lesbos, from which comes the term "lesbian," after Sappho's reputed love for young girls. Whether or not this is accurate is much debated; she was probably married, and a few poems refer to her daughter Cleis: "I have a beautiful child who looks like golden flowers, my darling Cleis, for whom I would not (take) all Lydia or lovely . . . [missing text]" (Sappho 132).

Sappho's poems, like those of Anacreon, deal with subjective feelings, usually her own. In that way they are both personal and universal in their themes, the most consistent theme being love. Most of Sappho's poems were solos sung to the lyre, but some were written for female choral groups. Little is known of Sappho's life. She had a reputation for being quite ugly, which may have inspired her appreciation of beautiful girls. Her conviction that women should be educated suggests that she came from an aristocratic family and was herself well educated. In the following fragment, Sappho addresses a woman who lacked education:

> But when you die you will lie there, and afterwards there will
> never be any recollection of you or any longing for you since
> you have no share in the roses of Pieria [the nine Muses];
> unseen in the House of Hades also, flown from our midst,
> you will go to and fro among the shadowy corpses.
>
> (Sappho 55)

In at least one fragment, the speaker declares her love for a boy: "Truly, sweet mother, I cannot weave my web, for I am overcome with desire for a boy because of slender Aphrodite" (Sappho 102).

In most of her poems, however, Sappho declares her erotic feelings for her female students. It is possible that they lived together only temporarily before marriage and that the homosexual aspects of this arrangement were conventional—as was the case generally with homosexual activity in ancient Greece (see Box). In the following relatively long fragment, Sappho's speaker compares her love for a young woman to Helen's passion for Paris:

> Some say a host of cavalry, others of infantry, and others
> of ships, is the most beautiful thing on the black earth,
> but I say it is whatsoever a person loves. It is perfectly
> easy to make this understood by everyone: for she who far
> surpassed mankind in beauty, Helen, left her most noble
> husband and went sailing off to Troy with no thought at all
> for her child or dear parents, but (love) led her astray . . .
> lightly . . . (and she?) has reminded me now of Anactoria
> who is not here; I would rather see her lovely walk and the
> bright sparkle of her face than the Lydians' chariots and
> armed infantry.
>
> (Sappho 16)

Society and Culture

Homosexuality in Ancient Greece

Homosexuality in ancient Greece was not thought of as a clear-cut category either socially or psychologically, as it is today. Indeed, the term itself did not exist. The Greeks followed certain conventions about who should be the active partner and who should be the passive partner in sexual relationships. Women, boys, slaves, and foreigners were supposed to be passive toward adult Greek men. The ideal homosexual relationship in Greece was between a man and an adolescent, both from good families, with no implication of financial gain or political favor. Such relationships existed simultaneously with heterosexual marriages, so that an older married man might become involved with a young man without incurring disapproval.

Less is known about female homosexuality in ancient Greece, although it is mentioned in the poems of Sappho and in fragments by other lyric poets of the Archaic period.

Sappho's emphasis on emotion, like Anacreon's attention to non-heroic experience, reflects the increasing focus of Greek culture on humanity. Similarly, the philosophical search for empirical evidence and the trend toward naturalism in painting and sculpture express the Greek interest in explaining the world scientifically and portraying natural form, especially that of idealized male youth. The small scale of Greek temples compared with those of Egypt mirrors the interest in human scale and proportion. In the development of the *polis*, Greeks emphasized individual rights and the role of citizens in self-governance. Even the Olympian gods are human in form and character.

At the end of the Archaic period, Greece was beset by invasions from Persia (modern Iran). The Greeks viewed the Persians as decadent foreigners ruled by tyrants, and Greece valiantly resisted being absorbed into the Persian Empire (see map 5.1, p. 92). In 499 B.C., with the support of Athens, eastern Ionian Greeks rebelled against Persian efforts to impose taxes on them.

Nine years later, the armies of the Persian king Darius I (ruled 522–486 B.C.) invaded the Greek mainland. But the Greek phalanxes used superior military strategy and defeated Darius in 490 B.C. at the Battle of Marathon. Led by the general Miltiades (c. 554–c. 489 B.C.), who joined the Ionian rebellion against Persia, 10,000 Athenians and 1000 allies defeated 25,000 Persians. Miltiades encouraged the Persians to attack the center of the Greek ranks and then ordered the Greek warriors to surround the Persians from either side and destroy them.

Ten years later, in 480 B.C., Darius's son Xerxes I (ruled 486–465 B.C.) mounted another attack on Greece. He overran Athens and defeated a small band of three hundred Spartans

Thematic Parallels

Sun Tzu and *The Art of War*

The art of war, as we have seen, was an important part of ancient Greek culture. In China, sometime around 500 B.C., the great general Sun Tzu wrote thirteen chapters, entitled *The Art of War*, which have been widely praised as a work of military genius and a guide to victory on the battlefield. The book has also been recommended as a roadmap to success in finance and in the art of love.

According to a second-century-B.C. Chinese chronicler, Sun Tzu demonstrated the effectiveness of his theories by training a group of ladies from the royal court of the King of Wu. At first, the ladies giggled instead of obeying orders, and Sun Tzu blamed himself for their inattention. But when they giggled a second time, he blamed the officers (the two leading ladies, who were the king's favorite concubines). Sun Tzu ordered the women to be executed. At this, the king protested, but Sun Tzu replied that a good general takes precedence over a king in military matters.

The two concubines were beheaded, and Sun Tzu appointed new leaders. The ladies stopped giggling and followed the commands of their officers. Sun Tzu then informed the King of Wu that his troops were properly trained and ready to be inspected. But the king declined to inspect the new battalion of well-trained ladies. When Sun Tzu accused him of being a man of words but not of action, the King of Wu recognized the general's genius and appointed him commander of his entire army.

Sun Tzu believed that the art of war is crucial to the safety of the state and that the real aim of war is peace. The calculations of the general, he said, determine the outcome of any conflict. Among Sun Tzu's strategic precepts, the following stand out: speed is essential, because weapons and morale grow dull with time; when an enemy is captured, he should be well treated; it is better to win without fighting and to seize the enemy's territory without destroying it; battles are won by avoiding mistakes and by creating tactical advantage.

In addition, there are only two kinds of attack in Sun Tzu's view: direct and indirect. Yet their combinations are infinite, and the element of surprise is important whatever the situation. Sun Tzu discussed the effect of terrain and weather on tactics, the crucial role of spies and intelligence, the use of fire, and the weak and strong characteristics of an army. Above all, he wrote, if you know your enemy and yourself, you need not fear a hundred battles.

China remained a warrior society for centuries after Sun Tzu wrote on the art of war. One of the most spectacular examples of this was discovered in 1974, when peasants in Xian, in Shaanxi Province, found fragments of a burial near an earth mound. When archaeologists excavated the site, they unearthed the burial of Emperor Qin ("Qin" being the source of the name "China"), who ruled from 221 to 210 B.C. The actual tomb chamber has still not been excavated because of fears that it may have been booby-trapped. But what has been unearthed has revealed an army of more than 7000 lifesize terra-cotta warriors dressed according to their rank, and horses (figure **5.27**). Among the warriors are infantrymen, archers, officers, and cavalrymen. At present, the site has been enclosed and turned into a vast museum open to visitors, who can observe the ongoing excavation and restoration of the figures. Qin's terracotta army was apparently not intended to be seen by the living; its function was to protect the emperor in the afterlife.

5.27 Emperor Qin's bodyguard, 221–210 B.C. Terra-cotta, lifesize. Emperor Qin's tomb, Lintong, Shaanxi Province, China.

and seven hundred allies who resisted at Thermopylae. The Persians then invaded and sacked Athens, but the citizens had already fled to the island of Salamis. Cornering the Persian ships between Athens and Salamis, the Athenians destroyed the invaders with their superior ***triremes*** *(warships with iron-covered prows). The final blow to the Persian invaders came in 479 B.C. at the Battle of Plataea, after which they retreated, and though they continued to threaten Greece, their strength was greatly reduced. This ended the Archaic chapter of Greek history.*

KEY TERMS

abacus the square element of the Doric capital.

agora an open public space in a city.

architrave the lowest long horizontal part of the entablature, which rests directly on the capital of a column.

burin a sharp instrument used for incising.

cornice the topmost horizontal part of an entablature.

echinus (Greek, "hedgehog") part of the Greek Orders above the abacus.

encaustic a type of paint in which beeswax is mixed with pigment.

entablature the portion above the capital on a column; it includes the architrave, the frieze, and the cornice.

entasis (Greek, "stretching") the bulge in the shaft of a Greek column.

frieze the central section of an entablature, often containing relief sculpture.

gorgoneion the severed head of the Gorgon Medusa.

helot a member of the native population enslaved by the Spartans.

hoplite a heavily armed foot-soldier who fought in close formation (phalanx).

hoplon a shield carried by a hoplite.

krater a vessel in which wine and water are mixed.

metope the square area between the triglyphs of a Doric frieze, often containing relief sculpture.

misogynist someone who dislikes and distrusts women.

necking the lowest of three elements comprising the capital of a Greek column.

oligarchy a form of government by a few people.

oracle the revelation of a god, the person who utters the revelation, or the place the revelation is spoken.

Order one of the architectural systems—Doric, Ionic, Corinthian—used by the Greeks to build their temples.

pediment the triangular section at the end of a gable-roof, often decorated with sculpture.

peristyle the freestanding columns surrounding a building.

phalanx a military formation in which heavily armed soldiers lined up close together in deep ranks, defended by a wall of shields.

polis (plural **poleis**) a city-state in ancient Greece.

precinct a sacred area.

prothesis the lying-in-state of the dead.

Pythagorean theorem a theory developed by Pythagoras: the square of the hypotenuse of a right-angled triangle equals the sum of the squares of the other two sides.

stylobate the top step from which a Doric column rises.

symposium a type of Greek banquet.

triglyphs in a Doric frieze, the three verticals between the metopes.

trireme an ancient Greek warship with an iron-covered prow.

tyranny a form of rule in which power is concentrated in a single person.

tyrant an illegitimate leader who exercises absolute power, often oppressively.

KEY QUESTIONS

1. The notion of citizenship evolved in the *polis*. Who were citizens and what was required of them?
2. How did the Olympic Games achieve a sense of cultural unity between warring *poleis*?
3. The *Theogony* reflects the Greeks' interest in __________.
4. The *Chigi Vase* is the earliest surviving representation of a hoplite phalanx. Describe the distinguishing features of a hoplite phalanx illustrated on this vase.
5. Compare the political organizations of Athens and Sparta.

SUGGESTED READING

Boardman, John. *Athenian Red Figure Vases. The Archaic Period.* London: Thames and Hudson, 1989.

——. *Athenian Black Figure Vases.* London: Thames and Hudson, 1974.

——. *Greek Sculpture. The Archaic Period.* London: Thames and Hudson, 1978.

▸ All of the above are standard surveys.

Brilliant, Richard. *Arts of the Ancient Greeks.* New York: McGraw-Hill, 1973.

▸ A survey of Greek art.

Carpenter, Rhys. *The Architects of the Parthenon.* Baltimore: Penguin, 1970.

▸ Architecture and aesthetics of the Parthenon.

Fullerton, Mark D. *Greek Art*. Cambridge, U.K.: Cambridge University Press, 2000.
- A general introduction to Greek art.

Murray, Oswyn. *Early Greece*. New York: Prometheus Books, 1979.
- Greece in the early stages of development.

Onians, John. *Classical Art and the Cultures of Greece and Rome*, New Haven, CT, and London: Yale University Press, 1999.
- An introduction to Greek and Roman art.

Pedley, John Griffiths. *Greek Art and Archaeology*. New York: Harry N. Abrams, 1997.
- A general introduction.

Pomeroy, Sarah, Stanley M. Burstein, Walter Donlan, and Jennifer Tolbert Roberts. *Ancient Greece: A Political, Social, and Cultural History*. New York and Oxford: Oxford University Press, 1999.
- Greek art in its social and political context.

Renault, Mary. *The Praise Singer*. New York: Pantheon Books, 1978.
- A popular historical novel about a sixth-century-B.C. singer in the age of the Archaic tyrants.

Scully, Vincent. *The Earth, the Temple, and the Gods: Greek Sacred Architecture*, rev. ed. New Haven, CT: Yale University Press, 1979.
- Greek architecture in the context of landscape.

Spivey, Nigel. *Greek Art*. London: Phaidon Press, 1997.
- A general survey.

Sun Tzu. *The Art of War*, trans. James Clavell. London: Hodder and Stoughton, 1981.
- A classic work on military strategy by a fifth-century-B.C. Chinese general.

SUGGESTED FILMS

1954 *Ulysses*, dir. Mario Camerini

1960 *The Giant of Marathon* (*La battaglia di Maratone*), dir. Jacques Tourneur

1963 *Jason and the Argonauts*, dir. Don Chaffey

1967 *Oedipus Rex* (*Edipo re*) (based on Sophocles), dir. Pier Paolo Pasolini

6 Ancient Greece: Classical to Hellenistic

"*What Herodotus the Halicarnassian has learnt by inquiry is here set forth: in order that so the memory of the past may not be blotted out from among men by time, and that great and marvellous deeds done by Greeks and foreigners and especially the reason why they warred against each other may not lack renown.*"

(HERODOTUS, BK. I, I)

With the defeat of the Persians in 479 B.C., Greece entered the Classical period. This was a time of great achievement in politics, philosophy, the visual arts, and theater, all of which have had a lasting impact on Western history. Poleis of different types had been established throughout mainland Greece and the Greek colonies, although, with a few exceptions, Greece maintained its agricultural base.

The Classical period is generally divided into Early Classical (c. 480–450 B.C.), High Classical (c. 450–400 B.C.), and Late Classical (c. 400–323 B.C.). Athens was the most important, and one of the most urbanized, of the fifth-century-B.C. poleis, and it was the focus of Greek cultural activity. After the Persian sack of Athens in 480 B.C., the city undertook building programs designed to revive confidence and project an image of cultural superiority. Athenian citizens enjoyed music, attended some of the most famous plays ever written, and participated in city-wide religious festivals. Poets thrived, and the philosophical interest in empirical observation that had begun in the Archaic period spread to medicine and science. For the first time in the West, historians such as Herodotus (c. 490–c. 425 B.C.), who is quoted at the opening of the chapter, began to record first-hand the events of their time and to explore their meaning.

The cultural expansion of Greece continued in the fourth century B.C. (the Late Classical period). In the latter decades of this century, Greece produced Alexander the Great of Macedon (356–323 B.C.), the greatest conqueror the world had ever known. His armies marched east to the Punjab, in modern Pakistan, where the influence of Classical style may be seen in Indian sculpture. Following Alexander's death in 323 B.C., his generals vied for power and broke up the unity of his empire. This ushered in the Hellenistic period, which lasted to the turn of the first century A.D., and the rise of the Roman Empire. During the Hellenistic period, new ethnic groups, especially from the east, infiltrated Greek territory. The scale of architecture increased, religious cults offered the possibility of a more appealing afterlife than Hades, and rule by kings replaced the polis.

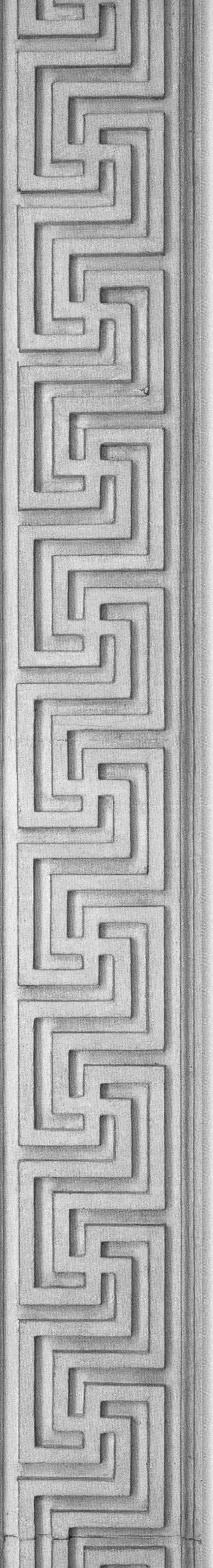

Key Topics

High Points of Greek Civilization

The Parthenon

The age of Pericles

Socrates, Plato, and Aristotle

Theater

The Real and the Ideal

Philosophy in search of truth

Music and math

Science and medicine

Writing History

Herodotus

Thucydides

ANCIENT GREECE: CLASSICAL TO HELLENISTIC (dates B.C. unless otherwise indicated)

TIMELINE	EARLY CLASSICAL 480–450	HIGH CLASSICAL 450–400	LATE CLASSICAL 400–323	HELLENISTIC LATE 4TH TO 1ST CENTURY
HISTORY AND CULTURE	Persians defeated, 479 Delian League, 478 Hatred of tyranny Urbanization grows Beginning of cultural expansion	Age of Pericles History writing Athens the main *polis*; ruled by male citizens, 450–400 Peloponnesian War, 431–404	Philip II of Macedon Athens loses preeminent position Conquests of Alexander the Great Alexander the Great dies, 323	Rise of kings Main cities: Alexandria, Pergamon Libraries *Polis* declines, 1st century
RELIGION AND MYTH		Same as Archaic period (see Chapter 5)		Mystery cults expand Influence of eastern religions
ART	Kritios and Nesiotes, *Tyrannicides*, *c.* 477 Myron, *Discus Thrower*, *c.* 460 *Oedipus answering the riddle of the sphinx*, early 5th century	*Muse Playing a Kithara*, 445–430 Polykleitos, *Spearbearer*, *c.* 440	Praxiteles, *Aphrodite of Knidos*, *c.* 350 Caivano painter, *Birth of Helen*, *c.* 340	*Battle of Issos* (Roman copy of a Greek painting of *c.* 300) *Drunken Old Woman*, late 3rd century *Aphrodite of Melos*, *c.* 150 Agesander, Athenodorus, and Polydorus, *Laocoön Group*, early 1st century A.D. *Chiron Instructs Achilles*, 1st century A.D.
ARCHITECTURE	Temple building continues Theaters	Pericles' reconstruction of Acropolis, Athens: Phidias, Parthenon sculptures, *c.* 448–420 Temple of Athena Nike, *c.* 427–424 Erechtheum, *c.* 421–405	Large-scale architecture Temples	Pergamon Altar, *c.* 180–160 Olympeium, reconstructed 2nd century
LITERATURE, PHILOSOPHY, AND MEDICINE	Pindar (*c.* 518–after 446), *Odes* Parmenides (*c.* 515–after 450) Zeno (*c.* 490–after 445) Herodotus (*c.* 490–*c.* 425), "Father of History" Thucydides (*c.* 460/455–400)	Protagoras (*c.* 485–410): "Man is the measure of all things" Empedocles (*c.* 490–430) Herodotus, *History* Thucydides, *History of the Peloponnesian War* Hippocrates (*c.* 460–*c.* 377) (Hippocratic Oath) Democritus (*c.* 460–*c.* 370) Socrates (469–399)	Plato (*c.* 429–347), *The Republic; Dialogues; Apology* Aristotle (384–322), *Metaphysics; Ethics; Politics; The Poetics*	Epicurus (341–271) Diogenes (*c.* 404–325) Stoics Cynics Skeptics
THEATER	Great Dionysia, annual festival of Dionysos Development of tragedy Aeschylus (*c.* 525–456), *Oresteia* Beginning of comedy	Sophocles (*c.* 496–406), *Oedipus the King; Antigone* Euripides (*c.* 485–406), *Medea; The Bacchae* Old comedy: Aristophanes (*c.* 445–*c.* 388), *The Clouds; The Frogs; Lysistrata*	Old comedy continues	Decline of tragedy New comedy Poetry: Pastoral, Lyrical
MUSIC	No notation	Monophonic	Greek modes: Dorian, Phrygian, Lydian, Mixolodian	Accompanied theatrical performances

HERODOTUS: THE "FATHER OF HISTORY"

In contrast to the mythic grandeur of the Homeric epics and the intimacy of the lyric poetry of the Archaic period, literature in Classical Greece is famous for laying the foundations of modern historical inquiry. (The Greek word *historiai* means "inquiries.") The seminal figure in this new approach to history was Herodotus. He was born in Halicarnassus, a Greek colony in Asia Minor, traveled widely, and lived for a time in Athens. Called the "Father of History," Herodotus recorded the Persian Wars and reported on his extensive journeys from western Asia through Egypt, Greece, and southern Italy. In addition to his own observations, he recorded hearsay and gossip, local legends, and traditions. Herodotus is remarkable for recognizing that writing history preserves the past and offers insights into human motivation. In particular, he wanted to understand why the Persians invaded Greece. His *History* concludes with the Battle of Plataea (479 B.C.) and the final Greek victory over Persia.

Herodotus's approach to history writing is marked by the effort to be objective. He sought to verify the truth of events and to record everything he heard. In so doing, Herodotus made another landmark contribution to the Greek exploration of the nature of humanity.

READING SELECTION

Herodotus, *History*, Sparta's last stand at the Battle of Thermopylae, PWC1-039

ATHENS FROM THE LATE ARCHAIC TO THE EARLY CLASSICAL PERIOD: *c.* 500–450 B.C.

Situated near the port of Piraeus, on the eastern coast of the Greek mainland, Athens was the most important city-state in the Classical period. Athenian sea power dominated the Aegean for most of the fifth century B.C. Athens had colonies throughout the entire region and the greatest fleet of all the Greek city-states. But the city itself was not large by modern standards. By 429 B.C., the population of Athens, which was about 7 square miles (18.1 sq km), numbered just over 100,000. The Athenian economy was based mainly on textiles, pottery, grapes, olives, wheat, and maritime trade. As the most democratic of the city-states, Athens was ruled by an assembly and a council of five hundred male citizens and ten generals. The laws traditionally attributed to Solon continued to prevail, and legal verdicts were decided by a jury. Since jurors were paid, lower-income citizens could participate in the legal system without suffering financially.

The Athenians were proud of their democratic values. In the sixth century B.C., the general Peisistratus (*c.* 605–527 B.C.) had risen to prominence in Athens, seized power, and ruled as a tyrant. Beginning around 508 B.C., a new leader, the aristocratic Cleisthenes (*c.* 600–*c.* 570 B.C.), took up where Solon left off (see Chapter 5) and steered the Athenian laws further toward democracy. Cleisthenes feared that the *polis* risked domination by men of high social status backed by traditional tribal ties. To offset their power, Cleisthenes grouped male citizens according to where they lived (the **deme**), rather than according to their family of origin. He redefined the notion of kinship, challenging it as a justification for power. In a final effort to prevent tyranny, Cleisthenes is thought to have devised the system of ostracizing any man considered a danger to the state. This was carried out, beginning in 487 B.C., by asking citizens to write on a piece of pottery (an *ostrakon*) the names of men whom they believed to be inclined to usurp political power. When there was a clear choice, he was ostracized (exiled) for ten years.

THE EARLY CLASSICAL PERIOD: *c.* 480–450 B.C.

As internal Athenian politics progressed toward democracy, external politics continued to focus on the East. Despite having defeated the Persians, the Greeks still considered them a threat. In 478 B.C., therefore, the Greeks formed an alliance of city-states against Persia. This was called the Delian League, because the funds that supported it were kept on the island of Delos. Although all the *poleis* contributed to the league, Athens soon dominated it and eventually used the funds for its own benefit.

SCULPTURE

Early Classical sculpture continues the trend toward naturalism that we saw in the Archaic period (see Chapter 5). This is clear in the *Kritios Boy* (figure **6.1**). The Archaic smile has disappeared, making the youth seem more serious than, for example, the *Anavysos Kouros* (see thumbnail), and the *Kritios Boy*'s proportions and stance are more natural. Instead of standing stiffly to attention, the later figure is relaxed—he bends one knee and shifts slightly at the waist. This **contrapposto** pose shows that the Early Classical artist has rendered the natural movements of the body. In addition, the *Kritios Boy* is no longer frontal, for he turns his head slightly, and the surface stylizations of the *Anavysos Kouros* are replaced by a sense of organic structure.

In 477 B.C., in honor of two opponents of tyranny, Harmodius and Aristogeiton, Athens commissioned a pair of

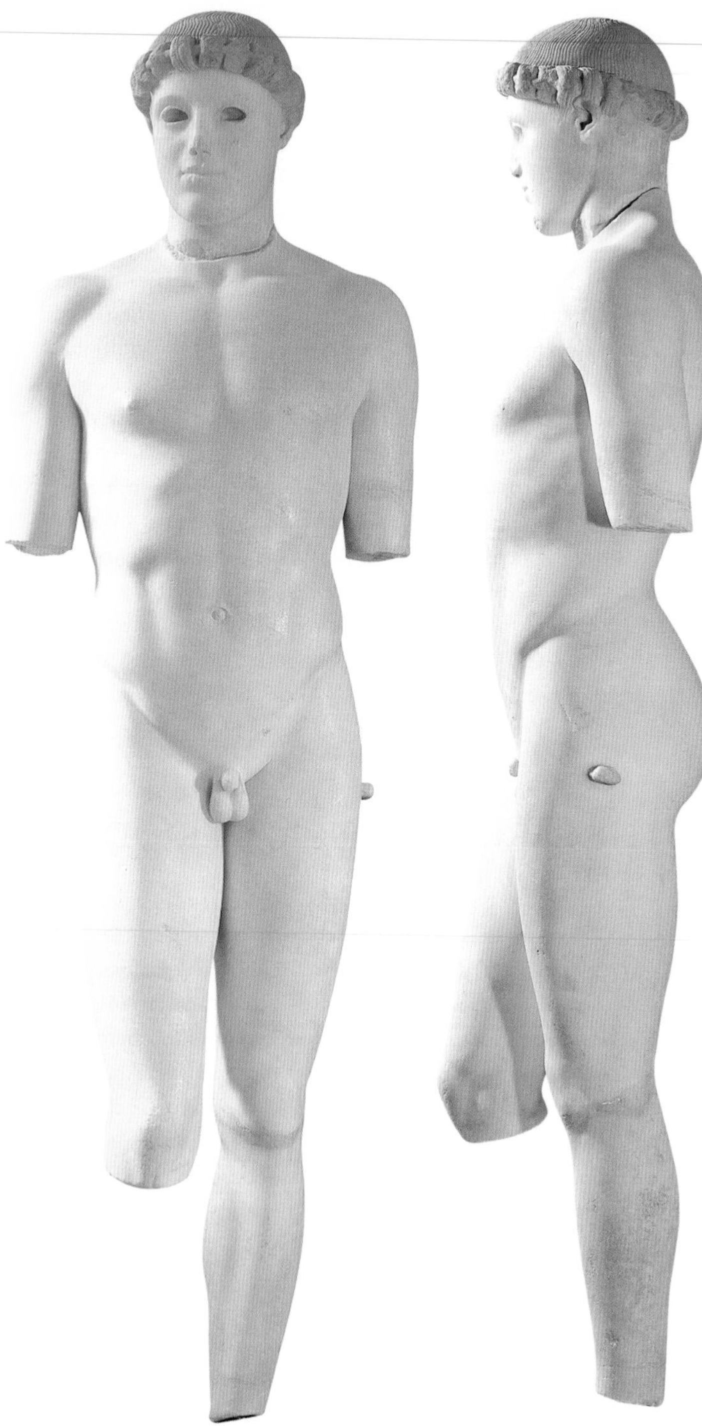

6.1 ***Kritios Boy*** **(front and side),** ***c.*** **480 B.C. Marble, 33⅞ in. (86 cm) high. Acropolis Museum, Athens.**

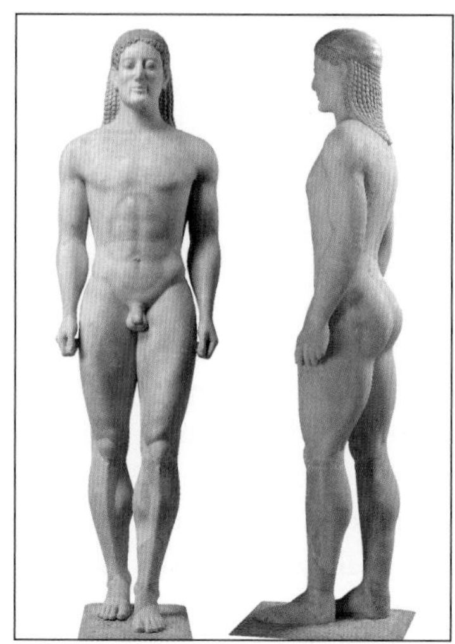

Anavysos Kouros see figure 5.15

bronze statues known as the *Tyrannicides* (tyrant-killers) (figure **6.2**) to replace an Archaic version that had been looted by the Persians. Note the change in the treatment of human form compared with the Archaic sculptures illustrated in the previous chapter. Although retaining some Archaic stylization, the *Tyrannicides* are structured organically and seem able to move freely in space. The statues were placed in the Athenian *agora*, marking the political use of statuary to project a democratic image of the Athenian *polis*.

A slightly later Early Classical bronze (now known only from Roman marble copies) that illustrated the transition to naturalism is Myron's *Discus Thrower* (*Diskobolos*) (figure **6.3**). This sculpture probably honored a victorious athlete, but

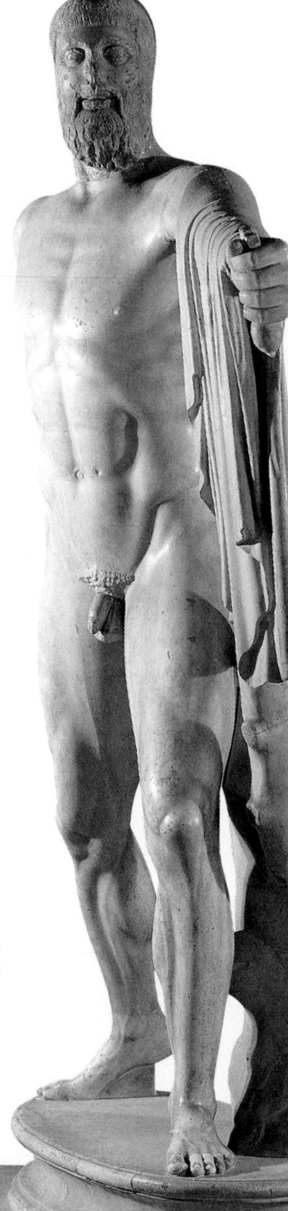

6.2 *right and opposite (p. 113)* **Kritios and Nesiotes,** ***Harmodius and Aristogeiton*** **(the** ***Tyrannicides*****), partially restored copies of bronze originals that were erected in Athens in 477 B.C. Marble, 6 ft. 4¾ in. (1.95 m) high. National Archaeological Museum, Naples.**
Although the rule of Peisistratus was relatively benevolent and he instituted much-needed reforms, his son and successor, Hippias, was unpopular. Two Athenians, Harmodius and Aristogeiton, had assassinated Hippias's brother in 514 B.C. For this act against tyranny they were honored with statues in the *agora*. But in 480 B.C., just before their defeat, the Persians overran Athens and carried off the statues. The pair illustrated here are the new statues, recommissioned in the fifth century B.C.

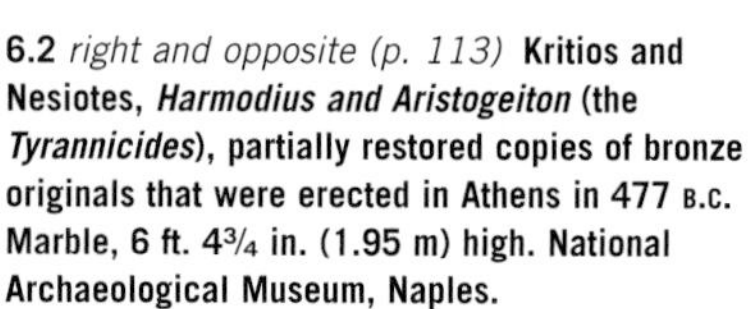

his identity is not known. The work reflects both the political and cultural importance that the ancient Greeks attached to athletic competition and shows how the human body works. Myron has designed the sculpture so that it echoes the circular movement the athlete will make when throwing the discus.

The figure is caught as he turns, gathering momentum before spinning and launching the discus. What we are seeing, therefore, is not a static pose, but rather a captured movement. As in the *Tyrannicides*, there are traces of stylization in the *Discus Thrower*—the patterned ribcage and the smooth hair—but the body works as a logical unit. The absence of a facial expression and of any indication of strain or effort, however, reveals the Early Classical tendency to idealize figures. Myron's sculptures are not based on the features of an actual human model, but on an ideal appearance of the male nude.

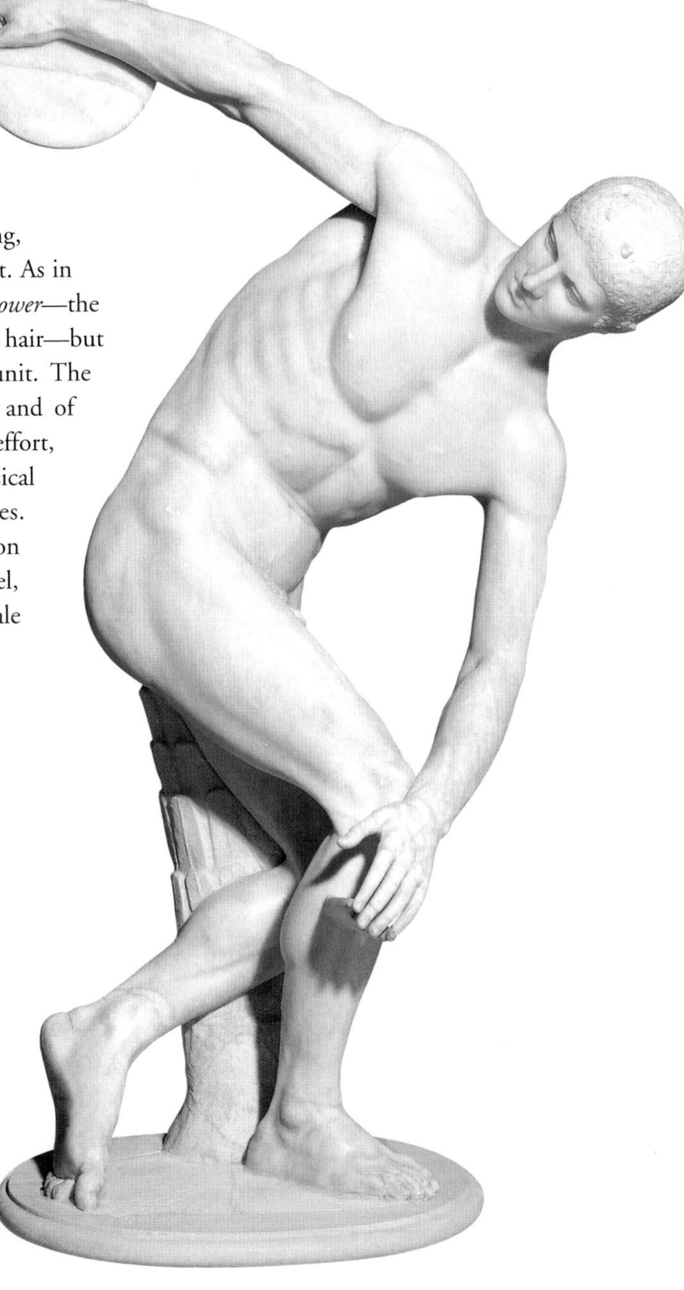

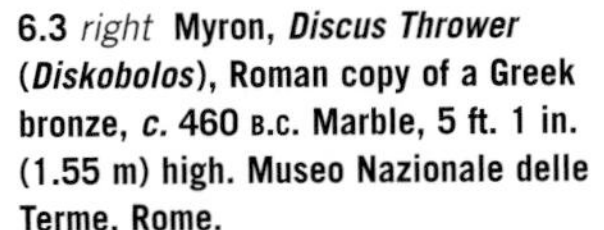

6.3 *right* **Myron, *Discus Thrower* (*Diskobolos*), Roman copy of a Greek bronze, *c.* 460 B.C. Marble, 5 ft. 1 in. (1.55 m) high. Museo Nazionale delle Terme, Rome.**
The original statue, which was cast in bronze by Myron, has disappeared. This version is one of several later Roman copies in marble, which is given extra support by the tree trunk next to the leg.

PHILOSOPHERS ON THE REAL AND THE IDEAL: PARMENIDES AND ZENO

Early Classical philosophy echoes the combination of nature (the real) with idealization (the ideal) that we can see in the sculpture of the period. This is reflected, for example, in the views of Parmenides (*c.* 515–after 450 B.C.), even though they survive only in fragments. Born in Elea, a Greek colony in southern Italy, Parmenides was the leading Eleatic (from Elea) philosopher in the early fifth century B.C. The Eleatics rejected both the empirical evidence of the senses and mathematical abstraction. Parmenides studied biology and considered the nature of the real; he concluded that reality, like mathematics, was timeless and without motion. Parmenides believed that the idea of a thing was inseparable from its physical reality, a belief made material in such sculptures as the *Diskobolos*. As in Myron's sculpture, the real was seamlessly merged with the ideal.

Another Eleatic philosopher and an admirer of Parmenides, Zeno (*c.* 490–after 445 B.C.), was interested in progression and motion, which is also characteristic of the *Diskobolos*. Zeno used a series of **paradoxes** (statements that seem to contradict common sense) to support the views of Parmenides. Taking the example of a runner, Zeno observed that he has to run a half length before he can run a whole length, and a quarter length before a half length, and so on forever.

In a similar paradox, Zeno noted that a fast runner will never catch up with a slower runner who starts first; the fast runner will halve the distance between himself and the slow runner, and then halve what remains, and then halve it again, and so on forever, without ever catching the slow runner. In the case of Myron's athlete, the figure is represented in motion, but, because he is fixed in stone, he, like Zeno's runner, will never achieve his goal of throwing the discus.

POETRY: PINDAR ON ATHLETES

The best preserved **odes** (lyric poems) of Pindar (518–after 446 B.C.), the most important Early Classical poet, are dedicated to victorious athletes, reflecting the high esteem in which Greece held sports. These were not the popular team sports of today, but rather sports in which individual excellence was honored and memorialized in poetry as well as in sculpture.

Pindar traveled widely, attending the four great ancient Greek athletic festivals—the Olympian, Nemean, Pythian, and Isthmian Games. His early success as a poet won him commissions throughout Greece. In all, some forty-four of his odes survive. They were sung to music, either at the end of a competition or after a winner had returned home.

Pindar's *Olympian Ode II* celebrates Theron of Acragas, the victor in a chariot race held at the Olympic Games in 476 B.C. Because these games were sacred to Zeus, whose precinct and great temple were located at Olympia, Pindar opens his ode by praising the god:

> Ye hymns that rule the lyre! what god, what hero, aye, and what man shall we loudly praise? Verily Zeus is the lord of Pisa [a Greek city]; and Heracles established the Olympic festival from the spoils of war; while Theron must be proclaimed by reason of his victorious chariot with its four horses, Theron who is just in his regard for guests, and who is the bulwark of Acragas, the choicest flower of an auspicious line of sires . . . But, O thou son of Cronus and Rhea [Zeus], that rulest over thine abode on Olympus, and over the foremost of festivals, over the ford of the Alphaeus [a river]!
>
> (lines 1–30)

Note that Pindar's verse is packed with background information. He tells us that Zeus, the son of Rhea and Chronos, rules the Olympic Games, presides over Mount Olympos, and is the patron god of Olympia. Pindar reminds us of the tradition that Heracles instituted the Olympic Games "from the spoils of war," alluding to the suspension of armed conflict so that Greek athletes could travel safely to the competition. Having paid homage to Zeus and Heracles, Pindar praises the family of Theron, a victor and an honor to his city.

THE HIGH CLASSICAL PERIOD: 450–400 B.C.

During the High Classical period, Athens was dominated by Pericles (*c.* 495–429 B.C.), a general and statesman who ruled the *polis* from 443 until his death (figure **6.4**). Under Pericles, the treasury of the Delian League was moved to Athens, and Pericles' political opponents accused him of diverting the funds to finance an Athenian building campaign. This aroused the anger of other city-states and eventually eroded Greek political unity.

6.4 Kresilas, *Pericles*, Roman copy of an original bronze of *c.* 429 B.C. Marble, 6 ft. (1.83 m) high. Vatican Museums, Rome.

6.5 **The Acropolis, Athens, Greece.**

Pericles presided over the rise of Athens to its central position in Greek art and politics. He used his power to finance works of architecture and sculpture designed to convey the importance of Athens. He decided to rebuild the Acropolis (literally the "upper city"), the elevated fortified rock that was the site of several temples and other important buildings (figures **6.5**, **6.6**, and **6.7**). But the Acropolis had lain in ruins since being sacked by the Persians. For Pericles, therefore, the reconstruction program celebrated the Athenian defeat of Persia and the cultural supremacy of Athens.

The reconstruction view in figure 6.6 conveys some idea of the original appearance of the Acropolis. Athenians proceeded to the Acropolis along the Sacred Way, which led to an impressive stairway. At the top of the stairs was the gateway called the Propylaia, which was begun in 437 B.C., with a Doric porch and an extension on either side. This structure marked a change from the previous function of the Acropolis—it had been a fortified citadel with a narrow entrance to deter invaders. But Pericles envisioned the area as a religious sanctuary. He wanted an imposing entrance, large enough to accommodate Athenians participating in religious processions and performing rituals dedicated to the gods.

6.6 **Peter Connolly, reconstruction of the Acropolis, Athens, at the beginning of the 4th century B.C. Watercolor.**

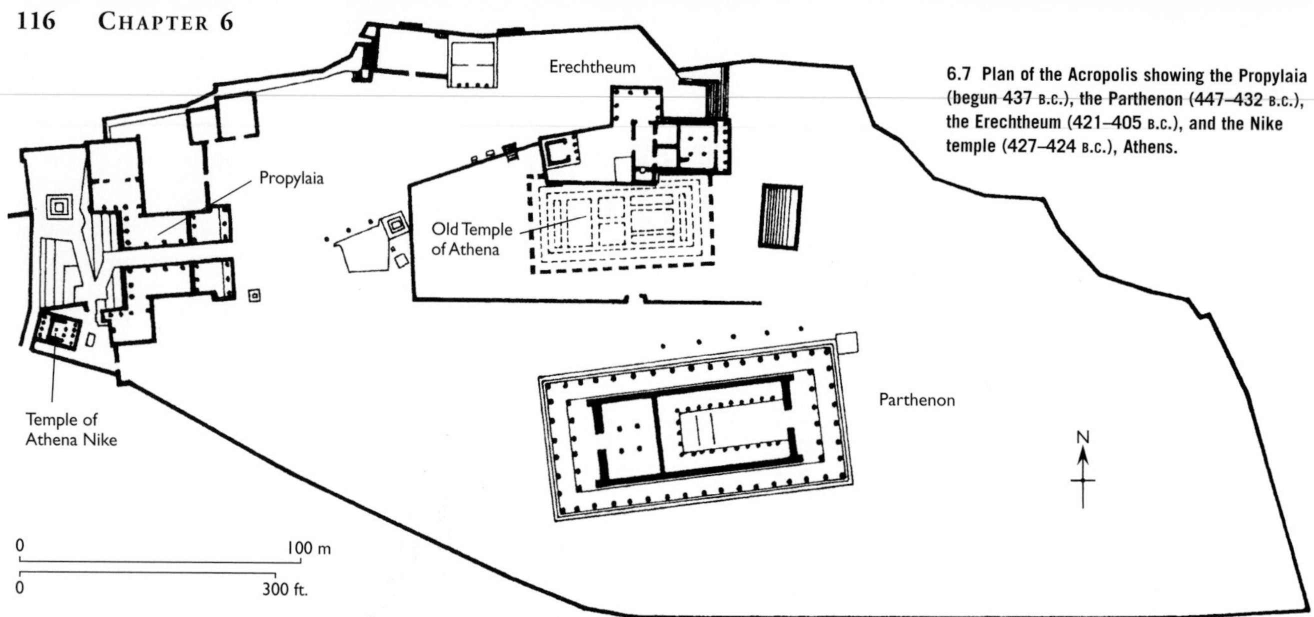

6.7 Plan of the Acropolis showing the Propylaia (begun 437 B.C.), the Parthenon (447–432 B.C.), the Erechtheum (421–405 B.C.), and the Nike temple (427–424 B.C.), Athens.

THE PARTHENON

To the east of the Propylaia on the Acropolis stands the Parthenon, a majestic temple dedicated to Athena (figure **6.8**). Figure **6.9** shows a cutaway reconstruction drawing.

The plan (figure **6.10**) shows the rectangular symmetry of the Parthenon, which has six columns on the front and back porches and a peristyle (a freestanding **colonnade**, or row of columns). Inside the peristyle is the *naos*, the main room containing the cult statue. To the west of the *naos*, a smaller room with four interior Ionic columns housed the Athenian treasury. Since the Doric Order was a western, mainland Order and Ionic was eastern, the use of both in the Parthenon suggested the global reach of Athens under Pericles.

The Parthenon was designed with several architectural refinements to improve its appearance. The corner columns, for example, are closer together than the center columns, creating an impression of stability (as well as increasing the actual structural support) at the ends of each wall. The peristyle

6.8 Iktinos and Kallikrates, the Parthenon, Athens, 447–432 B.C. Marble, 111 × 237 ft. (33.8 × 72.2 m).
In Greek, *parthenos* means "virgin," which was an aspect of Athena, who was also the patron goddess of Athens. Today, the Parthenon is in ruins, although its restoration is an ongoing process. It was converted to a church by the Christians and to a mosque under Turkish domination in the sixteenth century. The Turks used the building to store gunpowder, which exploded in the seventeenth century and destroyed the interior.

6.9 *above* **Peter Connolly, cutaway reconstruction of the Parthenon, Athens. Drawing with watercolor.**

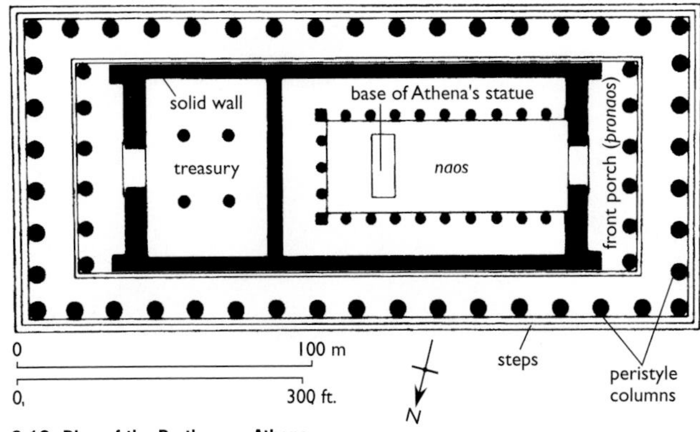

6.10 Plan of the Parthenon, Athens.

columns slant inward and the top step, the stylobate, is slightly convex. This corrects the natural tendency of the eye to perceive a long horizontal as concave.

THE SCULPTURAL PROGRAM OF THE PARTHENON The Parthenon sculptures were designed by Phidias (*c.* 490–432 B.C.), who was a close friend of Pericles. The sculptural **program** (its design and meaning) of the temple was intended to reflect the political, religious, civic, and artistic superiority of the Athenian *polis*. Phidias decorated four main areas of the Parthenon with brightly painted sculpture: the *naos*, the outer Doric frieze, the inner Ionic frieze (around the *naos*), and the two pediments. The *naos* itself housed the colossal cult statue of Athena; the flesh was made of ivory and the clothing and armor of gold (figure **6.11**).

The freestanding pediment sculptures illustrated two mythological events involving Athena. Her birth was shown on the east pediment, and her contest with Poseidon for the patronage of Athens was on the west pediment. The birth scene is diagrammed in figure **6.12**. Two of the most impressive figures from the east pediment are the reclining *Dionysos*, god of wine (figure **6.13**), and the *Horse of Selene* (figure **6.14**), a goddess of the moon.

The birth itself, which is now entirely missing, occupied the center of the pediment. According to Greek myth, Athena sprung full grown and armed for war from the head of Zeus—like an idea. On either side of Athena's birth, the gods await news of the event. The figure of Dionysos, who has not yet heard the news, faces the left corner of the pediment. He reclines in a relaxed manner, so that he fits naturally under the sloping frame of the pediment. His smooth, domed head, lack of facial expression, and youthful body are characteristic of the High Classical idealization of heroic male youth. The anatomical structure of the body is clearly visible, reflecting the Classical interest in human form.

At the left corner of the east pediment the horses of the sun god, Apollo, appear to be rising, an indication that Athena was born at dawn. At the far right corner, the *Horse of Selene* (a moon goddess) seems to descend, denoting the waning of the moon. This figure, like the *Dionysos*, creates a harmonious unity with its triangular space; note the curved triangle of the

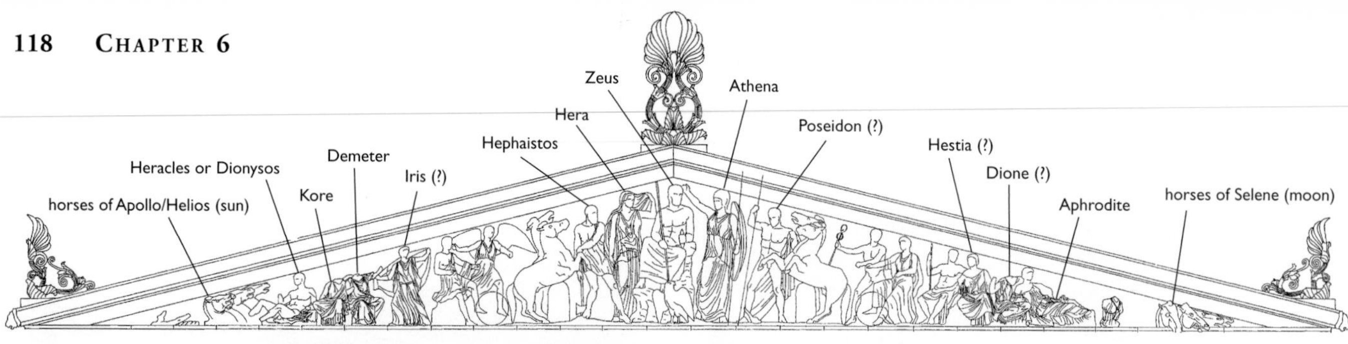

6.12 *above* **Figures on the east pediment of the Parthenon, Athens.**
Most of the Parthenon sculptures are now in London. In the nineteenth century, when Greece was under Turkish domination, the British ambassador, Lord Elgin, was given permission to remove the works from the Acropolis and ship them to London. Today they are referred to as the Elgin Marbles. One shipment sank and the sculptures were lost; the remainder were sold to the British Museum and have been a subject of international controversy ever since. The Greeks are pressing for their return, but the British argue that no laws were broken by the removal of the works, that they are available for study and viewing, and that they are safer in London than in air-polluted Athens.

6.11 Replica of Phidias's lost statue of Athena, from the *naos* of the Parthenon, Athens. Marble, 3 ft. 5¼ in. (1.05 m) high. Royal Ontario Museum.
It is most likely that the original statue was plundered for the value of its gold and ivory, but its appearance is known from descriptions and from ancient coins. Athena was shown armed for war, with a Gorgon head (the gorgoneion) on her breastplate. In her right hand she holds a Nike (goddess of victory), alluding to the Greek defeat of the Persians. Athena's imposing presence was a reminder of the invincible power of Athens protected by the goddess of war and wisdom. Athena was also a goddess of weaving, which was an artistic female pursuit in antiquity. She thus combined male and female qualities, as well as the ability to destroy (war), to create (the arts), and to administer justice (as in Aeschylus's *Libation Bearers*, in which she casts her vote for Orestes' acquittal).

6.13 *right* **Phidias, *Dionysos*, from the east pediment of the Parthenon, Athens, *c.* 420 B.C. Pentelic marble, over lifesize. British Museum, London.**

cheek plate, and the triangular space of the mouth. As with the human figure, the horse has a convincing organic structure.

The metope sculptures are carved in relief. Although in ruins today, they depicted four mythological battles, each shown as a series of single combats and chosen to project the image of Greek cultural dominance. The battle between the Gods and the Giants illustrated the triumph of the Olympians over the more primitive, pre-Greek Titans; the battle between the Greeks and the Trojans, and between the Greeks and the Amazons (eastern warrior women), connoted victories of western civilization over the east; and the battle between the Lapiths (a Greek tribe) and the Centaurs (creatures that were half-man and half-horse) demonstrated the superiority of Greek reason over animal instinct (figure **6.15**).

The Ionic frieze continued around the solid side walls of the *naos* and treasury and over the front and back porches. In contrast to the triglyphs and metopes separating the Doric narrative into individual frames (see Chapter 5), the Ionic frieze is continuous. As such, it is well suited to the depiction of a procession, in this case the Great Panathenaic Procession in which all of Athens participated. The Panathenaia was held every four years in honor of Athena.

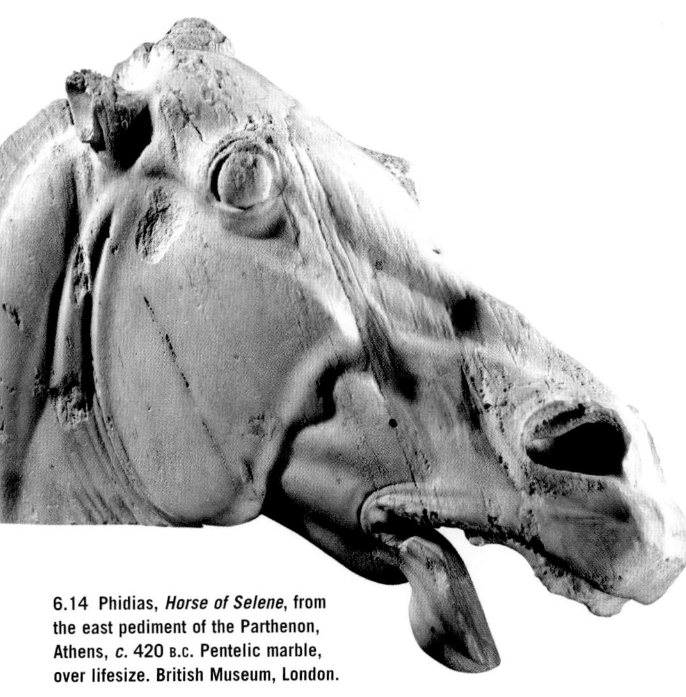

6.14 Phidias, *Horse of Selene*, from the east pediment of the Parthenon, Athens, *c.* 420 B.C. Pentelic marble, over lifesize. British Museum, London.

6.15 Phidias, *Lapith Battling a Centaur*, metope 30 from the Parthenon, Athens, *c.* 448–442 B.C. Pentelic marble, 4 ft. 4¾ in. (1.34 m) high. British Museum, London.

This illustrates the myth of the Lapiths and Centaurs. The Lapiths invited the Centaurs to a wedding, but the Centaurs became drunk and attempted to rape the Lapiths. The ensuing battle ended with the defeat of the Centaurs, indicating the victory of Greek civilization over the primitive, antisocial behavior of the Centaurs. In this metope, a Centaur temporarily has the upper hand. His horse part rears upward, and his entire body forms a series of energetic diagonals. Both figures show strain and tension, as they fight to the death.

Figure **6.16** shows a detail of the horsemen on the Ionic frieze. They are carved in different poses to convey a sense of variety within a unified whole. At the left, rearing horses prepare to gallop forward. At the right, a dismounted youth turns to gaze at the group proceeding slowly behind him. The procession ends with the gods awaiting the presentation of a sacred *peplos* to Athena (figure **6.17**).

6.16 *below* **Detail of the Great Panathenaic Procession, slabs 41 and 42, from the Parthenon frieze, Athens, *c.* 442–438 B.C. Marble, 3 ft. 5¾ in. (1.06 m) high. British Museum, London.**

Phidias introduced two refinements in the Ionic frieze that enhance its harmonious appearance. He maintained a horizontal unity by placing all the heads at a relatively equal height (**isocephaly**), and he carved the lower section in deeper relief than the upper section. This improved visibility from below and created the impression of swift movement in the legs of the horses and youths. Over time, the Parthenon marbles have suffered considerable damage, but originally the sections were so precisely cut that the separations between them were not visible.

6.17 Phidias, *Hera and Zeus with Iris*, slab 5/28–30, from the Parthenon frieze, Athens, *c.* 442–438 B.C. Marble, 3 ft. 5¾ in. (1.06 m) high. British Museum, London. Notice that Phidias has maintained the isocephaly here by making the seated figures of Hera and Zeus as high as the standing figure of Iris. The large size of the king and queen of Mount Olympos reflects their importance compared with Iris, the rainbow-messenger goddess, as well as with the human figures and horses in figure 6.16. Hera turns toward the bearded Zeus, her veil an attribute of marriage. As with the horsemen, Hera and Zeus turn freely in space, as if engaged in casual conversation with each other.

THE TEMPLE OF ATHENA NIKE

The small Ionic temple dedicated to Athena Nike (Athena as a goddess of victory) was not begun until 427 B.C., two years after the death of Pericles (figure **6.18**). This elegant building overlooks the southern edge of the Acropolis, discreetly but decisively standing for Greek victory. Its nearly square *naos* originally housed small golden Nike statues. The front and back porches have four columns resting on three steps, and the continuous frieze, which survives only in fragments, represented gods and battle scenes. In its small scale, harmonious proportions, and symmetry, the Nike temple embodies the Classical architectural ideal.

THE ERECHTHEUM

Opposite the Parthenon to the north stands the complex Ionic Erechtheum (figure **6.19**). This temple is named after Erechtheus, a legendary king of Athens, but is dedicated to Athena Polias (Athena as goddess of the city). The Erechtheum is on uneven ground and thus has an irregular plan. Its most

6.18 Temple of Athena Nike. Acropolis, Athens, *c.* 427–424 B.C. Marble.

6.19 View of the Erechtheum, Athens, *c.* 421–405 B.C. Marble.

interesting feature is the south porch, with six **caryatids** (female figures that function as architectural supports), who wear the traditional *peplos* and support the entablature (figure **6.20**). Their human form is combined with architectural elements—for example, the folds of their garments resemble the flutes (grooves) of columns. Their crowns, like the capitals of columns, create a visual transition from vertical to horizontal and also perform a similar support function. In these figures, the Classical artists made explicit the association of the column with human form.

CLASSICAL PAINTING AND SCULPTURE UNRELATED TO THE ACROPOLIS

The architecture and sculpture of the Acropolis were not the only expressions of High Classical style in Greece. Concurrent with Pericles' building program, other artists worked on commissions unrelated to the Parthenon.

By the first half of the fifth century B.C., a new type of vase painting known as "white ground" had developed. White ground allowed artists even more freedom to paint lifelike figures than was possible with the red-figure technique. Artists working in white ground outlined figures in black, red, or brown and filled them in with green, blue, yellow, and purple

6.20 A caryatid (front and side), from the Erechtheum, Athens, 421–405 B.C. Marble, 8 ft. 7 in. (2.31 m) high. British Museum, London.

6.21 Achilles painter, *Muse Playing a Kithara on Mount Helikon*, *c.* 445–430 B.C. White ground lekythos, terra-cotta, 16 in. (40.7 cm) high. Staatliche Antikensammlungen, Munich. How far vase paintings such as this one reflect the lost monumental wall paintings of the period is not certain. However, a number of anecdotes about Greek painters indicate that illusionism was highly esteemed. One famous story describes a painting by Zeuxis of a boy carrying a bunch of grapes. The painted grapes were so convincing that real birds tried to eat them. What is clear is that this and similar anecdotes suggest that naturalism led to a taste for illusionistic tours-de-force by Greek painters.

on a white background. White ground was most often used for *lekythoi*—tall, slim oil jars that were placed in graves. The scene in figure **6.21** shows a Muse sitting on a rock, playing a hand-held harp (*kithara*) and concentrating on the music; the little bird at her feet probably symbolizes the soul. The inscription *HELIKON* at the lower right refers to Mount Helikon, the mythological home of the nine Muses.

Perhaps the best-known High Classical work by an artist not involved in the Parthenon is the *Doryphoros* (*Spearbearer*) (figure **6.22**) by Polykleitos. He called his statue the *Canon*, indicating that it embodied his ideal of human **proportions**. In contrast to the stance of Archaic *kouroi*, the *Spearbearer* is relaxed, and he occupies a contrapposto pose, in which the waist twists slightly in response to the bent knee. Polykleitos believed that mathematical ratios determine order and harmony, and he represented this idea in the *Spearbearer*. The figure expresses the Classical ideal of youth and perfection of form and, at the same time, achieves a balanced harmony between motion and rest.

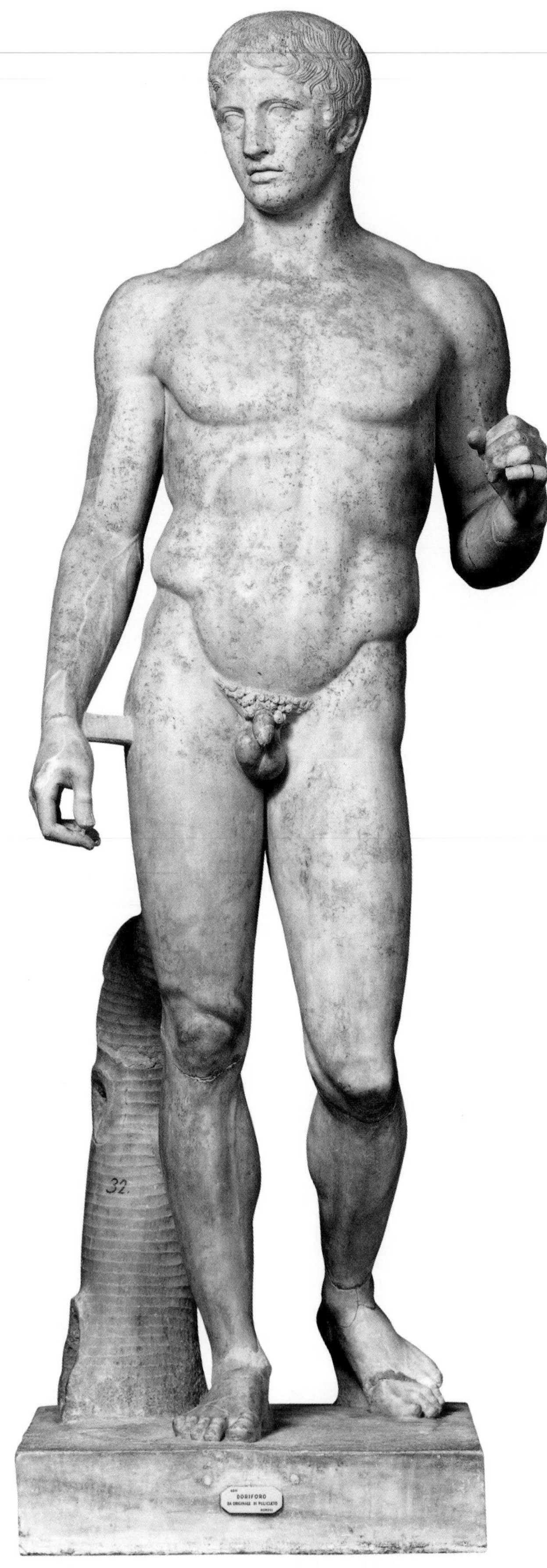

6.22 Polykleitos, *Spearbearer* (*Doryphoros*), Roman copy of a Greek bronze original, *c.* 440 B.C. Marble, 6 ft. 11½ in. (2.12 m) high. Archaeological Museum, Naples.

CLASSICAL PHILOSOPHY

Greek philosophy, which is first known from the Archaic period, continued to be an important part of Greek culture. During the fifth century B.C., a group of traveling philosophers hired to teach **rhetoric** (the art of eloquent argument), mathematics, and politics became popular. These were known as the Sophists—literally, "men of wisdom." They did not advocate any single philosophical point of view, but prided themselves on being able to argue any side of an issue. Eventually, however, the substance of their arguments gave way to artificial rhetoric, and they began to stress stylish form over content. The modern term "sophistry," referring to an argument that seems reasonable but is actually invalid, comes from the rhetorical style of the Greek Sophists.

PROTAGORAS Born in Thrace, in northern Greece, Protagoras (*c.* 485–410 B.C.) was the most famous Sophist. He was acquainted with Pericles and achieved fame in Athens, but was eventually exiled for questioning the existence of the gods. His main argument was that truth varies according to what each individual concludes from his own experience. This is a relativist view, which does not impose an objective set of rules defining the "real" and the "ideal," as had the Eleatic school. Protagoras thus exemplifies the Classical Athenian sense that men, not gods, are the standard by which everything is measured. He stated this notion explicitly in the famous saying attributed to him: "Man is the measure of all things."

EMPEDOCLES The philosopher Empedocles (*c.* 490–430 B.C.) of Sicily identified the four basic elements of matter as air, fire, water, and earth. He believed that the forces of love and strife caused evolution and that the most adaptive organisms would survive. In this view, he prefigured Darwin's theory of evolution (see Chapters 1 and 19). Empedocles' theory of four elements was applied by Greek physicians to the four humors (fluids) of the human body: blood, phlegm, yellow bile, and black bile.

DEMOCRITUS Democritus (*c.* 460–*c.* 370 B.C.), like Protagoras and in contrast to the Eleatics, was a relativist. Because he believed that atoms were the basic unit of matter, he is known as an Atomist (from the Greek word *atomos*, meaning "uncuttable"). Atoms, he thought, were unchanging, indivisible, and forever moving through space. They made up all physical matter, including the human body, but did not deteriorate with age. He also held that the soul was made of fire and was similar to the atom in that both animated the body, but also outlasted it.

The works of Democritus do not survive, but he is known to have described the physical universe and to have written about natural science, astronomy, mathematics, literature, and ethics. He believed that moderation (*metron*, or "measure") was the most ethical position and would lead to a happy life, hence the Greek maxim *metron ariston*—"measure is best." Later authors describe Democritus as the "laughing philosopher" because he laughed at the extremes of human frailty even as he recommended a life based on moderation.

6.23 Attributed to Lysippos, *Socrates*, Roman copy of a 4th-century-B.C. Greek original. Marble, 10 in. (27.5 cm) high. British Museum, London. Note that this Late Classical statue has a portrait-like quality absent in Early and High Classical style. Socrates is shown with his proverbial short stature, pug nose, fat torso, and beard, which fostered his reputation for ugliness.

SOCRATES AND PLATO Socrates (469–399 B.C.) and his student Plato (*c.* 429–347 B.C.) were the two leading Classical philosophers in Athens. Socrates was the son of a sculptor and a midwife; he was married to Xanthippe, whose nagging became legendary. (Today, therefore, a shrewish woman may be referred to as a "Xanthippe.") Unlike the Sophists, Socrates was not paid for his philosophy. He preferred to wander around Athens discussing philosophical issues with other citizens. Pretending to know nothing himself ("Socratic irony"), Socrates used a dialectic process of question and answer to elicit truth from his questioners. He was interested in inductive argumentation—that is, arriving at generalities from particular instances—which he used to lead his followers to conclusions he himself had already reached. This so-called "Socratic method" became a foundation of Western philosophy and the cornerstone of Plato's *Dialogues*.

Socrates did not write down his philosophy. His views are known mainly from what his most famous student, Plato, says he said. Plato presents Socrates as a man dedicated to pursuing the nature of the Good, the True, and the Beautiful, although Socrates, himself, was notoriously ugly (figure **6.23**). In this pursuit, Socrates discussed a wide variety of topics, ranging from the nature of love (*The Symposium*), rhetoric (*Phaedra* and *Giorgias*), metaphysics (*Parmenides*), death and the immortality of the soul (*Phaedo*), to the ideal state (*The Republic*, and later *The Laws*). In *Protagoras*, Socrates argues against the Sophists' view that there is no absolute truth and concludes that knowledge of the Good is the basis of virtue. And the deepest wisdom, according to Socrates, is insight into oneself. In his view, no one who knew right would act wrongly, making virtue synonymous with wisdom. To this end, he cites the wisdom of the inscription carved in stone at Delphi—"Know thyself"—which is also a cornerstone of Socratic philosophy.

Socrates' unconventional ideas led to his arrest in 399 B.C. for corrupting the youth of Athens and denying the existence of the gods. In his own defense, which is recorded in Plato's *Apology*, Socrates cross-examines his accusers. How, he asks, could he not believe in the gods, since it is well known that he believes in demi-gods, the illegitimate offspring of the gods? He points out, "You might as well affirm the existence of mules, and deny that of horses and asses" (*Apology*, 27).

The court found Socrates guilty and gave him a choice of exile from Athens or death by drinking the poison, hemlock. He chose death:

> . . . the difficulty, my friends, is not to avoid death, but to avoid unrighteousness; for that runs faster than death. I am old [he was seventy at the time] and move slowly, and the slower runner has overtaken me, and my accusers are keen and quick, and the faster runner, who is unrighteousness, has overtaken them.
>
> (*Apology*, 39)

Plato's *Crito* is set in the Athenian prison with the hour of Socrates' death approaching. His followers try to persuade him to escape and appeal to his obligations to his children. But Socrates replies that the issue is law and justice, not family. Having lived under Athenian law for seventy years, he refuses to escape on the grounds that he would be exchanging one evil for another—that is, escape and exile from Athens are as bad as death. He cannot break with the city-state that has nourished him his entire life and thus decides to obey the verdict of the court. Another reason for Socrates' decision to die was his refusal to do evil, even if others had been evil in their actions toward him.

THE REPUBLIC Plato's most famous dialogue, *The Republic*, outlines an ideal society based on justice and reason, but not on democracy. Plato's ideal state is authoritarian, and its rulers (guardians) require a lengthy period of education. He divides his state into three main classes: artisans (crafts workers) who labor and produce, soldiers who have physical power, and philosopher-kings who have wisdom. This social structure is a model of Plato's ideal individual—someone who is capable of productive work, who is morally and physically strong, and who is ruled by wisdom.

Plato's recommendations emphasize the importance of order and harmony in all areas of life. He bans from his Republic any person or activity that disrupts order or causes disharmony. For example, because music arouses the emotions, Plato outlaws all but martial music, which inspires soldiers in battle. He urges training the body as well as the mind, educating women along with men, and raising children in communal settings.

Plato believed in the existence of a realm of ideas, separate from the material world. This rather mystical notion of an ideal realm distinguished Plato's philosophy from both the empiricists and the relativism of the Sophists. The realm of ideas also had a bearing on Plato's view of visual artists. He believed that artists, unlike artisans, create illusions, which are a danger to the Republic because they are false.

The Platonic view—that the real world is merely a shadow of truth and that illusion is dangerous—has influenced thinkers and inspired metaphors throughout Western history. This notion is illustrated in the famous Allegory of the Cave (Book VII), in which Plato juxtaposes knowledge with illusion, comparing the former with light and the latter with darkness. Those who are chained inside the cave see only shadows, like screen puppets, but they believe the shadows to be real. When they leave the cave, they are dazzled by the brightness, but as their eyes grow accustomed to the light, they become capable of achieving true knowledge. Enlightenment, according to Plato, comes from intellectual rather than emotional knowledge. On occasion, he says, the enlightened must renounce intellectual pleasure and return to the cave, which they rule in order to improve the general condition of the state and not just that of the most educated citizens.

Plato taught in an olive grove near Athens, where he founded the Academy in 387 B.C. After his death in 347 B.C. his followers continued to teach there.

READING SELECTION

Plato: *Phaedo*, the body imprisons the soul, PWC1-145; *The Symposium*, on cosmic love, PWC1-158-C; *Apology*, "Know Thyself" and the Delphic Oracle, PWC1-141-A; *The Republic*, the Myth of Er, PWC1-127; *The Republic*, Allegory of the Cave, PWC1-122

MEDICINE

During the Classical period, Greek medicine, like Greek philosophy, marked a break from purely religious thinking, even though faith and prayer were still seen as aids to healing. Whereas pre-Greek medicine had used magic, ritual, and herbal potions to promote healing, the historical Greeks began to study empirical evidence based on clinical observation. From around 500 B.C., groups of doctors were practicing on the island of Cos and in Greek areas of western Anatolia.

HIPPOCRATES The best known Greek physician is Hippocrates (*c.* 460–*c.* 377 B.C.), who is called the "Father of Medicine." His name lives on in the Hippocratic Oath, which is taken by contemporary Western physicians before starting to practice medicine. They promise, among other things, to honor their teachers, to do no harm to their patients, and to respect confidentiality. A large body of Hippocratic texts, written by Hippocrates or based on his ideas, still survives. Their focus on observing and describing symptoms laid the foundation for later medical practice. The Hippocratic method of diagnosis reflects the Greek interest in the individual and in empirical inquiry.

In treating serious illness, Hippocrates recommends the following:

> examine the face of the patient, and see whether it is like the faces of healthy people, and especially whether it is like its usual self. Such likeness will be the best sign, and the greatest unlikeness will be the most dangerous sign.

In order to arrive at a diagnosis Hippocrates recommends questioning patients about their symptoms. He says that physicians should find out whether a patient has trouble sleeping or eating. They should also observe whether a patient's eyes are red, the complexion sunken, or the lips white. A bent nose, in the view of Hippocrates, indicates that death is near. When patients with fever grind their teeth and are delirious, according to Hippocrates, madness and death are imminent.

READING SELECTION

Hippocrates, *Hippocratic Writings*, the Oath, PWC1-529

Many Hippocratic texts deal with women and gynecology, but because women did not speak freely with male doctors, the information is less empirical and, therefore, less likely to be accurate than medical texts on other subjects. Greek women were not allowed to study medicine beyond the profession of midwife, but deliveries were performed more often by midwives, mothers, and grandmothers than by male doctors. The dangers of childbirth in historical Greece are clear from the high death rate of women aged sixteen to twenty-six, especially in Athens. Additionally, the social restrictions on Athenian women, who were confined to the house or accompanied by chaperones, were not conducive to healthy exercise.

Some of Hippocrates' views about female health stem from the inferior status of women and the idealization of young men. He asserts, for example, that pregnancy bestows a good complexion on the expectant mother if she is carrying a boy but a bad one if it is a girl. Male fetuses, he says, lean to the right of the uterus and females to the left; this reflects the age-old preference for right over left (consider, for example, the Latin word *sinister*, meaning "left").

Hippocrates differed from Mesopotamian and Egyptian physicians in taking a holistic approach to food. He believed that good health resulted from a proper balance of the four humors. He recommended that people suffering from wounds eat nothing and drink only water and vinegar. Plasters (salves) made from boiled beets, celery, and olive leaves could be applied to wounds, but fats, he said, should be avoided. Barley, millet, and flour are good for all diseases, he maintained, and lentils are indicated if a fever arises after taking a medication. Dry, strong meats help to restore a patient when a disease has subsided, and liquids should be added to the diet slowly.

In general, Hippocrates believed that healthy food and drink taken in small quantities best satisfied hunger and thirst. To build strength, he recommends eating dense flesh, such as pork and beef, because they thicken the blood. Fish, dog, fowl, and rabbit, on the other hand, were considered lighter meats. Best of all for humans, whether sick or healthy, in Hippocrates' view, are wine and honey, provided they are taken in moderation (see Box).

Society and Culture

A Greek Dinner Party: The Menu

The ancient Greeks took eating very seriously. Believing that body and mind are related, they felt that a good diet led to physical health. Phyllis Pray Bober, a modern scholar, has reconstructed a Greek symposium, complete with recipes and a menu based on the Greek ideal of a well-balanced diet.

Guests arrived wearing garlands and wreaths and washed their hands in bowls of scented water. They reclined on couches and were served and entertained (as in the Archaic period; see Chapter 5) by musicians and acrobats. The symposium began with a libation to the gods, but drinking during the main meal was generally restricted to honey water lightly flavored with vinegar; wine was saved for later. Appetizers included lamb meatballs, stuffed figs, toasted walnuts (the "acorns of Zeus") in a honey glaze, sausage, olives, and smoked eel and mackerel.

Lentil was a favorite type of soup (also recommended by Hippocrates). It was flavored with onion, parsnip, olive oil, thyme, and parsley and served with crusty bread. Sow's womb, stuffed with nuts, cracked wheat, calves' brains, onion, sausage, liver, and egg, was served with a balsamic vinaigrette containing olive oil and red wine. Additional meats included squid, whole pig, and hare with date sauces. Among the vegetables were stuffed fig leaves, turnips, cabbage, chard, leeks, artichokes, cucumber, zucchini, radishes, dandelion, nettles, and black-eyed beans.

For dessert, diners had flat cake poached in sweet wine, water, and honey. The top was embellished with fruit, and the cake was baked in the oven; once cooked, it was garnished with almonds. Honey and nut cake was made from almonds, hazelnuts, and walnuts mixed with honey. Generally, cheeses, fruits, and nuts were the dessert staples in ancient Greece.

MUSIC

Very little ancient music has been preserved, although it was an important part of everyday life. The Greeks believed that music had divine origins, and they associated the sun god Apollo with music. Music was thought capable of working miracles, of healing, of purifying, and of transporting listeners into states of ecstasy. Greeks performed religious rituals and recited poetry to music. In addition, music theory was an aspect of Greek philosophy and mathematics.

For the philosopher Pythagoras, music, like the cosmos, was organized according to a mathematical structure. He speaks of the musical **modes**, or scales, each consisting of an **octave** (the span between one note and the next of the same name). Octaves were divided into **tetrachords** of four notes each, with the notes separated by **intervals** (differences in pitch) of either whole or half steps. The feeling of the modes varied according to the order and sequence of its whole-step and half-step intervals. The native Greek Dorian mode, preferred by Plato because it inspired soldiers in battle, was strong and warlike. The more eastern Phrygian and Lydian modes came from Anatolia; the for-mer aroused the passions, and the latter was plaintive. The Mixolydian mode was elegiac.

Despite attempts to reconstruct ancient Greek music, nobody really knows how it sounded. It appears to have been **monophonic**—that is, consisting of a single line of melody. We do know, however, that music was an important part of Greek theater.

GREEK THEATER

Greek theater became a foundation of Western theater. Many Homeric myths and legends, such as the story of Agamemnon and the House of Atreus, were first dramatized in ancient Greece but later found their way into modern plays. Inspired by the rhythms of lyric poetry, Greek actors sang their lines, and music enriched the text. But much more is known about Greek theater than about the music that accompanied it.

In the Classical period, plays were performed throughout Greece, with the most important playwrights centered in Athens. Plays were performed at religious festivals, notably at the Great Dionysia, the festival of Dionysos (the wine god), which was held in Athens every year on March 10, and a prize was awarded for the best trilogy.

The Great Dionysia had evolved from outdoor cult performances in honor of the god. A chorus of singers and dancers performed in a horseshoe-shaped space (the *orchestra*, or

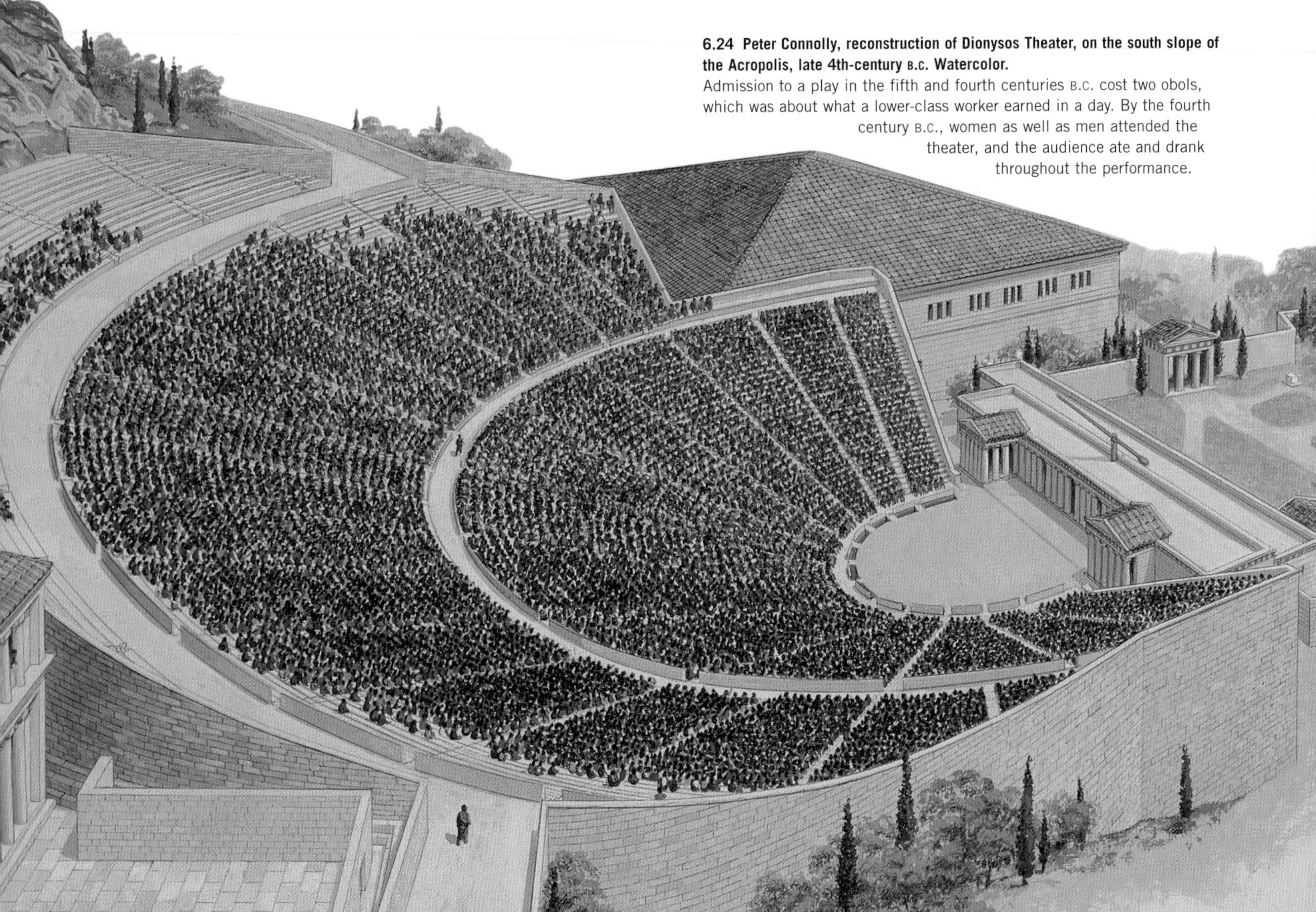

6.24 Peter Connolly, reconstruction of Dionysos Theater, on the south slope of the Acropolis, late 4th-century B.C. Watercolor.
Admission to a play in the fifth and fourth centuries B.C. cost two obols, which was about what a lower-class worker earned in a day. By the fourth century B.C., women as well as men attended the theater, and the audience ate and drank throughout the performance.

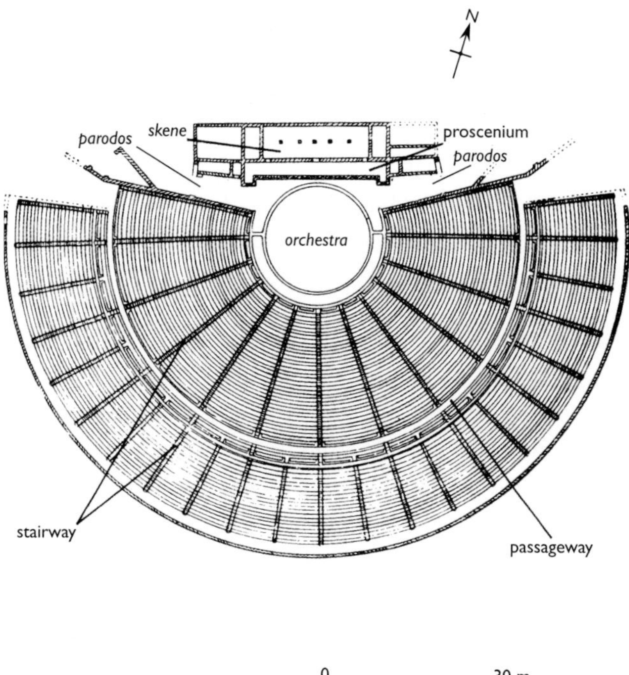

6.25 Plan of the theater at Epidauros, Greece, 4th century B.C.

"dancing place"). At the center of the orchestra stood the god's altar. The theater itself (the *theatron*) was at first merely the slope of a hill and later stone seats were added. This arrangement grew into the modern theater-in-the-round, in which the audience sits around the stage in a semicircle rather than opposite the stage in rows.

The cult of Dionysos inspired the development of theater because, in addition to music, sacrifice, and ritual, it included mythological and heroic narratives. Dionysos was an orgiastic god, and the participants in his rites drank wine to increase their range of emotion and induce states of ecstasy. The rites themselves later became organized into theater and the participants in the rites became the actors.

The earliest festivals of Dionysos were accompanied by a **dithyramb** chorus (a group of actors who performed the dithyramb, a type of lyric poem sung and accompanied by flute music). In the sixth century B.C., according to tradition, the actor Thespis (from whose name derived the word "thespian," meaning "actor") began to converse with the chorus, thus introducing spoken dialogue and essentially inventing theater. Later, two actors and then three took on individual roles, and the chorus, usually representing a group of local townspeople, reacted to events as they unfolded.

Thespis is also credited with having introduced masks, for all Greek actors wore either a tragic or a comic mask, depending on their role. Masks consisted of linen strips glued together, slightly stiffened, and attached to the actor's face. As with Greek sculptures, the masks were painted to produce a lifelike impression. They also disguised the fact that female as well as male roles were performed by men.

Figure **6.24** shows a reconstruction of a typical Greek theater. The large number of seats reflects the importance of the Great Dionysia. Superior acoustics made it possible to hear a pin drop on the stage from every seat. The area behind the orchestra was the *skene* (from which comes the word "scene"), a structure with three entrances, giving the actors access to the orchestra. The plan of the actual surviving theater at Epidauros, on the Greek mainland, is shown in figure **6.25**.

Some time in the early fifth century B.C., a crane-like device was created so that actors playing gods could be lowered onto the stage as if descending from the sky. Called by the Romans a *deus ex machina* ("god from a machine"), the term stuck and now means "out of the blue," referring to something that arrives at the last minute. Today we speak of a *deus ex machina* when a playwright (or film scriptwriter) resolves a plot complication by introducing some entirely unanticipated, and often jarring, element (character or event). In ancient Greek theater, the *deus ex machina* was always a god.

Another feature of Greek theater was the satyr play, from which we get the English word "satire." Satyr plays, which were performed for comic relief, made fun of the main tragedy and its heroic characters. The chorus was composed of satyrs—men with the ears and tail of a horse—who behaved in grotesque or obscene ways. Sometimes Silenus, the obese, drunken, orgiastic father of the satyrs, was also a character in the play. All three of the great Greek tragedians—Aeschylus, Sophocles, and Euripides—wrote satyr plays.

THE TRAGIC PLAYWRIGHTS

Playwrights in ancient Greece wrote tragedies and comedies. The term "tragedy" comes from *tragos*, meaning "one who wears a costume to perform in a ritual of Dionysos." Tragedies were usually written in verse form and dealt with serious, universal themes. The main character is generally a person of importance who falls by virtue of a character flaw. Fate, or destiny, is a crucial aspect of Greek tragedy. In refusing to accept fate, Greek tragic heroes often suffer from **hubris**, a word that denotes arrogant grandiosity.

AESCHYLUS The only surviving work by Aeschylus (c. 525–456 B.C.) is the trilogy, *Oresteia* (see Chapter 4). Aeschylus won his first victory at the Great Dionysia in 468 B.C. and was the leading Greek playwright until his death at the dawn of the High Classical period. His themes emphasize human frailty and its consequences, but his plays generally end on an optimistic note. At the conclusion of the *Oresteia*, Orestes is absolved of his crime by an Athenian court and the favorable vote of Athena, the city's patron goddess. This outcome is a mirror of the moral evolution of the *polis* and is intended to show that Athens is ruled by divine as well as by human justice.

The organization of the *Oresteia* reflects certain Classical ideals and conventions. It avoids violence on the stage by the device of a messenger, who brings news of what has happened off-stage. Thus the audience, like the actors, is told of violent acts, but does not witness them. This allows the playgoers to visualize events for themselves and requires that the author use words to depict events. Aeschylus's success in creating such images comes from the power of his language and the simplicity of Greek tragic form. By restricting the number of actors on stage to two or three, Greek Classical theater intensified emotions in both the characters and the audience.

SOPHOCLES The next great Athenian playwright of the fifth century was Sophocles (*c.* 496–406 B.C.). Only seven of his 123 plays survive, and all deal with heroes who struggle against themselves, against their fate, and against adversity. The story of Oedipus was well known to Greek audiences and is the subject of Sophocles' most famous play, *Oedipus the King*. It is the first of three in a trilogy dealing with the tragic fate of Oedipus. According to an oracle, Oedipus was destined to murder his father, King Laios of Thebes, and marry his mother, Queen Jocasta. To avoid this fate, Oedipus's parents take the infant to the mountains, drive a stake through his foot (Oedipus means "swollen foot"), and leave him to die. But he is discovered and reared by a shepherd and his wife. Later, when Oedipus learns of the oracle, he leaves home to avoid killing the shepherds, whom he believes to be his real parents.

Arriving at a crossroads, Oedipus argues with an older man over who will pass first, and he kills him. He journeys on and reaches the outskirts of Thebes, where a sphinx is terrorizing the countryside. According to Greek myth, the sphinx posed a riddle to all who passed its way: "What walks on four legs in the morning, two legs in the afternoon, and three legs in the evening?" Oedipus gives the correct answer—"Man"—which destroys the sphinx (figure **6.26**). When Oedipus reaches the court of Thebes, he receives the hand of the widowed queen, Jocasta, as a reward for solving the riddle of the sphinx, and becomes king. The play opens after Oedipus has fathered several children with Jocasta and a plague has fallen on the city of Thebes. A blind messenger, Teiresias, informs Oedipus that he has committed parricide and incest and that these crimes are the cause of the plague. At first appalled by the news, Oedipus finally realizes that the man he killed at the crossroads was his own father and that Jocasta is his mother. In a frenzy of guilt, spurred by the climactic discovery of his true identity, Oedipus blinds himself.

Sophocles' play exemplifies the vexing Greek notion that man has free will but is also ruled by fate. Dramatically, this sets up an ironic situation, because the audience understands the meaning of the oracle before the characters do. The **irony** of Oedipus's behavior is that he suffers the very fate he leaves home to avoid. In *Oedipus*, as in Greek tragedy generally, the oracle represents the power of the unconscious mind, whereas free will is conscious choice. Because Oedipus does not understand the hidden meaning of the oracle—that is, because he lacks insight into his unconscious motivation—he is doomed to fulfill its prophecy. The blindness he inflicts on himself is retribution both for his refusal to see the truth and for his crimes. It is the result of his tragic insight (*anagnorisis*) and initiates the **falling action** of the play. At the end of the play, the **resolution** occurs when Oedipus goes into exile, which restores order to Thebes.

In *Antigone* (performed in 442 B.C.), Sophocles deals with the fate of Oedipus's daughter Antigone. After Oedipus goes into exile, his two sons, Eteocles and Polyneices, agree to take turns ruling Thebes, each for a year at a time. But Eteocles refuses to cede the throne to his brother when his year is up, leading Polyneices to form an alliance with an enemy of Thebes. He and Eteocles kill each other in the ensuing civil war. Their uncle Creon becomes king and orders proper funeral rites for Eteocles but not for Polyneices, whom he considers a traitor. Creon decrees that Polyneices' body be left unburied for animals to feed on, thus condemning his shade to wander forever.

Antigone defies her uncle Creon's order and secretly places earth over Polyneices. When Creon discovers that she

6.26 *Oedipus answering the riddle of the sphinx*, interior of a red-figure cup, from Vulci. Vatican Museums, Rome.
The sphinx is tensely perched on an Ionic column as a relaxed Oedipus ponders the riddle. He is shown wearing the hat and boots and carrying the stick of a traveler. The meaning of Oedipus's solution to the riddle is explained as a baby crawling on all fours, an upright adult on two legs, and an old person whose cane is the third leg.

has disobeyed him, he threatens her with death, even though she is engaged to marry his son, Haemon. But no amount of pleading sways Creon. He imprisons Antigone, who hangs herself. When Haemon also commits suicide, Creon repents of his decree and renounces the throne of Thebes.

In this story, Sophocles explores the conflict between Creon's blind tyranny and the rights of the individual, which was an important theme in the early days of the Greek *polis*, especially in Athens. Antigone is determined to obey the laws of the gods, which in her view take precedence over human law. She thus assumes the proportions of a tragic heroine. At the end of the play, Creon, like Oedipus, achieves self-knowledge, which evokes guilt and leads to atonement. He, too, therefore, fulfills the requirements of a tragic hero. Creon is, metaphorically, blinded by his own arrogance and places himself above divine law. He changes only when events force him to recognize his hubris, and insight overcomes his refusal to see.

EURIPIDES In contrast to Sophocles, Euripides (*c.* 485–406 B.C.) explores individual personal feelings. He is also known for his heroic female characters, in whom he juxtaposes extremes of human passion with the intimacy of softer emotions. The moods of his plays vary, often according to aspects of contemporary society he criticizes. In *Medea*, for example, which was produced in 431 B.C., the main character is a foreign enchantress who destroys her own family to rescue and follow the Greek hero Jason. Jason brings Medea to Corinth, where they have two sons. But when Jason decides to take a new wife, the daughter of the king, Medea is consumed with rage and insults the king, who banishes her from his land. Nor is she persuaded by Jason's argument that he loves her, but is marrying the princess only to improve the status and security of his existing family. Medea sends the princess a poisoned robe, which burns her flesh, and kills the king as he tries in vain to save his daughter. Finally, Medea takes revenge by murdering her two young sons to prevent the continuation of Jason's line.

A major theme of *Medea* is the tension between Greeks and foreigners. Medea embodies the Greek view of non-Greeks as irrational and driven by passion rather than by reason. She bemoans her fate as an outsider and a woman, with nowhere to go. As a woman, Medea is also a vehicle for Euripides to comment on Greek misogyny. His views angered a number of his contemporaries, and he later accepted voluntary exile from Athens.

Euripides' last play, *The Bacchae* (produced in 405 B.C.), deals with the power of emotion to engulf and destroy reason, possibly referring to ongoing wars on Greek soil. He increasingly believed that Athenians were unable to think for themselves.

In *The Bacchae*, the legendary Theban king Pentheus mocks Dionysos and his religious cult. The god takes revenge by tricking Pentheus into spying on his female followers (the Bacchae or Maenads), who are in a state of ecstatic frenzy. One of these is Pentheus's own mother, Agave. When she and the other women discover Pentheus, they are deluded into thinking that he is an animal and they tear him to pieces (figure **6.27**). Agave, like Oedipus, is ignorant of her victim's identity until it is too late.

6.27 *Death of Pentheus*, House of the Vettii, Pompeii. Roman painting after a Greek prototype, mid-1st century A.D. 3 ft. 5½ in. (1.05 m) high.
This shows Pentheus kneeling before the frenzied Bacchae as they tear him limb from limb. His mother, at the right, ignores his pleas for mercy and tears out his shoulder.

Euripides' description of the frenzied murder is delivered by a messenger:

> the swiftness of their [the Bacchae's] feet
> Was as of doves in onward-straining race—
> His mother Agave and her sisters twain,
> And all the Bacchanals. Through torrent gorge,
> O'er boulders, leapt they, with the God's breath mad.
>
> . . . .
>
> Agave cried, "Ho, stand we round the trunk,
> Maenads, and grasp, that we may catch the beast
> Crouched there, that he may not proclaim abroad
> Our God's mysterious rites!" Their countless hands
> Set they unto the pine, tore from the soil:—
> And he, high-seated, crashed down from his height;
> And earthward fell with frenzy of shriek on shriek
> Pentheus, for now he knows his doom at hand.
>
> His mother first, priest-like, began the slaughter,
> And fell on him: . . .
> . . . with foaming lips and eyes that rolled
> Wildly, and reckless madness-clouded soul,
> Possessed of Bacchus . . .
> . . . his left arm she clutched in both her hands,

And set against the wretch's ribs her foot,
And tore his shoulder out—not by her strength,
But the God made it easy to her hands.
. . . .
In mangled shreds: with blood-bedabbled hands
Each to and fro was tossing Pentheus' flesh.
. . . His miserable head,
Which in her hands his mother chanced to seize.

(*Bacchae*, lines 1080–1140)

COMEDY

Comic theater originated in the Greek colonies of Sicily, where comic actors roamed the countryside, singing bawdy songs and participating in revels and processions in honor of Dionysos. Comedy (from *komos*, meaning "a light-hearted parade in honor of Dionysos") did not become part of the Great Dionysia until the 480s B.C., when five poets were permitted to compete. Greek comedy combined social, literary, and political satire and buffoonery with aspects of religious ritual.

ARISTOPHANES The most famous of the Greek comic playwrights is Aristophanes (*c.* 445–*c.* 388 B.C.), who makes fun of social and intellectual pretensions. *The Clouds*, produced in 423 B.C., satirizes Socrates and the false arguments of the Sophists. A potential student has the following exchange with his father about Socrates' theory of the gnat:

FATHER: . . . and what said your Master of the gnat?
STUDENT: . . . the entrail of the gnat
Is small: and through this narrow pipe the wind
Rushes with violence straight toward the tail;
There, close against the pipe, the hollow rump
Receives the wind, and whistles to the blast.
FATHER: So then the rump is trumpet to the gnats!
O happy, happy in your entrail-learning!
Full surely need he fear nor debts nor duns,
Who knows about the entrails of the gnats.
STUDENT: And yet last night a mighty thought we lost
Through a green lizard.
FATHER: Tell me, how was that?
STUDENT: Why, as Himself [Socrates], with eyes and mouth wide open,
Mused on the moon, her paths and revolutions,
A lizard from the roof squirted full on him.

(*Clouds*, lines 154–169)

In *The Frogs*, produced in 405 B.C., Aristophanes satirizes the Athenian tradition of dramatic competition. He places Aeschylus and Euripides in Hades, where they compete for the crown of tragedy. Each criticizes the other, but Aeschylus wins because his poetry is weightier—it literally weighs more—than that of Euripides. Aristophanes' chorus is composed of frogs, who sing in the Underworld. Their **onomatopoeic** refrain (in which words sound like the very thing to which they refer), "brekekekax, koax koax," replicates the natural sounds made by croaking frogs. It also reflects the musical basis of choral commentary and conveys some idea of the play's poetic rhythms.

THE PELOPONNESIAN WAR: 431–404 B.C.

Despite remarkable Athenian achievements during the High Classical period, conflicts with other Greek city-states, notably Sparta, arose in the second half of the fifth century B.C. One source of dissatisfaction stemmed from events following the Persian Wars, when Athens established the Delian League (477 B.C.). Sparta and other cities feared the power of the Athenian navy and the city's expansionist political ambitions; Corinth considered Athens a threat to its primacy in commerce and trade. In 431 B.C. the Peloponnesian War broke out between Athens and Sparta.

Pericles led Athens until his death only two years into the war. The best surviving primary source for the Peloponnesian War is the *History* written by the Athenian general Thucydides (460/455–400 B.C.). He fought in the war and contracted the plague, which had broken out in 430 B.C. Unlike Pericles, who died of the plague, Thucydides recovered. One of the most vivid passages in his account of the war is the description of the "plague of Athens." This epidemic entered the city in waves, coming first from Ethiopia, then from Egypt, and finally from the Persian Empire. In all, it killed 4400 hoplites, 300 cavalrymen, and an unknown number of the lower classes. By 427 B.C., one-third of the Athenian population had died and the city was seriously weakened.

Thucydides also recorded Pericles' stirring funeral oration praising Athenian soldiers killed in the fighting. From even the brief passage quoted here, it is clear that Pericles was a great orator and a charismatic leader. Rallying support for the war, Pericles extols the fallen fighters and the city of Athens for which they fought:

> "We live under a form of government," he declares, "which does not emulate the institutions of our neighbors; . . . our government is called a democracy, because its administration is in the hands, not of the few, but of the many; yet while as regards the law all men are on an equality for the settlement of their private disputes."
>
> (Thucydides, *History*, Bk. II. 36)

In addition to Athens being a democracy, in which all men were equal before the law, Pericles points out that the city is beautifully adorned. Games and sacrifices, he says, are provided for relaxation, Athenians are better trained for war than their enemies, and they honor the wisdom of their philosophers. Pericles implores the survivors to honor the dead and to celebrate the freedoms enjoyed in Athens. He argues that Athenians should not fear war, because they have the most to lose if they lose liberty.

Defining Moment

The Classical Ideal and Its Decline: The Peloponnesian War

In the history of Western civilization, one of the major defining periods was the brief moment in which Classical Athens rose to prominence. This period lasted about seventy-five years, from the Greek defeat of Persia in 479 B.C. to the devastation wrought by the Peloponnesian War, 431–404 B.C. The seeds of democracy, which had been sown by certain lawmakers and a general aversion to tyranny in the Archaic period (see Chapter 5), came to fruition in the fifth century B.C.

Athens specifically and the very notion of the *polis* differed from all previously known Mediterranean cultures. Greeks generally opposed kings and tyrants and evolved a political ideal requiring free male citizens to govern themselves. In Athens, this ideal in politics developed alongside vast building programs under the leadership of Pericles that were designed to embody the superiority of Athens. In addition to sculpture and painting, artists strove for the ideal representation of the human figure, especially the male nude (figure **6.28**).

6.28 *Warrior*, from Riace, Italy, 5th century B.C. Bronze with bone, glass paste, silver and copper inlaid, 6 ft. 6¾ in. (2 m) high. Museo Nazionale, Reggio Calabria, Italy.

Eventually, however, other city-states began to resent Athenian power and its abuses of that power. *Poleis* allied themselves either with Sparta, which had a strong land army, or Athens, which had become a naval power. In 431 B.C. these alliances went to war, called "Peloponnesian" after the peninsula forming the southern part of Greece, which was united in a league headed by Sparta. The war strained the financial resources of Athens, which had been supplied by the Delian League. Pericles, in his famous funeral oration, had exhorted Athens to defend its democracy, though nobody could have predicted the length or eventual costs borne by either Athens or Sparta. Unfortunately, Pericles died of plague early in the war and it cannot be known how the outcome might have been different had he lived.

Critical Question What, if any, similarities can you describe between the political situation in fifth-century-B.C. Athens and the United States today?

READING SELECTION

Thucydides, *History of the Peloponnesian War*: Pericles' funeral oration and the plague, PWC1-066-B; Pericles' last speech, PWC1-067-A

One of the most entertaining antiwar works of literature dates to 411 B.C., twenty years into the Peloponnesian War. Written by Aristophanes, *Lysistrata* is about women who rebel against war by witholding sexual favors from their husbands. The main character, Lysistrata, instructs the women of Sparta and Athens to join in the following oath:

I will abstain from Love and Love's delights.
And take no pleasure though my lord invites.
And sleep a vestal [i.e., a virgin] all alone at nights.
. . . .
I will abjure the very name of Love.
So help me Zeus, and all the powers above.
If I do this, my cup be filled with wine.
But if I fail, a water draught be mine.

(*Lysistrata*, lines 213–228)

The women persist in their plan and eventually take over the Acropolis, effecting a humorous exchange of male and female roles. At the end of the play, once an agreement is in place, Athenians and Spartans dance to celebrate the peace.

In reality, however, Sparta defeated Athens in 404 B.C., and Athens lost its political and military power. However, this did not end Athenian supremacy in the arts, literature, and philosophy. After the war, new styles began to develop in the visual arts and fresh philosophical ideas emerged. The period following the Peloponnesian War, which occupied most of the fourth century B.C., is termed Late Classical.

THE LATE CLASSICAL PERIOD: *c.* 400–323 B.C.

Before the middle of the fourth century B.C., the powerful king of Macedon (north of Greece), Philip II (ruled 359–336 B.C.), rose to power. He quelled decades of political conflict, improved weaponry, disciplined the army, and instituted reforms that unified Macedon. By 338 B.C. Philip controlled most of Greece and had advanced to the Black Sea. In 337 B.C., he established the League of Corinth, an alliance designed to maintain Greek unity and prepare for an invasion of Persia. By this tactic, Philip projected his image as the legitimate ruler and defender of Greece.

Philip was assassinated in 336 B.C., at least in part because of an unpopular seventh marriage. He was succeeded by his son Alexander (356–323 B.C.), then nineteen years old (see Box). With a large army and new weapons, Alexander went on to conquer most of the known world, including Greece, Egypt, Mesopotamia, and the Persian Empire as far as the Punjab region of modern India. He had at his disposition 37,000 troops, 3000 royal guards, 1800 cavalry, a Greek army 9000 strong, and a fleet of nearly 200 ships (see Box).

Society and Culture

The Myth of Alexander's Birth

Alexander's mother, Olympias, was a foreigner, known in Greece for her violent and ambitious character. A worshipper in the cult of Dionysos, Olympias participated in the ecstatic frenzies of the Bacchantes. She kept pet snakes, which, as symbols of the earth, were used in the Dionysian nature cult. Olympias herself used the snakes in rites designed by women to frighten men.

When Philip II took a new wife, Alexander quarreled with him and left the court with his mother. When Philip's new wife gave birth to a son, Alexander's status as heir to the throne of Macedon was in jeopardy. Philip's assassination and the subsequent murder of his infant son were fortuitous for Olympias and Alexander, although their responsibility for these deeds has never been established.

In order to reaffirm her own relationship to Greece and Alexander's inheritance, Olympias traced her ancestors to Achilles and Helen of Troy. She wove mythical accounts of Alexander's birth, which were designed to legitimize his kingship and distance him from Philip. Olympias spread the rumor that when she became pregnant, her womb was sealed with a lion's mark, ensuring that Alexander would have the courage of a lion. She also claimed that she had been impregnated by Zeus's thunderbolt, which meant that Alexander was the son of the god rather than of Philip. This enabled Alexander, like many of the Homeric heroes, to boast a divine parentage.

Society and Culture

Warfare Technology and Science

The development of new weaponry and military engineering increased Philip of Macedon's power and that of his successors. Under Alexander, engineers devised mobile siege towers and long-distance catapults. Later engineers improved the accuracy of missiles by calculating the relationship of their weight to their range.

Hellenistic science was less innovative than its technology, but there were a few important scientists, notably Euclid (active *c.* 300 B.C.) and Archimedes (*c.* 287–212 B.C.). Euclid developed plane geometry in his *Elements.* He codified and systematized proofs and the form of reasoning in which a proof is logically deduced from a series of axioms. Archimedes wrote on the circle, the sphere, and the cylinder, and invented the compound pulley. The so-called Screw of Archimedes enabled water in irrigation canals to be raised for use on higher ground.

The Battle of Issos, in northern Syria, at which Alexander defeated the armies of the Persian king, Darius III, in 333 B.C., is memorialized in a Roman **mosaic** thought to be a copy of an original Greek painting of around 300 B.C. (figure **6.29**). The Greek conqueror is shown launching a frontal attack at the center of Darius's troops at the turning point of the battle. Darius wears a Persian helmet and towers over the fray as his charioteer attempts a retreat. Alexander, his breastplate decorated with a gorgoneion, charges in from the upper left on a powerful war horse. He raises his long Macedonian spear, which pierces a Persian soldier. This image of Alexander, as an energetic young man with flowing hair, became a model for portraits of rulers in Western art.

The Issos mosaic exemplifies the Greek interest in creating lifelike figures and natural, three-dimensional space. Shading and cast shadows reflect the fact that form in nature is made visible by shifts in light and dark. The rumps of the horses appear rounded as the lighter areas gradually shift to darker ones. Several figures, as well as horses, are **foreshortened** (shown in perspective)—that is, we see them as if they move spatially from front to back rather than from side to side. Note that the frame design is **illusionistic**—that is, it creates the illusion of three-dimensional geometric shapes, even though it is flat.

In addition to these formal techniques, the artist shows the psychological intensity of battle. In the foreground, a Persian watches himself die in the mirror reflection of his convex shield. The horses are visibly frightened and in disarray, and the anguished expressions of Darius and his men indicate their awareness of defeat. The artist thus evokes sympathy with the panic of the defeated Persians as well as admiration for the heroic Greek victory.

6.29 *The Battle of Issos*, from the House of the Faun, Pompeii, 1st century B.C. Mosaic, 8 ft. 10¾ in. × 16 ft. 9⅓ in. (2.71 × 5.12 m). Archaeological Museum, Naples.
A mosaic is an arrangement of small, colored stones or tiles called *tesserae*, which are embedded into a flat surface. In this example, the arrangement of the stones was termed "worm work" because they form curves similar to those made by crawling worms.

Alexander's vast empire (map **6.1**) reached to the western border of India. This laid the foundation for a period of Hellenization, a process by which Greek culture spread throughout the Mediterranean world and Greek became the dominant language. At the same time, however, cross-cultural influences in politics, religion, and the arts led to new developments and widespread assimilation (see Box, p. 134). The death of Alexander in Babylon, in 323 B.C., marks the beginning of the Hellenistic period.

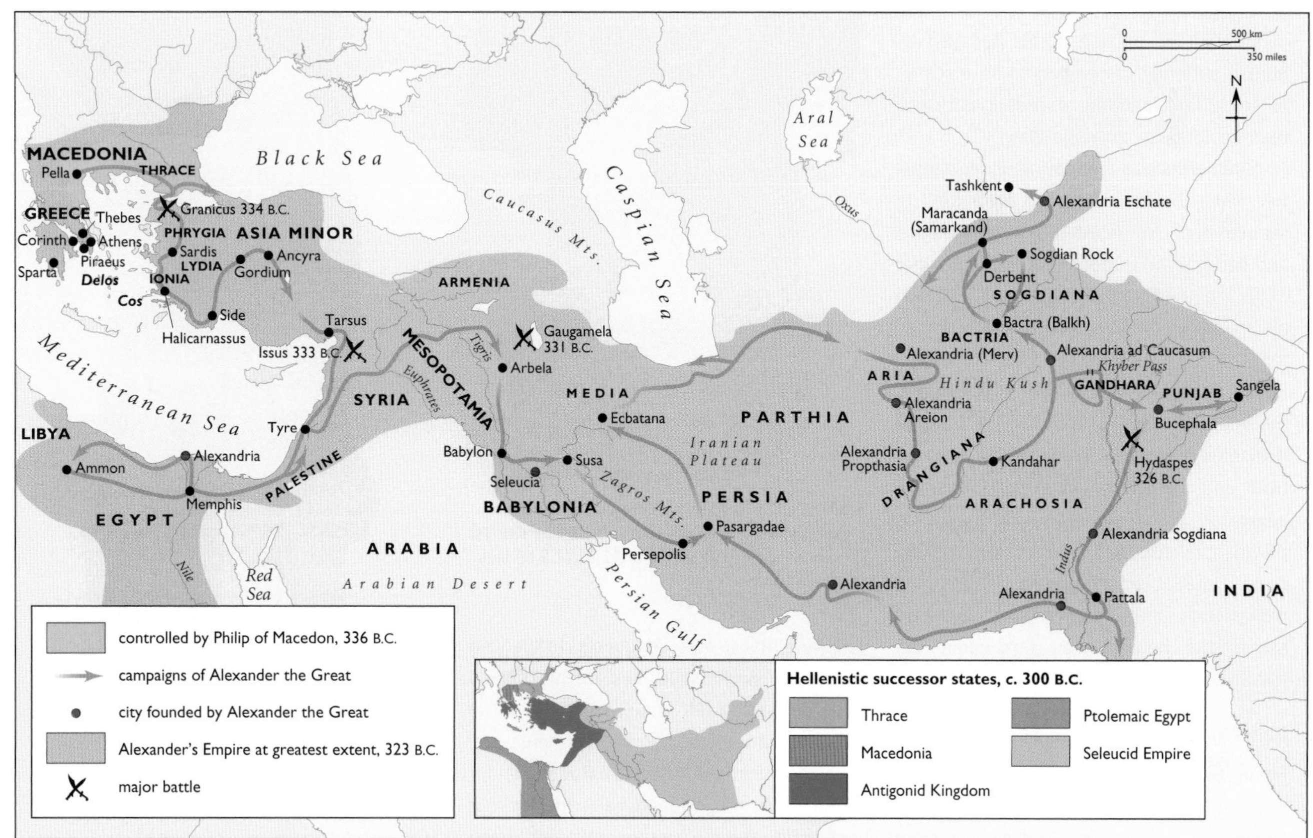

Map 6.1 Alexander's Empire, 323 B.C.

Cross-cultural Influences

Hellenism and the Far East

As Alexander the Great conquered the world, he spread Greek culture (Hellenism) to the Indian subcontinent (see map 6.1). Before turning back, Alexander founded the city of Karachi, now in Pakistan. Some of his soldiers remained in Bactria (parts of modern Afghanistan and Pakistan), located between the Hindu Kush and the Oxus River, which flows into the Aral Sea. Throughout the regions Alexander conquered, there is evidence of Greek art and architecture, but the clearest instance of Greek stylistic influence is found in the Buddhist art of Gandhara, across the Khyber Pass just north of the Indus River.

Siddhartha and the Origin of Buddhism

Buddhism, one of the world's great religions, arose in the region of modern Nepal. The sixth-century-B.C. prince Siddhartha Gautama (*c.* 563–483 B.C.), whose father was head of the Shakya clan, was raised in courtly luxury. But, at the age of twenty-nine, Siddhartha left the palace grounds and confronted the outside world. Appalled by human suffering, he embarked on a search for truth, first following an ascetic path and then deciding on a Middle Way.

Siddhartha was meditating under a pipal tree when the female demon Mara tried to seduce him. He resisted her temptations and became the Buddha. For the remainder of his life, the Buddha pursued a life of self-discipline, meditation, and quest for knowledge. He preached his first sermon in the Deer Park at Sarnath, which set in motion the Buddhist Wheel of the Law. The Buddha dedicated himself to the pursuit of spiritual truth and the alleviation of social ills. He advocated enlightenment as a means of providing release from reincarnation, making *nirvana* available to everyone. He founded monasteries and his missionary followers spread the new religion throughout the Far East.

Gandharan and Mathuran Sculpture

Figure **6.30** illustrates the impact of Hellenism on Far Eastern art. It shows a standing Buddha in a style prevalent in Gandhara following Alexander's conquests. Influenced by the Classical style, the deeply carved folds define the left knee, and the head is depicted naturalistically. The garments and pose, however, are distinctly Buddhist—for example, the large round halo, the topknot (*ushnisha*), and the gesture of the right hand (which is now missing). The Buddha's plain robe and lack of ornamentation signify his renunciation of the material world.

6.30 ***Standing Buddha*, from the Bactro-Gandhara region, Pakistan, Kusana period, 1st century B.C.–1st century A.D. Schist, approx. 4 ft. 11 in. (1.5 m) high. Lahore Museum.**

The Mathuran style, in contrast to the Gandharan, shows no evidence of Western Classical influence. Enormous figures of the Buddha from Mathura (between modern New Delhi and Agra, in India) convey a sense of monumental, otherworldly power (figure **6.31**). The imposing Mathuran Buddha has broad shoulders, little open space, and flat patterned drapery curves. Its rigid pose and aloof character are quite distinct from the more three-dimensional naturalism of Gandharan sculpture.

6.31 ***Standing Buddha*, from Sarnath, *c.* A.D. 100. Red sandstone, 8 ft. 10¼ in. (2.70 m) high. Sarnath Museum.**

READING SELECTION

Arrian, *Campaigns of Alexander*: cutting the Gordian Knot, PWC1-022; conquering an Indian army fighting with elephants, PWC1-023

After the Peloponnesian War and the conquests of Philip II and Alexander the Great, Athens was no longer the dominant military power in Greece. In philosophy and the arts, however, Athens retained its preeminent position. Styles of painting and sculpture became more illusionistic and emotional: the idealization of the young male hero began to wane as new, more specific types of representation evolved. The greatest fourth-century-B.C. philosopher was Aristotle, who wrote on a wide variety of topics, including the theater.

ARISTOTLE

Aristotle (384–322 B.C.) was born in Stagira, Macedonia, and moved to Athens to study with Plato. In 343 B.C. Aristotle left Athens for the Macedonian court of Philip II, where he became tutor to Alexander until Alexander came to power in 336 B.C. Aristotle then returned to Athens and founded the Lyceum, a school of philosophical studies based on his own, rather than on Plato's, ideas.

Unlike Plato, who believed in an immaterial realm of ideas, Aristotle was an empiricist. He believed that an idea and the thing to which the idea refers were one and the same. For Aristotle, nature and the physical world, including human experience, constituted reality. He discusses his quarrel with Plato's ideal realm primarily in the *Metaphysics*. In other works, Aristotle systematizes the study of nature by classifying and describing what can be observed. His writings include such topics as ethics, politics, rhetoric, logic, and science.

In the *Politics* and the *Ethics* (also called the *Nicomachean Ethics*), Aristotle sets out the ethical aspects of his political theory. In the *Ethics*, he argues that the aim of all conduct is the Good, which is a state of happiness, and that the greatest happiness lies in contemplating philosophical truth. He opens the *Ethics* as follows:

> Every art and every investigation, and likewise every practical pursuit or undertaking, seems to aim at some good: hence it has been well said that the Good is that at which all things aim.
>
> (*Ethics*, I, i)

The *Politics*, in which Aristotle famously calls man a "political animal," focuses on the city-state, its development, its citizens, and its constitution. For Aristotle the *polis* should be ruled not by the rich or the many, but by the good. He concludes that monarchy is the ideal political system, as long as the ruler is a good one. If there is no such ruler, Aristotle recommends government by an aristocracy of virtuous citizens. However, given the reality of contemporary Greece and its aversion to tyranny, Aristotle admits that the political system closest to the Good is a relative democracy.

READING SELECTION

Aristotle: *Politics*, on the political animal, PWC1-505-B; *Poetics*, comparing the epic with tragedy, PWC1-014

Aristotle codifies the rules of tragedy in the *Poetics*, and he takes the example of Sophocles' *Oedipus* as a model. The basic elements of Greek tragedy, according to Aristotle, are unity of action, place, and time. This means that the action unfolds in a single location and that it is a continuous narrative within a short space of time. In addition, the personalities of the characters should be consistent with their behavior. Aristotle insists on the importance of language and plot: a plot should stand on its own as a powerful narrative, so that even without seeing the play readers would be affected by the story.

These requirements are met in the *Oedipus*. The action unfolds in Thebes within a brief period, and past events are reported by the characters. The messenger who informs Oedipus that he is the cause of the Theban plague is the seer Teiresias, whose physical blindness ironically highlights the psychological blindness of Oedipus and also foreshadows Oedipus's act of self-blinding. Oedipus is consistent in his willful refusal to see, whereas Teiresias, although blind, never fails to see clearly.

Aristotle states that tragic characters must be larger than life, just as the portrait-painter conveys a likeness:

> Since tragedy is a representation of men better than ourselves we must copy the good portrait-painters who, while rendering the distinctive form and making a likeness, yet paint people better than they are. It is the same with the poet. When representing people who are hot-tempered or lazy, or have other such traits of character, he should make them such, yet men of worth.
>
> (*Poetics*, xv, 15)

In other words, Greek tragic heroes are complex and neither perfectly virtuous nor entirely evil. They are generally the victim of a **tragic flaw**, which plunges them from a high station in life into misfortune. In *Oedipus*, the tragic flaw is the hero's *hubris* (grandiose pride), which convinces him of his ability to outwit fate. In attempting to avoid his fate rather than understand it, Oedipus inevitably brings it about. Once he comprehends what he has done, he undergoes a **catharsis** (literally an emotional "cleansing")—that is, he experiences fully his own responsibility for his actions and their consequences. He then works through his guilt and accepts the power of fate, which resolves the tragedy. The viewers of the play also experience a catharsis so that they, as well as the hero, gain insight into the human condition.

PAINTING AND SCULPTURE

In the fourth century B.C., the Greek interest in lifelike representation increased. Artists expanded the range of emotion, age, and character in their paintings and sculptures. With this expansion of types, the idealized male youth gave way to greater variety, and comic scenes appeared more frequently than before.

A Late Classical bell-krater of around 340 B.C. depicts the birth of Helen of Troy (figure **6.32**) in a humorous way. It shows a miniature nude Helen emerging like a movie starlet from a large egg as her mother and mortal father look on. She is no longer either a heroine of epic proportions or an ideal Classical figure.

If the Late Classical *Aphrodite of Knidos* (figure **6.33**) is compared with the *Spearbearer* (see figure 6.22), it is clear that the proportions have changed in the later work. Aphrodite is fleshier than Polykleitos's youth—her neck and waist are thicker—and her contrapposto (the shift at the waist) is slightly more pronounced. She stands by a *hydria* (water jar) and grasps her garment, to cover her nudity as if suddenly aware that she is being observed.

Praxiteles was the first Greek artist who consistently portrayed the female nude. This particular example was rejected by the Greeks, who commissioned it, as being overly erotic and it was purchased instead by the Knidians, the inhabitants of the island of Knidos, in Ionia. They built a temple for the statue, which attracted many admirers. Some men were reported to have hidden in the precinct so that they could spend the night with the statue.

6.33 Praxiteles, *Aphrodite of Knidos*, *c.* 350 B.C. Marble, 6 ft. 8¾ in. (2.05 m) high. Vatican Museums, Rome.
According to the first-century A.D. Roman author Pliny the Elder, this statue was equally beautiful from all points of view and made Knidos famous. He relates the tale of a man who fell in love with the statue and embraced it. His act of passion was betrayed by a lustful stain left on the marble.

6.32 Caivano painter, *Birth of Helen*, red-figure bell-krater, from Campania, southern Italy, *c.* 340 B.C. National Museum, Naples.
According to Greek myth, Helen was the daughter of Zeus-disguised-as-a-swan and the mortal woman, Leda. The egg is thus the egg of a swan, hence its size. Leda's mortal husband was Tyndareus, whose stepdaughter was sought after by so many suitors that he feared the anger of those who would be rejected. Odysseus proposed that Tyndareus leave the decision to Helen, provided that all the suitors swore to avenge any affront to her chosen husband. They all agreed, and Helen picked Menelaus, the wealthy king of Sparta and Agamemnon's brother.

THE HELLENISTIC WORLD: 323 TO FIRST CENTURY B.C.

Alexander's untimely death at the age of about thirty-three left no obvious heir to rule his empire. At the beginning of the Hellenistic period, the empire was divided into three main areas by Alexander's generals: the Ptolemaic dynasty (which originated with Ptolemy I) ruled Egypt, the Seleucids (founded by Alexander's officer Seleucus I) ruled Persia, and Antigonus, called the One-Eyed, ruled Greece.

Throughout Greece, the *polis* gave way to kingship and small towns and cities became international urban centers. These benefited economically and were enriched culturally by thriving trade with the east, Africa, and Italy. Social divisions, ranging from royalty to an ever-increasing slave population, became more pronounced as the ideal of democracy faded. Women, on the other hand, especially in the upper classes, were accorded more social and economic freedom than they had enjoyed in Classical Athens.

In theater, tragedy ceased to be a popular form of entertainment. It was replaced by so-called New Comedy—usually light romances designed to distract audiences from the tensions of urban life.

Two main centers of Hellenistic culture were Alexandria, in Egypt, and Pergamon, on the west coast of modern Turkey. Alexandria was founded by Alexander the Great, after whom the city was named, and Pergamon adopted Classical styles and traditions. The latter city rose to power after its king, Attalos I (ruled 241–197 B.C.), vanquished the barbarian Gauls (in modern France and the Low Countries), who invaded in 238 B.C.

With an increase in literacy and developments in science, two huge libraries were established in Alexandria and Pergamon. The Pergamon library, rivaling that of Alexandria, housed some 200,000 texts written on calf-skin parchment ("pergamene paper"). In Alexandria, the Ptolemies encouraged scholars, scientists, physicians, and poets by building the Museum (Temple of the Muses), an institution dedicated to research. In conjunction with the Museum, Alexandria boasted the Great Library, which housed 700,000 papyrus manuscripts. The library's aim was to acquire every known Greek text.

MYSTERY CULTS

One source of Eastern influence in the Hellenistic world was the expansion of mystery cults. The Greeks had had mystery cults at Eleusis and Samothrace, as well as the cult of Dionysos, since the Bronze Age. In contrast to Olympian religion, however, these cults had a mystical flavor, practicing magic to protect against evil and performing secret rites. By the later fourth century B.C., aspects of Eastern religions began to infiltrate Greece.

Cults involving astrology came from Babylon, Zoroastrianism (see Chapter 2) came from Persia, and the pre-Greek belief in a Great Goddess began to be revived. The Egyptian mother-goddess, Isis, was worshipped first at Delos and later throughout the Mediterranean. Her role in the resurrection of Osiris (see Chapter 3) appealed to the new interest in life after death. The enormous attraction of immortality increased the power of such cults and later influenced the spread of early Christianity.

PHILOSOPHY IN THE HELLENISTIC PERIOD

Encouraged by wealthy and powerful rulers, Hellenistic philosophy flourished, although it has not exerted as strong an impact on Western thought as that of the Classical and Late Classical philosophers. Nevertheless, Hellenistic philosophers were influential later, especially during the Roman period. Terms used to describe Hellenistic schools of philosophy—Cynicism, Skepticism, Epicureanism, and Stoicism—live on in modern English nouns and adjectives. All denote ways of viewing human life.

The Cynics valued independence from desire and materialism, and they rejected religious and political institutions. In the view of the Cynics, traditional values of civilization were worthless. The most famous Cynic was Diogenes (*c.* 404–325 B.C.), who was known for public displays of vulgar behavior. He reportedly carried a lantern through the streets of Athens in search of an honest man. Today, we call someone a cynic if he or she tends to believe the worst about people, just as Diogenes thought he would never find the honest man.

The Skeptics questioned the basis for all conclusions, hence the English word "skeptical." They challenged the findings of science and prevailing philosophical ideas and argued that these disciplines could not furnish adequate explanations of reality. Because there is no certainty, according to the Skeptics, reality is relative and absolute judgments should be avoided.

In contrast to the Skeptics, the Stoics and the Epicureans did believe in certainty and were convinced of their respective approaches to life. Both were essentially materialists. The Stoics believed that universal reason, the *logos* (or "word" of God), determined the order of life. Thus, the ideal Stoic was disciplined and prepared to accept any fate. Epicureanism is named for Epicurus (341–271 B.C.), who advocated a calm mind, a healthy body, and a proper attitude toward the gods and death. Epicureans believed that sensory experience was superior to the intellect, that the gods were indifferent to humans, and that death was nothing more than a rearrangement of the body's atoms. As a result, since it is impossible to know the future, Epicureans devoted their lives to pleasure in the present.

HELLENISTIC POETRY

The main Hellenistic contributions to poetry were the **pastoral** (a poem dealing with the life and loves of shepherds) and the **idyll** (a short descriptive poem describing rural life). These poetic types were developed by Theocritus (*c.* 310–250 B.C.), a native of Syracuse, in Sicily, who wrote in hexameter verse (lines of six metrical feet). His pastorals describe the bucolic life and romances of rural dwellers, and his idylls create concise images of daily life and mythological tales. Theocritus's subject matter and poetic rhythms inspired the English Romantic poets in the eighteenth and nineteenth centuries (see Chapter 18).

In *Idyll* XI, entitled "The Cyclops," the one-eyed giant Polyphemus is a youth in love with the beautiful Galatea. Blinded by Odysseus (see Chapter 4), the Cyclops sits on a rock and finds consolation in music and song. Woefully aware of his ugly appearance, Polyphemus woos Galatea with his skill as a shepherd, feeding his sheep, making cheese, and producing the best milk in the land:

O Galatea fair and white, white as curds in whey,
Dapper as a lamb a-frisking, wanton as calf at play,
And plump o' shape as ruddying grape, O why deny thy lover?
. . . .
I've loved ye true; but Lord! to you my love as nothing is.
O well I wot pretty maid, pretty maid, for why thou shun'st me so,
One long shag eyebrow ear to ear my forehead o'er doth go,
And but one eye beneath doth lie, and the nose stands wide on the lip;
Yet be as I may, still this I say, I feed full a thousand sheep,
And the milk to my hand's the best i' the land, and my cheese 'tis plenty also;
Come summer mild, come winter wild, my cheese-racks ever o'erflow.
And, for piping, none o' my kin hereby can pipe like my piping,
And of thee and me, dear sweet-apple, in one song oft I sing,
Often at dead of night.

(Theocritus, "The Cyclops")

In *Pastoral* I, the shepherd Thyrsis sings of Daphnis, another shepherd, who died of love. In the section cited here, Thyrsis complains that the wood nymphs ignored Daphnis:

Country-song, sing country-song, *sweet Muses.*
'Tis Thyrsis sings, of Etna, and a rare sweet voice hath he.
Where were ye, Nymphs, when Daphnis pined? ye Nymphs, O where were ye?
. . . .
When Daphnis died the foxes wailed and the wolves they wailed full sore,
The lion from the greenwood wept when Daphnis was no more.

(Theocritus, *Pastoral* I)

DEVELOPMENTS IN ARTISTIC STYLE

In the visual arts, the Hellenistic period brought about a further increase in the range of age, subject, and personality types. In Hellenistic sculpture and painting, figures move with increasing freedom as the space opens and expands. Hellenistic artists rejected Classical symmetry and created a greater variety of pose and gesture.

Compare, for example, the Hellenistic *Drunken Old Woman* (figure **6.34**) with the mid-second-century-B.C. *Aphrodite of Melos* (figure **6.35**). The former clutches a jug of wine and rolls her head backward in a stupor. Gone are all traces of Classical idealization, as wrinkles pattern the aged face. The figure evokes the belief in the Dionysian promise of immortality, which is indicated by the ivy (an attribute of the wine god) on the jug. The woman's drunken state signifies the experience of ecstasy in the afterlife.

6.34 *above* ***Drunken Old Woman,*** **late 3rd century B.C. Marble, 3 ft. (92 cm) high. Glyptothek, Munich.**

6.35 *right* ***Aphrodite of Melos, c.*** **150 B.C. Marble, 6 ft. 8¼ in. (2.04 m) high. Louvre, Paris.**

The *Aphrodite of Melos* retains idealized, although not Classical, form. Her youthful figure flows into an elegant S-shaped curve, and the smooth flesh merges gracefully into her garment. In contrast to the sense of weight conveyed by the old woman firmly planted on the ground, the Aphrodite swivels as if in continuous motion.

The Greek sculpture in which motion assumes its most powerful

6.36 *above* **Agesander, Athenodorus, and Polydorus of Rhodes, *Laocoön Group*, early 1st century A.D. Marble, 7 ft. 10½ in. (2.44 m) high. Vatican Museums, Rome.** Carved on the island of Rhodes, which was a major center of culture in the second century B.C., this sculpture disappeared in the fifth century A.D. and was rediscovered only in the sixteenth century. It was excavated in Rome and made a forceful impression on Michelangelo. The *Laocoön* influenced Western art and aesthetic theory for centuries to come.

emotional character is the Late Hellenistic *Laocoön Group* (figure **6.36**), which illustrates an event from the end of the Trojan War that is related in the *Odyssey*. Laocoön was a Trojan seer (prophet) who warned his fellow citizens not to admit the great wooden horse, which was filled with Greek soldiers, past the gates of Troy. When the gods sent huge serpents from the sea to devour Laocoön and his two sons, the Trojans concluded that Laocoön must be mistaken. They opened the gates to admit the horse, and the Greeks sacked Troy. In the statue, the curvilinear serpents weave among the human figures, strangling and biting them. In their struggle to escape, Laocoön and his sons echo the winding serpentine forms and grimace in pain.

In painting, as in sculpture, Hellenistic style increases formal movement as it turns away from Classical idealization. The wall painting depicting the centaur Chiron instructing Achilles on the lyre (figure **6.37**) shows the continuing taste for illusionism in the background architecture. Similarly, the use of shading, instead of line, to create form conveys the impression of the figures' three-dimensional volume. In the foreground, the rather uncomfortable-looking centaur tries to accommodate his horse part as he demonstrates on the strings of a lyre. Achilles does not conform to the proportional canon of Polykleitos, but his pose resembles that of the *Spearbearer* (see figure 6.22).

In accord with the large-scale political ambitions of rulers, Hellenistic architecture is generally monumental. One example of Hellenistic grandeur is the Great Altar at Pergamon, a section of which is illustrated in figure **6.38**. Constructed in the early second century B.C. under the ruler

6.37 *below* ***Chiron Instructs Achilles in Playing the Lyre*, from the Basilica, Herculaneum, 1st century A.D. Roman copy of a Hellenistic fresco. National Museum, Naples.**

6.38 North projection of the Pergamon Altar, *c.* 180/160 B.C. Marble, frieze 7 ft. 6½ in. (2.30 m) high. Pergamon Museum, Berlin.

6.39 Olympeium, Athens, reconstructed 2nd century B.C. Marble, 354 × 135 ft. (108 × 41.1 m); columns 55 ft. 5 in. (16.9 m) high.

Eumenes II (ruled 197–*c.* 160 B.C.), the altar celebrated the triumph of Greek civilization. Its vivid frieze, in which the Olympian gods battle the Titans, shares with the *Laocoön* a taste for violent struggle. The depiction of the battle was a metaphor for the recent defeat of the Gauls by the king of Pergamon, but it also alluded to the Greek victory over the Persians, which had remained in the cultural consciousness of Greece for centuries.

In temple architecture, too, scale increased and buildings became monumental. At the same time, the last of the three main Greek architectural Orders, the Corinthian, originally used only for interiors, now appeared on exterior columns. This more ornate Order had **foliate** (leaf-shaped) capitals, whose decorative qualities relieved the massive scale of Hellenistic temples.

In Athens, in the mid-second century B.C., the Seleucid ruler Antiochus IV (ruled 175–164 B.C.) commissioned the first use of the Corinthian Order in a large-scale building in the reconstruction of the Olympeium, a temple dedicated to Zeus. Originally a Doric temple built in the Archaic period (figure **6.39**), the surviving remains belong to a later reconstruction. The Olympeium today has only thirteen columns left, but even in its ruined state the monumentality of the temple is impressive.

Alexander's conquests bequeathed to the Hellenistic period a melting pot of cultural ideas and forms. Because of the new political climate in which kings held sway and democracies waned, the arts were used in the service of power. In 146 B.C., the Romans conquered Corinth and subordinated Greece to Roman rule. By 100 B.C., Greece was a province of Rome and in 86 B.C. the Romans sacked Athens. At the same time, however, Greek culture continued to exert an enormous influence on Rome and its vast empire, which are the subjects of the next chapter.

KEY TERMS

caryatid a supporting column carved to represent a woman; the male equivalent is an *atlantis* (plural *atlantes*).

catharsis "cleansing"; a term used by Aristotle to describe the emotional effect of a tragic drama on the audience.

colonnade a row of columns.

contrapposto a type of pose characterized by a twist at the waist.

deme a unit of local government.

dithyramb a type of lyric poem sung and accompanied by flute music.

falling action the means by which a complication in a literary work is unraveled and resolved.

foliate leaf-shaped.

foreshortened shown in perspective.

hubris arrogant grandiosity, often characterizing Greek tragic heroes.

idyll a short descriptive poem describing rural life.

illusionistic a type of representation in which objects appear real.

interval in music, a difference in pitch between two notes.

irony a literary device in which the implication of the words is the opposite of their literal meaning.

isocephaly the horizontal alignment of heads in a painting or sculpture.

mode in ancient music, an arrangement of notes forming a scale; Dorian mode: strong and military; Phrygian mode: passionate; Lydian mode: mournful; Mixolydian mode: elegiac.

monophonic consisting of a single line of music.

mosaic an image on a wall, ceiling, or floor created from small pieces of colored tile, glass, or stone.

octave in music, the interval between two notes of the same name, twelve semitones apart; in poetry, a stanza of eight lines.

ode a lyric poem.

onomatopoeic the use of words that sound like the objects to which they refer.

paradox a statement that seems to contradict common sense.

pastoral a poem dealing with the life and loves of shepherds.

program in art, a series of related images.

proportion the relation of one part to another and of parts to the whole in terms of scale.

resolution the outcome of a literary narrative.

rhetoric the art of eloquent argument.

tetrachord a series of four notes, with the first and last separated by the interval of a perfect fourth.

tragic flaw in theater, a characteristic of a hero that causes his or her downfall.

KEY QUESTIONS

1. Discuss the myths narrated in scenes on the Parthenon sculptures and their cultural meaning.
2. What theory of Empedocles prefigured Darwin's theory of evolution? What theory of Democritus prefigured atomic theory? Are these philosophers important because they are forerunners of modern thought or for other reasons?
3. What qualities did Plato wish to find in an ideal state (as outlined in his *Republic*)? Would his ideal state be a democracy?
4. What Classical ideals are seen in the *Oresteia*?
5. Compare two works of sculpture that show the differences between the Classical and Hellenistic ideals.

SUGGESTED READING

Bober, Phyllis Pray. *Art, Culture, and Cuisine. Ancient and Medieval Gastronomy*. Chicago and London: University of Chicago Press, 1999.
- A survey of feasts and menus from antiquity to the Middle Ages.

Carpenter, T. H. *Art and Myth in Ancient Greece*. London: Thames and Hudson, 1998.
- A general survey of Greek art and mythology.

Connolly, Peter, and Hazel Dodge. *The Ancient City*. Oxford and New York: Oxford University Press, 1998.
- Ancient architecture illustrated with clear, colorful reconstructions of ancient buildings in context.

Fox, Robin Lane. *Alexander the Great*. London: Allen Lane, 1973.
- A biography of Alexander the Great.

Hartnoll, Phyllis, *The Theater*. New York and London: Thames and Hudson, 1998.
- A brief history of the theater from Greek and Roman times to the present.

Kagan, Donald. *The Outbreak of the Peloponnesian War*. Ithaca, NY: Cornell University Press, 1994.
- A classic study of the causes of the Peloponnesian War.

——. *The Peloponnesian War*. New York: HarperCollins, 2003.
- A one-volume version of the author's standard four-volume study of the war.

Plato. *Apology*, in *Dialogues of Plato*, trans. B. Jowett. New York: Random House, 1932.
- Plato's account of Socrates' defense against the charge that he corrupted the youth of Athens.

Pomeroy, Sarah B. *Women in Hellenistic Egypt: From Alexander to Cleopatra*. New York: Schocken Books, 1988.
- An account of the role of women in the Hellenistic period.

Renault, Mary. *The Mask of Apollo*. New York: Longmans Green, 1966.
- A historical novel about an actor in the fourth century B.C.

——. *Fire from Heaven*. New York: Pantheon Books, 1969.
- A historical novel that brings to life Alexander the Great and his times.

Sophocles. *Oedipus the King*, trans. F. Storr. Loeb Library Edition. Cambridge, MA: Harvard University Press, 1981.
- Sophocles' play about the king of Thebes and his downfall, based on the myth that corresponds to Freud's account of the child's Oedipus Complex.

SUGGESTED FILMS

1939 *Trial and Death of Socrates* (in Italian), dir. Corrado d'Errico

1956 *Alexander the Great*, dir. Robert Rossen

1960 *Never on Sunday*, dir. Jules Dassin

1961 *Antigone*, dir. George Tzavellas

1962 *300 Spartans*, dir. Rudolpph Maté

1970 *Socrates*, dir. Roberto Rossellini

2004 *Alexander*, dir. Oliver Stone

7 Ancient Rome

"*Arms I sing and the man who first from the coasts of Troy, exiled by fate, came to Italy and Lavinian shores; much buffeted on sea and land by violence from above, through cruel Juno's unforgiving wrath, and much enduring in war also, till he should build a city and bring his gods to Latium; whence came the Latin race, the lords of Alba, and the walls of lofty Rome.*"

(VIRGIL, *Aeneid* BK. 1, LINES 1–7)

The early history of Rome is complex. Originally a village composed of huts by the River Tiber, Rome grew into a powerful city. Beginning in the Hellenistic period, Rome began its rise, and by the second century A.D. it had become a huge empire (see map 7.4, p. 163). The Roman Empire lasted for around five hundred years and stretched from Britain in the north to northern Africa and Egypt in the south, and from western Europe as far east as Mesopotamia, Assyria, and Armenia (in southern Russia). Because of its size and power, Rome was able to impose its language (Latin) on conquered territories—most of western Europe had no writing system until the Roman conquest in the first century A.D. At the same time, Rome was a vast melting pot; both the city and the empire absorbed influences from cultures throughout the Mediterranean region and beyond.

Several early kings of Rome—including the last three—were Etruscans, a people native to the Italian peninsula. They ruled from the ninth century B.C. until 509 B.C., a period corresponding to the evolution of Greece from the Dark Age through the Archaic era. In 509 B.C. Rome overthrew the last Etruscan king and became a republic, inspired in part by the democratic ideals of the Greek polis. *The Roman Republic lasted until 27 B.C., when Octavian (63 B.C.–A.D. 14) came to power. Four years later, he changed his name to Augustus and became the first Roman emperor. The empire came to an end in A.D. 476, when barbarian tribes (Goths) from the north overran the city of Rome.*

Key Topics

Beginnings

- Etruscan opulence
- The Roman senate
- Internal power struggles lead to civil war
- The eloquence of Cato, Cicero, and Caesar
- The Roman Republic

The Empire

- Architecture for entertainment, daily life, worship, and power
- The Colosseum
- Trajan's Column
- The Basilica Ulpia
- The Pantheon
- Apartments
- Villas
- Life in Pompeii

Walls, Roads, and Water

- Aqueducts
- The Appian Way
- Walls and arches

TIMELINE	ETRUSCAN CIVILIZATION 1000–509 B.C.	ROMAN REPUBLIC 509–27 B.C.	ROMAN EMPIRE 31 B.C.–A.D. 476
HISTORY AND CULTURE 	Villanovan culture, 1000 B.C. Kings rule Etruria Powerful trading nation, 8th century B.C. Large naval fleet Advanced urban planning Irrigation Aristocratic, fashion-conscious, literate society Greek influence in art and architecture Improved status of women	Influence of Greek *polis* Latin language Ruled by senate and assembly of patricians Law of the Twelve Tables, *c.* 450 B.C. *Paterfamilias* and piety Punic Wars Caesar and the Gallic Wars, 58 B.C.: *Commentaries* Caesar crosses the Rubicon River, 49 B.C. Caesar killed, 44 B.C.	Octavian becomes Augustus, 27 B.C. *Pax Romana*: Rome "head of the world" (*caput mundi*) Latin language Rome falls to the Goths, A.D. 476
RELIGION AND MYTH	Greek gods given Etruscan names Belief in material afterlife Burials in the form of houses Borrowed Greek myths	Lares and Penates—household gods Roman names for Greek gods *Pontifex maximus* Ancestor worship	Founding myths: Aeneas, Romulus and Remus
ART	Bronze mirrors used by women *Achilles Ambushes Troilus,* *c.* 540 B.C. Cerveteri sarcophagus, *c.* 520 B.C. *Capitoline Wolf*, *c.* 500 B.C. Bronze hoplite, *c.* 450 B.C.	Sarcophagus of Lucius Cornelius Scipio Barbatus, *c.* 200 B.C. *Street Musicians* mosaic, *c.* 100 B.C. Wall-painting, Villa of the Mysteries, *c.* 60 B.C.	*Ara Pacis Augustae*, 13–9 B.C. Boscotrecase Villa wall-painting, *c.* 12 B.C. Patrician with two portrait heads, 1st century A.D. *Augustus of Prima Porta*, early 1st century A.D. *Gemma Augustea*, *c.* A.D. 10 Flavian woman as Venus, late 1st century A.D. Equestrian portrait of Marcus Aurelius, A.D. 164–166 Head of Constantine's colossal statue, A.D. 313
ARCHITECTURE 	Temple of Apollo, Veii, *c.* 500 B.C. *Necropoleis* (cities of the dead)	Roman arches Appian Way, 312 B.C. Temple of Portunus, late 2nd century B.C. Pont du Gard, near Nîmes, late 1st century B.C. Roman forum Domestic buildings: villas and *insulae*	Colosseum, *c.* A.D. 72–80 Arch of Titus, *c.* A.D. 81 Trajan's Column, A.D. 113 Basilica Ulpia Pantheon, A.D. 125–128 Imperial forums
LITERATURE	Language not translated	Catullus (*c.* 84–*c.* 54 B.C.), poetry Virgil (70–19 B.C.), *Aeneid; Georgics; Eclogues* Horace (65–8 B.C.), lyric odes	Livy (59 B.C.–A.D. 17), *The History of Rome* Ovid (43 B.C.–A.D. 17), *Metamorphoses; Art of Love* Petronius (d. A.D. 65), *Satyricon* Tacitus (*c.* A.D. 56–120), *Annals; Histories* Juvenal (*c.* A.D. 55/60–after 127), *Satires* Suetonius (*c.* A.D. 69–after 122), *The Twelve Caesars*
THEATER 		Comedy: actors masked Plautus (*c.* 250–184 B.C.), comedies Terence (*c.* 195–159 B.C.), comedies	
PHILOSOPHY, AND RHETORIC	Lost	Cicero (106–43 B.C.) Lucretius (98–*c.* 55 B.C.), *On the Nature of Things*	Marcus Aurelius (ruled A.D. 161–180), *Meditations* Seneca (*c.* 4 B.C.–A.D. 65), *Letters*, tragedies
MUSIC 	No notation Music at dinner Music while cooking	Pipes (*auloi*), tambourines, cymbals	

MYTHS OF THE FOUNDING OF ROME

This chapter opens with the first seven lines of the *Aeneid*, an epic poem written by Virgil (70–19 B.C.). They allude to the two origin myths of Roman culture: Greek and native Italic. The Greek myth focuses on the tradition of Aeneas, the hero of the *Aeneid*, who linked Rome to the Homeric heroes and the gods. The Italic myth attributes the founding of Rome to Romulus and Remus and emphasizes the period of the republic.

7.1 Copy of a statue group of Aeneas, Ascanius, and Anchises.
The original group stood in the Roman forum of Augustus. Aeneas carries a small figure of Anchises, gazes back on his past as Troy burns, but strides forward toward his future destiny. Ascanius wears a cap from Phrygia, a civilization of ancient Anatolia; his elaborate costume, including the Phrygian cap, denotes the eastern locale of Troy.

VIRGIL'S *AENEID*

Virgil wrote the *Aeneid* to celebrate Rome's origins and to locate them within the Greek heroic tradition. Composed in hexameter verse (its lines have six metric feet) like Homer's *Iliad* and *Odyssey*, the *Aeneid* traces the long journey of the Trojan hero Aeneas, the "man" of whom Virgil sings. Virgil explains that he "sings arms and the man" to evoke the ancient oral traditions of the Homeric epics and link them with the founding of Rome.

The *Aeneid* begins with the end of the Trojan War and Aeneas's escape from the burning city of Troy after its sack by the Greeks. He carries his aged father, Anchises, and leads his young son, Ascanius, from the ravaged city (figure **7.1**). The fugitives carry away statues of the household gods, the **Lares and Penates**—spirits who protected Roman farms and homes. Romans worshipped these gods at certain times of year, at wedding festivals, and at meals. In Roman houses, statues of the Lares and Penates were placed over the hearth, where a fire burned steadily as a sign of family continuity from one generation to the next.

Like Odysseus, who also embarks on a journey after the Trojan War, Aeneas travels great distances and has many adventures before reaching his destination. Virgil relates that Aeneas arrives in Italy, where his descendants found Rome. His wife, Creusa, has died, but her shade (ghost) appears to Aeneas and informs him that a great destiny awaits him. The notion of divine destiny, like Rome's mythic descent from the gods, is a main theme of the *Aeneid*.

Aeneas was himself of divine origin: his mother was the goddess Venus. His father, the mortal Anchises, was a cousin of King Priam of Troy. The myth of Aeneas's parentage thus provided Rome with the desired link to the gods, and his heroic journey with a heritage of epic proportions.

Aeneas sets sail for Sicily, but a storm unleashed by the goddess Juno forces him off course to the northern coast of Africa (modern Libya). There, he and his men are welcomed by Dido, the Phoenician queen of the newly founded city of Carthage. Dido falls in love with Aeneas, who relates his adventures to her, just as Odysseus had described his adventures to the princess Nausicaa after being shipwrecked on her father's island. Both Homer and Virgil use a similar literary device—that of making the hero rather than the author seem to be the narrator.

Like Nausicaa, Dido tries to keep the man she loves at her court with an offer of marriage. But Jupiter reminds Aeneas of his destiny and orders him to cut short his dalliance with Dido. Dido kills herself in despair as Aeneas sails from Carthage. In Book VI of the *Aeneid*, Aeneas returns to Italy—to Cumae, south of Rome. There he meets the Cumaean Sibyl, one of the female oracles who foretold the future in antiquity. She reveals Aeneas's destiny, which, like that of Gilgamesh (see Chapter 2), is to found a city. Then she escorts Aeneas to the Underworld, where he meets his father's shade. Anchises introduces his son to the future heroes of Roman history and describes Rome's destiny:

> Others, I doubt not, shall beat out the breathing bronze with softer lines; shall from marble draw forth the features of life; shall plead their causes better; with the rod shall trace the paths of heaven and tell the rising of the stars: remember thou, O Roman, to rule the nations with thy sway—these shall be thine arts—to crown Peace with Law, to spare the humbled, and to tame in war the proud!
>
> (*Aeneid*, Bk. VI, lines 847–853)

The "others" are Greeks. They are poets and philosophers, and their artists cast in bronze and carve in marble lifelike figures that seem to breathe. But the Romans will rule an empire, and their rule will be just, for they will "crown Peace with Law."

Not only is Rome descended from the gods and destined to command a mighty empire, therefore, but it will also gain legitimacy by imposing the rule of law.

In Book VII, Aeneas reaches Latium (where Latin was spoken), and marries Lavinia, the daughter of the king. A period of warfare follows (Books VIII–XI), until the gods preside over a truce between the Trojans and the Latins. In the final book (Book XII), Aeneas kills the local Latin king and founds the city of Lavinium (modern Pratica di Mare, on the west coast of Italy).

Ascanius assists his father in the struggle against the Latins. He is credited in Roman legend with being the founder and first king of Alba Longa, the city that preceded Rome—the "lords of Alba [Longa]" mentioned by Virgil were considered the descendants of Ascanius.

Romulus and Remus

The second, native Italic (non-Greek) myth deals directly with the founding of Rome, traditionally dated April 21, 753 B.C. The last king of Alba Longa had usurped power from the rightful king, Numitor, and sent Numitor's daughter, Rhea Silvia, to live with the Vestal Virgins, guardians of the hearth. In so doing, the king wanted to ensure that Numitor would have no descendants to reclaim Rome. Rhea Silvia would devote her life to keeping alive the fire in the temple of Vesta and preparing cakes for religious festivals. However, she is impregnated by Mars and gives birth to twin sons, Romulus and Remus. The role of the war god in creating the ancestry of Rome foreshadows the power of the Roman armies and the vast extent of their conquests. Numitor's usurper orders that the twins be killed, but, instead, the executioner abandons them on the banks of the Tiber. A she-wolf rescues Romulus and Remus, nursing them until, like the Greek king Oedipus, they are found and reared by a shepherd couple.

When Romulus and Remus grow up, they overthrow the usurper and restore Numitor to the throne. They decide to found a new city and mark out its boundaries on the Palatine (one of Rome's seven hills; see Box). They agree that one of them will rule the new city and that the choice will depend on an omen read from the flights of birds. But, in an act of arrogance, Remus shows contempt for his brother by jumping over the newly plowed foundations of the city walls. In revenge, Romulus kills Remus.

Society and Culture

The Seven Hills of Rome

Seven hills up to 150 feet (45 m) high stand near the River Tiber (map **7.1**). Rome's first settlement was on the Palatine, where Augustus, the first Roman emperor, built his house. Opposite the Palatine were the Quirinal and Viminal Hills. The remaining four are the Aventine, Capitoline, Caelian, and Esquiline.

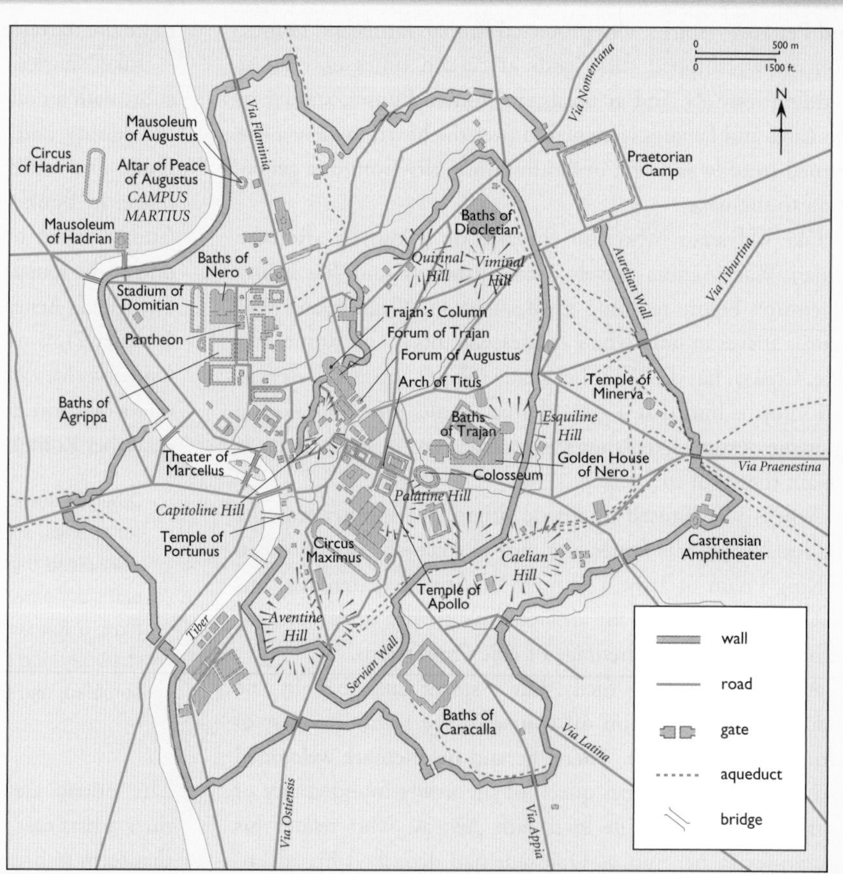

Map 7.1 Ancient Rome.

For Romans, the story of Romulus and Remus, like the epic account of Aeneas, reinforced a sense of destiny and divine lineage. Such founding myths would continue to define the self-image of Rome throughout its history. They connected Rome to the heroic Greek past and made its imperial expansion appear to have been decreed by the gods. As with Virgil's *Aeneid*, these ideas influenced the art, literature, and politics of both the republic and the empire.

The remainder of this chapter is divided into three historical periods: Etruscan civilization (ninth century to 509 B.C.), the Roman Republic (509–27 B.C.), and the Roman Empire (31 B.C.–A.D. 476).

THE ETRUSCANS: NINTH CENTURY TO 509 B.C.

The Etruscans inhabited most of the Italian peninsula between Florence and Rome (map **7.2**, p. 148). The region is known as Etruria, or Tuscany, after the Roman terms *Tusci* and *Etrusci*, designating the Etruscans. The ancestors of the Etruscans belonged to the Villanovan Iron Age culture, which flourished around 1000 B.C. Named after the town of Villanova, near Bologna, in northern Italy, this culture produced the earliest known evidence of Etruscan civilization. Archaeologists have discovered Villanovan burials of both men and women dating from as early as the ninth century B.C. These burials contained valuable personal possessions, including armor, elaborate jewelry, bronze mirrors, and everyday household objects. Such works reflect the high level of Etruscan craftsmanship and indicate a belief in a material afterlife.

From the eighth century B.C., Etruria became a powerful nation with a large naval fleet. Natural resources of iron ore, silver, and copper made Etruria an important center of trade in the Mediterranean. Abundant forests in the region provided wood for shipbuilding and houses, as well as for processing iron ore into metal. The Etruscans were pioneers in urban planning and skilled in augury (the ability to foretell the future from natural phenomena, such as the flights of birds, animals' entrails, and the weather).

Etruscan civilization was known in the Mediterranean world for its aristocratic taste. People enjoyed the cultural benefits of leisure time and were quite fashion-conscious. Little is known of Etruscan theater or music, but the Romans described their modes of entertainment. According to Roman accounts, the Etruscans were skilled dancers and cooked their meals to music. Etruscan wall-paintings show banquets with diners being entertained by dancers, musicians, and jugglers. They also depict sports and games.

GREECE AND THE ETRUSCANS

Etruscan civilization was influenced by Greek culture. The Etruscans adopted the names of the Greek gods and illustrated Greek myths. They borrowed elements of Greek architecture and sculpture, and imported thousands of Greek vases. The Etruscans also used the Greek alphabet, but their language was different from any other in their time or ours. They were literate, but their literature has not survived. As a result, much of what we know about the Etruscans comes from accounts by Greek and Roman writers.

The bronze statuette of a hoplite (figure **7.2**) shows the influence of Greek art and culture on the Etruscans as well as the evolution of an individual Etruscan style. Although the aristocratic hoplite originated in the Greek Archaic period, this figure wears tight-fitting Etruscan armor and a large helmet. It was made in around 450 B.C., which corresponds to the Greek Classical period. But the distinctively Etruscan character of the hoplite's slim proportions and flat surface patterns have more in common with Archaic than with Classical style. The lively, energetic stride that creates the impression of a warrior advancing into battle is typical of Etruscan sculpture. In addition, the delicate form reflects the skill of Etruscan artists in casting bronze.

7.2 Statuette of a hoplite, *c.* 450 B.C. Bronze. Archaeological Museum, Florence.

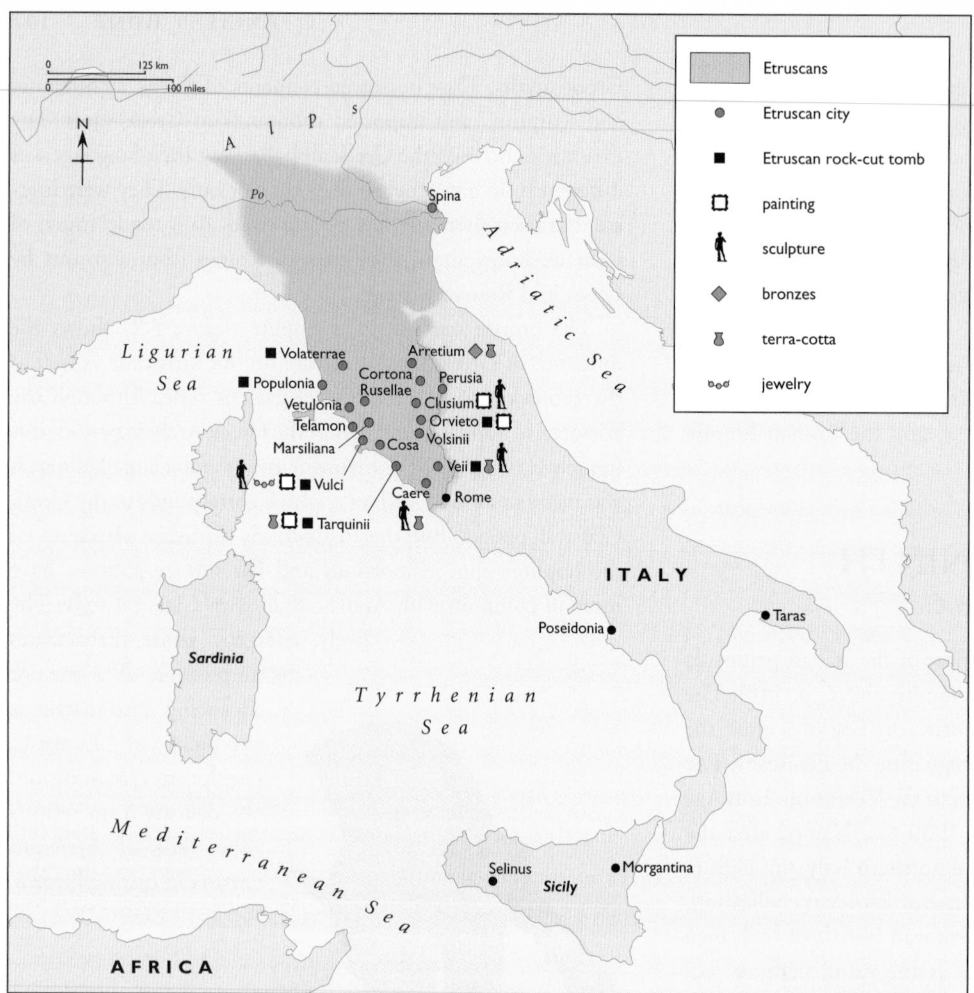

Map 7.2 Etruscan Italy, *c.* 500 B.C.

In temple architecture as in sculpture, the Etruscans developed their own forms but borrowed certain features from Greece. The favorite Etruscan building materials, in contrast to the Greek preference for marble, were wood, terra-cotta, and **tufa** (a soft, easily workable, volcanic rock that dries when exposed to the air). Figure **7.3** shows a reconstructed Etruscan temple dedicated to Apollo at Veii, northeast of Rome. The front porch (*pronaos*) has **Tuscan columns**, which are a form of Doric to which a round base has been added. The *pronaos* leads into the *cella* (the Roman equivalent of the Greek *naos*), which housed the cult statue. Unlike Greek temples, Etruscan ones are accessible only by a narrow flight of steps at the front.

The Veii temple stands on a raised platform (the **podium**), rather than at the top of steps

7.3 Reconstructed model of the temple of Apollo, Veii, Italy, *c.* 500 B.C.
The reconstruction is based on descriptions of Etruscan temples by the Roman architect Vitruvius (30 B.C.–A.D. 14). His treatise on architecture was written, like the *Aeneid*, in Augustan Rome.

that continue around the building and form a base, as in Greek temples. It has a broader, more gradually sloping roof than was found in Greece. Terra-cotta statues, some representing Greek gods in lively poses, were placed on the roof—a distinctive Etruscan practice not found in Greece.

ETRUSCAN WOMEN: THE ENVY OF ATHENIAN WOMEN

The aristocratic character of Etruscan society is related to the elevated position of women compared with Greece, especially Athens. In contrast to Athenian women, Etruscan women went out in public with their husbands and could attend theatrical performances, sporting events, and religious festivals. In art, scenes show women performing as athletes.

The attention to fashion among Etruscan women is indicated by the many bronze mirrors that have been excavated exclusively from female graves. Etruscan mirrors are typically decorated with mythological scenes, and the fact that they are inscribed with texts indicates that the women who used them could read (Figure **7.4**).

7.4a Etruscan mirror with Bellerophon and the Chimera, 4th century B.C. Bronze, 9 in. (22.8 cm) high. The Metropolitan Museum of Art, New York.

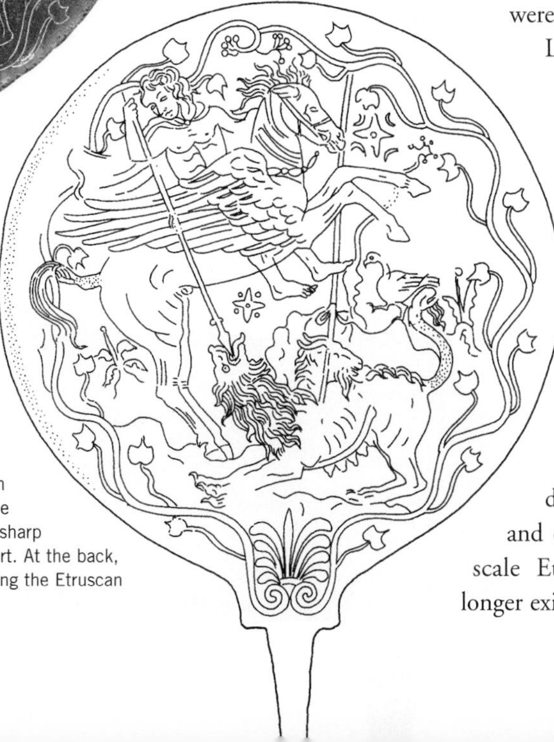

7.4b Diagram of mirror. The delicate engraving on this mirror shows the Greek hero Bellerophon riding the winged horse, Pegasus, and thrusting his spear into the upturned lion head of the monstrous chimera. The chimera's goat head has already been killed, but its snake part is unaware of the impending attack. The lion body is female, as indicated by the udders, which is an Etruscan element. Bellerophon's flowing hair, the lion's mane, the elaborate wings of Pegasus, and the sharp diagonals create the lively forms typical of Etruscan art. At the back, a single duck surrounded by foliage strolls by, reflecting the Etruscan interest in landscape.

Because women went out in public, they wore mantles over their shirt-like *chitons*, as well as hats, boots, and elaborate jewelry. In the early periods of Etruscan history, women wore long braids tied with decorative clasps, often reaching to their feet. In the fifth century B.C., their shoes had gold laces and were elevated with wooden soles attached by hinges. To the dismay of Greek men, Etruscan footwear was particularly admired by Athenian women.

Literary accounts by Greek men confirm that they were offended by the fashionable dress and luxurious tastes of Etruscan women. For example, a fourth-century-B.C. Greek Sophist, Theopompus of Chios (active *c.* 380 B.C.), described Etruscan women as shamefully loose, lustful, given to appearing nude in public, and obsessed with opulence. The entire culture, he asserted, tolerated improper heterosexual and homosexual behavior. At the same time, however, Theopompus admitted that their attention to physical appearance made the Etruscans pleasing to look at, and he noted with amazement that Etruscans even frequented barber shops.

One distinctive way in which Etruscans improved their appearance was with the most advanced dental care of the time. From the seventh century B.C., Etruscans made dental bridges and dentures attached with gold wires to the jaw bone. (These are still studied by modern dentistry students.) False teeth were made of human teeth and, in at least one case, the tooth of an ox. These skills impressed the Romans, who themselves adopted dental care. In 450 B.C., Rome forbade burying the dead with gold in their teeth.

ETRUSCAN FUNERARY ART

Much of what is known about the Etruscans comes from their funerary art. They believed that demons escorted the dead to the Underworld and that the afterlife was a material one. In the Villanovan period, small funerary urns were designed to resemble houses. Later, much larger tombs were built in the form of houses and equipped with household furniture made of stone. Objects of everyday use, including mirrors and jewelry for women, armor for men, and toys for children, were buried with the deceased. Tombs were arranged in groups that resembled cities. These **necropoleis** ("cities of the dead")—at Cerveteri, Tarquinia, and elsewhere—resemble the large-scale Etruscan architecture that no longer exists.

7.5 *Achilles Ambushes Troilus*, Tomb of the Bulls, Tarquinia, Italy, *c.* 540 B.C. Fresco.
Troilus was a son of the Trojan king, Priam. In this scene, Troilus stops his horse at a date-palm tree. Achilles hides behind a large fountain, preparing to ambush and kill Troilus. Both Achilles and the horse are portrayed in a lively manner; the horse is enlarged, which compresses the figure of Troilus. This disregard for naturalistic proportions, together with the patterned fountain and stylized trees, is typical of Etruscan style in the sixth century B.C.

Tomb interiors were decorated with reliefs or paintings. Such images, especially in the sixth century B.C., typically illustrated aristocratic Etruscan banquets or Greek myths. The oldest excavated tomb site is at Tarquinia, northwest of Rome. There, in the Tomb of the Bulls, the rear interior wall is painted with a scene from the Trojan War (figure **7.5**). In Etruscan tomb paintings of banquets, diners recline on couches according to Greek custom. But unlike the Greeks, Etruscan husbands and wives dined together. This custom is reflected in the distinctive Etruscan ash-urns with sculptures of the deceased on the lid (figure **7.6**).

THE END OF ETRUSCAN RULE

Etruscan kings ruled Rome until 509 B.C., when Tarquin the Proud (Tarquinius Superbus) was expelled and a constitutional republic was established. Over the next two hundred years, Rome gradually assimilated elements of Etruscan culture, a process that was completed by the end of the first century B.C. Nevertheless, during the nearly five hundred years of republic and another five hundred years of empire, Etruscan ideas and art continued to influence Roman civilization. The Etruscans taught the Romans techniques of reading omens, engineering, and irrigation. They also provided a bridge between Roman and Greek culture by importing vases, borrowing architectural forms, and adopting the names of Greek gods and the Greek alphabet. In addition, according to literary sources, the Roman public theater traditions and gladiatorial combats were imported from Etruria.

7.6 Sarcophagus, from Cerveteri, *c.* 520 B.C. Terra-cotta, 6 ft. 7 in. (2 m) long. Museo Nazionale di Villa Giulia, Rome.
Etruscans cremated their dead and placed the ashes in urns of various sizes. Wealthier people commissioned the largest urns, most of which represented the deceased on the lid. As if to deny the fact of death, the Etruscans show the deceased couple very much alive. In this example, they share a blanket and recline on a dining couch. They seem engaged in lively conversation, an impression enhanced by the animated gestures, and stylized patterns in the hair and feet. Both husband and wife have Archaic smiles, which enliven the figures and reflect Greek influence.

THE ROMAN REPUBLIC: 509–27 B.C.

The geographical position of Rome (map 7.3)—at a crossroads of trade between the Mediterranean, the Greek settlements in Sicily (Magna Graecia), and the Etruscans—proved commercially and politically advantageous in the coming centuries. What began as a small village on the banks of the Tiber grew into the capital of a vast empire (figure 7.7). By the late republic, the population of Rome had grown to around one million, international trade was thriving, and a large number of people had grown wealthy through trade and commerce. Grains were imported from Africa, and oil from Spain. Generally these were shipped in large Greek amphorae, reflecting Rome's commercial ties with Greece and other Mediterranean regions. Wine came from Campania, a fertile area in the south of the Italian peninsula, where many prosperous Romans had country houses.

7.7 *Capitoline Wolf, c.* 500 B.C. Bronze, 33½ in. (85.1 cm) high. Capitoline Museum, Rome. The Italic legend of Rome's founding inspired the image of the she-wolf nursing Romulus and Remus. This became the symbol of Rome and it remains so today. During the republic and the empire, other versions of the subject were exhibited on the Capitoline Hill, which also housed a live wolf. In this particular statue, the wolf is an original Etruscan bronze guardian figure, but the twins were added during the Renaissance. Nevertheless, the twins were also added in antiquity, as is evident from Roman coins.

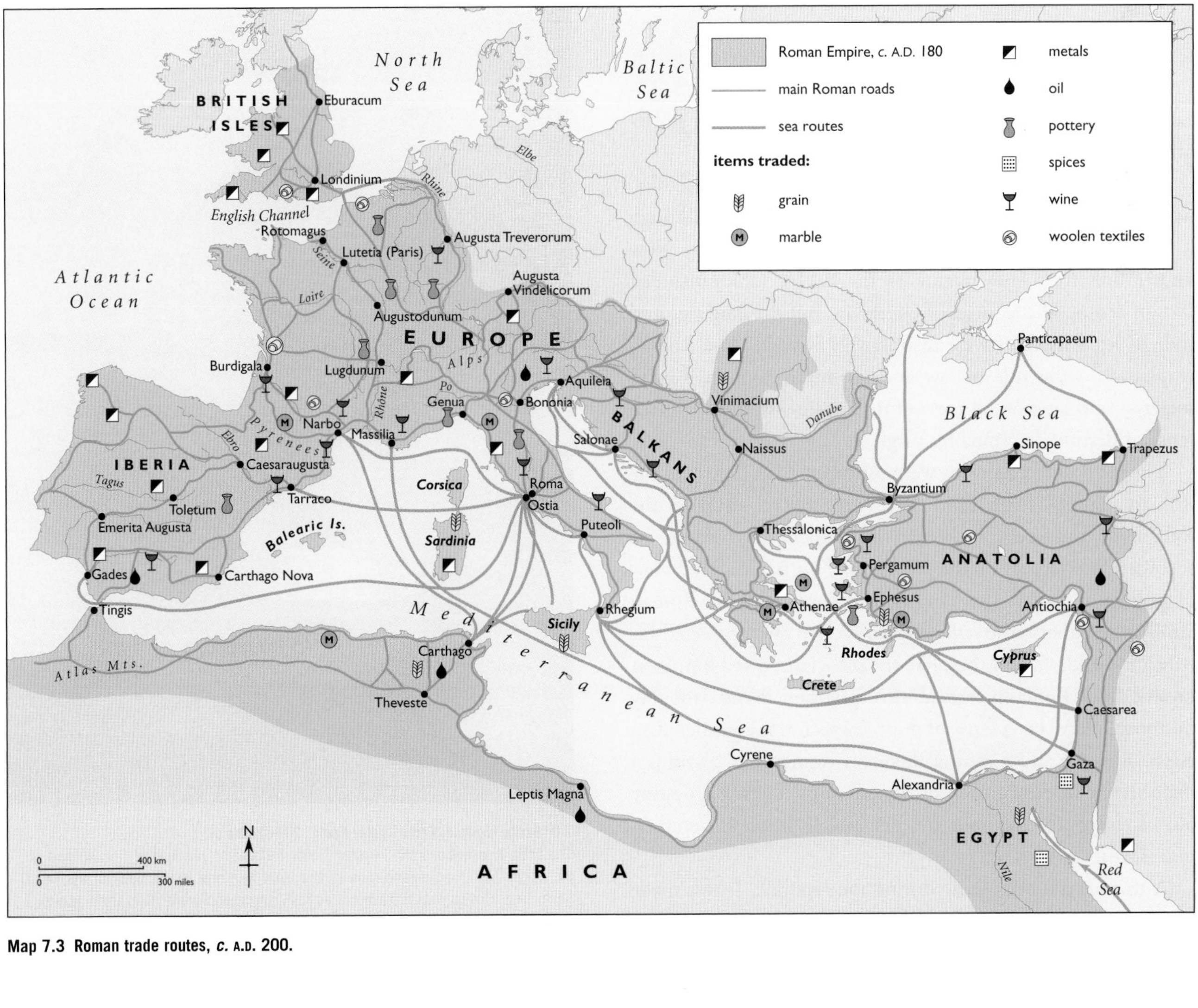

Map 7.3 Roman trade routes, *c.* A.D. 200.

CHRONOLOGY AND HISTORY

The traditional date of Rome's founding is 753 B.C., but it remained a small village until the late sixth century B.C., when Etruscan rule transformed it into a great city. After the ousting of the last Etruscan king in 509 B.C., Rome established a republic comparable to the oligarchies in some of the Greek city-states.

The political divisions of the Roman Republic were based largely on the class structure of Roman society. The two main governing bodies were the aristocratic, patrician senate (*senatus*) and the plebeians, who made up the popular assembly of citizens (*comitia centuriata*). Two patrician magistrates (later called consuls) were elected each year (up to around 300 B.C.) by male citizens. Most of the power, however, lay with the senate, which had grown to three hundred members by the third century B.C. A senator indicated his rank by wearing a white toga (an Etruscan style) with a purple band.

The senate was located in the **forum**, originally an open market area and public meeting-place derived from the Greek *agora* (see Chapter 5). Under the Etruscans, the forum contained the king's palace and the temple of the Vestal Virgins. During the republic, however, the forum expanded. It became a political center, where citizens gathered to hear announcements from the senate. They worshipped in shrines and temples located in the forum and did their marketing in the shops. During the empire, the number of forums increased as each emperor built a new one in his own name to glorify himself and the power of Rome.

Around 450 B.C. Rome issued the Law of the Twelve Tables, which granted all citizens equal rights before the law, although it prohibited marriage between patricians and plebeians. Now known only from later fragments, the Twelve Tables included certain democratic features of Greek law, but the language and style of legal thought were distinctively Roman. The Roman emphasis on the rule of law and its imposition on Roman society—and later on all parts of its empire—were part of the sense of destiny described by Virgil.

The governing patricians were conceived of as fathers of the Roman "family." Patricians were expected to oversee the welfare of the state, in return for which they would be accorded due respect by the plebeians. This paternalistic view of politics mirrored the view of the family. In the Roman family, the father—the *paterfamilias*—ruled and protected his wife and children, and they, like the plebeians, owed him their loyalty. The Romans termed this devotion *pietas* (roughly meaning "piety" or "a sense of duty"), which was considered an essential virtue and a central theme of Roman life. *Pietas* is a main theme of the *Aeneid*, for Aeneas must follow his destiny out of respect for the gods and his father—hence his epithet, *pius Aeneas*.

A third social class arose during the republic. It was made up of families of *equites* (knights, or horsemen), who were wealthy enough to own horses. As part of the Roman cavalry, the *equites* were important to the army, and, as their power increased, they demanded more rights. From the early second century B.C., the *equites* were a class with a high economic and political status, second only to the senatorial class. However, their military function was phased out in favor of more expert horsemen. Despite the social stratification, in 90 and 88 B.C. the senate enacted legislation granting equal rights and citizenship to every free man in Italy.

The history of Rome's rise from a small settlement to a world power is one of continual warfare and conquest. In 390 B.C., Rome was attacked by Gauls, a northern tribe that eventually settled in the area that became modern France. In response, Rome built tufa walls around the city to improve its defense. Figure **7.8** shows a wall constructed during the republic of ashlar tufa blocks, each about 18 inches (45 cm) high. Cut into the wall is a round arch (figure **7.9**), a structural system first devised in ancient Babylon (see Chapter 2), used in the Hellenistic period, and developed by the Romans for many types of architectural construction. In this case, the arch

7.8 Santa Maria di Falleri gate, Rome, 241–200 B.C.
The little head above the keystone may be that of Janus, the Roman god of gateways. His double face (one in the front and one in the back of his head) permitted him to watch travelers as they came and went. It is from Janus that we call the first month of the year "January," when we look forward to the New Year and back over the past year.

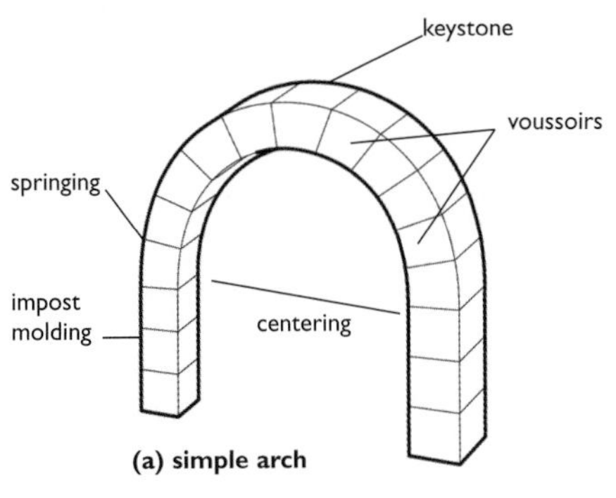

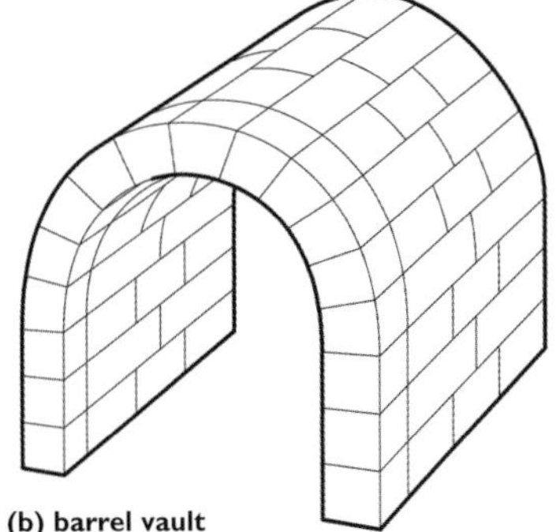

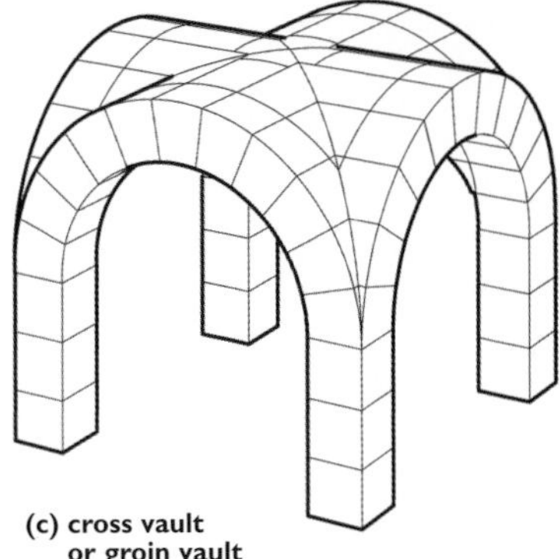

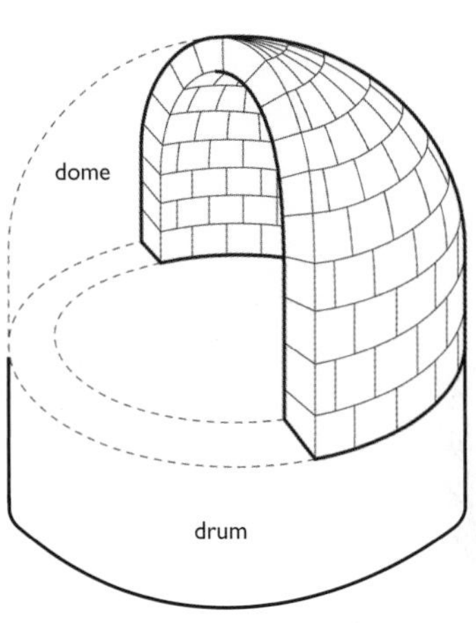

7.9 Roman arch construction.
The simple arch (a) is composed of wedge-shaped stones (**voussoirs**), which seem to spring upward from the **impost** molding to form the curve of the arch. They are held in place at the center by the **keystone**. The extension of the simple arch through space creates the **barrel vault** (b), and two intersecting barrel vaults create a **cross-vault** (also called a groin vault) (c). When a simple arch is rotated, the result is a **dome**, which in Rome rested on a round supporting structure called a **drum** (d). In the round arch, the weight is transferred from the keystone outward and downward to the **springing** points, which push outward on the piers. The **centering** holds each stone in place while the arch is being completed and makes it possible to cap large interiors with domes. Such techniques reflect the Roman interest in the utilitarian use of space in contrast to the Greek emphasis on the exterior appearance of its architecture.

spans a road, one of many built by the Romans—hence the popular expression, "All roads lead to Rome."

Roads were one of the most important features of ancient Rome. They linked different parts of the empire, making trade and travel relatively easy and encouraging cultural unity. The most famous of the roads leading to Rome is the Appian Way (figure **7.10**), which was constructed in 312 B.C.

7.10 The Appian Way, constructed 312 B.C.

7.11 Pont du Gard, over the Gardon River, near Nîmes, France, late 1st century B.C. Stone, 162 ft. (49.38 m) high, 883 ft. (269 m) long.
Aqueducts served the combined purpose of transporting water over long distances and providing a bridge for travel. The Pont du Gard, made of large stones assembled without mortar, was designed to carry water through a pipe, or channel, at the top. Located 13 miles (21 km) from Nîmes, in the south of France, the Pont du Gard is one of many surviving aqueducts built outside Rome.

By the end of the fourth century B.C., Rome had developed sophisticated engineering techniques that made possible not only an elaborate system of roads, but also impressive **aqueducts** (figure **7.11**) that brought water to homes and public baths. The earliest aqueduct, which carried water to Rome from a spring over 7 miles (11.3 km) away, the Aqua Appia, was built on the Appian Way. Eleven aqueducts were built between 312 B.C. and A.D. 226, the longest being 59 miles (95 km) long. The Segovia aqueduct in Spain, still functioning today, is built of around 20,400 stone blocks.

In the course of the fourth century B.C., Rome took control of the Latin League, a group of settlements allied against the Greeks and the Etruscans. Rome later conquered the Greek area of southern Italy (called Magna Graecia) and, by 275 B.C., controlled all of Italy south of the Po valley.

The Punic Wars

During the second and third centuries B.C., Rome fought three wars against Carthage, which was a major naval power and controlled trade throughout the western Mediterranean. These were called the Punic Wars, after *Poeni*, meaning "Phoenicians," people from the Arabian peninsula who had settled in parts of northwest Africa. The first war (264–241 B.C.) was a struggle for control of Sicily, which Rome feared it would lose to the Carthaginian Empire. In the second war (219–202 B.C.), Rome aimed to prevent Carthage from dominating Spain. The Carthaginian general Hannibal (247–183 B.C.) invaded the Italian peninsula from Spain and reportedly led a herd of elephants over the Alps. But Rome defeated Hannibal and took control of parts of Spain.

Rome's leading orator (public speaker), Marcus Porcius Cato, known as Cato the Censor (234–149 B.C.), fought in the second Punic War. He was elected censor in 184 B.C.; as censor he devoted himself to a program of moral reform among the aristocracy and advocated conservative values. Cato's writings, some of which survive, as well as his public speeches, urged Rome to return to a simpler, agricultural way of life. Cato visited Carthage after the war and was impressed by its prosperity. He believed that the city still posed a serious threat to Rome's independence.

Cato's declaration *Carthago delenda est* ("Carthage must be destroyed") was fulfilled when Rome defeated and sacked Carthage at the end of the third Punic War (149–146 B.C.). With the threat of Carthage removed, Rome stepped into the power vacuum left by the death of Alexander the Great in 323 B.C., and by 129 B.C., it controlled provinces in the eastern Mediterranean, Macedonia, and parts of western Asia. Internal power struggles and civil wars had marked much of the first century B.C. For the next hundred years, Rome permitted temporary dictatorships as a means of dealing with political crises. One of the final contenders was the Roman patrician general Gaius Julius Caesar (100–44 B.C.).

JULIUS CAESAR

In 58 B.C., Julius Caesar launched a series of conquests in western Europe against the Gauls and Goths that took Roman culture and the Latin language as far north as Britain. He memorialized his military campaigns in his *Commentaries on the Gallic War*, which describe life in the Roman army in a matter-of-fact style and offer detailed, sometimes entertaining, accounts of the peoples he conquered.

Caesar writes in the third person, creating an impression of objectivity. For example, after a difficult, stormy crossing of the English Channel, he describes how the Britons fought with chariots:

> First of all they drive in all directions and hurl missiles, and so by the mere terror that the teams inspire and by the noise of the wheels they generally throw ranks into confusion. When they have worked their way in between the troops of cavalry, they leap down from the chariots and fight on foot . . . Thus they show in action the mobility of cavalry and the stability of infantry.
>
> (*Gallic War*, Bk. 4.33)

Caesar describes the inhabitants of Kent, in southeastern England, as "by far the most civilized." Clearly impressed by their customs, he writes:

> Of the inlanders most do not sow corn, but live on milk and flesh and clothe themselves in skins. All the Britons, indeed, dye themselves with woad, which produces a blue color, and makes their appearance in battle more terrible. They wear long hair, and shave every part of the body save the head and the upper lip. Groups of ten or twelve men have wives together in common, and particularly brothers along with brothers, and fathers with sons; but the children born of the unions are reckoned to belong to the particular house to which the maiden was first conducted.
>
> (*Gallic War*, Bk. 5.33)

In 49 B.C. Caesar crossed the River Rubicon in northern Italy, which was then the boundary of the corporate Roman state, and declared war on the senate. He defeated his rival, the general Pompey (106–48 B.C.), and took control of Rome. Caesar pursued Pompey to Egypt, where he met Queen Cleopatra (see Box). Their celebrated affair produced a son, Caesarion, who was later murdered by Octavian.

As ruler of Rome, Caesar instituted a number of civic improvements. Streets were cleaned, heavy daytime traffic was banned, and traders were forbidden to display their wares in public. Caesar reformed the Roman calendar, introducing the 365-day year we use today and adding an additional day every four years. One of his greatest achievements was unifying the civil law code, called the *Ius Civile*. The laws of the Twelve Tables had become complex and disordered, and Caesar enlisted legal experts to unify and simplify them. On the military front, he extended Roman conquests to parts of Asia Minor, and in 47 B.C. he uttered the famous words: *Veni, Vidi, Vici* ("I came, I saw, I conquered").

Caesar's power in Rome increased to the point where the senate suspected that he planned to become king. In 44 B.C., on the Ides of March (the 15th of the month), a group of senators gathered to assassinate him. When he recognized his friend Marcus Junius Brutus (*c.* 78–42 B.C.), who was a committed republican, Caesar uttered the well-known phrase *Et tu Brute!* ("You, too, Brutus!"). It was this event that gave rise to the expression "Beware the Ides of March" (from Shakespeare's *Julius Caesar*; see Chapter 15).

Society and Culture

Cleopatra, Queen of Egypt

Cleopatra (*c.* 68–30 B.C.), the Egyptian queen celebrated in plays, operas, songs, and films throughout Western history, was, like Helen of Troy, renowned for her beauty. But she was also a shrewd politician. She became queen in 51 B.C. and co-regent with her younger brother, Ptolemy XII. Although engaged to marry her brother, Cleopatra fell in love with Julius Caesar. She contrived to meet him in a scene famous in cinema history by arranging to be carried into his presence rolled up in a carpet. Their son, Caesarion, was named after his Roman father. Cleopatra left Egypt and went to Rome to live with Caesar, but after Caesar's murder in 44 B.C., she returned to Egypt and resumed her role as queen.

In 41 B.C., Cleopatra met the Roman leader Mark Antony, who had married the sister of Octavian (later Augustus). Mark Antony, a rival of Augustus, deserted his wife and went to live with Cleopatra in Egypt; they had three sons. When Rome declared war on Cleopatra and defeated her forces in 31 B.C. at the Battle of Actium (on the west coast of the Greek mainland), Cleopatra managed to escape with sixty Egyptian boats, and Mark Antony again followed her to Egypt. The Romans attacked Alexandria in 30 B.C., and, seeing no hope of winning, Antony and Cleopatra committed suicide.

According to tradition, Cleopatra died by placing a poisonous asp on her breast, but there is no evidence that this was in fact her method of suicide. In Egypt she was remembered as a great queen and associated with Isis as a goddess who gave birth to kings.

RELIGION AND ART

Roman ceremonies and festivals were important from earliest times. Presiding over the rituals was the *pontifex maximus*. This official title translates literally as "the greatest bridge-builder," but its original meaning is not known. In the early period, when Rome was ruled by kings, the *pontifex maximus* was the highest priest. He assisted the king in matters relating to the state cult, advised on religious rituals, established certain important dates, and supervised the Vestal Virgins. At first the *pontifex* was a patrician, but the position was later open to plebeians as well. The title was conferred on every emperor, and in the late fifth century A.D. on the Christian pope. The solemn nature of Roman religion meant that vows made to the gods were taken very seriously. Obligations to the divinities were mirrored by the sense of *pietas* toward the state and the *paterfamilias*.

Roman religion was **syncretistic**—that is, it assimilated features of other belief systems. Like the Etruscans, the Romans adopted the Greek pantheon, but they gave the gods Roman names and a Roman character (see Box). As Rome overran more and more territory, it absorbed customs from different cultures and borrowed from local religious cults, such as the Egyptian cult of Isis and the Phrygian cult of the Mother Goddess. This openness to assimilation both appealed to the conquered people and infused Roman religion with new ideas.

Romans cremated their dead and placed them in ash-urns or buried them in stone sarcophagi. Unlike the Etruscans, however, Romans rarely included effigies on the lid (figure **7.12**). In this example, the influence of Greek motifs is readily apparent. The ends of the flat lid curve into Ionic volute shapes, and the side is decorated with a Doric frieze. Triglyphs alternate with rosette designs in the metopes, below which an inscription proclaims the virtuous life of the deceased.

Ancestor worship was an important part of Roman religion. For centuries, the inhabitants of Italy had made death masks of their ancestors and displayed them during funerals. Under

Society and Culture

The Roman Gods

Roman God	*Greek Equivalent*
Jupiter	Zeus
Hera	Juno
Neptune	Poseidon
Pluto	Hades
Ceres	Demeter
Vesta	Hestia
Venus	Aphrodite
Cupid	Eros
Vulcan	Hephaestos
Minerva	Athena
Mars	Ares
Phoebus	Apollo
Diana	Artemis
Hermes	Mercury
Bacchus	Dionysos

7.12 Sarcophagus of Lucius Cornelius Scipio Barbatus, from the graves of the Scipios, Via Appia, near Rome, *c.* 200 B.C. Tufa, 4 ft. 7 in. (1.4 m) × 9 ft. 1 in. (2.77 m). Vatican Museums, Rome.

7.13 Patrician with two portrait heads, copy of a republican statue, 1st century A.D.; the patrician head is a later addition. Marble, 5 ft. 5 in. (1.65 m) high. Palazzo dei Conservatori, Rome.
Republican portraits were typically individual marble busts (showing the figure from the head to the shoulders). But this is a more complex example, illustrating a patrician wearing a toga and carrying two ancestor busts to show the importance of his family. They are carved to reveal their actual features and somber expressions. The pose of the patrician suggests that he is walking slowly, as if in a funeral procession, but the one bent leg combined with the straight, support leg is reminiscent of the Greek *Spearbearer* (see figure 6.22).

7.14 Temple of Portunus, Rome, late 2nd century B.C. Stone.

Augustus, Virgil wrote the *Aeneid* to demonstrate the divine ancestry of Roman culture. And Roman portraits, influenced by Hellenistic realism, express a desire to keep alive the memory of the deceased through a lifelike image (figure **7.13**).

Roman temples, such as the late second-century-B.C. Temple of Portunus (the god of harbors), combine elements of Greek and Etruscan architecture (figure **7.14**). The temple is rectangular and accessible only by steps at the front. Surrounding the solid walls of the single *cella* are **engaged columns** (columns attached to a wall); the only freestanding columns, which are Ionic, are located on the *pronaos*. In contrast to Greek temples, which were designed in relation to the surrounding landscape, the Roman temple, like the Etruscan, stands on a podium and dominates an urban space.

ART AND ARCHITECTURE OF EVERYDAY LIFE

The Romans devoted a great deal of time, energy, money, and engineering to domestic architecture. Inside the city, most people lived in apartment blocks, called *insulae* ("islands"; see Box, p. 158, and figure 7.15). The poorer classes occupied low-lying *suburbia*, literally the area "below the city" (compare the word "suburbs"). Those who could afford it built second homes (**villas**) in the countryside.

Much of our knowledge of Roman domestic architecture and everyday life (see Box, p. 158, and figure 7.16) comes from the ruins of Pompeii and Herculaneum. These two towns south of Rome were completely buried in volcanic ash in A.D. 79, when Mount Vesuvius suddenly erupted. People were literally stopped "in their tracks" as the lava flowed over them. They remained buried until the eighteenth century, when an Italian farmer accidentally discovered traces of the cities on his land.

Defining Moment

Rome Builds in Concrete

As the hub of a vast and long-lasting empire built on conquest and assimilation, Rome and its territory needed large-scale buildings to accommodate crowds of people. Huge audiences filled the Colosseum, aqueducts carried water over long distances, public baths provided recreation and relaxation spaces, and domestic architecture (both urban and in the country) came into its own. The Greeks had built mainly in marble, the Egyptians in limestone, sandstone, and granite, and the Mesopotamians had imported much of their stone. When the Romans developed the inexpensive and easily acquired material of concrete, they made possible new types of building on a scale that corresponded to their imperial ambitions.

Roman concrete was a mixture of rubble and gravel combined with mortar made from *pozzolana* (volcanic ash) and water. It could be shaped around a wooden frame and reinforced with stones and bricks. Large spaces could thus be enclosed, as is evident in buildings such as the Pantheon, basilicas, country villas, and apartment blocks (figure **7.15**). Limestone was generally used for solid foundations, and tufa was available when a soft material was required.

The use of concrete expanded in the early years of the Roman Empire under Augustus, Vespasian, and Hadrian. Architects constructed arches, vaults, and domes in concrete and reinforced them with brick facing. As concrete is not an attractive material, the Romans faced the exteriors of these structures with tile and **travertine** (a type of limestone that turns yellow as it ages). Later, colored marble, from the Aegean and North Africa, was used to decorate private houses and some public buildings. White marble was a Greek-inspired fashion. It was quarried at Carrara, in Italy, from around 50 B.C. and became the favorite facing material of the empire. Hence the assertion that Augustus found Rome a city of brick and left it a city of marble.

Critical Question Do all innovations in technology and science improve cultural development? Is there a necessary link between developing technological innovations and using these innovations?

7.15 Reconstruction of an *insula* (apartment block), Ostia, near Rome, 2nd century A.D. Brick and concrete.

Society and Culture

A Roman Bakery

Except for the occasional banquet, dining in ancient Rome was a simple affair. The average Roman ate a breakfast of bread and cheese, had a quick lunch at a food-stand, and for dinner had a two-course meal. Meat, fish, fruit, and cakes were standard fare. The main drink was wine diluted with water, which could be sweetened with honey. Romans did not drink tea, coffee, or hard liquor.

Bread was one of the most popular foods, originally baked at home and, from the second century B.C., in bakeries. It could then be delivered to a house or purchased directly from the shop. Figure **7.16** shows a reconstructed bakery at Pompeii. At the right, the hour-glass-shaped mill made of volcanic stone stands on a round base. Grain was poured into the top, ground into flour by turning the upper section against the lower section, and made into dough.

Brick ovens had a space for storing fuel and a chimney. For good luck, Romans often placed a relief or a painting of an erect phallus on the wall by their ovens.

7.16 Peter Connolly, detail of reconstructed baker's shop, Pompeii. Watercolor.

7.17a
Peter Connolly, reconstruction of an upper-class Roman house based on examples from Pompeii. Watercolor.

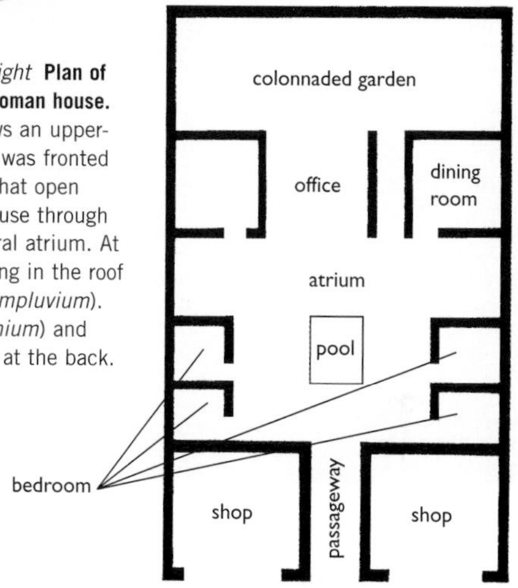

7.17b *right* **Plan of an upper-class Roman house.** This reconstruction shows an upper-class house built on one floor. It was fronted by shops (*tabernae*, compare "taverns") that open onto the street. One entered the interior of the house through a passageway between the shops, coming first to the central atrium. At the center of the atrium, a pool collected rain water from an opening in the roof (the *compluvium*) and drained it into a cistern under the floor (the *impluvium*). On either side of the atrium were bedrooms. The dining room (*triclinium*) and office (*tablinum*) were behind the atrium, with a colonnaded garden at the back.

colonnaded garden
office
dining room
atrium
pool
bedroom
shop
passageway
shop

WALL-PAINTINGS Upper-class houses in Pompeii were decorated with wall-paintings and mosaics. Surviving Roman wall-paintings are divided by scholars into four Pompeian styles based on their chronology. The first two styles belong to the republic and the last two to the empire. The earliest style is the First, or Masonry, Style, which can be seen in figure **7.17**. It consists of imitation marble, which enlivened the walls with rectangles of color.

Second Style paintings were three-dimensional and often created architectural illusions (figure **7.18**). Here, the artist makes the wall appear to extend into a deep space defined by a receding row of columns, which cast shadows. To the left, a striking mask reflects the Roman fascination with theater and suggests that the scene represents a stage set. The peacock enhances the illusion of depth, as its tail seems to fall out of the picture into the real space of the viewer.

At the Villa of the Mysteries, on the outskirts of Pompeii, there is a group of paintings illustrating a mysterious initiation ritual. Lifesize figures are shown against a background of Pompeian red (figure **7.19**). They turn freely on an illusionistic ledge that seems to occupy a real space between the actual wall and the painted wall. Painted architectural divisions, such as the **pilasters** (square columns) and the geometric horizontal frieze above them, are characteristic of the Second Style.

Third Style painting (see figure 7.27) tends to depict either tiny scenes surrounded by broad monochrome spaces framed with thin, decorative architectural motifs or large-scale villas and landscapes. In the Fourth Style, artists used features of all three previous styles.

7.18 *right* **Second Style Roman painting, from the villa at Oplontis, Italy, 1st century B.C. Fresco.**

7.19 **Fresco, Villa of the Mysteries, south wall, outside Pompeii, *c.* 60 B.C., 5 ft. 3 in. (1.62 m) high.**

A MUSICAL MOSAIC The mosaic in figure **7.20** decorated a villa in Pompeii. It shows street musicians from a Roman comedy and is thought to illustrate a scene in a play. It also depicts some of the musical instruments popular in Rome. Roman actors, like their Greek counterparts, wore masks, and Roman musicians played Greek instruments. Here, the woman wears a white mask and plays a double flute (the *aulos*, which the Romans called a *tibia*). The men wear darker masks and dance to the music of a large tambourine and small cymbals. As in Greek theater, Roman performances included music, but in the absence of musical notations, it is not known how Roman music sounded.

7.20 ***Street Musicians*, from the Villa of Cicero, Pompeii, *c.* 100 B.C. Mosaic, $16^{7}/_{8} \times 16^{1}/_{8}$ in. (42.5×41 cm). National Museum, Naples.**

PHILOSOPHY: LUCRETIUS

Romans were more legally than philosophically inclined. They were interested in civic and military duty rather than abstract philosophical thought. Nevertheless, they adapted from Greece the Stoic and Epicurean philosophies—although the latter had few followers. Stoicism, which was the prevailing philosophy during the empire, is discussed later in this chapter.

The only significant Roman follower of Epicurus during the republic was the poet Lucretius (98–*c.* 55 B.C.). His long work, *On the Nature of Things* (*De rerum natura*), combines verse with philosophy. He concludes from the atomism of Democritus (see Chapter 6) that it is best to follow the live-and-let-live attitude of Epicurus. For example, Lucretius argues that human autonomy makes happiness possible, that religion is superstition, and that the gods—should they exist—do not affect the course of human life.

His disregard of the gods notwithstanding, Lucretius opens his poem with a passionate appeal to the goddess Venus to inspire the work. It is a hymn to the beauty of nature and to the creative powers of the goddess. Like Virgil, Lucretius links Venus to the founding of Rome:

> Mother of Aeneas and his race, darling of men and gods, nurturing Venus, who beneath the smooth-moving heavenly signs fill with yourself the sea full-laden with ships, the earth that bears the crops, since through you every kind of living thing is conceived and rising up looks on the light of the sun: from you, O goddess, from you the winds flee away, the clouds of heaven from you and your coming; for you the wonder-working earth puts forth sweet flowers, for you the wide stretches of oceans laugh, and heaven grown peaceful glows with outpoured light.
>
> (*On the Nature of Things*, Bk. I.1–10)

Lucretius's purpose is extensive. He describes the behavior of atoms (the basic unit of nature) and conceives of the universe as composed of matter and void:

> For since the first-beginnings of things wander through the void, they must all be carried on either by their own weight or by a chance blow from another atom. For when in quick motion they have often met and collided, it follows that they leap apart suddenly in different directions; and no wonder, since they are perfectly hard in their solid weight and nothing obstructs them from behind.
>
> (Bk. II.80–88)

According to Lucretius, atoms alone comprise the mind and the spirit and themselves have no feeling. There is, therefore, no need to fear death. "The sum of things," he writes,

> is ever being renewed, and mortal creatures live dependent one upon another. Some species increase, others diminish, and in a short space the generations of living creatures are changed and, like runners, pass on the torch of life.
>
> (Bk. II.76–80)

THEATER: ROMAN COMEDY

As the Roman Republic declined, literature flourished. New genres developed, in part as a result of Greek influence. One example of this is the popularity of Hellenistic New Comedy (see Chapter 6), which influenced the early Roman comedies of Plautus (*c.* 250–184 B.C.) and Terence (*c.* 195–159 B.C.). Terence was the more elegant of the two; Plautus was known for his bawdy, slapstick humor, verbal punning, stock characters, and lively plots. The lyrics of both Plautus and Terence were set to music.

The first lines of *The Braggart Soldier* (*Miles Gloriosus*), convey a sense of Plautus's literary style. The scene opens in front of two houses on a street in the Greek colony of Ephesus, in modern Turkey. A pompous Pyrgopolynices is proud of his huge shield and claims to be a brave soldier. He enters with Artotrogus, who portrays the popular stock character of a flatterer.

> PYRGOPOLYNICES: Look lively—shine a shimmer on that shield of mine
> Surpassing sunbeams—when there are no clouds, of course.
> Thus, when it's needed, with the battle joined, its gleam
> Shall strike opposing eyeballs in the bloodshed—bloodshot!
> Ah me, I must give comfort to this blade of mine
> Lest he lament and yield himself to dark despair.
> Too long ere now has he been sick of his vacation.
> Poor lad! He's dying to make mincemeat of the foe.
> . . . Say, where the devil is Artotrogus?
> ARTOTROGUS: He's here—
> By Destiny's dashing, dauntless, debonair darling.
> A man so warlike, Mars himself would hardly dare
> To claim his powers were the equal of your own.
> PYRGOPOLYNICES [preening]: Tell me—who was that chap I saved at Field-of-Roaches?
> Where the supreme commander was Crash-Bang-Razzle-Dazzle
> Son of Mighty-Mercenary-Messup, you know, Neptune's nephew?
> ARTOTROGUS: Ah yes, the man with the golden armour, I recall.
> You puffed away his legions with a single breath
> Like wind blows autumn leaves, or straw from thatch-roofed huts.
> PYRGOPOLYNICES: A snap—a nothing, really.
>
> (*The Braggart Soldier*, lines 1–17)

READING SELECTION

Plautus, *The Pot of Gold*, on why it is best to marry a poor wife, PWC1-220

RHETORIC: CICERO

The art of rhetoric (logical argument) was an important part of Roman education. The greatest and most influential Roman orator of the first century B.C. was the upper-class citizen Marcus Tullius Cicero (106–43 B.C.). He began his career as a lawyer, and his courtroom arguments, especially those defending accused murderers, made his reputation as a master of rhetoric. He published his legal speeches as well as works on religion, and moral and political philosophy.

In 63 B.C. Cicero was elected consul, and he became famous for his political speeches. After his death, some nine hundred of his letters, which reveal an intimate picture of his personality, were also published. Cicero had studied Greek, but his culture was thoroughly Roman. A strong supporter of the republic and its laws, Cicero hated tyranny and had the following to say after the assassination of Julius Caesar:

> We recently discovered, if it was not known before, that no amount of power can withstand the hatred of the many. The death of this tyrant [Caesar], whose yoke the state endured under the constraint of armed force and whom it still obeys more humbly than ever, though he is dead, illustrates the deadly effects of popular hatred; and the same lesson is taught by the similar fate of all other despots, of whom practically no one has ever escaped such a death. For fear is but a poor safeguard of lasting power; while affection, on the other hand, may be trusted to keep it safe forever.
>
> (Cicero, *On Duties*, Bk. II.23:7)

READING SELECTION

Cicero, *Select Political Speeches*, the value of literature, PWC1-040

THE POETS

One of Rome's major poets, Gaius Valerius Catullus (*c.* 84–*c.* 54 B.C.) was born in Verona, in northern Italy. He moved to Rome around 62 B.C. and frequented an upper-class, somewhat degenerate social set. He fell in love with Clodia, the sister of one of Cicero's enemies and the wife of a consul. Their romance, as reflected in Catullus's brief poems, was fraught with heights of passion, bouts of distrust, and despair caused by Clodia's infidelities. He addresses her in the poems as Lesbia. Here Catullus is at his most ardent:

> We should live, my Lesbia, and love
> And value all the talk of stricter
> Old men at a single penny.
> Suns can set and rise again;
> For us, once our brief light has set,
> There's one unending night for sleeping.
> Give me a thousand kisses, then a hundred,
> Then another thousand, then a second hundred,
> Then still another thousand, then a hundred;
> Then, when we've made many thousands,
> We'll muddle them so as not to know
> Or lest some villain overlook us
> Knowing the total of our kisses.
>
> (Catullus, No. 5)

In this famous poem, Catullus is tormented by ambivalence:

> I hate and love. Perhaps you're asking why I do that?
> I don't know, but I feel it happening and am racked.
>
> (No. 85)

The other major Roman poet of the period was Virgil (see p. 145), whose bucolic *Eclogues* were influenced by the idylls of Theocritus, and whose *Georgics* praise country life. The following passage from the *Georgics* describes the orderly lifestyle of bees:

> They alone have children in common, hold the dwellings of their city jointly, and pass their life under the majesty of law. They alone know a fatherland and fixed home, and in summer, mindful of the winter to come, spend toilsome days and garner their gains into a common store. For some watch over the gathering of food, and under fixed covenant labour in the fields; some, within the confines of their homes, lay down the narcissus' tears and gluey gum from tree-bark as the first foundation of the comb, then hang aloft clinging wax; others lead out the full-grown young, the nation's hope; others pack purest honey, and seal the cells with liquid nectar. To some it has fallen by lot to be sentries at the gates, and in turn they watch the rains and clouds of heaven . . . All aglow is the work, and the fragrant honey is sweet with thyme . . . The aged have charge of the towns, the building of the hives, the fashioning of the cunningly wrought houses . . . All have one season to rest from labour, one season to toil.
>
> (Virgil, *Georgics*, 4:152–184)

Virgil's friend and fellow poet Quintus Horatius Flaccus (65–8 B.C.), known as Horace, wrote odes inspired by Greek lyrics. He found a wealthy backer, Maecenas, to whom he dedicated his first ode. He compares different paths to fame and glory, beginning with Olympic athletes and Roman politicians, and concluding with lyric poets:

> Maecenas, sprung from an ancient line of kings,
> my stronghold, my pride, and my delight,
> some like to collect Olympic dust
> on their chariots, and if their scorching wheels
> graze the turning-post and they win the palm of glory
> they become lords of the earth and rise to the gods;
> one man is pleased if the fickle mob of Roman citizens
> competes to lift him up to triple honors;
> . . . .
> As for me, it is ivy, the reward of learned brows,
> that puts me among the gods above. As for me,
> the cold grove and the light-footed choruses of Nymphs
> and Satyrs set me apart from the people

if Euterpe lets me play her pipes, and Polyhymnia*
does not withhold the lyre of Lesbos.
But if you enrol me among the lyric bards
My soaring head will touch the stars.

*Euterpe and Polyhymnia are two of the nine Muses

(Horace, Ode I)

READING SELECTION

Horace, *The Art of Poetry*, on how to write poetry, PWC1-235

THE END OF THE REPUBLIC

Several factors led to Rome's evolution from a republic to an empire. One was an increase in economic and social conflicts between the patricians who were in control of the senate; another was the rise of the *equites*, who were opposed to the senators; and a third problem arose as small farmers were forced by wealthy landowners to sell their farms. When the small farmers then migrated from the country to the city, they lost their livelihoods and created a new, impoverished class. Civil war, following Caesar's assassination in 44 B.C., added to the unrest until Octavian defeated his rival Mark Antony and took control of Rome. Octavian claimed to be in favor of the republic and promised to restore order, but in fact he became the first of a long line of emperors. Some emperors were good rulers, a few were dissolute or insane, or both; others were merely incompetent. All had absolute power.

Octavian was Caesar's grandnephew and had been adopted as his son so that he could inherit Caesar's fortune and power. In 27 B.C. Octavian took the title *Augustus*, which combines connotations of dignity, reverence, divinity, and prosperity. He maneuvered to have Caesar deified (declared a god), making himself *divi filius* ("son of the god"). The republic drew to a close when Augustus assumed the power of veto over all laws passed by the senate. In 12 B.C., Augustus was declared *pontifex maximus*.

THE ROMAN EMPIRE: 27 B.C.–A.D. 476

Augustus succeeded in restoring peace. Known as the *Pax Romana* ("Roman Peace"), this lasted for two hundred years, during which time Rome became *caput mundi* ("head of the world") (map **7.4**) and survived the worst of its emperors. Peace freed the Romans from having to finance wars, permitting them to undertake cultural programs—in the arts, architecture, and literature—of

Map 7.4 The expansion of the Roman Empire, 133 B.C.–*c.* A.D. 180.

monumental dimensions. Even the distant provinces of the empire recognized the benefits of Roman rule, which included economic prosperity and the increasing ease of attaining Roman citizenship.

Society and Culture

Greek and Roman Coinage

Coins are more than units of monetary exchange. They are also a relatively inexpensive means of circulating images to an entire population. Ancient Greeks and Romans understood this, as we do today (see the symbols on the U.S. quarter, for example). Among the Greek coins were the Owls of Athena, showing the profile head of the goddess of wisdom on the **obverse** (the front), and an owl, an attribute of Athena, on the **reverse** (the back) (figure **7.21**). Then, as now, the owl was a symbol of wisdom—hence the term "wise old owl." Next to the owl is an olive branch, Athena's gift to Athens, whose economy depended on the olive tree. The *A TH E* alludes to both the goddess and her city.

7.21 Athenian tetradrachm, *c.* 530–490 B.C. Silver, 1 in. (2.4 cm) diameter. Museum of Fine Arts, Boston.

Figure **7.22** shows a Roman coin minted by Augustus. Following the Greek model, the Augustan coin depicts the emperor's profile on the obverse and an emblematic image on the reverse. The emblem consists of an elephant on a triple arch surmounting an aqueduct. Both structures refer to the architectural achievements of Rome and its vast empire. Elephants, which were imported from Nubia and India, symbolized strength and long life. In Rome they were the exclusive property of the emperor.

7.22 Roman coin with the head of Augustus, and Augustus and an elephant on an arch resting on an aqueduct, 17 B.C. British Library, London.

IMPERIAL AUGUSTAN IMAGERY

Augustus was a genius in the use of imagery for political propaganda. One particularly successful technique was aligning himself in the public mind with his adoptive father, Julius Caesar. To this end, Augustus completed the building projects begun by Caesar and added new ones of his own. He built theaters, aqueducts, roads, race tracks, temples, and other public buildings throughout Roman territory. He also built the forum of Augustus in Rome and minted coins showing himself as a just and benevolent ruler (see Box).

A major example of Augustan iconography is the *Augustus of Prima Porta* (figure **7.23**). This large-scale portrait idealizes the new emperor. He appears handsome and youthful in a pose reminiscent of Polykleitos's *Spearbearer* (see figure 6.22). The meaning of this statue is intentionally political, for it depicts Augustus in the role of a victorious general, an *imperator*—the title Julius Caesar had earned with his military victories. Unlike Caesar, Augustus was not a great general, but he

7.23 *Augustus of Prima Porta*, after a bronze of *c.* 20 B.C., early 1st century A.D. Marble, 6 ft. 8 in. (2.03 m) high. Vatican Museums, Rome.

7.24 *Ara Pacis Augustae*, Rome, 13–9 B.C. Marble, outer wall approx. 34 ft. 5 in. × 38 ft. × 23 ft. (10.5 × 11.6 × 7 m).

nonetheless adopted the title for himself. From that time on, only the emperor was allowed to celebrate military triumph as commander-in-chief.

The breastplate of the statue is decorated with reliefs referring to Augustus's defeat of the Parthians (a Near Eastern culture inhabiting Bactria, in modern Afghanistan) in 20 B.C. Augustus raises his right arm as he addresses the troops. The little Cupid by his right leg alludes to the *Aeneid* and the legend that Rome was founded by the son of Venus (who was also Cupid's mother). Both Augustus and Cupid are thus shown as having a divine genealogy—Cupid by virtue of Greek and Roman myth, and Augustus through Rome's descent from Aeneas.

Augustus created his most outstanding example of political imagery, the *Ara Pacis Augustae* (Altar of Peace of Augustus), between 13 and 9 B.C. (figure **7.24**). The *Ara Pacis* was constructed on the Campus Martius (Field of Mars) in Rome. It conveyed the impression of Augustus as the man who brought peace through military triumph. The altar itself is enclosed in a rectangular wall decorated with a frieze glorifying Augustus and his reign.

The detail of the frieze in figure **7.25** illustrates a procession of the imperial family and court. This evokes the characteristic Roman link between rulers and the *paterfamilias* and reflects Augustus's campaign to restore family values to the city. Children are shown together with adults, including senators

7.25 Detail of the procession from the *Ara Pacis*, Rome, 13–9 B.C. Marble, 5 ft. 3 in. (1.6 m) high. Rome.

7.26 ***Gemma Augustea*, c. A.D. 10. Onyx cameo, 7½ in. × 9 in. (19 × 23 cm). Museum of Art History, Vienna.** The iconography of this cameo reflects Augustus's desire to ensure the succession of his stepson Tiberius. The surface of the "gem" is divided into two registers. At the top, Augustus is enthroned in the center beside the helmeted personification of Rome. Rome gazes at Augustus, who looks toward Tiberius as he leaves his chariot at the far left. The armed figure beside Rome is the young Germanicus, Tiberius's adopted son and a renowned warrior ready to fight for the empire. At the right, Augustus is crowned with the symbol of the city of Rome, and a personification of Italy sits on the ground with images of plenty. In the lower register, Roman soldiers defeat a group of foreigners and take them prisoner.

wearing togas—a reminder that Augustus encouraged large families because Rome's elite population had been decimated by civil war. At the left of the procession, an elderly Augustus, his head covered, wears the priestly costume of *pontifex maximus*. This alludes to his piety, which provides yet another link between the emperor and Aeneas.

Augustan imagery not only harks back to his divine descent, it also looks forward to his future successor. When Augustus died in A.D. 14, his wife, Livia (58 B.C.–A.D. 29), received the title *Julia Augusta*, designating her power and influence. Her administrative skill and commitment to civic virtue endeared her to the Romans. Although she had no children by Augustus, she did have two sons, Tiberius and Drusus (who died in 9 B.C. after falling from a horse), by her previous marriage. For political stability as well as dynastic continuity, both Livia and Augustus wanted to ensure that Tiberius would be the next emperor.

Announcing the end of Augustus's reign and the beginning of the next is the imagery on the so-called *Gemma Augustea* (Gem of Augustus) (figure **7.26**). A summation of Augustan propaganda, this large cameo shows Augustus ruling over a loyal, victorious army and a prosperous land. His reputation for maintaining civic order extends to the order of imperial succession, which is blessed by the gods. Augustus himself is compared to the supreme god, Jupiter, in whose guise he is shown. Note the eagle, Jupiter's emblem, beneath Augustus's throne. This foreshadows his own posthumous deification, and that of all subsequent emperors.

AUGUSTUS AS A PATRON OF LITERATURE As with visual imagery, Augustus patronized literature in the service of politics. He welcomed Virgil's *Aeneid* and became a friend and patron of the historian Titus Livius, known as Livy (59 B.C.–A.D. 17). Born in Padua, in northern Italy, Livy wrote a history of Rome in 142 books, which describes the mythic founding of the city, its kings, the early republic, and the beginning of the empire up to 9 B.C.

Livy idealized Roman tradition and wanted to record the events that had led to the rise of the greatest city in the world. At the same time, he criticized the social unrest of his own time, which he attributed to moral decline.

READING SELECTION

Livy, *The History of Rome from Its Foundation*, Romulus and Remus and the wolf, PWC1-042

Augustus also befriended Horace and Maecenas and on several occasions asked Horace to write for him. The poet obliged with a *Secular Hymn* and a new collection of odes. Both praise Rome and refer to its divine origin. In the third stanza of the *Secular Hymn*, Horace addresses the Sun:

Life-giving Sun, who with your gleaming chariot
display and then conceal the day, born for ever new
and for ever the same, nothing can you see greater
than the city of Rome.

(Horace, *Secular Hymn*, lines 9–12)

And later in the same poem:

O you gods, since Rome is your work, since through you
Trojan troops once reached the Etruscan shore, that small band
Commanded to change its city and household gods
and find safety in flight
when the chaste Aeneas, who outlived his fatherland,
and carved a free path for his people,
unscathed through the burning city [Troy] to give them
more than they had lost—
O you gods, grant good character to our young,
and peace and quiet to the old, and to the race of Romulus
prosperity, posterity,
and every glory,
and whatever the noble blood of Anchises and Venus
prays for with offerings of white oxen,
let Rome receive, first in war, but merciful
to a fallen enemy.

(lines 37–52)

The third major poet of the Augustan period was Publius Ovidius Naso (43 B.C.–A.D. 17), known as Ovid. He studied rhetoric—his father wanted him to be a lawyer—but decided to write poetry instead. Ovid's *Metamorphoses* has become a standard source for Greek and Roman mythology and has inspired later poets and artists. The *Metamorphoses* deals with the transformations of the gods, including the disguises assumed by Zeus in his pursuit of mortal women. For example, Ovid gives his own account of Zeus's abduction of Europa, which had previously been described by Hesiod (see Chapter 4):

Majesty and love do not go well together, nor tarry long in the same dwelling place. And so the father and ruler of the gods, who wields in his right hand the three-forked lightning, whose nod shakes the world, laid aside his royal majesty along with his sceptre, and took upon him the form of a bull . . . His color was white as the untrodden snow, which has not yet been melted by the rainy south-wind. The muscles stood rounded upon his neck, a long dewlap hung down in front; his horns were twisted, but perfect in shape as if carved by an artist's hand . . . Agenor's daughter [Europa] looked at him in wondering admiration, because he was so beautiful and friendly . . . The disguised lover rejoiced and, as a foretaste of future joy, kissed her hands . . . And now he jumps sportively about on the grass, now lays his snowy body down on the yellow sands . . . The princess even dares to sit upon his back, little knowing upon whom she rests. The god little by little edges away from the dry land, and sets his borrowed hoofs in the shallow water; then he goes further out and soon is in full flight with his prize on the open ocean. She trembles with fear and looks back at the receding shore, holding fast a horn with one hand and resting the other on the creature's back. And her fluttering garments stream behind her in the wind.

(Ovid, *Metamorphoses*, 2.845–875)

Ovid's knowledge of the arts of seduction, among other things, inspired his *Art of Love* (*Ars Amatoria*), which opens as follows:

If anyone among this people knows not the art of loving, let him read my poem, and having read be skilled in love. By skill swift ships are sailed and rowed, by skill nimble chariots are driven: by skill must Love be guided.

(Ovid, *The Art of Love*, I.1–4)

For this poem, or for other reasons Ovid never acknowledged, he was banished by Augustus to Tomi (modern Constanza), a town on the west coast of the Black Sea. He died there after ten unpleasant years of exile, during which he continued to write poetry.

READING SELECTION

Ovid: *The Art of Love*, on where to find women, PWC1-250; *Metamorphoses*, Caesar becomes a god, PWC1-260

PAINTING IN THE AGE OF AUGUSTUS Under Augustus, painters developed the Third Pompeian Style of wall painting. Like the First and Second Styles, the Third survives on walls of villas that belonged to wealthy Romans. The best early Third Style paintings are from a dismantled villa at Boscotrecase (figure **7.27**). They consist mainly of delicate landscapes framed by thin painted architectural dividers and flat rectangles of solid red or black.

ART AND ARCHITECTURE AFTER AUGUSTUS

The use of art and literature for political purposes continued throughout the Roman Empire. After the death of Augustus, with the succession of Tiberius, the Julio-Claudian dynasty (named for Julius Caesar and the later emperor, Claudius) was in place (see Box, p. 169).

THE JULIO-CLAUDIANS Late in the Julio-Claudian dynasty, around A.D. 60, the Fourth Style of wall-painting appeared and continued for several generations. It combines elements of the Second and Third Styles, and shows the influence of Hellenistic art in the lifelike figures and three-dimensional space. Fourth Style subject matter was often taken from Greek myths or Homeric epics, which reinforced perceptions of Rome's heroic ancestry (figure **7.28**).

Nero (ruled A.D. 54–68) was the last emperor of the Julio-Claudian dynasty. He is famous for both his artistic interests and his delusions of grandeur. The allegation that Nero "fiddled while Rome burned" alludes to a fire that swept the city in

7.27 Red room, north wall, from Boscotrecase Villa, near Pompeii, *c.* 12 B.C. Fresco, 10 ft. 10¼ in. (3.31 m) high. Archaeological Museum, Naples. Note the fine detail in the framing and in the foliage above the scene. Perspective lines at the top contribute to the three-dimensional illusion of the wall, and enhance the impression that the viewer is looking through the wall at figures in a distant countryside.

A.D. 64. Instead of rebuilding the destroyed houses of the general population, Nero constructed for himself a huge country villa. It was known as the Golden House, because of its beauty and lavish gold decoration. The original design consisted of an octagonal core, from which radiated numerous rooms embellished with gems and mother-of-pearl. The entrance portico was a mile (1.6 km) long, the pool was set in a space as wide as a pasture, and baths were equipped with saltwater from the ocean and sulphur water from natural springs. In the dining room, a golden dome revolved above

7.28 *Iphigenia Carried to her Sacrifice*, fresco after a 4th-century-B.C. Greek painting, from A.D. 63. National Museum, Naples.
This shows Agamemnon's daughter Iphigenia being carried to her sacrifice (see Chapter 4). Her frantic gestures are characteristic of Hellenistic style. An old priest stands at the right looking skyward at Artemis riding a stag, a reminder that the goddess demanded Iphigenia's death as recompense for Agamemnon's having killed her sacred stag. A statue of Artemis, flanked by a pair of animals, stands on a column. At the left, Agamemnon covers his head and turns from the sight of Iphigenia's forthcoming death.

Society and Culture

Reign Dates of the Major Roman Emperors

Augustus (27 B.C–A.D. 14)
Julio-Claudian Dynasty
Tiberius (A.D. 14–37)
Caligula (37–41)
Claudius (41–54)
Nero (54–68)
Flavian Dynasty
Vespasian (69–79)
Titus (79–81)
Domitian (81–96)
Adoptive Emperors
Nerva (96–98)
Trajan (98–117)
Hadrian (117–138)
Antonine Dynasty
Antoninus Pius (138–161)
Marcus Aurelius (161–180)
Commodus (180–192)
Severan Dynasty
Septimius Severus (193–211)
Caracalla (211–217)
Severus Alexander (222–235)
Period of Anarchy (235–284)
Tetrarchy under Diocletian (284–306)
Late Empire
Constantine I (306–337)
313 Constantine issues the Edict of Milan, granting tolerance to all religions, especially Christianity.
330 Constantine makes Byzantium a new Roman capital.
Visigoths Sack Rome (410)
Goths Sack Rome (476)

an ivory ceiling. At the emperor's command, perfume and flowers floated down from the ceiling onto the guests.

Nero also commissioned a colossal, 120-foot (36-m)-high statue of himself, which was known as the Colossus. But his self-aggrandizing character so offended the Romans that he was forced to commit suicide. A period of civil disruption followed, during which three generals became emperor in the space of a year.

In A.D. 69, Vespasian assumed power and tried to correct the abuses of Nero's reign. The senate officially damned Nero's memory and dismantled both his Golden House and the colossal statue. Vespasian decapitated the Colossus and replaced Nero's head with that of the sun god. He also turned Nero's vast private gardens into a public park. For these and similar actions, Vespasian was said to have given Rome back to the Romans.

THE FLAVIANS Vespasian (ruled A.D. 69–79) was a member of the plebeian Flavian dynasty, who wanted to be thought of as a man of the people. The crowning architectural achievement of his reign was the enormous Colosseum (figures **7.29** and **7.30**), which was designed for violent public entertainments. As an affront to the memory of Nero, the Colosseum stood on the site of his pond and was named after his colossal statue.

On the exterior (see figure 7.29) the first three stories are composed of rows of round arches separated by decorative, engaged columns belonging to three different Orders. Each set of columns appears to support an entablature, but in fact both

7.29 *below* **Colosseum, Rome, *c.* A.D. 72–80. Stone and concrete, originally faced with travertine and tufa, 159 ft. (48.5 m) high.**
This huge oval amphitheater has a concrete core that was originally faced with tufa and travertine. The bloodthirsty tastes of Roman spectators were satisfied by combat between gladiators or between gladiators and lions and other wild animals kept in cages below the central floor. The Colosseum could also be flooded for mock naval battles, and a sophisticated drainage system allowed for the removal of water and blood after the spectacles. In case of inclement weather, awnings were stretched across the top of the amphitheater.

7.30 Interior of the Colosseum, Rome.

columns and entablature are part of a decorative façade and are attached to the underlying arch and pier. At ground level the Order is Tuscan Doric, which conveys an impression of sturdy support. The lighter, more elegant Ionic and Corinthian Orders are on the second and third tiers, respectively. The top level is a solid wall pierced by small square windows.

Romans entered the Colosseum through one of seventy-six ground-level arches into barrel-vaulted (see figure 7.9) corridors, which permitted an easy flow of human traffic. Spectators, fashionably dressed women and men (see Box), ascended a stairway to their seats, of which there were some 50,000. At the end of a gladiatorial contest, one of the twelve Vestal Virgins seated near the imperial box would signal whether the loser should be spared or killed by the gesture of a thumbs up or a thumbs down.

Vespasian's successor, Titus (ruled A.D. 79–81), is known for his victory over the Jews and his destruction of Solomon's Temple (previously rebuilt by King Herod) in Jerusalem (see Chapter 2). After his death and deification, Titus was honored by his brother Domitian (ruled A.D. 81–96), the last of the Flavian emperors, with an imposing triumphal arch (figure **7.32**). This typically Roman structure marked a place of passage through which a triumphant emperor entered the Roman forum. The Arch of Titus celebrated his sack of Jerusalem, and it is decorated with reliefs depicting his army carrying off the spoils of war. Such triumphal arches with single openings were constructed throughout the Roman Empire, and among their later descendants are the Triumphal Arch in Paris, the Washington Square Arch in New York City, and Marble Arch in London.

Society and Culture

The Flavian Coiffure

Under the Flavian emperors (ruled A.D. 69–96), elegant hairstyles became popular. Figure **7.31** shows a Flavian woman as Venus. Her hair is piled on top of her head in a mass of neatly arranged curls. Her perfectly coiffed portrait head is juxtaposed with a semi-nude torso, reminiscent of Greek sculpture—a merging of Greek and Roman traditions typical of the Roman Empire. Note also that wide hips, a departure from the proportions of the Classical ideal, are accentuated by the sharp contrapposto. The stance and gesture convey self-confidence and assertiveness, which were characteristic qualities of Roman matrons. And such elaborate attention to the hairstyle reflects the more public lifestyle of Roman women compared to their Greek counterparts. Upper-class Roman wives owned more slaves than Athenian women, which freed them to shop, attend performances, accompany their husbands on social occasions, and even pursue intellectual achievement and the arts.

7.31 Portrait of a Flavian woman as Venus, late 1st century A.D. Marble, over lifesize. Capitoline Museum, Rome.

7.32 **Arch of Titus, Rome, *c.* A.D. 81. Marble, 50 ft. (15 m) high.**

7.33 *below* **Trajan's Column, Rome, A.D. 113. Marble, 125 ft. (38 m) high.**

TRAJAN: *OPTIMUS PRINCEPS* The emperor Trajan (ruled A.D. 98–117) rose in the ranks of the army and became a Roman consul. Because of his reputation as a good emperor, he was known as *optimus princeps* ("best leader"). He was celebrated for his victory over the Dacians, a tribe that inhabited the region of modern Romania along the Danube River and was known for its goldwork. With the proceeds of his booty, Trajan built a huge retirement colony for his soldiers in North Africa and his forum in Rome.

Dominating Trajan's forum is a monumental freestanding column (figure **7.33**) symbolizing Trajan's defeat of the Dacians. It rests on a podium and is decorated with an innovative spiral frieze of historical reliefs (figure **7.34**). Figure **7.35** shows the section of Trajan's forum containing the Basilica Ulpia, named for Trajan's family. The basilica, a characteristic Roman structure, was a large rectangle with a wide central aisle (the **nave**) separated from the side aisles by rows of columns, with an **apse** (the curved section) at each end. Basilicas were used for social gatherings, business transactions, administration, and law courts (figure **7.36**), and took their name and design from Hellenistic royal audience halls.

In the next chapter, we shall see that the Roman basilica became the basis for the architectural design of early Christian churches.

7.34 *above* **Detail of the frieze, Trajan's Column, Rome.**
This segment of Trajan's Column illustrates a Roman military tactic called the *testudo*, or "turtle." As the soldiers besiege a Dacian fort, they raise their shields to create a protective shell against enemy weapons. Peering over the walls at the onslaught are small Dacian soldiers whose oval shields seem flimsy compared with those of the powerful Roman formation. Dead soldiers lie on the ground below.

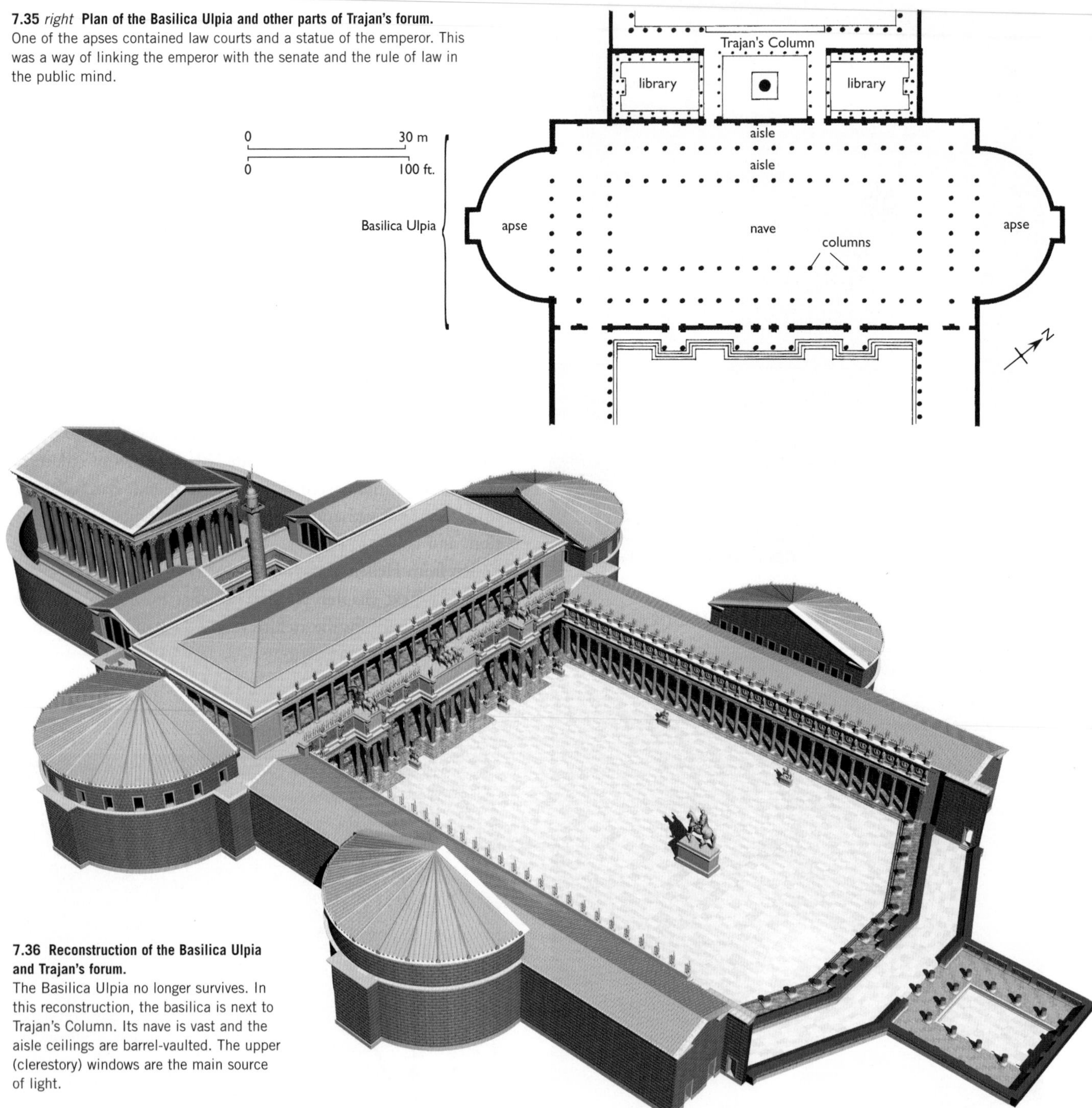

7.35 *right* **Plan of the Basilica Ulpia and other parts of Trajan's forum.**
One of the apses contained law courts and a statue of the emperor. This was a way of linking the emperor with the senate and the rule of law in the public mind.

7.36 Reconstruction of the Basilica Ulpia and Trajan's forum.
The Basilica Ulpia no longer survives. In this reconstruction, the basilica is next to Trajan's Column. Its nave is vast and the aisle ceilings are barrel-vaulted. The upper (clerestory) windows are the main source of light.

HADRIAN: THE PANTHEON Trajan was succeeded by the emperor Hadrian (ruled A.D. 117–138), whose admiration for the Greeks influenced art styles during his reign. He built an enormous villa at Tivoli, outside Rome, and decorated it with copies of Greek statues and floor mosaics.

In Rome, Hadrian commissioned the Pantheon (meaning "all the gods"), a large, round temple dedicated to the five known planetary gods plus the sun and the moon and a remarkable feat of engineering. In the exterior view (figure **7.37**), the large round **drum** (the central space), the **dome** at the top, and the Greek temple front are visible (figure **7.38**).

The interior (figure **7.39**) is a huge circular space. The curved walls are decorated with Corinthian columns and pilasters, niches containing statues of the gods, and different colored stone—tufa, travertine, brick, and pumice. The Pantheon's unique feature is the huge dome, whose square **coffers** (the recessions in the ceiling) decrease its weight. At the center is the round **oculus**, 27 feet (8.23 m) in diameter, designed to allow outdoor light into the interior. The light circles the interior as the earth rotates around the sun, evoking the sun's journey across the sky.

7.37 *left* **Exterior of the Pantheon, Rome, A.D. 125–128. Marble, brick, and concrete.**

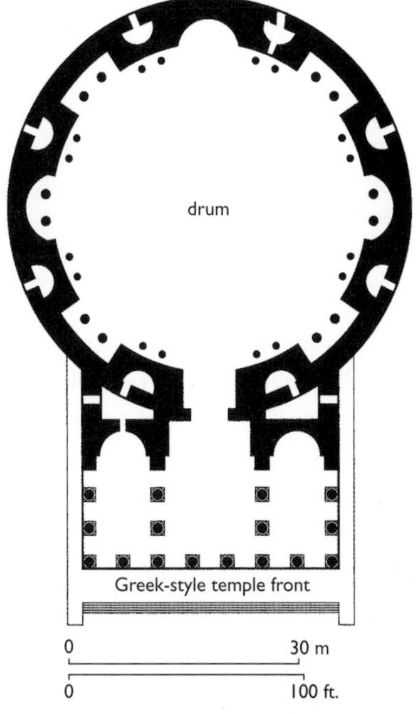

7.38 *above* **Plan of the Pantheon, Rome**

MARCUS AURELIUS: EMPEROR AND STOIC PHILOSOPHER

Marcus Aurelius (ruled A.D. 161–180) was the second member of the Antonine dynasty. He is the subject of the major surviving **equestrian monument** (figure on horseback) of ancient Rome (figure **7.40**), which portrays him as a victorious fighter crushing his enemies. Originally, a small figure of a defeated enemy cowered beneath the raised foreleg of the horse. The emperor was, in fact, continually fighting Germanic, barbarian invaders. Like Hadrian, Marcus Aurelius admired the Greeks, which is reflected in his Greek-style beard. At the same time, however, as with the *Augustus of Prima Porta* (see figure 7.23), Marcus Aurelius wears a Roman military mantle and gestures as if speaking to his troops.

Marcus Aurelius wrote a collection of thoughts that reflect Roman Stoicism. Known as the *Meditations* and written in Greek, these are short instructions to himself. They recommend that he accept his fate with the dignity expected of a loyal Roman:

> Begin each day by telling yourself: Today I shall be meeting with interference, ingratitude, insolence,

7.39 *right* **G. P. Pannini, *Interior of the Pantheon*, c. 1734. Oil on canvas, 4 ft. 2 in. × 3 ft. 3 in. (1.28 m × 0.99 m). National Gallery of Art, Washington, D.C.**

disloyalty, ill-will, and selfishness—all of them due to the offenders' ignorance of what is good or evil. But for my part I have long perceived the nature of good and its nobility, the nature of evil and its meanness . . . therefore none of those things can injure me, for nobody can implicate me in what is degrading.

(Marcus Aurelius, *Meditations*, 2.1)

Hour by hour resolve firmly, like a Roman and a man, to do what comes to hand with correct and natural dignity, and with humanity, independence, and justice. Allow your mind freedom from all other considerations. This you can do, if you will approach each action as though it were your last.

(*Meditations*, 2.5)

Marcus Aurelius's dissolute and depraved son, Commodus, did not live up to his father's ideals. He was murdered in A.D. 192, and a new dynasty, the Severans, came to power.

7.40 Equestrian portrait of Marcus Aurelius, Rome, A.D. 164–166. Gilded bronze, 11 ft. 6 in. (3.5 m) high.

Roman Authors after Augustus

During the reign of the Julio-Claudian dynasty (A.D. 14–68), Rome entered its Golden Age of literature. But praise of Augustus gave way to a somewhat anti-imperial tone, because many authors were aristocrats who resented imperial rule. They believed that the emperors had usurped the power wielded during the republic by the patrician senate.

HISTORY: TACITUS The greatest historian after Livy was Publius Cornelius Tacitus (*c.* A.D. 56–120), who was born two years after Nero became emperor. Tacitus was a member of the provincial aristocracy of the region that now includes southern France and northwest Italy. He became a Roman orator and a provincial governor in Anatolia. Like Livy, Tacitus was devoted to Rome but favored the republic over the empire. Tacitus's *Annals* trace Roman history from the reign of Tiberius to Nero's death in A.D. 68. His *Histories* begin with the death of Nero and end with the assassination of Domitian in A.D. 96. Book I of the *Annals* criticizes Roman history writing as biased, first by fear of an emperor's power and then by hatred of his deeds:

while the glories and disasters of the old Roman commonwealth have been chronicled by famous pens, and intellects of distinction were not lacking to tell the tale of the Augustan Age, until the rising tide of sycophancy deterred them, the histories of Tiberius and Caligula, of Claudius and Nero, were falsified through cowardice while they flourished, and composed, when they fell, under the influence of still rankling hatreds. Hence my design, to treat a small part (the concluding one) of Augustus' reign, then the principate of Tiberius, and without partiality, from the motives of which I stand sufficiently removed.

(*Annals*, I.1)

READING SELECTION

Tacitus, *Annals*, Nero and the burning of Rome, PWC1-010

BIOGRAPHY: SUETONIUS Another type of literature that became prominent in imperial Rome was biography. Gaius Suetonius Tranquillus, known as Suetonius (*c.* A.D. 69–after 122), was secretary to Hadrian and thus had access to state archives. He wrote a series of highly entertaining biographies, *The Twelve Caesars*, which are filled with historical and personal anecdotes. Suetonius depicts the ambivalent character of the Roman emperors, who could be fair and generous, but even the best of them could at any moment switch into the hubristic grandiosity that comes with absolute power.

Suetonius had the greatest admiration for Augustus, describing him as a talented youth fully deserving of Julius Caesar's confidence. According to Suetonius, Augustus had simple tastes, even as emperor, living in a plainly furnished household, sleeping on an ordinary bed, and wearing homemade clothes. He also wore the white toga with a purple stripe of the republican senate and, reflecting a touch of vanity, kept a pair of thick-soled shoes to make him appear taller than he was. Physically, according to Suetonius, Augustus was:

> remarkably handsome and of very graceful gait even as an old man; but negligent of his personal appearance. He cared so little about his hair that, to save time, he would have two or three barbers working hurriedly on it together, and meanwhile read or write something, whether they were giving him a haircut or a shave.
>
> (*The Twelve Caesars*, "Augustus," 79)

READING SELECTION

Suetonius, *The Twelve Caesars*, "Augustus," PWC1-050-B

Suetonius begins the life of Nero by listing his accomplishments. He then proceeds to his follies and vices, including the ridiculous musical ambitions that gave rise to his reputation for fiddling while Rome burned. Suetonius says that Nero tried to develop his singing voice:

> He would lie on his back with a slab of lead on his chest, use enemas and emetics to keep down his weight, and refrain from eating apples and every other food considered deleterious to the vocal chords. Ultimately, though his voice was still feeble and husky, he was pleased enough with his progress to nurse theatrical ambitions.

When singing in Naples, then a Greek city, Nero became so

> captivated by the rhythmic applause of some Alexandrian sailors from a fleet which had just put in, that he sent to Egypt for more. He also chose a few young knights, and more than 5000 ordinary youths, whom he divided into claques to learn the Alexandrian method of applause—they were known, respectively, as "Bees," "Roof-tiles," and "Brick-bats"—and provide it liberally whenever he sang.
>
> (*The Twelve Caesars*, "Nero," 20)

On the subject of Nero's insane vices, Suetonius is eloquent:

> Not satisfied with seducing free-born boys and married women, Nero raped the Vestal Virgin Rubria . . . Having tried to turn the boy Sporus into a girl by castration, he went through a wedding ceremony with him—dowry, bridal veil, and all—which the whole court attended; then brought him home, and treated him as a wife . . .
>
> The passion he felt for his mother, Agrippina, was notorious; but her enemies would not let him consummate it, fearing that, if he did, she would become even more powerful and ruthless than hitherto. So he found a new mistress who was said to be her spit and image; some say that he did, in fact, commit incest with Agrippina every time they rode in the same litter—the state of his clothes when he emerged proved it.
>
> Nero practiced every kind of obscenity, and at last invented a novel game: he was released from a den dressed in the skins of wild animals, and attacked the private parts of men and women who stood bound to stakes . . . According to my [Suetonius's] informants he was convinced that nobody could remain sexually chaste, but that most people concealed their secret vices; hence, if anyone confessed to obscene practices, Nero forgave him all his other crimes.
>
> ("Nero," 28–29)

Nero was alleged to have murdered his adoptive father (the emperor Claudius), his mother, an aunt, at least one wife, and several other family members. Shortly before his own death at the age of thirty-two, Nero had changed the name of the month of April to Neroneus after himself and was about to change the name of Rome to Neropolis. When he finally killed himself, the senate rejoiced.

STOIC PHILOSOPHY: SENECA Stoic philosophy was introduced to Rome in the late republic by Greek philosophers, but it took on a new cast during the empire. The major Roman Stoic author was Lucius Annaeus Seneca (*c.* 4 B.C.–A.D. 65), who was born in Spain to a wealthy Roman family. He was educated in Rome, where he learned philosophy and rhetoric, and for a time he was a senator. Seneca wrote tragedies inspired by Greek plays, moral essays in the form of letters, and Stoic treatises on nature.

Seneca had the misfortune of being hired as Nero's tutor, and there is some controversy over the degree to which he compromised his moral principles in order to survive. For example, in his letter *On Anger*, Seneca advises his nephew Novatus on how to allay anger, "the most hideous and frenzied of all the emotions." Throughout, Seneca subtly warns of the political dangers in expressing anger against imperial abuse.

Nonetheless, Seneca tried to improve Nero's character by comparing the ruler to a physician and to a ship's captain. He observes that a wise man is "kindly and just toward errors," and a "reformer of sinners," just as a physician tries to heal the sick. Similarly, according to Seneca, when a "skipper finds that his ship has sprung her seams," he does not become angry at the ship or the crew but, rather, rushes to the rescue.

Seneca cites the example of another insane emperor, Caligula, who murdered the son of a Roman soldier because he disliked his appearance. When the soldier, Pastor, pleaded for his son's life, Caligula sentenced him to death as well. Then, in order not to appear completely callous, Caligula invited Pastor to dinner on the very day of his son's burial. Pastor accepted the invitation, because, writes Seneca, he had another son. Pastor was thus an ideal Stoic, capable of restraining his anger in order to save the life of his second son.

Seneca's tragedies reflected his philosophy and influenced Classical theater in fourteenth-century Italy (see Chapter 13), later inspiring Shakespeare as well (see Chapter 15). In A.D. 65,

Seneca was accused of conspiring against Nero and was forced to commit suicide.

READING SELECTION

Seneca, *Moral Epistles*, on whether philosophers should withdraw from the world, PWC1-525-C

SATIRE: JUVENAL AND PETRONIUS The leading Roman author of satirical poems, Decimus Junius Juvenalis, better known as Juvenal (*c.* A.D. 55/60–after 127), wrote sixteen lengthy satires during the reigns of Trajan and Hadrian. His attacks on life in Rome are strongly ironic and pessimistic. Juvenal insulted and reviled the rich, women, homosexuals, foreigners, and inferior literature. At the same time, he idealized the republic. In the third satire, Juvenal attacks the Greeks for being foreigners:

> And while we're discussing Greeks, let us consider
> not the gymnasium crowd, but some bigwig philosophers,
> like that elderly Stoic informer who destroyed his friend and
>   pupil:
> *he* was brought up in Tarsus, by the banks of the river
> where Bellerophon fell to earth from the Gorgon's flying nag
>   [Pegasus].
> No room for honest Romans when Rome's ruled by a junta
> of Greek-born secret agents, men who—like all their race—
> never share friends or patrons, but keep them to themselves.
>
> (Juvenal, Satire 3.114–121)

On the infidelity of women, Juvenal writes:

> The bed that contains a wife is always hot with quarrels
> and mutual bickering: sleep's the last thing you get there.
> In bed she attacks her husband, worse than a tigress
> robbed of its young, and to stifle her own bad conscience
> bitches about his boy-friends, or weeps over some fictitious
> mistress. She always keeps a big reservoir of tears
> at the ready, and waiting for her to command in which
> manner they need to flow: so you, poor worm, are in heaven,
> thinking this means she loves you, and kiss her tears away—
> but if you raided her desk-drawers, the letters, the
>   assignations
> you'd find that your green-eyed adulteress has amassed!
>
> (Satire 6.268–278)

READING SELECTION

Juvenal, *Satires*, on sex-crazed women, PWC1-242

The other leading satirist, Petronius Arbiter (died A.D. 65), was a member of Nero's inner circle and the emperor's authority on taste. He was falsely accused of disloyalty and exiled to Cumae, where he killed himself. His colorful and obscene *Satyricon* contains descriptions of life under Nero and reflects his talent for capturing local speech patterns and conveying humorous images of Roman society. In the "Eumolpus" (part of the *Satyricon*), one of Petronius's characters recites a short verse on hair as a metaphor for growing old:

> Poor boy,
> One moment your hair
> Was shining gold
> And you were more beautiful
> Than Phoebus or his sister [Diana].
> Now you are shinier
> Than a bronze
> Or the round cap
> Of a mushroom after rain.
> You run nervously
> From the laughter of ladies.
> Death's sooner than you think,
> You must believe—
> See now, Death has begun at the top.
>
> (Petronius, *The Satyricon*, "Eumolpus")

In another section of the *Satyricon*, "Dinner with Trimalchio," Petronius satirizes the host's vulgar display of wealth. Trimalchio epitomizes the newly rich social climber:

> The orchestra played, the tables were cleared, and then three white pigs were brought into the dining-room, all decked out in muzzles and bells. The first, the master of ceremonies announced, was two years old, the second three, and the third six. I was under the impression that some acrobats were on their way in and the pigs were going to do some tricks, the way they do in street shows. But Trimalchio dispelled this impression by asking:
>
> "Which of these would you like for the next course? Any clodhopper can do you a barnyard cock or a stew and trifles like that, but my cooks are used to boiling whole calves."
>
> ("Dinner with Trimalchio")

READING SELECTION

Petronius, *Satyricon*, an extravagant banquet, PWC1-237

THE DECLINE AND FALL OF THE ROMAN EMPIRE

For generations, historians have argued about the reasons for the decline of the Roman Empire. If Roman literature is any indication, it would appear that moral corruption and depraved rulers had a hand in the fate of Rome. But other factors also contributed, including the barbarians beyond the boundaries of the empire and the internal anarchy that erupted when the last Severan emperor died in A.D. 235. In an effort to quell civil unrest and restore imperial control, the emperor

Diocletian established a **tetrarchy** of four co-rulers. But the turmoil persisted, and several emperors were assassinated by the army, which was itself in disarray. At the same time, the rise of Christianity (see Chapter 8) provided an alternative to paganism and posed a challenge to the empire.

The late empire begins with the rule of Constantine I (ruled A.D. 306–337). He legalized Christianity and in A.D. 330 established a new capital in Byzantium (Istanbul, in modern Turkey). Under Constantine, who tried to assimilate the popular appeal of Christianity, Christian churches began to be constructed in Rome. We can see how different Constantine's political image was from that of Augustus by comparing the head and hand of his colossal marble statue (figure **7.41**) with the more human scale of the *Augustus of Prima Porta* (see figure 7.23).

Not even Constantine, however could maintain the Roman Empire as it had been since 27 B.C. In A.D. 410, a German tribe, the Visigoths, took advantage of the weakened empire and sacked Rome. This was followed by a period of invasion throughout Europe and a second sack of Rome in A.D. 455. Rome's final demise came in A.D. 476, when the city fell to barbarian Goths. In the next chapter we turn to the development of Christianity and its roots in Judaism, against the background of pagan cults prevalent in the Mediterranean world.

7.41 Elbow, head, knee, and hand of Constantine's colossal statue, Palazzo dei Conservatori, Rome, A.D. 313. Marble, head 8 ft. 6 in. (2.6 m) high.

This statue once stood in the apse of Constantine's Basilica. At over 30 ft. (9 m) high, with stylized hair patterns, an abstracted gaze, and an upwardly pointing finger, the statue was an image of awe-inspiring, divine power.

Thematic Parallels

Deadly Games: Gladiators and Mesoamerican Ball-players

There is little question that the gladiatorial games held at the Roman Colosseum and attended by thousands were often deadly. To the degree that they pleased the crowds, these events may be considered to have been popular entertainment. But the games had originated as religious rituals, perhaps as substitutes for human sacrifices offered to the gods.

Another deadly contest, which remained explicitly religious, took place in some early Mesoamerican cultures (map **7.5**), especially during the Classic and early post-Classic periods (600–1200). This was the ritual ball game, the meaning of which is debated by scholars. Both the Roman and the Mesoamerican contests had elements of theater, spectatorship, and ritual violence. But the ball courts do not appear to have had seats; spectators would have had to watch from the walls surrounding the court (figure **7.42**).

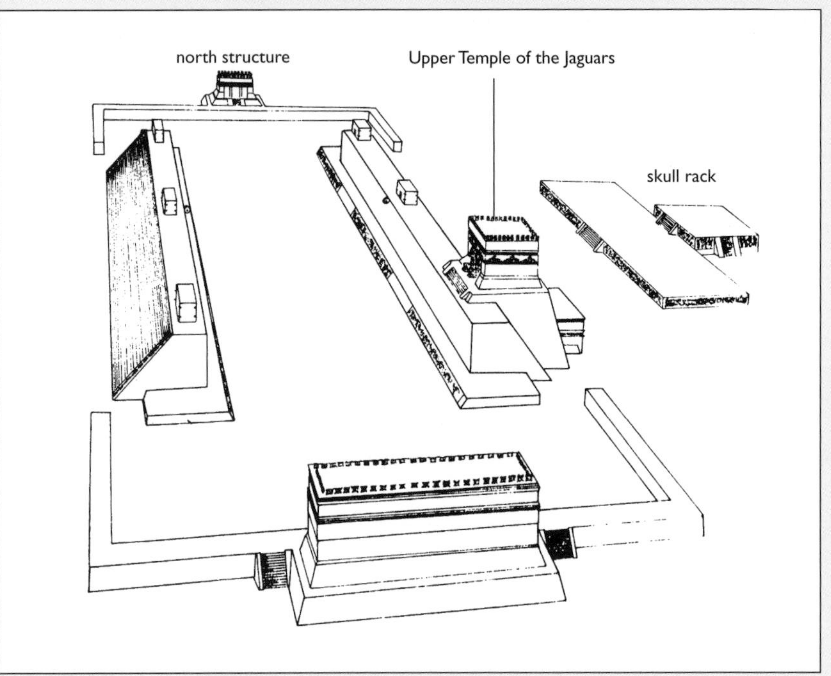

7.42 Diagram of the ball court at Chichén Itzá, Mexico.

The nature of the sites also differed. The Roman Colosseum was built over Nero's pond largely for political reasons; the ball courts were oriented according to the symbolic meaning of a local landscape. Often they continued a natural line of sight from a nearby mountain.

According to descriptions of the Mesoamerican ball game by Spanish conquerors, players wore heavy padding and used only their hips and arms (not their hands or feet). The object was to knock a heavy rubber ball through elevated narrow hoops attached to the inner walls of the court. The ball game appears to have combined athletic skill with

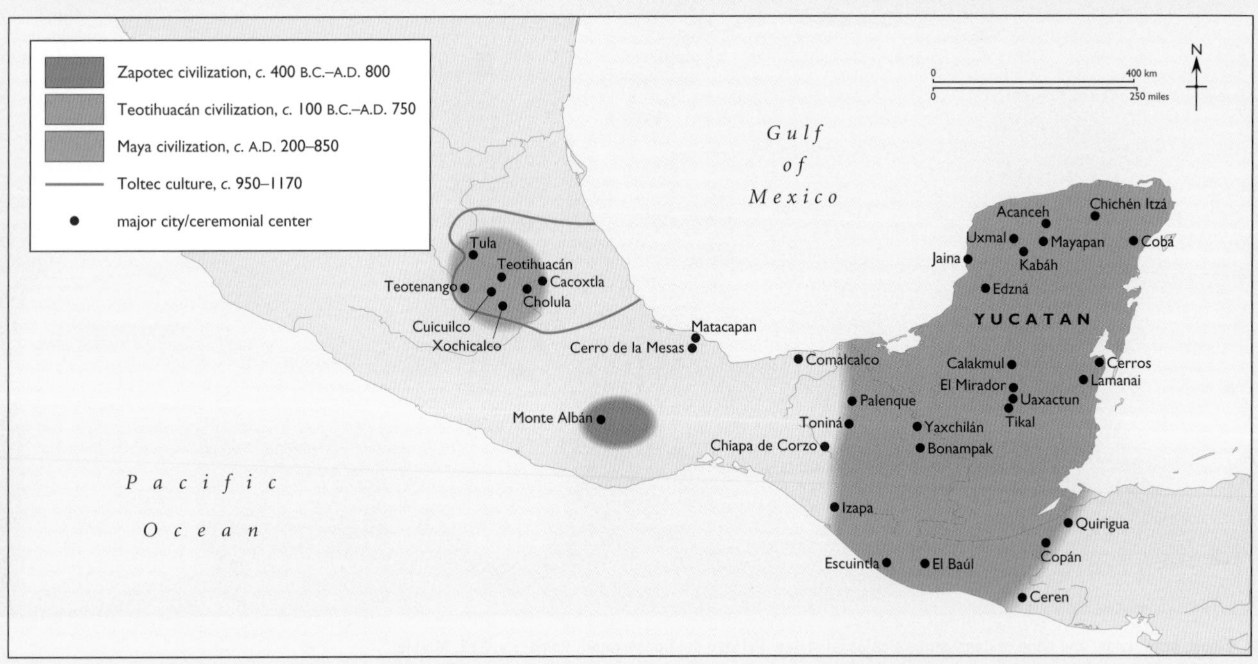

Map 7.5 Classic cultures of Mesoamerica, *c.* 400 B.C.–A.D. 1170.

ritual. Sacrifices involved offering human blood to the gods, and allusions to war suggest that captives might have been players. In some cases people gambled on the outcome of a game. The Mesoamerican ball game was also played by the Native American Hohokam culture of Arizona, suggesting cultural interchange between the two regions.

The game itself is described in the pre-Columbian Mayan creation epic, the *Popol Vuh*, which, like *The Epic of Gilgamesh* and the Homeric tales, was transmitted orally for centuries and written down only much later (in the seventeenth century). According to the *Popol Vuh*, the ball game, played by two sets of Hero Twins against the lords of Xibalba (the Underworld), is a metaphor for life and death. A first set of twins, One-Hunahpu and Seven-Hunahpu, had angered the lords of Xibalba (One Death and Seven Death) because their game made too much noise. One and Seven Death complain:

What's happening on the face of the earth? They're just stomping and shouting. They should be summoned to come play ball here. We'll defeat them, since we simply get no deference from them. They show no respect, nor do they have any shame. They're really determined to run right over us!

(*Popol Vuh*)

The twins were invited to play against the gods and were killed. The head of One-Hunahpu was hung from a calabash tree and caused it to bear fruit. Blood Gatherer, the daughter of an Underworld god, passed by, and the head impregnated her with its spit. The head then addressed Blood Gatherer as follows:

7.43 *above* **Bilbao Monument 3, from Guatemala, *c.* A.D. 600. Stone, 9 ft. 6 in. (2.9 m) high. Ethnographic Museum, Berlin.**

It's just a sign I have given you, my saliva, my spittle. This, my head, has nothing on it—just bone, nothing of meat. It's just the same with the head of a great lord: it's just the flesh that makes his face look good. And when he dies, people get frightened by his bones. After that, his son is like his saliva, his spittle, in his being, whether it be the son of a lord or the son of a craftsman, an orator. The father does not disappear, but goes on being fulfilled. Neither dimmed nor destroyed is the face of a lord, a warrior, craftsman, orator. Rather he will leave his daughters and sons. So it is that I have done likewise through you.

(*Popol Vuh*)

(Note the image of spittle as an impregnating force; hence the modern term to be "the spitting image" of a parent.)

Blood Gatherer was exiled from the Underworld and gave birth to a new set of Hero Twins (Hunahpu and Xbalanque), who are doubles of the first twins and the heroes of the Maya creation myth. These new twins have magic powers. When they reach adulthood, they become famed ball-players and call for a rematch against the Underworld gods. This time, the Hero Twins win by trickery and skill. Eventually they are transformed into heavenly bodies.

In the actual ball games of Mesoamerica, losers appear to have been sacrificed, whereas in Roman gladiator contests life or death could depend on the "thumbs up or thumbs down" of a Vestal Virgin or the will of an emperor. The player in figure **7.43** wears a yoke around his waist and offers a human heart to a god. Echoing his gesture is the small skeleton beside him. A large figure with flames and rays resembling the sun hovers over the scene.

Decorating the walls of the ball courts were complex, flat reliefs illustrating various stages of the games and their aftermath (figure **7.44**). This drawing of a scene depicted on a ball court shows a figure at the left holding the severed head of another. At the right, the decapitated body kneels with serpents, symbolizing blood, and a large flower extending upward from his neck. This imagery reflects the Mesoamerican notion that life and death are intermingled rather than being two completely different states.

7.44 Drawing of a relief illustrating the ball game in the Great Ball Court of Chichen Itzá, Mexico.

KEY TERMS

apse the curved section at the end of a nave.

aqueduct a structure designed to transport water.

barrel vault a vault made by extending a round arch through space.

centering a means of holding stones in place during the construction of an arch.

coffer a recessed geometric panel in a ceiling.

cross-vault (or **groin vault**) a vault made by the intersection of two barrel vaults.

dome a hemispherical roof or ceiling; made by rotating a round arch.

drum the circular support of a dome.

engaged column a column that is attached to a wall.

equestrian monument a portrait of a ruler on horseback.

forum the public center of an ancient Roman city.

impost the support of an arch attached to a wall.

keystone in a round arch, the top center stone holding the voussoirs in place.

Lares and Penates Roman household gods.

nave in basilicas, a wide central aisle separated from the side aisles by rows of columns.

necropolis (plural **necropoleis**) a city of the dead.

obverse the front of a coin.

oculus a round opening in a wall or ceiling.

pilaster a square column.

podium (plural **podia**) the masonry forming the base (usually rectangular) of a temple, arch, or other building.

reverse the back of a coin.

springing the upward thrust of an arch.

syncretism a process through which differing belief systems are assimilated.

tetrarchy a form of government by four co-rulers.

travertine a type of pale limestone, used in Roman building, that turns yellow as it ages.

tufa soft, easily workable, volcanic rock, used in Etruscan building.

Tuscan column a form of Doric style, used by the Etruscans.

villa a country estate.

voussoir a wedge-shaped stone used in round arches.

KEY QUESTIONS

1. Judging from the funerary art, what view of the afterlife was held by Etruscans?
2. What aspects of Roman life and Roman art reinforce the concept of *paterfamilias*?
3. What military action did Cato and Caesar consider essential for Rome's rise to power?
4. How were Roman buildings constructed to accommodate large crowds, and how were they used?
5. When Aeneas meets his father in the Underworld, what does Anchises predict for Rome's future? Is his prediction correct? How does Virgil's characterization of Rome differ from his characterization of Greece?
6. Why is Aeneas called *pius Aeneas* by Virgil?
7. How does Caesar describe the Britons?

SUGGESTED READING

Balsdon, J. P. V. D. *Life and Leisure in Ancient Rome*. London: Weidenfeld and Nicolson, 2002.
▸ A study of everyday life in Rome.

Bonfante, Larissa (ed.). *Etruscan Life and Afterlife*. Oxford: Aris and Phillips, 1986.
▸ Everyday life and religion in ancient Etruria.

——. *Etruscan Dress*, 2nd ed. Baltimore: Johns Hopkins University Press, 2003.
▸ A study of form and meaning in Etruscan dress.

Brendel, Otto. *Etruscan Art*. Harmondsworth, UK: Penguin, 1978.
▸ A classic work on Etruscan art.

Brilliant, Richard. *Roman Art from the Republic to Constantine*. London: Phaidon, 1974.
▸ An account of Roman art in context.

——. *Pompeii A.D. 79*. New York: Outlet, 1979.
▸ An account of Pompeii and the eruption of Mount Vesuvius.

Brown, Frank E. *Roman Architecture*. New York: George Braziller, 2000.
▸ A brief interpretive study of Roman architecture.

Chauveau, Michel. *Cleopatra: Beyond the Myth*, trans. David Lorton. Ithaca and London: Cornell University Press, 2002.
▸ A brief biography of the Egyptian queen.

Friedel, David, Linda Schele, and Joy Parker. *Maya Cosmos.* New York: William Morrow, 1993.
- On the religion of the ancient Maya.

Harris, Robert. *Pompeii.* London: Hutchinson, 2003.
- A historical novel about an aqueduct engineer sent to investigate suspicious water activity just before the eruption of Mount Vesuvius.

Johnston, D. *Roman Law in Context.* Cambridge, UK: Cambridge University Press, 1999.
- A study of ancient Roman law in its social, political, and economic context.

Lyttleton, Margaret, and Werner Forman. *The Romans: Their Gods and Their Beliefs.* New York: Orbis Publications, 1984.
- An introduction to ancient Roman religion.

Miller, Mary Ellen. *The Art of Mesoamerica.* London, 1996.
- A survey of Mesoamerican art.

Noble, David Grant. *Ancient Ruins of the Southwest.* Flagstaff, AZ: Noble Northland Publishing, 2000.
- A survey of the surviving ruins of the Native American Southwest.

Pasztory, Esther. *Pre-Columbian Art.* London: Weidenfeld and Nicolson, 1998.
- A general introduction to pre-Columbian art.

Popol Vuh, trans. Dennis Tedlock. New York: Simon and Schuster, 1996.
- A translation of the major Mayan epic.

Ramage, Nancy H., and Andrew Ramage. *Roman Art.* London: Laurence King Publishing, 1996.
- A general introduction to Roman art in context.

Shelton, Jo-Ann. *As the Romans Did.* New York: Oxford University Press, 1988.
- A study of Roman life and culture.

Zanker, Paul. *The Power of Images in the Age of Augustus.* Ann Arbor, MI: University of Michigan Press, 1990.
- A study of the political role of imagery under Augustus.

SUGGESTED FILMS

1917 *Cleopatra*, dir. J. Gordon Edwards

1934 *Cleopatra*, dir. Cecil B. de Mille

1946 *Caesar and Cleopatra*, dir. Gabriel Pascal

1951 *Quo Vadis?*, dir. Mervyn Leroy

1953 *Julius Caesar* (based on Shakespeare), dir. Joseph Mankiewicz

1959 *Ben Hur*, dir. William Wyler

1959 *Spartacus*, dir. Stanley Kubrick

1963 *Cleopatra*, dir. Joseph Mankiewicz

1964 *The Fall of the Roman Empire*, dir. Anthony Mann

1973 *Antony and Cleopatra*, dir. Charlton Heston

1976 *I Claudius* ("Masterpiece Theater" television series)

1979 *Caligula*, dir. Tinto Brass, Giancarlo Lui, and Bob Guccione; screenplay by Gore Vidal

1999 *Titus* (based on Shakespeare), dir. Julie Taymor

2000 *Gladiator*, dir. Ridley Scott

8 Pagan Cults, Judaism, and the Rise of Christianity

"*For unto us a child is born, unto us a son is given: and the government shall be upon his shoulder: and his name shall be called Wonderful, Counsellor, The mighty God, The everlasting Father, The Prince of Peace.*"

(ISAIAH 9:6)

As the Roman Empire was beginning its rise to power, a new religion, Christianity, was taking root in the Mediterranean region. The pivotal figure of the new faith was Jesus, who died around A.D. *33. According to the Christian religion, Jesus was crucified outside Jerusalem, which was then part of the Roman Empire. At first, the followers of Jesus seemed to be members of one of the many cults flourishing throughout the Near East in the Hellenistic period. But, like the Roman Empire, Christianity grew into a powerful force. Eventually it spread to Rome itself, outlasting the empire and becoming central to Western civilization.*

Christianity stems in large part from Judaism, especially the Hebrew Scriptures (written texts). The opening quotation of this chapter is from Isaiah, a prophetic book in the Hebrew Bible (called the Old Testament by Christians). Writing in the eighth century B.C.*, the prophet Isaiah declared that the birth of a child would usher in a new era and an age of peace. This child would be the Jewish Messiah. The word* Messiah, *meaning "anointed" in Hebrew and translated as* Christos *in Greek, at first meant someone who had been given special powers by God. It later came to mean "savior" or "deliverer."*

Isaiah's imagery associates the notion of a child's birth with the beginning of a new age. This idea was basic to both Judaism and Christianity, and it echoes the theme of rebirth after death found in the Egyptian myth of Osiris (see Chapter 3). The thematic similarities between these religions are another example of cross-cultural influences in the Mediterranean region, but before we discuss these world religions, we will consider a few of the pagan cults popular during the period of the Roman Empire.

Key Topics

Syncretism

- Mystery cults
- Mithraic baptism by blood
- The Hebrews
- Christian rites

Martyrs and Heretics

- Persecution of Christians
- The Passion
- Constantine's Edict of Milan

Interpreting God's Word

- Iconography
- Typology
- Gospels
- Gnosis
- Logos

Early Monasticism

- St. Anthony
- Pachomius
- Basil the Great
- Gregory of Nazianus

The Four Doctors of the Church

- Ambrose
- Jerome
- Gregory I
- Augustine

TIMELINE	PAGAN CULTS	JUDAISM	EARLY CHRISTIAN PERIOD A.D. 33–600
HISTORY AND CULTURE	Cults throughout the Mediterranean Syncretism Astrology Osiris and Isis Cybele and Attis Greek mysteries: Eleusinian, Orphism Mithraism (Persia) Animal sacrifice	4000 years old Abraham, Moses Ten Commandments Prophets, Twelve Tribes Rule of kings: Saul, David, Solomon, Herod the Great Assyrian conquest, 722 B.C. Babylonian Captivity, 586 B.C. Jews return to Jerusalem, 538 B.C. Theocracy Diaspora	Life of Jesus (d. A.D. 33) Titus razes Temple of Solomon, A.D. 70 Zealots at Masada Teachings of Jesus Mission of Paul, Acts of Apostles Roman persecutions of Christians Constantine's new eastern capital at Byzantium, A.D. 330 Edict of Milan, A.D. 313 Christianity established as official religion of Rome under Theodosius
RELIGION 	Mysticism Neoplatonism	Covenant, Ark of the Covenant Exodus One God, Yahweh (Jehovah)	Death and Resurrection of Christ Christ as Messiah Typology Creeds established Missionaries and monasteries Heresies: Aryan, Manichean Gnosticism Transubstantiation Trinity Baptism
ART 	*Mithras Slaying the Sacred Bull*, *c.* A.D. 200	Wall-painting of a menorah, 3rd century A.D. *Moses and the Crossing of the Red Sea*, *c.* A.D. 250	Relief from the Arch of Titus, A.D. 81 *Token of St. Agnes*, 4th century A.D. *Good Shepherd*, *c.* A.D. 300 *The Sacrifice of Isaac*, *c.* A.D. 320 Sarcophagus of Junius Bassus, *c.* A.D. 359
ARCHITECTURE 		First Temple of Solomon, Jerusalem, 10th century B.C. Second Temple of Solomon, Jerusalem, 516 B.C.	Old St. Peter's, Rome, *c.* A.D. 330 Santa Costanza, outside Rome, *c.* A.D. 350 Santa Maria Maggiore, Rome, A.D. 432–440
LITERATURE 	Plotinus (*c.* A.D. 205–269/270), *Enneads*	Hebrew Bible: 39 books, including Genesis, Exodus, Psalms, Song of Solomon, Isaiah, Ezekiel Dead Sea Scrolls	New Testament: 27 books–4 gospels, Acts, 21 epistles, Revelation Gnostic Gospels St. Augustine, *Confessions*, *c.* A.D. 397; *The City of God*, A.D. 413–426 St. Ambrose (A.D. 339–397), *De officiis ministrorum* St. Jerome (*c.* A.D. 347–*c.* 420), Vulgate St. Gregory (*c.* A.D. 540–604), *Book of Pastoral Rules*
MUSIC	Used in rituals	Used in liturgy (religious services) Lyre, harp with Psalms of David Responsorial singing	Used in Mass and other church services Ambrose founds Latin hymnody Gregorian chant: monophonic plainsong for liturgy

PAGAN CULTS

Rome assimilated many different cultures under the mantle of its huge empire. It also tolerated various religious cults, as long as they did not interfere with the authority of the emperor.

From ancient Babylon came an interest in astrology, which was also popular in Rome. From Egypt came the cult of Isis, who had restored her brother-spouse, Osiris, to life after his murder and dismemberment by Set (see Chapter 3). Images of Isis nursing the infant Horus made her a popular maternal figure, and the Romans dedicated a temple to her as early as the second century B.C. From Phrygia, in modern Turkey, came the cult of Cybele, the Great Mother Goddess, who was believed to have power over life and death. Her cult, which centered around the myth of Attis, was present in Rome by the late third century B.C. Cybele fell in love with Attis, a handsome mortal youth. When he died, she restored him to life, just as Isis had restored Osiris. But Attis betrayed the goddess, and she had him castrated.

MYSTERIES

From Greece came secret religions, called **mysteries**, or mystery cults. Unlike other cults that welcomed any believer, the mysteries were accessible only to the initiated. The Eleusinian Mysteries, for example, were celebrated in honor of the agricultural goddess, Demeter, and her daughter, Persephone. Orphism was based on the myth of Orpheus, a legendary musician torn to pieces by Maenads (frenzied female followers of Dionysos; see Chapter 6) when he tried to interfere with their cult. Adherents of Orphism believed in reincarnation and in retribution in Hades for those who had led immoral lives.

In general, the mystery cults used agricultural cycles and seasonal rebirth as metaphors of everlasting life. They promised immortality for all people, not only for the deified emperor, and they satisfied the natural wish to see justice done—which could not always be fulfilled in one's lifetime—by promising reward or punishment after death. Rituals performed in the mystery religions included communal meals, in which the body of a god was symbolically eaten; animal sacrifice; initiation and purification ceremonies; and entering into ecstatic, visionary states.

MITHRAISM

The most prevalent religion in Persia (modern Iran) was Mithraism, whose hero, Mithras, was born on December 25. Mithras killed a sacred bull (figure **8.1**) and fertilized the earth with its blood. Followers of Mithras were thus baptized in the blood of a bull. Mithraism's emphasis on masculinity and its exclusion of women appealed to the ideals of Roman soldiers. By the third century A.D., the cult had spread to North Africa and to Europe, as far north as Britain. Under the emperor Commodus (ruled A.D. 180–192), Mithraism became an imperial cult, but by the fourth century A.D. it began to die out.

8.1 *Mithras Slaying the Sacred Bull*, from the mithraeum at Marino, south of Rome, *c.* A.D. 200. Fresco.
One of many images of Mithras slaying the sacred bull, this shows the hero wearing a Phrygian cap, ankle-length, baggy trousers, a short tunic, and a flowing cape decorated with a star-studded night sky. He kneels on the bull, pulls back its head, and plunges a knife into its neck, while a dog and a snake eagerly lick the blood dripping from the wound. To the left and right of a cave entrance are torchbearers; one torch points upward and the other downward. (On Roman sarcophagi, the upright torch symbolized eternal life and the downward one death.) Faces of the sun and moon are visible above vertical rows of Mithraic scenes. Mithras exchanges a glance with the sun, reflecting the association of light with the forces of good in Mithraism. The migration of this motif to the art of the Roman Empire reflects the widespread influence of Mithraic religion.

NEOPLATONISM

Another source of religious thought was Neoplatonism, which was based mainly on the writings (*Enneads*) of the Egyptian philosopher Plotinus (*c.* A.D. 205–269/270), who settled in Rome. His views were mystical both in his sense of the divine and in his Platonic notion of a higher Good, which he called the One. For both Plato and Plotinus, the material world was a mere reflection of the Good and the One, or God. Through meditation, Plotinus believed, it was possible to unite with God. But he also considered God to be beyond the reach of human language and indefinable, except by what he is not.

READING SELECTION

Plotinus, *Enneads*, treatise on beauty, PWC1-072

THE ISRAELITES AND JUDAISM

Judaism has been in existence for around 4000 years. The Hebrew Bible (see Box) begins with the beginning: "In the beginning God created the heaven and the earth," making creation the result of God's Word: "And God said, Let there be light: and there was light." "And God said, Let the waters under the heaven be gathered together unto one place, and let the dry land appear: and it was so" (Genesis 1:1, 3, 9).

The word "Judaism" refers to the belief system of the Hebrews; the word "Israelites" refers to the inhabitants of ancient Israel, who shared certain beliefs with other Mediterranean peoples but differed from them in important ways. At first, the Israelites believed in more than one god, but later, from around the eighth to seventh century B.C., they were monotheistic. Their one god was Yahweh (Jehovah), the one and only God. The name *Yahweh* was so revered that it could not be spoken, nor could images of him be created, which inhibited the development of Jewish pictorial art. Other Mediterranean religions at the time had no such prohibitions.

Prophecy was part of Israelite practice, especially from the eighth to the fifth century B.C., which is reflected in the writings of Isaiah and others. Some warned that the end of time was near and that there would be a final day of judgment. The prophets were united by a shared hope for a better future at the coming of a Messiah and by a belief in living an ethical life. These general principles evolved over a long period, during which history, tradition, faith, fact, and fiction converged.

HISTORY, CHRONOLOGY, AND TRADITION

Much of early Jewish history is unknown. The first biblical figure who can, to some degree, be located in a historical context is Abraham. According to tradition, around 2000 B.C. Abraham was a Hebrew who led his people from their home, believed by some to have been the Sumerian city of Ur (see Chapter 2). Tradition also has Abraham settling in Canaan, an area later called Palestine (see map 8.1, p. 189). Abraham's grandson, Jacob, changed his name to Israel; his twelve sons produced descendants who became the Twelve Tribes of Israel, and the Hebrews became the Israelites.

According to the biblical book of Genesis, Jacob's son Joseph was sold by his brothers into slavery in Egypt, where he became renowned as the pharaoh's dream interpreter. Joseph interpreted

Society and Culture

The Hebrew Bible and the Dead Sea Scrolls

There are three main parts to the Hebrew Bible: the Torah, the Prophets, and the Writings. The first five books—Genesis, Exodus, Leviticus, Numbers, and Deuteronomy—make up the Torah, which is also called the Law or the Pentateuch. The Pentateuch, accepted as divinely inspired from the fifth century B.C., begins with the Creation and the Fall of Man, and concludes with the early history of the Jewish people.

The books of the Prophets, accepted in the first century B.C., elaborate on Jewish history and develop religious ideas. The early Prophets are Joshua, Judges, 1 and 2 Samuel, and 1 and 2 Kings. The later Prophets are Isaiah, Jeremiah, Exekiel, Hosea, Joel, Amos, Obadiah, Jonah, Micah, Nahum, Habakkuk, Zephaniah, Haggai, Zechariah, and Malachi.

The Writings consist of wisdom and visionary texts, poetry, stories, and histories. These are Psalms, Proverbs, Job, Song of Songs, Ruth, Lamentations, Ecclesiastes, Esther, Daniel, Ezra, Nehemiah, and 1 and 2 Chronicles. Most of the Writings were accepted in A.D. 90, but the Psalms were not considered divinely inspired until ten years later.

The books of the Apocrypha were written between 200 B.C. and A.D. 100. These are wisdom texts, stories, and histories that are not accepted as sacred. Later, however, the Catholic Church included them in the Greek version of the Hebrew Bible, known as the Septuagint. Literally the "Seventy," the Septuagint was, according to tradition, commissioned by Ptolemy II of Egypt (ruled 285–246 B.C.). He reportedly asked seventy-two Hebrew elders to translate the Bible into Greek in seventy-two days.

In 1947, a startling new discovery revealed a group of writings hidden in eleven caves near the Dead Sea, in modern Jordan (see map 8.1, p. 189). Written in Hebrew, Aramaic, and Greek on papyrus scrolls, these works have been dated by carbon-14 to between 250 B.C. and A.D. 70. They contain sections of the Hebrew Bible, two versions of Isaiah, and apocryphal and non-sacred writings. The authors of the texts belonged to the militant monastic Qumran community, which lived apart from the Jewish community in Jerusalem. This group is identified with the Essene sect, to which Jesus is thought by some to have belonged.

two of the pharaoh's dreams as omens of widespread famine and instructed him to store food for the future. When Joseph's prediction came to pass, the pharaoh invited his family to Egypt, where they prospered and multiplied. But a new pharaoh came to power and enslaved the Israelites. Eventually, around 1250 B.C., Moses, who had grown up at the pharaoh's court, led the Israelites on a forty-year journey—the **Exodus**—out of Egypt, to freedom. According to the Bible, they traveled through the Sinai Desert to the Promised Land of Canaan.

MOSES Moses is associated with one of the most important tenets of Judaism, namely the **covenant**, a solemn pact between God and the Jews. The covenant established an exclusive relationship, in which God chose the Jews to be his people (hence the expression "Chosen People") and the Jews promised fidelity to God. They agreed that Yahweh would be their one and only God and that they would worship only him. This notion is reflected in the first of the Ten Commandments, a set of religious and ethical rules that God is believed by Jews and Christians to have given to Moses (see Box). Like Hammurabi, who received the laws of Babylon from the sun god Shamash (see Chapter 2), Moses went up a mountain (Mount Sinai) to receive the **Tablets** (also called the **Tables**) **of the Law**.

8.2 ***Wall-painting in a Jewish catacomb*, Villa Torlonia, Rome, 3rd century A.D. 3 ft. 11 in. × 5 ft. 9 in. (1.19 × 1.8 m).**
A menorah, with illuminated candles, stands on either side of the Ark of the Covenant, which is below a painted curtain. This corresponds to God's instructions in Exodus (26:1), where he calls for "ten curtains of fine twined linen, and blue, and purple, and scarlet." Note that the Ark resembles a miniature temple with a crowning pediment, indicating the influence of Greek and Roman architecture on this artist's conception of the Ark.

The Ten Commandments

The Ten Commandments embody the ethical and religious rules of Judaism. The first four describe the relationship between God and the Israelites:

1. *Thou shalt have no other gods before me.*
2. *Thou shalt not make unto thee any graven image, or any likeness of any thing that is in heaven above, or that is in the earth beneath, or that is in the water under the earth.*
3. *Thou shalt not take the name of the Lord thy God in vain.*
4. *Remember the Sabbath day, to keep it holy.*

(Exodus 20:3–8)

The last six commandments establish social order:

5. *Honor thy father and thy mother.*
6. *Thou shalt not kill.*
7. *Thou shalt not commit adultery.*
8. *Thou shalt not steal.*
9. *Thou shalt not bear false witness against thy neighbor.*
10. *Thou shalt not covet thy neighbor's wife . . . nor any thing that is thy neighbor's.*

(20:12–17)

To house the Tablets of the Law, Moses and his followers built a sacred container, the **Ark of the Covenant**, and carried it with them to the Promised Land. The Ark also housed a **menorah** (a candelabrum with seven candlesticks, three on each side and one in the center) and other holy objects (figure **8.2**). In the book of Exodus, God tells Moses how to design the menorah:

> And thou shalt make a candlestick of pure gold: of beaten work shall the candlestick be made . . . And six branches shall come out of the sides of it . . . Three bowls made like unto almonds [almond blossoms], with a knop [calyx] and a flower [petal] in one branch; and three bowls made like almonds in the other branch, with a knop and a flower; so in the six branches that come out of the candlestick.
>
> (Exodus 25:31–33)

One of the most dramatic events in Exodus is the parting of the Red Sea, a miracle that allowed the Israelites to escape their Egyptian pursuers:

> And Moses stretched out his hand over the sea; and the Lord caused the sea to go back by a strong east wind all that night, and made the sea dry land, and the waters were divided.
>
> And the children of Israel went into the midst of the sea upon the dry ground and the waters were a wall unto them on their right hand, and on their left.
>
> And the Egyptians pursued, and went in after them to the midst of the sea, even all Pharaoh's horses, his chariots, and his horsemen . . .

> And the Lord said unto Moses, Stretch out thine hand over the sea, that the waters may come again upon the Egyptians, upon their chariots, and upon their horsemen . . .
>
> And the waters returned, and covered the chariots, and the horsemen, and all the host of Pharaoh . . .
>
> But the children of Israel walked upon dry land in the midst of the sea; and the waters were a wall unto them on their right hand, and on their left.
>
> (Exodus 14:21–29)

Although figurative imagery was prohibited, the parting of the Red Sea was nonetheless illustrated in a monumental wall-painting of around A.D. 250 in Dura Europos, a town in modern Syria where Roman soldiers were garrisoned. The work is a major example of the presence of a Jewish pictorial tradition under Roman rule. Several Mithraic and Roman shrines, in addition to Christian and Jewish places of worship, were discovered at Dura Europos, indicating a mix of different religions.

The *Crossing of the Red Sea* (figure **8.3**) illustrates the biblical text. Moses and his brother Aaron stand firmly on dry land, their togas reflecting Roman influence. Above, the hand of God descends from heaven to divide the water. At the right, the pursuing army, stripped of its arms, begins to drown. Leaping fish add an element of lively visual description.

MONARCHY AND CONFLICT Over the next two centuries, the Twelve Tribes established a monarchy with Saul as its first king. His armies defeated the Philistines, thought to have been a Sea People who settled in the Near East around 1100 B.C. Under David (ruled *c.* 1000–960 B.C.) and his son, Solomon (ruled *c.* 960–933 B.C.), the Israelites prospered. Solomon built the Temple, which is described in detail in the Bible. Located on the site of the Temple Mount in modern Jerusalem, it was rectangular and constructed of cedar wood from Lebanon. A front porch led to a holy inner sanctuary that contained the Ark of the Covenant. Two bronze columns flanked the entrance, and the entire surface of the Temple was covered with gold.

Solomon instituted certain repressive financial policies that led to class conflict and caused Israel to split into two kingdoms. After his death, ten of the tribes formed the kingdom of Israel in the north, while the remaining two tribes retained the kingdom of Judah in the south, with Jerusalem as its capital (map **8.1**). This division weakened the power of Israel.

In 722 B.C. the kingdom of Israel was conquered and its people were dispersed by the Assyrians (see Chapter 2). In 586 B.C., Nebuchadnezzar II of Babylon attacked Jerusalem and razed the Temple. He exiled the citizens of Judah to Babylon, hence the term for this period—the Babylonian Captivity (also known as the Babylonian Exile). In 538 B.C., the Persians conquered Babylon and permitted the Israelites (now called Jews) to return to Jerusalem. Those who chose to return rebuilt the Temple in 516 B.C., were ruled by a theocracy (government by priests), and accepted the visionary and prophetic texts written before the period of exile as the word of God. Those who did not return from exile are known as the Jews of the Diaspora (the Dispersion). They remained in Babylon and eventually spread to different regions of the ancient world.

Between the fourth and first centuries B.C., Judah was conquered first by Alexander the Great, who Hellenized the region, and later by the Romans. Rome placed Judah under the rule of local kings. Among these was Herod the Great (ruled 37–4 B.C.). He expanded the second Temple of Solomon, a reconstruction of which is shown in figure **8.4**.

8.3 ***Moses and the Crossing of the Red Sea*, detail, from Dura Europos, Syria, *c.* A.D. 250. Fresco. National Archaeological Museum, Damascus.**

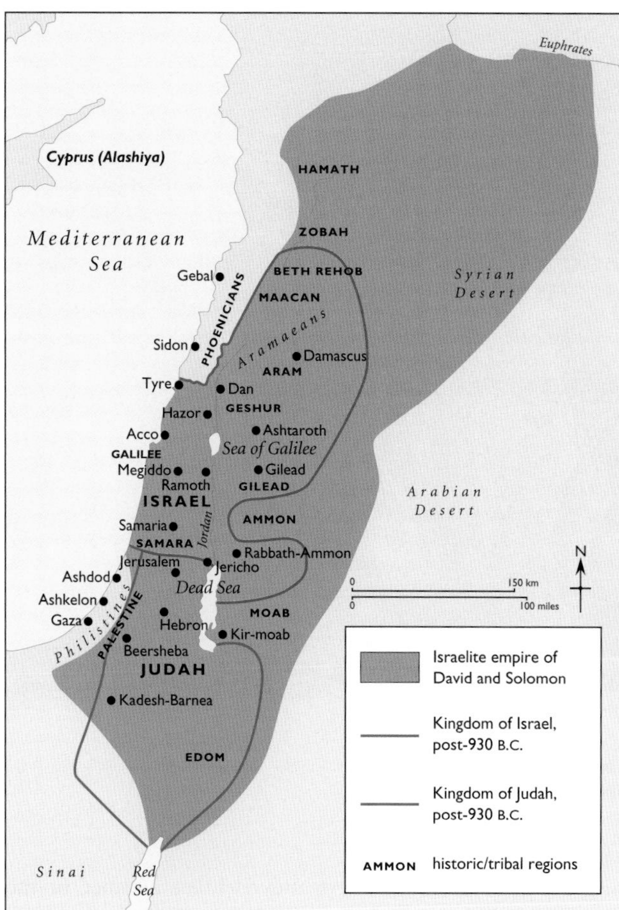

Map 8.1 Ancient Israel.

THE SECOND TEMPLE DESTROYED The Jews rebelled against Roman domination in A.D. 66 and fought until A.D. 70, when the Roman emperor Titus (see Chapter 7) defeated them and destroyed the second Temple. Only one group of so-called Zealots continued to resist. They held out at Masada, a mountain fortress near the Dead Sea. Rather than submit to Roman rule, the Zealots committed suicide.

Like all victors in the ancient world, Titus looted the city, an action memorialized in a relief from the interior of his triumphal arch in Rome (figure **8.5**). The destruction of the Temple was recorded by Flavius Josephus (*c.* A.D. 37–100), a Jewish soldier and statesman who wrote in Greek. He had impressed the emperors Vespasian and Titus and was granted Roman citizenship. According to Josephus, the Temple was destroyed against the wishes of Titus:

> As the legions charged in, neither persuasion nor threat could check their impetuosity: passion alone was in command. Crowded together round the entrances many were trampled by their friends, many fell among the still hot and smoking ruins of the colonnades and died as miserably as the defeated. As they neared the Sanctuary they pretended not even to hear Caesar's commands and urged the men in front to throw in more firebrands . . . everywhere was slaughter and flight. Most of the victims were peaceful citizens, weak and unarmed, butchered wherever they were caught. Round the Altar the heap of corpses grew higher and higher, while down the Sanctuary steps poured a river of blood and the bodies of those killed at the top slithered to the bottom. The soldiers were like men possessed and there was no holding them, nor was there any arguing with the fire.
>
> (Josephus, *The Jewish War*)

READING SELECTION

Josephus, *The Jewish War*, on religion in Roman Judea, PWC1-011

8.4 Reconstruction model of the second Temple, Jerusalem.
Note the engaged Corinthian columns and pilasters, reflecting Hellenistic elegance. Decorating the upper section of the building is a continuous gilded frieze, with finials crowning the projecting cornice.

8.5 Relief from the Arch of Titus, Rome, A.D. 81. Marble, 6 ft. 7 in. (2 m) high.
This shows Titus's soldiers carrying off the spoils of war as they head for the triumphal arch at the far right. Prominently depicted is the large menorah, whose capture symbolizes the triumph of Rome over the Jews.

One wall of the Temple escaped destruction; in modern Jerusalem it is called the Wailing Wall, because it remains a place of mourning. Following the Temple's destruction, the surviving Jews were again dispersed, this time by the Romans, who wanted to avoid future rebellion. Nevertheless, the Jews maintained their cultural unity and, in the absence of a great temple, began to worship in synagogues, led by rabbis (teachers).

With the institution of the synagogue came new religious views and practices. Forms of worship changed from sacrifice to prayer and religious study. Previously, presiding over worship had been restricted to a small number of priests, but it now became a possibility for more people. In contrast to ancient Egypt, where worshippers were relegated to a courtyard, and Greece, where worship was held outside the temple, Jewish ceremonies took place inside the synagogue, and rituals were enacted in the presence of the congregation. The synagogue remains the typical Jewish place of worship today.

THE HEBREW BIBLE AS LITERATURE

The Bible, like the *Iliad* and the *Odyssey*, has had an enormous influence on Western literature. Parts of the Hebrew Bible were first written down in around the tenth century B.C., having been transmitted orally prior to that date. The Bible includes a number of different genres and literary devices. In Exodus, for example, the device of repetition enhances the poetic quality of the story of the crossing of the Red Sea, suggesting the rushing waters and relentless advance of the Egyptian army. Repetition also creates the impression of a divinely inspired **litany** (a form of prayer in which a leader and a congregation speak alternately during a service).

Poetry is the genre of the Psalms of David and the Song of Solomon. Perhaps the best known psalm is the twenty-third:

> The Lord is my Shepherd; I shall not want.
> He maketh me to lie down in green pastures: he leadeth me beside the still waters.
> He restoreth my soul: he leadeth me in the paths of righteousness for his name's sake.
> Yea, though I walk through the valley of the shadow of death, I will fear no evil: for thou art with me; thy rod and thy staff they comfort me.
> Thou preparest a table before me in the presence of mine enemies: thou anointest my head with oil; my cup runneth over.
> Surely goodness and mercy shall follow me all the days of my life: and I will dwell in the house of the Lord forever.

The Song of Solomon (also called the Song of Songs) is essentially a collection of love poems. They are lyrical in style, obscure in meaning, and rich in pastoral metaphor:

> I am the rose of Sharon, and the lily of the valleys.
> As the lily among thorns, so is my love among the daughters.
> As the apple tree among the trees of the wood, so is my beloved among the sons. I sat down under his shadow with great delight and his fruit was sweet to my taste.
> (2:1–3)

And the beginning of Chapter 4:

> Behold, thou art fair, my love; behold thou art fair; thou hast doves' eyes within thy locks: thy hair is as a flock of goats, that appear from mount Gilead.
>
> Thy teeth are like a flock of sheep that are even shorn, which came up from the washing; whereof every one bear twins, and none is barren among them.
>
> Thy lips are like a thread of scarlet, and thy speech is comely; thy temples are like a piece of a pomegranate within thy locks . . .
>
> Come with me from Lebanon, my spouse, with me from Lebanon; look from the top of Amana, from the top of Shenir and Hermon, from the lions' dens, from the mountains of the leopards.
>
> (4:1–3, 8)

There is a great deal of mythic grandeur in the Hebrew Bible, as there is in epic poetry. One cultural purpose of myths is to explain what otherwise seems inexplicable. For example, in Genesis, the story of the Tower of Babel—a Mesopotamian ziggurat (see Chapter 2)—explains why people around the world speak different languages. This was not, however, always the case:

> And the whole earth was of one language, and of one speech.
>
> And it came to pass, as they journeyed from the east, that they found a plain in the land of Shinar; and they dwelt there.
>
> And they said to one another, Go to, let us make brick, and burn them thoroughly. And they had brick for stone and slime had they for mortar.
>
> And they said, Go to, let us build us a city and a tower, whose top may reach unto heaven; and let us make us a name, lest we be scattered abroad upon the face of the whole earth.
>
> And the Lord came down to see the city and the tower, which the children of men builded.
>
> And the Lord said, Behold, the people is one, and they have all one language; and this they begin to do: and now nothing will be restrained from them, which they have imagined to do.
>
> Go to, let us go down, and there confound their language, that they may not understand one another's speech.
>
> So the Lord scattered them abroad from thence upon the face of all the earth: and they left off to build the city.
>
> Therefore is the name of it called Babel; because the Lord did there confound the language of all the earth: and from thence did the Lord scatter them abroad upon the face of all the earth.
>
> (Genesis 11:1–9)

To punish the human race for its hubris in daring to invade the sky, God made its speech garbled so people could no longer communicate with each other. As a result, cooperation came to an end, work stopped, and the tower was never completed. The builders scattered over the earth and formed different language groups. The story of the Tower of Babel demonstrates God's power to destroy as well as to create. In order to reaffirm his supremacy in a universe created by his Word, he reduced the power of human speech by breaking up its unity.

The writings of the prophet Ezekiel are visionary in nature and are said by the Bible to have been directly inspired by God's own Word:

> The word of the Lord came expressly unto Ezekiel the priest, the son of Buzi, in the land of the Chaldeans by the river Chebar; and the hand of the Lord was there upon him.
>
> And I looked, and, behold, a whirlwind came out of the north, a great cloud, and a fire infolding itself, and a brightness was about it, and out of the midst thereof as the color of amber, out of the midst of the fire.
>
> Also out of the midst thereof came the likeness of four living creatures. And this was their appearance; they had the likeness of a man.
>
> And every one had four faces, and every one had four wings.
>
> And their feet were straight feet; and the sole of their feet was like the sole of a calf's foot: and they sparkled like the color of burnished brass.
>
> And they had the hands of a man under their wings on their four sides; and they four had their faces and their wings.
>
> Their wings were joined one to another; they turned not when they went; they went every one straight forward.
>
> As for the likeness of their faces, they four had the face of a man, and the face of a lion, on the right side: and they four had the face of an ox on the left side; they four also had the face of an eagle.
>
> (Ezekiel 1:3–10]

Ezekiel's poetic vision of four divine creatures, part human and part animal, would inspire later Christian imagery.

CHRISTIANITY: THE BIRTH OF JESUS THROUGH THE FOURTH CENTURY

The period of Rome's decline roughly corresponds to the rise and spread of Christianity. It is a religion grounded in Judaism and, like Judaism, has a strong ethical message and is based on Scripture. The Christian texts reflect a belief in the power of God's Word and its sacred character. As with Judaism, the power and promise of faith is a central feature of Christianity. But in contrast to the Jews, who are still awaiting the Messiah, Christians believe that the Messiah is Jesus, a Jew born between 6 and 4 B.C., who died at the age of thirty-three.

The life and teachings of Jesus were not recorded until between A.D. 70 and 100. There is thus no first-hand account of him. His life marks the major division of the traditional Western calendar into B.C. (Before Christ) and A.D. (*anno domini*, Latin for "in the year of our Lord," denoting the time after the birth of Jesus). The main Christian text is the New Testament, which takes Jesus to be the Messiah prophesied by Isaiah and builds on the foundation of the Hebrew Bible (see Box).

Although Jesus did not leave any writings, his message and life are recorded in the four Gospels of the New Testament—Matthew, Mark, Luke, and John. Jesus preached the Jewish belief in a single God who created the human race, but he went beyond contemporary Jewish thinking by placing greater emphasis on faith and forgiveness, on the promise of eternal life, and on God's compassion. Christians are thus expected to perform works of charity in the community. Jesus gathered around him his twelve devoted apostles, performed miracles, and claimed to be the Messiah prophesied by Isaiah.

In the Sermon on the Mount, recorded in the Gospel of Matthew, Jesus sets forth his ethical principles. He promises the poor and unfortunate a blessed future in heaven, he revises Old Testament law, and he advances the notion that one can sin in thought as well as in deed. He also announces that he has come to fulfill the prophecy of a Messiah (see Box):

Society and Culture

The New Testament

The New Testament was written in Greek and accepted as **canonical** by the middle of the second century A.D. It is organized into the Gospels, the Acts, the Epistles, and the Apocalypse (or Revelation).

The four Gospels were written by the Evangelists (literally "bearers of good news"), Matthew, Mark, Luke, and John. The first three are biographies of Jesus. They are called **synoptic** ("seen together") because they are similar enough to be placed side-by-side and viewed together at a glance. Matthew opens with the genealogy (the "begats") of Jesus to demonstrate his descent from the House of David. Mark focuses on the miracles of Jesus. Luke describes Jesus' childhood in the most detail and includes the miraculous birth of John the Baptist.

John's is the most philosophical gospel. It opens with: "In the beginning was the Word, and the Word was with God, and the Word was God." Jesus is thus the *Logos*, the Word of God made flesh (human) by the power of God's speech. John conveys the originality of Jesus' message and the ways in which it departs from traditional thinking. He uses the metaphor of light to express the intellectual newness of Jesus' teachings: "That was the true Light, which lighteth every man that cometh into the world" (1:9). John the Baptist, by contrast, was not *the* light, but rather, "He was . . . sent to bear witness of that Light" (1:7). And whereas Moses had introduced the law, Jesus brought grace and truth: "For the law was given by Moses, but grace and truth came by Jesus Christ" (1:17).

The Acts of the Apostles, written by Luke toward the end of the first century A.D., span a period of some thirty years. They chronicle the apostles' mission to spread Christianity to the world beyond Jerusalem. They include miracles performed by the apostles and end with Paul under house arrest in Rome.

The Epistles are in the form of letters, the first fourteen of which are attributed to Paul. They are Romans, 1 and 2 Corinthians, Galatians, Ephesians, Philippians, Colossians, 1 and 2 Thessalonians, 1 and 2 Timothy, Titus, Philemon, Hebrews, James, 1 and 2 Peter, 1, 2 and 3 John, and Jude.

The Apocalypse, from the Greek word for "revealing," or Revelation, is a visionary book and the last of the New Testament. It was written between A.D. 75 and 90 by John the Divine on the Greek island of Patmos. The Apocalypse is a vision of the end of the world and the Second Coming of Christ. John describes seeing the enthroned Christ surrounded by fire and light, twenty-four elders clothed in white and wearing gold crowns, and four beasts that echo those envisioned by Ezekiel (see p. 191):

> *And before the throne there was a sea of glass like unto crystal: and in the midst of the throne, and round about the throne, were four beasts full of eyes before and behind.*
>
> *And the first beast was like a lion, and the second beast like a calf, and the third beast had a face as a man, and the fourth beast was like a flying eagle.*
>
> *And the four beasts had each of them six wings about him; and they were full of eyes within.*
>
> (Revelation 4:6–8)

The enthroned Christ in the form of a Lamb holds a book with seven seals. When they are opened, the cataclysm at the end of time is revealed. The first four unleash the Four Horsemen: Conquest, War, Famine, and Death.

> *And I saw . . . a white horse: and he that sat on him had a bow; and a crown was given unto him: and he went forth conquering, and to conquer . . .*
>
> *And there went out another horse that was red: and power was given to him that sat thereon to take peace from the earth, and that they should kill one another: and there was given unto him a great sword.*
>
> *And when he had opened the third seal . . . I beheld . . . a black horse; and he that sat on him had a pair of balances in his hand.*
>
> *And I heard a voice . . . say, A measure of wheat for a penny, and three measures of barley for a penny; and see thou hurt not the oil and the wine . . .*
>
> *And I looked, and behold a pale horse: and his name that sat on him was Death, and Hell followed with him. And power was given unto them over the fourth part of the earth, to kill with sword, and with hunger, and with death, and with the beasts of the earth.*
>
> (6:2–8)

Finally John envisions the New Jerusalem, illuminated by God's light and "prepared as a bride adorned for her husband" (21:2).

And seeing the multitudes, he went up into a mountain: and when he was set, his disciples came unto him:

And he opened his mouth, and taught them, saying:

Blessed are the poor in spirit: for theirs is the kingdom of heaven . . .

Blessed are the meek; for they shall inherit the earth.

Blessed are the peacemakers; for they shall be called the children of God . . .

Think not that I am come to destroy the law, or the prophets; I am not come to destroy, but to fulfil.

(Matthew 5:1–9, 17)

And referring to the Old Law, he says:

Ye have heard that it hath been said, An eye for an eye, and a tooth for a tooth:

But I say unto you, That ye resist not evil: but whosoever shall smite thee on thy right cheek, turn to him the other also . . .

Be ye therefore perfect, even as your Father which is in heaven is perfect.

(5:38–39, 48)

Jesus also teaches his followers how to pray and recites what is known as the Lord's Prayer:

Our Father which art in heaven, Hallowed be thy name.

Thy kingdom come. Thy will be done in earth, as it is in heaven.

Give us this day our daily bread.

And forgive us our debts, as we forgive our debtors.

And lead us not into temptation, but deliver us from evil: For thine is the kingdom, and the power, and glory, for ever. Amen.

(6:9–13)

In the last verses of the Sermon, Jesus offers some of his most famous lessons for right conduct, some direct and others as allegories (stories told in symbolic form):

Judge not, that ye be not judged . . .

And why beholdest thou the mote that is in thy brother's eye, but considerest not the beam that is in thine own eye? . . .

Give not that which is holy unto the dogs, neither cast ye your pearls before swine, lest they trample them under their feet . . .

Ask, and it shall be given you; seek, and ye shall find; knock, and it shall be opened unto you:

. . . whatsoever ye would that men should do to you, do ye even so to them: for this is the law and the prophets.

Enter ye in at the strait gate: for wide is the gate, and broad is the way that leadeth to destruction . . .

Beware of false prophets, which come to you in sheep's clothing, but inwardly they are ravening wolves.

Ye shall know them by their fruits . . .

A good tree cannot bring forth evil fruit, neither can a corrupt tree bring forth good fruit.

(7:1–18)

Society and Culture

The Typological Reading of History

In the Christian typological view of history, events and personages of the Old Testament are interpreted as prefigurations, or types (from the Greek *tupoi*, meaning "examples"), of corresponding events and personages of the New Testament. Jesus, for example, calls himself the New Solomon in the Gospel of Matthew. Jesus is also called the New Adam and was, according to tradition, crucified on the site of Adam's burial. Both Solomon and Adam, therefore, are types for Christ.

Mary is the New Eve and redeemed Eve's sin as Jesus redeemed Adam's. Moses receiving the Tablets of the Law on Mount Sinai is compared with Jesus delivering the Sermon on the Mount. The parting of the Red Sea is paired with the rite of baptism, because both are miracles involving water. And the story of Jonah's three days in the whale and release is paired with the resurrection of Jesus after three days in the tomb.

Typology became so widespread that ever-increasing numbers of events and personages from the Old Testament were paired with those in the New Testament. The underlying purpose of the typological system was to demonstrate God's divine plan encompassing all of time. According to this plan, Jesus fulfills the prophecy of a Messiah.

DEATH AND RESURRECTION

One of the basic original tenets of Christianity was the sacrificial death and resurrection of Jesus. Through his sacrifice, he was believed to have redeemed humanity from Original Sin, which had caused the Fall of Man. The Fall, according to the Bible, alienated people from God, from their original state of grace, and from the paradise that Adam and Eve enjoyed in the Garden of Eden. God sent his "only begotten son," Jesus, conceived through the Incarnation and born to the Virgin Mary, to assume the fate of humanity. As a man, Jesus was destined to suffer and die on the Cross (see Box, p. 194). Christians believe that, in so doing, he took on the sins of Adam and Eve and the guilt of the human race and reconciled the faithful to God. This reconciliation included the promise of an afterlife.

BAPTISM AND THE EUCHARIST

As Christianity evolved, a number of rites became basic to Christian worship. Two of the most important, though neither was entirely new, were baptism and the Eucharist. Baptism had been practiced in Mithraism; but in Christianity, water rather than blood was used. Jesus himself was baptized in the River Jordan by John the Baptist. For Christians, the rite of baptism came to symbolize rebirth into the faith.

Society and Culture

Principal Events in the Life of Jesus

Childhood

Annunciation: The angel Gabriel announces Jesus' birth to the Virgin Mary and tells her that Jesus' father is God (celebrated on March 25). Joseph is Jesus' earthly father; Mary, Joseph, and Jesus constitute the Holy Family.

Visitation: Mary is three months pregnant when she visits her cousin Elizabeth, who is six months pregnant with John the Baptist.

Nativity: Jesus is born in Bethlehem (celebrated on December 25).

Adoration of the Magi: Three wise men, often described as kings, are led to Bethlehem by a star. They bring gifts of gold, frankincense, and myrrh (celebrated on January 6).

Presentation in the Temple: Jesus is presented to Simeon, the old priest at the Temple in Jerusalem. God has promised Simeon that he will see the Savior before he dies.

Massacre of the Innocents: King Herod decrees the murder of all boys under the age of two in Bethlehem and its vicinity because of a prophecy that one will destroy his kingdom.

Flight into Egypt: Warned by an angel of Herod's plans to massacre the infants, the Holy Family escapes to Egypt.

Jesus among the Doctors: At twelve, Jesus astounds the Temple priests with his wisdom.

Adult Life

Baptism: Jesus is baptized by John the Baptist in the River Jordan.

Temptation of Jesus: Jesus rejects the Devil's offer of wealth and earthly power.

The Calling of the Apostles: Jesus calls the twelve apostles (his followers) to his service. He calls Matthew the tax collector and the brothers Peter and Andrew, who are fishermen. Jesus promises to make them "fishers of men."

Miracles: In the Marriage at Cana, Jesus turns water into wine. In the Transfiguration, Jesus appears in glory in a blaze of light on Mount Tabor, in Galilee, and God announces that Jesus is his son. In the Resurrection of Lazarus, Jesus restores the brother of Mary and Martha to life.

The Passion

The events leading to, and including, the death of Jesus are:

Entry into Jerusalem: Jesus enters Jerusalem on a donkey. This begins his approach to death and is celebrated on Palm Sunday, a week before the Resurrection.

Last Supper: Jesus' last meal with his apostles. He tells them to remember him by eating bread (his body) and drinking wine (his blood), which institutes the ritual of the Mass (the Eucharist).

Betrayal of Judas: The apostle Judas Iscariot accepts thirty pieces of silver in exchange for identifying Jesus to the Romans.

Kiss of Judas: Judas identifies Jesus with a kiss in the Garden of Gethsemane.

Jesus Before Pilate: The Roman governor of Jerusalem, Pontius Pilate, condemns Jesus to death.

Flagellation: Jesus is whipped by Roman soldiers.

Mocking: Jesus is taunted for his claim to be King of the Jews. He is made to wear a crown of thorns and a scarlet robe.

Way to Calvary: Jesus is made to carry his own cross to Calvary (Golgotha, the Hill of the Skulls outside Jerusalem), where he will be crucified.

Crucifixion: Jesus is executed on the Cross between two thieves.

Lamentation: Mourning over Jesus' body. In art, this usually includes Mary his mother, Mary Magdalene, and the youngest apostle, John.

Entombment: Jesus is placed in the tomb, later called the Holy Sepulcher.

Resurrection: Jesus rises from the tomb, which is guarded by Roman soldiers.

Three Marys at the Tomb: The three Marys discover that the tomb is empty.

Noli me tangere: Mary Magdalene sees the risen Jesus and reaches out to touch him. He commands her not to touch him. (*Noli me tangere* is Latin for "do not touch me.")

Ascension: Jesus ascends to heaven.

Pentecost: The apostles are given the gift of tongues so that they can travel the world spreading Jesus' message to communities speaking different languages.

Christianity eliminated the orgies and animal sacrifices of paganism and established rituals that were more symbolic. From early worship in private houses, the table became the altar, and Jesus' Last Supper was reenacted in the central rite of the Mass, or Communion—that is, the Eucharist, which means "thanksgiving" in Greek. During Mass, the bread (or a wafer) is transformed into Jesus' body, and red wine becomes his blood. This miracle later came to be known as transubstantiation.

THE MISSION OF ST. PAUL

St. Paul (died *c.* A.D. 67) was a crucial figure in the spread of Christianity. Originally named Saul, he was born in Tarsus, in Cilicia (now in Turkey). He was a Jew and a Roman citizen who persecuted Christians, but he became a Christian after hearing the voice of Jesus asking why he was persecuting him. Saul was on the way to Damascus, in Syria, and in some accounts he saw a bright light and fell from his horse. On conversion, Saul changed his name to Paul. He believed in the Incarnation (that Jesus was born as a human being), the Trinity (three equal parts of the godhead—Father, Son, Holy Ghost), and redemption (that Jesus saved humanity by assuming

Original Sin). For Paul, therefore, Jesus was both human and divine and equal to God.

In his devotion to Jesus, Paul undertook to spread the Christian message to Jews and gentiles (non-Jews) throughout the Mediterranean world (map **8.2**). Beginning around A.D. 40, Paul traveled to Syria, Cyprus, Asia Minor, Greece, and Rome, where, emphasizing the importance of faith and the love of God, he converted many gentiles. In addition to preaching, Paul wrote the Epistles, which are letters to groups of believers and Christian leaders to reinforce previous teaching and overcome immorality. The Epistles are now part of the New Testament and a foundation of Christian religion. When Paul arrived in Rome, according to tradition, he was imprisoned and beheaded in the persecution of Christians ordered by the emperor Nero.

EARLY CHRISTIANITY IN ROME

Like Judaism, Christianity was considered a threat to the power and authority of Rome. Adherents of both faiths were persecuted for refusing to worship pagan gods and for denying the divinity of the emperor. The times of greatest persecution of Christians in the first century A.D. were under Nero in 64 and Domitian in 93. Later, in 111, Trajan declared Christians traitors to the Roman Empire; in 250 Decius (ruled 249–251) ordered Christians to be executed for refusing to sacrifice to the emperor; and in 257 Valerian (ruled 253–260) launched a full-scale persecution, burning and beheading thousands of Christians.

In 284, Diocletian (ruled 284–305) tried to stabilize the empire by instituting a **tetrarchy**. This form of governance established four equal rulers at the far ends of the empire. The tetrarchy lasted for ten years but failed to re-establish Rome's former power. At first, Diocletian tolerated Christianity, but when Christians refused to join the Roman army, he turned against them. In 303, Diocletian ordered the destruction of all Christian places of worship and Christian texts, and in 304, he demanded the death or imprisonment of anyone known to be a Christian. This created a large number of **martyrs** (people who die for their beliefs). Eventually, the Church conferred sainthood on most martyrs as well as on other Christians considered to have led holy lives.

In its early stages, Christianity appealed to the lower classes of Roman society, including slaves. But from the second century, the middle class, intellectuals, and aristocrats—more women than men—were drawn to the new religion. The broad appeal of Christianity came in large part from its advocacy of universal equality before God. The promise of salvation was not restricted by gender or class; Jesus himself had had prominent female followers. In addition, women were integrated with men during services, and some assumed leadership roles in the new cult. In Paul's Epistle to the Romans (16:1–15), he mentions a number of female as well as male followers of Christ who help him spread the gospel (see Box, p. 196).

Although under continual threat of persecution, Christians could safely worship in the **catacombs**, underground burial places that the Romans held sacred. Built by law outside the city walls, the catacombs consisted of complex passageways and up to four stories of small chambers. Bodies were placed in niches in the walls and sealed in with tiles or blocks of stone.

Because of the restrictions placed on Christians, their art developed only minimally before the fourth century. In fact, it

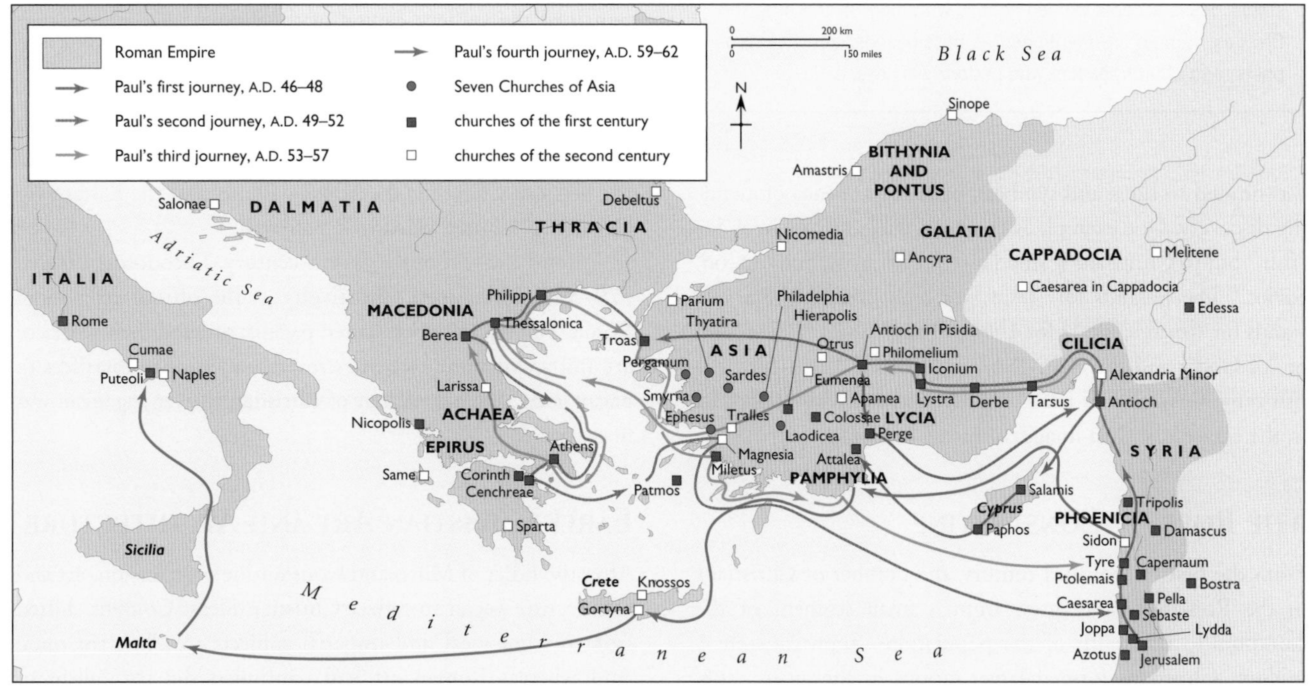

Map 8.2 Paul's missionary journeys, A.D. 46–62.

Society and Culture

Women in the Bible

The role of women in the Bible is complex and varied and has been reinterpreted many times. In addition, the biblical narrative is interwoven with cultural and political histories that influence views of women in different times and places. Nevertheless, there are some important general observations to be made. Women in the Bible have many symbolic meanings and can personify wisdom, compassion, and even nations.

Typically of lower status than men, a number of women—for example Delilah, in the story of Samson and Delilah—control men through the power of seductiveness. In the Hebrew Bible, foreign women are seen as especially dangerous in this respect unless, like Ruth, they accept the covenant with Yahweh. Ruth was a Moabite who not only assumed her husband's culture and religion but also followed her mother-in-law, Naomi, after her husband's death: (". . . Whither thou goest, I will go . . . thy people shall be my people, and thy God my God"; Ruth 1:16). In contrast, when Israelite women marry foreign men and adopt different religions, they are compared to treacherous nations. Women are thus described as devious as well as faithful.

Royal women, priestesses, widows, and temple prostitutes sometimes escape the traditional status imposed by their gender. Queen Esther, for example, personifies the wise, devoted, and courageous spouse who saves her people. The same may be said of the apocryphal heroine Judith, who rescued the Hebrews from the Assyrian army, although she did so by deception and seduction.

The four Gospels of the New Testament, in which women are the first witnesses to the Resurrection, accord women a new status. Jesus accepts women equally with men. In the Acts and Epistles, women are mentioned as missionaries, apostles, prophets, and church leaders who perform services.

was limited to signs and symbols, partly as a means of avoiding discovery. One example is the word *ICHTHUS*, Greek for "fish," but to Christians it stood for "Jesus Christ, Son of God, Savior." The I stands for "Jesus," or *Iesus* in Greek; the CH stands for *Christos*; the U for *Uios*, or "Son"; the TH for *theou*, or "of God"; and the S for *Soter*, or "Savior." Eventually, the fish came to symbolize the Eucharist, and the symbol appears in the catacombs with images of bread and wine.

The Role of Constantine

From the first to the third century, the number of Christians in the Roman Empire grew from a small segment of the community to a tenth of the population—approximately 5 million. Christians formed larger groups in the cities, especially Rome, and smaller ones along the borders of the empire. In 313, Constantine (ruled 306–337) issued the Edict of Milan, which granted tolerance to all religions, especially Christianity. The edict essentially ended persecutions and paved the way for Christianity to become the official religion of Rome. According to Constantine's biographer, the Palestinian theologian Eusebius (*c.* 260–*c.* 339), who was the bishop of Caesarea (in modern Israel), the emperor was himself converted and baptized. The event believed to have inspired Constantine's conversion is part of a complex Christian narrative known as the Legend of the True Cross.

According to the legend, in 312, when Constantine was preparing for battle, he had a vision (or a dream, depending on the text). He saw an angel carrying a small cross with the words *in hoc signo vincis* ("In this sign, you conquer"). True to the vision, Constantine carried a small cross before him into battle and routed the enemy without effort.

Although the only source for Constantine's conversion is the account of Bishop Eusebius, which could be considered biased, it is clear that Constantine made it possible for Christianity to expand and develop throughout and beyond the Roman Empire. Constantine also took as his emblem the *Chi-Rho*, "Chr" in Greek and the first two letters of Jesus' Greek name, Christos. It is written as a superimposed *X* (*Ch* in Greek) and *P* (*R* in Greek). The emblem adorned Constantine's shield and became a motif in Christian art. In addition, Constantine encouraged the construction of many churches, freeing Christians to worship openly, seek converts, publish texts, and create large-scale works of art.

In the year 330, Constantine established a new capital at the port city of Byzantium to take advantage of its potential as a center of commerce. Changing the name of the city to Constantinople, he made it his eastern capital, while Rome remained the western capital of the empire. The two centers gave rise to differences in doctrine as well as to divergent artistic styles. The western style, discussed below, is generally referred to as Early Christian; the eastern style, known as Byzantine, is explored in the next chapter. Today, the head of the Western Church is the pope in Rome, and the Eastern (or Orthodox) Church is led by a patriarch.

Toward the end of the fourth century, Theodosius I (ruled 379–395) proclaimed Christianity as the official religion of Rome. The emperor persecuted pagans, ordered their works of art and architecture to be destroyed, and banned sacrifices to pagan gods. The ascendancy of Christianity over paganism was now complete.

Early Christian Art and Architecture

After the Edict of Milan and Constantine's conversion, art and architecture began to reflect Christian ideas. Content shifted from mythological and imperial subjects to Christian ones. And whereas Roman art had continued the naturalism of Hellenistic Greece, Early Christian art became progressively two-dimensional. Striving to express a spiritual rather than a material realm, Christian artists moved away from naturalism by flattening space and increasing the stylization of their figures. The transition was gradual but steady, and many Early Christian images have traces of Roman features.

PAINTING AND SCULPTURE Because Christian art is highly symbolic, any discussion of it must include the iconographic aspect of its imagery as well as its style. The word **iconography** means how the subject matter is "written." It relates not only to the apparent meaning of an image, but also to its themes and underlying symbolism.

A good example of a Christian image with both a surface meaning and a symbolic meaning is the little disk called the *Token of St. Agnes* (figure **8.6**). Originally from the inside of a cup or bowl, this was found in the catacombs. It shows a frontal figure of St. Agnes, a popular martyr in Rome, with outstretched arms. She is flanked by two columns, each surmounted by a dove.

The symbolic meaning of the image on the disk is more complex than what we see at first glance. The saint's pose is one of prayer, a type known as an *orans* (a praying figure). But in a Christian context, this pose alludes to the Crucifixion, because Agnes's outstretched arms visually echo Christ's arms on the Cross. In Christian art, the dove stands for the Holy Ghost,

8.6 *below* ***Token of St. Agnes*, Catacomb of San Pamfilo, Rome, 4th century A.D. Gold-glass.**

Polykleitos, *Spearbearer*
see figure 6.22

8.7 ***Good Shepherd*, c. A.D. 300. Marble, 39 in. (99 cm) high. Vatican Museums, Rome.**

and the architectural columns can refer to the church building. The symbolic meaning of the image is thus that St. Agnes is a mirror of Christ in having died for her faith and that faith, like a column, is supportive. In this context, faith supports the Christian Church and is reinforced by the Holy Ghost.

Another image that alludes to Christ is the Good Shepherd, whose flock symbolizes the Christian congregation (figure **8.7**). This was derived in part from the pastoral traditions of Greece and Rome and from the Archaic Greek type of a youth carrying a sheep on his shoulders. Classical influence can be seen in the contrapposto stance, which is reminiscent of the *Spearbearer* (see thumbnail). The shepherd is beardless, which is a Roman rather than Greek fashion, and he wears a Roman

8.8 *The Sacrifice of Isaac*, Via Latina Catacomb, Cubiculum C, Rome, *c.* A.D. 320. Fresco.
The sacrificial meaning of this event is accentuated by the central position of the altar and wood-burning fire. Themes of obedience and the sacrifice of a son by a father recur in the New Testament story of Jesus. His death, like Isaac's, is presented as the will of God; and both are saved by God, though in different ways. Isaac became a type for Jesus, and his potential sacrifice was seen as a prefiguration of Jesus' actual sacrifice on the Cross. The man and the donkey may simply be a scene of everyday life, or they may refer to Jesus' entry into Jerusalem.

tunic. The artist has emphasized the intimate relationship between the shepherd and his sheep (and implicitly between Jesus and his followers), which endows the original Greek subject with a Christian meaning. In John 10:11 Jesus says, "I am the good shepherd."

After the Edict of Milan, the number and scale of Christian paintings increased. The *Sacrifice of Isaac* (figure **8.8**) from the catacombs illustrates a well-known event from the Old Testament book of Genesis. It shows Abraham preparing to sacrifice his son Isaac as a sign of obedience to God. In the biblical text, Isaac is saved when an angel intervenes. Although the figure of the angel in the painting has faded, Abraham can be seen gazing toward either the angel or the hand of God staying Isaac's death. Isaac kneels at the right, and the ram, which will be sacrificed in his stead, is at the left.

Note the transitional nature of this painting, which is partly Roman in style and partly Early Christian. Abraham wears Roman costume and is shown in a contrapposto stance. Foreshortening (rendering in perspective) creates the illusion of depth: by turning the ram so that it is seen from the rear, the artist compresses its form and makes it appear to occupy three-dimensional space. The cast shadows add to the impression of a natural, horizontal surface. At the same time, however, the altar tilts unnaturally upward, which flattens the space. This shift in perspective reveals the tension between naturalism and the Early Christian preference for the flat space of a spiritual world.

Another expression of the transition between Roman and Early Christian style can be seen in the fourth-century sarcophagus of the Roman consul Junius Bassus (figure **8.9**). The style is primarily Roman, but the iconography is Christian. Like the Romans, the early Christians did not include an image of the deceased on the lids of their sarcophagi. Instead, they carved narrative scenes on the sides. The figures resemble Roman sculpture, and the head types are reminiscent of Roman portrait busts. In some cases, however, such as the Adam and Eve in the lower tier (second from the left), the proportions are not Classical. The architectural divisions consist of different Orders of Greek columns, but the twisted columns allude to Solomon's Temple.

ARCHITECTURE There are two main types of Early Christian church plan: the longitudinal basilica and the centrally planned building. Although there are no surviving fourth-century basilican churches, there are drawings that show the typical plan (figure **8.10**) that evolved from the Roman basilica (see Chapter 7). Figure **8.11** is a diagram of the interior and elevation of Old St. Peter's, which remained the most important Christian church in the West until the sixteenth century.

The plan was in the form of a Latin cross, with an atrium at the entrance, as in Roman domestic architecture (see figure 7.17). The large central nave, side aisles, and **clerestory** (upper story) windows of the Roman basilica were retained. A new feature, the **transept** (the cross-section corresponding to the arms of the cross), separated the nave from the curved apse. In contrast to pagan temples, the interior of the church building,

8.9 Sarcophagus of Junius Bassus, *c.* A.D. 359. Marble, 3 ft. 10½ in. (1.18 m) high. Lateran Museum, Rome.

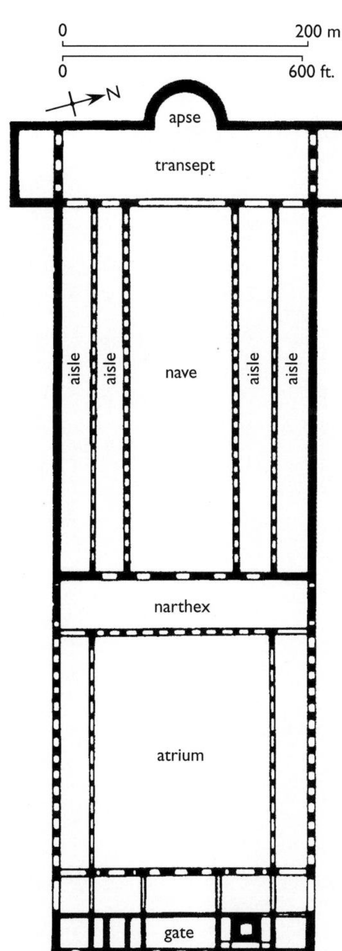

8.10 *Plan of Old St. Peter's*, Rome, *c.* A.D. 330.
In Matthew 16:18–19, Jesus tells Peter: "Thou art Peter, and upon this rock I will build my church; and the gates of hell shall not prevail against it. And I will give unto thee the keys of the kingdom of heaven." Because the Greek word for "rock" is "petros," Jesus' declaration is grammatically ambiguous. Tradition has maintained that Jesus gave Peter the keys to heaven and the mission to found the Church. As a result, Peter is considered to have been the first Roman pope and Old St. Peter's stood on the traditional burial site of St. Peter.

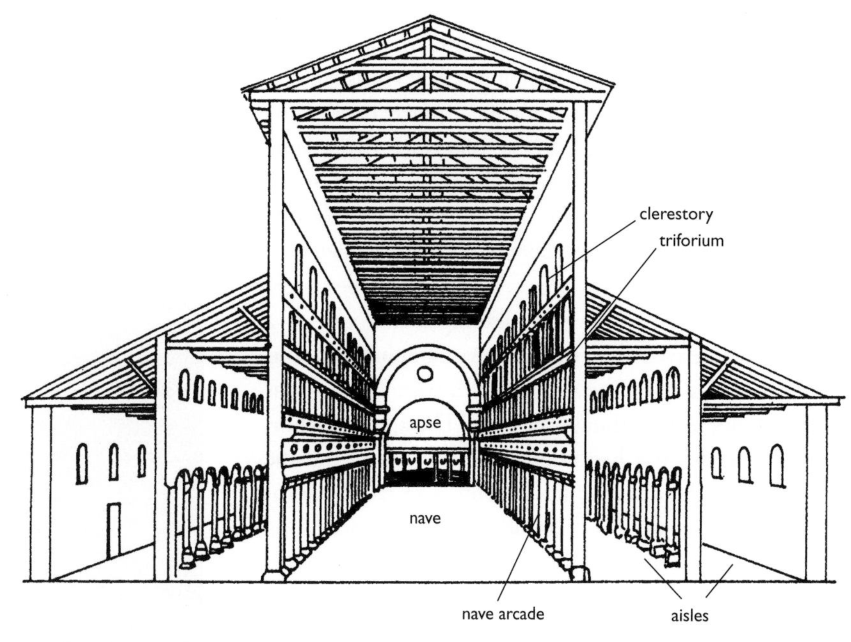

8.11 Section showing the interior and elevation of Old St. Peter's, Rome, *c.* A.D. 330.

8.12 Interior of Santa Maria Maggiore, Rome, A.D. 432–440.

like the Roman basilica, was designed to accommodate large crowds.

Old St. Peter's was destroyed in the sixteenth century to make way for the present church, New St. Peter's. But the appearance of an early Christian basilican church can be gained from the interior view of Santa Maria Maggiore in Rome (figure **8.12**). It combines Early Christian elements with those derived from the Roman basilica. As in Old St. Peter's, Santa Maria Maggiore has a large central nave, side aisles, a transept, and an apse. But the coffered ceiling, similar to that in the dome of the Pantheon (see figure 7.39), differs from the wooden roof of Old St. Peter's.

At the far end of the nave, leading to the apse, is a round arch derived from the Roman triumphal arch. But instead of signifying the triumph of a pagan emperor, it now alludes to the triumph of Jesus. The apse, which in the Roman basilica had housed the law courts and the emperor's colossal statue, has become a sacred space for the Christian altar. The long horizontal of Santa Maria Maggiore's nave draws the gaze of the worshipper toward

8.13 Exterior of Santa Costanza, outside Rome, *c.* A.D. 350.

8.14 Interior of Santa Costanza, outside Rome, *c.* A.D. 350.
The two visible sections showing the ceiling mosaics reflect the Christian assimilation of pagan iconography. Cupids, birds, and animals are juxtaposed with a scene of grape-harvesting. The grapes refer both to the wine of the Eucharist and to the orgiastic cults of Dionysos. This use of the grapes as an allusion to two religious rites is a good example of iconographic syncretism.

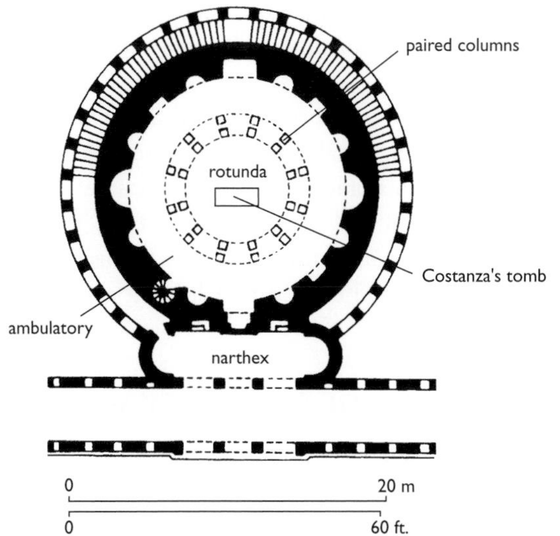

8.15 Plan of Santa Costanza, Rome, *c.* A.D. 350.

the apse, and the gold mosaics on the walls reflect light, denoting the presence of the divine.

The second type of church design is based on the Greek cross, which has four arms of equal length. Such centrally planned buildings had traditionally been used as **baptisteries** (where baptisms are performed), **martyria** (built over tombs of martyrs), and **mausolea** (large round tombs). Thus the fourth-century church of Santa Costanza was originally built by Constantine to mark his daughter's tomb but was later converted to a church. Its monumental, imposing exterior (figure **8.13**) contrasts with the lighter, more decorative interior (figure **8.14**). The vaulting is brick, and twelve pairs of smooth-shafted columns ring the domed core (figure **8.15**). Colored granite columns support miniature entablatures; their ornate marble capitals combine Ionic volutes with Corinthian foliage. The interior is designed so that worshippers enter first into a darkened space. They are then drawn toward the center, where light from the clerestory windows dramatically illuminates Costanza's tomb.

THE SPREAD OF CHRISTIANITY

As Christianity expanded, the Church established **creeds**, or doctrines, and disseminated them throughout the Mediterranean world. Christianity was less tolerant of other religions than paganism was. Since Christians were convinced of the truth of their beliefs and the reality of their experience of God, they sent missionaries to share their message and convert people to their faith. In the second century, missionaries traveled as far east as India, and by the fifth century, according to tradition, St. Patrick had converted Ireland, and St. Columba, Scotland. Beginning in the fourth century, the Church convened numerous councils to plan ways of combating **heresy** (belief or practice that is contrary to established Church teaching).

THE ARIAN HERESY

One of the most vexing problems of early Christianity concerned the nature of Jesus. According to the Libyan priest Arius (*c.* 250–*c.* 336), who preached and wrote songs, Jesus was less divine than God and his nature was different. Arius argued that Jesus was God's instrument and was created by God, which meant he was not eternal. In effect, Arius was challenging the Trinity by denying Jesus' equality with God. To resolve this controversy, in 325, Constantine convened the Council of Nicaea, in Bithynia (in modern Turkey) and exiled the Arian leaders. But Arianism remained popular, prompting further councils—in 343, 351, 353, 355, 357, 359, and 362. Finally, in 381, the emperor Theodosius convened the Council of Constantinople, and the Trinity was proclaimed doctrine. Nevertheless, the Arian heresy persisted for nearly a hundred years more.

MANICHEES, BOGOMILS, CATHARS, AND ALBIGENSIANS

Heresies have continued to challenge Church doctrine throughout its history. Manichaeism, founded by Mani in the third century (see Chapter 2), argued that conflict between good and evil was derived from the light and dark forces of Zoroastrianism. Mani taught that Satan had stolen light particles from the world and imprisoned the human mind. The aim of religious practice was to release these particles of light. In order to bring this about, according to the Manichees, the Hebrew prophets, the Buddha, and Mani himself, as well as Jesus, had been sent by God.

The Bogomil heresy developed in the eighth century in the Balkans, in eastern Europe. Originally a Manichee sect, the Bogomils believed that the world and its inhabitants had been created by Satan and that only the soul was God's creation. The Bogomils were declared heretics in the tenth century but were not completely eradicated until the fifteenth.

In the twelfth century, the Cathars, in the south of France, Germany, and northern Italy, took up Mani's notion of the duality of good and evil. They taught that material things, including the established Christian rites, were evil. Cathars living around Albi were called Albigensians; they believed that Jesus was an angel and thus neither God nor human. They denied the doctrine of the Resurrection and Jesus' assumption of human sin. Such heresies, like Arianism, were enormously popular. They were eradicated only after numerous Church councils and, eventually, the massacre of their followers.

GNOSTICISM

At first, Gnosticism was considered a heresy by the Church, but by the second century, it had become a separate Christian sect. It was an extremely complex version of Christianity, and its origins and beliefs are still being studied. The name comes from the Greek word *gnosis*, meaning "knowledge." Gnosticism developed over a long period and was influenced by both Judaism and the New Testament. It, in turn, influenced Zoroastrianism, Manichaeism, and the early heresies.

Gnosticism, like the mystery religions, held that secret wisdom possessed by ascetics could lead to salvation. The source of knowledge, however, was not a pagan god or a state of ecstasy, but the wisdom of the apostles transmitted by teachers from one generation to the next. Gnosticism distinguished between a Demiurge (creator god) and a Supreme Divinity (Divine Being). Jesus was seen as the messenger of *gnosis*, or divine knowledge. He was not believed to have been "God made Man" but, rather, a phantom who assumed a human shape or a being who entered the body of a human. Gnosticism attempted to solve contradictions between good and evil. According to the Gnostics, evil did not come from the Supreme Divinity or from Original Sin, but from the Demiurge, who trapped humanity in ignorance. Their goal was thus to seek the knowledge that would bring them to a state of pure spirituality.

The Gnostics wrote gospels that differ from those in the Bible and the Apocrypha. In the Gnostic Gospel of Thomas there are secret sayings attributed to Jesus, which are metaphorical, and often enigmatic. One of the main themes is enlightenment.

Gnosticism differed from orthodox Christianity in according equality to women. For although we have seen that during the second century in Rome, the Christian message included equality between men and women (see p. 196), this later changed. One of the main forces in this change was the misogyny of St. Paul and other early Christian authors who postdate the Bible.

THE BEGINNINGS OF MONASTICISM

An important development in the early Church was the growth of monasticism, beginning around 300. The monastic movement originated with the conviction that to achieve salvation one must withdraw from the corrupt world. Although he did not establish a formal monastery, St. Anthony of Egypt

Defining Moment

St. Anthony and the Beginnings of Monasticism in the West

The idea of monasticism apparently originated in India and infiltrated the West through monks traveling along trade routes. The origins of Christian monasticism are attributed to St. Anthony, whose life is known mainly from a biography by the Greek author St. Athanasius.

Anthony was born in Koma, in Egypt. His parents died when he was around twenty years old. About six months later, he entered a church and heard a reading from the Gospel of Matthew: "If thou wilt be perfect, go and sell all thou hast" (19:21). Anthony was struck by the words and renounced his worldly possessions.

Anthony withdrew from the world around 270 and went to live an isolated existence in a tomb near Koma. Visited by visions of demons, he suffered extreme moral conflict for some fifteen years (figure **8.16**). Around the age of thirty-five, he left the tomb and retired across the River Nile to the mountain of Pispir (modern Der-el-Memum), living in an ancient fortress. He remained there for twenty years, resisting all human contact. But his holiness and learning attracted ascetics who looked to him for spiritual leadership, and finally he emerged.

Anthony then spent time organizing groups of monks, and these would later develop into great monastic communities during the Middle Ages. He also fought heresy—especially the Arian heresy—and the Roman persecution of Christians. According to Athanasius, Anthony preached lengthy sermons on the ascetic life and on his own battle with demons. He died at the age of 105, having spent his last forty-five years in relative isolation.

Critical Question Is the task of the journey or is the reward of finding the right goal more important? Would it matter if one were never to reach a desired goal? Would the journey still have meaning?

8.16 Paul Cézanne, *Temptation of St. Anthony*, 1874–1877. Oil on canvas, 18½ × 22 in. (47 × 56 cm). Musée d'Orsay, Paris.
Cézanne produced several pictures on the theme of St. Anthony's temptation. This one is the third in his series and shows the saint at the left cowering beneath an overpowering horned red devil. The real source of the temptation, however, is the large Venus-like woman surrounded by small boys, who exposes herself to Anthony.

(*c.* 251–355) is generally considered the founder of monasticism in the Roman Church (see Box). He renounced his possessions in his early twenties and for the next thirty-five years lived as a hermit. His resolve in resisting attacks from demons has been the subject of many later creative works, notably, paintings by the nineteenth-century French artist Paul Cézanne (see figure 8.16) and Gustave Flaubert's novel *The Temptation of St. Anthony.* Anthony's piety attracted scores of disciples eager to learn from him, and so, in 305, he reluctantly returned to the world.

During the next several hundred years, as Christians followed Anthony's example, monasticism grew. Separate religious communities were established, where monks lived, worked, and prayed according to a particular **rule** (a systematic regimen).

Anthony's counterpart in the Eastern Church was Pachomius of Egypt (*c.* 290–346). Born a pagan, Pachomius converted to Christianity and founded a monastery near the River Nile, at Tabennisi. A few decades later, Basil the Great, bishop of Caesarea (*c.* 330–379), and his friend Gregory of Nazianus (*c.* 329–*c.* 389) preached against Arianism and urged Christians to take up the monastic life. They built hospitals, churches, and living quarters for the poor. The rule of Basil became the basis of monasticism in the Eastern Church. Community life was rigorous and founded on obedience, daily routines of prayer and worship, manual work, poverty, chastity, and charity.

CHRISTIAN AUTHORS: THE FOUR DOCTORS OF THE CHURCH

Because Christianity is based on Scripture, early Christian writers were enormously important in establishing Church doctrine. Four of these writers are known as the Four Doctors of the Church, because they laid down the most fundamental precepts of Christianity. They are Ambrose, Jerome, Pope Gregory I, and Augustine, all of whom were classically educated. They warned against heresy and paganism, and wrote extensively.

Ambrose (339–397), born in Trier, in modern Germany, was the son of a Roman administrator in Gaul. He became a lawyer and practiced Roman law before converting to Christianity. In 374, when he was thirty-four, he became bishop of Milan, in northern Italy, a post he held until his death. Ambrose had a strong social conscience, caring for the poor and preaching against injustice. He particularly objected to the abuses of the Roman emperors. Of his many writings, the most significant is *De officiis ministrorum*, which is influenced by the rhetorical style of Cicero and emphasizes the importance of leading an ethical Christian life.

Jerome (*c.* 347–*c.* 420) was born in Italy, south of Rome. He is considered the most distinguished scholar of the early Church. He wrote treatises attacking heretics and pagans and commentaries on the Bible. He also translated the Bible from Hebrew and Greek into Latin. At the time, Latin was the *volgare*, or common, everyday speech—Jerome's translation is thus called the "Vulgate" and is still the standard Bible of the Roman Catholic Church. Jerome traveled widely, and founded a monastery in Bethlehem. He led the life of a hermit, practicing asceticism and self-denial.

Gregory the Great (*c.* 540–604) was the son of a Roman senator, but he renounced his wealth and gave his belongings to the poor. He was committed to monasticism, founding six monasteries in Sicily and one, St. Andrew's, in Rome, which he joined at the age of thirty-four. Gregory believed that bishops were shepherds of souls, and he described the life they should lead in *Liber regulae pastoralis* (*Book of Pastoral Rules*). His belief in the notion of Purgatory—a place where souls can be purged of sin in preparation for entry into heaven—became part of Church doctrine. Gregory's social, political, and economic skills, combined with his piety, led to his being elected pope as Gregory I in 590.

READING SELECTION

Gregory the Great, *Dialogues*, St. Benedict, the father of western monasticism, struggles against sin, PWC2-101-B

The most influential of the Four Doctors was Augustine (354–430). Born in Tageste, in modern Algeria, to a Christian mother and a pagan father, Augustine studied Plato and Plotinus in Carthage. He led a dissolute life, and was fascinated by magic and astrology. At first an adherent of Manichaeism, Augustine went to Rome and met Ambrose, who inspired him to become a Christian. He was baptized in 387. Augustine then returned to North Africa to preach, entered the administration of the Church, and became bishop of Hippo in 396.

Around 397, Augustine wrote the *Confessions*, an autobiography of his spiritual journey from paganism to Christianity. He was eloquent and charismatic, and believed that God's grace, more than good works, determined salvation. For Augustine, evil was created by the human race, not by God. No doubt drawing on his own experience as a sinner, Augustine argues the power of Original Sin and insists that faith is the best weapon against evil. In describing his boyhood, he enumerates his sins and his curiosity, implores God, and shrewdly observes the hypocrisy of parents:

> And yet I sinned, O Lord my God, creator and arbiter of all natural things, but arbiter only, not creator, of sin. I sinned, O Lord, by disobeying my parents and the masters of whom I have spoken . . . I was disobedient, not because I chose something better than they proposed to me, but simply from the love of games. For I liked to score a fine win at sport or to have my ears tickled by the make-believe of the stage, which only made them itch the more. As time went on my eyes shone more and more with the same eager curiosity, because I wanted to see the shows and sports which grown-ups enjoyed. The patrons who pay for the production of these shows are held in esteem such as most parents would wish for their children. Yet the same parents willingly allow their children to be flogged if they are distracted by these displays from the studies which are supposed to fit them to grow rich and give the same sort of shows themselves. Look on these things with pity, O Lord, and free us who now call upon you from such delusions.
>
> (Augustine, *Confessions*, 1.10)

READING SELECTION

Augustine, *Confessions*, on his conversion, PWC2-009-C

Augustine's other great work is *The City of God*, written in twenty-two books, after the Visigoths sacked Rome in 410. He wrote partly in response to pagans, who blamed the destruction of Rome on the Christian God. Augustine argued that Rome's destruction was simply another event on the way to the Second Coming of Christ. *The City of God* is based on the architectural metaphor of dividing the universe into two cities. The City of God is inhabited by those destined for eternal life in heaven; the City of Man is inhabited by those destined for hell. Throughout, Augustine alludes to Classical works such as the *Aeneid*, to Roman history, to the Bible, and to contemporary Christian authors. Book One opens with God's divine plan:

> Most glorious is and will be the City of God, both in this fleeting age of ours, wherein she lives by faith, a stranger among infidels, and in the days when she shall be established in her eternal home.
>
> (*The City of God*, Preface)

The City of Man, on the other hand, is the source of the pagan enemy:

> For it is from this earthly city that the enemies spring against whom the City of God must be defended.
>
> (*The City of God*, 1.1)

The City of God concludes with Augustine's lengthy discourse on the end of time. He does not claim to know exactly how things will be, but he is certain that the virtuous will see God in the heavenly city:

> Therefore it is possible, and very probable, that we shall see the corporeal bodies of the new heaven and the new earth in such as way that, wherever we turn our eyes, we shall, through our bodies that we shall be wearing and plainly seeing, enjoy with perfect clarity of vision the sight of God everywhere present and ruling all things, even material things.
>
> (*The City of God*, 22.29)

READING SELECTION

Augustine, *The City of God*, on the two cities, PWC2-001

MUSIC IN THE EARLY CHURCH

Music had been an important part of Jewish services in the Temple of Solomon and continued to be so in the synagogues. A **cantor** chanted Bible readings, and psalms were sung **responsorially**—a soloist alternated with congregational responses. This involved the congregation in the service, creating an atmosphere for worship and reinforcing a sense of religious community. As described in the Psalms of David, the lyre and harp sometimes accompanied singing. The early Church discontinued this use of instruments in worship, on the grounds that they were pagan and could incite passion; the Church Fathers were particularly opposed to anything associated with luxury. However, the chanted style of singing was to develop into the most important form of early Christian music, namely, **plainsong** (or **plainchant**).

Two forms of service developed in the early Church. The first was a reenactment of Jesus' Last Supper, and gradually a standard text narrating the Eucharist or Mass was established. Much of this was chanted to music. Some sections—known as the "Ordinary"—always used the same words, but other parts—known as the "Proper"—changed according to the Church year and its feasts. The second type of service was a meeting devoted to singing psalms, reading the Bible, and prayer.

At first, the language of worship was Aramaic, but as the apostles and missionaries of the Church began to spread the gospel, Greek, the international language of the time, was adopted. It was not until the fourth century that Latin came to be used in the Western Church, a usage that persisted in Roman Catholicism until the 1960s. Thus the texts of the main body of Western religious music are in Latin.

Little remains of early church music, partly because notation did not come into use anywhere until at least the seventh century—songs and chants were transmitted orally from generation to generation. However, it is known that Ambrose wrote Latin hymns, and several have survived. He is considered the founder of Latin hymnody. There is also a body of plainsong called Ambrosian chant, which he may have developed.

It is Pope Gregory I whose name has gone down in history for his contribution to the Church's **liturgy** (form of worship). During his reign, the chants used in the Western Church were collected and standardized for use in the Mass and throughout the Church year, for celebrations such as Easter and saints' days. Now known as "Gregorian chant," this body of some 3000 melodies is a highly significant part of church music.

Plainsong, as the term suggests, is a plain line of music, sung unaccompanied. Like earlier forms of chant, it is monophonic (it has a single strand of melody). Its range of **pitch** (height or depth of notes) is small, and it has no **meter** (regular divisions into set numbers of rhythmic beats). Gregorian chant has an austere, timeless quality, with phrases rising and falling gently in patterns somewhat like speech. In some chants there is one note per text syllable ("syllabic chant") and in others the syllable is held for several notes ("**melismatic** chant"). This distinction between syllabic and melismatic music would later become a major issue in church music, as the authorities sought to cut down on musical diversions so as to assert the primacy of the religious text.

In the next chapter we follow the development of the Christian Church, which eventually split into Eastern and Western factions, each with its own version of doctrine and liturgy. During the seventh century, under the influence of Muhammad in Saudi Arabia, a new world religion—Islam—would arise. This, in turn, would lead to new forms of art and architecture.

KEY TERMS

Ark of the Covenant the original container for the Tablets containing the Ten Commandments.

baptistery a building in which baptisms are performed.

canonical authorized; used with reference to a collection of writings or works applying to a particular religion or author.

cantor in Jewish worship, the singer who chants Bible readings, prayers, or parts of the liturgy.

catacomb an underground burial place or cemetery, held sacred by the Romans.

clerestory in a church or temple, an upper story of the nave, above the aisle, that is pierced with windows to admit light.

covenant a formal agreement; the conditional promises made between God and his people in the Bible.

creed a formal statement of the beliefs of a particular religion or philosophy.

Exodus the forty-year journey made by the Israelites, led by Moses, out of Egypt to freedom; also, the second book of the Hebrew Bible.

heresy a belief or practice that is contrary to established Church teaching.

iconography the apparent meaning of an image and its underlying symbolism.

litany a type of prayer in which a leader and a congregation speak alternately.

liturgy rites of worship.

martyr a person who dies for his or her beliefs (the meaning of the Greek word is "witness").

martyrium (plural **martyria**) a structure built over the tomb of a martyr.

mausoleum (plural **mausolea**) a large, elaborate round tomb.

melismatic music in which several notes are sung to one syllable.

menorah a candelabrum with seven candlesticks, three on each side and one in the center.

meter in music, regular division into set numbers of rhythmic beats.

mystery (or **mystery cult**) cultish religion, based on ancient myths, of a type that was common in Greece and throughout the Roman Empire.

pitch in music, height or depth of a tone.

plainsong (sometimes called **plainchant** or **Gregorian chant**) unaccompanied monophonic music sung to Latin texts as part of a church service.

responsorial a style of music in which a soloist alternates with congregational or choral responses.

rule in monasteries, a systematic regimen.

synoptic referring to three books of the New Testament, the Gospels of Matthew, Mark, and Luke, which are considered to form a group.

Tablets (Tables) of the Law the stones on which were inscribed the laws given to Moses on Mount Sinai.

transept in a church, the cross-section corresponding to the arms of the Cross.

KEY QUESTIONS

1. What rituals did Christianity borrow from mystery cults and Judaism? What term is used to describe these borrowings?
2. Why did Rome consider both Judaism and Christianity as threats?
3. What sources do scholars use for the life of Jesus? When were these sources written?
4. What is a good example of a Christian image with both a surface meaning and symbolic meaning?
5. What changes in art occurred when its content shifted from mythological and imperial subjects to Christian subjects?
6. How would you distinguish between a valid original source, tradition, legend, myth, and literature?

SUGGESTED READING

Augustine, St. *The City of God*, ed. D. Knowles. New York: Penguin Books, 1972.
- ▸ The classic work by the Bishop of Hippo on his vision of salvation.

——. *Confessions*, trans. R. S. Pine-Coffin. New York: Dorset Press, 1986.
- ▸ An autobiography of the saint from his early childhood through his conversion to Christianity.

Brown, P. *Power and Persuasion in Late Antiquity: Towards a Christian Empire*. Madison, WI: University of Wisconsin Press, 1992.
- The relationship of early Christianity to imperial Rome.

——. *The Rise of Western Christendom*. New York: Blackwell, 1996.
- On the transition from pagan Rome to the rise of the Western Church.

Elsner, Jas. *Imperial Rome and Christian Triumph*. New York: Oxford University Press, 1998.
- On the transition from the Roman Empire to early Christianity in art and culture.

Fox, Robin Lane. *Pagans and Christians*. Harmondsworth, U.K.: Penguin Books, 1986.
- On paganism in the ancient world and the rise of Christianity.

Frend, W. H. C, *The Rise of Christianity*. Philadelphia: Augsburg Fortress, 1983.
- A history of early Christianity.

Geist, Sidney. *Interpreting Cézanne*. Cambridge, MA: Harvard University Press, 1988.
- An original, biographical approach to Cézanne's imagery that includes the *Temptation of St. Anthony* pictures.

Grabar, André. *The Beginnings of Christian Art, 200–395*, trans. Stuart Gilbert and James Emmons. London: Thames and Hudson, 1967.
- A standard work on early Christian art.

Pagels, Elaine. *The Gnostic Gospels*. New York: Vintage Books, 1989.
- A study of the Gnostic Gospels.

Pritchard, J. B. *Ancient Near Eastern Texts Relating to the Old Testament*. Princeton, NJ: Princeton University Press, 1969.
- A compilation and discussion of ancient Near Eastern texts relating to the Hebrew Bible.

Smart, Ninian (ed.). *Atlas of the World's Religions*. Oxford and New York: Oxford University Press, 1999.
- A survey of the major world religions showing their geographical spread and development.

SUGGESTED FILMS

1932 *The Sign of the Cross*, dir. Cecil B. de Mille

1953 *The Robe*, dir. Henry Kosta

1956 *The Ten Commandments*, dir. Cecil B. de Mille

1959 *Solomon and Sheba*, dir. King Vidor

1966 *The Bible*, dir. John Huston

1972 *Augustine of Hippo* (*Agostino di Ippo*), dir. Roberto Rossellini

1981 *Raiders of the Lost Ark*, dir. Steven Spielberg

1988 *The Last Temptation of Christ*, dir. Martin Scorsese

2000 *Joseph—King of Dreams*, dir. Robert C. Ramirez and Rob La Duca

9 The Byzantine Empire and the Development of Islam

"*The entire ceiling is overlaid with pure gold . . . Who can recount the beauty of the columns and the stones with which the church is decorated: One might imagine that he had come upon a meadow with its flowers in full bloom. For he would surely marvel at the purple of some, the green tints of others, and at those from which the white flashes, and again, at those which Nature, like some painter, varies with contrasting colors.*"

(PROCOPIUS OF CAESAREA, *The Buildings*, I.1)

The end of the Pax Romana in A.D. 193 was followed by decades of civil war until Diocletian became emperor in 284. Among the formidable challenges he faced in stabilizing the Roman Empire were the Germanic tribes to the north (see Chapter 10). By 300, the Huns, Vandals, and Goths had reached the boundaries of the empire along the Danube and Rhine rivers. The Goths then separated into Visigoths in the west and Ostrogoths in the east.

In 330, in another attempt to stabilize the declining Roman Empire and protect its wealthier eastern regions, Constantine established a new imperial capital in Byzantium, which he renamed Constantinople. But in 410 the Visigoth king Alaric attacked and plundered Rome. The sixth-century Byzantine historian Procopius of Caesarea (c. 500–565) described the brutality of the Visigoths, who slaughtered men, women, and children, and burned and looted the city. What is now known as the Byzantine Empire is the Eastern Roman Empire that persisted after the fall of Rome itself in 476. People in the Eastern Empire considered themselves Romans and their culture as a continuation of that of Rome.

In 451–452, Attila, king of the Huns (ruled 434–453), invaded Germany, Gaul, and northern Italy, but he did not advance on Rome. Three years later the city was invaded by the Vandal leader Gaiseric (ruled 428–477), who further impoverished Rome by blocking a grain shipment from North Africa. In 476, the official date of the fall of Rome, the German Goth Odoacer (ruled 476–493) dealt the city a devastating blow and took control of the entire Italian peninsula. He ruled from the strategically important Italian port city of Ravenna, on the Adriatic coast. In 493, the king of the Ostrogoths, Theodoric (ruled 493–526), killed Odoacer and seized power in Ravenna. Under Theodoric, Ravenna began its political, religious, and artistic rise to prominence.

In the quotation that opens this chapter, Procopius is describing the interior of the church of Hagia Sophia in Constantinople. The splendor of this huge Byzantine church, with its gold mosaics, reflective light, and expansive space, was meant to project the piety, wealth, and power of the ruler. A similar taste for elaborate surface decoration characterized Islamic design, despite profound differences between the Christian and Muslim religions, their cultures, and their approaches to imagery.

Key Topics

The Byzantine Empire

- After the fall of Rome
- The founding of Constantinople
- Justinian and Theodora
- Nika Riots
- Law Code of Justinian
- Art as power
- Church music

The Development of Islam

- Muhammad's vision
- A succession of caliphs
- Schisms in the Islamic world
- Islamic philosophy and science
- Islamic poetry and art
- The Five Pillars and *jihad*

Controversies

- *The Consolation of Philosophy*
- Popes and patriarchs
- Iconoclasm
- *The Incoherence of the Incoherence*
- *The Guide for the Perplexed*

TIMELINE	END OF THE WESTERN ROMAN EMPIRE AND OSTROGOTHIC RULE 193–526	BYZANTINE EMPIRE 476–1453	ISLAM *c.* 600–*c.* 1700
HISTORY AND CULTURE 	Diocletian becomes emperor, 284 Constantine's eastern capital renamed Constantinople, 330 Alaric sacks Rome, 410 Attila the Hun invades, 451–452 Odoacer causes the fall of Rome, 476 Theodoric comes to power, 493 Ravenna rises to prominence	Capital Constantinople Justinian comes to power, 527 (rules with Theodora) Arab and Bulgarian encroachments, 7th–8th century Golden Age begins under Basil I (ruled 867–886) Army in power: Comnenus (ruled 1081–1118) Michael Palaeologus (ruled 1259–1282) Ottoman Turks begin to erode Byzantine power, c. 1302 Turks sack Constantinople, 1453; rename it Istanbul	Muhammad (*c.* 570– 632) Muhammad leaves Mecca: *Hijra*, 622 Succession of caliphs, from 632 Umayyad dynasty founded, 661 Abbasid dynasty in power, 750–1258 Islam spreads, 8th century Muslims ousted from Spain, 1492
RELIGION	Arianism under Theodoric Boethius (*c.* 480–524) on theology	Eastern Orthodox Christianity Patriarch as head of Church Iconoclastic Controversy, 726–843	Allah, the one true God of Islam Qur'an (Koran) (114 *suras*) Hadith Five Pillars of Islam *Ka'bah*, Mecca Sunnis and Shi'ites Mystical devotional movement: Sufism
ART 	Mosaics in Sant' Apollinare Nuovo, Ravenna, early 6th century	Mosaics in San Vitale, Ravenna, 6th century Icon showing Christ blessing, 6th century *Barberini Ivory*, late 6th century	Calligraphy from the Qur'an, 11th or 12th century Glass bottle, mid-14th century Kashani, Ardabil carpet, 16th century
ARCHITECTURE 	Mausoleum of Theodoric, Ravenna, early 6th century Sant' Apollinare Nuovo, Ravenna, early 6th century	San Vitale, Ravenna, 6th century Monastery of St. Catherine, Mt. Sinai, 530 Hagia Sophia, Constantinople, 537 Mt. Athos monastery, 963 St. Mark's, Venice, begun 1063	Dome of the Rock, Jerusalem, completed 691 Córdoba Mosque, 786–987 Alhambra, Granada, 1343–1391 Tomb of Timur Leng, Samarkand, *c.* 1403 Taj Mahal, Agra, 1630s
LITERATURE		Procopius (*c.* 500–565), *History of the Wars of Justinian; Secret History* Justinian Law Code, 534 Icasia (poet) (born *c.* 810) Michael Psellus (1018–1078) Anna Comnena, *Alexiad*, *c.* 1148	*The Thousand and One Nights*, recorded by late 8th century Omar Khayyam (*c.* 1048–*c.* 1131), *Rubáiyát* Sufi poets: Jalal al-Din Rumi (*c.* 1207–1273) Hafiz (1326–1390)
PHILOSOPHY	Boethius, *The Consolation of Philosophy*, *c.* 523		al-Kindi (*c.* 800–*c.* 870) al-Farabi (*c.* 870–*c.* 950), *The Ideas of the Inhabitants of the Virtuous City* al-Ghazali (1058/9–1111), *Deliverance from Error* Averroës (1126–1198), *The Incoherence of the Incoherence* Maimonides (1135–1204), *The Guide for the Perplexed*
MATHEMATICS AND MEDICINE 	Boethius on mathematics and music		Mathematics: al-Khwarizimi (*c.* 780–*c.* 850) Medicine: al-Razi (c. 865–932) Avicenna (980–1037), *Canon of Medicine* al-Hazen (d. 1038)
MUSIC	Boethius on mathematics and music	Eastern (Orthodox) liturgy (hymns and psalms) Western (Roman) liturgy (the Mass and Divine Office) Plainchant Responsorial and antiphonal performance	Chanting of Qur'an, call to prayer Sufism: whirling dervishes, *qawwâli* Court music: *maqams, taqsims*

RAVENNA UNDER THEODORIC

Since A.D. 404, Ravenna had been an alternative capital to Rome on the Italian peninsula. In addition to its strategic location on the coast, Ravenna was smaller than Rome and was not the center of the empire. As a result, barbarian tribes were less likely to attack Ravenna than Rome. Under Theodoric, Ravenna was a thriving center of culture and an Ostrogoth capital until 526. In 510, Theodoric appointed the statesman and philsopher Anicius Manlius Torquatus Severinus Boethius (*c.* 480–524) to a consulship. Boethius wrote the last great theological treatise in the tradition of imperial Roman literature.

BOETHIUS ON THEOLOGY

Boethius became Theodoric's adviser. But when he defended a former consul charged with treason, Theodoric arrested him and condemned him to death. While he was in prison Boethius wrote *The Consolation of Philosophy*, which became enormously popular in the West. Boethius argued that through philosophy one could arrive at a vision of God. In this view, he was influenced by Plato, Aristotle, Cicero, and Augustine. Boethius attempted to resolve the long-standing conflict between the notion of free will and an omnipotent divinity by distinguishing between human time and divine time. God, according to Boethius, sees all of time simultaneously, whereas people experience time sequentially—as past, present, or future. The fact that God has foreknowledge does not, therefore, eliminate human choice. The *Consolation* is written in the form of a dialogue between the author and the fictional speaker, Lady Philosophy. This literary device allowed Boethius to address various sides of philosophical issues and also to feel less isolated by conversing with an imaginary companion.

READING SELECTION

Boethius, *The Consolation of Philosophy*, on the wheel of Fortune, PWC2-012

BOETHIUS ON MUSIC

In addition to philosophy, Boethius wrote on physics, astronomy, and music. His treatise on music, *De institutione musica*, was influenced by Plato's theories, especially the notion that music and mathematics are related. He organized music according to a three-tiered hierarchy. At the top was the "unhearable" music of the planetary spheres described by Greek philosophers (see Chapter 5). Then came human music based on Platonic "harmonia" and finally, of lesser value in Boethius's view, instrumental music and popular songs. His treatise on music, like the *Consolation*, was extremely influential during the Middle Ages, providing something of a synthesis and a transition between Classical and Christian ideas.

THEODORIC AND THE VISUAL ARTS

Theodoric's reign was, on the whole, prosperous, and relatively tolerant of religious minorities. He instituted social reforms and patronized the arts. Two of his major artistic commissions in Ravenna were his own tomb (figure **9.1**) and the Palace Church of Sant' Apollinare Nuovo (figure **9.2a**). The church walls are decorated with mosaics designed to express the piety of Theodoric. The detail of the nave wall shown here depicts a long row of male saints wearing Roman togas. They are proceeding toward an enthroned Christ flanked by angels. Figure **9.2b** shows the palace of Theodoric, its frontal white columns echoing the saints' togas. This visual correspondence between the saints and the architecture reflects the combined secular and religious significance of the palace. Above the triple-arched entrance, alluding to Roman triumphal arches, is the inscription *PALATIUM* (meaning "palace"). Behind the palace the rooftops of Ravenna can be seen.

9.1 Mausoleum of Theodoric, Ravenna, early 6th century.
Theodoric's mausoleum is the typically round funerary structure of antiquity. Its massive dome measures 36 by 10 feet (11 × 3 m) and rests on a circular drum. Note the round exterior arches resting on narrow projecting ledges in the manner of Roman arches cut into city walls (see figure 7.8). The tomb itself, which was destroyed in the Middle Ages, was made of porphyry, a stone traditionally reserved for emperors.

9.2a *above* **Mosaics on the south wall of the nave, Sant' Apollinare Nuovo, Ravenna, early 6th century.**
St. Apollinaris was the first bishop of Ravenna. He was martyred and venerated in the nearby port city of Classe.

9.2b Theodoric's palace, detail of the mosaics on the south wall of the nave, Sant' Apollinare Nuovo, Ravenna, early 6th century.

THE BYZANTINE EMPIRE: AN OVERVIEW—FOURTH TO THIRTEENTH CENTURY

Constantine planned to take advantage of the strategic position of his new capital, Constantinople. Byzantium was located on the Bosphorus, between the Black Sea and the Aegean Sea (see map 9.1), which flows into the Mediterranean. Constantine believed that from Byzantium he would benefit from readily accessible trade routes and be better able to defend the declining Roman Empire. In fact, however, his move laid the foundation for the rise of the Byzantine Empire. It also reinforced the division between the Eastern and Western Churches, which led to the final schism in 1054.

In 527, a powerful new emperor came to power in Constantinople. Justinian I (ruled 527–565) succeeded his uncle, Justin I (ruled 518–527), who had come from a peasant family in Macedonia. But Justinian was well-educated and had worked in the imperial administration. He ruled together with his empress, Theodora, and greatly expanded the empire. In 562, he conquered Italy, and eventually he controlled the Near East, North Africa, Egypt, Asia Minor to the west coast of the Black Sea, and Greece to the Danube River (map **9.1**). The Byzantine Empire flourished, and Justinian presided over a vast artistic program, which included church building, mosaic decoration, and other works.

During the seventh and eighth centuries, Arabs and Bulgarians conquered parts of the Byzantine Empire. This led to a repressive social and economic system, with private armies in control of most of the land. In the ninth century, however, a period known as the Golden Age of the empire began when Basil I (ruled 867–886) established the Macedonian dynasty. He improved the economy, encouraged the development of an intellectual community, and sent missionaries to eastern Europe. By the tenth century, Russia had adopted Christianity.

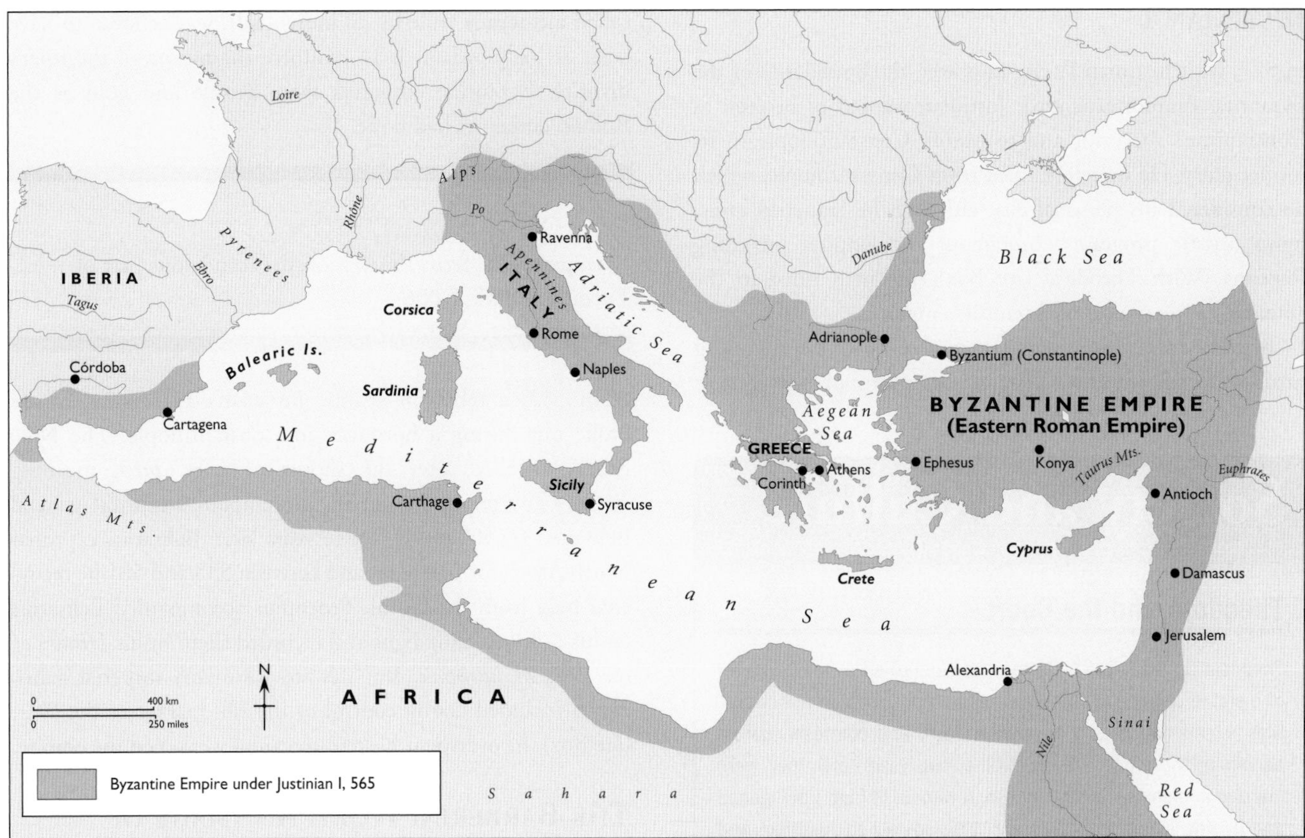

Map 9.1 The Byzantine Empire, 565.

At the end of the eleventh century, the army took over the administration of the empire. Its economy was primarily agrarian, with **serfs** (peasant workers) living on the land and turning over a portion of their income to the landowners. In 1081, another new dynasty of rulers, the Comneni, led by General Alexius I Comnenus (ruled 1081–1118), gained power. His daughter, Anna Comnena (1083–*c.* 1153), wrote the *Alexiad*, which is a biased account of his reign (see Box).

READING SELECTION

Anna Comnena, *Alexiad*, Byzantium meets the crusaders, PWC2-200-A

In 1261, after nearly a century of unrest, a new dynasty was founded by the aristocratic Michael VIII Palaeologus (ruled 1259–1282). A ruler in Nicaea, he blinded the legitimate emperor and seized control of Constantinople. His successors maintained power for two hundred years. But beginning around 1302, the Ottoman Turks (named for their leader, Osman) gradually eroded Byzantine power and encroached on its territory. This culminated in the sack of Constantinople in 1453 and the establishment of the Ottoman Empire. The Ottomans renamed the city Istanbul.

Society and Culture

Byzantine Scholarship, Ninth to Eleventh Century

Byzantine scholars, among them the clergy and educated aristocrats, kept alive the Classical Greek texts. Michael Psellus (1018–1078), a statesman who wrote on science, mathematics, history, law, and rhetoric, was particularly devoted to the works of Plato and Aristotle. In general, Byzantine scholarship was not innovative. Its main contribution was in preserving, editing, and commenting on Classical literature. During the eighth century, the principal innovations in philosophy and science came from the Arab world.

A few women, despite severe social and legal restrictions on their freedom, also participated in Byzantine intellectual life. One was the poet Icasia (born *c.* 810), who was celebrated at court but eventually retired to a convent. Anna Comnena studied Classical literature, and her history of her father's reign is evidence of a high level of literacy and strong, independent opinions. According to the *Alexiad*, Comnenus shared power with his mother; he made the military decisions and she administered the civil service and ran the finances of the empire. Anna Comnena's secret efforts to eliminate her brother, John II Comnenus, so that she herself could rule, failed. He became co-emperor with his father in 1092, and she entered a convent.

JUSTINIAN I

In 527, with Justinian I's rise to power, the boundaries of the Byzantine Empire expanded. Justinian wanted to be seen as Constantine's successor and to restore Constantinople to its former glory. He therefore ruled from Constantinople, which he considered his personal city, although he launched enormous artistic programs throughout the empire, including Ravenna. With Theodora (see Box), Justinian ruled in the autocratic style typical of Byzantine emperors.

Byzantine rulers considered themselves God's emissaries on earth, and their power was absolute. This form of government, called **autocracy** (rule by an individual), was believed to have been divinely ordained. To reinforce the notion of the ruler's divinity, Byzantine emperors wore purple and gold as the Roman emperors had done.

Society and Culture

Theodora and the Court

Theodora (*c.* 500–548) is sometimes identified as the daughter of a stable owner, sometimes of an animal trainer in the circus. She herself had been a dancer, actress, and courtesan before becoming the emperor's concubine; two years later they were married and she became empress. A woman of high intelligence and driving ambition, she was a close adviser to Justinian and urged him to exert his power. During the Nika riots, Theodora reportedly said to Justinian, "there is the sea, and there are the ships," should he wish to escape the mob. She herself, ever vain, would stay, because "purple makes a superb shroud."

Like Justinian, Theodora opposed paganism and approved the shutting down of Plato's Academy and Aristotle's Lyceum in Athens. Her early life notwithstanding, as empress she was engaged in moral reform, and she founded a home for rehabilitated prostitutes. Theodora also influenced certain laws in the Justinian Code that benefited women. At the time, marriage between people of different social classes was illegal—which made it impossible for Justinian to marry Theodora. That law had been eased before the new laws were issued, but with the Code, any woman who renounced the theater could marry a high-ranking man. The Code also ended all proscriptions on marriages between the upper and lower classes.

The lavish life at Justinian's court contrasted markedly with the style of Theodora's humble beginnings. Some 4000 servants attended the imperial couple, and access to them was guarded by eunuchs and slaves. A huge civil service, composed of well-educated men, administered the empire. Justinian's otherwise faithful historian Procopius (*c.* 500–565) chronicled the rampant abuses at court in a *Secret History*, which was not intended for publication. Procopius objected to a woman of low-class origin ascending the throne and believed Theodora had bewitched Justinian. As an actress, she was naturally viewed at the time as a prostitute. She was well known for her striptease and her talents as a comic mime and contortionist. Procopius, who was not only elitist but also a misogynist, thoroughly disapproved of Theodora and was extremely hostile to her.

READING SELECTION

Procopius, *The Secret History*, on the scandalous past of Theodora, PWC1-006

In 532, a rebellion against Justinian's autocratic policies broke out during a horserace in Constantinople. The Nika Riots, so-called after the shouts of *nika*, *nika*, meaning "victory," were suppressed by the emperor's faithful general Belisarius (*c.* 505–565). Three years later, Belisarius captured North Africa for Justinian, and between 535 and 561 he recovered Italy from the Goths. Procopius accompanied Belisarius on his military campaigns and recorded them in his *History of the Wars of Justinian.* But despite Justinian's imperial gains, which included taking control of the silk market in the West (see Box), he overspent his resources and weakened the empire.

THE BARBERINI IVORY: AN IMAGE OF IMPERIAL TRIUMPH

A good example of Justinian's political iconography can be seen in the *Barberini Ivory* (figure **9.3**). This carving shows

9.3 *Barberini Ivory*, late 6th century. 3³/₈ × 10⁹/₁₆ in. (34.2 × 26.8 cm). Louvre, Paris.

Society and Culture

Justinian and the Silk Routes

The Silk Routes (map **9.2**) had long been traveled by merchants and caravans bringing silks, ceramics, lacquer ware, and furs from Asia to Rome. They also took Western gold, ivory, glass, and wool to the East. The particularly profitable silk trade was controlled by a Persian monopoly. With a view to improving his own economy, Justinian persuaded Indian Buddhist monks to teach him the secret of making silk. He hired the monks to transport mulberry trees and worms' eggs to Constantinople. By learning how to feed the silkworms on mulberry leaves, he broke the Persian monopoly on silk in the West.

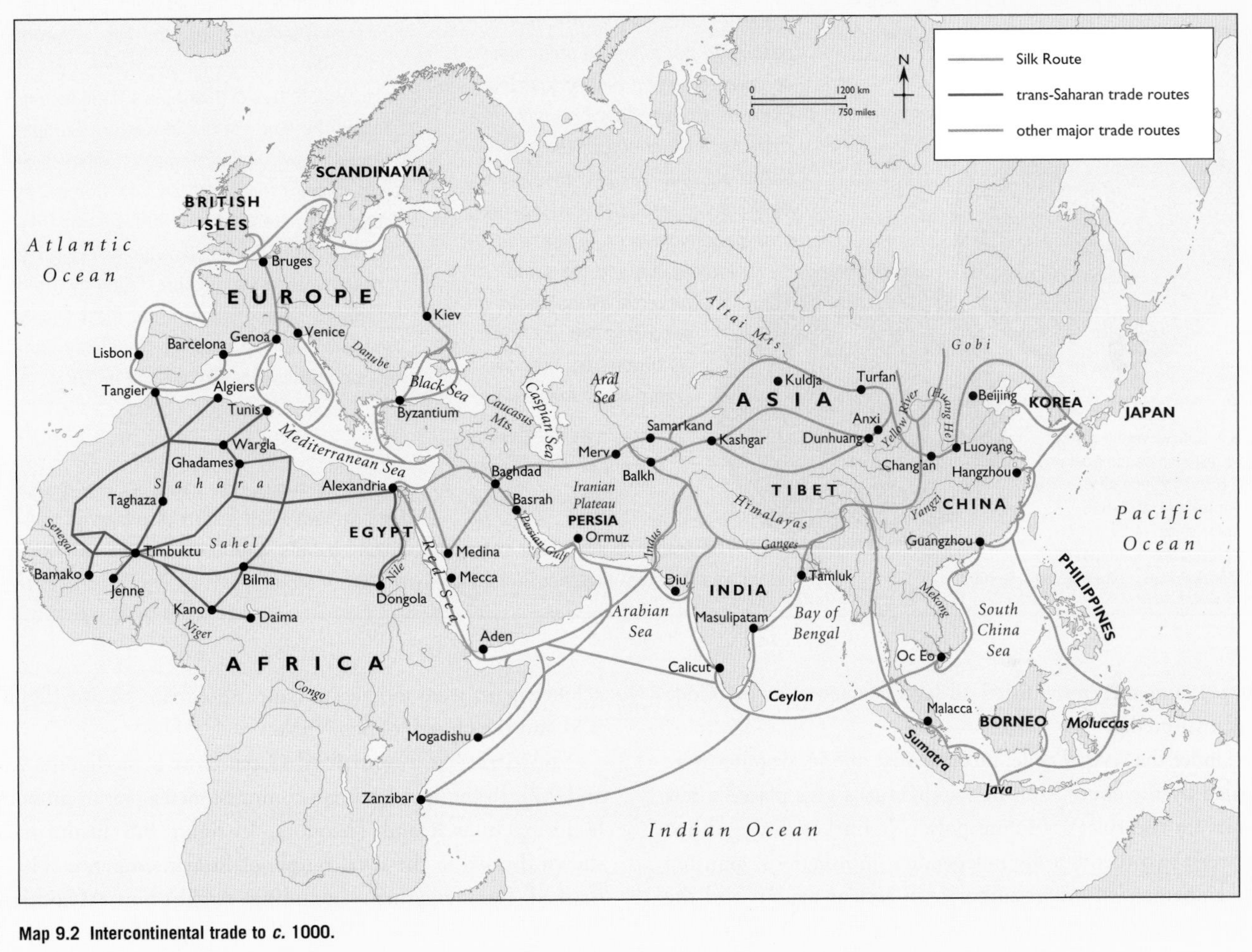

Map 9.2 Intercontinental trade to *c.* 1000.

the emperor as an equestrian in the tradition of Roman emperors such as Marcus Aurelius (see figure 7.40). Justinian wears a jeweled crown and controls a vigorous horse rearing over a female figure. She personifies fertility and prosperity, which are indicated by her pendulous breasts and the fruit in her lap. To the left, a Roman soldier carries a small figure of Nike offering a laurel wreath to the emperor, and an Asiatic prisoner follows behind the horse. Above Justinian, a young Christ in beardless Roman tradition is flanked by angels.

The lower tier of the ivory is filled with defeated enemies. Among these are Asians wearing Phrygian caps and leggings and an African carrying a large tusk. The Asians are accompanied by a lion and the African by an elephant; both are bearing tribute. Another Nike dominates the center, alluding to Justinian's military and imperial triumphs.

Justinian's Law Code

One of Justinian's most lasting accomplishments was commissioning a revision of the Roman law code, which had grown exceedingly complex since the republic and needed reorganizing. The revision consisted of four parts: the *Codex* reviewed all imperial decrees from Hadrian to Justinian; the *Digest* summarized past legal opinions and arguments; the *Institutes* were laws that dealt with people, things, actions, and crimes against

Defining Moment

The Code of Justinian

The legal code that was to become the foundation of law in most western European countries during the twelfth to eighteenth centuries was initiated by the Emperor Justinian (figure **9.4**). In February 528, Justinian appointed a commission of ten headed by the pagan legal scholar Trebonianus (d. 545) to devise new imperial constitutions. His aim, as asserted in the preface of the Code, was that:

> *Imperial majesty should not only be adorned with military might but also graced by laws, so that in times of peace and war alike the state may be governed aright and so that the Emperor of Rome may not only shine forth victorious on the battlefield, but may also by every legal means cast out the wickedness of the perverters of justice, and thus at one and the same time prove as assiduous in upholding the law as he is triumphant over his vanquished foes.*
>
> (Justinian, *The Digest of Roman Law: Theft, Rapine, Damage, and Insult*)

The result of some ten years of labor was to gather together Roman law into one body, known as the Justinian Code or the *Corpus Iuris Civilis* (*Body of Civil Law*). Justinian's code was a compilation of early Roman laws and legal principles, illustrated by individual cases, and combined with new laws. Significant as the Code was in its own time, it achieved even greater significance thereafter. In the late eleventh century, the discovery of two manuscripts of the complete text of Justinian's Code revolutionized the study of law in western Europe. Comprehensive and systematic Roman civil law became a model for western Europeans struggling to create their own legal systems. The view that law should be based on a philosophical system comes directly from Justinian's Code. This was the most widely used law until the emperor Napoleon commissioned the Napoleonic Code in 1804.

9.4 Solidus with a portrait of Justinian on the front and a representation of Victory on the reverse, 527–565. Gold, 1/8 oz. (4.27 g). Preussischer Kulturbesitz, Münzkabinett, State Museums, Berlin.

Critical Question How can a society devise fair civil laws? Is it just to base laws on traditional beliefs and the customs of those already in power?

people; and the *Novels* listed all laws enacted after the Code was instituted.

Under the revised code, promulgated in 534, disputes were settled by the courts, and new individual rights placed a few limits on the ruler's absolute power. It further distinguished between two theoretically independent jurisdictions, granting the emperor (*imperium*) authority in secular matters and the clergy (*sacerdotum*) authority in matters pertaining to the Church. Justinian, however, remained the head of both Church and state.

READING SELECTION

Justinian, *Digest of Roman Law*, on sexual harassment in ancient Rome, PWC1-045

THE ARTS IN RAVENNA

Although Justinian never visited Ravenna, his artistic program was designed to make his presence and his image known in that part of the Byzantine Empire. Two of Justinian's major achievements were mosaics at Sant' Apollinare Nuovo (figure **9.5**) and the church of San Vitale.

San Vitale has a centralized Greek cross plan (figures **9.6** and **9.7**). In the apse Justinian commissioned a pair of mosaics honoring himself and Theodora. In figure **9.8** Justinian is shown dressed in the royal purple of Roman emperors. He is flanked by clergymen, including Archbishop Maximian holding a jeweled cross. All wear Roman togas. To the left, Justinian's soldiers carry a shield with the *CHI-RHO* monogram, reflecting Justinian's role as Constantine's legitimate successor and showing that his power is sustained by the army as well as by the Church. His central position and direct frontal gaze convey his power, just as the halo denotes his divine status.

The figures in Theodora's mosaic (figure **9.9**) are set slightly back in space, which makes her appear less imposing than the emperor. She, too, wears purple and has a halo. At her left is a group of richly clothed and elaborately jeweled ladies-in-waiting, and at her right are clergymen. One of them pushes aside a curtain to reveal a baptismal fountain. Theodora herself offers a gold chalice, a gesture echoed by the three Magi embroidered at the bottom of her robe. Her mosaic, like Justinian's, projects an image of wealth, power, and piety—all of which served the political purpose of empire.

9.5 North wall of Sant' Apollinare Nuovo, Ravenna, early 6th century.
A long procession of virgin saints and martyrs approaches the enthroned Virgin Mary. She wears a toga and holds Jesus on her lap. In this iconography, Mary is the Queen of Heaven and Christ its King. His small size and adult appearance embody the notion of the miraculous baby-king, which is a fundamental aspect of Christian imagery. Leading the procession are the three Magi. Their names, like those of the virgins, are inscribed above each one: Balthasar, Melchior, and Caspar. Note their Asiatic costume—red Phrygian caps, flowing capes, and patterned leggings—denoting the luxury of the East. Their bowed poses indicate that they are paying homage to Christ. Palm trees identify the locale as the Near East.

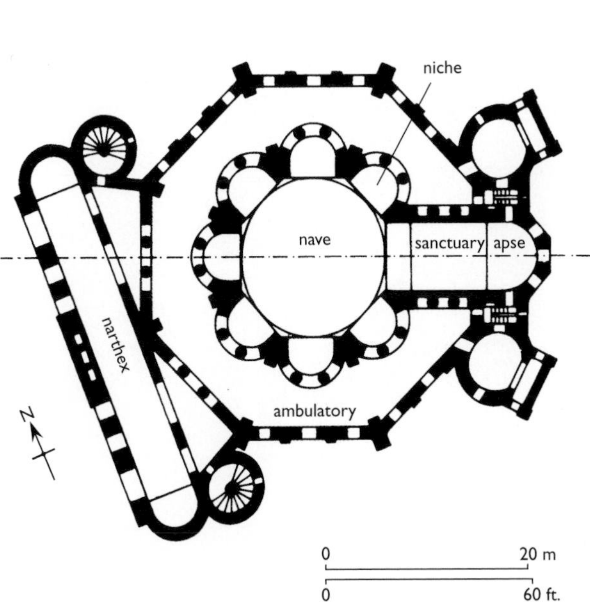

9.6 Plan of San Vitale, Ravenna, 6th century.

9.7 Exterior of San Vitale, Ravenna, 6th century.
San Vitale is a small, complex, octagonal church, with a brick exterior. It has a circular nave surrounded by seven niches, which are fronted by arches and surrounded by an ambulatory. Opposite the **narthex** on the west side is the apse at the east end.

9.8 *above* **Mosaic of Justinian, apse of San Vitale, Ravenna, 6th century.**

9.9 Mosaic of Theodora, apse of San Vitale, Ravenna, 6th century.

MUSIC IN THE WESTERN AND EASTERN CHURCHES

There are no surviving musical notations from sixth-century Ravenna. Nevertheless, as the liturgy in the Western Church differed from that in the Eastern Church, and as manuscripts do survive from later periods, one can assume that their music was also different. Both Western and Eastern church buildings had been constructed in Ravenna—Theodoric's basilican, Latin cross plan in Sant' Apollinare Nuovo and Justinian's centralized Greek cross plan in San Vitale—reflecting the city's status as a meeting point of the cultures of West and East.

Since the fourth century, when Christianity had been legalized and encouraged under Constantine, increasingly large gatherings had been assembling for services. Gradually the great urban centers—especially Rome, Byzantium, Antioch, and Alexandria—began to develop their own forms of worship. Liturgical texts were written down, standardized, and circulated. The Western Church, led from Rome, focused primarily on the Mass. In the sixth century the essential structure of the Roman liturgy was established, specifying, for example, set forms for the prayers of the officiating priest in the Mass, and the texts of Bible readings for different times of the year. The second important liturgical and musical element in the Western Church was the Divine Office—meaning other regular church services, both monastic and non-monastic. The most significant, musically speaking, were Matins, Lauds, and Vespers.

The Mass was still heavily based on plainchant, enhanced by **antiphonal** singing (alternation of two groups of singers) as the choir processed in at the start of the service and again for the offertory and communion within the Mass. After the Bible readings, solo chants were sung with simple congregational or choral responses. Psalms continued to form a regular part of services; they were performed either responsorially (a soloist alternated with the congregation or choir) or antiphonally. The latter style led to the development of a new genre, the **antiphon**—a separate chant with a Latin text and a simple melody to be sung with the psalm.

Antiphonal psalm singing was also characteristic of the Eastern Church as its liturgies developed in Byzantium, Antioch, and Alexandria. But, unlike the Western Church, the Eastern Church assigned a prominent and permanent place to the hymn. Early hymn tunes probably had semipopular origins, deriving from secular songs or folk music. Thus their melodies were simpler and their style more rhythmic than other church music. Hymn texts were written in short stanzas, so within a hymn each verse had the same number of lines, the same pattern of stresses, and sometimes the same rhyming scheme. One hymn tune could be used for all the texts with a matching poetic structure, an interchangeability that still applies to the hymnals of the twenty-first century.

HAGIA SOPHIA

Justinian's personal church and the main church of Constantinople was Hagia Sophia ("Holy Wisdom") (figure **9.10**). It was designed by two Greek mathematicians—Anthemius of Tralles and Isidorus of Miletus. Their interest in circular form is apparent in the medley of domes, curved arches, and **lunettes** (half-moon shaped wall sections), which give the building a

9.10 Anthemius of Tralles and Isidorus of Miletus, exterior of Hagia Sophia, Constantinople (Istanbul), Turkey, finished 537. 184 ft. (55.2 m) high.
Note the four minarets, which were added after Constantinople fell to the Ottoman Turks in 1453. The church was then converted to a mosque.

9.11 Anthemius of Tralles and Isidorus of Miletus, interior of Hagia Sophia, Constantinople.

dynamic, organic character. The plan in figure **9.12** gives some idea of its size and complexity. At 184 feet (55.2 m), it is taller than the Roman Pantheon (see figure 7.37), and, like large basilican churches, it has an arcade on either side of the nave.

The dazzling splendor of the interior (figure **9.11**) is achieved with gold mosaics and reflected light. Procopius described the huge dome as a suspended gold sphere. In contrast to the Roman Pantheon, the huge dome of Hagia Sophia towers over a cubed space. To make a graceful transition from the round dome to the square cube, Byzantine architects devised a feature called the **pendentive**. This is a curved triangle between the lunettes and the dome, which leads from the outline of the dome to the solid cubed base. Since the two

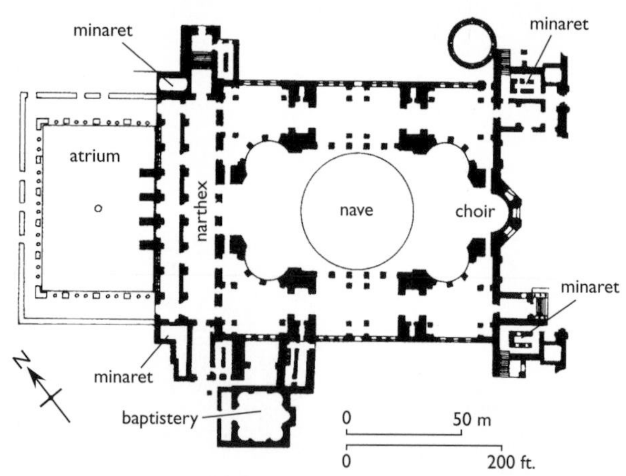

9.12 Plan of Hagia Sophia, Constantinople.

lower stories belong to the cube, the lunettes, which have one horizontal and one curved border, are shared by the rectangular wall and the dome.

ICONS AND THE MONASTERY OF ST. CATHERINE

Justinian built many churches throughout his empire. On Mount Sinai, in the Sinai Desert where Moses is believed to have received the Ten Commandments, Justinian commissioned a monastic church dedicated to St. Catherine (figure **9.13**). The church, the *Katholikon*, visible behind the fortified wall, was built in 530 for hermits who had been living on the mountain. Members of the monastery, located in the valley below the fortress, not only worked and prayed, but also painted **icons**. The Byzantine icon was typically a painting that represented Christ, an individual saint, or a religious event. Icons were usually on wood panel and shown against a rich, gold background.

9.13 Fortress enclosing the monastery of St. Catherine, Sinai Desert, Egypt, 6th century.

9.14 Icon showing Christ blessing, monastery of St. Catherine, Mount Sinai, 6th century. Encaustic on board, 33 × 18 in. (84 × 45.5 cm).

This type of Christ—the *Pantokrator*, Greek for "Ruler of All"—emphasizes Christ's universal power. From the ninth century, bust-length figures of the *Pantokrator* appear on interiors of domes, where they tower over the space below just as Christ dominates the universe.

During church services, icons were a means of reinforcing the worshipper's identification with holy figures. These are usually frontal, gazing directly at the viewer. In figure **9.14** a Greek-style, bearded Christ looks at us as if through a window. His large scale and gesture of blessing convey his power as well as his compassion. The jeweled book with a cross embedded in the cover reminds the viewer of Christianity's basis in Scripture and of Jesus' teachings. Traces of shading on Christ's face reflect the continuing impact of Roman and Hellenistic traditions of naturalism.

THE EASTERN ORTHODOX CHURCH

Christianity had been practiced as early as the second century in Byzantium, and with Constantine's move there in 330 the city became predominantly Christian. In 451, the bishop of Constantinople assumed the office of patriarch, and the patriarch of Constantinople would vie with the Roman pope for power for centuries to come. Although Latin was the official language of the whole Western Church, the Eastern (also called Orthodox) Church used different languages in different areas. In Constantinople, Greek was the official Church language; Syriac was used in regions influenced by Syria, and Egyptians used Coptic; Armenians and Georgians similarly worshipped in their own local languages; and in the Caucasus, there was an Albanian liturgy. These variations in the use of language influenced the evolution of different forms of worship. Nevertheless, the Greek rite of Constantinople remained the major Eastern liturgy.

One example of a difference between Roman and Eastern liturgy can be seen in events celebrated to commemorate Christ's birth. Christ's Nativity, celebrated on December 25, is the more important event in the Roman Church calendar, whereas in the Eastern Church it is the Epiphany, celebrated on January 6. This date was in some cases associated with Christ's baptism, and in others with the journey of the Magi. As a result, in Byzantine church decorations, scenes of the Magi bearing gifts for Christ are more often represented than the Nativity.

Orthodox priests, unlike those of the Western Church, were allowed to marry. But as in the Roman Church, some chose to set themselves apart for divine service. Some Eastern Orthodox monastics adhered to the ascetic ideal of isolation, whereas others formed communities of monks. The Eastern Church's monasteries, which consisted of independent self-governing units, grew wealthy and powerful in the course of its history. The most famous Greek Orthodox monastery was founded in 963 and is located on Mount Athos (known as Holy Mountain) in northeastern Greece. By the thirteenth century, the monastery could accommodate up to 8000 monks, who lived, worked, prayed, and painted holy images inside its walls. Today it consists of some twenty individual monasteries. Women were, and still are, excluded from the peninsula on which Mount Athos is located, a regulation that extends even to female animals.

THE ICONOCLASTIC CONTROVERSY

One of the most heated debates between the Eastern and Western Churches, the Iconoclastic controversy, raged for over a century, from 726 to 843. In 726, as the new religion of Islam threatened Christianity, the Byzantine emperor Leo III (ruled 717–741) decreed the destruction of all icons and other images of holy figures. Evoking the authority of the second commandment against graven images, Leo hoped that **iconoclasm** (literally "breaking of images") would attract converts from among the Jews and the Muslims (followers of Islam), both of whom discouraged figurative art. One argument against representational art, especially sculptures of human figures, was that people would worship images of saints rather than the saints themselves. As a rule, iconoclasm was supported by the emperors, the bishops, the army, and members of the civil service. Monks and the Roman Church, on the other hand, were in favor of images.

Leo III's son, Constantine V (ruled 741–775), continued his father's policies and persecuted **iconophiles** (those who supported religious imagery). Between 775 and 780, the Empress Irene, who was regent for Constantine VI until he was old enough to assume the throne, reversed the iconoclastic policy. In 787, the Council of Nicaea decreed that icons could be displayed in private houses and churches. But when Constantine VI (ruled 780–797) assumed power in 790, he placed his mother under house arrest. In 797, Irene took back the throne, had her son blinded and killed, and ruled until she was herself deposed and exiled in 802.

Despite the efforts of Irene and the Council of Nicaea, a second wave of iconoclasm swept the Eastern Church when the Armenian general Leo V (ruled 813–820) was elected emperor by the army. Leo removed icons from all public buildings, including churches, and persecuted iconophiles. After Leo's assassination in 820, his successor, Michael II (ruled 820–829), relaxed the persecutions. But they were again revived by his son Theophilus. With the death of Theophilus in 842, his mother, acting as regent, influenced the election of an iconophile monk, Methodius, as patriarch in 843. He held a celebration of icons on the first Sunday of Lent in the year of his election, thereby ending the Iconoclastic controversy. The intense debate over this issue, however, reinforced the split between the Eastern and Western Churches.

THE PERSISTENCE OF BYZANTINE STYLE

With the resolution of the Iconoclastic controversy, there was a revival of image-making in the Byzantine Empire. Byzantine style continued to influence church architecture in northeastern Italy and central and eastern Europe. One of the most impressive cities to have been influenced by Byzantium is Venice, on the northeast coast of Italy. Its Cathedral of St. Mark, begun in 1063, dominates the main square, the Piazza San Marco (figure **9.15**). Based on a centralized Greek cross plan, Saint Mark's has five gilded domes. The spectacular interior of the main dome is decorated with creation scenes from Genesis (figure **9.16**).

9.15 *above* **Exterior of St. Mark's, Venice, begun 1063.**

9.16 Creation Dome of St. Mark's, Venice.

The Byzantine Empire had various periods of growth and decline, but its culture persisted until 1453—well into the Renaissance period (see Chapter 13). With the fall of Constantinople, Greek scholars emigrated to Italy and other areas of western Europe. Their departure contributed to a revival of interest in Greek Classical texts, which had an enormous influence, first in Italy and eventually throughout the Western world. In Russia, the Byzantine style lasted well into the sixteenth century.

THE RISE AND EXPANSION OF ISLAM: SEVENTH TO SEVENTEENTH CENTURY

One of the major challenges to the Byzantine Empire had been the rise to power of the new religion of Islam in the seventh century. It originated on the Arabian peninsula, an impoverished area surrounded by several large empires. In the fifth and sixth centuries, Arabia had been primarily a desert, nomadic culture, although some regions were ruled by kings.

Islam is the most recent of the world's major religions. It began with the prophet Muhammad (*c.* 570–632) and expanded rapidly. By 750 Islam dominated the area from the Indus River, Central Asia, and the borders of China to North Africa, Spain, and Portugal (map **9.3**). In 725, Muslim armies reached Tours, in central France, but were repelled by Frankish forces. Islamic rulers controlled most of Spain, however, until the fall of Granada in 1492. Some of the greatest examples of Western Islamic art and architecture can be found there today.

THE LIFE OF MUHAMMAD

Since Islam begins with Muhammad, we begin with his life. He was born a member of the Quraysh tribe in Mecca, the most prosperous Arabian city. His father died before his birth, and his mother died when he was still a child. He was raised by a grandfather and an uncle among Bedouin nomads but later returned to Mecca. Muhammad worked for several years as a merchant and at the age of twenty-five married his wealthy, forty-year-old employer, Khadijah, with whom he had six children. Their daughter Fatima later married a religious leader and was venerated by Muslims. After Khadijah's death in 619, Muhammad married Ayisha, who was to play an active role in early Islam. In 632, Muhammad died in her house, which later became a major Islamic shrine.

In the late sixth century, hundreds of pagan gods, the god of the Hebrews and the Christians, the Zoroastrian Ahura Mazda, and the Arabian Allah were worshipped in the Near East. It was in this context that Muhammad, then around the age of forty, began praying in isolation and had a dream vision in which the voice of the archangel Gabriel called on him to "recite." Muhammad asked what he should recite, and Gabriel instructed him to recite in the name of the Lord Allah, who created the human race from clots of blood.

Gabriel also told Muhammad to repeat that Allah (which means "the one God") was the most bountiful, and by the pen taught people what they did not know. According to the traditional account of this event, Muhammad awoke convinced that Gabriel's words had been inscribed on his heart. The emphasis on the pen in Muhammad's vision is of interest in the light of the tradition that he himself could not read or write. He, as well as the religion he founded, attributed enormous importance to the power and beauty of the written word.

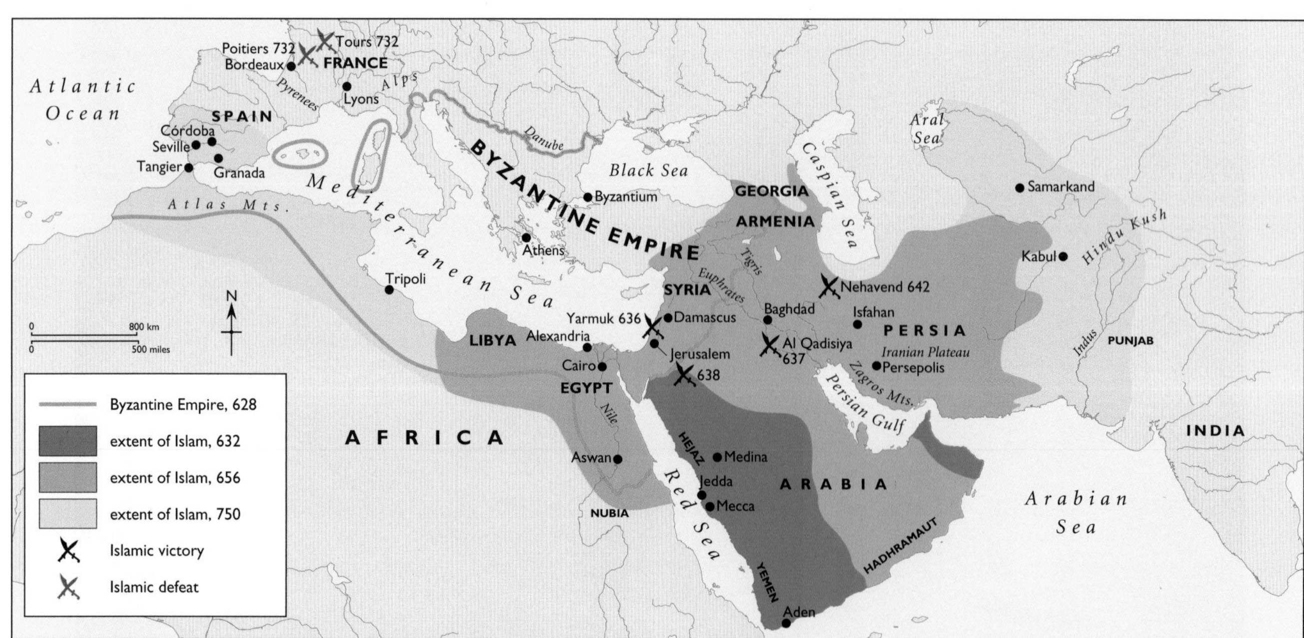

Map 9.3 The Byzantine Empire and the expansion of Islam, 622–750.

Muhammad's vision was followed by twenty years of revelations from Allah, which Muhammad memorized and scribes recorded. In 610, Muhammad declared Islam the last and final of God's three revelations of truth, the first being Judaism and the second Christianity. He taught that the Jews had corrupted the Scriptures, that the Christian belief that Jesus was the son of God was blasphemous, and that the Trinity was a false concept. Islam honors Abraham, Moses, and Jesus as prophets, but considers Allah the one true God. Islam's unquestioning submission to Allah is consistent with Judaism's story of Abraham's strict obedience to God's will, even to the point of being ready to sacrifice his son Isaac. The term *Islam*, in fact, means "submission." Muslims trace the genealogy of Islam, through Muhammad, to Abraham's other son, Ishmael.

Muhammad preached his message and was gradually accepted in Mecca as Allah's prophet. But his stance against idolatry and his growing influence alarmed the ruling classes. In 622, in the face of overt hostility, Muhammad left Mecca and went to Yathrib, later called Medina. His departure is known as the *Hijra* ("Great Emigration") and marks the opening date of the Islamic calendar—the Muslim year 1 corresponds to the Western year 622.

Eight years later, in 630, Muhammad returned to Mecca with an army, fought three successive battles, and converted most of the population to Islam. He transformed the pagan *Ka'bah* ("Cube") into the central and most holy site of the new religion. The *Ka'bah* itself is a sacred black stone believed to have been first erected by Adam. Abraham and Ishmael, according to Islam, then fulfilled God's order to construct a sanctuary around it.

In 632, Muhammad died without an heir. A succession of **caliphs** (Muslim rulers, or delegates of Allah) then led the Islamic world.

SUNNIS AND SHI'ITES

Soon after Muhammad's death, Islam split into two main factions—the Sunni and the Shi'ites—which led to a struggle for power. The Sunnis, who were in the majority, venerated the first three caliphs: Abu Bakr, who died in 634; Umar, the ally of Abu Bakr (ruled 634–644); and Uthman (ruled 644–656). Sunnis believed that religious guidance came from the Qur'an (Koran), the sacred text of Islam. They also believed that leaders should be chosen on the basis of piety and competence but not necessarily because of blood ties to the prophet.

Within the Sunni faction, a mystical, devotional movement arose called Sufism. Its followers were named for the rough woolen cloth worn to denote their ascetic lifestyle. The Sufi believed in emotional union with God, which was achieved through meditation and prayer, but this was considered by orthodox Muslims to border on blasphemy. Sufism has been a force in the arts, especially poetry and music.

The Shi'ites (from the term "Shi'a" of Ali, or faction of Ali) rejected the authority of the three caliphs and followed Muhammad's first cousin Ali (*c.* 600–661). He had married Muhammad's daughter Fatima and became caliph in 656 after Uthman was assassinated. The Shi'ites believed that religious guidance must come from a leader who, like Ali, had blood ties with Muhammad and thus shared in his religious charisma.

Ali and Fatima are considered by Shi'ites to embody the Islamic ideals of wisdom, humility, spirituality, and willingness to wage war to gain converts. But Ali's legitimacy as caliph was challenged by Mu'awiya, who was related to Uthman. A military leader in Syria and a member of the wealthy Umayyad clan from Mecca, Mu'awiya asserted his own legitimacy on the grounds of family prominence and military and leadership credentials.

Mu'awiya succeeded in undermining Ali's authority and in 661 Ali was assassinated by an angry follower. One of Ali's sons, al-Hasan, ruled for six months but resigned in the face of Mu'awiya's superior strength. With Mu'awiya's assumption of the caliphate—he ruled from 661 to 680—the Umayyad dynasty was founded. In 680, Mu'awiya was attacked by Ali's other son, al-Hasayn, who was killed by Umayyad forces at Karbala. He became the first martyr commemorated by the Shi'ites.

Both the Shi'ites and Sunnis believed in conquest to put other nations under Islamic rule, but they did not generally conquer to make converts. From 661 to 750, the Umayyad dynasty ruled from Syria and spread Islam through military conquest to Pakistan in the east and Spain in the west. The Umayyads encouraged scholarship, founded schools and libraries, and commissioned translations of Greek texts—especially Aristotle—into Arabic. In 750, the Umayyads were overthrown by the Sunni Abbasid dynasty, which moved the capital of Islam to Baghdad, in modern Iraq, and retained power until it was conquered by the Mongols in 1258. The Abbasid period, lasting from 750 to 1258, is sometimes called the Classical period of Islam.

THE FIVE PILLARS OF ISLAM

Muhammad is considered the "Seal of the Prophets"—that is, he is the final prophet of Allah and his law. Muslims believe that Muhammad transmitted Allah's code of ethics and the basic tenets of Islam. These include the conviction that the world is Allah's creation and a reflection of his presence. People are made in Allah's image, and their immortal souls are received into heaven if they have followed Islamic law. This law is stated in the Five Pillars of Islam; note the architectural metaphor used to describe the base on which the religion rests:

1. Repeat the creed (*shahada*) daily: there is no God but Allah and Muhammad is his prophet.
2. Pray to Allah five times a day in the direction of Mecca (the *salat*)—at daybreak, noon, mid-afternoon, sundown, and nightfall.

3. Give to charity (*zakat*); Muslims are required to donate a percentage of their income to the poor.
4. During the holy month of Ramadan (the ninth of the lunar year), refrain from food and drink, medicine, tobacco, and sex during daylight hours (*sawm*).
5. Make at least one pilgrimage to Mecca (*hajj*) in a lifetime and pray at the *Ka'bah*.

Early in the history of Islam, men were required to join the *jihad*, or holy war, against "infidels" (non-Muslims). For some Muslims, *jihad* is an additional "pillar," of which there are two types. The Greater Jihad is the individual's personal struggle to achieve a state of piety; the Lesser Jihad is Holy War. It obliges Muslims to combat pagans, Jews, and Christians and force them to accept an Islamic state. This belief and subsequent armed warfare in Allah's name has proven extremely effective. Aside from Spain and Portugal, the areas of the world conquered by Lesser Jihad in the seventh and eighth centuries are still largely Muslim today.

THE QUR'AN (KORAN) AND THE HADITH

The Qur'an, or Koran, is the most sacred Islamic Scripture. Literally "the Recital," the Qur'an was completed after Muhammad's death under Umar, the second caliph. By around 650 it was declared official by the third caliph, Uthman. The Qur'an is composed of 114 *suras* (chapters), each opening with the *basmala*: "In the name of Allah, the Compassionate, the Merciful." The *suras* are written in verse (*aya*) form, and become shorter as the text proceeds. The longest sura has 286 *ayas*, and the last has three. The Qur'an was originally written in Kufic script, which has only a few vowels and does not differentiate between certain consonants. This has given rise to various interpretations (figure **9.17**).

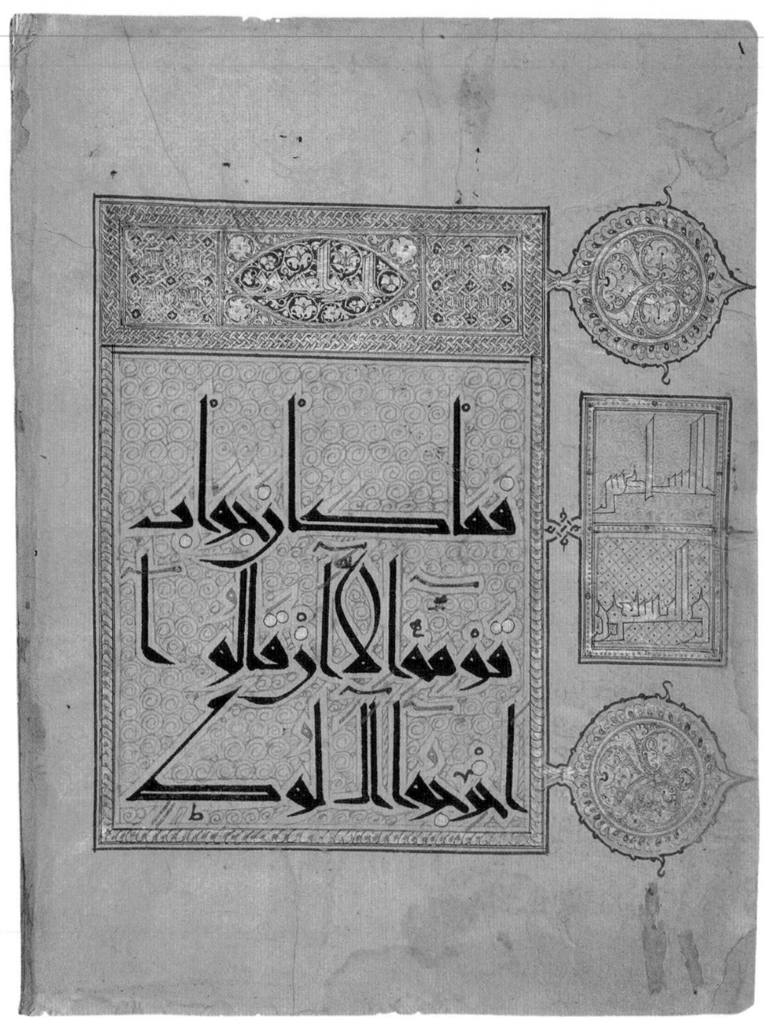

9.17 Page from the Qur'an, 11th or 12th century. 9¾ × 7⅜ in. (24.7 × 18.7 cm). Bayerische Staatsbibliothek, Munich.
To express the truth of the Qur'an Muslims have evolved a high level of calligraphy (literally, "beautiful writing"), through which Allah's Word is conveyed. The striking black, angular Kufic script is particularly elegant. Framing the page is a pattern of spirals; rich gold designs are found in the top panel and in the shapes to the right.

Whatever the interpretation of particular passages in the Qur'an, however, the text is considered the concrete revelation of Allah's eternal Word in Arabic. Ideally it should not be translated or read in any other language. Verse 43:1 of the Qur'an, for example, reads as follows:

> In the Name of Allah, the Compassionate, the Merciful
> *Ha mim.* By the Glorious Book!
> We have revealed the Koran in the Arabic tongue that you may grasp its meaning. It is a transcript of Our eternal book, sublime, and full of wisdom.
>
> (Qur'an, 43:1)

The Hadith, which are later than the Qur'an, are a collection of Muhammad's sayings and include accounts of his life. They are meant to instruct the faithful in how to live an ethical life according to the precepts of Islam.

The Qur'an, like the second commandment of the Hebrew Bible, forbids figurative imagery because it is seen as a route to idolatry. Although Muslim rulers have often been patrons of figurative painting, especially for courtly audiences, Islamic devotional art completely avoids the figure. Islamic styles are characterized by elaborate designs and countless varieties of pattern. The abstract quality of the written word and of calligraphy shown in figure 9.17 recurs in most Islamic works, including monumental architecture, crafts, and the decorative arts.

READING SELECTION

The Qur'an: the believer's duties, PWC2-212; on women, PWC2-213; on Jews and Christians, PWC2-214

ISLAMIC ART AND ARCHITECTURE

The most important type of Islamic architecture is the mosque. But Muslims have also built shrines, monumental tombs, and elaborate palaces. These, like Islamic pictorial images, are typically decorated with complex surface patterns and rich color.

THE DOME OF THE ROCK

The late-seventh-century Dome of the Rock on Temple Mount in east Jerusalem is the earliest surviving Islamic shrine and the second most important Islamic site after Mecca (figure **9.18**). Its plan, like that of San Vitale in Ravenna, is octagonal (figure **9.19**) with four entrances, and a tall, gilded dome towers over the sacred rock inside (figure **9.20**). Elaborate arches resting on multicolored columns surround the rock. The walls are covered with inscriptions from the Qur'an. The patterns, typical of Islamic decoration, consist mainly of floral forms and the merging of repetition and variety reflects the Islamic concept of the infinite and the oneness of the universe.

A shrine rather than primarily a place of community worship, the Dome of the Rock has no large space for prayer. It was built by Abd al-Malik (ruled 685–705), a caliph of the Umayyad dynasty, and designed to serve a political as well as a religious function. It was meant to proclaim that just as Muhammad, the true prophet of Allah, had superseded Abraham, Moses, and Jesus, so Islam had superseded Judaism and Christianity as the definitive world religion.

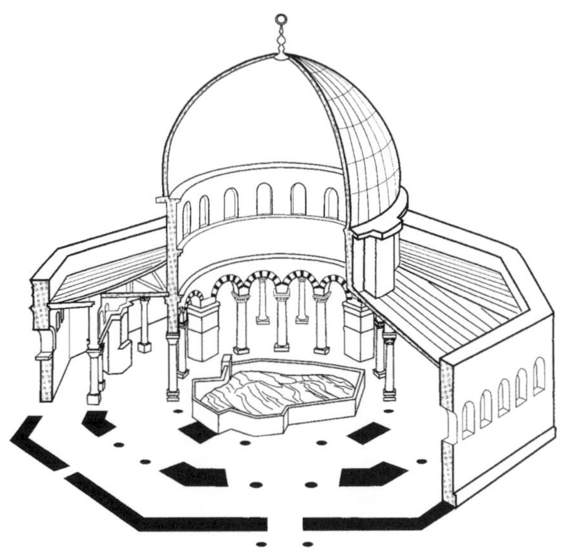

9.19 Cutaway drawing of the Dome of the Rock, Jerusalem.

9.18 Exterior of the Dome of the Rock, Jerusalem, completed 691.
For Muslims this is the site from which Muhammad rose to the Seventh Heaven, passing on his way his predecessor prophets Abraham, Moses, and Jesus. Later commentators claimed that Muhammad ascended to heaven on the winged horse Buraq. For Jews, Temple Mount is the site of the Sacrifice of Isaac and the first Temple of Solomon.

9.20 Interior of the Dome of the Rock, Jerusalem.

MOSQUES

Like the early Christians, Muslims first worshipped in private surroundings, notably the court of Muhammad's house in Mecca. Later the mosque became the main Islamic structure of Islam. Mosques, of which there are two main types, are oriented so that worshippers pray facing the direction of Mecca. Masjid mosques are for daily prayer, and Jami, or Friday mosques, are used on the Muslim holy day, which is Friday. The latter contain a *minbar* (pulpit), from which the *imam* (spiritual leader) preaches. The *minbar* is the only piece of furniture inside the mosque. Fountains are used for ritual purification and prayer rugs are placed on the floor—people have to remove their shoes before entering. The exteriors of most mosques have tall, thin towers (**minarets**), from which a **muezzin** (crier) calls the faithful to prayer five times a day.

A good example of a mosque in the West can be seen in the Great Mosque at Córdoba, in Spain (figure **9.21**). The plan shows the large open space of the *sahn* (courtyard), which had been a feature of Muhammad's own house. At the far end, a *mihrab* (niche) is set into the *qibla* (prayer wall) facing Mecca.

Although converted to a church after the Christian reconquest of Spain, the Córdoba Mosque retains its original two-tiered, horseshoe-shaped arches on the interior. They were designed for increased height and enhanced illumination (figure **9.22**). The alternating red and white voussoirs of the arches create a lively formal pattern typical of Islamic taste. Further elegant ornamentation can be seen in the *mihrab* (figure **9.23**), which was added in the tenth century.

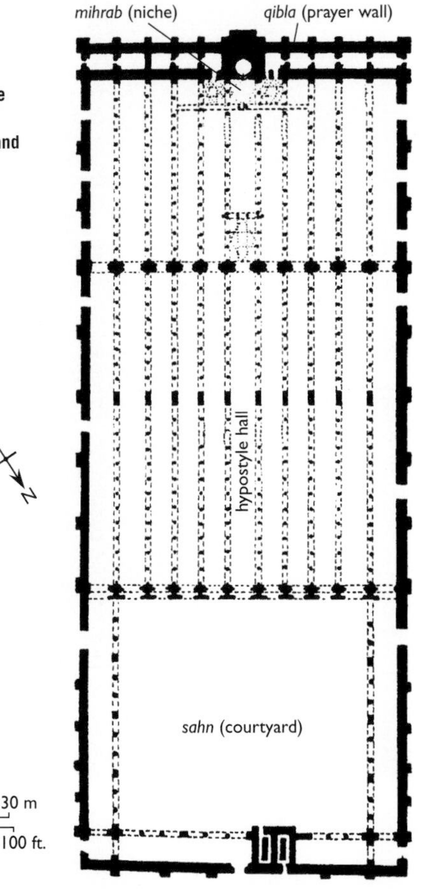

9.21 Plan of the Córdoba Mosque, Spain, built in three stages; originally 786–787, with additions in 832–848 and 961–987.

9.23 *above* ***Mihrab*, Córdoba Mosque, 10th century.**

9.22 Arches of the Córdoba Mosque, 8th century. Columns 9 ft. 9 in. (2.97 m) high.

TOMBS

The melon- or slightly more elongated onion-shaped domes of mosques are a distinctive feature of Islamic architecture also used in tombs. The fifteenth-century mausoleum of Timur Leng, or Tamerlane (*c.* 1336–1405), in Samarkand, Uzbekistan, supports a dome over 30 feet (9.1 m) high (figure **9.24**). The rich colors of the dome and exterior walls were created using the vivid glazed tiles that are typical of much Islamic architecture. Kufic script on the dome proclaims that Allah alone is eternal.

Perhaps the most famous of all Islamic mausoleums is the seventeenth-century Taj Mahal (figure **9.25**). It was built by the Mughal ruler Shah Jahan in honor of his wife Mumtaz (the "chosen one of the palace"), who died in childbirth. The Taj Mahal sits like a jewel on the banks of the River Jumna, near

9.24 *right* **Mausoleum of Timur Leng (Tamerlane), Samarkand, Uzbekistan, *c.* 1403.**
Timur Leng was a much-feared Mongol conqueror who defeated the Mongol empire originally established by Jenghis (Genghis) Khan (*c.* 1162–1227). In 1398, Timur's armies invaded the Punjab and overran the Muslim areas of north India. He also conquered Persia, Armenia and Georgia in southern Russia, Syria, and parts of Asia Minor. From 1369 until his death in 1405 he ruled at Samarkand, in Uzbekistan.

9.25 Taj Mahal, Agra, India, 1630s.

Agra, in India. It is a graceful, octagonal structure, with four minarets and four pavilions, surrounded by gardens. The white marble facing, accented with color and patterns carved and inlaid into the surface, exemplifies the rich artistic culture that flourished in India under the Mughal dynasty.

SECULAR ART

Islamic palace architecture is highly complex and lavishly decorated. At the Alhambra in Granada, in southern Spain, the fourteenth-century Court of the Lions is particularly elaborate (figure **9.26**). As at the Córdoba Mosque, the arches rest on short columns, but here some are paired for extra support. The plaster and wood carvings around the arches and on the walls and ceilings are more complex than at Córdoba. They are enhanced by shimmering, outdoor light. The Alhambra is actually two palaces, the Palace of the Myrtles, which was used for public receptions, and the private Palace of the Lions. Throughout the complex, fountains serve the practical purpose of cooling the air and the aesthetic purpose of reflecting light and creating the murmur of rushing water.

Islamic attention to minute, decorative detail lends itself to certain types of crafts, notably glasswork and carpets. The carpet in figure **9.27** shows the taste for intricate design patterns and rich color. This is one of

9.26 *above* **Court of the Lions, Granada, Spain, 1343–1391.**
The architecture of the Alhambra and its surrounding stark landscape and hardy peasants inspired the nineteenth-century American author Washington Irving (1783–1859). He memorialized the Alhambra in his engaging classic work of fantasy, *Tales of the Alhambra.*

9.27 Masaud Kashani, Ardabil carpet, from northwest Iran, 16th century. Silk and wool, 30 ft. 5¾ in. × 17 ft. 6¼ in. (10.51 × 5.34 m). Victoria and Albert Museum, London.

9.28 Bottle, from Syria, mid-14th century. Glass with enamel and gilt, $19^{1/2}$ in. (49.7 cm) high, $9^{3/4}$ in. (24.8 cm) diameter. Freer Gallery of Art, Smithsonian Institution, Washington, D.C.

the earliest surviving knotted carpets of Middle Eastern origin. Its layout is related to book design, having a central medallion in a field of nearly symmetrical patterns.

Glasswork is an ancient technology some 4000 years old; it reached a high degree of development in Syria under the Roman Empire. Made by heating and fusing sand and silicates and adding magnesium for transparency, glass was cooled slowly in an oven. It was shaped by blowing through a long tube, and threads of color could be added (figure **9.28**). In this example, areas of design are set off from the elegant enamel used to decorate the surface. A rich blue forms the background for calligraphic inscriptions, and the red rosettes in white circles are the emblem of the Syrian ruler who commissioned the work.

ISLAMIC MUSIC

Orthodox Islam frowns on music as a distraction from piety. As an institutionalized religion, therefore, Islam has not encouraged music, apart from its use in chanting the Qur'an or the call to prayer, both of which have a musical quality and are suited to the patterns of Arabic melody. Music and dance are not permitted in mosques.

MUSIC LISTENING SELECTION
Islamic call to prayer (*Adhan*). CD track 2

However, music is widely used in devotional contexts throughout much of the Islamic world. Music has been cultivated with particular enthusiasm by members of Sufi sects, who regard song as a means of intensifying devotional fervor and, ideally, attaining a state of mystical union with God. The **whirling dervishes** associated with the Mevlevi Sufis of Turkey represent one example of such practices. In India and Pakistan, many Muslims are also fond of **qawwâli** (devotional song), which originated in Sufi tradition and is regularly performed at Muslim shrines, stage concerts, and other events. Further, many kinds of sung poetry in the Muslim world (including those used in *qawwâli*) can be interpreted—often depending on performance context—as expressing either worldly, romantic love, or else mystical love for God. In that sense, the range of Muslim devotional music, everywhere from Morocco to Bangladesh, is in fact vast.

Muslim rulers have been patrons of secular music, which is an important artistic medium of the courts. Inspired by Greek musical texts, Muslim scholars wrote treatises on music theory, which became a branch of Islamic science and philosophy. Regional music, both Classical and folk, also flourished throughout the Muslim world.

By the twelfth century, according to treatises, Arabic music was based on a system of melodic modes, later called **maqam** (a specific scale having certain phrases and patterns). Popular instruments at the time included the stringed *'ud*, from which the later Western lute was derived, and the *nay* (a cane flute), still in use today.

Improvised preludes often preceded fixed compositions and evolved into **taqsim** (an improvised elaboration of *maqams* in a free-rhythmic style). It is possible that modern *taqsims*, even those played on a recently invented instrument like the steel-stringed *bouzouq*, might sound like older Arabic music. This is not certain, however, because there are no surviving notations of ancient Arabic music.

ISLAMIC LITERATURE

The collection of prose stories from the Arabic world perhaps best known to Westerners is *The Thousand and One Nights* (*The Arabian Nights*). The tales were originally transmitted orally and probably derived from Indian and Persian traditions. The basic core of some eleven stories was written down by the late eighth century, with elements of folktales and legends added over time. The earliest surviving complete manuscript is from fourteenth-century Syria, but tenth-century Arab historians refer to collections of a thousand stories, which no longer exist. Some of the most popular tales, such as "Aladdin and the Magic Lamp," were not known until the eighteenth century. In any case, what is now called the *Arabian Nights* developed from a long tradition of lively and imaginative narrative that interwove fantasy with details of everyday life.

The story of the *Arabian Nights* is, itself, about story-telling. Its narrator is Shahrazad, wife of the Persian king Shahrayar. The king had killed all of his previous wives on their wedding night because he believed that all women were unfaithful. Shahrazad stays alive by entertaining the king with a story each night until he finally learns to trust her.

The pace of the narrative is regularly varied with verse, and throughout there is a whimsical sense of enchantment. Each tale opens with a statement designed to engage the king, who is called "O happy King"—for example, the One Hundred and Sixty-First Night: "I heard, O happy King, that the tailor told the king of China that the barber told the guests that he had said to the caliph . . ." The Forty-Sixth Night begins:

> "I heard, O happy King, that the second dervish said to the girl:
>
> "When I took the sword and went up to her, she winked at me, meaning, 'Bravo! This is how you repay me!' I understood her look and pledged with my eyes, 'I will give my life for you.' Then we stood for a while, exchanging looks, as if to say:
>
> Many a lover his beloved tells
> With his eyes' language what is in his heart.
> 'I know what has befallen,' seems to say,
> And with a glance he does his thoughts impart.
> How lovely are the glances of the eyes,
> How graceful are the eyes with passion fraught.
> One with his looks a lover's message writes,
> Another with his eyes reads what his lover wrote.
>
> (*The Arabian Nights*)

Islam has an extensive poetic tradition. One of the best known Persian poets in the West is Omar Khayyam (*c.* 1048–*c.* 1131). He was also an astronomer, as much of his imagery shows. His *Rubáiyát*, here freely translated by Edward Fitz-Gerald, consists of individual quatrains, rich in metaphor; the work later influenced English poetry. Note that the first, second, and fourth lines rhyme:

> Awake! for Morning in the Bowl of Night
> Has flung the Stone that puts the Stars to Flight:
> And Lo! the Hunter of the East has caught
> The Sultan's Turret in a Noose of Light.

Many verses recommend enjoying the fleeting pleasures of life:

> Dreaming when Dawn's Left Hand was in the Sky,
> I heard a Voice within the Tavern cry,
> "Awake, my Little ones, and fill the Cup
> Before Life's Liquor in its Cup be dry."
>
> Ah, my Beloved, fill the cup that clears
> Today of past Regrets and future Fears—
> *Tomorrow?*—Why, To-morrow I may be
> Myself with Yesterday's Sev'n Thousand Years.

On philosophers and philosophy:

> Oh, come with old Khayyam, and leave the Wise
> To talk; one thing is certain, that Life flies;
> One thing is certain, and the Rest is Lies;
> The Flower that once has blown forever dies.
>
> Myself when young did eagerly frequent
> Doctor and Saint, and heard great Argument
> About it and about: but evermore
> Came out by the same Door as in I went.
>
> With them the Seed of Wisdom did I sow,
> And with my own hand labour'd it to grow:
> And this was all the Harvest that I reap'd—
> 'I came like Water, and like Wind I go.'

And on the inevitable march of time:

> The Moving Finger writes; and, having writ,
> Moves on: nor all thy Piety nor Wit
> Shall lure it back to cancel half a Line,
> Nor all thy Tears wash out a Word of it.

Sufi poetry, which is less familiar to Westerners than the *Arabian Nights* and the *Rubáiyát*, emphasizes mystical union with God. This union is sometimes achieved through ecstasy and intoxication from wine and love. Both are generally seen as metaphors for the intense love of God. Wine-drinking is also celebrated as a way of flouting the strict rules of orthodox Islam, which prohibits all alcohol. The Sufi combination of secular and religious images of love is reminiscent of the Song of Songs in the Hebrew Bible (see Chapter 8).

The Sufi poet Jalal al-Din Rumi (*c.* 1207–1273) was born in Balkh, in modern Afghanistan, and moved to Konya, in what is now Turkey. He wrote around 30,000 verses and performed ecstatic dances while reciting poetry, and it was his followers who set up the Sufi sect of whirling dervishes that still exists today. In the poem "Only Breath," Rumi describes a universal state of being:

> Not Christian or Jew or Muslim, not Hindu, Buddhist, sufi, or zen. Not any religion
> or cultural system. I am not from the East or the West, not out of the ocean or up
> from the ground, not natural or ethereal, not composed of elements at all. I do not exist,
> am not an entity in this world or the next, did not descend from Adam or Eve or any
> origin story. My place is placeless, a trace of the traceless. Neither body or soul.
> I belong to the beloved, have seen the two worlds as one and that one call to and know,
> first, last, outer, inner, only that breath breathing human being.
> There is a way between voice and presence where information flows.
> In disciplined silence it opens.
> With wandering talk it closes.
>
> (Rumi, "Only Breath")

The Persian Sufi poet Hafiz (1326–90) wrote **ghazals**, which had been popular at Middle Eastern courts before Islam.

They are written in concise lyrical couplets with strict meter and a double rhyme scheme. *Ghazals* are typically about love, which is interpreted either as divine or romantic love. In "The only dervish in the world who can't dance," Hafiz bewails his distance from the "Beloved," which in this translation means "God." Note that each couplet has a separate theme:

> I am perhaps the only dervish in the world who can't dance,
> Because my heart is like a frightened deer.
>
> In Winehouse Street I walk around weeping, with hanging head,
> Ashamed of how little I've accomplished and how little I have done.
>
> The Golden Age of Egypt didn't last forever and neither did Alexander's reign.
> O dervish, don't add your troubles to an already troubled world.
>
> Friend, face it, you're a slave, so don't go complaining about
> The lack of love in your life: move on!
>
> Hafiz, it's not every beggar who has touched the hem of the Beloved's shirt:
> All the gold in the Sultan's bank wouldn't fit into His hand.
>
> (Hafiz, "The only dervish in the world who can't dance")

ISLAMIC SCIENCE, MEDICINE, AND PHILOSOPHY

From their beginnings, Islamic philosophy and science were linked as a single discipline. They flourished in the Golden Age that lasted from around the ninth to the end of the twelfth century under the Abbasids. Academic centers in Seville and Córdoba (Spain), Cairo (Egypt), Baghdad (Iraq), and Damascus (Syria) revived Greek texts of Aristotle, Plato, and the Neoplatonists through Arabic translations. Islamic scholars also studied Indian and Chinese texts, and Christian theology was another important source of influence. Like their Western contemporaries, Islamic philosophers sought to reconcile reason and revelation. However, they did not make logic an end or a discipline in its own right, as Western philosophers later began to do.

SCIENTISTS AND PHYSICIANS

The Islamic view of God as an architect and mathematician inspired an interest in mathematics and astronomy. Geographers and astrologers studied the earth and the movements of the planets and stars. A leading Islamic mathematician, al-Khwarizimi (*c.* 780–*c.* 850), made several important contributions that are still in use today. He introduced the concept of algorithms and helped bring the Indian development of the concept of zero and Arabic numerals to the West. Al-Khwarizimi also invented algebra.

During the period of intellectual expansion from the ninth through the twelfth century, Islamic medicine and medical schools were among the most progressive in the world. Islamic physicians studied infectious diseases, particularly of the eye, and learned to perform cataract surgery. In the eleventh century, the Egyptian al-Hazen (d. 1038) improved the practice of optics and devised new ways to grind lenses. He also measured the density of the earth's atmosphere and investigated how it affected astronomy.

Physicians studied drugs and their properties and encouraged clinical observation. Al-Razi (Rhazes) (*c.* 865–932), a physician who ran the hospital in Baghdad, wrote the first known clinical account of the difference between measles and smallpox. Like the Greek philosopher Socrates, whom he greatly admired, al-Razi believed in the importance of detailed study and precise description. His major work was a medical encyclopedia, which he filled with his own clinical observations and conclusions as well as with comparative medical views of physicians in Iran, Syria, India, and Greece.

The Persian physician Avicenna, or Ibn Sina (980–1037), was also a philosopher who studied Aristotle and Plato as well as the Qur'an. His approach to philosophy and religion was from a scientific point of view. For example, Avicenna defined prophecy as a form of knowledge through which one could describe visionary experience. In medicine, Avicenna discovered a relation between pulse beats and diagnosis. He believed that in medicine, as in philosophy, reality is observable. He constructed a hierarchical system to demonstrate that reality could be ranked according to ontology: that is, each entity is responsible for the existence of the entity below it. Because this is observable, he argued, there can be no infinity and no vacuum. And he concluded that existence is, itself, the equivalent of proof. Avicenna founded the medical curriculum that prevailed in the West until the nineteenth century. His *Canon medicinae* (*Canon of Medicine*) became a standard medical text (figure **9.29**).

Moses ben Maimon, known as Maimonides (1135–1204), was a Jewish physician, philosopher, and jurist trained in Islamic medicine. Originally from Córdoba, he was forced from Spain by persecutions of the Jews and went to Egypt as personal physician to the vizier (Muslim state minister) of the sultan (Muslim ruler) Saladin. An authority on Jewish Law, Maimonides understood the then unknown importance of hygiene in warding off disease. Influenced by the philosophy of Aristotle, Maimonides wrote *The Guide for the Perplexed* around 1204. This was an attempt to resolve the apparent conflict between theism and paganism, which he considered primitive. Revelation requires that through the quest for human perfection we approach God's likeness, he argued. For Maimonides, it is God who demands continual moral and intellectual improvement in people, which can be obtained by seeking God through nature and the laws of mathematics.

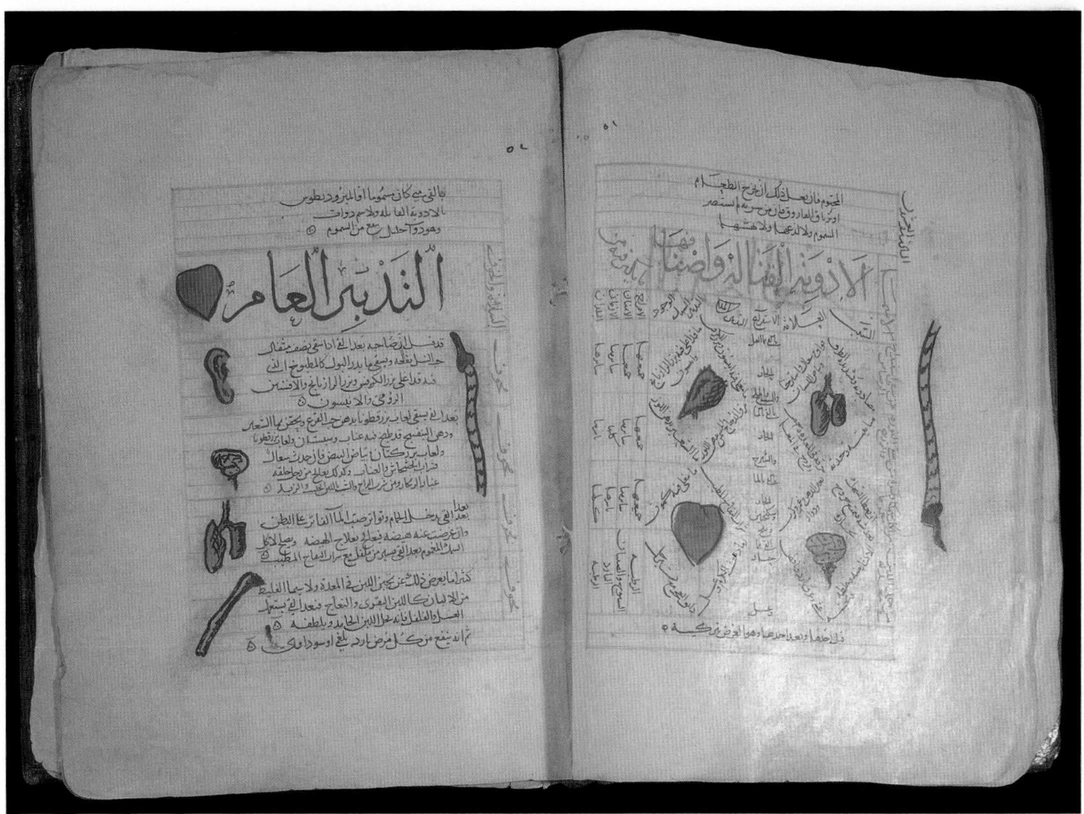

9.29 Page from Avicenna, *Canon medicinae*, with text and anatomical drawings, fourteenth-century copy in Al Quanum manuscript. National Museum, Damascus, Syria.

Philosophers

From the late eighth to the middle of the ninth century, Islamic philosophy was centered in Baghdad's House of Wisdom, a hub of scholarship under the patronage of the caliphs. The House of Wisdom welcomed thinkers from around the Islamic world and encouraged them to find ways to increase the power of the Islamic Empire. A leading philosopher of this period, al-Kindi (*c.* 800–*c.* 870), argued that although the concept of scriptural revelation was valid, it needed to be demonstrated. In this he was influenced by Neoplatonism and Plotinus's notion of the One (see Chapter 8), which stated that original creation emanated from nothing (*ex nihilo*). Al-Kindi also studied Greek musical theory and wrote on the ways in which people could be affected by music. He recorded properties of medicines and perfumes and conducted experiments in physics, optics, and pharmacology.

The philosopher al-Farabi (*c.* 870–*c.* 950) commented on Aristotle and wrote on linguistics. He also produced the first work discussing Islamic political theory in relation to Islamic religion. In *The Ideas of the Inhabitants of the Virtuous City*, which was influenced by St. Augustine's *City of God*, al-Farabi attempted to reconcile secular law with divine law.

Two major Islamic thinkers of the twelfth and thirteenth centuries with opposing views were the Persian theologian al-Ghazali (1058/9–1111) and the Arabic philosopher Averroës (1126–1198). Al-Ghazali's autobiographical *Deliverance from Error* has similarities with the *Confessions* of Augustine. Both authors repented their earlier views and dedicated their lives to the study of God and visionary revelation. Al-Ghazali says that his teaching had been motivated by ambition rather than by the wish to serve God. Following a mental breakdown, al-Ghazali resigned as a college professor in Baghdad and became a Sufi. He argued in favor of the Sunni against the Shi'ites and believed that although philosophy could assist math and logic, it could not lead to a knowledge of God. His *Incoherence of the Philosophers* recommended that theologians use logic to rebut heresy, thus placing philosophy in the service of theology. Reason and philosophical logic, in al-Ghazali's view, should be subordinated to revelation, because God can only be known by emotional and spiritual experience. His theological position, published in *Revival of the Religious Sciences*, earned him the reputation of having revived the power of Islam.

Averroës was born in Córdoba and became a judge in Seville, in southern Spain. He took issue with al-Ghazali's views and argued in *The Incoherence of the Incoherence* that theology can neither lead to empirical knowledge nor correctly interpret divine law. Accused of heresy, Averroës was banished in 1195. The last of the great medieval Islamic philosophers, Averroës wanted to draw a clear distinction between theology and philosophy. He recommended a return to Aristotelianism and the elimination of Neoplatonic mysticism from Islamic philosophy. His work had a more profound impact on later Christian thinkers than on Islamic theologians, and his commentaries on Aristotle and Plato's *Republic* became well known in the West.

For several centuries after the fall of Rome, when western Europe was beset by turmoil from barbarian invasions and urban culture was in decline, Islamic philosophy and science were highly developed. For a time, Classical thought was kept alive through Arabic translations of ancient Greek texts. Later, during the Middle Ages, Aristotle's logic and Plotinus's mysticism began to appeal to Christian thinkers. With the dawn of the Italian Renaissance beginning in the fourteenth century (see Chapter 12), however, there would be a widespread revival of interest in the philosophy of Plato and in Classical culture.

KEY TERMS

antiphon in music, a liturgical chant with a Latin text sung with a psalm.

antiphonal in music, a style of composition using two or more groups of performers to create effects of echo or contrast.

autocracy absolute rule by one person.

caliph a Muslim ruler or leader.

ghazal a Middle Eastern poem in couplets having strict meter and a double rhyme scheme.

icon a sacred image.

iconoclasm the destruction of religious images.

iconophile someone who supports religious imagery.

lunette a half-moon shaped wall section.

maqam in Arabic music, a specific scale having certain phrases and patterns.

minaret a thin tower on the exterior of a mosque.

muezzin in Islam, a crier who calls the faithful to prayer from a minaret.

narthex a vestibule or porch across the west end of a church.

pendentive an architectural feature resembling a curved triangle between the lunettes of a dome.

qawwâli a genre of Muslim devotional song, generally with lyrics in Urdu, popular in north India and Pakistan, typically sung by two to four vocalists, with hand-clapping, harmonium, and barrel-drum accompaniment.

serf a peasant worker unable to leave the land.

taqsim in Arabic music, an improvised elaboration of *maqams* in a free-rhythmic style.

whirling dervish a Sufi ascetic who seeks divine ecstasy through whirling to music.

KEY QUESTIONS

1. Byzantine rulers considered themselves God's emissaries. Their power was absolute. This form of government is called _______ and literally means _______.
2. How might a ruler enforce such a concept through art and architecture?
3. What were the arguments that led to the Iconoclastic controversy? What was its resolution?
4. What schisms developed in the Islamic world after the death of Muhammad?
5. What is the most important type of Islamic architecture? Why?
6. What interests developed in the academic centers of the Islamic world from around the ninth to the end of the twelfth century under the Abbasids? Why is this age considered a Golden Age?

SUGGESTED READING

Boethius. *The Consolation of Philosophy*, trans. V. E. Watts. New York: Penguin Books, 1969.
- ▸ An account of Boethius's philosophy.

Comnena, Anna. *The Alexiad of Anna Comnena*, trans. E. R. A. Sewter. London: Penguin Books, 1969.
- ▸ A translation of Comnena's biased view of Byzantine history.

Demus, Otto. *Byzantine Art and the West*. New York: New York University Press, 1970.
- ▸ A study of Byzantine style in art.

Elias, Jamal J. *Islam*. London: Routledge, 1999.
- ▸ A general overview of Islam.

Evans, James Allan. *The Empress Theodora: Partner of Justinian*. Austin, TX: University of Texas Press, 2002.
- ▸ A brief, up-to-date study of Theodora and her time.

Graves, Robert. *Belisarius.* London: Penguin Books, 1975.
▸ An interpretive account of the life of Belisarius.

Hourani, A. *A History of the Arab Peoples.* London: Faber and Faber, 1991.
▸ The beginnings of Islam and its early development.

Irwin, Robert. *Islamic Art in Context.* New York: Harry N. Abrams, 1997.
▸ A study of Islamic art in its cultural context.

Khayyam, Omar. *Rubáiyát of Omar Khayyam,* trans. Edward FitzGerald. Edinburgh: Riverside Press, n.d., and New York: Thomas Y. Crowell, 1859.
▸ The loosely translated poems of Omar Khayyam.

Kitzinger, Ernst. *Byzantine Art in the Making: Main Lines of Stylistic Development in Mediterranean Art, 3rd–7th Century.* Cambridge, MA: Harvard University Press, 1978.
▸ A survey of the development of Byzantine art.

The Koran, trans. and ed. N. J. Dawood. London: Penguin Books, 1956.
▸ A standard translation.

Lowden, John. *Early Christian and Byzantine Art.* London: Phaidon, 1997.
▸ A well-illustrated account of early Christian and Byzantine art.

Mainstone, Rowland J. *Hagia Sophia: Architecture, Structure and Liturgy of Justinian's Great Church.* London: Thames and Hudson, 1988.
▸ A thorough discussion of Hagia Sophia's architecture and its relationship to liturgy under Justinian.

Manuel, Peter. *Popular Musics of the Non-Western World.* New York and Oxford: Oxford University Press, 1988.
▸ A general introductory survey.

Mathews, Thomas. *Byzantium.* New York: Harry N. Abrams, 1998.
▸ Places the art of Byzantium in its cultural context.

Nett, Bruno, Charles Capwell, Philip V. Bohlman, Isabel K. F. Wong, and Thomas Turino. *Excursions in World Music.* Englewood Cliffs, NJ: Prentice Hall, 1992.
▸ A survey of Western and non-Western music.

Rumi. *The Essential Rumi,* trans. Coleman Barks and John Moyne. New York: HarperCollins, 1995.
▸ Rumi's poems in English translation.

Von Simpson, Otto G. *Sacred Fortress: Byzantine Art and Statecraft in Ravenna.* Princeton, NJ: Princeton University Press, 1987.
▸ On politics and art in Ravenna during the Byzantine period.

Walther, W. *Women in Islam.* Princeton, NJ: Markus Wiener Publishers, 1995.
▸ The effect of Islam on women.

Weitzmann, Kurt, et al. *The Icon.* New York: Marboro Books, 1982.
▸ A study of the style and meaning of Byzantine icons.

SUGGESTED FILMS

1910 *Justinian and Theodora,* dir. Otis Turner

1924 *The Thief of Bagdad,* dir. Raoul Walsh

1940 *The Thief of Baghdad,* dir. Michael Powell, Ludwig Berger, and Tim Whelan

1958 *The Seventh Voyage of Sinbad,* dir. Nathan Juran

1973 *The Golden Voyage of Sinbad,* dir. Gordon Hessler

10 The Early Middle Ages and the Development of Romanesque: 565–1150

"The Emperor Charles [Charlemagne], who left us in command
Of twenty thousand he chose to guard the pass,
Made very sure no coward's in their ranks.
In his lord's service a man must suffer pain,
Bitterest cold and burning heat endure;
He must be willing to lose his flesh and blood.
Strike with your lance, and I'll wield Durandel [Roland's sword]—
The king himself presented it to me—
And if I die, whoever takes my sword
Can say its master has nobly served his lord."

(*Song of Roland*, VERSE 88)

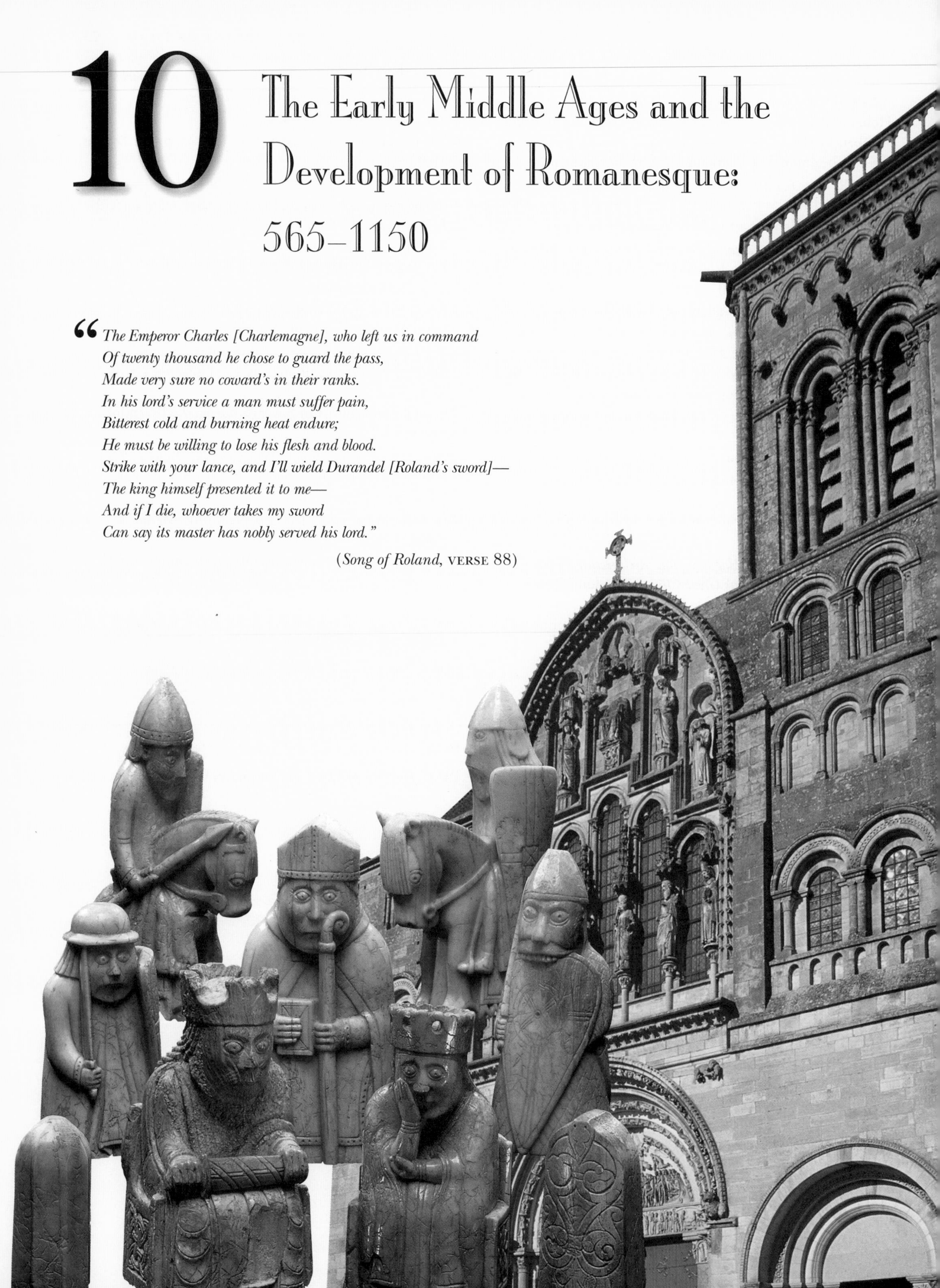

In western European history the term "Early Middle Ages" refers to the period from the end of Justinian's reign (565) to around 1000, when the Romanesque style of architecture began to emerge. From the sixth through the ninth centuries, Europe's economy declined. This was largely a result of weakened, decentralized government within the lands of the Roman Empire, and of invasions of that empire by Germanic tribes and Vikings from the north. Poverty and disease were widespread. Monumental architecture and other costly pursuits declined along with the general economy. Literacy also declined and the largest segment of society consisted of farmers, landowners, and local warlords.

Early medieval society was dominated by the Church, with its increasing power and expanding network of monasteries. From the ninth century, two complex but loosely organized social systems, **manorialism** *and* **feudalism**, *also became important. The Church was the primary spiritual force and to some degree it influenced politics. Manorialism guaranteed the basic needs of everyday life, while feudalism protected people from external dangers. These systems continued in some form to the end of the thirteenth century.*

The quotation that opens this chapter is from the French epic poem the Song of Roland, *which was inspired by wars fought by Christian soldiers. A work of literature rather than of history, the poem exemplifies the medieval code of* **chivalry**, *in which men promised service and loyalty to a lord in return for protection. Such men evolved into a warrior class and followed certain rules of behavior.* ***Vassals*** *had land in return for duties involving allegiance to their lords and* **knights** *performed military service for the right to own land. The loyalty of knights to their lords provided armies that defended a lord's power and territory. In the episode cited above, the French knight Roland has pledged his allegiance to the emperor Charlemagne. Roland thinks of dying with honor as he prepares to fight Muslim forces amassing on the border between France and Spain.*

Key Topics

Religion

- Monasticism
- Missionaries
- Pilgrimage
- Crusades

Structuring Society

- Feudalism
- Manorialism
- The code of chivalry
- The palace school

Structuring Power

- Charlemagne's Classical revival
- Ottonian rulers
- Northern Europe: Vikings and Goths

The Arts

- Literature: sagas and epics
- Music: antiphonal singing
- Mystery, miracle, and morality plays
- Secular theater: Hroswitha of Gandersheim
- Visual arts: manuscripts, metalwork, churches, monasteries

TIMELINE	EARLY MIDDLE AGES 565 TO *c.* 1000	ROMANESQUE PERIOD *c.* 1000–1150
HISTORY AND CULTURE 	Economic and cultural decline No central government Agrarian economy Feudalism and manorialism Growth of monasteries Merovingian and Carolingian dynasties Charles Martel stops Muslim invasion of France, 734 Charlemagne (768–814) Carolingian Renaissance Viking, Magyar, and Muslim invasions Ottonian rule, from 936	Revival of monumental architecture Improved technology and commerce Urbanization Capetian dynasty founded in France, 987 Pilgrimage roads Crusades
RELIGION AND MYTH	Norse myth Christianity Bede, *Ecclesiastical History of the English People*, 731 Monastic schooling: Alcuin of York adopts *trivium* and *quadrivium*, late 8th century Alcuin reforms monasteries, late 8th century	Norse myth Christianity
ART 	Sutton Hoo purse cover, 7th century Book of Kells, late 8th century Cross of Muriedach, early 10th century	Rune stones, *c.* 1000 Picture stones, *c.* 1000 Gospel Book of Otto III, *c.* 1000 Bayeux Tapestry, *c.* 1070–1080 Chessmen, 12th century Reliquary of Thomas à Becket, *c.* 1190 Hildegard of Bingen illumination, *c.* 1200
ARCHITECTURE	Charlemagne's Palace Chapel, Aachen, 792–805 Benedictine monasteries	Sainte Marie Madeleine, Vézelay, *c.* 1089–1206 Cluny monastery reconstruction, *c.* 1157
LITERATURE	Legend of King Arthur Oldest-known English poem: "Caedmon's Hymn," 7th century Einhard (*c.* 770–840), *Life of Charlemagne* *Beowulf*, 7th–10th century *Song of Roland*, late 8th century, first recorded 11th or 12th century Icelandic sagas: *Njal's Saga*, 10th century	*Mabinogion*, recorded by 1100 Romances Herrad, *The Garden of Delights*, 12th century Hildegard of Bingen (1098–1179), *Scivias; Book of Divine Works* Geoffrey of Monmouth, *History of the Kings of England* (1135–1139) Snorri Sturluson (1179–1241), *Edda*
THEATER	Traditions of Roman comedy, pagan festivals, and Christian liturgy German *scop* (5th–7th century) Feast of Fools Boy Bishop ritual Theatrical elements in the Mass Mystery, miracle, and morality plays Secular theater: Hroswitha (*c.* 935–*c.* 1002)	*Play of Adam*, 12th century *Everyman*, recorded 15th century
MUSIC 	Charlemagne adopts Gregorian chant, 8th century Parallel organum develops, 9th century Antiphonal singing Tropes added to existing chants, by 925 Notation using neumes	Gregorian chant Melismatic organum develops, 11th century Guido of Arezzo (*c.* 991–1050) invents four-line staff for notation

THE EARLY MIDDLE AGES

MONASTERIES

The Christian monastic movement, which had begun in the third century with St. Anthony (see Chapter 8), underwent a period of expansion during the Early Middle Ages. Monasteries became cultural centers, encouraging the arts and the study and preservation of religious texts. Their ordered way of life consisted of communal worship, prayer, and contemplation, which provided a spiritual model for society at large.

Monasteries were self-supporting communities of monks and nuns, supervised by abbots and abbesses, respectively. In addition, some members of the monastic community worked as clerks, secretaries, accountants, and lawyers, running day-to-day operations. The administrative skill of the monastic workers and their ability to use successful farming practices to good effect made many monasteries wealthy. Their increasing wealth enabled them to provide social services, such as caring for the poor and the sick. These good works, in turn, led more people to enter monasteries, inspired more converts to Christianity, and increased the importance of the Church in medieval society.

EARLY MEDIEVAL SOCIAL STRUCTURE

The social structures that developed in the Early Middle Ages were a response to the problems of decentralized government. They represented an effort to create stability and order after the fall of Rome.

FEUDALISM Feudalism evolved from the sixth and seventh centuries when **freemen**, who lacked social or political ties, sought protection from more powerful people. The word "feudalism" refers to a fluid political, military, and social organization based on mutual obligations between warlords, or princes, and vassals, who swore allegiance (**fealty**) to them. The vassals could be summoned at any time to fight for the lord, and they eventually developed into a knightly warrior class that followed a code of chivalry. Groups of vassals thus amounted to standing armies, maintaining horses, arms, and armor in case of war. Both the lord and the vassal were bound to each other through honor and loyalty. By the ninth century even clerics, including abbots and bishops, swore allegiance to local lords. This led to new sources of conflict, because the Church, although pleased to receive the protection that feudalism provided, objected to its clergy becoming vassals to a secular authority.

MANORIALISM The manorial system of the Early Middle Ages was organized around the **manor**. This was a group of farms and villages, including grazing land for animals and forests for hunting. A landowner (the lord) allowed peasants to live and work on the land, and to collect wood for their fires, in exchange for a percentage of their produce and other obligations. By the ninth century, peasants had split into two main classes: the freeman and the serf. The freeman owned property, but turned it over to the lord in return for protection and certain economic and legal rights. The serf, who was tied to the land, could own animals but not the land he cultivated.

Peasants made up nearly 90 percent of the medieval population. They typically lived at or below subsistence level in small one-room houses. Women and girls did most of the weaving and spinning to produce textiles. They also helped to farm the land, baked bread, salted meat in order to preserve it, and brewed ale. Peasant families were the most susceptible to famine and disease. Their poor living conditions led some peasants to enter monasteries, while others took up a wandering life of begging or searched for more generous lords.

Later in the Middle Ages, the manor coalesced into a one-family property. As the working population grew and the lord's territory diminished in size, peasants worked more for themselves and less for the lord. This resulted in individual families owning more property, which they could pass on to their descendants.

GERMANIC TRIBES

In addition to the uncertain lives of medieval peasants, the nomadic lifestyle of Germanic tribes contributed to the weakened social and political structure in the Early Middle Ages, as it had previously contributed to the fall of Rome. Although the skilled, non-urban, Germanic fighters were sometimes tolerated and occasionally used by Rome to fend off other attackers, they were generally considered to be barbarians. Forced westward by the warlike Huns of what is now Mongolia, these tribes moved rapidly through Europe. The Goths were divided into Visigoths (west Goths) who went to Spain and France, and Ostrogoths (east Goths), who moved into the Balkans and thence to Rome. Franks went south and west into what is now France; Burgundians and Alemanni moved into Burgundy and part of modern Germany; Angles, Saxons, and Jutes migrated from what are now Denmark and the Netherlands to England; and Vandals moved west across the Rhine, through Spain, across North Africa and Sicily, and up through Italy (map **10.1**, p. 242). The Huns reached as far as northern France by around 450.

The Goths and Vandals became Christian, but because they were Arians (see Chapter 8), they came into conflict with the Roman Church. The Franks were to have the most significant impact on Western history, for they gave rise to the Merovingian and Carolingian dynasties.

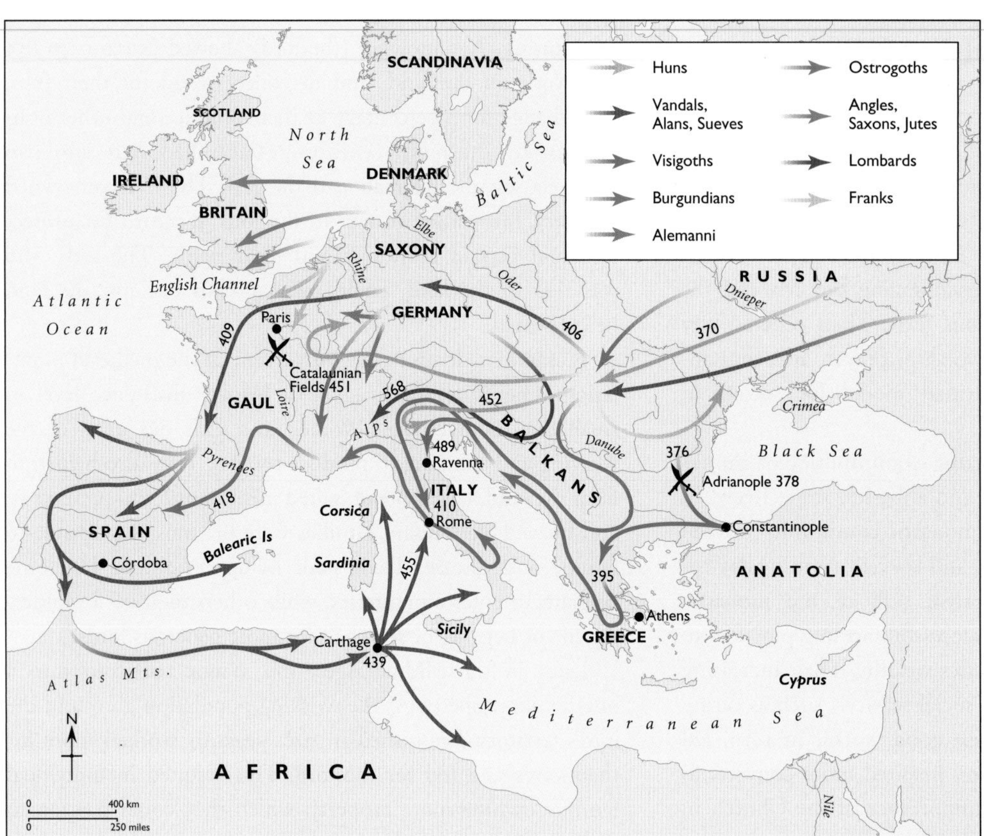

Map 10.1 Movements of Germanic tribes, 370–568.

THE MEROVINGIAN AND CAROLINGIAN DYNASTIES

The Franks, a Germanic people from what is now Belgium and from the lower Rhine, occupied Gaul (modern France, Belgium, the Netherlands, part of Germany, and north Italy). Four Frankish rulers were particularly influential for the development of Western culture: Clovis, Charles Martel, Pepin the Short, and Carolus Magnus, who became known as Charlemagne. Clovis was a warlord who belonged to the Merovingian dynasty; the other three were in the Carolingian line.

Clovis (ruled 481–511) was the first Frankish king and founder of the Merovingian dynasty, which was named after his ancestor Merovich. According to Church tradition, Clovis was a pagan when he ascended the throne, but he called on Christ to aid him in battle and his victory inspired him to become a Christian. His Christian wife, Clotilde, encouraged him to convert to Christianity by inviting the bishop of Reims (in northern France) to teach Clovis the gospel. His conversion is described in the *History of the Franks* by the bishop of Tours, Gregory (*c.* 538/539–593), although some historians consider Gregory's account biased.

READING SELECTION

Gregory, *History of the Franks*, the conversion of Clovis, PWC2-056-C

In 732, Charles Martel (Charles the Hammer) (*c.* 688–741), who was **mayor of the palace** of Austrasia (the eastern part of the Frankish kingdom), raised an army and took Neustria and Burgundy from the Church. This action angered the Church, but in fact it gave Charles the means to defend the Church from attacks by the Lombards, another Germanic tribe, who came from the Danube region and ruled in northeast Italy. Charles Martel's most significant military triumph was the defeat of Muslim armies moving northward in their campaign of conquest, having conquered most of North Africa and Spain. In 734, he stopped their advance at Tours, near Poitiers, in central France. With this victory, Charles Martel enabled most of Europe to remain Christian.

The Carolingian rulers developed an administrative system designed to restore centralized power to their domain and at the same time maintain the feudal system of allegiances. They also standardized the obligations of counts and dukes in exchange for a **benefice** (originally land granted for services, but later extended to ecclesiastical offices as well). However, the real administrative officers were household ministers known as *missi domini*.

Map 10.2 Europe on the death of Charlemagne, 814.

The ruler gave land to the counts and dukes and in return expected loyalty. In fact, however, the counts and dukes were themselves ambitious and amassed their own followers, often having different aims than the ruler. Further weakening the ruler was the system of succession: instead of transferring power and territory to his eldest son, the ruler divided his land among all his legitimate sons.

By the eighth century, the holder of the office of mayor of the palace wielded more power than the counts. In 751, one of Charles Martel's sons, Pepin the Short (*c.* 714–768), used that office to overthrow the last Merovingian king, Childeric III (ruled *c.* 743–751). Pepin established the Carolingian dynasty, which was named for his father. He seized parts of Italy (later called the Papal States) from the Germans and the Lombards and returned them to the pope. In recognition of Pepin's service to the Church, the pope proclaimed him the first legitimate Carolingian king.

The Carolingian ruler who had the greatest impact on medieval culture was Pepin's son Charlemagne (768–814). He expanded the borders of the Frankish lands and forced his conquered enemies to become Christian. When he died, his empire included most of continental western Europe (map **10.2**).

CHARLEMAGNE AND THE CAROLINGIAN RENAISSANCE

Charlemagne was inspired by the achievements of Rome, notably in law, politics, literature, and the visual arts. He saw himself as a ruler in the imperial Roman tradition (figure **10.1**) and accordingly launched a Classical revival, now known as the Carolingian Renaissance (rebirth). Although he himself could not write, Charlemagne promoted literacy and encouraged the accurate use of Latin in official documents. He also improved the economy and standardized coinage and church music.

Charlemagne's life and achievements are recorded in the *Vita Caroli* (*Life of Charlemagne*), a biography by the Frankish scholar Einhard (*c.* 770–840). Modeled on Suetonius's *Lives of the Caesars* (see Chapter 7), Einhard's account includes personal observations and historical facts. He writes as follows of the impressive appearance of Charlemagne, who stood over 6 feet 3 inches (1.9 m) tall:

> He used to wear the national, that is to say, the Frank, dress—next his skin a linen shirt and linen breeches, and above these a tunic fringed with silk; while hose fastened by

10.1 Equestrian statuette of Charlemagne, from Metz (the capital of Austrasia), 9th century. Bronze with traces of gilt, 9½ in. (24.1 cm) high. Louvre, Paris.

bands covered his lower limbs, and shoes his feet, and he protected his shoulders and chest in winter by a close-fitting coat of otter or marten skins. Over all he flung a blue cloak, and he always had a sword girt about him, usually one with a gold or silver hilt and belt; he sometimes carried a jeweled sword, but only on great feast days or at the reception of ambassadors from foreign nations.

(Einhard, *Life of Charlemagne*, 23)

Charlemagne fought the Lombards in northern Italy, the Saxons in Germany, and the Muslims who were expanding into southern Gaul. He instituted a program aimed at converting as many people as possible to Christianity and sought to protect Christian shrines, such as the Holy Sepulcher (Christ's tomb), that were located in Muslim-ruled Palestine. At the same time, however, he maintained diplomatic ties with the court of Harun-al-Rashid, the Abbasid caliph of Baghdad (the caliph of the *Arabian Nights*; see Chapter 9). Within his own borders, Charlemagne encouraged the presence of Jews, who, he believed, would promote commerce. In recognition of Charlemagne's efforts on behalf of Christianity, Pope Leo III (papacy 795–816) crowned him Holy Roman Emperor on Christmas Day in the year 800 (see Box).

Defining Moment

The Coronation of Charlemagne

The only time that a pope has ever bowed to an "earthly king" was at the coronation of Charlemagne on Christmas Day in 800 (figure **10.2**). The coronation of Charlemagne is significant because it marked the arrival of a new inheritor of the Roman legacy and a competitor of the Byzantine Empire. The event also marked the union of the Roman and the German, of the Mediterranean and the northern civilizations—the beginning of a concept of nations unified by a common culture. The Holy Roman emperors strengthened the power of the popes to enthrone, and at times to dethrone, emperors.

10.2 *The Coronation of Charlemagne as Holy Roman Emperor by Pope Leo III in Rome (25 December 800)*, from the *Grandes Chroniques de France, 1375–1379*. Illumination, Bibliothèque Nationale, Paris.

After inheriting the kingdom of the Franks, Charlemagne worked toward bringing order to what is now called Europe. In Charlemagne's realm, the Franks had been regressing toward barbarianism and neglecting education. In 771, the northern half of Europe was still pagan and lawless under the Saxons and the Norse tribes; meanwhile, in the south, the Roman Church strove to assert its power against the Lombard kingdom on the Italian peninsula.

In 772, Charlemagne launched a thirty-year campaign, during which he conquered and Christianized the powerful Saxons in the north. He subdued the Avars, a Tatar tribe on the Danube, and compelled the rebellious Bavarian dukes to submit to him. When possible, however, he preferred to settle matters peacefully. For example, Charlemagne offered to pay the Lombard king, Desiderius, for return of lands to the pope. But Desiderius refused, and Charlemagne seized his kingdom in 773–774.

By the year 800, Charlemagne was the undisputed ruler of western Europe. His vast realm covered what are now France, Switzerland, Belgium, the Netherlands, half of present-day Italy, Germany, part of Austria, and the Spanish March ("border"), which reached to the Ebro River. By establishing a central government in western Europe, Charlemagne restored much of the unity of the old Roman Empire and sowed the seeds of modern Europe.

Critical Question Why is a county, district, or municipality officer who inquires into deaths called a coroner? How does "coroner" relate to "coronation"?

READING SELECTION

Einhard, *Life of Charlemagne*, the coronation of Charlemagne, PWC2-032

LITERARY EPIC: *SONG OF ROLAND*

Despite Charlemagne's ultimate victory over the Muslims, his forces were defeated in 778 by the Basques at the Battle of Roncesvalles in northern Spain. This episode is included in the epic *Chanson de Roland* (*Song of Roland*), an anonymous poem of 4000 ten-syllable lines. It glorifies the loyalty and bravery of Charlemagne's commanders as well as Charlemagne's determination to rout the Muslims and preserve Christianity.

The *Song of Roland* is the most famous example of the *chanson de geste* (literally a "song of deeds"), and the name suggests that the deeds in question are heroic and therefore worthy of being told and retold. In keeping with medieval ideals, the heroes of these *chansons* fight in service to a lord and are devout Christians. Although not written down until the eleventh century, the *Song of Roland* had been recited orally at early medieval courts ever since the time of Charlemagne. Wandering performers, among them **minstrels** who sang secular songs, kept alive the heroic deeds of Charlemagne's French knight, Roland, who warned his lord of the Muslim threat.

As with many epics, the *Song of Roland* is a mixture of tradition and legend. Its heroes perform larger-than-life deeds, their faith is unwavering, and their loyalty to Charlemagne is unquestioning. The epic is composed from the point of view of the French, and it exalts Christianity while depicting the Muslims as evildoers. It also extols the virtue of chivalry, the code of behavior that required knights to fight and die for their lord and have faith in God. In the eyes of the poet, Roland exemplified the chivalric code.

In one of the most dramatic episodes in the poem, Charlemagne has crossed the Pyrenees from Spain back into France. Arrayed along the border are troops chosen by Charlemagne as a rearguard. His trusted count, Oliver, overlooks Spain from a hilltop and sees that the Saracens (Muslims) have assembled a great force:

> Their helmets gleam with gold and precious stones.
> Their shields are shining, their hauberks [chain mail coats]
> burnished gold,
> Their long sharp spears with battle flags unfurled.
>
> (verse 81)

Defending his king and Christendom, Roland attacks. But he loses his warhorse, Veillantif, and is forced to proceed on foot. When he sees the corpses of his friends strewn over the battle field, Roland recognizes the imminence of his own death. As he dies, his last thoughts are of honor, penance, and faith in God:

> His ears give way, he feels his brains gush out.
> He prays that God will summon all his peers;
> Then, for himself, he prays to Gabriel.
> Taking the horn, to keep it from all shame,
> With Durandel clasped in his other hand,
> He goes on, farther than a good cross-bow shot,
> West into Spain, crossing a fallow field.
>
> (verse 168)
>
> In the green grass he lies down on his face,
> Placing beneath him the sword and Oliphant [an elephant-
> tusk horn];
> He turns his head to look toward pagan Spain.
> He does these things in order to be sure
> King Charles [Charlemagne] will say, and with him all
> the Franks,
> The noble count conquered until he died.
> He makes confession, for all his sins laments.
> Offers his glove to God in penitence.
>
> (verse 174)

READING SELECTION

Song of Roland, the death of Roland, PWC2-163-B

CHARLEMAGNE'S PALACE

Charlemagne's palace was located at Aachen, near the border between modern France and Germany. It was designed by his chief architect, Odo of Metz. In contrast to the Merovingian kings, Charlemagne wanted one palace identified as the cultural center of his kingdom. This, he believed, would be an advantage in maintaining political stability—and, indeed, the Palace (or Palatine) chapel would remain the site of German coronations until the sixteenth century.

Although the fortress-like palace was destroyed, it is thought to have had a huge royal hall, some 140 by 60 feet (42.7 × 18.3 m), lavishly decorated on the interior. A long gallery connected the hall to the royal chapel. All that remains of the original royal complex is the chapel (figures **10.3** and **10.4**). Its centralized, octagonal plan and interior design were inspired by the Church of San Vitale in Ravenna (see Chapter 9). Charlemagne had visited Ravenna, and he instructed Odo to take mosaics from San Vitale and use them at Aachen.

THE PALACE SCHOOL

In order to revive learning and literacy, Charlemagne established a palace school and staffed it with outstanding scholars from different parts of Europe. The most important of these scholars was Alcuin of York (*c.* 732–804), an Anglo-Saxon from Northumbria, in England. Alcuin had been educated at

10.3 Odo of Metz, interior of Charlemagne's Palace Chapel, Aachen, 792–805.
This section of the octagonal interior of Charlemagne's Palace Chapel shows the massive squared piers on the ground floor supporting round arches inspired by Roman architecture, with voussoirs of alternating color. Behind the arches is the ambulatory, which supports the second-story gallery, from where Charlemagne could view Mass being celebrated. Outdoor light enters the chapel from the upper clerestory windows.

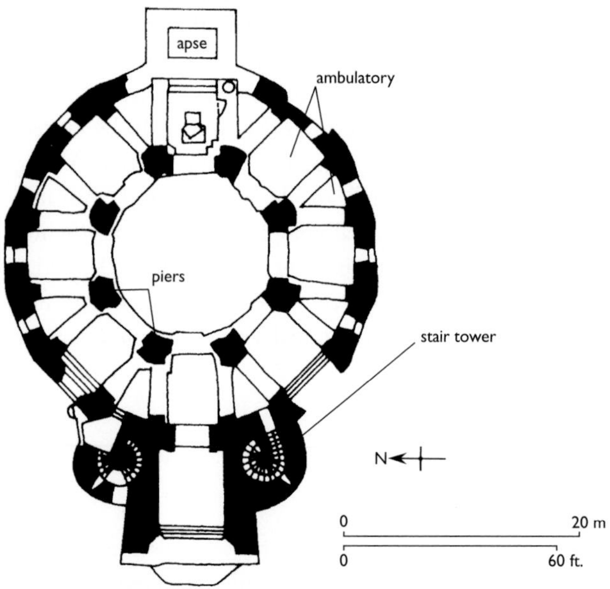

10.4 Odo of Metz, Plan of Charlemagne's Palace Chapel, Aachen (Aix-la-Chapelle), Germany, 792–805.
Note that the chapel's exterior wall is composed of sixteen segments.

the cathedral school in York and was appointed its master in 766. In 782 Alcuin moved to Aachen, where he established the curriculum at the palace school and promoted similar curricula throughout Charlemagne's empire.

At York, Alcuin had been influenced by the writings of the Venerable Bede (*c.* 673–735), a biblical scholar, known as the "Father of English History." Bede had written on language and science, lives of saints, and monastic histories. He completed his *Historia Ecclesiastica Gentis Anglorum* (*Ecclesiastical History of the English People*) in 731.

Alcuin was also influenced by Classical texts. He studied the Latin grammar of the Roman scholar Aelius Donatus and adopted his curriculum: the *trivium*, which consisted of grammar, rhetoric, and dialectic (logical argument) and the *quadrivium*, which consisted of arithmetic, geometry, music, and astronomy. This became the standard medieval course of study in schools until the Renaissance, some four hundred years later. Alcuin himself read Greek authors on philosophy, rhetoric, history, mathematics, and Greek musical theory.

CAROLINGIAN MANUSCRIPTS

Medieval manuscripts, often containing religious texts, were books written by hand. They played a key role in Charlemagne's cultural revival and helped to keep literacy alive throughout the Middle Ages. Biblical and other sacred texts were frequently **illuminated** (decorated with painted images). The most valuable manuscripts had pages of purple **parchment** (the treated and dyed skin of a sheep or calf), on which texts were copied in letters of gold and silver. Manuscript illumination was not only a significant art form in its own right, but was considered a way of enhancing and honoring God's Word.

Under Alcuin, penmanship was simplified and made more readable than the unpunctuated Roman **cursive** script used in the Merovingian era. The new Carolingian **minuscule** resembled modern-day lowercase writing. As a result, it was possible for Charlemagne to improve communication throughout his empire and make administration more efficient. In addition, more people, especially the clergy, learned to read and write.

Figure **10.5** shows a page from a manuscript produced at Charlemagne's palace school. St. Mark is seated at his desk before a parted curtain. He is in the process of writing his Gospel, which lies open on the desk. At the same time, he turns to receive the first words of the text from a lion (Mark's iconographic symbol), depicted as if dictating the already-written text from heaven. The two realms, heaven and earth, are separated by the rod holding a curtain, which opens to reveal the evangelist as the lion reveals the Word of God. At the corners above the arch (the **spandrels**), the artist has illustrated an angel at the left and John the Baptist at the right. The figure of St. John probably alludes to the description of Christ's Baptism in the Gospel of Mark.

The style of the illumination reflects the influence of various cultures. Patterning and stylization combine elements from Byzantium and Ireland (see below), but suggestions of organic form and perspective indicate some knowledge of Greco-Roman naturalism. Such cross-cultural infusions, especially when applied to different disciplines, tend to encourage periods of high cultural achievement. This was true of Charlemagne's reign, and it would occur again on an even grander scale during the Renaissance in Italy (see Chapters 13 and 14).

MUSIC IN THE CAROLINGIAN PERIOD

Charlemagne's approach to music, especially church music, was another expression of his interest in assembling the best minds from different regions of Europe. He brought Roman monks to Aachen to revise the liturgy and develop musical accompaniment. He believed that music as well as literacy would inspire the faithful.

10.5 ***St. Mark*, from the Gospel Book of St. Médard of Soissons, France, early 9th century. Gold ink on vellum, 14$^{3}/_{8}$ × 10$^{1}/_{4}$ in. (36.5 × 26 cm). Bibliothèque Nationale, Paris.**

Society and Culture

St. Benedict and the Benedictine Rule

Benedict was born in Nursia, in southern Italy, and studied in Rome. Around 500, he retired from the world to live as a hermit in a cave, but his piety attracted a group of followers. In 525, Benedict went to Monte Cassino, near Rome, and founded the Benedictine Order, to which he imparted a set of rules for monastic living. He required that members of his Order take vows of poverty and chastity, agree to live communally in one place, and obey the abbot. The daily schedule in a monastery was governed by routines to be followed at designated times during the day. These included a series of daily prayers, scriptural readings, celebration of Mass, and manual labor. Monks would rise at two in the morning and retire around five or six in the evening.

Benedict's sister, St. Scholastica (*c.* 480–543), also chose a religious life. She founded a convent of Benedictine nuns near her brother's monastery and met with him on a yearly basis to discuss issues relating to the rule.

Charlemagne adopted plainsong, sung without instrumental accompaniment, as his official church music (see Chapter 8). Singing in church was reserved for men, and the emperor himself participated. There are no surviving examples of musical notation from Charlemagne's court, but one can imagine how the haunting rise and fall of Gregorian chant filled the chapel.

During the ninth century, a new musical style known as **organum** developed. Whereas plainsong was monophonic ("single-sounded"), consisting of a single melodic line sung by one or more persons, organum was **polyphonic** ("many-sounded"), with two or more melodic lines performed at once. The result, documented in *Musica enchiriadis*, a musical handbook of around 900, was a fuller texture. In the earliest form of organum, two voices moved in parallel, simultaneously singing the same piece of plainsong and using the same rhythms, but with one voice four or five notes lower than the other. Later, a third or fourth vocal line was added at the octave. These particular intervals between the lines of music—fourths, fifths, and octaves—sound bare and melancholy to modern ears.

In the eleventh and twelfth centuries, the style evolved. A lower voice sang the plainsong melody in long notes; this was named the **tenor**, from the Latin *tenere*, "to hold." Above it, a higher voice sang shorter notes in melismatic style—that is, with several notes sung to a single syllable (see Chapter 11).

MONASTICISM UNDER CHARLEMAGNE

By Charlemagne's era, monastic communities had been established throughout Europe. The monks, and to some degree the nuns, who lived in monasteries and convents, composed sacred music. Through copyists and illuminators in the monastic **scriptoria** (rooms for writing), Classical and Christian texts remained in circulation. Charlemagne encouraged the expansion of monastery and church schools with their own libraries throughout the empire. Further, since the standard of monastic life had declined by the beginning of his reign, Charlemagne decided to institute reform. In particular, he wished to implement the early-fifth-century rule of St. Benedict (*c.* 480–547; see Box). The task fell to Alcuin of York, who was a member of the Benedictine Order.

The earliest surviving Benedictine monastery plan is preserved at St. Gall, in Switzerland (figure **10.6**). No known monastery actually adheres to this plan; it may be that of an ideal monastery. This complex design shows all the buildings necessary for the community of monks, including a church, cloister, school, living quarters, stables, land for the monks to work, an infirmary, and a cemetery. The typical monastery was thus a self-sufficient community. Its economy was based on agriculture, though the monks often made craft items and wine, which could be sold outside the monastery.

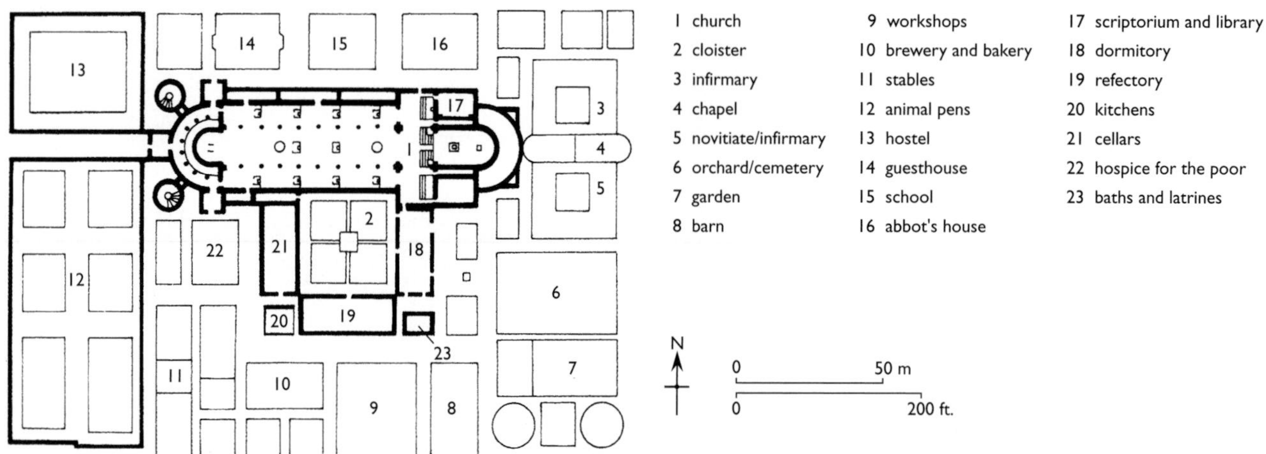

10.6 Plan of the Benedictine monastery of St. Gall, Switzerland, *c.* 820, drawn from five pieces of parchment.

Cross-cultural Influences

Monasticism

Monasticism began in the Far East before taking hold in the West. It was practiced in India in the first millennium B.C. and was espoused by the Buddha in the sixth century B.C. as a way of achieving spiritual enlightenment. From the third century B.C., there were Buddhist missionaries in the Near East and Greece, where they influenced the development of Christian monasticism.

In India, monks and nuns inhabited living spaces (*viharas*) cut into caves. These were located outside the main cities, but close to small villages and trading routes. Because monks did not own land or personal possessions, many begged for support and food.

The thirty Buddhist *viharas* at Ajanta, northeast of Bombay, are the best-known monastic quarters in India. Inside the *viharas*, Buddhists built *chaitya* halls with columns and a curved apse (figure **10.7**). The apse contained a statue of the Buddha and a **stupa**, a round structure that evolved from the Buddha's burial mound. Relief sculptures decorating the capitals of the columns and the walls illustrate important Buddhist events.

As Buddhism spread throughout the Far East, the number of monasteries increased. In Japan, for example, the best-known Buddhist monastery complex is Horyu-ji in Nara (figure **10.8**). This view shows the elaborate architectural design of the monastery, which includes temples, *kondos* (halls), **pagodas** (tiered towers that contained relics), cloisters, and living spaces.

Like Christian monastics, Buddhist monks at first espoused poverty and isolation from society, but as the movement grew, they formed self-sufficient communities owning land and the buildings on it. Buddhist monks also spent time in prayer, study, and work.

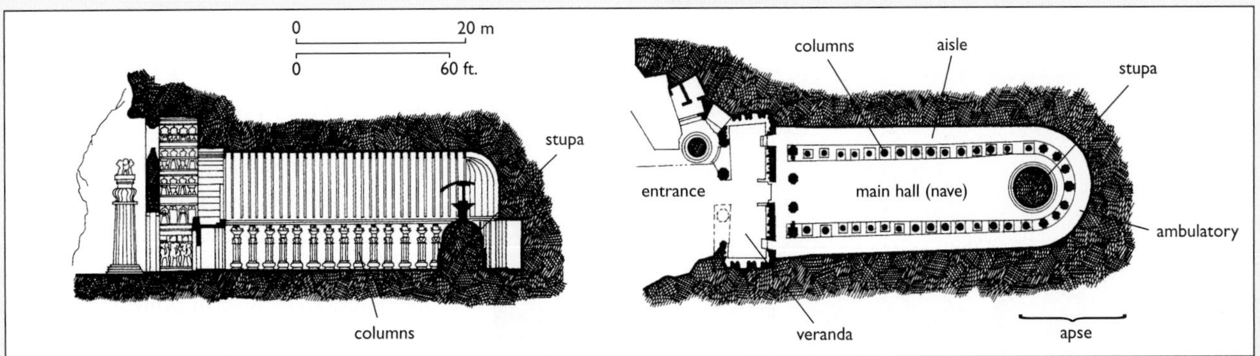

10.7 *above* **Generic plan and section of a *chaitya* hall.**

10.8 Horyu-ji monastery complex, Nara, Japan, 7th century.

FROM THE CAROLINGIAN TO THE OTTONIAN PERIOD

When Charlemagne died in 814, his only surviving son, Louis I, the Pious (ruled 814–840), came to power. Louis did not want to weaken the empire by dividing it equally among his three sons by his first wife. Instead, he appointed the eldest, Lothair (d. 855), as his imperial successor and gave parts of France and Germany to his other two sons. But Louis remarried and, in 823, had a fourth son, Charles the Bald, who was also entitled to a share of the kingdom. This further division of the imperial realm diminished the power of the empire and left it open to waves of invasion from Vikings, Magyars (modern Hungarians), and Muslims. A dark age followed, which was a period of illiteracy and widespread poverty, and it saw a decline in monumental architecture. Charlemagne's achievements receded into legend, and his reign reemerged in works of literature, such as the *Song of Roland*, as a time of mythic grandeur.

In the tenth century, a more stable government took hold in Germany under a series of rulers, three of whom were named Otto, giving rise to the term Ottonian Empire. Otto I, the Great (ruled 936–973), expanded his power base by defending the pope and being proclaimed emperor in return. Like Charlemagne, Otto encouraged a revival of ancient Roman culture, including the arts and literature. A page from the *Gospel Book of Otto III* gives some idea of the artistic revival in the Ottonian period (figure **10.9**).

Despite the relative political stability and cultural achievements promoted by the Ottonian rulers, rivalry between Rome and the Eastern (Byzantine) Empire continued. As a result, the Ottonian Empire never truly evolved into an independent political state. The conflict was only partly resolved in 1122 by the Concordat of Worms, which ended the Investiture controversy. Thereafter, the pope had the authority to invest clergy with control of spiritual matters, while the emperor could bestow secular authority and land.

10.9 *Jesus Washing the Feet of Peter*, from the *Gospel Book of Otto III*, *c.* 1000. Tempera on vellum, image 8³⁄₈ × 6 in. (21.3 × 15.2 cm). Bayerische Staatsbibliothek, Munich.

In this scene, St. Peter protests the humility of Jesus, who washes the feet of his followers. Jesus reprimands the apostle and glares sternly at him. Their gestures and glances animate their exchange and energize the narrative. At the left, eight apostles await their turn, while, at the right, one apostle laces his sandal as another arrives with a fresh basin of water. Jesus is a commanding presence, centered between two colorful green columns and towering over the apostles. Byzantine influence can be seen in the re-use of Greco-Roman art, which the Ottonian illuminator has flattened and thus made less three-dimensional.

THEATER IN THE EARLY MIDDLE AGES

Like literacy, theater declined after the fall of Rome. Invasions and political instability had made organized theater difficult to maintain. Nevertheless, the traditions of Roman comedy, pagan festivals, and Christian liturgy all provided sources from which theater began to revive. In addition, there were traveling entertainers, such as minstrels, jugglers, acrobats, and animal-trainers, who performed in public squares and at the courts. The most popular performing animals were bears and apes.

From the fifth to the seventh centuries, a type of German performer called a **scop** sang tales of Germanic heroes. The *scop* tradition died out in the eighth century, when the

Church declared it a threat to the Christian faith. Pagan seasonal rites, on the other hand, were absorbed into the liturgical calendar. Thus the spring maypole festival coincided with the Resurrection of Jesus, and the date of the Nativity, December 25, was associated with pagan rites of winter. Comedy and revelry were also incorporated into the Church from popular rites, including the burlesque Feast of Fools celebrated by minor clerics. On Holy Innocents' Day (December 28 in the liturgical calendar), equality was celebrated in the Boy Bishop ritual, when choirboys impersonated members of the clergy.

LITURGY AND DRAMA

Certain aspects of Church liturgy lend themselves to the establishment of a dramatic tradition. The prime example is that liturgy marks religious events cyclically—that is, according to days of the calendar—rather than according to historical chronology. Thus the Nativity is celebrated *every* December 25 without fail, year after year. Congregations would build up the expectation of revisiting each such story annually. In addition, priests began to introduce visual elements into the liturgy—symbolic gestures, such as making the sign of the Cross—which could easily be recognized by a congregation unable to read. In the performance of Mass itself, the priest created an atmosphere of dramatic expectation, engaging the congregation in the narration of the events of Jesus' Last Supper, acted out with bread and wine. Enhancing the drama were antiphonal songs, sung either by two alternating groups of singers or by a group of singers and an individual.

Antiphonal singing eventually led to inserting, first, music and, later, music with words into the text of a service. These insertions, called **tropes**, consisted of newly composed verses with melodies, and they were added between sections of existing chant. An Easter trope from around 925 is the earliest to have survived. This exchange between angels and the Three Marys who discover the empty tomb of Jesus is both dramatic and direct:

ANGELS: Whom seek ye in the tomb, O Christians?
THE THREE MARYS: Jesus of Nazareth, the crucified,
O Heavenly Beings.
ANGELS: He is not here, he is risen as he foretold.
Go and announce that he is risen from the tomb.

(Easter trope)

By the late tenth century, liturgical theater had become widespread in Europe. Over the next two hundred years, plays would be performed, first inside the church and then, from the twelfth century, outside in the square in front of the church. Attributes such as the keys of St. Peter, wings of angels, and the devil's horns, tail, and pitchfork allowed viewers to identify stock characters. There were three main types of religious plays performed in the Middle Ages. **Mystery plays** dramatized biblical events, **miracle plays** focused on miraculous events, and in **morality plays** the human struggle between good and evil was given dramatic form.

The twelfth-century *Play of Adam*, a mystery play, presents the Creation and Fall of Man. In "Creation," God makes the earth and animals but wants a creature to worship him and keep his world in order:

To keep this world, both more and less,
A skillful beast then will I make
After my shape and my likeness,
The which shall worship me to take.

(*Play of Adam*, lines 21–24)

In the "Fall of Man," responsibility for sin falls squarely on Eve, through the guile of Satan. She tells Adam that they will be as great as God if they eat the apple:

We shall be as gods, thou and I,
If that we eat
Here of this tree. Adam, forthy [therefore]
Let not that worship for to get,
For we shall be as wise
As God that is so great,
And as mickle [worthy] of price;
Forthy eat of this meat [i.e. the apple].

(lines 92–99)

The most widely known medieval morality play is *Everyman*. This was not written down until the fifteenth century, but had already been performed for centuries. It is composed in rhyming couplets, combining allegorical characters and personifications with moral lessons. The plot is simple: the life of Everyman is a pilgrimage from the earthly world to death and salvation. As with Greek tragedy (see Chapter 6), a prologue introduces the main theme. Here, the words of the Prologue are spoken by a messenger:

I pray you all give your audience,
And hear this matter with reverence,
By figure [in form] a moral play:
The *Summoning of Everyman* called it is,
That of our lives and ending shows
How transitory we be all day [always].

(*Everyman*, lines 1–6)

At the outset of the play, God is displeased with the behavior of mankind. He summons Death to instruct Everyman in the pilgrimage he must make. Death is only too willing to oblige:

Lord, I will in the world go run overall [everywhere],
And cruelly outsearch both great and small;
Every man will I beset that liveth beastly
Out of God's laws, and dreadeth not folly.
He that loveth riches I will strike with my dart,
His sight to blind, and from heaven to depart [separate]—
Except that alms be his good friend—
In hell for to dwell, world without end.
Lo, yonder I see Everyman walking.

Full little he thinketh on my coming;
His mind is on fleshly lusts and his treasure,
And great pain it shall cause him to endure
Before the Lord, Heaven King.

(lines 72–84)

Everyman gradually comes to realize that friends, relatives, and worldly possessions will not bring salvation. Rather, the only way to satisfy God at the reckoning of the Last Judgment is with Confession, Good Deeds, and Christian Knowledge, all of which are personified in the play. Having learned his moral lesson, Everyman is received into heaven:

ANGEL: . . . Hereabove thou shalt go
Because of thy singular virtue.
Now the soul is taken the body fro [from],
Thy reckoning is crystal-clear.
Now shalt thou into the heavenly sphere,
Unto the which all ye shall come
That liveth well before the day of doom.

(lines 895–901)

Non-Liturgical Drama: Hroswitha of Gandersheim

Only one group of non-liturgical plays has survived from the tenth century. These are of interest partly because they were written by the first female playwright on record, and partly because they are the earliest known examples of non-liturgical drama. The author is Hroswitha (*c.* 935–*c.* 1002), a canoness at Gandersheim Abbey in northern Germany. She came from an aristocratic family and, as her plays indicate, had received a Classical education.

Hroswitha was a prolific author, but her works were not published until the sixteenth century. She wrote two historical epics praising Otto I and Otto II, eight legends in verse, and six morality plays in rhymed prose. Inspired by the Roman comedies of Terence (see Chapter 7), Hroswitha intended to use the appeal of sophisticated, worldly dialogue to convey the moral lessons of the Bible and Christianity.

In *Dulcitius*, for example, Hroswitha engages the reader in the ecstasy of martyrdom with humor bordering on slapstick. The setting is the palace of Diocletian during the fourth-century Christian persecutions. Governor Dulcitius, having heard that Christians indulge in exotic orgies, attempts to seduce three recently converted Christian virgins: Agape, Chione, and Irena. But when he approaches them, he becomes delusional and kisses pots and pans instead of the girls. When he comes to himself and sees that the pots have blackened his face, he sends the young women to their death.

Hroswitha was the first author in the West to use the Faust legend, in which a man sells his soul to the devil for earthly wealth and power. This, as we shall see, became a popular theme in Western literature.

NORTHERN EUROPE: BRITAIN, IRELAND, SCANDINAVIA, AND ICELAND

Christianity arrived in northern Europe somewhat later than in central and southern Europe. Roman missionaries had brought the faith to Britain in the second or third century A.D. However, in the fifth century, the pagan Germanic Angles, Saxons, and Jutes invaded England and wiped out most of the Christians. Then, in 596, Pope Gregory I, who was devoted to the spread of monasticism, dispatched Augustine (d. *c.* 604), the prior of St. Andrew's monastery in Rome. Augustine, later known as Augustine of Canterbury, went with forty missionaries to reestablish Christianity in England.

Augustine arrived in Kent, in the southeast, the following year. He converted the king of Kent, Ethelbert (d. 616), whose Frankish wife Bertha was herself a Christian. Ethelbert was thus England's earliest Christian king. Augustine founded an abbey at Canterbury and became its first archbishop. By the seventh century, monasticism was well established in England.

The *History* of the Venerable Bede describes these events, including the story told in the oldest-known English poem, "Caedmon's Hymn." According to Caedmon (650?–680?), an illiterate cowherd and lay brother (an unordained member of a monastery) at Whitby, a voice instructed him to sing of the Creation. Whitby, a dual monastery housing both men and women, was founded and ruled by the abbess St. Hilda (614–668).

READING SELECTION
Bede, *Ecclesiastical History of the English People*, Augustine's conversion of King Ethelbert, PWC2-051-C

Ireland and the Book of Kells

Because of its isolation and distance from the main centers of European power, Ireland remained Christian even when England was dominated by the pagan Anglo-Saxons. According to Irish tradition, St. Patrick (*c.* 390–*c.* 461) Christianized the country in the early fifth century. Monasticism took hold in the sixth century and became a strong force. Two saints were particularly important in the monastic movement of Ireland and Scotland. St. Brigid, the abbess of Kildare (d. *c.* 525), was believed to have performed many miracles during her lifetime and is credited with expanding monasticism in Ireland. St. Columba (543–615), whose rule was extremely strict, left Ireland around 563 to convert the pagan Picts of Scotland. He founded a monastery on the island of Iona.

10.10 ***Canon Table*, Book of Kells, late 8th century. Illumination on vellum, 13 × 9½ in. (33 × 24 cm). Trinity College, Dublin.**
Note the appearance of the four Evangelists in symbolic form. The upper corners are formed by the stylized wings of the angel of Matthew and the eagle of John. The lion of Mark and the bull of Luke are shown in the space between the two small arches.

Irish monasteries maintained a high level of learning. They kept alive the Latin language by reading and copying Classical as well as Christian texts. As the number of monasteries expanded, they became repositories of texts and housed some of the greatest examples of manuscript illumination. Those that have survived managed to escape the Viking raids.

The best-known Irish manuscript is the Book of Kells, generally dated to the late eighth century. It contains the four Gospels, whose text pages, designed to enhance the Word of God, are richly decorated. But there are also pages that completely or primarily consist of images. It is likely that the Book of Kells and other important manuscripts were placed on altars for special occasions.

The page illustrated in figure **10.10** depicts a Canon Table, a type of image created by Eusebius, the fourth-century bishop of Caesarea (see Chapter 8), to demonstrate parallels between the Gospels. The texts are arranged in four vertical rows separated by columns filled with colorful, intertwined designs. Intricate patterns above the columns include fanciful, interlacing animal, human, and abstract forms. Some are pagan and some are Christian.

A characteristic example of Irish art that predates Christianity is the simple, upright stone marker, generally placed in a graveyard or near a monastery. After the conversion of the Irish, these markers were made in the form of the Cross and decorated with Christian scenes, for instructive purposes

10.11 Cross of Muriedach, Monasterboice, County Louth, Ireland, early 10th century. Stone.
This view shows the Crucifixion, framed by a circle symbolizing the universal Church at the crossing point.

(figure **10.11**). Here, as in the Book of Kells, the surfaces are filled with interlace ornament.

Anglo-Saxon Metalwork and Literature

The Anglo-Saxon invaders of England brought with them great skill in metalworking and a particular style of animal art. Examples of both can be seen in the Sutton Hoo purse cover, which was discovered in East Anglia (figure **10.12**). The purse was filled with gold coins and was one of several objects found in a pagan ship burial. Such elaborate burials were reserved for Anglo-Saxon kings and the nobility. A similar rite, in which the deceased is placed in a ship and sent out to sea, is described in the oldest surviving Anglo-Saxon epic poem, *Beowulf.*

Beowulf

The epic of *Beowulf* is a heroic narrative of some 3000 lines. It was composed between the seventh and tenth centuries in Anglo-Saxon (Old English). Although the setting is the warrior culture of medieval Scandinavia, strains of Christian morality permeate the text. *Beowulf* is the story of a Geat (Swedish) prince who travels to Denmark, where most of the action takes place. His mission is to destroy Grendel, the monster ravishing the land, devouring its inhabitants, and attacking the royal hall of Denmark:

> So times were pleasant for the people there
> until finally one, a fiend out of hell,
> began to work his evil in the world.
> Grendel was the name of this grim demon
> haunting the marches, marauding round the heath
> and the desolate fens.
>
> (lines 99–104)

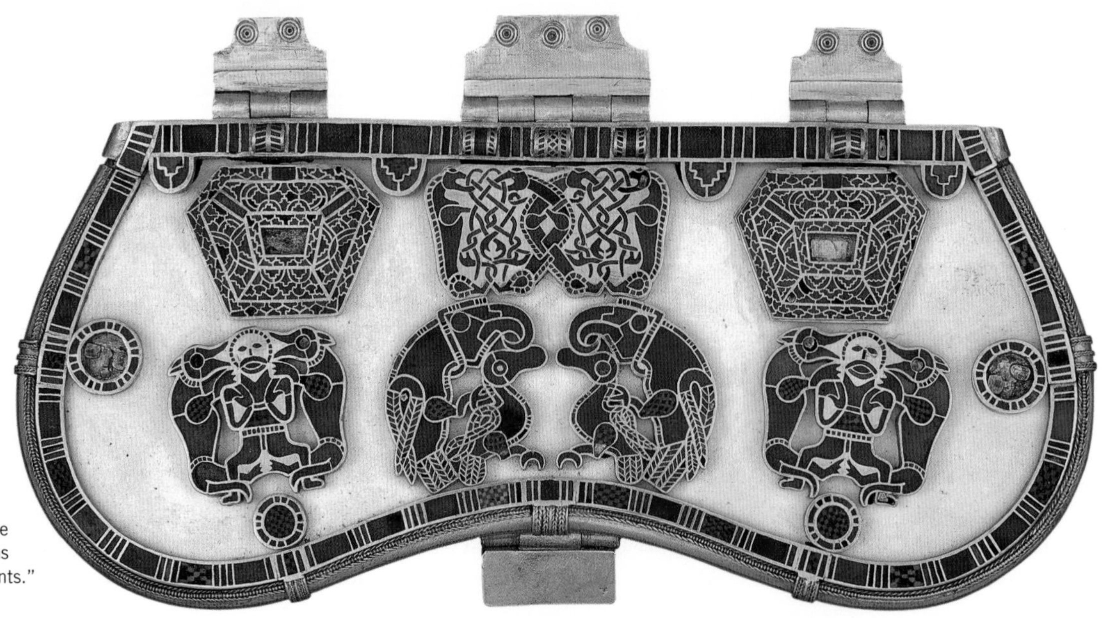

10.12 Purse cover, from Sutton Hoo, East Anglia, 7th century. Gold, garnets, and enamel, 8 in. (20.3 cm) long. British Museum, London.
The intricate interlace and animal designs are made of sections of gold and garnets held in place by gold strips. The individual sections are known as *cloisons,* meaning "compartments."

Grendel is descended from Cain, the first man to commit murder in the Bible, which links him to a genealogy of evil:

he had dwelt for a time
in misery among the banished monsters,
Cain's clan, whom the Creator had outlawed
and condemned as outcasts.

(lines 104–107)

So, after nightfall, Grendel set out
for the lofty house, to see how the Ring-Danes
were settling into it after their drink,
and there he came upon them, a company of the best
asleep from their feasting . . . Suddenly then
the God-cursed brute was creating havoc:
greedy and grim, he grabbed thirty men
from their resting places and rushed to his lair,
flushed up and inflamed from the raid,
blundering back with the butchered corpses.

(lines 115–125)

Beowulf is committed to defending his men, reflecting the bond between the Germanic chieftain and his band of warriors. Like Roland, Beowulf is motivated by bravery and honor. When Beowulf kills Grendel, the monster's mother takes revenge by killing several of Beowulf's men. Beowulf then pursues Grendel's mother to a swamp, destroys her, and returns home to rule for fifty years. When a dragon preys on his subjects, Beowulf is driven to fight by pride, a fatal flaw like the hubris of the Greek tragic heroes that results in his death.

The poetic power of *Beowulf* comes from its skillful use of language. The narrative is enriched by the use of concrete, compound words called **kennings**—the "Spear-Danes," the "Ring-Danes," the "shadow-stalker" (Grendel), the "poison-breather" (Grendel's mother), the "Weather-Geats" (Swedes), and the "tail-turners" (cowards who run from battle), to cite but a few. Subhuman monsters inhabiting murky swamps, a sense of impending doom, the strident clash of battle, larger-than-life heroism, and majestic royal feasts create an atmosphere of poetic mystery.

The epic concludes with Beowulf's warrior funeral and the recognition that with the death of their lord his people face an uncertain, dreary future:

The Geat people built a pyre for Beowulf,
stacked and decked it until it stood four-square,
hung with helmets, heavy war-shields
and shining armour, just as he had ordered.
Then his warriors laid him in the middle of it,
mourning a lord far-famed and beloved.
On a height they kindled the hugest of all
funeral fires; fumes of woodsmoke
billowed darkly up, the blaze roared
and drowned out their weeping, wind died down
and flames wrought havoc in the hot bone-house,
burning it to the core. They were disconsolate
and wailed aloud for their lord's decease.

(lines 3137–3149)

THE LEGEND OF KING ARTHUR

One of the most popular stories of the Early Middle Ages is the legend of King Arthur and his knights of the Round Table. The literary origins of the Arthur legend are found in pre-Christian Britain, but aside from brief references in several sources to a brave warrior called Arthur, the earliest written account in which he is a king presiding over a group of loyal followers is the Welsh *Mabinogion.* This collection of tales, written down by 1100, is filled with mystery, magic, folklore, and echoes of Irish and Welsh myth. Arthur appears in five of the stories; his queen is Guinevere (Gwenhwyvar in Welsh). He rules over the most virtuous and splendid court in an uncertain setting, somewhere in Britain (see Box).

The following passage from "The Dream of Rhonabwy" gives some idea of the imaginative atmosphere pervading these tales. A rider from an opposing army approaches Arthur and

Society and Culture

The Legend of King Arthur through Time

Arthur's first recorded appearance as a king occurs in the Welsh *Mabinogion*, but Arthurian themes later appeared in France and Germany, where they were interwoven with local legends. The French author Chrétien de Troyes wrote four poems about Arthur in the second half of the twelfth century. He added the story of the knight Percival and the search for the Holy Grail—the cup used by Christ at the Last Supper. Geoffrey of Monmouth's *History of the Kings of England* (1135–1139) presents an extensive account of King Arthur as a heroic warrior who brought peace and prosperity to Britain. He also describes Arthur's murder by his evil nephew Mordred.

In the thirteenth century, the *Prose Lancelot* became popular. Lancelot, Arthur's French knight, was associated with the Holy Grail through his pure son, Sir Galahad. (Lancelot had fallen from grace because of his adulterous affair with Arthur's queen, Guinevere.) In the fifteenth century, there was a resurgence of interest in the legend in Britain with Thomas Malory's *Le morte d'Arthur* (*The Death of Arthur*) (1469–1470), and in Victorian England in the late nineteenth century, it was revived again with Alfred, Lord Tennyson's long poem *The Idylls of the King* (1885).

In the twentieth century, the American poet Edwin Arlington Robinson wrote an Arthurian trilogy. The English author T. H. White retold the legend in *The Once and Future King* (1939–1958), which would form the basis for Alan J. Lerner and Frederick Loewe's musical, *Camelot* (1960), named for the legendary seat of Arthur's court. To the present day, King Arthur and his court are associated with the political ideals of even-handed justice and peace maintained by a force of knightly, chivalrous warriors. And Camelot has become a generic term for a Golden Age in which government is fair and just.

asks him to call off the flock of ravens that are killing his troops and devouring his dead knights. Note the use of vivid, fanciful color—especially gold and black—to convey the mystery of the setting:

> After that came a rider on a handsome black high-headed horse: from the top of its left leg it was pure red, and from the top of its right leg down to the hoof pure white, and both horse and rider were clothed in spotted yellow armour speckled with Spanish linen; his cloak and that of the horse were in halves, white and pure black with purple-gold fringes. He carried a gleaming gold-hilted three-grooved sword, with a belt of yellow gold-cloth and a clasp from the eyelid of a pure black whale with a tongue of yellow gold; on his head he wore a helmet of yellow linen with gleaming crystals, and on the crest the image of a griffin with a powerful stone in its head, while in his hand he carried a ridge-shafted ash spear coloured with blue lime, the blade covered with fresh blood and riveted with pure silver.
>
> (*The Mabinogion*, "The Dream of Rhonabwy")

Chivalry and Medieval Paradigms of Women

According to the chivalric code depicted in romances, the knight was not only brave and loyal to his lord and faithful to God, but he was devoted to a particular woman—his lady. The woman in question was most likely of noble or royal status. "Romantic" knights performed feats of valor to impress their ladies and defend their lords.

The chivalric code was related to the Christian cult of the Virgin Mary that developed around 1050. As the mother of Jesus, the Virgin became a maternal ideal—nourishing, compassionate, willing to intercede with God on behalf of humanity, and free of sin. Eve had disobeyed God and eaten the forbidden fruit, thus causing the Fall of Man and becoming the paradigm (model) of the sinful woman. The Virgin had obeyed God and was thus seen as sinless—a "new Eve."

The third female paradigm was Mary Magdalene, a composite of several women in the Bible and medieval glosses. She, like the Virgin, was the object of a growing cult, in her case because she exemplified the average woman. Mary Magdalene was given special status as the first person to see Christ after his Resurrection. She thus combined Eve's sinfulness with redemption, offering a model for human imperfection and the possibility of human salvation.

In romance literature, as in the medieval code of chivalry, women tended to be seen in terms of religious, secular, or legal paradigms. The religious models were Eve, the Virgin Mary, and Mary Magdalene; the secular models were the queen, the lady, and the commoner; and the legal models depended on the social status of maiden, wife and mother, and widow.

From the sixth or seventh century, the Arthurian legend was elaborated, Christianized, and romanticized on the European continent, first in France and then in Germany. From around 1150, the legend appealed to the growing taste for the literary form known as the **romance**, which was distinct from the *chanson de geste*. The romance, so-called because it was thought (incorrectly) to have originated in Roman tradition, was a long tale, in which a knight performed heroic feats to impress his lady. Ideally, in terms of setting up emotional tension, the knight's lady was married to someone else and thus unattainable (see Box).

READING SELECTION

Geoffrey of Monmouth, *History of the Kings of Britain*, King Arthur, PWC2-063-C; Malory, *Death of Arthur*, Arthur becomes king, PWC2-316-B

THE VIKINGS: NINTH TO TWELFTH CENTURY

The Vikings, who repeatedly invaded Europe during the Early Middle Ages, belonged to the heroic cultures described in *Beowulf.* They came from Norway, Sweden, and Denmark. With longboats propelled by oars and equipped with square sails, the Vikings could navigate rough waters fairly easily. In the ninth century, they overran northern Britain and France, parts of Spain, and central and eastern Europe. On the north coasts of Europe they established trading centers, but they were also pirates, raiding, looting, and kidnapping (map **10.3**). Like the Anglo-Saxons, the Vikings were literate. They used the runic alphabet, which consisted of sixteen letters, to inscribe records, memorials, and poetry on large upright **runestones** (figure **10.13**).

When Christian missionaries arrived in the Viking lands, they brought the scripts used for manuscripts, and the unconnected runic letters gradually fell into disuse. Before 965, when Harald Bluetooth of Denmark converted to Christianity, the Vikings were pagans. Their mythology mirrored both their Nordic climate and their warrior culture.

NORSE MYTHOLOGY Like other pagan cultures, the pre-Christian Norse were polytheists. As we saw in Chapter 1, the Norse creation myth begins when frost from the north and fire from the south meet and produce Ymir, the ice giant, and a cow. The cow licks off Ymir's ice, and his children are born.

The Norse universe was divided into three tiers, with spaces between them. Asgard, at the top, was the home of the Aesir, the warrior gods, who inhabited the halls of Valhalla (figure **10.14**). There, deceased warriors feasted and fought while awaiting Ragnarök, the great battle at the end of time. The ruler of Valhalla was Odin, god of wisdom and poetry; his

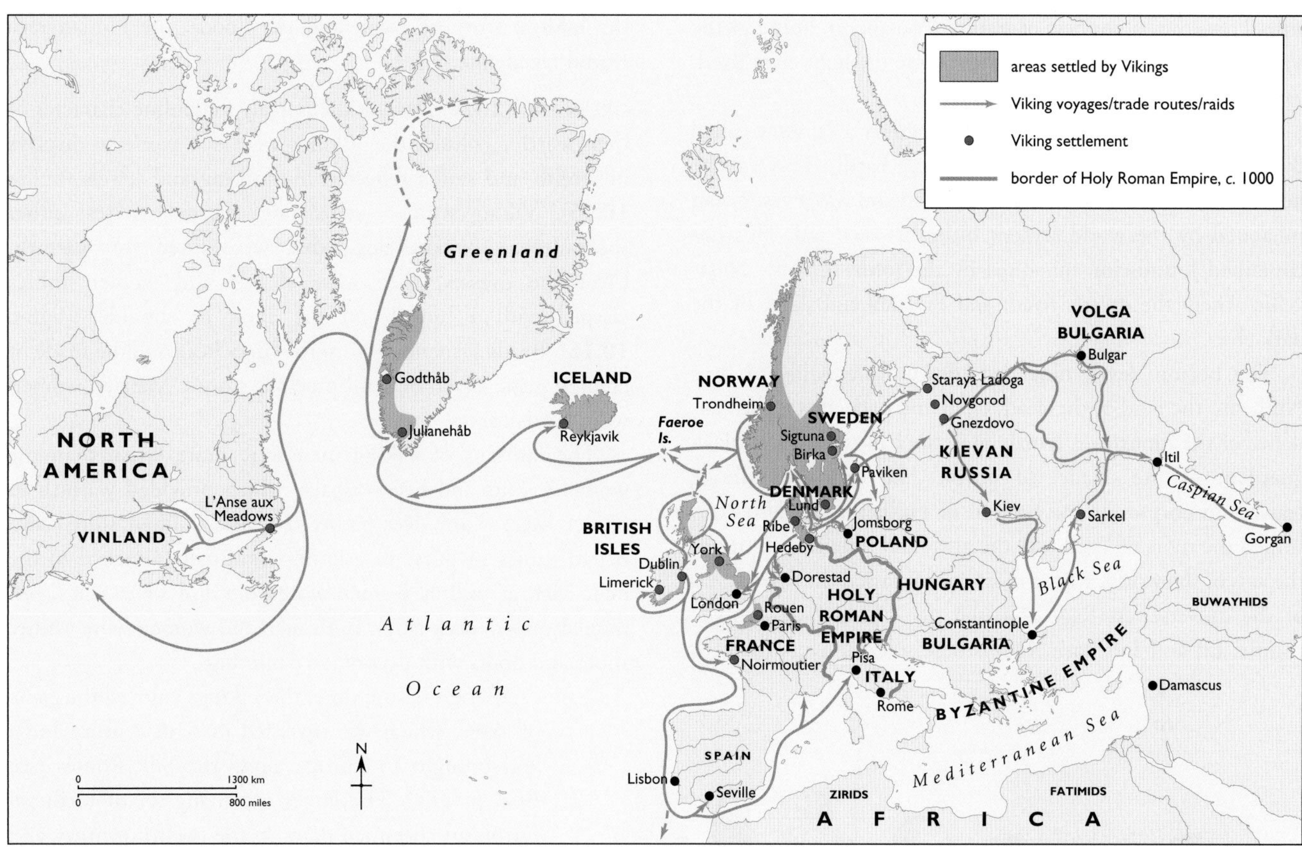

Map 10.3 The Viking world, *c.* 1000.

10.13 Rune-stone, Karlevi, Öland, Sweden, *c.* 1000.
This rune-stone was raised in memory of a Viking chieftain and contains a runic text in verse.

10.14 *right* **Memorial picture stone, from Lillbjärs, Sweden. Paint on stone (the paint is modern), 33¾ in. (86 cm) high. National Antiquities Museum, Stockholm.** Like rune-stones, many picture stones were memorials. This one illustrates the deceased in the guise of a mounted warrior being welcomed to Valhalla. At the right, a woman offers him a drinking horn. Below, two men ride in a Viking ship—possibly a reference to a ship burial. Both scenes are framed with an interlace pattern.

wife, Frigg, was a goddess of fertility. Vanaheim, home of the Vanir (fertility gods), and Alfheim, where the light elves lived, were also in Asgard.

The second level, connected to Asgard by a rainbow called the flaming bridge, was Midgard (Middle Earth). This was the home of the human race. Encircling Midgard was a vast ocean inhabited by the world serpent biting its own tail. This tier contained Jotunheim, inhabited by the Jotun (giants); Nidavellir, where the dwarfs lived; and Svartalfheim, land of the dark elves.

The bottom level, nine days down from Midgard, was Niflheim, the land of the dead. Cold and dark, it was the residence of the monstrous female Hel, the half-white, half-black guardian of the citadel of death. The dragon Nidhogg feasted on corpses at the bottom of Niflheim. He also consumed the roots of Yggdrasil, the great and timeless ash tree at the axis of the world, whose roots encompassed the three levels of the universe. At Ragnarök, the tree would hide a single couple, Lif and Lifthrasir. From these sole survivors (as with the biblical story of Noah and the flood), the human race would regenerate.

DRESS AND CHESS Despite the fiercely masculine character of their warrior culture, the Vikings were not averse to displays of wealth and status reflected in clothing and jewels (figure **10.15**). Viking women wore long, pleated dresses, either short-sleeved or sleeveless, that were lined for warmth. Over the dresses, they wore shawls and woolen tunics clasped with a brooch on the chest or shoulder (figure **10.16**). Beads suspended from the brooches could be made of colored glass, silver, or semi-precious stones. Married women wore head-scarves.

The fashions of Viking men were more lavish than the women's. Furs and heavy cloaks, which provided warmth in winter, were worn over gathered trousers, linen shirts, and belted tunics. A purse or a knife was usually attached to the belt. Men as well as women wore gold and silver rings, but men also wore neck rings. Both men and women wore leather shoes and boots with decorative trimmings.

In their leisure time, the Vikings enjoyed the game of chess, which was invented in sixth-century India and brought to Europe along the Silk Routes (see Box, p. 215). The largest surviving set of medieval European chessmen dates to the twelfth century and comes from the Outer Hebrides, islands off Scotland but then part of Norway (figure **10.17**).

10.15 Viking dress.

10.16 Trefoil brooch, from Oslo, Norway. Bronze, gold, and silver, 20½ in. (8.1 cm) high. National Antiquities Museum, Stockholm.
This elaborate silver and bronze brooch, decorated with interlaced patterns, is in the shape of a box. The cross at the center indicates that it was made for, or by, a Christian.

10.17 Chessmen, from the island of Lewis, Outer Hebrides, Scotland. 12th century. Walrus ivory, tallest figure 26 in. (10.2 cm) high. British Museum, London.
The design of the pieces, particularly the foliate interlace on the pawn, reflects the cross-cultural influences that resulted from continual invasions, colonization, and trade. Norway itself was a center of trade in walrus ivory, of which the chessmen are made.

ICELAND AND THE SAGAS: NINTH TO TWELFTH CENTURY

Around 870, not wishing to live under King Harald Fairhair of Norway or pay the taxes he levied on them, many Vikings departed in search of new land. They settled in Iceland, northwest of Britain, where they established a society of landowning farmers, including people from Ireland, northern Britain, and the Hebrides Islands. Much of the work was done by slaves, who had been captured from different parts of Europe in Viking raids. Many of the women had been kidnapped from Scotland and Ireland.

The Icelandic settlers pushed westward. In the tenth century, Erik the Red founded a colony on Greenland, and his son, Leif Erikson (called Leif the Lucky), sailed to the east coast of Newfoundland, where Norse settlements have been discovered. Icelanders also went to North America (now New England), as is recorded in the *Vinland Sagas*. Named "Vinland," or "Wineland," after the abundance of grapes, New England impressed the Icelanders with its fields of grass and wheat, rivers rich in fish, and climate warmer than their own.

READING SELECTION

Vinland Sagas, the Norse discovery of America, PWC2-108-B

Iceland was first ruled by an oligarchy of clans (family groups), headed by a chieftain. Around 930, they established a parliamentary government and instituted the **Althing**. This was a general assembly governed according to a law code prepared by an expert on Norwegian law. The Althing convened every year on the plain of Thingvellir, about 30 miles (48 km) east of Reykjavik, to resolve disputes and decide judicial and constitutional issues. Thirty-nine chiefs held power, which could be inherited, bought, or even borrowed. At the time Icelandic religion was pagan, but by 1000 Christianity had been officially adopted.

As in Scandinavia, Christian missionaries to Iceland brought a new script that made it easier to write down traditional stories previously transmitted orally. As a result, the rich Norse poetic tradition was committed to parchment and preserved. The two main types of verse are **scaldic** and **eddaic**. Scaldic recounts tales of kings and heroes, and eddaic relates myths and legends.

Snorri Sturluson (1179–1241), a politician, historian, and poet, is best known for the *Poetic Edda*, a group of poems setting forth the Norse creation myths. At the beginning of the "Prophecy of the Seeress," for example, the narrator announces that she will set forth the fate of the world:

> Hear me, all ye hallowed beings,
> both high and low of Heimdall's children:
> thou wilt, Valfather, that I well set forth
> the fates of the world which as I first recall.
>
> (*Poetic Edda*, verse I)

The children of Heimdall comprised members of three social classes: nobility, freemen, and slaves. Valfather is Odin, the "father" of the deceased in Valhalla. The poet thus calls on all of society to hear the will of Odin. As in *Beowulf*, the use of kennings—such as "Valfather," a combination of father and Valhalla—enriches the language.

Kennings are also a feature of the Icelandic **sagas**. The sagas are a mix of history, legend, myth, and folk tradition written down after Iceland converted to Christianity. Like the *Song of Roland*, they purport to record heroic events of the past—in this case, the settlement of Iceland in the ninth century. The most famous of the sagas, *Njal's Saga*, is a good example of the genre. Direct and straightforward, it reflects the rugged, warrior-based, agricultural lifestyle of the Icelanders. After being introduced, characters may be either dropped or carried through the tale, but their inner motivations are never identified. What motivates them is implied through descriptive detail, such as a raised or lowered eyelid, an action, or a brief comment. The sagas reflect the harsh landscape, blood-feuds, fears of eerie pagan spirits, and sense of fate that characterized the heroic period of Iceland.

The basic plot of *Njal's Saga* is simple. It recounts the events leading to Njal Thorgeirsson's death, when enemies trap him and his family and burn them alive in their home. The opening of Chapter 25 shows how characters are introduced by their genealogy, a reflection of the family-based organization of Icelandic society. Note, too, the use of kennings in the names:

> A man called Valgard the Grey lived at Hof, beside Rang River. Valgard the Grey was the son of Jorund the Priest, the son of Hrafn the Fool, the son of Valgard, the son of Ævar, the son of Venumd the Word-Master, the son of Thorolf Creek-Nose, the son of Thrand the Old, the son of Harald War-Tooth, the son of Hraerek the Ring-Scatterer and of Aud, the daughter of Ivar-of-the-Long-Reach, the son of Halfdan the Brave.
>
> He had a brother called Ulf Aur-Priest. Ulf Aur-Priest was the ancestor of the Oddi family. He was the father of Svart, the father of Lodmund, the father of Sigfus, the father of Saemund the Learned. One of Valgard the Grey's descendants was Kolbeing the Young.
>
> (*Njal's Saga*)

Descriptions of battle are brutal and matter-of-fact:

> Kol lunged at him with a spear. Kolskegg had just killed someone, and had no time to raise his shield; the spear struck the outside of his thigh and went right through it. Kolskegg whirled round and leapt at him, swung at his thigh with the short-sword, and cut off Kol's leg.
>
> "Did that one land or not?" asked Kolskegg.
>
> "That's my reward for not having my shield," said Kol. He stood for a moment on one leg, looking down at the stump.
>
> "You don't need to look," said Kolskegg. "It's just as you think—the leg is off."
>
> Then Kol fell dead to the ground.

And a few lines later:

> Gunnar . . . hurled himself at the Easterner; with one sweep he sliced him in two at the waist. Next he threw the halberd at Bork, sending it right through him and pinning him to the ground. Kolskegg cut off Hauk Egilsson's head, and Gunnar sliced off Ottar Egilsson's forearm.

Farming—New Technology and Inventions

A major technological development that benefited the medieval peasant was the moldboard plow. This type of plow was drawn by oxen or horses and could penetrate the soil more deeply than the older scratch plow. The moldboard plow turned over the soil, forming ridges and impressions in which seeds could be more deeply planted. The newer plow was particularly effective in northern Europe, where rain made the soil heavier and more compacted than in the south. Another advantage of the moldboard was its impact on crop rotation. Previously, peasants rotated crops by leaving one out of every two fields fallow each year. The new system used three fields, only one of which was left fallow. This meant that more land could be cultivated.

The waterwheel had been invented in China and carried west by Muslim traders, but was not commonly used in Europe before the eighth century. Then it was employed to power mills, and eventually it would also facilitate brewing, fulling cloth, and making paper.

Europeans in the Early Middle Ages also discovered how to make their horses work more efficiently. From the horseriders of the Asian Steppe Westerners learned to harness their horses with stiff, padded collars, which enabled the horses to draw heavy weights without choking. As in Asia, horses in Europe began to be shod with iron nailed to their hoofs, protecting their feet and lengthening the time they could work. Stirrups, also known in China from the fourth century, began to be used in Europe during the Middle Ages.

ROMANESQUE ON THE EUROPEAN CONTINENT: ELEVENTH AND TWELFTH CENTURY

The term Romanesque, or "Roman-like," refers to the period of architectural revival that began before the new millennium, in the tenth century. Invasions had died down somewhat, and new social and political structures evolved from feudalism. The Church was to remain the most stabilizing force in western Europe for several more centuries.

Centers of commerce, banking and manufacturing enterprises, and organizations (**guilds**) of workers in particular crafts arose. Guilds were established as a means of ensuring that workers were well trained and that their families were protected if a worker died. These organizations would grow and become a central aspect of the medieval economy. During the Gothic period, when cities competed to build great cathedrals (see Chapter 11), the guilds took on an even more important role.

Trade also expanded during the early medieval period. Cloth was imported from the north, silks from China, and spices from the Middle East. As the economy improved, populations increased. Towns began to emerge, gradually leading to the growth of cities. Meanwhile, new plowing and farming techniques improved the life of the peasants (see Box).

ROMANESQUE ART AND ARCHITECTURE

Romanesque architecture first developed in France, where Hugh Capet (ruled 987–996) founded the Capetian dynasty, which lasted over three hundred years. From around 1000,

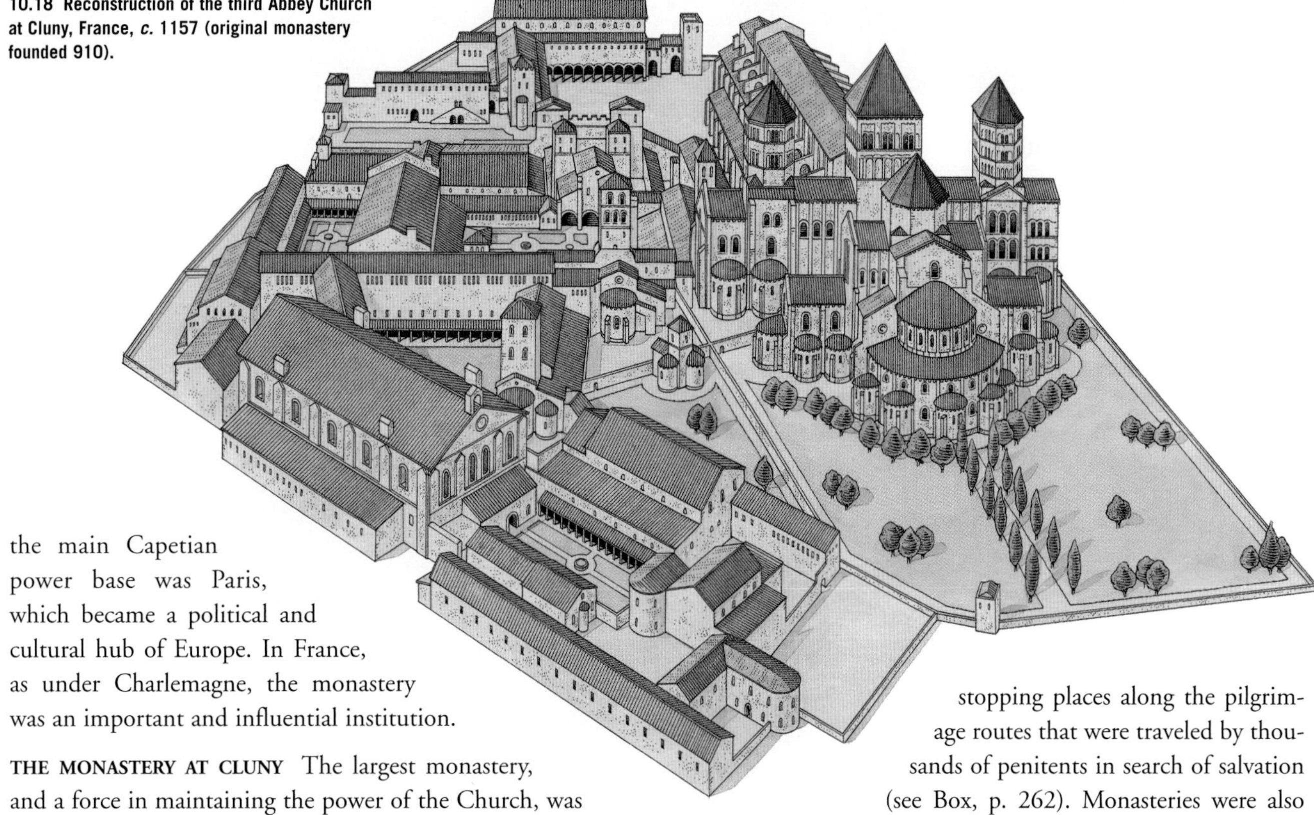

10.18 Reconstruction of the third Abbey Church at Cluny, France, *c.* 1157 (original monastery founded 910).

the main Capetian power base was Paris, which became a political and cultural hub of Europe. In France, as under Charlemagne, the monastery was an important and influential institution.

THE MONASTERY AT CLUNY The largest monastery, and a force in maintaining the power of the Church, was the French Benedictine monastery founded at Cluny, in Burgundy (figure **10.18**). The monastery was rebuilt twice after being destroyed by fire and invasion. This third version, destroyed in 1798 after the French Revolution (1789), has been reconstructed to show its elaborate twelfth-century complex. Members of the Order worshipped in the large church, which was considered an expression of Heavenly Jerusalem on earth. They held meetings in the chapter house where the archives were kept, ate in the refectory, and sang in the choir of the church. Scribes and illuminators worked in the scriptorium. Other buildings included the pantry, a warming room (calefactory), a hospital, and an inn for visitors. Like St. Gall, Cluniac monasteries were self-sufficient communities run by an abbot.

Beginning around 900, the Cluniacs set out to standardize monastic practices. They insisted on strict ethics, devotion to spiritual rather than worldly pursuits, and a celibate clergy. They were also against the selling of spiritual **benefices** (a practice known as **simony**).

Some of the popes elected in the eleventh century supported the reforms advocated at Cluny. One of the major papal decisions, made in 1059, was to form the College of Cardinals, which ensured that popes would be elected by members of the Church acting independently of national politics. And from 1073, when Gregory VII (papacy 1073–1085) was elected, the Cluniac reforms were instituted in Rome and officially adopted by the Church.

The Cluniac Order, which broke away from the Benedictine Order, spread throughout Europe as its reforms gathered support. Many of its churches and abbeys became stopping places along the pilgrimage routes that were traveled by thousands of penitents in search of salvation (see Box, p. 262). Monasteries were also havens for people hiding from political enemies. And children from large aristocratic families were often urged into the religious life, so they would renounce their claim to a share of the family's inheritance.

Early Benedictines emphasized the importance of manual labor, but the Cluniacs were more interested in learning, art, and music. In the tenth century, Odo of Cluny (abbot 927–942) encouraged his monks in choral singing, himself composing hymns and antiphons. At that date plainsong was notated using **neumes** (diagonal marks placed over the word to be sung, each indicating a note or group of notes). As pitch and intervals were not specified in this system, training took years and monks had to memorize long passages—the notation was just a memory aid. Later, in the early eleventh century, another Benedictine monk and musician, Guido of Arezzo (*c.* 991–1050), immeasurably improved notation by inventing a four-line staff on which to place the notes, so it was clear when the melody went up or down (figure **10.19**).

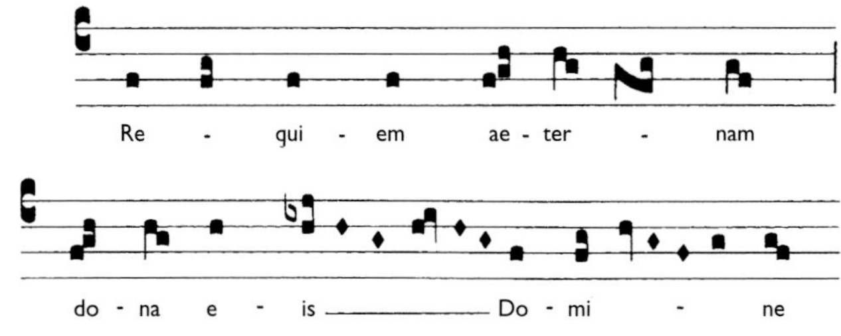

10.19 Guido of Arezzo's musical staff.

Society and Culture

The Pilgrimage Roads

In the course of the Middle Ages, large numbers of Christians made pilgrimages to holy sites. The most important of these sites was the Holy Sepulcher in Jerusalem. But Jerusalem was a long and arduous journey from western Europe, and many pilgrims traveled instead to nearer sites. In Europe, the two main destinations were Rome and Santiago de Compostela, in northwest Spain. Rome was the Christian capital of western Europe, and the church in Santiago was dedicated to St. James, the first of Christ's apostles to be martyred. Beheaded in A.D. 42 by King Herod Agrippa I (ruled A.D. 41–44), James's body was said to have been miraculously moved (**translated**) to Santiago de Compostela.

Many other churches throughout Europe contained sacred **relics**, which are either the physical remains of saints or martyrs, or items associated with them. These objects were enshrined in **reliquaries** (sacred containers) and venerated by the faithful. Relics were believed capable of bringing about miracles, but one had to see or touch the actual object.

The cathedral of Canterbury, in the English county of Kent, became a major pilgrimage site after its archbishop, Thomas à Becket, was assassinated there on December 29, 1170. Becket had been appointed chancellor to King Henry II (ruled 1154–1190) in 1155 and archbishop in 1162. Once the closest of companions, the two men fell out over matters of taxation and judicial authority. Henry, who had overhauled the entire legal and administrative systems of his kingdom, wanted power over the Church courts, an ambition that was vigorously opposed by Becket and the Church. Four of Henry's knights killed the archbishop as he worshipped at the altar of Canterbury Cathedral. After negotiating with the Church, Henry performed a penance that would absolve him of Becket's death. Becket's remains were removed to the Trinity Chapel in Canterbury Cathedral and venerated by thousands of people. The Church canonized Becket in 1173 (figure **10.20**).

10.20 Reliquary of Thomas à Becket, *c.* 1190. Limoges *champlevé* enamel, 11¼ × 15½ × 4⅝ in. (28 × 38.5 × 11.5 cm). Private collection.
Limoges, in France, was famous for its enamel workmanship. *Champlevé* is a technique in which shallow indentations are made in a metal surface, filled in with ceramic, and fired in a kiln. In use since Roman antiquity, the process was typically reserved for reliquaries and other liturgical objects during the Middle Ages. The scenes on this reliquary are divided into two horizontal narratives. Below, Becket is attacked by three knights as he prays at the altar; at the far right two clergymen raise their hands in horror. Above, Becket is lowered into his tomb, and to the right he ascends to heaven accompanied by angels.

Guido's staff made it possible for the singers to sight-read the notes of music they had never previously heard.

The integration of sculpture with architecture and piety at Cluny is reflected in the decoration of its Abbey Church. By adorning architectural surfaces with sculpture, as well as by encouraging music and illuminating manuscripts, the members of the Cluniac Order expressed their belief that the arts should engage worshippers and strengthen their faith. One example can be seen in the capitals that depict musical tones (figure **10.21**). Music, a subject of philosophical and mathematical enquiry for Plato and the Neoplatonists, here becomes an expression of God's presence on earth.

Not all clerics approved of the time, money, and work that the Cluniac Order put into the arts. The influential abbot Bernard of Clairvaux (1090–1153) took an opposing view. He established a monastery at Clairvaux in France that demanded a rigorous lifestyle of prayer and self-denial. Bernard held that mystical experience and the power of grace and free will in

10.21 *right* **Third Musical Tone, capital from the Abbey Church, Cluny, 1088–1095. Farinier Museum of the Abbey, Cluny.**
The third tone is personified as a musician playing a hand-held harp, or lyre. As in illuminated manuscripts, text and image here reinforce each other. The inscription identifies the third tone with Christ's Resurrection. The harp itself had been the instrument of David, who was seen as a typological precursor of Christ. Harps were also Christian symbols of the Cross.

attaining salvation were of paramount importance. His treatise on monastic decadence, claiming that the arts distracted from piety, was specifically directed against Cluny.

READING SELECTION

Bernard of Clairvaux, *An Apologia for Abbot William*, monastic decadence, PWC2-155-B

MONASTICISM AND WOMEN IN THE ARTS A significant result of monasticism in the twelfth century was the increasing literacy of certain women. Some women, especially aristocrats, became patrons of the arts and there are records of women, such as Ingeborg of Denmark (wife of Philip II Augustus, king of France) and Melisende (queen of the crusader state of Jerusalem), who commissioned **psalters** (psalm books). Matilda of Canossa, who ruled the Italian regions of Emilia and Tuscany, commissioned an illustrated book of Gospels.

But it was in the convents that women, freed from the constraints of marriage and the dangers of childbirth, had the greatest contact with learning and the arts. Christina of Markyate (d. *c.* 1155) was prioress of a convent near London and a visionary. The St. Albans Psalter is thought to have been a gift to her from the abbot of St. Albans. As such, it would indicate her refined taste in works of art. Herrad, the twelfth-century abbess of Hohenberg, in Alsace, wrote an encyclopedia of world history entitled *The Garden of Delights* for her nuns to read.

Perhaps the best-known religious woman of the twelfth century was the noble German mystic Hildegard of Bingen (1098–1179). Instructed by a vision to found a community of nuns in the Rhineland, she composed music to accompany hymns and wrote Latin poetry and treatises on herbs and medicine. Her morality play, *Ordo virtutum*, also in Latin, deals, like *Everyman*, with the conflict between good and evil. Her two visionary books are *Scivias* (a composite of two Latin words "you know" and "the way," meaning "the ways of God") and *Liber divinorum operum* (*Book of Divine Works*).

Hildegard is also credited with supervising the illustration of her books and, although the originals have been lost, later copies exist (figure **10.22**). The visionary character of the image is clear, as a red-skinned woman in a long red robe with

10.22 Hildegard of Bingen, illustration from a 13th-century copy of "The Vision of Divine Love, who holds the Lamb of God, and Tramples upon Discord and the Devil," from the *Book of Divine Works*, *c.* 1200. Illumination on parchment, 13¾ × 6½ in. (34.5 × 16 cm). Biblioteca Statale, Lucca, Italy.
In the small rectangle below the main image, Hildegard's vision descends in the form of red flames through an opening in the frame. Seated between her confessor and a nun wearing black, Hildegard writes her vision on a tablet.

gilded folds stands on a serpent (Satan) and a monster (Discord). She carries the Lamb of God and a scroll of prophecy. Emerging from the top of her head is the head of an older, protective male figure. At the sides are elaborate wings, in which appear the head of an eagle (left) and a woman's red face (right). The flattened gold space thrusts the figures forward and accentuates the otherworldly character of the scene.

MUSIC LISTENING SELECTION
Hildegard of Bingen, "O viridissima Virga." Oxford Camerata, conductor Jeremy Summerly, CD track 4

SAINTE MARIE MADELEINE AT VÉZELAY The Romanesque church at Vézelay, in Burgundy, France, is known for its sculptural decoration and elaborate vaulted ceiling. It was designed by an architect who trained at Cluny and is dedicated to Mary Magdalene, whose relics were housed there. (Vézelay is one of two French churches claiming to have Mary Magdalene's entire, intact body.) An important church on the pilgrimage routes, it had to accommodate the large crowds traveling to venerate her relics. Figure **10.23** shows a generic Romanesque church plan derived from the Roman basilica (see Chapter 7).

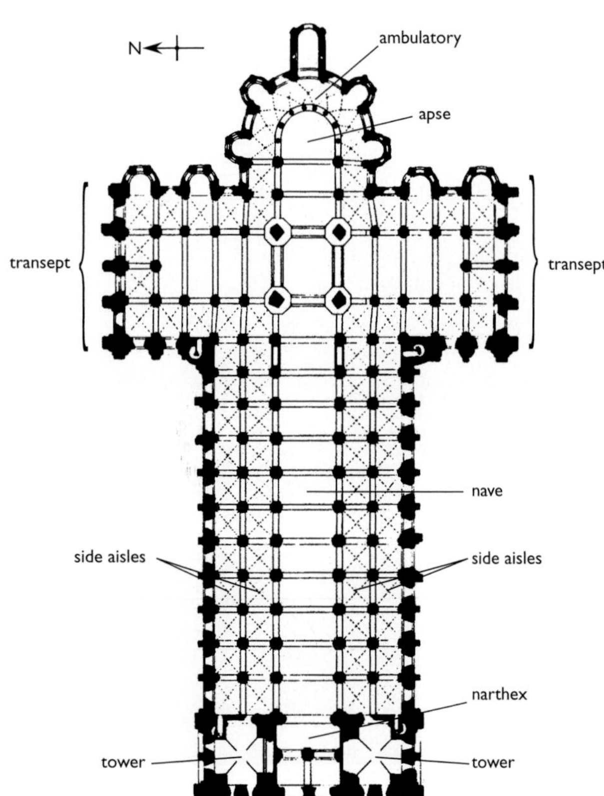

10.23 Plan of a typical Romanesque church.

10.24 Church of Sainte Marie Madeleine. Vézelay, France, *c.* 1089–1206.

The addition of an **ambulatory** (the curved passageway that surrounds the apse) allowed pilgrims to proceed from the side aisles of the apse, leaving the clergy to worship undisturbed at the high altar.

Vézelay, like most Christian churches, is oriented with its apse to the east and the main entrance to the west. This expresses the idea that the church building is a metaphor of the Christian world, with the Holy Land in the east and Europe to the west. The main altar, with a crucifix placed on or above it, was located in the apse, corresponding to Jerusalem as the site of Christ's Crucifixion.

The façade at Vézelay retains the Roman round arch and the massive walls and small windows that are found in contemporary castles and palaces (figure **10.24**). The interior view of the nave (figure **10.25**) shows the groin-vaulted ceiling—again, a style developed by the Romans. The alternating brown and white voussoirs of the **transverse arches** create an impression of lightness, despite the massive Romanesque walls. Each arch, which rests on a pier support consisting of **column clusters**, frames a **bay** (the repeated section of the wall). Second-story clerestory windows are the main source of natural light.

In addition to being an important pilgrimage site, Vézelay was a crusade church. It encouraged the first two of the eight crusades undertaken by the Western Church between 1095 and 1291 against the Muslims (see Box). Pope Urban II planned to preach the First Crusade at Vézelay in

10.25 Nave looking east, Church of Sainte Marie Madeleine, Vézelay, 1135–1140.

Society and Culture

The Crusades

The crusades originated as armed pilgrimages to rescue lands from various non-Christian cultural groups, and crusaders believed they would receive pardons and improve their chances of salvation. In eastern Europe, crusaders campaigned against the Slavs, in Livonia against the Bulgars, and, to a lesser degree, they campaigned against the Jews throughout Europe. Associated with notions of chivalry, the crusades were related to stories of the Holy Grail (the cup that Christ used at the Last Supper) and its quest. But the major crusades were launched to rescue the Holy Land from the Muslims.

In 638 the Muslims had conquered Jerusalem, where they built several mosques. In 1091, the Byzantine emperor asked Pope Urban II (papacy 1088–1099) for help in recapturing Jerusalem. Four years later, Urban II proclaimed the First Crusade in a rousing anti-Muslim sermon. Thousands of soldiers from France, Italy, and Germany answered his call and traveled to Constantinople to join forces with Orthodox Christians. Every Muslim living in Jerusalem was killed, and the Dome of the Rock (see Chapter 8) was converted to a church. Many crusaders remained in the Holy Land, building castles and becoming wealthy through international commerce.

By the middle of the twelfth century, Muslims had begun to retake the Holy Land. This led to the Second Crusade (1147–1149), preached by Bernard of Clairvaux. Led by King Louis VII of France (ruled 1137–1180) and the Holy Roman Emperor, this crusade ended in failure. Nearly forty years later, in 1187, Jerusalem was reconquered by the Muslims. The Third Crusade (1189–1192) also failed, mainly because of political rivalry between the European rulers leading it.

The Fourth Crusade (1202–1204) was launched against Egypt, but Venice wanted to protect its profitable Egyptian trade and thwarted the crusaders. Instead of attacking Egypt, they sacked Constantinople, even though it was a Christian city. This led to a fifty-year period during which the West controlled Byzantium.

The strange Children's Crusade (1212) was undertaken by thousands of children between the ages of ten and fourteen. They set out for Palestine, but most died or were captured and sold into slavery.

In the Fifth Crusade (1218–1221), Egypt was captured, but only temporarily. The Holy Roman Emperor Frederick II (ruled 1212–1250) captured Jerusalem in the Sixth Crusade (1228–1229), but lost it again in 1244. The Seventh (1249–1254) and Eighth (1270–1272) Crusades were led by Louis IX of France (ruled 1226–1270), later St. Louis. Both failed, and by 1300 interest in the crusades had subsided.

Although at first fought in the name of religion, the crusades were motivated partly by political and economic considerations. One factor was colonialism, similar to the Germanic impulse to dominate the Slavs, the English to control the Irish, and, in 1492, the reconquest of Muslim Spain by Christians. Despite overt animosity, however, the crusades were a source of cultural contact between Islam and the West. Muslim science, math, philosophy, and elements of Muslim architecture began to infiltrate and influence west Europeans in those fields. Economically the crusades were sometimes enormously rewarding, for successful crusaders returned home with huge amounts of booty, including fruits, spices, and other luxurious materials from the East. Crusades, like pilgrimages, could also be an excuse for travel at a time when many Europeans wished to see more of the world.

10.26 Central entrance, Church of Sainte Marie Madeleine, Vézelay, 1130s.

10.27 *The Mystical Mill*, capital from the Church of Sainte Marie Madeleine, Vézelay, 1104–1120.
An Old Testament prophet pours grain into a wheel-powered mill and St. Paul receives the flour. The meaning of this image is typological: Old Law becomes New Law through the teachings of Christ, just as the rough grain is transformed into refined flour.

1095 (he actually preached it elsewhere). Then, in 1146, Bernard of Clairvaux preached the Second Crusade at Vézelay; and forty-four years later the English king, Richard the Lion Heart, and the French king, Philip II Augustus, departed for the Third Crusade from the church.

Vézelay's role as a crusade church is reflected in the iconography of its sculptural decoration. The façade sculpture is concentrated around the central entrance (figure **10.26**). The **tympanum** merges two scenes—Christ's Ascension (when he rises to heaven) and Pentecost (when the Holy Spirit descends on the apostles to empower them for their mission to spread the gospel, as told in Acts, Chapter 2). The flame-like designs represent the tongues of fire that came down from heaven and gave the apostles the miraculous ability to speak in different tongues, and they allude to the fiery character of the Holy Spirit's inspiration. Each apostle holds a book, indicating that the Christian message is based on Scripture.

Christ dominates the scene. Framed by a **mandorla** (an oval of light around the entire body), he is the central figure and by far the largest. His frontality and extended arms, from which rays of light emanate, indicate that he is welcoming the faithful to his mission and to the church. The flat, stylized, rhythmic curves of Christ's draperies are typical of Romanesque sculpture.

Illustrated in the **archivolts** (the attached arches around the tympanum) are signs of the zodiac and the labors of the months (depicted either as seasonal workers or as their tools). The horizontal **lintel** shows people from around the world awaiting conversion. At the far right, for example, members of an imaginary Indian race have large ears, signifying that though they can hear sound, they are deaf to moral truth. To their left, a Pygmy tries to mount a horse with the help of a ladder. The figures at the left include a group with bows and arrows—weaponry no longer in general use in Europe. Next to them a bull is being led to a pagan sacrifice.

Below the lintel, on the **trumeau** (the vertical stone between the doors), John the Baptist stands with the Lamb of God. He refers to the rite of baptism as the sign of accepting the Christian faith. Positioned at the church entrance, the sculpture conveys the message that salvation is to be found within.

The decoration of capitals with narrative reliefs was a Romanesque development (figure **10.27**). Such scenes functioned as sermons in stone for the illiterate population. In the course of the Middle Ages, as we shall see in the next chapter, these visual sermons became more numerous and more elaborate.

THE BAYEUX TAPESTRY: ROMANESQUE NARRATIVE

One of the most significant historical events of the Romanesque period was the Norman conquest of England in 1066. William the Conqueror, ruler of Normandy in France, was descended from Viking invaders, and when he defeated the Anglo-Saxons at the Battle of Hastings, he established the rule of Norman kings in Britain. This event is recorded in the remarkable work of embroidery known as the Bayeux Tapestry (figures **10.28** and **10.29**).

It is not known who designed or executed the tapestry, but it may have been commissioned by William's half-brother, Bishop Odo of Bayeux, for the cathedral. The narrative, which reads from left to right, occupies the central field, with a Latin text explaining what is happening. Above and below the main narrative are fallen warriors and fanciful animals like those seen in manuscripts such as the Book of Kells (see figure 10.10).

Like the *Song of Roland*, the Bayeux Tapestry is an epic, but it is a visual rather than a literary epic. Both works are lengthy, secular narratives. The Tapestry is some 230 feet (70 m) long, its heroic characters change the course of history, it combines fact with fiction, and it presents the French view of events. Both works are also expressions of the impulse to make artistic records of significant historical and religious experiences, which is particularly characteristic of the Romanesque period.

10.28 Bayeux Tapestry, detail showing William of Normandy giving the order to build a fleet, *c.* 1070–1080. Wool stitching on linen, 20 in. (50.8 cm) high. Musée de l'Evêché, Bayeux, France.

The inscription reads: "King William ordered ships to be built." William can be seen enthroned inside his castle with Bishop Odo. A courtier at the left gestures in response, and a man with a carpentry tool receives the order and turns to go. He points toward the figure outside the castle, who is chopping down a tree.

10.29 Bayeux Tapestry, detail showing the longboats landing on the south coast of England, *c.* 1070–1080. Wool stitching on linen, 20 in. (50.8 cm) high. Musée de l'Evêché. Bayeux.

This scene shows William's arrival in England. The inscription says that the soldiers and horses are disembarking. The longboats used by William to cross the rough waters of the English Channel were similar to those used by the Vikings. Men lower the sails as the horses are led from the boats. At the right, a series of empty boats indicates that they arrived earlier and their passengers are now on dry land. At the left, a boat is just arriving as its prow and lead warrior come into view. By this technique of showing different stages of arrival, the artist creates a sense of narrative time.

In the next chapter, we survey the Gothic period that evolved from Romanesque. New architectural developments led to taller, wider cathedrals decorated with huge, elaborate stained glass windows. In sculpture, a new naturalism prefigured the Renaissance. In English politics, the king's absolute power was limited officially so that he had some responsibility to certain of his subjects. And as churches and cathedrals took over education, there was a gradual rise in literacy and the beginnings of a professional class.

Thematic Parallels

Pilgrimage

We have seen that the notion of pilgrimage, whether conceived of as a literal or a spiritual journey, occurs across cultural boundaries. Christian pilgrimages inspired the construction of numerous churches to accommodate the large crowds traveling through Romanesque Europe. In addition to churches, inns and hostels were required, which led to thriving economic activity along the pilgrimage roads.

We have also seen the importance of pilgrimage in Islam, where the *hajj* is one of the Five Pillars (see Chapter 9). Figure **10.30** shows a view of the *Ka'bah* at the Great Mosque of Mecca, illuminated at night. Muslims perform the *tawaf*, a ritual in which they circumambulate (proceed around) the *Ka'bah* seven times. (Circumambulation is also a feature of Buddhism, whose adherents circumambulate the stupa, and some Christians circumambulate while praying or meditating.)

Another pilgrimage that draws millions of people is the Indian *Kumbh Mela* (figure **10.31**). This ancient festival is mainly a Hindu event, but it is open to all faiths. Its dates vary with astrological signs and the summer and winter solstices. The main site of the *Kumbh Mela* is at the meeting-point of the Yamuna and Ganges rivers at Allahabad in Uttar Pradesh. But it is also celebrated on the Ganges at Hardwar, at Ujjain on the banks of the Shipra, and at Nasik on the River Godavari. The pilgrims bathe in the river's holy water, which washes away sin and leads to salvation. As such, the *Kumbh Mela* can be compared with the Christian rite of baptism, originally performed by John the Baptist in the River Jordan. In both faiths, the symbolic notion of spiritual cleansing is expressed by literal cleansing—whether by bodily immersion in a holy river or by sprinkling holy water on a person's head.

10.31 *Kumbh Mela* celebrations, Hardwar, India.

10.30 The Ka'bah, Great Mosque of Mecca, Saudi Arabia.

KEY TERMS

Althing in medieval Iceland, a general assembly governed according to a law code.

ambulatory in a church, the curved passageway that surrounds an apse.

archivolts the attached arches around the tympanum.

bay a space in a building defined by piers.

benefice originally land granted for services, the word later included ecclesiastical offices.

chivalry a code of values in which knights promised service and loyalty to a lord in return for protection.

column cluster a group of attached columns.

cursive handwriting in flowing strokes with the letters joined together.

edda a type of Icelandic poetry that recounts myths and legends.

fealty an oath of allegiance sworn by a vassal to a lord.

feudalism in medieval Europe, a fluid political, military, and social organization based on mutual obligations between lords and their vassals, who swore allegiance to them.

freeman a property-owning peasant, who turned the property over to a lord in return for protection and certain economic and legal rights.

guild an organization of workers within a particular craft.

illumination the decoration of biblical and other sacred manuscript texts with painted images.

kennings concrete, compound words used to enrich a narrative.

knight in the Middle Ages, a man who carried out military service in return for the right to hold land.

lintel a horizontal cross-beam.

mandorla an oval of light around the entire body.

manor in the Middle Ages, a group of farms and villages.

manorialism in medieval Europe, a social system organized around a manor in which a landlord allowed peasants to live and work on the land in exchange for a percentage of their produce and other obligations.

mayor of the palace in Merovingian France, the king's major-domo (prime minister) and often the real ruler.

minstrel a wandering performer who sang secular songs in medieval courts.

minuscule a small cursive script.

miracle play a medieval religious play dramatizing miracles.

morality play a medieval religious play that gives dramatic form to the human struggle between good and evil.

mystery play a medieval religious play based on a Bible story.

neume in plainsong, a diagonal mark indicating a note or group of notes over the word to be sung.

organum a form of plainsong in which two or more melodic lines are sung at once; a type of polyphony.

pagoda in Buddhist architecture, a multi-tiered tower that contains relics.

parchment the treated and dyed skin of a sheep or calf used for manuscripts.

polyphony a form of music in which two or more melodic lines are sung at once.

psalter a psalm book.

relics the physical remains of saints and martyrs or objects associated with them.

reliquary a container housing a sacred relic.

romance a medieval tale in a Romance language depicting heroic deeds.

rune-stone a large, upright memorial stone engraved with runic text.

saga an Icelandic story that mixes history, legend, myth, and folk tradition.

scaldic a type of Norse poetry that recounts tales of kings and heroes.

scop a type of German performer who sang tales of Germanic heroes in the fifth to seventh centuries.

scriptorium (plural **scriptoria**) a room for writing, usually in a monastery.

simony the selling of spiritual benefices.

spandrel in architecture, the triangular area between (1) two adjacent arches or (2) the side of an arch and the right angle that encloses it.

stupa in Buddhist architecture, a round structure derived from the Buddha's burial mound.

tenor in medieval music, the low voice singing long held notes of plainchant in polyphonic pieces.

translate in religion, to transfer or remove to another place.

transverse arch in a church or cathedral, an arch that spans the nave.

trope a passage, with or without words, inserted in Gregorian chant.

trumeau the central vertical support of a lintel or tympanum above a wide doorway.

tympanum in Christian architecture, the curved triangular area between an arch and the lintel below it.

vassal in the Middle Ages, a man who held land in return for duties of allegiance to a lord.

KEY QUESTIONS

1. How and why was the feudal system of allegiances maintained in the Middle Ages?
2. What actions of Charlemagne influenced learning in medieval culture?
3. How does the fact that the *Song of Roland* was written from the French point of view affect the portrayal of the Muslims?
4. How do plainsong and organum differ?
5. How did Irish monasteries help keep Classical learning alive during the Middle Ages? What other functions did monasteries perform?
6. Summarize the heroic qualities of *Beowulf*.

SUGGESTED READING

Alexander, Jonathan J. G. *Medieval Illuminators and their Methods of Work*. New Haven, CT, and London: Yale University Press, 1993.
▸ A well-illustrated study of manuscript illumination.

Beowulf: A New Verse Translation, trans. Seamus Heaney. New York: Farrar, Straus and Giroux, 2000.
▸ A modern translation of *Beowulf* by a Nobel prize-winning poet.

Bragg, Melvyn. *Credo*. London: Hodder and Stoughton, 1996.
▸ A fictional account of the Early Middle Ages and Romanesque period.

Braunfels, Wolfgang. *Monasteries of Western Europe*. London: Thames and Hudson, 1972.
▸ A basic study of monasticism and its art.

Cahn, Walter. *Romanesque Bible Illumination*. Ithaca, NY: Cornell University Press, 1983.
▸ A scholarly study of manuscript painting.

Cawley, A. C. (ed.). *Everyman and Medieval Miracle Plays*. London: Orion, Phoenix Editions, 1993.
▸ A study of *Everyman* and medieval theater.

Diebold, William. *Word and Image*. Boulder, CO: Westview Press, 2000.
▸ A brief, original approach to early medieval art.

Einhard. *The Life of Charlemagne*, with a Foreword by Sidney Painter. Ann Arbor, MI: University of Michigan Press, 2001.
▸ A brief, early medieval biography of Charlemagne.

The Mabinogion, trans. Jeffrey Gautz. London: Penguin Books, 1976.
▸ A translation of the Celtic tales.

Mâle, Emile. *Religious Art in France, the Twelfth Century: A Study of the Origins of Medieval Iconography*. Princeton, NJ: Princeton University Press, 1978.
▸ A classic study of medieval art and iconography.

McKitterick, R. (ed.). *Carolingian Culture: Emulation and Innovation*. London: Cambridge University Press, 1993.
▸ On the origins and rise of Carolingian art and culture.

Njal's Saga, trans. Magnus Magnusson and Hermann Pálsson. London: Penguin Books, 1960.
▸ The most popular of the Norse sagas.

Petzold, Andreas. *Romanesque Art*. New York: Pearson, 1995.
▸ A general introduction to Romanesque art and its context.

The Plays of Hroswitha of Gandersheim, trans. Larissa Bonfante with the collaboration of Alexandra Bonfante-Warren. Wauconda, IL: Bolchazy-Carducci Publishers, 1986.
▸ An annotated edition of the plays of Hroswitha.

The Poetic Edda, trans. Lee M. Hollander. Austin, TX: University of Texas Press, 1986.
▸ A translation of the Norse poem.

Sawyer, P. *The Oxford Illustrated History of the Vikings*, Oxford: Oxford University Press, 1997.
▸ A well-illustrated survey of Viking history, culture, and art.

Schapiro, Meyer. *Romanesque Art: Selected Papers*. New York: George Braziller, 1976.
▸ A classic work of medieval scholarship.

Stokstad, Marilyn. *Medieval Art*. Denver, CO: Westview Press, 2004.
▸ A standard survey of medieval art.

SUGGESTED FILMS

1931 *A Connecticut Yankee in King Arthur's Court* (based on Twain), dir. David Butler

1933 *Charlemagne*, dir. Pierre Colombier

1942 *Arabian Nights*, dir. John Rawlins

1949 *A Connecticut Yankee in King Arthur's Court* (based on Twain), dir. Tony Garnett

1951 *Murder in the Cathedral*, dir. George Hoellering

1953 *Knights of the Round Table*, dir. Richard Thorpe

1964 *Becket*, dir. Peter Glenville

1968 *The Lion in Winter*, dir. Anthony Harvey

1978 *La Chanson de Roland* (*The Song of Roland*), dir. Frank Cassenti

1987 *Juniper Tree* (old Icelandic tale), dir. Nietzcha Keene

1998 *Canterbury Tales*, dir. Jonathan Myerson

11 The Development and Expansion of Gothic: 1150–1300

> *"We will not sell, refuse, or delay right or justice to anyone . . . We will appoint only such justices, constables, sheriffs, or bailiffs as know the law of the realm and intend to obey it."*
>
> (*Magna Carta*, 1215)

The term Gothic refers to a style of art and architecture and to the period of their development in western Europe, which lasted from the middle of the twelfth century into the fourteenth century in Italy and later in other European countries. Today, the term is purely descriptive, but when it was first coined, in early-sixteenth-century Italy, the word Gothic had negative connotations associated with the Germanic Goths, who had sacked Rome. To the Italians, Gothic style seemed "barbaric" but, in fact, Gothic style is one of the most remarkable Western achievements. The term is now associated with the towering cathedrals that first appeared in France in the mid-twelfth century and rapidly spread throughout Europe.*

The Gothic period is also significant for developments in economics, religion, philosophy, and literature, as well as in society and politics. One example of a small but important step forced on the English king in the early thirteenth century can be seen in the above quotation. The Magna Carta *(*Great Charter*) marks the first time that a king's power was officially limited so that he was no longer above the law. The two clauses of the* Magna Carta *cited above are a small part of a much larger document, but they clearly reflect the demand to be ruled by law rather than by royal whim.*

Scholasticism

- Gothic cathedrals as mirrors of the Christian universe
- Peter Abelard: *Sic et non*
- St. Thomas Aquinas: *Summa theologiae*

Conflict

- King John versus the nobility
- Dominicans and Franciscans
- Faith versus reason
- Realists versus nominalists

The Written Word

- *Magna Carta*
- Suger on embellishing the cathedral
- St. Francis: "Canticle of the Sun"
- Dante: *Divine Comedy*

Music

- *Cantus firmus*
- Léonin
- Pérotin
- The motet

Timeline

Gothic Period 1150–1300

History and Culture

Towns become cities
Emergence of merchant class
Population of western Europe rises to 70 million
Magna Carta in England, 1215
Paris political and artistic center of western Europe
Founding of medieval universities: Paris, Bologna, Oxford, and Cambridge

Religion

Establishment of cathedral schools, including lay education
Power of popes increases
Lay sisterhood of Beguines formed, *c.* 1170
Inquisition established, 1184
Lay brotherhood of Beghards formed, early 13th century
St. Francis of Assisi founds Franciscan Order, *c.* 1208
Foundation of Poor Clares, *c.* 1212
St. Dominic founds Dominican Order, *c.* 1214
Cult of the Virgin takes on new importance
Church institutes Seven Sacraments, by 1215

Architecture

Abbot Suger renovates St. Denis, Paris, from 1124
Development of exterior buttressing, 12th century
Notre Dame, Paris, begun *c.* 1163
Sainte-Chapelle, Paris, 1241–1248
Cathedrals: Chartres, begun 1194; Amiens, begun 1220; and Reims, begun *c.* 1230–1240
Late Gothic: Cologne Cathedral, begun 1228, towers *c.* 1350
Use of stained glass: north rose window, Notre Dame, Paris, *c.* 1255

Literature and Philosophy

Scholasticism
Abelard (1079–1142), *Sic et non*
Suger (1080–1151), *Book of Suger*
St. Francis of Assisi, "Canticle of the Sun," *c.* 1224
Aquinas, *Summa theologiae*, 1266–1274
Dante, *Divine Comedy*, *c.* 1308–1321

Theater

Mystery, miracle, and morality plays performed inside churches and cathedrals
Plays move outside church: liturgical drama declines and secular drama expands

Music

Cathedral school of Notre Dame, Paris, becomes music center
Melismatic organum using *cantus firmus*, late 12th century
Discant, late 12th century
Léonin, *Magnus liber organi*, *c.* 1170
Pérotin (d. *c.* 1238): counterpoint
Motet developed, 13th century

THE ECONOMY, POLITICS, AND RELIGION

The Gothic period saw an increasing trend toward the urbanization that had begun in the Romanesque era. As trade and commerce expanded, towns began to grow into cities. Old Roman cities, in decline since the fall of the empire, became revitalized. Early medieval manors attracted fairs and markets, which encouraged commerce, improved the economy, increased the population, and spurred the development of yet more towns. From 1000 to 1300, the population of western Europe doubled, rising to about 70 million. By 1300, western Europe had become a network of small cities. The biggest, with populations of 100,000 or more, were in Italy—especially Milan, Venice, Genoa, Naples, and Florence. In France, Paris had a population of 80,000 in 1300. In the Netherlands (Holland and Belgium), too, cities soon became thriving centers of commerce and trade.

In this new economic atmosphere, people became more entrepreneurial. A rural society based on networks of loyalty and allegiance to a lord was replaced by towns, by workers demanding better working conditions, and by individual ambition. A new merchant class evolved, with bankers, moneylenders, and other wealthy businessmen enjoying lives of luxury. But conflicts also arose—between the landowners and the city dwellers, between the rich and the poor, and between different groups within the clergy.

The role of the monastery as a center of learning was taken over by cathedral schools, especially in France. These schools had been established to teach the liberal arts to members of the clergy, but in the late twelfth century the pope required that lay people (those not ordained) be admitted to the schools free of charge. This improved literacy among the population, which helped promote a higher level of professional life. In addition, the cathedral schools were centers of intellectual debate. Scholars argued about the validity of faith versus reason, about whether literature should be written in Latin or the vernacular (everyday language), and about the nature and value of Arabic contributions to learning. Eventually, universities would replace cathedral schools as the main centers of learning in Europe.

In England, in 1215, after King John (ruled 1199–1216) had lost English territories in France, dissatisfied barons wanted to retain their power. They forced the king to sign the *Magna Carta*, the first document to recognize that kings as well as their subjects (in this case the nobility) had moral and social responsibilities and were subject to certain laws. Taxes, according to the *Magna Carta*, could be levied only by general consent, and freemen could no longer be arrested, imprisoned, or exiled without due legal process.

The Church consolidated its power through the papacy, sometimes antagonizing rulers by encroaching onto the secular arena. Innocent III (papacy 1198–1216) wielded significant political influence, especially in England, France, and the territories around Rome. He supported crusades to the Holy Land and Egypt (see Chapter 10) and fought heresy in Europe. In an effort to combat the Albigensian heresy (see Chapter 8), Innocent sent preachers to persuade the Albigensians to accept the doctrines of the Roman Church. In 1208, when this failed, he launched a crusade against them.

In 1215, Innocent convoked the Fourth Lateran Council, the largest in the Middle Ages. It was attended by over 1200 bishops and abbots, two Eastern patriarchs, and many representatives of secular rulers. The Council passed seventy decrees and condemned two sects for heresy—Cathars and Waldensians. The latter originated in France and followed the Bible but opposed the Church hierarchy. Among the doctrinal issues covered, the Council decreed that all adult Christians should attend Mass and confession at least once a year.

By 1215, the Church had instituted the Seven Sacraments: Baptism (by which one enters the faith), Confirmation (by which one is confirmed in the faith), the Eucharist (the Mass, in which bread and wine are transformed into Christ's body and blood, a process known as **transubstantiation**), Penance (confession and atonement), Marriage, Last Rites, and Ordination (for the priesthood). These Sacraments were conceived of as points of progression in the Christian faith.

At the close of the thirteenth century, Boniface VIII (papacy 1294–1303) was elected to the papacy. He believed in the absolute power of the Church and demanded authority over secular rulers. His views angered the French king, Philip IV, the Fair (ruled 1285–1314), also called Philip the Handsome—in French, Philippe le Bel—who ordered his arrest. Boniface barely escaped, but he was captured in 1302 by Philip's army and severely beaten before being allowed to return to Rome. He died the following year, and the power of the papacy began to decline.

MONASTIC DEVELOPMENTS IN THE THIRTEENTH CENTURY

One result of urbanization was the development of the **mendicant** (literally "begging") Orders, which consisted of **friars** (brothers) who wandered from town to town. In contrast to monks, who isolated themselves in self-sufficient monastic communities, the friars worked in the outside world. They did not own possessions, and relied on townspeople for their subsistence. The two main figures in this new movement were Dominic Guzmán (*c.* 1170–1221) of Old Castile, in Spain, and Francis (*c.* 1182–1226) of Assisi, in Italy.

ST. DOMINIC

Dominic was a nobleman who espoused poverty and founded the Dominican Order, also called the Black Friars because of their black robes. He traveled through Italy, Spain, France, and Hungary, establishing friaries. The Dominican Order was devoted to intellectual work, especially preaching and studying religious texts. The Order was forbidden to have possessions—except its churches and residences—and thus had to beg. Dominican friars followed a strict rule requiring a Spartan, regulated regimen of prayer, worship, abstinence, and self-denial. Since they espoused a strictly orthodox view of Christianity, the Dominicans became zealous **Inquisitors** (officials appointed to combat heresy) (see Box). In their zeal, the Dominicans established an institute designed to save women from the dangers of Albigensian ideas.

ST. FRANCIS OF ASSISI

St. Francis espoused a different approach to Christianity from that of St. Dominic. According to traditional accounts of the life of St. Francis, he defied his wealthy father by publicly renouncing his possessions and removing his clothes in the market square of Assisi. He thus rejected both his father and

Defining Moment

The Inquisition

The Inquisition was an official body established in 1184 under Pope Lucius III by the papal bull *Ad abolendum* to combat heresies that had been plaguing the Church since the fourth century. This was a defining moment in Western history, for the Inquisition would become a source of fear and terror in the countries where it thrived. For the arts and sciences, the Inquisition represented a regressive, conservative force that discouraged innovation, empiricism, and intellectual inquiry. Judicially, the Inquisition embodied everything that goes against the grain of modern democracy.

In 1232, under Frederick II, Holy Roman Emperor and king of Sicily, the Inquisition was empowered to pursue, arrest, and bring to trial heretics throughout Frederick's empire. But the extent of its zeal alarmed Gregory IX (papacy 1227–1241), who insisted that campaigns against heresy were the province of the Church. He therefore appointed the mendicant Orders, especially the Dominicans, to comb Church territory and warn heretics to repent.

Heretics were tried before a jury of clerics and laymen based on the evidence of two witnesses. The accused had no right to counsel, and sentences could not be appealed. At first the identity of the accusers was kept secret, but under Boniface VIII (papacy 1294–1303) this was changed.

Beginning in 1252, under Innocent IV (papacy 1243–1254), torture was permitted as a means of forcing the accused to confess. Penalties ranged from making pilgrimages or wearing the cross of infamy to the loss of all possessions or life imprisonment. And when the inquisitors handed heretics over to the civil authorities, it was tantamount to a demand that the accused be put to death.

In 1484, Innocent VIII, in his bull *Summis desiderantes* of December 5, describes the motives for establishing the Inquisition:

Desiring with supreme ardor, as pastoral solicitude requires, that the Catholic faith in our days everywhere grow and flourish as much as possible, and that all heretical depravity be put far from the territories of the faithful, we freely declare and anew decree this by which our pious desire may be fulfilled, and, all errors being rooted out by our toil as with the hoe of a wise laborer, zeal and devotion to this faith may take deeper hold on the hearts of the faithful themselves.

It has recently come to our ears, not without great pain to us, that in some parts of upper Germany, as well as in the provinces, cities, territories, regions, and dioceses of Mainz, Köln, Trier, Salzburg, and Bremen, many persons of both sexes, heedless of their own salvation and forsaking the Catholic faith, give themselves over to devils male and female, and by their incantations, charms, and conjurings, and by other abominable superstitions and sortileges, offences, crimes, and misdeeds, ruin and cause to perish the offspring of women, the foal of animals, the products of the earth, the grapes of vines, and the fruits of trees, as well as men and women, cattle and flocks and herds and animals of every kind, vineyards also and orchards, meadows, pastures, harvests, grains and other fruits of the earth; that they afflict and torture with dire pains and anguish, both internal and external, these men, women, cattle, flocks, herds, and animals, and hinder men from begetting and women from conceiving, and prevent all consummation of marriage; that, moreover, they deny with sacrilegious lips the faith they received in holy baptism; and that, at the instigation of the enemy of mankind, they do not fear to commit and perpetrate many other abominable offences and crimes, at the risk of their own souls, to the insult of the divine majesty and to the pernicious example and scandal of multitudes.

The notorious Spanish Inquisition was not instituted until the late fifteenth century under Ferdinand V and Isabella (the rulers who financed the voyage of Columbus to the New World). Initially, Jews were the target, then the Moors who had been forcibly converted, and finally Protestants (from the sixteenth century). The Spanish Inquisition, which was independent of Rome, was a tightly run, highly efficient organization under the leadership of an Inquisitor General. In Spain, the Inquisition instituted *autos-da-fé* (burnings of heretics), but in northern Europe and England the Inquisition had little influence. When the French overran Spain in the early nineteenth century, the Inquisition was finally suppressed.

Critical Question What is "due process"? Why would "due process" be incompatible with the practices of the Inquisition?

his father's profession—that of a textile merchant. Instead, Francis identified with Jesus, and sought a new father in God. He founded the Franciscan Order and established a convent in Portiuncula, near Assisi. He traveled through the towns of Italy, preaching poverty and asserting God's presence in nature. In 1224, while praying on Mount La Verna, Francis saw a vision of the crucified Christ in the form of a seraph (a type of angel). Marks resembling Christ's Crucifixion wounds—called the **stigmata**—miraculously appeared on Francis's hands, feet, and side.

After receiving the stigmata, Francis wrote the "Canticle of the Sun," praising God in nature as a metaphor of the human family:

Praised be You, my Lord, with all your creatures, especially
 Sir Brother Sun, . . .
Praised be You, my Lord, through Sister Moon and the
 stars, . . .
Praised be You, my Lord, through Brother Wind, . . .
Praised be You, my Lord, through Sister Water, . . .
Praised be You, my Lord, through Brother Fire, . . .
Praised be You, my Lord, through our Sister Mother Earth, . . .
Praised be You, my Lord, through our Sister Bodily Death.

("Canticle of the Sun")

READING SELECTION

St. Francis of Assisi, "Canticle of the Sun," In Praise of God's Creation, PWC2-148

From the thirteenth century, St. Francis became a popular subject of painting. His love of nature and his genius as a communicator extended to birds and other animals, and this aspect of his character is reflected in the iconography of many Franciscan works of art (figure **11.1**).

Despite Francis's insistence on poverty, the Franciscan Order became wealthy. It then split into two groups: Conventualists and Observants. The Conventual Franciscans accepted their wealth and managed their money well. But the Observant Franciscans followed the original rule and refused to have possessions or own land. The pope sided with the Conventualists, largely because the papacy itself and the Church in Rome were enormously wealthy and wanted their wealth to grow.

WOMEN MONASTICS IN THE THIRTEENTH CENTURY

Inspired by the message of St. Francis, the noblewoman Clare (1194–1253) followed his teachings and attracted a group of her own followers, known as the **Poor Clares**. In 1215, Francis established her as the abbess of a convent, also at Portiuncula. Like the Franciscans, the Clares followed a strict rule and expanded in the fourteenth century. In contrast to the Franciscans, however, the Poor Clares were confined to convents and did not wander from town to town as the Franciscans did.

In late-twelfth-century Belgium, a group of lay women, the **Beguines**, formed a sisterhood, which quickly spread to France, Germany, and the Netherlands. Although not nuns,

11.1 Master of the Bardi Saint Francis Dossal, *Saint Francis Preaching to the Birds*, Bardi Chapel of Saint Francis, Church of Santa Croce, Florence, *c.* 1250. Tempera on panel.
In the company of two other friars, Francis preaches to a group of alert birds standing up and taking notice of the saint's words. Today, visitors to Assisi are invariably struck by the thousands of birds flying around the city.

they established Christian centers devoted to prayer, education, social work, and helping the poor and the dying. In addition, the Beguines worked as weavers, fullers (workers who increased the weight of cloth by shrinking and pulling it), and dyers of cloth. Unlike the Poor Clares and other monastic communities, the Beguines had no abbess and they worked in the outside world. They could also own property and were allowed to marry as long as they lived outside the beguinage. A male counterpart of the Beguines, the **Beghards**, was also dedicated to doing good work for the community and to leading a spiritual life. The establishment of such lay groups reflected an expansion of religious life among the laity in northern Europe during the later Middle Ages.

THE CENTRAL ROLE OF PARIS

In the Gothic period, the city of Paris was the political and artistic center of western Europe. It was the residence of the king, a commercial hub, and the site of an important university as well as a cathedral and its school. Nearby, at St. Denis, was a royal Benedictine monastery, the burial place of French kings and associated in the popular imagination with Charlemagne. The monastery's abbey church was dedicated to the fifth-century martyr St. Denis, traditionally identified as the first bishop of Paris, and contained his relics. St. Denis was, therefore, a major pilgrimage site. In addition, a large trade fair of considerable commercial importance was held in the area every year. For all these reasons, crowds of visitors flocked to the church of St. Denis, which soon needed more space to accommodate them.

ABBOT SUGER AND ST. DENIS

The abbot of St. Denis in the early twelfth century was Suger (1080–1151). He came from a poor family that pledged him to the Church when he was ten. Suger attended school with the future king, Louis VI (ruled 1108–1137), and became his friend and adviser, remaining as adviser to Louis VII (ruled 1137–1180). He was named abbot of St. Denis in 1122. Influenced by Bernard of Clairvaux's call for monastic reform (see Chapter 10), Suger tightened discipline at the abbey and insisted on following a strict version of the Benedictine rule.

A man of small stature but great intelligence, political skill, and vanity, Suger decided in 1124 to rebuild the abbey church of St. Denis. This proved to be a momentous decision that changed the course of intellectual and artistic history in the West. Unlike Bernard, who opposed the display of art in churches, Suger believed that the more lavish the art, the more inspiring it was to the faithful. His views were reinforced by reading Neoplatonic texts, which extolled light as an expression of the divine. (At the time these writings were mistakenly believed to be by St. Denis himself.) Suger also, of course, realized that his building program would increase the power and popularity of his king.

Suger documented the renovation in his *Book of Suger, Abbot of Saint Denis*. He added two towers at the entrance and a triple portal (figure **11.2**), and extended the length of the nave. The enlarged choir was surrounded with a double ambulatory to permit an easy flow of pilgrims (figure **11.3**). The outer ambulatory had seven **radiating chapels**, which allowed Masses to be celebrated and relics to be displayed without interfering with the services that were taking place at the high altar. Each chapel had two tall, pointed windows, called **lancets**, so that outdoor light could stream into the interior (figure **11.4**).

Suger's alterations included two of the most important structural developments of Gothic style. The first was the design of the vaults of the ambulatory, which, in contrast to the heavy vaulting systems of the Romanesque period, were **rib vaults**, made by the intersection of pointed arches (figure **11.5**). The pointed arch permitted greater height and a sense of greater delicacy than the Romanesque round arch. The second development was an increase in the size of windows

11.2 Façade of St. Denis, Paris, mid-12th century.

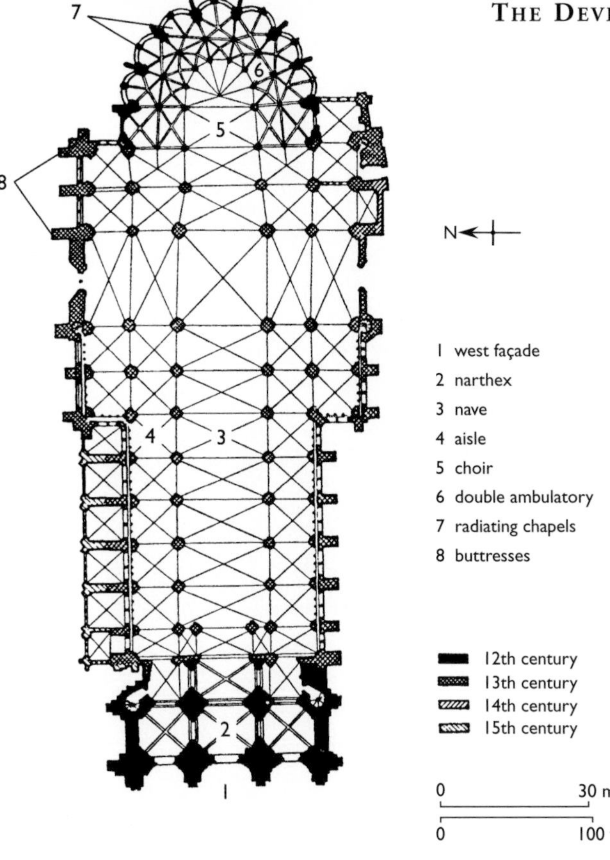

11.3 Plan of St. Denis, Paris.

11.4 Interior of the ambulatory, St. Denis, Paris.

made possible by the ribbed vault construction. Coupled with greater use of **stained** (colored) **glass**, it flooded the interior with light and color.

For Suger, the dazzling play of light and color indicated God's presence at St. Denis. To this, he added his own taste for precious gems and gold decoration. And, indeed, he did transform St. Denis into a vision that elevated the soul to new heights of mystical experience. Suger defended the expense of his project as a necessary aid to salvation.

The door to the church was a metaphor for the entrance to heaven. Accordingly, Suger decorated the central portals on the west façade with gilded bronze reliefs. These he described in the following verse:

> Whoever thou art, if thou seekest to extol the glory of these doors,
> Marvel not at the gold and the expense but at the craftsmanship of the work.
> Bright is the noble work; but, being nobly bright, the work
> Should brighten the minds so that they may travel, through the true lights,
> To the True Light where Christ is the true door.
> In what manner it be inherent in this world the golden door defines:
> The dull mind rises to truth through that which is material
> And, in seeing this light, is resurrected from its former submersion.

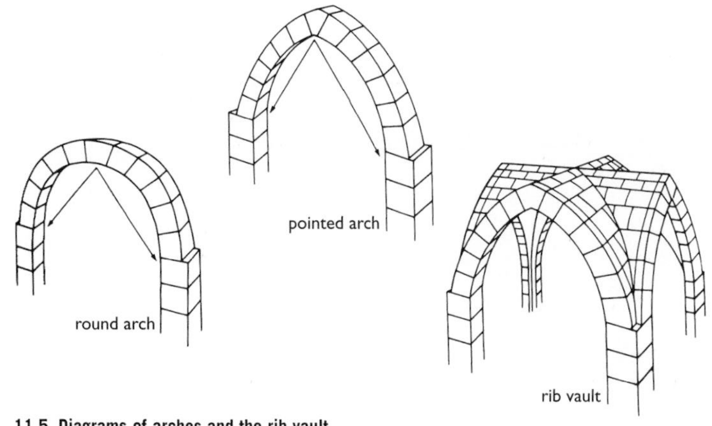

11.5 Diagrams of arches and the rib vault.

THE CATHEDRAL OF NOTRE DAME IN PARIS

Suger's ideas about light, color, and space launched the Gothic style. In addition to expanding the window area and using pointed arches (rather than the round Romanesque arch), Gothic builders after Suger developed flying buttresses. These are visible in the side view of the cathedral of Notre Dame, Paris (figure **11.6**). They were added around 1200, when the thrust (the downward and outward force) of the interior arches began to make the walls buckle.

Notre Dame is located, as was the king's palace, on the Ile de la Cité, a small island in the River Seine, which divides Paris into its Left and Right Banks. Notre Dame was begun around 1163 and consecrated in 1177. Its towers were added from 1220 to 1225, but the building was not completed until the second half of the thirteenth century. Note the curve of the apse at the eastern (back) end to the right, the elaborate transept wall, and the towers at the western entrance

11.7 *above* **West façade of Notre Dame, Paris, 1220–1250.**

11.6 Notre Dame, Paris, 12th century.

11.8 Nave of Notre Dame, Paris, 1180–1250.
The nave wall is three stories high. The lower story (the nave arcade) consists of heavy piers supporting pointed arches. The second story, called the triforium, is a series of shorter pointed arches, and the third story, called the clerestory, is the main source of light. The clerestory windows are larger than their Romanesque predecessors, and the proportions are taller and thinner (see thumbnail). In this view we are looking east, toward the curved apse illuminated by three stories of windows, reflecting Suger's philosophy that light and color glorify the interior of the church building.

Romanesque nave of Sainte Marie Madeleine, Vézelay
see figure 10.25

(to the left). The slim projections at the top of the buttresses are called flyers, because they resemble wings.

The façade of the cathedral (figure **11.7**) is symmetrical, with tall towers and pointed arches that carry our gaze heavenward. Compared with St. Denis, the wall surface decoration is more animated, and it is also divided into geometric sections. Triple portals are surmounted by a **gallery** (row of figures) of Old Testament kings, including Christ's typological precursors David and Solomon. Above these, the **rose window** (a large, round window in Gothic cathedrals) is flanked by double lancets framed by a larger single arch.

In the interior (figure **11.8**) soaring vaults are locked in place by circular keystones. Note that the wall of the nave is divided into repeated sections, called bays. Each bay is separated from its neighbor by a pier and slim columns rising from the capital of the pier and continuing into the ribs of the vaults. The reconstruction in figure **11.9** shows how the buttressing system is designed to counter the thrust of the ceiling vaults. The bay is shown in relation to the aisle and the entire exterior buttress in the sectional drawing in figure **11.10**.

11.9 Reconstruction showing the Gothic system of buttresses and flying buttresses.
At each point of contact at the inside wall, the thrust is carried on the exterior by the buttress.

By the time the north rose window (figure **11.11**) was in place, Gothic builders had developed the **rayonnant** (radiant) style, in which shapes of glass seem to radiate from the small circle at the center. The area occupied by supporting architectural elements has been reduced and the glass windows now take up more space. The geometric regularity of the design creates the impression of an ordered universe. By filtering outdoor light through colored glass, Gothic cathedrals suggested the transforming power of faith.

Gothic cathedrals were thought of as mirrors of the Christian universe. As such, they devoted space to the grotesque, the deformed, and the monstrous aspects of nature and human fantasy. Such images appear on capitals and under the feet of holy personages. But they are most consistently represented as **gargoyles** (figure **11.12**).

BUILDING THE CATHEDRAL

Building a Gothic cathedral was a major architectural, economic, and social undertaking. Reflecting the hierarchical structure of the Church, a cathedral is the seat of a bishop and has authority over a larger territory than a parish

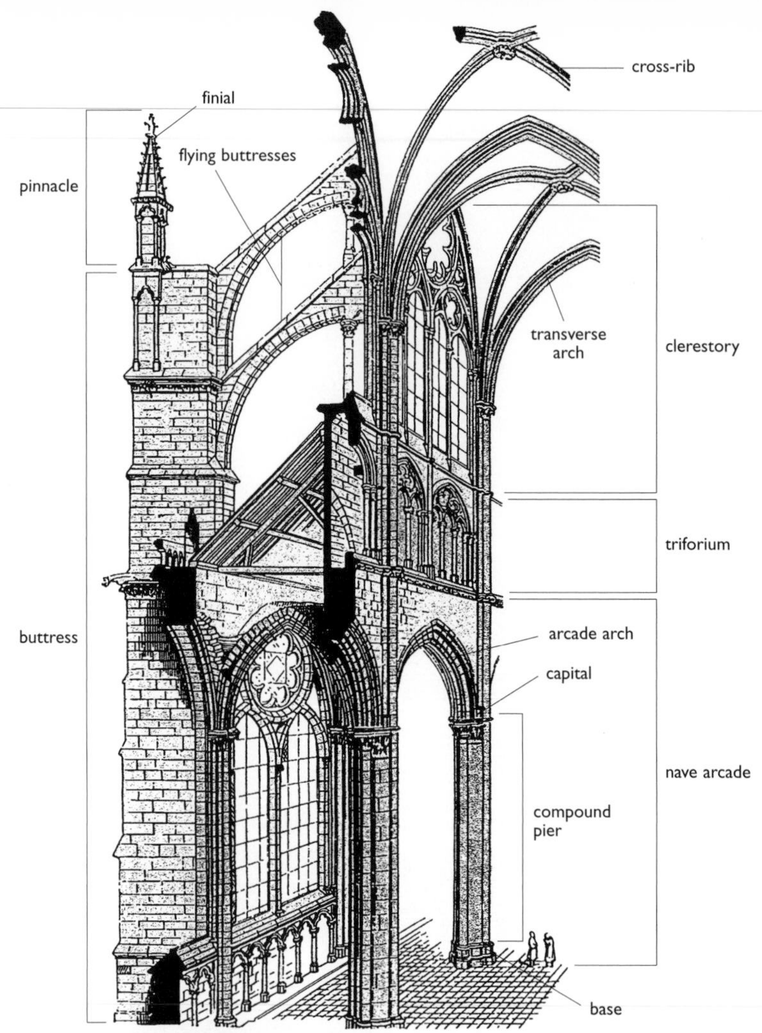

11.10 *above* **Sectional diagram of Notre Dame, Paris.**

11.11 *left* **North rose window, Notre Dame, Paris, *c.* 1255. 43 ft. (13.1 m) diameter.**

11.12 *above* **Gargoyle on the balustrade of the Grande Galerie, Notre Dame, Paris, 19th-century replica of a 12th-century original. Stone.**
Gargoyles originally served as water spouts of the cathedral's drainage system, keeping water from eroding the walls—water is expelled through their mouths. The term itself is related to "gargle," which comes from the French word *gorge*, meaning "throat." Their exclusion from the sacred space of the interior, like their monstrous forms, reflects their association with evil.

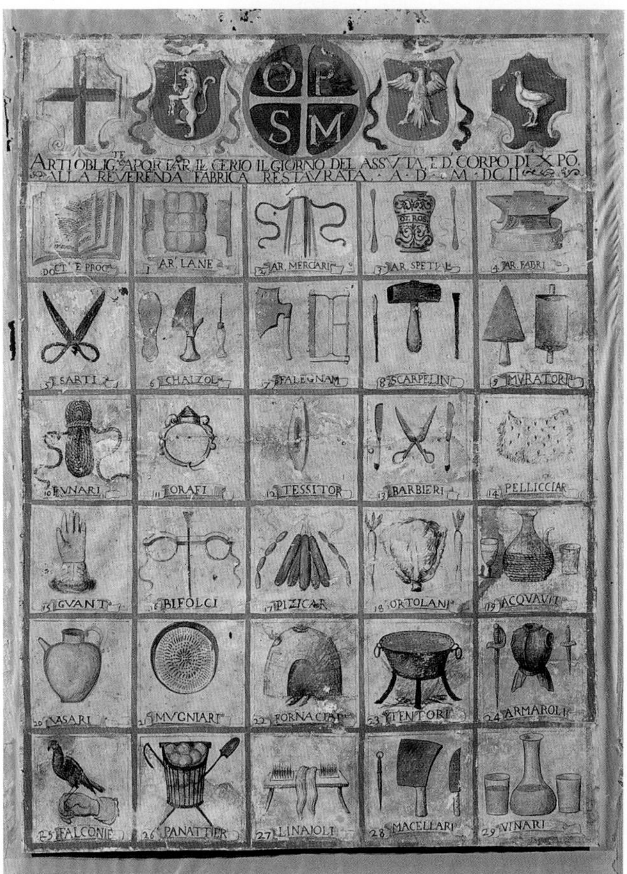

11.13 *above* **Table of guilds, from Orvieto, Italy, 14th century. Museo dell'Opera del Duomo, Orvieto.**
The table shows various trade guilds, including tailors, barbers, bread-makers, vintners, and eyeglass makers, whose workers and their families benefited from the building of a cathedral.

church or an abbey church. The greater size of the cathedral thus indicates its greater importance in the Church hierarchy. Generally, the site chosen for a cathedral in the Middle Ages was the high point of a town, so that the building would be visible from a distance. In addition, the bells, located in the towers, could be heard for miles around, announcing the hours of worship.

Constructing a cathedral usually brought prosperity to a medieval town. The work created jobs for a large number of workers and a stream of income for their families. Patronage of the cathedral was also a community affair. Some of the financing came from the royal family, some was provided by contributions from the clergy, and some came from local people wishing to atone for their sins or hoping for a miracle. Contributions from the associations of craftsmen who worked on the project provided another source of money. These associations were the guilds (see Chapter 10), which oversaw the training, maintenance, and population of specific trades and industries (figure **11.13**). Guilds also provided care and education for the families of workers if a worker died. Each guild had a patron saint, and each worker learned his trade by a system of apprenticeship.

Figure **11.14** shows builders at work. Stonemasons on top of the wall lay and level the bricks; at the left, a man operates a pulley lifting mortar to the masons. In the center, a carver completes a capital, and at the right, a woodcutter removes the bark of a log on a sawhorse.

11.14 Matthew Paris, *Building a Cathedral*, from the *Life of Saint Alban and Saint Amphibalus*, *c.* 1250. Trinity College, Dublin.

11.15 Thomas de Cormont, interior of Sainte-Chapelle, Paris, 1241–1248. 32 ft. × 99 ft. 6 in. (9.75 × 30.3 m).

Supervising the enormous numbers of workers was the master mason—the **master-builder**. Since building a cathedral could take several generations, the master-builder worked from **templates**—diagrams of architectural sections, which could be passed on to a successor. Thus if one master-builder died or retired, a new one was able to continue building according to the original design.

Sainte-Chapelle: The King's Chapel

One of the greatest Gothic expressions of mystical atmosphere created through light and color is the French royal chapel, Sainte-Chapelle, in Paris (figure **11.15**). It was commissioned by Louis IX (later St. Louis, ruled 1226–1270) and was adjacent to the king's palace on the Ile de la Cité. The chapel was divided into a lower section, dedicated to the Virgin Mary and used by members of Louis's household, and an upper section for the royal family. The upper section is composed of tall, thin, gilded columns extending to the blue, star-studded, vaulted ceiling. Visible on the lower piers are statues of the twelve apostles. At the far end is the gilded reliquary tabernacle for which Sainte-Chapelle was built. It contains relics of the Crucifixion—the Crown of Thorns, the sponge (Jesus was given a sponge filled with vinegar to drink while he was on the Cross), and fragments of the lance that pierced his side and the True Cross.

With its nearly transparent wall of red and blue glass and its tall, slim, gilded columns, Sainte-Chapelle embodies Suger's conception of a church interior. Indeed, in this chapel, which is clearly fit for a king, the mystical treatment of light espoused by Suger and by the Neoplatonists he read marks a high point of Gothic style.

MUSIC AT THE CATHEDRAL SCHOOL OF NOTRE DAME

The cathedral school in Paris followed the curriculum that Alcuin of York had developed for Charlemagne (see Chapter 10), which included the study of Aristotle and the Church Fathers. It was also an important center of music in the twelfth and thirteenth centuries. Traditional church music had been the plainchant sung responsively by a chorus (the choir) and an individual or by two choirs. In the early tenth century, the trope had been inserted into the liturgy.

Composers at Notre Dame brought earlier organum techniques (the earliest form of polyphony) to fruition in the late twelfth century. In the organal or melismatic style, a chant melody (the *cantus firmus*) was sung by the tenor voice, with each note held for several seconds, like a drone. Above the chant, another voice sang an elaborate faster moving line, with several notes to each syllable of text.

11.16 Miniature from a Book of Hours, showing a church service with singing, from Paris, 15th century. Illuminated manuscript, decorated area $6\frac{1}{2}$ in. (16.7 cm) high. British Library, London. The integration of music in church services is shown here as a priest prays before the altar surrounded by a choir of singing monks. At the left, a group reads from an open book, the notes clearly visible on the page. The exuberance of the music is shown not only by the singers around the altar, but also by the seated figure in the initial D and the monks in the border area. The border is filled with floral and foliate designs, indicating that music both fills space and flows through it.

A second style was known as **discant** (from the Latin for "singing apart"). In this, the tenor voice sang shorter notes, while one or more higher voices sang only slightly more rapid notes above it. These parts, rather than rising and falling at the same time (as in earlier parallel organum), often moved in different directions, and functioned as simultaneous melodies. The technique came to be called *punctus contra punctum*, literally "point against point," or counterpoint.

The most important new musical form developed in the thirteenth century was the **motet**. Just as extra words had earlier been added to plainchant to create tropes, now new text was added to the upper voice (or voices) of organum to create the motet. (The term derives from the French *mot*, meaning "word.") Both sacred and secular motets were composed, and the religious and profane could be combined within one work—so, for example, the tenor might perform the notes and Latin text of a chant while a higher voice sang the words of a French poem. By the fifteenth century the motet would evolve into a polyphonic setting of a Latin religious text, normally in three parts.

The increasing complexity of church music in this period can be compared with the new, more complex architecture of cathedral interiors. Both the music and the architecture were designed to express the soaring quality of faith and the expansiveness of God's presence in the universe (figure **11.16**).

The two main figures associated with church music in the late twelfth and early thirteenth centuries are Léonin (*c.* 1163–1190) and Pérotin (d. *c.* 1238). They and their contemporaries at the Notre Dame School standardized the use of six regular rhythmic patterns, which replaced the free-flowing earlier chant styles. Units of three formed the basis of all the patterns—like the triple architectural sections of Gothic cathedrals, anything structured in threes was considered sublime because it mirrored the Trinity.

Léonin compiled the *Magnus liber organi (The Great Book of Organum)* (*c.* 1170), the most important collection of Gothic liturgical music. It contained over a hundred pieces of organum interleaved with plainsong, arranged, for maximum convenience, in the order of the Church year. Pérotin, who became head of the music school at Notre Dame Cathedral toward the end of the twelfth century, is believed to have revised and re-notated the *Magnus liber.* While Léonin's organum was florid and generally for two voices (tenor and *duplum*, or "second"), Pérotin often used three or four voices, with shorter melismas. As all the singers were men, the vocal parts lie at roughly the same pitch and weave in and out, sometimes imitating each other's melodies. One consequence of having four simultaneous lines of music within a narrow range is that the interest begins to switch from the horizontal strands of music to the vertical—to the way the notes coincide as chords. Regular, persistent rhythms give the music a hypnotic quality that is enhanced by the scale of the later pieces; some last for twenty minutes and in their grandeur match the magnificence of the architectural setting in which they were sung.

THE UNIVERSITY OF PARIS

Our modern universities originated in the Middle Ages and were products of urbanization. With the rise of cities, administrative workers who could read and write were needed. These, along with a new interest in legal studies, science, and mathematics, contributed to the growth of an educated class.

The medieval university was more organized than the informal schools of Aristotle, Plato, and other ancient philosophers. At first, students and teachers came together as a group, like masters and apprentices in an academic guild. But soon universities were granted charters and became official institutions that could borrow and invest money. Students who had a reading knowledge of Latin entered university as early adolescents. They usually spent four years there. When students finished a course of study they were awarded certificates and

Society and Culture

Medicine in the Middle Ages

As in ancient Greece and Rome, the practice of medicine in the Middle Ages was a mix of tradition, superstition, folklore, astrology, and ignorance of human anatomy. Medical ingredients consisted mainly of herbs and ointments sold in apothecary shops (pharmacies). Textbooks were in Latin, which most people could not read, and only a few doctors who treated the wealthy had university training in Hippocratic medicine. Some, especially surgery students, were apprenticed to a practicing doctor. Barber-surgeons, who treated more people, formed a guild-based profession.

The majority of the population was treated by herbalists, midwives, and healers, who had no university training. Through the fourteenth century, only midwives dealt with women in childbirth, but with the invention of forceps men began delivering babies. Although monks cultivated herbs for medicinal purposes, the Church barred the clergy from medical studies. It also discouraged empirical investigations of the human body.

Most doctors diagnosed illness by examining a patient's urine. Because the body was believed to be composed of four humors (fluids)—blood, phlegm, yellow bile, and black bile—it was assumed that an imbalance of the humors would show itself in the urine. Doctors also examined blood to see how it flowed and clotted. As a result, it was generally believed that blood-letting could bring the humors into the correct balance (figure **11.17**). In fact, however, blood-letting often resulted in death from loss of blood.

11.17 Aldobrandino of Siena, blood-letting scene, from *Li livres dou santé* (*The Books of Health*), France, 13th century. Manuscript illumination, initial box 2⅛ in. (5.5 cm) wide. British Library, London.
This illustration from an Italian health manual was published in thirteenth-century France. It shows a doctor, wearing a professional cap and long gown, cutting a patient just above the elbow. The patient looks away, apparently to avoid the sight of blood, which flows into a bowl on the floor. Medieval manuals on surgery and the treatment of broken and dislocated bones also survive.

could go on to complete the level of Master. Thereafter they could pursue a doctorate (the ancestor of the PhD degree) in law, theology, or medicine (see Box, p. 286). The requirements were rigorous and a degree in theology could take over twenty years of study.

By the end of the twelfth century, the University of Paris was an intellectual center, and it is still, as the Sorbonne, the major university in France. Other important medieval universities that are well known today include Bologna (in northern Italy), and Oxford and Cambridge (in England). Students at these medieval universities were exclusively men. Although they enrolled for the benefits of having a degree, they criticized the poor living conditions and the lack of money for books, food, and lodging. They had no heat or hot water, and only candlelight to read by.

As with the cathedral schools, the curriculum in medieval universities was based on the one devised by Alcuin of York for the palace school of Charlemagne (see Chapter 10). In the Gothic period, Alcuin's focus on rhetoric and dialectic became the basis of a system of thought called **scholasticism**.

SCHOLASTICISM: PETER ABELARD AND THOMAS AQUINAS

Scholasticism tried to impose a sense of order on the world and to deal with the apparent contradiction of faith and reason. This was a form of logic inspired by the writings of Aristotle and Augustine. Aristotle's works had been preserved in Arabic commentaries and in translations made from Greek into Arabic by Arabic scholars. Eventually these texts were translated into Latin and could be read by Western scholars.

The scholastic method began with a question and sought the answer by demonstrating a series of incorrect or contradictory responses. Its approach to questioning an idea consisted of three steps: (1) posing a question, (2) discussing different aspects of the question based on Classical and Christian authors and biblical texts, and (3) achieving a resolution. Scholasticism was thus a closed system, designed to uphold Church doctrine rather than to explore new ideas.

Within scholasticism, there were two main points of view: the **realist** and the **nominalist**. Realists based their arguments on Plato's notion that universal ideas exist separately from the physical world and the mind. The nominalists disagreed with Plato and argued that only some things are real. An accomplished lecturer at the Paris Cathedral School, William of Champeaux (*c.* 1070–1121), espoused realism. His brilliant student Peter Abelard (1079–1142) claimed that universal ideas did exist but could be understood only by being expressed in language. He exposed contradictions in Church doctrine and in the scriptures by using the scholastic method of logic. He argued, for example, that three and one could never be the same. By this reasoning, Abelard concluded that the concept of the Trinity as three persons in one was not logical (see Box).

Society and Culture

Abelard and Héloïse

Peter Abelard was the major figure in the growth of the University of Paris. He began teaching at the cathedral school in 1113, lecturing on logic and theology. He challenged the Church in *Sic et non* (*Yes and No*), in which he brilliantly demonstrated contradictions in the Bible and in the writings of Christian authors and brought to light the differences between faith and reason. But instead of trying to reconcile the contradictions, he allowed them to remain as open questions.

Abelard's challenge to the Church was not only intellectual, it was also personal. While he was teaching in Paris he met and fell in love with Héloïse (*c.* 1098–1164), an accomplished theologian. She was a brilliant and beautiful young woman, who was living with her uncle, Fulbert, a canon (church official) of Notre Dame Cathedral, and was being tutored by university scholars. Abelard rented a room from Fulbert and began an affair with Héloïse. Their son, Astralabe, was born around 1118 after Héloïse went to live with Abelard's family. At first, Héloïse refused Abelard's offer of marriage on the grounds that a scholarly life was preferable to a domestic one. Eventually, however, they did marry, so enraging Canon Fulbert that Abelard sent Héloïse to the safety of a convent. Soon thereafter Fulbert's men attacked and castrated Abelard.

Abelard entered the monastery of St. Denis in Paris, but he was expelled by Suger when he challenged the monks on a matter of historical accuracy. He continued to teach, but was accused of heresy by both Bernard of Clairvaux and Pope Innocent II. The abbot of Cluny, Venerable Peter, defended Abelard, who then joined the abbey. When Abelard died, Peter sent his body to Héloïse for burial. Héloïse, meanwhile, had become abbess of her convent. Astralabe was raised by Abelard's sister, who lived in Brittany, and he became a canon at the cathedral of Nantes. Abelard recorded his affair with Héloïse in his *Historia calamitatum* (*Story of My Misfortunes*).

READING SELECTION

Héloïse, *The Letters of Abelard and Héloïse*, on the hypocrisy of religion and discrimination against women, PWC2-021; Abelard, *Story of My Misfortunes*, on his love affair with Héloïse, PWC2-018

Abelard's views were taken up by the leading proponent of scholasticism of the thirteenth century, Thomas Aquinas (*c.* 1225–1274). Born in Italy to a noble family, he became a Dominican friar, wrote extensively, and is widely considered the greatest of the medieval philosophers. His most influential work is the *Summa theologiae*. Aquinas sought to resolve the conflicts between faith and reason, and reason and revelation. He argued that because some aspects of Christian doctrine—such as the immortality of the soul, the existence of God, the Trinity, and the notion of Christ as God who became human—are not empirically (through the five senses) or logically provable, we must go beyond reason and embrace faith. In other words, the knowledge we acquire from our senses leads us to intuit the existence of God and the immortal soul.

Aquinas was the first thinker to propose a systematic reconciliation of Christianity with the philosophy of Aristotle. His aim was not only to resolve the dualisms inherent in the Church—faith, reason, revelation—but also to synthesize the ideas in the Bible and in the writings of Christians, Muslims, and Aristotle. He argued for faith as an absolute and for accepting God's revealed truth. His well-known statement, quoted from Tertullian, *Credo quia absurdum est* ("I believe because it is absurd"), sums up his conviction that reason alone is not sufficient to account for the mysteries of the universe.

READING SELECTION

Aquinas, *Summa theologiae*, on natural law, PWC2-007-C

Thomas Aquinas and the scholastic system of thought were in conflict not only with Abelard but also with Duns Scotus (*c.* 1265–1308). An Oxford-educated Franciscan friar, Duns Scotus challenged Aquinas's synthesis of faith and reason. According to Duns Scotus, Christian mysteries, such as the existence of God and the Holy Ghost, are not provable. Rather, faith was the only route to understanding such mysteries. Duns Scotus proposed the preeminence of free will and the notion that human behavior is determined by a sense of justice, which is a matter of secular reason rather than faith. He argued that people act out of a motivation combining what is good for the individual with the common good.

In these various approaches to understanding the nature of the world, medieval thinkers were attempting to reconcile what they could observe and prove with what seemed inexplicable. They wanted to explicate Church doctrine to the point where there was no further room for questioning. Like the Gothic cathedral, followers of scholasticism combined hierarchy, structural logic, and mysticism with reason. On the other hand, some scholars, such as Peter Abelard and Duns Scotus, resisted the closed scholastic system and sought new ways of thinking about the world. As we will see in the next chapter, these thinkers were laying the foundation for the deeper questioning stance that would lead to the development of the Renaissance.

THE DEVELOPMENT OF GOTHIC STYLE OUTSIDE PARIS

The Gothic style in architecture quickly spread beyond Paris. If we compare the façades of three French cathedrals—at Chartres (begun 1194), at Amiens (begun 1220), and at Reims (façade begun *c.* 1230–1240)—we can see that they share basic structural elements (figures **11.18**, **11.19**, **11.20**). All have triple portal entrances and are divided horizontally and vertically into three sections; two soaring towers flank the center, which contains a rose window.

11.18 Façade of Chartres Cathedral, France, begun 1194.

11.19 Façade of Amiens Cathedral, France, begun 1220.

11.20 Façade of Reims Cathedral, France, begun *c.* 1230–1240.

11.21 Central portal of Chartres Cathedral, France, *c.* 1194.

As the style progresses, the pointed arches become increasingly vertical, the amount of glass increases as the amount of solid wall decreases, and spaces become deeper. There is also much more surface decoration.

In every case, the portals are surrounded by sculptures designed to create a transition from the material world outside to the sacred space inside. Conceived of as the Heavenly Jerusalem on earth, the Gothic cathedral was a vision of eternity in stone and glass. The portal sculptures, for example, were designed to inspire worshippers to deepen their faith. A case in point is the central portal on the entrance façade of Chartres Cathedral (figure **11.21**).

THE CENTRAL PORTAL OF CHARTRES: A VISION OF THE END OF TIME

The sculptures that embellish the center door of Chartres's west façade are divided into two main groups. The vertical figures at the door jambs represent Old Testament kings and queens. The relief sculptures above the door come from St. John the Divine's apocalyptic vision described in Revelation, the last book of the Bible. Christ appears on the tympanum in a mandorla of light, surrounded by the four symbols of the Evangelists—Matthew the angel, Luke the bull, Mark the lion, and John the eagle. Below, on the lintel, are the twelve apostles. Carved on the three archivolts are one set of twelve angels and the twenty-four Elders of the Apocalypse. This is John's vision of the Second Coming of Christ, who returns to earth to judge humanity for all time. He holds a book in his left hand, alluding to the textual basis of his teaching, and blesses with his right.

The typological iconography is based on the notion of prophecy and prefiguration on the one hand and fulfillment on the other (see Chapter 8). Old Testament royalty prefigures Christ the new king and, by extension, Mary the new queen, to whom the cathedral is dedicated. The door jambs and their statues comprise a literal and symbolic foundation on which the New Testament rests. In this case, the end of the world and of time reminds viewers of their own mortality and cautions them to follow the teachings of the Church.

THE CULT OF THE VIRGIN

Although the cult of the Virgin developed in the Romanesque period, it took on new importance in the Gothic period. Chartres had been a pilgrimage site since the ninth century when King Charles II, the Bald, donated a relic of the tunic worn by the Virgin at the Nativity. In the stained glass window known as the *Belle Verrière*—literally, "beautiful stained glass window" (figure **11.22**)—Mary is shown as the Queen of Heaven. She is enthroned and crowned, with the Holy Ghost (the white dove) suspending a halo behind her head. She is the largest and most important figure, befitting her lofty position in the hierarchical structure of the Church. Three angels kneel on either side of her, four swinging censers (incense containers) and two holding large candlesticks. The architectural detail above the Holy Ghost identifies Mary as a symbol of the church building itself.

In this complex iconography, Mary is not only the Queen of Heaven and the church building, she is also the throne of Christ. He, in turn, is suspended between her knees, defying gravity and occupying a flattened, non-material space. His depiction as a miniature man exemplifies the Christian notion of Christ as a miraculous baby-king.

11.22 ***Notre Dame de la Belle Verrière*, Chartres Cathedral, *c.* 1220.**
Stained glass windows were made by fitting together pieces of colored glass and fusing them with lead strips. A few details, such as facial features, were painted in, and the glass sections were set in frames and held in place by vertical and horizontal rods. The rich blues and reds are characteristic of the windows at Chartres.

11.23 ***Vierge dorée* (*The Gilded Virgin*), south portal, Amiens Cathedral, France, *c.* 1250. Stone, over lifesize.**

Another image of the Virgin and Christ, created some thirty years after the *Belle Verrière*, shows an increasing concept of Mary's humanity in her relationship to her son (figure **11.23**). She is still a queen; three angels in a cruciform arrangement support her halo, and an architectural detail appears over her head. Although the symbolism here is similar to that of the *Belle Verrière*, Mary now holds a more baby-like Christ and turns to face him. She responds to him as an infant rather than as a king. There is even the suggestion of a turn at her waist, indicating a human body beneath the clothing. Compared with the regal, hierarchical figures of the *Belle Verrière*, these are more human and interact as would a normal mother and child.

11.24 Cologne Cathedral, Germany, begun 1228, towers planned *c.* 1300 and built *c.* 1350.

LATE GOTHIC: COLOGNE CATHEDRAL

Although Gothic style began in France, it soon spread throughout western Europe, especially to England, Germany, the Netherlands, Italy, and the non-Muslim parts of Spain. The basic French style was retained, but certain national characteristics were added. In some countries, the style lasted for several centuries. In Cologne in Germany, for example, a cathedral was begun in 1228, but its towers were not constructed until around 1350 (figure **11.24**). (The entire cathedral was in fact completed only in the nineteenth century.) The towers demonstrate the Late Gothic taste for tall, thin spires and animated surfaces.

Gothic style became international in scope and expanded beyond Church patronage to regional courts. The courtly Gothic style, called International Gothic, continued in parts of northern Europe well into the fifteenth century.

THEATER AND LITERATURE IN THE GOTHIC PERIOD

From the middle of the eleventh century to around 1300, liturgical drama continued to develop. Mystery, miracle, and morality (*Everyman*) plays were performed inside churches and cathedrals throughout Europe, although in Muslim Spain such drama was forbidden.

According to surviving manuals, plays were acted by males only—either choirboys or members of the clergy. Lines were chanted rather than spoken, generally in Latin. Because the cathedral was considered a microcosm of the universe, it was easily transformed into a vast theatrical environment. The choir loft became the setting for heaven and the underground crypt for hell. Staging used mechanical apparatuses to move the star leading the three kings to Bethlehem, to lower a dove or the angel Gabriel when re-enacting the Annunciation, or to create tongues of flame for Pentecost.

As dramatic productions moved outside the church, liturgical plays began to decline and secular drama expanded. Comedy, as we saw in Chapter 10, grew out of liturgical events such as the Feast of Fools. But the full expansion of comedy would not come until the late Middle Ages, when theater had become more detached from both the liturgy and the church interior.

In literature as in theater, Romanesque themes and genres continued to flourish in the Gothic era, even as new ones developed. In the eleventh century, troubadours recited poetry and wandering minstrels sang *canzoni* (love poems) in Provençal, the language of the south of France. *Canzoni* were popular at the courts, as was the **lay** (*lai*, in French), a short poem sung to the accompaniment of the harp. The earliest surviving lays are by Marie de France (active *c.* 1170), a poet born in Brittany who lived mainly in England. She wrote twelve lays in Old French rhyming couplets. They were inspired by the legends of Lancelot and King Arthur, and their themes were love, infidelity, and moral conflict.

Marie de France also composed *Ysopet*, seventy-five tales based on the ancient Greek fables of Aesop. According to the Greek historian Herodotus (see Chapter 6), Aesop was a slave in sixth-century-B.C. Egypt. His fables, in which the characters are animals rather than people, contain moral messages. Marie de France's *Ysopet* thus reflects her acquaintance with Classical authors.

READING SELECTION

Marie de France, "Lanval" and "Les Deus Amanz" ("The Two Lovers"), PWC2-169

DANTE AND THE *DIVINE COMEDY*

In Italy, Dante Alighieri (1265–1321) wrote the great medieval poem, which he titled *Commedia*, now known as the *Divine Comedy*. It is an epic vision of a journey in three parts through hell (*Inferno*), purgatory (*Purgatorio*), and heaven (*Paradiso*). Each of these three parts of the Christian universe is divided into nine regions. Dante calls his traveler the Pilgrim, although it is clear that the Pilgrim represents the author.

The poem is composed of one hundred *cantos*, thirty-three in each section and a prologue. Dante wrote the *Divine Comedy* in the vernacular (called *volgare* in Italian)—that is, in Italian, not Latin. He used a verse form known in Italian as *terza rima*, in which each stanza has three lines (*terzine*, or tercets) with a rhyme scheme of ABA, BCB, CDC. The line that does not rhyme in one stanza thus recurs and *does* rhyme in the next stanza. For example, the non-rhyming B of ABA rhymes in BCB; then the C, which does not rhyme in BCB, becomes the rhymed line in CDC. This strictly controlled poetic structure reflects the influence of Thomas Aquinas and the hierarchy of scholasticism. The repeated groupings of three also echo the Trinity and the three-part organization of Gothic cathedrals.

Dante was born in Florence, and he was devoted to the city. His family saw to it that he was well educated. He studied rhetoric at the University of Bologna, read Classical and Christian texts, knew the leading intellectuals of his time, and was deeply involved in politics. His marriage to Gemma Donati was arranged by the couple's parents when he was eleven years old and she was around ten. They had three children. In 1302, Dante was exiled from Florence for political reasons.

DANTE AND BEATRICE Dante was nearly ten years old when he first saw Beatrice Portinari, who was about a year younger than he. For the rest of his life he was infatuated with her, and she inspired much of his poetry. Aside from a few passing remarks, Dante and Beatrice were involved only in the poet's imagination, where he raised Beatrice to a level of divine perfection that exists only in myth and art.

In 1287, when she was twenty-one, Beatrice married a member of the wealthy Bardi family and went to live in the countryside. Dante then addressed a number of poems to her, but he was rebuffed and decided to devote himself solely to writing about her. In 1290, when she was twenty-four, Beatrice died and thereafter, for Dante, resided in heaven. In the *Divine Comedy*, it is Beatrice who guides the Pilgrim through paradise and sends Virgil to guide him through hell and purgatory.

THE POEM The *Divine Comedy* was written between about 1308 and 1321, during Dante's exile from Florence. It is, first and foremost, a pilgrimage of the poet's soul. Dante the author writes about Dante the pilgrim, fusing present and future time just as the cathedral expressed both earthly and spiritual time.

The poem is also a rich tapestry of medieval politics, for along the way Dante mentions events in Florentine history and describes encounters with famous political and religious figures, meting out the punishments or rewards he thinks they deserve.

The *Divine Comedy* opens on Good Friday in the year 1300. The events are condensed into a single liturgical week, beginning on the day of the Crucifixion. On Easter Sunday morning, Dante emerges from hell (as Christ rose from the dead) into purgatory. Three days later, on the Wednesday after Easter, Dante enters paradise, and he concludes his journey on Thursday. Throughout, the poet uses the metaphor of light and dark to symbolize good and evil, salvation and damnation, enlightenment and sin, the divine and the primitive, respectively. At the outset of the first *canto*, which opens like a dream, Dante writes:

Midway along the journey of our life
    I woke to find myself in a dark wood,
    for I had wandered off from the straight path.

How hard it is to tell what it was like,
    this wood of wilderness, savage and stubborn
    (the thought of it brings back all my old fears),

a bitter place! Death could scarce be bitterer.
    But if I would show the good that came of it
    I must talk about things other than the good.

(*Inferno*, Canto I, lines 1–9)

Dante sees a figure approaching and asks if he is a shade (ghost) or a living man:

"No longer living man, though once I was,"
    he said, "and my parents were from Lombardy [in
        northern Italy]
    both of them were Mantuans by birth.

I was born, though somewhat late, *sub Julio* [late in the reign
        of Julius Caesar]
    and lived in Rome when good Augustus reigned,
    when still the false and lying [pagan] gods were worshipped.

I was a poet and sang of that just man [Aeneas],
    son of Anchises, who sailed off from Troy
    after the burning of proud Ilium [another name for Troy]."

(Canto I, lines 67–75)

The former man is Virgil, the Roman poet from Mantua and author of the *Aeneid* (see Chapter 7), who will be Dante's guide. Dante thus suggests that his journey through hell is inspired by the journeys of Aeneas and Odysseus, making himself an epic hero traveling through a Christian universe.

THE CIRCLES OF HELL Dante's hell is a hierarchy arranged in descending circles of sin and ascending degrees of punishment. The first circle is Limbo, which is inhabited by the unbaptized, including the great figures of pagan antiquity. In the second circle, Dante sees carnal sinners whirling in eddies of uncontrollable winds. Among them are the famed adulterous lovers Paolo and Francesca, whose romance was inspired by the Arthurian story of Lancelot and Guinevere. The third circle contains gluttons, who are condemned to roll in mud; in the fourth circle are the avaricious (money-hungry), and in the fifth are the wrathful. In the sixth circle, heretics are burned alive. The seventh circle contains people who have committed suicide and those who have sinned against their neighbors and against God, art, and nature.

In the eighth circle, containing the fraudulent, Dante notices dark compartments in which different tortures are carried out. Seducers are whipped by demons, and those who bought their clerical offices are held upside down and the soles of their feet are burned. People guilty of giving evil counsel are engulfed in flames; among them is Odysseus, the wily strategist of the Homeric epics. He is punished in Dante's Christian hell for deceiving the Trojans with the wooden horse (see Chapter 4).

Nearing the lowest depths of hell in the ninth circle, Dante encounters the Lake of the Treacherous. Their sins range from betrayal of family, nations, and guests to treason against lords and benefactors. Among the treacherous, Dante sees one of the most despicable and dramatic figures in Western literature—Count Ugolino of Pisa—who is embedded in ice. Ugolino had been a traitor during his lifetime, and in hell he eats the brain of his partner in treachery, the archbishop Ruggieri. Ugolino had been imprisoned along with his sons, who had died of starvation. In hell, too, Ugolino sees his sons die, and then returns to his own gruesome meal. Dante gives him the words: "hunger proved more powerful than grief" (Canto XXXIII, line 75).

He spoke these words; then, glaring down in rage,
    attacked again the wretched skull with his teeth
    sharp as a dog's, and as fit for grinding bones.

(Canto XXXIII, lines 76–78)

Dante and Virgil finally reach Satan's realm in Canto XXXIV, the conclusion of the *Inferno*. This is the center of the earth, the location of the worst betrayers, including Brutus and Cassius, who betrayed Julius Caesar, and Judas, who betrayed Christ. Satan himself has three heads and is half wedged in ice. Here is Dante's lurid description:

If once he was as fair as now he's foul
    and dared to raise his brows against his Maker,
    it is fitting that all grief should spring from him.

Oh how amazed I was when I looked up
    and saw a head—one head wearing three faces!
    One was in front (and that was a bright red),

the other two attached themselves to this one
    just above the middle of each shoulder,
    and at the crown all three were joined in one:

The right face was a blend of white and yellow,
    the left the color of those people's skin
    who live along the river Nile's descent.

11.25 Detail of Hell, from a mosaic in the vault of the Baptistery. Florence, Italy, 13th century.
In this image, located in the Baptistery of Dante's native Florence, Satan is surrounded by flames and has features similar to the Satan of the *Inferno.* He has a distorted human face with large horns, and two serpents emerge from his ears and thighs. Souls are being chewed, swallowed, and expelled only to suffer the same fate over and over. Some are tortured by dozens of little devils, lizards, and toads, while others are engulfed in flames. At the left, appearing particularly downcast, are a few souls who have just begun to confront their unfortunate future.

Beneath each face two mighty wings stretched out,
the size you might expect of his huge bird
(I never saw a ship with larger sails):

Not feathered wings but rather like the ones
a bat would have. He flapped them constantly . . .

In each of his three mouths he crunched a sinner,
with teeth like those that rake the hemp and flax,
keeping three sinners constantly in pain.

(Canto XXXIV, lines 34–57)

Satan's hideous appearance is the opposite of his former beauty. Whereas he had been Lucifer (God's bearer of light) in heaven, he is now immersed in the darkness of hell. His former beauty has become monstrous, and his angel wings have turned into bat wings. His triple head is an intentional reversal of the Holy Trinity. Satan is thus an eternal, cannibalistic torturer who has sunk to the depths of evil. Such imagery abounded in the Middle Ages, both as a warning to would-be sinners and as a means of rich literary and artistic expression (figure **11.25**).

Having confronted the full force of Satan's hideous nature, Dante is told by Virgil that they must depart. For the first time, at the end of the *Inferno*, the travelers rise rather than descend. They climb through a hole and welcome the sight of the night sky. Each of the three main sections of the *Divine Comedy* ends with the image of a star, denoting a hopeful outcome.

PURGATORY Dante's purgatory is reserved for souls on their way to heaven. They have died in a state of grace but need time, often hundreds of years, to atone for their sins. Purgatory is a mountain island arranged, like hell, in levels, but it begins with the gravest sins at the bottom—pride is the first sin and lust is the last. Now Dante and Virgil are on the ascent. At the summit of purgatory, Virgil can go no further, for it marks the limit of human wisdom and he is among the unbaptized. From here on Dante is in paradise, the site of divine revelation, wisdom, faith, and purity of soul.

Just before the summit of purgatory, Dante is terrified by a wall of flame. Virgil reassures him that the wall is all that separates him from Beatrice and that beyond the wall lies the last stairway to the top of purgatory. Dante and Virgil fall asleep (note that at the opening of the *Inferno*, Dante awoke from sleep) and awaken to ascend the summit.

The conclusion of the *Purgatorio* takes place on the mountaintop and lasts for six *cantos*. Here Dante sees a figure associated with Countess Matilda of Canossa, who had ruled parts of Italy from around 1065 to 1115 and was a patron of the arts (see Chapter 10). She enchants Dante with her singing.

As Matilda fades, a vision of St. John the Divine from the book of Revelation comes into view. The twenty-four Elders parade before him, followed by Ezekiel's vision of the four creatures with six wings (see Chapter 8). Two additional groups, one, dancing personifications of the theological virtues—faith, hope, and charity—and the other of the cardinal virtues—prudence, temperance, justice, and fortitude—surround a chariot. Dante sees that Beatrice rides in the chariot, and he hears angels singing verses from the *Aeneid.* Virgil, denied the vision of paradise for having lived in a pagan era, is forced to depart.

PARADISE Beatrice, who resides in the ninth heaven, takes over from Virgil and guides the poet through paradise, which is based on the seven planets described in medieval astronomy.

These are the Sun and Moon, Mercury, Venus, Mars, Jupiter, and Saturn. Beyond the planets are the fixed stars and, further still, the Empyrean Heavens. This final segment of the *Divine Comedy* opens, like the *Iliad* and the *Odyssey*, with an invocation of the gods and Muses:

> O good Apollo, for this last task, I pray
> you make me such a vessel of your powers
> as you deem worthy to be crowned with bay . . .
>
> O power divine, but lend to my high strain
> so much as will make clear even the shadow
> of that High Kingdom stamped upon my brain,
>
> and you shall see me come to your dear grove
> to crown myself with those green leaves [the poet's laurel]
> and my high theme shall make me worthy of.
>
> (*Paradiso*, Canto I, lines 13–27)

Now Dante is in the realm of visionary light and weightlessness. He no longer climbs against the force of gravity, but ascends the planets from the moon to Saturn, and finally to the ninth sphere—the Empyrean Heavens. He does this without physical effort or travel time, listening along the way to the Platonic music of the spheres (see Chapter 6). Throughout the *Paradiso*, Dante is struck by the power of God's divine light that pervades the heavens. As in hell and purgatory, Dante meets historical personages; but now they are immaterial spirits. Among these are the Roman emperor Constantine, the Byzantine emperor Justinian, the Dominican Thomas Aquinas, and St. Benedict, whose monastic rule spread throughout Europe. Higher spheres are inhabited by the apostles, Christ, the Virgin Mary, and the hierarchy of angels.

At the summit of paradise, Dante again receives a new guide, St. Bernard of Clairvaux. Bernard shows the poet his last vision of Beatrice, who resumes her place at God's eternal fountain. Bernard had been a most devoted follower of the Virgin, and the fact that he is Dante's guide demonstrates the power of Mary's cult in the Middle Ages. Dante has Bernard name the Virgin

> The Queen of Heaven, for whom in whole devotion
> I burn with love, will grant us every grace
> because I am Bernard, her faithful one.
>
> (Canto XXXI, lines 101–103)

Thematic Parallels

Views of Paradise

Most religions have a view of life after death. But the image of that life, whether based on reward and punishment as in Christianity, or a more neutral view, varies. Paradise is generally the destination of those who are rewarded for a lifetime of faith and good works. But this too differs according to a particular religion and, to some extent, according to the culture in which that religion arose. For example, in Greek mythology there is no paradise or immortality for ordinary mortals. These are the province of the gods and the Muses, with the exception of Heracles, who was admitted to Mount Olympos. Indeed, one of the reasons Christianity appealed to the pagan Mediterranean world was its promise of paradise for the faithful.

In Norse myth, paradise is Valhalla—the destination of brave warriors who await Ragnarök, the battle at the end of time. This image is consistent with Viking warrior society.

In Hinduism, first practiced in India, there is no paradise in the Western sense. Instead there is nirvana (a state of perfect bliss). Most Hindus believe in reincarnation, which is a cycle of rebirth depending on one's behavior in a previous life. Related to the strict caste system of India, reincarnation accounts for one's birth into a particular level of society—Brahmins, the spiritual and social elite, are at the top. Each class is seen as merely one step in the long cycle of reincarnation, which ends with release from the cycle. When Hindus attain nirvana, their souls become one with the cosmos, and they are freed from the material constraints of the world. Outside the caste system are the Untouchables, or "outcastes."

When Buddhism originated in India in the sixth century B.C., the notion of nirvana was adopted. Later, however, around the fifth century A.D., a number of sects arose that sought to avoid the repeated cycles of rebirth and to simplify the route to nirvana. These sects promised an afterlife in a splendid paradise, which could be attained directly through faith rather than having to endure several lifetimes of reincarnation.

Muslims, like Christians, believe that the end of the world will come and that there will be a final judgment according to the way one has lived life. The Qur'an describes the last day as filled with noise and disruption. Those who have led a good life will be rewarded with an afterlife of pleasure, whereas those whose lives are found wanting will be committed to a dark abyss (or hell). In contrast to Christianity, however, Muslim souls are not eternally damned. They spend time in hell according to the amount and nature of their sins but can eventually enter heaven. Only heretics burn forever in hell. According to the Qur'an, paradise is a lush garden, flowing with rivers and filled with fruit, flowers, and beautiful virgins. A more mystical view interprets heaven as closeness to God and a state of eternal spiritual well-being. The Islamic paradise is not necessarily high up in the heavens, but can be interpreted as being on a transformed earth.

READING SELECTION

The Qur'an, on infidels burning in hell and dark-eyed virgins attending the faithful in heaven, PWC2-220

Bernard asks the Virgin to intercede on behalf of Dante so that he might see God. The vision of God swells Dante's soul, but he cannot describe it, for human words are dark compared to God's light. He concludes the *Paradiso* with the following verse:

> Here my powers rest from their high fantasy,
> but already I could feel my being turned—
> instinct and intellect balanced equally
>
> as in a wheel whose motion nothing jars—
> by the Love that moves the Sun and the other stars.
>
> (Canto XXXIII, lines 142–146)

Dante is considered the most important figure in Italian literature, and his influence on later Western authors has been enormous. The *Divine Comedy* is the poetic equivalent of the *Summa* of Thomas Aquinas. But Dante's creation is imaginative—a personal, historical, and artistic vision—whereas Aquinas's *Summa* is a compendium of his philosophical and theological thought. Dante's poetry, like the Gothic cathedral, gives concrete expression to the universe of the Christian spirit. It also embodies Suger's notion that the arts, the experience of the senses, and human creativity are ways of understanding the divine. Dante's poetry is as rich in metaphor and allusion as Suger's church was in gold, gemstones, stained glass, and light.

READING SELECTION

Dante, *Divine Comedy*, Vol. 1, *Inferno*: Canto I, Dante begins his journey through hell and meets Virgil, PWC2-022-B; Canto III, the gates of hell, PWC2-023-B; Canto V, Paolo and Francesca, PWC2-024

In Italy, Dante and the Divine Comedy *can be seen as occupying a pivotal place in the gradual transition from the Middle Ages to the early Renaissance period. On the one hand, he writes in the hierarchical tradition of the medieval scholastics and on the other he conveys a sharp sense of personality and history. In addition, by choosing Virgil as the guide on his epic journey, he heralds the fourteenth-century revival of Classical texts that would propel Italy and, later, parts of northern Europe into a new era.*

KEY TERMS

Beghards in medieval northern Europe, a group of lay men dedicated to leading a spiritual life and working for the community.

Beguines in medieval northern Europe, a group of lay women who established spiritual centers.

discant in medieval music, a style in which the lower, tenor voice sings in a steady rhythm, while one or more higher voices sing slightly faster melodies above.

friar a member of a mendicant ("begging") Order.

gallery a row of figures.

Inquisitors officials appointed by the Roman Church to combat heresy.

lancet a tall, narrow arched window.

lay a short poem, sung to the accompaniment of a harp.

master-builder one who supervises the building of a cathedral.

mendicant a member of a religious order who wandered from town to town begging.

motet a polyphonic choral work, generally written in Latin for church performance; some early motets were secular and multilingual.

nominalism in philosophy, the belief that universals (general ideas, abstract concepts) are nothing more than names; the opposite of realism.

Poor Clares nuns who belong to the Order of Abbess Clare.

radiating chapels chapels placed around an ambulatory.

rayonnant a style in Gothic rose windows in which shapes of glass radiate from the small circle at the center.

realism in philosophy, the belief that universals (general ideas, abstract concepts) have an objective existence; the opposite of nominalism.

rib vault a vault made by the intersection of pointed arches.

rose window a large, round window in Gothic Cathedrals.

scholasticism a system of thought developed in the Gothic period that addressed the apparent contradiction of faith and reason.

stained glass pieces of colored glass held in place in windows by strips of lead.

stigmata marks resembling Christ's wounds on the Cross.

template a diagram of an architectural section used by master-builders.

transubstantiation in the Mass, a process in which bread and wine are believed to be transformed literally into Christ's body and blood.

KEY QUESTIONS

1. What document was the first to recognize that kings as well as their subjects had moral and social responsibilities and were subject to certain laws?
2. Explain the relationship between the crusades, the concept of heresy, and the Inquisition.
3. Whose ideas about light and color launched the Gothic style? What were these ideas, and how does the construction of the Gothic cathedral illustrate them?
4. Summarize the controversy between the realists and the nominalists.
5. Who was the first thinker to propose a systematic reconciliation of Christianity with the philosophy of Aristotle? Summarize what the statement *Credo quia absurdum est* means and how it relates to this reconciliation.

SUGGESTED READING

Baldwin, J. W. *The Scholastic Culture of the Middle Ages: 1000–1300*. New York: Houghton Mifflin, 1971.
▸ A discussion of medieval scholasticism.

Branner, Robert. *Chartres Cathedral*, New York: Norton, 1969.
▸ A classic study of the cathedral: style and iconography.

Burge, James. *Héloïse and Abelard: A New Biography*. San Francisco: HarperSanFrancisco, 2004.
▸ An account of the famous medieval romance.

Camille, Michael. *Gothic Art: Glorious Visions*. New York: Harry N. Abrams, 1996.
▸ A survey of Gothic art in Europe.

Clanchy, M. T. *Abelard: A Medieval Life*, Oxford: Blackwell Publishers, 1997.
▸ A biography of Abelard.

Dante. *The Inferno of Dante*, trans. Robert Pinsky. New York: Farrar, Straus and Giroux, 1996.
▸ A modern verse translation juxtaposed with the original.

Follet, Ken. *Pillars of the Earth*. London: Pan Books, 1990.
▸ A historical novel about the lives and families of cathedral builders, by an author of popular thrillers.

Gilson, Etienne. *Héloïse and Abelard*. Ann Arbor, MI: University of Michigan Press, 1960.
▸ A discussion of the story of Héloïse and Abelard in its social context.

Herlihy, D. *Medieval Households*. Cambridge, MA: Harvard University Press, 1985.
▸ Everyday life in the Middle Ages.

Hollister, C. Warren. *Medieval Europe*. New York: McGraw-Hill, 1997.
▸ A general survey of the period.

The Lais of Marie de France, trans. R. Hanning and J. Ferrante. Durham: Labyrinth Press, 1982.
▸ A modern translation in free verse of the *lais* of Marie de France.

Mâle, Emile. *Religious Art in France: the 13th Century—A Study of Medieval Iconography and its Sources*. Princeton, NJ: Princeton University Press, 1984.
▸ A classic study of Gothic iconography.

Panofsky, Erwin. *Gothic Architecture and Scholasticism*. New York: Meridian Books/London: Thames and Hudson, 1957.
▸ On the relationship between Gothic architecture and scholastic thought.

——. *Abbot Suger on the Abbey Church of St. Denis and its Art Treasures*, Princeton, NJ: Princeton University Press, 1979.
▸ An account of Suger's innovations and the origin of Gothic style.

Shahar, S. *The Fourth Estate: A History of Women in the Middle Ages*. London: Methuen, 1983.
▸ On the roles and lifestyles of medieval women.

Stock, B. *The Implications of Literacy*. London: Methuen, 1983.
▸ The effect of literacy on the Middle Ages.

Voelkle, William. *The Stavelot Triptych: Mosan Art and the Legend of the True Cross*. New York: The Pierpont Morgan Library, 1980.
▸ A monograph on one of the central reliquaries of medieval art.

Von Simpson, Otto. *The Gothic Cathedral: Origins of Gothic Architecture and the Medieval Concept of Order*. Princeton, NJ: Princeton University Press, 1988.
▸ A study of the sources of Gothic style in the context of medieval thought.

SUGGESTED FILMS

1938 *Alexander Nevsky*, dir. Sergei Eisenstein
1950 *The Black Rose*, dir. Henry Hathaway
1950 *Francis, God's Jester* (*The Flowers of St. Francis*), dir. Roberto Rossellini
1961 *Francis of Assisi*, dir. Michael Curtiz
1971 *Blanche*, dir. Walerian Borowczyk
1972 *Brother Sun, Sister Moon*, dir. Franco Zeffirelli
1986 *The Name of the Rose*, dir. Jean-Jacques Arnaud
1993 *Anchoress*, dir. Chris Newby
1993 *Francesco*, dir. Liliana Cavani
1993 *The Hour of the Pig*, dir. Leslie Megahey

12 The Transition from Gothic to Early Renaissance: 1300–1450

"*The impulse to make the climb . . . took hold of me while I was reading Livy's History of Rome . . . and I happened upon the place where Philip of Macedon . . . climbed Mount Haemus in Thessaly . . . I could see the clouds under our feet, and the tales I had read of Athos and Olympus seemed less incredible as I myself was witnessing the very same things from a less famous mountain.*"

(PETRARCH, *Familiares*, BK. 4.1)

The fourteenth century was a period of sharp contrast and transition in art, literature, and music, as well as in society. In art, the Gothic style expanded in some regions and declined in others. Authors increasingly depicted everyday life, and composers wrote more secular music than before. Cities continued to grow, guilds became more powerful, and a significant merchant class developed. At the same time, however, Europe struggled with a series of catastrophes. War and famine ravaged the countryside, peasant rebellions eroded the feudal and manorial systems, banks failed, and plagues wiped out a large percentage of the population.

New challenges to the authority of the Church arose not only from theologians and scholars but also from ambitious kings. As political power became more centralized under aggressive rulers, a sense of national identity emerged. This was reinforced by the increasing use of the vernacular in literature and theater.

On the Italian peninsula, which was culturally and geographically identified with Rome, a new interest in the Classical tradition appeared in the late thirteenth century, and in the following two centuries it became the basis of a complex intellectual and artistic trend called **humanism**. *With the Classical revival, Italy led Europe into the Renaissance.*

The quotation that opens this chapter embodies the transition from the Middle Ages to the early Renaissance in Italy. It comes from the Italian author Francesco Petrarca (Petrarch, in English; 1304–1374). On reading Livy's History of Rome *(see Chapter 7), Petrarch felt impelled to climb Mount Ventoux, in the south of France. There, exhilarated by the vista below, Petrarch recalls the past. In a single moment, the view from the French mountain reminds him of three mountains famous in antiquity: Mount Haemus (scaled by Philip of Macedon, the father of Alexander the Great), Mount Athos (the site of a Byzantine monastery), and Mount Olympos (the home of the Greek gods). Petrarch's rapturous response to nature and antiquity exemplifies the ideals of the humanist movement and heralds Renaissance culture.*

Key Topics

Religion and Politics

- Hundred Years War
- Popes and princes compete for power
- The Great Schism: popes and antipopes
- The Ciompi rebellion

Philosophy

- William of Ockham's razor
- John Wycliffe questions transubstantiation
- The humanist movement

Style and Iconography

- Dance of Death
- Classical revival
- Cimabue and Giotto
- Ambrogio Lorenzetti
- Andrea da Firenze

Literature

- Chaucer
- Christine de Pisan
- Petrarch
- Boccaccio

Music

- *Ars nova*
- Machaut
- Landini

TIMELINE	LATE MIDDLE AGES 1300–1450	EARLY RENAISSANCE IN ITALY 1300–1450
HISTORY AND CULTURE 	Rise in urban populations Guilds become more powerful Increase in international trade Bubonic plague devastates Europe, 1348 Political power more centralized under kings Peasant revolts in France, 1356, and England, 1381 Ciompi rebellion in Italy, 1378 Hundred Years War (1337–1453) between England and France	Emergence of humanism Interest in original Latin and Greek texts Revival of Classical tradition New educational curriculum developed Italy divided into regions with courts, monarchies, and republics
RELIGION	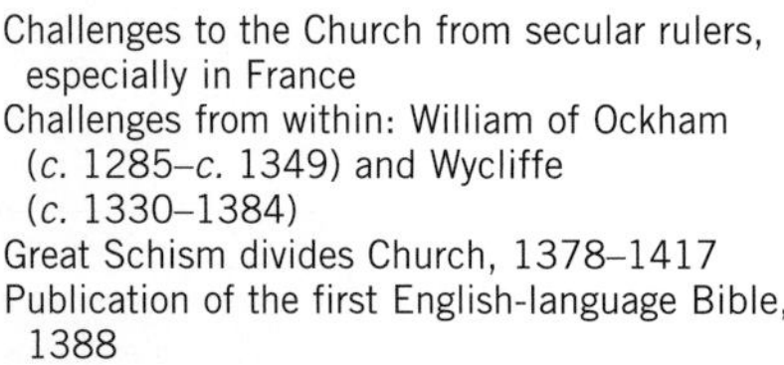Challenges to the Church from secular rulers, especially in France Challenges from within: William of Ockham (*c.* 1285–*c.* 1349) and Wycliffe (*c.* 1330–1384) Great Schism divides Church, 1378–1417 Publication of the first English-language Bible, 1388	Scholasticism persists The effects of the plague
ART 	Pisano, *Adoration of the Magi*, *c.* 1260 Cimabue, *Enthroned Madonna and Child*, *c.* 1285 Traini, *Triumph of Death*, 1330s Limbourg brothers, *Très riches heures du duc de Berry*, *c.* 1415	Giotto, *Enthroned Madonna*, *c.* 1310; Arena Chapel frescoes, *c.* 1305–1310 Duccio, *Maestà*, 1308–1311 Lorenzetti, Palazzo Publico frescoes, 1338–1339 Andrea da Firenze, *Triumph of St. Thomas Aquinas*, *c.* 1365
ARCHITECTURE	Palazzo Publico, Siena, completed 1309 House of Jacques Coeur, Bourges, 1443–1451	
LITERATURE AND PHILOSOPHY 	Chaucer, *Canterbury Tales*, *c.* 1386 Christine de Pisan, *Book of the City of Ladies*, 1405	Petrarch, *Africa*, 1343 Boccacio, *Decameron*, 1349–1351
THEATER	Folk comedy introduced into liturgical drama Wakefield Master, *The Second Shepherds' Play*, early 15th century Plays begin to be set in the present Theater becomes more independent of the Church	Mussato, *Ecerinis,* 1314
MUSIC 	Development of *ars nova*, 14th century Music becomes increasingly secular Machaut (*c.* 1300–1377), *Mass of Notre Dame*, secular songs	Landini (*c.* 1325–1397), secular love-songs

THE LATE MIDDLE AGES

The late Middle Ages witnessed an increase in international trade that promoted the economies of medieval cities. At the same time, many peasants renounced farming, preferring to work for hard currency rather than in exchange for low-level subsistence. Some, recognizing that new opportunities were opening up in towns, set out to learn a trade. Larger numbers of skilled laborers increased the economic power of the guilds, which also benefited as their members demanded a role in the political life of the city.

A merchant class developed as enterprising individuals took advantage of the opportunities in trade and commerce. To facilitate the new merchant economy and to regulate the workday, clocks, which were invented in the thirteenth century, were installed in the major cities. No longer were church bells the primary markers of time.

Along with a rise in urban populations, the growth of monumental church architecture, which had begun in the Romanesque period, continued. In addition, secular building increasingly included hospitals, orphanages, and public bath houses (which required bringing in water supplies). Guildhalls and town halls also sprang up. After 1300, secular universities supplanted cathedral schools as the primary centers of higher learning, and they attracted more students to the cities. Bridges and paved roads made travel and trade easier.

But urbanization brought its own problems. Fires destroyed houses made of wood, crime was on the rise, and disease became more prevalent, especially in crowded areas. In Venice, the first public houses of prostitution opened in 1360.

Causing further disruption in the late Middle Ages, workers began staging social protests. Many demanded better pay and more political rights. In 1356, for example, French peasants revolted against excessive taxation levied on them by wealthy landowners. In Italy, the Ciompi rebellion of 1378 was the most important of several workers' revolts. Wool-workers in Florence, the Ciompi—like their counterparts in Germany and France—wanted membership in the guilds and access to guild privileges. The Ciompi were successful, and three new guilds were established for wool-workers, making them eligible for political office and improving their social status (see Box). Three years after the Ciompi rebellion, peasants in England rose up against laws that kept them bound to landowners. Indirectly, their anger was fueled by a religion that preached submission and poverty while ambitious popes sought worldly power and enriched the Church.

Society and Culture

The Wool Industry in Florence

In the fourteenth century, the most sophisticated textile production was located in Florence, in Tuscany. High-quality English wool and dyes were imported and used in the manufacture of cloth. Workers washed the wool in the Arno, the river that runs through Florence, and sent the clean wool to the countryside for carding, combing, and spinning. Carding and combing cleaned the fibers and removed knots from the threads to prepare them for spinning. The spun wool was then returned to weavers in the city. Wool was dyed in separate workshops, fulled in nearby mills, and then packaged for export.

In the thirteenth century, the spinning wheel, which had previously been used in the East, was brought to Europe. In figure **12.1**, the spindle is hand-held instead of being attached to a wheel. The woman at the lower right combs the wool, the central figure holds two cards (flat boards with sharp projections), and the third works a hand spindle. At the top, a fourth woman weaves on a loom. Patterns on the wall and floor allude to those created by cloth-makers, particularly the weavers.

12.1 ***Carding, spinning, and weaving,*** **from Boccaccio, *Le Livre des cleres et nobles femmes*, early 15th century. Manuscript illustration, 2⅝ in. (6.6 cm) wide. British Library, London.**

THE HUNDRED YEARS WAR

The late Middle Ages unfolded against the backdrop of a long and devastating war between England and France. Called the Hundred Years War, it was actually fought from 1337 to 1453. At dispute were the succession to the French throne and the control of territory and industry in northern Europe.

In 1328, the French king Charles IV died leaving no heir to the throne. The English king, Edward III (ruled 1327–1377), then fifteen years old, was the grandson of Philip IV, the Fair, of France. On the grounds of his heritage, at a time when the immediate French successors had died out, Edward claimed the French throne. But the French nobility and Church instead appointed Philip VI, a member of the Valois dynasty (to which Philip IV had belonged). Philip VI ruled from 1328 to 1350, and the Valois remained on the French throne for nearly three hundred years.

Joan of Arc

Although Joan of Arc, Jeanne d'Arc in French (1412–1431), lived in the fifteenth century, she is essentially a figure of the late Middle Ages. She was born to a peasant family in the French village of Domrémy during the Hundred Years War. As an illiterate girl of twelve, she heard voices from God instructing her to remain a virgin and rescue France from the English. This meant defending Charles VII's claim to the French throne. When she was seventeen, Joan persuaded a neighboring lord to present her to the king. At first, the king doubted that her voices were really sent by God, but his cause seemed doomed, so he was willing to try anything and agreed to equip her with armor and weapons. She rode into battle with the French troops at Orléans, giving them a new sense of national pride and inspiring them to victory. In Reims, she personally crowned Charles king.

Joan's subsequent battles were less successful, and in 1430 she was captured by the Burgundians (English allies from Burgundy, in central France), sold to the English, and handed over to the Inquisition in Rouen, in northern France. Charles did nothing to help her. The transcript of her trial has survived, showing that she was questioned about her voices, accused of heresy, witchcraft, idolatry, and transvestitism, and tortured. Condemned as a heretic, she was burned at the stake in the public square of Rouen.

Very much too late—in 1456—King Charles reviewed Joan's trial and declared her innocent. In 1920, Pope Benedict XV made Joan a saint. The appeal of her story has inspired many literary works, including Christine de Pisan's hymn (1429), George Bernard Shaw's play *Saint Joan* (1923), and several twentieth-century films.

England and France also vied for control of Flanders (modern Belgium, Holland, and part of northern France) and its profitable wool industry. Battles ravaged the countryside and mercenary soldiers looted villages. Peasants who survived the war often lost their homes and animals. Adding to the number of deaths among both the combatants and the civilians was the use of gunpowder. It had been known in China as early as the third century B.C., was perfected in the Far East by A.D. 1000, and by 1313 traders had imported large amounts of it to Europe.

As the Hundred Years War continued into the early decades of the fifteenth century, it looked as if France had lost. But unexpected help arrived in 1429 when a young peasant, Joan of Arc, rallied the dispirited French troops and defeated the English at the Battle of Orléans, a city south of Paris (see Box). The English were forced to renounce most of their claim to French land, which made France more secure. In the end, France and England consolidated their national boundaries as growing nationalist sentiments on both sides reinforced their long-standing animosity, and both countries established strong, centralized monarchies.

CONFLICT IN THE CHURCH

Challenges to the Church were another source of unrest in the late Middle Ages. In the fourteenth century, these challenges were both political and philosophical. Secular rulers, particularly the French king, objected to the political claims of the pope. In addition, two English philosophers, William of Ockham and John Wycliffe, took issue with prevailing Church thought.

THE GREAT SCHISM Boniface VIII was elected pope in 1294. Six years later, in 1300, he proclaimed a Jubilee Year (Holy Year). Thousands of pilgrims, drawn by the promise of pardon for their sins, flocked to Rome, where the spectacle of large crowds created the impression that the city, the papacy, and Boniface himself were comfortably in power. But Boniface's political ambitions threatened Philip IV, the Fair, of France, who ordered the pope's death (see Chapter 11). Philip then saw to it that Boniface's successor was a Frenchman, Clement V (papacy 1305–1314). In 1309, Clement moved the papal court from Rome to Avignon, a city in the south of modern France, which at the time belonged to the Angevin king of Naples. With the papacy now in Avignon, it was strongly influenced by France.

The popes remained at Avignon for nearly seventy years (from 1309 to 1377), a period that came to be known as the Church's "Babylonian Captivity"—a reference to the Babylonian exile of the Israelites (see Chapter 8). Finally, in 1377, the Avignon pope Gregory XI (papacy 1370–1378) returned to Rome. When Gregory died, the College of Cardinals elected an Italian pope, Urban VI (papacy 1378–1389).

Soon after his election, Urban tried to curtail the power of the cardinals (Church officials appointed by the pope). In return, the cardinals—who were mainly Frenchmen—claimed that Roman mobs had forced them to elect Urban because he was Italian. The cardinals then elected a new pope, Clement VI (papacy 1378–1397), who was French. Now there were two popes, one claiming authority from Avignon and the other from Rome, causing the division in the Church known as the Great Schism.

The popes struggled for control for the next thirty-five years, until the Avignon pope John XXIII convened the Council of Constance (1414–1418) in Switzerland at the instigation of Sigismund, who had become Holy Roman Emperor in 1411. Determined to reform the Church, combat heresy, and end the Great Schism, the council elected Martin V (papacy 1417–1431) and returned the papal court to Rome. The Avignon popes, called **antipopes**, were never legitimized in the eyes of the Roman Church, and the papacy in Rome continued to abuse its office by seeking wealth and secular power.

PHILOSOPHICAL CHALLENGES TO THE CHURCH As the Church faced external political threats, tensions increased from within. The English philosopher William of Ockham (*c.* 1285–*c.* 1349) was, like Duns Scotus (see Chapter 11), an Oxford-educated Franciscan friar, who took issue with Thomas Aquinas. Ockham denied the existence of universals except as they are constructed by the human mind. He also disagreed that a divine spark could ignite faith and an understanding of God. Nor did he accept the relationship between faith and reason that Aquinas proposed. Rather, he thought that these were completely separate.

In Ockham's view, facts could be determined only from empirical observation and should not be taken on pure faith. This idea was, of course, an attack on the unquestioned authority of the Church. At the University of Paris, Ockham openly challenged the scholastic realists. He considered their ideas needlessly complex, especially the **syllogistic** system of Aquinas, in which a formal argument is analyzed according to a major and minor premise and a conclusion that follows logically from them. He argued the merits of shaving down every issue to its simplest form, a concept known as **Ockham's razor**. Ockham's emphasis on experience was, in part, inspired by the ideas of St. Francis, and he was excommunicated for advocating the Franciscan rule of poverty at a time when the Church sought more and more wealth and power.

Another influential fourteenth-century Englishman was John Wycliffe (*c.* 1330–1384), who taught at Oxford University. Objecting to the rampant corruption of the Church and rejecting scholasticism, he preferred the simplicity of the Bible's message over the dialectic of theologians. Furthermore, he questioned the infallibility of the pope and denied the doctrine of transubstantiation (the belief that the wafer and wine are transformed into Christ's body and blood during Mass). The Eucharist, he argued, should be understood symbolically and spiritually, and he dismissed the Church's literal view as pure superstition.

Wycliffe was condemned, but not otherwise punished, by the Church because he was protected by the duke of Lancaster, John of Gaunt. Later he was accused of having incited the English Peasants' Revolt of 1381 and was forced to retire from teaching. Nonetheless, he continued preaching until the end of his life. When Gaunt died, Wycliffe was posthumously convicted of heresy, and his corpse was exhumed and burned. One result of Wycliffe's influence and his appeal to the common people was the publication of the first English-language Bible.

THE BLACK DEATH

By 1346, Europe had received news of a virulent plague raging in the Far East and spreading through the Middle East. The following year, ships from the East brought rats carrying infected fleas to Sicily. From there, the plague spread through mainland ports of Italy to overcrowded cities. A panicked population fled to the countryside, carrying the infection with them. The so-called Black Death would ravage Europe for the next several years (see map 12.1, p. 305).

Even before the arrival of the Black Death, parts of Europe from Spain to Scandinavia were suffering severe food shortages. A number of harvests had failed, and bad weather with little sunshine (needed for evaporation) limited salt production. Without salt, meat could not be preserved. At the worst, famine led to a few documented instances of cannibalism. Several important Italian banks failed, which caused severe economic problems. Meanwhile, the plague tore across Europe, and by the time it subsided a huge percentage of the population of Europe had died (see Box, p. 304).

Reactions to the plague vacillated between a *carpe diem* (seize the day and enjoy life) attitude and a fervent belief that penance and atonement were the only routes to salvation. In the absence of medical knowledge, the plague was attributed to astrological occurrences, polluted water, an angry God, heretics, Arabs and other foreigners, and people with deformities or leprosy. In Germany, Jews were blamed for the epidemic and thousands were massacred (figure **12.2**).

One result of the Black Death was a new interest in medicine. Another was increased religious fervor and a preoccupation with death. At the height of the plague, a belief that the dead danced on their graves to entice the living intensified. This is reflected in the popular image of the *danse macabre*, or Dance of Death, which was a feature of many fourteenth-century theatrical productions.

12.2 The burning of lepers as mass poisoners on behalf of the Jews, from *Chroniques de France ou de St. Denis*, late 14th century. Manuscript illumination, 7 in (17.8 cm) wide. British Library, London.
Even before the Black Death, Jews were accused of using lepers to poison wells owned by Christians (leprosy cannot in fact be transmitted via water). In this illustration from a French manuscript, lepers are burned at the stake as punishment for allegedly spreading the plague.

Defining Moment

Plague Devastates Europe

Plague is a great equalizer, killing rich and poor alike. Some scholars argue that the plague of 1348 altered the economic and social structures of Europe and led to the rise of cities, capitalism, and belief in individual freedom. Others argue that the arts witnessed a conservative backlash in Italy, from which art styles did not recover until around 1400. Some who survived the plague began to question traditional beliefs, and a new skeptical attitude toward the Church emerged. Some adopted a philosophy of enjoying life while there was still time. And others became fearful and more devout.

The Black Death, according to some accounts, arose in Asia by around 1346 and was brought to Europe from the Genoese trading station of Kaffa in the Crimea (on the coast of the Black Sea). Another account suggests that the Mongols were besieging Kaffa when disease broke out among their forces and compelled them to abandon the siege. This account further says that the Mongol commander catapulted some of the plague victims into the town. As soon as the Mongols had departed, merchants who left Kaffa for Constantinople carried the plague with them. It then spread from Constantinople along the trade routes to Italy. Another version of the origins of the Black Death attributes it to an outbreak of the plague in China. In October 1347, several Italian merchant ships returned from the Black Sea, one of the key trade links to China. When the ships docked in Sicily, many of those on board were already dying.

Plague mainly affected rodents, but fleas also transmitted the disease to people, who, once infected, rapidly communicated it to others. Symptoms included high fever, vomiting, hemorrhaging, and a painful swelling (or bubo, hence the term "bubonic plague") of glands and lymph nodes. Bleeding under the skin produced spots that were red at first and then turned black (hence the name "Black Death"). Contemporary chroniclers observed different symptoms but did not know that they were part of the same disease. A pneumonic form spread into the lungs and caused vomiting of blood. Another form, called septicemia, was caused by bacilli entering the bloodstream. A rash appeared within hours, and death occurred in a day, even before the swellings appeared. Boccaccio, in the Introduction to the *Decameron*, wrote of the devastation caused by the plague in Florence, and of the speed with which it took people to their death:

What more remains to be said, except that the cruelty of heaven (and possibly, in some measure, also that of man) was so immense and so devastating that between March and July of the year in question, what with the fury of the pestilence and the fact that so many of the sick were inadequately cared for or abandoned in their hour of need because the healthy were too terrified to approach

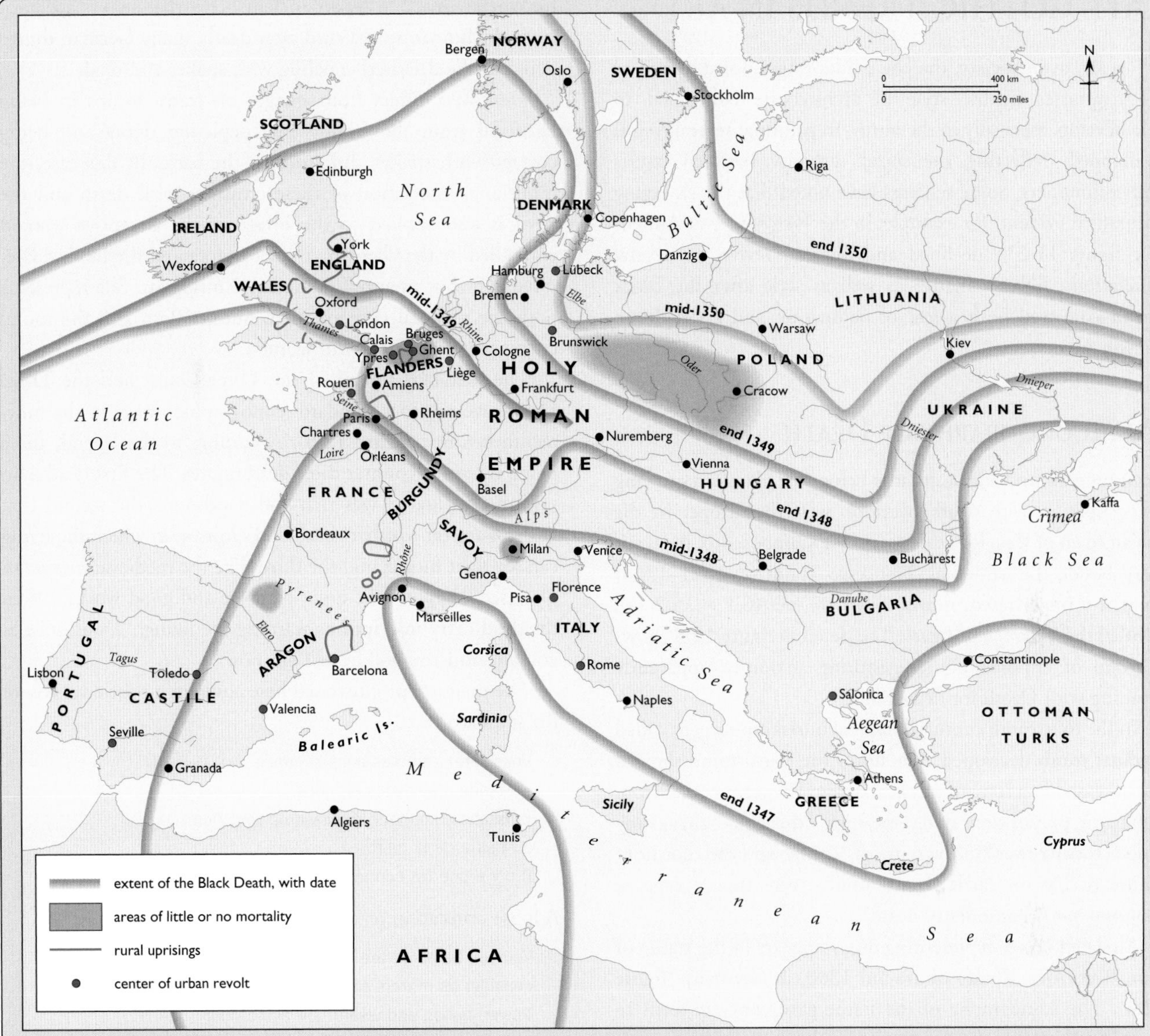

Map 12.1 The Black Death in fourteenth-century Europe.

them, it is reliably thought that over a hundred thousand human lives were extinguished within the walls of the city of Florence? Yet before this lethal catastrophe fell upon the city, it is doubtful whether anyone would have guessed it contained so many inhabitants.

Ah, how great a number of splendid palaces, fine houses, and noble dwellings, once filled with retainers, with lords and with ladies, were bereft of all who had lived there, down to the tiniest child! How numerous were the famous families, the vast estates, the notable fortunes, that were seen to be left without a rightful successor! How many gallant gentlemen, fair ladies, and sprightly youths, who would have been judged hale and hearty by Galen, Hippocrates, and Aesculapius (to say nothing of others), having breakfasted in the morning with their kinfolk, acquaintances, and friends, supped that same evening with their ancestors in the next world!

(Boccaccio, *Decameron*, Introduction)

In the winter of 1348, the disease seemed to disappear, but only because fleas were dormant. The following spring, the plague attacked again, killing new victims. After five years 25 million people were dead—one-third of Europe's population in the fourteenth century (map **12.1**).

The death of such a large proportion of the population tore apart the existing economic and social structures. A shortage of peasants and laborers caused wages to rise as peasants and serfs gained greater bargaining power. For the first time in history, wealthy landlords were at the mercy of those who survived and were healthy enough to work their land. Without the many architects, masons, and artisans who had been killed by the plague, cathedrals and castles remained unfinished for decades. Governments lacked officials, since priests and scholars were in short supply, ancient manuscripts were put to one side, and documents began to be written in the vernacular.

Critical Question What is cognitive dissonance? Does it take an extreme event to cause cognitive dissonance or does it often happen when ideas conflict?

LATE GOTHIC TRENDS IN ART

In art, as in society, the late Middle Ages was a period of contrasts. Gothic style in architecture continued to develop, especially in the north. In painting, several trends overlapped, reflecting the social disparity between courts and commoners. Some scholars have noted that the emerging naturalism evident, for example, in the *Vierge dorée* at Amiens (see figure 11.23), declined and did not revive for several generations. Subject matter as well as style after the Black Death conveyed both a fear of damnation and a delight in worldly luxury.

THE ICONOGRAPHY OF DEATH

Beginning around 1300, decades before the plague, a growing preoccupation with death overtook western Europe. In the Italian town of Pisa, for example, in the Camposanto, the cemetery beside the cathedral, Francesco Traini (*c.* 1321–1363) painted a huge fresco, nearly 20 by 50 feet (6.1 × 15.2 m), entitled the *Triumph of Death*. The detail in figure **12.3** shows a group of crippled figures gesturing anxiously, apparently pleading with Death for deliverance.

In the fourteenth century, a type of burial monument called a **transi tomb** developed. The lid of the transi tomb showed the deceased in a state of physical decay. The term comes from the Latin preposition *trans*, meaning "through," suggesting both "crossing over" in the sense of "dying" and the transitory nature of life on earth. Transi tombs were thus a type of *memento mori* (reminder of death).

A related image representing decay appears in the statue of *Frau Welt* (*Mrs. World*) of around 1300, in Germany (figure **12.4**). The iconography of the statue gave concrete form to fire-and-brimstone sermons warning that unrepentant souls would suffer the fires of hell, and all flesh would become food for worms. Inspired by an ancient belief that snakes are born from the human spinal cord after death, many German tombs depicted the deceased crawling with snakes and toads.

Frau Welt differs from images on transi tombs in being beautiful from the front while depicting decay and being covered with snakes and toads at the back. In this case, the traditional association of these creatures with death and the devil is also applied to the image of the deceptive woman embodied by the Greek myth of Pandora and the biblical Eve. *Frau Welt* thus exemplifies medieval misogyny. She represents both the physical corruption of human flesh and the moral corruption associated with women.

The medieval legend of the Three Quick and the Three Dead gave rise to a standard iconographic image in the fourteenth century (figure **12.5**). According to the legend, three living figures encounter three dead figures. The first dead man says that in life he was rich and handsome; the second that death is a great equalizer and God's mirror, in which the living can see their future; and the third, like the medieval *Everyman* play (see Chapter 10), urges penance and good works. Often the dead carry inscriptions warning the living: "I was once as you are, and you will be as I am now."

The manuscript illustrated here contains a poetic version of the standard text:

> Vous serez commes nous sommes
> d'avance mirez-vous en nous
> puissance, honneur, richesse ne sont rien
> à l'heure de la mort
> il n'y a que les bonnes oeuvres qui comptent.

A loose translation reads:

> You will be as we are
> consider us mirrors of your future.
> Power, honor, and wealth are as nothing
> at the hour of death;
> only good works count.

12.3 Francesco Traini, *Triumph of Death*, detail showing cripples and an inscription, Camposanto, Pisa, Italy, 1330s. Fresco, entire painting approx. 20 × 50 ft. (6.1 × 15.2 m).

12.4 *right and far right*
***Frau Welt* (side and back), Worms Cathedral, Germany, *c.* 1300.**

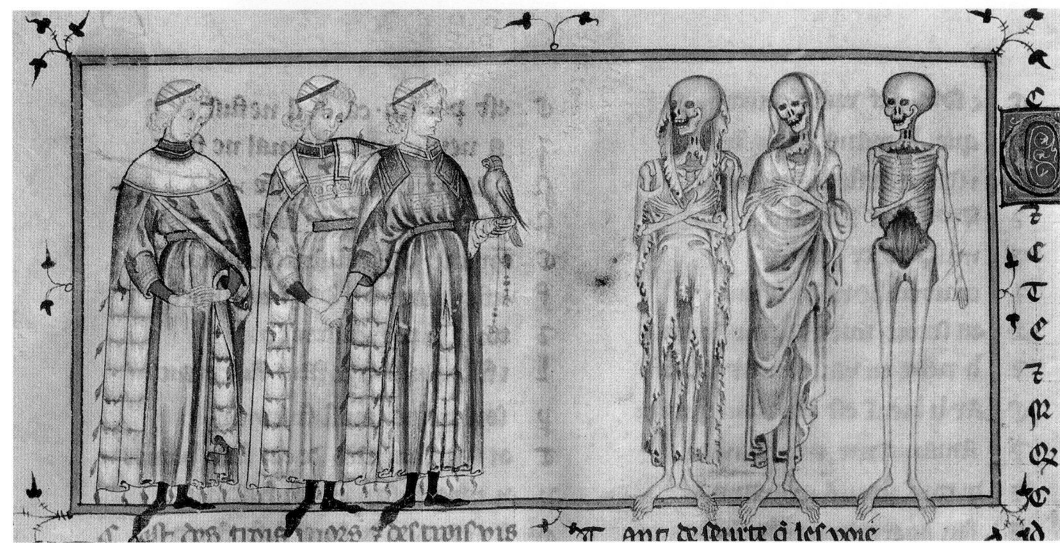

12.5 *The Three Quick and the Three Dead*, from the Psalter of Maria of Brabant, *c.* 1300. Bibliothèque Nationale, Paris.
Three living figures confront three grinning skeletons, two in rags and one a mere "bag of bones." Note that the feet overlap the lower frame, which is characteristic of flattened medieval style. But there is also some shading in the draperies and the skulls, reflecting an emerging interest in naturalism.

THE ICONOGRAPHY OF WEALTH

Among the royal courts, the late Gothic style of painting evolved into the International Gothic style, which appealed to courtly tastes and continued into the fifteenth century. Although the subject matter of International Gothic painting was often Christian, it reflected the opulence of the European courts. One of the most luxurious regional courts where International Gothic flourished was that of Jean, duc de Berry, brother of the French king, Charles V (ruled 1364–1380). Jean levied outrageously high taxes on his subjects to finance his passion for collecting works of art, jewels, and other objects of value. His most famous commission is the Book of Hours (an illustrated prayer book) known as the *Très riches heures du duc de Berry* (*The Very Rich Hours of the Duke of Berry*). It was richly illuminated in the International Gothic style by the Limbourg brothers (active 1400–1415).

Figure **12.6** is typical of International Gothic style north of Italy. It shows the rich detail of Jean's castle, the surrounding landscape, and contains his royal emblems. The wealth reflected in the illuminations stood in stark contrast to the everyday existence of the average person. Courts, especially north of the Alps, were centers of artistic and musical patronage, but they also indulged a last gasp of medieval excess, including extravagant dress and cuisine (see Box, p. 310), in the lifestyle of the very wealthy.

To a great degree, the courts set an example of taste that was emulated by the wealthiest commoners (see Box). With the rise of international trade in the late Gothic period, some merchants amassed large fortunes as a result of their skill in business. By the fifteenth century, one such merchant in France, Jacques Coeur (*c.* 1395–1456), lived in truly luxurious surroundings (figure **12.7**).

From Bourges, an important city in the cloth trade, Jacques Coeur ran a successful international enterprise between the Middle East and western Europe. He oversaw some three hundred agents, who managed his warehouses, messengers, and a carrier pigeon service. He also owned a fleet of boats for trading and shipping in the Mediterranean. Coeur was a skilled financier, who loaned money to King Charles VII of France (ruled 1422–1461) when the Hundred Years War with England depleted the treasury. In this capacity, Coeur frequented the French court and his house reflects his taste for late Gothic International style luxury.

12.6 Limbourg brothers, *The Temptation of Christ*, from *Très riches heures du duc de Berry*, *c.* 1415. Illumination on vellum, $6\frac{3}{4} \times 4\frac{1}{2}$ in. (17 × 11.4 cm). Musée Condé, Chantilly, France.
Christ stands on a tall rock, alluding to the future Church as the "Rock of Ages." He confronts a black, winged Satan and rejects the offer of worldly wealth. The elaborate castle with its turrets, delicate crenellations (the notches along the top of the wall), and moat, belonged to the duc de Berry. The swans gliding along the stream are one of Jean's royal emblems, and, at the lower right, a lion seems to have treed a creature that is part bear and part ape. The bear was also a Berry emblem.

12.7 House of Jacques Coeur, Bourges, France, 1443–1451.
Jacques Coeur's house in Bourges, in northeastern France, is a good example of late Gothic-style domestic architecture. The entrance wall is decorated with elaborate windows and turrets. Two simulated balconies show servants depicted in relief gazing at the street below. Delicate stone tracery designs are carved on the archivolts of the double entrance, the narrower one for pedestrians and the wider one for horses. The entrance leads to a courtyard, around which were arranged the living spaces and Coeur's private chapel. Reinforcing his identification with royalty, Coeur commissioned an equestrian portrait of himself on an interior portal. He thus projected the image of his house as both his home and his castle. In 1450, after being accused of poisoning the king's mistress, however, Coeur was banished from the country.

Society and Culture

Daily Life in the House of a Prosperous Merchant

In the Middle Ages, housing was relatively rudimentary. There was little heat, windows were openings in the wall, and entire families slept together. But at the end of the thirteenth century, as wealthy merchants came in contact with the courts and began to want more creature comforts and privacy for themselves, domestic interiors improved. More bedrooms were constructed for the family as well as for the servants, fireplaces improved heating, doors were sturdier, and windows were covered with oil cloth or shutters. Instead of remaining plain stone or wood, interior walls were plastered or paneled and some were hung with tapestries, which added insulation and improved the decor. In the absence of plumbing, people washed in portable basins, and each morning chamber pots were emptied from a window.

Merchants and their wives were generally literate, which was useful for accounting and record-keeping. Children were educated at home for a few years and then sent to school. The literate populace began buying and reading books, the favorites being romances and the chivalric tales of Roland, Arthur, and the Holy Grail. Lives of the saints, prayer books, health manuals, and cookbooks were also popular.

If the owner of the house was a merchant or craftsman, a shop and an office usually occupied the ground floor. Households were led by the husband, who was expected to work hard to support his family. The housewife had to clean the bedchamber and make sure her husband had clean linen and clean feet. She kept the fire going without letting smoke build up in the house, cared for the children and servants, stocked what was needed to run the house, did the spinning and weaving, and entertained guests. Families who could afford it had their infants fed by wet nurses.

Husbands were permitted to beat their wives for disobedience but did not have the right to kill them. However, women could face death for infanticide or witchcraft. In addition, sumptuary laws (which determined appropriate dress) were applied more strictly to women than to men. Dressing lavishly or above one's social position was unacceptable.

Society and Culture

A Late Gothic Feast

The discussion and sample meals are based on Phyllis Pray Bober's *Art, Culture, and Cuisine.*

As the period of opulence in Gothic courts waned, rulers indulged in unrestrained displays of wealth, including lavish banquets and rich cuisine. Exotic spices, herbs, and other delicacies imported from the East were popular. Surviving cookbooks and health manuals based on ancient Greek medicine reflect increasing culinary sophistication, especially among the upper classes.

Forks were not in general circulation in the late Middle Ages, but the use of spoons replaced drinking soup directly from the bowl. Male diners no longer sliced their own meat from a communal roast; instead, carving was the function of a separate carver. Vegetables and fruit were considered good for the health. The best wines were said to come from Greece and Cyprus, and in addition to wine, the French drank cider. The English preferred mead (an alcoholic honey drink), ale, and beer. Children also drank alcohol.

A late Gothic English court banquet might look as follows: the table is set with a different tablecloth for each course. Large napkins, spoons, and knives are laid at every place. A basin of scented water is provided for washing one's hands. Married couples share a wine goblet; each spouse drinks from one side only. The same goes for soups and stews, which means that spouses have to be seated next to each other. If children are present, they are dressed up to serve, and they sound a trumpet to announce the arrival of each new dish.

Royal banquets could have from three to five main courses. In England, such feasts usually began with a roast (beef or lamb), boiled for a short time and then cooked on a spit. The meat was served with a sauce made of currants, hazelnuts, cloves, ginger, mace, cinnamon, peppercorns, salt, breadcrumbs, red wine, and vinegar. Next, to balance the heated roast, came minced and strained chicken, colored with saffron (an expensive condiment derived from the crocus), and served cold with a mixture of fruit, nuts, and cinnamon.

A capon served with a sauce made of herbs, goose fat, liver, onion, and sugar might follow, and it could be accompanied by a peas pudding pie, wholemeal breads, fritters, wines from Bordeaux, and a gingerbread house or castle, made in the manner of a Middle Eastern honey cake.

Other popular roasted dishes were salmon and venison. Salmon was served with the medieval version of potato chips (*cryspes*), which were made of flour, egg whites, and yeast deep-fried in fat. Other accompaniments were salad (with oil and vinegar, salt, onion, garlic, shallots, fennel, and herbs), almond custard, pears in syrup, dried fruits, and quail pie. Venison roasts were served with currant jelly and red wine vinegar sauce.

A particularly impressive course was the cockentrice, the front half of a capon attached to the rear of a piglet and served as if it were a single species. Figure **12.8** illustrates the custom of "endoring" meats and fowl—that is, reconstituting them with their skin and feathers after they have been cooked. The feet and beaks were usually gilded. Such dishes were designed to arouse the admiration of the diners as well as to whet their appetites.

Banquets usually concluded with hot or cold spiced wine, named Hippocras, after the Greek physician Hippocrates (see Chapter 6), who believed that certain foods were necessary to balance the body's humors.

Of course, a Gothic feast was less pleasurable to a creature on the menu. Here is the "Minstrel's Song of the Swan," an example of medieval irony illustrating the point of view of the cooked bird:

Once I was white as snow
by far the fairest high and low
Now I'm darker than a crow.

REFRAIN: *Alas, alack, I am black,*
to repeat burned to a crisp.

Once I swam upon a lake
all my beauty wide awake
I was a pretty swan.

On the water I should lie
bare below the airy sky
Not spiced with peppercorn.

How the searing fire burns
as the spit turns and turns
So to table I must go.

Laid out on a silver platter
I liked flying high much better
than the teeth of hungry eaters.

12.8 ***Presenting the Peacock*, detail of miniature in the *Histoire du Grand Alexandre* (*The Romance of Alexander the Great*), late 14th century. Illumination on parchment. Musée du Petit Palais, Paris.**

THEATER IN THE FOURTEENTH CENTURY

Liturgical drama continued to be performed in the fourteenth century, but the weakened position of the Church caused by the Schism, as well as by the political and philosophical challenges to its power, led to some major new developments. Most importantly, folk comedy was introduced and mixed with the more pious message of a play. This can be seen in the best-known mystery play of the period, *The Second Shepherds' Play*, which is attributed to the Wakefield Master and was performed in England in the early 1400s. The play is divided into two parts. In the first, a scoundrel steals a sheep. When the shepherds discover a sheep in the thief's house, his wife claims it is her own infant. The shepherds bring gifts to the child, but soon realize that it is actually their stolen sheep. They retaliate by swaddling the thief in a blanket and hurling him back and forth between them. In the second part of the play, an angel appears to the shepherds and announces the birth of Christ.

The slapstick humor in the first part of the play engages the audience; the second part leaves the audience with the uplifting message that Christ is born. The two parts of the play are linked by the simple motifs of sheep and shepherds, both of which can allude to Christ. Christ is at once a sacrificial lamb and the shepherd of a flock, giving the play a symbolic typological character. The opening farce prefigures the more serious second part, thereby combining popular drama with liturgical drama.

Comic scenes were also incorporated into Passion plays. In addition, choral segments called *laude* ("praises") were integrated into the narrative. Thus, even the tragic events leading to Christ's death might now include music and humor.

A second development in late medieval theater was setting plays in the present. This technique encouraged viewers to identify with the time and place of the story. In *The Second Shepherds' Play*, for example, shepherds and sheep were familiar parts of village life, and most people had, at some time, come across a scoundrel or a thief.

In a third development, the idea that a play could be an entertainment independent of the Church gained acceptance. Even in miracle plays celebrating the Feast of Corpus Christi ("body of Christ," held in honor of the Eucharist) there was more community participation than before. For example, processions of guild members carried the Host (the wafer representing the body of Christ) through the city. In addition, as lay people became involved in theater, secular drama began to evolve.

With the increase in the use of the vernacular, Latin declined as the primary language of theater, including liturgical drama. This shift to everyday speech led to a greater use of spoken dialogue (Latin had been chanted). Laymen who did not speak Latin could now participate in liturgical as well as secular plays. Also, by virtue of the vernacular, national differences began to infiltrate theater, and individual plays started to reflect the culture of the language in which they were written.

Among the few surviving records of how plays were performed in the medieval period is a director's scroll listing actors' cues and stage directions from a play in fourteenth-century Germany. Elaborate portable staging devices were moved from town to town, assembled in the public square, and dismantled at the end of the performance. Scenery was designed in individual units to accompany specific scenes and could be reused from one play to another.

MUSIC

Music continued to play a prominent role in Christian liturgy, but, as in theater, the most important late medieval innovations lay in secularization. In England, for example, a secular song that dates to around 1250, "Sumer is icumen in" ("Summer is a-coming in"), has survived:

Sumer is icumen in,
Lhude sing cucu,
Groweth sed and bloweth med,
And springth the wde nu.
Sing cucu.

This brief text is significant because its subject is nature rather than liturgy. Also, it was written in English instead of Latin and is the earliest known polyphonic song for six voices. The words are sung in a **round**, a form in which each voice enters in turn with the same music after the previous one has sung several measures.

ARS NOVA

Ars nova, literally "new art," is the term used to describe the new, more secular musical style of fourteenth-century music. The term comes from a treatise of the same name, written around 1322 by the French composer, poet, and theorist Philippe de Vitry (1291–1361). One innovation described both in *Ars nova* and in another treatise of around 1330, *Ars novae musicae (The Art of New Music)*, is dividing a beat into two, rather than three. This new rhythmic structure was a departure from the triple division preferred by the Church. De Vitry also codified recent developments in notation.

The leading composer of *ars nova* was Guillaume de Machaut (*c.* 1300–1377), who was an ordained priest, a politician, and a poet as well as a musician. He traveled widely in France and Bohemia, working for the Church and noble patrons, including King John of Bohemia and Jean, duc de Berry. Eventually Machaut became canon of Reims Cathedral in northern France.

Machaut's music reflects the prevailing contemporary taste for secular compositions and the new interest in nature. In addition to traditional motets and early medieval lays, Machaut composed romantic ballads for three voices and wrote rounds, love songs, and drinking songs, which were enormously popular with courtly audiences.

Machaut's compositions illustrate an important feature of *ars nova*—namely, the attempt to create a formal structure. In place of the loose, open-ended, meandering chants or repetitive melodies of earlier styles, *ars nova* composers wrote fixed song-like pieces. One technique for achieving a more unified composition was the use of repeated rhythmic patterns, or **isorhythms**. Machaut's *Messe de Notre Dame* (*Mass of Our Lady*) shows careful attention to formal unity. It was written for the Ordinary of the Mass (the part of the Mass that is unchanging; see Box). It is polyphonic, written for four voices, and thematically cohesive. In general, Machaut's polyphony, with its greater use of thirds, has a soft, warm sound, which is more pleasing to the modern ear than the earlier, austere organum styles.

Society and Culture

The Ordinary of the Mass

The Ordinary of the Mass consists of the following sections:

1. Kyrie eleison, which translates as "Lord have mercy on us. Christ have mercy on us."
2. Gloria, which is a hymn praising God and Christ.
3. Credo, which means "I believe"; the words of the creed, or belief statement of the Church, follow.
4. Sanctus and Benedictus, which are based on praise in Isaiah 6:3 and Psalm 118:26, respectively.
5. Agnus Dei, meaning "Lamb of God," which is sung at the opening of communion.

Musical instruments used in the fourteenth century included strings, percussion, and wind, as shown in figure **12.9**. The two women at the top play a lute (on the right) and a viol (on the left). The lower figures, from left to right, play bagpipes, drums, and trumpets. In the center, flanked by a tambourine-player on the left and a clapper-player on the right, is the personification of Music herself. She plays a hand-held organ and, like King Solomon, sits on a lion throne. Above the figure of Music, in a round frame, is Solomon's father, King David, who plays a psaltery (a type of harp). By placing David in a separate frame, the artist removes him in time and space from the contemporary figures on the page. David also serves as a reminder of the tradition that he introduced music into Jewish religious services.

12.9 ***Music and Her Attendants*, from Boethius, *De arithmetica*, 14th century. Manuscript illumination. Biblioteca Nazionale, Naples.**

LITERATURE IN ENGLAND AND FRANCE

As with music, fourteenth-century literature in England and France became increasingly secular. The greatest author in England, Geoffrey Chaucer, depicted characters drawn from everyday life. And in France, the Italian-born Christine de Pisan wrote seriously about women in a way that reflected the Classical tradition and has been seen as a forerunner of feminism.

GEOFFREY CHAUCER

Geoffrey Chaucer (*c.* 1342–1400) grew up in London, where his father, John Chaucer, was a vintner who bought wine for King Edward III (ruled 1327–1377). Through his connections, John arranged for his son to become a page at court. In 1359, Geoffrey fought with Edward's troops against the French and was captured and ransomed (with the king's help) the following year. He married, had a family, and traveled around Europe in the king's service.

Chaucer read widely in the Classics and was familiar with recent Italian authors, including Dante. A prolific writer, he began his classic work, *The Canterbury Tales*, around 1386 when he moved to Kent (the county in which Canterbury is located) to serve in parliament. He was the first commoner to be buried in London's Westminster Abbey.

Chaucer sets *The Canterbury Tales* in 1386 and uses the context of a pilgrimage to examine life in medieval England. Each character represents a particular social class or profession and as such is a window into society. The work begins in the spring and the opening lines, like "Sumer is icumen in" and Petrarch's account of climbing Mount Ventoux, exemplify the emerging interest in nature:

When in April the sweet showers fall
And pierce the drought of March to the root, and all
The veins are bathed in liquor of such power
As brings about the engendering of the flower . . .

(Prologue, lines 1–4)

Chaucer is about to embark on a pilgrimage when a group of twenty-nine "sundry folk" arrives at the Tabard Inn where he is staying in Southwark, by the River Thames. Their destination is Canterbury and the relics of Thomas à Becket (see Chapter 10). Each pilgrim recounts a tale that reveals the character and status of the teller. Thus "The Knight's Tale" is a chivalric romance, the Pardoner (a cleric who pardons people's sins for money) tells an exemplary story, and the Parson sermonizes. The Miller (one who grinds grain into flour) and the Reeve (an officer on a medieval English manor) are exuberantly bawdy. The Prioress is inspired by legends of the saints, and the Wife of Bath (a Roman town in England) exposes social hypocrisy.

These people are not, however, entirely stock characters. They have well-rounded personalities with good and bad qualities. Chaucer makes this clear as he introduces each one in the Prologue. He also takes the opportunity to criticize hypocrisy and corruption in the Church. The Nun Prioress, for example, appears dainty, pious, and well-mannered, but under her habit she wears a necklace and a gold brooch inscribed with the words *Amor vincit omnia* ("Love conquers all"). The Monk adorns his robe with fur and a gold clasp and eats and drinks to excess:

I saw his sleeves were garnished at the hand
With fine grey fur, the finest in the land,
And on his hood, to fasten it at his chin
He had a wrought-gold cunningly fashioned pin;
Into a lover's knot it seemed to pass.
His head was bald and shone like looking-glass;
So did his face, as if it had been greased.
He was a fat and personable priest.

(Prologue, lines 193–200)

The Friar is charming but corrupt, a tippler and a womanizer who prefers the material benefits of wealth to the spiritual rewards of caring for the sick and the poor:

He knew the taverns well in every town
And every innkeeper and barmaid too
Better than lepers, beggars and that crew,
For in so eminent a man as he
It was not fitting with the dignity
Of his position, dealing with a scum
Of wretched lepers; nothing good can come
Of commerce with such slum-and-gutter dwellers,
But only with the rich and victual-sellers.

(Prologue, lines 240–248)

Chaucer uses humor and a vivid sense of irony to expose human foibles. A good example is the Wife of Bath. She has made three pilgrimages to Jerusalem, but has been widowed five times because of her habit of marrying old men for their money. Chaucer describes her unappealing appearance and her seductive ways: "Her hose were of the finest scarlet red." She had "gap-teeth," "large hips," and a red face, "And knew the remedies for love's mischances,/An art in which she knew the oldest dances . . ." (Prologue, lines 475–476).

In the end, Chaucer completed only twenty-three tales. All are rooted in medieval society and set in the religious context of a pilgrimage, but they are down-to-earth rather than romantic or chivalric. Chaucer's women are not idealized, his men are not heroic, and his nuns and priests are corrupt. He wrote in the vernacular, in a local London dialect (now called Middle English) from which modern English evolved. The following, which can be compared with the first quotation in this section, are the first four lines of the Prologue in the original:

Whan that Aprille with his shoures sote
The droghte of Marche hath perced to the rote,
And bathed every veyne in swich licour,
Of which vertu engendred is the flour . . .

(Prologue, lines 1–4)

READING SELECTION

Chaucer, *The Canterbury Tales*, Prologue, PWC2-324-B

12.10 ***Christine de Pisan presenting her poems to Queen Isabel,*** ***c.*** **1410–1415. Manuscript illumination, 7 in. (17.7 cm) wide. British Library, London.**
The setting is an intimate interior inhabited by women. Christine kneels before Isabel and presents her with a large book of poems, implying that both are literate. The room is filled with rich, royal details. Patterns of gold fleurs-de-lis (emblems of French royalty) are embroidered in the blue wall hanging, the women wear the latest fashion, and the ceiling is gilded. On the back wall, an open window shows the type of small panes of glass used in the Middle Ages. One dog sleeps at the foot of the bed and another sits by Isabel. The elaborate, delicate detail of this manuscript reflects the wealth and luxury of International Gothic style that also characterized the illuminations of the Limbourg brothers (see figure 12.6).

CHRISTINE DE PISAN

Christine de Pisan (1364–*c.* 1430) was a scholar and poet who was born in Venice. When her father was appointed astrologer and physician to Charles V of France (ruled 1364–1380), she accompanied him to the court. There she learned to write and to read Latin. She married a court notary when she was fifteen, and, when he died, she wrote to support their three children. She published a world history of women from antiquity to the fourteenth century (1404), a defense of women against misogyny, and a poem about Joan of Arc. Between 1399 and 1415 she wrote fifteen books, including a history of Charles VII and a treatise on weaponry. Among her best-known works is the *Cité des dames* (*Book of the City of Ladies*) (1405), a history of powerful and virtuous women (figure **12.10**).

Christine de Pisan was very much a figure of the late Middle Ages. To a degree, she accepted the traditional role of the woman, instructing women how to advise their husbands in business and how to be loving enough to keep them at home. She recommended that wives focus on the household, treat their husbands well, and avoid wasting money. At the same time, however, she herself was quite independent, well educated, and aware of the benefits of literacy. Without them, she could not have supported her family by writing. Furthermore, she cited as models examples of educated women and powerful goddesses of antiquity. In so doing, she exhibited intellectual affinities with the new humanist developments that emerged in Italy at the turn of the fourteenth century.

READING SELECTION

Christine de Pisan, *Book of the City of Ladies*, refuting ideas of ancient authors alleging the inferiority of women, PWC2-190

HUMANISM IN ITALY

Humanism was an intellectual and cultural movement that began in Italy in the late thirteenth century, and was manifested in an interest, first, in original Latin and, later, in Greek texts. In Padua, in northeastern Italy, a group of lawyers started to examine Roman law. They read Cicero, the great Roman orator, and studied his summation courtroom speeches. Around the same time, also in Padua, the plays of the Roman Stoic philosopher Seneca were revived. The fascination with antiquity grew and spread, so that by the early fourteenth century a few intellectuals were beginning to build libraries of Classical texts. The texts they sought were not the Arabic translations and commentaries that had been carried to Europe in the Middle Ages. Rather, the humanists set out to rediscover Greek and Roman authors in their original form. In addition to searching for the great Classics in law and literature, humanists collected works of philosophy, history, biography, and autobiography.

Reading the Classical texts in the original languages was an aspect of the new interest in chronological, rather than liturgical, time and in understanding human motivation. Humanity and its place in nature became the focus of inquiry, as it had been in ancient Greece. Intellectuals turned from Aristotle to Plato and revitalized the intellectual spirit by opening up the fixed dialectic of scholasticism. The rediscovery of Plato's dialogues, with Socrates as the spokesman, sparked an interest in the human mind. Stepping back from the medieval emphasis on faith, humanists (who were usually devout Christians) sought knowledge through experience. Eventually, this new view of humanity led to a spirit of exploration in science, medicine, mathematics, philosophy, and geography.

The Byzantine and Gothic styles were rejected sooner in Italy than in the rest of western Europe. Humanist artists began to study Roman architecture and sculpture and revived the Classical approach to human form. By the beginning of the fifteenth century, wealthy collectors were sending agents to Greece to buy original Greek sculpture and Classical Greek manuscripts.

Despite the focus on antiquity, however, aspects of Byzantine and Gothic style continued to appeal to those of conservative taste. The Dominicans, for example, preferred more decorative artists who emphasized mysticism and, following St. Dominic, the authority of the Church hierarchy. The Franciscan Order, in contrast, tended to favor monumental artists who were interested in humanity and the natural world. This was consistent with the teachings of St. Francis and his devotion to nature.

In education, a new curriculum developed as humanism evolved. Classical as well as Christian texts supplemented Alcuin's more limited early medieval *trivium* and *quadrivium* (see Chapter 10). The idea that women should be educated and literate gained credence from the early fourteenth century, and in the most enlightened humanist schools of the fifteenth century, girls were educated along with boys (see Chapter 13).

Politically, fourteenth-century Italy was not the unified nation it is today (see map **12.2**). Some regions were governed by princely and ducal courts, others were monarchies, and a few were republican communes with guild members participating in self-rule. The last of these, modeled on the Roman Republic, was the system of choice for the humanists. Among the main centers of humanism were Padua (the site of a distinguished university founded in 1222), Florence (whose *studium*—university—had a chair of Greek studies by 1390), and Naples and Rome (where ancient ruins were most in evidence). Siena was also an important artistic and theological

Map 12.2 Fourteenth-century Italy.

center in the fourteenth century. But as a city dedicated to the cult of the Virgin, Siena adhered more closely to Byzantine style in the visual arts.

LITERATURE AND MUSIC

As the humanist revival developed in Padua, dramatists began writing plays inspired by Roman theater. In 1314, for example, the author Albertino Mussato (1261–1329) produced *Ecerinis*, a tragedy in the style of Seneca (see Chapter 7). The subject, however, was not Roman; it was the story of a tyrant, Ezzelino da Romano, who had ruled Padua. Mussato, inspired by the humanist preference for republicanism, used the play to warn against the dangers of tyranny. Later, in imitation of an ancient Roman ceremony, Mussato was crowned poet laureate of Padua.

In music, the late medieval trend toward secularization continued. The leading Italian musician of the fourteenth century was Francesco Landini (*c.* 1325–1397). Although he was blind, he excelled as a poet, composer, and performer on the lute, organ, and flute. Most of Landini's compositions were *ballate* —that is, secular love-songs in two or three parts, which could be rendered vocally or instrumentally. They are distinguished for their suave-sounding harmonies, which anticipate the chord-based, "common-practice" tonal system of later periods.

PETRARCH AND BOCCACCIO Dante, as we have seen, was a man of the Middle Ages. He created an *Inferno* that mirrored the scholastic hierarchy and the soul's journey from sin to salvation. At the same time, Dante chose as his guide the Roman poet Virgil; both convey a sharp sense of history and politics as they travel through the circles of hell. Dante is thus a pivotal figure, at once immersed in medieval culture and an admirer of his pagan predecessor who was denied salvation by the Church.

The first thoroughly humanist literary giant was Petrarch (1304–1374). He was born in the central Italian town of Arezzo but lived primarily in Avignon, in the south of France. Although he studied law, he settled on a career as a writer and amassed a large private library of Classical manuscripts. He was a prolific writer, whose works include poetry, prose, songs, and letters to dead authors such as Seneca, Cicero, Virgil, and Homer. Although he himself never learned Greek, he recommended that others do so. In 1341, he was crowned poet laureate in Rome.

As Dante had his Beatrice, so Petrarch had his Laura. This was his pseudonym for a married woman with whom he fell in love at a glance. They never met, and Laura died of the plague in 1348. She was the object of most of Petrarch's love poetry, mainly sonnets. Each Petrarchan sonnet is composed of fourteen lines, beginning with an eight-line octave followed by a six-line sestet. The octave poses a question and describes a situation, or expresses a set of feelings, and the sestet offers a comment or conclusion. The main themes are female perfection and the tortures of love.

In the following sonnet, Petrarch questions his intensely conflicted reaction to love and its power over him. For Petrarch, love is a series of apparent contradictions (**oxymorons**)—a living death, a sweet torment—and he the lover is adrift at sea, buffetted by the wind, wise and foolish, hot and cold:

> If it's not love, then what is it I feel:
> but if it's love, by God, what is this thing?
> If good, why then the bitter mortal sting?
> If bad, then why is every torment sweet?
>
> If I burn willingly, why weep and grieve?
> And if against my will, what good lamenting?
> O living death, O pleasurable harm,
> how can you rule me if I not consent?
> [end of octave]
>
> And if I do consent, it's wrong to grieve.
> Caught in contrasting winds in a frail boat
> on the high seas I am without a helm,
>
> so light of wisdom, so laden of error,
> that I myself do not know what I want,
> and shiver in midsummer, burn in winter.
> [end of sestet]
>
> (Petrarch, "If it's not love, then what is it I feel?")

Compared with Dante's mystical account of Beatrice in paradise, Petrarch's sonnet describes love on a more human level. He is unsure, ambivalent, and confused, echoing the psychological exploration of love that characterizes his poetry.

Petrarch's humanism is also evident in his passionate response to nature. The quotation that opens this chapter is taken from an allegorical letter that he wrote in 1336, describing his ascent of Mount Ventoux after reading Livy. Petrarch's account of breathing the pure air, surveying the vast expanse of landscape, and watching the clouds below him inspired wealthy Italians to build country villas giving onto distant scenic views.

In 1343 Petrarch completed a draft of his epic poem *Africa*. Inspired by Homer and Virgil, *Africa*, like the *Iliad*, the *Odyssey*, and the *Aeneid*, opens with an invocation of the Muse. Petrarch asks for inspiration in telling the story of a great cultural hero.

> Muse, you will tell me of the man renowned
> for his great deeds, redoubtable in war,
> on whom first noble Africa, subdued
> by Roman arms, bestowed a lasting name.
>
> (Petrarch, *Africa*, lines 1–4)

The hero of the epic is Scipio Africanus the Elder, who defeated Hannibal in the Second Punic War between Rome and Carthage (see Chapter 7). Of two possible heroes, Julius Caesar and Scipio, Petrarch chose the more republican-minded Scipio over the more tyrannical Caesar. Petrarch's Scipio combines the characteristics of a Christian saint and a triumphant Roman general.

Petrarch drew on Livy for historical background and on Virgil for epic style, thus departing from literary practice for medieval romances, *chansons de geste*, and chivalric legends.

Stylistically, *Africa* exhibits the humanist interest in models and ideas drawn from Classical antiquity. It is filled with allusions to Roman myth and history, and it is also meant to demonstrate the virtues of the Roman Republic.

Reading Livy inspired Petrarch to write *De viribus illustribus* (*On Famous Men*), which heralded another feature of Renaissance humanism—namely, the interest in fame. In the Middle Ages, immortality was conceived of mainly in spiritual terms, but humanists strove for worldly fame and the promise that their achievements would live on in the cultural memory. Petrarch describes his own moral struggle between earthly ambition and spirituality in his autobiographical *Letters of Old Age*.

READING SELECTION

Petrarch, *Canzoniere*, lyric poetry, PWC3-073-C

Petrarch's younger contemporary and friend Giovanni Boccaccio (1313–1375) shared his humanist philosophy and credited Petrarch with having restored ancient Rome to its rightful place in the heritage of Italy. He also took Petrarch's advice and learned Greek. Boccaccio was the illegitimate son of a Florentine banker employed by the prominent Bardi bank and an unknown mother. His father later married a distant relative of Dante's Beatrice Portinari.

When Boccaccio was thirteen, his father was transferred to the Naples branch of the bank. At the time, Naples was one of the preeminent intellectual centers of Europe; an interest in classicism had emerged some years previously at the court of Holy Roman Emperor Frederick II (ruled 1212–1250). In the early fourteenth century, the king of Naples was Robert the Wise (ruled 1309–1343), a serious patron of the arts. Boccaccio worked alongside his father at the bank in Naples where, though he disliked the job, he met people from all walks of life. Later he drew on them to create the characters in his stories.

Boccaccio's most famous work is the *Decameron*, written in the vernacular and set at the time of the Black Death. Ten (whence the title *Deca*, meaning "ten") young people depart for the countryside to escape the plague. They pass the time telling stories that include vivid, satirical descriptions of contemporary society and the Church. In particular, the stories condemn the Inquisition and discrimination against women. For Boccaccio, nature meant human nature as well as landscape, and his tales thus reflect various psychological reactions to the Black Death.

READING SELECTION

Boccaccio, *Decameron*: Day 1, Story 6, criticizing the Inquisition in Rome, PWC3-103; Day 3, Story 1, on the custom of placing young women in convents against their will, PWC3-104

THE VISUAL ARTS

The visual arts, like literature, were invigorated by humanism. For example, the sculpture of Nicola Pisano (*c.* 1220/1225–*c.* 1284) demonstrates the developing taste for naturalism (figure **12.11**), although Gothic elements persist. Pisano's name indicates that he spent most of his career in Pisa, but he was originally from the south of Italy, where he came into contact with Classical taste at the court of Naples. In painting, the shift away from medieval style is illustrated by a comparison of two altarpieces depicting the Virgin and Christ—one by Cimabue and the other by Giotto.

12.11 Nicola Pisano, *Adoration of the Magi*, baptistery pulpit, Pisa, *c.* 1260. Marble, approx. 34 in. (86.4 cm) high.
Pisano retains Gothic patterning in the beards, the horses' manes, and the angel's wings, but the draperies now define the organic structures of the body. Mary, who resembles a Roman matron more than a medieval Queen of Heaven, occupies a believable three-dimensional space. Christ is himself a believable infant, with his pudgy proportions and eagerness to receive the king's gift. He sits firmly on his mother's lap as she rests her hand protectively on his shoulder. Evidence of medieval style can still be seen in the unnatural scale of the horses compared with the human figures and in the angular drapery folds.

PAINTING: CIMABUE AND GIOTTO The last great Byzantine painter in Italy was Cenni di Pepi, known as Cimabue (*c.* 1240–*c.* 1302). His monumental *Enthroned Madonna and Child* of around 1285 was commissioned for the high altar of the church of Santa Trinità in Florence (figure **12.12**). Its large size and imposing grandeur convey the power of Byzantine imagery. The Virgin and Christ are seated on a jeweled throne held aloft by eight angels in a flattened gold space. Below the throne, four Hebrew figures—Abraham, David, Jeremiah, and Isaiah—are shown with scrolls signifying prophecy. The message here, as on the central west portal of Chartres Cathedral (see figure 11.21), is that the new era ushered in with the birth of Christ rests on the foundation of the Old Testament. Christ and *his* message are thus seen typologically as the fulfillment of prophecy.

The predominance of gold, not only in the background and on the throne, but also in the drapery folds, is characteristic of Byzantine style. In addition, the proportions of Christ are more adult than baby like. He thus retains the medieval character of a miraculous infant, small in size but endowed with adult form and intelligence.

Cimabue, and his place in the history of Italian art, inspired the following lines in the eleventh *canto* of Dante's *Purgatorio*:

> O empty glory of human powers! How short the time
> its green endures at its peak, if it be not
> overtaken by the crude ages! Cimabue thought to hold
> the field in painting, and now Giotto has the cry,
> so that the fame of the former is obscured.
>
> (Dante, *Purgatorio*, Canto XI, lines 91–95)

In this passage, Dante laments the fact that earthly fame is short-lived. He notes that Cimabue's reputation as the greatest living painter in Italy was soon overshadowed by that of his successor, Giotto di Bondone (*c.* 1266–1337). A comparison of Giotto's *Enthroned Madonna* of around 1310 with Cimabue's makes clear why Dante thinks Giotto is the greater artist (figure **12.13**). Similar though these altarpieces are in serving a devotional purpose, a careful viewing of Giotto's reveals several innovations that struck his contemporaries—and future art historians—as revolutionary.

Giotto has retained the gold background characteristic of Byzantine altarpieces, and the throne, with its pointed arches and tracery, is Gothic in style. However, in comparison with Cimabue's work, Giotto represents space in a more three-dimensional way, and the throne does not appear to move upward. Giotto's Christ is more naturally baby-like than Cimabue's. He sits solidly on his mother's lap, and she holds him rather than presenting him to the viewer, as Cimabue's Virgin does. Giotto's Christ is nevertheless a miraculous baby, wise beyond his years, for he carries a scroll and blesses the faithful. But his proportions are more naturalistic, and rolls of baby fat are visible around his neck and wrists.

12.12 Cimabue, *Enthroned Madonna and Child*, *c.* 1285. Tempera on panel, 12 ft. 7 in. × 7 ft. 4 in. (3.84 × 2.24 m). Galleria degli Uffizi, Florence.
The favorite medium for altarpieces was tempera on wood panel. Tempera paint is a mixture of pigments with water thickened with egg yolk. The technique was painstaking, requiring months of preparation. First the wood (usually poplar) had to be cut, reinforced with glue, sized to prevent warping, and sanded. The artist then drew in, and inked, the outlines of the image. Gold leaf was applied to background areas, halos, and other decorative details, and then polished. When the picture had been completely painted, it was left to dry. Once dry, the surface was varnished.

The Virgin, as in Nicola Pisano's relief (see figure 12.11), is a solid, matronly figure. Her drapery is heavy, and it defines her form by a new technique of shading called "chiaroscuro" (literally "light-dark"). Chiaroscuro makes form visible, as it is in nature, by gradations in light and dark rather than through outlining (there are no outlines in nature), as in Byzantine style. Looking closely at the folds of Mary's white robe, one can see that they curve as if she is shifting her torso to one side, which suggests the contrapposto pose of antiquity (see Chapter 5). Like the more natural depiction of light and dark, the weightier figures reflect the force of gravity. The depiction of three-dimensional space and the use of contrapposto indicate a revival of Classical naturalism. Giotto thus pierced the picture plane, which had been two-dimensional for nearly the first thousand years of Christian style. He conceived of a painting not as a flat devotional space, but as a stage on which human characters perform and human as well as divine events unfold.

PETRARCH AND BOCCACCIO ON GIOTTO In his last will and testament, Petrarch proudly bequeathed a painting of the Virgin and Christ by Giotto to his patron, Francesco da Carrara. Petrarch wrote that although the ignorant (unenlightened) may not understand its beauty, "masters of the art will marvel at it." In other words, Petrarch applies a light–dark metaphor to intelligence and ignorance while also alluding to Giotto's use of chiaroscuro.

Boccaccio echoes these sentiments in the sixth story of the *Decameron*. Citing the Western theme of the ugly genius (such as Socrates), he writes: "Nature has frequently planted astonishing genius in men of monstrously ugly appearance." Giotto, who was known for his ugliness, was, according to Boccaccio,

> a man of such outstanding genius that there was nothing in the whole of creation that he could not depict with his stylus, pen, or brush . . . Hence, by virtue of the fact that he brought back to light an art which had been buried for centuries beneath the blunders of those who, in their paintings, aimed to bring visual delight to the ignorant rather than intellectual satisfaction to the wise, his work may justly be regarded as a shining monument to the glory of Florence.
>
> (Boccaccio, *Decameron*, 6.5)

GIOTTO'S NARRATIVE PAINTING Giotto's most famous and best-preserved fresco cycle is located on the walls of the Arena Chapel in Padua. It testifies to his reputation for returning naturalism to painting. The chapel was commissioned by Enrico Scrovegni, the richest man in Padua, whose father Dante had confined to hell for the sin of usury. Enrico financed the chapel as a means of atonement and to ensure his own entry into heaven.

12.13 Giotto di Bondone, *Enthroned Madonna* (*Ognissanti Madonna*), *c.* 1310. Tempera on panel, 10 ft. 8 in. × 6 ft. 8¼ in. (3.25 × 2.03 m). Galleria degli Uffizi, Florence.
Giotto was a Florentine, although his reputation as the greatest living artist took him to many Italian cities. He was also a skilled businessman, earning money on the side from real estate. The father of some six children, Giotto was one of the first Christian artists to portray children as they look and behave in the real world.

Figure **12.14** shows the chancel arch and part of the side walls as seen on entering the chapel. The barrel-vaulted ceiling is painted to resemble a star-studded blue sky. On the side walls, the top row of narrative scenes portrays the lives of Mary and her parents (Anna and Joachim), and the life of Christ is depicted in the second and third rows. The scenes on the chancel arch are like the prologue of a play: they announce the beginning of the narrative and foreshadow future events.

Above the opening of the arch, God is shown summoning the host of heaven, including Gabriel, and setting in motion the story of Christ. On either side of the arch opening is the *Annunciation*, split into two panels, with Gabriel at the left and Mary at the right. Below the *Annunciation*, at the right, is the *Visitation* (when Mary, who is three months pregnant, visits her cousin Elizabeth, who is six months pregnant); and the *Betrayal of Judas* is at the left. The former scenes foreshadow the

12.14 Giotto, Arena Chapel, looking toward the chancel arch, Padua, Italy, *c.* 1305–1310. Frescoes.

births of Christ and John the Baptist and the latter shows Judas receiving a bag of silver to betray Christ. The remainder of the narrative unfolds horizontally on the side walls in chronological sequence.

12.15 Giotto, *Last Judgment*, Arena Chapel, Padua, *c.* 1305–1310. Fresco.
To the left of the Cross below Christ, the penitent figure of Enrico Scrovegni presents a model of the chapel to three holy figures. Including the patron in a work he financed would become standard practice in Renaissance art. Notice as evidence of Giotto's wit that a little soul is trying to hide behind the Cross and sneak from hell over to the side of the saved. Evidence of Giotto's taste for illusionism appears in the painted white cloak of the monk assisting Scrovegni. It seems to overlap the doorway arch as if actually falling out of the fresco into the space of the viewer.

12.16 Giotto, *St. Francis rejecting his father's wealth*, Bardi Chapel, Church of Santa Croce, Florence, *c.* 1318. Fresco. The preferred technique for painting walls in the Renaissance was fresco, in which waterpaint is applied to damp lime plaster. It is a durable technique requiring speed and skill. Because plaster dries within twenty-four hours, the artist has to prepare only that part of the wall to be covered in one day. A layer of lime and sand is applied, a coat of plaster is added, and then the surface is painted. As the plaster dries, the paint is absorbed and bonds with the wall.

Turning to leave the chapel, viewers confront the huge *Last Judgment* on the entrance wall (figure **12.15**). This is Giotto's vision of the end of time, which corresponds to the conclusion of the viewer's visit to the chapel. Its structure follows the conventional arrangement of the Last Judgment in Western art. Christ occupies a central position in heaven, surrounded on either side by apostles and angels. In the lower section to the right of Christ (our left), the saved climb from their tombs and ascend to heaven in an orderly manner. On the lower right (Christ's left), a fiery hell awaits the damned who tumble downward in disorder. A monstrous Satan simultaneously swallows and expels several souls, while devils torture others. A number of figures are shown hanging, a form of death that depends on gravity and thus emphasizes that hell is down.

Giotto's genius for conveying human drama can be seen in his later fresco cycle illustrating the life of St. Francis of Assisi (figure **12.16**). Located in Florence, in a chapel commissioned by the Bardi banking family, it reflects the irony of wealthy citizens who idealize the vows of poverty taken by the saint. In this scene, Francis rejects his father's wealth. He has removed his clothes and is wrapped in a bishop's cloak, signifying his transition from the everyday world to the Church. His father's rage is shown by his jaw jutting forward in fury, and his separation from Francis by an empty space. Giotto thus juxtaposes the solid form of the building with the literal and figurative void between father and son.

Here, as in the Arena Chapel frescoes, Giotto places his figures in a solid, three-dimensional setting. In contrast to Early Christian and medieval figures, these turn freely in space and interact with each other rather than facing the viewer directly. They participate, like actors on a stage, in a dramatic narrative, combining Christian subject matter with natural human emotion.

PAINTING IN SIENA Florence's rival city was Siena, which considered itself the city of the Virgin. It was ruled by a Council of Nine, the *Nove*, who represented the city's wealthy merchants. Like Florence, Siena supported the arts for both religious and political purposes. The cathedral was the main source of religious patronage, and the town hall—the Palazzo Pubblico—of political patronage.

The leading painter in Siena was Duccio di Buoninsegna (*c.* 1260–*c.* 1319). He was commissioned in 1308 to produce a large altarpiece, the *Maestà* ("majesty"), for the cathedral. Rather than standing with its back to a chapel wall like the enthroned madonnas of Cimabue and Giotto, the *Maestà* was placed under the dome and was visible from all sides. The back was decorated with scenes of Christ's Passion and the front with the enthroned Virgin, saints, and angels (figure **12.17**).

12.17 *above* **Duccio, *Maestà*, 1308–1311. Tempera and gold leaf on panel, 7 × 13 ft. (2.13 × 3.96 m). Museo dell'Opera del Duomo, Siena.**
Note the predominance of gold, the rich color, and the elaborate detail of the throne. Although Duccio has eliminated the gold drapery folds used by Cimabue and there is some evidence of chiaroscuro, the flavor of the image is Byzantine. Related to the powerful cult of the Virgin, the work was intended to evoke a devotional response and to emphasize the compassion of the Virgin rather than to create a dramatic narrative.

Mary is shown as a queen surrounded by a heavenly court, the sides of her throne expanding outward as if to embrace the faithful. In the inscription on the base of the throne, Duccio asks her to bring peace to Siena and long life to himself as recompense for his altarpiece.

Siena's town hall (figure **12.18**), completed in the first decade of the fourteenth century, is an imposing structure with Gothic arches, a tower, and fortress-like crenellations. For the interior of the Palazzo Pubblico the Council of Nine commissioned frescoes that were politically motivated and designed to suggest that their rule was fair. The humanist commitment to just government can be seen, for example, in the frescoes by Ambrogio Lorenzetti (*c.* 1290–1348), who died during the Black Death. In *The Effects of Good Government in the City* (figure **12.19**), the bustling merchant town of Siena can be seen

12.18 Palazzo Pubblico, Siena, completed 1309.

12.19 Ambrogio Lorenzetti, *The Effects of Good Government in the City*, Palazzo Pubblico, Siena, 1338–1339. Fresco, total length approx. 23 ft. (7 m).

in full swing. Under good government, according to Ambrogio, there is peace and prosperity. Traders offer their wares for sale, students attend school, shops are open for business, musicians and dancers perform in the street, and builders are hard at work on the roof tops. To show the effects of bad government, Ambrogio painted the allegory in figure **12.20**, which personifies Tyranny and its evil companions. By juxtaposing two types of government, Ambrogio exemplifies humanist political philosophy and projects the image of Siena as a well-ruled commune under the Council of Nine.

12.20 Ambrogio Lorenzetti, *Allegory of Bad Government*, Palazzo Pubblico, Siena, 1338–1339. Fresco.
Tyranny is the large central figure with fangs and a horned black hood. Surrounding his head are the vices of Avarice, Pride, and Vainglory. Seated on his right (reading from the viewer's left) are Cruelty, with an infant killed by a snake; Treason, holding a creature that is part-lamb, part-scorpion; and Fraud, with cloven feet. On Tyranny's left, an agitated, wolf-headed centaur represents Frenzy, Discord saws herself in half, and War is armed for battle. The figure in white is labeled Justice; she has been tied up and her scales broken.

DOMINICAN ICONOGRAPHY AND SCHOLASTIC RESISTANCE TO HUMANISM

After the Black Death, there was no fourteenth-century artist who rivaled the innovations of Giotto, Duccio, or Ambrogio Lorenzetti. At the same time, scholasticism persisted amid the widespread anxiety and preoccupation with death that followed the plague. The scholastic concern for salvation is portrayed in a set of huge frescoes by Andrea da Firenze (Andrea di Bonaiuti; *c.* 1337–1377). They are located in the Spanish Chapel, a Dominican chapter house in the Florentine church of Santa Maria Novella.

Andrea's *Triumph of St. Thomas Aquinas* of around 1365 is organized hierarchically and has none of Giotto's dramatic narrative, Duccio's compassion, or Ambrogio's humanist politics (figure **12.21**). Below an angel-filled sky sits St. Thomas Aquinas in direct confrontation with the viewer. He presides over the scene, flanked on his left by Old Testament figures and by New Testament figures on his right. Below, a long arcaded bench decorated with delicate tracery and pinnacles is occupied by personifications of the Virtues, the Liberal Arts, and the Sciences. In these three tiers—the heavens, St. Thomas, and the earthly world—Andrea has produced the pictorial equivalent of an orderly scholastic dialectic. His image conveys the power of the Church as the route to salvation.

It would take Italy a few more generations to recover fully from the devastating effects of the Black Death, which had added to the problems already besetting Europe. With recovery would come a cultural, intellectual, and artistic expansion that began at the turn of the fifteenth century. Throughout Europe, despite lingering Gothic influence, the Renaissance style would broaden the innovations introduced by the early humanists.

12.21 Andrea da Firenze, *Triumph of St. Thomas Aquinas*, Spanish Chapel, Santa Maria Novella, Florence, *c.* 1365. Fresco, approx. 38 ft. (11.58 m) wide.

KEY TERMS

antipope the name given to a rival pope, often resident in Avignon, but not legitimized by the Roman Church.

humanism an intellectual and artistic trend, beginning in the late thirteenth century and based on a renewed interest in the Classical tradition.

isorhythm in fourteenth-century music, the use of a repeated rhythmic scheme, usually applied to a plainsong melody.

Ockham's razor the principle of reducing—shaving—an assumption to its simplest form.

oxymoron a figure of speech using an apparent contradiction.

round a musical form in which each voice enters in turn with the same music after the previous one has sung several measures.

syllogism a logical system of deductive reasoning, in which a conclusion follows from a major and a minor premise.

transi tomb a tomb with an effigy of the deceased in a state of decay.

KEY QUESTIONS

1. What does the term "Great Schism" mean? Summarize the main problems present in this schism.
2. How did the Black Death affect the visual art and literature of this period?
3. What qualities make *ars nova* a new, more secular musical style?
4. How does Chaucer satirize society through his characters?
5. How did humanism affect the visual arts and literature of this period?

SUGGESTED READING

Allmand, C. *The Hundred Years War: England and France at War, c. 1300–1450.* Cambridge, U.K.: Cambridge University Press, 1988.
- A survey of the origins and effects of the war.

Barolsky, Paul. *Giotto's Father and the Family of Vasari's Lives.* University Park, PA: Pennsylvania State University Press, 1992.
- A brief interpretive view of Giotto's relationship to his father and its implications for his art.

Baxandall, Michael. *Giotto and the Orators.* Oxford: Oxford University Press, 1971.
- A study of Giotto and literature relating to him.

Bober, Phyllis Pray. *Art, Culture, and Cuisine.* Chicago and London: University of Chicago Press, 1999.
- Feasts and menus from the fourteenth century.

Boccaccio, *The Decameron*, trans. G. H. McWilliam. London: Penguin Books, 1972.
- Ten tales set at the time of the Black Death.

Burckhardt, Jacob C. *The Civilization of the Renaissance in Italy*, trans. S. G. C. Middlemore, 3rd rev. ed. London: Phaidon, 1950.
- A classic study of the Italian Renaissance

Chaucer, Geoffrey. *The Canterbury Tales*, trans. Nevill Coghill. London: Penguin Classics, 1977.
- A long poem in which pilgrims pass the time by recounting the stories of their lives. A window on medieval society.

Christine de Pisan. *The Book of the City of Ladies*, trans. Earl Jeffrey Richards. New York: Persea Books, 1982.
- A book by a medieval woman on the position of women during the Middle Ages.

Cohen, Kathleen. *Metamorphosis of a Death Symbol.* Berkeley and Los Angeles: University of California Press, 1973.
- A study of medieval transi tombs, their iconography, and meaning.

Cole, Bruce. *Giotto and Florentine Painting, 1280–1375.* New York: Harper and Row, 1975.
- A brief study of Giotto and his impact on Florentine painting.

Gordon, Mary. *Joan of Arc.* New York: Viking Press, 2000.
- A brief biography of St. Joan by a well-known author.

Meiss, Millard. *Painting in Florence and Siena after the Black Death.* Princeton, NJ: Princeton University Press, 1951.
- A classic account of the character of the Black Death and its effects on art and society.

——. *French Painting in the Time of Jean de Berry: The Late Fourteenth Century and the Patronage of the Duke.* London: Thames and Hudson, 1975.
- A study of International Gothic painting in France.

Schneider, Laurie (ed.). *Giotto in Perspective.* Englewood Cliffs, NJ: Prentice Hall, 1974.
- A critical history of the artist, from the fourteenth to the twentieth century.

Tierney, B. *The Crisis of Church and State 1050–1300.* Englewood Cliffs, NJ: Prentice Hall, 1964.
▸ Annotated original documents of the period.

Tuchman, Barbara. *A Distant Mirror.* New York: Alfred A. Knopf, 1978.
▸ An account of the Middle Ages.

White, John. *The Birth and Rebirth of Pictorial Space*, 2nd ed. Boston: Faber and Faber, 1967.
▸ On the development of linear perspective.

Ziegler, Philip. *The Black Death.* London: Penguin Books, 1991.
▸ A recent account of the Black Death.

SUGGESTED FILMS

1922 *Robin Hood*, dir. Allan Dwan

1928 *The Passion of Joan of Arc* (*La Passion de Jeanne d'Arc*), dir. Carl Theodor Dreyer

1938 *The Adventures of Robin Hood*, dir. Michael Curtiz and William Keighley

1948 *Joan of Arc*, dir. Victor Fleming

1952 *Ivanhoe*, dir. Richard Thorpe

1957 *Saint Joan*, dir. Otto Preminger

1962 *Procès de Jeanne d'Arc* (*The Trial of Joan of Arc*), dir. Robert Bresson

1991 *Robin Hood*, dir. John Irvin

1991 *Robin Hood: Prince of Thieves*, dir. Kevin Reynolds

1999 *The Messenger: The Story of Joan of Arc*, dir. Luc Besson

13 The Early Renaissance in Italy and Northern Europe

"*How great and wonderful is the dignity of the human body . . . how lofty and sublime the human soul, and . . . how great and illustrious is the excellence of man himself made up of these two parts.*"

(GIANNOZZO MANETTI, *On the Dignity of Man*)

The word Renaissance (meaning "rebirth") refers to the revival of interest in, and admiration for, Greek and Roman antiquity. This began in the late thirteenth century in Italy and appeared somewhat later in northern Europe, contributing to the waning of the Middle Ages. History evolves slowly, however, and the medieval worldview persisted throughout Europe even after the beginnings of Renaissance thought.

It took several generations for Europe to recover from the Black Death of 1348, from bank failures, and from the other economic problems of the fourteenth century. But by the turn of the quattrocento *(1400s), a new era was emerging. Economic recovery, resulting from increasing trade between Italy and the north of Europe (see map 13.1) and a rise in banking, improved living conditions for all social classes. Prosperity, in turn, led to an expansion of artistic patronage, which was no longer restricted to the Church and the courts, as it had been during the Middle Ages. New patrons appeared, especially among wealthy merchants, guilds, and individual families, who were ambitious for power and prestige. These new sources of secular patronage reflected new ideas about the role of the individual in society and in the cosmos.*

The city of Florence, in Tuscany, was the center of the humanist movement in the early decades of the fifteenth century. Humanist chancellors who ran the city favored a form of government that was based on the republic of ancient Rome and fifth-century-B.C. Athenian democracy. Eventually, however, Florence became an oligarchy, ruled by a few families, notably the Medici, who dominated the political, financial, intellectual, and artistic life of Florence for most of the century. Having amassed a vast fortune through banking and moneylending, the Medici spent huge sums on art and architecture, helping to establish Florence as the cultural center of Italy. They also supported humanist poets, musicians, and philosophers.

Outside Florence, too, humanist Italian courts patronized artists, architects, and writers, as well as scientists and philosophers. Like the Medici, these rulers, who included the popes, used the arts to express their wealth, power, and intellectual ambition.

Although humanism emerged first in Italy with the revival of Classical antiquity, it soon spread to parts of northern Europe, especially Germany and the

Key Topics

New Developments

- Linear perspective
- Dissection of human bodies
- Perfection of the printing press

The Effects of Change

- Naturalism in the arts
- Humanism in art, music, and literature
- Renewed Platonism
- Rise in literacy
- Conservative backlash

Explorers, Patronage, and Competition

- Christopher Columbus, Vasco da Gama, Henry the Navigator, John Cabot
- Competition for the Florence baptistery doors, 1401
- Brunelleschi's dome
- The Medici family

Music

- Isaac
- Dunstable
- Dufay
- Josquin

TIMELINE	ITALY 1400–1500	NORTHERN EUROPE 1400–1500
HISTORY AND CULTURE 	Economic recovery Mercantile economies City-states and courts Florence key cultural center Turks take Constantinople, 1453 Trade and exploration Production of books; increase in literacy Spread of humanism Patronage by Church, wealthy individuals, and guilds Medici family: rulers and patrons	Economic recovery Mercantile economies Countries ruled by monarchs Bruges leading commercial city Trade and exploration Gutenberg perfects printing press, 1440s Expansion of humanism Patronage by Church, wealthy individuals, and guilds
RELIGION	Dominican backlash against humanism: Antoninus (1389–1459) and Savonarola (1452–1498) Humanist popes	
ART 	Brunelleschi/Ghiberti, *Sacrifice of Isaac* reliefs, 1401–1402 Donatello, *John the Evangelist*, *c.* 1409–1411; *David*, 1420–1440 Masaccio, *Trinity*, 1425–1428; *Virgin and Child*, 1426; *Tribute Money*, 1420s Fra Angelico, *Mocking of Christ with the Virgin and St. Dominic*, 1438–1445 Uccello, *Battle of San Romano*, 1440s Rossellino, tomb of Leonardo Bruni, begun 1444 Gozzoli, *Procession of the Magi*, 1459 Piero della Francesca, *Battista Sforza* and *Federico da Montefeltro*, *c.* 1472 Botticelli, *Birth of Venus*, *c.* 1480 Verrocchio, *Colleoni*, *c.* 1481–1496 Leonardo, *Last Supper*, *c.* 1495–1498	van Eyck, Ghent altarpiece, 1432; *Man in a Red Turban*, *c.* 1433; *Arnolfini Portrait*, 1434 Petrus Christus, *St. Eloy in His Studio*, 1449 Fouquet, *Portrait of Charles VII*, after 1451 Schongauer, *Elephant*, *c.* 1485
ARCHITECTURE 	Brunelleschi, dome of Florence Cathedral, begun 1420 Rossellino, plan of Pienza, 1460s Mantegna, Camera Picta, Mantua, 1474 Giuliano da Sangallo, Santa Maria delle Carceri, Prato, 1485–1490	
LITERATURE	Bruni, *Panegyric of the City of Florence*, 1401; *History of the Florentine People*, 1415 Manetti (1396–1459), *On the Dignity of Man* Ficino (1433–1499), commentaries on Plato and translations of Plotinus Alberti, *On Painting*, *c.* 1435; *Book of the Family*, 1436; *On Architecture*, 1452 Pico della Mirandola, *Oration on the Dignity of Man*, 1486	Gutenberg Bible, 1450s William Caxton (*c.* 1422–1491), illustrated books
THEATER	Merging of Classical subject matter and form Laschi, *Achilles*, 1390	Increased use of farce and comedy *Pierre Pathelin*, *c.* 1470 Morality plays increasingly portray human nature
MUSIC 	Humanist tastes encourage listener response Move from sacred to secular Lorenzo de' Medici founds music school Isaac spends ten years in Florence under Lorenzo's patronage, from 1485 *Intermedio* and *frottola*	Main center of music patronage: court of Philip the Good (1396–1467) in Burgundy Secular song: *chansons* Dunstable (*c.* 1390–1453), motets, secular songs Dufay (*c.* 1400–1474), development of "cyclic Mass," motets, chansons Josquin Desprez, *Ave Maria . . . virgo serena*, *c.* 1485 Four-voice texture becomes the norm

Netherlands. Nevertheless, the visual arts of the north retained a more Gothic flavor than in Italy. In music, on the other hand, the north was more innovative than the south, as patronage became increasingly secular and composers developed new styles.

As the quotation by the humanist philosopher Giannozzo Manetti at the opening of this chapter suggests, the essence of humanism is its interest in man. Whereas medieval thinkers made a sharp distinction between the body and the soul, fifteenth-century humanists conceived of man as a totality—which includes the physical appearance, the mind, and the soul. Manetti argued that because man was made in God's image, he must also be endowed, like God, with a creative mind and a "sublime soul." This Renaissance view of humanity was consistent with the revival of Classical culture.

THE EXPANSION OF HUMANISM

The development of humanism (see Box, p. 333) coincided with advances in technology, new approaches to the arts and sciences, a greater awareness of the world through geographic exploration, and an expansion of international trade (map **13.1**).

ADVANCES IN TECHNOLOGY

In 1425, in the German city of Mainz, Johannes Gutenberg (*c.* 1398–1468) perfected movable type, and by the 1450s, he had printed the entire Bible on a printing press. The technology of printing enabled ideas to circulate at a faster rate than previously, which had enormous cultural ramifications. Books, which had hitherto been painstakingly copied by hand, could now be replicated and printed in large quantities. The increase in the number and availability of books was accompanied by a gradual rise in literacy as the reading public grew (see Box, p. 332).

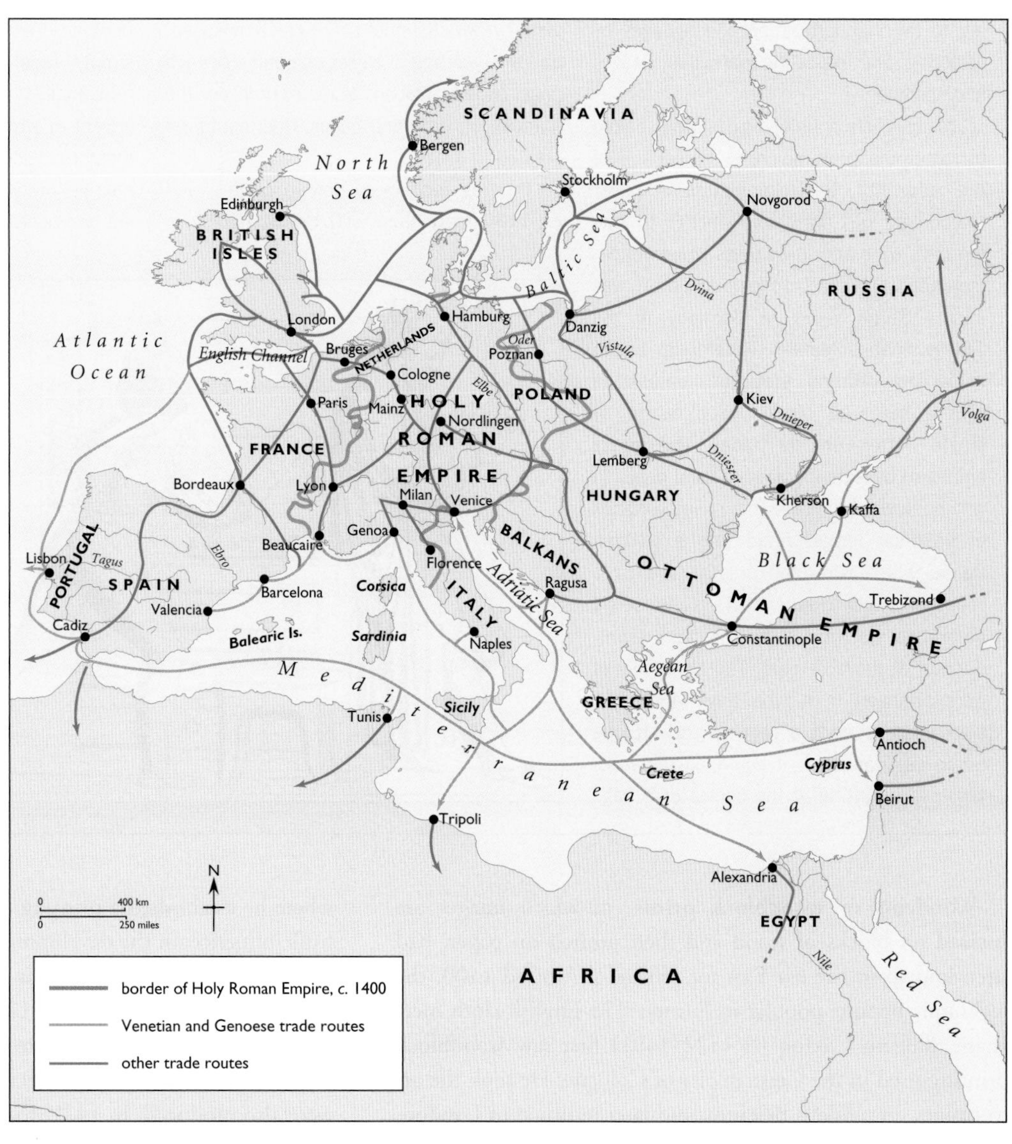

Map 13.1 European trade in the fifteenth century.

Defining Moment

The Printing Press

In the early fifteenth century, commercial centers of business, royal courts, and banks needed scribes to record transactions. Scribes, however, were expensive and few were available. The improvement of the printing press in mid-fifteenth-century Europe solved this problem and brought about one of the most radical changes in Western intellectual and commercial history. The printing revolution made reading a part of everyday life and changed the face of education, law, and politics. It popularized the discoveries of the New World and contributed to the reproduction of more accurate charts and maps, which, in turn, facilitated further discovery. Printing also led to the standardization of languages by selecting and repeating particular usages and spellings.

Many existing technologies were linked to foster the printing press: the punch of the goldsmith, the manufacture of paper (parchment was not porous enough to take the ink), wine and linen press construction, metallurgy, ink and oil production. It was in the Rhine Valley in Germany in the 1440s that Johannes Gutenberg began using the printing press in conjunction with a series of blocks, each bearing a single letter on its face. The press employed by Gutenberg was a hand press, in which ink was rolled over the raised surfaces of hand-set letters fitted into a wooden frame, which was then pressed against a sheet of paper (figure **13.1**). Gutenberg's innovative system allowed the mass reproduction of movable type. The letter blocks were arranged in a type tray, which was then used to print a page of text. If one letter was damaged, it could be replaced. When the printing of the copies of a page was finished, the type could be reused for the next page or, indeed, the next book.

At first, typefaces imitated hand lettering. However, as humanists rediscovered works from Classical antiquity, they popularized new typefaces modeled after the curved, more readable letters of the Romans.

Before the invention of the printing press, books had been copied mainly in monasteries, where monks wrote them out. Books were scarce, because it could take a year to copy a Bible by hand. With the Gutenberg press plus two or three people who could read and a few operatives to work the machinery, it was possible to create several hundred copies of the Bible—or any other long text—in a year. Each sheet of paper still had to be fed into the press individually, which limited reproduction speed, and the type had to be set manually for each page, which placed a restriction on the number of different pages that could be created in a day.

Printing technology spread rapidly, and by 1480 more than 110 towns, mainly in Italy and Germany, had established presses. The printing press helped to spread intellectual ideas across Europe. Because many craftsmen had died of the plague, the European economy needed "how to" books, and the printing press made pos-sible the transmission of accurate technical information. At the same time as the concept of authorship emerged, writers could be sure of reaching readers, who would then hold them responsible for information. Printing also made possible new forms of cross-cultural exchange independent of travel and generally contributed to greater knowledge among the populations of Europe.

Critical Question If a new technology becomes popular, do old technologies simply fade away or do they find new relevance? (For example, before the advent of writing and books, people had to memorize poetry if it was to pass to the next generation. Now that we have computers, are books becoming obsolete?)

13.1 Artist's impression of Johannes Gutenberg, based on the carvings on his tomb, showing him reading proofs while his assistant works the printing press. Woodcut.

Woodcuts or **woodblock prints**, in which images are **incised** on blocks of wood and then printed on paper, had been known in the Far East for centuries. Around 1400, the technique became popular in Europe. The English cloth merchant William Caxton (*c.* 1422–1491) first saw woodblock printing used in the German city of Cologne. He took the art to Bruges, in modern Belgium, and later returned to London, where he established a printing concern in Westminster. Caxton's influence on the development of printing was enormous; and his woodcut illustrations of texts such as Chaucer's *Canterbury Tales* (see Chapter 12) are still popular today.

At first, religious texts were the most commonly printed books, but in time popular secular works and Classical texts were also produced. In 1429, for example, twelve hitherto lost

Society and Culture

The Humanist Movement

The origins of the intellectual movement known as humanism are found in the late thirteenth century, when a group of attorneys in the northern Italian city of Padua became interested in Roman law, especially the works of Cicero. Dramatists revived the Roman plays of Seneca, and a new interest in ancient texts, stored but neglected in monasteries, emerged. Philologists (those who study language) began to analyze texts as a means of interpreting ancient thought. This thirst for the original writing of Greek and Roman authors led some to collect and translate texts and eventually to amass large libraries of Classical manuscripts.

For the humanists, man and his place in the world were a focus of attention and inquiry, just as they had been for the ancients. The authors Petrarch and Boccaccio were the leading figures in fourteenth-century humanism. They extolled the benefits of studying Latin and Greek, and their own writings reflect the influence of Classical thought. In addition, they admired new developments in the arts, especially the painting of Giotto (see Chapter 12), which represented the human figure more naturalistically than medieval artists had done. In the view of Petrarch and Boccaccio, Giotto revived the art of painting, which had lain buried after the fall of Rome, and returned it to the light of day. Humanists used the metaphor of light and dark to suggest that the Classical revival brought with it a renewal of intellectual enlightenment and the creative arts.

As the humanist movement expanded in the fifteenth century, a new educational curriculum evolved, in which Classical texts were included along with Christian ones. In a few of the most enlightened humanist schools of Italy, girls as well as boys studied works on geography, history, politics, philosophy, mathematics, rhetoric (the art of persuasive argument), and the arts and music. In Italy as well as in northern Europe, Plato became a central source for humanists and gradually overshadowed the important role that Aristotle had played in medieval scholasticism.

plays by Plautus were located and printed. Soon the revival of Classical Roman authors extended to Greek texts, and after the fall of Constantinople (modern Istanbul) to the Turks in 1453, many Greek scholars emigrated to Italy. By 1518, every known Roman and Greek play had been published.

ARTS AND SCIENCES

The humanist emphasis on individual personality had begun to appear in the late medieval works of Dante, Chaucer, and Christine de Pisan (see Chapter 12). In the fourteenth century, Petrarch and Boccaccio wrote of a new view of man's place in the world, focusing on personality and advocating fame through achievement as a route to immortality. In the fifteenth century, this new humanist perspective influenced the writing of history, which strove to understand human motivation and to explain the relationship of the present to the past. The fresh historical perspective was accompanied by a new grasp of the third dimension in art (see Box, p. 341) and of greater depth in music.

In theater, plays increasingly focused on everyday life. A merging of Classical subject matter and style expanded the depth of plays and of their characters. For instance, whereas the tragedy *Ecerinis* by Mussato (see Chapter 12) followed the form of Seneca's plays, its subject matter was twelfth-century Italian politics. In 1390, however, in Antonio Laschi's play *Achilles* both the style and the subject of the play were Classical. By coordinating content with style, authors began to grapple more thoroughly with the psychology of their characters, who acted and reacted in a historical context consistent with a specific dramatic form.

Farce and comedy, which had been performed on a small scale in the late Gothic period, became more popular in the fifteenth century. In around 1470, for example, a French dramatist wrote the play *Pierre Pathelin*, in which a lawyer cheats a merchant out of his cloth only to be cheated himself by a peasant. German farces, called Shrovetide plays, were derived from folk festivals and revels during Shrovetide (the period preceding Lent). Even the traditional morality plays increasingly portray human nature.

Humanism in music developed later than in the visual arts. In music, humanist tastes encouraged listener response and a move away from the sacred toward the secular. Flowing rhythms displaced the more stylized, repetitive church music of the Middle Ages, and the hierarchy of musical lines gradually altered. Where previously the tenor part was the basis of the texture and structure, now the voices tended toward equality, interweaving like threads of a tapestry and creating a sense of balance and symmetry.

These changes in the arts signaled a new naturalism emphasizing the human experience—inspired by the ancient Greek maxim, "Man is the measure of all things" (see Chapter 6). The drawing of *Vitruvian Man* (figure **13.2**) by Leonardo da Vinci (1452–1519), for example, illustrates the notion of man's centrality, which the Renaissance adopted from Classical philosophy. Vitruvius was a Roman architect under the emperor Augustus; his *De architectura* (*On Architecture*) was recovered in Italy in 1414. Like Plato, Vitruvius believed that the circle was the ideal shape, and he related human symmetry to architectural harmony. In the Middle Ages, on the other hand, theologians had conceived of the circle not in human terms but rather as symbolizing the perfection of God, the cosmos, and the universal nature of the Church.

During the Renaissance, the status of artists, who in the Middle Ages had been considered artisans (skilled or semi-skilled manual laborers) rose to that of educated gentlemen

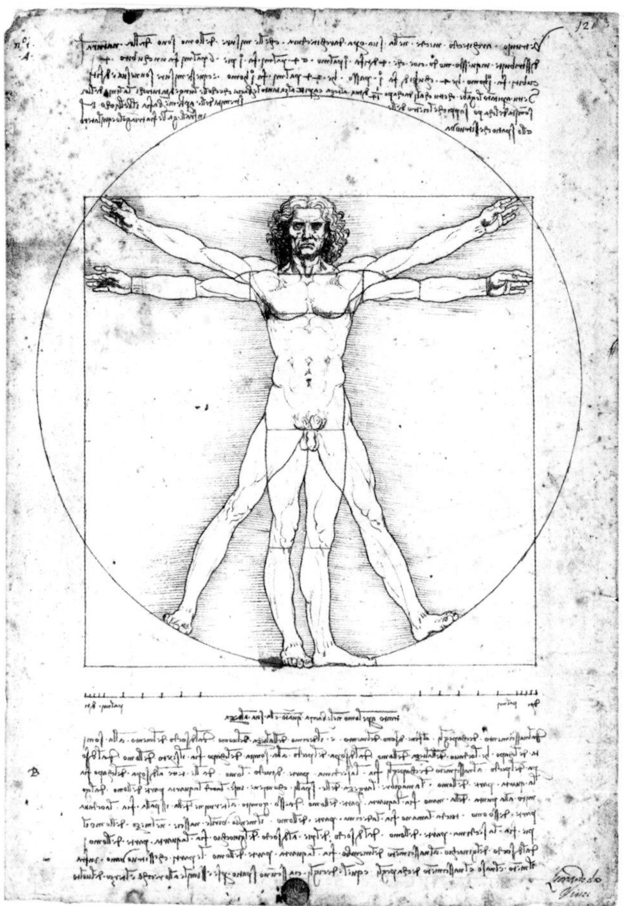

13.2 Leonardo da Vinci, *Vitruvian Man*, c. 1485–1490. Pen and ink, $13^{1}/_{2} \times 9^{5}/_{8}$ in. (34.3 $\times$ 24.5 cm). Gallerie dell' Accademia, Venice.
In this drawing, Leonardo illustrates Vitruvius's assertion that the navel of a man standing inside a circle with arms and legs extended will be placed at the center. Man's central position in nature is thus reflected in the relation of the human navel to the Platonic notion of a geometric harmony regulating the universe. Leonardo has added the square to reinforce the Classical theory of Plato and Vitruvius.

and academicians. The notion of the academy as a place of formal art training and intellectual exchange—based on the informal academies of antiquity (see Chapter 6)—began in the late fifteenth century. Eventually, painting and sculpture (which are now considered to be art) would rise from being mere handicrafts to the higher status of the liberal arts—that is, disciplines capable of freeing or liberating the mind. The Renaissance enlarged the scope of the medieval *trivium* (grammar, rhetoric, and dialectic) and *quadrivium* (arithmetic, geometry, music, and astronomy), adding, among other disciplines, the newly invented practice of linear perspective as well as philosophy and theology.

As an expression of the new sense of authorship, Renaissance painters, sculptors, and architects practiced the ancient genres of biography and portraiture. During the Middle Ages, biography had been largely restricted to lives of saints, and portraiture was the exception rather than the rule. In contrast, Renaissance artists painted many portraits and self-portraits (figure **13.3**) and signed their works (a rare occurrence in the Middle Ages). Similarly, musicians sometimes introduced themselves into the lyrics of their compositions. In a religious work, for example, a composer might ask the Virgin Mary to remember him and pray for his soul. These practices express the general interest in earthly achievement as a route to salvation.

Together with the exploration of human nature, the early Renaissance witnessed a new attitude toward science. Emphasizing observation and experiment rather than theory, science became more empirical than it had been in the Middle Ages. The Renaissance emphasis on empiricism reflected new methods of exploring the world. Artists wishing to render human form began to dissect cadavers and study anatomy. The anatomical drawings of Leonardo da Vinci, whose work marks the transition from the early to the High Renaissance (see Chapter 14), are a case in point (figure **13.4**).

13.3 Jan van Eyck, *Man in a Red Turban*, c. 1433. Tempera and oil on wood, $13^{1}/_{8} \times 10^{1}/_{8}$ in. (33.3 $\times$ 25.8 cm). National Gallery, London.
Although there is some disagreement among scholars as to whom this represents, it is generally thought to be one of the earliest self-portraits of the Renaissance. The Netherlandish artist Jan van Eyck depicts the face in detail, along with an elaborate headpiece and fur collar. The headpiece, usually called a turban, is actually a *chaperon*—a long cloth wrapped around a padded support. As it was worn at the time, the two ends of the cloth hung down. Here, however, they do not, and this has been explained as indicating the artist's need to keep his face clear in order to paint it.

Pinpoints of reflected light in the eyes and the direct gaze animate the expression, while the gradual shading of the flesh creates a strong sense of surface texture. Van Eyck, assuming it is he, communicates with the viewer through his image as well as through the text inscribed on the frame, *Als ich kan* ("as I can"), meaning that he did the best he could, but would have done better had he been able to do so.

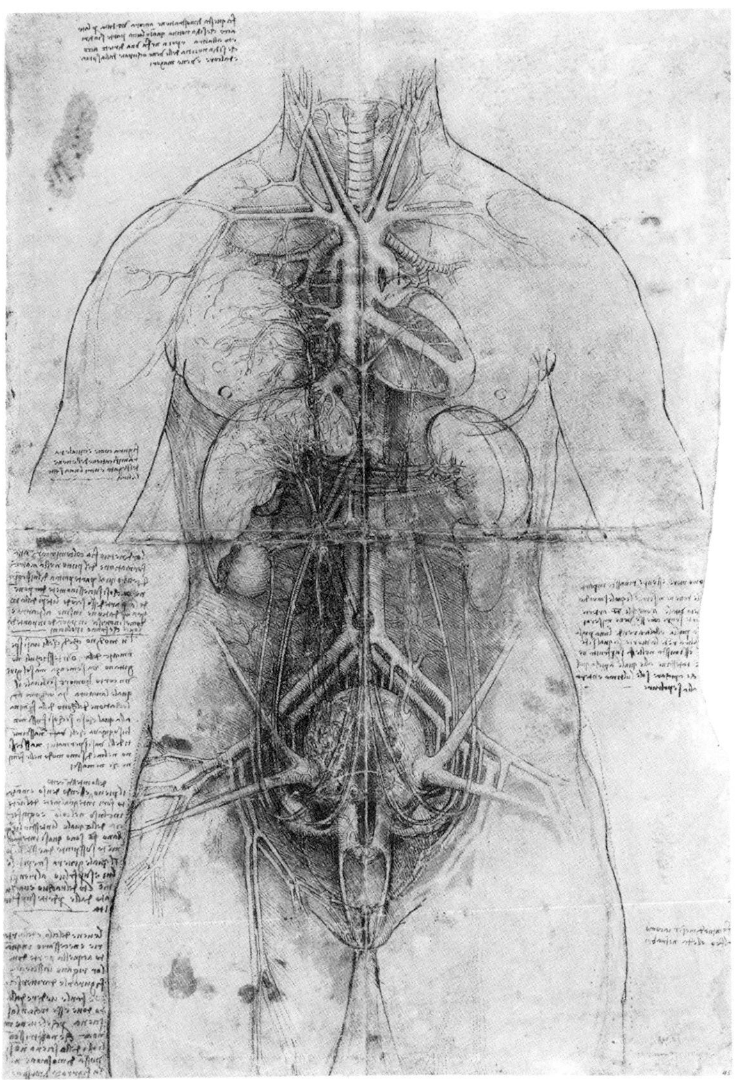

13.4 Leonardo da Vinci, dissection of principal organs and arterial system of a female figure, *c.* 1510. 18³/₈ × 13 in. (46.7 × 33 cm). The Royal Collection, Windsor, U.K.
Leonardo's notes show that he was influenced by the Greek physician Galen, with whom he shared some misconceptions. For example, both believed that human anatomy mirrored animal anatomy and that it was possible to reason from one species to another. Nor did Galen or Leonardo understand the workings of the heart or the circulatory system. Nevertheless, in the light of medieval medicine, drawings based on actual observations were revolutionary.

Although medical training in the fifteenth century was essentially a continuation of medieval training, certain developments required physicians to learn new techniques. With the advent of gunpowder, for example, instruments had to be invented for extracting bullets. This led to a new medical specialty—the army surgeon.

EXPLORATION

A corollary to the interest in human nature and anatomy was an exploration of the world at large. Although there had been world travelers during the Middle Ages and even earlier, in the fifteenth century explorations of the globe began in earnest. Backed by Spain and sailing in ships paid for by the Medici, Christopher Columbus (1451–1506) discovered the New World in the last decade of the fifteenth century. Spain tried to claim the West Indies (Hispaniola) and, later, most of South America. The Portuguese explorer Prince Henry the Navigator (1394–1460) devised a better compass, built more seaworthy ships, and learned how to use the Arabic astrolabe to calculate latitude. In 1497 the Portuguese Vasco da Gama (*c.* 1460–1524) sailed to India, the first person to do so by rounding the Cape of Good Hope on the southern tip of Africa. The Italian John Cabot (1450–1498) sailed to Labrador, on the east coast of Canada, and to New England, claiming North America for England.

As European rulers vied for the potential riches on other continents, they embraced colonialism and planted the seeds of later turmoil. By papal decree (the Treaty of Tordesillas) in 1494, Africa and Brazil were awarded to Portugal; the rest of South America remained with Spain. At the end of the fifteenth century, the known world was larger than it had ever been.

FLORENCE IN THE FIFTEENTH CENTURY

When the fifteenth century dawned, the Italian peninsula was the most commercial, urbanized region of western Europe. Enormous wealth in private hands encouraged the notion that material success was a virtue. More than in any other Italian city, wealth and art converged to produce the greatest innovations in Florence. For the mercantile Florentines, amassing wealth was something devoutly to be wished. They not only enjoyed the benefits of riches on a personal level, but they believed that spending money on art to adorn their city was a virtue. They called this *magnificentia*—the virtue of magnificence.

Located in Tuscany, Florence was the focal point of the Italian Renaissance. Its spoken dialect was Tuscan, the same vernacular in which Dante, Petrarch, and Boccaccio had written. Florence was a leader in the textile trade, especially in the manufacture of wool, which was the original source of Florentine wealth (see Chapter 12). The city also established its financial influence internationally in 1252 by minting the florin (a coin worth about one hundred dollars in today's value and named "the flower" after Florence). This provided a stable monetary system in the city as well as other parts of Europe. Double-entry book-keeping, in which debits are listed with equivalent credits, was invented in the 1300s by Florentine businessmen and is still in general use today.

Society and Culture

The Medici Family in the Fifteenth Century

The origins of the Medici family are not known precisely. According to one legend, a distant ancestor had been a knight of Charlemagne. While traveling to Rome, this knight encountered and fought a giant whose mace dented the knight's shield. Charlemagne, impressed with the knight's bravery, awarded him a coat of arms of three gold balls (derived from the dents) on a gold field. This became the Medici coat of arms. More plausible accounts trace the coat of arms either to the pills dispensed by apothecaries (*Medici* is related to *medico*, meaning "physician") or to the triple balls of pawnbrokers (denoting the moneylending practices of the family).

What *is* known is that the Medici came from the Mugello valley outside Florence. The first wealthy member of the family, Giovanni di Bicci de' Medici (1360–1429), was notoriously ugly. He established the family fortune and the Medici bank through moneylending. Giovanni di Bicci also established the *Monte delle doti*, a bank in which fathers deposited money at high interest rates in order to build up dowries for their daughters.

Giovanni married the beautiful Piccarda de' Bueri, who belonged to an old noble family. Their sons, Cosimo (1389–1464) and Lorenzo (1395–1440), added to the family fortune, and Cosimo became the *de facto* (actual) ruler of Florence in the 1430s. He loaned money to the most important citizens and, by never calling in the loans, maintained both their dependence on him and his influence over them. Cosimo married the dutiful but boring Contessina de' Bardi, a member of the banking family that had commissioned Giotto's St. Francis cycle in Santa Croce (see Chapter 12). When Cosimo died, he was awarded the honorific *Pater patriae*, "Father of his country."

Cosimo's handsome son Piero (1416–1469), who suffered from gout, married the remarkable Lucrezia Tornabuoni. They had two sons, Giuliano and Lorenzo. Giuliano was killed in the Pazzi conspiracy, a plot organized in 1478 by the Pazzi family against Medici control of the city. Lorenzo (1449–1492), known as *Il Magnifico* (The Magnificent), continued the brilliant rule and lavish patronage of his grandfather Cosimo. His mother Lucrezia, herself a successful business entrepreneur and author of plays and musical *laude*, was his most trusted political adviser. She arranged Lorenzo's marriage to the Roman aristocrat Clarice Orsini, with a view to extending Medici influence to the highest circles in Rome.

When Lorenzo died in 1494, he left a weak son and a city that had grown tired of the family's autocratic rule. The Medici were expelled from Florence, though they returned to rule as dukes in the sixteenth century. Over the course of time there would be two Medici popes—Clement VII and Leo X—and members of the family would marry into several royal houses of Europe.

In the early fifteenth century there are estimated to have been at least seventy bankers operating in Florence. One of the leading banking families was the Medici, who had started as wool merchants and moneylenders. By the mid-fifteenth century the Medici bank had a network of branches in London, Antwerp (Belgium), Bruges (Belgium), Cologne (Germany), Geneva (Switzerland), and Lyons (France), as well as other major Italian cities, including Rome, Naples, and Venice.

Twelve trade guilds (*arti*) wielded political power in Florence. Guild members participated in the government, which was at first a republic. But Florence soon evolved into an oligarchy, controlled by a few prominent families, particularly the Medici, who dictated city policy throughout most of the fifteenth century (see Box). Nevertheless, outwardly at least, Florence was determined to maintain the image of a republic.

In the early fifteenth century, Florence was under military threat from the powerful northwestern city-state of Milan. Ruled by the Visconti family, Milan threatened the independent position of Florence and planned an invasion in 1402. The attack was thwarted when an outbreak of plague killed the Milanese leader, Giangaleazzo Visconti (1351–1402). Twenty-five years later, in 1427, Giangaleazzo's son Filippo Maria Visconti (1392–1447) again threatened Florence, though he never invaded the city. This threat prompted Florence to institute the *catasto*, a survey of the citizenry for the purpose of levying a new tax on property to provide funds for defense. Male heads of households had to list their assets, investments, family members, and other dependents. This information, which the meticulous Florentines kept with great care, has proved a rich source of information for historians.

HUMANISM AND THE STATE

At the time of the first Visconti threat, the chancellor (political head of the city) of Florence was Coluccio Salutati (1331–1406). A friend of Petrarch, Salutati was a dedicated humanist. He appointed Manuel Chrysoloras (*c.* 1350–1415), a Greek scholar from Constantinople, to teach Greek at the University of Florence, and in his personal correspondence he advocated reading the Classics. As chancellor, Salutati argued in favor of Florentine political freedom, and in his public speeches he compared the city to the Roman Republic.

READING SELECTION

Salutati, *Letters*, in defense of liberal studies, PWC2-153

In 1427, Leonardo Bruni (*c.* 1370–1444), the first official historian of Florence, became chancellor of the city. Born in Arezzo, in central Italy, Bruni was a humanist who translated Plato and Aristotle and worked as a papal secretary. He subscribed to Cicero's ideal of the philosopher-statesman, and

13.5 Bernardo Rossellino, tomb of Leonardo Bruni, Santa Croce, Florence, begun 1444. Marble, 20 ft. (6 m) high.
Like many Renaissance artists, Rossellino was trained in his family's workshop, which specialized in stonecutting and sculpture. He also worked as an architect and urban designer (see figure 13.27), especially on humanist commissions.

in his *Panegyric of the City of Florence* (1401) he extolled the city's republican government and its cultural ties to Greece and Rome.

Bruni's *History of the Florentine People* (1415) exemplifies the humanist approach to recording history. Taking the Classical past as a model for the present, the *History*, which is imbued with humanist rhetoric, traces the origins of Florence to the ancient Roman Republic.

When Bruni died, he was honored with a new type of sculptural installation placed against the wall of a church—the so-called humanist tomb (figure **13.5**). Unlike the medieval transi tombs, which had effigies of decaying, worm-eaten bodies on their lids (see Chapter 12), Bruni's tomb idealizes the image of the deceased. It shows him fully clothed, sleeping peacefully, and holding a copy of his *History of the Florentine People*. A Roman round arch has replaced the Gothic pointed arch, and it rests on fluted Corinthian pilasters (rectangular columns), reflecting the revival of the ancient Orders of architecture. At the same time, the tomb design includes Christian elements such as the figures of Mary and Christ flanked by angels in the round frame, forming a **tondo**, inside the arch.

Humanists, who were, by and large, devout Christians, welcomed such combinations of pagan and Christian iconography as are incorporated into Bruni's tomb. At the very top, two winged nude boys (*putti*), which derive from Roman sarcophagi, display a laurel wreath, the ancient sign of triumph. Inside the wreath is the lion symbol of Florence (the *Marzocco*), which alludes to Bruni's position as the city's chancellor. A pair of eagles, suggesting the Roman Jupiter and the Greek Zeus, support his bier. On the sarcophagus two winged Victories carry an inscription announcing that the Greek and Roman Muses, even history itself, mourn the loss of Bruni's eloquence. The base of the sarcophagus is sculpted in the form of lion's paws. Below, on the plinth, reliefs of dancing *putti* carrying garlands frame another lion head. The repetition of the lion motif alludes to Bruni's name (Leo, short for *leone*, which means "lion" in Italian).

A third humanist chancellor of Florence, Poggio Bracciolini (1380–1459), was a distinguished antiquarian. Following Petrarch, Bracciolini searched for ancient texts that had lain forgotten in monastic libraries and amassed a large collection of books. His best writings, most of which were in Latin, were dialogues using the Socratic method after the manner of Plato. This marked a departure from scholastic dialectic, because Socrates sought truth in human discourse rather than through a superimposed, hierarchical system of reasoning based on faith.

THE PLATONIC ACADEMY

Inspired by Cosimo de' Medici's ambition to establish a Platonic Academy, Lorenzo did so in 1469 to encourage the study of Plato. The Academy was headed by Marsilio Ficino (1433–1499), the son of Cosimo's physician and an ordained priest who had also studied medicine, magic, and astrology. Above all, Ficino was a follower of Plato's philosophy.

Cosimo had commissioned Ficino to translate Plato's known works from Greek into Latin. Ficino's discussion of Plato's *Symposium* (the dialogue on love) distinguishes two aspects of Venus—profane and divine. He argues that physical love can lead to spiritual love.

Ficino also translated Plotinus, the third-century-A.D. commentator on Plato. At the core of Ficino's philosophy, which is based on Plotinus's Neoplatonism ("new Platonism"), is the notion of a divine chain of being. In the chain of being, the lowest form of divisible matter is at the bottom, and the indivisible, perfectly unified God is at the top. At the center is the human soul, which strives toward God's perfection through reason, will, and contemplation. Ficino believed that Plato, more so than Aristotle, could be reconciled with Christianity, and he advocated the inclusion of Plato in the Christian curriculum.

Human potential similarly influenced the ideas of Ficino's student, Giovanni Pico della Mirandola (1463–1494), who came from Lombardy in northern Italy. Pico studied philosophy in Paris and advanced a system of thought that combined Greek, Arabic, and medieval Jewish philosophy with Christianity. Although Pico believed Christianity to be the highest of these, his views offended the Church; only the intervention of Lorenzo the Magnificent saved him from arrest. Pico became part of the Medici circle of Platonists, arguing for the inherent value of man. His *Oration on the Dignity of Man* (1486) exemplifies the humanist view that man is rational, endowed with free will, and capable of determining his own destiny.

READING SELECTION

Pico, *Oration on the Dignity of Man*, the humanist view of man, PWC3-075

DECORATING THE CITY

The first generation in fifteenth-century Florence produced several artists of unusual genius. Foremost among these were Ghiberti and Donatello in sculpture, Brunelleschi in architecture, and Masaccio in painting. All received commissions that enhanced the appearance of the city and enriched its civic and religious institutions. The competition held in 1401 exemplifies the new approach to patronage and its relation to civic pride.

13.6 The cathedral, bell tower, and baptistery, Florence, Italy.
From 1294, the old cathedral of Florence was rebuilt and gradually enlarged. This building is faced with bands of green and white marble and has a dome over the crossing. The single bell tower (campanile) was designed by Giotto in the fourteenth century. The round windows in the dome's octagonal drum and the clerestory windows are the main sources of light, but surmounting the dome is a new Renaissance feature, the lantern, which is a further source of light.

13.7 **Filippo Brunelleschi, *Sacrifice of Isaac*, 1401–1402. Gilt bronze, 21 × 17½ in. (53.3 × 44.4 cm). Museo Nazionale del Bargello, Florence.**

13.8 **Lorenzo Ghiberti, *Sacrifice of Isaac*, 1401–1402. Gilt bronze, 21 × 17½ in. (53.3 × 44.4 cm). Museo Nazionale del Bargello, Florence.** Note that Brunelleschi's relief is more powerful, as Abraham's knife is about to pierce his son's neck and the angel intervenes just in time to save Isaac. Ghiberti's relief is more graceful, and there is more attention to patterns of landscape, which reflects the influence of International Gothic style. Isaac is modeled after a Classical nude, its organic form and contrapposto indicating that Ghiberti had studied Greek sculpture.

THE COMPETITION OF 1401 At the center of Florence stood the huge Gothic cathedral, Santa Maria del Fiore (also called the Duomo), and the octagonal baptistery dedicated to John the Baptist (figure **13.6**). In 1401, the board of the cathedral held a competition for the commission of a pair of doors for the baptistery. Sculptors submitted bronze reliefs illustrating the biblical story of the Sacrifice of Isaac, in which Abraham is about to obey God's command to sacrifice his son. Judging the reliefs were clerical and lay people under the supervision of the wool refiners' guild. Only two of the submissions survive, one by Filippo Brunelleschi (1377–1446) and one by Lorenzo Ghiberti (*c.* 1378–1455) (figures **13.7** and **13.8**). Ghiberti was awarded the commission for the doors, which he completed around 1424.

BRUNELLESCHI'S DOME In 1417 the cathedral of Florence was still without a dome. The nearly 140-foot (42.6-m) diameter of space that had to be covered was the largest span since the construction of the Roman Pantheon, whose dome was 142 feet (43.28 m) in diameter (see Chapter 7). But the Pantheon was a hemisphere and rested on a round drum, whereas Florence cathedral needed a dome to cover an octagonal space.

In 1418, Brunelleschi, who had renounced sculpture and dedicated himself to architecture, submitted a model for the dome. His model was accepted and he began construction in 1420. The splendid result illustrates Brunelleschi's genius for architectural engineering and design (figure **13.9**). Ghiberti claimed to have been Brunelleschi's equal partner in constructing the dome. But Ghiberti probably exaggerated his role, given that he was dismissed from the work on the dome in 1425, after Brunelleschi objected to his participation.

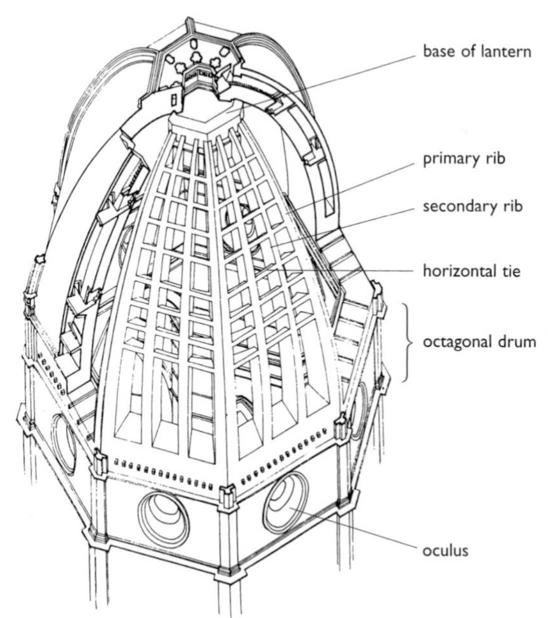

13.9 **Axonometric section of the dome of Florence Cathedral.** Having studied the Pantheon in Rome, Brunelleschi knew that a space of this size could be spanned, but there were no trees large enough to permit the type of centering used in the Middle Ages. Further, the octagonal drum was not as strong as the round drum of the Pantheon. Brunelleschi therefore devised a system in which eight large ribs extend from the base of the lantern to an angle of the octagon. These are visible on the exterior of the dome, but they alternate with pairs of smaller ribs, which are not visible. Reinforcing the vertical ribs are nine horizontal ties, which absorb the thrust of the ribs and prevent the wall of the dome from buckling outward. Additional support is provided by the herringbone pattern of the outer brick shell. By doubling the shell, Brunelleschi created an interior space that relieved the weight of the structure. Finally, by using brick, which is lighter than stone, he further reduced the weight borne by the skeleton.

Giotto, *Enthroned Madonna*
see figure 12.13

DONATELLO'S *JOHN THE EVANGELIST* In 1409, the guild of manufacturers of woolen cloth commissioned seated statues of the four Evangelists for the cathedral's façade. The most innovative sculptor of his generation, Donatello di Niccolò Betto Bardi (*c.* 1386–1466), executed the statue of John the Evangelist. After the 1401 competition Donatello had accompanied Brunelleschi to Rome, where he absorbed the principles of ancient statuary such as naturalism and idealization evident in figure **13.10**. This commission, like the competition for the baptistery doors, reveals the influence of guilds in the artistic and political life of Florence.

MASACCIO The leading painter of the early Renaissance was Tommaso di ser Giovanni, known as Masaccio (1401–1428). Although he died at the age of twenty-seven, in a few short years he developed Giotto's approach to the picture plane and created a new pictorial style. His *Virgin and Child*, the central panel of the Pisa altarpiece of 1426, shows the enthroned Virgin and Christ according to a new system of perspective attributed to Brunelleschi (figure **13.11**) (see Box). Compared with Giotto in the *Enthroned Madonna* (see thumbnail), Masaccio has eliminated the Gothic pointed arches and delicate Gothic tracery of the throne. Instead, he has revived the

13.10 Donatello, *John the Evangelist*, *c.* 1409–1411. Marble, 6 ft. 11 in. (2.1 m) high. Museo dell'Opera del Duomo, Florence.
The elongated torso and heavy drapery folds compensate for the placement of the statue above the entrance, where it would have been seen from below. The evangelist holds his gospel and gazes upward, enrapt in a vision. Compared with medieval sculptures, this has organic form and individual character.

13.11 Masaccio, *Virgin and Child*, central panel of the Pisa altarpiece, 1426. Tempera on wood panel, 53 3/8 × 28 3/4 in. (135.5 × 73 cm). National Gallery, London.

Classical Orders of architecture (see Chapters 5 and 6), which appear on the sides and back of the throne. His use of chiaroscuro creates gradual shifts of light and dark that define the forms.

Masaccio's Christ exemplifies a new approach to depicting children, which is unlike the medieval baby-king. In the more natural form and childlike behavior of Masaccio's Christ, the figure has a miraculous nature as well as an infant's normal impulse to put things in its mouth. But this child is eating grapes, which an average infant would not be allowed to do. Masaccio's image thus conflates the reality of childhood with a symbolic allusion to the wine of the Eucharist.

In the monumental fresco of the *Trinity* (figure **13.14**), which is on the nave wall of the church of Santa Maria Novella in Florence, Masaccio again implemented Brunelleschi's perspective system. He assumed a viewer whose eye level is at

Society and Culture

Linear Perspective

Renaissance artists conceived of the picture plane as a window giving onto a view of three-dimensional space. Brunelleschi is credited as the inventor of rendering this view mathematically from the fixed position of an observer. Figure **13.12** shows Brunelleschi's conception, designed for architects, which assumes a person standing on the ground looking up at a building. Figure **13.13**, on the other hand, is designed for paintings and relief sculpture, and illustrates one-point perspective. In this system, the floor plan of the picture or relief is a grid and the sides of the squares (**orthogonals**) appear to recede toward a horizon. The squares diminish in size as they approach the horizon, creating the impression of increasing distance. When the image is symmetrical, the orthogonals meet at a single central point, known as the **vanishing point**. With this system, artists were able to replicate three-dimensional space on a flat surface and also to control the viewer's line of sight.

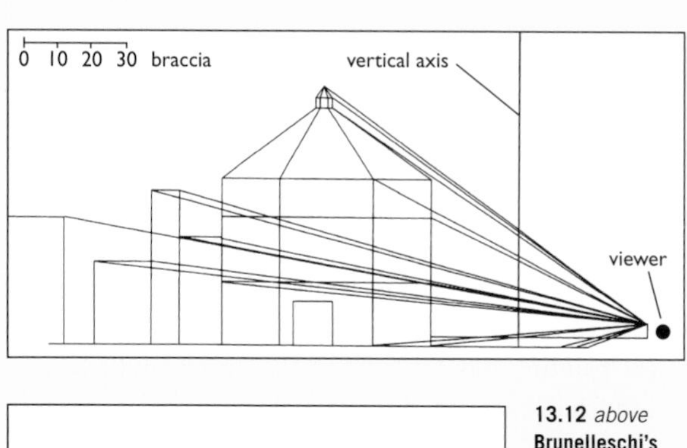

13.12 *above* **Brunelleschi's perspective system.**

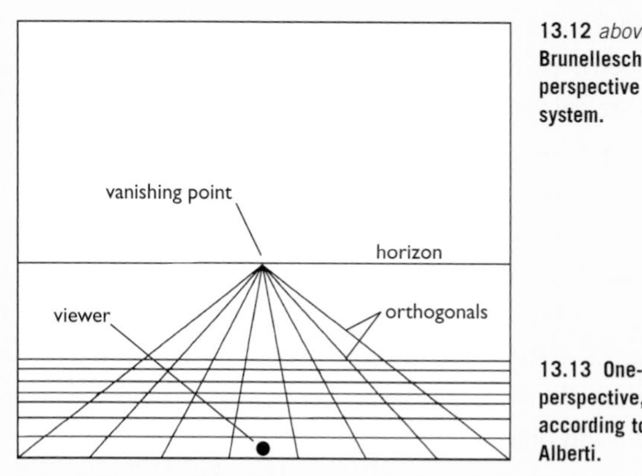

13.13 One-point perspective, according to Alberti.

the center of the lower step, which is also the location of the vanishing point. Looking up at the image, therefore, one sees the patrons—members of the influential Lenzi family—kneeling on the outer step. Their placement in the transitional space between the viewer and the Trinity identifies them as the donors and reflects their wish for salvation. The interior sacred space, occupied by the three persons of the Trinity, seems projected into an area beyond the wall. God stands on the back ledge, Christ hangs on the Cross, and a dove representing the Holy Spirit hovers above Christ's head. Mary is to the viewer's left and St. John is to the right.

Just below the steps is a foreshortened ledge supported by Corinthian columns. Between the columns, a painted sarcophagus supports an extended skeleton. The inscription over the skeleton reads: "I was once what you are, and what I am you will also be." Continuing the medieval tradition of the Quick

13.14 Masaccio, *Trinity*, 1425–1428, Santa Maria Novella, Florence. Fresco, 21 ft. 10⅝ in. × 10 ft. 4¾ in. (6.67 × 3.17 m).
The architectural rendering reflects several Renaissance developments. The round arch and barrel vault were inspired by ancient Rome, and the coffers by the Pantheon. Following the recommendations of Brunelleschi, Masaccio uses fluted pilasters and smooth-shafted columns. The capitals of the former are Corinthian, and the latter combine the Ionic volute capital with the Doric abacus.

13.15 Masaccio, *Tribute Money*, Brancacci Chapel, Santa Maria del Carmine, Florence, 1420s. Fresco, 8 ft. 1¼ in. × 19 ft. 7 in. (2.47 × 5.97 m).
At the center of the fresco, Christ is surrounded by apostles as the tax collector of Capernaum, seen in rear view, demands payment. Because Christ has no money, he instructs Peter to go to the Sea of Galilee and to extract a coin from the mouth of a fish. Peter's conflicted response is shown in his ambivalent gestures: he draws back his left hand in protest, while simultaneously echoing Christ's pointing right hand. At the far left, in the distance, Peter kneels at the edge of the sea and removes the exact amount of tax due from the fish's mouth. At the right, in the foreground, he places the money in the tax collector's hand.

and the Dead (see Chapter 12), the skeleton admonishes the viewer that death and decay are the future of the human condition. Faith in Christ, the image implies, is the route to salvation.

Masaccio's next major contribution to the city of Florence was the fresco cycle in the Brancacci Chapel illustrating the life of St. Peter. The large scene entitled the *Tribute Money* is divided into three narrative events based on the Gospel of Matthew (figure **13.15**). The monumental figures, whose heads resemble ancient Roman portrait busts, dominate the landscape. Each one shows by his expression or gesture a certain astonishment at Christ's words.

ALBERTI: A RENAISSANCE MAN Leon Battista Alberti (1404–1474) epitomizes what we today call a "Renaissance Man," a person who is highly accomplished in many fields. He was born in Florence, the illegitimate son of a wealthy merchant who was exiled from Florence for political reasons. Alberti himself studied law and classics and worked as a papal secretary in Rome. He did not return to Florence until the early 1430s.

Alberti's influential work *On Painting* (*Della pittura*), of around 1435, is the earliest Renaissance treatise on art theory. The text opens with the author's impression that the arts in Italy were in decline. After coming to Florence and seeing the work of Brunelleschi, Donatello, Masaccio, and others, however, Alberti realized that a Classical revival was taking place. He described Greco-Roman antiquity as "glorious days," when marvelous works of art and architecture were produced.

Alberti's writing is filled with Classical allusions, for he believed that Classical culture, which inspired the new generation of artists in Florence, was the ideal model. He credited Brunelleschi's system of perspective with having revived the illusion of three-dimensional space achieved by Classical Greek painters; and he credited Giotto and Masaccio with having created convincing figures to inhabit that space.

Nature, in Alberti's view, was the source of art, and art, therefore, should reflect nature. He cited the ancient myth that the first painting was made when the Greek youth Narcissus saw, and fell in love with, his own reflection in a pool of water. For Alberti, painting consists of embracing nature, just as images are reflected on the surface of water. Because the figures created by Giotto, Masaccio, and Donatello appear natural in both form and character, they conform to Alberti's ideal.

Alberti compared painting to a window. The picture plane was equivalent to the flat surface of the window, so that looking at a picture is like looking through a window. Both views, Alberti believed, should replicate what one actually sees—three-dimensional space containing figures behaving naturally and objects appearing as they would in reality.

Alberti's learning was prodigious. He wrote on many topics other than painting, including sculpture, architecture, and society. Like Ghiberti, Alberti wrote an autobiography. Published anonymously, Alberti's account describes the difficulties of being illegitimate and boasts of his physical and intellectual achievements. Most influential of all his work during the fifteenth century was the *Book of the Family* (*Della famiglia*), copies of which could be found in most of the major fifteenth-century humanist libraries. The book, which was written in the form of a dialogue, set out Alberti's ideal view of the Florentine family.

In the *Book of the Family*, Alberti uses an architectural metaphor to equate the father of the family with an architect. A father, he wrote, is responsible for guiding the development of his sons, just as an architect supervises a building. Alberti feared women's evil influence on men and recommended that they be silent and obedient. He advised husbands against sharing secrets with their wives, lest they reveal them to others. Men were to be educated and to work outside the home, Alberti wrote, but women were to tend to the servants and other household matters. When a man was selecting a wife, Alberti declared, it was better if the prospective bride had many brothers and no sisters. He also wrote a number of misogynistic short stories in which women are described in virulently negative terms.

To a considerable degree, Alberti's views were consistent with those of his time. In one respect, however, he was progressive, even by modern standards: he firmly believed that mothers should breast-feed their own infants, rather than hiring wet nurses, as was the prevailing custom. Assuming that a husband had chosen his wife well, Alberti believed that the wife's good character would thus be transferred to her children. Among the women who followed Alberti's advice was Lucrezia Tornabuoni, the wife of Piero de' Medici and mother of Lorenzo the Magnificent.

ALBERTI'S ARCHITECTURE When he was around the age of forty, Alberti became a practicing architect and embarked on an architectural treatise, *De re aedificatoria libri X* (*On Architecture in 10 Books*). This work, as well as the buildings he designed, had a lasting influence on Renaissance and later styles. From 1446 to 1451, he supervised the construction of the Rucellai Palace in Florence (figure **13.16**). This enormous palace exemplifies the virtue of *magnificentia*, for it decorated the city and also proclaimed the wealth and status of the owner. Stylistically, the Rucellai Palace reflects Alberti's ambition to integrate Classical with Renaissance architecture. Following the principles he saw in the Colosseum in Rome (see figure 7.29), Alberti emphasized the structural logic of the building by making the ground floor appear heavier than the top two floors. The ground floor is taller, made with heavier blocks, and has smaller windows than the floors above it.

Like the Colosseum, the Rucellai Palace uses progressively lighter Orders as the building ascends. Alberti employed the heavier Tuscan Doric Order for the ground-floor pilasters, a version of the lighter Ionic Order on the second floor, and the more elaborate Corinthian Order on the third floor. In addition to adopting the Orders, which were derived from antiquity, Alberti designed a diamond pattern at the base of the ground floor. This derived from ancient Roman buildings, where a similar pattern, called *opus reticulatum*, emphasized the structural solidity of the base of a wall.

13.16 Bernardo Rossellini, after Alberti's design, Rucellai Palace, Florence, 1446–1451.
This palace was commissioned by Giovanni Rucellai, who had made a fortune manufacturing the red color (*oricello*) used in dyeing cloth. A supporter of the Medici, Rucellai's son married a sister of Lorenzo the Magnificent. In honor of their marriage, the frieze is decorated with Rucellai and Medici emblems. Medici coats of arms are visible over two of the second-story windows.

13.17 Alberti, façade of Sant' Andrea, Mantua, begun 1472.

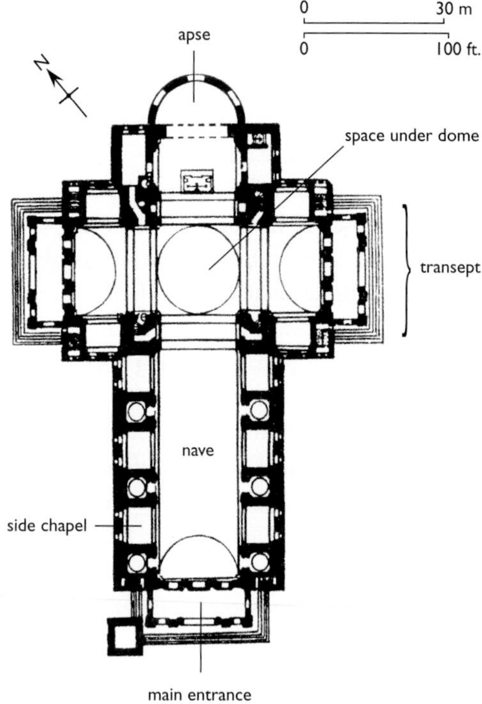

13.18 *above* Plan of Sant' Andrea, Mantua.

In church architecture, too, Alberti combined Classical with Renaissance features. His late (and unfinished) church of Sant' Andrea in Mantua (figures **13.17** and **13.18**) shows the influence of Classical symmetry, harmonious proportions, and the use of the Roman round arch and barrel vault. Giant Corinthian pilasters rest on podia reminiscent of those found on Roman triumphal arches and support an entablature based on ancient Greek and Roman prototypes. Crowning the entablature is a wide pediment, also derived from ancient temples. Like a Roman temple, Sant' Andrea seems to dominate the urban space before it. Note also the symmetry and harmonious regularity of the plan (see figure 13.18).

MEDICI PATRONAGE

Not only were the Medici the *de facto* rulers of Florence for most of the fifteenth century, they were also the city's most generous patrons of the arts. They financed works for religious Orders, for churches, and for civic buildings. They commissioned book dealers to buy Classical and Christian texts and established humanist libraries. The Medici palace was both a private residence and a showcase of the family's power. Inspired by Petrarch's description of Mount Ventoux (see Chapter 12) and by the ancient Roman preference for the countryside as respite from urban tensions, the Medici commissioned several country villas. These proved particularly useful as places of refuge during outbreaks of the plague.

DONATELLO'S *DAVID* Sometime between 1420 and 1440, Cosimo de' Medici commissioned Donatello's bronze statue of *David* (figure **13.19**), which stood on a pedestal in the courtyard of the Medici palace. David was a paradigm of Florentine resistance against tyranny, which was symbolized by the Philistine giant, Goliath. David's role as an ancestor of Christ also made his victory over Goliath a symbolic triumph over the devil. As a victor, David exemplified the Renaissance notion of fame achieved through success, in this case overpowering a stronger enemy through intelligence and skill rather than by brute force.

The effeminate quality of the *David* is unusual in a male biblical hero, though it was perhaps less surprising to the humanists, who read Plato and were familiar with his argument that homosexual men make the bravest soldiers, because

Polykleitos, *Spearbearer*
see figure 6.22

13.19 Donatello, *David*, 1420–1440. Bronze, 5 ft. $2\frac{1}{4}$ in. (1.58 m) high. Museo Nazionale del Bargello, Florence.
This is an early Renaissance nude sculpture inspired by Classical style (see thumbnail). Note the revival of contrapposto, the convincing organic quality of the body, and the relaxed pose. These characteristics of the Classical canon indicate Donatello's study of Classical sculpture. In breach of Classical style, however, Donatello gives David a distinctive personality. His smug expression signals his easy victory, as his toe plays casually with Goliath's mustache.

they fight to impress their lovers. Plato further says that republics—of which Florence was one—tolerate homosexuality, whereas tyrannies do not.

FRA ANGELICO IN SAN MARCO Cosimo de' Medici, a Christian as well as a humanist, financed the Dominican convent of San Marco in Florence and commissioned frescoes and altarpieces for the interior. Most of these were executed by Fra Angelico (*c.* 1400–1455), a pious Dominican friar, manuscript illuminator, and painter. His most monumental works are the frescoes on the walls of the friars' cells and in the corridors of San Marco (figure **13.20**). Fra Angelico's style combines the perspectival construction devised by Brunelleschi and the naturalism of Giotto and Masaccio with the intellectual and spiritual focus of the Dominican Order. In this work, the Virgin, who was the spiritual abbess of San Marco, occupies a pose of mourning, as if meditating on her son's death. The figure of St. Dominic, in contrast, reads a text, reflecting the Order's devotion to study.

INSIDE THE MEDICI PALACE As a frequent destination of visiting dignitaries, ambassadors, and other political figures, the Medici palace was decorated to enhance its image in the outside world. One series of prominently displayed paintings

13.20 Fra Angelico, *Mocking of Christ with the Virgin and St. Dominic*, cell 7, San Marco, Florence, 1438–1445. Fresco, 6 ft $1\frac{5}{8}$ in. × 4 ft. $11\frac{1}{2}$ in. (1.87 × 1.51 m).
In each cell of San Marco, Fra Angelico painted an event from the life of Christ. In keeping with the Dominican Order's rigorous emphasis on asceticism, the images evoke identification with the suffering of holy figures. Here Christ is mocked and tortured by disembodied heads and hands in the background.

13.21 *above* **Paolo Uccello, *Battle of San Romano*, 1440s. Tempera on wood panel, 6 ft. × 10 ft. 6 in. (1.82 × 3.20 m). National Gallery, London.**

13.22 **Benozzo Gozzoli, *Procession of the Magi*, east wall of the Medici chapel, Medici Palace, Florence. 1459. Fresco.**

represents three scenes from the Battle of San Romano. In this battle, fought in 1432, Cosimo's ally, the **condottiere** (mercenary soldier) Niccolò da Tolentino, defeated the Sienese army. The episode in figure **13.21** was designed to show the association of the Medici family with the military triumphs of Florence. Riding the rearing white horse and brandishing his sword is Niccolò da Tolentino. The greater force of his army as compared with the Sienese is shown by the prominent lances, waving flags, and central position of the *condottiere*. Visible on the background trees are apples (despite their orange color), known as *mala medica* ("medicinal apples"), which were a symbol of the Medici family. Note the abrupt shift in perspective from the foreground to the distant landscape, where tiny figures continue the battle. The radical foreshortening of the fallen knight is characteristic of Uccello, who was known for his interest in perspective.

The frescoes by Benozzo Gozzoli (*c.* 1420–1497) that illustrate the Procession of the Magi reflect the enormous wealth of the Medici family. The scene covers an entire wall of the chapel in the Medici palace but is only one segment of a long and elaborate procession, painted as if leading toward the altar to worship before a painting in which Mary and Joseph adore the infant Jesus. The part of the procession shown in figure **13.22** contains a number of portraits of family members as well as of important political visitors to the palace. The lead Magus is the young Caspar, who has occasionally been identified as Lorenzo the Magnificent. In fact, however, Lorenzo was only eleven in 1459 and is shown with his brother Giuliano at the center of the retinue. At the head of the group are Cosimo (in black) and his son Piero (wearing a brocade coat). Note that one figure gazes at the viewer. This is the artist, who has signed the picture in gold on his red hat—OPUS BENOTII ("the work of Benozzo"). The predominance of gold, the attention to details of costume, and the variety of figure types and animals is characteristic of International Gothic style (see Chapter 12). It is also consistent with the Medici practice of using their palace as a political center where the arts reflected their wealth and power.

BOTTICELLI'S *BIRTH OF VENUS* While collecting and translating Classical texts, humanists also revived mythological subject matter and commissioned artists to illustrate scenes from Greek and Roman mythology. Around 1470 to 1480, a cousin of Lorenzo the Magnificent commissioned Botticelli's impressive *Birth of Venus* (figure **13.23**). The goddess, in Greek myth, was

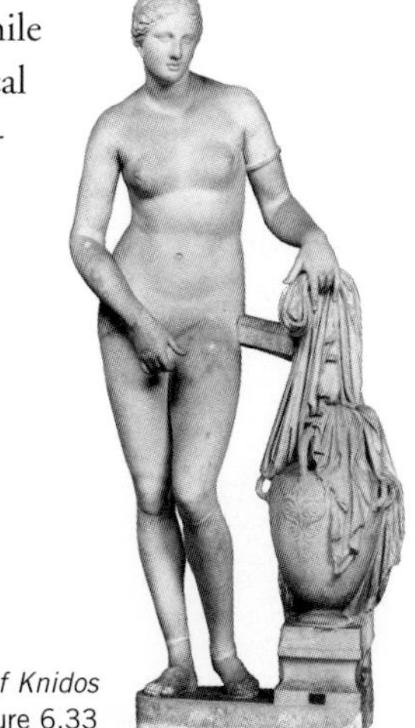

Praxiteles, *Aphrodite of Knidos*
see figure 6.33

13.23 Sandro Botticelli, *Birth of Venus*, *c.* 1480. Tempera on canvas, 5 ft. 9 in. × 9 ft. 2 in. (1.73 × 2.77 m). Galleria degli Uffizi, Florence.

born from the foam of the sea and is shown here drifting ashore, blown by a gentle breeze from the wind gods. She is welcomed by a personification of Spring, who carries a floral robe. Venus's languid, modest pose is reminiscent of Hellenistic statues (see thumbnail), indicating that Botticelli (1445–1510) was a humanist who studied both the form and content of ancient art.

ARCHITECTURE: GIULIANO DA SANGALLO The Medici commissioned churches as well as urban palaces and country villas. Lorenzo supported the work of Giuliano da Sangallo (*c.* 1445–1516), a leading humanist architect of the late fifteenth century (figure **13.24**). In the church of Santa Maria delle Carceri (St. Mary of the Prisons), built in the small town of Prato, near Florence, Sangallo revived the centralized Greek cross plan (figure **13.25**). Although this was a Byzantine type of plan, in the Renaissance centralized church plans were associated with the Platonic perfection of the circle and *Vitruvian Man* (see figure 13.2). The exterior view of Santa Maria delle Carceri shows the use of Greek pediments and the simple geometric forms that had appealed to Brunelleschi. Like the Colosseum in Rome, this church uses the heavier Doric Order for the first floor and the lighter Ionic Order above. With the revival of the Greek cross plan, Sangallo introduced a new type of Renaissance church that would influence architecture in the sixteenth century (see Chapter 14).

MUSIC IN FLORENCE UNDER THE MEDICI Music and dance were popular features of Florentine festivals, pageants, and weddings (figure **13.26**). Lorenzo the Magnificent founded a music school, which, like the fifteenth-century courts, drew talent from other parts of Europe. The Flemish composer Heinrich Isaac (*c.* 1450–1517), for example, spent ten years working under Lorenzo's patronage in Florence. He was later appointed court composer to the Holy Roman Emperor Maximilian I in Innsbruck, Austria. Isaac wrote secular as well as church music, with texts in German, French, and Italian.

In Florence, the *intermedio*, which combined music with dance and poetry, became popular. Florentines also devised a

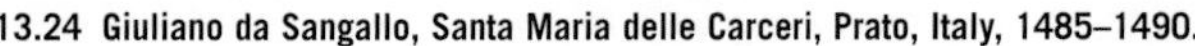

13.24 Giuliano da Sangallo, Santa Maria delle Carceri, Prato, Italy, 1485–1490.

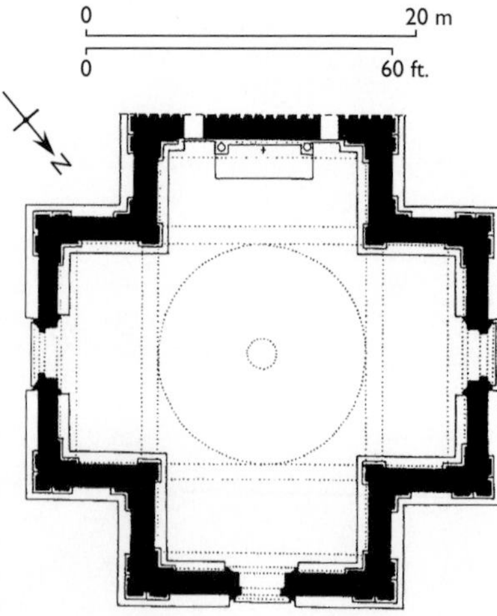

13.25 Plan of Santa Maria delle Carceri, Prato. Note the plan's regular symmetry, which appealed to the Classical taste.

13.26 Giovanni di Ser Giovanni (lo Scheggia), Adimari wedding *cassone* panel, detail, *c.* 1450. 24¾ in. (63 cm) high. Galleria dell'Academia, Florence.
This panel from a *cassone* (wedding chest) is decorated with a scene showing the types of musical instruments that were played at such events. The setting is a tent, with a receding street and buildings in the background. Elegantly attired couples dance to the music of three shawms with fleurs-de-lis banners and a slide trumpet, as older women sit gossiping to one side. A young page and a servant carrying a wine bottle attend to the guests.

characteristic version of the **frottola**, a lighthearted, generally amorous poem for three or four voices with instrumental accompaniment. The carnival song (a type of *frottola*), or *canto carnascialesco*, was especially popular during the pre-Lenten carnival season. Some of these were written by Isaac during his stay in Florence, and Lorenzo himself composed a famous carnival song reflecting the philosophy that one should enjoy one's youth:

Quant' é bella giovanezza,
Che si fugge tuttavia!
Chi vuol esser lieto, sia:
Di doman ne c'è certezza.

How beautiful is youth,
Which quickly flies away!
Whosoever wishes for happiness, let him:
For tomorrow is never certain.

(Stanza 1)

There was also a more serious, theoretical side to music in fifteenth-century Florence. The philosopher Marsilio Ficino, for example, wrote on musical topics, referring to the practices of antiquity and in particular to Pythagoras. Contemporary accounts relate that Orpheus was an inspiration for songs Ficino performed, improvising (inventing) his own accompaniment on the "lyre." The *lira da braccio*, a bowed string instrument, was widely used by poet-musicians to accompany recitations of lyric and narrative poetry.

CONSERVATIVE BACKLASH: ANTONINUS AND SAVONAROLA

Although fifteenth-century Florence was progressive in many ways, some conservative clerics perceived humanism as a threat to the Church. They objected to the view of man's centrality in the universe and argued for greater emphasis on the power of faith. Two orthodox Dominicans took particularly strong stands on this issue. One was Antonio Pierozzi (1389–1459), a friend of Cosimo de' Medici, who was appointed San Marco's prior in 1439 and in 1446 became archbishop of Florence. A number of miracles were attributed to him, and he was canonized as St. Antoninus in 1523.

Antoninus preached fire-and-brimstone sermons, threatening Florentines with damnation if they failed to repent of their sins. Using the model of Mary Magdalene as a sinner saved through penance, he warned of a coming apocalypse and vividly described everlasting tortures in hell. The dire predictions of Antoninus took on additional force in 1448, when an outbreak of plague swept through Florence. To the populace it seemed that the apocalypse had arrived.

In 1491, another fiery, charismatic Dominican monk, Girolamo Savonarola (1452–1498), became prior of San Marco. Although he had been a friend of the Medici—Lorenzo the Magnificent had arranged for his transfer from his native Ferrara to Florence—Savonarola railed against the family. He convinced the Florentines that the Medici had abused their political power, so much so that in 1494, two years after Lorenzo's death, Savonarola managed to oust the Medici and take control of the government.

Preaching austerity, Savonarola objected to gambling, popular music (including carnival songs), and all displays of material ostentation. He banned carnival celebrations because of their burlesque eroticism. Savonarola presided over two "bonfires of the vanities," in which paintings depicting nudes and mythological subjects were publicly burned. In addition, the citizens of Florence threw into the bonfires articles of clothing, jewels, and playing cards deemed to reflect vanity. Unfortunately for Savonarola, he made the mistake of criticizing Pope Alexander VI, and he was excommunicated. In 1498, Savonarola was hanged. His body was taken down while he was still alive and burned; his ashes were scattered in the River Arno.

THE ARTS OUTSIDE FLORENCE

Although Florence was the preeminent artistic city in fifteenth-century Italy, important works of art were produced elsewhere as well. In Rome, progressive popes were influenced by humanist ideas and encouraged the revival of Classical texts and the stylistic innovations of early Renaissance artists. Nicholas V (papacy 1447–1455), for example, created the core of the Vatican library with Classical and Christian texts. Sixtus IV (papacy 1471–1484) enlarged the library and built the Sistine Chapel. Pius II (papacy 1458–1464) oversaw the development of the first Renaissance ideal city by replanning his native Corsignano (figure **13.27**). He renamed the city Pienza, after himself.

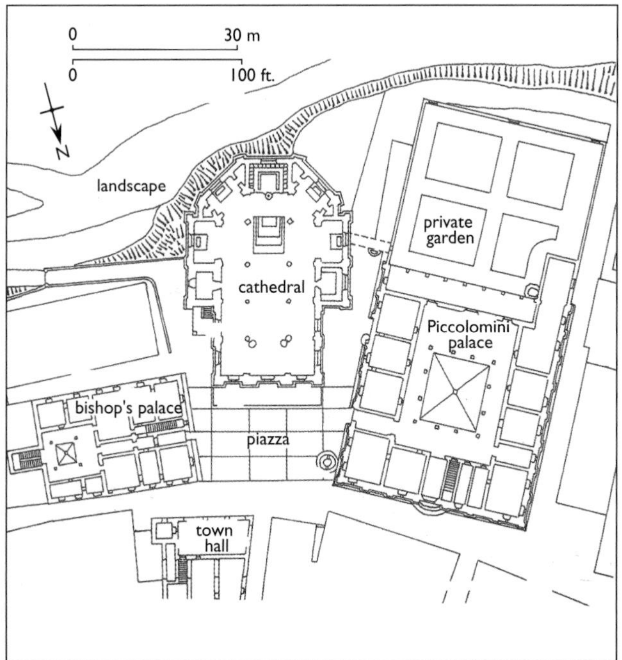

13.27 Bernardo Rossellino, plan of Pienza, Italy, 1460s.
This shows the design of the central area of Pienza. The townhall, cathedral, bishop's palace, and Piccolomini palace (the residence of the pope, named for his family) radiate from the piazza. The centralized design is related to both the Greek cross and Leonardo's *Vitruvian Man* (see figure 13.2). At the back of the Piccolomini palace, Rossellino designed a garden giving onto a landscape view inspired by Petrarch's description of Mount Ventoux (see Chapter 12).

Rulers of humanist courts in Italy—the Aragon in Naples, the Este in Ferrara, the Gonzaga in Mantua, the Malatesta in Rimini, and the Montefeltro in Urbino—competed for artists and writers to convey their political images. At the humanist court of Urbino, Federico da Montefeltro (1422–1482) spent more money on the arts than any other fifteenth-century lord. He imported artists, architects, and tapestry-makers from the Netherlands and central Europe as well as from different parts of Italy. Italian courts thus became centers of humanist patronage, financing musical and theatrical performances and pageants, and staging triumphal processions in imitation of the ancient Roman emperors. A few courts also established humanist schools, where, aside from the martial arts, women were educated equally with men (see Box).

Society and Culture

Women and their Education in Early Renaissance Italy

Most women in fifteenth-century Italy were thought of as wives, mothers, grandmothers, sisters, daughters, and so forth, rather than as individuals. They were defined in terms of their husbands and their husbands' families. In the *catasto* (tax) records, women (and children) are referred to as *boche* ("mouths") to be fed. Daughters were valuable as marriage prospects; their main asset was the dowry (property or money brought by a bride to her husband). Wives were expected to produce children, especially sons, and were continually subjected to the dangers of childbirth. Upper-class women who did not marry usually became nuns. Lower- and middle-class women were often unceremoniously placed in convents, which required smaller dowries than husbands did.

As early as the fourteenth century, Boccaccio had advocated educating women and included them among famous historical personages. The Gonzaga court at Mantua established a humanist school in 1423 open to both boys and girls: the Gioiosa was run by Vittorino da Feltre (1378–1446) according to a humanist curriculum that included Classical and Christian texts. Inspired by the Greek physician Hippocrates (see Chapter 6), Vittorino stressed physical as well as intellectual development. Aside from the martial arts, which were reserved for boys, girls and boys studied together, and scholarships were awarded to talented children who could not afford the tuition. As the humanist movement gained momentum in the fifteenth century, more and more women were educated, some by tutors at home, others at humanist schools.

THE STATE PORTRAIT

Like other Renaissance rulers, Federico da Montefeltro commissioned state portraits that reflected his desired political image. Around 1472, he commissioned Piero della Francesca (*c.* 1420–1492) to paint a pair of portraits of himself and his wife, Battista Sforza (figure **13.28**). Piero was the leading painter in central Italy in the mid-fifteenth century. He worked for a time at Federico's court and is known for his monumental style and his Latin texts on perspective and mathematics. In this **diptych** (two-paneled painting), Piero shows the couple gazing intently at each other, as if oblivious to the viewer. He captures their mutual devotion, evidenced by Federico's refusal to remarry after Battista's death.

Visible in the distance is a landscape view of the territory they ruled around Urbino. The formal posture of the figures conveys their moral uprightness. Note that despite the apparent equality of the couple, Federico appears larger and his geometric hat elevates him above Battista, reminding the viewer that the right to rule is his, even though Battista often ruled in his absence. The red color of Federico's dress, as well as his strict profile, shows his identification with ancient Rome: imperial Roman statuary typically depicted the emperor in a red porphyry garment, and on coins the emperor was similarly shown in profile.

THE EQUESTRIAN PORTRAIT

Another Roman motif revived in fifteenth-century Italy was the equestrian portrait. Inspired by the *Marcus Aurelius* (see thumbnail) in Rome, Renaissance *condottieri* such as Niccolò da Tolentino were honored with images depicting them on horseback. One of the most powerful of these portraits is the bronze *Colleoni* (figure **13.29**) by the Florentine artist Andrea del Verrocchio (1435–1488).

The monument was commissioned by the family of Bartolommeo Colleoni, who came from Bergamo, in northern Italy. He had defended the Venetian republic and is shown here as a fierce, dynamic fighter riding his powerful warhorse into battle. He sits upright in the saddle and turns abruptly, as if

13.28 Piero della Francesca, *Battista Sforza* and *Federico da Montefeltro* (after restoration), *c.* 1472. Oil and tempera on panel, each panel 18½ × 13 in. (47 × 33 cm). Galleria degli Uffizi, Florence.
Federico ran a highly organized court, which he supported by fighting as a *condottiere*. After the death of his first wife, he married Battista Sforza of Pesaro and supervised her humanist education. Their first six children were girls. Finally, at the age of twenty-six, Battista gave birth to a son, Guidobaldo, but she died shortly thereafter. Judging from her pallor compared to Federico, it is likely that she was already dead when Piero painted the portraits.

13.29 Andrea del Verrocchio, *Colleoni*, Campo Santi Giovanni e Paolo, Venice, *c.* 1481–1496. Bronze, about 13 ft. (4 m) high.

Equestrian portrait of Marcus Aurelius
see figure 7.40

catching sight of the enemy. Verrocchio has thus represented Colleoni on the alert and prepared for battle, protecting the republic against invasion.

THE STATE BEDROOM AT MANTUA

The northern Italian city of Mantua was ruled in the fifteenth century by the Gonzaga family. Andrea Mantegna (1431–1506), the court painter to three generations of Gonzaga rulers, decorated the state bedroom of the ducal palace (figure **13.30**). In this view of the fireplace wall, Lodovico Gonzaga (at the left) turns to receive a message. He is seated on an army field-stool, indicating that he fought for Mantua as a *condottiere*. His wife, the German princess Barbara of Brandenburg, is beside him, along with family members, courtiers, a dwarf, and Lodovico's faithful dog.

The combination of painted and actual architectural surfaces merges reality with illusion, dissolving the entire wall into a painted fiction. The ceiling, only part of which is visible here, is painted as if adorned with marble busts of Roman emperors framed in laurel—an allusion to the Gonzaga family's wish to be associated with the rulers of antiquity.

13.30 Andrea Mantegna, Camera Picta (Camera degli Sposi), Ducal Palace, Mantua, 1474. Fresco, entire room about 26 ft. 6 in. (8.1 m) square.

LEONARDO IN MILAN

The northwestern city of Milan had attracted humanists, including Petrarch, since the fourteenth century. From 1287 to 1447, Milan was ruled by Visconti despots and allied with France and the Holy Roman Empire. The Visconti steered the city through a period of strife lasting to the middle of the fifteenth century. In 1443, one of the daughters of the family married the renowned *condottiere* Francesco Sforza (1401–1466), who ruled Milan until 1466. He and the subsequent Sforza dukes continued a despotic style of rule that placed Milan at odds with republican Florence. Lodovico Sforza (1452–1508), called Il Moro (The Moor) because of his dark complexion, became regent for his nephew, probably had him killed, and ordered the beheading of his own mother. He then seized power and used the arts to reinforce his political legitimacy.

Lodovico hired a number of artists, among them Leonardo da Vinci, who had written to the duke offering his services as a military engineer and describing his abilities in painting, sculpture, and architecture. Lodovico appointed Leonardo court artist and engineer in around 1482. This position entailed devising weapons, producing works of art, and designing scaffolds and other devices for theatrical pageants.

READING SELECTION

Leonardo, *Notebooks*, including his letter to Lodovico Sforza, PWC3-076

Leonardo's most famous work in Milan is the *Last Supper* (figure **13.31**). The fresco was painted opposite a Crucifixion scene on a wall of the original refectory of Santa Maria delle Grazie. Jesus was thus depicted as if facing his own death, which he foretells in the *Last Supper*. Leonardo has represented a sequence of reactions to Jesus' announcement that one of his apostles will betray him. Despite the damaged condition of the work, we can see the quick-tempered St. Peter grabbing a knife in his right hand, Thomas raising his finger in doubt, James the Less (called the Lord's brother) echoing Jesus' cruciform gesture, and the young St. John fainting on hearing Jesus' words. All the apostles gesture and converse in ways that reveal their inner distress. Judas, leaning firmly on the table to the right of Jesus, is marked as the betrayer by his sharp withdrawal and by the bag of silver he holds in his right hand.

The mathematical symmetry of the painting and its perspective is designed to focus the viewer on Jesus (see thumbnail). He is placed at the center, framed by the window, symbolically haloed by the round arch, and illuminated by the natural light of the sky. His extended arms form a triangle, alluding to the doctrine of the Trinity. Jesus is flanked by apostles arranged in four groups of three, echoing the four tapestries on the side walls and the triple window on the back wall. Like Masaccio's *Trinity* (see figure 13.14), the *Last Supper* is constructed illusionistically as if it takes place in a room beyond the actual wall. The orthogonals (see Box, p. 341) converge at a vanishing point on Jesus' eye, making him the psychological as well as the mathematical center of the fresco. The placement of the eye on the horizon can be associated with the setting sun and thus with the death of Jesus (who is traditionally associated with the sun).

Leonardo da Vinci, *Last Supper*, with superimposed orthogonals

13.31 Leonardo da Vinci, *Last Supper* (before last restoration), refectory of Santa Maria delle Grazie, Milan, *c.* 1495–1498. Fresco, oil, and tempera on plaster, 15 ft. 1⅛ in. × 28 ft. 10½ in. (4.6 × 8.6 m).
The triple arch above the painting contains the arms of Lodovico Sforza and his wife Beatrice d'Este, a member of the ruling family of Ferrara. They were married in 1491, when she was fifteen, but she died six years later. The coats of arms are thus both a memorial to Beatrice and Lodovico's statement of his patronage of the work.

THE EARLY RENAISSANCE IN THE NORTH

Like Florence, northern Europe—especially the Netherlands (Low Countries) and Germany—consisted of essentially bourgeois societies. Bankers and merchants flourished, and artistic patronage expanded beyond the Church to include wealthy individuals and civic institutions. Commerce and trade between Italy and the north were extensive, with Italian businessmen working in the Netherlands, and Netherlandish artists and musicians employed in Italy. At the same time, a few important painters were active in France, and the graphic arts, such as woodcut and engraving, were popular in Germany.

After 1415, when the English king Henry V won a decisive battle against the French at Agincourt, the French economy weakened, and France lost its important role in art patronage. Thereafter, the center of art patronage north of Italy shifted to the Netherlands.

13.32 Jan van Eyck, *Arnolfini Portrait*, 1434. Oil on wood, 32¼ × 23½ in. (81.8 × 59.7 cm). National Gallery, London.

This painting has been the subject of extensive scholarly debate, interpretation, and reinterpretation since the 1930s. It has been called a straightforward double portrait of a merchant and his wife, and a wedding document witnessed formally by the artist's signature. Van Eyck signed the picture in Latin, *Johannes de eyck fuit hic* ("Jan van Eyck was here"), just above the mirror on the back wall and dated it 1434. If the artist is among the figures reflected in the mirror, this would mean that he signaled his presence through both his image and his name.

PAINTING

Painters in the north favored the medium of oil over the fresco and tempera preferred by their Italian contemporaries in the fifteenth century. Oil paint is made by grinding **pigment** (color) in linseed oil and in this period was applied to a wood panel coated with **gesso** (chalk and plaster thickened with glue). Among the advantages of oil are rich color and a slow drying time. The medium allows the artist to build up layers of paint, to revise the work over a long period, and to depict minute details with a fine brush.

The most important Netherlandish painter in the early fifteenth century was Jan van Eyck (*c.* 1380/1390–1441), whose self-portrait was discussed earlier (see figure 13.3). Among his patrons were Philip the Good in Bruges and John of Bavaria in The Hague. Van Eyck's famous and much discussed *Arnolfini Portrait* (figure **13.32**) indicates that he also worked for wealthy individual patrons. This painting was commissioned by a member of the Italian Arnolfini family from Lucca, who worked for the Medici in the Netherlands.

An influential article published in the 1930s by the eminent art historian Erwin Panofsky identified the painting as a wedding document, made at a time when marriages were sealed by mutual declaration. He took the signature and the inscription to confirm that the artist had indeed been present at the marriage as a witness and that his self-portrait is among the figures in the mirror. Later, however, in a number of studies by subsequent art historians, Panofsky's views were challenged. His primarily iconographic reading was followed by economic, social, political, feminist, and psychological interpretations, all of which attest to the complexity of this enigmatic work. Recent archival research by the British scholar Lorne Campbell has shown that the wedding in question did not take place until 1447; in his view the painting is a double portrait of Giovanni di Nicolas Arnolfini and an unidentified second wife. Whichever of the many readings of this picture is the true one, we can conclude that portraiture (and probably self-portraiture, if we accept the view that the *Man in the Red Turban* is indeed van Eyck himself) was of paramount importance to the artist and his patrons.

Van Eyck's largest and most spectacular work, filled with rich detail, is the *Altarpiece of the Lamb* (figures **13.33** and **13.34**). Also known as the Ghent altarpiece, this work reflects the Netherlandish delight in rich texture and different perspectival viewpoints. The main panels, visible when the altarpiece is closed, represent the Annunciation, the donors, and statues of John the Evangelist and John the Baptist. The small panels at the top depict Old Testament prophets and pagan sibyls, with scrolls foretelling the coming of Christ.

The New Testament figures—Mary, Gabriel, and the two Saints John—are shown in *grisaille* (imitation stone). The donors, on the other hand, are shown in flesh and blood and they wear fifteenth-century dress. Van Eyck uses this distinction between biblical figures and the contemporary donors to suggest that the message of Christianity is like stone: it will last.

When opened, the Ghent altarpiece presents a vast panorama of time and space. Beginning with the Fall of Man, it

13.33 *right* **Jan van Eyck, *Altarpiece of the Lamb* (Ghent altarpiece), exterior, Cathedral of St. Bavon, Ghent, 1432. Oil on panel, closed 11 ft. 6 in. × 7 ft. 7 in. (3.5 × 2.33 m).**

13.34 *below* **Jan van Eyck, *Altarpiece of the Lamb* (Ghent altarpiece), interior, Cathedral of St. Bavon, Ghent, 1432. Oil on panel, open 11 ft. 6 in. × 14 ft. 5 in. (3.5 × 4.4 m).**

13.35 Petrus Christus, *St. Eloy (Eligius) in His Studio*, 1449. Oil on panel, 39 × 33½ in. (99 × 85 cm). The Metropolitan Museum of Art, New York.
St. Eloy is in his shop, dressed as an artisan, talking with a pair of customers. A ledge containing Eloy's wares occupies the foreground, while the shelves on the wall are filled with rings, vases, and other objects. He appears to be selling a wedding ring to the woman, a reading that is reinforced by the bridal girdle on the ledge. The rich colors and reflective light are characteristic of north European painting. The inscription on the front of the ledge reads: "Master Petrus Christus made me in 1449."

shows Adam and Eve occupying the upper panels at each end, with small *grisaille* scenes of Cain and Abel. Choirs of angels separate the primal couple from the three central panels, arranged hierarchically: God is in the center, flanked by the Virgin and John the Baptist. God wears a papal tiara, and a royal crown is placed at his feet.

The large central panel below depicts the Adoration of the Lamb. A sacrificial lamb, signifying Christ, stands on an altar surrounded by angels. Beyond the altar to the left is a group of confessors; to the right are virgin martyrs carrying palms (an iconographic allusion to triumph over death). In the far distance, the towers of the Heavenly Jerusalem are visible. On either side of the baptismal fountain in the foreground, groups of pilgrims arrive and kneel in adoration. The side panels show the pilgrims journeying toward the more sacred space of the center.

The Ghent altarpiece is filled with richer color and a greater abundance of minute detail than Italian paintings of the same period. Van Eyck's figures, although naturalistic, appear less Classical than those in Italian paintings. And despite the grid pattern on the floor in the upper center panels, which reflects the use of linear perspective, there are shifts in points of view from panel to panel.

The complex iconography of *St. Eloy in His Studio* (figure **13.35**) by Petrus Christus (*c.* 1420–1475/6), who worked mainly in Bruges, has—like the *Arnolfini Portrait*—made the work the subject of several interpretations. Because the painting represents St. Eloy, a Merovingian martyr, mintmaster, and patron of goldsmiths, scholars assume that it was commissioned by the guild of goldsmiths.

Petrus Christus's style reflects the north European tendency to merge secular and religious content in a single work. For example, the coral on the shelf is both a material used in making jewelry and a Christian symbol of rebirth and resurrection. The presence of a scale and weights, used in determining the value of jewels, also alludes to the weighing of souls at the Last Judgment. The convex mirror at the right was a standard means of deterring shoplifters, but, as it is cracked, it suggests *vanitas*—a warning to those who create and wear expensive jewels that death and decay are the inevitable future.

In France, the leading court painter of the second half of the fifteenth century was Jean Fouquet (*c.* 1420–*c.* 1481). Born in Tours, in central France, Fouquet is best known for his miniature portraits. His depiction of Charles VII (figure **13.36**), with its parted curtain revealing the king, exemplifies the Renaissance notion of painting as a window.

13.36 Jean Fouquet, *Portrait of Charles VII*, after 1451. Oil on wood panel, 33⅞ × 28⅜ in. (86 × 72 cm). Louvre, Paris.
Downcast and gloomy, Charles seems overwhelmed by his dark red, fur-trimmed coat, and his hat is too large for his narrow face. Nevertheless, the inscription asserts his power and his lineage: "The very victorious king of France" above, and "Charles, the seventh of the name" below. Charles owed his crown to Joan of Arc.

13.37 Martin Schongauer, *Elephant*, *c.* 1485. Engraving, 4¼ × 5¾ in. (10.8 × 14.6 cm). Cleveland Museum of Art, Ohio.

Graphic Art

With the introduction of illustrated books, printing became a major source of imagery. Woodcut, the earliest technique, was used for illustrating both books and playing cards. It was followed by engraving, in which lines are cut or incised into a metal plate and then inked. When a sheet of paper is pressed onto the plate, the design is transferred to the paper.

Martin Schongauer (*c.* 1450–1491), a painter who worked in Colmar, in Alsace, was also a leading printmaker. He is known for the tactile quality of his images and his ability to convey three-dimensional form through modeling. His *Elephant* (figure **13.37**) of around 1485 combines naturalism with fanciful features. Note the seashell shapes of the ear, the spiral patterns on the trunk, and the round feet.

In the north, elephants were considered exotic, and, judging from this print, one wonders whether Schongauer had ever seen one. The elephant carries a tower with figures peering out, alluding to medieval manuscripts showing warrior elephants. The derivation of this motif from India, where elephants were used in battle, reflects a migration of imagery from the East. In the West, elephants symbolized strength and long life—Schongauer's elephant is literally a "tower of strength."

Music

The most innovative fifteenth-century music was composed in northern Europe. As with the visual arts, secular patronage increased and individual musicians, like artists, worked for courts and for the Church in various countries. This greatly enriched their sources of influence and their compositions.

Composers began to move away from the rigid isorhythmic structures of fourteenth-century *ars nova* (see Chapter 12), writing music for three or four voices in a simpler polyphonic style. Of increasing concern and interest was the way the musical lines related to each other—how the notes coincided as chords and how the chords themselves fell into successions of harmonies, or **chordal progressions**. This period could thus be seen to mark the beginning of Western or "common-practice" harmony.

The trend toward secular song seen in the music of Machaut continued into the fifteenth century. The main form was the **chanson** (French for "song"). Usually written for three voices, these songs were often performed with one or two lines taken by instruments.

The greatest English composer of this period, John Dunstable (*c.* 1390–1453), wrote both French and English secular songs and was famed for his sweet style. Using the harmonious intervals of thirds and sixths rather more than his contemporaries, he became widely known as far afield as France and Italy and influenced other musicians. The major part of his output was sacred music; two complete Masses and over forty motets (polyphonic choral compositions for the Roman service) have survived. Most are written for three voices, rather than the four or five that would later become the norm. Although some of this music still uses medieval isorhythm, Dunstable unites it with lyrical melodies that prefigure the style of the High Renaissance.

GUILLAUME DUFAY North of the Alps, the main center of music patronage was the court of Philip the Good in Burgundy—an independent region until the death of Charles the Bold in 1477. The most important early-fifteenth-century composer—Guillaume Dufay (*c.* 1400–1474) of Cambrai, in northern France—worked for Philip for several years. Dufay also studied in Italy, was employed by Italian courts, sang in the papal choir in Rome, and was choirmaster at the Savoy court. Some two hundred works by him survive, including over eighty *chansons*, eight Masses, and numerous motets.

During his lifetime, Dufay was considered the greatest composer of his day. Although the majority of his works were written for three voices, he was one of the first musicians to write skillfully for four. He was also a key figure in the development of the so-called "cyclic Mass," a musically unified setting of the Ordinary of the Mass. Unity was achieved by repeating the same tenor theme in each movement and, sometimes, by beginning sections with the same musical motif in all parts.

Most of Dufay's motets were composed to celebrate particular political or social events. One of the best-known pieces was written for the consecration of Brunelleschi's dome in 1436. In accord with the concerns of early Renaissance artists with harmony and balance, the rhythmic proportions and other elements of Dufay's motet correspond to the structural features of the dome itself.

Dufay's secular music was written for performance at banquets and other social events at the various European courts where he worked. In 1423, for example, he was employed at Pesaro in Italy, where he was required to compose a *chanson* celebrating the marriage of Carlo Malatesta, the future lord of Rimini, to the pope's niece. The song's refrain praises Dufay's patron as "Charles gentil, qu'on dit de Malateste" ("Fair Charles, called Malatesta"). Note that although it was written for an Italian audience, the French language was used. Such pieces were performed by skilled solo singers and instrumentalists. Most were for one vocalist with two accompanying players.

The influence of humanism can be seen in many of Dufay's *chansons*. "Ce moys de may" ("Ce Mois de Mai," "This Month of May") of around 1440, for instance, celebrates the coming of spring and reflects the new enthusiasm for nature. It begins:

This month of May let us be happy and joyous
And banish melancholy from our hearts.
  Let us sing, dance and make merry.
  To spite these base, envious creatures.

Let each one try more than ever
To serve his fair mistress well:
This month of May let us be happy and joyous
And banish melancholy from our hearts.

Another humanist element is Dufay's insertion of his name into the text of a few of his songs. In the last stanza of "This Month of May" and in the motet *Ave regina coelorum* ("Hail Queen of Heaven"), he asks the Virgin to have pity on him. This increasing presence of the author, whether by signature, self-portrait, or musical text, was part of the Classical revival and would be a feature of the Western humanities from the Renaissance forward.

JOSQUIN DESPREZ The interest in individual genius was an aspect of Renaissance culture related to the humanist emphasis on fame. The first musician described in terms of genius by his contemporaries was Josquin Desprez (*c.* 1440–1521). Born in northern France, Josquin sang at Milan Cathedral from 1459 to 1472, and he spent one year at the Sforza court and thirteen years with the papal choir in Rome. From 1499 to 1503 he lived in France, and in April 1503 he was appointed music director at the Este court of Duke Ercole I in Ferrara. Josquin returned to France in 1504 and became canon of the collegiate church of Condé-sur-l'Escaut, where he remained until his death.

Josquin composed over a period of about sixty years, and more works by him survive than by practically any of his contemporaries. During Dufay's lifetime, the Mass had become established as a musical form with five linked movements setting the Ordinary of the Mass. Josquin's twenty Masses, all with the richer four-voice texture that was becoming the norm, consolidate this. The fact that the Italian music printer Petrucci chose to publish three volumes of Josquin's Masses and no more than one by anyone else is an indication of the esteem in which the composer was held.

Josquin's originality can be seen particularly in his motets, of which he wrote over eighty. Compared with motets of the fourteenth century, Josquin's break free from the confines of isorhythm, with flowing melodies and clearer chordal progressions. Harmony and texture are richer—in part due to the fact that at least four voices are used, and sometimes as many as six. Moreover, there is a definite attempt to express emotion in music. Josquin's *Ave Maria . . . virgo serena* ("Hail Mary . . . serene Virgin") of around 1485 is a prayer to the Virgin. Written for four voices, it uses the technique of imitation between the parts that became fundamental to later Renaissance music. The opening words, "Hail Mary," appear first in the highest voice, and are then sung by each lower part in turn to the same music. The voices overlap partially in such a way that all four singers combine only briefly to bring the phrase to a climax and conclusion. Elsewhere in the motet there are "full" sections where all four voices weave together in imitation, and lighter ones where two voices are picked out in a duet. The conclusion, "O Mother of God, remember me," is peaceful; it is also another example of an author's presence in his own work.

Josquin wrote some seventy *chansons*. In "Woodland Nymphs," he introduces a personal note again as he laments the death of the Flemish composer who may have been his teacher, Johannes Ockeghem (*c.* 1410–*c.* 1497). A loose translation of the French text reflects the inspiration of Classical myth:

Nymphs of the woods, goddesses of fountains,
Expert singers from every nation,
Transform your strong voices, clear and high
Into trenchant cries and lamentations,
Because the ravages of Atropos [one of the three Fates of
  Greek mythology]
Have ensnared your Okeghem [the Fates were believed to
  control life by a thread, which they cut to signal death]
The real treasure and master of music
Who no longer escapes death
And who, to great sorrow, lies covered with earth.

Clothe yourself in mourning,
Josquin, Brumel, Pierchon, Compère [names of musicians]
And let the tears fall from your eyes
For you have lost a good father
May he rest in peace [in Latin in the original].
Amen.

The early Renaissance, affected by the Black Death of 1348, peasant rebellions, the Great Schism in the Church, and economic changes, witnessed a vast expansion in the arts. As the culture of the Middle Ages waned, a new, more questioning approach to the world developed, which extended outward to geographical exploration and inward to human character. As we will see in subsequent chapters, these developments would not be without backlash of the kind seen in fifteenth-century Florence.

Thematic Parallels

The Classical Tradition: Revival and Opposition

As we have seen, the Classical tradition that began with the culture of fifth-century-B.C. Athens was reborn during the Renaissance. Although the Italian Renaissance has proved to be the most far-reaching revival of Greek and Latin culture, such revivals have recurred intermittently in Western history, from Charlemagne to the present day. The language of Classical architecture has been particularly vital in Western history, and elements of it are still used in building design today. However, there have also been periods of conscious rejection of the Classical tradition, when artists tried to free themselves of its influence.

Each revival has adapted classicism to its own context, altering aspects of its style and thought. The ancient Romans, for example, so admired Greek sculpture that they devoted an enormous industry to making copies. Indeed, much of what we know about Greek sculpture comes from Roman copies, because many of the Greek originals have not survived. In the realm of political organization, republican Rome based its notion of elected government on Athenian democracy, in which male citizens were required to participate in self-governance. Even the Roman emperors, mindful of the tradition of republicanism, tried to maintain an impression of fair and just rule, false though that impression often was. In turn, later periods of Western history looked to imperial Rome as a source of the "Classical tradition."

Charlemagne, crowned Holy Roman Emperor in A.D. 800, wanted to be regarded as a new Roman emperor. This, he believed, would benefit his image as the ruler of a great empire. One visual expression of this notion was his equestrian portrait, which was based on those commissioned by the emperors of Rome (see figure 10.1). Similarly, the design of his palace chapel in Aachen derived, via the centralized Greek cross plan of Byzantine churches, from the round temples of Greece and Rome. Charlemagne's educational reforms consciously emphasized Latin language and culture, as exemplified by his adoption of Roman grammar.

13.38 Charles Bulfinch, Massachusetts State House, Boston, 1795–1797. Charles Bulfinch, the son of a wealthy merchant in Boston, studied classics at Harvard, traveled in Europe, and was an amateur architectural designer. When his family lost its fortune, Bulfinch found work as the Boston police superintendent, becoming active in politics and earning extra money as an architect.

Arch of Titus, Rome, *c.* A.D. 81
see figure 7.32

In the eighteenth century the Classical tradition once again inspired democratic reform. This time, violent revolutions in America and France looked to Classical models of constitutional government to overturn the "divine right" of kings. In architecture, the Neoclassical style was introduced in France as a style of revolution; ironically, after the French Revolution it was adopted by Napoleon as a style of empire. Napoleon revived architectural expressions of Roman imperial power—such as the triumphal arch (see thumbnails) and the freestanding monumental column—as a way of proclaiming the legitimacy of his power by linking himself to ancient rulers.

In the United States, Thomas Jefferson (1743–1826) promoted the Neoclassical style, renamed the Federal style, as the type of architecture best suited to the new American republic. The effects of this can be seen today in the many Federal and public buildings—the White House, state capitols, banks, courthouses, libraries, etc.—that are inspired by the Classical Orders of architecture. A good example is the Massachusetts

Arc de Triomphe, Paris, 1806–1836
see figure 18.3

State House in Boston (figure **13.38**), which was designed by Charles Bulfinch (1763–1844) in the late eighteenth century. His use of the dome, inspired by Roman and Renaissance architecture, has become characteristic of government buildings in the United States.

Despite the persistence of the Classical tradition, there have been times of outright rebellion against it. In sixteenth-century Europe, for example, as the High Renaissance evolved into Mannerism, artists subverted the Classical taste for symmetry, harmony, and an impression of stability. While using the language of classicism, they rearranged elements, creating a sense of instability, tension, and compression. Sometimes these rearrangements had a humorous quality, but more often they represented an effort to achieve new architectural solutions.

During the second half of the nineteenth century, as enthusiasm for Neoclassicism declined, European and American artists and architects began to look for alternatives to the Classical tradition. Around the turn of the twentieth century, the modernist **avant-garde** advocated newness in place of traditional forms. Artists found new formal solutions in non-Western art—African, Oceanic, Native American, pre-Columbian, and others—which came to light as a result of colonialism, archaeological and anthropological missions, international cultural exhibitions, and increasing global travel and trade.

Despite modernist efforts to escape the Classical tradition, it persists in one form or another. Recently, Postmodernists (like the Mannerists before them) have appropriated Classical forms but have altered them in ways that defy historical meaning and structural logic. In the Piazza d'Italia, in New Orleans (see thumbnail), for example, the architects reused the grammar of Classical Orders and the round arch, accenting them with color created by neon lighting. The interest lies in the way they place them in a new context and in new relationships to each other.

Piazza d'Italia, New Orleans, 1978–1979
see figure 23.31

KEY TERMS

avant-garde newness for its own sake.

chanson (French, "song") a secular polyphonic song in the Middle Ages and Renaissance; the form includes rondeaux, ballades, and virelais.

chordal progression a sequence of chords.

condottiere in medieval and Renaissance Italy, a soldier of fortune.

diptych a two-paneled painting.

frottola a lighthearted, generally amorous poem for three or four voices sung to instrumental accompaniment, usually chordal in style.

gesso a white coating of chalk, plaster, and resin that is applied to a surface to make it more receptive to paint.

incise to cut designs or letters into wood or metal with a sharp instrument.

orthogonal consisting of, or relating to, right angles, or a line perpendicular to the plane of a relief or a picture.

pigment a substance used to give color to paints, inks, and dyes.

tondo a painting or relief sculpture having a round frame.

vanishing point in linear perspective, the point at which the orthogonals meet.

woodcut or **woodblock print** an image incised on a block of wood and printed on paper.

KEY QUESTIONS

1. Define humanism. What three characteristics would have to be included in this definition if it were to apply to the Renaissance period?
2. Cite instances of Renaissance works that contain the following:
   a. Architectural Orders derived from antiquity
   b. Linear perspective
   c. Psychological insight and motivation
   d. Emphasis on authorship
   e. Human anatomy
3. Describe Ghiberti's and Brunelleschi's submissions (figures 13.7 and 13.8) for the baptistery door of Santa Maria del Fiore. What traits of each submission show the artist's innovative approach?
4. How does Donatello's *David* illustrate the Renaissance interest in antiquity and in personality?
5. Prove or disprove the following statement: "The Medici and other rulers, including popes, used the arts to express their wealth, power, and intellectual superiority."

SUGGESTED READING

Adams, Laurie Schneider. *Italian Renaissance Art.* Boulder, CO: Westview Press, 2001.
- ▸ A well-illustrated survey of Italian Renaissance art from the thirteenth to the sixteenth century.

——. *Key Monuments of the Italian Renaissance.* Boulder, CO: Westview Press (Icon edition), 2000.
- ▸ Major monuments of the Italian Renaissance in context.

Alberti, Leon Battista. *On Painting*, trans. John R. Spencer. New Haven, CT, and London: Yale University Press, 1996.
- ▸ The first treatise on Renaissance art theory.

——. *The Family in Renaissance Florence*, trans. R. N. Watkins. Colombia, SC: University of South Carolina Press, 1989.
- ▸ A translation of Alberti's advice on family life and child-rearing.

Antal, Frederick. *Florentine Painting and its Social Background.* Boston: Boston Book and Art Shop, 1965.
- ▸ A history of Florentine painting in the Renaissance in its social context. A Marxist approach to art history, focusing on the economic forces behind the arts.

Barolsky, Paul. *Infinite Jest: Wit and Humor in Italian Renaissance Art.* Columbia, MO: University of Missouri Press, 1978.
- ▸ A witty study of humor in Italian Renaissance art.

Baron, Hans. *In Search of Florentine Civic Humanism*, 2 vols. Princeton, NJ: Princeton University Press, 1988.
- ▸ A classic study of the humanist movement.

Baxandall, Michael. *Painting and Experience in 15th-century Italy*, 2nd ed. Oxford: Oxford University Press, 1988.
- ▸ The relationship of society and money to painting.

Brown, Patricia Fortini. *Life and Art in Renaissance Venice.* New York: Harry N. Abrams, 1997.
- ▸ Venetian art in the context of its time.

Cole, Alison. *Virtue and Magnificence: Art of the Italian Renaissance Courts.* New York: Harry N. Abrams, 1995.
- ▸ A nicely illustrated study of court patronage during the Italian Renaissance.

Cuttler, Charles D. *Northern Painting from Pucelle to Bruegel.* New York: Henry Holt and Co., 1968.
- ▸ A standard survey of painting in northern Europe.

Harbison, Craig. *The Mirror of the Artist: Northern Renaissance Art in its Historical Context.* New York: Harry N. Abrams, 1995.
- North European art in context.

Herlihy, D., and C. Klapisch-Zauber. *Tuscans and Their Families.* New Haven, CT: Yale University Press, 1985.
- Life and society in fifteenth-century Italy.

Hibbert, Christopher. *The House of Medici: Its Rise and Fall.* New York: Morrow Quill, 1980.
- A study of the Medici family and its financial fortunes.

King, Margaret. *Women of the Renaissance.* Chicago and London: University of Chicago Press, 1991.
- On the roles and status of women in the Renaissance.

Lane, Barbara. *The Altar and the Altarpiece: Sacramental Themes in Early Netherlandish Painting.* New York: Grafton Books, 1984.
- A study of the role and meaning of the altar and the altarpiece in north European painting.

Panofsky, Erwin. *Early Netherlandish Painting,* 2 vols. New York: HarperCollins, 1971.
- A classic study of north European painting.

——. *Meaning in the Visual Arts.* New York: Viking Press, 1974.
- Art and meaning in the Renaissance.

Roover, Raymond de. *The Rise and Decline of the Medici Bank, 1397–1494.* Cambridge, MA: Harvard University Press, 1963.
- The history and influence of the Medici bank.

Seidel, Linda. *Jan van Eyck's Arnolfini Portrait: Stories of an Icon.* Cambridge, U.K.: Cambridge University Press, 1993.
- One of several methodological studies of van Eyck's painting.

Trexler, Richard. *Public Life in Renaissance Florence.* Ithaca, NY, and London: Academic Press, 1980.
- A study of Renaissance Florence from the point of view of society, politics, and everyday life.

SUGGESTED FILMS

1964 *The Masque of the Red Death,* dir. Roger Corman

1968 *Andrei Rublev* (*Andrei Rublyov*), dir. Andrei Tarkovsky

1971 *The Canterbury Tales,* dir. Pier Paolo Pasolini

1989 *Henry V,* dir. Kenneth Branagh

1992 *Christopher Columbus,* dir. John Glen

14 The High Renaissance in Italy and Early Mannerism

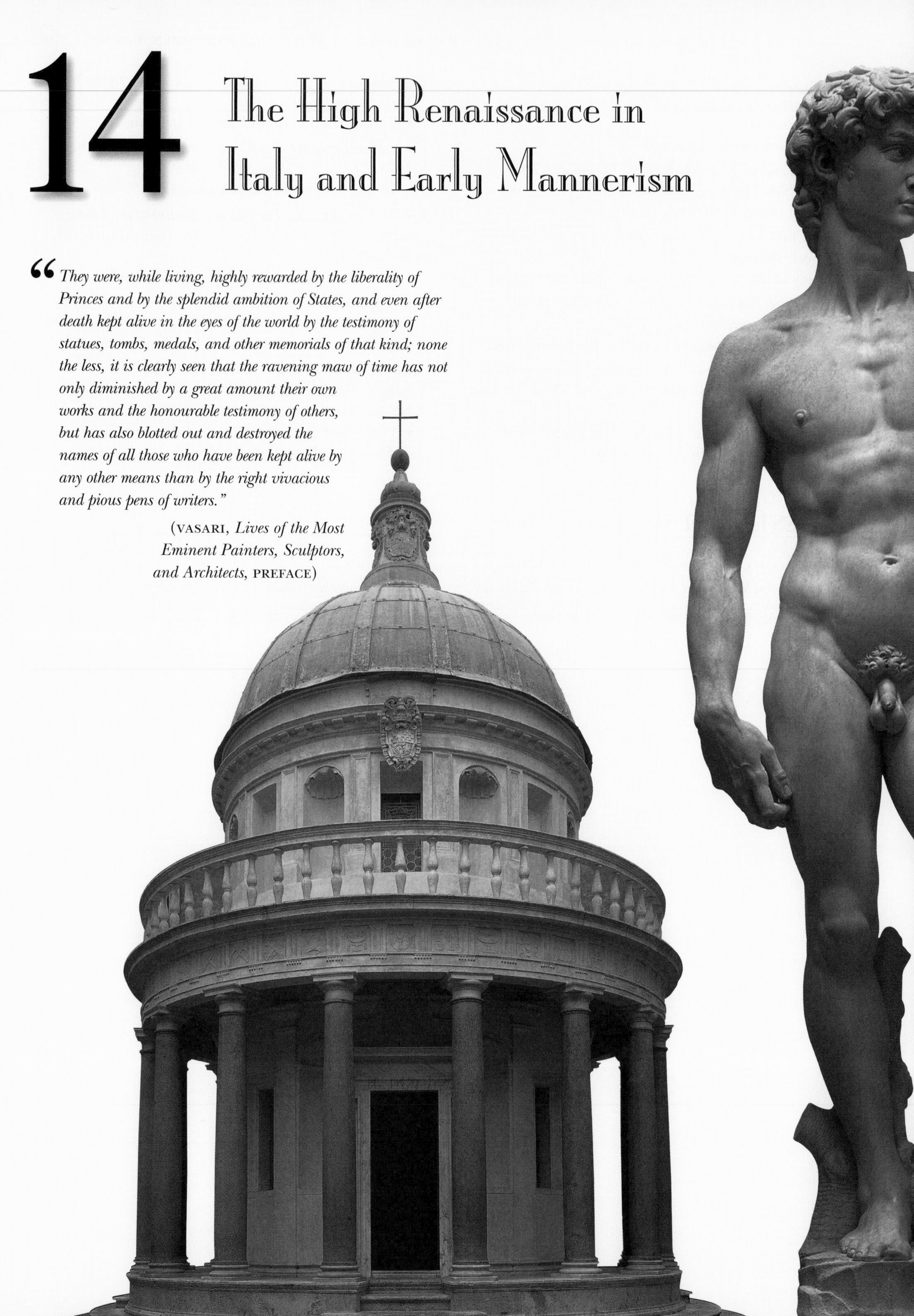

"They were, while living, highly rewarded by the liberality of Princes and by the splendid ambition of States, and even after death kept alive in the eyes of the world by the testimony of statues, tombs, medals, and other memorials of that kind; none the less, it is clearly seen that the ravening maw of time has not only diminished by a great amount their own works and the honourable testimony of others, but has also blotted out and destroyed the names of all those who have been kept alive by any other means than by the right vivacious and pious pens of writers."

(VASARI, *Lives of the Most Eminent Painters, Sculptors, and Architects*, PREFACE)

The High Renaissance in Italy lasted from around 1494, when the Medici were expelled from Florence, to around 1520, when the artist Raphael died. At the turn of the sixteenth century, the center of patronage shifted from Florence to Rome, where humanist popes and other wealthy individuals financed innovative artistic projects, although major works continued to be produced in Florence. Venice, too, was an important center of cultural innovation, not only in the visual arts but also in music and the new printing technology. In addition to Raphael (1483–1520), the great artists of the High Renaissance include Donato Bramante (1444–1514), Leonardo da Vinci (1452–1519), and Michelangelo Buonarroti (1475–1564); and the Venetian painters Giovanni Bellini (c. 1435–1516), Giorgione da Castelfranco (c. 1477–1510), and Tiziano Vecelli, known in English as Titian (c. 1487–1576).

Literary figures contributed significantly to the High Renaissance. The Prince (Il principe) by Niccolò Machiavelli (1469–1527) remains a classic work of political theory. The Courtier (Il cortegiano) by Baldassare Castiglione (1478–1529) combines philosophy and politics with manners in describing the ideal education of a gentleman. And the literary epic Orlando furioso by Lodovico Ariosto (1474–1433) reflects the persistence of chivalric and pastoral traditions. Dramatists continued to revive genres of Classical theater, often placing Greek and Roman plot structures in contemporary settings.

A few visual artists also produced important written works. Leonardo's extensive notebooks cover aspects of nature, science, technology, and the arts. They include a treatise on painting and the Paragone, in which he compares the relative merits of different art forms. Michelangelo wrote sonnets, which reveal his personal psychology and his views on art.

Around the time of Raphael's death in 1520, the High Renaissance style began to evolve into Mannerism.

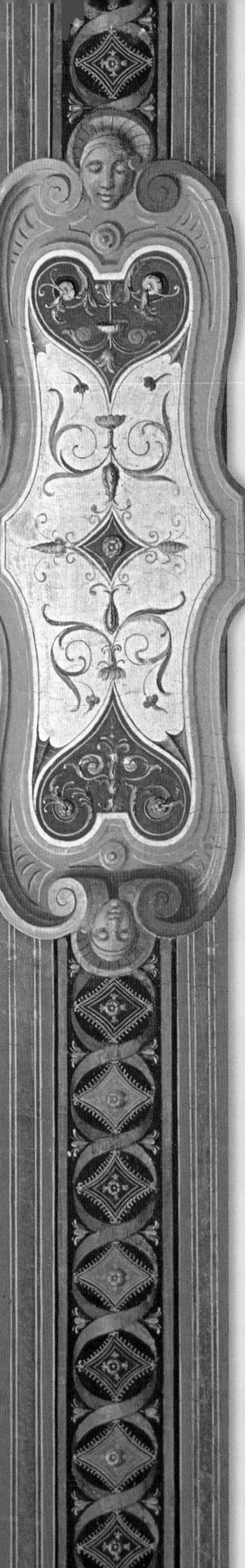

Key Topics

The High Renaissance

- Papal patronage
- Extending the vernacular
- Biography and autobiography: Vasari
- Michelangelo's sonnets
- Machiavelli: *The Prince*

Contrasts

- Innovation and revival
- Secular and sacred iconography
- Painting: handicraft or liberal art
- Leonardo: *Paragone*
- Humanism versus conservative backlash
- Cellini: *Autobiography*

Mannerism

- Anti-Classical proportions
- Mysticism
- Saints and martyrs
- Eroticism
- Cellini: *Autobiography*

Music

- Willaert
- The Gabrielis
- The madrigal

TIMELINE	HIGH RENAISSANCE *c.* 1494–1520	MANNERISM *c.* 1520–1590
HISTORY AND CULTURE	Center of patronage shifts from Florence to Rome Venice: cultural center for music Aldine Press, Venice, produces inexpensive small-scale books, from late 15th century Italy invaded by French, 1494 Magellan circumnavigates the globe, 1519–1521 Holy Roman Emperor Charles V fights French, 1522 Treaty of Cambrai, 1529, brings in period of prosperity Population of western Europe rises to nearly 90 million Antwerp and London become mercantile centers Trafficking in slaves *Conquistadores* seek silver and gold from New World, early 16th century	The Medici return to Florence, 1512 Style spreads to France, Spain, and northern Europe Political and religious turmoil
RELIGION	Humanist pope: Julius II (papacy 1503–1513) Martin Luther launches Protestant Reformation in Germany, 1517	
ART 	Giovanni Bellini, *Madonna of the Meadow*, *c.* 1500–1505 Michelangelo, *David*, 1501–1504; Sistine Chapel ceiling, 1509–1512; *Last Judgment*, 1534–1541 Leonardo, *Mona Lisa*, *c.* 1503–1515; drawings Raphael, *Madonna and Child*, *c.* 1505; *School of Athens*, 1509–1511; *Baldassare Castiglione*, *c.* 1514 Giorgione, *Fête Champêtre*, *c.* 1510 Titian, *Assumption of the Virgin*, 1516–1518; *Venus of Urbino*, *c.* 1538; *Charles V Seated*, 1548	Raphael, *Fire in the Borgo*, from 1514 Pontormo, *Portrait of a Halberdier*, *c.* 1528–1530 Parmigianino, *Madonna of the Long Neck*, *c.* 1535 Cellini, saltcellar of Francis I, 1543; *Perseus*, 1545–1554 Anguissola, *Self-portrait at a Spinet*, after 1550
ARCHITECTURE 	Bramante, Tempietto, Rome, *c.* 1502 Plans of New St. Peter's, Rome: Bramante, Antonio da Sangallo, Michelangelo	Romano, Palazzo del Tè, Mantua, 1527–1534 Palladio, San Giorgio Maggiore, Venice, begun 1565; *The Four Books of Architecture*, 1570
LITERATURE 	Machiavelli, *The Prince*, 1513 Ariosto, *Orlando furioso*, 1516 Castiglione, *The Courtier*, 1528	Vasari, *Lives of the Most Eminent Painters, Sculptors, and Architects*, 1550; autobiography added 1568 Cellini, *Autobiography*, 1558
THEATER	Court patronage Increased use of the vernacular Ariosto, *The Casket*, 1508 Machiavelli, *The Mandrake*, 1513–1520 Trissino, *Sofonisba*, 1515	
MUSIC 	Venice in the forefront of music printing Musical instruments developed Organ used in liturgy Split choir Adrian Willaert (*c.* 1490–1562) chapel master of St. Mark's Cathedral, Venice The Gabrielis: grand choral works New Renaissance form: madrigal Music for instrumental ensembles	

This refers both to an artistic style that continued to the end of the century and to a worldview that rejected the humanist classicism, symmetry, and use of linear perspective that characterize Renaissance style. Michelangelo and Titian lived well into the Mannerist period, and there are discernible elements of Mannerism in their late styles. In the case of Michelangelo, his late work reflects his sense of spiritual conflict which, in turn, conformed to political and religious tensions in the sixteenth century.

The quotation that opens this chapter is taken from the Preface to the Lives of the Most Eminent Painters, Sculptors, and Architects *by Giorgio Vasari (1511–1574). First published in 1550 and revised and expanded in 1568, the* Lives *reflects the Renaissance preoccupation with fame and individual genius. Vasari reports that Renaissance artists were well paid by ambitious rulers and remembered through their works, but he notes that time destroys or diminishes the reputation of those not kept alive by the written word. Vasari thus takes as his mission the preservation of the memory of Renaissance artists by writing about them. He also included an autobiography in the revised edition of 1568.*

Although there is much to be learned from Vasari, his Lives *often contains misinformation, either because he is mistaken about certain facts and events or because he wishes to embellish them. For example, Vasari describes Leonardo's death as if the French king, Francis I, rushed to the artist's bedside, when in fact he was not there at all. We may know (or discover through further research) that such stories are not literally true. Nevertheless, Vasari's distortions often contain an implied truth—in this case, Vasari conveys Francis I's devotion to Leonardo and his work.*

Beginning with Cimabue (see Chapter 12) and concluding with Vasari's autobiography, the Lives *provides a framework of Italian art from the late thirteenth to the mid-sixteenth century. It contains a wealth of source material on artists, descriptions of works of art, gossip, and anecdotes that bring the social context of the Renaissance to life. Throughout the* Lives, *Vasari makes clear his opinions of art and artists—their characters and their talent. Above all he admires Michelangelo, who was his personal friend. For Vasari, Michelangelo is* Il divino *("The divine one"), a reflection of the Renaissance view that genius is an inborn, God-given gift.*

POLITICAL AND ECONOMIC DEVELOPMENTS

By the late Middle Ages, the modern nation-state, defined by national boundaries, had begun to evolve more or less into its present form. France and England had been ruled by single kings for centuries. Spain had been divided into different kingdoms until the marriage of Isabella of Castile (ruled 1474–1504) and Ferdinand of Aragon (ruled 1479–1516), who reigned jointly from 1479. In a show of Christian unity and political might, they expelled the Muslims, whom they defeated in Granada in 1492, and the Jews. In addition, they solidified their power through the Spanish Inquisition, which persecuted anyone suspected of disloyalty to the Church or the Crown.

The Holy Roman Empire—which encompassed most of modern Austria and Germany, the Netherlands, the southern half of Italy, and Sicily—continued to be a force in Europe and remained so through the High Renaissance. By 1500, the dominant European powers were England, France, Spain, and the Holy Roman Empire. The rest of Europe also had more or less established national boundaries.

The High Renaissance was a period fraught with continual political turmoil. Repeated invasions of the Italian peninsula disrupted the power of the Church. In 1494, the armies of the French king, Charles VIII (ruled 1483–1498), invaded Italy on the grounds that France had long-standing claims to Milan and Naples through marriage. Italy's defense depended on support from Venice, the pope, the Holy Roman Empire, and Spain. In 1499 the French under Louis XII (ruled 1499–1515) invaded Milan—continuing to attack Italy despite, and perhaps because of, their admiration for Italian culture. The Valois king Francis I (ruled 1515–1547), for example, hired Leonardo to work at the French court in 1516.

In addition to trying to secure Milan and Naples for himself, Francis I wanted to obtain the Holy Roman Empire. His failure to do so led to years of war against Charles V (of the House of Habsburg) (figure **14.1**), whose reign as emperor lasted from 1519 to 1556 (map **14.1**, p. 369).

Charles V was born in 1500 to Philip I, king of Castile, and Queen Joanna, who went insane. When he was fifteen, Charles was named regent of Castile in central Spain, and in 1516, when his maternal grandfather, Ferdinand II, died, he became Charles I of Spain. In 1519 his paternal grandfather, the Habsburg Holy Roman Emperor Maximilian I, died, and Charles was elected Holy Roman Emperor as Charles V. By the age of nineteen Charles was on his way to leading the world's largest empire.

Charles was unable to control his kingdom as tightly as he wished, and his ambition to rule a unified Christian empire was never realized. In 1522 he fought the French in Italy, and he sacked Rome five years later. This led to a decline in papal patronage and weakened the papacy itself. In 1529, the Treaty

14.1 Titian, *Charles V Seated*, 1548. Oil, 6 ft. 8¾ in. × 4 ft. (2.05 × 1.22 m). Alte Pinakothek, Munich.
This portrait reflecting Charles V's imperial status also suggests the burdens of the cares of state. A genius in conveying character and aware of the importance of flattering his imperial patrons, Titian manages to make the emperor's unattractive jutting jaw contribute to a pensive expression. The silhouetting of the black stockings and shoes against the red carpet gives the emperor an appearance of strength, while the red color and the imposing column indicate that Charles wished to be linked with the Roman emperors.

of Cambrai brought about a period of relative peace after thirty-five years of hostilities. But threats to Charles's power came from France in the west, the Ottoman Empire in the east, and North Africa in the south.

Charles also faced unrest within the Holy Roman Empire as princes of the principalities vied for power during Charles's frequent absences. Compared with the tight organization of France under Francis I, the Holy Roman Empire remained bogged down in disarray. Charles was further frustrated by protests within the Roman Catholic Church (see Chapter 15), which would become a source of major upheaval. He abdicated in 1556 and spent the remainder of his life in a monastery.

Despite warfare and religious conflict, the early decades of the sixteenth century were a time of relative prosperity in western Europe. The population rose to nearly 90 million in the course of the century, and cities such as Antwerp and London became large centers of commerce. Raw materials from the New World—including South American gold and silver (see Box)—increased trade and manufacturing. Prosperity brought more people to the cities in search of work.

Another development that benefited commerce was the entry of several European countries into the already existing West African slave trade. The Portuguese had begun importing African slaves in the mid-fifteenth century, and for over a hundred years they monopolized the European end of such trafficking. Meanwhile Arab traders were shipping central African slaves to the Middle East and India. During the sixteenth century the Portuguese began to supply slaves to the Spanish colonies in the Americas to work on plantations. Then England entered the slave trade, followed by France, Holland, and Denmark. The practice brought profit but inevitably sowed seeds of future conflict over the morality of owning human beings and forcing them to work without pay.

By the middle of the sixteenth century, Europe's prosperity began to decline. Inflation rose and poverty and begging became serious social problems. Spain depended on gold and silver from the New World and launched religious wars before financing was actually available. Thus, in the 1570s, when the Spanish king Philip II (ruled 1556–1598) was unable to pay his soldiers, they rebelled and destroyed Antwerp. Nevertheless Philip II was able to fight wars against England and France and was successful against the Ottomans.

Map 14.1 The Holy Roman Empire under Charles V, 1526.

Cross-cultural Influences

Exploration and Colonialism

The sea voyages that had begun late in the fifteenth century increased during the sixteenth, resulting in a global expansion of exploration and trade. The Spanish explorer Vasco Nuñez da Balboa (1475–1517) discovered the Pacific in 1513, and the Portuguese explorer Ferdinand Magellan (*c.* 1480–1521) departed to circumnavigate the globe in 1519. Magellan was killed in the Philippines in 1521, but his ships sailed on and returned to Spain the following year. The French explorers Jacques Cartier (1491–1557) and Samuel de Champlain (*c.* 1567–1635) secured France's claim to territory in North America. Spain and Portugal were the first to control the seas, but the English and French soon rivaled them.

Expanding exploration resulted in conquest and colonialism. In the first half of the sixteenth century, Hernando Cortés (1485–1547) and Francisco Pizarro (*c.* 1475–1541), two Spaniards known as *conquistadores* (foreign conquerors), unleashed their troops on two New World empires. Seeking gold, silver, and other raw materials for the king of Spain, Cortés and Pizarro decimated the Aztec Mexica and the Inka civilizations, respectively. And most of those who escaped immediate death soon succumbed to measles and other diseases brought to the Americas by the invaders.

The Aztec Mexica had flourished from the middle of the fourteenth century; by the sixteenth they were a powerful empire. Their capital, Tenochtitlán, with a population of around 100,000, was located at what is now Mexico City. Extensive building programs had transformed the capital into a thriving city, with temples, palaces, schools, and gardens. A network of roads and bridges tied the empire together. The Aztec were literate and had a rich tradition of art and poetry. Their religion was polytheistic and they practiced human sacrifice, believing that the gods demanded human blood.

Despite being a warrior culture (figure **14.2**), the Aztecs found that their spears and slings were no match for Spanish pistols. In 1519, Cortés arrived in Tenochtitlán with an army of six hundred men and was welcomed as the Aztec god-king, Quetzalcoatl. But fearing that the Aztecs would attack him, Cortés captured the king, Montezuma II (ruled 1502–1520). Cortés razed the city and destroyed Aztec religious texts. In an effort to impose Christianity on the native population, the Spanish conqueror built churches and a cathedral on the sites of ruined Aztec temples.

The Inka—which is both the designation of the people and their term for "king"—rose to imperial power around the same time as the Aztec Mexica. The Inka capital was at Cuzco, a highland city in the Andes Mountains of present-day Peru. Comprising an empire of several million people inhabiting a 2000-mile (3220-km) stretch of territory, the Inkas built some 20,000 miles (32,200 km) of roads. The empire controlled all agriculture, which used irrigation and was the basis of the economy. The Inka ruler was an absolute monarch, venerated as a god. An elite priesthood controlled the temples, but, unlike the Aztecs, the Inka had no writing system and therefore no religious texts.

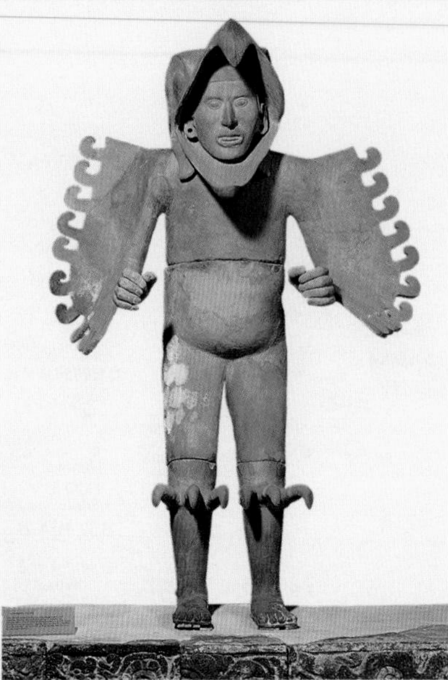

14.2 *Eagle Warrior*, from Tenochtitlán, Aztec culture, 15th century. Terra-cotta, 67 × 46½ × 21½ in. (170 × 118 × 55 cm). Museo del Templo Mayor, Mexico City.
The eagle warriors were an elite, aristocratic military group, dedicated to capturing their enemies alive so they could offer their blood to the gods. Eagle imagery characterizes the costume: a beak functions as a helmet, wings spread out at the arms, and claws project from the knees.

When Pizarro arrived in 1531 with 168 men, he, like Cortés, was dazzled by the abundance of gold and silver. Lacking iron tools, the wheel, and modern weapons, the Inka were annihilated by the *conquistadores*. In 1532, Pizarro destroyed the empire using brutal tactics, including torture. One of the few sites to escape destruction was the secluded mountaintop city of Machu Picchu (figure **14.3**). Probably the royal enclave of an Inka king, Machu Picchu is built of huge blocks of stone without mortar.

Despite the devastation of the Aztec Mexica and the Inka civilizations by the Spanish *conquistadores*, there were positive results from contacts between Europe and the New World. The two regions exchanged aspects of their culture, food, and technology. In the future these contacts would broaden the outlook of both Europe and the Americas.

14.3 Machu Picchu, near Cuzco, Peru, Inka culture, 15th–16th century.

FLORENCE IN THE HIGH RENAISSANCE

In 1492, when Lorenzo the Magnificent died, his weak son, Piero di Lorenzo (1471–1503), called Piero the Unfortunate, became head of the Medici family. Piero made several poor political decisions, including granting concessions to Charles VIII of France. In 1495, under the influence of Savonarola (see Chapter 13), the citizens of Florence forced the Medici from the city. After Savonarola's execution four years later, a brief period of turmoil ensued.

At the turn of the century, Florence was in political disarray. In 1502, in an attempt to restore order and stability, the Florentines elected Piero Soderini (1452–1522), a member of a patrician family with political influence, to the lifetime mayoral position of *gonfaloniere* (literally "standard-bearer"). But he was forced into exile in 1512, and the grandson of Lorenzo the Magnificent, also called Lorenzo, was installed as *gonfaloniere*.

Expelled from Florence in 1527 by citizens who wanted to preserve a republic, the Medici returned again in 1530 when the Holy Roman Emperor Charles V installed Alessandro de' Medici, Lorenzo's illegitimate son, as hereditary ruler of Florence. Alessandro dismantled all traces of republicanism and ruled as duke until 1537, when he was assassinated by a cousin. Alessandro was succeeded by Cosimo I de' Medici (1519–1574), a ruthless but effective ruler and, like the earlier Medici, an important patron of the arts. He was crowned grand duke of Tuscany by the Dominican pope, Pius V (papacy 1566–1572), and his descendants ruled Florence until nearly the middle of the eighteenth century.

MACHIAVELLI

The political intrigues of Renaissance Italy inspired the best known political theorist of the period, Niccolò Machiavelli (1469–1527). Machiavelli had had a long political career, but he was accused of plotting against the Medici and exiled from Florence in 1513. Machiavelli was a political realist. He studied the Roman histories of Livy in the belief that it was possible to learn how to function politically in the present from knowing about past political events. In his classic work *The Prince* (1513), Machiavelli describes a shrewd statesman as one who follows the dictates of strategy and tactics. He also advocates the appearance, if not the practice, of morality. The modern word "Machiavellian" connotes ruthless deceit purely for the pursuit of power, but that is a distortion of the author's point of view and does not convey the nuances of his thinking. In addition to *The Prince*, Machiavelli wrote *Discourses on the First Decade of Livy* (*c.* 1516), *The Art of War* (1519–1520), and *The History of Florence* (1520–1525).

READING SELECTION

Machiavelli, *The Prince*: how to hold onto power by understanding and manipulating the desires of the nobility and the people, PWC3-085; whether it is better to be loved than feared, PWC3-088-B

MICHELANGELO'S *DAVID*

By the turn of the century, Michelangelo had already made his name as an emerging genius in sculpture. In 1502, at the age of twenty-six, he was commissioned by the guild of cloth manufacturers to produce a statue of David for the exterior of Florence Cathedral (figure **14.4**). For three years the artist worked on the enormous

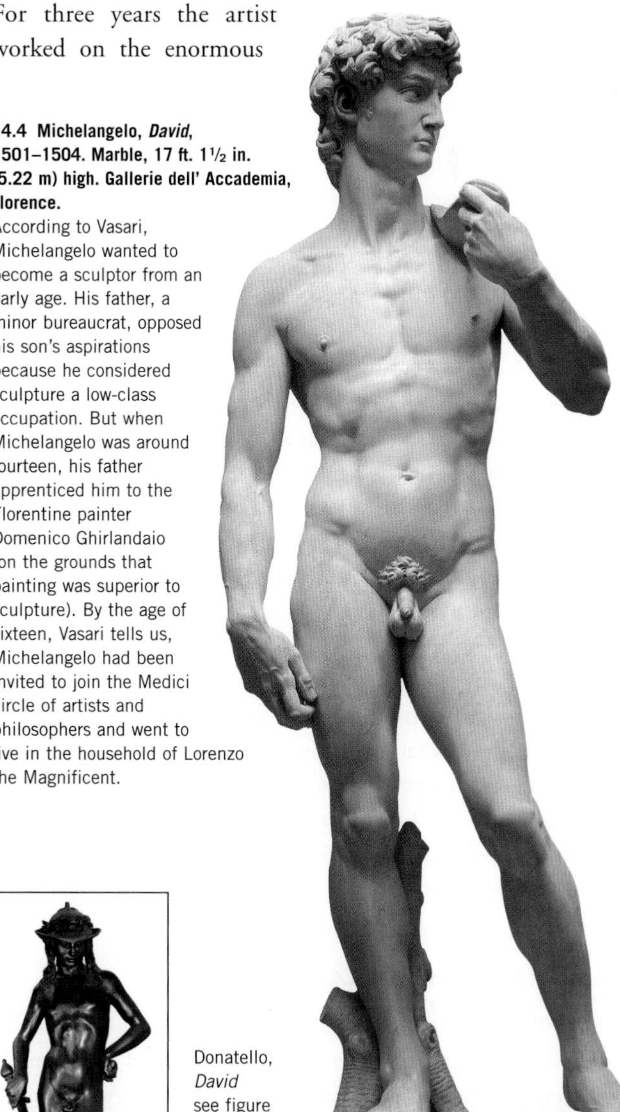

14.4 Michelangelo, *David*, 1501–1504. Marble, 17 ft. 1½ in. (5.22 m) high. Gallerie dell' Accademia, Florence.
According to Vasari, Michelangelo wanted to become a sculptor from an early age. His father, a minor bureaucrat, opposed his son's aspirations because he considered sculpture a low-class occupation. But when Michelangelo was around fourteen, his father apprenticed him to the Florentine painter Domenico Ghirlandaio (on the grounds that painting was superior to sculpture). By the age of sixteen, Vasari tells us, Michelangelo had been invited to join the Medici circle of artists and philosophers and went to live in the household of Lorenzo the Magnificent.

Donatello, *David* see figure 13.19

sculpture, which he carved from a single block of marble from the quarry in Carrara, near Lucca, that had supplied ancient Roman builders. Michelangelo's marble block, which had been abandoned by a previous sculptor because of a flaw, was nicknamed "the Giant." A surviving preliminary sketch of the *David* depicts the figure and a detail of an arm. Written on the sketch is the phrase "David with his sling and I with my bow," referring to the hand-drill used by sculptors. In 1504, when the *David* was completed, city leaders persuaded the guild to place the statue at the entrance to the Palazzo Vecchio, Florence's town hall, instead of outside the cathedral.

This decision reflected Florence's identification with the David and Goliath story. Like Donatello's *David* (see thumbnail), Michelangelo's figure symbolized the republican spirit of the city. In this case, however, there is no Goliath, and David, at 17 feet (5.22 m) tall, has become the giant. Michelangelo's *David* "stands guard" over Florence, tensely alert, watching out for the safety of the city and ever ready to defend it from tyranny.

Stylistically, the *David* shows the influence of Hellenistic sculpture (see Chapter 6). The figure is posed in the relaxed contrapposto stance of Classical figures, but the torso is tense, which is more characteristic of Hellenistic than Classical style. The proportions, notably the large right hand and the slightly awkward youthfulness, are also more Hellenistic than Classical. In addition to being a structural reinforcement, the little tree trunk support behind the figure alludes to Roman marble copies of Greek sculpture.

In his *Lives*, Vasari says that the *gonfaloniere* Piero Soderini asked Michelangelo to reduce the size of the *David*'s nose, which he found offensively large. Accordingly, Michelangelo climbed the scaffold with a handful of marble dust. Pretending to chip away at the nose, he dropped some dust to the ground. Soderini, believing that the artist had complied with his wishes, was satisfied.

In this story (which may or may not be true), the humanist Vasari conveys two aspects of art and artists. On the one hand, he shows that art is illusion and that the artist, like a magician, can make viewers believe a fiction. On the other hand, he reminds his readers that the viewer's suspension of reality and willingness to believe the fiction is a necessary component of art appreciation.

LEONARDO'S *MONA LISA*

In 1508, after working for several years for the duke of Milan, Leonardo returned to Florence, where he painted an enigmatic portrait that has intrigued viewers for centuries. According to Vasari, the *Mona Lisa* (figure **14.5**) depicts the wife of the Florentine aristocrat Francesco del Giocondo. As a result, the woman in the painting is sometimes called "La Gioconda," or "the smiling one." Although she is famous for her smile, it is not clear that she actually is smiling. The impression that her

14.5 Leonardo da Vinci, *Mona Lisa*, *c.* 1503–1515. Oil on wood, 30¼ × 21 in. (76.7 × 53.3 cm). Louvre, Paris.

lips curve upward is created by the artist's subtle use of chiaroscuro and soft, smoky lighting, or *sfumato*, which define the features as well as the expression.

As a portrait, the *Mona Lisa* is innovative. The figure's three-quarter view and length—from the head to below the waist—were new. Previous portraits tended to be either frontal or profile views like Piero della Francesca's diptych of the Urbino rulers (see figure 13.28). Leonardo's Mona Lisa sits on a balcony overlooking an imaginary landscape in the distance; our view of her is head on, whereas we have a bird's eye view of the background.

This portrait identifies the figure with the landscape through a series of formal parallels. Her pyramidal form echoes the rock formations; her veil filters light as does the misty horizon; the aqueduct at the right curves into the fold over her left shoulder; and the spiral road at her right repeats the folds of the sleeves. These parallels correspond to Leonardo's famous metaphor comparing the earth to the human body: the rocks, he wrote, are the bones, the waterways are the veins and arteries, and the soil is the flesh.

Little is known of the *Mona Lisa*'s patron, but he apparently never received the portrait. Even less is known of the sitter. However, it is clear that the painting was of great importance to Leonardo. He took it with him when he went to the court

Society and Culture

Technology and the Inventions of Leonardo da Vinci

The greatest inventive genius of the High Renaissance was Leonardo da Vinci. Besides painting, sculpture, and architecture, his fields of study included geology, physics, alchemy, botany, geology, anatomy, optics, astronomy, and music. He worked as an engineer for Lodovico Sforza of Milan, for whom he devised tanks, catapults, multiple-barrel guns, and cannons. Leonardo drew up plans for draining marshes, designed underwater machines for attacking boats, and proposed the use of the Screw of Archimedes (see Chapter 6) for raising the level of water.

In his drawing of a helicopter-like flying machine, Leonardo envisioned the principle of a screw rising in the air (figure **14.6**). According to the drawing, the machine was powered by the pedaling man at the center. Although Leonardo never succeeded in creating a machine that could actually fly, he was intensely interested in flight and wrote extensively on the physics of flight and the movement of bird wings.

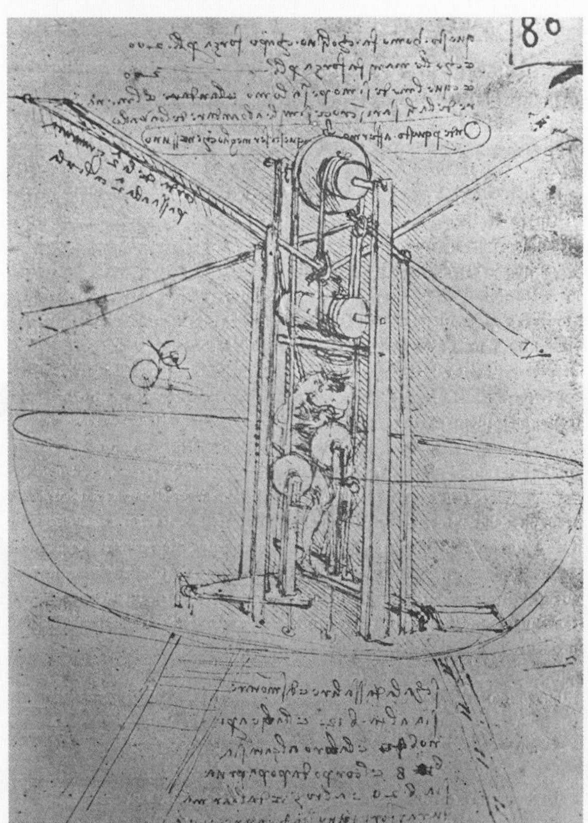

14.6 Leonardo da Vinci, drawing study for a flying machine, *c.* 1490. Pen and ink. Institut de France, Paris.
Leonardo's notebook drawings are accompanied by detailed texts in mirror writing—that is, they have to be read in a mirror. To date, there is no explanation for this unusual practice; it is not due to left-handedness. In addition to machines, Leonardo designed a number of musical instruments and was an accomplished musician.

of Francis I and kept it until his death. From the French court, the painting entered the French national art collection that is housed today in the Louvre, in Paris.

LEONARDO ON THE ART OF PAINTING VERSUS SCULPTURE AND POETRY

The *Mona Lisa* exemplifies Leonardo's genius for visual metaphor. In his writings, he also uses metaphor to convey his artistic, philosophical, and scientific theories (see Box). His passion for imagery pervades the *Paragone*, in which he compares the art of painting with sculpture and poetry. Leonardo personifies Nature, which he believes to be the inspiration for art. Art itself he considers a "science." In Leonardo's view, painting is the most noble of the arts, because it is closest to nature.

> The divinity of the science of painting considers works both human and divine, which are bounded by surfaces, that is to say the boundary lines of bodies, with which she [Nature] dictates to the sculptor the way to perfect his statues. Through her principle, that is to say, draughtsmanship, she teaches the architect how to make his buildings convey pleasure to the eye; she teaches the potters about the varieties of vases, and also the goldsmiths, the weavers and the embroiderers. She has invented the characters in which the various languages are expressed; she has given numerals to the mathematicians; she has taught the drawing of figures to the geometrician; she has taught the students of optics, the technicians and the engineers.
>
> (*On Painting*)

Leonardo notes that poets use words to praise poetry. But the impact of painting, he says, is more direct and immediately understood by the viewer because it is an image. He says that "painting does not speak, but is self-evident through its finished product." Engaging in the ongoing quarrel over the merits of poetry, which was considered a liberal art, and painting, which was still considered a manual craft, Leonardo strove to raise the social position of painting and to elevate artists to the status of gentlemen. "With justified complaints," Leonardo concludes:

> painting laments that it has been excluded from the number of the liberal arts, since she is the true daughter of nature and acts through the noblest sense. Therefore it was wrong, O writers, to have left her outside the number of the liberal arts, since she embraces not only the works of nature but also an infinite number that nature never created.
>
> (*On Painting*)

RAPHAEL

Raphael (Raffaello Sanzio) was born at the court of Urbino, then ruled by Guidobaldo da Montefeltro, the son of Federico da Montefeltro and Battista Sforza (see Chapter 13). Raphael's own father, Giovanni Santi, was Urbino's court poet and painter and the author of an epic poem praising Federico.

14.7 Raphael, *Madonna and Child* (*The Small Cowper Madonna*), *c.* 1505. Oil on wood panel, 23³/₈ × 17³/₈ in. (59.5 × 44 cm). National Gallery of Art, Washington, D.C.

Santi apprenticed Raphael to Pietro Perugino (*c.* 1450–1523), the leading Umbrian painter, when his son was eleven years old. Raphael went on to become a prolific artist, known for his charm, political skill, and classically harmonious style. His brilliant career, however, was cut short by his death at the age of thirty-seven.

From 1504 to 1508, Raphael worked in Florence, painting mainly Madonnas and portraits. The *Madonna and Child* (figure **14.7**), known as the *Small Cowper Madonna* after the family that once owned it, is typical of his numerous early Madonnas. Raphael's Mary is a simple, everyday mother supporting a squirming infant. The only indications that the figures are sacred are the faint, translucent haloes and the distant church building. Like most of Raphael's Madonnas, this one has delicate features and a downcast expression—the latter a convention of Christian art alluding to her foreknowledge of her son's Crucifixion.

Raphael's reputation for personal grace seems reflected in his painted figures, especially the Madonna and Christ. At the Urbino court, Raphael had been exposed to the Classical texts in Federico's vast library and to the artists, writers, scientists, and philosophers who lived and worked there. His own enthusiasm for humanist thought and the revival of antiquity became an important force in his future career in Rome.

HIGH RENAISSANCE PATRONAGE IN ROME

The High Renaissance in Rome is linked with the patronage of a few wealthy bankers and humanist popes and with the artists who worked for them. The most extensive patronage was that of Giuliano della Rovere, who chose the name Julius II (papacy 1503–1513) because he admired Julius Caesar. Julius II was a warrior pope—a skilled military strategist who led the armies of the Papal States and was admired by Machiavelli for his political acumen. Despite his career in the Church, Julius II was a man of the world who had fathered three illegitimate children while still a cardinal. As pope, he hired the greatest artists of the age. His acquisition of Classical and Christian manuscripts enriched what later became the Vatican library, and his passion for collecting launched the vast papal collection of Greek and Roman sculpture.

A New St. Peter's

One of Julius II's first decisions as pope was to replace the Early Christian basilica of Old St. Peter's (see Chapter 8), which had been built near the Vatican Hill under Constantine in the fourth century. Julius entrusted the commission to Donato Bramante, who had worked in Milan and been in contact with Leonardo. In Rome, Bramante achieved fame with the Tempietto (figure **14.8**).

14.8 Bramante, Tempietto, San Pietro in Montorio, Rome, *c.* 1502.
This little round *martyrium* (a building over the tomb or relics of a martyr) was commissioned by Ferdinand and Isabella of Spain. The cella, which contained an altar, was placed over the traditional site of St. Peter's martyrdom. The peristyle columns are Doric, as is the frieze with alternating triglyphs and metopes. Bramante has combined Classical with Christian features and has surrounded the drum with a balustrade.

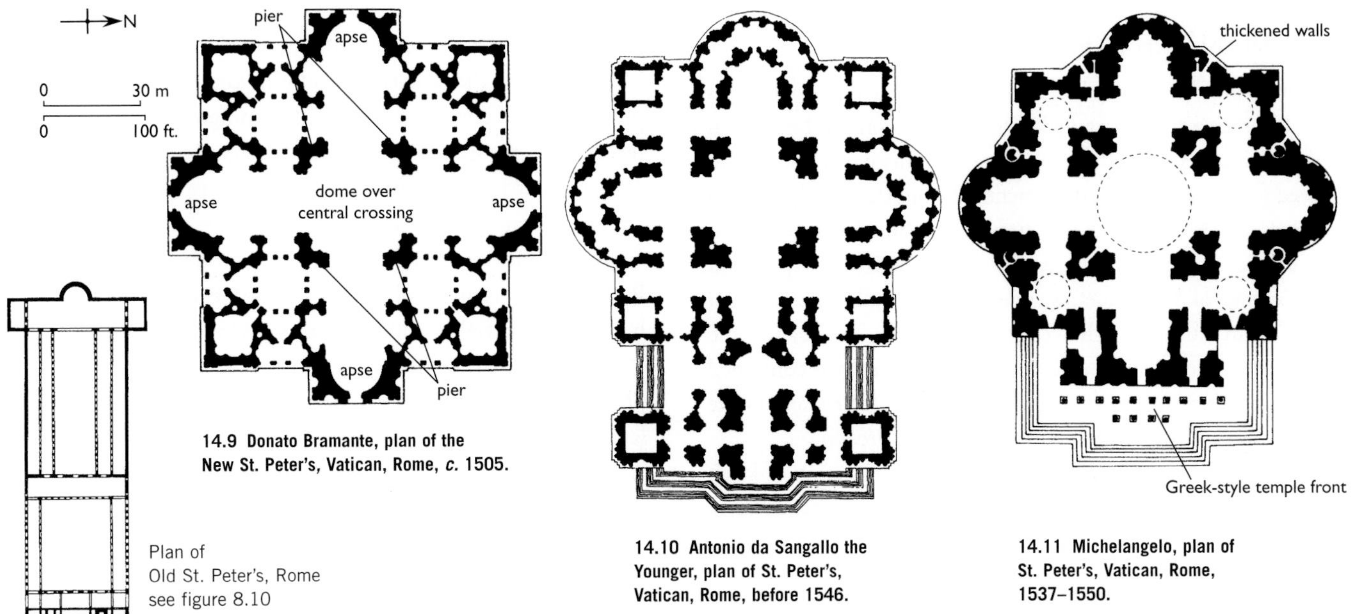

Plan of Old St. Peter's, Rome see figure 8.10

14.9 Donato Bramante, plan of the New St. Peter's, Vatican, Rome, *c.* 1505.

14.10 Antonio da Sangallo the Younger, plan of St. Peter's, Vatican, Rome, before 1546.

14.11 Michelangelo, plan of St. Peter's, Vatican, Rome, 1537–1550.

Bramante's interest in humanism is reflected in his plan for the New St. Peter's (figure **14.9**). Whereas the old basilica had a longitudinal Latin cross plan (see thumbnail), Bramante envisioned a perfectly symmetrical, centralized Greek cross plan of the type preferred by Leonardo, Alberti, and Vitruvius (see Chapter 13). Bramante designed a central nave surmounted by an enormous dome and surrounded by four apses connected by piers. The pier vaults would carry the weight of the dome.

The project was cut short by Bramante's death in 1514, but the foundations were in place, and the dimensions and general shape of the church were fixed before he died. Other architects worked on the New St. Peter's for over a century. Raphael was the first to succeed Bramante, but his plan did not progress very far. Leo X (papacy 1513–1521), a member of the Medici family, commissioned the nephew of Giuliano da Sangallo (see Chapter 13), Antonio da Sangallo the Younger (1485–1546), to continue the project. Sangallo's plan (figure **14.10**) extended the nave, but little else was achieved before his death in 1546.

A year after Antonio's death, Paul III (papacy 1534–1549) appointed Michelangelo architect of St. Peter's, and he devised a simplified version of Bramante's Greek cross plan (figure **14.11**). Michelangelo increased the dome's support, thickened the walls, and added a Greek temple front to the façade. The exterior view from the south (figure **14.12**) shows the giant, two-story Corinthian pilasters, the pedimented windows, and the dome that Michelangelo planned as a hemisphere but that was slightly elongated after his death. The entire structure was not completed until the seventeenth century, when a new style and new religious requirements would call for further alterations (see Chapter 16).

14.12 Michelangelo, St. Peter's from the south, Vatican, Rome, 1546–1593.

RAPHAEL'S *SCHOOL OF ATHENS*

From around 1509 until 1511, Raphael worked for Pope Julius II decorating the Stanza della Segnatura (Room of the Seal) in the Vatican. A huge chamber containing the papal library and used for signing official documents, the Stanza, like the Medici palace in Florence and the ducal palace in Milan, was both a public and a private space. Raphael designed a program consisting of four lunettes, one on each wall; two depicted Christian subjects (the *Dispute over the Eucharist*—the *Disputà*—and the *Three Cardinal Virtues*) and two contained pre-Christian and mythological iconography (*Parnassus*, home of Apollo and the Muses, and the *School of Athens*).

The *School of Athens* (figure **14.13**) is a summation of High Renaissance Classical humanism. It combines Renaissance perspective and architecture with Classical subject matter and is imbued with the Renaissance admiration for Greek philosophy. The setting is a barrel-vaulted, symmetrical space, which recedes, like the grid pattern on the floor, according to the laws of linear perspective. The central dome, inspired by Roman and Renaissance buildings, is indicated by the architectural curve behind the foreground vault. Statues of Greek and Roman gods occupy wall niches—at the left is Apollo with his lyre and at the right, Minerva with her Gorgon shield.

Occupying the central space of the fresco is an assembly of philosophers whose texts had been recovered, collected, translated, and studied throughout the Renaissance. Plato and Aristotle are the central figures on the top step. Plato points upward toward the realm of ideas and carries the *Timaeus*, the

14.13 Raphael, *School of Athens* (after restoration), Stanza della Segnatura, Vatican, Rome, 1509–1511. Fresco, 16 × 18 ft. (7.92 × 5.49 m).

dialogue in which he discusses the cosmos. Aristotle holds his *Ethics* and points toward the space of this world, a gesture consistent with his empiricism.

A few other philosophers can also be identified; they appear to be arranged more or less with the idealists on Plato's side and the empiricists on Aristotle's. On the left is Pythagoras outlining his proportional system. Peering over his shoulder is Averroës, the turbaned Arabic scholar. Behind Averroës are Zeno, the Stoic philosopher, and Epicurus, the founder of Epicureanism. Diogenes, the Cynic who roamed the streets of Athens with a lantern in search of an honest man, sprawls across the steps. On the right, a group of scholars includes Euclid drawing a circle with a compass, the Persian astronomer Zoroaster with a celestial globe, and the Greek philosopher Ptolemy with an earthly globe.

Raphael's fresco blends portraits of his contemporaries with those of the ancient philosophers. Plato resembles a self-portrait by Leonardo da Vinci, his questioning gesture reflecting the artist's passion for inquiry and investigation. The bald-headed Euclid is a portrait of Bramante, Raphael's mentor and the first architect appointed to design the New St. Peter's. He is shown drawing a circle with a compass, reflecting his preference for centralized church plans and echoing his own domed head. At the far right, wearing a black hat and peering at the viewer, is Raphael himself. Brooding in the central foreground is the portrait of Raphael's rival in Rome, Michelangelo. His stonecutter's boots show that he is a carver of marble, and his detached, inner contemplation conforms to his depiction as the Greek philosopher Heraclitus. Raphael's Michelangelo is writing and thinking at the same time, a visual metaphor for the obscure, "either-or" philosophy of Heraclitus (see Chapter 5).

In these and other portraits, Raphael follows Alberti's principle that images keep a person alive in the cultural memory. The artist has "memorialized" ancient philosophers and famous contemporary figures, including himself, with his brush. Raphael's inclusion of written texts in the *School of Athens* shows that they were a cornerstone of the humanist revival of Classical antiquity.

MICHELANGELO ON ART

As a humanist and member of the Medici intellectual circle in Florence, Michelangelo held views that were influenced by Plato's notion of a pre-existing realm of ideas. He believed that the raw material of art, such as stone or wood, contained an inherent form that the artist reveals. For Michelangelo, the artist's mind, which has access to the realm of ideas, guides his hand.

He left a sizable body of poetry, in particular sonnets inspired by Dante and Petrarch (see Chapters 11 and 12). These sonnets, many of them autobiographical, cover a range of subjects, including love, death, and the nature of art. Michelangelo believed that art mediates the human struggle with love and death. He observed that artistic creations are fixed, outlast nature, and do not age. Art, therefore, resists time:

> Not even the best of artists has any conception
> that a single marble block does not contain
> within its excess, and *that* [the conception] is only attained
> by the hand that obeys the intellect.
> The pain I flee from and the joy I hope for
> are similarly hidden in you, lovely lady,
> lofty and divine; but, to my mortal harm,
> my art gives results the reverse of what I wish.
> Love, therefore, cannot be blamed for my pain,
> nor can your beauty, your hardness, or your scorn,
> nor fortune, not my destiny, nor chance,
> if you hold both death and mercy in your heart
> at the same time, and my lowly wits, though burning,
> cannot draw from it anything but death.
>
> (Sonnet 51)

Note the comparison of the image inherent in the marble block with emotions hidden in a "lovely lady," which relates the passion of art with the passion of love.

THE SISTINE CHAPEL

Both Raphael and Michelangelo worked for Julius II. Michelangelo designed Julius's monumental tomb and much of the New St. Peter's, and he was commissioned to paint the interior of the Sistine Chapel. The chapel had been built from 1473 by Pope Sixtus IV, the uncle of Julius II. In accordance with Sixtus IV's wishes, its proportions match those of Solomon's Temple (see Chapter 8)—the length is double the height and triple its width. The pope commissioned frescoes to decorate the side walls with Old Testament scenes on the left and New Testament scenes on the right. These were in place when Michelangelo began his work, decorating the rest of the chapel from the level of the windows upward. The view of the ceiling in figure **14.14** gives some idea of the complexity of the artist's conception (see Box, p. 380). He has filled the space with figures, each engaged in its own narrative. Aside from the spandrels (curved triangles) over the window lunettes, the architectural sections dividing the scenes are painted illusions.

The diagram in figure **14.15** shows the disposition of the paintings. The best-known scene on the ceiling is the *Creation of Adam* (figure **14.16**), the first man and the typological ancestor of Christ. Michelangelo shows Adam as a monumental nude inspired by Hellenistic naturalism. Adam has been formed but not yet brought to life: between God's energetic forefinger and Adam's more relaxed finger there is a space. Michelangelo has thus painted the moment before Adam comes to life, fixing an image of tension between the creator God and his creation. God himself is a powerful patriarchal figure, whose flowing hair and drapery indicate his swift movement through space.

14.14 Michelangelo, Sistine Chapel ceiling frescoes, Vatican, Rome, 1509–1512.

Death of Haman
Jeremiah
Salmon
Persian Sibyl
Roboam
Ezekiel
Ozias
Eritrean Sibyl
Zorobabel
Joel
David and Goliath
Jonah
Separation of Light and Dark
Creation of Sun, Moon and Planets
Separation of Land and Water
Creation of Adam
Creation of Eve
Temptation and Expulsion
Sacrifice of Noah
The Flood
Drunkenness of Noah
Zacharias
N
Moses and the Serpent of Brass
Libyan Sibyl
Jesse
Daniel
Asa
Cumaean Sibyl
Ezekias
Isaiah
Josiah
Delphic Sibyl
Judith and Holofernes

14.15 Diagram of Michelangelo's scenes in the Sistine Chapel, Vatican, Rome.

Dynamic monumentality also characterizes the *Libyan Sibyl* (see Box, p. 380, and figure 14.17). Her twisting pose, robust muscularity, and sculpturesque drapery create a sense of massive energy and power. The rich orange color accentuates her vigor. She holds up an enormous open book, which alludes to her oracles foretelling the coming of Christ. She, like the other sibyls and prophets, is framed by illusionistic *putti* who support an entablature that seems to project from the ceiling.

14.16 Michelangelo, *Creation of Adam*, Sistine Chapel, Vatican, Rome, 1510. Fresco.

Defining Moment

The Sistine Chapel Ceiling: Imagery for the Ages

On May 10, 1506, Michelangelo received an advance payment from Pope Julius II to paint frescoes on the ceiling of the Sistine Chapel. This would prove to be one of the great defining moments in the history of Christian art. Michelangelo built his own scaffold for the project, but he complained bitterly about the physical discomfort of painting a ceiling. Vasari, in his *Lives*, describes how difficult it was:

> *He executed the frescoes in great discomfort, having to work with his face looking upwards, which impaired his sight so badly that he could not read or look at drawings save with his head turned backwards; and this lasted for several months afterwards. I can talk from personal experience about this, since when I painted five rooms in the great apartments of Duke Cosimo's palace if I had not made a chair where I could rest my head and relax from time to time I would never have finished; even so this work so ruined my sight and injured my head that I still feel the effects, and I am astonished that Michelangelo bore all that discomfort so well. In fact, every day the work moved him to greater enthusiasm, and he was so spurred on by his own progress and improvements that he felt no fatigue and ignored all the discomforts.*
>
> (Vasari, *Lives*)

The frescoes, blackened and dulled by centuries of incense and candles, were recently cleaned—a restoration that has provoked intense controversy. Those in favor admire the bright colors that have been revealed. Those who opposed the cleaning regarded the materials used as too abrasive. They have shown that much of the chiaroscuro has been removed, flattening the artist's powerful, muscular three-dimensionality. Nevertheless, today the Sistine Chapel is one of the world's most visited sites.

When Michelangelo arrived in Rome in 1508, the pope suggested that he paint the Twelve Apostles and a few customary ornaments on the ceiling. But Michelangelo envisioned a larger project. He created a grand view of the beginning of time, the creation of the world and the human race, and God's wrath in destroying what he had made. The window lunettes and the spandrels depict the ancestors of Christ listed in the "begats" at the beginning of the Gospel of Matthew. In the spaces between the windows, twelve Old Testament prophets alternate with twelve pagan sibyls—women of Classical antiquity said to possess prophetic powers. Four Old Testament scenes fill the corner spandrels. Nine scenes from Genesis—three depicting the Creation, three showing the life of Adam and Eve, and three telling the story of Noah—occupy the central area of the barrel-vault ceiling. Although Christ himself does not appear, Michelangelo's iconography alludes to his birth through prophecy and figures such as Adam, Noah, and Jonah, who were seen as his typological precursors. By the end of October 1512, the artist had painted more than three hundred lifesize or overlifesize figures on the Sistine Chapel ceiling.

Michelangelo began slowly, not having painted frescoes before. The work suffered numerous setbacks, such as mold and damp weather that interfered with the drying of the plaster and its bonding with the paint. In addition to having to learn the medium, Michelangelo had the challenge of making his figures look "correct" on curved surfaces, viewed from nearly 60 feet (18 m) below (figure **14.17**).

The project was frequently in jeopardy while Julius was at war or near death. It was also risky for Michelangelo perched high above the floor on scaffolding while he worked. The scaffolding itself was difficult to secure because Michelangelo did not want to leave holes in the ceiling. But once the ceiling was painted, in Vasari's opinion, other painters could lay down their brushes and renounce their art, for no one would ever equal the genius of Michelangelo's Sistine Chapel frescoes.

Critical Question Is the purpose of art to provide viewers with concrete images or abstract ideas? What are other functions of art? What "use" is the Sistine Chapel ceiling?

14.17 Michelangelo, *Libyan Sibyl*, Sistine Chapel, Vatican, Rome, 1509. Fresco.

14.18 Michelangelo, *Last Judgment* (after restoration), Sistine Chapel, Vatican, Rome, 1534–1541. Fresco, 48 × 44 ft. (14.6 × 13.4 m).

Michelangelo focuses on the attributes of martyrs in heaven with the instruments of their torture and death. St. Sebastian, for example, kneels at the far right and holds a set of arrows. Next to him, St. Catherine carries a broken wheel, while an angry St. Peter faces Christ and brandishes the keys to the gate of heaven. Seated on a cloud below and to the right of Christ, St. Bartholomew displays the knife with which he was flayed alive. The flayed skin drooping from his other hand contains Michelangelo's distorted self-portrait.

More than twenty years after completing the frescoes, Michelangelo was commissioned by Pope Paul III to paint a huge *Last Judgment* on the altar wall of the Sistine Chapel (figure **14.18**). This is the artist's vision of Christ's Second Coming. Compared with Giotto's vision in the Arena Chapel (see figure 12.15), Michelangelo's image is agitated, filled with nude figures, and pervaded by terror. Michelangelo's *Last Judgment* reflects the political and religious uncertainties of the times and the artist's own spiritual conflicts. He envisions a cataclysm at the end of time, filled with souls either straining to reach heaven or struggling against eternal damnation.

The hell to which the souls descend is the Greek Hades. The boatman of Greek myth, Charon, ferries the damned across the River Styx and then swings his oar to beat them from his boat. Presiding over Michelangelo's hellfire and darkness is a horned creature entwined by a serpent, a monstrous combination of Minos (see Chapter 4) and Satan. Here again Michelangelo combines Classical myth and Christianity—a hallmark of Renaissance humanism.

VENICE IN THE HIGH RENAISSANCE

The port city of Venice, on Italy's northeast coast, is built on a network of canals flowing into the sea. At the dawn of the High Renaissance, Venice had been an independent republic for some eight hundred years. It was ruled by an oligarchy consisting of an elected doge (senator), a patrician Council of Ten, and the Great Council (also composed of patricians). But its independent status was threatened in 1509 by the League of Cambrai, in which the pope, the Holy Roman Emperor, Milan, France, and Spain united to strip Venice of all its territory outside the city. Not until the Treaty of Cambrai was signed in 1529 was Venice allowed to keep most of its possessions.

As a result of this reprieve, a myth evolved in Venice celebrating its steadfastness in the face of external danger. Venice depicted itself as a tolerant republic, ruled by just leaders, free of social unrest, and protected by its patron, St. Mark. This self-image was not restricted to the political and social arenas. The city's waterways produce an atmosphere of shimmering light and luxurious color, and are often enveloped by mist from the sea. These qualities are reflected in Venetian painting, especially oil painting. Artists used canvas sooner in Venice than elsewhere in Italy as a support for oil paint. The medium of oil had long been known in Italy. It was used on panel paintings in Florence, admired in the imported works of van Eyck and other north European painters (see Chapter 13), and was a favorite in Venice. Oil paint was particularly suited to the depiction of subtle atmospheric effects as it enabled artists to build up layers of paint to enrich color and light.

THE ALDINE PRESS

Venice was a publishing center, the home of the Aldine Press, which printed practical, pocket-size books for a growing readership. The owner of the press, Aldus Manutius (1450–1515), was a humanist who had learned Greek from scholars emigrating to Venice after the fall of Constantinople in 1453. He arranged for Greek manuscripts to be edited and then printed them in the original, for which he commissioned a Greek typeface. From 1494 onward, Manutius printed all the existing manuscripts of Greek dramatists, poets, philosophers, and historians. He also published revised editions of Latin and Italian authors, including Dante and Petrarch. Manutius's introduction of italic type (slanted, thinned lettering) in 1500 was important in the production of inexpensive, small-scale books that were affordable for students.

The advent of printing in fifteenth-century Europe had made books more widely available (see Chapter 13). This, combined with increasing literacy among the general population, led to a demand for reading material. With the establishment of Gutenberg's press in Mainz, Caxton's printing concern in London, and the Aldine Press in Venice, several million books had been printed by 1500.

VENETIAN PAINTING

Venice's connections with the East meant that the Byzantine style persisted longer in that city than elsewhere in Italy. Venice also retained the medieval tradition of family workshops, in which artists were thought of as artisans rather than as intellectuals. The leading artist-family was the Bellini family; the career of Giovanni Bellini (*c.* 1430–1516) embodies the transition from early to High Renaissance.

Little is known of Giovanni's personal life. At first influenced by the linear style of his brother-in-law Andrea Mantegna (see Chapter 13), he soon turned to more textured surfaces and richer colors. His landscape backgrounds became vehicles for studying the atmospheric effects of light and shade.

Giovanni's *Madonna of the Meadow* (figure **14.19**), which was painted at the turn of the sixteenth century, shows Mary humbly seated on the ground, praying over the sleeping infant Jesus. Her large scale and the arch formed by her hands allude to her symbolic role as the church building—the "House of God." In Venice, the association of sleep and death (twins in ancient Greek mythology) was often used by artists to foreshadow the future of Jesus. Here, the sleeping infant (like the dead trees and the crow at the upper left) refers forward in time to his death, and his mother's melancholy expression suggests mourning. The landscape extends to the blue hills of the horizon, and rolling clouds form leisurely curves across the sky. Soft lighting bathes the scene, emphasizing the subtle modeling of the figures.

In the following decades, the two most important High Renaissance painters in Venice were Giorgione da Castelfranco (*c.* 1477–1510), a student of Giovanni Bellini who died young of the plague, and his pupil Titian (*c.* 1487–1576), who had a long and prolific career. Both Giorgione and Titian used oil paint and **glazes** (coats of translucent paint) to produce the rich colors and textures characteristic of Venetian style.

According to Vasari, Giorgione was sociable and musical and frequented a humanist circle in Venice. His interest in music and the pastoral tradition of antiquity is evident in his *Fête Champêtre*, or *Pastoral Concert* (figure **14.20**). This work conveys the sense of a dream unfolding in an idyllic, atmospheric landscape. There is no apparent explanation for the nudity of the two women, whose soft flesh and voluptuous proportions are no longer strictly Classical. Nor is their interaction with the clothed men made clear. The men seem to be conversing as one woman pours water into a well and the other holds a flute. In the distance, a shepherd tends his flock.

The lack of a readily identifiable narrative and the unanswered iconographic questions are typical of Giorgione. Softened contours, velvet textures, and muted lighting create a

14.19 Giovanni Bellini, *Madonna of the Meadow*, *c.* 1500–1505. Oil and tempera on wood panel, 26½ × 34 in. (67.3 × 86.4 cm). National Gallery, London.

dream-like quality and, as with dreams, much of the artist's imagery has remained a mystery.

The work of Titian is no less complex than Giorgione's and includes a wide range of subject matter—mythological and Christian scenes, portraits, and allegories. At the age of nine, Titian left his native town of Pieve da Cadore and went to Venice to study painting. Later in life, he numbered among his patrons the leading churches of Venice, Paul III (papacy 1534–1549), and Charles V. Charles's son, Philip II of Spain (ruled 1556–1598), commissioned Titian to paint several pictures based on Greek mythology. Also famous for his portraits, Titian produced several of the Holy Roman Emperor Charles V (see figure 14.1), who knighted him in 1533.

Some sense of Titian's artistic range can be gleaned from a comparison of his colossal *Assumption of the Virgin* (figure **14.21**) with his *Venus of Urbino* (figure **14.22**). The *Assumption* is a religious, Christian painting, whereas the *Venus* is erotic and inspired by Classical mythology (see thumbnail). The *Assumption* was commissioned for the altar of Santa Maria Gloriosa dei Frari, in Venice, to be viewed publicly, whereas the *Venus* was a private commission from a duke of Urbino.

The minimal setting of the *Assumption* focuses attention on the miracle of Mary's Assumption into heaven and on the

14.20 Giorgione, *Fête Champêtre*, *c.* 1510. Oil on canvas, approx. 3 ft. 7¼ in. × 4 ft. 6⅛ in. (1.05 × 1.38 m). Louvre, Paris.

14.21 **Titian, *Assumption of the Virgin*, Santa Maria Gloriosa dei Frari, Venice, 1516–1518. Oil on panel, 22 ft. 7½ in. × 11 ft. 9¾ in. (6.9 × 3.6 m).**
The apostles occupy the lower, darkened area of the picture, forming a transition from the earthly space of the viewer to the dazzling light of heaven. Their agitated poses and gestures are accentuated by the intense reds of the draperies. A radically foreshortened God the Father, surrounded by angels, sweeps across the top of the picture. The divine connection between the gazes of God and the Virgin bridges the yellow light of heaven. Unveiled in 1518, this picture established Titian's reputation as the greatest painter in sixteenth-century Venice.

astonishment of the apostles who witness the event. The woman in the *Venus of Urbino*, on the other hand, occupies the carefully depicted room of an aristocratic Venetian palace. In contrast to the *Assumption*, the *Venus of Urbino* is languid and calm. It reflects the influence of Giovanni Bellini and Giorgione in the voluptuousness of the nude, the textural variations, and the filtered light of the sky.

Music in High Renaissance Venice

Music in High Renaissance Venice was more innovative than elsewhere in Italy. In addition to housing the Aldine Press, Venice was in the forefront of the printing of music. The first chant books had been published in 1473, and polyphonic music became available from 1501. The violin was invented and other types of musical instruments developed. The violin was derived from the Arabic rebec (a bowed instrument with a pear-shaped body and three strings based on the lute-like medieval Arabic *rebab*) and from the Western fiddle used in the Middle Ages. The viola da gamba (a bowed string instrument with frets) was played widely, and **consorts** (families of instruments) were developed. The string and wind instruments of this period would eventually led to the instrumental groupings of modern orchestras.

In liturgical music, the **split choir**—in which groups of singers sing against, or in response to, each other—increased musical variation and complexity. Venice spearheaded the use of the organ in the liturgy, which led to new genres of composition. Among the types of organ work that became standard before a church service are the *intonazione* (which sounds improvised, or invented on the spur of the moment) and the *toccata* (which displays the instrumental potential of the organ and the dextrous "touch" of the performer—the Italian word meaning "to touch" is *toccare*).

The leading musician in Venice was Adrian Willaert (*c.* 1490–1562). He had been a student of Josquin Desprez (see Chapter 13) and was Netherlandish by birth. He visited Rome in 1515, and then worked at the Este court and in Milan. His success in Venice, where he was chapel master of St. Mark's (San Marco) from 1527, exemplifies the international flavor of the city.

Using the two organs in St. Mark's and writing for split choirs, Willaert took advantage of the layout of St. Mark's to create music that echoed back and forth across the cathedral. His basic polyphonic style uses a four-voice texture, but sometimes he wrote more sumptuous works using up to seven voices. Willaert composed over 170 motets, and in the later ones he abandons the *cantus firmus* structure that had been the foundation of polyphony throughout the medieval period. Now the voices are treated equally when they are woven together in polyphony, and there are contrasting chordal sections using the **triadic** harmony that became the basic language of Western music. Rhythms are less intricate than in medieval music, and where all the voices coincide, there can be an almost declamatory feeling. For the Church, Willaert also composed Masses, hymns, and psalms; his collection of psalms for double chorus published in 1550 was to foster a tradition of such psalms for the next fifty years.

14.22 *above* **Titian, *Venus of Urbino, c.* 1538. Oil on canvas, 3 ft. 11 in. × 5 ft. 5 in. (1.19 × 1.65 m). Galleria degli Uffizi, Florence.**

There are several interpretations of this painting, but none is definitive. They range from considering the woman a high-class courtesan to a bride awaiting her husband. The roses and myrtle are attributes of Venus. The dog symbolizing marital fidelity and the two maidservants removing clothes from a *cassone* (marriage chest) would seem to reinforce the latter interpretation. But the mood of the painting is decidedly erotic, as the gaze of the nude, her slightly parted lips, and the placement of her left hand are designed to entice a male viewer.

Botticelli, *Birth of Venus*
see figure 13.23

Willaert's secular music includes pieces for instrumental ensembles, *chansons*, and the Italian equivalent, **madrigals**. Unlike the *chanson*, which had a history dating back to the minstrels of the twelfth and thirteenth centuries, the madrigal was a new form in the Renaissance. Originating in Italy, it later spread across Europe, in particular to England. One of its characteristics was **word painting**—the musical illustration of the meaning of a word. Thus, a text about ascending a hill would be set to a rising scale, the words "running down" would be sung to fast, descending notes, all the voices but one would drop out for a phrase such as "all alone," and so forth. Such techniques brought into the musical arena the concept that art imitates nature; composers strove to express the ideas and emotions contained in their texts.

THE GABRIELIS The Gabrielis were the most prominent family of musicians in sixteenth-century Venice. Andrea Gabrieli (*c.* 1510–1586), a native of the city, worked for a time at the court of Bavaria. He returned to Venice in 1566 and was hired as one of the two organists at St. Mark's. His compositions, especially light madrigals, were extremely popular. They move away from polyphony toward homophony, and the setting of words is often virtually syllabic. Andrea's most monumental work was the ceremonial sacred music he composed for St. Mark's. By using the upper galleries of the cathedral as spaces for choirs accompanied by instruments, Andrea created music that flowed expansively from different directions, creating a new depth of sound.

Andrea's developments in sacred music were elaborated by

his nephew, Giovanni Gabrieli (*c.* 1554–1612), who became the greatest composer of his generation in Venice. Like his uncle, Giovanni had been a court organist in Bavaria before settling in 1585 in Venice as one of the organists of St. Mark's. His output includes a greater proportion of instrumental music than was usual at the time, both solos for organ and ensemble music for instruments. Venice had a particularly rich pool of players from which he could draw, with a nucleus of six instrumentalists employed at St. Mark's, and up to about twenty being engaged for grand festivals to perform with a choir of about thirty. Giovanni innovatively transferred the methods of writing for split choirs to instruments. Some of the music has elaborate solo writing, particularly for cornetts (a form of trumpet) and violins.

Giovanni is most famous for his sacred choral music. Like Willaert and Andrea Gabrieli, Giovanni composed a large number of grand motets for split choirs accompanied by a range of instruments. Increasingly, he contrasted different groups, for example, alternating choirs of high and low voices in dialogue. This produced a new formal coherence. In developing the practice of contrasting and opposing different sonorities, Giovanni is considered a forerunner of seventeenth-century Baroque music (see Chapter 16). Interestingly, he was always more admired by contemporaries in Germany than in Italy.

LITERATURE AND THEATER

Italian literature in the High Renaissance continued to expand the use of the vernacular and reflect the influence of humanism. Although not generally ranked among the greatest Western drama, Italian theater was enormously influential. The introduction of vernacular dialogue and the revival of Classical genres brought about a total break with medieval theater.

CASTIGLIONE'S *BOOK OF THE COURTIER*

Baldassare Castiglione (1478–1529) (figure **14.23**) wrote the classic High Renaissance treatise on manners. Born near Mantua to a family of small landowners and administrators at the Gonzaga court, Castiglione had a humanist education. He traveled to various courts as an ambassador and was known for his gentlemanly demeanor. From 1504 to 1517, he was at the Montefeltro court in Urbino.

In 1528, Castiglione published *The Courtier* (*Il cortegiano*), which is imbued with humanist ideas and meant for courtly audiences. Plato's influence is evident in the author's use of the dialogue form. *The Courtier* takes place during four evenings at the court of Urbino, which was so vast that Castiglione compares it to a small city. Actual historical characters engage in imaginary conversations on subjects ranging from the formation of an ideal courtier and the relative merits of monarchies and republics, to the meaning of love. Discussions of contemporary controversies include arguments over whether texts should be written in the vernacular or in Latin and whether the ideal education of a gentleman should emphasize the arts and humanities or physical training for war. Castiglione concluded that, as in the humanist curriculum of Mantua's Gioiosa (see Chapter 13), both should be included. The courtier should be skilled in horsemanship and sword play, and in all things his demeanor should be elegant and appear effortless.

The Courtier also had something to say about the formation of the ideal lady. Castiglione attributes to women the ability to civilize men. His ideal lady is attractive and well educated and a witty hostess, endowed with grace and charm. As for relationships between men and women, Castiglione preferred that they be Platonic, which was consistent with the medieval tradition of courtly love.

As regards the visual arts, *The Courtier* remarks that in ancient Greece aristocratic children were trained in drawing and painting. He notes that drawings of military installations

14.23 Raphael, *Baldassare Castiglione*, *c.* 1514. Oil on canvas, 32¼ × 16½ in. (81.9 × 67.3 cm). Louvre, Paris.
Raphael's genius for incorporating the innovations of important artists in his work is apparent in the influence of *Mona Lisa*. Note the three-quarter view, the seated pose, the folded hands, and the soft lighting. Castiglione exudes an air of understated sophistication. The rich black of the velvet hat, the voluminous fur sleeves, and the white silk shirt reflect courtly style. At the same time, the minimal background and crisp edges have the direct clarity for which Raphael is famous. Castiglione's slightly cocked head and penetrating gaze suggest the careful social observation that informs his descriptions of courtly life.

and of potential military targets, such as bridges and fortresses, serve practical political purposes. In accord with Leonardo, Castiglione says that since the art of painting both represents and is inspired by nature, it should be ranked among the highest human achievements.

The ideal outcome of the courtier's education, in Castiglione's view, is the creation of a *uomo universale* ("universal man"). In 1561, *The Courtier* was translated into English. It was considered the paradigm of elite courtly behavior and of the qualities of the Renaissance *uomo universale.* The treatise influenced Shakespeare (see Chapter 15) and by 1600 had been translated into most European languages.

READING SELECTION

Castiglione, *The Courtier*: the ideal courtier and the ideal court, PWC3-001; what women want from their lovers, PWC3-010

ARIOSTO'S *ORLANDO FURIOSO*

Lodovico Ariosto (1474–1533) came from an aristocratic family in Reggio Emilia and moved to Ferrara when he was ten. He received a humanist education, studying law, Latin, and Greek, and in 1503 became a courtier at the Este court. Fifteen years later, he went to work for the duke of Ferrara. While at the court of Ferrara, Ariosto wrote his classic epic *Orlando furioso* (published in 1516, 1521, and 1532), a long poem in octaves (stanzas of eight lines).

Written in the tradition of medieval legend, the work also has elements inspired by Roman poets, as well as by Dante, Petrarch, and Boccaccio. While focusing on Charlemagne, *Orlando furioso* alludes to contemporary figures as it interweaves two distinct narratives. In one, Orlando falls passionately in love with a princess and descends into madness (*furioso*) when she fails to return his affections. In the other, a pagan prince becomes a Christian, marries a virgin warrior, and founds the Este line of Ferrara, under whose patronage the poem was written. *Orlando furioso* is remarkable for its versatile style, combining different literary genres with various time periods, plots and subplots, and widely divergent characters.

Like the musicians and artists of the Renaissance who included references to themselves in their work (see Chapter 13), Ariosto fills *Orlando furioso* with autobiographical allusions. He makes his identification with its hero explicit, particularly in the maddening effects of unrequited love. The poem was an immediate success and came to exemplify one side of a new aesthetic quarrel, for advocates of the type of Classical unity recommended by Aristotle (see Chapter 6) objected to the discursive variety of Ariosto's style.

THEATER IN HIGH RENAISSANCE ITALY: FROM LATIN TO THE VERNACULAR

Most fifteenth-century plays were written in Latin, but in the early sixteenth century this began to change. With court patronage, vernacular theater was aimed at aristocratic audiences. Plays were often performed as segments of festivals, pageants, and courtly entertainments.

While he was at the Este court, Ariosto staged comedies by the Roman dramatists Terence and Plautus (see Chapter 7). Ariosto himself wrote the first vernacular play of the Renaissance, *The Casket* (*La cassaria*), which was produced in 1508. He used a standard Roman comic plot, in which a pair of servants arrange marriages for their masters, but the setting is sixteenth-century Italy. This combination of Classical and contemporary features, common today, was at the time a new idea—and one that quickly caught on.

Between 1513 and 1520, Machiavelli wrote *The Mandrake* (*La mandragola*). In this case, the plot was original, but the form was based on Roman comedy. *The Mandrake* is a farce, in which a foolish, doting husband is cuckolded by his young wife. By 1540, Italian comedy in the vernacular had become an established genre, and Italian theater was soon influencing dramatists in France and England.

Italy's first important tragedy in the vernacular was written by the humanist Giangiorgio Trissino (1478–1550). Entitled *Sofonisba* and published in 1515, it is the story of the beautiful and virtuous queen of Carthage who chooses suicide over defeat during the Punic Wars (see Chapter 7). Her history was first recorded by the Roman author Livy and then taken up in fourteenth-century Italy in Petrarch's *Africa* (see Chapter 12).

Trissino added another layer to the Latin-versus-vernacular controversy (see Chapters 12 and 13). He preferred Greek to Roman drama, the latter mainly known by way of Seneca. By using the Greek chorus and obeying Aristotle's rules of tragedy, Trissino's work led to arguments over whether Greek or Roman drama provided the better model for contemporary theater.

EARLY MANNERISM

In the visual arts, High Renaissance style was supplanted by Mannerism, which rejected Classical proportions, symmetry, and linear perspective, although mythological subjects were often represented. Mannerist artists preferred odd, agitated poses (especially the *serpentinata*, a sharply twisted, serpentine pose), spatial exaggeration, and jarring, incongruous color schemes. Although very much a style of the courts, Mannerism also appealed to Church patrons. The style first appeared in Florence after the return of the Medici in 1512 and eventually spread to France, Spain, and northern Europe. In architecture, Mannerists self-consciously tried to subvert the Classical Orders that had been revived during the Renaissance.

Paintings for private or court patrons tended to have erotic, even perverse overtones, often exhibited with considerable humor. And sculptures emphasized open space, an impression of instability, and spiraling motion. To what degree the Mannerist style reflected political and religious turmoil is a matter of debate. But that Mannerism and the turmoil of the time coincided is certain, which argues for some cause-and-effect relationship between what artists were doing and broader contemporary developments.

PAINTING

In Rome, early manifestations of Mannerism appear in the late work of Raphael (figure **14.24**). This is one of a series of frescoes that he completed under the Medici pope, Leo X (papacy

14.25 *right* **Jacopo Pontormo, *Portrait of a Halberdier, c.* 1528–1530. Oil (or oil and tempera) on panel transferred to canvas, $36^{1}/_{4} \times 28^{3}/_{8}$ in. (92.1 × 72.1 cm). The J. Paul Getty Museum, Los Angeles.**
Note the bulky arms and ballooning upper torso, which seem mismatched with the slim hips. Despite the large halberd and prominent sword hilt, the boy seems too refined for his profession. The slim red hat and light feather, the gold chain, and ruffled sleeves convey an air of delicacy. The slightly parted lips curve downward, creating a wistful expression that contradicts the self-assured pose.

14.24 Raphael, *Fire in the Borgo*, Stanza dell'Incendio, Vatican, Rome, from 1514. Fresco, 22 ft. 1 in. (6.7 m) wide at base.
Note the young man at the left carrying an old man on his shoulders with a young boy beside him. This detail quotes the ancient Roman sculpture group depicting Aeneas escaping from the burning city of Troy with Anchises and Ascanius (see figure 7.1).

1513–1521). It alludes to a ninth-century event in the life of Pope Leo IV (papacy 847–855), whose gesture of blessing miraculously extinguished a fire raging in Old St. Peter's. Compared to the restrained *School of Athens* (see figure 14.13), this fresco is filled with animated, muscular figures in a state of panic. The contorted poses, frantic gestures, and agitated draperies are keynotes of Mannerist style.

The early Mannerist painter Jacopo Pontormo (1494–1557) was born two years after the death of Lorenzo the Magnificent. An outstanding draftsman and painter of altarpieces and fresco cycles, he was also in demand as a portraitist. The odd proportions of his *Portrait of a Halberdier* (figure **14.25**), the varied surface textures, and the ambiguous characterization of the figure are typical of Mannerist style.

Madonna and Christ with Angels, also called *The Madonna of the Long Neck* (figure **14.26**), by Parmigianino (1503–1540), was commissioned for a private chapel. It juxtaposes large foreground figures with an illogically small prophet at the lower right. A truncated column without a capital was probably a reference to the Virgin as a metaphor for church buildings; in hymns her neck is sometimes compared to a column. In that metaphor, Mary is not only the sacred building, she is also its supporting member. Parmigianino's Mary and Christ defy Classical proportions: she is elongated from her waist down, and Christ is unnaturally contorted. His sleeping state alludes to his death and especially to *pietà* scenes, where Mary supports his dead body. Observing Christ at the left is a group of leering angels, who imbue the picture with a perverse cast.

14.26 Parmigianino (Francesco Mazzola), *Madonna of the Long Neck*, *c.* 1535. Oil on panel, approx. 7 ft. 1 in. × 4 ft. 4 in. (2.16 × 1.32 m). Uffizi, Florence.

14.27 Sofonisba Anguissola, *Self-portrait at a Spinet*, after 1550. Oil. Museo di Capodimonte, Naples.

Sofonisba, named after the Carthaginian queen, was one of six sisters from a noble family in Cremona. All six were encouraged by their father to become painters. While Sofonisba worked at the court of Philip II of Spain, she was commissioned by Pope Pius IV to paint a portrait of the Spanish queen. In 1570, the artist married a Sicilian and went to live in Palermo. Widowed four years later, Sofonisba next married a sea captain and settled in Genoa. The self-portrait conveys the sense of a serious, introspective young woman.

The *Self-portrait at a Spinet* (figure **14.27**) by Sofonisba Anguissola (1527–1625) reveals Mannerist tendencies in the fussiness of the lace collar and cuffs, as well as in the details of the spinet. Sofonisba was one of the first women to have a successful international career as a painter. She was admired by Vasari, and her success was unusual for a woman at the time. Traditionally excluded from artistic training, women were at a disadvantage unless they came from artist families and could study at home. However, in the sixteenth century women gradually began to be taken seriously as professional artists.

SCULPTURE: BENVENUTO CELLINI

One of the most elegant examples of Mannerist sculpture is the gold and enamel saltcellar in figure **14.28**, made by Benvenuto Cellini (1500–1571). Trained as a goldsmith and sculptor, Cellini worked in Florence for the grand duke of Tuscany, Cosimo I de' Medici, and in France for Francis I. The saltcellar, which was made for the French king, exemplifies the complex iconography, unstable poses, and erotic overtones of Mannerist court art. In this case, the mythological figures probably allude to the king and his amours. The sea god Poseidon holds a trident and leans so far backward that he seems about to topple over. The same is true of the woman, an earth goddess, who tweaks her breast and seductively extends her leg toward Poseidon.

14.28 Benvenuto Cellini, saltcellar of Francis I, finished 1543. Gold and enamel, $10\frac{1}{4} \times 13\frac{1}{8}$ in. (26 × 33.3 cm). Stolen from the Kunsthistorisches Museum, Vienna.

When he was fifty-eight and under house arrest, Cellini wrote an autobiography. He describes a life of art, crime, and sexual experimentation. On the run from the law, he racked up debts, committed acts of violence, and was accused of murder. He was bisexual and an occasional transvestite. Having studied for the priesthood, Cellini finally married the mother of two of his children.

Cellini's major large-scale bronze sculpture is the *Perseus* in Florence (figure **14.29**). Commissioned by Cosimo I de' Medici, the 18-foot (5.48-m) high statue portrays the Greek hero Perseus displaying the severed head of Medusa. The statue is located in front of the town hall, thereby associating Cosimo with the heroism of Perseus. Perseus extends his sword and carefully looks down to avoid being turned to stone by gazing at the head. The self-conscious pose, animated surface patterns, and elaborate winged cap are typical of Mannerism. Similarly, the depiction of Medusa's blood dripping downward in waves of bronze from the head and sideways from the neck exemplifies the Mannerist taste for disturbing imagery (see Box).

14.29 Benvenuto Cellini, *Perseus*, Loggia dei Lanzi, Piazza della Signoria, Florence, 1545–1554. Bronze, 18 ft. (5.48 m) high.

Society and Culture

Cellini on the Casting of the *Perseus*

In his autobiography, Cellini describes casting the bronze *Perseus* as an exciting and harrowing process that could have been accomplished only by a genius such as himself. While preparing his chisels for the job, he tells us, a splinter flew into his eye and was removed when a surgeon spilled pigeon blood over the eye. In gratitude Cellini thanked St. Lucy, who had gouged out her own eyes on discovering that a Roman taken with her beauty could not help looking at her with desire.

After casting the Medusa, Cellini covered the model of Perseus in wax in preparation for making a mold of it. Thereupon his patron Cosimo de' Medici said that he did not believe it could be made in bronze. In Cosimo's view, it would not be possible to cast the head at a height of 18 feet (5.48 m). Cellini replied that Cosimo, being a patron rather than an artist, could not possibly understand the extent of his genius. He reminded Cosimo of his remarkable saltcellar for Francis I (see figure 14.28) and of the king's generosity. He did acknowledge, however, that the foot of the sculpture would be a problem.

When Cosimo left the artist's house, Cellini set to work, creating the mold, drawing off the wax, using pulleys and ropes to lift sections of the sculpture, and forcing himself to continue despite a raging fever. He soon took to his bed, leaving instructions for his assistants to finish the work. But they were unable to do so and declared the task impossible. Newly propelled into action, Cellini overcame fires, furnace explosions, and curdling metal until the finished bronze was unveiled. At that point, every feature except the toes was perfect, and Cellini completed them with a little more work. When the duke came to view the statue, he was impressed with the result—even more so because, as Cellini had predicted, the foot was not quite right and had to be redone.

ARCHITECTURE: GIULIO ROMANO AND ANDREA PALLADIO

Mannerist architecture used the Classical Orders, but it changed the relationships between their individual parts. This is evident, for example, in the work of Raphael's pupil Giulio Romano (*c.* 1499–1546). From 1527, Romano was in the employ of the Mantua court, designing the villa known as the Palazzo del Tè, which served as both the court's horse farm and a place for royal entertainments. The view of the courtyard façade (figure **14.30**) illustrates the Mannerist disruption and reconfiguration of the Classical tradition and Renaissance style. The pediment above the round-arched entrance is no longer supported by columns and an entablature. Instead, it rests on scroll-shaped brackets above an open wall space. The pediments over the blind niches lack horizontal bases and also rest on brackets.

Although the columns of the façade support a Doric entablature, some of the triglyphs dip below the narrow architrave as if falling from the wall. The columns stand on narrow podia (projecting bases) formed by rectangular blocks repeated on the entire surface of the wall. This heavy **rustication** (rough masonry blocks having beveled, or sloping, edges and recessed joints), alternating with the opened architectural spaces, dominates the wall surface. Compared with the canonical Classical Orders, those at the Palazzo del Tè create an impression of instability by increasing spatial movement, opening space, and altering the expected arrangement of forms. There is a playful quality in these forms that conforms to the purpose of the Palazzo as a place of entertainment.

In the churches of Andrea di Pietro (1508–1580), known as Palladio, the Classical Orders of the façade are rearranged in order to unify the tall nave with the shorter side aisles. This is the case with San Giorgio Maggiore in Venice (figure **14.31**), where the façade is composed of a double portico. The taller

14.30 Giulio Romano, courtyard façade, Palazzo del Tè, Mantua, 1527–1534.

14.31 Andrea Palladio, San Giorgio Maggiore, Venice, begun 1565.

portico, consisting of four Corinthian columns on podia supporting an entablature and a pediment, corresponds to the nave. The wider portico behind it is framed by pilasters, and the wall surface is animated by pediments and round-arched niches containing statues. As in Romano's Palazzo del Tè courtyard, Palladio has used elements of the Classical Orders but juxtaposed them in new ways.

Palladio was the author of an important architectural treatise, the *Quattro libri dell' archittetura* (*The Four Books of Architecture*), which would influence architects in eighteenth-century Britain and the United States. In particular, the buildings designed by Thomas Jefferson (see Chapter 17), who was himself a student of Classical architecture, show evidence of Palladio's style.

As the High Renaissance and then Mannerism were developing in Italy, cultural changes were unfolding elsewhere in Europe. The Renaissance arrived north of the Alps, where it took on a different shape than in Italy. In northern Europe, where Christian humanism dominated progressive thinking, one of the most significant events in the history of the West came as a protest to corruption in the Roman Church. In the next chapter we focus on northern Europe and consider the northern Renaissance and the movements known as the Protestant Reformation and the Catholic Counter-Reformation.

KEY TERMS

consort a set of musical instruments of the same family for playing music composed before about 1700.

glaze a translucent paint layer that enriches colors.

madrigal a secular contrapuntal song for several voices, from the Renaissance.

rusticate to give a rustic appearance to masonry blocks by roughening their surface and beveling their edges.

split choir a choir in which groups of singers sing against, or in response to, each other.

triadic based on the three notes of the "common" chord in Western music, using notes 1, 3, and 5 of the scale.

word painting in a vocal work, the musical illustration of the meaning of a word.

KEY QUESTIONS

1. What was the result of the exploration and colonization of the New World for those living in the conquered lands?
2. Portraits were a popular subject in an age of patronage and a source of commissions for artists. Name three other genres or subjects found in the High Renaissance period and explain their particular relevance in this era.
3. Why is the *School of Athens* called "a summation of High Renaissance humanism"? Explain how Raphael creates the illusion of a real space containing historically significant figures—what techniques were used?

4. In what ways did music and literature "extend the vernacular" and include humanist interests? Does *The Courtier* illustrate these concerns? What two other works show extensions of the vernacular and humanism?

5. What are the characteristics of Mannerism? What stylistic features would a person who had never seen a Mannerist work look for?

SUGGESTED READING

Ariosto, Ludovico. *Orlando furioso*, trans. Barbara Reynolds. London: Penguin Classics, Vol. 1 1975, Vol. 2 1977.
▸ Ariosto's classic tale in translation.

Barolsky, Paul. *Michelangelo's Nose: A Myth and its Maker.* University Park, PA: Pennsylvania State University Press, 1990.
▸ Based on Vasari's account of Michelangelo reducing the size of the nose on the *David.*

——. *Why Mona Lisa Smiles and Other Tales by Vasari.* University Park, PA: Pennsylvania State University Press, 1991.
▸ A discussion of the meaning of the smile in words and images.

Castiglione, Baldassare. *The Book of the Courtier*, trans. G. Bull. New York and London: Penguin Books, 1967.
▸ A study of manners and society in the Renaissance.

Cellini, Benvenuto. *Autobiography*, trans. J. A. Symonds, ed. John Pope-Hennessy. New York: Modern Library, 1985.
▸ Cellini's lively autobiography, through which a picture of his life and times emerges.

Cole, Bruce. *Titian and Venetian Painting: 1450–1590.* Boulder, CO: Westview Press, 1999.
▸ A brief account of Titian and the High Renaissance Venetian painters.

Hall, Marcia (ed.). *Raphael's School of Athens.* Cambridge, U.K.: Cambridge University Press, 1998.
▸ A collection of essays on the painting from different viewpoints.

Hauser, Arnold. *Mannerism: The Crisis of the Renaissance and the Origin of Modern Art.* Cambridge, MA: Harvard University Press, 1986.
▸ A Marxist history of art that looks at works in their economic context.

Kemp, Martin (ed.). *Leonardo on Painting*, trans. Martin Kemp and Margaret Walker. New Haven, CT: Yale University Press, 1989.
▸ An edition of Leonardo's writings on the art of painting.

Machiavelli, Niccolò. *The Prince*, trans. George Bull. London: Penguin Classics, 2003.
▸ A classic view of Renaissance politics.

Meilman, Patricia (ed.). *The Cambridge Companion to Titian.* New York: Cambridge University Press, 2004.
▸ Essays on Titian.

Ruggiero, Guido. *The Boundaries of Eros: Sex, Crime, and Sexuality in Renaissance Venice.* New York: Oxford University Press, 1985.
▸ A study of sexual crime and punishment in Venice.

——. *Binding Passions: Tales of Magic, Marriage, and Power at the End of the Renaissance.* New York: Oxford University Press, 1993.
▸ A social and psychological account of the late Renaissance.

Saslow, James M. *The Poetry of Michelangelo.* New Haven, CT, and London: Yale University Press, 1991.
▸ A translation of the artist's poetry.

Shearman, John K. G. *Mannerism.* Baltimore: Pelican Books, 1967.
▸ A survey of the style and the ideas behind it.

Vasari, Giorgio. *The Lives of the Most Eminent Painters, Sculptors, and Architects*, trans. Gaston du C. de Vere. New York: Random House, 1979.
▸ Biographies of Italian Renaissance artists from Cimabue to Vasari; concludes with Vasari's autobiography.

SUGGESTED FILMS

1950 *The Story of Michelangelo*, dir. Robert J. Flaherty and Richard Lyford

1965 *The Agony and the Ecstasy*, dir. Carol Reed

1969 *The Royal Hunt of the Sun*, dir. Irving Lerner

1990 *Cabeza de Vaca*, dir. Nicolás Echevarria

15 Reformation and Reform in Sixteenth-century Europe

> "*Why should I want a temple, since the whole world, unless I am badly mistaken, is a splendid temple dedicated to me? Nor will there ever be a lack of worshippers, as long as there is no lack of men. Moreover, I am not so foolish as to require stone statues decked out in gaudy colors. For sometimes these are a drawback to the worship of us gods—that is, when stupid numbskulls adore the figures instead of the divinities, and then we are left in the position of those who have been edged out by substitutes.*"
>
> (ERASMUS, *The Praise of Folly*)

While Pope Julius II and his successors were rebuilding St. Peter's in Rome, northern Europe grew restive. Since the mid-fifteenth century critics inside and outside the Church had been calling for reform. The most forceful challenge to the Church came from Martin Luther (1483–1546), whose protests against corruption would eventually lead to the religious upheaval known as the Protestant Reformation.

Further challenges to Church authority came from science and the visual arts. Physicians, relying on empirical evidence rather than faith, wrote and illustrated books on anatomy. New instruments enabled astronomers to make discoveries that contradicted entrenched religious beliefs. In the visual arts, Gothic elements persisted in the North, even though leading humanist painters were drawn to naturalism and Classical as well as Christian subject matter continued to interest certain artists.

The response of the Catholic Church to these challenges is called the Counter-Reformation by scholars who view the Church's response as a reaction against criticism coming from the outside, and the Catholic Reformation by scholars who see the Church's response as a push for reform from within. Whatever the cause, Pope Paul III convened the Council of Trent, which met from 1545 to 1563 and codified the views of the Church. The Council reaffirmed the authority of the Roman Catholic Church and advocated measures that discouraged scientific inquiry and humanism. It also drew up rules for depicting Christian subject matter in the arts and literature that would inspire viewers to identify with the suffering of saints and martyrs.

*In the quotation that opens this chapter, the Dutch humanist Desiderius Erasmus (*c. *1469–1536) personifies Folly as a conceited woman. Spoiled but charming, Folly is the narrator and leading lady of* The Praise of Folly *(*Encomium moriae*), a satire published in 1509. Erasmus's Folly makes fun of the clergy, the professions, and other classes of society; she is an illusion that makes life bearable. Folly, he says, drives men to admire, even worship, beautiful women, while such worship gives women the illusion of power and men the illusion of satisfaction.*

The Praise of Folly *combines criticism, humor, and paradox while denouncing ignorance, corruption, superstition, and war. As a humanist, Erasmus was influenced by Plato and other Classical authors, whom he reconciled with Christian thought. Humanism in northern Europe is often called "Christian humanism," which*

Key Topics

The Reformation

- The sale of indulgences
- Satire and skepticism
- Sacraments simplified
- Translations of the Bible in the vernacular

Counter-Reform

- The Council of Trent
- Monastic Reform
- Society of Jesus
- The Inquisition

Elizabethan England

- Secular music
- Shakespeare
- The Globe Playhouse

TIMELINE	REFORMATION	COUNTER-REFORMATION
HISTORY AND CULTURE 	Henry VIII ascends to English throne, 1509 Vesalius (1515–1564), first anatomical textbook, 1543 Copernicus (1473–1543) argues for heliocentrism, 1543 War between Holy Roman Emperor Charles V and German Lutherans, 1546 Independence of English and French kings from pope Peace of Augsburg, 1555 Elizabeth I rules England, 1558–1603 Drake circumnavigates the globe, 1577–1580 England defeats the Spanish Armada, 1588	Council of Trent reaffirms authority of Catholic Church, 1545–1563 Philip II rules Spain, 1556–1598 *Index of Forbidden Books*, 1557 The Netherlands resist Spanish invasion, 1585
RELIGION 	Erasmus, *Adagia*, 1500; *Julius Excluded from Heaven: A Dialogue*, 1503; *The Praise of Folly*, 1509 More publishes *Utopia* criticizing corruption of English society, 1516 Luther, 95 theses, 1517 Luther excommunicated, 1520; Lutheran Church formed Reformation spreads to Switzerland; main advocate John Calvin (1509–1564) Calvinism spreads across Europe, particularly to Scotland and the Netherlands Act of Supremacy establishing monarch as head of Church of England, 1534; destruction of the monasteries, 1535; More executed for refusing to take Oath of Supremacy, 1535 Knox, *First Blast of the Trumpet against the Monstrous Regiment of Women*, aimed at Catholic regent of Scotland, Mary of Guise, 1558 Elizabeth I presides over passage of Act of Uniformity, establishing Anglican Church, 1559	New religious Orders: Jesuits, Ursulines Jesuit missionaries visit East Indies, China, Japan, and Ceylon Mystic saints: Teresa of Avila (1515–1582) and John of the Cross (1542–1591) Power of Inquisition expanded Pope Paul IV first Counter-Reformation pope, 1555–1559 St. Bartholomew's Day Massacre in Paris, in pursuit of heretics, 1572 Henry IV of Navarre (Henry IV) converts to Catholicism, 1594; issues Edict of Nantes, granting freedom of worship throughout France
ART 	Bosch, *The Cure of Folly*, *c.* 1490; *The Garden of Earthly Delights*, *c.* 1510–1515 Dürer, *Self-portrait*, 1500; *The Last Supper*, 1523 Grünewald, Isenheim Altarpiece, 1515 Holbein the Younger, *Portrait of Erasmus Writing*, 1523; *Henry VIII*, *c.* 1540; *Head of a Young Man*, early 16th century Bruegel the Elder, *The Big Fish Eating the Little Fish*, 1556; *Hunters in the Snow*, 1565 Hilliard, *Ermine Portrait of Queen Elizabeth I*, 1585 Housebook Master, *Coat of Arms with a Peasant Standing on His Head*, 16th century van Mander, *The Painter's Book*, first northern compilation of art and artists, 1604	Veronese, *The Last Supper (The Feast in the House of Levi)*, 1573 El Greco, *The Burial of Count Orgaz*, 1586–1588; *Laocoön*, *c.* 1610/1614 Tintoretto, *The Last Supper*, 1590s
ARCHITECTURE		Giacomo da Vignola, Il Gesù, Rome, *c.* 1565–1584
LITERATURE AND PHILOSOPHY 	Rabelais, *The Histories of Gargantua and Pantagruel*, 1532–1534 Montaigne, *Essays*, 1572–1580 Elizabethan poets: Marlowe (1564–1593): lyrical poetry in pastoral tradition; *The Passionate Shepherd to his Love* Shakespeare (1564–1616), sonnets Sidney, *Astrophel and Stella*, 1582; *Arcadia*, 1590; *Apology for Poetry*, first work of literary criticism in England, 1595 Spenser, *The Faerie Queen*, 1617	
THEATER	Elizabethan theater: Marlowe, *Tamburlaine*, 1587; *Dr. Faustus*, 1604 Shakespeare, the Globe Playhouse, 1599–1613: *Richard III*, *c.* 1593; *Romeo and Juliet*, *c.* 1595; *Julius Caesar*, *c.* 1599; *Hamlet*, *c.* 1600; *Twelfth Night*, *c.* 1600; *Othello*, *c.* 1602; *Macbeth*, *c.* 1605; *The Tempest*, 1611	
MUSIC	Luther (1483–1546) believes music essential aspect of worship Luther's chorales: "Ein' feste Burg ist unser Gott" Marenzio (*c.* 1553–1599) composes madrigals Elizabethan music influenced by composers from the Netherlands, Germany, France, and Italy Italian madrigals become popular in England Byrd (1543–1623) greatest English composer of Elizabethan period; "This sweet and merry month of May" Morley (*c.* 1557–1602) popularizes madrigal; *The Triumphes of Oriana* Weelkes (1575–1623) madrigals: "As Vesta was from Latmos hill descending" Bull (1562–1628) leading keyboard musician Dowland (1563–1626), somber airs for lute Campion (1567–1620), light pieces for lute	Council of Trent reverses secular trends in music Palestrina (1524–1594) in Rome embodies spirit of Catholic reform Lasso (1532–1594), religious and secular works Victoria (1548–1611), sacred music in Spain

differed from Italian humanism in its use of proverbs and satire to comment on the morals of society. Whereas Italian humanism originated in the revival of Classical culture, northern humanism strove for a "back to basics" form of Christianity. Many northern humanists, including Erasmus, remained Catholic and strove for Church reform from within.

THE PROTESTANT REFORMATION

Although corruption in the Catholic Church is traditionally cited as the cause of the Reformation, the movement coincided with other significant developments in western Europe. One was the growing sense of nationalism engendered by more stable national boundaries (see Chapter 14). The relative independence of the English and French kings made them resent the pope's efforts to control political decisions and his demands for money. In England Henry VIII broke with the pope over his wish to divorce his wife and remarry in order to have a male heir. In the Holy Roman Empire, which was still largely under papal domination, rulers of the various states objected to paying Church taxes and to the fact that the Church appointed local clergy without consulting the rulers. In Germany, in addition to rooting out corruption, Martin Luther wanted to simplify the Church hierarchy and make Christianity more direct and accessible to worshippers. In Switzerland and Germany reformers wanted **vernacular** translations of the Bible as a means of reaching the common people, which spurred printing and encouraged literacy. John Calvin (1509–1564) sought the moral reform of society. The popes themselves were preoccupied with politics and a pressing need for money. All of these conflicts between the Church and various states were reflected in the writings of Erasmus.

15.1 Housebook Master, *Coat of Arms with a Peasant Standing on His Head*, 16th century. German engraving, 5³/₈ × 3¹/₄ in. (13.7 × 8.4 cm). Rijksmuseum, Amsterdam.

Satirical images were especially popular in Nuremburg, Germany. This print conveys the fear that women were becoming too dominant. It shows a woman mounted on her unhappy husband as he steadies the distaff used for spinning. The figure on the coat of arms below represents the theme of the world turned upside-down as a result of disrupting the natural order of male domination and female submission.

ERASMUS AND REFORM

Satire was often used to express the push for reform in sixteenth-century northern Europe (figure **15.1**). The engraving illustrated here reflects a trend that began in the fifteenth century and grew in the sixteenth, in which images of a "world turned upside-down" became widely popular.

The illegitimate son of a priest, Erasmus was born in the Dutch port of Rotterdam. He was educated at the University of Paris, knew Latin and Greek, and was, like his father, an ordained priest. Erasmus traveled in Italy, lived much of his life in England, and wrote extensively. Although a devout Catholic, he objected to Church corruption and was one of many northern thinkers who criticized the Church while remaining Catholic.

Erasmus was a master of satirical writing (figure **15.2**). In 1500 he published *Adagia* (*Adages*), a book of proverbs that speak, like Folly, in double meanings and teach moral lessons. Three years later Erasmus brought out a scathing attack on Pope Julius II entitled *Julius Excluded from Heaven: A Dialogue, "You're All Belches and You Stink of Boozing and Hangovers."* In this satirical story, when the pope dies and arrives at heaven's gate he finds his way barred and complains that the lock has been changed. A divine attendant observes that Julius must have the wrong key, remarking that the key to a treasure chest will not open the door to heaven. St. Peter asks the pope to identify himself. Julius replies that Peter will surely recognize him as P.M., a reference to the title Pontifex Maximus ("Highest Priest"), bestowed on the Roman emperor

15.2 Hans Holbein the Younger, *Portrait of Erasmus Writing*, 1523. Panel, 16½ × 12⅝ in. (42 × 32 cm). Louvre, Paris.
Holbein shows Erasmus writing his *Paraphrase of the Gospel of Mark*, a commentary on the biblical text, which he completed in 1523. Note the use of highlight to emphasize the face, hands, and paper. The portrait conveys the calm determination of the scholar who embodied the sixteenth-century spirit of reform.

Augustus (see Chapter 7) and later adopted by the popes. But St. Peter misunderstands, concluding that P.M. refers to *Pestis Maxima* ("Biggest Pest"), and denies Julius entry. Casting his eyes over the pope's entourage, St. Peter declares: "You've brought twenty-thousand men with you, but not one of the whole mob even looks like a Christian to me. They seem to be the worst dregs of humanity, all stinking of brothels, booze, and gunpowder."

Erasmus particularly objected to the sale of indulgences. These were letters of credit toward redemption sold by the Church to people who wanted to reduce their time in purgatory. Traditionally, a sinner had to perform acts of penance, ranging from saying Hail Marys and the Lord's Prayer to taking on harsh tasks or even self-flagellation. Indulgences allowed sinners to avoid performing acts of penance and also enabled them to show appreciation to God for having granted salvation. People who bought indulgences—whether for themselves or for others—were promised that they would not suffer for their sins after death on their way to be with God.

Thousands of people, terrified that salvation might elude them, purchased indulgences, and the money went into Church coffers. Julius II, in Erasmus's view, was preying on superstition to raise money for the rebuilding of St. Peter's in Rome. Nonetheless, Erasmus remained a devout Catholic, but he was criticized not only by Catholics for his reformist position but also by Protestants for not being enough of a reformer.

READING SELECTION
Erasmus, *The Praise of Folly*, PWC3-051-B

MARTIN LUTHER

Born in Saxony to a family of successful miners, Luther attended the cathedral school of Magdeburg, in Eisenach. He studied philosophy for four years at the university in Erfurt. In 1505 he joined Erfurt's monastery of Augustinian Hermits and was ordained two years later. In 1508 he became a lecturer at the university in Wittenberg in central Germany. Endowed with a passionate temper and, like most of society, an obsessive concern with sin, Luther (see figure 15.3) lacked the detachment and composure of the scholarly Erasmus. Above all, Luther was concerned with how to attain forgiveness and salvation. In 1510 he traveled to Rome on monastic business and was appalled by the religious corruption he saw there, especially the sale of indulgences. He was particularly enraged by the Dominican friar Johann Tetzel, who took advantage of the poor and the ignorant, threatening them with damnation but promising salvation if they purchased "letters of safe conduct" (indulgences) into heaven. In 1511 Luther returned to Wittenberg, where he became a doctor of theology and was appointed professor of scripture. His beliefs began to differ from traditional teaching and took on a pessimistic cast. He soon arrived at the conclusion that faith and God's grace, rather than good works, determined salvation.

Tradition has it that in 1517 Luther nailed ninety-five theses, written in dialogue form in Latin, to the door of the Castle Church in Wittenberg (see Box, p. 400). In fact, the theses may have been circulated for discussion at Wittenberg University and printed by someone else. The printing presses established throughout Europe disseminated the theses, propelling Reformation ideas to a wide audience. The following excerpts from two of the theses illustrate Luther's view:

> 21. . . . those preachers of indulgences are in error who say that by the indulgences of a pope a man is freed and saved from all punishment.
> 28. It is certain that, when the money rattles in the chest, avarice and gain may be increased, but the effect of the intercession of the Church depends on the will of God alone.

Luther urged that the Church hierarchy and its monasteries be reformed and that the Sacraments be simplified by confining them to Baptism and the Eucharist. Arguing that the clergy and the pope had corrupted the true Church, Luther preached a form of Christianity based on the original text of the Bible rather than on layers of Church doctrine. He envisioned a return to the piety of the early Christian period and rejected the authority of parts of the Septuagint (see Chapter 8), which, he believed, should be excluded from the Hebrew Bible. By preaching in German and translating the Bible into German, Luther sought to make religion accessible to the average person. The availability of printed books and increasing literacy spread his ideas throughout Europe.

Luther recognized the potential of music in making Christian worship more accessible to the people. He wanted members of the congregation to take part in the singing of the services and to understand what they were singing, rather than leave this to professional choirs, who sang in Latin. To achieve this Luther wrote many hymns, known as **chorales** or *kirchenlieder* (church songs), in German. He either used existing tunes which the congregation already knew or composed new music. For simplicity these chorales were sung in **unison** (with all voices singing the same melody) by the congregation rather than in harmony, without accompaniment. Perhaps the best-known of Luther's chorales is "Ein' feste Burg ist unser Gott" ("A Mighty Fortress Is Our God"). The chorale is the most important musical contribution of the Lutheran Church and it had a major impact on later composers.

Driven by a sense of human weakness in the face of God's omnipotence, Luther sought spiritual communication free of the Church hierarchy and its rites. He objected to the use of priests as intermediaries between God and people, and to having to pray to saints and martyrs. He believed that men are slaves to desire and have no free will, arguing that salvation depends entirely on faith and the grace of God. In this Luther diverged from Erasmus, who *did* believe in free will, although he agreed that the Church was in need of moral and educational reform.

Luther renounced his vow of chastity and was excommunicated in 1520 by the Medici pope Leo X. Luther publicly burned the excommunication document and was declared a heretic. Five years later he married Katherine von Bora, a former nun, and had several children. He eluded the wrath of the Church through the protection of the Elector of Saxony, Frederick the Wise, who faked Luther's kidnapping and housed him in his castle in the Thuringian forest. There Luther translated the Bible into German.

Luther's ideas led to the formation of the Protestant (the "protester's") Church, and Lutheran churches began to be built around 1521. In contrast to Catholic churches and cathedrals, Lutheran churches had little decoration, especially in France and Switzerland, although in Germany the attitude toward the arts in churches was less austere. In general, however, reformers opposed lavish works of art and decoration as a form of idolatry, much as the Iconoclasts had done in the eighth century (see Chapter 9). As a result, artistic patronage in the Protestant north of Europe became increasingly secular.

In 1546 war broke out between Holy Roman Emperor Charles V and German Lutherans. Fighting continued until 1555, when the Peace of Augsburg recognized Lutheranism and Catholicism, but not Calvinism (see below). The peace treaty determined that the religion of each ruler (prince or bishop) would be followed within his own territory. People who opposed this decision were free to sell their property and move elsewhere. The agreement governed ecclesiastical matters in the Holy Roman Empire until the middle of the seventeenth century.

READING SELECTION

Luther, *Ninety-five Theses*, against the sale of indulgences, PWC3-037

JOHN CALVIN

The Protestant Reformation spread to Switzerland, where its main advocate was the Frenchman John Calvin. In 1533, while studying law and Classics in France, Calvin began to campaign for Church reform. To avoid persecution, he left France for the Swiss city of Basel and then moved to Geneva, which became the center of his movement. When he was twenty-seven, Calvin published *The Institutes of the Christian Religion*, in which he argued for faith over free will and which he continued to revise until his death.

Like Luther, Calvin believed that God predestined some people to be saved and others to be damned. He also shared Luther's view that faith rather than works justified and that scripture was the basis of faith. But he diverged from Luther in denying grace and in his absolute certainty of salvation and of predestination. According to Calvin, God had willed the Fall of Man, which drove humanity toward sin and made people evil by nature.

In contrast to Luther, who believed in the supremacy of the state over the Church, Calvin's political ideal was **theocracy** (rule by the Church rather than by secular authority). His ideal state would be run according to strict ethical principles, where citizens would work hard, avoid the temptations of the arts, and renounce frivolity. Calvin's views spread across Europe, and were the basis of the beliefs of French Protestants (called Huguenots). In the Netherlands Calvinism became the official religion, and in Scotland it was the basis of Presbyterianism. The doctrine of the virtue of hard work led to the notion that wealth was comparable to salvation in that it came directly from God. This influenced the Puritan view of Christian capitalism and the belief that poverty was divine punishment whereas wealth was God-given.

Defining Moment

Martin Luther and the Ninety-five Theses

Although Martin Luther (figure **15.3**) was not the first person who wished to reform the Catholic Church, he was the first to have such an enormous impact on the future of Christianity. His reforms led to the founding of a new, Protestant Church. Before Luther, Erasmus had taken issue with the secular pursuits of the papacy and challenged the practices of fasting, worshipping relics, celibacy, selling indulgences, pilgrimages, burning heretics, and praying to saints. Although Erasmus believed that education could change the world, his actual audience was the intellectual elite. Convinced of the need for reform, Erasmus nevertheless remained within the Catholic Church.

Luther never anticipated the revolutionary effects of his ideas or his actions. As a professor of theology at the University of Wittenberg, Germany, he had become alarmed at what he considered to be doctrinal flaws in Church teaching, but none was more repugnant to him than the selling of indulgences. An indulgence was an extra-sacramental declaration of absolution of sin, which allegedly reduced the amount of time one had to spend in purgatory.

As a priest in Wittenberg listening to the confessions of his parishioners, Luther was dismayed at how little remorse they showed for their sins and how eagerly they looked for means to escape punishment. He was also plagued by worries about his own salvation. Then, he found in the Book of Romans the word "justice," which he interpreted as "righteousness." Luther associated the righteousness of God with the eternal condemnation of the damned. But the words of St. Paul—"The just shall live by faith"—gave him new insight. He concluded that God's righteousness was not based on condemnation but rather on mercy. He was convinced that God alone could bestow grace and that it could not be bought.

In 1517 the Dominican Johann Tetzel sold indulgences during flamboyant performances near Wittenberg. Luther's anger at Tetzel's conduct led him to explain formally his concerns. Since it was then customary for scholars to post their ideas in public places, tradition has it that Luther chose the north door of the Castle Church of Frederick the Wise, Elector of Saxony, on October 31, 1517. He also sent a copy to his bishop and one to friends. Luther's expectations of a quiet, scholarly discussion of his grievances were confounded when copies of the theses were circulated throughout Europe. Tetzel read them and declared that he would throw Luther "in the fire."

15.3 Lucas Cranach the Elder, *Martin Luther*, 1533. Oil on panel, 8 × 5¾ in. (20.5 × 14.5 cm). City of Bristol Museum and Art Gallery, England. Luther's plain black robe and intent expression convey a sense of determination. In contrast to Holbein's Erasmus (see figure 15.2), Cranach's Luther is unshaven and appears unconcerned with finery and grooming. A personal friend of Luther, Cranach was a witness at his wedding.

Some of the theses were definitions; some posed questions. They conveyed the message that no one, not even the pope, had jurisdiction over purgatory, and therefore sellers of indulgences were deceiving people. Following are ten of the ninety-five theses:

1. *When our Lord and Master Jesus Christ said, "Repent" (Matthew 4:17), he willed the entire life of believers to be one of repentance.*
2. *This word cannot be understood as referring to the sacrament of penance, that is, confession and satisfaction, as administered by the clergy.*
3. *Yet it does not mean solely inner repentance; such inner repentance is worthless unless it produces various outward mortifications of the flesh.*
4. *The penalty of sin remains as long as the hatred of self (that is, true inner repentance), namely till our entrance into the kingdom of heaven.*
5. *The pope neither desires nor is able to remit any penalties except those imposed by his own authority or that of the canons.*
6. *The pope cannot remit any guilt, except by declaring and showing that it has been remitted by God; or, to be sure, by remitting guilt in cases reserved to his judgment. If his right to grant remission in these cases were disregarded, the guilt would certainly remain unforgiven.*
7. *God remits guilt to no one unless at the same time he humbles him in all things and makes him submissive to the vicar, the priest.*
8. *The penitential canons are imposed only on the living, and, according to the canons themselves, nothing should be imposed on the dying.*
9. *Therefore the Holy Spirit through the pope is kind to us insofar as the pope in his decrees always makes exception of the article of death and of necessity.*
10. *Those priests act ignorantly and wickedly who, in the case of the dying, reserve canonical penalties for purgatory.*

In 1520 Luther released three long doctrinal treatises, which were indictments of Church teaching. Shortly afterward, in the Edict of Worms, Luther was condemned as a heretic.

Critical Question Are unintended consequences of an action sometimes more historically significant than intended consequences? What were the unintended consequences of Luther's actions?

HENRY VIII AND CHURCH REFORM

Protestantism was established in England more for the political and personal convenience of the king than as a result of moral conviction. In 1485 the first Tudor king, Henry VII (1457–1509), became king of England. The Tudors dominated Renaissance England and brought new stability to the country.

Henry VIII (1491–1547; figure **15.4**), the son of Henry VII, was originally a devout Catholic. His first wife, the Spanish Catherine of Aragon, produced six children, of whom only one daughter survived. But Henry wanted a male heir and asked the pope to annul his marriage (see Box). The pope refused, as did Holy Roman Emperor Charles V, because Catherine was his aunt and annulling the marriage would make Catherine's daughter illegitimate. Nevertheless, Henry was determined to marry the young English woman Anne Boleyn, who, he hoped, would give him a son.

An enraged Henry VIII broke with the Medici pope Clement VII (the illegitimate grandson of Lorenzo the Magnificent), who excommunicated him. In 1533 Henry was granted a divorce by the English Parliament, which passed the Act of Supremacy the following year. This established the monarch as head of the Church of England. In 1535 Henry

15.4 Hans Holbein the Younger, *Henry VIII*, c. 1540. Oil on panel, 34¾ × 29½ in. (88.3 × 74.9 cm). Galleria Nazionale d'Arte Antica, Rome. Born in Augsburg, in southern Germany, Hans Holbein the Younger (*c.* 1497–1543) traveled to the Swiss city of Basel, where he painted Erasmus's portrait (see figure 15.2). Erasmus recommended him to England, where he was Henry VIII's court painter from 1532. Holbein shows Henry in all his bulk and finery, with rings, a large chain, a hat decorated with pearls and a feather, and an authoritative, regal stance that generously fills the picture.

Society and Culture

The Six Wives of Henry VIII

Henry VIII's six wives are the subject of the popular rhyme:

Divorced, beheaded, died.
Divorced, beheaded, survived.

Catherine of Aragon (1485–1536), the daughter of Ferdinand and Isabella of Spain, became engaged to the eleven-year-old future Henry VIII after the death of her first husband (Henry's elder brother). When Henry was crowned king in 1509 he married Catherine, but she failed to produce a male heir who survived. The marriage was annulled, and the former queen was kept a virtual prisoner for the remainder of her life. Her one surviving daughter, Mary, became famous as the Catholic "Bloody Mary" who had 287 Protestants burned at the stake and inspired hundreds more to flee England.

Henry's second wife, Anne Boleyn (*c.* 1507–1536), was lady-in-waiting to Catherine of Aragon and soon caught Henry's eye. She, too, failed to have a son. Henry accused Anne of adultery and she was beheaded at the age of twenty-nine. Anne Boleyn did bear Henry a daughter, however, who came to rule as the great queen, Elizabeth I.

Jane Seymour (*c.* 1509–1537), Henry's third wife, led a brief, quiet life at court. She had been Anne's lady-in-waiting before marrying the king. She had a son, who became a radical Anglican and later ruled as Edward VI (1537–1553), but she died around the age of twenty-eight from complications of childbirth.

Henry's marriage to Catherine of Aragon had been a political arrangement with Catholic Spain, but after Jane's death he was advised to marry a Protestant. Accordingly, Henry married the German princess Anne of Cleves (1515–1557). He sent Hans Holbein to Germany to paint her portrait and was pleased by the image. Anne arrived in England in 1539 and married the king in 1540, but, Holbein's portrait notwithstanding, Henry found Anne physically unattractive and supposedly never consummated the marriage. She herself was skilled in domestic duties but was uneducated. When Henry asked for an annulment, she readily agreed, and he awarded her a large income and a high status for life.

Henry's lively fifth wife, Catherine Howard (*c.* 1520–1542), was Anne Boleyn's second cousin. More attractive than Anne of Cleves, to whom she was a lady-in-waiting, Catherine came from an impoverished aristocratic family. She was much younger than the obese king and known for her flirtatious character. In 1542, when she was about twenty-one, Catherine was beheaded for adultery.

The following year Henry married Catherine Parr (1512–1548). She was twice widowed and childless, but was devoted to her stepchildren, Edward, Mary, and Elizabeth. When Henry died, Catherine Parr married her first love, Thomas Seymour, the brother of Jane.

ordered the destruction of every monastery and religious image in the country, including the shrine of Thomas à Becket in Canterbury (see Chapter 10). But despite his break with the Catholic Church, Henry did not completely alter the liturgy. He followed Luther in the use of English vernacular, although he retained much of the flavor of Catholic services and traditional church music.

The seriousness of Henry's conflict with the pope can be seen in his treatment of the devoutly Catholic humanist Sir Thomas More (1478–1535). At first More fared well under Henry, serving as a diplomat, becoming Speaker of the House of Commons in 1523, and being appointed Lord Chancellor in 1529. In 1516 he published *Utopia*, a humanist work written in Latin. Its title, which is Greek for "Nowhere," refers to an ideal socialist state—influenced by Plato's *Republic*—located somewhere in the New World. More's criticism of the corruption of English society in *Utopia* was influenced by Erasmus (who had dedicated *The Praise of Folly* to him). When More opposed Henry's marriage to Anne Boleyn and refused to take the Oath of Supremacy to Henry, he was tried and executed in 1535.

RELIGIOUS CONFLICT IN FRANCE

Turmoil between Catholics and Protestants plagued Europe for most of the sixteenth century. In France the majority of Protestants (Huguenots) lived in the south, the home of two leading authors, François Rabelais (*c.* 1494–1553) and Michel Eyquem de Montaigne (1533–1592). Though both men remained Catholic, they were critics of Church corruption. Both were well-educated humanists and sympathetic to contemporary reform movements. Like Luther, they urged the Church to return to what they considered the simple and straightforward message of early Christianity found in the Bible.

FRANÇOIS RABELAIS

François Rabelais became a monk and then decided to study medicine. His classic work, *The Histories of Gargantua and Pantagruel* (1532–1534), is a burlesque epic about a family of friendly giants. In it Rabelais satirizes the Church, the clergy, war, the justice system, and the faculty of theology at the University of Paris. Condemned by the Sorbonne (then a residential college at the university), Rabelais was protected by the influential humanist Cardinal Jean du Bellay and by Queen Marguerite of Navarre, sister of King Francis I. Marguerite herself was a humanist and author of the *Heptameron*, a compilation of seventy stories inspired by Boccaccio's *Decameron* (see Chapter 12). The *Heptameron* reveals the taste of French courts for overt sexuality in literature. A similar taste is evident in Rabelais, whose use of obscenity and profanity (language we now call Rabelaisean), as well as his skepticism, distinguishes him from northern humanists such as Erasmus and Sir Thomas More.

READING SELECTION

Rabelais, *Gargantua and Pantagruel*, a giant's education, PWC3-053

MICHEL EYQUEM DE MONTAIGNE

As a child, Montaigne learned to speak Latin and French. As an adult, he served as a mayor and a judge, but around the age of forty he came into an inheritance and retired to write. First as a Stoic influenced by Seneca (see Chapter 7) and gradually as a skeptic, Montaigne sought the truth about life from his own experience.

Montaigne asks the recurring question *Que sais-je?* ("What do I know?"), which reflects his skepticism. The development of his thought is recorded in his *Essays*, which are the earliest examples of the genre. (The English word "essay" comes from the French verb *essayer*, meaning "to try." An essay is thus an attempt to "try out" or "test" an idea by writing about it.)

Montaigne wrote in a clear, direct style. "The speech that I like," he declared, "is plain and simple, whether it comes from one's mouth or is written on paper." Montaigne remained a Catholic, but he advocated both clerical reform and moral education for all students. He also had strong political views. Drawing on his experience as a magistrate, he repudiated judicial abuse and torture. He deplored the manner in which the Europeans had conquered and colonized the New World, suggesting that Europe had a lot to learn from the cannibals of Brazil.

Montaigne's essay on cannibals, published in 1580 and translated into English in 1603, expresses his aversion to dogmatic thinking, to the belief that Europe's culture was superior to that of the New World, and to the atrocities committed by Catholics against Protestants and by Protestants against Catholics. In his admiration for the natives of Brazil, he observes with bitter irony that their Portuguese conquerors buried them to the waist, shot them full of arrows, and hanged them while they were still alive. Much better, Montaigne wrote, to do what the natives do to their enemies: they kill them first and roast them only after they are dead.

READING SELECTION

Montaigne, *Essays*, on what Brazilian cannibals could teach the French, PWC3-175-B

THE CHALLENGE OF SCIENCE

The pressure for reform in sixteenth-century Europe came from scientific discoveries as well as from humanists, ambitious kings, and disenchanted monks. Traditional Church control of ideas about the nature of the universe and prohibitions against human dissection gradually began to dissolve. In 1543, for example, Andreas Vesalius (1515–1564) published the first anatomical textbook, the *Seven Books on the Structure of the Human Body* (figure **15.5**). A native of Brussels, in modern Belgium, Vesalius studied at the University of Padua, which had been a center of fourteenth-century humanism (see Chapter 12), although even there only animals could be dissected in the great anatomy theater. (Secretly, however, some human bodies were also brought in.) Vesalius introduced scientific biology by basing his conclusions on empirical observation and the dissection of human cadavers. The following is an example of his precise, scientific writing style:

> By professors of dissection the brain is customarily divided into an anterior part, which they call *cerebrum*, and a posterior, the *cerebellum*, the anterior [being divided] into right and left . . .
>
> The cerebellum is a tenth or eleventh part of the cerebrum. Together with the origin of the medulla dorsalis, it occupies that part of the cranial cavity which is bounded in front by the posterior part of those ridges for the organs of hearing which project into the great cavity of the head, and behind by two fossae hollowed into the occipital bone which are bounded by the grooves for the first two sinuses. No part of the cerebellum trespasses beyond this circumscription, which limits it completely.

Among other things, Vesalius disproved the popular belief that women have one more rib than men (a belief based on the biblical story that God used one of Adam's ribs to create Eve). He also contradicted Aristotle by arguing that the mind and the emotions are located in the brain and nervous system rather than in the heart. Vesalius's textbook made future physicians aware of the importance of accurate illustrations and hands-on experience (see Box, p. 404).

Additional challenges to entrenched beliefs came from astronomers. The Polish physician and astronomer Nicolaus Copernicus (1473–1543) published *On the Revolutions of the Heavenly Spheres* (*De revolutionibus orbium coelestium*) in 1543, the same year as Vesalius's treatise. Copernicus replaced the anthropocentric (human-centered) view of the universe with **heliocentrism** (sun-centered view of the universe). He argued that the Earth revolves once around the sun each year, while also rotating on its own axis once each day. Although we now take this for granted, at the time it was a revolutionary idea, shattering the age-old notion that Earth and humanity occupied the center of the universe.

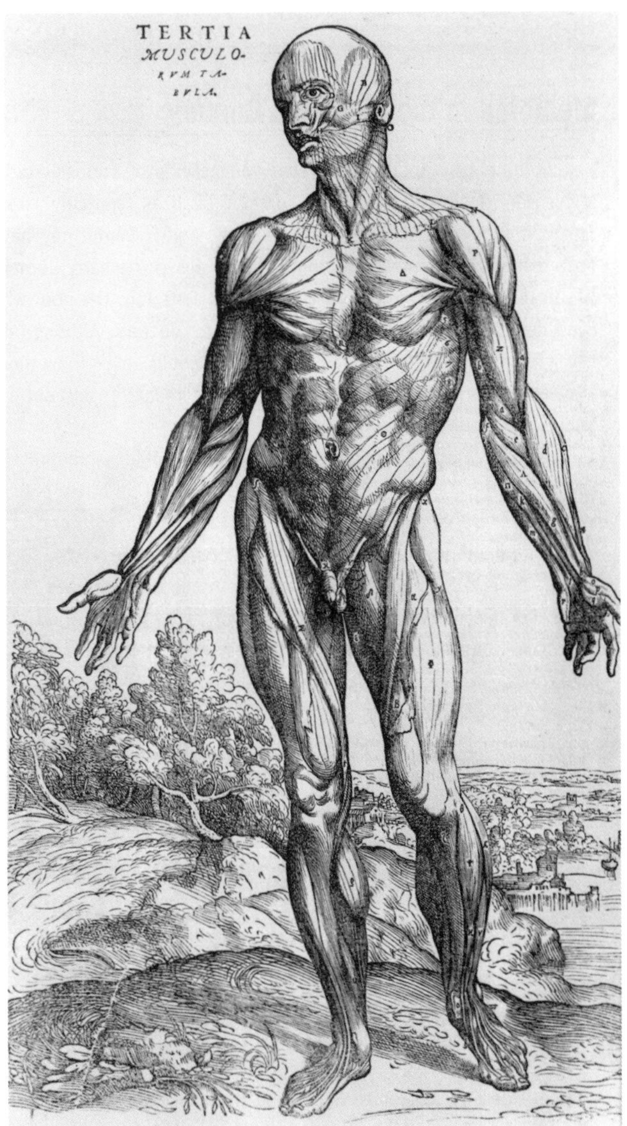

15.5 Andreas Vesalius, "Third Musculature Table" from *De humani corporis fabrica*, Brussels, 1543. National Library of Medicine, Bethesda, Maryland.

The Danish astronomer Tycho Brahe (1546–1601) applied empirical observation to the stars even before the invention of the telescope. In 1572 he reported sighting a supernova (the explosion that occurs when a star dies) and published the first modern catalogue of stars. Five years later he proved that comets orbit among the planets; this was in opposition to Aristotle, who believed that comets originate in the earth's atmosphere. Given an island by the king of Denmark on which to build an observatory, Brahe produced the most accurate descriptions of stars and planets of his time. In 1599 he moved to Prague, in the modern Czech Republic, and was appointed mathematician to the court.

Society and Culture

Medicine in the Sixteenth Century

Sixteenth-century apothecaries sold concoctions of various kinds. Many were devised from foreign sources, such as "mummy" from Egyptian tombs and plants from the New World. Some may have been effective, but most were not, which caused the early humanists to make fun of the medical profession. Petrarch, the poet who lived during the Black Death, had no use for doctors. Although he had a few physician friends, he said that he would never allow them to attend him. He preferred to let nature take its course and entrust himself to God.

Erasmus wrote about the first known syphilis epidemic in Europe. He recommended that the sick be quarantined, like lepers, to protect the public. Holbein's drawing of a syphilitic youth reflects the contemporary interest in the new disease (figure **15.6**). Montaigne, in his autobiographical essays, describes kidney stones, from which he suffered, and his dislike of doctors. He complained that they took financial advantage of the sick, without knowing how to cure them.

Despite such recurring commentaries, ethical doctors did exist in sixteenth-century Europe. The French surgeon Ambroise Paré (1510–1590), for example, was known for his humanitarian approach to medicine. His *Ten Books of Surgery* describes his surgical methods and reveals a personal interest in helping patients who had lost limbs in battle. He devised artificial arms and legs as well as prosthetic noses to replace those lost as a result of mercury treatments for syphilis. In an age before anaesthesia, Paré believed that a good surgeon does not allow a patient's suffering to interfere with his medical judgment.

15.6 Hans Holbein, *Head of a Young Man*, early 16th century. Black and colored chalks, black ink, and yellow and gray wash on cream antique laid paper, 8⅛ × 6 in. (20.6 × 15.2 cm). Fogg Art Museum, Harvard University, Cambridge, Massachusetts.

PAINTING IN THE NORTH

Signs of the Protestant Reformation's impact on art in the North emerged around 1520. A few artists embraced Protestantism, and their imagery reflects Protestant ideas. As in the fifteenth century, northern European artists in the sixteenth century were affected by developments in Italy, but they evolved their own style. Sixteenth-century art in the North is typically linear, which is consistent with the growing popularity of woodcuts and engravings. Although the woodcut technique had been used in China since the fifth century, engraving was first developed in Germany. The two leading artists working in Germany were Albrecht Dürer (1471–1528) and Matthias Grünewald (died 1528).

In the Netherlands artists were influenced by the taste for satire, and to some degree their work was more somber than that of their Italian counterparts. The most important Netherlandish painters were Hieronymus Bosch (*c.* 1450–1516) and his follower, Pieter Bruegel the Elder (1525–1569). They illustrated popular proverbs, types of folly, and depicted the "world upside-down." In addition, Bruegel painted landscapes that reflect human activities, especially the lives of peasants.

As with the revival of artists' biography, culminating in Italy with the writings of Vasari, the North also took an interest in the personal and professional lives of artists. In 1604 the Netherlandish biographer of artists, Karel van Mander (1548–1606), published the first northern compilation of art and artists, *The Painter's Book* (*Het Schilderboeck*). Van Mander discussed artistic principles and promoted the view advocated in Italy that painting should be considered a Liberal Art. Like Vasari, van Mander cited Classical texts, in particular Ovid's *Metamorphoses* (see Chapter 7), as sources of Greek and Roman myth and culture.

ALBRECHT DÜRER

The German artist Albrecht Dürer became a Protestant late in life (figure **15.7**). The son of a prominent goldsmith in Nuremberg, Dürer studied wood engraving and painting and traveled to Italy where he met the leading Renaissance artists of the day. Although influenced by Italian Renaissance style, Dürer retains the linear quality characteristic of German art.

Dürer's imagery in his 1523 woodcut *The Last Supper* (figure **15.8**) presents a reformist approach to Christian

15.7 *right* **Albrecht Dürer, *Self-portrait*, 1500. Oil on panel, 26¼ × 19¼ in. (64 × 48 cm). Alte Pinakothek, Munich.**
This self-portrait is the last of many by the artist. Dürer has depicted himself in a striking frontal pose, reminiscent of icon painting (see Chapter 9). The painting shows the influence of Italian art and suggests the ancient association of artists with divine creators. Note the right hand touching the fur, a reminder that the artist's hand is the instrument of his mind. At the upper left, Dürer's signature monogram—a *D* inside an *A*—is visible.

subject matter. He reinforces Luther's call for a simple, direct relationship between Christians and their God, and his iconography reflects the rejection of the Eucharist as the literal body and blood of Christ in favor of a more general remembrance.

The artist "foregrounds" the issue of the Eucharist—as it was in the forefront of contemporary controversy—by placing a bread basket and wine pitcher at the lower right. A liturgical chalice stands prominently on the table. The charger on the floor traditionally held a dead lamb, alluding to Christ's sacrifice as the Lamb of God, but in Dürer's Protestant version, the charger is empty. This iconography indicates that such allusions more properly exist as a commemoration in the mind of the worshipper.

15.8 Albrecht Dürer, *The Last Supper*, 1523. Woodcut, 8⅜ × 11¹³⁄₁₆ in. (21.3 × 30 cm). British Museum, London.
As in Leonardo's *The Last Supper* (see Chapter 14), Dürer's apostles react to Christ's words with animated gestures that contrast with the inner calm of Christ himself. Above, the bright light of the round window refers to Christ as the sun, while his halo is an illuminated cross. Dürer's monogram and the date, 1523, are inscribed in the square plaque on the floor. The development of printing made such images available to a wide audience and assisted in the dissemination of Luther's ideas.

MATTHIAS GRÜNEWALD

Little is known about the life of Matthias Grünewald, the other major German artist of the period. He may have been born in Würzburg, but this is not certain. In his approach to Christian themes Grünewald appears to have been less influenced by the Reformation than Dürer was, and there is no evidence that he was conversant with the Classical revival. He is best known for his impressive and original evocations of Christ's suffering and for the dark mood of his paintings.

Grünewald's best-known work is the Isenheim Altarpiece (figure **15.9**), painted for the chapel of St. Anthony's hospital in Isenheim. Patients prayed in front of the altarpiece for miraculous cures from skin diseases, which was the specialty of the hospital. Particularly painful was ergotism, known as St. Anthony's Fire, caused by a poisonous fungus in grains that resulted in lameness and necrosis of the hands and feet.

Grünewald alludes to ergotism in the gangrenous discoloration of Christ's body and the distortion of his extremities. The bowed Cross and Christ's taut musculature emphasize the weight of his body and the force of gravity. The blood dripping from his wounds is echoed by the reds in the draperies. The letters above the Cross, *INRI*, stand for "Jesus of Nazareth, King of the Jews." Kneeling in prayer is Mary Magdalene, her long hair a sign of penitence. To Christ's left, John the Baptist holds a text and speaks the words written in red against the black sky: "He must increase and I must decrease." The sacrificial lamb at the feet of John the Baptist stands for Christ (compare van Eyck's *Altarpiece*, figure 13.34), while the water behind him refers to the rite of baptism.

HIERONYMUS BOSCH

Hieronymus Bosch is the most enigmatic of the northern painters: the details of his life are as elusive as his iconography. His masterpiece is the large triptych known as *The Garden of Earthly Delights* (figure **15.10**). The imagery in this work derives from multiple sources, including the Bible, popular proverbs, traditional folklore, and unknown sources of the artist's imagination. The painting has also been interpreted as alluding to alchemy, the process by which people tried to make gold from base metal. This is suggested by the globular forms that are reminiscent of the alchemist's retort. The eggs might refer to the alchemical egg, which alchemists believed could return them to the origins of mankind, and to the Garden of Eden in its primal state before the Fall.

In the left panel God presents the newly created Eve to Adam in a fanciful landscape. The center panel seems to represent an orgy of pleasure, including elaborate towers by a pool of water, enlarged succulent berries, and erotic, cavorting nudes. The right panel is a dark, fiery vision of hell. Musical instruments, traditional symbols of lust because of their association with song and romance, have become machines of torture. Toward the lower right Satan swallows and expels souls into a dark hole. At the center of hell a curious "egg man," sometimes identified as Bosch himself, has tree-trunk legs and balances a bagpipe on his head.

15.9 Matthias Grünewald, Isenheim Altarpiece: *Crucifixion with St. Sebastian, St. Anthony, and a Lamentation*, 1515. Oil on panel, center panel of the Isenheim Altarpiece 9 ft. 9½ in. × 10 ft 9 in. (2.98 × 3.28 m). Musée d'Unterlinden, Colmar, France.
Of the nine panels that make up the altarpiece, those illustrated here show the altarpiece closed. The wings depict St. Anthony at the right and St. Sebastian at the left. Because he was shot through with arrows, Sebastian was a plague saint, reflecting the fact that symptoms of plague include severe skin sores. Represented on the base is the Lamentation over Christ's body. The distant winter landscape, like the black sky in the main panel, symbolizes the death of Christ. When opened, on Sundays and feast days, the panels show Christ resurrected in a blaze of light.

15.10 *above* **Hieronymus Bosch, *The Garden of Earthly Delights*, *c.* 1510–1515. Oil on panel, center panel 7 ft. 2 in. × 6 ft. 4 in (2.18 × 1.93 m); side panels 7 ft. 2 in. × 3 ft. (2.18 × 0.91 m). Prado, Madrid.**

15.11 Attributed to Hieronymus Bosch, *The Cure of Folly*, *c.* 1490. Oil on panel, $18\frac{3}{4} \times 13\frac{1}{4}$ in. (48.1 × 35 cm). Prado, Madrid.

The Cure of Folly (figure **15.11**), which is usually attributed to Bosch, satirizes human folly. A bogus surgeon removes folly (madness) in the form of a small flower from a patient. The surgeon cuts into the patient's forehead, and folly flies out; the "folly" here, Bosch seems to be saying, is that a mental condition is treated as if it were a physical one. Observing the operation are a priest and a melancholic woman with a book on her head, symbolizing false knowledge. The church in the background and the vast landscape probably refer to the clergy and the world, both of whose folly is enacted in the foreground.

Pieter Bruegel the Elder

Pieter Bruegel the Elder worked in the port of Antwerp (now in Belgium). As the financial hub of Europe, Antwerp was also an artistic center where prints and paintings were in great demand. Little is known of Bruegel's life, but the moral tone of his iconography and his depiction of proverbs reflect humanist sympathies (figure **15.12**). His imagery suggests an awareness of authors such as Petrarch, who praised nature, and Erasmus, who used a similar satirical style. Inspired by a trip through Italy in 1552, Bruegel painted a number of scenes in which landscape predominates. *Hunters in the Snow* (figure **15.13**), which comes from his series of paintings depicting the months of the year, is a recollection of the alpine landscapes he saw in Italy. It also exemplifies his interest in peasants and their lives of hard work. Hunters in the foreground return home

15.12 Pieter Bruegel the Elder, *The Big Fish Eating the Little Fish*, 1556. Drawing, 8½ × 12 in. (21.6 × 30.5 cm). Albertina, Vienna.
Like many of Bruegel's drawings, this was made for a series of prints. It depicts in allegorical form the proverb of the title. A big fish on dry land is cut open by a man with a large knife. Tumbling out of the big fish are smaller fish, which, in turn, have swallowed even smaller fish. Echoing the curved back of the big fish is the foreground boat occupied by fishermen. One cuts open his catch to reveal another small fish as the others gesture toward the big fish. The scene emphasizes the message of the proverb: men are like fish; their greed drives them to devour lesser men who stand in the way of their ambition. At the upper right, the fish with human legs and a smaller fish in his mouth confirms the metaphor.

15.13 Pieter Bruegel the Elder, *Hunters in the Snow*, 1565. Oil on wood, approx. 3 ft. 10 in. × 5 ft. 4 in. (1.17 × 1.63 cm). Kunsthistorisches Museum, Vienna.

with their dogs and prey. On the distant frozen pond, ice-skating villagers enjoy a respite from their daily routines. At the far left a group of figures stokes a fire, the only suggestion of heat in the picture. Bruegel minimizes color just as the sunless sky drains the colors of nature.

THE COUNTER-REFORMATION: CATHOLIC REFORM

Confronted by the challenge of the Reformation, the Catholic Church launched an internal program of reform. Although strongest in Italy and Spain, the Catholic reaction affected all of Europe. The Church attempted to root out corruption among the clergy and to reassert its authority in matters of doctrine, science, literature, and the arts. To this end, Pope Paul III (papacy 1534–1549) convened the Council of Trent, which met three times between 1545 and 1563 at Trento in northern Italy.

THE COUNCIL OF TRENT: 1545–1563

In its meetings the Council of Trent reaffirmed the power and authority of the Catholic Church. It advocated a better-educated clergy, vows of chastity, and new religious communities. In contrast to Protestant iconoclasm, relics were to be venerated, and vernacular translations of the Bible were condemned. In direct opposition to Martin Luther, the Council included the Septuagint as part of the Bible. The Seven Sacraments were retained, and the doctrine that salvation could be achieved by faith and good works was reaffirmed.

One outcome of the Council was the *Index of Forbidden Books*, published in 1557 to stem the swelling tide of progressive ideas. The first version of the *Index* banned the writings of Luther, Calvin, and Copernicus. It remained in effect, adding new authors, until 1966.

MONASTIC REFORM

An important aspect of the Counter-Reformation was the institution of new religious Orders. The Society of Jesus (the Jesuits), founded by the Spanish nobleman Ignatius Loyola (*c.* 1493–1556) and approved by Paul III in 1540, had an enormous impact on Church reform. Loyola began his career as a soldier, but he was crippled by a leg wound and started reading the Bible and lives of the saints. When he recovered, he changed his life. He lived as a beggar, devoting himself to prayer and mortification of the flesh (self-inflicted physical suffering).

Determined to counteract the inroads made by Martin Luther and the Protestant Reformation, Loyola ran the Society of Jesus with military discipline, becoming the proverbial Christian Soldier. To educate his followers in meditation, he wrote *Spiritual Exercises*, a treatise on rules for contemplating sin and suffering designed to control the emotions and conquer the fear of death:

> Listen to the monotonous sound of the clock which measures your last hours, and says at each movement, Behold yourself a second nearer to the tribunal of God; the sound of your painful labored breathing, and that terrible rattle, the forerunner of death.

At first dedicated to educational reform and aiding the poor, the Jesuits became a powerful missionary force and combated Protestantism.

With the work of Francis Xavier (1506–1552), one of the original Jesuits and a personal friend of Ignatius Loyola, Jesuit missionaries traveled to the East Indies, Japan, Ceylon (now Sri Lanka), and China. Both Xavier and Loyola were canonized in 1622.

The Ursuline Order (the Company of Saint Ursula) was named for a legendary figure associated with the medieval city of Cologne, in Germany, who, together with 11,000 virgins, was said to have been martyred by the Huns. The Ursuline Order was founded in 1535 in Brescia, Italy, by Angela Merici (*c.* 1474–1540), later St. Angela. As a lay person associated with the Franciscan Order, Angela tended the sick, and in the 1520s she made a pilgrimage to Palestine, where she became temporarily blind. Inspired by visionary experiences, she founded a new Order, which was approved by Pope Paul III in 1544. Originally a community of lay women sworn to chastity and devoted to Christian education, the Ursulines were forced in the seventeenth century to take vows, live in convents, and submit to male authority.

Two particularly zealous mystics who contributed to monastic reform were St. Teresa of Avila (1515–1582) and St. John of the Cross (1542–1591). They founded the Discalced (barefoot) Carmelite Order, whose members wore either sandals or, in some cases, no shoes at all. This practice, which originated with the Eastern Orders, was introduced to the West by St. Francis and followed by the most orthodox Western Orders. The Discalced Carmelites came into conflict with the Calced Carmelites, who did wear shoes.

St. John wrote extensively about his mystical way of life and composed spiritual poetry. He describes the soul's detachment from the senses and its union with the divine through suffering. St. Teresa wrote *The Way of Perfection*, an autobiography, and several shorter books to instruct her nuns. Her works are detailed accounts of the relationship between ecstatic and meditative experiences.

READING SELECTION

St. Teresa, *The Life of St. Teresa of Avila*, on spiritual ecstasies, PWC3-050

THE INQUISITION

The Council of Trent also increased the power of the Inquisition (see Chapter 11), which was mainly concerned with heretics and apostates. In addition, witch-hunts reached their peak from around 1570 to 1680 in western Europe and resulted in the torture and execution of thousands of people. Recent scholarship indicates that some 35,000 "witches" were killed, of whom 29,000 were women. Four out of five of this number were killed in what roughly corresponds to modern Germany. The Inquisitors referred to *The Witches' Hammer* (*Malleus Maleficarum*), which had been published in 1498 by two Dominicans, James Sprenger and Heinrich Kramer. This book was a detailed account of witches, their appearance, behavior, alleged Satanic rites, and associates (called "familiars"). Included were instructions on how to torture witches in order to extract confessions:

> The method of beginning an examination by torture is as follows: First, the jailers prepare the implements of torture, then they strip the prisoner . . . lest some means of witchcraft may have been sewed into the clothing—such as often taught by the devil, they prepare from the bodies of unbaptized infants . . . if he will not confess, [the] attendants make the prisoner fast to the strappado* or some other instrument of torture . . .
>
> The judge shall see to it . . . that [in between episodes of torture] guards are constantly with the prisoner, so that she may not be left alone; because she will be visited by the devil and tempted into suicide.

*An instrument in which the wrists are strapped to a rope. The prisoner is yanked suddenly upward and then dropped to just above the floor.

Figure **15.14** illustrates the prevailing view of the witches' Sabbath which, like the coat of arms in figure 15.1, was a projection of the popular fear of women.

15.14 Hans Baldung Grien, *Witches' Sabbath*, 1510. Chiaroscuro woodcut with orange tone block, $14^7/_8 \times 10^1/_4$ in. (37.9 × 26 cm). British Museum, London. Hans Baldung Grien (*c.* 1485–1545) was a prominent German printer. This woodcut shows a coven of frenzied hags conducting a Witches' Sabbath. One rides backwards on a flying goat, signifying perverse sex with the devil. The night-time setting suggests forbidden activities and alludes to ominous "familiars," such as black cats. The central woman, with sagging breasts, raises a communion plate containing a lizard—an image of the religious perversion attributed to witches.

CONTINUING CONFLICT

Throughout the sixteenth century Catholics and Protestants vied for the minds, hearts, and souls of the population. Each tradition wished to affirm its own doctrines and to expand its influence in Europe and the New World. By the seventeenth century it was clear that much of northern Europe would become Protestant, while the south, especially Spain and Italy, but also France, the area that would become Belgium, and parts of Germany and Ireland, would remain Catholic.

In France on August 24, 1572, thousands of Protestants were murdered in what is called the St. Bartholomew's Day Massacre. Although there are no surviving documents of the event, it is known that an assassination attempt against a Protestant noble, possibly at the behest of a member of the Catholic nobility or even the royal family, led to rumors that sparked mob violence. Over three thousand people were killed in Paris in a single night. The event was celebrated in Spain and in Italy. Efforts at reconciliation did not emerge until the Protestant Henry of Navarre became the king of France, as Henry IV, in 1594. Five years into his rule, in the face of persisting opposition, Henry famously declared *Paris vaut bien une messe* ("Paris is well worth a Mass"). He converted to Catholicism and issued the Edict of Nantes, which granted tolerance to Protestants and freedom of worship throughout France.

Philip II of Spain (ruled 1556–1598) inherited the crown from his father, Charles V. He married the Catholic Tudor queen of England, Mary I ("Bloody Mary"), daughter of Henry VIII and Catherine of Aragon, but the brevity of her rule (1553–1558) cut short his ambition to annex England to Spain. Enriched by New World plunder, Spain annexed Portugal and took control of the Netherlands. But the Netherlands formed an alliance with the new English queen, the Protestant Elizabeth I (ruled 1558–1603), daughter of Henry VIII and Anne Boleyn. With the help of thousands of English reinforcements, the Netherlands resisted the Spanish invasion and by 1609 was independent.

In 1588, partly motivated by rivalry for territory in the Americas, Spain sent an Armada of 130 ships to invade England. Setting out from Lisbon (in modern Portugal), the fearsome Armada reached the English Channel, but the Spanish ships were decisively outmaneuvered by the smaller, lighter, and faster ships of the English navy under the command of Sir Francis Drake (*c.* 1540–1596) and were blown off course by adverse winds. The defeat left the English navy a dominant force in Europe and reduced the power of Spain.

THE IMPACT OF CATHOLIC REFORM ON THE ARTS

In 1563 a meeting of the Council of Trent took steps to reverse secular trends and restore spirituality in the arts. They forbade the use in church of "those musics where something lascivious and impure mixes with the organ or the singing." The Council banned church music based on secular tunes, especially bawdy songs, and required that the words be easily comprehensible, rather than obscured by elaborate polyphonic music. The use of instruments in church music, other than the organ, was not permitted. Architecture had to be conducive to worship, and sacred paintings and sculptures had to observe certain proprieties. The main purpose of imagery was to inspire viewers to identify with the suffering of saints and martyrs. Even when the life of a saint or martyr had involved sinful actions—for example, Mary Magdalene—the character had to be depicted as holy and pure and without erotic allusions. In addition, artists were required to illustrate Christian miracles rather than pagan myths and appeal to the emotions rather than the intellect. These rules were rigorously enforced by the Inquisition, especially in Italy and Spain.

The first Counter-Reformation pope, Paul IV (papacy 1555–1559), objected to Michelangelo's *Last Judgment* (see figure 14.18) in the Sistine Chapel. The pope wanted the entire painting removed on the grounds that it did not conform to the rules of the Council of Trent. Eventually, the painting was allowed to remain, but draperies were painted over the nude figures. These draperies were not removed until the chapel was restored in the 1990s.

Counter-Reformation painting is notable for its mystical emphasis on the spiritual qualities of divine light. Subject matter dealt with miracles and the suffering of saints and martyrs.

PAOLO VERONESE

In 1573 Paolo Caliari, better known as Paolo Veronese (1528–1588), the great Venetian painter of the late sixteenth century, ran afoul of the Inquisition when he unveiled his huge *Last Supper* (figure **15.15**). The Inquisitors brought Veronese to trial, alleging that his painting was heretical. The painter's accusers objected to the presence of Germans on the grounds that Germany was riddled with Lutheran heresy. They pointed to the dwarfs, buffoons, and the man with the nosebleed as unsuitable guests at "the Lord's" last meal. The inclusion of St. Peter was required by the biblical narrative, but the Inquisitors were offended that he was shown picking his teeth.

15.15 Paolo Veronese (Paolo Caliari), *The Last Supper* (renamed *The Feast in the House of Levi*), 1573. Oil on canvas, 18 ft. 3 in. × 42 ft. (5.56 × 12.8 m). Gallerie dell' Accademia, Venice.
Born in Verona, Veronese moved to Venice where he had a successful career. This picture shows his taste for illusionistic architectural settings and rich material textures. The stairways lead to a balcony with a triple arched wall alluding to the triumph of Christ. The use of the Corinthian Order and the Winged Victories in the spandrels of the arches reflect Veronese's use of Classical motifs. The setting is Venice, which is visible in the background.

Veronese argued that in the Bible the Last Supper takes place in a rich man's house, where servants and visitors are to be expected. He also admitted that he had used artistic license in certain details. The Inquisitors were unconvinced and ordered the artist to alter the picture in accord with the Council of Trent or face the consequences. Not wishing to repaint his picture, Veronese satisfied his accusers by changing its title to *The Feast in the House of Levi.*

TINTORETTO

The Italian painter who most embodied Counter-Reformation ideals in Italy was Jacopo Robusti, known as Tintoretto (1518–1594). He worked in Venice, where he succeeded Titian as the republic's official painter. Tintoretto's *Last Supper* (figure **15.16**) takes place in a darkened room, which is illuminated not by the natural outdoor light of Veronese's picture but by a mystical, miraculous light. Instead of being symmetrically organized, with a table parallel to the picture plane and orthogonals leading to a vanishing point, like Leonardo's *Last Supper* (see thumbnail), Tintoretto's version thrusts the table back into space on a sharply receding diagonal. The gestures and poses of the apostles, their heads framed in rings of diaphanous yellow light, are intended to evoke our identification with their impassioned responses to Christ's statement that one of his apostles will betray him. The servants at the right add to the agitation of the scene by the Mannerist exaggeration of their poses. Hovering over the entire scene are disembodied, ethereal angels outlined in light rather than shown in Renaissance chiaroscuro.

Leonardo da Vinci, *Last Supper* see figure 13.31

GIACOMO DA VIGNOLA

The church of Il Gesù designed by Giacomo da Vignola (1507–1573) (figures **15.17** and **15.18**) conforms to the architectural requirements of the Council of Trent. Commissioned to be the new Mother Church of the Jesuit Order in Rome, Il Gesù uses the longitudinal Latin cross plan of the Early Christian basilica, which had been prevalent in the Middle Ages. Vignola's plan rejects the symmetrical, centralized designs preferred by Renaissance humanists (see thumbnail and Chapter 13).

By focusing on the eastern apse, rather than on a central space, the interior of Il Gesù draws the attention of the

15.16 Jacopo Tintoretto (Jacopo Robusti), *The Last Supper*, 1590s. Oil on canvas, 12 ft. × 18 ft. 8 in. (3.66 × 5.69 m). Choir, San Giorgio Maggiore, Venice.

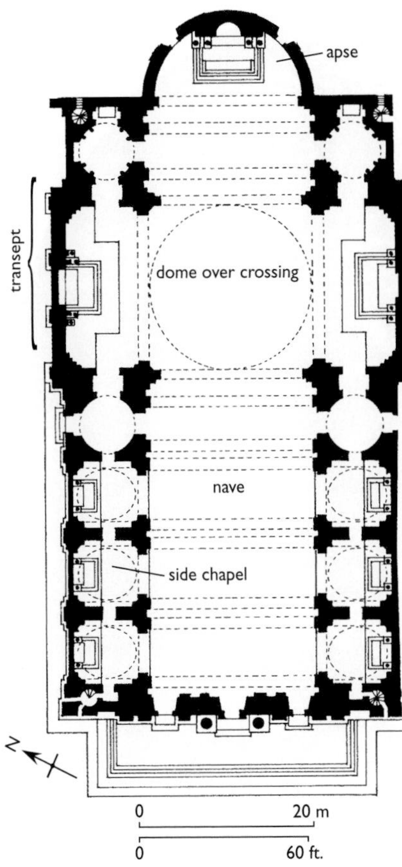

15.17 Giacomo da Vignola, plan of Il Gesù, Rome, *c.* 1565–1584.

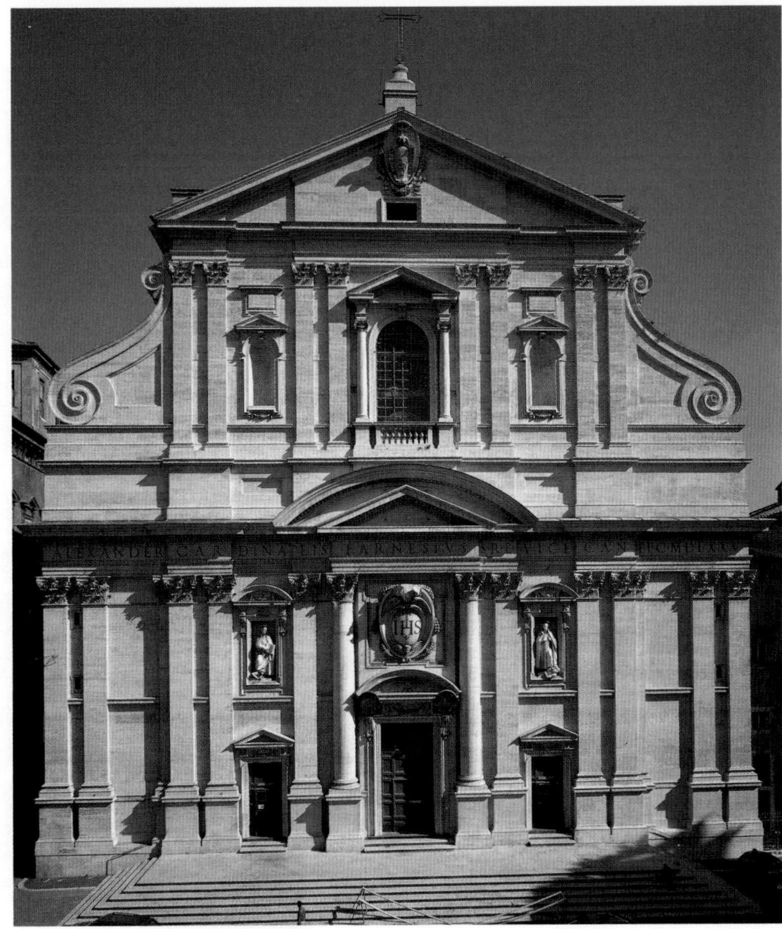

15.18 Façade of Il Gesù, Rome, *c.* 1565–1584, completed by Giacomo della Porta.

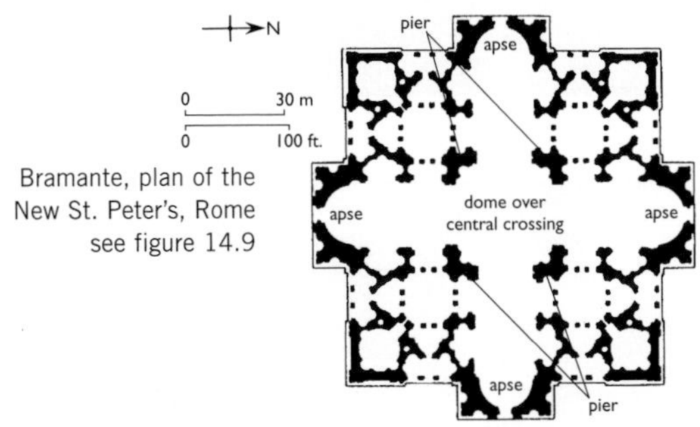

Bramante, plan of the New St. Peter's, Rome see figure 14.9

congregation toward the altar. Like an audience watching a play, worshippers focus on the movements of the priest and the drama of the Mass. In accord with the decrees of the Council, Vignola's architectural divisions correspond to the notion of hierarchy: lay people occupy the nave; clergy the choir; and the priest presides over the Eucharist in the apse.

The façade uses Classical features: engaged Corinthian columns flank the central door and second-story window, and pilasters support entablatures. But the surface is flattened, and this, with the crowning pediment, creates an impression of imposing height, which dominates the open square before it. Il Gesù became a model for Counter-Reformation churches in the next century and influenced church designs carried around the globe by Jesuit missionaries.

El Greco

The leading Counter-Reformation painter in Spain, Domenikos Theotokopoulos (1541–1614), was born on Crete—hence his Spanish nickname, El Greco ("The Greek"). He went to Venice, where he was influenced by the reds of Titian and the mystical light of Tintoretto. From Venice he traveled to Toledo, in Spain, and worked mainly for the Church. His most famous painting, *The Burial of Count Orgaz* (figure **15.19**), is in the burial chapel of Ruiz González, Count of Orgaz, in Toledo's church of Santo Tomé. The scene celebrates a miracle reported to have occurred in 1323: when the count died, he was placed in his tomb by Sts. Stephen and Augustine.

The burial, in the center foreground, is highlighted by the gold brocade cloaks of the saints lowering the count's lifeless, pallid body. St. Stephen, the first Christian martyr, has the scene of his martyrdom by stoning sewn into his cloak, whereas St. Augustine's cloak is bordered with images of individual saints. His mitre identifies him as a bishop.

Surrounding the burial are portraits of El Greco's contemporaries. The count's small, disembodied soul is received by an angel above the row of portraits. Mary (in blue and red), John the Baptist (wearing only a loin cloth), and St. Peter (holding a set of keys) lead the viewer's gaze toward Christ. His white robe and illumination show him as the radiant "Light of the

World." The heavens are filled with figures enveloped in ethereal clouds filtering the flickering light characteristic of El Greco's style. The excitement generated by the count's miraculous burial is shared by the living figures as well as by the host of heaven.

El Greco's *Laocoön* (figure **15.20**), his only mythological picture, dates to the last year of his life. Bearing in mind the Council of Trent's prohibition against pagan subject matter, El Greco transformed the mythological event into one that evokes Christian martyrdom. That is, rather than struggling against the serpents as in the Greek Hellenistic statue (see thumbnail), El Greco's Laocoön lies on his back and merges suffering with mystical ecstasy. Laocoön is not the forceful figure seen in the ancient statue but has the quality of a Christian martyr, passively accepting his fate. Nevertheless, the *Laocoön* indicates El Greco's awareness of humanist themes

15.19 *right* **El Greco (Domenikos Theotokopoulos),** ***The Burial of Count Orgaz*****, 1586–1588. Oil on canvas, 15 ft. 9 in. × 11 ft. 10 in. (4.8 × 3.6 m). Church of Santo Tomé, Toledo, Spain.**
Note the portrait at the lower left of El Greco's son, who directs the viewer to the miracle. His handkerchief bears the artist's signature, the inscription "Domenikos Theotokopoulos made me," and the date of his son's birth.

Agesander, Athenodorus, and Polydorus of Rhodes, *Laocoön Group*
see figure 6.36

15.20 *right* **El Greco (Domenikos Theotokopoulos),** ***Laocoön*****,** ***c.*** **1610/1614. Oil on canvas, 4 ft. $6^1/_8$ × 5 ft. $7^7/_8$ in. (1.38 × 1.73 m). National Gallery of Art, Washington, D.C.**
The ancient city of Troy, where Laocoön was Apollo's priest, and Rome, where the Laocoön sculpture had been excavated in the sixteenth century, are here merged with El Greco's adoptive Toledo. The artist thus continues the Classical tradition while showing that it has been subsumed by Christianity.

MUSIC

By the sixteenth century, patronage had become increasingly international, enabling musicians to travel and work in different cities and countries. Most composers wrote secular as well as religious works, but in Catholic countries religious music predominated, and Rome was the center of Church patronage.

Orlando di Lasso (1532–1594), a Franco-Flemish composer, worked in Mantua, Florence, and Naples before arriving in Rome in 1553, where he was appointed choirmaster of the large basilica church of St. John Lateran. In 1556 he was invited to sing at the court of Bavaria in Munich, later becoming choirmaster there. Lasso was a prolific composer of religious and secular works, including German *lieder* (songs), French *chansons* (songs), and Italian madrigals, as well as Latin Masses and motets (see Chapter 13). His cosmopolitan experience enabled him to draw on a wide variety of styles, from the lighthearted *chanson* or madrigal in French or Italian style for his secular music to the sumptuous and expressive polyphony of his church music. This reflected the polyphonic techniques that had been developed in northern Europe by composers such as Josquin and Willaert (see Chapters 13 and 14).

Wealthy private individuals and clergy were patrons of Luca Marenzio (*c.* 1553–1599), from Brescia, in northern Italy. He traveled to Poland and visited a number of Italian cities before finally settling in Rome. Marenzio is best known for his madrigals, in which he showed particular mastery of word painting, influencing late-sixteenth-century English composers such as Thomas Weelkes (see p. 417).

The most important composer of church music in late sixteenth-century Rome was Giovanni Pierluigi da Palestrina (1524–1594). Apart from a period as cathedral organist in his native town of Palestrina, his career was spent entirely in Rome. He sang in the choir of Santa Maria Maggiore, later becoming director of the Cappella Giulia—a musical establishment at St. Peter's—and a member of the Sistine Chapel. This was followed by a brief period as choirmaster at St. John Lateran (the post held two years earlier by Lasso).

Palestrina's church music embodies the Catholic spirit of reform. The words of his religious choral music are set to the music in a way that makes them as intelligible as possible. Each successive element of the melody normally contains a complete phrase of the text. Syllables stressed according to their meaning may be set at a higher pitch than those around them or at a strong point in the rhythm. Musical **cadences** (the close of musical phrases) match the punctuation of the text. Phrases are carefully shaped and well balanced—a melodic leap in one direction is usually followed by stepwise, flowing notes in the other direction. Palestrina avoided **chromatic** harmony (harmony containing notes that do not belong to the key in which the music is written) in his composition and his use of **dissonance** (clashing sounds) for expressive purposes is limited and carefully resolved. The overall effect is pure, serene, and devotional, with melodies often based on plainsong and never on secular tunes. Of over a hundred settings of the Mass that Palestrina composed, the Pope Marcellus Mass is one of the best-known examples of his mature style. The Music Listening Selection is of the words "Kyrie eleison" ("Lord, have mercy") at the beginning of the Mass.

MUSIC LISTENING SELECTION

Palestrina, Pope Marcellus Mass, "Kyrie." Oxford Camerata, conductor Jeremy Summerly, CD track 7

Catholic reformist ideas were also reflected in the music of the Spanish composer Tomás Luis de Victoria (1548–1611). Victoria wrote only religious music, including some fifty motets, more than twenty Masses, and music for Holy Week comprising two Passions, nine Lamentations, and various other pieces. His style resembles that of Palestrina but is distinguished from it by a fervent, emotional intensity not present in Palestrina's restrained and controlled music. Victoria infuses his music with a mystical quality that corresponds to the sense of drama evident in the church design of Vignola or the religious passion in the art of El Greco.

ELIZABETHAN ENGLAND

Despite political and religious entanglements with continental Europe, international dynastic marriages, and cultural exchange, England's status as an island kept it apart from other European countries. During the reign of Elizabeth I (1558–1603) (figure **15.21**) the English court was a lively humanist center, more innovative in music, literature, and drama than in the visual arts.

ELIZABETH I

Elizabeth survived the beheading of her mother, Anne Boleyn, and became queen of England in 1558 on the death of her Catholic half-sister, Mary Tudor. As a child, Elizabeth was well treated by Henry's last wife, Catherine Parr, and was tutored for two years by the Reformation scholar Roger Ascham in the manner he recommended for gentlemen in his book *The Scholemaster*. Ascham described the adolescent Elizabeth as gentle and dignified, and endowed with the intelligence of a man. She learned to read and speak French, Latin, and Italian and could read Greek. In addition to studying Classical philosophy, history, and the Bible, Elizabeth translated several works into English.

In 1559 Elizabeth presided over Parliament's passage of the Act of Uniformity, which eliminated the Catholic Mass and established the Anglican Church once and for all. For some three hundred years afterwards, Catholics were excluded from holding public office in England. Although Anglicans did not recognize the pope, they nevertheless retained a good amount of Catholic ritual in their services.

Elizabeth was a highly skilled ruler who surrounded herself with shrewd advisers (see Box). Among them was her discerning secretary, Sir Francis Walsingham (1530–1590), who uncovered plots against her life and thus preserved the crown. Sir William Cecil (1520–1598) helped her to maintain religious stability, avoiding the extreme conflict between Catholics and Protestants that plagued the rest of Europe. Sir Francis Drake, who circumnavigated the globe from 1577 to 1580, helped establish England's naval supremacy against Spain.

15.21 Attributed to Nicholas Hilliard, *Ermine Portrait of Queen Elizabeth I*, 1585. Oil on canvas, 41¾ × 35 in. (106 × 89 cm). Hatfield House, England. Nicholas Hilliard, best known for his miniature portraits, was the leading painter in Elizabethan England. In this regal image, the artist shows the queen tightly restrained by a large lace collar, elaborate wig, and weighty velvet dress. The confined atmosphere highlights Elizabeth's intelligent face and her hands. Perched on her left arm, an ermine symbolizes virginity, which was an important part of the queen's political image. Elizabeth never risked her position by marrying, although she was rumored to have been romantically involved with several of her courtiers, including Sir Francis Drake.

Society and Culture

John Knox on Female Rulers

Sixteenth-century philosophers considered female rulers unsuitable. In 1558, the year of Elizabeth's accession to the English throne, the Scottish Puritan John Knox (*c.* 1514–1572), who had met John Calvin in Geneva, published the *First Blast of the Trumpet against the Monstrous Regiment of Women.* This was directed mainly at the Catholic regent of Scotland, Mary of Guise, ruling for her daughter, Mary, Queen of Scots (1542–1587), who later became the mother of the future James VI (also James I of England). Knox objected to Mary of Guise's Catholic views. He generalized from her case to argue that women are naturally defective and incompetent and that rule by a woman is contrary to God and nature:

> *The empire of a Woman is a thing repugnant to Nature . . . For their sight in civil regiment is but blindness; their strength, weakness; their counsel, foolishness; and judgment, frenzy.*

Like the female pharaohs of ancient Egypt (see Chapter 3), Elizabeth I assumed a male persona and often referred to herself as a king or a prince. Offended by Knox, she refused him the right to travel on English soil.

In France, a woman could rule only as regent for a son who was heir to the throne; otherwise female rulers were forbidden under French law. These misogynist attitudes persisted and became more intense in the next century.

MUSIC AT THE ELIZABETHAN COURT

Less insular than English painting, Elizabethan music was influenced by composers from the Netherlands, Germany, France, and Italy. Church music was simplified in accordance with Protestant ideas and Gregorian chant was reduced to one note per syllable of text to make it more intelligible. The madrigal became popular in England in the sixteenth century. Italian madrigals were translated into English, inspiring English composers to write madrigal settings of English poetry. These ranged from lighthearted and rapidly paced to serious and melancholic. They were performed either by unaccompanied voices or with accompaniment by an instrumental consort. Composers of English madrigals, like their Italian counterparts, attached great importance to the pictorial and expressive setting of the texts to music.

WILLIAM BYRD Byrd (1543–1623) was the greatest English composer of the Elizabethan period. He was raised during the reign of the devout Mary Tudor, but his career flourished under the more worldly Elizabeth. Reflecting his own times,

Byrd composed church music for both Catholics and Protestants, and for Latin as well as for English texts. He also aroused increased interest in secular music toward the end of Elizabeth's reign. A singer and organist in the Chapel Royal, Byrd was perhaps the most distinguished of the English composers writing for keyboard instruments, including the organ, but especially harpsichord-type instruments such as the virginal and spinet. He also wrote instrumental music and secular music for voices, but his Latin Masses and motets are considered his best vocal compositions.

Among Byrd's secular compositions is "This sweet and merry month of May," a lighthearted madrigal demonstrating his inventive use of word painting and counterpoint. The phrase "and birds do sing" imitates the sound of chirping birds; rapid dipping and rising notes suggest flight. In contrast, "and beasts do play" is set to a jumpy, dotted rhythm, and the text addressing the queen conveys respect with its rich chordal style before the madrigal draws to a playful close.

THOMAS MORLEY Composer and publisher Thomas Morley (1557–1602) was important in popularizing the madrigal. He published several collections of madrigals by a range of English composers, the best-known being *The Triumphes of Oriana.* All twenty-five pieces praise Elizabeth and end with the words "Long live fair Oriana"—a name from pastoral poetry that was often applied to the queen. Morley's own madrigals were in lighter vein, typified by the dance-like, lilting Italian **ballett** (balletto) form. Livelier than the madrigal, the ballett is made up of verses ending in a "fa-la" refrain:

> Now is the month of maying,
> When merry lads are playing, fa la,
> Each with his bonny lass
> Upon the greeny grass. Fa la.

Morley's "Now is the month of maying," quoted here, deals with the same theme as Byrd's "This sweet and merry month of May." Both are sprightly and have great popular appeal.

THOMAS WEELKES The madrigals of Thomas Weelkes (*c.* 1575–1623), organist at Winchester College and Chichester Cathedral, were particularly influenced by Italian word painting. His own contribution to *The Triumphes of Oriana*, the madrigal "As Vesta was from Latmos hill descending," is a good example:

> As Vesta was from Latmos hill descending,
> She spied a maiden Queen the same ascending,
> Attended on by all the shepherds swain,
> To whom Diana's darlings came running down amain.

MUSIC LISTENING SELECTION

Weelkes, "As Vesta was from Latmos hill descending." Oxford Camerata, conductor Jeremy Summerly, CD track 6

In the first line the melody rises like the hill itself, then descends to match the word "descending." The melody again rises in the second line to represent the ascent of Latmos Hill by the "maiden Queen" (Elizabeth). In the fourth line notes descend dramatically on the words "running down amain." Composed in honor of Elizabeth, the madrigal reveals humanist leanings in its references to Diana, the virgin Roman goddess of the hunt and the moon, and to Vesta, goddess of the hearth, who presided over the Vestal Virgins tending Diana's sanctuary. The "shepherds swain" refers to the queen's courtiers, among whom were several unsuccessful suitors.

In the course of Elizabeth's reign keyboards and lutes found new solo roles as music began to be composed specifically for those instruments. John Bull (1562–1628) was the leading keyboard musician, developing a genre in which the basic melody was repeated in sets of elaborate variations characterized by **trills** and other musical ornaments. The ayres (airs) composed for the lute by John Dowland (1563–1626) are somber and gloomy. The very title of his "In darknesse let me dwell" reflects the moodiness of his work. Thomas Campion (1567–1620) wrote light pieces for the lute, and poetry as well as music.

POETRY AND THEATER

During the reign of Elizabeth I, poetry flourished and theater was enormously popular, with actors traveling from town to town in groups, or companies. Poetry was enriched by incorporating traditional genres, such as the medieval romance, the pastoral, and the epic. The greatest poets, Philip Sidney (1554–1586) and Edmund Spenser (*c.* 1552–1599), along with Christopher Marlowe (1564–1593) and William Shakespeare (1564–1616), made this one of the most illustrious periods of English literature.

Many people attended plays, and the most important companies were invited to perform at court. The humanism of the best Elizabethan theater is reflected in its Classical inspiration, depiction of universal human themes, enormous range of characterization, and wide appeal to the imagination. The emphasis on music at the Elizabethan court is evident not only in its poetry, but also in theater, in which songs often play a role.

PHILIP SIDNEY AND EDMUND SPENSER Philip Sidney and Edmund Spenser were influenced by the amorous exuberance of Ariosto (see Chapter 14) and the pastoral genres of ancient Rome. Sidney was a soldier, member of Parliament, and an author of important sonnets. He wrote the romance *Arcadia* (1581, revised in 1590), in which he combined dramatic dialogue and pastoral eclogues (see Chapter 7) inspired by Virgil with a complicated narrative filled with intrigue.

Sidney's sequence of 108 sonnets entitled *Astrophel and Stella* (1582) was inspired by Petrarch's sonnets (see Chapter 12). It recounts the story of the love of Astrophel (meaning "star's lover") for Stella (the star). Some scholars believe that

Astrophel was actually Astrophil, alluding to the name "Philip" and hence to Sidney himself as lover of the heavens, with Stella as his star. The model for Stella is thought to have been Penelope Rich, the sister of Queen Elizabeth's last favorite courtier, the Earl of Essex. Penelope was a famous beauty in her day, the mother of seven children by Lord Rich and five or six more by the Earl of Devonshire, whose mistress she was, but her actual relationship with Sidney is not known. In his sonnets, she is a distant and unattainable star.

Sidney's essay *Apology for Poetry* (also called *Defence of Poesie*) (1595), itself imbued with a poetic quality, is the first example of literary criticism in England. In it, Sidney observes that poetry is an ancient art produced by every culture and a foundation of future learning. Sidney believed that poetry combined the best features of philosophy and history and was the most effective route to virtue. He claims that whereas other arts and sciences are based on works of nature, poetry is subject only to the poet's imagination. Sidney's poet creates "another nature," which is "better than Nature," for the poetic imagination creates a timeless world filled with epic gods and heroes, myths, personifications, monsters, and fairies.

When Sidney died, Edmund Spenser published a commemorative elegy entitled *Astrophel.* Spenser's most famous work is the epic poem of six complete books, *The Faerie Queene*, which combines medieval romance with Christian allegory, Celtic myth, and the pastoral. The hero of Book One is a Knight of the Red Cross who proves himself through a variety of challenges in Faerie Land. Like Homer and Virgil, Spenser begins by invoking the Muse:

Lo! I, the man whose Muse whylome [formerly] did mask,
As time her taught in lowly shepherd's weeds,
Am now enforced, a far unfitter task,
For trumpets stern to change mine oaten reeds,
And sing of knights' and ladies' gentle deeds;
Whose praises having slept in silence long,
Me, all too mean, the sacred Muse areeds [declares]
To blazon broad [spread abroad] amongst her learned throng:
Fierce wars and faithful loves shall moralize my song.

CHRISTOPHER MARLOWE The son of a shoemaker in Canterbury, Christopher Marlowe was educated at Cambridge. Although he died young, killed in a bar-room brawl before the age of thirty, Marlowe translated Ovid, wrote memorable lyrical poetry in the pastoral tradition, and produced plays. His poem *The Passionate Shepherd to his Love* invites a nymph to share the joys of love:

Come live with me and be my love,
And we will all the pleasures prove [try]
That valleys, groves, hills, and fields,
Woods, or steepy mountains yields.

And we will sit upon the rocks,
Seeing the shepherds feed their flocks,
By shallow rivers to whose falls
Melodious birds sing madrigals.

Marlowe's two major plays are *Tamburlaine* (about the Mongol leader now known as Timur Leng, see Chapter 9), the theme of which is power, and *Dr. Faustus.* Based on a German legend in which a man sells his soul to the devil for riches on earth, the Faust story has become a persistent theme in Western literature, opera, and theater (see Chapter 18). The most famous passage in the play occurs when Dr. Faustus first looks on Helen of Troy in astonishment:

Was this the face that launch'd a thousand ships,
And burnt the topless towers of Ilium?
Sweet Helen, make me immortal with a kiss!

Marlowe's works exemplify the secular character of drama in the Elizabethan period. A pioneer of blank (unrhyming) verse, he was greatly admired by his contemporaries and had an enormous influence on English poets, particularly Shakespeare.

READING SELECTION

Marlowe, *Dr. Faustus*, Faustus's bargain with the devil, PWC3-312-B

WILLIAM SHAKESPEARE

William Shakespeare (figure **15.22**), the great poet and dramatist of Elizabethan England, is widely considered the finest writer of the English language. An extensive debate about Shakespeare's identity has never been resolved. Some scholars doubt that one man could have written all thirty-seven plays or commanded a vocabulary vastly larger than any other on record. Some of the plays are clearly less good than others, which has led to speculation that more than one author may have written them. Candidates for "the real Shakespeare" have included Christopher Marlowe and Edward de Vere, Earl of Oxford, the latter on the grounds that the author of the plays must have been highly educated and familiar with the court.

The Shakespeare we know does not fit that profile. He was born at Stratford-upon-Avon, in the Midlands of England, and probably attended the local grammar school. It is assumed that he had no further formal education, although this is not documented. He married Anne Hathaway when he was eighteen, and they had three children. Within ten years, an actor named William Shakespeare was writing plays performed in London. By the time he retired to Stratford some nineteen years later, at the age of forty-seven, Shakespeare is thought to have written 154 sonnets and thirty-seven plays.

15.22 *Page of the first Folio*, 1623. Folger Shakespeare Library, Washington, D.C.

Shakespeare's sonnets transposed Petrarchan style into the English sonnet form. The sonnets are composed in four-line stanzas (**quatrains**), an alternating rhyme scheme of ABAB, CDCD, EFEF, and a final rhyming **couplet** (two lines), GG. In Sonnet 29 the poet reminds himself that when ill-fortune and the disapproval of his fellow-man plunge him into despair, he has only to think of his beloved to revive:

When in disgrace with Fortune and men's eyes [A]
I all alone beweep my outcast state, [B]
And trouble deaf heaven with my bootless [useless] cries, [A]
And look upon myself and curse my fate, [B]

Wishing me like to one more rich in hope, [C]
Featur'd like him, like him with friends possess'd, [D]
Desiring this man's art, and that man's scope, [C]
With what I most enjoy contented least; [D]

Yet in these thoughts myself almost despising, [E]
Haply I think on thee, and then my state [F]
(Like to the lark at break of day arising [E]
From sullen earth) sings hymns at heaven's gate, [F]

For thy sweet love rememb'red such wealth brings, [G]
That then I scorn to change my state with kings. [G]

READING SELECTION

Shakespeare, *Sonnets*, on love, PWC3-182

Shakespeare's plays are based on Classical sources, medieval chronicles of English history, Italian *novellae* (short stories), and other plays, and epitomize the humanist spirit of the sixteenth century. They reflect a familiarity with Ovid, Virgil, the tragedies of Seneca, Roman comedy, and especially the biographies of famous Greeks and Romans—called *Parallel Lives*—by the first-century-A.D. author Plutarch. Shakespeare was versed in Chaucer, Montaigne, and contemporary English authors. He read Petrarch, Boccaccio's *Decameron*, and Castiglione's *Courtier*, and he used stock characters derived from the Italian comic theater.

Shakespeare's plays have an enormous range of theme, setting, character, and plot, and they portray conflict, humor, tragedy, and frivolity. They employ dramatic devices such as poetry and song, plays within plays, disguise, and self-conscious shifting between reality and illusion. The plays are at once universal and reflective of their time and place. Shakespeare's appeal is universal—he has been called a playwright not only of an age, but for all ages. His themes—love, death, hate, revenge, jealousy, ambition, folly—are as relevant today as they were in the sixteenth century. A character in *As You Like It* presents the theater as a metaphor of the world:

All the world's a stage
And all the men and women merely players:
They have their exits and their entrances;
And one man in his time plays many parts,
His acts being seven ages.

(Act 2, scene 7)

THE GLOBE PLAYHOUSE The original Globe Playhouse, where Shakespeare's plays were performed, was built in Bankside (today the Borough of Southwark in London), beside the River Thames (figure **15.23**). Bankside was known for its brothels, animal-baiting rings, and sewers, as well as its playhouses, and was readily accessible by boat and London Bridge. The Globe's design resembled the courtyard of an inn with galleries facing an open courtyard. The upper classes sat in the upper galleries, where they had a clear view of the stage, whereas the lower classes (called **groundlings**) stood in the **pit** at ground level. Based in part on ancient amphitheaters, such as the Roman Colosseum (see Chapter 7), the stage projected into the audience. Doors on stage provided entrance and exit points for the actors, and rooms backstage offered space for costume changes and storage. Below the stage was the area known as Hell, which was used for playing music or for ghostly effects and was accessible by trapdoors.

Because scenery was kept to a minimum, the lines and characterizations had to carry the play. Shakespeare's plays were addressed to people from all walks of life and depicted characters with whom they could identify—from kings and queens to sots, fools, and clowns. Other characters such as elves, fairies, ghosts, and witches appealed to the popular imagination. All the parts were acted by men or boys.

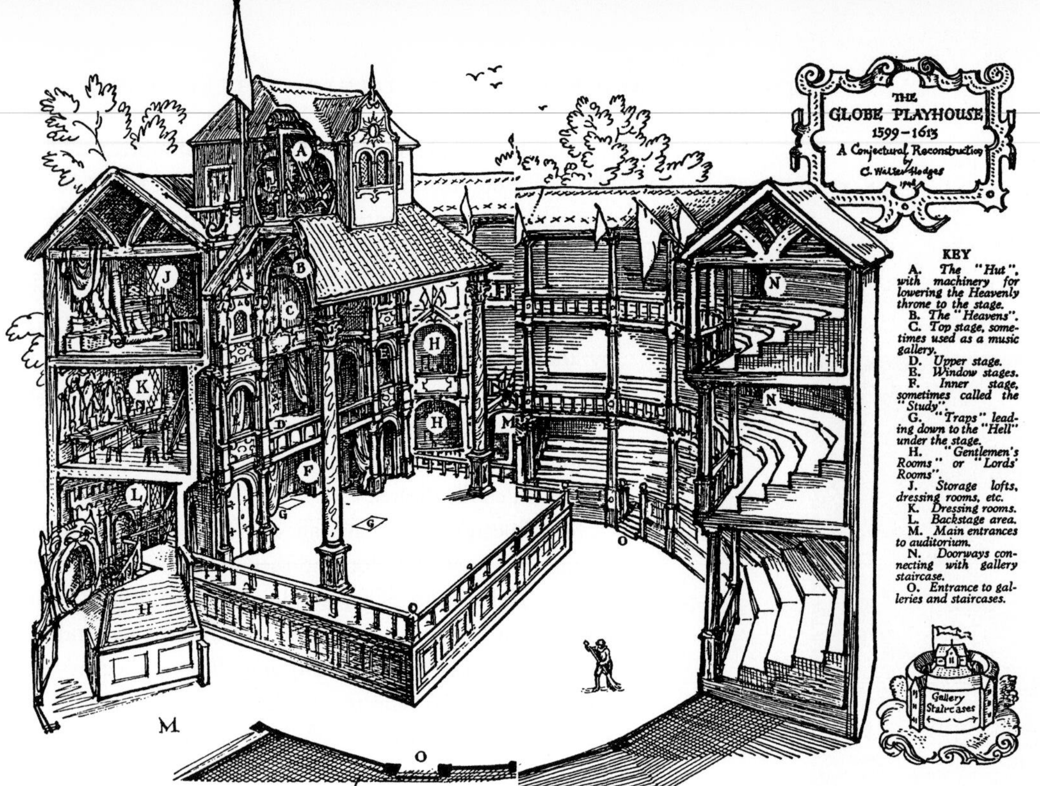

15.23 The Globe Playhouse, London, 1599–1613, reconstruction by C. Walter Hodges as it was during the lifetime of Shakespeare. Surrounding an outdoor stage the original Globe had a diameter of 80–100 feet (24.5–30.5 m) with an audience capacity of up to 3000 people. The general admission price was traditionally a penny (approx. 10 percent of a worker's daily wage). Women and men of all social classes were avid theater-goers during the reign of Elizabeth I and the subsequent rule of James I, which began in 1603.

In Shakespeare's day a group of actors, including Shakespeare himself, jointly owned the Globe Playhouse. The theater burned down in 1613 and underwent several stages of reconstruction. In 1999 a modern replica, constructed according to studies of the original Globe, was opened on Bankside.

THE PLAYS Shakespeare's plays have been staged and re-staged, reinterpreted, and transposed into contemporary settings. They have been turned into opera and film versions and have inspired works of art. Performed throughout the world in many languages, the plays retain their freshness after four hundred years and provide meaningful roles for each new generation of actors.

Shakespeare wrote comedies, histories, and tragedies. His first great tragedy, *Romeo and Juliet* (*c.* 1595), is perhaps the most famous story of star-crossed lovers. Its tale of ideal love struggling against the demands of society is a recurring theme in Shakespeare (figure **15.24**). The play opens and the audience learns that two leading families of Verona (in northern Italy), the Montagues and the Capulets, have long been feuding. But what begins as a romantic comedy, with the Montague Romeo falling in love with the Capulet Juliet, turns to tragedy when Tybalt, Juliet's kinsman, kills Romeo's friend Mercutio in a street brawl. Romeo takes revenge by killing Tybalt and is exiled by the prince of Verona.

Romeo and Juliet contains the famous "balcony scene," in which Romeo finds Juliet at her window:

> But soft, what light through yonder window breaks?
> It is the east, and Juliet is the sun.
>
> (Act 2, scene 2)

Juliet laments that she and Romeo are forbidden to be together because of their names:

> Oh Romeo, Romeo, wherefore art thou Romeo?
> Deny thy father and refuse thy name:
> Or, if you wilt not, be but sworn my love,
> And I'll no longer be a Capulet . . .
> What's in a name? that which we call a rose
> By any other name would smell as sweet.
>
> (Act 2, scene 2)

Juliet's father, unaware of her love for Romeo and convinced that the Montagues are his enemies, wants her to marry someone else. At the end of the play, when the young lovers are dead, the heartbroken families recognize their folly and agree to set aside their feud.

Shakespeare's comedies are fast-paced and incorporate pastoral and romantic genres as well as elements of farce. Influenced by Roman comedy, his plots often include stock characters, such as the parasite, the braggart, and the cuckold.

Twelfth Night (*c.* 1600) deals with mistaken identity and disguised gender, which were among Shakespeare's favorite themes. The play opens with Viola shipwrecked on the coast of Illyria, on the east of the Adriatic Sea. She has been separated from her twin brother, Sebastian, and believes that he is dead. Disguised as a boy, Viola seeks employment at the court of Duke Orsino. The duke has fallen in love with Countess Olivia, who spurns him, and he sends Viola to Olivia's house with a message of his love. But Olivia is attracted to Viola (who is still disguised as a boy), while Viola is falling in love with Orsino. Unknown to Viola, her twin brother is safe and arrives in Illyria with his friend Antonio. In the happy conclusion, Olivia marries Sebastian and Orsino marries Viola, but the confusion is resolved only in the last scene when the twins appear together on stage.

15.24 Royal Shakespeare production of *Romeo and Juliet* with Zoe Waites and Ray Fearson, 1998.
In this production *Romeo and Juliet* was reinterpreted according to modern racial issues. Here, Romeo's family is black and Juliet's is white. In addition to theatrical revisions of the play, five popular movies of *Romeo and Juliet* have been made, including one set in Verona Beach, California. The musical *West Side Story* (see Chapter 23) shifts the setting to the slums of New York, where the conflicts are between gangs, between criminals and the police, and between whites and Hispanics.

The subplot of *Twelfth Night* provides a comic thread dealing with members of Olivia's household. They include Olivia's uncle, the knight Sir Toby Belch, Toby's milktoast friend (the pallid Sir Andrew Aguecheek), Olivia's egoistic steward Malvolio, her maid Maria, and her clown, Feste. Malvolio is tricked into believing that Olivia is in love with him and, when he foolishly courts her, he is imprisoned as a madman. The Clown Feste sings a metaphor of human life and concludes with a reminder that he is but an actor in a play:

When that I was and a little tine [tiny] boy,
  With hey, ho, the wind and the rain,
A foolish thing was but a toy,
  For the rain it raineth every day . . .

A great while ago the world begun,
  With hey, ho, the wind and the rain,
But that's all one, our play is done,
  And we'll strive to please you every day.

(Act 5, scene 1)

Shakespeare wrote dramatic cycles about English kings. In *Richard III*, about evil coming to power in the absence of opposition from the good, Shakespeare created a villain without remorse. Richard's deformed hunchback is a metaphor for his corrupt character and empty spirit.

As King Edward IV lies dying, Richard, duke of Gloucester, vows to usurp the throne. He kills his rivals, including his brother and his nephews, and marries the sister of the murdered nephews. Once in power, however, Richard III antagonizes his former ally, the duke of Buckingham, who raises an army against him. Fighting with Buckingham is the earl of Richmond, who, according to an old prophecy, is destined to be king. Buckingham is captured and killed, but Richmond's army defeats Richard at the Battle of Bosworth, when Richard famously declaims: "A horse, a horse! my kingdom for a horse!" At the end, Richmond becomes King Henry VII, the first of the Tudor line and the father of Henry VIII.

In their combination of formal genius and psychological insight, Shakespeare's later tragedies are on a par with the great tragedies of Aeschylus, Sophocles, and Euripides (see Chapter 6). Events lead to disaster when lofty figures fall because of a moral flaw and we identify with their internal conflicts, even as we are riveted by the inexorable unfolding of doom. In *Othello* (*c.* 1602), the Moor (dark-skinned Arab) of Venice is led by unreasonable jealousy to kill his devoted wife, Desdemona, whom he dearly loves. In *Macbeth* (*c.* 1605) the hero and his wife are ruined by grandiose ambition, greed for power, and a misunderstood prophecy. *King Lear* (*c.* 1605) is the story of an old man destroyed by foolish vanity.

Julius Caesar (*c.* 1599), based on Plutarch, is set in Rome at the end of the Republic (see Chapter 7). The play shows how political ambition and disregard for popular sentiment can cause even the most powerful leaders to fall. Caesar's assassination by a group of Roman senators fearing that he wants to be king is an allusion to England's own conflicts between its kings and Parliament, and to the wider conflict between tyranny and democratic ideals. Although warned by an oracle to "beware the Ides of March," Caesar disregards the prophecy. His friend Brutus joins the senators, and Caesar declares: "*Et tu, Brute*? [You too, Brutus?]—then fall Caesar!" Themes of friendship and betrayal are interwoven throughout the play, affecting rulers, their families, and their subjects.

Another theme in *Julius Caesar* is the fickleness of a crowd. When Brutus addresses the Romans, he convinces them that Caesar's death was for the good of the Republic; but when Mark Antony takes the stage, the crowd is swayed to outrage by his oratory. He asserts that Caesar's death spared Rome a tyrant's rule:

Friends, Romans, countrymen, lend me your ears!
I come to bury Caesar, not to praise him.
The evil that men do lives after them,
The good is oft interred with their bones;
So let it be with Caesar. The noble Brutus
Hath told you Caesar was ambitious . . .
And Brutus is an honorable man.

(Act 3, scene 2)

But Antony's emphasis on Brutus's honor is ironic, for by the end of the speech he has made it clear that Caesar's killer is every bit as ambitious as his victim. In so doing, he turns the crowd against Caesar's murderers, who are forced to flee Rome.

The greatest of Shakespeare's tragedies—certainly the most frequently performed—is *Hamlet* (*c.* 1600), the story of a young man's indecision and thirst for revenge. Hamlet, prince of Denmark, has returned home from university to find that his recently widowed mother has married his uncle. He meets his father's ghost, who reveals that he was murdered by his ambitious brother and asks Hamlet to avenge his death. Hamlet agonizes over the choices before him:

> To be, or not to be, that is the question:
> Whether 'tis nobler in the mind to suffer
> The slings and arrows of outrageous fortune,
> Or to take arms against a sea of troubles,
> And by opposing, end them.
>
> (Act 3, scene 1)

Weakened by indecision, Hamlet becomes dysfunctional. He rejects Ophelia ("Get thee to a nunnery"), and the girl he purports to love drowns herself after her father's death. He feigns madness and finally seizes on the device of a play-within-a-play to trap his uncle into revealing himself:

> The play's the thing
> Wherein I'll catch the conscience of the king.
>
> (Act 2, scene 4)

In the final scene, Hamlet kills his uncle, his mother dies by poison, and Ophelia's brother kills Hamlet in a duel.

Shakespeare's last and most "theatrical" play, *The Tempest* (1611), is influenced by the pastoral tradition of ancient Rome. Set on a magic island, the play is populated by spirits, monsters, characters who become invisible, and masquerades of goddesses. The hero of the *Tempest* is also its director.

Prospero, the duke of Milan, was overthrown by his brother Alonso and cast adrift at sea with his young daughter, Miranda. They land on a magic island previously occupied by an Algerian witch. Prospero, an impresario of magic himself, releases the spirits imprisoned by the witch and becomes their master. The spirit Ariel serves Prospero but wants his freedom. The witch's monstrous son, Caliban, whose name is a play on "cannibal" inspired by Montaigne's essay on cannibals, is under Prospero's orders.

After twelve years on the island, Prospero uses his magic to arrange for a ship carrying Antonio (his ally, the king of Naples), his brother, Alonso, and Alonso's son, Ferdinand, to be shipwrecked on the island. Ferdinand and Miranda (now grown up) fall in love, and after Ferdinand proves himself, Prospero agrees to their marriage. Prospero and Alonso are reconciled, and Ariel is freed, providing he summons a wind that will enable the mortals to sail home.

In writing about a magic island, Shakespeare reveals aspects of the real world in the early 1600s. Influenced by reports of the Americas, Shakespeare depicts Caliban as a natural man, freed from the constraints and corruption of "civilized" society. Prospero, like a god and a poet, plays with the boundary between reality and illusion. He sums up the metaphor in which life is a dream and by extension a play, which soon comes to an end:

> We are such stuff
> As dreams are made on, and our little life
> Is rounded with a sleep.
>
> (Act 4, scene 1)

The religious upheavals of the sixteenth century were consolidated in the course of the seventeenth century, although conflicts would continue. Similarly, advances in science continued to be opposed by the Catholic Church. In the arts and philosophy the seventeenth century would be enormously prolific, building on sixteenth-century developments and ushering in the eighteenth-century Enlightenment.

KEY TERMS

ballett (balletto) in Italian music, a lilting, dance-like song.

cadence the close of a musical phrase.

chorale a congregational hymn in the German Protestant church.

chromatic harmony harmony containing notes that do not belong to the key in which the music is written.

couplet two consecutive lines in a poem that rhyme or have some other correspondence.

dissonance the effect produced when musical notes that clash with each other are sounded simultaneously.

groundling in Elizabethan theater, a spectator standing in the area (the pit) in front of the stage.

heliocentrism the notion that the sun is at the center of the solar system.

pit the ground-level area in front of a stage.

quatrain a four-line stanza (verse) in a poem.

sonnet a fourteen-line poem, typically composed of four-line stanzas with an alternating rhyming scheme and final rhyming couplet.

theocracy rule by a religious leader or group of leaders.

trill a musical ornament consisting of the rapid alternation of two adjacent notes.

unison voices singing (or instruments playing) the same melody, rather than performing different lines to make harmony.

vernacular the language of a particular country or region.

KEY QUESTIONS

1. Discuss the power of satire to criticize society's institutions. Who were the most significant satirists in this period and who and what were their targets?
2. Luther sought direct spiritual communication with God, free of the Church hierarchy and its rites. What steps did he take to accomplish these goals?
3. What forms of literature developed in response to the struggles of this period? What are the goals of satire?
4. What measures of the Council of Trent influenced the visual arts? Give two examples.

SUGGESTED READING

Bloom, Harold. *Shakespeare: The Invention of the Human.* New York: Riverhead Books, 1998.
- ▸ A study of Shakespeare by a distinguished literary critic.

Bradley, A. C. *Shakespearean Tragedy*, ed. John Bailey. London: Penguin Books, 1991.
- ▸ A classic work on Shakespeare's tragedies by a twentieth-century critic.

Cameron, E. *The European Reformation.* Oxford: Clarendon Press, 1991.
- ▸ A description of Europe during the turmoil of the sixteenth-century Reformation.

Eisenstein, E. *The Printing Revolution in Early Modern Europe.* Cambridge, U.K.: Cambridge University Press, 1984.
- ▸ On the importance and influence of printing and the printing press in Europe.

Harbison, Craig. *The Mirror of the Artist: Northern Renaissance Art in its Historical Context.* New York: Abrams, 1995.
- ▸ A brief illustrated overview of northern Renaissance art.

Newman, J. *Renaissance Music.* Englewood Cliffs, NJ: Prentice-Hall, 1963.
- ▸ A survey of Renaissance music.

Oberman, Heiko. *Luther: Man Between God and the Devil.* New Haven, CT: Yale University Press, 1990.
- ▸ A biography of Martin Luther.

Starkey, David. *Elizabeth: The Struggle for the Throne.* London: HarperCollins: 2000.
- ▸ Queen Elizabeth I, her life and times, with an emphasis on her relationship to politics and power.

Tey, Josephine. *The Daughter of Time.* London: Penguin Books, 1990.
- ▸ A twentieth-century mystery-writer solves the murder of the princes in the tower in *Richard III.*

SUGGESTED FILMS

1936 *Mary of Scotland*, dir. John Ford

1966 *A Man for All Seasons*, dir. Fred Zinnemann

1969 *Anne of the Thousand Days*, dir. Charles Jarrott

1998 *Shakespeare in Love*, dir. John Madden

Based on Shakespeare:

1945 *Henry V*, dir. Laurence Olivier

1948 *Hamlet*, dir. Laurence Olivier

1948 *Macbeth*, dir. Orson Welles

1953 *Kiss Me Kate* (musical based on the *Taming of the Shrew*), dir. George Sidney

1955 *Richard III*, dir. Laurence Olivier

1966 *Chimes at Midnight* (*Campanadas a medianoche*) (version of Shakespeare's *Henry IV* Parts 1 and 2), dir. Orson Welles

1968 *Romeo and Juliet*, dir. Franco Zefferelli

1993 *Much Ado about Nothing*, dir. Kenneth Branagh

1996 *Hamlet*, dir. Kenneth Branagh

1996 *Looking for Richard III*, dir. Al Pacino

1999 *Titus*, dir. Julie Taymor

2005 *The Merchant of Venice*, dir. Michael Radford

16 Absolutism and the Baroque

"*It is God who establishes kings . . . the royal throne is not that of a man, but the throne of God himself.*"

(JACQUES-BÉNIGNE BOSSUET)

"*Every man, by consenting with others to make one body politic under one government, puts himself under an obligation to every one of that society to submit to the determination of the majority, and to be concluded by it; or else this original compact, whereby he with others incorporates into one society, would signify nothing.*"

(JOHN LOCKE)

The seventeenth century in Europe is often called the Age of Absolutism because monarchs attempted to exercise total control over their states and claimed to rule by divine right. The three most powerful rulers in the seventeenth century were Philip IV of Spain (ruled 1621–1665), Louis XIV of France (ruled 1643–1715), and Charles I of England (ruled 1625–1649). In order to concentrate their power, these monarchs insisted on greater centralization of the institutions governing finance, the military, and religion. In fact, however, they were unable to exercise real control in the provinces and relied on the nobility as well as on some commoners to implement their policies. Although they hired ministers of culture to promote themselves as icons of power, Louis XIV, Philip IV, and Charles I also used political persuasion and military force.

Seventeenth-century Europe continued to experience the religious turmoil that resulted from the Protestant Reformation and the Counter-Reformation (see Chapter 15). The first half of the century was beset by the Thirty Years War (1618–1648), which was sparked by conflict between Catholics and Protestants. One result of the war was that states began to build up national armies, which not only intensified the unrest but also reinforced centralization in Britain, France, and Spain.

In philosophy and science the seventeenth century was an age of dissent. Scientific discoveries contradicted entrenched beliefs, and new philosophical ideas advocating tolerance challenged notions of divine right.

The arts reflected the turbulence and uncertainty of the period. The conflict between maintaining Classical models and newer forms was known as the quarrel between the Ancients and the Moderns. To a large degree, although framed as an artistic and literary quarrel, this argument reflected the tension between traditional ideas and new challenges from philosophy and science.

In Rome, a new artistic style evolved, and it spread throughout Europe, adapting itself along national and religious lines. The style was called Baroque by later artists and scholars after the Portuguese word barroco *("an irregular pearl"). In Italy the term* barocco *meant "convoluted logic," but the style itself is*

Key Topics

Style and Conflict

- The Ancients versus the Moderns
- Illusionism and realism
- The Baroque

Politics and Philosophy

- Absolute monarchy
- Divine right of kings versus the social contract
- Thirty Years War: Catholics versus Protestants
- Philosophical doubt

Science and Superstition

- Kepler
- Galileo
- Newton
- Boyle
- Leeuwenhoek

TIMELINE	SEVENTEENTH-CENTURY EUROPE	THE NEW WORLD
HISTORY AND CULTURE 	Absolute monarchs in Europe: Philip IV of Spain (r. 1621–1665); Charles I of England (r. 1625–1649); Louis XIV of France (r. 1643–1715); Peter I, the Great, of Russia (r. 1682–1725) Persecution of witches in Europe and New England intensifies Rise and modernization of military in Sweden, Prussia, Russia Dutch East India Company founded, 1602 James I ascends to English throne, 1603 Thirty Years War, 1618–1648 Richelieu (in office 1624–1642) establishes absolute power of French king Charles I suspends Parliament, 1642; executed, 1649 Charles II rules in England, 1660–1685; the Restoration James II deposed, 1688; William III of Orange (r. 1689–1702)	Increased colonization of New World Jamestown, Virginia, founded, 1607 First Africans brought to Virginia by Dutch traders, 1619; development of slave trade Anglicans found Plymouth Bay Colony, Massachusetts, 1620 Puritans establish Massachusetts Bay Colony, 1630 Abel Tasman (*c.* 1603–*c.* 1659) discovers New Zealand, 1642
RELIGION	Thirty Years War, 1618–1648 Church in conflict with science and philosophy King James Bible, 1611	
SCIENCE AND TECHNOLOGY 	Bacon (1562–1626), *Novum Organum*, 1620 Galileo (1564–1642) establishes that light travels at measurable speed Kepler (1571–1630) formulates three laws of planetary motion Harvey (1578–1657) discovers blood circulation Telescope invented in the Netherlands, 1609 Boyle (1627–1691), Boyle's Law, 1662 van Leeuwenhoek (1632–1723) improves magnification of microscope Newton (1642–1727), *Mathematical Principles of Natural Philosophy*, 1687 Leibniz (1646–1716) proposes that all laws of the universe are mechanical	
ART 	Baroque style Caravaggio, *Bacchus*, *c.* 1596; *The Conversion of St. Paul*, 1601 Gentileschi, *Judith Slaying Holofernes*, 1612–1613 Rubens, *The Marie de' Medici Cycle*, 1622–1625 Hals, *Officers of the Haarlem Militia Company of St. Adrian*, 1627 Leyster, *Self-portrait*, *c.* 1630 Lorrain, *Landscape with Merchants*, *c.* 1630 Rembrandt, *The Anatomy Lesson of Dr. Nicolaes Tulp*, 1632; *Self-portrait with Saskia*, 1636; *Aristotle with a Bust of Homer*, 1653 van Dyck, *Henrietta Maria, Queen of England*, *c.* 1632 Poussin, *Et in Arcadia Ego*, 1638–1639 Bernini, *David*, 1623; *The Ecstasy of St. Teresa*, 1645–1652 Velázquez, *Philip IV at Fraga*, 1640s; *"El Primo,"* 1644; *Las Meninas*, 1656 Vermeer, *Girl with a Pearl Earring*, *c.* 1665; *The Astronomer*, 1668 Gaulli, *The Triumph of the Name of Jesus*, 1676–1679	Mission Church of San Estevan, Acoma, New Mexico, *c.* 1629 Mexico City Cathedral, 1656–1671
ARCHITECTURE	Maderno (1556–1629), façade of St. Peter's, Rome Bernini (1598–1680), piazza of St. Peter's, Rome Borromini, San Carlo alle Quattro Fontane, Rome, 1665–1667 Palace of Versailles, late 1670s Wren, St. Paul's Cathedral, London, 1675–1710	
LITERATURE AND PHILOSOPHY	Philosophers question existence of God Cervantes, *Don Quixote*, 1605–1615 Donne, *Holy Sonnets*, *c.* 1610 Letters of Mme de Sévigné, 1626–1696 Descartes, *Discourse on Method*, 1637 Milton, *The Doctrine and Discipline of Divorce*, 1643; *Paradise Lost*, 1667 Hobbes, *Leviathan*, 1651 Pascal, *Lettres provinciales*, 1656–1657; *Pensées*, 1670 Mme de Lafayette, *La Princesse de Clèves*, 1678 Locke, "Essay Concerning Human Understanding," 1690 Bossuet, *Politics Drawn from the Holy Scriptures*, 1709	
THEATER	Corneille, *Le Cid*, 1636 Molière, *L'École des femmes*, 1662; *Le Bourgeois Gentilhomme*, 1670 Racine, *Andromaque*, 1667; *Britannicus*, 1670; *Phèdre*, 1677 La Comédie Française established, 1687	
MUSIC	Monteverdi (1567–1643), *Orfeo*, 1607 Lully (1632–1687) establishes *tragédie lyrique* style of French opera Vivaldi (1678–1741), solo concertos; operas; *The Four Seasons*, 1725 Bach (1685–1750), fugues; Passions; *Brandenburg Concertos*, 1721 Handel (1685–1759), operas; oratorios; *Messiah*, 1742	

characterized by theatrical, expansive, and even violent subject matter and the disruption of Renaissance order and symmetry. By eliminating the regulated linear perspective used in the Renaissance, Baroque artists achieved a new sense of dynamic tension. Nevertheless, Baroque style was not as convoluted as Mannerism, its color was less jarring, and its poses were less exaggerated. In addition, Baroque had a more Classical flavor than Mannerism, especially in its formal structure. Baroque music was rich and varied, and the range of musical expression expanded greatly. Theater, like the other arts, expressed a new emotionalism, and **opera**, *a new genre combining music with theater, was created.*

The two quotations that open this chapter embody the era's divergent views of how people should be governed. At one extreme was the notion of the divine right of kings articulated by Jacques-Bénigne Bossuet (1627–1704). The court preacher to Louis XIV and a major Catholic philosopher, Bossuet wrote Politics Drawn from the Holy Scriptures. *He asserted that monarchs have a hereditary right to kingship and that to rebel against the monarch is a crime against God. This view accords few rights to the common person. At the other extreme was the notion of a "compact" between the ruler and the ruled—government as a social contract—which was advocated by the English political philosopher John Locke (1632–1704). Locke held that citizens agree to be ruled, and that the ruler retains his rights as long as he provides practical benefits, such as protection and order. If the ruler breaks the contract by abusing his subjects' trust, they have the right to rebel.*

These developments aroused an intense backlash in certain quarters. The Catholic Church fought the scientists, the monarchs fought new ideas about government, and the persecution of witches that had begun in the sixteenth century (see Chapter 15) was intensified. As both Catholic and Protestant elites began to police popular beliefs and religious practices more closely than before, they focused on so-called witches as a threat to religious orthodoxy. In the seventeenth century, the witch "craze" spread to the American colonies in New England, where over two hundred people, mainly women, were tried as witches and thirty-six were executed. Eventually, as science increasingly relied on empirical evidence, traditional proofs of witchcraft seemed unconvincing. By around 1700 the persecution of alleged witches had virtually died out.

POLITICS AND RELIGION

Politics and religion were the primary issues at work in the notion of absolute rule. Whereas medieval rulers had been controlled to a large extent by the Church, Louis XIV of France (figure **16.1**), Charles I of England (figure **16.2**), and Philip IV of Spain (figure **16.3**) saw themselves as divinely appointed to rule. All three became fascinated by their own political power and worldly ambition. Changes in society and administration fuelled the impulse for the king's greater control of his people. With university study and an expanding professional bureaucracy, more middle-class citizens rose in the ranks as the medieval lords declined. The monarchs looked beyond their own borders and exerted their influence through ambassadors and diplomats stationed in foreign cities. Rulers also formed national armies to reinforce their political aims.

16.1 Hyacinthe Rigaud, *Louis XIV*, 1701. Oil on canvas, 9 ft. 1½ in. × 6 ft. 2⅝ in. (2.78 × 1.9 m). Louvre, Paris.
Louis XIV, like Philip IV, used the sun as a metaphor for his political power. He proclaimed himself the sun king—*le roi soleil*. In Rigaud's portrait, Louis is surrounded by signs of kingship: the blue royal robe embroidered with gold fleurs-de-lys (emblems of French royalty), the crown and scepter, and the throne-like chair at the top of the steps. As Louis declared to his heirs, "I was king and born to be one."

16.2 Anthony van Dyck, *Charles I with M. de St. Antoine* (after restoration), 1633. Oil on canvas, 12 ft. 1 in. × 8 ft. 10¼ in. (3.68 × 2.7 m). Royal Collection.
Armed and mounted on a powerful warhorse, under a stormy sky, Charles I rides through a triumphal arch like a Roman emperor. He is revealed by a drawn curtain, and surrounded by allusions to kingship—the courtier, the crown, and the coat of arms.

16.3 Diego de Velázquez, *Philip IV at Fraga*, 1640s. Oil on canvas, 4 ft. 5 in. × 3 ft. 2½ in. (135 × 98 cm). Frick Collection, New York.
This portrait shows Philip IV during a military campaign of 1644 at the Spanish town of Fraga. His illuminated face, richly embroidered costume, and projecting staff convey an impression of imposing self-confidence. Philip IV has the same jutting jaw as his father, Charles V (see figure 14.1). Called the Planet King after the sun, which was number four in the hierarchy of planets, Philip IV is shown shining forth from a dark background.

The Netherlands, together with England, were the main economic force in the seventeenth century. With the opening of the Bank of Amsterdam in 1609, the establishment of a stock exchange, and the wealth to underwrite insurance, the city of Amsterdam became a financial hub of Europe. Dikes and windmills kept the sea at bay, crop rotation made agriculture increasingly prosperous, and the Dutch shipping industry made the Netherlands into a major international trading nation. The Dutch East India Company was founded in 1602 to encourage trade in the Far East. Overseas, colonization increased, notably in the Americas. The colonial practice of transporting slaves from Africa to the "New World" sowed seeds of later social, political, and economic conflict.

The political and religious struggles of the seventeenth century encouraged European nations to unite against each other, leading them to improve their armies and maintain their borders. Late in the century, in eastern Europe, Russia began to be more accessible to Western influences, especially under Peter I (ruled 1682–1725), but in western Europe the first half of the seventeenth century was dominated by the Thirty Years War.

The Thirty Years War

Sparked by Bohemian resistance to the Holy Roman Emperor, the Thirty Years War (which was actually a series of wars) began in Prague in 1618 and spread to most of Europe. It was a conflict mainly over religious domination and political power. By 1648, when the war came to an end, several million soldiers had lost their lives. The Habsburgs (the Holy Roman Emperors, together with Philip II and Philip IV of Spain) wanted to retain control of their territory and impose Catholicism on the rest of Europe, but the German princes and Protestant Denmark, Sweden, and the Netherlands united against them. Supporting the Protestant countries, and eventually turning the tide in their favor, was the Catholic Bourbon monarchy of France. Efforts by Spain under Philip IV to dominate the Netherlands were quelled with the assistance of England and France. Thus the power of Spain and the Holy Roman Empire (by now confined largely to modern Austria) began to wane as that of France and England rose. The Treaty of Westphalia (1648) concluded the war and set the religious boundaries for Europe. Although religious strife within the Holy Roman Empire ceased, the empire remained decentralized, unlike England, France, and Spain.

Sweden, under King Gustavus II Adolphus (ruled 1611–1632), fought on the side of the Protestants and emerged from the war as a strong military force. He established a national standing army, rather than using mercenaries as had been customary in Europe. He also raised the moral standards of his army by forbidding his soldiers to loot or rape their defeated enemies. Gustavus was succeeded by his daughter, Queen Christina (ruled 1632–1654, d. 1689), who inherited the throne at age six and abdicated at twenty-two.

Under the Great Elector, Frederick William (ruled 1640–1688), Prussia also established a strong military presence in Europe. Frederick William allocated most of Prussia's finances to the army, on which his power rested, and by the end of his rule the Prussian army was a fighting force of 40,000 men.

Under Habsburg rule the Netherlands had been made up of seventeen provinces. In 1581 the seven northern provinces, which were Protestant, declared their independence from Catholic Spain. This action sparked a war that lasted until 1609, when the Netherlands was divided along religious lines. The southern Netherlands (also called the Spanish Netherlands) remained Catholic and today comprises modern Belgium. The Protestant northern Netherlands became the Dutch Republic (modern Holland). This division was made official in 1648 by the Treaty of Westphalia, which left Sweden the major European state, France more powerful than Spain, and Germany in decline (map **16.1**).

EASTERN EUROPE: PETER THE GREAT

In the late seventeenth century eastern Europe began to witness significant changes, which continued into the eighteenth century. Under the absolute rule of Peter I, the Great (ruled 1682–1725), Russia was opened to Western ideas. Coming after centuries of powerful, medieval tsars—Ivan III in the fifteenth century and Ivan IV, the Terrible, in the sixteenth—Peter the Great was the first tsar of the Romanov line, which lasted until the Revolution of 1917 (see Chapter 21). Peter brought a measure of stability to Russia and sought to adopt the economic and cultural advances he observed in

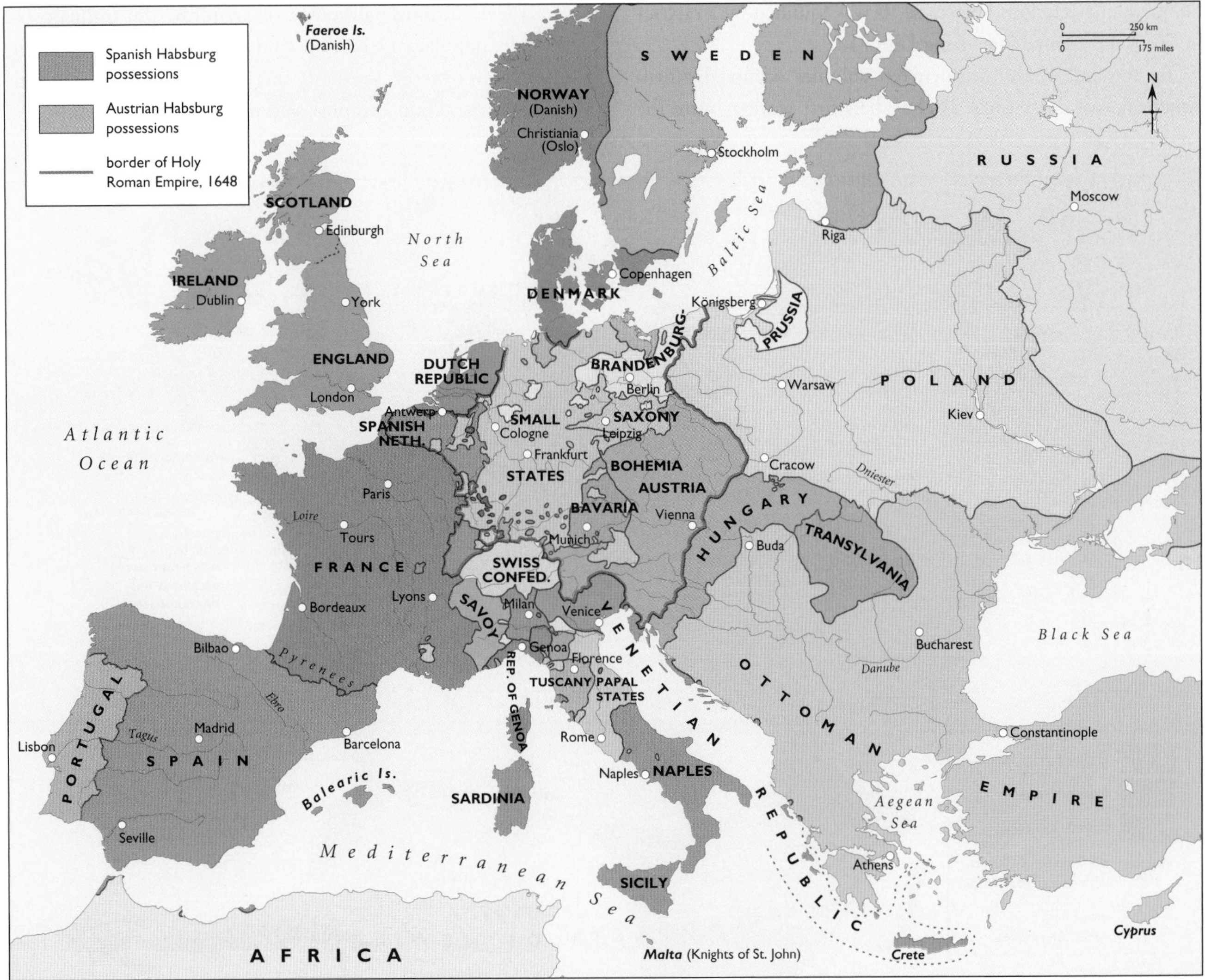

Map 16.1 The division of Europe according to the Treaty of Westphalia, 1648.

western Europe. He required, for example, that the sons of aristocrats be given a west-European-style education and encouraged the publication of printed materials that circulated in west-European capitals. Peter also improved the Russian army and expanded the navy in the Baltic. When his son opposed the modernization of Russia, Peter had him killed.

THE "NEW WORLD"

As the European countries most skilled at trade and cloth manufacturing recognized the potential for acquiring raw materials, colonization of the "New World" gained momentum. In Spain and France, which wanted to ensure Catholic domination in their colonies, prospective settlers had to prove their adherence to the Church before being allowed to emigrate. In England, on the other hand, emigration was largely motivated by the search for religious freedom, especially by the Puritans. They split from the Anglicans and founded the Plymouth Bay Colony in Massachusetts in 1620. Ten years later Puritans established the Massachusetts Bay Colony. Jamestown, Virginia, however, was established as a commercial rather than a religious enterprise. It was founded by a charter in 1607 and named after King James I.

By the end of the century, ten colonies occupied North America's east coast (map **16.2**). Their first workers were the immigrants themselves. But soon convicted felons from Europe could have their sentences commuted if they agreed to work in the colonies. Indentured servants received passage to the New World, room and board, and training in a trade in exchange for several years of unpaid labor. The first Africans were brought to Virginia by Dutch traders as indentured servants in 1619. As the tobacco industry developed in Virginia, however, so did the slave trade. With the cultivation of rice in the Carolinas, the economic advantages of slavery became even more apparent. By the eighteenth century slave labor had become the economic base for much of the American South.

SCIENTISTS

Seventeenth-century science built on the discoveries of the late Renaissance. Improvements in lenses facilitated research by mathematicians and physicists. The telescope, invented in the Netherlands around 1600, was used to study astronomy, whereas microscopes led scientists to the study of invisible life on earth. Among the forces counteracting science were the traditional ignorance of anatomy, the influence of Aristotle, popular superstition, and the Church and the Inquisition. Nevertheless, scientists increasingly based conclusions on experimentation and observation rather than on faith.

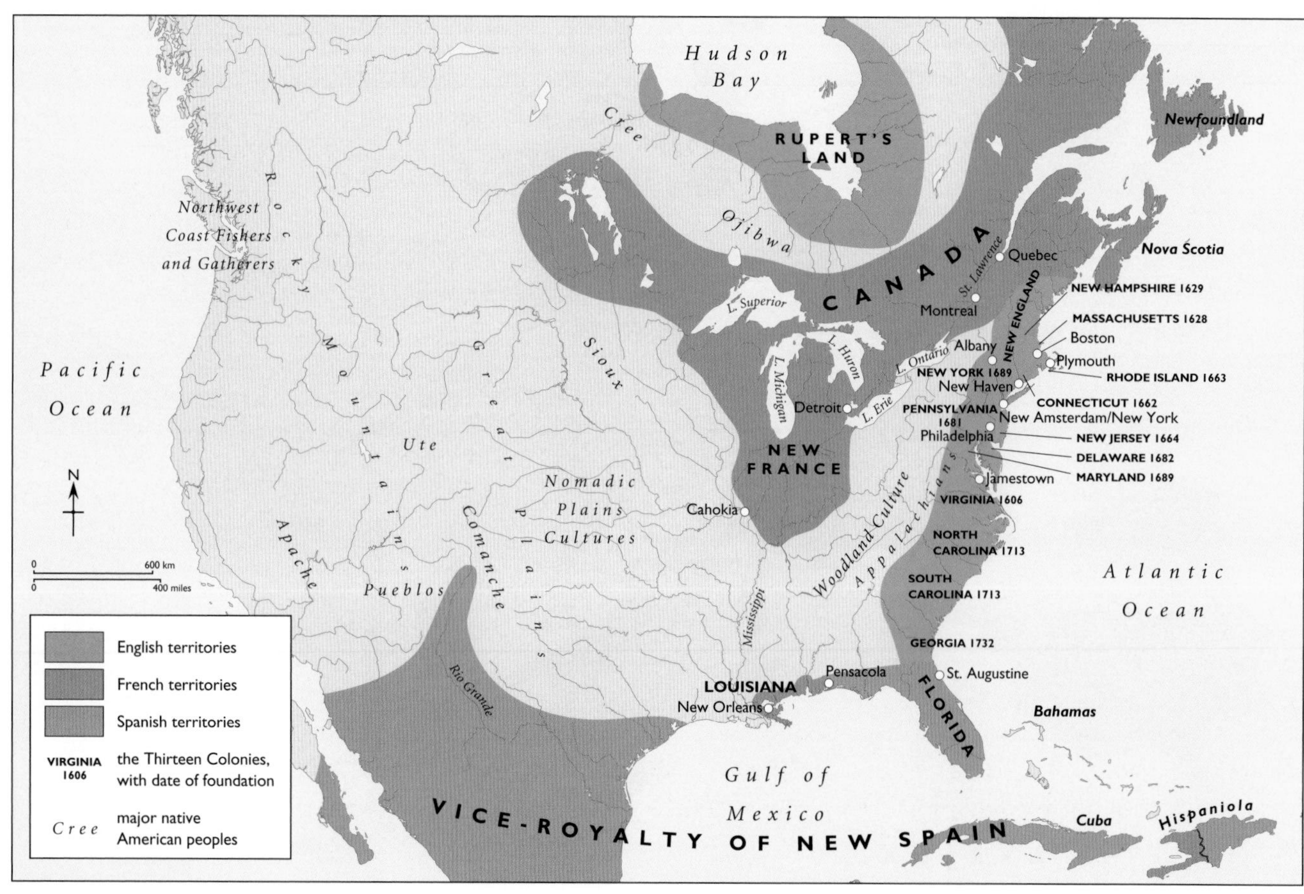

Map 16.2 Early European settlement of North America.

JOHANNES KEPLER

The German astronomer and mathematician Johannes Kepler (1571–1630) reaffirmed the heliocentrism of Copernicus (see Chapter 15). Kepler recognized that the eye is an optical instrument and was the first to describe the optics of vision accurately. He studied Tycho Brahe's measurement of planetary motion (see Chapter 15) and formulated three laws of planetary motion:

1. Planets orbit the sun in an elliptical, not a circular, motion; the sun is at one of the short ends of the ellipse.
2. The sun controls the orbits of the planets, which move faster the closer they are to the sun.
3. The squares of the periods of the planets are proportional to the cubes of their mean distances from the sun. Therefore, the amount of time it takes a planet to orbit the sun is related to its distance from the sun.

Kepler's study of Brahe's measurements led him to produce a set of astronomical tables, which permitted the accurate calculation of the positions of planets at any given time.

GALILEO GALILEI

Kepler's friend and fellow scientist Galileo Galilei (1564–1642) improved the Dutch telescope. This allowed him to observe the phases of Venus, from which he concluded that the Earth and other planets travel in different orbits and revolve around the sun. His telescope enabled him to see galaxies (which he called *nebulae*, or "clouds"), lunar craters, sunspots, and the four main moons of Jupiter. Galileo theorized that light travels at a measurable speed and demonstrated that objects of different weights fall at the same velocity. He proved that the time it takes an object to fall is governed by gravity, not by weight.

Galileo's views, especially his support of the Copernican notion that planets orbit the sun, angered the Church, which had previously been more open to new ideas. Now, however, the Church declared heliocentrism heretical and placed Galileo's *Two Chief Systems of the World* on the *Index of Forbidden Books*. Summoned to Rome by the Inquisition to defend his ideas, Galileo failed to persuade Urban VIII (papacy 1623–1644). He was forced to recant, condemned to life in prison, and later banished to a villa in Tuscany.

BACON, HARVEY, BOYLE, AND NEWTON

In 1620 the English thinker Francis Bacon (1562–1626) published *Novum Organum* (*New Organon*), written in aphorisms, which challenged the **deductive** logic of Aristotle. Noted for his clear writing style, Bacon insisted on the preeminence of observation and experimentation over faith. He foresaw that science would ultimately provide systems that could be used to control nature. Using an inductive method, Bacon began with empirical observation and evolved theories based on what he observed and tested. He thus rejected the medieval approach, which began with a theory and then tried to prove it with certain examples.

Another English scientist, William Harvey (1578–1657), discovered that blood is pumped by the heart and circulates through veins and arteries. Shortly after Harvey's discovery, the Italian scientist Marcello Malpighi (1628–1684) used the newly invented microscope to see that capillaries connect the arteries and veins.

The Irish Robert Boyle (1627–1691) worked as a chemist, although chemistry was not yet considered a separate discipline (see Box). Like Bacon, Boyle emphasized the importance of experimentation and observation, and his study of gases led him to formulate Boyle's Law in 1662:

> The volume of a mass of gas at the same temperature is inversely proportional to its pressure. If the pressure of a gas is doubled, for example, its volume decreases by one half.

Sir Isaac Newton (1642–1727), the greatest scientist of the period, was professor of mathematics at Cambridge University and a natural philosopher. His *Mathematical Principles of Natural Philosophy* (1687) applies mathematical principles to nature. Newton's interest in nature and religion and in combining earthly with outer-space-related science led to his unified theory of physics. This theory, in turn, led to a quest for a science of human nature and the notion of a "complete" science, which would integrate the study of man with that of nature and the universe.

Among other things, Newton discovered differential calculus (see Box, p. 432) and demonstrated that white light is composed of the colors of the spectrum, which can be seen by passing light through a prism. He is best known for his study

Society and Culture

Alchemy

In the seventeenth century the nearest thing to chemistry was alchemy, which sought to transmute base metals into gold and silver. An ancient pursuit that persisted into the Middle Ages and the Renaissance, alchemy was based on the conviction that the so-called Philosopher's Stone held the secret of immortality. Combined with astrology, magic, and philosophy, alchemy was practiced by many reputable intellectuals, including Marsilio Ficino (see Chapter 13) and Leonardo da Vinci (see Chapter 14). Its hold on the popular imagination was enormous and it was not until the development of chemistry, largely at the instigation of Robert Boyle, that alchemy fell into disuse. This heralded the transition from centuries of "pseudo-science" to "real" science as it is conceived of by most modern scientists.

Defining Moment

Newton and Leibniz: A Momentous Quarrel

Today, Newton and Leibniz are considered the co-inventors of calculus, but in the late seventeenth and early eighteenth centuries a heated debate arose between these two scientists as to who first developed this mathematical system.

The theory of universal gravity, developed by Isaac Newton, challenged the medieval view of a world moved by the unseen but ever-present hand of God. The new vision described the Earth as only one small planet in a vast universe, which functioned according to laws that could be calculated. In his statement, "Every body attracts every other with a force directly proportional to the product of the masses and inversely proportional to the square of the distance between them," Newton provided a method for analyzing planetary motion. Mathematics was the tool that, for Newton, could explain the "hows," if not the "whys," of the workings of the universe.

To study problems of motion, Newton needed a mathematical means of measuring variable rates of change. The term used for this kind of calculation was "fluxions" (from the Latin word *fluxus*, meaning "flow"). Newton developed two kinds of calculus: differential calculus, which measures different rates of change of functions, and integral calculus, which shows how rates of change vary with each other.

Newton's great discoveries in physics were not published until 1687. In *Philosophiae Naturalis Principia Mathematica* (usually called *The Principia*, figure **16.4**), Newton explains how to calculate the masses of planets from their orbital behavior. He also demonstrates that irregularities in the moon's behavior are due to the pull of the sun, that the moon causes the earth's tides, that comets are part of the solar system, and that the earth tilts on its axis by 66½ degrees to the plane of its orbit.

Some people criticized Newton's theory as "occult." Indeed, following Descartes and other materialists, Gottfried Wilhelm Leibniz (1646–1716) believed that all laws of the universe are mechanical. Leibniz had an additional quarrel with Newton. In the late 1690s British scientists began accusing Leibniz of having plagiarized Newton's discovery of calculus. Actually, Newton was the first to make the discoveries, but he waited twenty years to publish them. Leibniz did not delay as long and published his results first. Consequently, the followers of Newton and Leibniz became involved in heated nationalistic arguments over who invented calculus. In 1711 Leibniz appealed to the Royal Society of London, of which he was a member and of which Newton was President, to resolve the allegations of plagiarism. In public, Newton abstained from the controversy and remained silent, but it seems that he was the secret motivating force behind the accusations. The Royal Society appointed a commission and essentially found Leibniz guilty of plagiarism.

By siding against Leibniz, Newton and his followers refused to use Leibniz's superior notation. As a result, British mathematicians ignored fruitful developments in mathematics on the continent, and mathematics there stagnated for almost a century.

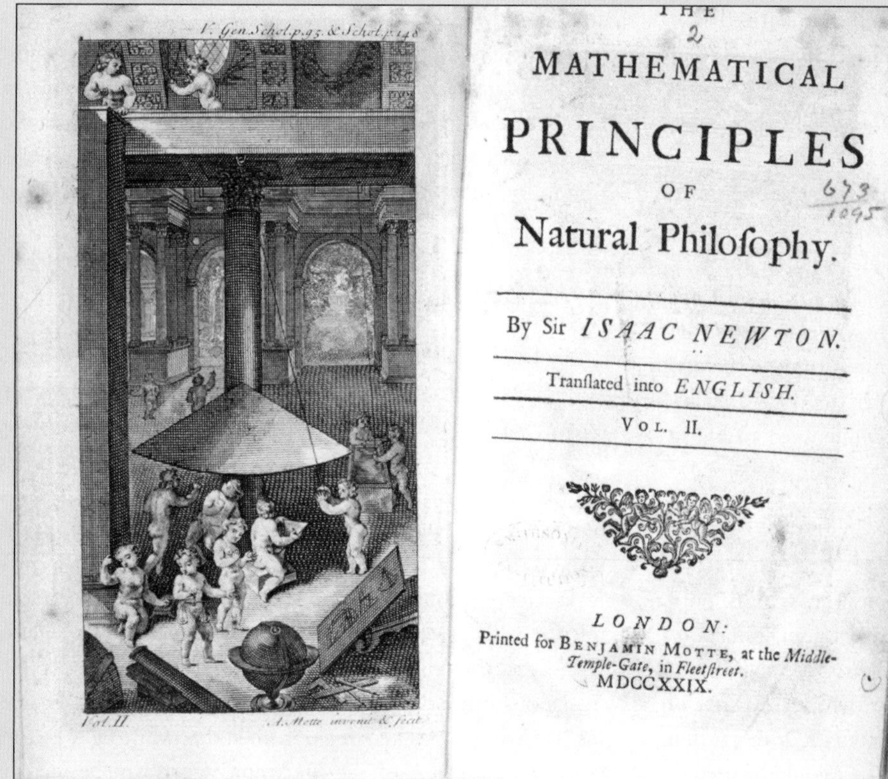

THE MATHEMATICAL PRINCIPLES OF Natural Philofophy.

By Sir ISAAC NEWTON.

Tranflated into ENGLISH.

VOL. II.

LONDON:
Printed for BENJAMIN MOTTE, at the Middle-Temple-Gate, in Fleetftreet.
MDCCXXIX.

16.4 Isaac Newton, *Mathematical Principles of Natural Philosophy*, title page of Volume 2 of the English translation of *The Principia*, 1729.

Critical Question It is known that Newton was a devout Christian. He might, it is speculated, have felt that universal gravity was not just an abstract force but was the force of God holding all elements of the universe together in an orderly path. Which explanation of this force works better with Ockham's razor? Which theory needs fewer components to complete its explanation?

of gravity and the apocryphal story of an apple falling on his head as he sat under a tree. It was through his knowledge of gravity that Newton was able to explain Kepler's laws of planetary motion.

Newton's belief in God was based on the order of the universe. He considered God to be supreme and felt that people owed him submission, but he rejected the Trinity, the Incarnation, the Resurrection, and Christ's divinity as not demonstrable by reason. These doctrines, in Newton's view, were unrelated to the harmony of the universe, which he believed proved the existence of God.

ANTON VAN LEEUWENHOEK

The Dutch were particularly skilled in making and grinding lenses. Anton van Leeuwenhoek (1632–1723) of Delft earned his living grinding lenses for microscopes. He improved the magnifying glass so that it could enlarge objects up to 270 times their actual size. As a result, van Leeuwenhoek was the first to describe red blood cells and to see protozoa and bacteria. He came to the fanciful conclusion that each sperm contains a fully formed person in miniature.

PHILOSOPHY

Seventeenth-century philosophers began to question the existence of God. Reflecting on the workings of the human mind, they concluded that empirical observation cannot always account for truth. Philosophers also questioned the nature of government and raised such questions as who should rule? and by what right, human or divine? These issues became heated topics of discussion for the first time since antiquity. In England the political philosophers Thomas Hobbes (1588–1679) and John Locke (1632–1704) debated these questions. In Holland, the ideas of Hugo Grotius (1583–1645) led to the development of international law. And in France René Descartes (1596–1650) and Blaise Pascal (1623–1662) were more concerned with the morality of religion than of politics.

THOMAS HOBBES AND JOHN LOCKE

Thomas Hobbes applied empirical observation to society. His classic work, *Leviathan*, is named for the Old Testament sea-monster in the Book of Job, who rules over "the children of pride." *Leviathan* was published in 1651 as a defense of monarchy, and the sea-monster personified powerful government capable of maintaining social order.

On the assumption that human life is dominated by a thirst for power and the fear of death, Hobbes concluded that, left to their own devices, people would produce a lawless, disordered society driven by base instinct. In Hobbes's view, people renounce certain rights in exchange for peace and social order. Hobbes called this a "social contract," a term that is still used in discussions of political philosophy.

READING SELECTION

Hobbes, *Leviathan*, on forms of government, PWC4-003

Hobbes's pessimistic view of human nature was challenged by John Locke, who believed that people should rule themselves. In his "Essay Concerning Human Understanding," published in 1690, Locke argued that environment is more defining than heredity and that faith and reason are linked. He believed that salvation depends on the individual, but, like Newton, he rejected the Trinity, the Incarnation, the Resurrection, and the divinity of Christ.

Locke's *Second Treatise on Government* was also published in 1690. There he claimed that people are naturally free. They accept government because it is practical, not because they require or wish to be subjected to a higher authority. For Locke, therefore, the social contract does not mean that citizens renounce their rights. Instead, the ruler is obligated to protect citizens *and* their rights. Rulers who fail to do so break the contract and invite rebellion. Locke's contract thus limits the authority of the ruler.

READING SELECTION

Locke, "An Essay Concerning Human Understanding," on ideas, PWC4-103-B

HUGO GROTIUS

In the Netherlands, the humanist leanings of certain reformers led to a revival of Roman law. Hugo Grotius, a poet, theologian, and lawyer, believed that reason should dominate law. He wanted to incorporate Roman legal philosophy into European law. Ever since the Middle Ages Roman law had been used to reinforce the power of rulers, but Rome had also made a distinction between national laws, which citizens had to obey, and natural law. Grotius argued that natural law, which he preferred, recognizes actions as moral or immoral according to whether they conform to rational and social nature. Natural law was thus independent of national law and systems of religious belief. This notion was consistent with international law, which, with Grotius, became a discipline in its own right. His emphasis on the international character of natural law can be seen as a reflection of Dutch colonial expansion in the New World and its commercial ventures in the Far East.

René Descartes and Blaise Pascal

The French philosopher and mathematician René Descartes was educated by Jesuits and studied law and medicine. In 1637 he published *Discourse on Method*, which sought to establish the relationship between reason and science and concluded that nothing is true unless it is knowable. In his 1648 *Treatise on the Passions of the Soul* Descartes explored the relationship between reason and wisdom. He identified six basic passions: admiration, love, hate, desire, joy, and sadness. These are good or not, he said, according to the degree to which they are consistent with reason. Thus, for example, love is good if what is loved is worthy; hate is good if what is hated merits hatred.

Descartes's thought begins with doubt. He asked: "What can be known for certain?" Perception, he noted, is not sufficient to prove reality, for a distant object can be perceived as small when, in fact, it is large. The color of an object varies in different lighting conditions, and food tastes differently in combination with other foods. In other words, since perception is relative, it is not a reliable source of absolute knowledge.

Descartes's famous assertion *Cogito, ergo sum* ("I think, therefore I am") was the solution of his efforts to reconcile the material world with the human mind, or soul. He was certain that the mind existed, but he was not certain *how* he knew that it did. If he could think, he reasoned, then he must exist as a thinking person, and from this he concluded that since God is imaginable, then God too must exist.

Blaise Pascal wanted to prove the truth of Christianity. He was a member of the Catholic Jansenist movement, which followed the doctrine of predestination, believed in Original Sin, and denied the existence of free will. Pascal broke his leg at the age of twenty-three and suffered ill health for the remainder of his short life. He spent much of his time at the Abbey of Port-Royal, a Jansenist community that attracted lay Christians who led lives of extreme austerity.

When he was thirty-one Pascal barely escaped death in a road accident, which he considered an act of divine providence. His first work, *Lettres provinciales* (1656–1657), was written to defend Jansenism against the Jesuits. Returning to the ideas of St. Augustine, St. Jerome, and Calvin, Pascal argued that grace is necessary for salvation, which God awards regardless of a person's virtue or sinfulness. In this way, Pascal attempted to prove that God's power is all-mighty and human responsibility inconsequential.

In his last work, *Pensées* (*Thoughts*), published posthumously in 1670, Pascal is more skeptical than Descartes and more fervent in his faith. Pascal believed that nature and man are unknowable, although nature can be somewhat comprehended through mathematics and geometry. As for God, Pascal argued that he can be known only through emotion: *Le coeur a ses raisons que la raison ne connait pas* ("The heart has its reasons that reason does not know").

ITALY: BIRTHPLACE OF THE BAROQUE

Seventeenth-century Italy, especially Rome, was the birthplace of Baroque art and music. The style was expansive, energetic, and melodramatic compared with the ordered classicism of the Renaissance and less "mannered" than Mannerism.

The main artistic patronage in Italy came from the Catholic Church, which adhered to the rules of the Council of Trent (see Chapter 15). But individual patrons often wanted imagery of a more personal nature, freeing artists to produce works with non-Christian subject matter. There is thus considerable variety within Baroque style.

Church patrons preferred narrative works with theological themes—including guilt, penance, and martyrdom—that exalted the Christian faith. In architecture the centralized plans designed by Renaissance humanists were supplanted by longitudinal Latin cross plans, especially in Catholic countries. With the surge in missionary activity, notably by the Spanish, the Baroque style was exported around the world, as an expression of the power of Christianity.

Architecture in Rome: Bernini and Borromini

The most monumental architectural expression of Church power in the seventeenth century was the completed New St. Peter's in Rome, with its imposing façade and dynamic square (figure **16.5**). The plan (figure **16.6**) shows the elongation of the nave, a revision of the original centralized Greek cross plan. This alteration was the work of Carlo Maderno (1556–1629) under the Counter-Reformation pope, Paul V (papacy 1605–1621). Maderno was also responsible for the new façade, which retains Michelangelo's original two-story Orders and crowning pediment. But Maderno added the sections on either side of the steps and a balcony to dramatize the pope's public appearances.

The architect Gianlorenzo Bernini (1598–1680), who designed the **piazza** (large square) with its two huge, curved colonnades, was also in charge of the interior renovations. He described the curved colonnades metaphorically as the welcoming arms of Mother Church. The practical function of his colonnade was to permit the easy circulation of the vast crowds —over 250,000—that can be accommodated by the piazza.

Bernini's grand square is typically Baroque in its pulsating design. The trapezoidal space in front of the steps narrows as it approaches the broad oval framed by the colonnade where it expands dramatically. This use of shifting spaces, like the curved wall, was a Baroque innovation that animated its architectural forms.

16.5 Giovanni Piranesi, *View of the Façade and Square of St. Peter's*, 1750. Engraving.

N
0 100 m
0 400 ft.

1 dome
2 sacristy
3 nave
4 Sistine Chapel
5 papal palace
6 piazza of Saint Peter
7 obelisk
8 fountain

16.6 *right* **Plan of St. Peter's, the square, and surrounding area.**

The sense of dynamic movement in Baroque architecture characterizes the buildings of Bernini's rival and Maderno's nephew, Francesco Borromini (1599–1667). His church of San Carlo alle Quattro Fontane (figures **16.7** and **16.8**), named for the four fountains at the intersection of the street, belongs to the Trinitarian Order. The undulating façade is decorated with the Corinthian Order on two stories and a balustrade over the cornice. A large oval, seemingly held aloft by two angels, surmounts the façade and crowns a wall animated by statues, niches, and other decorative elements. The plan shows the oval shape and curved walls of the nave, which expands at the center and contracts at the entrance and the apse.

Although Borromini was a highly original architect, he could not rival Bernini in patronage. Apparently inclined to depression, Borromini committed suicide.

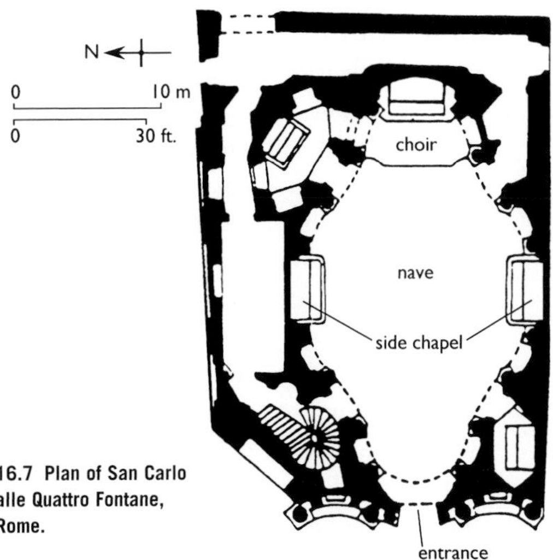

16.7 Plan of San Carlo alle Quattro Fontane, Rome.

16.8 Francesco Borromini, façade of San Carlo alle Quattro Fontane, 1665–1667.

SCULPTURE: BERNINI

Gianlorenzo Bernini was the leading sculptor, as well as the leading architect, in seventeenth-century Rome. In the course of his enormously successful career he numbered among his patrons members of the aristocracy, high-ranking clergy, and the pope. Cardinal Scipione Borghese, nephew of Pope Paul V, commissioned many works from the artist, including portraits and biblical and mythological subjects. Bernini's preferred medium, like Michelangelo's, was marble.

In the marble *David* (figure **16.9**), commissioned by Scipione Borghese, Bernini represents the biblical hero at the moment he launches the fatal stone against Goliath. Compared with the vertical mass and pent-up tension of Michelangelo's *David* (see thumbnail), Bernini's is more Baroque in its diagonal movement, open spaces, and dynamic narrative. The armor that David rejects in the biblical story lies on the ground behind him. His determined facial expression was derived from Bernini's study of his own features, for he made several drawings of himself as David.

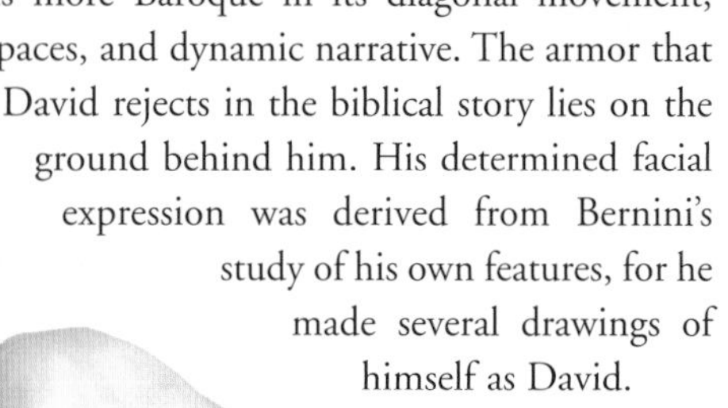

16.9 *left* Gianlorenzo Bernini, *David*, 1623. Marble, 5 ft. 6¼ in. (1.7 m) high. Borghese Gallery, Rome.

16.10 Gianlorenzo Bernini, *The Ecstasy of Saint Teresa*, 1645–1652. Marble, 11 ft. 6 in. (3.51 m) high. Cornaro Chapel, Santa Maria della Vittoria, Rome.

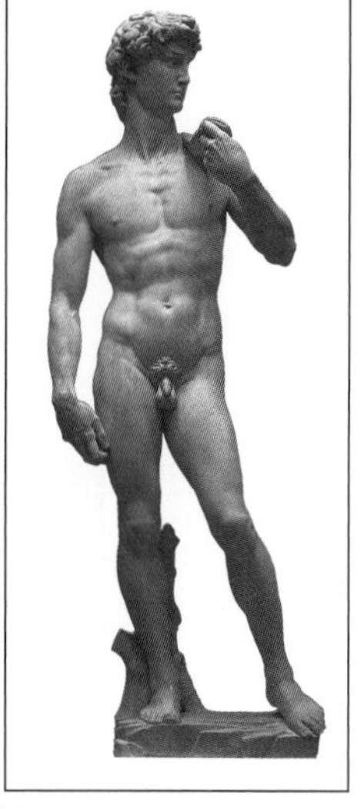

Michelangelo, *David*
see figure 14.4

Drama merges with mystical rapture in Bernini's famous *The Ecstasy of St. Teresa* (figure **16.10**). Inspired by St. Teresa's account of her mystical experiences, Bernini shows the saint in the midst of an ecstatic swoon, infused with erotic excitement. The angel is calm as he prepares to pierce Teresa with an arrow, but the saint, her lips slightly parted, is enveloped by turbulent drapery expressing her agitated state. Her ability to levitate, which she describes in her memoirs, is indicated by cloud formations and the fact that she seems to rise above the ground. Behind the figures, gilded rods denote rays of heavenly light entering the chapel and illuminating the miraculous event.

PAINTING

Illusionistic paintings on church ceilings appealed both to the Baroque taste for drama and to Counter-Reformation ideology. Church patronage was much sought after, especially by artists whose talents and religious beliefs were consistent with the aims of Church reform.

GIOVANNI BATTISTA GAULLI An example of mystical illusionism in the service of the Catholic Counter-Reformation can be seen in *The Triumph of the Name of Jesus* (figure **16.11**) by Giovanni Battista Gaulli (1639–1709) on the barrel-vaulted ceiling of Il Gesù, the Mother Church of the Jesuit Order in Rome. The painting combines the power of God's Word with elements of the Last Judgment and the bright light of divine space with the darkness of human space. The whitest light is used for the *IHS*, the first three Greek letters of *JESUS* and the monogram of the Jesuit Order. Saved souls are drawn toward the dazzling light surrounding the *IHS*, which appears to dissolve into eternal timelessness. The damned, in contrast, seem to tumble out of the oval frame into the darkness below. The fact that they are depicted as if falling into the time and space of the viewer reminds worshippers that through faith they can attain salvation.

16.11 Giovanni Battista Gaulli, *The Triumph of the Name of Jesus*, 1676–1679. Fresco with stucco figures. Ceiling vault, Il Gesù, Rome. Gaulli came to Rome from Genoa and studied with Bernini. He shared the older artist's devout Catholicism, taste for illusionism, and genius for creating dramatic environments.

CARAVAGGIO Michelangelo Merisi (1573–1610), called Caravaggio after his native town in northern Italy, was famous for his realism. Although more down-to-earth than Gaulli, Caravaggio produced many works with spiritual meaning. However, he had frequent brushes with the law, and his propensity for violence is as evident in his imagery as in his lifestyle (see Box). On the one hand, Caravaggio painted Christian scenes for the Church (figure **16.12**), including commissions for Scipione Borghese, and on the other he painted homosexual subjects for private viewing (figure **16.13**). The hallmarks of Caravaggio's style are his **tenebrism**, in which figures emerge from a darkened background, and a new intensity in the use of chiaroscuro. Light is used for symbolic as well as formal drama. The close study of nature, evident in the precise rendering of the fruit and leaves, the transparency of the glass, and the psychological portrayal of the boy, justify the artist's reputation for realism.

16.12 Caravaggio (Michelangelo Merisi), *The Conversion of St. Paul*, 1601. Oil on canvas, 7 ft. 6⅝ in. × 5 ft. 8⅞ in. (2.3 × 1.75 m). Cerasi Chapel, Santa Maria del Popolo, Rome.
Saul of Tarsus was a Jew who persecuted Christians. While traveling to Damascus, he heard the voice of Jesus asking why he persecuted him. Saul beheld a bright light and fell from his horse. Although blinded, Saul continued on his way, and when he reached Damascus, an apostle of Christ touched him and he regained his sight. Saul was then baptized a Christian and became the apostle Paul. This episode is described in Acts 9:3–9.

Society and Culture

Caravaggio: Artist and Criminal

Caravaggio's criminal record is well-documented. He began as a petty crook, given to minor acts of violence. At various times between 1600 and 1605 he was arrested for street fighting, for insulting an officer, and for throwing a plate of artichokes at a waiter. He was also sued for libel and non-payment of rent and jailed for carrying a dagger and sword without a license. In 1606 he killed a man over a tennis match and fled Rome. He escaped to Malta and in 1608 was made a Knight of Malta, an eleventh-century Order of knights dedicated to John the Baptist, which had its headquarters in Jerusalem. The Order had crusaded against the Turks and in 1530 the Holy Roman Emperor Charles V had conferred the sovereignty of Malta on the knights. The knights admired Caravaggio's work and commissioned several portraits from him, but he again became embroiled in a dispute and was expelled from the Order. Imprisoned in the Maltese jail, he escaped to Sicily and was killed in a brawl on the west coast of Italy when he was around thirty-seven years old.

Karel van Mander (1548–1606), the Flemish biographer of artists, remarked on Caravaggio's ambivalent character, which alternated between bouts of creative genius and criminality:

> *He does not study his art constantly, so that after two weeks of work he will sally forth for two months with his rapier at his side and his servant-boy after him, going from one tennis court to another, always ready to argue or fight, so that he is impossible to get along with. This is totally foreign to art; for Mars [the war god] and Minerva [goddess of war, wisdom, and weaving] have never been good friends.*

In *The Conversion of St. Paul* Caravaggio combines form with content in a miracle involving the symbolism of light. Here, light stands for eyesight, insight, and the presence of the divine. The rich red fabric intensifies the color, and the changes from light to dark are abrupt. Spatially, Caravaggio conveys the new violence of Baroque painting as Paul tumbles from his horse. He seems to fall nearly out of the picture into the space of the viewer.

Caravaggio's theatrical involvement of the viewer in the drama of the event is characteristic of Baroque style. As with Bernini's *David*, Caravaggio brings the viewer into the space and narrative of the image. The impact of Caravaggio's work was felt throughout western Europe; painters who absorbed his taste for dramatic tenebrism, tension, dynamic diagonal movements, and contrasts of light and color are known as *Caravaggisti*.

ARTEMISIA GENTILESCHI Among the *Caravaggisti*, Artemisia Gentileschi (1593–1652), daughter of the Roman painter Orazio Gentileschi, studied art at home. When she was raped

16.13 Caravaggio (Michelangelo Merisi), *Bacchus*, *c.* 1596. Oil on canvas, 3 ft. 1½ in. × 2 ft. 9½ in. (95 × 85 cm). Galleria degli Uffizi, Florence.
Caravaggio has dressed up an effeminate boy as the Roman wine god. The patron, Cardinal del Monte, encouraged Caravaggio in the early part of his career, when he painted a series of androgynous boys. This figure, with his powdered face, made-up eyebrows, and seductive gestures, flirts with a presumed male viewer to whom he offers a glass of red wine. The arrangement of the toga, leaving one shoulder bare, was a convention for seductiveness. A dish in the foreground is filled with fruit that is beginning to rot, a metaphor for the passage of time.

16.14 Artemisia Gentileschi, *Judith Slaying Holofernes*, 1612–1613. Oil on canvas, 5 ft. 6⅛ in. × 4 ft. 2¼ in. (1.68 × 1.28 m). Museo di Capodimonte, Naples.
According to the Book of Judith, the Hebrew widow of Bethulia rescued her people from the Assyrians. As the army threatened the city, Judith summoned her maidservant Abra and went to the Assyrian camp. She impressed Holofernes with her beauty, and he invited her to join his generals at dinner. Afterward, Holofernes led Judith to his tent, but he had drunk too much wine and fell into a stupor. Judith and Abra then took up his scimitar and beheaded him. They returned to Bethulia, displayed the severed head on the city wall, and the Assyrian army dispersed in terror at the sight.

by her painting teacher, who refused to marry her, her father sued him. During the trial, she, rather than the accused, was tortured to prove the veracity of her story.

Themes of violence in Artemisia's paintings and her emphasis on heroines have been linked to her own experience (figure **16.14**). She painted several pictures of women being treated unjustly by men as well as pictures in which women inflict violence on men. The theme of Judith and Holofernes, also the subject of a painting by Caravaggio, was one of her favorites. In this version, Judith and her servant Abra are illuminated against a blackened background at the most violent moment of the story. Judith plunges the scimitar through her victim's neck, and his blood flows over the sheets. Intensifying the impact of the scene is the foreground placement of Holofernes' head and its abrupt twist to one side. In addition, Holofernes is still alive enough to react to what is happening. His mouth is open as if protesting his fate, and his forehead wrinkles as his eyes gaze in horror at the very moment that they roll back in death.

MUSIC

Baroque music, like Baroque art, was expansive and dramatic. Both reflect the seventeenth-century taste for lavish, grandiose expression. "Contrast" is a key concept in understanding the music of this era—in music, usually taken to span the period from 1600 to 1750. There are contrasts between melody and accompaniment, full orchestra and soloist, loud and soft, fast and slow, declamatory and lyrical. These opposing textures and moods reflect the basic feeling of the period; its emotionalism and energy contrast with the cool classicism of the Renaissance.

BAROQUE STYLE In the Baroque era the modern system of **tonality** emerged: major and minor keys replaced the earlier modes. Standard patterns of three-note chords came to be used. They are familiar today, as they are the basis of the Classical and Romantic repertory as well as most pop music. Their sounds create a sense of momentum, with one chord seeming to push toward the next, always returning finally to the key note. Composers began to **modulate**—to change from one key to another, and back—within a piece. The effect was to establish a feeling of "home," depart from it into a contrasting realm, and then experience a sense of homecoming at the end.

With a chordal system shaping the writing of music, the idea of accompanying a melody came into its own. While there had been solo songs with lute accompaniment in the Renaissance, the basic musical texture of that period was polyphonic—with interwoven strands of melody, all of equal importance. Now the essential texture became melody plus an accompaniment provided by the **continuo** part. Continuo players were given chords to perform that would support the music above.

THE RISE OF OPERA The most important musical genre to develop in the Baroque period was opera—theater in which actors sing rather than speak their lines and music flows throughout the entire performance. Sets and costumes, lighting and stage machinery, orchestral and vocal sound merge in a grand spectacle.

Opera combined elements from various types of drama, including the *intermedio* (see Chapter 13) and the pastoral play. But it actually arose as a new genre toward the end of the sixteenth century in Florence, with a group of intellectuals—the *Camerata*—who wanted to recreate Greek drama, in which roles were sung and music was part of the performance. They composed a style of music called **monody**: solo singing with inconspicuous accompaniment. The musical line was principally meant to express the "affect" or emotional content of the words. Sometimes it was florid and **virtuosic**, at other times it declaimed the text.

Monody did not last, but from it developed a similar semi-spoken rhythmically free style known as **recitative**. Used for dialogue and narrative, lightly accompanied by continuo or by punctuating orchestral phrases, it enabled the words to be followed easily by the audience. Interspersed among the recitative were **arias**—melodic solo songs with orchestral support. Here the action stopped and a character reacted emotionally to a situation, expressing one "affect."

The typical story line was derived from Classical myth or ancient history. Initially the Greek myth of Orpheus was the most common plot, because it dealt with the power of music, which is what musicians were eager to demonstrate. Orpheus descends to Hades and tames the Furies with his singing and playing in order to win back his dead wife, Eurydice. The gods have promised him that Eurydice will be permitted to follow him out of the Underworld on condition that he does not turn and look at her. But Eurydice demands that he does look at her, Orpheus responds, and thus he loses her forever.

At first, opera was presented to courtly, aristocratic audiences, but it soon became popular outside the courts. In the course of the Baroque period, opera spread from Italy throughout Europe, especially to Germany, Austria, France, and England. Opera houses were constructed in many major European cities. Most were designed according to the social hierarchy of the audience—as in Shakespeare's Globe Playhouse (see Chapter 15): aristocrats sat in elevated boxes, whereas the general public (the groundlings) occupied the ground level.

The first great composer of opera was the Italian Claudio Monteverdi (1567–1643). His earliest opera, *Orfeo* (*Orpheus*), was composed in 1607 for the Duke of Mantua. Most of it consists of expressive dialogue, using the monodic style to convey the story of Orpheus's fear and hope as he uses his musical skill to rescue his wife from death. Dissonances and leaps convey his uncomfortable emotions; virtuosic flourishes embellish his solos, which contrast with gentle pastoral music. Monteverdi used a large, varied orchestra for *Orfeo*, including several continuo instruments, seventeen string instruments, trumpets, trombones, and recorders. It is likely that he was one of the first composers to specify particular combinations of players at certain points in the music, aiming to create specific tone colors to enhance the mood.

BAROQUE INSTRUMENTAL MUSIC Several new instrumental genres arose in the Baroque period, including the **trio sonata** and the **concerto**. The word "sonata" describes a piece to be sounded (played) rather than sung. Trio sonatas feature two melody instruments (usually violins) and continuo (generally cello and harpsichord). A seminal figure in their development was Arcangelo Corelli (1653–1713), who wrote forty-eight trio sonatas. Half of these fall into four movements—slow, fast, slow, fast—with at least one movement where the instruments take the same theme in turns and interweave it. The other twenty-four sonatas use dances derived from the folk traditions of Europe as the basis for each movement: slow, dotted rhythms in an *allemanda* (from Germany), for example, and lively triple meter in a *giga* (the jig came from Ireland and England). The dances have a simple **binary** (two-part) structure, changing key by the halfway point, and returning to the original key at the end. Music for small groups of this sort is known as **chamber music** (literally, "room music") and was written as much for the enjoyment of the players as for anyone who might listen to it.

Concertos, however, are for public performance. The earliest type, which developed in the Baroque period, was the **concerto grosso**. A small group of solo instruments (the *concertino*, often two violins and continuo) is set against the full orchestral sound (the *ripieno*) for a piece in three movements—fast, slow, fast. The fast movements form the bulk of the *concerto grosso*, with the slow section acting as a lyrical interlude. The first movement, and sometimes the last, is structured in **ritornello** form, which takes full advantage of the Baroque love of drama and contrast. A ritornello is an orchestral passage that begins a work and is then repeated, in whole or in part, between episodes where the soloists perform, usually in a more virtuosic, complex style. This is the essence of a concerto—conflict between orchestra and soloists, stable orchestral refrain versus fanciful soloistic display.

The Venetian priest Antonio Vivaldi (1678–1741) wrote about eighty *concerti grossi* and composed hundreds of solo concertos (concertos with just one solo instrument set against the orchestra). Working from 1703 as music master at a school for orphaned girls, he wrote many of these pieces for his pupils. Although Vivaldi also composed vocal music and over forty-five operas, it is for his concertos that he is primarily known. He was a skilled violinist, and about 230 of his concertos are for violin. They are energetic and sometimes technically demanding pieces with great rhythmic vitality.

Vivaldi's most widely known composition is probably *The Four Seasons* (1725). Four violin concertos represent the four seasons, musically illustrating the text of a set of sonnets. Such **program music**—instrumental music representing a non-musical idea or story—is unusual for the Baroque period (see Chapter 18). Vivaldi creates the atmosphere of each season by replicating the natural sounds associated with it. After the first ritornello of "Spring," trills of birdsong ring out on the solo violin, imitated below in the orchestra, and later in the movement thunder and lightning break through in showers of repeated notes and rapid scales. The cuckoo's call is built into the solo violin line in its first appearance in "Summer." In "Fall," the sounds of harvesting are heard, followed by drunken revelry and then a peaceful, muted slow movement as the drunkards sleep soundly and the peasants rest. "Winter" evokes shivering and scenes of skating. Whether or not one knows the poems, what they describe is clear from the music alone. *The Four Seasons* are expressive, brilliant, and memorable, and along with the rest of Vivaldi's output they would influence subsequent composers, including those as far afield as Germany.

THE BAROQUE IN SPAIN

The most important patron of the arts in Baroque Spain was King Philip IV (ruled 1621–1665). In addition to ruling as an absolute monarch and attempting to expand his influence in Europe and the New World, Philip IV was a discerning art collector who recognized genius when he saw it. He established his court in Madrid and renovated the medieval Alcázar Palace, which he used as his primary royal residence. Throughout his reign, Philip used artistic imagery to promote his political image as a powerful monarch.

LITERATURE: CERVANTES

In late-sixteenth-century Spain, the main literary form was the picaresque novel (from the Spanish word *picaro*, meaning "rogue"). This was a rambling tale in which the hero is a rogue engaged in various swindles and illicit romances. The best-known Spanish novel is *Don Quixote*, which uses some picaresque devices but which has more emotional depth and a more complex construction than the typical picaresque work. *Don Quixote*'s emphasis on the psychology of character, on the forces that motivate behavior, and on the juxtaposition of universal ideals with down-to-earth realism makes it a paradigm of the modern novel.

Miguel de Cervantes Saavedra (1547–1616), known as Cervantes, was educated by Jesuits, fought as a mercenary soldier in Italy, joined the last crusade against Muslims in Turkey, and was captured by Algerian pirates. After spending five years as a slave in Algeria, Cervantes settled into life as an administrator but was arrested for mismanaging funds. He was excommunicated and twice sent to prison, where he began writing *Don Quixote* (1605–1615).

The modern word "quixotic," meaning idealistic, optimistic, and impractical, derives from the hero of Cervantes' masterpiece. A courtly old fool searching in vain for the medieval chivalric ideal, Don Quixote meets people from all walks of life. His adventures provide the reader with a window onto Spanish society shown from two opposing viewpoints—his own rose-colored view and the realistic view of his side-kick, the peasant squire Sancho Panza. Don Quixote's eternal optimism continually clashes with the negative aspects of human nature, the truth of which escapes him but is evident to his companion. The discrepancy between Don Quixote's illusions and reality is a metaphor for the author's play with the boundaries of art and life.

Don Quixote's ideal lady, Dulcinea del Toboso, exists only in his imagination. In the following excerpt Don Quixote is determined to remain faithful to Dulcinea when he finds himself tempted by whores at an inn. He imagines that the inn is a castle and the daughter of the innkeeper a fine lady:

> Forcing her to sit down upon the bed, he [Don Quixote] began fingering her nightgown, and although it was of sack cloth, it impressed him as being of the finest and flimsiest silken gauze. On her wrists she wore some glass beads, but to him they gave off the gleam of oriental pearls. Her hair, which resembled a horse's mane rather than anything else, he decided was like filaments of the brightest gold of Araby whose splendor darkened even that of the sun. Her breath without a doubt smelled of yesterday's salad, but for Don Quixote it was a sweet and aromatic odor that came from her mouth. The short of it is, he pictured her in his imagination as having the same appearance and manners as those other princesses whom he had read about in his books.

READING SELECTION

Cervantes, *Don Quixote*, a deluded Spanish gentleman becomes a knight, PWC3-321-B

PAINTING: VELÁZQUEZ

Philip IV's court painter, Diego Rodríguez de Silva y Velázquez (1599–1660), was one of the greatest seventeenth-century artists. His wide-ranging subject matter includes genre scenes from early in his career, myth pictures, Christian events reflecting Counter-Reformation taste, and portraits of members of the royal court.

The eldest of seven children from Seville, Velázquez received a Classical education that was unusual in Spain, where 80 percent of the population was illiterate. He studied art with the humanist Francisco Pacheco, who advocated elevating painting to the status of a Liberal Art (a status already enjoyed in Spain by literature). Pacheco introduced Velázquez to the court, where he was awarded the important position of Usher of the Privy Chamber in 1627.

Velázquez's masterpiece, *Las Meninas*, also called *The Maids of Honor* (figure **16.15**), depicts a room in the Alcázar, where members of the court are assembled. The complexity of the picture has made it the subject of extensive scholarly discussion. Placed in the center is the infanta (the five-year-old daughter of Philip IV and Mariana of Austria). She commands our attention by her central placement, by the light color and intricate textures of her royal dress, and by the fact that she is the focus of two young maids. At the far right are a male and a female dwarf, and a dog. Behind this group are two more attendants, and silhouetted in the doorway is the court tapestry-master—himself a weaver of pictures. Velázquez, holding a brush and palette, depicts himself as a member of the court and as the painter of the painting. He peers at the viewer from a huge canvas, the front of which we cannot see.

Las Meninas is also a painting about the art of painting. Reflected in the mirror on the back wall are the king and queen. They seem to be watching the scene from the position of the viewer, suggesting that they, too, are in the room. If so, then,

16.15 Diego Velázquez, *Las Meninas*, 1656. Oil on canvas, 10 ft. 6⅜ in. × 9 ft. 2⅝ in. (3.21 × 2.81 m). Prado, Madrid. The red cross of the noble Order of Santiago on the artist's coat is a mark of aristocratic distinction. Since Velázquez completed the painting in 1656 and was admitted into the Order in 1658, it would appear that he added the cross later. Knighthood was consistent with his ambition—for his art as well as for himself—to be elevated to noble status.

16.16 Diego Velázquez, *Diego de Acedo, called "El Primo,"* 1644. Oil on canvas, 6 ft. 5½ in. × 2 ft. 9 in. (1.97 × 0.84 m). Prado, Madrid.

they simultaneously observe from the front and back of the scene. This gives them an implicit power as both viewers and participants, while also conveying the dynastic importance of the infanta. The circular shape of the red curtain over Philip's head (note that he is in front of the queen, showing his higher status) alludes to his political image as the solar Planet King.

On the walls are pictures from the royal collection, which seem to continue in the rectangular mirror and doorway. By this arrangement, Velázquez plays with the theme of paintings within paintings (on the walls), of mirror images (the king and queen), and of the framed tapestry-master.

Among the most popular figures at the Spanish court were dwarves, who became a rich source of individual portraits by Velázquez (figure **16.16**). In the portrait of Diego de Acedo, known as El Primo, the dwarf is pensive, his gaze downcast. The silhouetting of the hat and coat is juxtaposed with El Primo's illuminated face and hands, and the large book accentuates his small size. Shifting, muted browns and yellows in the overcast sky reflect the dwarf's inner turmoil.

SPANISH ARCHITECTURE IN THE NEW WORLD

Philip IV's expansionist ambitions extended to the New World. He coveted raw materials, including gold and silver, from South America and also wanted to impose Spanish culture on the native populations. This is reflected in the missionary zeal of the Spanish Jesuits, which led to extensive church-building in the New World. In the American Southwest, mission churches combined the building material and style of Native American Pueblos with the Latin cross basilica plan of western Europe. In Acoma, New Mexico, the Mission Church of San Estevan (figures **16.17** and **16.18**) was built under the supervision of the Spanish missionary Fray Juan Ramirez, who arrived in Acoma in 1629, eight years after Philip ascended the throne.

The plan shows the long nave, with an altar at one end and the entrance at the other. The façade, like church façades in Europe, is divided into three sections: a central door and window are surmounted by a cross, with a sturdy, imposing tower on either side. The square cloister, also a European feature, has projecting wooden beams characteristic of the American Southwest.

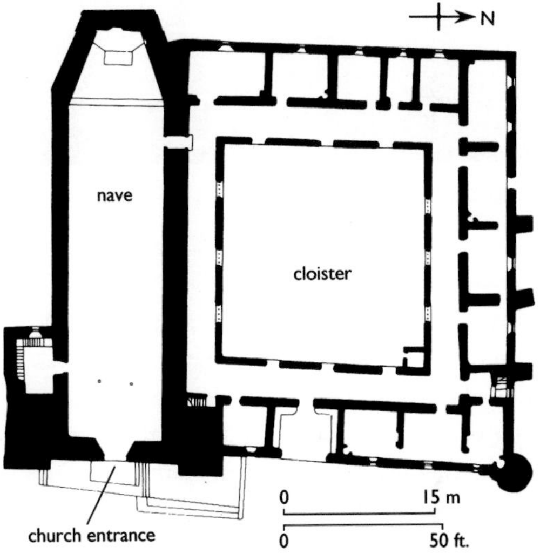

16.17 *above* Plan of Mission Church of San Estevan, Acoma, New Mexico.

16.18 Mission Church of San Estevan, Acoma, *c.* 1629.

16.19 Mexico City Cathedral, 1656–1671.

In Mexico City, the Spanish built a huge cathedral (figure **16.19**) on the ruins of the Templo Mayor, which was a double pyramid dedicated to the Aztec gods of water and war in the Aztec city of Tenochtitlán. In so doing, the Spanish emphasized the destruction of Tenochtitlán by the *conquistadores* (see Chapter 14) and the imposition of Christianity on the conquered culture. Mexico City and its cathedral became central to the New Spain established in the New World. The cathedral combined Italian prototypes and forms derived from Classical models with a superimposed, elaborate stucco design. Its cross-plan structure is symmetrical and expands horizontally to accommodate the five naves. The lower section is more Baroque in its ornate character than the sturdy, square bell towers, which are surmounted by bell-shaped features.

ABSOLUTISM AND THE FRENCH COURT

Louis XIV of France (ruled 1643–1715) was the seventeenth century's most powerful monarch, and his seventy-two year reign was the longest in the history of France. Since antiquity, rulers had used the sun as an image of royal power and divine right, but Louis XIV took the symbolism to new heights. He developed a royal iconography depicting himself as the Sun King—solar center, fertilizing power, and light of the universe. Each day visiting dignitaries, together with Louis's courtiers, were accorded the honor of attending the king as he rose, like the sun, from bed in the morning (the ritual of *lever*) and retired with the sun to bed in the evening (the ritual of *coucher*). According to tradition, the Sun King also proclaimed *l'état, c'est moi* ("I am the state").

Louis XIV, a member of the French Bourbon dynasty, was four years old in 1643 when his father, Louis XIII (ruled 1610–1643), died. Louis XIII's reign had been dominated by his chief minister, Cardinal Richelieu (in office 1624–1642), one of the greatest forces in establishing the absolute power of the French king. He not only made alliances with Protestants when necessary, but also was determined to minimize the influence of the Holy Roman Empire. Inside France, Richelieu advocated a strong centralized government, persecuted the Huguenots, and created a large army.

Louis XIV's mother, Anne of Austria, ruled as regent until he assumed sole power in 1661. As a child, Louis XIV was tutored by the court preacher and Catholic philosopher Bossuet, who engrained in the young heir the legitimacy of divine right and the importance of political control, which became the hallmark of Louis XIV's style. Bossuet also urged the revocation of Henry IV's relatively tolerant Edict of Nantes of 1685 (see Chapter 15), resulting in the departure of several hundred thousand Huguenots for England, Holland, and Switzerland. Louis's ministers revamped the French army, standardizing uniforms, imposing rigorous training, and organizing the military hierarchy. By the end of the seventeenth century France had the largest army and was the most powerful nation in Europe.

Much of Louis's success in controlling France was due to the skill of his ministers. After Richelieu's death in 1642, Cardinal Mazarin, an Italian by birth, became the court's main adviser, a position he held from 1643 to 1661. He supervised the king's political education and taught him how to rule. Mazarin also controlled internal unrest among the peasants and quelled a revolt among the nobles known as the Fronde. At first launched by the parliament of Paris (a law court), the Fronde spread to the high nobility who opposed Anne's regency and Mazarin's control of the young king.

When Mazarin died in 1661, Louis was twenty-three. He then assumed personal rule of France—that is, he ruled without a prime minister—although he did appoint Jean-Baptiste Colbert (1619–1683) minister of finance. Colbert improved the economic independence of France, promoted **mercantilism**, and supervised developments in the arts.

16.20 **Jean Lepautre, a performance of Lully's *Alceste* in Louis Le Vau's Marble Court at Versailles, day one of a series of six prints recording a fête held in 1674 by Louis XIV to celebrate France's reconquest of the Franche-Comté, reprint of 1675–1676 plate. Engraving, plate 11⅞ × 16⅝ in. (30.2 × 42.2 cm), sheet 19¼ × 26¼ in. (48.9 × 66.7 cm). The Metropolitan Museum of Art, New York.** This particular play is based on Euripides' tragedy *Alcestis*, which opens with Apollo having been banished from Mount Olympos and forced to work for a mortal. The god admires his taskmaster, Admetus, and promises him that when it is his time to die the Fates will accept anyone willing to die in his place. When Admetus's wife, Alcestis, offers to die for him, he regrets the agreement. At the end of the play, Heracles restores Alcestis to life.

The Arts under Louis XIV

By 1635 Cardinal Richelieu had established the French Royal Academy to unify and standardize the language, create an official dictionary of the French language, and codify the rules of French grammar. In 1648 Mazarin founded the Royal Academy of Painting and Sculpture, which Colbert reorganized in 1663. Artists in the Academy had to be classically trained, and subject matter was ranked according to a hierarchy of importance, from still life on the lowest tier to landscape, genre, portraiture, history, and the Christian Sacraments in ascending order.

By establishing such rigid rules, the Academy incited opposition, leading to the quarrel between the Ancients and the Moderns. The Ancients argued that art should obey the Classical rules of order, symmetry, and clarity, whereas the Moderns wanted to relax the rules and explore new approaches to style and technique. Despite these Classical leanings, however, the culture of Louis XIV's court was Baroque in its insistence on spectacle and elaborate dramatic effects in all the arts.

Rules and royal academies were created for science, architecture, music, dance, and theater, as well as for languages and the visual arts. Louis XIV founded the Royal Academy of Music in 1669. His court composer, Giovanni Battista Lulli (1632–1687), like Mazarin a native of Italy, found it prudent to gallicize his name to Jean-Baptiste Lully. He established the style of French opera—spectacular courtly productions of tragic Greek or legendary plots, with big choral and ceremonial scenes including dance (figure **16.20**). Known as *tragédies lyriques*, these operas consisted of a prologue and five acts. Later in the Baroque period, the form was taken up by Jean-Philippe Rameau (1683–1764). He wrote some thirty operas, among them *Hippolyte et Aricie*, which has a Classical plot inspired by Racine's *Phèdre* (see p. 448). Musically, French opera differs from Italian opera: it has a more continuous flow, with less distinction between recitative and aria. French recitative is more declamatory than its Italian counterpart; arias are shorter and simpler.

Versailles

During the 1660s Louis moved his court from the Louvre in Paris to the small town of Versailles, about 15 miles (24 km) away. The size of Louis's court, which included the entire administration of government, accommodations for the royal family and its 4000 servants, horses, dogs, and the army (totaling over 9000 men), was unprecedented. In the late 1670s work began on a large palace at Versailles. The building itself is a long horizontal, with two stories of large, round-arched windows and a third story with square windows. Above, the space is animated by a balustrade decorated with statues.

The palace grounds at Versailles included some 1400 fountains and extensive formal gardens divided into geometric *parterres* (figure **16.21**)—flowerbeds framed by neatly trimmed hedges. The elaborate fountains associate the king with Apollo,

16.21 **North Parterre, Versailles.**

16.22 *left* **Balthasar and Gaspard Marsy, Latona Fountain, Versailles, 1668–1670. Marble. Revised by Jules Hardouin-Mansart, 1687–1689.**
In Greek myth, Apollo and his twin sister, Artemis (the moon goddess), were the children of Zeus and the mortal Latona. Fleeing Hera's jealousy, Latona was given sanctuary on the island of Delos, but when she stopped to drink at a lake, she was accosted by peasants who leaped up and down, stirring up mud and making the water undrinkable. When Latona called on the gods for assistance, they turned the peasants into frogs. These are represented, along with lizards and turtles, around the base of the fountain.

and the Latona Fountain (figure **16.22**), situated along the Allée Royale (Royal Way), is based on a description of Apollo's birth in Ovid's *Metamorphoses* (see Chapter 7). Latona, signifying Louis's divine lineage through Zeus, stands at the top, whereas the "sub-human" peasants below have been changed into croaking frogs. Like those who rebelled against the king, the frogs make noise but in the end are ineffective.

Louis XIV was not simply being an astute politician when he used the grounds and images at Versailles to glorify himself. He was also personally interested in the arts, which he lavishly promoted. His early education had included drawing, music, dance, and theater, and on more than one occasion he himself performed the role of Apollo (figure **16.23**). The importance of dance at Louis XIV's court is reflected in the social necessity of being an accomplished dancer. As a result, most aristocrats hired dance masters, which eventually led to the art of ballet as it is known today.

16.23 Louis XIV dancing the role of the Sun in the 1653 *Ballet de la Nuit*. $10^3/_4 \times 7$ in. (27.5×18 cm). Bibliothèque Nationale, Paris.

LITERARY REFLECTIONS OF THE FRENCH COURT: MME DE SÉVIGNÉ AND MME DE LAFAYETTE

Literature was highly regarded in the France of Louis XIV. At a time when letter-writing was an art, the letters of Mme de Sévigné (1626–1696) to her daughter create a vivid picture of French society. Born during the reign of Louis XIII and orphaned at the age of seven, Marie de Rabutin-Chantal was raised by relatives. When she was eighteen, she married Henri, Marquis de Sévigné, a brilliant but unfaithful husband. After her daughter married and went to live in the South of France, Mme de Sévigné wrote to her about the society in which she circulated. She describes urban and courtly lifestyles and comments on the leading intellectuals of the day.

READING SELECTION

Madame de Sévigné, *Letters*, an inside view of Louis XIV's court, PWC4-091

Mme de Sévigné's younger contemporary, Madame de Lafayette (1634–1693), was born Marie-Madeleine Pioche de La Vergne in Paris. She married the Count of Lafayette and frequented the literary and social circles of the city. In 1678 she published her classic novel, *La Princesse de Clèves* (*The Princess of Cleves*), which is set in the brilliant court of Henry II but actually reflects the court of Louis XIV. The plot revolves around the romantic life of the princess and explores the psychology of love. The princess, though married, falls in love with the duke of Nemours, which she confesses to her husband. When the Prince of Cleves dies of a broken heart, the princess confesses her love to Nemours but refuses his offer of marriage and ends her life in seclusion. Although Mme de Lafayette's court is populated with elegant characters circulating in resplendent settings, they obey the code of chivalry, leaving passions unsatisfied and the ideal of chastity upheld.

FRENCH THEATER

France witnessed a great revival of drama under Louis XIV, who enjoyed theater so much that he established La Comédie Française in 1687. All three giants of seventeenth-century French theater—Pierre Corneille (1606–1684), Jean Racine (1639–1699), and Jean-Baptiste Poquelin (1622–1673), known as Molière—were at times patronized by Louis XIV. When their plays included music and dance, they worked with the court composer, Lully.

Relaxing the ancient unity of action, Baroque plays often take place in several settings, and the action can extend over a period of days or even years. Baroque theater also introduced supernatural elements along with realistic narratives, and episodes of violence, combat, and assassinations were shown on stage. Although much of this was already present in the plays of Shakespeare, there was a new emphasis on the overt display of emotion and scenes of hysteria and madness.

PIERRE CORNEILLE Pierre Corneille dominated French theater during the first half of the century. He was born into a bourgeois family in Rouen, north of Paris, and was the eldest of seven children. Educated by Jesuits, Corneille studied law and worked as an attorney. After he began writing plays, mainly romantic comedies, he came to the attention of Cardinal Richelieu. The author's fortunes rose and fell in the course of his career depending on the reaction of the public and the court.

Corneille's characters are psychologically complex. Typically they are confronted with conflicts between such grand emotions as glory (*la gloire*), passion, faith, and loyalty. In his dramatic resolutions, Corneille shows himself to be a humanist and an advocate of free will.

His first major success, *Le Cid*, came in 1636, when he was thirty years old; it was translated into nearly every European language. The play is set in Spain and is based on a Spanish story, in which honor conflicts with romance to create an impossible situation for a pair of lovers. The hero, Rodrigue, is duty-bound to kill the father of his mistress Chimène, and she, in turn, is duty-bound to demand the head of Rodrigue. Chimène says:

> Tu t'es, en m'offensant, montré digne de moi:
> Je me dois, par ta mort, montrer digne de toi.
> ("In offending me, you showed yourself worthy of me:
> I must, by your death, show myself worthy of you.")

Figure **16.24** shows a scene from *Le Cid*, in which Don Diego, Rodrigue's father, hands over his sword to his son saying:

> My arm no longer has the strength to lift this sword, I entrust it to you [to use in meting out] vengeance and punishment.

Le Cid does not strictly follow the Classical rules of unity described by Aristotle. Although the characters are simple, the plot is complex and extends beyond twenty-four hours. The action takes place in the city of Seville, but the setting changes from scene to scene. These departures from the Classical unities unleashed a quarrel that raged among intellectuals well beyond France. Arguments reached such a pitch that the play was closed down. Eventually, in 1676, after Corneille had retired, he regained favor with the court and six of his tragedies were performed at Versailles.

JEAN RACINE Jean Racine's earliest and greatest plays are based on ancient history, legend, and myth, but after 1677 he turned to Christian subjects. His main theme is self-destruction caused by uncontrollable passion. Raised at Port-Royal and influenced by the Jansenist rejection of free will, Racine contemplated the consequences of human choice overcome by fate.

16.24 Act 5, scene 1, *Le Cid*.
In this photograph of Gérard Philipe (right) and Jean Vilar (left), two of the greatest twentieth-century French actors, the sword is transferred from father to son. The gesture is emblematic of family loyalty and vengeance, and the sword itself was a sign of noble prerogative.

In *Andromaque* (*Andromache*), produced in 1667, Racine's heroine is the widow of the Trojan hero Hector. She is entangled in issues involving the Greek treatment of captives, whether to marry a Greek warrior, and the fate of her son Astyanax, who is killed by the Greeks. *Britannicus* (1670) deals with an episode from the life of Nero and his mother, Agrippina, whom he eventually has murdered (see Chapter 7). In *Iphigénie* (*Iphigenia*), which was performed at Versailles in 1674, Racine revisits the tragedy of Agamemnon's daughter whose sacrifice enables the Greek ships to set sail for Troy (see Chapter 4).

Phèdre (1677) is based on a Greek myth about illicit passion on the part of an older woman for her stepson. Phèdre marries the Greek king Theseus but falls in love with his grown son Hippolytus. Enraged because her passion is unrequited, she falsely accuses Hippolytus to his father. Theseus kills his son, only to learn later of Phèdre's treachery.

MOLIÈRE Molière was born in Paris, where his father worked for the royal tapestry works. After an early start as an actor, Molière turned to writing and directing, though he continued to act in his own plays throughout his career. He was influenced by the tradition of Roman comedy, but his settings are French interiors rather than the street scenes typical of Terence and Plautus (see Chapter 7). Through what today would be called "drawing-room farce," enhanced by music and dance, Molière creates amusement in the most reprehensible characters, some of whom have become paradigms of their vice.

Molière's first major play, *L'École des femmes* (*The School for Wives*), appeared in 1662. A satire about an octagenarian who undertakes the education of a four-year-old girl to be the perfect wife, the play caused a scandal with its exposure of the folly of illusion and mockery of contemporary manners.

In *Le Bourgeois Gentilhomme* (*The Bourgeois Gentleman*, 1670) the main character, M. Jourdain, is satirized for social pretensions typical of the nouveau riche. In his efforts to become a gentleman Jourdain is astounded to discover that he has been speaking prose his entire life. His famous line, delivered with expansive, pompous authority, *Tout ce qui n'est point prose est vers, et tout ce qui n'est point vers est prose* ("All that is not prose is verse, and all that is not verse is prose"), sums up the pretensions of a man who aspires to rise above his station.

Molière's *Tartuffe* (1664) exposes hypocrisy. He was forced to rewrite the play after the Church declared it anti-Catholic and banned it. *Le Misanthrope* (1666) explores the misanthrope's disenchantment with humanity, and in *L'Avare* (*The Miser*, 1668) Harpagon embodies stinginess. Finally, in *Le Malade imaginaire* (*The Hypochondriac*), produced in 1673 at the end of his life, Molière deals with a hero haunted by the fear of death, who seeks solace in attention from others.

In exposing hypocrisy and revealing social pretension, Molière's plays caused more than one scandal. Nevertheless, Louis XIV liked Molière's work and hired his theatrical company, the King's Troupe. When Molière died, the Church denied him a Christian burial in retaliation for his criticism of the clergy. The king interceded and the Church relented, but agreed only to a small, insignificant service.

READING SELECTION

Molière, *Le Bourgeois Gentilhomme*, on how to become a gentleman, PWC4-094-B

16.25 Nicolas Poussin, *Et in Arcadia Ego*, 1638–1639. Oil on canvas, $33\frac{1}{2} \times 47\frac{5}{8}$ in. (85×121 cm). Louvre, Paris.
Three shepherds who live in Arcadia have come upon a tomb inscribed "I, too, [lived] in Arcadia [*et in Arcadia Ego*]." At their first premonition of death, the shepherds are frozen on learning that they, too, will die. One traces the inscription with his finger, his shadow cast on the stone a prefiguration of his own death. The woman is Clio, the Greek Muse of History, an allusion to the passage of time.

16.26 Claude Lorrain, *Landscape with Merchants*, *c.* 1630. Oil on canvas, $38^{1}/_{4} \times 56^{1}/_{2}$ in. (97.2 × 143.6 cm). National Gallery of Art, Washington, D.C. Minute figures of elegant merchants bringing their wares to the local inhabitants are barely visible in the foreground. The contrast between local and exotic costumes indicates that two worlds are crossing paths. Overwhelming the figures, however, is the vast landscape, with its harbors, and a mill and fortified tower in the distance. The idyllic present of the landscape is juxtaposed with a fading, misty horizon that seems to go on forever.

PAINTING: NICOLAS POUSSIN AND CLAUDE LORRAIN

Two major French painters of the seventeenth century preferred Rome to the court of Louis XIV. Nicolas Poussin (*c.* 1594–1665) found the intrigues of Versailles unbearable; Rome was more congenial to his clear, crisp manner of painting, which was a Classical form of Baroque. Poussin's *Et in Arcadia Ego* (figure **16.25**) combines Classical pastoral subject matter with traditional Christian iconography and warns that death is inevitable.

Claude Lorrain (1600–1682), originally Claude Gelée, also worked in Italy, living in Rome from the age of thirteen. He produced mainly landscape paintings, a genre that became popular in the seventeenth century. Lorrain's landscapes convey the atmospheric effects of transitional times of day—sunrise and sunset—reflecting the Baroque interest in the dramatic use of light and dark (figure **16.26**).

NORTHERN EUROPE

In 1566 William I, Prince of Orange, had led a rebellion in the Netherlands against Philip II of Spain. Although raised as a Catholic, Prince William converted first to Lutheranism and then to Calvinism. When Protestant Holland gained its freedom from Spain in 1609, a constitutional government was established that recognized the rights of citizens and limited the power of the state.

Although its small size and precarious geography below sea level were a constant concern, Holland was a prosperous mercantile, bourgeois society. Foreign trade and banking were the main sources of commerce, and when the Dutch East India Company was founded in 1602, the Netherlands quickly supplanted Portugal in the trade of spices, cotton, silks, and porcelain goods. In 1642 the Dutch explorer Abel Tasman (*c.* 1603–*c.* 1659) discovered New Zealand. The mercantile and colonial success of the Dutch led to commercial wars with England that lasted from 1652 to 1674.

In Flanders (modern Belgium), which remained Catholic after the Reformation, ties with Spain persisted. The leading Flemish painter was Peter Paul Rubens (1577–1640), who worked as a diplomat for the Spanish court and received commissions from the court of Versailles.

PETER PAUL RUBENS

A prodigious artist with a large workshop, Rubens traveled widely in Europe and spoke five languages. He was born in Germany to former Catholics who had converted to Calvinism. When his father died, his mother returned to the Catholic Church and moved to Antwerp. Rubens himself was a devout Catholic and produced many pictures for the Church, although he also executed mythological and political commissions. He worked for Philip IV of Spain, studied for years in Italy, and advised Velázquez to do likewise. One of his greatest series of paintings is the cycle celebrating Marie de' Medici.

16.27 **Peter Paul Rubens, *The Journey of Marie de' Medici*, 1622–1625. Oil on canvas, 14 ft. 11 in. × 9 ft. 6 in. (3.94 × 2.95 m). Louvre, Paris.**

husband and she the jealous wife. Below, a personification of France in the guise of Minerva (the Roman goddess of war and wisdom) encourages Henry's infatuation with his queen.

The voluptuous flesh, broad brushstrokes, and rich colors and textures of Rubens's style allied him with the Moderns. Soon the aesthetic quarrel that had originated at the Versailles court would become known as the *Rubénistes* versus the *Poussinistes*: the former championed the exuberant energy of Baroque, whereas the latter worked in a more subdued, Classicizing version of the style.

Painting in Holland

In Holland the decline of the Catholic Church and the rise of a middle class interested in decorating its homes, guildhalls, and other institutions led to increasingly secular patronage. Professional organizations often commissioned group portraits such as Frans Hals's (*c.* 1580–1666) *Officers of the Haarlem Militia Company of St. Adrian* (figure **16.29**) and *The Anatomy Lesson of Dr. Nicolaes Tulp* (figure **16.30**) by Rembrandt van Rijn (1606–1669). Note the typically Baroque diagonals, the

THE MARIE DE' MEDICI CYCLE Marie de' Medici was the widow of Henry IV, the mother and regent of Louis XIII, and the grandmother of Louis XIV. She commissioned twenty-four enormous paintings from Rubens to commemorate herself as the French queen. Between 1622 and 1625 Rubens took on the difficult task of transforming a plain and unpopular queen into a glamorous, fashionable, and politically attractive heroine.

In figure **16.27** Marie de' Medici, in a royal fleur-de-lys robe, rides a white horse, whose flowing mane echoes her own feathered headdress. Her retinue—a woman with a lion, a winged Victory with a laurel wreath, and a trumpeting sky god—proclaims her triumphant journey to France. In figure **16.28** a dazzled Henry IV is presented with Marie's portrait by Cupid and a god of marriage. Two small cupids play with the king's armor, indicating that he is disarmed by the beauty of Marie de' Medici. Juno with her peacock and Jupiter with his eagle enjoy marital bliss in heaven, which is actually a revisionist portrayal of the Olympian rulers. For, in Classical myth, Jupiter and Juno were at odds—he the philandering

16.28 *right* **Peter Paul Rubens, *Henry IV Receiving the Portrait of Marie de' Medici*, 1622–1625. Oil on canvas, 12 ft. 11 1/8 in. × 9 ft. 8 1/2 in. (3.94 × 2.95 m). Louvre, Paris.**

16.29 Frans Hals, *Officers of the Haarlem Militia Company of St. Adrian*, 1627. Oil on canvas, 6 ft. × 8 ft. 8 in. (1.83 × 2.67 m). Frans Halsmuseum, Haarlem, Holland.
This picture of a convivial militia company at one of its social gatherings is enlivened by the broad diagonals of the flags, sashes, ruddy complexions, and the detailed description of costume and still-life objects on the table. Some of the men converse, while others seem to enjoy posing for their portraits.

uncertain placement of the figures, and the highlights of light. The broad areas of dark in *The Anatomy Lesson* reflect the influence of Caravaggio's tenebrism in the North.

REMBRANDT VAN RIJN Rembrandt was born in Leiden, and studied Latin for seven years before deciding to be an artist. He moved to Amsterdam in 1631 and soon became the city's leading portrait painter. Most of his portraits were painted on commission, but other subjects, usually uncommissioned, include biblical and mythological scenes, and landscapes.

Rembrandt was unique in his time for his approach to patronage. He disliked working on commission, for which pictures were generally priced by subject or size. Instead, he wanted his work to be priced according to the reputation of the artist. In this regard, Rembrandt revised the essential nature of the art market. Thus, after he painted *Aristotle with*

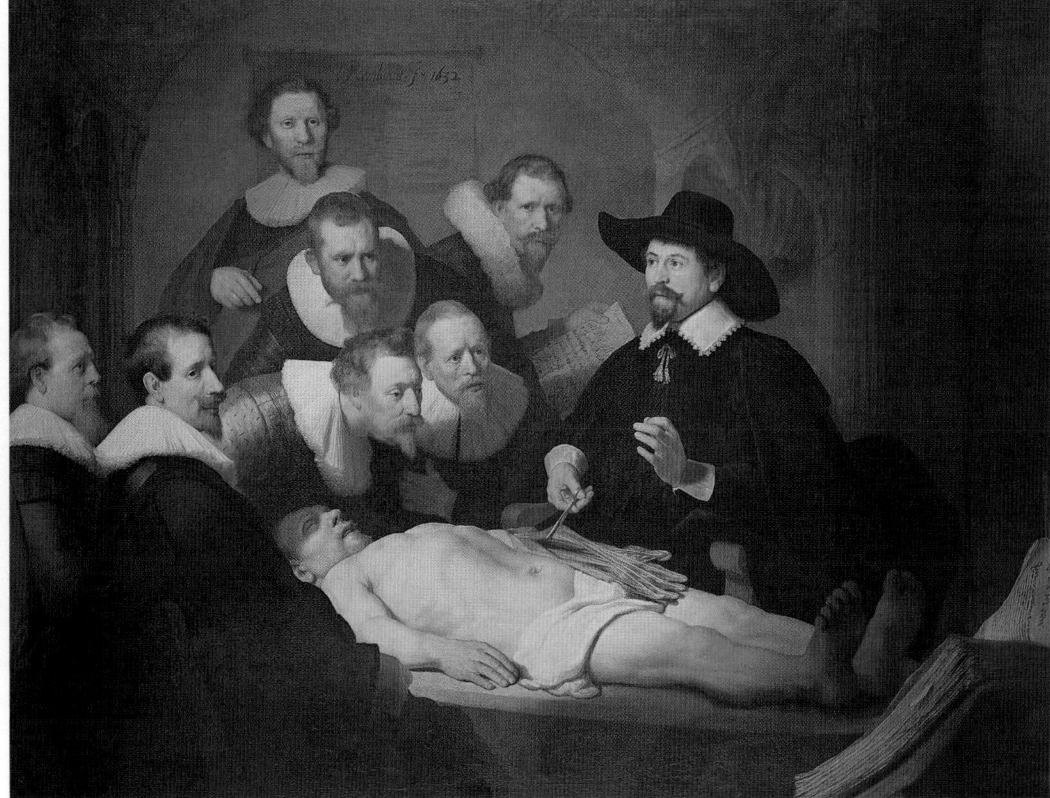

16.30 Rembrandt van Rijn, *The Anatomy Lesson of Dr. Nicolaes Tulp*, 1632. Oil on canvas, 5 ft. 3⅛ in. × 7 ft. 1¼ in. (1.16 × 2.17 m). Mauritshuis, The Hague.
This was Rembrandt's first major group portrait, painted in Amsterdam when he was twenty-six. It depicts members of the Guild of Physicians and Surgeons attending a dissection. The anatomy text at the right might be a copy of Vesalius's book, reflecting the new empirical approach to the human body that had been banned by the Catholic Church.

16.31 Rembrandt van Rijn, *Aristotle with a Bust of Homer*, 1653. Oil on canvas, 4 ft. $8\frac{1}{2}$ in. × 4 ft. $5\frac{3}{4}$ in. (1.43 × 1.36 m). The Metropolitan Museum of Art, New York.

Rembrandt shows Aristotle in contemporary Dutch costume. His broad gold chain and the gold threads of his sleeves reflect yellow light. The subtle shading that seems to reveal the inner psychology of Aristotle also reveals Rembrandt's genius for conveying character. The philosopher rests his hand meditatively on the marble bust of Homer, his great predecessor. Because Homer was blind, Aristotle contacts him through the sense of touch. The pile of books at the left alludes to Classical literary tradition.

a Bust of Homer (figure **16.31**) he sold it to a wealthy nobleman in Sicily for the large sum of 500 florins. The price reflected Rembrandt's high reputation in Italy.

Rembrandt is known for his skill in etching as well as in oil painting. In both media, he created numerous self-portraits, chronicling his features as he aged and as his fortunes changed. His *Self-portrait with Saskia* (figure **16.32**), for example, is an etching that shows an exuberant artist with his young wife. His hat tilts rakishly and his cheerful gaze is direct. Saskia, looking plump and contented, is seated at the other side of the table. Here Rembrandt varies the surface lights from pure white to solid black, with degrees of hatching and cross-hatching creating the shaded areas. The sharp contrasts of light and dark as well as the predominant diagonals are characteristic features of Baroque style.

Overlapping with part of the Baroque period in Europe, the Mughal dynasty in India promoted cross-cultural exchanges in art and also, contrary to more conservative Islamic practice, encouraged figurative art at the court. Some European rulers sent ambassadors to India and received Indian ambassadors at their courts. Indian artists borrowed Western motifs, and Western artists were aware of the Mughal style (see Box, p. 454).

JUDITH LEYSTER The Dutch portrait painter Judith Leyster (1609–1690) worked, like Frans Hals, in the small town of Haarlem, where she was the only woman in the painter's guild. Her *Self-portrait* (figure **16.33**) combines genre with

16.32 Rembrandt van Rijn, *Self-portrait with Saskia*, 1636. Etching, 4 × $3\frac{3}{4}$ in. (10.4 × 9.5 cm).

16.33 Judith Leyster, *Self-portrait*, *c.* 1630. Oil on canvas, $29\frac{3}{8}$ × $25\frac{5}{8}$ in. (74.6 × 65.1 cm). National Gallery of Art, Washington, D.C.

portraiture. She depicts herself as pausing to face the viewer while painting a musician wearing a richly colored blue outfit. Her face is highlighted and framed by a large lace collar and cap, and her lips are a striking highlight of red.

JAN VERMEER Jan Vermeer (1632–1675) of Delft is known for his interior scenes, striking pinpoints of light, detailed textures, and the contemplative intensity of his figures. Married with fifteen children, he remained a local painter his entire life and, unlike Rembrandt, was a Catholic. When Vermeer died, Anton van Leeuwenhoek, who ground lenses for microscopes (see p. 433), was appointed trustee of his estate.

Vermeer's imagery contrasts the intimacy of an enclosed setting with the sense that his figures participate in the world outside. This is particularly true of *The Astronomer* (figure **16.34**), which is signed and dated 1668. Although very much inside and surrounded by domestic objects, the astronomer studies the celestial globe—an actual globe currently in use—with a text by a contemporary scientist open on the table. The light shining through the window, illuminating the interior and highlighting the globe and the book, is a reminder of the vast spaces newly visible with the invention of the telescope.

The painting on the wall is the *Finding of Moses*, which at the time was paralleled typologically with the Nativity of Christ. This reflects the tradition of relating biblical events with the stars, indicating the continuing appeal of astrology. Just as Boyle's work led to the evolution of chemistry from alchemy, so the seventeenth century witnessed the development of astronomy, which gradually superseded the age-old practice of astrology.

16.35 Jan Vermeer, *Girl with a Pearl Earring*, *c.* 1665. Oil on canvas, 18¼ × 15¾ in. (45 × 40 cm). Mauritshuis, The Hague.

In the *Girl with a Pearl Earring* (figure **16.35**), which appears to be a portrait, the figure is set against a dark background, thereby increasing the three-dimensional effect. The close-up view adds to the intimacy between viewer and figure and accentuates the delicate lighting. Vermeer's characteristic pinpoints of light can be seen in the headdress, eyes, lips, and, especially, the earring. As the girl turns toward the viewer, she creates the impression that something, or someone, has caught her attention—but the artist does not identify who or what that might be.

16.34 *left* Jan Vermeer, *The Astronomer*, 1668. Oil on canvas, 20 × 18 in. (50.8 × 46.3 cm). Louvre, Paris.

Cross-cultural Influences

Mughal Art and Western Europe

Roughly contemporary with the Baroque period in Europe, three emperors of the Muslim Mughal dynasty in India—Akbar (ruled 1556–1605), Jahangir (ruled 1605–1627), and Shah Jahan (ruled 1627–1658)—encouraged narrative art and naturalism rather than adhering to the Islamic proscription against figurative images. Akbar collected Western art and hired Hindu artists to combine Eastern and Western themes, especially in miniatures created for the court (figure **16.36**). In 1580 he invited a group of Jesuit missionaries to his court, and they brought with them examples of Western art, which influenced Indian painters.

Tolerance remained characteristic of the Mughals in India until 1658, when Shah Jahan was ousted by his more traditional Muslim son, who put an end to figurative, Western-influenced imagery. Indian artists then returned to traditional Islamic forms.

Rembrandt's copy of a Mughal miniature (figure **16.37**) reflects the cross-cultural influence between East and West at a time when Europe, especially the Netherlands, was involved in establishing commercial trading companies in Asia. Note the artist's attention to the figure's Eastern costume and physiognomy.

16.36 *left* **Basawan, *The Virgin and Child*, from a Muraqqa Album, Mughal, reign of Akbar *c.* 1590. Opaque watercolor and gold on paper, full page 15¾ × 9¾ in. (40 × 24.7 cm.) San Diego Museum of Art.**
In this example, the Virgin nurses Christ in a Far Eastern setting. Whereas the figures are naturalistic and rendered three-dimensionally, they occupy a space flattened by the patterned Persian rug.

16.37 Rembrandt van Rijn, *Shah Jahan*, copy of a Mughal miniature, 1654–1656. Drawing, pen and bistre sepia wash, 8⅞ × 6¾ in. (22.5 × 17.1 cm). Von Hirsch Collection, Basle.

MUSIC

In Germany in the year 1685, two boys were born who would prove to be among the greatest composers ever: Johann Sebastian Bach (1685–1750) and George Frideric Handel (1685–1759). Between them they wrote in all the major musical genres of the time, sacred and secular, vocal and instrumental. Bach is probably most noted for his **fugues**, his **cantatas** and **Passions** for the Church, and orchestral works such as the Brandenburg Concertos. Handel was celebrated in his day as an opera composer of international standing; today his best-known work is the **oratorio** *Messiah*.

The fugue is an important Baroque musical form. Originating in the polyphony of earlier eras, it was brought to perfection by Bach in his compositions for organ and for harpsichord. In a fugue, each voice or instrument enters in turn with the same theme (known as the subject). As the music proceeds, the texture grows fuller and more complex. Once all the parts have entered, the composer uses various ingenious techniques to adapt the subject, like stretching it out in longer notes or turning it upside-down; often, the subject is firmly restated in the final section of the fugue.

Fitting the different strands of music together in a fugue is a difficult technical exercise, but Bach brings it off to rewarding musical effect, for example, in *The Well-Tempered Keyboard*. This collection of forty-eight preludes and fugues was composed between around 1722 and 1742 to demonstrate developments in tuning keyboards that enabled music to be performed in any key. (Today pianos are tuned in "equal temperament," with the octave split equally into twelve semitones. In the well-tempered system, some intervals were tuned "pure," in exact mathematical ratios, and others were not, creating a slightly different character for each key.)

Fugal writing also played an important part in church music, sometimes as the structure of a whole movement, and on other occasions forming a contrasting section within, for example, a chorus of an oratorio. The oratorio had originated during the Counter-Reformation as a spiritual drama—the word "oratorio" means "prayer hall"—and the earliest works were performed in prayer halls for the spiritual benefit of listeners. At first an Italian genre, the oratorio spread throughout Europe, and became widely popular. Featuring solo arias, recitative, and choruses, it was somewhat like opera, but without its theatricality. Oratorios were performed in public concert halls, not in theaters, and the plot unfolded in song, without being acted out. Similarly, the story of Christ's Passion was dramatized by composers of the Baroque period in powerful musical settings that were not intended for staging, but rather for performance during a church service.

Another major type of sacred vocal work in the Baroque period was the church cantata. Such pieces were written for Lutheran services as a focus for devotion and generally consisted of several movements: an opening chorus, several arias linked by recitative, and a closing chorale. As part of Bach's terms of employment, he had to write a cantata each week, plus extra ones for church festivals. The music of over two hundred of them has survived, including one based on Luther's chorale "Ein' feste Burg ist unser Gott" (see Chapter 15).

JOHANN SEBASTIAN BACH Bach was born to a Lutheran family of musicians in Eisenach, Germany, orphaned at the age of ten, and raised by an unsympathetic older brother. He worked as an organist, violinist, and harpsichordist in various German towns, and for twenty-seven years was music director of St. Thomas's church school in Leipzig. He was deeply religious and a devoted family man: he married twice and had twenty children.

Bach's work as a church organist shaped much of his output. Organ music was needed for services and study material was required for his pupils. For the organ he wrote over six hundred **chorale preludes** (organ pieces based on chorale themes) as well as fugues, pieces in a freer improvisatory style known as fantasias, and sonatas. Technically demanding to perform, many of these works are startling in their grandeur and their sense of impetus. For harpsichord, Bach was among the first to write concertos, and his other keyboard writing includes **suites** of dances, variations, and a set of four books entitled *Keyboard Exercises*.

In addition to his enormous number of church cantatas, Bach wrote three notable large-scale choral works: the B minor Mass (1749), which harks back to the polyphonic Masses of earlier generations, and two Passion settings based on the gospels of John and Matthew. The better known of these is the *St. Matthew Passion* (1727). About three hours in performance, it takes listeners on an emotional journey that begins with Jesus predicting his betrayal and death and ends with his burial. One soloist takes the part of the Evangelist, narrating the story through recitative, and other soloists enact other characters—among them Jesus, Peter, Judas, and Pilate. Many performers are needed, as Bach scored the work for double orchestra and double chorus, who begin and end the work majestically. Interspersed in the drama are contemplative moments: mournful solo arias and chorales for the audience to sing as a religious response.

Bach wrote no operas, but his secular works range from chamber music, such as the suites for solo cello, to orchestral pieces such as the six *Brandenburg Concertos* (1721). While Vivaldi's *concerti grossi* are for string soloists accompanied by string orchestra, Bach uses a different combination of soloists in each of the *Brandenburg Concertos*—a violin and two recorders in No. 4, for example, and two violas and a cello in No. 6, creating a dark sonority. No. 2 is one of the most vivid *Brandenburg Concertos*, with a solo group of high trumpet, recorder, oboe, and violin. The Music Listening Selection presents the last movement of this concerto. Listen for the fanfare-type theme at the beginning, played first on the trumpet, then copied in turn by oboe, violin, and recorder in the style of a fugue. After the opening solo section the full orchestra enters with a busy bass line on the cellos. Note how the texture changes, and how the harpsichord can be heard throughout, as it provides continuo backing.

MUSIC LISTENING SELECTION

Bach, Brandenburg Concerto No. 2 in F major, third movement, Allegro assai. Cologne Chamber Orchestra, conductor Helmut Muller-Bruhl, CD track 8

GEORGE FRIDERIC HANDEL Handel was born in Halle, Germany, where his father discouraged him from pursuing a career in music. At seventeen he went to university to study law, but at the same time he became organist at the Calvinist cathedral in Halle. A year later he left the city to take up a job as violinist at the opera house in Hamburg. Opera would later be one of the mainstays of his life as a composer. In 1706 he traveled to Italy, meeting Corelli and Vivaldi and immersing himself in the lyrical style of Italian music. Handel visited London for the first time in 1710, settling there two years later and eventually becoming a British citizen.

In the course of his career, Handel wrote harpsichord suites, trio sonatas, *concerti grossi*, ceremonial orchestral music for royal performance, secular cantatas, and anthems for the Church. But it is for his dramatic music that he is most noted. His first opera, *Almira*, was produced in 1705, when he was nineteen, and over the next thirty-six years he composed another forty operas—first for German audiences, then Italian, and finally English. He brought Italian-style opera to London, where he was a great success, and in the 1720s and 1730s he composed many operas for the London stage. So-called "serious opera" of the late Baroque was made up of arias expressing emotion interspersed with recitative that advanced the plot. The typical structure of the arias was **ternary** (three-part) form, with the first section repeated at the end

(*ABA*). Handel composed with great skill, characterizing the members of the cast through the style of their music. Plots were often based on Classical or historical subjects. But despite the enthusiasm of London audiences for opera, its organizing body, the Royal Academy, continually lost money and eventually collapsed.

As his career in opera waned, Handel moved on to oratorio. Most of these works relate Old Testament stories through arias and recitative, interspersed with choral items. Unlike his operas, they were written in English and, despite the drama of their subjects, they were not acted. His most famous oratorio—indeed the most famous choral work written to date—is *Messiah* (1742). Filled with a profound sense of religious faith, *Messiah* is a masterpiece of Baroque writing. It plumbs the range of human emotion, from bitterness in the chorus "Surely he hath borne our griefs and carried our sorrows" to anger in the aria "Thou shalt break them with a rod of iron" and triumph in "If God be for us, who can be against us?"

The majestic Hallelujah Chorus that closes the second of *Messiah*'s three sections illustrates the different types of Baroque choral texture. After the opening three bars of orchestral introduction the full choir enters, repeatedly singing "Hallelujah." All the singers punch out the same rhythm in this section. At the words "For the Lord God Omnipotent reigneth," all voices sing a rising figure in unison. Later, these two ideas are put together **contrapuntally**. One of the most exciting moments in the movement is when the parts come together again for the words "The Kingdom of this world is become . . .," sung quietly and low, before everyone leaps triumphantly onto high, loud notes to proclaim "the kingdom of our Lord and of His Christ." Listen also for the rising **sequence** of long notes in the soprano line to the text "King of Kings, and Lord of Lords," building to a climax.

MUSIC LISTENING SELECTION

Handel, *Messiah*, Hallelujah Chorus. Scholars Baroque Ensemble, CD track 9

ENGLAND

During the seventeenth century, England witnessed political turmoil that led to the dissolution of absolutism and divine right and the development of a constitutional monarchy. Like the monarchs of Spain and France, Charles I used the arts to promote his royal image. Literature in England continued to display a humanist interest in Classical tradition but was also infused with religious Christian themes.

FROM DIVINE RIGHT TO CONSTITUTIONAL MONARCHY

The Protestant James VI ruled Scotland from 1567 to 1625. In 1603, on the death of Queen Elizabeth I, he ascended the throne of England and ruled as James I. The first in the line of Stuart kings, he was a firm believer in divine right. Despite being a Protestant himself, James antagonized the Puritans, who, he felt, threatened the unity of the Church of England. As a result, many Puritans left England for the New World, founding the American colony of Plymouth, on Massachusetts Bay, in 1620 and soon thereafter the Massachusetts Bay Colony.

James also tried to curtail the freedoms of Catholics and to ignore Parliament, which was composed of the House of Commons and the House of Lords. His court was notorious for moral and financial corruption, but his reign saw at least one positive outcome: a translation of the Bible was compiled in 1611 by a commission James hired to standardize the text and reinforce Anglican unity. This became known as the King James Bible.

READING SELECTION

James I, *The True Law of a Free Monarchy*, on the divine right of kings, PWC3-180

The reign of James's son, Charles I (ruled 1625–1649), was beset by continual crisis. Charles married the Catholic Bourbon Henrietta Maria (figure **16.38**), daughter of Marie de' Medici and Henry IV of France, which distressed his Protestant subjects. Since Charles needed money for war with England and Spain, he levied new taxes and introduced the so-called forced loan (a tax that would supposedly be repaid at a later date). In 1628 Parliament passed the Petition of Right which stipulated that taxes could be levied only with its consent. Parliament also objected to what it called Charles's "popery"—his sympathetic attitude toward Catholicism and the influence of the pope. Charles reacted by dismissing Parliament in 1629 and launching a period of personal rule, which lasted until 1640, when he needed Parliament to approve funds for war with Scotland. Parliament agreed to grant new funds only if Charles would redress its grievances against him.

In 1642 civil war broke out after Charles again suspended Parliament. Two issues were at stake: whether England would be governed by an absolute monarch or a parliamentary system, and whether the Church of England would be controlled by a king suspected of "popery" or by decentralized governance. Charles's supporters, the Cavaliers, were mainly centered in northwestern England. His opponents, primarily Puritans, favored a parliamentary system. They were based in

16.38 Anthony van Dyck, *Henrietta Maria, Queen of England*, c. 1632. Oil on canvas, 43 × 34 in. (109 × 86.2 cm). Royal Collection, Windsor Castle.
Rubens's student Anthony van Dyck (1599–1641) left Flanders and became painter to Charles I of England. His affinity for courtly tastes is apparent in the elegant satin dress, the precise curls, the pearls, and hair piece. Henrietta Maria stands by an open window, the very image of composure, her right hand resting by the crown.

southeastern England and were called Roundheads because their hair was cropped short.

The parliamentarians won for two main reasons. First, they had the support of Scotland, and second, their leader, the Puritan country squire Oliver Cromwell (1599–1658), created a well-disciplined New Model Army. Cromwell introduced an innovative military tactic in which troops were arranged in closely knit squares with pikes projecting at an angle. This effective fighting force, known as the Ironsides, ensured Cromwell's victory.

In 1649 Charles was brought to trial and executed, and the monarchy was abolished. However, Cromwell, the leader of the new republic, proved to be a repressive ruler. In 1653 he dissolved the House of Commons and imposed a military dictatorship. His puritanical policies resulted in a ban on artistic extravagance. He remained in power until his death, and two years later Parliament invited Charles I's son to return from exile and restored him to the throne.

The new king, Charles II, ruled for the next twenty-five years (1660–1685)—a period known as the Restoration. He made peace with Parliament and revived artistic patronage, but, like his father, he aroused the displeasure of Protestants with his pro-Catholic leanings. He was also an advocate of absolutism.

Having failed to produce a legitimate heir, Charles II left the succession to his Catholic brother, James II. But the English did not want a Catholic king and they deposed James II in the "bloodless" Glorious Revolution of 1688. He was succeeded by his Protestant daughter Mary II and his son-in-law William III of Orange (ruled 1689–1702). They recognized parliamentary and citizens' rights, and England became a constitutional monarchy.

THE ARTS IN ENGLAND

Like the absolute monarchs of France and Spain—but lacking their political acumen—Charles I used art in the service of the state. One vehicle for projecting his political image was the court **masque**, a performance designed to show that the king created civil order and social harmony (figure **16.39**). But the aloof Charles I was unaware of his own disengagement from his subjects, which is clear from this masque.

16.39 Inigo Jones, costume design for Charles I as Philogenes in *Salmacida Spolia*, 1640. Pen and brown ink, 11¼ × 6⅛ in. (28.6 × 15.5 cm). Devonshire Collection, Chatsworth.
This is the costume designed for Charles I in the role of Philogenes in the last masque before the outbreak of the Civil War in 1642. The masque opened with a storm and the Furies rejecting the king's peace. Then the scene shifted to the English countryside with Concord and the Genius of Britain riding through clouds in a silver chariot. Philogenes was seated on a golden chair; the queen descended from a cloud to join him, and together they danced a ballet. The scene shifted again to a city, where a harmonious vision of the gods was accompanied by music.

CHRISTOPHER WREN: ST. PAUL'S CATHEDRAL In 1666, following an epidemic of plague in 1664–1665, the Great Fire of London burned more than two-thirds of the old city. Three years later Charles II appointed Christopher Wren (1632–1723), a professor of astronomy at Oxford, Surveyor-General of the King's Works. Wren's task was to rebuild London.

He rebuilt some fifty-two churches for which he combined new forms with traditional features. His most famous project was the Anglican Cathedral of St. Paul, today in London's financial district (figure **16.40**). The towering dome (figure **16.41**) is second in size only to that of St. Peter's in Rome. It was constructed with a triple shell of brick, wood, and lead.

Although Wren had never been to Italy, he visited France, where he met Bernini and saw many Baroque churches with domes. St. Paul's has a lantern, suggesting the influence of Italian Renaissance design. Wren, like Bramante, Raphael, and Michelangelo in their plans for the New St. Peter's (see

16.40 *left* **Christopher Wren, west façade of St. Paul's Cathedral, London, 1675–1710.**
The central portion of the façade contains double-story Corinthian columns supporting entablatures, the upper one crowned by a pediment. Imposing square towers with curved walls in the upper sections have complex surface designs and gilded pineapples at the pinnacles. The combination of Gothic towers with Classical Orders, symmetry, and new elements is characteristic of Baroque inventiveness.

16.41 John Coney, rotunda of St. Paul's Cathedral, London, 1818. Engraving, 16½ in. (42 cm) high. Victoria and Albert Museum, London.

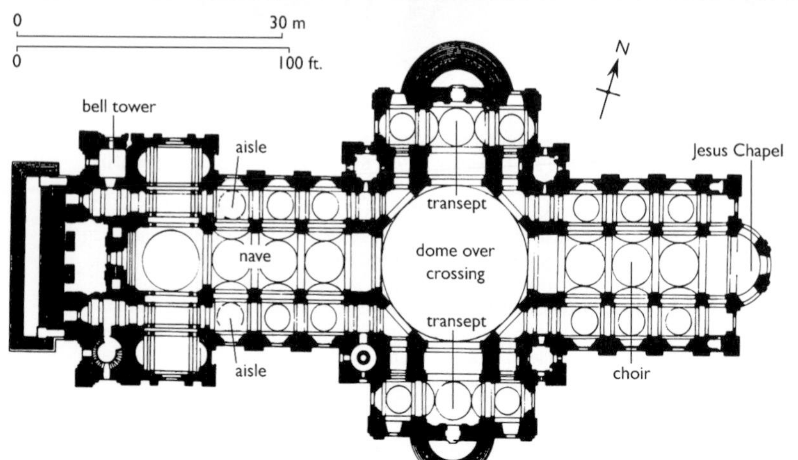

16.42 Plan of St. Paul's Cathedral.

Chapter 14), wanted a centralized Greek cross plan and a Greek temple front at each entrance, but the conservative Anglican clergy preferred a longitudinal plan (figure **16.42**) with a long nave for large crowds of worshippers facing the altar in the choir.

LITERATURE: DONNE AND MILTON England continued to produce great literature (particularly poetry) in the seventeenth century. The two leading poets of the period are the lyrical, sometimes enigmatic John Donne (1572–1631) and John Milton (1608–1674), who is best known for his epic *Paradise Lost*.

John Donne was raised a Catholic but later converted to Protestantism and became a highly regarded Anglican preacher. His sermons are considered models of seventeenth-century religious prose. In 1621, Donne was named Dean of St. Paul's. He is noted for the *Holy Sonnets* of around 1610, which address religious themes, as well as for lyrical, colorful imagery, the meaning of which can be difficult to understand. His poetry is characterized by passion, eroticism, and the use of **conceits**, which make extended comparisons and explore themes in witty and complex ways. In his poem entitled "Song," Donne infuses nature with the supernatural:

Go, and catch a falling star,
  Get with child a mandrake root [used to aid in conception]
Tell me, where all past years are,
  Or who cleft the devil's foot,
Teach me to hear mermaids singing
  Or to keep off envy's stinging,
    And find
    What wind
  Serves to advance an honest mind.

In "Death, be Not Proud," as in much of his poetry, Donne deals with the theme of death. He personifies death, addressing it directly and challenging its power. For, although death can fell all of mankind, Donne says, in the end it is death that will die and humanity that will awaken to eternal salvation.

Death, be not proud, though some have callèd thee
Mighty and dreadful, for thou art not so;
For those whom thou think'st thou dost overthrow
Die not, poor Death, nor yet canst thou kill me.
From rest and sleep, which but thy pictures be,
Much pleasure; then from thee much more must flow,
And soonest our best men with thee do go,
Rest of their bones, and soul's delivery.
Thou art slave to fate, chance, kings, and desperate men,
And dost with poison, war, and sickness dwell,
And poppy or charms can make us sleep as well
And better than thy stroke; why swell'st thou then?
One short sleep past, we wake eternally
And death shall be no more; Death, thou shalt die.

Donne's preoccupation with the theme of mortality is reflected in the fact that he preached a sermon on his own death in 1631, just two days before he died.

John Milton was born in London, where his father worked as a scrivener and composer. In preparation for the ministry, Milton studied Latin and Italian poetry at Cambridge, but he soon became involved in politics and from 1640 wrote pamphlets and essays on religious and political issues. Milton, who believed that people have a right to overthrow unjust kings, supported Cromwell's rebellion. He was appointed Latin Secretary under Cromwell, a post he kept until Charles II ascended the throne.

In 1643 Milton wrote *The Doctrine and Discipline of Divorce* after his seventeen-year-old wife left him. (She returned two years later.) This work was suppressed by government censors for immorality and threatening social stability because it advocated divorce. In 1644 Milton responded with the *Areopagitica*, which championed freedom of speech and of the press.

Milton's work combines Christian morality with the Classical tradition. He wrote a number of sonnets, perhaps the most famous being on his blindness, which developed in the 1640s and became total by 1652:

When I consider how my light is spent
  Ere half my days, in this dark world and wide,
  And that one talent which is death to hide*
  Lodged with me useless, though my soul more bent
To serve therewith my Maker, and present
  My true account, lest he returning chide;
  "Doth God exact day-labor, light denied?"
  I fondly ask; but Patience to prevent
That murmur, soon replies, "God does not need
  Either man's work or his own gifts; who best
  Bear his mild yoke, they serve him best. His state
Is kingly. Thousands at his bidding speed
  And post o'er land and ocean without rest:
  They also serve who only stand and wait."

* A reference to the parable in Matthew 25:14–30, in which a servant is given a talent and buries it. He is cast into darkness as a result.

With the Restoration and Charles II's accession to the throne, Milton retired from court and was briefly imprisoned. After his release, in the decade before his death, Milton published his great work, *Paradise Lost* (1667) in twelve books. In this epic poem, Milton relates the story of Man's Fall and Redemption. Inspired by Virgil's *Aeneid* and rich in Classical and biblical imagery, *Paradise Lost* embodies the principles of Christian humanism. It is also dramatic, emotional, moody, and imbued with conflict and struggle, all of which place *Paradise Lost* squarely in the style of Baroque grandeur. Like Virgil and Homer before him, Milton begins with the Muse, but Milton's muse differs from the Classical Muse in being the Holy Spirit, rather than a pagan deity.

Thematic Parallels

In Search of Outer Space

Today we think of outer space as a new frontier of discovery and exploration, made possible by advances in technology and science. Early cultures conceived of outer space in mythological terms. In ancient Greece, for example, philosophers believed in the harmony of the cosmos and the music of the planetary spheres, and in ancient Egypt and Babylon, astrology accounted for the movement of the stars and planets. The invention of telescopes in the seventeenth century allowed the study of outer space to begin its journey from speculative myth to observational science, bringing it into conflict with religious dogma and traditional beliefs.

Since antiquity, people have marveled at the motions of the stars, the sun, and the moon. (Indeed, the English word *planet* comes from a Greek word meaning "wanderer.") In many cultures, planets and stars were named for gods, and in Greek myths heroes and demigods were transformed into constellations when they died. Constellations, in turn, inspired countless myths.

For many centuries people in the West assumed that the sun orbited the earth (the **geocentric** view of the universe), but in the sixteenth century the Polish astronomer Copernicus challenged this view in favor of heliocentrism by demonstrating that the earth revolves around the sun and that the sun is the center of our solar system. In the seventeenth century Galileo used the telescope to confirm the findings of Copernicus. Since that time, outer space has continued to intrigue scientists, poets, philosophers, and artists.

In the twentieth century American and Soviet scientists led the world in early space exploration. In 1957 the Soviet Union launched *Sputnik* I, the first man-made satellite to orbit the earth. A month later, *Sputnik* II carried a live dog into orbit. In 1958, the first American satellite, *Explorer* I, was launched. The competition in space continued, and in 1961 a Soviet spaceship carried the first cosmonaut, Yuri Gagarin, the first man in space, once around the earth and Alan Shepherd made the first space flight for the United States. In 1962 the United States sent John Glenn into orbit (the first of his four space missions), and that same year the *Telstar* communications satellite transmitted the first live television images between Europe and the United States. In 1969 the American astronaut Neil Armstrong became the first man to walk on the moon. He trained for this mission in, among other venues, Iceland, whose barren lava fields resemble the terrain of the moon. Two years later the Soviets launched the first orbital space station, while the American Skylab module enabled astronauts to live and work in space for extended periods of time. Finally, in 1975, the two countries launched a joint mission, linking separate spaceships in orbit.

In 1990 the United States launched the Hubble Space-based Telescope, which, unhindered by the earth's atmosphere, could detect celestial data seven times further away than any earth-based telescope. The Hubble produced enormous amounts of new information, including photographs of the births and deaths of stars (figures **16.43** and **16.44**). In 1997 the telescope recorded a black hole with a mass 300 million times that of the sun, some 50 million light years from earth in Galaxy M84. Astronauts have made four visits to the Hubble to correct flaws and make improvements. After the Shuttle disaster in 2003 the Hubble Telescope was slated to be abandoned, but later it was decided to keep Hubble active. As of this writing, the fate of Hubble is still under discussion. In 2004 British and American Rovers (unmanned vehicles equipped with robots) landed on Mars. The American Rover sent back photographs of Mars and searched for evidence that life once existed there.

The exploration of outer space reflects the human impulse to explore. Despite a few disastrous failed missions, astronauts continue to brave the unknown in the pursuit of knowledge. Their courage, like that of Galileo and Copernicus, is a tribute to the human spirit.

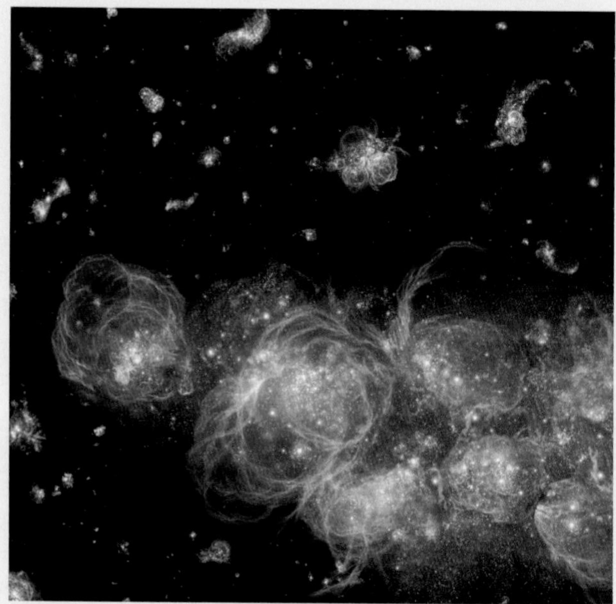

16.43 Birth of a star, from the Hubble telescope.

16.44 Light from a dying star, from the Hubble telescope.

Of Man's first disobedience, and the fruit
Of that forbidden tree whose mortal taste
Brought death into the World, and all our woe,
With loss of Eden, till one greater Man
Restore us, and regain the blissful seat,
Sing, Heavenly Muse . . .
what in me is dark
Illumine, what is low raise and support;
That, to the height of this great argument,
I may assert Eternal Providence,
And justify the ways of God to man.

READING SELECTION
Milton, *Paradise Lost*, the Redemption, PWC4-016

Milton thus takes on the enormous and ambitious task of explaining what the Bible left unexplained—that is, the ways in which humanity has been treated by its creator. The argument opens with the Fall, presented as Satan's revenge against God for banishing him from heaven. The images in Book I in which Satan awakens his rebellious cohorts as they lie in hell on a lake of fire are characteristic of the epic's striking visual impact. In the depiction of Adam and Eve as vulnerable to Satan's deception, Milton creates a powerful human drama and evokes the identification of his readers with his characters. At the conclusion, the archangel Michael tells Adam the future, beginning with the Fall and ending with the Second Coming of Christ, which redeems the Fall. The primal couple are reassured that there is a paradise within themselves and that they can regain it through obedience to God.

In the seventeenth century the notion of divine right dominated western Europe, and the arts were used by rulers in the service of that idea. At the same time, however, the stirrings of change appeared in the philosophy of John Locke and other thinkers. In the eighteenth century, Locke's followers would overturn the notion of divine right and set in motion the events leading to the French and American revolutions.

KEY TERMS

aria a composition for solo voice with orchestral accompaniment; usually part of an opera or oratorio.

binary the form of a piece of music in two sections, *AB*.

cantata a composition for one or more voices with instrumental accompaniment; church cantatas are sacred pieces, but there are also secular cantatas.

chamber music (literally, "room music") music for a small number of instruments.

chorale prelude an organ piece based on a chorale theme.

conceit in literature, a witty and complex turn of phrase.

concerto a musical work for soloist (or soloists) and orchestra, exploiting the contrast between small and large forces.

concerto grosso in the Baroque period, a musical composition for a small group of solo instruments accompanied by an orchestra.

continuo a type of accompaniment in Baroque music that uses a keyboard or plucked instrument to play chords, often with a low sustaining instrument playing the bass line of the music.

counterpoint (adj. **contrapuntal**) performing two or more melodies simultaneously; polyphony.

deductive method a method of reasoning in which the conclusion follows logically from a given premise.

fugue a type of polyphonic musical composition with a formal structure that uses imitation between voices systematically.

geocentrism the view that the sun orbits the earth.

masque a short dramatic composition of allegorical content, usually performed as court entertainment and consisting of mime, music, and dancing.

mercantilism the belief that a nation's wealth depends on the possession of precious metals and that, to achieve this, a government must encourage overseas trade and the foundation of colonies.

modulate in music, change from one key to another.

monody a style of music in which a single voice carries a melody.

opera a dramatic performance set to music, for vocal soloists, chorus, and orchestra.

oratorio an unstaged dramatic religious text set to music, for vocal soloists, chorus, and orchestra.

Passion an unstaged musical setting of the story of the events leading up to Jesus' Crucifixion, for vocal soloists, chorus, and orchestra, originally performed within church services.

piazza an open square in an urban area.

program music instrumental music representing a nonmusical idea or story.

recitative a vocal passage in an opera or oratorio that has the inflections and rhythms of speech, sung by a soloist with light accompaniment.

ritornello in Baroque music, an orchestral passage that begins a work and is then repeated, in whole or in part, between episodes performed by soloists.

sequence a pattern of notes repeated at higher or lower pitch than the original.

suite in Baroque music, an instrumental work in several movements based on different dance meters.

tenebrism a style of painting, associated with Caravaggio and his followers, in which certain features of a scene are dramatically illuminated while the rest are in darkness.

ternary the form of a piece of music in three sections, *ABA*.

tonality in music, a system of keys, which gives the feeling of a "home" pitch.

trio sonata a Baroque musical genre in several movements, normally written for two melody instruments and continuo.

virtuoso a performing artist (usually a musician) of outstanding skill.

KEY QUESTIONS

1. What forces opposed science in the seventeenth century? What methods did scientists use to seek truth?
2. How did Baroque plays favor modernism in the quarrel between the Ancients and the Moderns? What new techniques did playwrights use?
3. How did seventeenth-century thinkers dispute such concepts as absolute power and divine right of kings? How did Louis XIV's iconography illustrate absolutism?
4. How did Bernini and Caravaggio involve the viewer in their art? What formal and narrative techniques did they use?
5. What kinds of questions do political philosophers ask? What kinds of questions did Descartes and Pascal ask? Were they political philosophers?

SUGGESTED READING

Adams, Laurie Schneider. *Key Monuments of the Baroque*. Boulder, CO: Westview Press (Icon edition), 1999.
▸ A brief introduction to major works of Baroque painting, sculpture, and architecture.

Alpers, Sveltana. *The Art of Describing: Dutch Art in the Seventeenth Century*. Chicago: University of Chicago Press, 1983.
▸ A new approach to seventeenth-century Dutch art and society.

——. *Rembrandt's Enterprise: The Studio and the Market*. Chicago: University of Chicago Press, 1988.
▸ Rembrandt's role in creating the modern art market.

——. *The Making of Rubens*. New Haven, CT: Yale University Press, 1995.
▸ A study of Rubens and his times.

Ashton, Robert. *Counter-Revolution: The Second Civil War and Its Origins, 1646–1648*. New Haven, CT: Yale University Press, 1994.
▸ England's development from absolute to constitutional monarchy.

Barry, J., M. Hester, and G. Roberts (eds.). *Witchcraft in Early Modern Europe: Studies in Culture and Belief*. Cambridge, U.K.: Cambridge University Press, 1998.
▸ A series of essays on witchcraft.

Berger, R. W. *A Royal Passion: Louis XIV as Patron of Architecture*. New York: Cambridge University Press, 1994.
▸ The design and construction of Versailles as the embodiment of absolutism.

Blunt, Anthony. *Art and Architecture in France, 1500–1700*, 4th ed. London: Penguin Books, 1980.
▸ French architecture in the sixteenth century.

Brown, Jonathan. *The Golden Age of Painting in Spain*. New Haven, CT, and London: Yale University Press, 1991.
▸ A study of seventeenth-century Spanish painting.

Buckley, Veronica. *Christina, Queen of Sweden*. New York: HarperCollins, 2004.
▸ A biography of the erratic queen.

Chevalier, Tracy. *The Girl with a Pearl Earring*. London: HarperCollins, 2003.
▸ A historical novel about the life and times of Vermeer.

Collinson, P. *The Religion of Protestants: The Church in English Society 1559–1625*. Oxford: Oxford University Press, 1984.
▸ A basic study of Puritanism.

Corneille, Pierre. *Le Cid*, trans. John Cairncross. London: Penguin Books, 1975.
▸ French tragedy based on Classical form.

Duran, M. *Cervantes*. Farmington Hills, MI: Twayne Publishers, 1975.
▸ A biography of the Spanish author.

Hall, A. R. *The Revolution in Science: 1500–1750*. London: Longman, 1983.
▸ New developments in science from 1500 to the mid-eighteenth century.

Haskell, Francis. *Patrons and Painters: A Study in the Relations between Italian Art and Society in the Age of the Baroque*. New Haven, CT, and London: Yale University Press, 1980.
▸ A study of Baroque patronage in Italy.

Hibbard, Howard. *Caravaggio*. New York: HarperCollins, 1974.
▸ A monograph on the artist.

Garrard, Mary D. *Artemisia Gentileschi*. Princeton, NJ: Princeton University Press, 1989.
▸ A study of the life, art, and times of Artemisia Gentileschi.

Kahr, Madlyn Millner. *Dutch Painting in the Seventeenth Century*, 2nd ed. New York: HarperCollins, 1993.
▸ A survey of seventeenth-century Dutch painting.

Machamer P. (ed.). *The Cambridge Companion to Galileo*. Cambridge, U.K.: Cambridge University Press, 1998.
▸ Essays on the impact of Galileo on science.

Milton, John. *Paradise Lost*. London: Penguin Books, 2003.
▸ The major English epic poem of the seventeenth century.

Monod, P. K. *The Power of Kings: Monarchy and Religion in Europe, 1589–1715*. New Haven, CT: Yale University Press, 1999.
▸ A study of the origins of royal power and the transition to modern Europe.

Nicolson, Adam. *God's Secretaries*. New York: HarperCollins, 2003.
▸ On the making of the King James Bible.

North, M. *Art and Commerce in the Dutch Golden Age*. New Haven, CT, and London: Yale University Press, 1997.
▸ Art and finance in seventeenth-century Holland.

Orrey, L. *Opera: A Concise History*, rev. R. Milnes. London: Thames and Hudson, 1987.
▸ A basic history of opera.

Racine, Jean. *Phèdre*, trans. Ted Hughes. New York: Farrar, Straus and Giroux, 1999.
▸ French tragedy based on Classical theater.

Ranum, O. *The Fronde: A French Revolution, 1648–1652*. New York: W. W. Norton, 1994.
▸ A study of the Fronde.

Treasure, Geoffrey. *Louis XIV*. London: Longman, 2001.
▸ A biography of the French king.

Wittkower, Rudolf. *Sculpture, Processes, and Principles*. New York: Viking Press, 1977.
▸ A classic work on approaches to sculpture, especially during the Baroque period.

——. *Gian Lorenzo Bernini, The Sculpture of the Roman Baroque*, 2nd ed. Baltimore: Penguin Books, 1973.
▸ A monograph on all aspects of Bernini's life and art.

——. *Born Under Saturn: The Character and Conduct of Artists—a Documented History from Antiquity to the French Revolution*. New York: W. W. Norton, 1969.
▸ An innovative biographical approach to major artists linking their lives with their art.

SUGGESTED FILMS

1933 *Queen Christina*, dir. Rouben Mamoulian

1935 *Carnival in Flanders* (*La Kermesse héroïque*), dir. Jacques Feyder

1940 *L'Ecole des femmes* (based on Molière; uncompleted), dir. Max Ophüls

1942 *Ivan the Terrible*, dir. Sergei Eisenstein

1966 *Rise of Louis XIV*, dir. Roberto Rossellini

1968 *Phèdre* (based on Racine), dir. Pierre Jourdan

1970 *The Last Valley* (about the Thirty Years War), dir. James Clavell

1975 *Galileo*, dir. Joseph Losey

1982 *Le Bourgeois Gentilhomme* (based on Molière), dir. Roger Coggio

1984 *Tartuffe* (based on Molière), dir. Gérard Depardieu

2003 *Girl with a Pearl Earring*, dir. Peter Webber

17 From Enlightenment to Revolution in the Eighteenth Century

"*The law is king.*"

(THOMAS PAINE, *Common Sense*)

The eighteenth century witnessed the decline of absolutism, which did not disappear without a struggle. Although monarchs and the nobility began to acknowledge some individual rights—such as free speech, expanded suffrage, and the abolition of slavery in France and its colonies—they did not willingly renounce privilege.*

In the course of the eighteenth century a number of elements converged to create a new view of the world and humanity's place in it. First among these were the ideas of John Locke, who had opposed the divine right of kings (see Chapter 16). Following his lead, many eighteenth-century thinkers advocated such civil liberties as basic judicial rights, the right to public assembly, and freedom of the press. Social and political factors affecting these new ideas included a rising middle class, which encouraged individual enterprise and led to an increase in professions, such as law, banking, and government administration.

After the death of Louis XIV in 1715 the cultural center of Europe moved from the Versailles court to the Paris salon, *literally a "reception room" but also a generic term for the private houses in which intellectuals gathered for social interchange and philosophical discussion. The typical* salon *was decorated in the ornate Rococo style that evolved from Baroque. Authors used satire to highlight the problems of the period, to further the cause of social justice, and to defend basic human rights.*

In music, the late eighteenth century was a tremendously significant and fruitful period. It witnessed the development of the Classical style used by some of the greatest Western composers—Haydn, Mozart, and Beethoven. Public concerts expanded rapidly and audiences increasingly included members of the middle classes. Thus the nature of music patronage was changing, and composers needed to write music with broad appeal to suit their new listeners. In addition, amateur music-making was on the rise, and music publishing flourished.

One particular group of intellectuals, known in both French and English as the Philosophes, *included novelists, philosophers, and naturalists. Among these were the group of Encyclopedists, who*

Key Topics

Age of Reason

- Science versus superstition
- Rights of citizens
- Law is king
- Satire

Age of Revolution

- Growth of secular education
- Constitutional monarchy
- Enlightened despotism
- "Man is born free and everywhere he is in chains"
- The Ancients restored
- Declaration of Independence
- U.S. Constitution and Bill of Rights

***Philosophes*, Philosophers, and Economists**

- The Social Contract
- Metaphysics
- Empiricism
- Laissez-faire versus mercantilism

TIMELINE	EIGHTEENTH-CENTURY EUROPE	THE NEW WORLD
HISTORY AND CULTURE 	War of the Spanish Succession, 1702–1713 War of the Austrian Succession, 1740–1748 Seven Years War, 1756–1763 Enlightened despotism: Frederick II of Prussia (r. 1740–1786); Catherine II of Russia (r. 1762–1796); Maria Theresa (r. 1740–1780) and Joseph II of Austria (r. 1780–1790) Enlightenment: advocacy of individual rights French Revolution: Declaration of the Rights of Man and Citizen, 1789; Storming of the Bastille, 1789; Reign of Terror under Robespierre, 1793–1795; Execution of Louis XVI and Marie-Antoinette, 1793; *Directoire*, 1795–1799 Britain becomes dominant European power Growth of middle classes in Europe	Franklin founds first American public library, 1731 Boston Massacre, 1767 Boston Tea Party, 1773 Declaration of Independence, 1776 American Revolution, 1776–1783; Peace of Paris, 1783 Constitution of the United States ratified, 1788 Washington becomes president, 1789 Bill of Rights, 1791 Jefferson becomes president, 1801
ART 	Rococo and Neoclassical styles Fashion for *chinoiserie* Watteau, *Les Bergers*, *c.* 1716 Chardin, *Young Man Blowing Bubbles*, *c.* 1734 Hogarth, "The Four Times of Day," 1738; "Marriage à la Mode," 1741 Boucher, *Odalisque*, 1745 Tiepolo, "America" fresco, 1750s Winckelmann publishes *The History of Ancient Art*, 1764 Royal Academy of Arts founded, London, 1768 Gainsborough, *The Blue Boy*, *c.* 1770 Houdon, *Diderot*, 1771 Vigée-Lebrun, *Marie Antoinette à la Rose*, 1783 Labille-Guiard, *Self-portrait with Two Pupils*, 1785 Kauffmann, *Cornelia, Mother of the Gracchi*, 1785 David, *The Oath of the Tennis Court*, 1789–1791	Trumbull, *General George Washington at Trenton*, 1792
ARCHITECTURE	Neumann, Würzburg Residenz, Würzburg, 1719–1753 Adam, Kenwood House, London, begun 1767	Jefferson, State Capitol, Richmond, Virginia, 1785–1789; Rotunda, University of Virginia, Charlottesville, 1817–1826
LITERATURE, PHILOSOPHY, HISTORY, AND ECONOMICS 	*Philosophes* and the French *salon* Dryden (1631–1700), translations, essays, poetry Leibniz, *Theodicy*, 1710 Pope, *The Rape of the Lock*, 1712–1714; translations: *Iliad*, 1713–1720; *Odyssey*, 1720s Defoe, *Robinson Crusoe*, 1719 Montesquieu, *Lettres persanes*, 1721; *The Spirit of Laws*, 1748 Swift, *Gulliver's Travels*, 1726 Fielding, *Tom Thumb*, 1730; *Tom Jones*, 1749 Voltaire, *Lettres philosophiques*, 1734; *Candide*, 1759 Hume, *A Treatise of Human Nature*, 1739–1740 Richardson, *Pamela*, 1740; *Clarissa*, 1748–1749 Diderot, *Encyclopédie*, 1750–1772; *Le Neveu de Rameau*, 1760s Johnson, *A Dictionary of the English Language*, 1755 Rousseau, *The Social Contract*, 1762; *Emile*, 1762; *Confessions*, 1770s Smith, *The Wealth of Nations*, 1776 Gibbon, *The History of the Decline and Fall of the Roman Empire*, 1776 Kant, *The Critique of Pure Reason*, 1787 Malthus, *Essay on the Principle of Population*, 1788 Wollstonecraft, *A Vindication of the Rights of Woman*, 1792	Franklin (1706–1790), *Poor Richard's Almanac*, 1733–1758; *Autobiography*, 1793 Paine (1737–1809), *Common Sense*, 1776
THEATER	Sheridan, *The Rivals*, 1775	
MUSIC	Birth of Classical style in music Development of comic opera Expansion of public concerts Musical *galant* Piano comes into common use Violin-makers: Amati, Stradivari, Guarneri Standardization of orchestra Classical instrumental forms: sonata, string quartet, concerto, symphony Development of sonata form Gluck (1714–1787), *Orpheus and Eurydice*, 1762; *Alceste*, 1767 Haydn (1732–1809), "The Father of Symphony": Symphony No. 94, the "Surprise," 1791–1792; *The Creation*, 1798 Mozart (1756–1791), *The Marriage of Figaro*, 1786; *Don Giovanni*, 1787; *Eine kleine Nachtmusik*, 1787; *The Magic Flute*, 1791 Beethoven (1770–1827) bridges Classicism and Romanticism in music	

wanted to classify all forms of existing knowledge. These thinkers shared a dedication to science over faith and superstition, to social, political, and judicial fairness, and to the rights of individual citizens. As a result of the influence of such ideas, the eighteenth century has been called both the Age of Reason and the Age of Enlightenment.

Toward the end of the century the notion that laws are made with the consent of the governed, rather than imposed by an absolute ruler, had become widespread and inspired two major upheavals—the American Revolution of 1776 and the French Revolution of 1789. These revolutions shattered the time-honored hold of the divine right of kings on Western politics.

The quotation at the beginning of this chapter is from Common Sense, *a political pamphlet written by the Englishman Thomas Paine (1737–1809) two years after he arrived in America in 1774. A staunch believer in human rights, Paine wrote anti-slavery tracts and supported the emancipation of women and the American and French revolutions. His assertion that "the law is king" reflected his conviction that legitimate laws are designed to protect individual citizens. Laws are "king" in the sense that they, rather than a hereditary monarch, are the rightful and just criteria by which a society is regulated.*

POLITICS AND WAR

Although a relatively peaceful period, the first half of the eighteenth century had its share of wars. Of the three major seventeenth-century monarchs, only Louis XIV of France was still alive in 1700. That same year, he inherited the estate of his grandfather, Charles II, the last Habsburg ruler of Spain. The idea that France and Spain might be united alarmed Britain and the Netherlands, and other countries allied with them against the French. This led to the War of the Spanish Succession, which was not settled until 1713 with the Treaty of Utrecht and which, with the Peace of Rastatt (1714), divided Europe in a new way. Philip of Anjou (grandson of Louis XIV) as Philip V now ruled Spain and Spanish territories in America. Habsburg Austria gained Italy and the Spanish Southern Netherlands. England won Gibraltar, parts of French Canada, and the right to transport slaves from Africa to Spanish colonies in the Americas. France agreed not to try to install a Catholic king on the English throne.

From 1740 to 1748 the War of the Austrian Succession was fought between Austria and Prussia mainly over the right to rule the hereditary Habsburg territories. The Seven Years War (1756–1763), which began as a conflict between Austria and Prussia, developed into a colonial struggle between Britain and France, with hostilities extending to Asia and North America. In America and Asia the conflict is known as the French and Indian War; it caused France to lose territory in North America, India, and Europe. From that time on, Britain was the dominant European power and remained so until World War I (1914–1918).

THE ENLIGHTENMENT

Eighteenth-century philosophers embraced the spirit of Enlightenment. They considered Britain a model of constitutional government. Enlightenment philosophers continued the previous century's advocacy of natural law and sought to make moral standards the basis for judicial and political decisions. Civil liberties, the rights of the individual, and a preference for scientific investigation over religious thinking and superstition also characterized Enlightenment thought.

A few monarchs began to be influenced by the Enlightenment. Rulers in Austria, Prussia (which now dominated large parts of Germany), and Russia came to be called "enlightened despots" because they wished to be seen as sympathetic to their people and were inclined to accept some reforms. Frederick II of Prussia, known as Frederick the Great (ruled 1740–1786), was such a despot. Although he established an organized, efficient army to maintain his power, he recognized that encouraging commerce would enrich his territory, and he allowed some religious tolerance. Catholic Austria, under Maria Theresa (ruled 1740–1780) and her son Joseph II (ruled 1780–1790), also enacted some reforms, including freedom for the serfs and economic modernization. Peter the Great continued to reform Russia, a policy also pursued by his effective and brilliant successor, Catherine II, the Great (ruled 1762–1796). She was a German princess and the widow of his assassinated grandson. She gained support from the population despite favoring the nobility over the serfs. Well-educated herself, Catherine believed in educating women, patronized the arts, and entertained west European intellectuals in St. Petersburg, the capital founded by Peter the Great.

PHILOSOPHY AND THE *PHILOSOPHES*

Several Enlightenment thinkers such as Thomas Paine and Benjamin Franklin embraced Deism—that is, they believed in God, but not in doctrine, prayer, or the Sacraments. Jesus, in contrast to the way he had been portrayed in Christian tradition, was seen as an ethical model rather than as the savior of humanity. In addition, the Deists wanted an educational curriculum independent of the Church. They adhered to the belief inspired by scientists such as Isaac Newton that God created the universe and then left his creations to evolve naturally. According to this view, God allowed the laws of nature to run the universe like a clock, which inspired the metaphor of God as clockmaker. This was among the Enlightenment views embodied by the French *Philosophes*, although Deism itself was not widely accepted. It was resisted in Europe and America, but reflected a gradual move from religious to secular thinking.

After the death of Louis XIV in 1715 and the succession of his ineffective great-grandson, Louis XV (ruled 1715–1774), the French aristocracy moved from Versailles to Paris. As the new center of intellectual life in Europe, Paris was home to the *salon*, an example of which is illustrated in figure **17.1**. In fact, the word *salon*, in addition to denoting a reception room, referred to a social gathering organized by a hostess (*salonnière*), usually in a *hôtel* (private house). The *salonnière*, typically an educated, wealthy woman, welcomed intellectuals and provided agreeable settings for lively intellectual conversation. The most influential thinkers in the Parisian salons were the *Philosophes*, including the French authors Denis Diderot (1713–1784), François-Marie Arouet (Voltaire; 1694–1778), and Baron de Montesquieu (1689–1755), and the Swiss author Jean-Jacques Rousseau (1712–1778). Their ideas spread to a wide audience in Europe and America through novels, essays, and political pamphlets.

DENIS DIDEROT Influenced by seventeenth-century discoveries in science, Denis Diderot (figure **17.2**) edited the *Encyclopédie* (*Enclyclopedia*), compiled from 1750 to 1772. He intended it to be a summation of Western knowledge, which it systematically classified in twenty-eight volumes of illustrated text. Politicians who felt threatened by Diderot's position on civil liberties and his criticism of divine right attempted to censor the *Encyclopedia*, but because it was privately funded (unusual at the time), its publication proceeded, and

17.1 Germain Boffrand, Salon de la Princesse, Hôtel de Soubise, Paris, *c.* 1740.
The ornate decoration of the Salon, designed by the French royal architect, is characteristic of Rococo style under Louis XV. Elaborate gilding frames the architectural spaces, stucco Cupids frolic at the edges of the ceiling, and paintings alternate with the arches of the mirrors. Reflecting outdoor light, the mirrors multiply the glittering atmosphere of the interior.

it had a large circulation. Diderot, who translated a number of Locke's works into French, repeatedly offended the Catholic Church by his emphasis on reason over faith and his advocacy of religious toleration. In the 1760s Diderot wrote *Le Neveu de Rameau* (*Rameau's Nephew*), a dialogue on the inevitable conflict between genius, tradition, and social convention.

17.2 Jean-Antoine Houdon, *Diderot*, 1771. Terra-cotta, 16⅛ in. (41 cm) high. Louvre, Paris.
This sculpture in the Neoclassical style embodies the admiration Enlightenment thinkers felt for the republican traditions of Greece and Rome. It recalls the busts of Roman emperors and portrays individual personality with stately dignity. Houdon's Diderot is a lively figure with raised eyebrows and a vivid expression that reflects the questioning spirit of the Enlightenment.

VOLTAIRE Voltaire admired England, especially its constitutional government. He considered Milton and Shakespeare among the greatest authors of western Europe and he translated Locke into the French *Lettres philosophiques* (*Philosophical Letters*), also called *Lettres anglaises* (*English Letters*), of 1734. Raised by Jesuits, Voltaire believed in God but advocated Church reform and was generally thought to be an atheist.

The title of Voltaire's well-known work *Candide* (*Optimism*, 1759) is ironic, because it is profoundly pessimistic. *Candide* recounts the far-flung adventures of its hero, conveying the absurdity of life, the incoherence of the world, the folly of mankind, and the evils of fanaticism and vice. Like Cervantes' Don Quixote (see Chapter 16), Voltaire's Candide encounters the horrors of the world but puts a positive gloss on them. His main companion is Pangloss, whose name conflates two Greek words: *Pan*, meaning "all," and *glossa*, meaning "tongue" or "language"; the French word *glose* has the additional meaning of criticism, commentary, and parody. These allusions are conflated in Pangloss's refrain, "this best of all possible worlds," which simultaneously echoes and satirizes Candide's eternal optimism.

Candide opens in the castle of Baron Thunder-ten-tronckh in Westphalia, where lives a gentle, absurdly optimistic youth. "His face," wrote Voltaire,

> was the expression of his soul. His judgment was quite honest and he was extremely simple-minded; and this was the reason, I think, that he was named Candide.

At the end of the tale, Candide and his companions consult an old Turk, who is indifferent to politics and leads a simple life. The Turk's advice becomes the basis of Candide's philosophy: *Il faut cultiver notre jardin* ("We must cultivate our garden"). Pangloss heartily agrees, pointing out that Adam and Eve were put in the Garden of Eden so they could tend it. Candide and his companions follow Pangloss and devote themselves to improving their lives, each according to his or her talents.

READING SELECTION

Voltaire, *Candide*, on the philosophy of Dr. Pangloss, PWC4-005

CHARLES-LOUIS DE MONTESQUIEU Baron Charles-Louis de Secondat, Baron de Montesquieu, a member of the French nobility and a local judge, wrote satires and political essays designed to convey a social message. His *Lettres persanes* (*Persian Letters*), published in 1721, satirizes French customs and institutions through the eyes of a Persian visitor to Paris. Montesquieu's Persian tourist sends his first impressions of Paris to a friend in Turkey:

> Paris is as big as Isfahan [in modern Iran]: the houses are so high that one would judge them inhabited only by astrologers. You realize that a city built in the air with six or seven houses one on top of the other is extremely populous. And when everyone is in the street, there is quite a to-do.
>
> You won't believe it, but I have been here a month and have yet to see anyone walk . . . They run, they fly: the slow caravans of Asia, their pace measured by our camels, would make them swoon.
>
> (Letter 24, lines 5–14)

Montesquieu advocated an English-style constitutional monarchy with the ruler's power balanced by the clergy, the nobility, and a parliament. In *Persian Letters* his allegory of the cave-dwelling Troglodytes portrays an ideal republic founded on moral principle. Montesquieu asks if people are happier leading lives of sensual pleasure or virtue. One of the Persian travelers recounts the fable of a small country in Arabia inhabited by a race of amoral, uncivilized Troglodytes. Having killed their king and elected ministers, they decide to live wild according to natural law. They work only for themselves without regard for their neighbors.

Two of the Troglodytes, however, live apart and agree to work together. They teach their children virtue and mutual cooperation. The children multiply and form a new society, learning to worship the gods, live frugally, and honor the common good. They find happiness in Montesquieu's virtuous society, which is based on the republican ideals of ancient Greece and Rome.

Montesquieu's interest in politics inspired him to travel for several years, two of which he spent in Britain. Aside from his curious notion that climate influences the style of a nation's government, Montesquieu's discussion, published in *The Spirit of Laws* (1748), of the different forms of political systems has become a classic of its kind. Following Locke, Montesquieu believed that republics are founded on virtue and that power ultimately rests with the citizens. Monarchy, he argued, is based on honor; citizens in a monarchy do not need virtue, because power is in the hands of the ruler and subjects are equal in their obedience to the crown. Despotism, he warned, is based on fear, which makes virtue unnecessary and honor dangerous. Citizens ruled by a despot are equal only in the degree of their servitude.

Montesquieu emphasized the importance of the balance of power, calling for separate jurisdictions divided among executive, legislative, and judicial branches of government. His ideas, which were directly critical of the divine right of kings, exerted a strong influence on the framers of the American constitution.

READING SELECTION

Montesquieu, *Persian Letters*, on the fable of the Troglodytes, PWC4-176

JEAN-JACQUES ROUSSEAU Rousseau was born to a Protestant family in Geneva but lived most of his life in France. A friend of Diderot, Rousseau wrote extensively on politics, education, and botany. He also wrote novels, one opera, and, in the last decade of his life, the *Confessions*. In 1762 Rousseau published *Emile* (on education) and *The Social Contract* (on politics). In *Emile* Rousseau expressed his belief in the natural freedom of the infant and the gradual acquisition of morality. He thought that children should be taught the principles but not the dogma of religion. Combining his ideas on education and politics, Rousseau argued that in nature people are immoral and that morality can be achieved only in states based on a social contract. Like Montesquieu, he opposed absolute monarchy and rule by divine right.

Rousseau contributed to the eighteenth-century notion of the "noble savage," a concept in part derived from the Classical myth of a "Golden Age." He argued that in a state of nature "primitive" humans are content, devoting themselves only to basic needs. Society's ills could thus be repaired by studying the model of people in nature.

Although Rousseau considered democracy the ideal form of government, he thought it was rarely attainable. Monarchy, he believed, was the strongest system but the least faithful to the general will. Rousseau's famous assertion, "Man is born free; and everywhere he is in chains," which became a rallying cry of revolution, reflects his conviction that society corrupts. After 1762, opposition to Rousseau's ideas caused him to leave Paris. His books were burned in Geneva and he did not return to France until 1770.

READING SELECTION

Rousseau, *The Social Contract*, on freedom in chains, PWC4-173

PHILOSOPHY IN GERMANY: GOTTFRIED LEIBNIZ AND IMMANUEL KANT

Unlike the *Philosophes*, German philosophers were mainly interested in **metaphysics** (an abstract approach to philosophy that considers the question of ultimate reality). Rather than focusing on political theory and the rights of citizens, German thinkers were concerned with God's relationship to Nature.

Gottfried Wilhelm von Leibniz (1646–1716), who was born in Leipzig, was a rationalist and an optimist. He argued that God had created a harmonious universe, which was perfectly ordered and composed of particles, which he called "monads." Each monad contained a reflection of the whole. In 1710 Leibniz published *Theodicy*, a justification of God's ways, including evil. Leibniz's interest in physics and mathematics also led him to develop what is now the standard version of calculus (see Chapter 16).

Immanuel Kant (1724–1804) lived in East Prussia, where he taught at the University of Königsberg. He established the idea that philosophy, as well as aesthetics and religion, should be organized systematically. He evolved a theory that divided the observable world from the spirit, or *noumena*. His greatest work, *The Critique of Pure Reason* (1787), argues that metaphysics can offer truth without empirical evidence. Although we begin to attain knowledge through experience and observation, Kant wrote, it is not possible to attain knowledge exclusively by observing and experiencing—for example, he said that we know God exists even though we cannot see him or demonstrate his existence. While Kant believed that Nature, the "phenomenal world," could be viewed scientifically through empirical observation and experimentation, he preferred a spiritual approach to understanding God.

One of Kant's most complex ideas involves transcendental metaphysics. On the one hand, he attributed meaning to the world and its creation, but did not believe that this is knowable. On the other hand, he argued that some things (the *noumena*) are real, but also transcendental, which means they have the potential for knowability. Kant's transcendentalism became enormously influential in the nineteenth century when it was adopted by the Romantic Movement (see Chapter 18) and applied more to social ideas than to philosophy.

BRITAIN: PHILOSOPHY, ECONOMICS, AND POLITICS

In Britain, where constitutional monarchy had supplanted absolutism, philosophers and political thinkers were generally more rational than transcendental in their views of the world. The Scottish philosopher and historian David Hume (1711–1776), for example, was, like Kant, interested in the limits of reason and the distinction between inner and outer experience. But unlike Kant, Hume believed that in addition to applying scientific study to the exterior world, the inner psychological world should be studied.

Hume was particularly concerned with morality and how people make judgments and arrive at conclusions. He viewed life as a struggle between reason, which he distinguished from illusion, and nature. As a skeptic, Hume was unconvinced by established proofs of God's existence and believed that there could be no certainty about what was unprovable. During a stay in France, Hume wrote *A Treatise of Human Nature* (published 1739–1740). His subsequent works were elaborations on the principles set forth in that treatise.

Eighteenth-century British economists began to develop theories that laid the foundations of political economy as a separate field of thought. The Scottish economist Adam Smith (1723–1790) opposed government control of commerce, advocating instead a system of laissez-faire (literally "let it be") over mercantilism, in which the economy was designed to benefit the state. He believed in the advantages of private property and in the notion that unregulated prices would nat-*urally adjust themselves to market forces. In An Inquiry into the Nature and Causes of the Wealth of Nations* (published in 1776 and generally known as *The Wealth of Nations*) Smith addressed agricultural economies. Nevertheless, the work became the basic text of free-market capitalism championed by nineteenth-century industrialists (see Chapter 19).

The economist Thomas Malthus (1766–1834), in his *Essay on the Principle of Population* (published 1788), focused on the economic and social dangers of overpopulation. Warning that the world's food supply could not keep pace with population growth, Malthus argued that famines, epidemics, and wars were inevitable. His views led to a commonly held notion that the immoral lifestyle of the lower classes caused their poverty.

The best-known work of history in the English language was written in the eighteenth century. Edward Gibbon (1737–1794) brought out the first volume of *The History of the Decline and Fall of the Roman Empire* in 1776 and the last volume twelve years later. The work is divided into three main sections—from Trajan to the fall of Rome, from Justinian to Charlemagne, and from the renewal of the West to the Fall of Constantinople in 1453. As with the historians of ancient Greece and Rome (see Chapters 6 and 7) and as was typical of the Enlightenment, Gibbon sought rational explanations for historical events, and he attributed the fall of Rome largely to the rise of moral decadence. Gibbon also tried to explain how and why Christianity came to dominate Rome and, like the humanists, explored the links between antiquity and the modern world.

A germ of the women's rights movement can be found in the late-eighteenth-century works of Mary Wollstonecraft (1759–1797). She believed that women should be educated and not subservient to men, and she was actively engaged in contemporary issues affecting women. She worked as a governess in Ireland, opened a school in Newington in 1783, and frequented intellectual circles in London and Paris. Her marriage to the radical William Godwin (1756–1836) produced a daughter, the future Mary Shelley, author of *Frankenstein* (see Chapter 18). In 1792 Wollstonecraft published *A Vindication of the Rights of Woman* in which she argued against the double standards that gave men more freedom than women.

READING SELECTION

Wollstonecraft, *A Vindication of the Rights of Woman*, on poor education as the primary source of woman's inequality, PWC4-074-B

ART IN THE EIGHTEENTH CENTURY

During the first half of the eighteenth century a growing aristocratic class patronized the arts. In painting, sculpture, and architecture the ornate Rococo style—from two French words, *rocaille* (rock) and *coquille* (shell)—evolved from the Baroque. Differing from the grandeur of Baroque, Rococo style appealed to the fanciful taste of upper-class patrons. Rococo works are typically decorative, depicting frivolous aristocratic subjects rather than retaining the dramatic quality and classicism of Baroque style. Color in Rococo painting tends to be pastel, and textures are usually soft and silky. Nevertheless, some Rococo artists increased the depth of their work with undercurrents of satire and social commentary. Rococo began in France, but achieved its most elaborate expression in Austria and Germany.

FRANCE

The main artistic style in eighteenth-century France was Rococo. It began in the *salons* of Paris after the death of Louis XIV in 1715. Since Louis XV was uninterested in art patronage, art ceased to be a political tool for the French royal court. Although the Rococo style evolved in Paris, it soon spread to Germany, Austria and, to a lesser degree, Italy.

JEAN-ANTOINE WATTEAU The most important Rococo painter in France was Jean-Antoine Watteau (1684–1721). He was born in Flanders, but lived and worked mainly in France. His paintings, known as *fêtes galantes*, depict the French aristocracy at leisure, often in pastoral or garden settings. Painting in the colorist tradition of his Flemish predecessors, Rubens and van Dyck (see Chapter 16), Watteau emphasized the elegance of the upper classes, yet his works contain an undercurrent of satire (figure **17.3**). Although he delighted in the portrayal of aristocratic finery and frivolity, Watteau's works hint at a subtext of loneliness, loss, and pessimism.

FRANÇOIS BOUCHER The French painter François Boucher (1703–1770) was less subtle than Watteau. His frank eroticism is conveyed by rich textures and flirtatious, fleshy nude women, which satisfied the taste of the French court. Boucher was a particular favorite of Mme de Pompadour, his most devoted patron and the mistress of Louis XV.

Boucher's *Odalisque* of 1745 (figure **17.4**) lies on Turkish pillows covered in blue silks. Her left foot falls casually onto the edge of a red Oriental carpet, which reinforces the harem setting. The white sheets are wrapped around her in a way that enhances her provocative pose.

ADÉLAIDE LABILLE-GUIARD A more stately but no less extravagant example of Rococo can be seen in the work of Adélaide Labille-Guiard (1749–1803). Her *Self-portrait with Two Pupils* (figure **17.5**) shows the artist in all her finery, seated before a canvas with a palette and brushes. Unlikely as it is that she would actually have painted in such an outfit, she is observed by two eager female students who are also rather too well-dressed to be working in a painting studio. The picture is thus a set piece, as the artist rests her

17.3 Jean-Antoine Watteau, *Les Bergers*, *c.* 1716. Oil on canvas, 22 × 32 in. (55.9 × 81.3 cm). Stiftung Preussische Schlösser und Gärten Berlin-Brandenburg, Schloss Charlottenburg.

Elegantly dressed figures enjoy themselves outdoors: a woman swings from a tree, pushed by a leering gentleman. Couples engage in amorous interchanges and dance. A flock of sheep is tended by a brooding shepherd. Nearly lost in shadow, his pensive expression contrasts with the frivolous pursuits of the aristocracy.

17.4 François Boucher, *The Odalisque*, 1745. Oil on canvas, 21 × 25⅜ in. (53.5 × 64.5 cm). Louvre, Paris.

slipper primly on the easel's support and gazes at the viewer. She, not her work, is the subject of the painting, although she has made her image a tour-de-force of the art of painting. The marble bust in the background alludes to the lingering Classical tradition.

17.5 Adélaide Labille-Guiard, *Self-portrait with Two Pupils*, 1785. Oil on canvas, 6 ft. 10¾ in. × 4 ft. 11⅞ in. (2.1 × 1.5 m). The Metropolitan Museum of Art, New York.

Labille-Guiard was interested in improving the status of women in the arts and in society. At the time, the French Academy of Painting and Sculpture admitted only four women to membership at any one time and they were not allowed to take up professorial appointments. Labille-Guiard helped persuade the Academy to lift these restrictions.

17.6 Balthasar Neumann, staircase of the Residenz from the northwest, Würzburg, Germany, 1752–1753.
The staircase is enlivened with ornate balusters, large kraters (Greek urns), and statues, and stucco Cupids decorate the cornices of the doors and windows. This view from the top of the staircase creates the impression that bright outdoor light animates the architectural forms.

17.7 Antonio Bossi, stucco detail from the Weisser Saal, the Residenz, Würzburg, 1744.
Bossi came from Italy and worked in Germany, where the Rococo style was supported by aristocratic taste. This detail is from the White Room, so called after its white and silver-gray color. The irregular curves, asymmetry, and spatial illusionism are typical of the most ornate Rococo designs. Fanciful creatures, Cupids, and foliage seem constantly in the process of transformation, merging into one another in endless revolutions of form.

Rococo in Germany: The Würzburg Residenz

A major expression of the Rococo in Germany, the Residenz in Würzburg, belonged to the hereditary prince-bishops (a German title combining the office of bishop with that of prince) of the Schönborn family. Designed by Balthasar Neumann (1687–1753) and built from 1719 to 1753, the Residenz was decorated with an elaborate staircase (figure **17.6**), illusionistic frescoes, and ornate stucco work (figure **17.7**).

The frescoes are the work of the Italian artist Giovanni Battista Tiepolo (1696–1770) and are typically Rococo in their pastel color and illusionism. Four large frescoes in the Stairway Hall represent Asia, Europe, Africa, and America, symbolizing the international power of the Schönborn family. The detail in figure **17.8** personifies America as a large female with a feathered headdress, a bow slung over her shoulder, and necklaces. The wildness of the New World is indicated by the ferocious crocodile on which America sits, its wealth by the cornucopia of fruit.

17.8 *left* **Giovanni Tiepolo, detail of "America," the Residenz, Würzburg, 1750s. Fresco.**

ROBERT ADAM The architecture of the Scottish designer Robert Adam (1728–1792) combined ancient Greek, Roman, and Etruscan designs with the pastel colors of Rococo. The excavation of Pompeii and Herculaneum fueled the interest in classicism and Adam incorporated aspects of the ancient ruins into his own designs. The Library at Kenwood House, London (figure **17.10**) has the barrel-vault ceiling and apse of a Roman basilica and painted architectural sections resembling those of Roman villas. Stately fluted Corinthian columns supporting an entablature recall Greek temples, but the abundance of gilding and the animated surface details are Rococo.

BRITAIN: ROCOCO, SATIRE, AND THE NEOCLASSICAL STYLE

Artists in Britain produced their own version of Rococo, which emphasized satire and portraiture rather than the frivolity of continental style. Figure **17.9** reflects the upper-class character of British patronage of eighteenth-century portraiture. By the second half of the century, in Britain as on the continent, Rococo began to give way to the more restrained Neoclassical style, although for a time the styles overlapped. The Royal Academy of Arts was founded in London in 1768, 120 years after the French Royal Academy. Its first director, Sir Joshua Reynolds (1723–1792), advocated the study of Greek and Roman art and the introduction of Classical features into English Rococo. Eventually, as the vogue for classicism spread, the Neoclassical style completely supplanted Rococo.

17.9 *right* **Thomas Gainsborough, *The Blue Boy*, c. 1770. Oil on canvas, 5 ft. 10 in. × 4 ft. (1.78 × 1.1 m). Huntington Art Collections, San Marino, California.** Gainsborough (1727–1788), who came from a middle-class family in Suffolk, was the leading portrait painter of eighteenth-century England. This represents Jonathan Buttall, whose father was a prosperous merchant and a friend of the artist. Gainsborough has dressed his sitter in the fashion of a van Dyck (see Chapter 16), whose work he admired. The rich blue crinkled silk outfit, feathered hat, and bows on the shoes reflect the aristocratic tastes of the previous century. The boy has a somewhat sullen arrogance, echoed by the moody landscape.

17.10 Robert Adam, Kenwood House Library, London, begun 1767.

WILLIAM HOGARTH The most popular artist of social satire in England was William Hogarth (1697–1764). He produced engravings of his work, which, because they were less expensive than paintings, were available to buyers from different social classes. Drawing on subjects from everyday life, Hogarth showed sympathy with the working class and aimed his satirical wit at the aristocracy—as in his series entitled "Marriage à la Mode."

Plate 1 of the series (figure **17.11**) attacks the custom of treating marriage as a purely business transaction. The fat Lord Squanderfield, a bankrupt merchant and the father of the groom, at the far left, elevates his foot, which is swollen with gout. He points proudly to his family tree, even though work on his new house (visible through the window) has stopped because he has run out of funds. At the right, the attorney Silvertongue addresses the bride, who barely listens. Her fiancé ignores her and admires himself in the mirror. At the lower right corner, a pair of chained dogs alludes to the couple's unfortunate future and the "imprisonment" of the bride.

The pictures on the wall reflect Hogarth's repulsion for such marriage arrangements. Most depict famous biblical and mythological calamities and conflicts—Pharaoh's armies drowning in the Red Sea, David battling Goliath, Judith beheading Holofernes, the martyrdoms of Sts. Sebastian and Lawrence (on a bed of coals), Prometheus tortured by the vulture, the Massacre of the Innocents, and Cain killing Abel.

17.11 William Hogarth, Plate 1 of "Marriage à la Mode," 1741. Etched from the painting, fifth state, $13^3/_4 \times 17^1/_2$ in. (35×44.5 cm).

17.12 William Hogarth, "The Four Times of Day" series plate IV, *Night*, second state, 1738. Etched from paintings, 17½ × 14½ in. (44.5 × 36.8 cm).
Signs on the buildings advertise a brothel and a tavern (the wine glass). Through an open window, we see an inebriated barber pulling a client's tooth. Dishes of blood on the ledge outside are reminders of previous surgeries performed that day. At the end of the street is the equestrian statue of King Charles I, recalling the ancient Roman emperors, but here presiding over chaos, poverty, and debauchery.

In an elaborate oval frame a raging Medusa head seems to scream in protest against the marriage.

In *Night*, from "The Four Times of Day" series (figure **17.12**), Hogarth addresses the social and moral problems of the urban street. Two men stagger home after a night of debauchery, as a chamber pot emptied from above spills its contents over the man at the left (see Box). Below the ledge next to him, a group of homeless people have settled in for the night. A fire in the middle of the street causes the carriage to crash and the distressed passengers to cry out in terror.

NEW ARTISTIC TRENDS IN THE EIGHTEENTH CENTURY

Artistic currents other than Rococo emerged in eighteenth-century Europe.

CHINOISERIE Beginning in the 1720s, a fashion for *chinoiserie* (Chinese elements inspired by both trade with Asia and Rococo opulence) developed (figure **17.13**). Another factor contributing to the interest in the East was the recent translation of the Persian collection of stories *The Thousand and One Nights* (see Chapter 9).

Society and Culture

Daily Life: The Chamber Pot

Chamber pots were the "plumbing" of choice in eighteenth-century Europe. Human waste was collected in pots—glass, copper, or ceramic pots for the lower classes, and solid, ornately decorated silver pots for the upper classes. The pots were generally emptied by servants, who threw the contents out of a door or window, as in Hogarth's engraving (see figure 17.12).

The history of the chamber pot is an old one. In ancient Greece the dramatist Aeschylus (see Chapter 6) referred to its contents as "missiles of mirth," and in Rome the Dejecti Effusive Act imposed a fine if the contents hit a passerby during daylight hours. The practice continued, and in France emptiers had to warn pedestrians by shouting *gardez-l'eau* ("watch out for water"), a phrase that became "gardy-loo" in Britain. The French chamber pot, called the *chaise percée* (pierced chair), was a chair with arms and a pot that slid on the seat. It was customary for Louis XIV and others of high status, including women, to receive visitors while using the chair.

Henry VIII's chamber pot was padded with black velvet adorned with ribbons and fringes attached with gilt nails, and King James I of England and Scotland traveled with a portable pot (the "potty"). The first toilet was designed for Queen Elizabeth I in 1596, but though she herself used it, the idea was generally ridiculed and failed to catch on. It was not until 1775 that the first patent for a toilet with a trap to retain water was granted. Three years later, hinges and two valves were added. Sanitary plumbing was not required by law in Britain until the nineteenth century.

17.13 Maison Chinoise, Désert de Retz, Seine-et-Oise, France. Engraving from *Le Rouge, Détails des Nouveaux Jardins* Vol. 13, 1785.
Chinoiserie, which was especially popular in France and England, inspired buildings, furniture, parks, and gardens in Chinese style. Gilded in places and decorated with curved roofs and finials, this three-story house was located in a large private French park.

17.14 Jean-Baptiste-Siméon Chardin, *Young Man Blowing Bubbles*, *c.* 1734. Oil on canvas, 24 × 25 in. (61 × 63 cm). The Metropolitan Museum of Art, New York.

CHARDIN AND BOURGEOIS STYLE A more bourgeois style in which artists emphasized the virtues of hard work and study also developed in the eighteenth century. The best-known painter in this style was Jean-Baptiste-Siméon Chardin (1699–1779), whose main subjects were genre and still life. His simply dressed figures engage in everyday activities. The darkened backgrounds and heavily textured paint (*impasto*) convey a sense of middle-class respectability and hard work (figure **17.14**). Here, however, there is a double message contained in the meaning of the term "bubble." An adolescent boy focuses intently on blowing a bubble as a smaller boy in shadow watches from behind the sill. But we know that the bubble will burst and that it is a transitory object. Chardin thus implies that the boy is engaged in a frivolous activity, without a practical outcome, that is contrary to the seriousness of the bourgeois work ethic.

THE VOGUE FOR CLASSICISM With the excavations of Pompeii and Herculaneum (see Chapter 7) and the publication in 1764 of *The History of Ancient Art* by the German scholar Johann Joachim Winckelmann (1717–1768), the fashion for antiquity grew in popularity. Winckelmann introduced a new approach to the study of art, leading to the academic discipline of art history. He believed that art was determined primarily by cultural factors and should be classified accordingly.

The reformist views of the Enlightenment used Greek and Roman subject matter with a political subtext that advocated republicanism. *Cornelia, Mother of the Gracchi*, by Angelica Kauffmann (1741–1807), for example, illustrates a famous event from Roman history (figure **17.15**). Born in Switzerland,

17.15 Angelica Kauffmann, *Cornelia, Mother of the Gracchi*, 1785. Oil on canvas, 3 ft. 4 in. × 4 ft. 2 in. (1.02 × 1.27 m). Virginia Museum of Fine Arts, Richmond.

Angelica Kauffmann became a leading Neoclassical painter. She joined a painting academy in Rome and helped establish the Royal Academy of Arts in London. Her version of the story of Cornelia takes place on a balcony overlooking the distant hills of Rome. The virtuous daughter of the republican leader Scipio Africanus (see Chapter 7), Cornelia had married the praetor Tiberius Sempronius Gracchus, who arranged a peace with Spain in 179 B.C. Their sons, known as the Gracchi, also became statesmen. When they were boys, their mother was asked to produce her family jewels. Cornelia produced her sons as exemplars of modesty and simplicity. Rome honored Cornelia with a statue inscribed "Cornelia, Mother of the Gracchi."

ENGLISH LITERATURE IN THE EIGHTEENTH CENTURY

As with the visual arts, Rococo and Neoclassical elements appear in the literature of eighteenth-century Europe. The most important fiction writers were English, and they combined aspects of Classical style and content with frivolity and satire.

POETRY: DRYDEN AND POPE

The poet John Dryden (1631–1700) founded the Augustans, a group of English authors who were inspired by literature from the period of the Roman emperor Augustus (see Chapter 7). Imbued with the spirit of Virgil and the *Aeneid*, Dryden wrote extensively on Roman subjects. He translated Latin poets into English and published essays, operas, plays, satires, and literary criticism. He supported the Restoration monarchy of Charles II because of the king's patronage of the arts, and when Charles died, Dryden eulogized him with an ode in the style of Pindar (see Chapter 7).

Another Augustan, Alexander Pope (1688–1744), combined Classics and a humanist outlook with Rococo levity. He translated the *Iliad* (1713–1720) and *Odyssey* (in the 1720s) and also admired Virgil and Horace, who inspired his poetry. Pope published a poetic version of Héloïse's letters to Abelard (see Chapter 11), moral essays in poetic form, epitaphs and odes, elegies, pastorals, and literary criticism.

Pope's most original genre was satire. He mocked the heroic epic styles of Homer and Virgil in *The Rape of the Lock* (1712–1714), in which he made fun of the fashionable world, including the social problems confronting women at the time. The inspiration for the poem was a real event: Lord Petre had cut off a lock of hair from Miss Arabella Fermor, which led to a feud between their families. Pope dedicated the poem to Arabella in an effort to mend the breach.

Invoking the Muse and applying the epic form to a lighthearted romp with underlying themes of social satire, in Canto I Pope asks:

> Say what strong motive, Goddess! [the Muse] could compel
> A well-bred Lord [Petre] t'assault a gentle Belle [Arabella]?
> O say what stranger cause, yet unexplor'd,
> Could make a gentle Belle reject a Lord?
> In tasks so bold, can little men engage,
> And in soft bosoms, dwells such mighty Rage?

Pope's Epitaph, "Intended for Sir Isaac Newton in Westminster Abbey" (1735), exemplifies his quick wit and admiration for the Enlightenment:

> Nature and Nature's Laws lay hid in Night:
> God said, *Let Newton be!* and all was Light.

PROSE: SWIFT AND JOHNSON

The fiercest satirical author of the eighteenth century was Jonathan Swift (1667–1745). Born in Dublin, he became an Anglican priest in England and later returned to Dublin as Dean of St. Patrick's Cathedral. Politically he was a monarchist and a conservative. Deeply pessimistic about human nature, Swift contended that, although it was possible for men to be reasonable, on the whole most were not. Women, Swift believed, were ridiculous and unreliable.

Swift's best-known satire, published in 1726, is *Gulliver's Travels*, in which the shipwrecked Gulliver lands in different countries that highlight the world Swift knows and disdains. Gulliver's first adventure takes place in the land of Lilliput, which is inhabited by small people who call Gulliver the "Man-Mountain." In the second voyage, Gulliver visits Brobdingnag, where he meets a race of Giants. In the third, he travels to Laputa, Balnibarbi, Luggnagg, Blubbdubrib, and Japan. In his fourth and final voyage Gulliver encounters the Houyhnhnms, a race of rational, civilized horses who rule their slaves, the despicable human Yahoos. The Houyhnhnms are appalled to learn that in Gulliver's world the situation is reversed and that humans ride, train, tame, and castrate horses.

Gulliver vividly describes humanity's physical flaws as seen through the eyes of the Houyhnhnms—the flatness of the face, the prominent nose, the eyes in the center of the face (which limits their range of vision), and their insecure step because they have only two, instead of four, feet. To the Houyhnhnms, humans are ugly, impractically formed, and wear clothes that they change according to the weather. Gulliver notes the astonishment of his hosts "that I was not able to feed myself, without lifting one of my Forefeet to my Mouth."

The Houyhnhnms are physically superior to humans, in Swift's view. More noble, temperate, and industrious, they practice superior hygiene. Their sense of social responsibility is reflected in their laws on reproduction. Each Houyhnhnm couple is permitted one child of each gender, whereas the Yahoos are known to have as many as three of each.

READING SELECTION

Swift, *Gulliver's Travels*, a giant's property in the land of Lilliput, PWC4-122

Samuel Johnson (1709–1784), the son of a bookseller, studied at Oxford and became a man of letters. He wrote extensively on various subjects, including politics, poetry, and theater. Whereas Diderot in France aimed to compile the *Encyclopedia* of all existing knowledge, and Gibbon recorded Western history from the fall of Rome to the fall of Constantinople, Johnson set out to catalogue the English language. His monumental work, *A Dictionary of the English Language* (1755), defined over 40,000 words, standardized pronunciation, and provided word derivations. Johnson was immortalized by James Boswell (1740–1795), whose *Life of Samuel Johnson* (1791) is widely considered the best biography in the English language.

DRAMA: SHERIDAN

Although English theater had suffered from censorship in the mid-seventeenth century under the puritanical rule of Oliver Cromwell (see Chapter 16), entertainment was revived under Charles II and his successors. Eighteenth-century audiences liked the fashionable dialogue peppered with brilliant wit that characterizes the comedies of Richard Brinsley Sheridan (1751–1816). His play *The Rivals* was produced in 1775, when he was only twenty-three.

The play is set in the old Roman city of Bath, in southwestern England. It is a farcical, frivolous tale, filled with word play. Sir Anthony Absolute, for example, is so-named because he requires absolute obedience, whereas Lydia Languish, his son's fiancée, lacks energy and spontaneity. She is the niece of Mrs. Malaprop, whose name has come to define a form of verbal error known as a "malapropism." Statements such as "He is the very pineapple of politeness" combine punning with Sheridan's satirical view of pomposity. In the first act of *The Rivals* Mrs. Malaprop regales Sir Anthony with her philosophy of the proper education for a lady:

> I would by no means wish a daughter of mine to be a progeny [malapropism for prodigy] of learning; I don't think so much learning becomes a young woman . . . she should have a supercilious [for superficial] knowledge in accounts; and as she grew up, I would have her instructed in geometry [for geography], that she might know something of the contagious [for contiguous] countries. But above all, Sir Anthony, she should be mistress of orthodoxy [for orthography], that she might not misspell and mispronounce words so shamefully as girls usually do, and likewise that she reprehend [for apprehend] the true meaning of what she is saying. This, Sir Anthony, is what I would have a woman know; and I don't think there is a superstitious [for superfluous] article in it.
>
> (Act 1, scene 2, lines 212–222)

THE MODERN NOVEL

The modern novel was born in eighteenth-century Britain where, as the middle class grew and literacy spread, narratives became popular reading matter, especially among women. Although generally read as entertainments, many stories taught manners and morality to their readers. Influenced by the Enlightenment interest in empiricism, this new genre focused on social and psychological observation. The plots unfold over time, and personality is minutely developed and described, which encouraged readers to identify with the characters and places they read about.

The first modern novelist is widely considered to be Daniel Defoe (1660–1731). Samuel Richardson (1689–1761) was the first British novelist to focus on the interior life of his characters, whereas the adventure stories of Henry Fielding (1707–1754) engage readers in the exterior events of his characters' lives.

DANIEL DEFOE Defoe began writing fiction in his late fifties. The son of a London butcher, Defoe was a Protestant who studied for the ministry and then became a hosiery salesman. He loved to travel and make detailed records of his observations. Among his more than five hundred works is a three-volume guide to Britain, written between 1724 and 1726. He also wrote hundreds of political pamphlets, for which he was imprisoned on more than one occasion.

Defoe's first novel is his best-known work—*Robinson Crusoe* (1719), published when he was fifty-nine years old. Based on a widely publicized shipwreck, the story is filled with realistic detail but is elaborated by Defoe's rich imagination. He describes Robinson Crusoe's existence on an island, where, having constructed a crude house furnished with odds and ends salvaged from the wrecked ship, he is disturbed by an encounter with cannibals. One of these becomes his assistant, and Crusoe names him "Friday." The juxtaposition of Crusoe with the inhabitants of the island is a reflection of the author's interest in current notions of the "noble savage" originally advanced by Rousseau (see p. 470). Crusoe and Friday remain on the island for several years until they are rescued by sailors. The work was immediately popular and translated into many languages, becoming widely known in Europe and America.

READING SELECTION

Defoe, *Robinson Crusoe*, on Crusoe's first years as a castaway, PWC4-007

SAMUEL RICHARDSON Richardson focused mainly on the psychology of his characters. In 1740 he published *Pamela*, the story of a servant who marries her employer. The subtitle, *Virtue Rewarded*, indicates that Pamela's refusal to succumb to her master's attempted seduction is rewarded with marriage. The plot revolves around six main characters, all of whom communicate through letters, and Richardson used the literary device of representing himself as the editor of letters that reveal his heroine's innermost thoughts. This type of novel, using letters or diaries to reveal character and to move the plot along, is termed **epistolary** (from the Latin word *epistola* meaning "letter"). *Pamela's* popularity reflected the rising importance of the English middle-class readership and the influence of women as a target audience.

In the eight-volume *Clarissa, or The History of a Young Lady* (1748–1749), more than twenty characters correspond in different writing styles, and their letters make up a third of the novel. Richardson deals with themes of love and deceit, identity and chastity, which for Clarissa are one and the same. When she is raped by the dashing cad Lovelace, Clarissa begins to go insane and ends up in debtor's prison. She recovers when she is rescued by the affectionate Belford, whose letters describe her preparation for a Christian death. The novel is unusual for its time in depicting the tragic inability of characters to resolve their conflicts.

HENRY FIELDING Whereas Richardson's novels are deeply psychological and take place in intimate domestic settings, Fielding wrote expansive adventures. Some of his plays were influenced by Molière, and he also wrote a dramatic tribute to Cervantes and a successful burlesque, *Tom Thumb* (1730). Fielding's taste for satire, leveled mainly at the upper classes, reflects his admiration for Swift and his friendship with Hogarth.

Fielding's popular novel *Tom Jones* (actually *The History of Tom Jones, a Foundling*) was written in 1749. Its adventuresome spirit, the exuberance of its hero, and its fast-paced narrative place it squarely in the picaresque tradition. The orphan Tom is a lusty, good-natured character who welcomes all that life has to offer. His penchant for getting into scrapes and his immoral behavior work out in the end. He inherits a fortune, marries, and settles down to enjoy a life of goodness and virtue.

READING SELECTION

Fielding, *Tom Jones*, Tom grows up, PWC4-109-B

MUSIC IN THE EIGHTEENTH CENTURY

The eighteenth century saw the birth of the Classical style in music. Classical music reflected the orientation of the Enlightenment toward the rational, secular, and "natural," as opposed to the enigmatic, mystical, and spiritual qualities valued in the Baroque period.

The context of music-making also changed. Much less centered on the Church and on aristocratic employers than in previous eras, music was now often written and performed for middle-class audiences. In large cities, orchestral concerts became a regular part of the social calendar, and successful composers mounted "benefit concerts"—concerts from which they took home the profits. Virtuoso players traveled from city to city to earn their living and gain acclaim. Meanwhile amateur music-making expanded with the cheaper production of musical instruments and more widely available published music. Often women learned the harpsichord or piano, and men tended to take up the violin or flute. Composers wrote chamber music and teaching material for this growing market. Music also began to be composed and performed for its own sake, rather than for specific occasions.

CLASSICAL STYLE

The style of Classical music differs markedly from that of Baroque music. As in the other arts, "Classical" in music refers to proportion, balance, and careful formal structuring. The genres of the Classical period—here taken to refer to the dates 1750–1810—work on standard principles of construction: repetition and reprise of themes; short, regular phrases; clearly demarcated sections; modulation from the home key to related tonalities and back again. For the listener, they contain easily recognizable moments of dramatic climax and repose. The melody-line dominates the texture, with slow-moving harmonies beneath.

THE MUSICAL *GALANT*

Musical styles do not switch neatly at a particular juncture in history; generally there is overlap between one era and another. While Bach and Handel were writing their masterpieces of the late German Baroque in the 1720s, a simpler and more delicate style was emerging, especially in France. The term **galant** (French for "gallant," but implying sensuous pleasure and worldliness) that had been used for the paintings of Watteau was applied to this music, with its flowing melodies, gently "sighing" phrases, and sometimes dancing rhythms. The musical *galant* shares lighthearted amorous content with Rococo.

OPERA IN TRANSITION

Nowhere can the taste for lighter music be seen more clearly than in the development of comic opera in the early eighteenth century. In France, *opéra comique* dramatized popular subjects in spoken dialogue alternating with catchy songs—unlike the formal *tragédies lyriques* of Lully and Rameau (see Chapter 16). In Italy, the equivalent was *opera buffa*, and in Germany, the *Singspiel* (literally "sung-tale").

Another response to the formal style and excessive vocal display that had overtaken serious Italian opera came from the German Christoph Willibald Gluck (1714–1787). Living for much of his career in Vienna, which was to become the center of late-eighteenth-century music, he came into contact with Enlightenment thinkers who sought to portray emotion truthfully. His opera *Orfeo ed Euridice* (*Orpheus and Eurydice*, 1762) is, like the earliest operas (see Chapter 16), based on a Greek myth in which music has power even over death. It is known as a "reform" work, abandoning showy *da capo* arias in favor of simpler formal structure and vocal style. Recitative and song flow into each other, both with orchestral backing. This avoids the abrupt changes of texture (from harpsichord alone to full orchestra) of Italian opera. As in Greek tragedy, Gluck emphasizes the chorus, bringing it into the action—first mourning the death of Eurydice, then as Furies, and later as Blessed Spirits.

In the Preface to a later opera, *Alceste* (1767), Gluck explained the thinking behind his new style of composition:

> When I undertook to write the music for *Alceste*, I resolved to divest it entirely of all those abuses, introduced into it either by the mistaken vanity of singers or by the too great complaisance of composers, which have so long disfigured Italian opera and made of the most splendid and most beautiful of spectacles the most ridiculous and wearisome. I have striven to restrict music to its true office of serving poetry by means of expression . . . I believed my greatest labor should be devoted to seeking a beautiful simplicity.

MUSICAL INSTRUMENTS OF THE CLASSICAL PERIOD

The piano was the most important instrument to come into use in the Classical period. Socially, this was a significant development, as the piano was reasonably priced and many families bought them to play at home. Previous keyboard instruments included the harpsichord and its small-scale counterparts, the virginal and spinet. All three produce sound by plucking, whereas the piano uses a small hammer to strike the string. Apart from making a different type of sound—the harpsichord has a tinkling quality—the piano is distinctive because it can be played loudly or softly. The performer controls volume by pressing the keys more or less forcefully (on the harpsichord this has no effect on the sound).

The Classical period was a time of technical advance among instrument makers. Seventeenth- and eighteenth-century violin-making has never been surpassed (see Box). In the woodwinds, the flute, oboe, and bassoon were improved by the addition of keys that made it easier to play in tune. Latest to arrive on the woodwind scene was the clarinet, which first appeared in the early eighteenth century and gained a regular place in the orchestra from around 1800. Brass instruments of the Classical period were restricted in the tones they could produce; extra lengths of tubing known as "crooks" were inserted into trumpets and horns to enable different pitches to be played, and it was not until the nineteenth century that the modern system of valves was invented.

In the mid-eighteenth century the orchestra began to take on a standard form. Prior to this it had been a flexible ensemble. Monteverdi's orchestra for his opera *Orfeo*, for example (see Chapter 16), had contained a wide variety of instruments, many of which fell out of use. The Classical orchestra (figure **17.16**) had as its basis a group of strings—from highest to lowest, violins, violas, cellos, and double basses. Supplementing this were wind instruments—two oboes and two French horns—and gradually further players were added: flutes, clarinets, and bassoons in the woodwinds; trumpets and trombones in the brass; and timpani in the percussion. In the early Classical period, the harpsichord continued to be used to support the harmony, often played by the conductor as he directed the musicians.

Classical composers took advantage of the particular characteristics of each instrument. Whereas a Baroque composer might have written the same pattern of notes for a violin, an oboe, or a voice, now more individual styles of writing emerged. Violins generally carried the melodic line in the orchestra, with their capacity to sustain and with their agility. Woodwinds were used for contrast, brass for expansive sound at climaxes. Trumpet and timpani were often paired, "punctuating" structural points within movements.

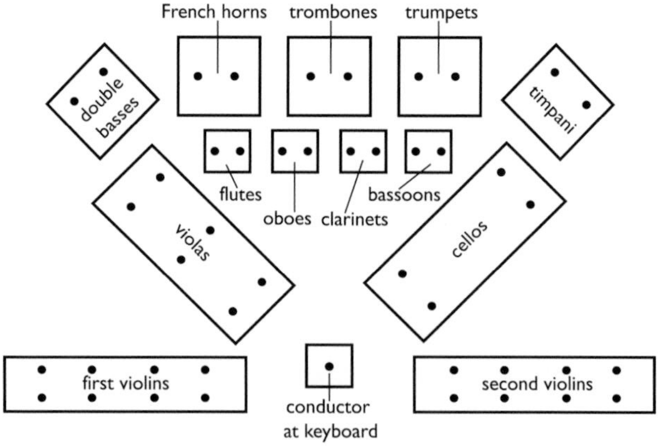

17.16 Diagram of a Classical orchestra.
The original arrangement of the symphony orchestra remains standard today. The layout is similar to ancient Greek theater design, hence the term *orchestra*, which denoted the Greek stage. There are four main families of instruments—strings, woodwinds, brass, and percussion—each grouped together.

Great Violin-makers of Italy: The Amati, Stradivari, and Guarneri

Most musical instruments have continued to evolve and improve up to the present day. The violin, however, reached its high point in the seventeenth and eighteenth century and has undergone only minor alterations since. At that time, great families of violin-makers, the Amati, the Stradivari, and the Guarneri, lived and worked in Cremona, in northern Italy. They created violins that have never been surpassed.

The violin is a shaped wooden box with a wooden neck attached to it. Four strings are fixed from pegs at the far end to run over a bridge to the tailpiece near the player's chin. Sound resonates in the wooden box when a bow is drawn across the strings, and different notes are produced when the player "stops" the string, placing a finger of the left hand on it to shorten it and thus raise the pitch. A well-made violin, competently played, produces a beautiful quality of sound—silvery on high notes and full and rich on lower ones.

Antonio Stradivari (1655–1737) was apprenticed to a member of the Amati family, and he modified their basic design by reducing the arching of the back and front panels of the instrument. One of the violins made by him—known as *the* Stradivarius—arguably produces the best sound to date, and an original Stradivarius is one of the most highly valued musical instruments in the world. No one has yet figured out how Stradivari made the distinctive soft varnish characteristic of his violins, about 650 of which are still in existence. He also made cellos, violas, harps, and guitars, in all totaling over 1100 instruments.

The Guarneri family produced five important violin designers, of whom the greatest was Giuseppe Guarneri (1698–1744). He signed his instruments with a cross and the monogram *IHS* on the labels, which gave rise to his nickname "del Gesù" ("of Jesus"). He is thought to have made 250 violins, of which 150 survive. They are known for their combination of strength of sound and tonal beauty.

Classical Instrumental Music

The most important forms of Classical instrumental music were the **sonata**, the **string quartet**, the concerto, and the **symphony**. The first two of these are types of chamber music, the latter are orchestral genres.

The sonata, like the trio sonata of the Baroque era, has several contrasting movements—usually three. Classical sonatas were most commonly written for solo piano or for piano with another instrument such as the violin. Generally the first movement is fast, the second slow, and the third fast. From the mid-eighteenth century onward, first movements were frequently structured to a plan that became known as **sonata form**. As this is the most important musical structure of the Classical and Romantic periods, we shall, despite its complexity, examine it briefly here. In its "textbook" form, it begins with the **exposition**, in which a first theme is introduced in the **tonic** or "home" key, followed by a second theme, often of a more lyrical nature, in a contrasting key. The **development** section follows, in which the two themes are elaborated, fragmented, and juxtaposed in passages that modulate to different keys. In the closing **recapitulation** section, the first and second themes are reintroduced, but this time both are in the tonic key. The movement is rounded off with a brief **coda**, or tailpiece. The overall sensation is that of a dramatic journey in which the two themes, once introduced, travel to unfamiliar surroundings and eventually return home, united in the same tonality. A parallel can be drawn with the novel, which appeared around the same time; it exhibits a similar sense of exposition, dramatic development to a climax, and resolution.

Sonata form was used by composers not just in sonatas, but for the first movements of most types of instrumental piece in the Classical period. This includes chamber music for various groupings of instruments, with and without piano—trios (for three players), quartets (for four), and quintets (for five). Most significant was the string quartet, for two violins, viola, and cello. It is an intimate form of chamber music, as much a pleasure to perform as to hear. The instruments work together as well as independently—like four individuals engaged in a discussion. Haydn wrote some seventy quartets, Mozart twenty-three, and Beethoven seventeen. Classical quartets are structured in four movements (with the exception of some late Beethoven), generally fast, slow, minuet, fast. Typically the opening movement is in sonata form. Sometimes the slow movement is a theme and variations, which gives each instrument in turn the chance to take the tune and perform it with whatever embellishment the composer has devised. The minuet is a stately dance in triple meter with a repetitive structure: the minuet is played first, then a trio section, followed by a reprise of the minuet. The last movement, or finale, may be in **rondo** form—this is a structure based on a recurrent theme with contrasting material presented between the recurrences.

The two main orchestral genres of the Classical period were the concerto and the symphony. Classical concertos are almost all in three movements, for one solo instrument with orchestra. As with the Baroque concerto, the essence of the Classical concerto lies in the interplay between soloist and large group.

The symphony (literally, a "sounding together"), a piece for orchestra, developed in the eighteenth century with the advent of public concerts. The earliest symphonies consisted of three or four movements. Typically, the first movement, the longest and most dramatic, is fast-paced and uses sonata form; the second is slow and meditative; a minuet and trio in dance meter sometimes follows as the third. The last is often the fastest, with a sprightly, less serious outlook than the rest of the work.

Franz Joseph Haydn

Franz Joseph Haydn (1732–1809), known as the "Father of the Symphony," was the first major Classical composer. As a child, he sang in the choir of St. Stephen's Cathedral, Vienna; as an adult, he was music director for the princely Esterházy family in Hungary for nearly thirty years. Enormously prolific, Haydn composed in all the main musical forms, among them symphonies, concertos, quartets, piano trios, piano sonatas, operas, oratorios, and Masses. The symphony is considered his greatest achievement: he wrote 108 in all.

The Listening Selection is an extract from the slow movement of a symphony Haydn wrote for a visit to London in 1791–1792. It was nicknamed "Surprise" because of its unexpected loud chord. The piece is written in theme and variation form; note the simplicity of the theme at the opening, broken into at midpoint by the "Surprise" chord. Another loud chord announces Variation 1, where the second violins take up the theme while first violins elaborate with graceful figuration above, sometimes doubled by woodwinds. Listen for the change in mood for Variation 2, a freer treatment of the theme as the key shifts from C major to the more forbidding C minor. A dramatic passage with rapid descending and ascending scales follows. (The extract fades out as the music leads toward the last two variations.)

MUSIC LISTENING SELECTION
Haydn, Symphony No. 94 in G major, the "Surprise," second movement, Andante. Capella Istropolitana, conductor Barry Wordsworth, CD track 11

Haydn's grand yet simple style heard in the "Surprise" Symphony is also a feature of his oratorio *The Creation* (1798), set to a text that draws on Milton's *Paradise Lost*. The first part, which tells the story of God's creation of the earth, opens with an orchestral depiction of chaos and concludes with an exuberant, joyful chorus, "The heavens are telling the glory of God." Songs of the newly created world depict the rhythms of the sea, the soaring flight of birds, and flowers opening up in the meadows. The second section describes the creation of life, with the music echoing the sounds of nature. Finally, in the third section, Adam and Eve appear and celebrate their love for each other.

Wolfgang Amadeus Mozart

Many musicians consider Wolfgang Amadeus Mozart (1756–1791) the most universal composer in the history of Western music. A child prodigy, he could play the harpsichord and the violin and had begun to write music and perform in public by the age of five. His father was a professional musician who promoted his talented children. Over a period of several years he took the young Wolfgang and his sister Nannerl touring across Europe from court to court, performing for the nobility and giving concerts in the major musical centers.

In 1769, in his early teens, Mozart was given the honorary title of concertmaster at the Salzburg court, and this became a formal salaried post in 1772—despite his efforts to find better employment. Increasingly frustrated by the limitations placed upon him by the archbishop of Salzburg, Mozart resigned from his service in 1781. Unlike Haydn, who was primarily a court musician—having security but essentially living as a servant—Mozart became a free agent. He composed and performed on commission, renting halls, hiring orchestras, and relying on ticket sales for his income. As one of the first composers to break with patronage, Mozart worked hard, earned well, but spent most of his income. He died in poverty in Vienna at the age of thirty-five.

As a composer, Mozart was inventive, versatile, and fluent in every musical form of the Classical period. He wrote over six hundred compositions, including operas, Masses, concertos, symphonies, string quartets, piano sonatas, and light pieces such as his well-known *Eine kleine Nachtmusik* (1787). It was not uncommon to compose in so many genres, but Mozart was exceptional in excelling in them all.

His twenty-one piano concertos range in mood from lyrical to brilliant, dramatic to richly expressive. They achieve a Classical balance between soloist and orchestra. Formally, they combine the ritornello structure of the Baroque with elements of sonata form—using contrasting thematic material and exploiting key relationships to build and release dramatic tension. The soloist sometimes shares and develops the orchestral material, sometimes departs into displays of technical skill. The first movement comes to a climax as the orchestra falls silent for the **cadenza**—a solo virtuosic display, sometimes improvised, before the final orchestral section.

In opera, Mozart took the forms of his day—*opera buffa*, serious Italian opera, *Singspiel*—and gave them a scale and expressiveness that make these dramas timeless. In his hands, comic opera moves away from a lighthearted romp of stock figures and becomes a human story. *The Marriage of Figaro* (*Le nozze di Figaro*, 1786), for example, is a play about servants outwitting the nobleman who employs them. Count Almaviva believes he has a right to seduce Susanna before her wedding to Figaro, but with the help of the neglected Countess they manage to prevent this.

Like other artists of the Enlightenment, Mozart satirizes the wealthy and points out social injustices. At the same time, he characterizes each personality in music. The Countess pines for her husband's love, yet is dignified; the Count's music portrays his power and expectation of having his own way. Lighter in style, Susanna's and Figaro's arias convey the quick wit they need to survive as servants. In the Listening Selection, a **duet** that opens the first scene of the opera, Figaro is measuring a room Count Almaviva has offered as a bedroom for the newlyweds. Figaro's voice can be heard counting out the measurements; Susanna is asking him to admire her new hat. Notice how the orchestra has a prominent role in the duet, providing a sustained backdrop of both harmony and melody. The vocal lines are quite unlike the set-piece arias of the Baroque; instead, they flow naturally from the script.

MUSIC LISTENING SELECTION

Mozart, *The Marriage of Figaro*, Act 1, scene 1, "Cinque . . . dieci." Patrizia Pace, soprano, Natale de Carolis, baritone, Hungarian State Opera Orchestra, conductor Pier Giorgio Morandi, CD track 12

Mozart followed *The Marriage of Figaro* with another Italian opera about social and sexual tensions. *Don Giovanni* (1787) takes the story of a Spanish nobleman who notches up a tally of women with whom he has scored. At the end of the opera he receives his come-uppance. Again, the comedy has serious undertones and the music a rich and dramatic score.

In the last year of his life, Mozart wrote an opera in the *Singspiel* tradition. The perennially popular *Magic Flute* (*Die Zauberflöte*) begins like a fairy tale, with a prince trying to rescue a princess from an evil magician. But all is not as it seems, and as the action continues, a moral tale of love tested emerges. The prince has to pass through fire and water, playing his magic flute for protection, before he can claim the princess's love. A sub-plot with a bird-catcher carrying magic bells provides comic relief, and the wicked Queen of Night contributes drama and vocal fireworks. *The Magic Flute* is a work of great variety in both form and content and its philosophical character reflects the ideas of the Enlightenment.

FROM CLASSICAL TO ROMANTIC: LUDWIG VAN BEETHOVEN

The German composer Ludwig van Beethoven (1770–1827) was born into a family of musicians in Bonn, but he spent most of his career in Vienna. At sixteen he performed for Mozart, who immediately recognized his genius, and for a time Beethoven studied with Haydn.

Beethoven's genius forms the bridge between Classical music and the Romantic style, and scholars continue to debate whether he is best considered in the light of classicism or of Romanticism. His structures and much of his technique are Classical, but his expansive, emotional moods and dramatic use of forceful rhythms are associated with Romanticism. Beethoven's life and work span both the styles and the periods in which they flourished. As most of his greatest music was composed in the first two decades of the nineteenth century, we consider him in the context of the Romantic Movement, which is the subject of the next chapter.

REVOLUTIONS IN AMERICA AND FRANCE

Both the American and French revolutions were fueled by Enlightenment ideas about constitutional government, civil liberties, and the rejection of the divine right of kings. The two revolutions occurred within thirteen years of each other, the former in 1776, the latter in 1789.

The American Revolution was fought by colonists against a foreign king, Britain's George III, whereas the French Revolution was essentially an internal conflict. Once the American colonies had defeated the British forces, they established a constitutional government and elected a president. The French king, Louis XVI (ruled 1774–1792), had sided with the American rebels against George III, but in France the change from monarchy to republic was more ambivalent than in America. The first phase of the French Revolution was followed by continued unrest before the monarchy ended permanently in the nineteenth century.

THE AMERICAN REVOLUTION: 1776–1783

The context of the American Revolution differed from that of the French Revolution. The American colonies had no state religion and no hereditary aristocracy. Revolutionary thinking in America was encouraged by a high rate of literacy and citizens acquainted with the *Philosophes* and the Classics. British authors who advocated the rights of individuals were read by intellectuals in America, notably Thomas Paine (1737–1809), Benjamin Franklin (1706–1790; see Box, p. 486), and Thomas Jefferson (1743–1826).

Before the outbreak of the Revolution in 1776, the population in the American colonies was approaching 5 million. At the top of the social hierarchy were plantation owners, lawyers, merchants, and the clergy. Following in descending order were land-owning farmers, artisans, craftsmen, day laborers, indentured servants, and working convicts. At the bottom of the socio-economic ladder were the slaves, on whom such economies as cotton and tobacco depended.

"NO TAXATION WITHOUT REPRESENTATION" In 1763, at the end of the Seven Years War, Britain received land stretching from the Appalachian Mountains to the Mississippi River, Quebec, and Florida. When King George III needed funds to pay debts amassed during the Seven Years War, he imposed new taxes on the colonists. Their objection was expressed in the rallying cry "No taxation without representation." The Stamp Act of 1765 required colonists to purchase a stamp or license for the right to read a newspaper, sign a legal contract, or send mail. Bowing to widespread protests, the king repealed the tax, but in 1767 colonists objected to the Townshend Duties levied on imports. This led to the Boston Massacre, in which British troops fired on colonists and killed five people.

By 1773 only the tax on tea, which helped to finance Britain's East India Company, remained. That year the Boston Sons of Liberty (colonists from Massachusetts) disguised themselves as Native Americans and threw tea from ships into the harbor. Known as the Boston Tea Party, this act of defiance resulted in the Coercive Acts of 1774, which closed Boston's harbor and imposed martial law on the city until the cost of the destroyed tea had been reimbursed. The same year, colonists responded with the Committees of Correspondence, which were designed to disseminate information throughout the colonies about events in Boston. The First Continental Congress met in Philadelphia, to which twelve of the thirteen colonies sent representatives; only Georgia declined to participate.

"THE SHOT HEARD AROUND THE WORLD" In 1775 Britain discovered that colonists had stored a cache of ammunition in the Massachusetts town of Concord and sent troops to confiscate it. On April 19, as the British marched through Lexington, a shot was fired—"the shot heard around the world." The Battles of Lexington and Concord followed, forcing the Continental Congress to take a position siding either with the colonists or with the British.

Benjamin Franklin and Poor Richard

Benjamin Franklin, scientist, inventor, diplomat, printer, statesman, and author, exemplifies the versatile talent and commitment to Enlightenment views of some eighteenth-century Americans. He was born in Boston, the tenth son of a candlemaker; he had some formal education but was largely self-taught. Franklin founded the University of Pennsylvania and the first American public library, and was the first person in the American colonies to publish newspaper cartoons.

Between 1733 and 1758 Franklin published monthly editions of the enormously popular *Poor Richard's Almanac*, whose main character is a dreamy astrologer in continual conflict with his practical wife. Franklin's sharp wit, influenced by reading Rabelais (see Chapter 15) and contemporary English satirists, is reflected in the almanac's epigrams:

> *May 1733: Beware of the young doctor and the old barber.*
> *June 1733: To lengthen thy life, lessen thy meals.*
> *September 1733: There is no little enemy.*
> *July 1749: If your head is wax, don't walk in the sun.*

In 1757 Franklin was sent to England to represent the colonists in matters of taxation. There, in 1771, he began his famous *Autobiography*, which was published in England in 1793 and in America in 1818. In 1776 he was appointed ambassador to France.

In 1776 the pamphleteer Thomas Paine published *Common Sense*, in which he declared that the American colonies were a new nation, free of tyranny, and entitled to pursue trade independently of Britain. That spring the Second Continental Congress formed a committee to draft a statement of independence. This document, the Declaration of Independence (see Box), was primarily drafted by Thomas Jefferson (1743–1826), a young lawyer from Virginia. It marked the establishment of the United States as a free and independent nation. The Declaration was signed July 4, 1776.

The principles of the Declaration echo Locke's notion of the rights of man and the social contract. It begins:

> When, in the Course of human Events, it becomes necessary for one People to dissolve the Political Bands which have connected them with another, and to assume among the Powers of the Earth, the separate and equal Station to which the Laws of Nature and of Nature's God entitle them, a decent Respect to the Opinions of Mankind requires that they should declare the causes which impel them to the Separation.
>
> We hold these Truths to be self-evident, that all Men are created equal, that they are endowed by their Creator with certain unalienable Rights, that among these are Life, Liberty, and the Pursuit of Happiness.

WAR Britain's response to the rebellious colonists—about 80 percent of the population—was swift and violent. Led by George Washington (1732–1799), the poorly trained American fighters were pitted against an efficient British army backed by naval support, an organized central government, and the assistance of colonial loyalists. However, the British were fighting on foreign territory, and they had to ship their supplies across the Atlantic Ocean. The rebels enjoyed the assistance of European nations seeking to restrain Britain's power, in particular France, Spain, the Netherlands, and parts of Germany.

Finally, after seven years of war, the Peace of Paris, partly negotiated by Benjamin Franklin (a signatory of the Declaration of Independence), was signed in 1783. The United States was granted its independence, along with territory stretching from the East Coast to the Mississippi River.

TOWARD A NEW GOVERNMENT: THE CONSTITUTION AND THE BILL OF RIGHTS In 1787 a Constitutional Convention met in Philadelphia to form a new government. Three important political figures collaborated on the Federalist Papers, which argued for a strong federal government—that is, one in which states are united under a central government but retain some measure of independence. The main author, Alexander Hamilton (1755–1804), had fought in the Revolution and was George Washington's secretary. After the war Hamilton became the first Secretary of the Treasury, establishing a national currency and the U.S. Bank. Assisting him were James Madison (1751–1836), later the fourth president of the

Defining Moment

The Declaration of Independence

The Declaration of Independence is one of the most important documents ever written. Its range of influence includes the French Revolution's Declaration of the Rights of Man and the Declaration of Sentiments by Elizabeth Cady Stanton for the Seneca Falls Convention of 1848 to advance women's rights. The lofty ideals of the Declaration of Independence have inspired countless writers, particularly the passage that states that all men are created equal, with certain unalienable rights.

Inspiring though it was, the Declaration was not legally necessary because the Philadelphia convention had passed a resolution of independence on July 2, 1776. However, the Declaration of Independence is far more than an announcement that thirteen English colonies in North America considered themselves free of allegiance to Britain and its king. The Declaration also states how free people should live, that all men have natural rights, the form their government should take, and the mutual responsibilities between a government and its citizens that ensure order and liberty.

The Declaration of Independence, John Adams later said, contained no new ideas. It borrowed from John Locke, from Montesquieu's *The Spirit of the Laws* (1750), and from other *Philosophes.* It reflected ideas circulated throughout the colonies in hundreds of pamphlets in the preceding fifteen years. The Declaration of Independence is clearly part of this pamphlet tradition and is, in fact, designed to justify a radical, unprecedented, and unlawful action by placing the blame on an incompetent king and Parliament. The colonists, the authors claimed, had done no more than protect their God-given rights.

The text of the Declaration has been compared to a legal brief. It presents a long list of grievances against George III, including taxation without representation, maintaining a standing army in peacetime, dissolving bodies of representatives, and hiring "large armies of foreign mercenaries." This analogy compares Thomas Jefferson, the chief author of the Declaration, to an attorney presenting his case before a world court.

Although the Declaration of Independence borrowed ideas, it effectively compresses a large amount of theory into a short space. The assertion that "all men are created equal" presents the basic principle of republican government. The notion that all men enjoy "unalienable rights" repudiates arguments by Thomas Hobbes and others that people surrender their natural rights outside the state of nature. When the Declaration states that governments are created by "the consent of the governed," it applies the social contract. And when it states that people retain the right "to alter or abolish" government when it violates its ends, it defines sovereignty.

Critical Question Should modern American citizens criticize the framers of the Constitution for not adhering to the spirit of the Declaration of Independence when they wrote the Constitution? What for example, did the word "equal" mean to the framers? What does the word "equal" mean today in America?

United States, and John Jay (1745–1829), the first Chief Justice of the Supreme Court. They wanted to convince New York to ratify the Constitution and accept the principle that political power would be shared by the federal and state governments. The introduction of the Federalist Papers, addressing the people of New York State, opens as follows:

> After an unequivocal experience of the inefficacy of subsisting federal government you are called upon to deliberate on a new Constitution for the United States of America . . . It has frequently been remarked that it seems to have been reserved to the people of this country . . . to decide . . . whether societies of men are really capable or not of establishing good government from reflection and choice, or whether they are forever destined to depend for their political constitutions on accident and force.

And in conclusion, Hamilton declares:

> A NATION without a NATIONAL GOVERNMENT is, in my view, an awful spectacle . . . I dread the more the consequences of new attempts because I know that POWERFUL INDIVIDUALS, in this and other States, are enemies to a general national government in every possible shape.

The Constitution ratified in 1788 combined the theories of Locke and Montesquieu. Following Locke, it established rule by an assembly of representatives; following Montesquieu it established a system of checks and balances among the legislature, the judiciary, and the executive branch of government.

The first ten amendments to the Constitution, added in 1791, make up the Bill of Rights. These guarantee freedom of speech, of assembly, and of the press; the right to bear arms (mainly for national defense); the sanctity of property and privacy; and freedom from self-incrimination. Finally, after centuries of torture and other judicial abuses in Europe, the American Bill of Rights forbade the use of "cruel and unusual punishment."

America was the first country in history to found its government on citizens' rights and to guarantee them in a written document. The Constitution precludes tyranny and establishes a balance of power. In place of divine right or hereditary rule, it establishes a system in which ordinary citizens are elected to govern for specified periods of time. Only the nine Supreme Court justices, nominated by the president and confirmed by Congress, have life terms. With the addition of the Bill of Rights and the possibility of further amendments, the

17.17 **John Trumbull, *General George Washington at Trenton*, 1792. Oil on canvas, 7 ft. 8½ in. × 5 ft. 3 in. (2.35 × 1.6 m). Yale University Art Gallery, New Haven, Connecticut.**

instrument of government had a built-in system for preserving flexibility as times change.

Despite the Enlightenment views of the framers of the Constitution, however, slavery was retained. Attempts by Jefferson to abolish slavery were blocked by Congress, and he compromised on the issue. By the end of the century states north of Maryland began to free their slaves, but the South did not follow suit until forced to do so by the Civil War (see Chapter 19). Nor did the Constitution give women the right to vote; that legislation was not enacted until the early twentieth century.

In 1789 George Washington declined the offer to become king and instead accepted the presidency. Washington has been represented in many ways by different artists: as a statesman, a general, a ruler, and an ordinary citizen. John Trumbull's full-length historical portrait, *General George Washington at Trenton* (figure **17.17**), was painted during the third year of Washington's presidency. He is shown in a pose inspired by Classical sculpture, leaning on his sword and surveying his troops. His elevated foreground position emphasizes his commanding presence. Washington's calm, dignified demeanor is conveyed by his juxtaposition with the distant battle, the soldier trying to control his rearing white horse, and the turbulent sky. It is likely that Trumbull's use of the Classical pose reflects the Classical spirit of the early American government and its Constitution.

THE FEDERAL STYLE Thomas Jefferson, who became America's third president in 1801, was an architect, violinist, inventor, author, diplomat, and statesman. As an architect, he established the Federal Style—the American version of Neoclassical architecture. As United States minister to France, Jefferson had been able to study at first hand the Roman ruins of western Europe and to travel to Rome. He also collected Neoclassical sculpture, and read Palladio's treatise on architecture (see Chapter 14).

When he returned to Virginia, Jefferson applied the principles of Neoclassicism to a number of new buildings. He designed the State Capitol in Richmond (figure **17.18**), which he based on Roman temples. The central part of the Capitol is rectangular (like the Roman *cella*) with a temple portico in the Ionic Order. Located at the top of a hill, Richmond's Capitol presides over the city just as the Roman temple was conceived of as presiding over the urban space before it.

A firm believer in public education and a humanist curriculum (see Chapter 12), Jefferson founded the University of Virginia, the first state-funded university in America. The epitaph on his tombstone reads: "Father of the University." Jefferson also designed the Rotunda (figure **17.19**), which was the original university library and is today used for special

17.18 Thomas Jefferson, State Capitol, Richmond, Virginia, 1785–1789.

17.19 Thomas Jefferson, Rotunda, University of Virginia, Charlottesville, 1817–1826.
This building was clearly inspired by the Roman Pantheon (see thumbnail), although the proportions of Jefferson's Corinthian portico are taller. Note the use of pediments over the door and ground-story windows, and the round clock, echoing the dome, in the main pediment. The walkway flanking the Rotunda is of red brick, surmounted by a balustrade and pierced with round-arched openings.

The Pantheon, Rome
see figure 7.37

lectures, meetings, and receptions. The Rotunda was part of a large quadrangle surrounded by the original dorms (which are still in use) and pavilions in the ancient Orders of architecture. Jefferson was the first rector of the school, which he called an "academical village."

THE FRENCH REVOLUTION: 1788–1799

In France the *Philosophes* argued for social reform and opposed the absolute power of decadent and abusive kings. Partly as a result of the Seven Years War and partly because of the rulers' own weaknesses, France lost its position as Europe's dominant power under Louis XV and Louis XVI. Domestic problems, especially the need to reform the tax system, were pressing. The government was on the verge of bankruptcy from its war debts (including, ironically, the cost of Louis XVI's support of the American revolutionaries). When the Catholic Church and the nobility refused to renounce the privilege that excluded them from paying taxes, the French aristocracy sided with the middle class against the king. More drawn out than the American Revolution, the French Revolution unfolded in two distinct phases: from 1789 to 1792 and from 1792 to 1795.

PHASE ONE: 1789–1792 Failure to push through tax reform in the French parliaments forced Louis XVI to convene the medieval assembly called Estates-General, which had not met since 1614. This group of representatives consisted of the Catholic clergy (the First Estate), nobles (the Second Estate), and commoners, which included peasants, artisans, and members of the middle class (the Third Estate). Traditionally, each Estate had one vote, which meant that the more privileged First and Second Estates could outvote the Third. But the deputies representing the Third Estate (mainly lawyers and lower level royal officials) successfully argued that the voting procedures of the Estates-General did not provide them with sufficient influence, and the king was forced to allow twice the number of delegates from the Third Estate.

The Estates-General met at Versailles between 1788 and 1789 and drew up a list of thousands of grievances against the monarchy, which represented the *Ancien régime* (Old Regime). Frustrated by resistance to the demands of the Estates-General, the Third Estate reassembled on June 20, 1789, on the site of the royal tennis court, the *Jeu de Paume*, in Versailles. Fired with revolutionary fervor, they proclaimed themselves the

National Assembly. Their demands reflected guarantees in the United States Constitution—freedom of the press, free trade, citizens' rights and representation, equality before the law, freedom of religion, and a constitution. The National Assembly swore an oath that its members would remain united until a new constitution had been drafted and accepted, an event memorialized by Jacques-Louis David (1748–1825), the leading pro-revolutionary painter, in *The Oath of the Tennis Court* (figure **17.20**).

That summer riots broke out in Paris as eighty thousand commoners, enraged at the high cost of grain and bread, stormed the Bastille prison in search of arms and ammunition. When guards fired on the crowd, the rebels killed six men, including the Bastille's commander, and publicly displayed his head on a stake.

In August the National Assembly wrote the Declaration of the Rights of Man and of the Citizen, which asserted citizens' rights to *Liberté, Egalité, Fraternité* ("Liberty, Equality, Brotherhood"). The clergy were reclassified as ordinary citizens rather than as the First Estate; the king was made chief executive but had no right to enact laws; slavery was abolished in France (and shortly thereafter in the French colonies), and property-owning males were given the right to elect legislators. Women could not vote but were granted new legal rights in marriage.

These inroads into royal authority led to further unrest in France and its colonies. In 1791, led by Toussaint L'Ouverture (1743–1803), the French colony of St. Domingue rebelled. Thirteen years later, in 1804, Haiti became the first independent black republic.

In June 1791, when Louis XVI and his queen, the unpopular Marie-Antoinette (1755–1793), finally realized the danger they were in, they tried to escape. Under cover of night they boarded a carriage with their children and were taken as far as Varennes in eastern France, but they were captured, taken back to Paris, and imprisoned.

Marie-Antoinette is remembered today for her retort to a starving crowd storming Versailles: "Let them eat cake." (In fact, she said "Let them eat brioche," which is a kind of rich breakfast bun popular in France.) The portrait of the queen (figure **17.21**) by Elisabeth Vigée-Lebrun (1755–1842) shows her self-absorbed attention to her own appearance rather than to the people she was meant to rule.

17.20 Jacques-Louis David, *The Oath of the Tennis Court*, 1789–1791. Pen and brown ink and brown wash on paper, 26 × 42 in. (66 × 107 cm). Louvre, Paris.
The crowd filling the enormous space creates a sense that the will of a people is being expressed. Grand gestures of defiance and triumphant embraces dominate the scene. Standing on the table in the center is the president of the National Assembly. His gesture alludes to the Roman generals addressing their troops as well as to the Roman orators in the senate. The light streaming through the windows is symbolically the light of reason and reform.

17.21 Elisabeth Vigée-Lebrun, *Marie-Antoinette à la Rose*, 1783. Oil on canvas, $51\frac{1}{2} \times 34\frac{1}{4}$ in. (131×87 cm). Musée du Chateau de Versailles.
The portrait, typical of the artist's refined, aristocratic style, emphasizes the royal textures of the queen's costume. Her blue silk dress matches her blue eyes—blue blood is a sign of nobility—and the delicate rose she holds matches her rouged cheeks. The powdered hair, feathered hat, and flowing lace contrast dramatically with the dark foliage behind the queen. There is no suggestion that the queen is aware of political reality in France.

PHASE TWO: 1792–1795 In the first phase of action the revolutionaries sought to create a British-style constitutional monarchy. A second revolution in August 1792 ushered in a republican government and a period of extreme violence that lasted for two years. Both the constitution and the monarchy were suspended, and the Reign of Terror began. Between 1793 and 1795, under the leadership of Maximilian Robespierre (1758–1794), hundreds of thousands of French citizens were murdered. Anyone suspected of monarchist sympathies, including members of the aristocracy and their acquaintances, was executed.

Victims of the Terror included the king and queen, who were publicly beheaded in 1793. Figure **17.22** shows Louis XVI's execution in the Place de la Concorde, to where the scaffold was moved for the occasion. The square is filled with revolutionary troops. Echoing the excitement of the event is the small dog racing with the white horse in the foreground. The king's decapitated body lies by the guillotine as a guard displays his severed head for all to see (see Box, p. 492). In this image, the artist emphasizes the detachment of the head from the body, a metaphor for the demise of the king as the "body politic" and "head of state."

Vigée-Lebrun, who witnessed the deaths of Louis XVI and Marie-Antoinette, wrote:

> It was the 5th of October, and the King and Queen were conducted from Versailles to Paris surrounded by pikes. The events of that day filled me with uneasiness as to the fate of Their Majesties and that of all decent people.

Robespierre was arrested in 1794 and condemned to death. France then entered the period known as the *Directoire* (Directory), ruled by moderate landowners from 1795 to 1799. The Directory came to an end with the rise of Napoleon Bonaparte (1769–1821).

17.22 *The Death of Louis Capet, January 21, 1793*, 1793. Colored etching, $11\frac{7}{8} \times 17\frac{3}{4}$ in. (30.3×45.2 cm). Musée Carnavalet, Paris.

Society and Culture

The Guillotine and the French Executioners

The guillotine derives its name from the physician Joseph-Ignace Guillotin (1738–1814), who either invented a new means of execution or sponsored the legislation that approved it. It was used for the first time in 1792, during the French Revolution. Executions in France had previously been carried out according to the social class of the condemned criminal: the nobility and royalty were beheaded by the sword; commoners were either hanged or beheaded with an axe. The guillotine was a great equalizer; nobles and commoners, as well as Louis XVI and Marie-Antoinette, were beheaded by the same method.

With a design derived from scientific experiments, the guillotine was considered a more humane way of executing criminals than the sword or the axe. The efficacy of swords and axes depended on the skill of the executioner, but the guillotine was a mechanical device; its sharp blade could sever a head quickly and cleanly.

From the seventeenth through the mid-nineteenth century, executions in France were carried out by members of a single family, the Sansons. A memoir left by Charles-Henri Sanson offers an unusual view of French history—from the point of view of a royalist who was also the executioner. During the Reign of Terror, Charles-Henri imagined himself regent of the scaffold. After beheading Louis XVI, Charles-Henri repented his act and prayed every night for the king's soul.

According to his memoirs, Charles-Henri sold or loaned cadavers to surgeons for dissection. He also loaned the heads of Louis XVI and Marie-Antoinette to Marie Grosholz, the future Mme Tussaud, who later used them for her museum in London—Madame Tussaud's Waxworks.

In France emblems of the guillotine became fashionable. Jewelers made earrings in its shape, gala dinner tables were decorated with guillotine-shaped cherry liqueur containers, and children played with toy guillotines.

The turbulence that accompanied the two phases of the French Revolution did not abate in the early nineteenth century. Conflicts continued until the country was temporarily stabilized under Napoleon. In the United States, on the other hand, the era of rule by monarchs was over. At the same time, however, there was unfinished business in the United States—in particular, issues of slavery and women's rights which had yet to be resolved.

KEY TERMS

cadenza a solo virtuosic display, sometimes improvised, near the end of an aria or a movement of a concerto.

coda a closing section of a piece of music, added to round it off rather than as a main part of the structure.

development in music, (a) a process of expanding, elaborating, and transforming a musical theme; (b) the section of a movement in which development occurs (commonly the middle section of a movement in sonata form).

duet a piece of music for two performers, or two soloists plus accompaniment.

epistolary a type of novel, which uses letters or diaries to reveal character and to move the plot along.

exposition the first section of a piece of music (especially a movement in sonata form), in which the principal themes are stated.

galant describing a light, elegant, tuneful, and relatively simple style of eighteenth-century music.

metaphysics a type of philosophy that deals with first principles, such as existence and understanding.

recapitulation in music, the third section of a movement in sonata form, in which the main themes are restated in the home key.

rondo a musical form based on a recurrent theme with contrasting material presented between the recurrences; often used for the last movements of Classical symphonies, sonatas, and chamber works.

sonata a musical composition in several movements for solo instrument, soloist with accompaniment, or ensemble.

sonata form a musical form used from the Classical period onward, particularly for the first movements of works such as symphonies, sonatas, and string quartets; it consists of exposition, development and recapitulation.

string quartet an ensemble of two violins, viola, and cello, or a piece of music written for those instruments.

symphony (literally, a "sounding together") an orchestral work, usually consisting of three or four movements.

tonic in music, the home key.

KEY QUESTIONS

1. If one had to choose the most important concept of political thought in the eighteenth century, that theme would be ______. What did that concept mean to three writers who used it?
2. Writers and visual artists use satire to portray society's flaws. Which flaws seemed to rally satirists in the eighteenth century? Suggest two satirists whose work illustrates these concerns.
3. Identify three eighteenth-century works that were influenced by ancient Rome. What events caused the resurfacing of interest in Roman artifacts and styles?
4. What is the social contract? Does the concept of *laissez-faire* relate to the social contract?

SUGGESTED READING

Alpers, Svetlana, and Michael Baxandall. *Tiepolo and the Pictorial Intelligence*. New Haven, CT, and London: Yale University Press, 1996.
▸ A detailed study of Rococo style as expressed at the Residenz, and especially the program of Tiepolo's Stairway Hall frescoes.

Antal, Frederick. *Hogarth and His Place in European Art*. London: Routledge and Kegan Paul, 1962.
▸ William Hogarth, style and context.

Black, J. *Eighteenth-century Europe, 1700–1789*. London: Palgrave Macmillan, 1990.
▸ A survey of the period.

Blackburn, R. *The Making of New World Slavery: From the Baroque to the Modern, 1492–1800*. London: Verso Books, 1997.
▸ A study of the origins and effects of slavery.

Bushkovitch, Paul. *Peter the Great: The Struggle for Power, 1671–1725*. Lanham, MD: Rowman and Littlefield, 2001.
▸ A biography of the life and times of Peter the Great of Russia.

Crow, Thomas E. *Painters and Public Life in Eighteenth-century Paris*. New Haven, CT: Yale University Press, 1985.
▸ Art and life in eighteenth-century France.

The Declaration of Independence and the Constitution of the United States. New York: Bantam Books, 1998.
▸ Primary source documents.

Doyle, W. *The French Revolution*. Oxford: Oxford University Press, 2001.
▸ A general introduction.

Ellis, Joseph J. *American Sphinx: The Character of Thomas Jefferson*. New York: Vintage Books, 1998.
▸ A biography of the American president.

Honour, Hugh. *Neoclassicism*. London: Penguin Books, 1987.
▸ A general survey of Neoclassical style.

Madison, James, Alexander Hamilton, and John Jay, *The Federalist Papers*. London: Penguin Books, 1987.
▸ The original text of the *Federalist Papers*.

McLaughlin, Jack. *Jefferson and Monticello: The Biography of a Builder*. New York: Henry Holt, 1888.
▸ Jefferson as architect.

Paine, Thomas. *Common Sense*. New York: Dover Publications, 1997.
▸ Paine's argument that the American colonies should be a nation independent of the British king.

Proctor, C. *Women, Equality, and the French Revolution*. Westport, CT: Greenwood Press, 1990.
▸ The effect of the Enlightenment and the revolution on the status of women.

Riley, P. *The Cambridge Companion to Rousseau*. New York: Cambridge University Press, 2001.
▸ A collection of essays on the philosopher.

Rushton, Julian. *Classical Music*. New York and London: Thames and Hudson, 1986.
▸ Survey from Gluck to Beethoven.

Vigée-Lebrun, Elisabeth. *Memoirs of Madame Vigée-Lebrun*, trans. Lionel Strachey. New York: George Braziller, 1989.
▸ The memoirs of a painter to European royalty, offering a close-up view of courts and rulers who patronized the arts.

Walzer, M. (ed.). *Regicide and Revolution: Speeches at the Trial of Louis XVI*. Cambridge, U.K.: Cambridge University Press, 1974.
▸ Primary documents and an introduction.

SUGGESTED FILMS

1934 *The Scarlet Pimpernel*, dir. Harold Young
1935 *A Tale of Two Cities*, dir. Jack Conway
1937 *Peter the Great*, dir. Vladimir Petrov
1938 *La Marseillaise*, dir. Jean Renoir
1958 *A Tale of Two Cities*, dir. Ralph Thomas
1979 *Don Giovanni* (film version of Mozart's opera), dir. Joseph Losey
1982 *La Nuit de Varennes* (*Night of Varennes*), dir. Ettore Scola
1984 *Amadeus*, dir. Milos Forman
1992 *Danton*, dir. Andrzej Wajda
1994 *The Madness of King George*, dir. Nicholas Hytner

18 The Early Nineteenth Century and the Romantic Movement

"That government is best which governs not at all."

(HENRY DAVID THOREAU, "CIVIL DISOBEDIENCE")

After the French Revolution Europe was in political turmoil over conflicts between monarchy, representational government, and various utopian social experiments. The dominant figure in early nineteenth-century politics was Napoleon Bonaparte (1769–1821). At first he supported the French Revolution, but he proclaimed himself emperor in 1804 and expanded French authority in Europe. He added new territory to France through conquest, placed monarchs friendly to him on the thrones of several European states, and forced others to comply with his political and economic demands. During the nineteenth century, France underwent a series of political shifts, from republics to restoration monarchies, becoming a modern democracy only after 1870.

Two new philosophical trends influenced by the political situation in Europe were liberalism and nationalism. Liberal thinkers, inspired by the Enlightenment, advocated the rights of citizens. This led to experiments in socialism, which became a force in nineteenth-century politics and inspired utopian communities. Some of the more conservative philosophers, appalled by the Reign of Terror (see Chapter 17), preferred more aristocratic forms of government. The nationalist trend affirmed the importance of national culture and independent statehood and contributed to cultural distinctions between evolving nations.

Industrialization had begun in the eighteenth century and with it came social, political, and economic change that had negative as well as positive effects. The impact of industry on western Europe and the United States became a force against which the Romantic Movement—the prevailing movement in the arts, literature, and music during the early decades of the nineteenth century—struggled. Even within the Romantic Movement, however, there were several currents of thought. Among these were nostalgia for an idealized past, an attraction to distant, exotic locales, a belief in the inherent goodness of humanity, an emphasis on nature, emotion, intuition, and imagination, and a commitment to political and social freedom. Several of these trends were in direct response to the encroachment of industry with its factories, mechanization, and abuses against the working classes.

The Neoclassical style, which we considered in Chapter 17 in the context of the French and American revolutions, was imbued with nostalgia

Key Topics

After the French Revolution

- Napoleon's rise and fall
- Enlightenment and reform

Romanticism and Revolution

- Restoration and revolution
- Individual rights
- Back to nature
- Heroes and monsters
- The sublime and the grotesque

Documents and Movements

- The Napoleonic Code
- Liberalism
- Nationalism
- Transcendentalism
- Exoticism

TIMELINE	EARLY-NINETEENTH-CENTURY EUROPE	THE NEW WORLD
HISTORY AND CULTURE 	Liberalism and nationalism Industrialization Napoleon Bonaparte (1769–1821) emperor of France, 1804 Parliament abolishes slavery in Britain, 1807; ban extended to colonies, 1833 Napoleon invades Russia, 1812 Restoration of Bourbon Monarchy in France, 1815 Napoleon dies in exile, 1821 Revolutions in France, 1830, 1848 Second Empire in France under Napoleon III, 1852–1870	Utopian communities Revolutions in the New World: Haiti, Mexico, Venezuela, Ecuador, and Bolivia
RELIGION	Concordat declares Catholicism France's primary religion, 1801	Unitarians reject Calvinism and religious orthodoxy Transcendental philosophy
ART 	Romanticism and Neoclassicism Turner, *Interior of Tintern Abbey*, 1794; *The Slave Ship*, 1840 David, *Napoleon at St. Bernard Pass*, 1800; *The Consecration of Napoleon I and the Coronation of the Empress Josephine*, 1805–1807 Blake, *Satan in his Original Glory*, *c.* 1805 Girodet-Trioson, *The Entombment of Atala*, 1808 Goya, *The Third of May, 1808*, 1814–1815 Géricault, *The Raft of the "Medusa,"* 1818–1819 Constable, *The Hay Wain*, 1821 Friedrich, *Moonrise Over the Sea*, 1822 Delacroix, *Liberty Leading the People*, 1830 Ingres, *Louis-François Bertin*, 1832	Hudson River School: Cole, *The Last of the Mohicans*, 1827 Luminism: Bierstadt, *Sunrise at Yosemite*, *c.* 1870
ARCHITECTURE	Chalgrin, Blouet, and Gilbert, Arc de Triomphe, Paris, 1806–1836 Nash, Royal Pavilion, Brighton, England, 1815–1818 Barry and Pugin, Houses of Parliament, London, 1836–1870	
LITERATURE AND PHILOSOPHY 	*Sturm und Drang* movement in Germany, late 18th century Burke, *A Philosophical Enquiry into the Origin of Our Ideas of the Sublime and Beautiful*, 1757 Goethe, *The Sorrows of Young Werther*, 1774; *Faust*, 1832 Wordsworth and Coleridge, *Lyrical Ballads*, 1798 Wordsworth, "Lines composed a few miles above Tintern Abbey," 1798 Coleridge, *The Rime of the Ancient Mariner*, 1798; "Kubla Khan," 1816 Chateaubriand, *Atala*, 1801; *The Genius of Christianity*, 1802 Blake (1757–1827), "Jerusalem" Hegel (1770–1831), *Lectures on the Philosophy of History* de Staël, *On Germany*, 1810 Austen, *Pride and Prejudice*, 1813 Mary Shelley, *Frankenstein*, 1818 Byron, *Don Juan*, 1818–1823 Shelley (1792–1822), "Ozymandias"; "Ode to the West Wind," 1819 Keats, "Ode to a Grecian Urn," 1820 Hugo, *Notre-Dame de Paris*, 1831; *Les Misérables*, 1862 Sand, *Indiana*, 1832; *Lélia*, 1833 Emily Brontë, *Wuthering Heights*, 1847 Charlotte Brontë, *Jane Eyre*, 1847 Anne Brontë, *The Tenant of Wildfell Hall*, 1847	Cooper, *The Last of the Mohicans*, 1826; *The Pathfinder*, 1840; *The Deerslayer*, 1841 Emerson (1803–1882), *Nature*, 1836; *Brahma* Poe, "The Raven," 1845; "Annabel Lee," 1849 Melville, *Typee*, 1846; *Omoo*, 1847; *Moby Dick*, 1851 Thoreau, "Civil Disobedience," 1849; *Walden, or Life in the Woods*, 1854 Hawthorne, *The Scarlet Letter*, 1850 Whitman (1819–1892), *Leaves of Grass*, 1855; *Memories of President Lincoln* Dickinson (1830–1886), *Poems on Nature, Poems on Life, Poems for Time and Eternity*
MUSIC 	Beethoven, "Pathétique" and "Moonlight" sonatas, 1799 and 1801; *Fidelio*, 1805–1814; "Eroica," 1803; Symphony No. 5, 1808; "Choral" Symphony, 1824 Schubert, "The Erlking," 1815; *The Beautiful Miller-Maid*, 1823; *The Winter's Journey*, 1827 Berlioz, *Symphonie fantastique*, 1830 Mendelssohn, "Italian" Symphony, 1833; "Scottish" Symphony, 1842 Schumann, *A Woman's Love and Life*, 1840; *A Poet's Love*, 1840 Liszt, *Hungarian Rhapsodies*, 1846–1885 Chopin (1810–1849), mazurkas, polonaises, nocturnes, *études* Brahms, four symphonies; *German Requiem*, 1860s; Violin Concerto in D major, 1878 Verdi, *Rigoletto*, 1851; *La Traviata*, 1853; *Aida*, 1871 Wagner, *Tristan and Isolde*, 1865; *The Nibelung's Ring*, 1848–1876 Mussorgsky, *Boris Godunov*, 1872; *Songs and Dances of Death*, 1877 Grieg, incidental music for *Peer Gynt*, 1876 Tchaikovsky, *Swan Lake*, 1877; *The Nutcracker*, 1892 Sibelius, *Kullervo*, 1892; *Finlandia*, 1899 Dvořák, Symphony No. 9, "From the New World," 1893	

for ancient Greece and Rome. As such, Neoclassicism can be considered an aspect of Romanticism. But despite thematic similarities between these two styles, the formal qualities and subject matter of the Neoclassical style differ from those that interested the Romantics. In contrast to Romanticism, which remained a movement congenial to proponents of intellectual, political, and artistic freedom, Neoclassicism was appropriated by Napoleon to promote his imperial image.

The quote that opens this chapter is from the political essay "Civil Disobedience" by the American author Henry David Thoreau (1817–1862). Thoreau espoused Transcendentalism, a Romantic philosophy that rejected religious orthodoxy and political dogma and advocated a return to nature. Because Thoreau believed in the natural goodness of humanity, he concluded that people are capable of governing themselves and that, therefore, the best form of government is no government at all.

FRANCE: AFTER THE REVOLUTION

The Reign of Terror was followed in France by the Directory (1795–1799), which seemed moderate by comparison. Commerce was promoted and the middle classes were favored. However, the Directory was beset by civil unrest, judicial corruption, pressure from those who had opposed the Revolution, an unstable currency, and a war with Austria that spread throughout Europe. These uncertain conditions continued until November 1799, when Napoleon Bonaparte (1769–1821) staged a coup d'état and took control of the French government, establishing the Consulate, with himself as First Consul.

NAPOLEON BONAPARTE

Born on the island of Corsica, off the west coast of Italy, Napoleon attended military school in France and was a general by the time he was twenty-four. In 1796–1797 he overcame Austria's ambition to dominate northern Italy, which he conquered for France. The following year, however, Napoleon failed in a campaign in Egypt against British control of the route to India through access to the Red Sea. In 1799 he returned to France to find Russia, Austria, Prussia, and Britain—all retaining some form of monarchy—allied against him.

Napoleon governed France as a military dictator. His centralized administration included a secret police corps, which he used to curtail the freedoms of the press and speech. In 1802 he appointed himself Consul for life, and two years later, by proclaiming himself emperor of France, he effectively restored the monarchy. His coronation is the subject of the enormous painting in figure **18.1**. Exhibited in 1808, this picture, like the event itself, records the transition from republic to empire in France, an echo of the reign of Augustus (see Chapter 7) that was not lost on contemporary viewers. Napoleon also wanted to create the impression that, with his assumption of power, France had once again entered a period of stability.

In fact, Napoleon's rule did benefit the French people in a number of ways. He maintained civil order, stabilized the

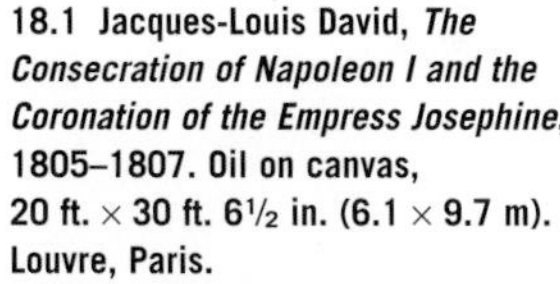

18.1 Jacques-Louis David, *The Consecration of Napoleon I and the Coronation of the Empress Josephine*, 1805–1807. Oil on canvas, 20 ft. × 30 ft. 6½ in. (6.1 × 9.7 m). Louvre, Paris.
This work conveys the grandiose splendor of Napoleon's coronation, which took place in the Cathedral of Notre Dame, Paris. Although the pope actually sat through the ceremony without participating, Napoleon instructed David to depict him blessing the occasion. Napoleon further slighted the pope by crowning himself emperor, traditionally a papal privilege. Napoleon is also shown crowning his empress, Josephine, who kneels before him beside a pillow embroidered with royal fleurs-de-lys. The large round arch framing her is an allusion to imperial Rome designed to legitimize Napoleon as a new emperor.

economy, and limited aristocratic privilege. Most importantly, he revised the French legal system and established the Civil Code (*Code civile*)—popularly called the Napoleonic Code—in 1804. This remains the basis of the legal system in France (and in the state of Louisiana) today, although in modified form.

Napoleon's legal system codified the idea of the secular state. In 1801 he confirmed the supremacy of the state over the Catholic Church when he concluded a Concordat with Pope Pius VII. This declared that Roman Catholicism was the primary religion of France, but it granted religious freedom to Protestants and Jews. It also required that the state appoint bishops and parish priests and pay their salaries.

Building on revolutionary reforms such as the abolition of serfdom and feudal property, the Napoleonic Code secured equal rights for large segments of society. However, the Code reversed some of the advances that women had made during the Revolution, including the right to own property without a husband's permission. Divorce was also made more difficult for women than for men, and there was less provision for women to become educated in 1815 than there had been in 1789. Although the Code instituted public education, Napoleon's curriculum was aimed at creating a professional male elite. He believed that a woman's primary function was to remain at home and take care of children.

As emperor, Napoleon launched a series of wars to strengthen France and weaken its enemies. He defeated Austria and Prussia and isolated Britain from the continent, installing his own relatives and generals as puppet monarchs in Italy, the Netherlands, and Spain (map **18.1**).

In 1812 Napoleon's grandiosity led him into a colossal error of judgment. He invaded Russia, believing that its small army would be easily defeated. But the Russians adopted a "scorched-earth" policy, destroying food supplies as they retreated toward Moscow. By the time Napoleon's troops reached the city, in October, Moscow was in flames. In December he abandoned the campaign and returned to Paris, but the Russian winter killed over two-thirds of his 600,000 troops as they struggled to return to France.

Napoleon's failed campaign inspired Austria, Britain, Prussia, and Russia to form a coalition against him, and they defeated what was left of the French army in 1814. Napoleon was exiled to Elba, a small island near his native Corsica, but he escaped the following year and returned to France to raise a new army. He was again defeated, this time at Waterloo (in Belgium) by a combined force of the British (under the Duke of Wellington) and the Prussians. Exiled for a second time, to the island of St. Helena in the South Atlantic Ocean, Napoleon died there in 1821.

Meanwhile, in 1814–1815, the Congress of Vienna met to ensure that no single nation would ever again dominate Europe as France had done under Napoleon. Territory controlled by France was reapportioned, and the Kingdom of the Netherlands was established. Austria gained control of northern Italy, and Prussia expanded along the River Rhine. The Holy Roman Empire finally disappeared as Austria and Hungary emerged as a dual monarchy, and the Bourbon monarchy was restored in France.

NEOCLASSICAL STYLE UNDER NAPOLEON

Napoleon's manipulation of power extended to the arts as he appropriated Neoclassicism in the service of a political image linking himself with imperial tradition (figure **18.2**, and see thumbnail). In addition to commissioning paintings that depicted him as emperor, Napoleon undertook a vast building program that evoked Roman power. He adopted Roman architectural forms such as the triumphal arch (figure **18.3**), which were designed to legitimize his imperial status. In the Arc de Triomphe, from which

Equestrian statuette of Charlemagne
see figure 10.1

18.2 Jacques-Louis David, *Napoleon at St. Bernard Pass*, 1800. Oil on canvas, 8 ft. 6¼ in. × 7 ft. 3 in. (2.6 × 2.2 m). Musée Nationale du Château de Versailles, France.

Painted in the tradition of imperial equestrian portraits, this work combines Neoclassical clarity with a Romantic taste for moody skies. The rearing white horse emphasizes the steep incline of the mountains as Napoleon urges his troops forward. His identification with famous generals of the past is shown by the inscriptions on the rock—Charlemagne and Hannibal.

Map 18.1 Europe at the height of Napoleon's power, 1812.

several grand boulevards radiate, a pair of winged Victories flanks the curve of the arch, an Ionic frieze wraps around the structure just below the cornice, and the rectangular attic has a Doric frieze with alternating triglyphs and metopes. The towering arch, the largest to date, was a monument to Napoleon's military victories and triumphant rule of France.

RESTORATION, REPUBLIC, AND EMPIRE

The Napoleonic period was followed in France by the restoration of a constitutional monarchy under the Bourbon Louis XVIII (ruled 1815–1824), brother of the executed Louis XVI, who guaranteed individual rights. However, in a bid to restore absolutism Charles X became king in 1824 and restricted the rights of citizens. When liberals won elections held in 1830, the king tried to usurp their power. On July 25 he issued the Four Ordinances, which limited freedom of the press, allowed

18.3 *left* **Jean-François-Thérèse Chalgrin, Guillaume-Abel Blouet, and Emile-Jacques Gilbert, Arc de Triomphe, Paris, France, 1806–1836. 164 ft. (50 m) high.**

only the wealthy to vote, called for new elections, and disbanded the democratically elected Chamber of Deputies.

The July Revolution of 1830 followed. Workers in Paris took up arms in protest against the Four Ordinances. Over 1800 protesters were killed by the king's troops, but the monarchy was overthrown, and Charles X abdicated on August 2. Louis-Philippe, Duke of Orléans (ruled 1830–1848), was installed by the Chamber of Deputies. He was called the Citizen-King because he headed a government controlled by a constitution and the middle classes.

In 1848 a revolution sparked by workers and middle-class liberals disillusioned by political corruption, made worse by agricultural and industrial depression, overthrew Louis-Philippe. Two years later, Louis-Napoleon Bonaparte, nephew of the emperor Napoleon, was elected president of the Second Republic. He instituted universal male suffrage and abolished slavery throughout the French colonies. A new constitution was written, and a National Assembly of representatives was elected. However, in 1852 Louis-Napoleon restored imperial rule and declared himself Napoleon III, launching the Second Empire. After his defeat in 1870 in the Franco-Prussian War, France entered the period of the Third Republic.

The impact of the revolutions of 1830 and 1848 in France was not lost on the rest of the world (see Box). Rulers in Prussia, Austria, and Russia maintained and strengthened their autocratic regimes to quell rebellion and stave off the influence of the Enlightenment. Britain, on the other hand, was becoming a modern constitutional monarchy, and, beginning in the 1820s, further reforms were enacted to encourage trade and liberalize the government.

Revolutions in the New World

Sparked by the French and American revolutions, people in Latin America rebelled against colonial rule. After the establishment of the Republic of Haiti (see Chapter 17), the priest Miguel de Hidalgo (1753–1811) led a peasant uprising in Mexico against the Spanish. He was executed by conservative Creoles (people of mixed ethnic heritage), but the spirit of revolution persisted in Mexico until 1821, when Augustín de Iturbide (1783–1824) proclaimed himself emperor and declared Mexico independent of Spain. In 1838 the Mexican Empire became a group of separate states, with Mexico in the north and, in the south, Costa Rica, Nicaragua, Honduras, Guatemala, and El Salvador.

In South America the revolutionary Creole Simón Bolívar (1783–1830), who was born in Venezuela, organized a coup to liberate Venezuela in 1810. This led to civil war (1811–1814), in which royalists fought slaves and cowboys. Bolívar fled first to Colombia and then to the West Indies, where he reorganized an army to invade Venezuela in 1816. By 1821 he had liberated Venezuela, of which he was named president, and Colombia; in 1822 he liberated Ecuador, and in 1824 Peru. The upper part of Peru was renamed Bolivia after him.

THE ROMANTIC MOVEMENT IN WESTERN EUROPE

The term Romantic is used to describe a revival of interest in literary works with medieval settings written in the Romance languages. As Romanticism developed, a number of revival styles emerged that reflected Romantic ideals of freedom and taste for the long ago and far away. Neoclassicism has been seen as the first of these revivals, beginning with the discovery of Pompeii and Herculaneum in the eighteenth century (see Chapter 17), but the style declined with the demise of Napoleon.

Romanticism originated in Paris and flourished during the restoration of the Bourbon monarchy and the rule of Louis-Philippe (called the July Monarchy). But enthusiasm for the Romantic Movement expanded beyond France, to Spain, the German states, Britain, Scandinavia, and Russia as well as to North America. In literature, and even more so in music, Romanticism continued to the end of the nineteenth century.

Romantic artists, writers, and musicians took a positive view of human nature. They were attracted by themes such as political freedom, social justice, and a new sense of national pride. The wish to escape the abuses of industry (see Box, p. 501) is reflected in the Romantic interest in the exotic East, nostalgia for an idealized Christian past and childhood, and a sense of oneness with nature. Romanticism also coincided with a new interest in psychology, which explored emotions, the unconscious mind, dreams, delusions, fantasies, and the supernatural.

PHILOSOPHY

Liberalism and nationalism, which emerged in the late eighteenth and early nineteenth century, contained aspects of Romantic thought. Liberalism was founded on the principles of a constitution, individual rights, and laissez-faire economics. Nationalism encouraged identification with a national culture —its folklore, arts, religion, and language. In Italy, Germany, parts of central Europe, and eventually Belgium and Holland, many liberals were inspired by nationalist sentiments. They wanted independence from Habsburg rule and papal domination and sought to establish constitutional governments.

These political ideas influenced the Romantic strain of philosophy and aesthetics. The Irish-born British statesman Edmund Burke (1729–1797) had a major impact on Romanticism in *A Philosophical Enquiry into the Origin of our Ideas of*

The Industrial Revolution and James Watt's Steam Engine

The Industrial Revolution began in Britain in the last quarter of the eighteenth century when agricultural productivity improved and the cotton and wool industries were mechanized. Factories mass-producing textiles drew people to the cities, increasing the rate of urbanization and opening up new consumer markets. However, children as well as adults were exploited by the factories, and pollution from burning coal caused widespread lung disease and other health problems (see Chapter 19).

One of the most significant inventions for the development of industry in Britain and later in western Europe and America was the steam engine. Recognizing that steam made by heating coal could be used to power the pumps that removed water from coal mines, inventors in the mid-eighteenth century had been working on a steam engine for some time. But problems arose because supplies of coal ran out and human pumping wasted time and energy.

In an effort to improve the effectiveness of the procedure, the Scottish inventor James Watt (1736–1819) spent the 1760s devising a steam engine that would burn less fuel and had uses other than mining. To this end, he approached gun designers to obtain high quality cylinders and added an insulated condensing chamber that would cool and recirculate the water by means of an air pump. Watt eventually produced the steam engine in 1774. It was later put to many industrial uses, including mining, textile manufacturing, grinding, brewing, and powering potters' wheels and printing presses. The invention was a crucial step toward nineteenth-century industrialization.

The modern term "watt," meaning a unit of power, as in a 60-watt lightbulb, is named after James Watt. He also measured the capacity of his engines in relation to the rate at which a horse works, and determined that this rate was 33,000 pounds raised through one foot per minute. Hence the term "horsepower" to denote the capacity of an engine.

the Sublime and Beautiful (1757). The sublime, Burke believed, evoked fear, hatred, love, and joy. Its power lay in its ability to produce primal terror, whether from loss, dissolution of the self, the eerie quality of the uncanny, or extremes of ugliness and beauty.

A belief in the power of nature, as we saw in Chapter 17, shaped Rousseau's concept of the "noble savage" and Kant's view of aesthetic response in the *Critique of Pure Judgment.* Kant argued that beauty produces delight, which stimulates understanding and imagination. Art, Kant believed, is capable of unifying opposites and thus has subjective as well as universal meaning. For Kant, as for Burke, beauty is finite and uplifting, whereas the sublime is without limit and terrifying.

Kant influenced the complex and intensely nationalistic German philosopher Georg Wilhelm Friedrich Hegel (1770–1831), who viewed art as a means of synthesizing the infinite (his "thesis") with the natural world (his "antithesis"). In *Lectures on the Philosophy of History* Hegel suggested that human thought is determined by history and argued that the philosopher is obligated to explain its rationale.

Enlightenment influence is clear in Hegel's discussion of Asian tyrants. He notes that under such rulers only the ruler himself is free. Hegel believed that the philosophy of Socrates (see Chapter 6) had introduced critical thought and the notion of individual freedom into Western history. And with the Reformation (see Chapter 15), Hegel argued, these freedoms were fully realized. He also considered it necessary to understand history in order to make informed choices, control one's destiny, and achieve intellectual and spiritual freedom. According to Hegel, what he called the World Spirit (a sense of the greater destiny of a historical period) achieves self-awareness through history. In Hegel's view, this consciousness—also called the World Soul—is first achieved through religion, then through art, and finally through philosophy.

PAINTING IN SPAIN AND FRANCE

Romantic painting in Spain and France was generally the province of liberal thinkers committed to political freedom and social justice and opposed to clerical abuses. In Spain, where the Inquisition had been rigorously enforced, the leading painter at the turn of the nineteenth century was Francisco de Goya (1746–1828). His painting *The Third of May, 1808* (figure **18.4**) was commissioned by the Spanish government six years after the expulsion of Napoleon's army from Spain. It illustrates an actual event, with a group of Madrileños (citizens of Madrid) facing a French firing squad. Rebel Spaniards had shot at fifteen French soldiers and, in response, the French killed nearly a thousand Spaniards. Goya's sympathy for the victims is characteristic of his belief that nations should be free from foreign occupation.

Although a strong proponent of liberty, Goya abhorred war. His series of anti-war etchings, entitled "Disasters of War," depicts the horrors of war with unprecedented intensity (figure **18.5**). In this image, Goya's message is that the cause of freedom is noble, but death in war is inevitable and ignoble. He illustrates the futile efforts of Spanish women who rose against Napoleon's troops in Zaragoza, using stakes, knives, bricks, and whatever else was available against the better equipped French soldiers.

In France the seminal Romantic painter was Théodore Géricault (1791–1824). He died at the age of thirty-three and produced the greatest painting of his career before he was twenty-one (figure **18.6**). His *Raft of the "Medusa"* documents a notorious contemporary event: the frigate *Medusa* hit a reef off the coast of Africa and sank. The ship was equipped

18.4 Francisco de Goya, *The Third of May, 1808*, 1814–1815. Oil on canvas, 8 ft. 9 in. × 13 ft. 4 in. (2.67 × 4.06 m). Prado, Madrid.
Goya evokes sympathy for the Spaniards by giving them individual identities and highlighting them in light, in contrast to the anonymous French soldiers in relative darkness. The man about to be shot raises his arms in a gesture that echoes Christ's Crucifixion, one hand leading the viewer's gaze toward the distant church. The blood of the man lying dead at the left soaks into the ground, suggesting that he has died to save Spanish soil.

with too few lifeboats, which were occupied by the captain, officers, and a few passengers. The rest of the passengers and the crew were placed on a wooden raft and assured that they would be towed to safety by the lifeboats. But the captain cut the cables, leaving those on the raft to die. Of the original 149 people on the raft, only fifteen returned to France alive. They reported a thirteen-day voyage of death, disease, insanity, and cannibalism.

Scandal broke out when it became known that the captain was not qualified for his job. He had been appointed for his monarchist sympathies rather than his merit. Géricault used the occasion to create a Romantic scene of human struggle against nature. In preparation for the task, he made many drawings, and studied the dying and dead in hospitals and morgues. The final painting sets the raft against a moody, darkened sky and turbulent sea. In the foreground the dead slide into the water, and an old man mourns his son. Behind them, an ironic crescendo of hope appears in the rising diagonal, which draws the viewer into the picture space. Figures strain and wave in vain toward a distant ship.

Eugène Delacroix (1798–1863), the most prolific of the French Romantic painters and a student of

18.5 Francisco de Goya, "Disasters of War" series, Plate 5, *And they are wild beasts!*, *c.* 1810–1814. Etching, burnished aquatint, and drypoint, $6^1/_4 \times 8^1/_4$ in. (15.8 × 21 cm). Museum of Fine Arts, Boston.
Note the romantically dying figure at the left as the woman behind her prepares to hurl a large rock. The central woman carries an infant in one hand, while attacking a soldier with a long stake. The inevitable death of all the women is implicit in the soldier at the far right who aims his rifle into the crowd.

18.6 Théodore Géricault, *The Raft of the "Medusa,"* 1818–1819. Oil on canvas, 16 ft. $1\frac{1}{4} \times 23$ ft. 6 in. (4.91×7.16 m). Louvre, Paris.

Géricault's, produced a stirring image of revolution in his *Liberty Leading the People* of 1830 (figure **18.7**). The scene shows people from all walks of life marching against the Bourbon king, Charles X, and willing to die for freedom. Liberty is an allegorical figure—a bare-breasted, barefoot heroine leading the crowd to freedom and raising the tricolor.

18.7 Eugène Delacroix, *Liberty Leading the People*, 1830. Oil on canvas, 8 ft. 6 in $\times$ 10 ft. 7 in. (2.59×3.23 m). Louvre, Paris.
Note the organization of the painting, with the French revolutionary flag at the apex of a large triangle. Called the tricolor (meaning three colors—red, white, and blue), the flag's colors are distributed throughout the scene, uniting the figures formally as well as politically. Through the mists of gunpowder, the skyline of Paris is visible in the distance.

She is a Romantic version of the Greek Winged Victory, part symbol and part comrade. The dead and dying in the foreground, like those in Géricault's *Raft of the "Medusa,"* directly confront the viewer with their plight and evoke sympathy with their cause.

The paintings of Jean-Auguste-Dominique Ingres (1780–1867), a student of David, combine the formal clarity of Neoclassicism with Romantic themes. Ingres worked for Napoleon and painted Classical subjects and exotic Turkish harems. His memorable portrait of *Louis-François Bertin* (figure **18.8**) depicts the successful business man and powerful journalist whose newspaper, *Journal des Débats*, supported the July Monarchy of Louis-Philippe. Bertin's restless energy is conveyed by his pose, somewhat disheveled hair, and overwhelming presence. By virtue of Bertin's monarchist views and his depiction of the king as an upper-middle-class figure, the painting came to embody the bourgeois rule of the Citizen-King.

18.8 Jean-Auguste-Dominique Ingres, *Louis-François Bertin*, 1832. Oil on canvas, 5 ft 6 in. × 3 ft. 1½ in. (1.93 × 1.16 m). Louvre, Paris.
The attention to detail is typical of Ingres. The careful shading, raised eyebrow, and downward curve of the mouth convey the stern, thoughtful character of Bertin. The artist's identification with Bertin, whom he had a great deal of difficulty painting, is shown by the pairing of their names. Ingres's Latin signature, INGRES PINXIT, and the date 1832 appear at the upper left, while L-F BERTIN is inscribed opposite at the right.

PAINTING AND ARCHITECTURE IN BRITAIN

The two leading English Romantic painters were John Constable (1776–1837) and Joseph Mallord William Turner (1775–1851), each of whom had a unique vision of nature. Constable is best known for his calm, pastoral landscapes, Turner for his turbulent scenes, thick brushwork, and dramatic color. In architecture the Romantic revival-style of John Nash (1752–1835) was inspired by Indian Gothic forms, whereas Sir Charles Barry (1795–1860) and Augustus W. N. Pugin (1812–1852) revived the Gothic style of medieval Europe.

THE ROMANTIC LANDSCAPE: TURNER AND CONSTABLE Constable's *Hay Wain* (figure **18.9**) is characteristic of his nostalgia for the landscape of his childhood. He was born in the Stour valley, in the English county of Suffolk, where his father owned a mill. The scene in this picture takes place at noon, by the edge of the River Stour. The land is quiet and still, a few farmers are visible, and a dog has paused to watch the hay wain as it crosses the river at a leisurely pace.

The colors—largely dark greens and browns—are varied only by an occasional red and areas of yellow light. The sky, filled with shifting blues, grays, and whites, is in constant motion and shows the changing aspect of nature. Constable was particularly attracted to clouds and their movements, their changing shapes, and their moods. He undertook a scientific study of clouds and weather, and his painting entered a period known as "skying" from 1821 to 1822, when he focused on cloud formations.

Turner's *Slave Ship* (figure **18.10**) reflects the artist's passion for nature and his abhorrence of slavery. Here the violence of the event, in which chained slaves (at the lower right) have been thrown overboard and struggle against the waves, is matched by nature's unpredictable and often dangerous energy. Sea and sky merge in a swirl of paint as the ship, silhouetted against the orange, sails off into a white foam. Turner's view of nature as depicted here allies its irrational character with the violence of slavery.

Opposition to slavery and the slave trade had begun with the Enlightenment. Abhorrence at the practice had been growing in Britain since the seventeenth century. In 1807 Parliament officially abolished slavery in Britain, extending the ban to all imperial possessions in 1833. One of the most forceful anti-slavery voices was that of the freed African Olaudah Equiano (*c.* 1745–1797), who had been a slave in America and who recorded a vivid description of conditions on the slave ships. Turner's sympathy with the Enlightenment is evident in his dramatization of the slaves' plight.

READING SELECTION

Equiano, *The Interesting Narrative and Other Writings*, on the horrors of a slave ship, PWC4-077-B

18.9 John Constable, *The Hay Wain*, 1821. Oil on canvas, 4 ft. 3 in. × 6 ft. 1 in. (1.3 × 1.85 m). National Gallery, London.

18.10 Joseph Mallord William Turner, *The Slave Ship*, 1840. Oil on canvas, 35¾ in. × 48¼ in. (90.8 × 122.6 cm). Museum of Fine Arts, Boston. Note the intensity of Turner's color and the thick impasto (paste-like) textures of his brushwork. The paint is thickest where the sun is brightest, giving off a white heat and descending into the fiery orange and red of the horizon. Both the doomed slaves and the ship are engulfed in dark browns and blacks. The ship's captain decided to throw overboard the sick and dying slaves because their condition made them unprofitable cargo.

Taj Mahal, Agra
see figure 9.25

18.11 John Nash, Royal Pavilion, Brighton, Sussex, England, 1815–1818.

GOTHIC REVIVAL ARCHITECTURE The Romantic taste for the exotic East can be seen in the Indian Gothic elements that John Nash introduced into the Royal Pavilion in Brighton, on the south coast of England (figure **18.11**). The surface patterns, minarets, and onion domes are features of Islamic architecture (see thumbnail), and the fanciful quality of the Pavilion is consistent with its function—to provide a place of entertainment for the Prince Regent (later King George IV) and his guests at a seaside resort.

Romantic nostalgia for the Christian past coincided with a revival of Western Gothic architecture. Thus, when the old Palace of Westminster in London was razed in a fire in 1834, it was replaced by new Houses of Parliament (figure **18.12**) in Gothic revival style. Some people preferred a Neoclassical style for the new Parliament, but Romanticism prevailed; Gothic was considered more Christian and more appealing to nationalistic taste.

Painting in Germany: Friedrich

Edmund Burke's notion of nature's sublime power to evoke a sense of mystery and loss of self is most consistently expressed in the paintings of the German Romantic artist Caspar David Friedrich (1774–1840). For Friedrich, the sublime included the appeal of lunar folklore, myth, and German nationalism. He was particularly attracted to the theme of figures contemplating the moon, which was popularly associated with the unconscious, "dark side" of the mind. His paintings convey his belief that divine power resides in nature and they reflect his deep religious faith (figure **18.13**).

18.12 Sir Charles Barry and Augustus W. N. Pugin, Houses of Parliament, London, 1836–1870. Although the buildings form a long horizontal on the bank of the Thames, repeated Gothic spires seem to pierce the sky. The Victoria Tower rises at the southern end, while Big Ben, the famous clocktower, rises at the north.

18.13 Caspar David Friedrich, *Moonrise over the Sea*, 1822. Oil on canvas, 21⅝ × 28 in. (55 × 71 cm). National Gallery, State Museums, Berlin.
It is sunset and a man and two women are seated on a rock contemplating the sea. Two sailboats approach the island, indicating the passage of time as the nearer one begins to lower its sails. The figures are silhouetted so that their identity becomes absorbed into the forms of nature. Their Romantic character is conveyed by the haunting setting and the sense that they have become one with nature.

ROMANTIC LITERATURE IN EUROPE

For many Romantics politics, philosophy, and literature overlapped. Authors focused on the power of imagination and an all-encompassing nature, exploring expressions of passion, mysticism, and a nostalgia for past and distant places. Most Romantics rejected the Classical literary rules and were drawn, like many liberal thinkers, to themes of nationalism and social justice.

GERMANY: GOETHE

In Germany the greatest Romantic writer was Johann Wolfgang von Goethe (1749–1832). Like Beethoven, Goethe wrote at first in a Classical mode, but he reached his greatest heights of passion as a Romantic. His renown was such that in his later years he was sought out for his wise advice by political leaders across Europe.

Goethe was born in Frankfurt am Main and studied law in Leipzig, but he soon turned to literature and wrote extensively on many subjects, such as botany and optics (*Treatise on Color*, 1810), and in several genres, including poetry, travel (*Italian Journey*, 1816–1817), fiction, and drama. Early in his career Goethe came to embody the literary *Sturm und Drang* ("Storm and Stress") movement, which began in Germany in the late eighteenth century. It was inspired by Rousseau's idealized view of nature, a rejection of the Classical unities in theater, and a belief in individuality and the cult of genius.

Goethe's greatest expression of *Sturm und Drang* is his semi-autobiographical early novel, *The Sorrows of Young Werther* (1774), a paradigm of Romantic melancholy and ill-ease with one's self and the world. The hero is a sensitive, idealistic youth driven to suicide by unrequited love. The enormous appeal of Goethe's book in Europe gave rise to the term *Wertherism*, denoting a fad in which young men, dressed as the hero, dashed off to commit suicide. Perfumes labeled *Werther* became popular, and scenes from the novel were widely illustrated.

Goethe's most famous later work, which occupied him from 1808 until 1832, is the verse play *Faust*. Based on the life of a sixteenth-century German magician (which had also inspired Christopher Marlowe, see Chapter 15), *Faust* is the story of a man who sells his soul to the devil (Mephistopheles)—signing a pact in blood—in exchange for power, riches, and knowledge. In the Prologue Mephistopheles asks God for permission to obtain Faust's soul, and the world-weary Faust opens the first act by proclaiming his disappointment with life. Led into temptation by Mephistopheles, Faust regains his youth and engages in carefree adolescent adventures, but despairs when he causes the deaths of his mistress and their illegitimate child.

Goethe wrote a sequel to *Faust*—Part II, which is more complex and difficult to fathom than Part I. It deals with Faust's redemption, death, and salvation and is filled with allusions to medieval folklore, Greek mythology, and Platonic philosophy. As in Marlowe's *Dr. Faustus*, Goethe's hero meets Helen of Troy, an encounter that takes up the entire third act.

READING SELECTION

Goethe, *Faust*, on Faust's pact with the devil, PWC4-041

FRANCE: DE STAËL, CHATEAUBRIAND, HUGO, AND SAND

In France the author Mme de Staël (1766–1817), daughter of a wealthy minister at the court of Louis XVI and wife of the Swedish ambassador to Paris, was a *salonnière* (see Chapter 17). She welcomed the French Revolution, was exiled from Paris

18.14 Anne-Louis Girodet-Trioson, *The Entombment of Atala*, 1808. Oil on canvas, 6 ft. 11¾ in. × 8 ft. 9 in. (2.13 × 2.67 m). Louvre, Paris.
The calm, Classical appearance of Atala and the overall clarity of form are characteristic of Neoclassical style. But Choctas's melodramatic embrace, his wavy black hair falling over Atala's white dress, and the medieval quality of the mission priest are decidedly Romantic. Reinforcing the sense of Christian power is the crucifix beside Atala and the large cross silhouetted against the distant sky. The spade quietly but pointedly directs our attention to the newly dug grave and the words carved into the cave wall: "I have died like the flower./I have become dry like the grass of the fields."

under Napoleon, and traveled extensively in Europe. Her most important work, *On Germany* (1810), explained the nature of German Romanticism and promoted its appeal in France. A Romantic herself, she extolled the lyrical qualities of poetic inspiration as an expression of genius and passion. Under the Bourbon restoration, she returned to Paris and re-established her *salon*.

Mme de Staël's contemporary, François-René de Chateaubriand (1768–1848), published *The Genius of Christianity* (*Le Génie du christianisme*) in 1802, four days after Napoleon had agreed the Concordat of Fontainebleau with the pope (see p. 498). The work appealed to the Romantic nostalgia for a Christian past, which in France had been overshadowed by the *Philosophes* and the French Revolution. Like Mme de Staël, Chateaubriand advocated the Moderns over the Ancients (see Chapter 16) and argued that beauty and morality were more congenial to Christianity than to paganism.

Chateaubriand's trip to America in 1791 inspired his popular novel *Atala* (1801), the story of an ill-fated romance between the Christian Atala and Choctas, a member of the Natchez Indian tribe. Chateaubriand describes the landscape around the Mississippi River in terms that convey the harmony of nature. The scene of the heroine's death is filled with Romantic emotion and is the subject of an intensely Romantic painting by the French artist Anne-Louis Girodet-Trioson (1767–1824) (figure **18.14**).

The French Romantic author Victor Hugo (1802–1885) wrote plays, poetry, and novels. His towering ambition, reflected in his statement of 1816, "I want to be Chateaubriand or nothing," was matched only by his massive literary production. In 1829 he published the play *Cromwell*, which stated his Romantic, anti-Classical literary principles. In the preface to the play *Hernani* (performed 1830), Hugo called Romanticism "literary liberalism." This work coincided with the July Revolution and seemed to the author's contemporaries to be its dramatic equivalent. The main character rebels against the king of Spain, who refuses to grant the outlaw Hernani the hand of his beloved, Doña Sol. In the end, the lovers die by drinking poison.

Hugo's great early novel *Notre-Dame de Paris* (also called *The Hunchback of Notre Dame*, 1831) combines the Romantic appeal of the sublime with the grotesque. The deformed hunchback, Quasimodo, who lives in the tower of Notre Dame Cathedral in Paris, is falsely accused of abduction. The beautiful gypsy Esmeralda is moved to pity by his plight, and Quasimodo, in turn, falls in love with her. Both die at the end—she is hanged for murder and he throws himself from the top of the cathedral.

Les Misérables (1862), Hugo's epic novel of social injustice, condemnation, and redemption, is written in a florid, Romantic style. Depicting the moral poverty of France after the fall of Napoleon, Hugo evokes enormous sympathy for his hero, Jean Valjean, who is jailed for stealing bread, escapes from prison, and then establishes his own prosperous business. But the law is relentless, and Valjean is eventually recaptured. Although he triumphs in the end, Jean Valjean stands for the oppressed citizens of France. Hugo thus championed individual freedom, opposed judicial abuses, and identified with the Romantic revolutionary spirit.

The Romantic lifestyle of Amandine-Aurore-Lucie Dudevant, known by her pseudonym George Sand (1804–1876), is reflected in her work. She assumed a male identity to facilitate her acceptance in the world of publishing. She flouted bourgeois propriety with public romantic liaisons, dressed as a man, and was actively committed to revolutionary politics. Her novel *Indiana* (1832) concerns an unhappily married woman who takes a lover and has to leave France. The heroine travels to a French island (modern Réunion) in the Indian Ocean, where she finds peace in nature with another man. Sand's *Lélia* (1833) criticizes the Church and the Napoleonic Code for advocating a subservient position for women. In all Sand wrote over eighty novels, twenty plays, a travelogue, and books for children. Her independent social spirit and enthusiasm for political rebellion were integral to her engagement with the Romantic Movement.

BRITISH ROMANTIC POETS

Britain's Romantic poets, like its painters and architects, were drawn to the exotic East and the antiquity of Greece and Rome. They were inspired by Gothic forms and medieval Christianity and reacted to industrialization either with direct condemnation or by evoking earlier, pre-industrial periods. They also emphasized the power of nature and the human imagination.

WILLIAM BLAKE William Blake (1757–1827) was a visionary artist and poet attracted to the theme of England's Christian past. He subscribed to Burke's notion of the sublime and was influenced by Milton's *Paradise Lost* (see Chapter 16). Blake believed in the power of imagination, which he called Poetic Genius. His poetry, like his drawings and paintings, expresses the mystical qualities of the mind (figure **18.15**).

18.15 William Blake, *Satan in his Original Glory, c.* 1805. Pen and ink and watercolor on paper, 16⅞ × 13⅜ in. (43 × 34 cm). Tate Gallery, London. Blake's Satan is shown here glorified in light. He is literally Lucifer, "the bearer of light," in heaven before his fall into darkness. Satan's expansive, bird-like wings wrap around his nude form and his features are not entirely human. This uncanny image was inspired by the visionary Book of Ezekiel (see Chapter 8).

Blake was captivated by the myth of Albion, the notion of a lost Christian era from the past, when Jesus was believed to have come to England. He expressed this in "Jerusalem":

And did those feet in ancient time
Walk upon England's mountains green?
And was the holy Lamb of God
On England's pleasant pastures seen?

And did the Countenance Divine
Shine forth upon our clouded hills?
And was Jerusalem builded here
Among these dark Satanic mills?

The "clouded hills" refer to the atmospheric pollution of industry, and the "dark Satanic mills" are factories responsible for the pollution. Albion thus transports the poet back to the time when England was green, filled with sunlight, and Christian.

WILLIAM WORDSWORTH AND SAMUEL TAYLOR COLERIDGE The publication of *Lyrical Ballads* in 1798 by William Wordsworth (1770–1850) and Samuel Taylor Coleridge (1772–1834) was a landmark of Romantic poetry (see Box, p. 510). The poets wanted to free poetry from the precious, stylized conventions of the eighteenth century.

Wordsworth was born in the scenic Lake District of northwestern England and attended Cambridge University from 1787 to 1791. A visit to France in 1790 inspired his sympathy for the Revolution, but later he was repelled by the Reign of Terror. In 1792 his French mistress gave birth to a daughter and, though hostilities between England and France kept them apart, Wordsworth did what he could to support them. He married Mary Hutchinson and had five more children, three of whom died early. In 1843 he was named Britain's Poet Laureate.

Wordsworth's poems are imbued with a love of nature, the appeal of simplicity, and emotional depth. His belief that God's presence is everywhere in nature was the inspiration for his famous poem entitled "Lines composed a few miles above Tintern Abbey, on revisiting the banks of the Wye during a tour, July 13, 1798." It combines a nostalgic mood with a landscape that evokes intense feelings and a sense of oneness with nature:

Five years have passed; five summers, with the length
Of five long winters! and again I hear
These waters, rolling from their mountain-springs
With a soft inland murmur. Once again
Do I behold these steep and lofty cliffs,
That on a wild secluded scene impress
Thoughts of more deep seclusion; and connect
The landscape with the quiet of the sky.

Defining Moment

The Romantic Lyrical Ballads of Wordsworth and Coleridge: 1798

A defining moment for the Romantic Movement, especially in Britain, came with the publication of the first edition of *Lyrical Ballads* on September 18, 1798. Although the collection was anonymous, the poems it contained were by William Wordsworth and Samuel Taylor Coleridge. Their stated aim was to free poetry from the precious, stylized conventions of eighteenth-century verse. The word "lyrical"indicates literary elevation and "ballad" reflects a basic simplicity.

Wordsworth wrote a "brief advertisement" in which he stated that: "It is the honourable characteristic of Poetry that its materials are to be found in every subject which can interest the human mind." He considered the poems "experiments," written "to ascertain how far the language of conversation in the middle and lower classes of society is adapted to the purposes of poetic pleasure." When the authors planned the collection, Coleridge wrote later, they agreed that Wordsworth would attempt to superimpose emotion, sensation, and imagination imbued with nostalgia for childhood onto images of everyday life, while Coleridge would focus on supernatural and exotic themes and locales.

This division can be seen in Wordsworth's "Tintern Abbey" (see p. 509), which is the subject of J. M. W. Turner's watercolor of 1794 (figure **18.16**). In his "The Thorn," Wordsworth took an everyday object and used language to elevate it to a poetic realm:

There is a thorn; it looks so old,
In truth you'd find it hard to say,
How it could ever have been young,
It looks so old and grey.
Not higher than a two-year's child,
It stands erect this aged thorn;
No leaves it has, no thorny points;
It is a mass of knotted joints,
A wretched thing forlorn.
It stands erect, and like a stone
With lichens it is overgrown.

The four poems by Coleridge, "directed to persons and characters supernatural or at least romantic," were *The Rime of the Ancient Mariner*, in the margins of which Coleridge wrote notes describing a spirit world parallel to the real world, "The Foster-mother's Tale," "The Nightingale," and "The Dungeon."

The second edition, which appeared under Wordsworth's name only, was published in 1800, and Wordsworth added a long Preface, explaining the aims of Romantic poetry:

> *The principal object . . . in these Poems was to choose incidents and situations from common life . . . in a selection of language really used by men, and, at the same time, to throw over them a certain colouring of the imagination, whereby ordinary things should be present to the mind in an unusual aspect; and, further, and above all, to make these incidents and situations interesting by tracing in them . . . the primary laws of our nature . . . Humble and rustic life was generally chosen, because, in that condition, the essential passions of the heart find a better soil in which they can attain their maturity, are less under restraint, and speak a plainer and more emphatic language.*

"Good poetry," according to Wordsworth, "is the spontaneous overflow of powerful feelings" and a poet "is a man speaking to men."

At the time of publication, the *Lyrical Ballads* were not generally well received; one critic called *The Rime of the Ancient Mariner* a strange "cock and bull" story. Nevertheless, the collection is generally regarded as marking the start of the Romantic Movement in Britain.

Critical Question Can you think of an example of contemporary writing that you consider important but that is critically out of favor? Explain your point of view.

18.16 Joseph Mallord William Turner, *Interior of Tintern Abbey*, 1794. Watercolor, $12^{5}/_{8}$ in × $9^{1}/_{8}$ in. (32 × 23 cm). Victoria and Albert Museum, London. Although Wordsworth's lines were composed "a few miles above" the abbey, it is clear from Turner's picture that the Gothic ruins appealed to the poet's Romantic nostalgia for the past.

In "The Daffodils" Wordsworth reveals his personal identification with nature and his ability to imagine it (the "inward eye"):

I wandered lonely as a cloud
That floats on high o'er vales and hills,
When all at once I saw a crowd,
A host of golden daffodils;
Beside the lake, beneath the trees,
Fluttering and dancing in the breeze . . .

For oft, when on my couch I lie
In vacant or in pensive mood,
They flash upon that inward eye
Which is the bliss of solitude;
And then my heart with pleasure fills,
And dances with the daffodils.

READING SELECTION
Wordsworth, "Composed upon Westminster Bridge," PWC4-168

Wordsworth's friend Coleridge was the son of a country vicar. He attended boarding school in London and studied at Cambridge from 1791 to 1794, but did not graduate. He founded and then abandoned a utopian community in Pennsylvania and was interested in German philosophy. Coleridge wrote on literary theory, theology, and philosophy, in addition to his poetry. From around 1796 he began taking opium as a painkiller and eventually became an addict.

Coleridge's complex, haunting poetry reflects the appeal of the exotic East, the Middle Ages, Shakespeare, and Homeric and Latin poetic meter. Some of his work was inspired by opium-induced visions. *The Rime of the Ancient Mariner*, written in ballad form, is permeated by the Romantic taste for the uncanny and the supernatural. It is the tale of a ship blown off course, its crew destroyed by ghostly forces, and its captain cursed and then redeemed. The opening verse sets the mysterious tone of the poem and the eerie determination of the Mariner, an unfortunate member of the crew, to tell his tale:

It is an ancient Mariner,
And he stoppeth one of three.
"By thy long grey beard and glittering eye,
Now wherefore stopp'st thou me?"

The expression "to have an albatross around one's neck" was inspired by Coleridge's poem. Through the fog, the crew sees a great, white seabird, an albatross, following the ship. It seemed to have a Christian soul, but the Mariner kills it just the same. Note the rhyming of "cross" and "Albatross," which suggests that killing the Albatross is a metaphor for Christ's Crucifixion: "—With my cross-bow/I shot the Albatross." The winds stop blowing, the sea is becalmed, and the ship runs out of supplies. The crew is thus punished for the death of the Albatross:

Day after day, day after day,
We stuck, nor breath nor motion;
As idle as a painted ship
Upon a painted ocean.

Water, water, every where,
And all the boards did shrink;
Water, water, every where,
Nor any drop to drink.

In "Kubla Khan" (1816), Coleridge describes his opium-induced vision of a palace and its gardens built by the khan Kubla in an imaginary Eastern setting:

In Xanadu did Kubla Khan
A stately pleasure-dome decree:
Where Alph, the sacred river, ran
Through caverns measureless to man
  Down to a sunless sea.

READING SELECTION
Coleridge, "Kubla Khan," PWC4-081

LORD BYRON, PERCY BYSSHE SHELLEY, AND JOHN KEATS Following the publication of the first edition of *Lyrical Ballads* in 1798 Britain produced two more generations of Romantic poets. Three of the first generation died young, which only added to their mystique, for they lived as romantically as they wrote. George Gordon, Lord Byron (1788–1824), who was criticized at home for his immoral lifestyle, died of a fever after joining the Greek uprising against Turkish rule. Percy Bysshe Shelley (1792–1822), the son of a baronet, died in a boating accident after visiting Byron in Italy. John Keats (1795–1821), who came from a working-class family and studied medicine before turning to poetry, died in Rome of tuberculosis at the age of twenty-five.

Byron's Romantic attraction to Greece and its Classical past is evident in "The Isles of Greece," which comes from his epic *Don Juan*. In it he laments the passing of Classical civilization:

The isles of Greece, the isles of Greece!
  Where burning Sappho loved and sung,
Where grew the arts of war and peace,
  Where Delos rose and Phoebus sprung!
Eternal summer gilds them yet,
  But all, except their sun, is set.

In the last stanza, Byron calls for freedom or death:

Place me on Sunium's* marbled steep,
Where nothing, save the waves and I,
May hear our mutual murmurs sweep;
There, swan-like, let me sing and die:
A land of slaves shall ne'er be mine—
Dash down yon cup of Samian wine!

*The site of a ruined Greek temple just outside Athens by the sea. Byron carved his initials in the marble, where they are still visible today.

This commitment to freedom characterizes the so-called Byronic Hero, whose unconventional behavior is driven by erotic passion and political causes. Byron's heroes tend to be inspired by the "romance" of the past, by distant, exotic places, and by a striving for social justice.

Shelley was well versed in the Classics, translated Plato's *Symposium* and parts of Homer, wrote verse tragedies based on Greek myth, and composed poems set in Italy, Egypt, Spain, and elsewhere. He championed liberty and fought injustice. His sonnet "Ozymandias" reflects the Romantic interest in ruins as reminders of distant civilizations lost in time:

I met a traveller from an antique land
Who said: Two vast and trunkless legs of stone
Stand in the desert. Near them on the sand,
Half sunk, a shattered visage lies, whose frown,
And wrinkled lip, and sneer of cold command,
Tell that its sculptor well those passions read
Which yet survive, stamped on these lifeless things,
The hand that mocked them, and the heart that fed:
And on the pedestal these words appear:
"My name is Ozymandias, king of kings:
Look on my works, ye Mighty, and despair!"
Nothing beside remains. Round the decay
Of that colossal wreck, boundless and bare
The lone and level sands stretch far away.

Shelley wrote a number of famous odes, a form inspired by antiquity. "Ode to the West Wind" (1819) was written in the woods by the River Arno near Florence. The poet's stated intention was to capture the shifting moods of weather, including fierce winds, mild temperatures, violent rain and hail, and thunder and lightning:

O wild West Wind, thou breath of Autumn's being,
Thou, from whose unseen presence the leaves dead
Are driven, like ghosts from an enchanter fleeing,
Yellow, and black, and pale, and hectic red,
Pestilence-stricken multitudes.

The odes and sonnets of Keats also exalt nature ("Ode to a Nightingale") and the lost civilizations of antiquity. His "Ode on a Grecian Urn" (1820) praises an Attic vase as a testament to ancient Greece and describes the orgiastic scene painted on its surface. Although silent, the vase communicates through time; its image is a window onto history:

Thou still unravish'd bride of quietness,
Thou foster-child of silence and slow time,
Sylvan historian, who canst thus express
A flowery tale more sweetly than our rhyme:
What leaf-fring'd legend haunts about thy shape
Of deities or mortals, or of both,
In Tempe or the dales of Arcady?
What men or gods are these? What maidens loth?
What mad pursuit? What struggle to escape?
What pipes and timbrels? What wild ecstasy?

The famous concluding lines summarize Keats's aesthetic philosophy: "'Beauty is truth, truth beauty,'—that is all/Ye know on earth, and all ye need to know."

READING SELECTION

Keats, "Ode on a Grecian Urn," PWC5-163

The English Novel in the Early Nineteenth Century

In addition to some of the greatest nineteenth-century poets, Britain produced major Romantic novelists. Jane Austen (1775–1817) was born in Hampshire, the seventh child of a clergyman and his wife. Austen herself never married, and unhappy romances are thought to have inspired the powerful emotional undercurrents of her novels, which she describes with Classical restraint. Austen was one of the first novelists to treat ordinary people in depth, and she is credited with originating the comedy of middle-class manners. Although Austen was not strictly a Romantic, she did implicitly criticize the status quo of British society.

Her most famous work, *Pride and Prejudice* (1813), depicts family life in provincial England as a microcosm of society at large. Austen portrays with crystalline precision the details of provincial behavior and social activity—from the excitement of a grand ball to intimate conversation and correspondence. The fragile nature of social ritual is shown by the disruptive effect of deviations from the norm.

Of particular concern to Austen were the social, legal, and educational restrictions placed on women. These are reflected in Mrs. Bennet's determination to find suitable husbands for her five daughters, which mirrors the prevailing notion that women should be brought up to be dependent on men, uneducated, and emotional rather than rational.

READING SELECTION

Jane Austen, *Pride and Prejudice*, on family obstacles, PWC5-066-B

Mary Wollstonecraft Shelley (1797–1851), daughter of the early feminist Mary Wollstonecraft (see Chapter 17), eloped to France in 1814 with Percy Shelley. She married him in 1816 after the suicide of his first wife. When he died in 1822 Mary returned to England to raise their son and published Shelley's *Posthumous Poems* (1824).

Mary Shelley's most famous novel, *Frankenstein, or the Modern Prometheus* (1818), was inspired by her liking for ghost stories. *Frankenstein* is about a young student of natural philosophy in Switzerland who constructs a human form of skin and bones and gives it life. But the creature is monstrous in size and appearance, and he is an outcast, shunned even by his creator. When Dr. Frankenstein refuses to fashion a female companion for him, the monster kills Frankenstein's brother, his best friend, and his new bride.

Several themes are evident in Mary Shelley's tale. Following the philosophy of Rousseau, Frankenstein's creature is a "noble savage" made monstrous partly by the abusiveness of a society that rejects him. The monster can also be seen as sounding an alarm bell warning of unregulated scientific experimentation.

Finally, the subtitle of Shelley's novel, *The Modern Prometheus*, alludes to the Greek myth of the Titan Prometheus whose *hubris* in stealing fire from the gods and breathing life into his clay sculpture resulted in eternal torture (see Chapters 5 and 6). In the case of Frankenstein, the monster, rather than the gods, turns on its creator and destroys his life.

READING SELECTION

Mary Shelley, *Frankenstein, or the Modern Prometheus*, on making a monster, PWC4-084-B

The three Brontë sisters, Charlotte (1816–1855), Emily (1818–1848), and Anne (1820–1849), daughters of an Anglican clergyman from Ireland, were born in Yorkshire, in northern England. Like George Sand, they published their works under pseudonyms—Currer, Ellis, and Acton Bell—which made it ambiguous whether they were male or female. Their novels, which are still popular, are permeated by Romantic moods and mysterious, Gothic atmospheres. The plots consist of complex Romantic situations and revolve around passionate characters. *Wuthering Heights* by Emily, *Jane Eyre* by Charlotte, and *The Tenant of Wildfell Hall* by Anne were all published in 1847. Emily died of tuberculosis the year after her book appeared, and Anne died of the same illness a year later.

Wuthering Heights relates the ill-fated romance between the well-bred Catherine and Heathcliff, an orphan brought home by her father to work as a stable boy. The very name Heathcliff echoes the wild, restless landscape of the Yorkshire moors where the Brontës lived. *Jane Eyre* is a tale of romance between the enigmatic Mr. Rochester, secretly burdened with an insane wife, and Jane Eyre, the witty, independent governess of his young ward, Adèle. Both works are imbued with emotional and sexual tensions boiling beneath a surface regulated by strict social convention.

THE ROMANTIC MOVEMENT IN AMERICA

American literature found its national voice in the Romantic Movement, strains of which persisted to the end of the nineteenth century. American Romantic authors emphasize nature, the individual, and themes of social justice. Their works are often colored by a patriotic fervor that echoes the nationalist strain of European Romanticism, but American authors were also drawn to the past, the exotic, and the supernatural.

TRANSCENDENTALISTS

The Transcendental school of philosophy developed in New England, and it was based largely on the Romantic idea that nature is the ideal environment and that people are inherently good. Most of the Transcendentalists were former Unitarians—Christians who believe in God but not necessarily in the divinity of Christ or the Trinity. In the nineteenth century Unitarians rejected Calvinism and religious orthodoxy in general. Influenced by Western as well as Eastern thought, the Transcendentalists believed in a universal spiritual unity and preferred intuition to logic. Some were involved in founding experimental communities and schools.

RALPH WALDO EMERSON AND HENRY DAVID THOREAU The two best-known American Transcendentalists, Ralph Waldo Emerson (1803–1882) and Henry David Thoreau (1817–1862), were Unitarians. Emerson became attracted to Eastern religions and moved away from Christianity, resigning his Unitarian pulpit and espousing the view that nature is pervaded by a universal spirituality. Emerson's essays and poems are thus imbued with the experience of nature. In *Nature* (1836) he wrote:

> The greatest delight which the fields and woods minister is the suggestion of an occult relation between man and the vegetable . . . They nod to me, and I to them.

The first and last stanzas of Emerson's poem "Walden" reflect his commitment to nature:

> In my garden three ways meet,
> Thrice the spot is blest;
> Hermit-thrush comes there to build,
> Carrier-doves to nest . . .
>
> What boots it [What is the relevance] here of Thebes or Rome
> Or lands of Eastern day?
> In forests I am still at home
> And there I cannot stray.

The appeal of Far Eastern religions among the Transcendentalists is conveyed in Emerson's well-known "Brahma":

If the red slayer think he slays,
  Or if the slain think he is slain,
They know not well the subtle ways
  I keep, and pass, and turn again . . .

The strong gods pine for my abode.
  And pine in vain the sacred Seven;
But thou, meek lover of the good!
  Find me, and turn thy back on heaven.

Thoreau, like Emerson, was interested in the mystical, nurturing qualities of nature and in political freedom. In 1849 Thoreau published the political essay "Civil Disobedience," which begins:

> I heartily accept the motto,—"That government is best which governs least;" and I should like to see it acted up to more rapidly and systematically. Carried out, it finally amounts to this, which also I believe,—"That government is best which governs not at all;" and when men are prepared for it, that will be the kind of government which they will have.

Thoreau's *Walden, or Life in the Woods* (1854) chronicles his two-year experiment of living self-sufficiently in a house he says he built himself by Walden Pond in the Massachusetts woods near Concord. The account of nature in and around the pond reflects Thoreau's powers of observation and attention to descriptive detail. Toward the end of the work, he describes the thaw of spring:

> At length the sun's rays have attained the right angle, and warm winds blow up mist and rain and melt the snow banks, and the sun dispersing the mist smiles on a checkered landscape of russet and white smoking with incense, through which the traveller picks his way from islet to islet, cheered by the music of a thousand tinkling rills and rivulets whose veins are filled with the blood of winter which they are bearing off.

With Emerson, who wrote that "Nature is the incarnation of thought," and Rousseau who advocated the "noble savage," Thoreau was anti-industrial and believed that God resides in nature. Thoreau's ideas about government, expressed in the quote that opens this chapter, reflected the Enlightenment's optimistic view of human nature and the conviction that people can and should govern themselves.

NOVELISTS

Nathaniel Hawthorne (1804–1864) wrote novels and short stories, in some of which he recreated seventeenth-century New England. His plots often deal with complex conflicts that reflect his admiration for certain Puritan qualities and his deep animosity toward others. The settings of his novels are sometimes inspired by Gothic architecture and a Romantic longing for a Christian past.

Hawthorne's *The Scarlet Letter* (1850) is set in Puritan New England, where Hester Prynne gives birth to an illegitimate daughter, Pearl. Cast out from society, Hester is forced to wear a scarlet *A*, signifying "Adulteress," on her chest. Hester refuses to identify Pearl's father, who turns out to be the popular local minister, Arthur Dimesdale. Despite his cowardice and descent into near madness, Dimesdale is reunited with Hester in a romantic conclusion and dies in her arms. In this novel, Hawthorne's exposure of hypocrisy and his sympathy for the social outcast has affinities with Romanticism.

James Fenimore Cooper (1789–1851) wrote historical novels of the American frontier and Native American life. In his books *The Last of the Mohicans* (1826), *The Deerslayer* (1841), and *The Pathfinder* (1840) Cooper chronicles the waning civilizations of the American Indians, who for him embody Rousseau's notion of the "noble savage."

Herman Melville (1819–1891) was attracted to the romance of the South Pacific and the sea, and he wrote about life in Polynesia in *Typee* (1846) and the South Seas in *Omoo* (1847). Melville's epic, *Moby Dick, or, The Whale* (1851), is the story of a physical and psychological struggle between man and beast, and between man and himself. The novel's opening line, "Call me Ishmael," evokes the biblical patriarchs. Ahab, captain of the *Pequod*, has lost his leg to Moby Dick, a demonic white whale, and undertakes a relentless, obsessive quest for revenge. The whale, according to some scholars, represents the dangerous forces of nature. Eventually Moby Dick destroys the ship and Ahab drowns. Only the sailor Ishmael lives to tell the tale.

POETS

American poetry came into its own in the course of the nineteenth century. Walt Whitman (1819–1892), born on Long Island and raised in Brooklyn, New York, worked as a printer, teacher, and editor, before serving as a volunteer nurse during the Civil War (1861–1865). In 1855 Whitman published the first edition of *Leaves of Grass*, a group of twelve poems to which he added in subsequent editions throughout his life. The poems are dedicated to the new American identity, freed from a European past with its history of tyranny, injustice, and intolerance. Whitman is known as an innovator in free verse and for his sexual frankness. He admired Emerson and the Transcendentalist view of nature and perceived a mystical quality in the spirit of America, its landscape, and its voices. This is conveyed, for example, in "I Hear America Singing," which also exemplifies his free verse style:

I hear America singing, the varied carols I hear,
Those of mechanics, each one singing his as it should be
  blithe and strong,
The carpenter singing his as he measures his plank or beam,
The mason singing his as he makes ready for work, or leaves
  off work,

The boatman singing what belongs to him in his boat, the
deckhand singing on the steamboat deck,
The shoemaker singing as he sits on his bench, the hatter
singing as he stands,
The wood-cutter's song, the ploughboy's on his way in the
morning, or at noon intermission or at sundown,
The delicious singing of the mother, or of the young wife at
work, or of the girl sewing or washing,
Each singing what belongs to him or her and to none else,
The day what belongs to the day—at night the party of young
fellows, robust, friendly,
Singing with open mouths their strong melodious songs.

Whitman particularly admired Abraham Lincoln, whom he celebrated in a number of poems after his assassination (see Chapter 19)—*Memories of President Lincoln*. In "When Lilacs Last in the Dooryard Bloom'd" Whitman calls Lincoln a "powerful western fallen star," and in "This Dust Was Once the Man" he describes him as "Gentle, plain, just, and resolute." The Romantic nostalgia for what is lost is combined with Whitman's exuberant praise of America and the ideals espoused by Lincoln in "O Captain! My Captain!" Note the use of the metaphor in which the ship is the ship of state and the president its captain:

O Captain! My Captain! our fearful trip is done,
The ship has weather'd every rack, the prize we sought is
won,
The port is near, the bells I hear, the people all exulting,
While follow eyes the steady keel, the vessel grim and daring:
But O heart! heart! heart!
O the bleeding drops of red,
Where on the deck my Captain lies,
Fallen cold and dead.

The poems of Emily Dickinson (1830–1886) are of an entirely different order than those of Whitman. They are brief and terse rather than expansive, though they, too, reflect the American landscape and the poet's relationship to it. Little is known of Dickinson's life. She lived quietly in Amherst, Massachusetts, becoming a recluse after graduating from college. During her lifetime only seven of her nearly two thousand surviving poems were published.

Her imagery often reveals an intense personal effort to grapple with violent undercurrents in nature as well as in her own psyche. Stylistically, Dickinson uses such innovative devices as dashes, unconventional uppercase nouns, and ungrammatical turns of phrase. Her metaphors can be striking and witty, and she uses concise, jewel-like imagery to convey universal themes such as love, death, and immortality.

Among her *Poems on Nature*, Number LVIII conveys her sense of communication with the forest:

The bee is not afraid of me,
I know the butterfly;
The pretty people in the woods
Receive me cordially.

The brooks laugh louder when I come,
The breezes madder play.
Wherefore, mine eyes, thy silver mists?
Wherefore, O summer's day?

Number LVII reveals the poet's personal vision of faith, which is inextricably tied to nature, but is also unconventional:

Some keep the Sabbath going to church;
I keep it staying at home,
With a bobolink for a chorister,
And an orchard for a dome.

In Number XLIII from *Poems on Life*, Dickinson echoes Whitman's exuberance for a distinctly American character. It is the speed of a train, a fast-moving, voracious creature proclaiming the dynamic power of industry, that inspires her. In contrast to the bee and the butterfly, the train can be seen as an image of the poet's desire for expressiveness:

I like to see it lap the miles,
And lick the valleys up,
And stop to feed itself at tanks;
And then, prodigious, step

Around a pile of mountains,
And, supercilious, peer
In shanties by the sides of roads;
And then a quarry pare.

One of Dickinson's primary themes is death. Her poetic encounters with death range from comic, to erotic, to macabre. In Number XXVII of *Poems for Time and Eternity* the meeting is a sedate, cordial affair:

Because I could not stop for Death,
He kindly stopped for me;
The carriage held but just ourselves
And immortality.

In Number X Dickinson echoes, in a dialogue between the dead, the aesthetic philosophy of Keats. But she also expresses the tension between living and dying and between fame and oblivion:

I died for beauty, but was scarce
Adjusted in the tomb,
When one who died for truth was lain
In an adjoining room.

He questioned softly why I failed?
"For beauty," I replied.
"And I for truth,—the two are one;
We brethren are," he said.

And so, as kinsmen met at night,
We talked between the rooms,
Until the moss had reached our lips,
And covered up our names.

Edgar Allan Poe (1809–1849) wrote horror stories and detective stories. In the former he evokes terror and the irrational, in the latter rational analysis. With Hawthorne, Poe is considered the "Father of the American Short Story." In 1842 Poe wrote a review of Hawthorne's *Twice-Told Tales* (1842), in which he provides rules for creating short fiction.

Many of Poe's poems are macabre and dream-like, plumbing the depths of the unconscious. Delusions, anxiety, and nightmares are depicted with a musical intensity that conveys both the author's genius and his tortured existence. Born to a family of actors, Poe's was a childhood of desertion, death, and tuberculosis. As an adult he struggled with poverty, alcoholism, drug addiction, and unhappy relationships with women.

In "Annabel Lee" (1849 version) Poe reflects with nostalgia on his dying wife:

It was many and many a year ago,
In a kingdom by the sea
That a maiden there lived whom you may know
By the name of ANNABEL LEE—
And this maiden she lived with no other thought
Than to love and be loved by me.

I was a child and *she* was a child,
In this kingdom by the sea,
But we loved with a love that was more than love—
I and my ANNABEL LEE—
With a love that the winged seraphs of heaven
Coveted her and me.

And this was the reason that, long ago
In this kingdom by the sea,
A wind blew out of a cloud, chilling
My beautiful ANNABEL LEE;
So that her highborn kinsmen came
And bore her away from me,
To shut her up in a sepulchre
In this kingdom by the sea.

In 1845 Poe published "The Raven," which established his reputation. It, too, is about the death of a beautiful woman, which Poe famously called "unquestionably, the most poetical topic in the world."

Once upon a midnight dreary, while I pondered weak and weary,
Over many a quaint and curious volume of forgotten lore—
While I nodded, nearly napping, suddenly there came a tapping,
As of some one gently rapping, rapping at my chamber door—
"'Tis some visitor," I muttered, "tapping at my chamber door
Only this and nothing more."

Poe's visitor is a raven, an uncanny, supernatural omen of evil and death. The poet asks the raven to identify itself, and the raven's response is the poem's refrain. It encapsulates the mystery, timelessness, and loss that characterize the Romantic aesthetic—"Nevermore":

Then this ebony bird beguiling my sad fancy into smiling,
By the grave and stern decorum of the countenance it wore,
"Though thy crest be shorn and shaven, thou," I said, "art sure no craven,
Ghastly grim and ancient Raven wandering from the Nightly shore—
Tell me what thy lordly name is on the Night's Plutonian shore!"
Quoth the Raven "Nevermore."

LANDSCAPE PAINTING: ROMANTIC VISIONS

In America, as in Britain, the Romantic Movement inspired landscape painting. Influenced by the Transcendental philosophy of nature and of God's omnipresence in it, American landscape painters celebrated the vast spaces and dramatic skies of a new, unsettled country. To a large extent, landscape, like the poetry of Walt Whitman, was associated with America's national identity. The first important group of American landscapists is known as the Hudson River School, after the Hudson River valley in upstate New York.

The leading Hudson River painter, Thomas Cole (1801–1848), was born in England and emigrated to the United States in 1819. In *The Last of the Mohicans* (figure **18.17**) he illustrates a scene of tribal judgment from James Fenimore Cooper's novel. The Mohicans have gathered in a circle on a mountain ledge. Their small size in relation to nature's vastness creates a sublime effect as the fading distant mountains disappear into the increasing haze of the horizon. Responding to the demise of a native civilization, Cole set the scene in autumn, when bright red and yellow foliage heralds the death of the year. The precariously positioned boulder behind the circle seems, like the Mohicans themselves, about to fall.

By the middle of the nineteenth century a group of painters known as Luminists took American landscape painting West. Luminism uses light in a new way to celebrate the dramatic grandeur of landscape untouched by modern industry; it has been called the first purely American style of painting.

Albert Bierstadt (1830–1902) was born in Germany but was raised in the whaling town of New Bedford, Massachusetts. He traveled west to the Rocky Mountains and the Yosemite Valley in California (figure **18.18**). Here, Bierstadt bathes the mountains in the yellow light of sunrise and dramatically silhouettes the foreground trees. In contrast to most Hudson River painters, Bierstadt and other Luminists generally omitted human figures, enabling the viewer to become absorbed in a vast stretch of land without human intermediaries or narratives. The contemplative mood of the landscape and its sense of vast, timeless power evoke Christian traditions in which light signifies the presence of the divine.

18.17 Thomas Cole, *The Last of the Mohicans*, 1827. Oil on canvas, 25 × 31 in. (64 × 79 cm). Fenimore Art Museum, Cooperstown, New York.

18.18 Albert Bierstadt, *Sunrise at Yosemite*, *c.* 1870. Oil on canvas, 36½ × 52⅜ in. (93 × 133 cm). Amon Carter Museum, Fort Worth, Texas.

ROMANTIC MUSIC IN EUROPE

The Romantic era in music began around 1810 and lasted to the end of the nineteenth century, producing a large number of important musicians in Europe. Their music, like Romantic painting and literature, emphasizes subjectivity and emotion. For the first time, music was generally perceived as a vehicle for self-expression. The graceful entertainment of the Classical period gave way to a personal outpouring of inspiration. Unlike earlier composers, who had expected their music to be eclipsed by future generations, Romantic musicians had a sense of writing for posterity.

It became common for music, even instrumental music, to carry extra-musical meaning—expressing, for example, universal brotherhood. Two areas of subject matter dominate. One is the supernatural, the mystical, the exotic, and awe-inspiring nature. "Exotic" may draw on a nostalgic past—Shakespeare's plays, medieval legends—or on foreign settings. The second area of inspiration was political. In line with Enlightenment thinking, and in part as a reaction to Napoleon's conquests, many composers were political idealists. Their compositions expressed national identity and freedom.

The shift in the social setting of music away from the Church and courts seen in the previous century continued. And as the population of Europe—especially the middle classes—increased, musicians had a wider audience for their concerts and operas. Far from being court servants, many composers were now regarded as geniuses or heroes. Virtuoso performer-composers attracted enthusiastic crowds for piano or violin recitals in a way that can be compared with pop musicians of today.

ROMANTIC STYLE

What we now recognize as Romantic music varies widely in style, ranging from late classicism in the symphonies of Beethoven and Schubert to full-blown Romanticism in the operas of Verdi and Wagner.

The nineteenth century was a time of instrumental development. The piano's volume and carrying power were boosted by a move from a wooden to a cast-iron frame, and its sound quality was altered by a change from leather to felt covering the hammers that strike the strings. The keyboard was lengthened, enabling composers to write for extremes of low and high pitch. A strong, resonant, bell-like sound replaced the piano's former delicate character. This fitted it for Romantic drama and passion, as well as for the larger sizes of concert halls and audiences.

String instruments were also modified to increase their carrying power: the bridge was raised, the fingerboard lengthened, and stronger strings were used. Wind instruments were improved, with new systems of keys that made possible greater agility and the full range of notes. New instruments such as harp, piccolo (a tiny, high flute with a shrill sound), tuba (the lowest in the brass family), and a greater range of percussion instruments were introduced into the orchestra. Exploitation of the different tone colors within the orchestra is a particular feature of Romantic music. Composers created powerful effects, such as huge walls of sustained sound, aggressive accents, *tremolo* (bowing strings so fast it sounds like trembling), crescendos (gradual increases in volume), and diminuendos (gradual reductions in volume).

Matching the expanded size and drama was the Romantic treatment of tonality. The key system remained in place, but composers increasingly explored more distant key relationships and chromatic harmonies (chord progressions that moved further and further from the primary key of the composition, increasing the sense of dissonance and the corresponding desire for resolution). This gave music a rich, emotional quality.

GENRES OF ROMANTIC MUSIC

The main musical forms of the Classical era—symphony, concerto, string quartet, opera—remained the main forms in the nineteenth century, but each became longer and grander. The symphony adopted the high-speed **scherzo** in place of the graceful minuet; the concerto moved from Classical balance to a Romantic battle between soloist and orchestra; and opera dealt with themes of freedom and human destiny. Within these large works, a significant new structuring principle emerged: the **motif**. Short rhythmic or melodic patterns were used recurrently to unify a movement, as Haydn had done in his Classical symphonies, sonatas, and string quartets, but such motifs now provided unifying material for a whole piece and were often identified with specific characters or ideas.

New forms also emerged. Short pieces for piano, often studies or miniatures based on folk dances, were composed by virtuoso pianist-composers. The equivalent of a short poem, each conveyed a particular emotion or atmosphere. The **art song**, often known by its German name *lied* ("song"), was written for a single voice accompanied by piano. These songs were sometimes grouped together in a narrative set to make a **song cycle**. Program music (see Chapter 16) came into its own in the nineteenth century. Sometimes the literary work that inspired it was used as the structural basis of the music, in a free one-movement form known as a **tone poem** (or **symphonic poem**). At other times the poetic element was imposed upon standard symphonic form or used for piano pieces. Poetry was considered the highest Romantic art form, and many argued that music, expressing emotion without words, was the purest means of poetic expression.

LUDWIG VAN BEETHOVEN

Ludwig van Beethoven (1770–1827) is considered the last of the great Classical musicians and a genius of early Romanticism

18.19 Carl Friedrich August von Kloeber, *Ludwig van Beethoven*, *c.* 1818. Pencil. Beethovenhaus, Bonn, Germany.
This typically Romantic portrait shows Beethoven with wavy hair and an intense expression. At the time of this drawing, he had been totally deaf for sixteen years. In the course of his life, Beethoven confronted not only deafness, but also family problems, unhappy love affairs, and bouts of depression.

(figure **18.19**). Growing up at court in Bonn, Germany, where his alcoholic father worked as a singer, Beethoven was pushed by him to learn the piano, organ, and violin in the hope that he would become a prodigy like Mozart (see Chapter 17). From the age of ten Beethoven studied composition and at thirteen he got his first job as an organist. In 1792 he went to study with Haydn in Vienna, where he would stay for the rest of his career.

At first patronized by several aristocrats, Beethoven subsequently decided to work on a freelance basis—a decision that was an inspiration to other composers seeking creative freedom. However, it was often difficult to earn a living this way. Beethoven began to establish himself as a pianist, performing in the houses of noblemen and playing concertos at public concerts. Consequently, much of his music composed during this period was for piano, most notably seventeen piano sonatas. These pieces are larger in emotional content, energy, and structure than Classical piano sonatas, with titles such as "Pathétique" (1799) and "Moonlight" (1801). Four years after his arrival in Vienna, the great tragedy of Beethoven's life began. He realized that he was becoming increasingly hard of hearing, and by 1802 he was stone deaf.

Now fully established as a major composer, Beethoven began a second, highly productive phase of his career in 1803, when he wrote the "Eroica" Symphony (No. 3 in E flat major). He originally titled the work "Bonaparte," dedicating it to the revolutionary heroism of Napoleon. But after Napoleon seized the throne, Beethoven tore out the dedication page and wrote on the score: "Heroic Symphony, composed to celebrate the memory of a great man."

The "Eroica" is a vast and complex creation in sound, forty-five minutes in performance. The first movement is in sonata form on a grand scale, with both first and second subjects made up of short themes that are suitable for breaking up into motifs that can be developed and woven into the orchestral texture. Driving rhythms, sudden contrasts of dynamics, and a long coda at the end of the movement are all typical of Beethoven. Next comes a slow movement—a somber funeral march in a minor key, with a lyrical central section featuring a musical conversation between oboe, flute, and bassoon. The scherzo, written in lively triple meter, starts low and quiet on strings alone, maintaining a mysterious mood until a sudden flare of sound as the whole orchestra enters. Cross rhythms (stresses against the regular main pulse) suggest elements of folk dance. The fourth movement is in variation form, on a theme Beethoven also used for the finale of his ballet music *The Creatures of Prometheus* (1801). In the myth, the Titan Prometheus sides with humanity against the gods and is consequently bound to a rock and condemned to have a vulture tear at his liver for all eternity. The Titan of Greek myth who created man and gave him life is thus revived in the titanic creative force of the "Eroica."

Beethoven's second phase included his only opera, *Fidelio* (1805–1814). The plot, which appealed to his revolutionary sympathies, is based on a French story. Florestan is jailed for his political beliefs, and his wife, disguised as the youth Fidelio, is hired to work in the prison. In a typically "Romantic" gesture, she flings herself between her husband and his would-be assassin. At the end, a government official arrives and releases all political prisoners. One of the emotional high points of the work is the Prisoners' Chorus, a musical portrayal of the wonderment of captives briefly allowed out of their cells to see the light of day and breathe fresh air.

In his Symphony No. 5 in C minor (1808), Beethoven continued to bring his genius to the symphonic form, creating a monumental and memorable work while breaking Classical rules of construction. For example, he foreshadows later Romantic practice by reusing themes and motifs from movement to movement. He builds and releases tension far beyond the Classical norms, as in the long coda section of the first movement, where he works up to cadences and then falls back and starts to build again, withholding resolution onto the key chord. Emotionally, too, the piece breaks with classicism. The minor key and driven rhythms give a sense of Beethoven's personal turmoil and stormy nature; the triumphant ending of the symphony, with blazing major chords, represents his triumph over adversity.

The first movement, featured in the Listening Selection, opens with an ominous representation of "fate knocking at the door"—a four-note motif that dominates throughout. Notice that the first few measures are strong, played in unison, with dramatic pauses. The motif is then tossed quietly between violins and violas before the full orchestra enters. The pattern is repeated: fate knocks forcefully, followed by quiet strings, building to a large orchestral climax. After a moment of silence, horns announce the start of the second subject, and the strings enter gently with a lyrical new theme. Rising sequentially in pitch and building in volume at the same time, it leads to another loud orchestral section, using the rhythm of the "fate" motif and bringing the exposition to a close. In the development there are key changes and various passages of dialogue between winds and strings. The recapitulation, as always, revisits the material of the exposition. Listen for the orchestra dropping out to leave one oboe playing for a moment of contemplation. The coda is a full-blown section of its own rather than a short tailpiece, with repeated chords and a sense of driving energy that are hallmarks of Beethoven's style.

MUSIC LISTENING SELECTION

Beethoven, Symphony No. 5 in C minor, first movement, Allegro con Brio. Nicolaus Esterházy Sinfonia, conductor Belah Drahos, CD track 14

In the third and final period of Beethoven's career, beginning in 1813, one year after Napoleon's retreat from Russia, the composer produced less music. His increasing personal conflict and misery are reflected in a number of his late works, including piano sonatas and the intense string quartets of the mid-1820s. In this period Beethoven often used fugal form to create dense textures or theme and variation form to work and rework one thematic idea.

A high point of the 1820s—and indeed of Beethoven's whole career—was the "Choral" Symphony, No. 9 in D minor (1824). Until this date, symphonies had not included voices. But here, in the fourth movement, the composer employed poetry to express the meaning of his music and celebrate the brotherhood of mankind. "Ode to Joy" is a sixteen-verse poem by a German author and friend of Goethe, Johann Christoph Friedrich von Schiller (1759–1805). Beethoven used six verses as the basis of complex orchestral variations with chorus and soloists that last for nearly thirty minutes. This work glories in the joyous triumph of international harmony after the French Revolution. Beethoven attended the first performance of the symphony without hearing a note. When it was over, a friend had to motion to him that the applause was overwhelming.

Despite his difficult personality, Beethoven was enormously admired. Fittingly for a Romantic, he died during a storm; his funeral was attended by about 10,000 mourners. By the time of his death in 1827, the Romantic era in music was firmly established. Initially the majority of the composers came from German-speaking countries, but gradually the new aesthetic appeared across Europe.

ART SONGS: SCHUBERT AND SCHUMANN

During his short life the leading Austrian-born Romantic composer, Franz Schubert (1797–1828), wrote more than six hundred songs, in addition to symphonies and exquisite chamber music. The son of a schoolteacher, Schubert sang in the chapel choir at the imperial court from the age of eleven and worked as a teacher from 1815 to 1818. Despite his job he was able to compose prolifically, writing 145 songs in 1815 alone.

One of his songs from that year was "The Erlking." Based on Goethe's ballad of the same name, it is imbued with supernatural mystery. It tells the story of a boy whose illness causes him to hallucinate visions of the elf-king, a symbol of death, which he describes to his father as they ride home through a storm. The child's high-pitched tones convey his fear, contrasting with the major-key melody of his father as he attempts to calm his son. When they arrive home, the lad is dead. Schubert skillfully uses the right hand of the piano accompaniment to convey the beating of the horse's hooves—and the mounting panic of the boy. Swirls of melody can be heard in the bass line of the piano part, and chromatic harmonies add to the sense of anxiety. In the Listening Selection, the song has been transcribed for piano solo by Franz Liszt (see p. 522).

MUSIC LISTENING SELECTION

Schubert, "The Erlking," transcribed by Liszt. Antii Siirala, piano, CD track 17

READING SELECTION

Goethe, "The Erlking," PWC4-034

While Schubert's individual art songs are masterful miniatures, his song cycles show how a group of poems can be set to create a compelling personal drama, using just one voice and piano. *Die schöne Müllerin* (*The Beautiful Miller-Maid*, 1823, twenty songs) and *Die Winterreise* (*The Winter's Journey*, 1827, twenty-four songs) each evoke a journey from joy and love to desolation and death. The vocal line is lyrical, the piano part descriptive—imitating the rippling stream in *The Beautiful Miller-Maid*, for example—and the use of nature to reflect emotion is typical of Romanticism.

Robert Schumann (1810–1856) continued the tradition of art song initiated by Schubert. A central figure in German Romantic music, he came from a literary family and worked as a music journalist as well as a composer. Although he wrote in many genres, including opera, symphony, piano concerto, cello concerto, and chamber music, his main contribution was in piano pieces and the art song. The titles of his piano works—such as *Scenes from Childhood* (1838), *Viennese Carnival Pranks* (1840), and *Album for the Young* (1848)—give an idea of the way he based pieces on pictorial or literary concepts, a common feature of Romantic music.

In 1840 Schumann married the virtuoso pianist Clara Wieck, the daughter of his piano teacher, after years of opposition from her father. Schumann's happiness seems to have inspired an outpouring of song, for in that year he composed almost 150, including two great song cycles. *Frauenliebe und -leben* (*A Woman's Love and Life*, eight songs) relates directly to his situation at the time; *Dichterliebe* (*A Poet's Love*, sixteen songs), like Schubert's song cycles, follows a journey from love to death. Again, a lyrical vocal line is underpinned by descriptive piano accompaniment expressing the emotion of the songs.

Like Schubert before him, Schumann's life was cut short by syphilis. By 1854, his mental health had failed. He became delusional, attempted suicide, and died at the age of forty-six in a mental hospital, leaving Clara with seven young children to care for. She did, however, continue to perform as a pianist, undertaking concert tours to England most years and receiving great acclaim.

SYMPHONIES: MENDELSSOHN, BRAHMS, AND BERLIOZ

Orchestral music of the Romantic period took two main directions. Many composers stayed with the tried and tested symphonic form in four movements, while the more experimental musicians wrote symphonic poems based on literary works.

Felix Mendelssohn (1809–1847), born in Hamburg and raised in Berlin, was a symphonist. By the age of fourteen he had written twelve symphonies as well as two concertos, piano sonatas, chamber music, and vocal pieces. As a boy he studied the music of Classical composers, and his own compositions reflect this in their clear structure, fluency, and grace. But there are Romantic elements to his music too, especially his use of literary subjects. Having had a good education in literature and philosophy, he drew frequently on the works of Goethe, who was a friend of his, and Shakespeare—for example, in his overture to *A Midsummer Night's Dream* (1826). This is descriptive music, where the fairies can be heard fluttering in the dainty notes of the violins, and Shakespeare's lovers are represented by flowing melody over sumptuous harmonies. The best-known of Mendelssohn's symphonies have titles—the "Italian" (1833) and the "Scottish" (1842)—and in both cases he succeeds in portraying something of the feel of these locations. The "Italian" Symphony is particularly sunny in its outlook.

Other high points of Mendelssohn's music are his Violin Concerto in E minor (1844)—the first of the great Romantic violin concertos, a lyrical, plaintive, and passionate piece—and his oratorio *Elijah* (1846). He was fascinated by Baroque music and was responsible for the "revival" of Bach's *St. Matthew Passion* in 1829 and some of Handel's oratorios in the 1830s.

Another great German composer, Johannes Brahms (1833–1897), was also involved in the revival of the music of Bach and Handel; conversely, he took some of their complexity of texture into his own music. Unlike many of the Romantic composers, he was a musical conservative and had no interest in using non-musical ideas in his compositions. His four symphonies are towering works, darker in mood than those of his contemporaries, conceived as following in the footsteps of Beethoven. Like Beethoven, he employed sonata-form structure, intensive development of themes and motifs, and extremes of mood, culminating in triumph.

Brahms pursued a career as a pianist as well as composing; he wrote several sonatas and shorter pieces such as rhapsodies, intermezzos, and ballades for piano. Like Mendelssohn, he composed a violin concerto, but Brahms's Violin Concerto in D major (1878) is a work of heroism and struggle—and indeed, it is a struggle for the solo violinist, with its enormous technical demands. It requires virtuosity, but virtuosity for musical purposes rather than simply to exhibit the capabilities of the player.

One of Brahms's best-loved compositions is his *German Requiem* of the late 1860s. Unlike most Requiem Masses, with their set Latin texts, it is based on Martin Luther's translation of the Bible (see Chapter 15). Some of the most poetic parts of Old and New Testament Scripture are used to meditate on death, comfort, and the hope of heaven. Aspects of the text—for example, "My soul longs and faints"—combine Christian spirituality with Romantic yearning. A songwriter as well as a symphonist, Brahms brought his lyrical skills to the *Requiem* in broad, singable melodies; he also used fugal form, and in the fifth movement he introduced a soprano soloist to soar over the chorus as he set words about the comfort of a mother.

The French Romantic composer Hector Berlioz (1803–1869) followed his father into medicine before turning to music. He was a passionate admirer of Shakespeare and married a Shakespearean actress. His love for her inspired the *Symphonie fantastique* (1830), a program symphony in five movements. The story involves a musician whose unrequited love drives him to opium, which sends him into a haunted, delusional sleep. In this symphony, Berlioz invented the **idée fixe** ("fixed idea"): he uses a recurring theme to represent his beloved. In the different movements it is transformed in various ways—put into other keys, played in different meters, decorated with trills, and so on—but it remains recognizable and effectively helps Berlioz tell his story.

The last movement, featured in the Listening Selection, is a dream of the Witches' Sabbath, evoking the supernatural and the macabre in true Romantic spirit. Beginning with a creeping effect, it builds up in volume and rises in pitch. Berlioz was interested in orchestral "color," and this movement exemplifies his use of contrasting groups of instruments. Listen for the roaring drums and brass, for a slow brass theme set against rushing strings, for ghostly percussive effects, and for the triumphant way the full orchestra rams home the final chord.

MUSIC LISTENING SELECTION

Berlioz, *Symphonie fantastique*, fifth movement, "Witches' Sabbath." San Diego Symphony Orchestra, conductor Yoav Talmi, CD track 15

18.20 *Liszt and the Women*, caricature from *Crazy Steven* (*Bolond Istók*), March 25, 1876.
Liszt has just risen from his seat at the piano and is presenting himself to the crowd as an egocentric matinée idol, feigning indifference to the attention he is receiving.

PIANIST-COMPOSERS: LISZT AND CHOPIN

Hungarian-born Franz Liszt (1811–1886), another major orchestral composer of the Romantic period, coined the term "symphonic poem" to describe pieces that rejected Classical form and were based instead on literary or pictorial ideas. Between 1848 and 1858, while working as musical director at the court of the Grand Duke of Weimar, he wrote twelve of these works. *Hunnenschlacht* (*Slaughter of the Huns*, 1857), for example, was inspired by a mural portraying a battle for the city of Rome in A.D. 451 between the Huns and Christian soldiers under Theodoric (see Chapter 9). The music represents the battle, with rival themes fighting for dominance until a Christian chorale breaks through in triumph; in keeping with the subject matter, the organ—an instrument rarely included in the orchestra—is used prominently in this symphonic poem.

Liszt based his two symphonies on great poetry: Goethe's *Faust* and Dante's *Divine Comedy*. The *Faust Symphony* (1854) is in three movements, each a character study—of Faust, Gretchen (the ideal woman), and Mephistopheles (the devil). Instead of using Classical sonata form structure, Liszt took a new approach that involved the transformation of a single theme—somewhat like Berlioz's *idée fixe*.

Liszt was the greatest piano virtuoso of his time. From the age of eleven he gave public concerts and wrote music for himself to perform. Piano works make up the majority of his compositions and fall into two categories: arrangements and original pieces. In transcriptions and fantasias on themes by other composers, Liszt spread knowledge of a wide range of styles, from Palestrina to Wagner and including Hungarian gypsy **folk music**. Interest in his Hungarian heritage, exemplifying Romantic nationalism, pervaded his original piano compositions. In the *Hungarian Rhapsodies* (1846–1885), using only a solo piano, he created the effect of a gypsy orchestra with its characteristic folk style of ornamentation.

Liszt's brilliance made him enormously attractive to women. A caricature entitled *Liszt and the Women*, published by the Hungarian journal *Crazy Steven* in 1876, shows him surrounded by female admirers (figure **18.20**). He had two prolonged love affairs—one with a countess, one with a princess—and several illegitimate children. Yet he also had a profound religious sense and seriously considered becoming a Catholic priest. Much of his later music is religious, including oratorios, Mass settings, motets, and even piano compositions such as "St. Francis of Assisi Preaching to the Birds" (1863).

The other great Romantic pianist-composer was Frédéric Chopin (1810–1849), the son of a French father and a Polish mother. He grew up in Warsaw and at the age of twenty-two moved to Paris, where he earned a good living teaching and performing privately in the *salons*. Less showy than the music of Liszt, but still virtuosic, Chopin's elegant, melodic style is characterized by the assimilation of dance and folk music.

Chopin wrote almost exclusively for piano, composing principally by improvising at the instrument. The majority of his works are miniatures for solo piano with dance titles (but not intended to accompany dancing). Two Polish forms dominate: the **mazurka** (a country dance in triple meter with offbeat accents) and the **polonaise** (a stately processional dance in triple meter). As well as pursuing this nationalistic element, Chopin composed waltzes and **nocturnes** (night pieces)—slow-paced works of lyrical, melancholic elegance that exploited the capabilities of the new pianos. The sustaining pedal allowed pianists to play chords larger than the reach of their hands by slightly spreading the notes out in time. Unlike music of earlier eras, these pieces could not equally well be played on another keyboard instrument; they are conceived entirely in terms of the piano's distinctive timbre.

Two other forms used by Chopin are the ballade (inspired by poems, but not narrating their content) and the **étude** ("study"). Liszt also wrote études, and both composers demonstrate how pieces originating as technical exercises can be creative and dramatic compositions. Written for their students, and to sell to the middle classes who were buying pianos as status symbols, such works mark the beginning of the piano culture. Amateurs—especially women—learned to play and to entertain, and composers took advantage of the rapidly growing domestic entertainment industry.

The Listening Selection is a study in left-hand agility. Listen for the rushing figuration low in the piano's register, set against an impassioned theme in the right hand. Toward the end the pattern is broken and the composer tricks us into thinking the piece will conclude softly on a major chord; but suddenly he reverts to the minor key and the aggression of the rest of the étude for its final chords.

MUSIC LISTENING SELECTION

Chopin, "Revolutionary" Etude in C minor, Opus 10. Idil Biret, piano, CD track 16

Chopin had a liaison with George Sand (see p. 508) that lasted from 1836 until 1847. It was the inspiration not only for Sand's autobiographical novel *Lucrezia Floriani* (1846) but also for much of Chopin's music. He composed very little after the relationship ended and died of tuberculosis at the age of thirty-nine.

GERMAN OPERA: RICHARD WAGNER

Richard Wagner (1813–1883) is extremely important in the history of opera. His concepts and musical style were revolutionary, and would permanently change the face of Western music—indeed, of the arts in the West. For Wagner's view of opera, or **music drama**, as he preferred to call it, was that it should be a *Gesamtkunstwerk*, a "total art work." Vocal music, instruments, poetry, dramatic action, and stage sets achieve unity as they bring to life mythical stories about the profoundest human emotions.

Born in Leipzig, Germany, Wagner studied music at Leipzig University and with the music director at St. Thomas's Church, where Bach had worked in the Baroque period. Wagner's career as conductor and composer took him to many European countries—Latvia, France, Switzerland, Austria—but in the early years he was forever in debt and fleeing his creditors. His revolutionary politics also landed him in trouble, and in 1848 he was banned from Germany for over ten years. Finally, in the early 1860s he achieved financial security in the form of patronage from King Ludwig II of Bavaria (ruled 1864–1886). This meant he could compose the music he wished, following his artistic ideals to their conclusion without continually having to break off to provide music his publishers judged saleable.

Wagner's first marriage, to a singer, was not much of a success. His second began in scandal—Liszt's daughter Cosima was at the time the court conductor's wife and Wagner's affair with her ran for some six years, producing three children, before they eventually married. Another relationship, with the wife of one of Wagner's most generous patrons, was the inspiration for his masterpiece *Tristan and Isolde* (1865), a drama about sexual love that has been called "the greatest of all love operas."

Wagner wrote his own **librettos** (texts for his operas), generally choosing medieval or supernatural settings. Some are based on Christian legends, some on Germanic or Norse myths. Redemption is the theme that runs powerfully through them—often, the redeeming love of a woman. His characters tend to be mythological rather than "real," embodying human ideals.

In addition to librettos, Wagner wrote copiously about music, publishing books and articles analyzing his and other composers' music and the ethos behind their work. Some of his ideas, not least the racist ones, are unacceptable today; others, as in his book *Opera and Drama* (1850), have changed the course of music history.

Lohengrin (1850), featured in the Listening Selection, is an epic Christian tale set in medieval Germany. Its hero, Lohengrin, is a mysterious knight of the Holy Grail (the chalice used by Jesus at the Last Supper, as told in the Gospels), who rescues Elsa from tyrants trying to seize power. Elsa, in return, has to promise never to ask his name or background. A royal decree instructs the couple to marry, and Lohengrin is told to lead the people to war against Hungarian invaders. But the tyrants egg Elsa on until she breaks faith and forces Lohengrin to disclose his identity. Without trust, the relationship ends: he leaves and she dies.

As the last of Wagner's early operas, *Lohengrin* still has recognizable sections of aria, recitative, and chorus. The Bridal

Chorus in the Listening Selection is often played in an organ transcription at weddings. The foursquare style, with a verse structure, was replaced in Wagner's later operas by a freer flow of music. Moments of orchestral accompaniment between the verses reflect this more flexible musical language.

MUSIC LISTENING SELECTION
Wagner, *Lohengrin*, Bridal Chorus. Slovak Philharmonic Chorus, Slovak Radio Orchestra, conductor Johannes Wildner, CD track 18

Wagner's later operas move away from set-piece songs and generally consist of narrative and dialogue supported by a rich orchestral texture. Wagner unifies the continuous flow of sound with **leitmotifs**, recurrent themes that can represent particular people, objects, or more abstract ideas such as places or emotions. This both binds the structure together and has dramatic impact. *Leitmotifs* are used straightforwardly—a sword motif if a sword is drawn—and more obliquely, for example when one character is thinking of another. Berlioz and Liszt had employed similar techniques, but Wagner develops the concept to a different degree and on a grander scale. Much twentieth-century film music has adopted this aspect of his music.

Wagner's harmonic style in his later works is extremely chromatic, loosening the sense of a home key and preparing the way for the complete breakdown of Classical tonality in the twentieth century. His chromaticism and dissonance give the music heightened emotion and sensuality. Similarly, orchestral color is exploited for dramatic purposes. In *Lohengrin*, strings refer to the Holy Grail, brass to the king. Wagner added to the orchestra of his day, particularly in the brass section. His cycle of operas *Der Ring des Nibelungen* (*The Nibelung's Ring*, 1848–1876) is scored for a massive string section of 32 violins, 12 violas, 12 cellos, and 8 double basses, which enables him to divide the sections into multiple parts and weave the musical lines into complex, delicate webs of sound. The woodwinds include extra instruments such as bass clarinet, and four of the sixteen brass players perform on the "Wagner tuba," constructed specially for the composer.

Wagner worked on the composition of his greatest work, *The Nibelung's Ring*, for several decades and founded a music festival at the small town of Bayreuth, Germany, so he could create the ideal conditions for its performance. Based on Nordic myth, it consists of four long operas and deals with great themes: lust for power, the corrupting effect of money, duty in conflict with love, redemption, ultimate disintegration. In *Das Rheingold* (*The Gold of the Rhine*, 1869), the Nibelung (dwarf) Alberich steals magic gold from the three Rhinemaidens, knowing that if he renounces love and makes it into a ring, he will become immensely powerful. Wotan, ruler of the gods (the Norse Odin), tricks him into giving up the Ring, and at that moment Alberich curses it and everyone who will own it. Next, the Ring passes to two giants in settlement of a debt; one kills the other to gain possession of it. Two-and-a-half hours of continuous music come to an end as the gods walk across a rainbow bridge to their heavenly castle, Valhalla, with the Rhinemaidens lamenting the loss of their treasure in the river below.

Die Walküre (*The Valkyries*, 1870), about five hours in performance, deals with Wotan's warrior-maiden daughters, the Valkyries. According to Norse myth, they brought brave warriors killed in battle to the banqueting hall of Valhalla. Wotan fathers two more children with a human woman in the hope of enlisting their help in regaining the Ring. Unaware of their sibling relationship, they enter into an incestuous romance, producing Siegfried, the hero of the third opera (*Siegfried*, 1876). It culminates in a blaze of passion as the fearless Siegfried crosses a ring of fire to awaken Wotan's favorite Valkyrie daughter, Brünnhilde. The fourth opera, *Götterdämmerung* (*Twilight of the Gods*, 1876)—the Norse Ragnarök (see Chapter 10)—concludes the cycle. Brünnhilde ends the violent quest for the Ring forever by wearing it as she rides into her lover's funeral pyre. Flames engulf Valhalla and the Rhine floods; the old order of gods, humans, and dwarfs is gone.

ITALIAN OPERA: GIUSEPPE VERDI

The greatest figure in Italian Romantic opera was Giuseppe Verdi (1813–1901). Born near Bussetto in northern Italy, Verdi was a gifted child who began learning the keyboard at the age of three. After studying locally and then in Milan, he became town music master in Bussetto, teaching and directing concerts. In 1839 he moved to Milan and his first opera was staged at the world-class opera house, La Scala. This led to commissions for further operas and interest from a publisher—vital for a musician trying to earn his living through composition. However, his next piece was not so well received, and since his wife and two children died around the same time, he sank into depression. Another commission from the director of the opera house set him back on the creative track, and with the opera *Nabucco* (1842) Verdi began to make an international name for himself. Opera houses all around Italy requested music from him, as well as London and Paris.

Verdi's glowing Romantic dramas, designed to appeal to the Italy of his day, form a peak in the long tradition of Italian opera. Full of passion and spectacle, they have an undercurrent of biting social and political criticism, which sometimes landed Verdi in trouble with the censors. A man of liberal views, he was anticlerical and fiercely opposed to tyranny. At this period, Italy was struggling toward nationhood after years of domination by Austria and Spain, and

Verdi was himself involved in the nationalist *Risorgimento* movement (see p. 531).

Verdi sought out subjects for his operas that were unconventional and would provide dramatic progression toward a climax. For example, *Rigoletto* (1851), inspired by a Victor Hugo story, is a dark tale dealing with a hunchback court jester involved in romantic intrigue, abduction, and murder at the sixteenth-century court of Mantua. A recurrent theme in Verdian opera is the conflict between love and loyalty to one's country, as in *Aida* (1871), where ill-fated love unfolds between the Egyptian general Radames and Aida, the daughter of his Ethiopian enemy. All but two of Verdi's operas are tragedies, and most end with a death. Some are overtly violent—*A Masked Ball* (1859), for instance—and others deeply poignant, such as the final scene of *La traviata* (*The Woman Gone Astray*, 1853), where the heroine dies of tuberculosis. If this all sounds somewhat gloomy, there are fun elements too: balls and parties, cross-dressing, elopement, gypsy scenes, exotic settings—and, above all, passionate hit tunes.

Verdi's musical structure is not ground-breaking like Wagner's. Verdi's early works use the standard elements of Italian opera: love duets, bold choruses, brilliant soprano arias, heroic tenor arias, and vigorous recitative. Each section is complete in itself and arias, especially, were often applauded in the nineteenth century as soon as they were finished. Over the years the composer developed greater continuity, so by the time he wrote his last opera, the comedy *Falstaff* (1893), there are few formal arias or ensembles, and conversation appears to flow freely between the characters. Musical recall—reusing a musical theme when a person or event is mentioned again—is used from time to time by Verdi, which has parallels with Wagner's *leitmotif*. But in Verdi, rather than being a structural principle, it is an occasional dramatic device.

Verdi retained the musical language of his day, his long, smooth vocal phrases forming expansive melodies that express the emotions of the characters and stir emotions in the audience. Key changes are generally conventional, with a leaning toward shifting to a key three notes from the original key at points of great expressiveness (one of the beautiful harmonic "tricks" characteristic of the Romantic period, giving a "melting" feeling). Rich orchestral harmonies support the voices and create atmosphere. Unlike Wagner, Verdi drew his characters as convincing people dealing with conflict, jealousy and hate, family ties, comradeship, and passion.

NATIONALISM IN MUSIC

We have seen that nationalism was an important strand in Romantic music, affecting the choice of operatic plots, musical forms (Chopin's polonaises), and styles (Liszt's gypsy melodies). In the later nineteenth century it became a distinctive feature of eastern and northern European music.

BOHEMIA: DVOŘÁK The son of a butcher in a small village in Bohemia (now the Czech Republic), Antonín Dvořák (1841–1904) studied music at the organ school in Prague from 1857, thereafter working as a viola player, teacher, organist, composer, and music college director. He composed in a wide range of forms including opera, Mass, symphony, and concerto; and on a smaller scale, string quartet, art song, and piano miniature.

Dvořák's *Slavonic Dances* (1878) were inspired by Bohemian folk music—they use typical folk rhythms and quote fragments of actual folk tunes. And even in his more Classically based works, Dvořák employed Czech forms. The polka (a couple dance in duple meter) might replace a scherzo and a *skočna* (a leaping dance) replace a finale. He frequently used the *dumka*, a lament, for his slow movements. Melodically, the influence of folk style can be seen in certain patterns: the repetition of the initial measure of a tune, or an upward leap followed by an immediate return to the same pitch, as in the third of the *Slavonic Dances*.

From the 1870s, Dvořák's music began to be published, and with support and encouragement from his friend Brahms the composer became an international success. Dvořák's compositions were especially popular in Britain, which he visited nine times. In 1891, he was invited to move to New York to direct the National Conservatory of Music. While living there he explored Native American folk traditions and African-American music, drawing from this research a **pentatonic** scale that can be heard in his String Quartet No. 12 in F major, the "American" (1893), and in the Symphony No. 9 in E minor, "From the New World" (1893). Tuneful and energetic, the symphony uses recurrent "motto" themes and melodies that sound like African-American spirituals—in particular, "Swing low, sweet chariot." However, Dvořák was quick to assert that all his New York compositions were "genuine Bohemian music."

RUSSIA: TCHAIKOVSKY AND MUSSORGSKY Pyotr Ilyich Tchaikovsky (1840–1893) is generally considered the greatest Russian Romantic composer. Lyrical and passionate, his music uses Classical forms—in particular the symphony—but still has Russian character. Some of his pieces are self-consciously nationalist: his Symphony No. 2 in C minor, the "Little Russian" (1872), is so-called because it quotes Ukrainian folksongs. At this period Tchaikovsky was particularly interested in nationalism and expressed it in two operas: *The Oprichnik* (1874), a grand historical drama, and *Vakula the Smith* (1876), a fairytale fantasy. His most enduring opera, *Eugene Onegin* (1879), is about a man who rejects a woman's love only to regret his decision later. As well as operas and symphonies, Tchaikovsky wrote a wonderful Violin Concerto in D major (1878) and evocative ballet music: *Swan Lake* (1877), *Sleeping Beauty* (1890), and *The Nutcracker* (1892).

Tchaikovsky's compatriot Modest Mussorgsky (1839–1881) was overtly nationalist, joining a group of composers known as "The Five" to pursue their Russian identity in music. He was inspired by older Russian culture—the music of the Orthodox Church and folksong—and by a type of musical realism that aimed to catch the nuances of the Russian language. In his solo songs, song cycles, and operas the vocal line thus simulates the inflections of speech while being pleasingly lyrical; the content is sometimes pessimistic (*Sunless*, 1874), sometimes ironic (*Songs and Dances of Death*, 1877). His small output of piano and orchestral music is descriptive, as is clear from titles like *Pictures at an Exhibition* (1874) and *St. John's Night on the Bare Mountain* (1867). His masterpiece is the opera *Boris Godunov* (1872), which he subtitled "A Musical Folk Drama." Based on a play by Pushkin, it deals with the guilt-ridden tsar who ruled Russia from 1598 to 1605, and it has a cast of distinctly local characters. This includes the old monk Pimen, who chants as he writes a history of Russia, and the People, a crowd that salutes Boris with a folk tune at his coronation but later turns against him. Musically, the mix of church-style music on a modal scale and lively folksong evokes the Russian setting.

SCANDINAVIA: GRIEG AND SIBELIUS In Scandinavia, as well, nationalism infiltrated music. The most important Norwegian composer of the period was Edvard Grieg (1843–1907). From the mid-1860s, he worked at developing a distinctive Norwegian style, and he was a founder member of Euterpe, a society for the promotion of Scandinavian music. First and foremost a lyrical Romantic composer, Grieg excelled in the composition of piano miniatures, such as the character pieces *Pictures from Country Life* (1870–1871). His 140 songs form an important part of his output. Some have texts modeled on Norwegian folk poetry, and they show how folk music can be transmuted into art song. Probably his best-known work is the **incidental music** written to accompany Ibsen's *Peer Gynt* (see Chapter 19), including numbers titled "Solveig's Song" and "In the Hall of the Mountain King." By turns melodious, angry, and excited, the music exemplifies descriptive orchestral writing.

The leading Finnish composer at the turn of the century was Jean Sibelius (1865–1957). Initially he hoped to become a virtuoso violinist, and judging by his Violin Concerto in D minor (1903)—the last of the great Romantic violin concertos—he had phenomenal technical ability. In 1885 he went to Helsinki University to study law, but after a year he decided to pursue composition instead. Sibelius's huge choral symphony (*Kullervo*, 1892) is the first of several works by him based on the Finnish national epic, the *Kalevala*. He had a strong sense of national identity and a preoccupation with Norse mythology and nature poetry that found musical expression in symphonic poems such as *Finlandia* (1899) and *Tapiola* (1926), an evocation of the northern forests. Principally an orchestral composer, he wrote seven symphonies of grand proportions, with broad melodies and slow-moving harmonies. Some of the later symphonies are at times intensely dissonant and use chromatic intervals that undermine the sense of tonality. His individual sound world includes open textures, sustained bass notes, and organic development of motifs.

While the symphonies of Sibelius are firmly rooted in a long tradition, the music of some of his contemporaries at the start of the twentieth century took an entirely different direction, which will be discussed in Chapter 21.

The Romantic Movement, which began in the late eighteenth century, flourished up to the latter years of the nineteenth century. But the nineteenth century witnessed several important trends that overlapped each other. In the next chapter we consider the Industrial Revolution, new social and economic theories that responded to industry, and the Realist style in the arts.

KEY TERMS

art song a composed song (as opposed to a folksong or popular song), often the concert setting of a poem; the term is commonly applied to the German *lied* of the Romantic period.

étude (French, "study") an instrumental piece written to develop or display playing technique.

folk music orally transmitted music of unknown origin.

idée fixe a term used by the composer Berlioz to describe a recurring theme in a large-scale work.

incidental music music composed as background or accompaniment to a stage production.

leitmotif in a dramatic musical work, a recurrent theme that can represent a particular person, object, or more abstract idea; a term used initially by Wagner, and by commentators on his music since.

libretto the text for an opera or oratorio.

mazurka a Polish country dance in triple meter with off-beat accents.

motif in music, a short rhythmic or melodic pattern used recurrently to unify a movement or a whole piece.

nocturne a musical composition that expresses the character of night, often written for the piano.

pentatonic a term used to describe a scale or mode consisting of only five notes.

polonaise a stately Polish processional dance in triple meter.

scherzo (Italian, "joke") a lively movement in triple meter that superseded the minuet in symphonies and string quartets in the early nineteenth century.

song cycle a set of songs composed as an ordered unit, often using texts by the same author or based on the same theme.

tone poem (symphonic poem) a one-movement orchestral composition based on a non-musical idea.

KEY QUESTIONS

1. How did Napoleon influence the visual arts and music in the nineteenth century?
2. Define the terms "liberalism" and "nationalism" as they were understood in Europe before 1848. Which political ideas influenced the Romantic strain of philosophy and aesthetics? Does Goya's *The Third of May, 1808* illustrate these ideas? Does Géricault's *Raft of the "Medusa"* illustrate these concerns or other Romantic concerns?
3. The theme of uncontrolled natural forces resulting in the sublime or the grotesque runs throughout Romanticism. How are these themes expressed in literature?
4. Nostalgia for the past is characteristic of classicism and Romanticism. How do artists use the past to present Classical or Romantic themes?
5. Define Transcendentalism. Does the term "sublime" apply to this concept? What ideas influenced Transcendentalism?

SUGGESTED READING

Ackroyd, Peter. *Albion*. London: Chatto and Windus, 2002.
- A study of the English myth of Albion.

Behler, E. *German Romantic Literary Theory*. Cambridge, U.K.: Cambridge University Press, 1993
- An introduction to the literary theory of the German Romantics.

Clark, Kenneth. *The Romantic Rebellion*. New York: Harper and Row, 1973.
- Ideas and styles of Romanticism.

Honour, Hugh. *Romanticism*. New York: Harper and Row, 1979.
- An introduction to the style.

Johnson, P. *Napoleon*. London: Weidenfeld and Nicolson, 2002.
- A brief biography.

Licht, Fred. *Goya: The Origins of Modern Temper in Art*. New York: Harper and Row, 1983.
- A monograph on the artist and his influence.

Luvaas, J. *Napoleon on the Art of War*. New York: Simon and Schuster, 2001.
- Napoleon's writings on war.

Nochlin, Linda. *The Body in Pieces*. London: Thames and Hudson, 1994.
- A brief study of fragmentation in nineteenth-century art.

Pinkney, D. H. *The French Revolution of 1830*. Princeton, NJ: Princeton University Press, 1973.
- The 1830 uprising in France.

Praz, Mario. *The Romantic Agony*. New York: Oxford University Press, 1983.
- A study of nineteenth-century Romantic ideas, themes, and iconography.

Thoreau, Henry David. *Walden and Other Writings*. New York: Bantam Books, 1981.
- Thoreau's "Walden Pond" and other essays.

Whittall, Arnold. *Romantic Music*. London: Thames and Hudson, 1987.
- A general overview from Schubert to Sibelius.

SUGGESTED FILMS

1913 *The Pit and the Pendulum* (based on Poe), dir. Alice Guy

1926 *The Scarlet Letter*, dir. Victor Sjostrom

1928 *The Fall of the House of Usher* (based on Poe), dir. Jean Epstein and Luis Buñuel

1934 *The Scarlet Letter*, dir. Robert G. Vignola

1940 *Pride and Prejudice*, dir. Robert Z. Leonard

1961 *The Pit and the Pendulum* (based on Poe), dir. Roger Corman

1964 *The Masque of the Red Death* (based on Poe), dir. Roger Corman

1994 *Immortal Beloved* (a life of Beethoven), dir. Bernard Rose

2000 *Pandaemonium* (about Coleridge and Wordsworth), dir. Julien Temple

19 Nineteenth-century Realism: Industry and Social Change

"Now, what I want is, Facts. Teach these boys and girls nothing but Facts. Facts alone are wanted in life . . . This is the principle on which I bring up my own children, and this is the principle on which I bring up these children. Stick to Facts, Sir!"

(CHARLES DICKENS, *Hard Times*)

A new trend in art, literature, and music emerged in western Europe in the mid-nineteenth century. This trend has been called Realism, and, as with Neoclassicism and Romanticism, it soon spread to the United States. Realist artists and writers presented panoramic views of society, reflecting a new interest in the working classes and in the economic problems brought about by the Industrial Revolution. Influenced to some degree by increasing empiricism in science and medicine, Realists also focused on precise depictions and descriptions of observed detail. Their works were inspired not by history, myth, or religion but by their own experience.*

In politics, rebellions throughout Europe were inspired by nationalist and class issues. In the United States the national conflicts that beset Europe were not an issue, although there were class conflicts. In both the United States and Europe, however, developments in technology, such as steel manufacture and railroads, held out a promise of progress; but they also created strife between the working classes and the wealthy. In architecture, technological innovations—especially steel manufacture—made it possible to construct tall buildings that could accommodate more people at lower cost than ever before. Science also made strides in the nineteenth century, often arousing criticism from religious quarters. Philosophers dealt with social and economic problems and proposed ways of improving conditions for the average worker.

The opening quotation of the chapter is from the novel Hard Times *(1854) by the British author Charles Dickens (1812–1870), who described the abuses of modern life. Whereas the Romantics reacted to the negative effects of industrialization by looking to the past and to the ideal of living in harmony with nature, to exotic locales, and to fantasy and imagination, Realist writers, artists, and musicians expressed the here and now of daily experience. The Italian term* verismo *(realism) refers to the portrayal in late nineteenth-century opera of intense, truthful emotions with contemporary stage sets. Realist works of art confront viewers with the bad as well as the good of "modern" life.*

Key Topics

Industry

- Railways
- Steamships
- Steel and the skyscraper
- Prefabricated architecture

Innovation in the Arts

- Literary Realism
- Slave narratives
- Social commentary
- Women strive for rights
- American Civil War
- Expansion of newspapers
- Photography

Science, Politics, and Philosophy

- Advances in medicine
- Pasteur discovers that germs cause disease
- Darwin's theory of natural selection
- Marx and Engels: *The Communist Manifesto*
- Utilitarianism and "empirical" philosophy
- Manifest Destiny

TIMELINE	NINETEENTH-CENTURY EUROPE	NINETEENTH-CENTURY UNITED STATES
HISTORY AND CULTURE 	Industrial Revolution Realism emerges in Europe Bismarck (1815–1898), Iron Chancellor of Prussia Crimean War, 1854–1856; Treaty of Paris, 1856 Italy unified, absorbing Papal States, 1861 Franco-Prussian War, 1870–1871 Queen Victoria (r. 1837–1901) proclaimed Empress of India, 1876 Dreyfus Affair, 1894	Lewis and Clark Expedition, 1804–1806 Indian Removal Act, 1830 Manifest Destiny, 1845 Underground Railroad Abraham Lincoln becomes sixteenth president, 1859 Civil War, 1861–1865; Battle of Gettysburg, 1863 Emancipation Proclamation, 1863 Gettysburg Address, 1863 Lincoln assassinated, 1865 Battle of Little Bighorn, 1876 Massacre at Wounded Knee, 1890
SCIENCE AND TECHNOLOGY 	Inventions: iron plow, reaper, flying shuttle, spinning jenny, power loom Development of steam-powered ships Jenner develops smallpox vaccine, 1798 First locomotive, 1814 Florence Nightingale (1820–1910) Pasteur (1822–1895) discovers that germs cause disease and invents pasteurization Darwin, *On the Origin of Species by Means of Natural Selection*, 1859 Suez Canal links Red Sea to Mediterranean, 1869 Mendel discovers genes and publishes *Experiments with Plant Hybrids*, 1869 Bell invents telephone, 1876	Morse sets up first telegraph line, 1844 Edison produces first commercial electric lightbulb, 1879
PAINTING AND PHOTOGRAPHY 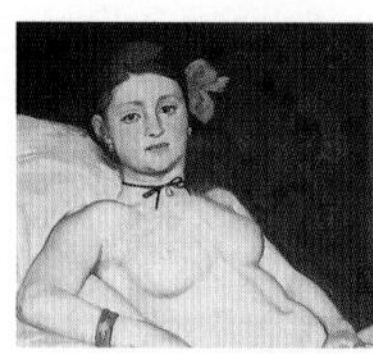	Daguerre invents daguerreotypes, 1830s Daumier, *Rue Transnonain, April 15, 1834*, 1834; *Third-class Carriage*, c. 1862 Fox Talbot, *The Pencil of Nature*, 1844–1846 Pre-Raphaelite Brotherhood, 1848 Courbet, *A Burial at Ornans*, 1849 Bonheur, *Plowing the Nivernais*, 1849 Hunt, *The Awakening Conscience*, 1853 Brady, *Lincoln, "Cooper Union Portrait,"* 1860 Manet, *Olympia*, 1865; *Portrait of Zola*, 1868 Bouguereau, *The Birth of Venus*, 1879	Catlin, *Keokuk (the Watchful Fox), Chief of the Tribe*, 1832 Mount, *California News*, 1850 Homer, *The War for the Union, 1862—A Bayonet Charge*, 1862; *Prisoners from the Front*, 1866 Riis, *Bandits' Roost*, 1888 Remington, *A Dash for the Timber*, 1889 Tanner, *Banjo Lesson*, 1893
ARCHITECTURE	Paxton, Crystal Palace, London, 1850–1851 Eiffel, Eiffel Tower, Paris, 1887–1889	Sullivan, Wainwright Building, St. Louis, Missouri, 1890–1891; "Form follows function"
LITERATURE AND PHILOSOPHY 	Utopianism and Marxism Owen (1771–1858) and Saint-Simon (1760–1825) Balzac, *Le Dernier Chouan*, 1829; *Le Père Goriot*, 1834–1835 Dickens, *A Christmas Carol*, 1843; *David Copperfield*, 1849–1850; *Hard Times*, 1854; *Great Expectations*, 1860–1861 Kierkegaard, *Either/Or*, 1843; *The Sickness unto Death*, 1849 Marx and Engels, *Communist Manifesto*, 1848 Mill, *Principles of Political Economy*, 1848; *On Liberty*, 1859 Tennyson, "The Charge of the Light Brigade," 1854 Flaubert, *Madame Bovary*, 1857 Goncharov, *Oblomov*, 1859 Eliot, *Adam Bede*, 1859; *The Mill on the Floss*, 1860 Tolstoy, *War and Peace*, 1863–1869; *Anna Karenina*, 1874–1877 Dostoyevsky, *Crime and Punishment*, 1866; *The Idiot*, 1868–1869; *Brothers Karamazov*, 1879–1880 Zola, *Les Rougon-Macquart*, 1871–1893; "J'Accuse," 1898 Butler, *Erewhon*, 1872 Nietzsche, *Thus Spake Zarathustra*, 1883–1892 de Maupassant, *The Horla*, 1887	Douglass, *Narrative of the Life of Frederick Douglass, An American Slave*, 1845 Truth, *Ain't I a Woman?* 1851 Stowe, *Uncle Tom's Cabin*, 1852 Twain, *The Adventures of Tom Sawyer*, 1876; *Life on the Mississippi*, 1883; *The Adventures of Huckleberry Finn*, 1884 Chopin, *Bayou Folk*, 1894; *A Night in Arcadie*, 1897; *The Awakening*, 1899 Crane, *The Red Badge of Courage*, 1895
THEATER	Ibsen, *Peer Gynt*, 1867; *A Doll's House*, 1879; *Ghosts*, 1881; *Hedda Gabler*, 1890 Strindberg, *Miss Julie*, 1888 Chekhov, *The Seagull*, 1896; *Uncle Vanya*, 1900; *The Three Sisters*, 1901; *The Cherry Orchard*, 1903	
MUSIC	*Verismo* opera Bizet, *Carmen*, 1875 Puccini, *La bohème*, 1896; *Tosca*, 1900	

POLITICAL DEVELOPMENTS

After the revolution of 1848 in France (see Chapter 18), workers' revolts spread across Europe to Prussia, Italy, and central Europe. The rebellions of 1848 not only altered national boundaries and national identities but also sought to redress class conflicts and social abuses (map **19.1**). In Prussia, however, the government's response was to establish a strong, anti-liberal regime. Known by the German term **Realpolitik**, this was a political philosophy based on practical rather than on moral or humanitarian considerations.

Otto von Bismarck (1815–1898), an advocate of Realpolitik, was called the Iron Chancellor of Prussia. He favored a constitutional monarchy and recognized the role that industry would play in modern society. He became Prussia's prime minister and foreign minister in 1862 and launched a program to unite the German states, which, by 1866, had been consolidated around Prussia to form the North German Confederation. With a view to strengthening Germany, Bismarck goaded France into declaring war on Prussia in 1870. After France was defeated and the Second Empire under Napoleon III collapsed (see Chapter 18), Germany absorbed Alsace-Lorraine and became the most powerful nation in Europe.

Austria, in contrast to Germany, lost power as nationalist Italian liberals began from the 1830s to foment rebellion. As a result, the Italian state of Piedmont-Sardinia (which included part of northern Italy and the island of Sardinia) emerged. This eroded Austria's position, because much of north Italy and Tuscany had formed part of the Austrian Empire.

The prime minister of Piedmont, Camillo Benso di Cavour (1810–1861), formed an alliance with Napoleon III to unify Italy, a process known as the *Risorgimento*. Cavour was aided by Giuseppe Garibaldi (1807–1882), whose army freed the southern Kingdom of the Two Sicilies from Spanish control. In 1861 most of Italy was unified under King Victor Emmanuel II (ruled 1861–1878) and absorbed the Papal States. By 1866 Austria ceded Venetia, in the northeast, and in 1870 Rome became the Italian capital.

Map 19.1 Europe, 1848–1849.

Politically, Russia was the least advanced European nation in the nineteenth century and the only one without some form of constitution by 1900. Absolute power remained in the hands of the tsars and efforts by Alexander I (ruled 1801–1825) to institute reforms failed. His successor, Nicholas I (ruled 1825–1855), wanted to control the Ottoman Empire, which caused France, Sardinia, and Britain to ally themselves with Turkey against Russia. The resulting Crimean War (1854–1856) was ill-conceived and poorly managed on both sides. Russia did not foresee the extent of the opposition to its territorial ambitions, and France and Britain misjudged the amount of troops and equipment necessary to fight the war. In 1855 French and British troops overran the Russian fortress at Sevastapol on the Black Sea, and the following year the war ended with the Treaty of Paris. Russia renounced all claims to the Ottoman Empire and agreed that the Black Sea would be neutral.

In one well-publicized skirmish of 1854 a tactical error on Britain's part led to the deaths of more than two hundred British soldiers and officers. This event was memorialized in "The Charge of the Light Brigade" by the late-Victorian poet Alfred, Lord Tennyson (1809–1892). The phrase "Someone had blundered" appeared in the London *Times* and inspired the poem's refrain, "Rode the six hundred":

Half a league, half a league,
Half a league onward,
All in the valley of Death
  Rode the six hundred.
"Forward the Light Brigade!
Charge for the guns!" he said.
Into the valley of Death
  Rode the six hundred . . .

Cannon to right of them,
Cannon to left of them,
Cannon behind them
  Volley'd and thunder'd;
Storm'd at with shot and shell,
While horse and hero fell,
They that had fought so well
Came thro' the jaws of Death,
Back from the mouth of Hell,
All that was left of them,
  Left of six hundred.

The Crimean War was the first conflict in which journalists and war photographers sent reports to the news media, informing the public of events more rapidly than before. Hence the account in the London papers that inspired Tennyson's poem.

Britain itself, with an established constitutional monarchy, avoided internal armed rebellions during the nineteenth century, although there were many workers' revolts and efforts to unionize. The greatest number of reforms were instituted under Queen Victoria, whose long reign lasted from 1837 to 1901. In this period more men won the right to vote and other democratic reforms improved social and economic conditions. Abroad, Britain was an imperial power, and in 1876 Queen Victoria was proclaimed Empress of India.

THE INDUSTRIAL REVOLUTION: TECHNOLOGY AND INVENTION

By 1800 the groundwork for the Industrial Revolution was already in place in Britain. The practice of enclosing open common land and separating it from that of small farmers increased agricultural productivity. Crop rotation, and improved techniques of mining coal and iron ore that led to the invention of the iron plow and the reaper, permitted more efficient farming. The textile industry benefited from the eighteenth-century invention of the flying shuttle, the spinning jenny, and the power loom for producing cotton goods. Although mechanizing the process destroyed the well-established cottage textile industry, there was a huge demand for labor—including child labor—in the factories.

Eventually, agriculture ceased to be Britain's main source of wealth and was replaced by mass-produced textiles. Urban factories drew people to the cities, but the quality of life for urban workers declined. Children as well as adults were exploited by the factories, with child labor constituting one of the greatest abuses of the Industrial Revolution. Another was pollution from burning coal, which caused lung disease and other health problems among urban populations.

Internationally as well as domestically, industry led to an increase in markets through the development of steam-powered ships and the expansion of the empire. Britain's colonies and former colonies provided raw materials—especially cotton from India and the American South—which were transported back to Britain for manufacture. Britain's factories were often located near rivers and used water to power steam engines. Railroads made it possible for people to live in one place and work in another. The first locomotive was built in 1814, and by 1850 most English cities were connected to each other by rail. In 1869 the Suez Canal linked the Red Sea to the Mediterranean, shortening the journey time from Europe to India. Now it was no longer necessary to sail around the Cape of Good Hope (at the southern tip of Africa) to ship goods to and from the Far East.

The Industrial Revolution soon spread from Britain to the continent, especially to France, Belgium, and Germany. Railroad networks in Europe created new routes for more efficient commerce and faster travel. By 1871 Paris and Brussels were linked by rail to Milan and Vienna. In North America, with its vast, unsettled spaces, the railroad was crucial to economic development (figure **19.1**).

The development of steel and iron allowed engineers and architects to invent new building techniques, which eventually changed the aesthetics of architecture and made decent

19.1 *American Express Train*, *c*. 1864. Color lithograph of Frances F. Palmer's painting, 17⅝ × 28 in. (44.8 × 71.1 cm). Museum of the City of New York. This lithograph conveys the energy and speed of the steam engine powering railroads in nineteenth-century America. The intense black smoke flowing from the sturdy smokestack merges into the mountain, leaving the sky an unrealistic clear blue. By making the colors of the cars echo those of the foliage, the artist depicts the train as an integral part of the American landscape. Note also the presence of the steamship, another industrial image, proceeding down the river at the right. Five years after this print was made, the first U.S. transcontinental railroad was completed.

housing and agreeable work spaces more widely available and affordable. Prefabrication made it possible to assemble structures from pre-made sections that could be transported to building sites, reducing the time and expense of construction. Sir Joseph Paxton (1803–1865), for example, built the 18-acre (7.3 ha) Crystal Palace (figure **19.2**) in London of cast iron and glass to house pavilions from all over the world during the Great Exhibition of 1851—the first "World's Fair"—inaugurated by Queen Victoria. After the exhibition the Crystal Palace was removed and reassembled outside London, where it stood until it burned down in 1936.

In contrast to the Crystal Palace, the Eiffel Tower in Paris is still standing. Intended as a temporary structure built of iron, it was designed for the 1889 World's Fair by Alexandre-Gustave Eiffel (1832–1923) (figure **19.3**) and at the time was the tallest building in the world. Although the French public disliked the tower and wanted it destroyed at the end of the fair, it survived because it could be used as a radio tower.

19.2 Joseph Paxton, Crystal Palace, London, 1850–1851. Iron and glass. Color lithograph by Joseph Nash, 1851. 35⅞ in. (91 cm) wide. Guildhall Library Print Room, London.

19.3 Alexandre-Gustave Eiffel, Eiffel Tower, Paris, 1887–1889. Iron structure on a concrete base, 984 ft. (300 m) high.
The tower is a metal truss of wrought iron, making the sky visible through its open lattice. The elevators were made by Elisha Otis (1811–1861), an American inventor who also made escalators.

Other inventions facilitated communication and the efficiency of labor. In 1844 Samuel Morse (1791–1872) set up a telegraph line between Washington and Baltimore. His system, the **Morse code**, uses dots and dashes in place of letters. In 1866 the first transatlantic cable was completed, followed ten years later by the invention of the telephone by Alexander Graham Bell (1847–1922). The Bell Telephone Company was founded in 1877. By 1879 the American inventor Thomas Alva Edison (1847–1931) had produced the first commercial electric lightbulb with a carbon filament. In 1892, after forming many companies to market his inventions, he merged them into General Electric. Edison also improved on the telephone and in 1877 invented the phonograph.

SCIENCE

The notion of "progress," encouraged not only by technology but also by science, had wide appeal from the mid-nineteenth century well into the twentieth. Discoveries in biology and related fields improved the lives of large numbers of people, but some of these discoveries also challenged traditional religious ideas.

In 1869 the Austrian biologist and monk Gregor Mendel (1822–1884) published *Experiments with Plant Hybrids*, which recorded his study of inherited characteristics in plants through certain factors, which are now called **genes**. Based mainly on studying peas in the garden of his monastery, he formulated two basic laws of heredity:

1. Both parent plants contribute a factor (the gene), which provides a particular trait, to the offspring.
2. Paired genes in the offspring do not result in a blend of traits.

Mendel also discovered that some genes are dominant and others are recessive. He noted that dwarf plants have only dwarf offspring, which in turn produce dwarfs. But tall plants can produce both tall and dwarf plants, leading to the conclusion that tallness is a dominant and dwarfism a recessive trait.

Advances in inoculations saved the lives of thousands of people and increased the life expectancy of children who would otherwise have died. In 1798 the British physician Edward Jenner (1749–1823) published his discovery of the smallpox vaccination after observing that cattle workers who had had cowpox never contracted smallpox. He devised a cowpox inoculation for children, followed by a smallpox injection, which produced immunity to smallpox. The term "vaccination" was coined from the Latin word *vaccinia*, meaning "cowpox."

In France the chemist and biologist Louis Pasteur (1822–1895) discovered that germs cause disease (see Box), a momentous finding that led to proposals for combating disease by practical methods such as washing one's hands and disinfecting medical instruments. Pasteur made vaccines against anthrax and rabies and developed the "pasteurization" of milk, a process of killing (through heating) microorganisms that cause typhoid, dysentery, diphtheria, and tuberculosis.

In the field of nursing, the British Florence Nightingale (1820–1910) recognized the importance of medical training for nurses while supervising nurses during the Crimean War and witnessing the dismal care and inattention to basic hygiene given to wounded soldiers. In 1860 she established the Nightingale School for Nurses' Training at St. Thomas's Hospital in London.

The scientist whose work posed the greatest challenge to traditional Christian beliefs was the British naturalist Charles Darwin (1809–1882). Studying animals on the Galápagos Islands, he noted that a single colony of finches could split into

Louis Pasteur and the Germ Theory of Disease

The French chemist Louis Pasteur (1822–1895; figure **19.4**) discovered that germs cause disease. Today we take this for granted, but before Pasteur's research no one understood what caused diseases or how diseases were transmitted. Pasteur demonstrated that germs live in the air and are spread through human contact, and he himself declined to shake hands with people to avoid infection. Modern hygiene evolved from his discoveries. He urged doctors to wash their hands before treating patients, especially in delivery rooms.

Pasteur invented pasteurization, a process that kills yeast in the aging of wine and protects milk from bacteria that cause tuberculosis, dysentery, diphtheria, and typhoid. He also made a number of ground-breaking discoveries, such as identifying the parasite infecting silkworms that threatened the lucrative French silk industry. He invented the anthrax vaccine by injecting weakened bacilli into sheep and pioneered the inoculation of fowl against a form of cholera affecting chickens.

Although viruses were not known at the time, in 1882 Pasteur set out to find a way to prevent rabies. Again, he isolated a weakened form of the virus, which he injected into humans. He achieved widespread fame in 1885 when he cured a boy who had been bitten by a rabid dog. In 1888 the Pasteur Institute in Paris was founded, and it remains an important French research center today.

Critical Question What do you consider today's most dangerous disease, and why?

19.4 Louis Pasteur in his laboratory, *c.* 1885. Engraving, 6 × 9 in. (15.2 × 22.9 cm).

fourteen finch groups that were not found on the mainland. Applying Malthus's theory of human population growth to animals (see Chapter 17), Darwin concluded that those species best adapted to their environment survive. After his voyage on the ship *The Beagle* (1831–1836), during which he studied flora and fauna around the world, Darwin developed his theory of animal and plant evolution by **natural selection**. In 1859 he published *On the Origin of Species by Means of Natural Selection.*

Darwin's three main principles are (1) that organisms increase geometrically, (2) that within a species the population is relatively constant, and (3) that there is a lot of variation within a single species. He concluded that, in the competition for survival among the young, only those who are most adaptable will survive (natural selection). These ideas reinforced the notion of progress because of their implication that complexity and improvement evolve over long periods of time.

In 1871 Darwin's *The Descent of Man and Selection in Relation to Sex* argued that humans were descended from a lower species. Since then, scientists have been searching for a so-called "missing link" connecting apes and humans, which Darwin believed shared a common ancestor. Darwin's theory of evolution offended many Christians by seeming to contradict the view that God created life on earth in a few days and by suggesting that people were descended from apes. In fact, however, Darwin claimed that he was a religious man and argued that his work on evolution actually demonstrated the existence of God. In Darwin's view, God had created the original organisms, which were then governed by the laws of natural selection.

READING SELECTION

Darwin, *The Origin of Species*, on natural selection, PWC5-055-B

ECONOMIC AND SOCIAL PHILOSOPHY

The growing class distinctions between those with access to capital—especially factory owners—and the working class that labored in the factories influenced nineteenth-century economic theories. Some economists began to question the laissez-faire philosophy of Adam Smith (see Chapter 17), which became the basis for capitalism, and the claim by Thomas Malthus that the poor conditions of the working classes resulted from their immoral lifestyle. These views were challenged in the mid-nineteenth century by two new social philosophies: **utopianism** and **Marxism**. The former, also called utilitarian socialism, was inclined toward economic and social reform in which class distinctions would be largely eliminated. The term socialism then came to be associated with communities in which the government assures a relative fairness in the social and economic lives of its citizens. A number of experimental, ideal communities based on utopian socialist ideas were established, but these generally failed. Marxism was a more aggressive form of socialism; it held that revolution was the only means of redressing social injustice and eradicating class distinctions.

BENTHAM, MILL, AND THE UTOPIANS

By the late eighteenth century the British thinker Jeremy Bentham (1748–1832) had formulated the philosophy of **Utilitarianism**. He believed that the effects of behavior, rather than behavior itself, should be considered in terms of moral value. At first a champion of laissez-faire economics, Bentham recognized that the pursuit of pleasure for some caused pain for others. He therefore concluded that the actions of governments and individuals should try to ensure that pleasure is provided to the greatest number of people. His ideas had much in common with socialism and became a basis for the twentieth-century welfare state in western Europe.

Bentham's most influential British follower was John Stuart Mill (1806–1873), who wrote *Principles of Political Economy* (1848), which favored laissez-faire. But he later modified this view and advocated individual freedom only so long as it did not impinge on the freedom of others. At the same time he warned against a "tyranny of the majority" in *On Liberty* (1859) and *Utilitarianism* (1861). Mill was unusual in his time for his enlightened views of women's rights. In *The Subjection of Women* (1869) he argued that women are the intellectual equals of men and should have the right to vote. He also believed in protecting the rights of children, aiding the poor, and freedom of religion. His essential optimism is evident in his conviction that happiness can be achieved given the right environment.

Two of the leading utopians—those who believe that an ideal state is possible—were the wealthy Welsh entrepreneur Robert Owen (1771–1858) and the French social philosopher Comte de Saint-Simon (1760–1825). Both advocated a fair distribution of goods between workers and the owners of production. In addition, they sought universal equality between all social classes and between the sexes. In 1800 Owen founded at New Lanark, Scotland, a community of workers who lived well and were able to educate their children. In the 1820s he went to America and set up another, less successful, experimental utopian community in New Harmony, Indiana, which was based on socialist ideas. Once back in Britain, Owen founded a national trade union that also failed.

Saint-Simon believed that socialism was the best form of government and that non-socialist societies were destined to decline to the degree that they ignored the needs of citizens. He influenced the French founder of **Positivism**, Auguste Comte (1798–1857), who argued that society passes through three stages of evolution: the theological, the metaphysical, and, finally, the positive. Comte's views were based on the laws of science, consistent with empirical study, and therefore related to the aims of Realism.

MARXISM

After 1848 the utopian ideals of early socialist thinkers were overshadowed by Marxism, named for the German philosopher Karl Marx (1818–1883). Born to a middle-class family in Trier, in the Rhineland, Marx studied at the University of Berlin, where he was inspired by the philosophy of Hegel (see Chapter 18). Marx joined forces with another German student, Friedrich Engels (1820–1895), whose father owned a textile factory in northern England.

Appalled by the dismal conditions in British factories and the poverty of their workers, Marx and Engels co-authored the *Communist Manifesto* (1848). In contrast to the beliefs of utopians and most socialists, communism advocated violent means to achieve an egalitarian society to which people would contribute according to their abilities and in which they would be taken care of according to their needs. Marx and Engels identified two main social groups: the **bourgeoisie**, who owned the "means of production"—the factories of the industrial economy—and the **proletariat** (the workers). The bourgeoisie, according to Marx and Engels, abused workers for profit. To redress this abuse, Marx and Engels believed that an international proletarian revolution was the inevitable—and desired—next step, followed by the dissolution of capitalism. Their exhortation to the world's workers had wide appeal:

> Let the ruling classes tremble at a Communist revolution.
> The proletarians have nothing to lose but their chains.
> They have a world to win.
> Working men of all countries unite!

Marx and Engels advocated specific measures to ensure social equality after the revolution of the proletariat. Among these were the abolition of private property and inheritance. Credit would be run by a central authority, which would also oversee communication, transportation, and agriculture. Further ideas that have become absorbed into many modern capitalist societies include free public education and graduated income taxes.

READING SELECTION

Marx and Engels, *The Communist Manifesto*, nothing to lose but their chains, PWC5-016

PHILOSOPHY AND MALAISE

The philosophers Søren Kierkegaard of Denmark (1813–1855) and Friedrich Wilhelm Nietzsche of Germany (1844–1900) viewed the problems of nineteenth-century society with despair. Kierkegaard was tormented by what he considered a decline in religion and spirituality that derived in part from the Realist emphasis on the here and now and on empiricism. In 1843 he published *Either/Or*, the very title of which conveys his struggle between two approaches to life—one based on enjoyment, the other on morality. In *The Sickness unto Death* (1849) Kierkegaard despairs at his failure to achieve either a synthesis of pleasure and morality or an integrated sense of self. As an antidote to despair, he recommends faith.

Nietzsche's response to contemporary life also had a religious character, and his despair resulted in his famous declaration that God is dead. In *Thus Spake Zarathustra* (1883–1892) he argues that religion, particularly Christianity, produces intellectual slaves, that democracy leads to mediocrity, and that morality is a way of keeping people in chains. Unlike Marx, Nietzsche believed that the impulse for power is ideal, as long as it leads to independence and the exercise of free will. Nietzsche was critical of bourgeois convention, which he felt had a limiting effect on society. Morality, in his view, was worthy only if it inspired freedom of thought, strength, and pride. To this end, he conceived the *Übermensch*, literally an "over person," but generally translated into English as "superman"—an exemplar of perfect strength, able to impose his desires on weaker, worthless members of society. Nietzsche, like Wagner (see Chapter 18), was intensely nationalistic, and his philosophy was imbued with a pessimistic view of humanity. Both Nietzsche and Kierkegaard can be seen as forerunners of twentieth-century existentialism (see Chapter 22).

LITERATURE IN EUROPE

The main genre of literary Realism was the novel. Whether set in the city or the country, surveying large segments of society or focusing on a single individual, Realist novels emphasize descriptive detail and the effects of society on character development. Realism in literature thus echoes the scientific emphasis on empiricism and philosophical approaches to problems caused by industry.

FRANCE

The Goncourt brothers, Edmond (1822–1896) and Jules (1830–1870), established many of the rules of Realism: methodical documentation, depiction of present-day society, the study of pathological personality, and the use of vivid, contemporary dialogue. When Edmond died, his will endowed the most elite French literary award, *le prix Goncourt* (the Goncourt Prize).

The leading French Realist authors were Honoré de Balzac (1779–1850) and Gustave Flaubert (1821–1880), both of whom portrayed society at large as well as the status and character of individuals. Literary Realism evolved into Naturalism, the main exponents of which were Emile Zola (1840–1902) and Guy de Maupassant (1850–1893).

HONORÉ DE BALZAC The ninety novels, thirty short stories, and five plays by Honoré de Balzac (figure **19.5**) create a panorama of nineteenth-century French society. Born in central France in the town of Tours, Balzac studied law and philosophy at the Sorbonne in Paris. After several literary failures he achieved success in 1829 with *Le Dernier Chouan* (*The Chouans*), part historical novel set at the time of the French Revolution, part romance, and part detective story. Balzac's assembled novels, known as *La Comédie humaine* (*The Human Comedy*), depict some two thousand characters. Taken together, they portray a range of human types, social classes, and contemporary settings. Influenced by the tradition of Molière (see Chapter 16), Balzac's characters personify certain traits, such as honesty, virtue, crime, greed, moral weakness, and self-deception.

Perhaps Balzac's best-known single work is *Le Père Goriot* (*Father Goriot*) of 1834–1835. Goriot lives with his daughters in a family-run inn in a working-class district of Paris. Balzac's Realism deals with the economic and emotional poverty of Goriot's existence. Although outwardly jovial, Goriot is deluded by his Romantic view of life. He fails to grasp his daughters' indifference until he is on his deathbed. When they desert him to attend a ball, he cries out in a state of semi-delirium:

> I hear them . . . they are coming. Oh yes, they will come.
> The law requires that one come to see a father die, the law
> is on my side . . . I want my daughters! I made them, they
> are mine! . . . [And] If they don't come? . . . But I will be
> dead, dead of rage, of rage! Rage is getting the better of me!
> At this moment, I see my whole life, I have been duped!
> they don't love me, they have never loved me!

The intensity of Goriot's emotion is a hallmark of Realist literature.

19.5 Edward Steichen, *Rodin's Monument to Balzac Seen at Night at Meudon*, 1908. Gelatin silver print.
Auguste Rodin's nearly 10-foot (3-m) high statue conveys Balzac's power as a stylist and observer of society. Looming upward, Balzac seems to survey the world. When Rodin saw Steichen's photographs of his sculpture, which emphasize the mysterious quality of Balzac's powerful genius, he compared the figure to "Christ walking on water." The statue was originally rejected by the Society of Letters that had commissioned it, but today a bronze version of Rodin's sculpture presides over the Boulevard Raspail in Paris.

GUSTAVE FLAUBERT Another outstanding French Realist author was Gustave Flaubert. Born in Rouen, in northern France, where his father had a medical practice, Flaubert disdained the hypocrisy of bourgeois morality and rejected literary convention. He believed that novels should address all aspects of society, including low-life subjects. He strove for objectivity, precision of detail, and rigorous psychological characterization. The publication of *Madame Bovary* (1857), the story of an adulterous wife, caused a scandal. Flaubert and his publisher were sued for offending public morals; both were acquitted.

Madame Bovary is the story of Emma Bovary, whose boring life as the wife of a country doctor in the bleak French provinces inspires her to escape first into Romantic novels and then into adulterous liaisons. Describing her despair after attending a country ball, Flaubert writes:

> In the depths of her soul . . . she waited for something to happen. Like sailors in distress, she strolled along the solitude of her life, her desperate eyes searching the distance for a white sail in the mists of the horizon.
>
> (Part 1, Chapter 9)

Unbeknownst to her trusting, hardworking husband, Emma takes lovers and racks up debts. In the end, forsaken by a lover and facing financial ruin, Emma commits suicide by drinking arsenic. The description of her death throes was based on Flaubert's study of medical texts. He describes her lips turning blue, the sensation of her body becoming ice, her flesh the pallor of white sheets, her metallic breath, and her convulsions. The account is Realist not only in its documentary character, but also in its emotional intensity. When Flaubert began the novel, he regarded Emma Bovary with disdain, but as he came to understand her and to present her more fully, he identified with her and finally projected his own personality into his characterization of her. He completed the novel after five years of strenuous work and famously declared to his friends: *Madame Bovary, c'est moi* ("Madame Bovary is me").

READING SELECTION

Flaubert, *Madame Bovary*, Emma's enchanted ball, PWC5-149

EMILE ZOLA Like Flaubert, Emile Zola was the son of a physician. He was a seminal figure in the Naturalist literary movement, which evolved from Realism. Like the Realists, Naturalists believed that scientific empiricism should be applied to the study of society. Zola defined the literary Naturalist as an author who documents the range of class from the lowest to the highest levels of society. His own subjects included the aristocracy, but also extended to prostitution, alcoholism (*L'Assommoir*, 1877), poverty, and industry. Zola's detached recording of society assumes that character is formed by a combination of heredity and environment. His twenty-novel sequence, *Les Rougon-Macquart* (1871–1893), chronicles a family during the Second Empire. Included in the series are *Nana* (1880), which deals with prostitution, and *Germinal* (1885), which is about the abysmal conditions of coal miners.

Zola was a socialist and believed that writing about social abuses would help to remedy them. In his view, the novel was as much a vehicle for political expression as the media. In 1898 he wrote to the press denouncing the government for the condemnation of the Jewish army officer, Alfred Dreyfus, who was wrongly accused of spying. This letter launched the tradition of writers' involvement in politics and was an important factor in the French scandal known as the Dreyfus Affair (see Box).

The Dreyfus Affair

In 1894 the French captain Alfred Dreyfus (1859–1935), a Jew, was convicted on the basis of a false handwriting analysis of selling secrets to the German army. France had been hostile to Germany since the end of the Franco-Prussian war (1870–1871), when France was defeated and forced to cede Alsace-Lorraine. Dreyfus was himself from Alsace, and Jews were suspected of having no loyalty to France—or to any other nation. Although Dreyfus insisted that he was innocent and the case against him was weak, he was sentenced to life imprisonment on Devil's Island, a penal colony in French Guyana off the coast of South America. Dreyfus was stripped of his medals and insignia, his sword was broken in two, and he was publicly shamed.

The affair exposed the depth of anti-Semitism in France. It split the country into Dreyfusards and anti-Dreyfusards. Monarchists, militarists, Catholics, and anti-Semites on the conservative side were generally against Dreyfus; republicans, intellectuals, socialists, and liberals supported him. In 1898 Dreyfus was granted a retrial and sent to a military prison in France, but his conviction was upheld and he was sentenced to another ten years in prison.

Dreyfus was championed by Emile Zola, who published his famous article, "J'Accuse" ("I Accuse"), in 1898 in the newspaper *L'Aurore*. Zola was convicted of libel, condemned to a year in jail, and fined. Eight years later Dreyfus was exonerated by a civil court and the evidence against him exposed as fabricated. He resumed his military duties, was awarded the Legion of Honor, and remained loyal to France.

The Dreyfus Affair has reverberated in French history up to the present. One important result was the decision in France to separate Church and State, which was achieved in 1905 as a victory for the liberal cause, in large part because of the involvement of the Catholic Church in fomenting the anti-Semitism that continues to be a problem in France today.

GUY DE MAUPASSANT The three hundred short stories (collected into six volumes) and six novels of Guy de Maupassant convey a pessimistic view of life. De Maupassant followed the literary philosophy of Flaubert and joined a group of Naturalists inspired by Zola. His direct style of story-telling and depiction of social classes—from the aristocracy to workers, to prostitutes and soldiers—reflect the influence of Flaubert and Zola.

A master of last-minute twists, de Maupassant's plots and characters are drawn with remarkable psychological insight. In addition to his perceptive view of human character, which is often not revealed until the end of a narrative, de Maupassant's realism is psychological as well as social. His story entitled *The Horla* (1887) is reminiscent of Poe's depictions of panic, anguish, and terror (see Chapter 18), but in de Maupassant, the effects of these emotions are those of a specific individual whose social class or profession is identified. The accuracy with which he records the uncanny sense of dread in *The Horla* is similar in its detailed precision to Flaubert's description of Emma Bovary's death by arsenic poisoning.

Possessed by an evil, unseen presence that has invaded his house, the narrator of *The Horla* conveys his own terror by displacing it onto his dog:

> for an hour the dog howled without moving; he howled as in the anguish of a dream; and fear, a crushing fear came over me; fear of what? Do I know? It was fear, that's all.
>
> We remained immobile, livid, in the apprehension of a horrible event, listening attentively, hearts beating, overwhelmed by the slightest noise. And the dog began to pace around the room, sniffing the walls and continually groaning. This animal drove us mad! Then the peasant who had led me here threw himself at the dog in a paroxysm of furious terror. He opened the door to a small courtyard and threw the animal outside.

Unable to master his terror or control the Horla, the narrator sets the house on fire and commits suicide.

BRITAIN

Some Realist novelists in Britain dealt with urban problems caused by the Industrial Revolution, while others wrote about country life and the conflicts between progress and tradition. Satire, as a means of highlighting the faults of contemporary society, was also a vehicle for Realists. Women writers were increasingly concerned with the role of women in society, while male authors often focused on issues such as politics and finance, thought to be of concern primarily to men.

CHARLES DICKENS Charles Dickens (1812–1870), the most popular nineteenth-century British author, used his childhood poverty as material for his enormous literary output. He championed social equality, the goals of the Enlightenment, and the French Revolution. He was a liberal, but was not involved in political or philosophical theorizing.

Dickens was born in Portsmouth, on the south coast of England, where his father was a navy clerk. When his father was imprisoned for debts, the twelve-year old Charles worked in a blacking warehouse (where black dye used for leather was made). He was later an office boy, and after studying shorthand was hired to report debates in the House of Commons. He began publishing in periodicals and had achieved success by the time he was twenty-five. Many of his novels were serialized in monthly journals, his readers eagerly awaiting the next installment.

Dickens's novels explore virtually every corner of English society and character. Contemporary issues are woven into vivid portrayals of time and place, which is the essence of his realism. His memorable characters are reinforced by their names, which often echo their personalities—for example M'Choakumchild's dismal and abusive school in *Hard Times*.

Some of Dickens's characters have become stereotypes of certain personalities. Uriah Heep in *David Copperfield* (1849–1850) exemplifies the ingratiating backstabber. Ebenezer Scrooge (*A Christmas Carol*, 1843) is the quintessential miser, who refuses to help the family of his dedicated clerk Bob Cratchit and his crippled son, Tiny Tim. Even today, the name "Scrooge" evokes the image of a stingy, small-minded individual. In Walt Disney's *Donald Duck* cartoons Uncle Scrooge is the mean-spirited, wealthy relative of Donald and his nephews. During the Christmas season, in community theaters and on television programs throughout the United States, modern audiences, like Scrooge, are haunted by the Ghosts of Christmas Past, Present, and Future. They terrify Scrooge, who changes into a kinder man and wakes up reformed on Christmas Day.

In *Hard Times* (1854) Dickens juxtaposes fact with fancy. He equates fact with Utilitarianism, and fancy with love and the imagination. A circus troupe of honest, warmhearted characters is contrasted with people who exemplify the evils of society—the fact-driven Blitzer, the acrimonious and snobbish housekeeper Mrs. Sparsit, and the hardware-merchant Thomas Gradgrind quoted at the beginning of the chapter.

Gradgrind lives in the fictitious city of Coketown in the industrial north of England. He raises his children entirely on fact, squashes all their flights of fancy, and shows them no affection. As a result of their upbringing, Gradgrind's children lead disastrous lives—his daughter makes a bad marriage to Josiah Bounderby, thirty years her senior, and his son becomes a thief. Gradgrind himself robs a bank and allows the honest mill-worker Stephen Blackpool to take the blame. Blackpool is ostracized for the crime and exonerated only after his death.

READING SELECTION

Dickens, *Hard Times*, Coketown, PWC5-246

Great Expectations (1860–1861) is widely recognized as one of Dickens's greatest achievements. Filled with minor comic characters from all walks of society, such as Pumblechook (an old imposter) and Wemmick (an eccentric), it is the story of Philip Pirrip's (Pip's) moral development. Pip is the narrator and hero, a village boy in Kent, where he is raised as an orphan by his sister and her blacksmith husband. Pip meets Miss Havisham, an elderly lady demented by having been jilted on her wedding day. She takes revenge by teaching her ward, Estella, to use her beauty to deceive men. Pip falls in love with Estella, who ignores him. He then decides to become a gentleman in order to be worthy of her.

As a young man, Pip receives financial support (and "expectations" that more will come later) from an unidentified source. He leaves his sister's house and leads an extravagant life in London, where he hypocritically tries to shed his old, working-class acquaintances. Estella, meanwhile marries an upper-class lout, who abuses her but soon dies.

Pip believes his benefactor to be Miss Havisham, but later discovers that his money comes from Abel Magwitch, an escaped convict whom Pip had helped as a boy. Magwitch also turns out to be Estella's father. When Magwitch dies, Pip loses his expectations of future wealth and returns to his sister's family, where he learns humility and loyalty. Dickens leaves it ambiguous whether or not Pip and Estella are ever reunited.

Though melodramatic and sentimental, *Great Expectations* has a serious purpose: to teach the value of human morality and the worthlessness of pretension and snobbery. Dickens shows the development of Pip's character from the poverty of his upbringing, through a period in which he is foolishly driven by social ambition, to his recognition that character is more important than status.

GEORGE ELIOT The popular novelist Mary Ann Evans (1819–1880), better known by her pen name George Eliot, grew up in Warwickshire, in the English Midlands. She was well educated, working as a translator from German into English and as an editor. She converted to Evangelicalism but was then influenced by free-thinking intellectuals. Throughout her life she struggled with the conflict between religious orthodoxy and dissent, which was intensified by the fact that she spent most of her adult life with a married man who could not divorce his wife.

In her first mature novel, *Adam Bede* (1859), Eliot applies a Realist approach to rural life. She juxtaposes two female characters: the vain, self-absorbed Hetty Sorrel and Dinah Morris, a Methodist preacher. Hetty is seduced and then deserted by a local squire of low moral character, who she deludes herself into believing will marry her. The honest carpenter Adam Bede falls in love with Hetty, and she agrees to marry him. But when she discovers that she is pregnant by the squire, she runs after him. Adam is devastated, but is consoled by Dinah, whom he later marries.

Hetty fails to find the squire, kills her infant, and is sentenced to death (later commuted to a prison term). Eliot's clinical description of childbirth combined the Realist interest in observed, scientific detail with a subject of particular concern to women. For Eliot, Hetty represents the impulsive individual who ignores convention to follow her own will. Dinah, on the other hand, conforms to the community and suppresses her will, and in so doing she reflects Eliot's view of ideal behavior; she believed that convention and the will of the community should prevail over the wishes of the individual.

Eliot explores the nineteenth-century theme of the deadening effect of a restrictive environment on a woman of intellect and intelligence in *The Mill on the Floss* (1860). In this novel Eliot contrasts Maggie and Tom Tulliver, the children of a local miller. Tom is dull and unimaginative, Maggie is rebellious, animated, and intelligent. Maggie loves her brother, but he fails to understand her, and she turns to a deformed young neighbor for companionship. But his father and Maggie's do not get along and find themselves on opposite sides in an acrimonious litigation. Tom reveals the friendship, and Maggie flees to St. Ogg's to visit her cousin. There, she becomes attracted to her cousin's fiancé and is publicly compromised. She is ostracized by the community and disdained by Tom. At the end, during a flood, Maggie rescues Tom from the mill. They are momentarily reconciled, only to drown together. As in *Adam Bede*, the consequences of defying the conventional wisdom of society are unhappiness and death.

SAMUEL BUTLER Samuel Butler (1835–1902) used satire to criticize contemporary society. The son and grandson of clergymen, Butler began to doubt his faith and instead of becoming a clergyman himself, went to New Zealand and became a successful sheep-farmer.

His letters home formed the basis of *Erewhon* (1872), an anagram of "nowhere" and the title of his satirical utopian novel critical of industrial Europe. The narrator crosses a mountain range and finds himself in the unknown country of Erewhon, where parents are selected by their unborn children and forced to live with them. Currency is not used, and foolish philosophers run the country. Machinery had formerly been used but has since been banned after causing civil war. Reflecting the hypocrisy of English society, *Erewhon* equates beauty with health and illness with crime. As a result, when the narrator comes down with measles, he risks being prosecuted as a criminal. To save himself, he escapes in a balloon and returns to England.

READING SELECTION

Butler, *Erewhon*, sickness and crime, PWC5-222

RUSSIA

In Russia, as in France and Britain, the novel was the main literary form of Realism. Russian Realist themes deal with the contemporary effects of war and social change and portray emotions with deep intensity. The satirical masterpiece *Oblomov* (1859) by Ivan Goncharov (1812–1891) is a classic depiction of neurasthenia, a psychological condition characterized by overwhelming fatigue, loss of memory, lethargy, and indifference to the world. *Oblomov* is written from the point of view of the neurotic, phlegmatic hero who is unable to motivate himself and spends his days in bed.

The two best-known Russian Realist authors are Leo Tolstoy (1828–1910) and Fyodor Dostoyevsky (1821–1881). Both wrote short novels and stories as well as works of epic grandeur. They shared the Realist interest in characters with psychological depth and in panoramic views of society.

LEO TOLSTOY Born to an aristocratic family in central Russia, Count Leo Tolstoy fought in the Crimean War (1854–1856), which enabled him to describe war in realistic detail. His two great novels are the epic *War and Peace* (1863–1869) and *Anna Karenina* (1874–1877). The former deals with the ruinous effects of Napoleon's invasion of Russia and its aftermath on an aristocratic family in Moscow. Using the literary technique of merging fact with fiction, Tolstoy interweaves historical figures with his own characters against the backdrop of a changing society devastated by war. The heroine is Natasha Rostov, who learns to navigate the turbulent world around her and finally triumphs over adversity.

Anna Karenina, an intensely personal novel, lacks the panoramic epic sweep of *War and Peace*. Instead it is a finely detailed psychological study of romance and adultery, culminating in suicide. Tolstoy echoed the behavior of Anna Karenina when he renounced his bourgeois family, gave up all claim to his property, and embarked on a vain search for an ideal love.

FYODOR DOSTOYEVSKY The son of a physician, Dostoyevsky grew up in Moscow. He was passionately interested in social justice and was arrested in 1849 for his anti-tsarist, socialist leanings and exiled to Siberia for four years. This experience inspired *Notes from the House of the Dead* (1861–1862). Dostoyevsky later renounced liberal politics and became deeply religious. His psychological portrayals of character are imbued with themes of guilt and redemption. He also drew on his own life, infusing his characters with aspects of himself. *The Gambler* (1866), for example, reflects his own addiction to gambling, and the hero of *The Idiot* (1868–1869), like the author, is an epileptic.

In *Crime and Punishment* (1866) Dostoyevsky's hero Raskolnikov is alienated by poverty and dissociation from society. He murders an elderly woman to achieve a feeling of power and control. Even more alienated by guilt and his unrelenting conscience, Raskolnikov finally confesses his crime to the police. In the *Brothers Karamazov* (1879–1880) three brothers, Ivan, Alyosha, and Dmitri, engage in complex love triangles that involve their father and at least two women. Intensely psychological in the interweaving of jealousy, rage, spirituality, and sexual energy, the dynamic quality of Dostoyevsky's characters and the tension between them are enormously compelling.

READING SELECTION

Dostoyevsky, *Crime and Punishment*, the murder of an elderly woman, PWC5-084-B

REALIST THEATER

Theater was a medium used by both Romantics and Realists. Realist playwrights, influenced by Modernism, represented contemporary life as it was lived. Dialogue mirrored everyday speech, actors performed in modern dress, and sets were designed in contemporary style. Non-traditional themes were introduced, including prostitution, venereal disease, the emancipation of women, and insanity. Many Realist plays offended convention and often avoided government censorship only by being performed in independent, privately funded theaters.

The three major Realist playwrights of the late nineteenth century credited with bringing Modernism to theater were Henrik Ibsen (1828–1906), August Strindberg (1849–1912), and Anton Chekhov (1860–1904). The nature of their Realism is both social and psychological, and their works portray the political and technological changes that affected society as well as the new interest in the mind that evolved over the course of the nineteenth century.

HENRIK IBSEN

The Norwegian author Henrik Ibsen wrote twenty-five plays as well as poetry. He has been called Realist, non-Realist, and the founder of Realism in theater. He was certainly influenced by Naturalism, especially his interest in heredity, which had been studied by Mendel (see p. 534). Some of his early plays—*Brand* (1866) and *Peer Gynt* (1867)—are filled with Romantic elements, such as fantasy, nationalism, and Scandinavian folklore. Among Ibsen's most radical plays engaged with contemporary social issues are *A Doll's House* (1879), *Ghosts* (1881), and *Hedda Gabler* (1890), each of which revolves around an unhappily married woman.

In *A Doll's House* the life of a doll is a metaphor for the life led by Ibsen's heroine, Nora Helmer. Nora is dependent on her husband, who treats her as his plaything rather than his equal. When she realizes this, she decides to leave. In *Ghosts*, on the other hand, Mrs. Alving remains with her husband, confronting his insanity and the fact that he has transmitted syphilis to their son. In this case, Ibsen uses inherited venereal disease as a metaphor for the moral corruption of society.

Hedda Gabler is the drama of a woman married to a dry pedant, George Tesman. She turns for companionship to Lovborg, her former admirer and an aspiring author. Lovborg lends her his manuscript, which she burns, and then shoots himself at her instigation. When a local judge recognizes Hedda's role in Lovborg's death, he threatens to expose her. Hedda fears scandal and commits suicide.

The women in Ibsen's plays suffer in some measure from moral and social repression in a patriarchal society. Like Nora Helmer, Hedda Gabler was considered by nineteenth-century critics to be an outrageously willful character, defying the ideal of the obedient, stay-at-home wife. Although Mrs. Alving remains with her family, the play's taboo subject of venereal disease was considered unacceptable, and *Ghosts* was banned throughout Europe.

AUGUST STRINDBERG

The Swedish playwright August Strindberg, the illegitimate son of a shipping agent and a barmaid, was born in Stockholm. His so-called dream plays incorporate the new understanding of psychic reality and coincide with the early discoveries of Freud (see Chapter 20). Strindberg wrote about contemporary characters and used dreams to portray unconscious fears and fantasies. He was involved in the Naturalist movement in literature and strove for realistic atmosphere in his plays. He used everyday objects as props, wrote dialogue that resembled everyday speech, and eliminated the artificial space of the intermission—he often filled the spaces between acts and scenes with pantomime or peasant dances.

Strindberg's best-known play, *Miss Julie* (1888), deals with exterior conflicts between convention and social impropriety and the interior conflicts of individuals. The two main characters are the spoiled, aristocratic Julie and her father's valet, Jean, with whom she has a brief romance. Julie thus tests the limits of her class, from which she is alienated. Jean is an unscrupulous social climber, although he recognizes the futility of a future without Julie. Unable to resolve the tension between her upbringing (the product of her environment) and the intensity of her emotions (which are her own), Julie commits suicide. In addition to containing explicit descriptions of sexual encounters, *Miss Julie* offended contemporary audiences by defying conventions of society and class. Julie herself embodies the declining morality and status of the aristocracy.

ANTON CHEKHOV

Anton Chekhov was the first important Realist playwright in Russia. He had studied medicine and was well known for his short stories. His four major plays were written at the turn of the twentieth century: *The Seagull* (1896), *Uncle Vanya* (1900), *The Three Sisters* (1901), and *The Cherry Orchard* (1903). Chekhov used more characters than Ibsen and Strindberg and involved them in complex subplots. He was also innovative in his combination of Naturalism with symbolic allusions and of comedy with tragedy in a single scene. His main theme was the conflict between tradition and contemporary life.

Chekhov depicts a stultified upper class and bored, inactive women. His plays have little narrative and focus instead on personality. The sense of stasis in his characters is reinforced by their inability to make decisions or define their emotions. In *The Cherry Orchard*, for example, the main character loses her family estate (including its cherry orchard) because she cannot deal with modernization.

The plays of Chekhov were staged primarily at the Moscow Art Theater, a leading center of Realism, where Constantin Stanislavski (1863–1938) originated the realistic acting style called **"method" acting**, which is still in use today.

READING SELECTION

Chekhov, *The Cherry Orchard*, on impoverished nobility, PWC5-123

REALISM IN MUSIC

In music, opera was the medium in which Realism could best be expressed. *Carmen* (1875), by the French composer Georges Bizet (1838–1875), is the tragic story of a passionate, sensual gypsy named Carmen in Spain in the 1820s. Her intense emotions and determination to love as she wishes rather than with any constancy result in her death at the hands of a jealous lover. Reviewers of *Carmen*'s first performance condemned the plot as obscene and the characters as repulsive.

In this opera, Bizet takes the light and sentimental form of nineteenth-century *opéra comique*, purges it of artificiality, and uses it to express the torment of sexual passion and jealousy. Typical of Realism are the local color and low-life scenes—outside a cigarette factory, in a tavern, at a smugglers' lair—as well as the true-to-life characters. José, for example, develops from an honest peasant soldier thinking only of his girlfriend Micaela into a murderer, going through various stages of temptation, insubordination, and desertion on his way finally to stabbing Carmen in the back. The power of the story and its vivid expression in music such as Carmen's "Flower Song" have made it one of the most popular French operas of all time.

Operatic Realism flourished principally in Italy, where it was known as **verismo**. It was set in train by Pietro Mascagni (1863–1945) with a one-act opera, *Cavalleria rusticana* (*Country Chivalry*, 1889). Another tale of infidelity and revenge, it brings to life the code of honor of village life in Sicily and again ends with the death of the unfaithful lover. It is usually performed with *Pagliacci* (*Clowns*, 1891) by Ruggiero Leoncavallo (1858–1919)—the pair of operas popularly referred to as "Cav and Pag." *Clowns* is a play within a play and once more a plot about love, adultery, and murder. A generation of Italian composers followed in the footsteps of Mascagni, but none of their works is performed today.

Giacomo Puccini (1858–1924) is considered by some the leading exponent of *verismo* opera. A great Italian melodist in the tradition of Verdi (see Chapter 18), he once wrote, "Without melody, fresh and poignant, there can be no music." His works exemplify the transition from Romanticism to Realism, with an increase both in sentimentality and in naturalism. Puccini still features vulnerable women who suffer and die for love: *La bohème* (1896), depicting Bohemian life in the Latin Quarter of Paris in around 1830, ends remarkably like *La traviata*, with a dying woman united with her lover. However, its strong emphasis on poverty reflects the Realist preoccupation with economic hardship and social class. The men struggle to succeed in the arts—Rodolfo as a poet, Marcello as a painter, Schaunard as a musician—while the heroine Mimi embroiders flowers in her chilly garret before succumbing to tuberculosis.

Realist in its gritty emotions is Puccini's *Tosca* (1900), an opera about political and sexual struggle in Rome in the year 1800. In one terrible scene the chief of police, Scarpia, forces the singer Tosca to listen to her lover being tortured until she can bear it no longer and betrays his secret. In another, Tosca bargains for her lover's life, the payment being sex with Scarpia—but once the deal is set up, she stabs him to death. The mixture of violence, sexual tension, religion, and political intrigue is typical of *verismo*; the music portrays it with expressive orchestration, plaintive, chromatic harmony, passionate outbursts, and soaring themes.

Puccini's musical language is more dissonant than Verdi's, his use of instrumental color more extreme. The pentatonic scale (a five-note scale that sounds approximately like the five black notes on a piano) is prominent in several of the operas, sometimes used simply to express bitter reality, at other times to evoke the Orient. These developments would be taken further in the next generation of musicians.

REALISM IN THE VISUAL ARTS

Official art exhibitions in nineteenth-century France were controlled by the government. Known as the Salon, after Louis XIV's hall dedicated to Apollo in the Louvre (the *Salon d'Apollon*), these exhibitions were held annually and the works were chosen by an official jury. In the seventeenth and eighteenth centuries the exhibitions had included works by progressive artists, but by the mid-nineteenth century the Salon had become conservative.

To a large extent Realism in painting was a reaction against the outmoded rules of the French Academy founded under Louis XIV (see Chapter 16). The best-known nineteenth-century academic artist was William-Adolphe Bouguereau (1825–1905), who appealed to conservative bourgeois taste (figure **19.6**). Although all artists strive to convey aspects of reality, in the nineteenth century Realism in art refers specifically to a commitment to painting social and psychological reality based on empirical observation. Artists rejected the Romantics' portrayals of fantasy, sentiment, and nostalgia. As with Realist novelists, the subject matter of Realist art was usually present-day society, an ideal reflected in the statement by the leading French Realist painter, Gustave Courbet (1819–1877): "Show me an angel, and I'll paint one."

19.6 William-Adolphe Bouguereau, *The Birth of Venus*, 1879. Oil on canvas, 9 ft. 10 in. × 7 ft. 1¾ in. (3 × 2.18 m). Musée d'Orsay, Paris.
Cupids and sea-creatures in mannered poses populate the painting. Their saccharine expressions seem detached from the narrative and are psychologically shallow. Although Bouguereau fills the image with observed detail, it is relevant neither to the mythic stature of the narrative nor to contemporary life.

GUSTAVE COURBET

Courbet was born in the French provinces but moved to Paris and launched the Realist movement in painting. It was Courbet's goal to present a visual panorama of contemporary society based on his own experience. His first great Realist painting, *A Burial at Ornans*, is over 20 feet (more than 6 m) long (figure **19.7**). It depicts a funeral in Courbet's native village and is filled with local figures in contemporary dress. On the scale of a large history painting, the *Burial* creates a horizontal frieze of provincial life. The intense relationship of the people to the land is shown by their unity with the stark landscape. Only the vertical of the crucifix breaks into the broad horizontal plane of the grim, dark sky. Similarly, only the red robes and hats of the beadles (local officials) and the green stockings of the man in the foreground vary the picture's chromatic tedium. Aside from the muted reactions of the women at the right, there is very little sense of emotion in the *Burial.* The painting's formal monotony and tight structure reflect the rigid, conventional, staunchly Catholic life of the French provinces.

ROSA BONHEUR

Rosa Bonheur (1822–1899) was the daughter of a Saint-Simon socialist and thus raised in an atmosphere of relative freedom for women. She dressed as a man and lived only with women. The first woman artist to receive the Legion of Honor, she was admired internationally for her paintings of horses: both Queen Victoria and Buffalo Bill Cody were among her patrons.

In the same year that Courbet painted *A Burial at Ornans*, Rosa Bonheur produced *Plowing in the Nivernais: The Dressing*

19.7 Gustave Courbet, *A Burial at Ornans*, 1849. Oil on canvas, 10 ft. 4 in. × 21 ft. 11 in. (3.15 × 6.68 m). Musée d'Orsay, Paris.

19.8 Rosa Bonheur, *Plowing in the Nivernais: The Dressing of the Vines*, 1849. Oil on canvas, 5 ft. 9 in. × 8 ft. 8 in. (1.75 × 2.64 m). Musée d'Orsay, Paris.

of the Vines (figure **19.8**). Note the Realist representation of the animals, which Bonheur studied and sketched in local butcher shops and slaughterhouses. Their slow pace, the turned up soil, and the sturdy peasants convey a sense of harmony with the crisp, clear landscape. As in Courbet's *A Burial at Ornans*, Bonheur creates a horizontal, frieze-like expanse of figures that live and work in the present.

HONORÉ DAUMIER

Honoré Daumier (1808–1879) published political and social caricatures in two Paris papers, the weekly *La Caricature* and the daily *Le Charivari*. He satirized many levels of society and the professions, taking aim especially at judicial and political corruption and all forms of hypocrisy. He was an astute observer of society and championed liberal causes, insulted the monarchy, and empathized with the poor. Using the medium of **lithography** (printing by means of a stone press), Daumier was able to reach a wide audience.

When a revolt against Louis-Philippe, the Citizen-King (see Chapter 18), broke out in April 1834, his troops overreacted. A boy locked in his room shot off a pistol, and the troops fired on a barricaded apartment building, killing innocent people. Daumier commemorated the incident in the lithograph entitled *Rue Transnonain* (figure **19.9**).

Though Daumier was also a painter, he did not have a one-man exhibition until he was seventy years old. His *Third-class Carriage* exemplifies the Realist observation of lower-class

19.9 Honoré Daumier, *Rue Transnonain, April 15, 1834*, July 1834. Lithograph, 17½ × 11½ in. (44.5 × 29 cm). Private collection, France. This print commemorates the family killed by Louis-Philippe's troops at 12 rue Transnonain in Paris. The father in his nightshirt, apparently having fallen from his bed, is reminiscent of Christian images of the dead Christ. His child lies crushed beneath him, his wife is in shadow at the left, and an old man lies dead by an overturned chair to the right.

19.10 **Honoré Daumier, *Third-class Carriage*, *c.* 1862. Watercolor on paper, 8 × 11⅝ in. (20 × 30 cm). Walters Art Gallery, Baltimore.**

social conditions (figure **19.10**). The occupants of the third-class railroad car are seated on hard wooden benches and the only source of light in the dingy interior comes from the windows at the left. One woman nurses her infant (not a fashionable practice in nineteenth-century France), and the other gazes blankly into space. The boy beside them has fallen asleep in an uncomfortable position. By encouraging the viewer's identification with the poor conditions of third-class travel, Daumier conforms to Zola's notion that portraying injustice is a step toward correcting it.

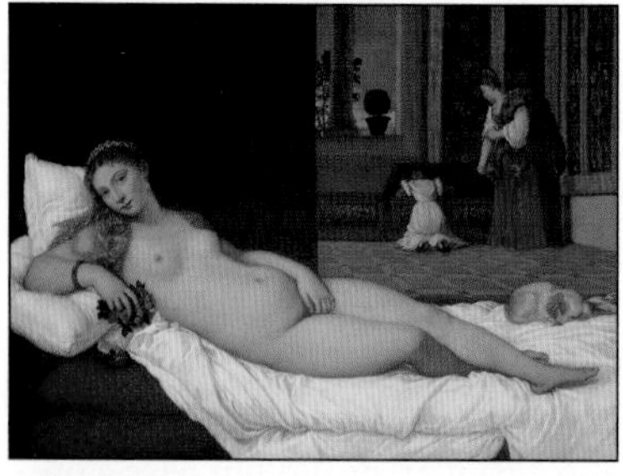

Titian,
Venus of Urbino
see figure 14.22

EDOUARD MANET

Edouard Manet (1832–1883) was a Realist in the 1860s, when he shocked Paris with his *Olympia* (figure **19.11**), a painting of a French prostitute. Alluding to the Classical tradition with the reclining nude and the mythological title, Manet challenged the French public to confront the here and now of contemporary life: Paris at the time was rife with venereal disease. His nude lies on rumpled sheets and a servant brings flowers from a male admirer. The shoes (denoting "streetwalking") and the black cat (compare "cat house," for "brothel") allude to her profession. Manet's flattened dark background forces Olympia toward the viewer, in contrast to the deeper picture space of Titian's *Venus of Urbino* (see thumbnail). Although the *Olympia* clearly refers to the *Venus of Urbino*, the bony proportions of Manet's nude are un-Classical and her meaning unambiguous.

One of Manet's greatest admirers was the critic and novelist Emile Zola (see p. 538). Zola wrote art criticism for the weekly *L'Evénement*, in which he praised Manet as the emerging artistic innovator of his generation. He agreed with Manet that artists have the right of free expression—to paint whatever and

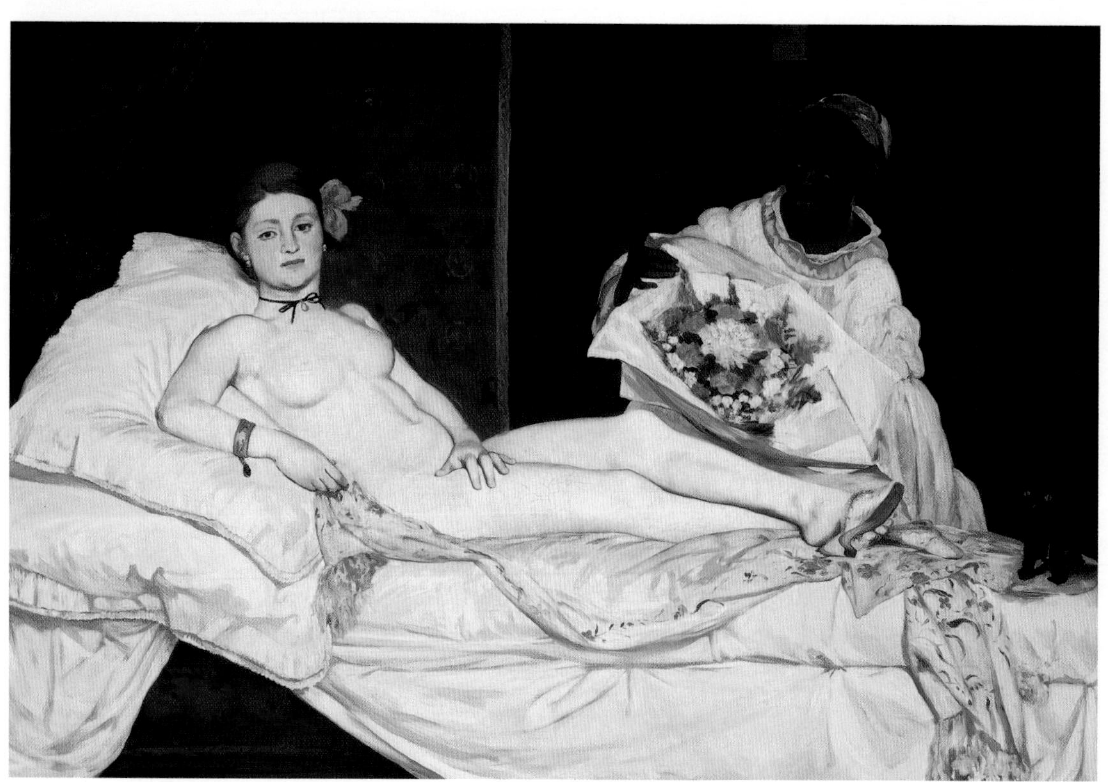

19.11 Edouard Manet, *Olympia*, 1865. Oil on canvas, 4 ft. 3 in. × 6 ft. 3 in. (1.3 × 1.9 m). Musée d'Orsay, Paris.

19.12 Edouard Manet, *Portrait of Zola*, 1868. Oil on canvas, 4 ft. 9 in. × 3 ft. 9 in. (1.44 × 1.14 m). Louvre, Paris.
Although a portrait of Zola, this painting is also about Manet. The books refer to the author, but the pictures in the background reflect influences on Manet's early style. The Japanese screen and Sumo wrestler refer to the contemporary taste for Japanese prints (see Chapter 20) and the black-and-white photograph of *Olympia* to the popularity of photography (see p. 548). The reproduction behind *Olympia* is of Velázquez's *The Drinkers*, a reflection of Manet's early interest in Spanish subjects and the impact of Velázquez on his artistic development. The fact that he has placed *Olympia* in front of *The Drinkers* is a metaphor showing Manet's ambition to surpass, literally "be in front of," his illustrious predecessor.

however they wish—but at the time this flouting of the established rules of the French Academy shocked the public. Manet returned the favor by painting Zola's portrait (figure **19.12**). As with *Olympia*, this picture projects forms through contrasting lights and darks, although with more iconographic details surrounding the figure. Zola is shown as something of a personified literary still life, holding an open book on a desk filled with books and pamphlets. The pamphlet visible behind the feathered quill pen is titled *Manet*, a reminder of Zola's praise for the artist and also an indirect signature.

BRITAIN: THE PRE-RAPHAELITE BROTHERHOOD

In Britain the early paintings of three artists—William Holman Hunt (1827–1910), John Everett Millais (1829–1896), and Dante Gabriel Rossetti (1828–1882)—portray certain Realist ideals. Their secret society, the *PRB* (for Pre-Raphaelite Brotherhood), was formed in London in 1848 and was dedicated to artistic change and social reform. They objected to social injustice and were inspired by revolutionary causes such as redressing the exploitation of women and industrial abuse. In matters of art the Pre-Raphaelites believed that the arts had been in decline since before Raphael's death in 1520 (see Chapter 14) and that the "truth" in painting had not flourished since the fifteenth century. They wrote poetry and published a magazine, *The Germ*, so named because they believed that contemporary attention to reality would provide the germ of an artistic revival.

In *The Awakening Conscience* (figure **19.13**) of 1853, William Holman Hunt shows a meticulously careful, even obsessive, study of the environment. It reflects the Brotherhood's admiration for the paintings of van Eyck (see Chapter 13), although its visual clutter creates a very different aesthetic impact. Psychologically as well as visually, Hunt was striving for a kind of "reality." Here it is the woman's realization of the man's sexual intentions that causes her anguish. She seems about to rise, wringing her hands and gazing out the window as if seeking freedom.

19.13 William Holman Hunt, *The Awakening Conscience*, 1853. Oil on canvas, 30 × 22 in. (76.2 × 55.9 cm). Trustees of Sir Colin and Lady Anderson.
The emphasis on bright reds, the man's open-mouthed leer, and the oddly staring cat under the table are signs of a dangerous sexuality. The piano and the sheets of music, especially when accompanied by a man and a woman, are traditionally erotic motifs. Confirming these implications is the painting-within-the-painting, *The Woman Taken in Adultery*, that hangs on the wall.

PHOTOGRAPHY

Today we take it for granted that photography can be an art form, but in the nineteenth century this was a controversial issue. Denied the status of art on the grounds that it was a mechanical process, photography was at first exhibited only in halls of science.

Literally "light writing," photography as an idea had been conceived in antiquity when Aristotle was watching an eclipse of the sun. He observed that the sun's crescent shape was reversed in its reflection on the ground. Medieval astronomers knew that rays of light entering a box through a round hole reversed images on the opposite side of the box. This box became known as a *camera obscura*, or "dark room." During the Renaissance Leonardo da Vinci described the principles of a dark room, noting that light entering a box through a hole produced an inverted imaged on the surface opposite. But it did not become possible to **fix** the image permanently to a surface until the nineteenth century. This was first achieved in the 1820s by Joseph-Nicéphore Niepce (1765–1833), but a disadvantage was the required exposure time of eight hours.

In the 1830s the Frenchman Louis-Jacques-Mandé Daguerre (1789–1851) reduced the exposure to fifteen minutes by using a silver-coated copper plate (figure **19.14**). The problem with daguerreotypes (named for Daguerre), however, was that they were unique images and they were reversed.

In Britain, the scientist Henry Fox Talbot (1800–1877) created negative film. He could then re-reverse the image to make a positive print. Between 1844 and 1846 he published in installments a classic work on photography entitled *The Pencil of Nature.* Talbot described not only his techniques but also the aesthetics of photography, comparing its conception and reception to that of painting.

19.14 Louis-Jacques-Mandé Daguerre, *The Artist's Studio*, 1837. Daguerreotype, 6¼ × 8⅜ in. (15.9 × 21.2 cm). Société Française de Photographie, Paris.

19.15 Mayall, Queen Victoria's *carte-de-visite*, March 1, 1861. 3½ × 2⅜ in. (8.9 × 6.1 cm). George Eastman House, Rochester, New York.
The visiting card photo was made by printing from eight to twelve poses on a single negative and then cutting them into individual pictures. Its inventor, Adolphe-Eugène Disdéri, became very successful but died penniless because his process was so easy to imitate. Visiting cards with photos were bought by the hundreds of thousands throughout Europe, including by the British royal family.

The excitement created by the potential of photography was enormous. For the first time in history, visual documents of current events could be made rapidly. During the Crimean War, for example, photographs of the fighting were sent to Britain, and the Franco-Prussian War was photographed by the French photographer Gaspard-Félix Tornachon (1820–1910), known as Nadar. He invented a balloon called "The Giant" (*Le Géant*), in which he could fly supplies to French troops and take aerial photographs of the fighting.

Photography influenced painters, many of whom were photographers themselves. Certain photographic viewpoints, such as the aerial view, the candid view, and the close-up, began to appeal to painters (see Chapter 20). The cropped viewpoint, as in Daumier's *Third-class Carriage* (see figure 19.10), gave the impression of a recorded "slice of life" and thus enhanced the illusion of realism.

In addition to aiding painters, who could now work from a photograph, portrait photography became a genre in its own right. Because photographs were less expensive than paintings, the demand for photographic portraits increased and included more social classes. Private portrait studios were set up, and in 1854 the *carte-de-visite* (visiting card) photograph was patented (figure **19.15**).

DEVELOPMENTS IN THE UNITED STATES

After gaining independence from Britain at the end of the eighteenth century the United States began to expand geographically and culturally. With the Industrial Revolution came factories, railroads, and more rapid communication, but it also led to new class divisions between workers and factory owners. Conflicts with Native Americans, who were less technologically advanced than the Europeans, was one source of tension. Another was the growing divide between the North and South, which erupted in civil war in 1861. The former resulted in part from the notion of "Manifest Destiny," a term first coined in 1845 by an American journalist and used to justify American expansionism.

MANIFEST DESTINY

After the Revolutionary War, the original thirteen states grew in number as settlers moved west (map **19.2**). In 1803 Napoleon needed money to support his monarchy and sold the Louisiana Territory (extending from the Mississippi River to the Rocky Mountains) to the United States government. Between 1804 and 1806 Meriwether Lewis and William Clark led an expedition westward (the Lewis and Clark Expedition), inspiring settlers to follow.

In 1819 Florida was purchased from Spain, and in 1845 Texas was annexed as a state. This sparked the Mexican–American War (1845–1848), which ended in defeat for Mexico, and the United States annexed California, New Mexico, and Texas north of the Rio Grande. The area that later became Idaho, Oregon, and Washington State was ceded by Britain in 1846. All of these gains reflected the notion of Manifest Destiny—namely, that the United States was destined to settle the North American continent from the East Coast to the Pacific (figure **19.16**).

CONFLICT BETWEEN SETTLERS AND NATIVE AMERICANS

The notion of Manifest Destiny resulted in conflict with the Native American population, who resisted the settlers' drive westward. The history of the conflict between white Europeans, Americans, and Native Americans is a history of broken treaties, mutual misunderstandings, and unresolved cultural differences. Native Americans boasted leaders of integrity and intelligence, as well as brave fighters, but they were unable to stem the tide of determined, technologically superior settlers and cavalry. In 1830 the Indian Removal Act required all Native Americans to relocate west of the Mississippi River into what is now Oklahoma. Only the Seminoles escaped and settled around the Florida swamps. From 1840 the Plains

19.16 Timothy O'Sullivan, *Desert Sand Hills near Sink of Carson, Nevada*, 1867. Albumen silver print, 8¾ × 11½ in. (22.4 × 29 cm). The J. Paul Getty Museum, Los Angeles. This photo shows the identification of America with its vast expanses of land. O'Sullivan (1840–1882) carried a darkroom in his wagon as he photographed western territories for the government. In this image, only a pair of tracks and the photographer's footsteps mark the desert sand.

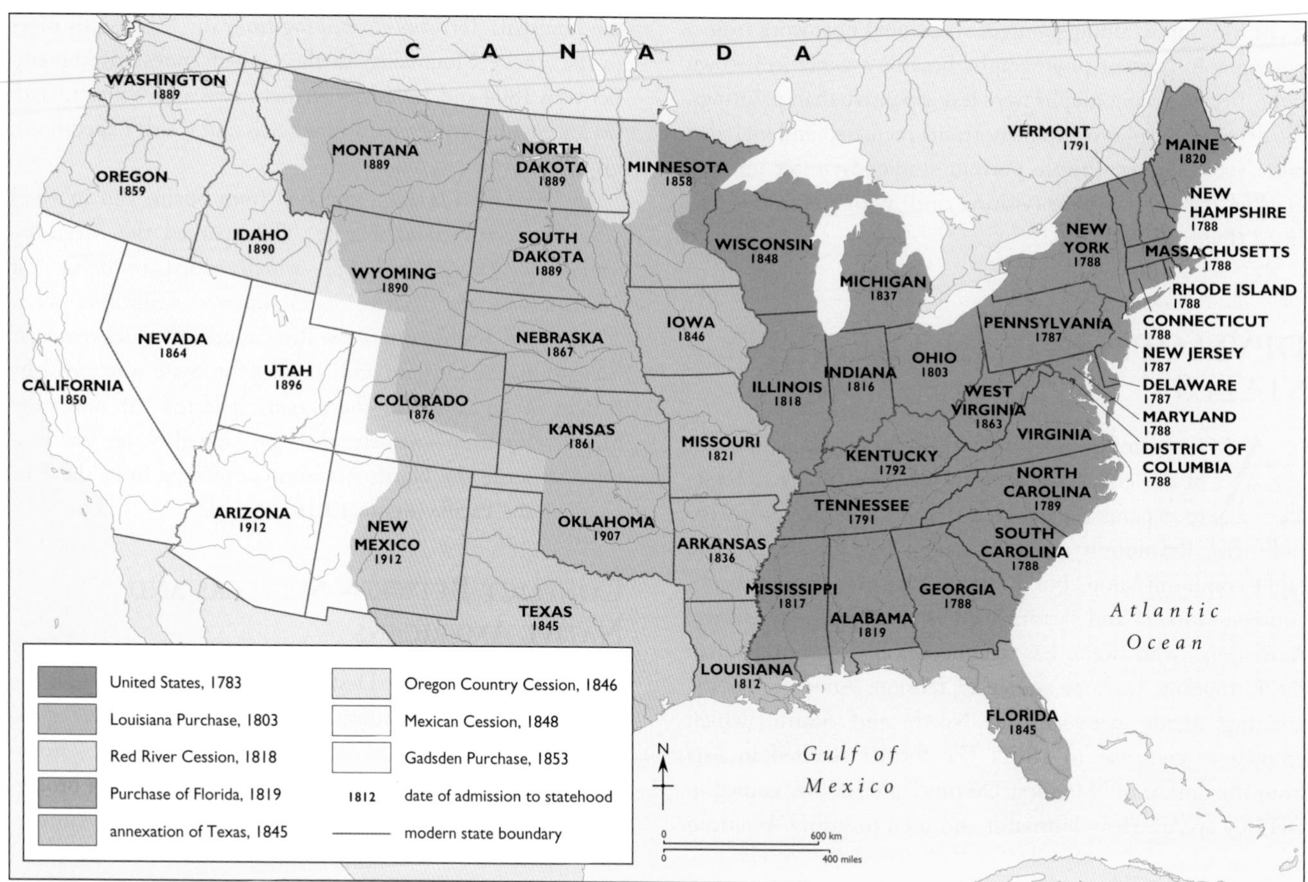

Map 19.2 Westward expansion of the United States from 1783.

Indians mounted the fiercest resistance, but failed nevertheless (figure **19.17**).

In 1876 one of the last and best-known battles between whites and Native Americans, the Little Bighorn, was won by the Sioux in Montana. Led by the skilled warrior Crazy Horse (*c.* 1842–1877) under Chief Sitting Bull (1831–1890), the Sioux destroyed the regiment and killed its commander, George Armstrong Custer (1839–1876). Despite the Sioux victory in what has come to be known as "Custer's Last Stand," the settlers continued to pursue their "Manifest Destiny." Crazy Horse was captured and killed a few months later.

As the Native Americans were pushed further and further west, in 1890 one shaman had a vision of a Ghost Dance, a ceremony that he believed would bring back the time before the arrival of the settlers. There would be no white men and the land would be filled with buffalo herds. As this notion caught on and spread through the Sioux and other tribes, the white settlers viewed the Ghost Dance as a threat. Fearful of an uprising, they sought the help of the tribal police, and Sitting Bull was killed while being arrested. The United States cavalry then intercepted a band of Sioux as they tried to make their way south to safety and ordered them to camp at Wounded Knee. According to many accounts, the following morning a soldier was attempting to disarm a man whose rifle went off. The cavalry opened fire and killed over three hundred people, many of them women and children. The massacre at Wounded Knee marked the end of the Ghost Dance movement and became a symbol of brutality against Native Americans.

In the far west the Apache tribe also mounted fierce resistance to white expansion. Chief Cochise (*c.* 1815–1874) was imprisoned by the army on false charges and several of his relatives were murdered. He escaped to Arizona and launched an eleven-year war against the army. Eventually Cochise agreed to a peace treaty and died on a reservation. The United States later broke the treaty and forced the Apaches to relocate once again. In Arizona the Apache chief Geronimo (1829–1909) refused to live on a reservation. Instead, he fought the settlers for ten years before surrendering in 1886. After several periods of imprisonment in the South, Geronimo became a farmer.

A Dash for the Timber (figure **19.18**) by Frederic Remington (1861–1909) shows the appeal of the west and romanticizes the brutal conflict with the Native Americans as a group of cowboys gallop away from their Apache pursuers. Although there are only eight cowboys, several turn to fire at the enemy. The white dust and purple shadows enhance the speed of the horses. We identify with the cowboys, who are in the foreground and more individualized than the anonymous band of distant Apaches. Remington's painting, and his later bronze sculptures, embody the emergence of the cowboy as a new American hero.

19.17 *left* **George Catlin, *Keokuk (the Watchful Fox), Chief of the Tribe*, 1832. Oil on canvas, 29 × 24 in. (73.7 × 60.9 cm). National Museum of American Art, Smithsonian Institution, Washington, D.C.**
This is one of many paintings of Native Americans by the lawyer-turned-artist George Catlin (1796–1872). It can be considered a Realist portrait for its closely observed detail and accurate portrayal. Reputed to be the greatest of the Plains chieftains, Keokuk carries an axe and a feathered staff and shield. These, together with his bear-claw necklace, beaded boots, and headdress, signify his tribal status.

CIVIL WAR: 1861–1865

Westward expansion increased conflicts among Americans over the issue of slavery and whether it should be allowed in new states. Objections to slavery had been raised since the eighteenth century, and in 1784 the Pennsylvania Abolition Society was formed to combat slavery. Benjamin Franklin was elected its president. **Abolitionists** (people seeking to abolish slavery), who were mainly Northerners, Quakers, slaves, and former slaves, fought to end slavery through rousing speeches, articles, and acts of violence. Northerners in general opposed extending slavery into any new states, though only abolitionists supported abolishing it in states where it already existed.

Abolitionism in the United States derived from the notion of equality espoused by the Declaration of Independence and a growing conviction that slavery was a moral wrong. Abolitionists also objected to the fact that the United States Constitution did not prohibit slavery and to the strong laws punishing runaway slaves. The Dred Scott case, which reached the Supreme Court in 1857, dramatized the conflict between slave owners and abolitionists. Scott was born into slavery and

19.18 Frederic Remington, *A Dash for the Timber*, 1889. Oil on canvas, 4 ft. 1/4 in. × 7 ft. 1/8 in. (1.23 × 2.14 m). Amon Carter Museum, Fort Worth, Texas.

moved to the Northwest Territory with his master's family. When his master died, Scott argued that he should be free, since he was living in a non-slave territory. But the Supreme Court denied his claim, and Scott was forced to return to slavery, a decision that further mobilized the abolitionists.

The issue of slavery was only one factor leading up to the Civil War, but it highlighted the issue of states' rights. Economics were also important, because the agricultural South relied on slave labor for much of its prosperity. The South also had a profound sense of cultural identity, as distinct from the more industrialized North, and was opposed to interference from the Federal government.

ABOLITIONISTS In 1831 Nat Turner (1800–1831), a Virginia slave and preacher, led some seventy followers in a rebellion. Convinced that God had chosen him to free the slaves, Turner killed over fifty white people and destroyed their plantations. Captured and sentenced to hang, he described the divine inspiration that motivated the rebellion, which his lawyer later published as the *Confessions of Nat Turner*.

In 1856 the abolitionist John Brown (1800–1859), a white man, led a massacre in Kansas in which five slave owners were killed. In 1859 he seized the government arsenal at Harper's Ferry, Virginia, but he was captured, convicted of treason, and hanged. The actions of John Brown were not successful in freeing the slaves, but the **Underground Railroad**, a network organized by freed blacks and other abolitionists through Ohio, Pennsylvania, and Indiana, helped slaves escape to Canada. Along the way, they found haven in safe houses (called stations), led by "conductors" such as Harriet Tubman (*c.* 1820–1913), who had herself escaped in this way. Of the several thousand slaves brought to freedom on the Underground Railroad, Harriet Tubman was probably responsible for about three hundred.

In literature a Realist genre known as the **slave narrative** (writings by freed slaves) brought the abuses of slavery to the attention of the general public. A classic example of a slave narrative is the autobiography of Frederick Douglass (*c.* 1817–1895). Born a slave, Douglass escaped in 1838. He went to New York and married a free woman he had met in Baltimore. They moved to Massachusetts, where he became an avid abolitionist, lecturing and writing on the degrading and dehumanizing facts about slavery. In his *Narrative of the Life of Frederick Douglass, An American Slave* (1845) Douglass begins by noting that he never knew his age:

> By far the larger part of the slaves know as little of their ages as horses know of theirs, and it is the wish of most masters within my knowledge to keep their slaves ignorant. I do not remember to have ever met a slave who could tell of his birthday. They seldom come nearer to it than planting-time, harvest-time, cherry-time, spring-time, or fall-time.

Douglass's determination to become literate and acquire knowledge was a driving force of his life. Recognizing that being unable to read and write, and remaining ignorant, would be another form of slavery, Douglass fought to learn. He describes his new mistress in Baltimore, one Mrs. Auld, who began teaching him to spell. When her husband found out, he forbade her to continue, saying, "Learning would *spoil* the best nigger in the world."

This experience, Douglass says, taught him a valuable lesson:

> From that moment, I understood the pathway from slavery to freedom . . . What he [Mr. Auld] most dreaded . . . I most desired . . . and the argument . . . against my learning to read, only served to inspire me with a desire and determination to learn.

In 1850 the autobiography of Sojourner Truth (*c.* 1795–1883) was published. Born a slave in New York, she was freed by state law in 1827. Though illiterate, she dictated her life story and became a forceful voice in the fight against slavery—and for the rights of women. In 1851 she delivered a speech to the Women's Rights Convention held in Akron, Ohio. Entitled *Ain't I a Woman?*, its transcription has been controversial, but it was clearly a masterpiece of oratory in a style influenced by the Bible and delivered in contemporary black dialect:

> Nobody eber help me into carriages, or ober mud puddles, or gives me any best place . . . and ar'n't I a woman? Look at me! Look at my arm! . . . I have plowed, and planted, and gathered into barns, and no man could head me—and ar'n't I a woman? . . . I have borne thirteen chilern and seen 'em mos' all sold off into slavery, and when I cried out with a mother's grief, none but Jesus heard—and ar'n't I a woman? . . . Whar did your Christ come from? From God and a woman. Man had nothing to do with him . . ." [and referring to Eve] if de fust woman God ever made was strong enough to turn the world upside down, all 'lone, dese togedder [the assembled audience of women] ought to be able to turn it back and get it right side up again, and now dey is asking to do it, de men better let 'em. Bleeged to ye for hearin' on me, and now old Sojourner ha'n't got nothing more to say.

A year after Sojourner Truth's speech, another abolitionist, Harriet Beecher Stowe (1811–1896), published *Uncle Tom's Cabin*, which was an immediate success. The hero is Uncle Tom, a slave sold to meet his owner's debts. His new owner lives in New Orleans, where a member of the household, Little Eva, befriends Tom. But she dies and Tom is sold to the heartless and vindictive plantation owner, Simon Legree, who beats him to death. Stowe's characters have become paradigms of certain traits—to call someone a "Simon Legree" denotes a cruel sadist, whereas an "Uncle Tom" is one who submits to his oppressor.

Stowe's subtitle, *Life Among the Lowly*, heralds the Realism of the story, despite its somewhat melodramatic style. Her emphasis on the practice of splitting up slave families and their harsh treatment by some plantation owners was a call to freedom. Enormously effective as an anti-slavery voice, *Uncle Tom's Cabin* concludes:

> A day of grace is yet held out to us. Both North and South have been guilty before God; and the *Christian Church* has a heavy account to answer. Not by combining together, to protect injustice and cruelty, and making a common capital of sin, is this Union to be saved,—but by repentance, justice and mercy; for, not surer is the eternal law by which the millstone sinks in the ocean, than that stronger law by which injustice and cruelty shall bring on nations the wrath of Almighty God!

WAR BREAKS OUT In 1859 Abraham Lincoln (1809–1865) became America's sixteenth president (see Box). He had made his opposition to slavery and to states' rights clear in his "House Divided" speech of 1858, when he denounced slavery and the exercise of Southern states' rights in continuing slavery. In addition, there were strong economic differences between the industrial North and the agricultural South. Soon after Lincoln's election, seven southern states (Florida, Louisiana, Georgia, Alabama, South Carolina, Mississippi, and Texas) invoked the principle of states' rights and seceded from the Union. They formed the Confederacy, also called the Confederate States of America, or CSA. Shortly thereafter, Arkansas, Tennessee, North Carolina, and Virginia also seceded; Missouri, Kentucky, Delaware, and Maryland—slave states that formed a border with the North—remained in the Union. These actions sparked the Civil War, which lasted from 1861 to 1865.

Society and Culture

Abraham Lincoln, Thinker, Writer, Orator

Abraham Lincoln (figure **19.19**) was born in a log cabin in rural Kentucky. Almost entirely self-educated, he passed the bar exam and began to practice law in Illinois. He was elected to the Illinois state legislature in 1834 and to the United States Congress in 1847. In 1856 he joined the new Republican party and was elected president in 1860.

Lincoln's speeches as a congressman, and later as the United States president, express his commitment to preserving the Union and the Constitution. He also denounced the institution of slavery as contrary to the principles of the Declaration of Independence. On October 16, 1854, in Peoria, Illinois, he asserted:

> *Let us re-adopt the Declaration of Independence . . . If we do this, we shall not only have saved the Union; but we shall have so saved it, as to make, and to keep it, forever worthy of the saving.*

On June 16, 1858, he told the Republican Convention that:

> *A house divided against itself cannot stand . . . this government cannot endure, permanently half* slave *and half* free. *I do not expect the Union to be* dissolved—*I do not expect the house to* fall—*but I* do *expect it will cease to be divided.*

19.19 Mathew Brady, *Lincoln, "Cooper Union Portrait,"* 1860. Photograph. Library of Congress, Washington, D.C.
Mathew Brady (*c.* 1823–1896), whose photographs constitute a comprehensive document of the American Civil War, was also Lincoln's photographer. In this portrait Brady shows Lincoln as a man of letters standing in a strong vertical pose that echoes the column. Both symbolize the Union and denote the upright honesty of Lincoln's political principles.

And declaring his commitment to peace, although admitting the necessity of war, to the New Jersey General Assembly on February 21, 1861:

> *The man does not live who is more devoted to peace than I am. None who would do more to preserve it. But it may be necessary to put the foot down firmly.*

In the Gettysburg Address of November 16, 1863, delivered after the Union army victory at Gettysburg, Lincoln spoke his most famous lines:

> *Four score and seven years ago our fathers brought forth on this continent, a new nation, conceived in Liberty, and dedicated to the proposition that all men are created equal.*

He called for a re-birth of freedom to honor those who fought and died in the Civil War:

> *we here highly resolve that these dead shall not have died in vain—that this nation, under God, shall have a new birth of freedom—and that government of the people, by the people, for the people, shall not perish from the earth.*

Although the North was technologically superior to the South, the bravery and commitment of southerners to their cause resulted in a fierce, four-year struggle. The Confederacy was commanded by General Robert E. Lee (1807–1870), but his defeat at the Battle of Gettysburg in July 1863 heralded the demise of the CSA. Thereafter, the Union army was commanded by General Ulysses S. Grant (1822–1885), who had served in the Mexican War and would later become the eighteenth U.S. president. Fighting continued for another two years after Gettysburg, until Lee's surrender to Grant at Appomattox (in Virginia), which effectively brought the war to a close.

Some seven months before Gettysburg, on January 1, 1863, Lincoln had issued the Emancipation Proclamation, officially freeing the slaves in rebellious states. On November 19, 1863, Lincoln delivered the Gettysburg Address. This momentous speech refocused the purpose of the Civil War as a struggle for the principles of individual freedom, based on the Declaration of Independence.

When the war ended in 1865, Congress passed the thirteenth amendment to the Constitution prohibiting slavery in all states. In addition, despite Lincoln's pleas for tolerance and compassion toward the South after its defeat, Congress imposed an abusive policy of **Reconstruction** on the South from 1867 to 1877. At the end of the period, however, backlash set in and former slaves continued to suffer economic hardship and discrimination. On April 14, 1865, as he sat in the John Ford Theater in Washington, D.C., Lincoln was assassinated by the Confederate sympathizer John Wilkes Booth (1838–1865).

19.21 William Sidney Mount, *California News*, 1850. Museums at Stony Brook, New York.
This scene conveys a microcosm of American life and shows the role played by the news media in nineteenth-century social consciousness. One man reads the *New York Daily Tribune*, which is reporting on the discovery of gold out west. Another already has his train ticket.

REALISM IN ART AND ARCHITECTURE

In the visual arts in the United States, as in Europe, Realists were interested in portraying and documenting everyday society and important contemporary events. A major subject was the Civil War, which was well documented in photographs by Mathew Brady (1823–1896), the best known of the war photographers, and in illustrations for *Harper's Weekly* magazine by Winslow Homer (1836–1910), who was a painter as well as an illustrator. His *Prisoners from the Front* (figure

19.20 Winslow Homer, *Prisoners from the Front*, 1866. Oil on canvas, 24 × 38 in. (61 × 96.5 cm). The Metropolitan Museum of Art, New York.
As with Courbet's *A Burial at Ornans*, Homer's figures are arranged in a frieze-like alignment against a stark landscape. In the background horses and dismounted soldiers go about their daily routines. The age range of the prisoners, from a gawky youth to an old, bearded man, reflects the universal call to serve the Confederacy. The two rifles lying on the ground denote both surrender and the land over which the two sides fought.

19.20), painted one year after the Civil War, was exhibited in Paris in 1867. It conforms to the Realist ideal of journalistic documentation. The atmosphere is calm and quiet as a Union officer encounters the bedraggled Confederate prisoners. There is no attempt to romanticize the war, only to record a simple event in its aftermath.

In 1850 William Sidney Mount (1807–1868) painted *California News* (figure **19.21**), reflecting the importance of newspaper reading as a means of learning about current events. Newspapers had been published in Europe in the eighteenth century and expanded in both Europe and America in the nineteenth century (see Box, p. 557). This meant there was a wider audience for editorializing through text as well as imagery and also increased communication in general. In *California News* several white men, one woman, and one black man gather at the entrance to a post office and join in the excitement of reading about the California Gold Rush.

The low-life and dismal conditions of the urban street, rife with poverty and crime, appealed to the Realism of the Danish immigrant Jacob Riis (1849–1914), whose photographs convey the reality of the worst elements of the city (figure **19.22**). The author of *How the Other Half Lives* (1890), Riis worked as a police reporter in New York City. In this photograph, Riis captures the run-down tenement buildings, smoke-filled back alley lined with open garbage, stray animals, and suspicious, unsavory characters riveted on the eye of the camera.

19.22 Jacob Riis, *Bandits' Roost, Mulberry Street, New York*, c. 1888. Photograph. Museum of the City of New York.

19.23 Henry Ossawa Tanner, *Banjo Lesson*, 1893. Oil on canvas, 49 × 35½ in. (124.5 × 90.2 cm). Hampton University Museum, Hampton, Virginia.

The living conditions of black Americans interested Henry Ossawa Tanner (1859–1937), who worked as a photographer in North Carolina. But Tanner lived mainly in France, where he became the first African American to exhibit with the Impressionists (see Chapter 20). The son of a bishop, Tanner traveled to the Middle East in 1897, which inspired a number of religious paintings in a Realist mode. His *Banjo Lesson* (figure **19.23**) conveys the intimate relationship between a grandfather and his grandson whom he is teaching to play the banjo. They are linked by their merged forms and the diagonal of the banjo, which connotes the transmission of cultural expression from one generation to the next. Despite the bare wooden floors and simple stove, the glowing light in the background bathes the figures in warmth.

In America, as in Europe, industrial innovations, especially steel manufacture, led to new architectural ideas related to Realist ideals. The Middle West was the home of the early American skyscraper, notably those designed by members of the Chicago School founded by Louis Henry Sullivan (1856–1924). He designed the Wainwright Building in St.

19.24 Louis Sullivan, Wainwright Building, St. Louis, Missouri, 1890–1891. The building has a steel skeleton hidden by the exterior. The lower stories are sturdy, consistent with their support function. The upper stories' vertical sweep is emphasized by the smooth walls and recessed windows. Strong verticals frame the corners and lead the viewer's eye toward the crowning projecting cornice, which is decorated with a foliate frieze.

Louis, Missouri (figure **19.24**) according to his architectural philosophy that "form follows function." By this Sullivan meant that the form of a building should reflect its purpose and that function and style reinforce each other. In the case of the skyscraper, less land is required for the foundation and the height of the building can accommodate more space and larger numbers of people at lower cost than a one-story structure of the same square footage. As a result, skyscrapers became the building of choice for cities, where land is typically more expensive than in the country. In taking into account such social and economic issues, the skyscraper is itself part of the Realist trends of the nineteenth century.

Literature

One of the most convincing accounts of the Civil War was written by a man who had never seen fighting. The novel *The Red Badge of Courage* by Stephen Crane (1871–1900) has been in print since its publication in 1895, when the author was twenty-four years old. Crane, who had heard accounts of the Civil War from veterans, used local speech patterns and accurate settings to create the impression that he was writing from personal experience. Historical facts provided the inspiration for the events in the novel. *The Red Badge of Courage* has been praised for its photographic imagery, an example of which occurs in the opening sentence: "The cold passed reluctantly from the earth and the retiring fog revealed an army stretched out on the hills, resting."

The post-Civil War author Samuel Langhorne Clemens, better known as Mark Twain (1835–1910), was an enormously prolific author and one of the earliest to write in the American vernacular (everyday speech). He was born in Missouri and when he was four, his family moved to Hannibal, on the Mississippi River. He left school when he was twelve, traveled throughout the United States and Europe, and briefly fought on the Confederate side in the Civil War. His childhood along the Mississippi inspired his most famous novels depicting the voices of rural America—*The Adventures of Tom Sawyer* (1876), *Life on the Mississippi* (1883), and *The Adventures of Huckleberry Finn* (1884).

Huckleberry Finn is the story of Huck Finn and his life on a raft with the runaway slave, Jim. At the opening of the story, Huck is taken in by the pious Widow Douglas, but Huck's alcoholic father abducts him. Huck then escapes and travels down the Mississippi River with Jim. The descriptions of the Mississippi and its rural environs are carefully observed and described with remarkable wit. Throughout the novel Twain's direct, satirical social commentary is conveyed in precise local dialect. For example, when Huck tells Jim about the harem of wise King Solomon—"he had about a million wives"—Jim replies:

> Why, yes, dat's so; I—I'd done forgot it. A harem's a bo'd'n-house, I reck'n. Mos' likely dey has rackety times in de nussery. En I reck'n de wives quarrels considable; en dat 'crease de racket. Yit dey say Sollermun de wises' man dat ever live'. I doan' take no stock in dat. Bekase why: would a wise man want to live in de mids' er sich a blimblammin' all de time? No—'deed he wouldn't. A wise man 'ud take en buil' a biler-factry; en den he could shet *down* de biler-factry when he want to res'.

During Huck's journey down the Mississippi he meets characters from all walks of life. In the guise of an adventure story, Twain comments on American society and criticizes the institution of slavery. His use of the vernacular and his refreshing approach to places and people offended some readers, but his novels remain memorable portraits of America in the late nineteenth century.

Kate Chopin (1851–1904) takes another view of the American scene in her stories of Creole and Cajun life in Louisiana. Born in St. Louis and married to a Creole cotton trader, Chopin was the mother of six children. Her interest in various

News

In the mid- to late nineteenth century, the Realist emphasis on facts and improvements in technology led to a surge in popular demand for information about newsworthy events. As a result, newspaper reading became more widespread in America as well as in Europe.

People in all cultures have always wanted "news" of important—and not so important—events. In cultures without writing, news is transmitted orally, and even literate cultures have produced messengers, town criers, carrier pigeons, and local gossips who make news available to a general audience.

In ancient Rome, from the first century B.C. until the third century A.D., the government posted *acta* (proceedings) in the forum to announce political decisions, results of trials, executions, and military victories and defeats. Around the same time in China *tipao* (news sheets) were circulated among government officials. By the seventh century *tipao* were printed, but modern newspapers were introduced into China only in the nineteenth century, mainly by foreign travelers and missionaries.

The notion of the modern newspaper originated in Europe, after Gutenberg perfected movable type (see Chapter 13) for printing in the mid-fifteenth century. In Italy, Germany, France, and England, weekly newspapers containing local and international news became available during the sixteenth and seventeenth centuries. The earliest surviving English newspaper (1621) was called *Corante, or weekely newes from Italy, Germany, Hungary, Poland, Bohemia, France and the Low Countreys*. England also produced papers with headlines, advertisements, and illustrations. English papers hired newsboys and newsgirls to sell papers on the streets and women—called "she-intelligencers"—to collect news.

The first American newspapers appeared during the colonial period. In 1690 Boston's *Public Occurrences, Both Foreign and Domestick* carried a lead story on Christian Indians in Plymouth who dedicated a day of thanksgiving to God. In the years leading up to the American Revolution newspapers rebelled against the Stamp Act and the Townshend Acts (see Chapter 17), both of which taxed papers and thus limited readership to the wealthier classes.

Freedom of the press also became a heated issue at the time. In 1787 Thomas Jefferson said that he would prefer newspapers without government to government without newspapers, and the following year George Washington praised the news media as a way of preserving liberty, stimulating industry, and improving the morals of free people. The first amendment to the U.S. Constitution, written in 1789 and ratified in 1791, guarantees freedom of the press.

In 1833 the penny press (inexpensive papers) became popular, further expanding readership. The cylinder press, invented in Germany and improved in England, followed by steam-powered presses, made printing faster and easier. Papers were soon selling thousands of copies a day. Inventions such as the telegraph, wire services, and the transatlantic cable allowed news to travel quickly across the ocean.

Papers became politically engaged, reporting on current events and issues, such as abolitionism and the Civil War. Winslow Homer's engravings for *Harper's Weekly* left a vivid pictorial record of that conflict (figure **19.25**) as well as of other aspects of mid-nineteenth-century American society.

By the second half of the twentieth century, especially after World War II (see Chapter 23), advances in technology led to forms of media that competed with printed news. Many newspapers went out of business as radio and television supplanted newspaper reading as a traditional evening activity. Whereas 85 percent of the American population read papers in 1946, only 55 percent did so in 1985. Today, newspapers have to compete with twenty-four-hour national and international news channels and easily accessible news on the worldwide web.

19.25 Winslow Homer, *The War for the Union, 1862—A Bayonet Charge*, July 12. *Harper's Weekly* wood engraving, 13⅝ × 20⅝ in. (35 × 52.3 cm). The Metropolitan Museum of Art, New York. Homer uses strong diagonals and silhouetting to convey the violence of battle. By crowding the picture he emphasizes the number of casualties, and by showing the figures in the foreground individually, Homer evokes the viewer's identification with them.

cultural and racial combinations—English, French, Spanish, African—local color, and local dialects of Louisiana, are evident in *Bayou Folk* (1894) and *A Night in Acadie* (1897). Her controversial novel *The Awakening* (1899) was banned in St. Louis for its explicit approach to female sexuality. Her heroine, Edna, like Ibsen's Nora Helmer and Flaubert's Emma Bovary, is bored with a meaningless marriage and flouts convention by seeking fulfillment through infidelity.

Nineteenth-century Realism began to evolve in the 1840s. It overlapped with Romanticism, which we discussed in the previous chapter. In the 1860s, new artistic styles that overlapped with Realism began to emerge, especially in Paris. Although influenced by industry, each of these styles responded differently to the changing face of society. In the next chapter we consider the Impressionist and Post-Impressionist styles and the Symbolist Movement.

KEY TERMS

abolitionist an advocate of the abolition of slavery.

bourgeoisie in Marxist theory, the upper-middle classes who own the means of production.

fix in photography, to make an image permanent.

gene a unit of heredity by which characteristics are transmitted from parents to their offspring.

lithography a printing medium using a stone press on which areas are made receptive to ink.

Marxism the political, economic, and social principles advocated by Marx, Engels, and their followers.

"method" acting a school of acting, based on the theory of Stanislavsky, in which actors identify with their characters' inner motivations.

Morse code a code (invented by Samuel Morse) in which letters, numerals, and other symbols are represented by dots and dashes.

natural selection a process described by Charles Darwin in which individuals or groups survive only if they can adapt to their environment.

Positivism a philosophical movement that recognizes only positive facts and observable phenomena.

proletariat in Marxist theory, the working class, which is hired and exploited by those who own the means of production.

Realpolitik the belief that the only realistic policies for a state are those that serve that state's interests.

Reconstruction the period (1867–1877) following the American Civil War during which the seceding states were reestablished in the Union.

slave narrative a genre of literature by freed slaves highlighting the abuses of slavery.

Underground Railroad the clandestine network in the United States that helped fugitive slaves to reach the North or Canada.

Utilitarianism a political philosophy that holds that the aim of all action should be the greatest happiness for the greatest number of people.

utopianism a philosophy that proposes ideal (and often impractical) schemes for the perfection of social and political conditions.

verismo (Italian, "realism") a term applied to late-nineteenth-century operas with contemporary settings, true-to-life characters, and strongly expressed emotions.

KEY QUESTIONS

1. Discuss three Realist works that illustrate Zola's notion that portraying injustice is a step toward correcting it. What reforms did such works advocate?
2. Realist artists exercised their right of free expression. What artistic innovations flouted the established rules of the French Academy?
3. Define Manifest Destiny. How did it arise and where did it lead?
4. What techniques of artistic expression were used in photography that influenced other media?
5. The statement "a house divided against itself cannot stand" describes more than one controversy in the mid- to late part of the nineteenth century. Discuss two of these controversies to show the effects of divisions within countries. Is the statement relevant to contemporary politics?

SUGGESTED READING

Barnes, D. S. *The Making of a Social Disease: Tuberculosis in Nineteenth-century France*. Berkeley: University of California Press, 1995.
▸ A study of the disease and its social effects in France

Boime, Albert. *A Social History of Modern Art*. Chicago: University of Chicago Press, 1987.
▸ A Marxist view of modern art.

Desmond, A., and J. Moore. *Darwin*. London: Penguin Books, 1992.
▸ A biography of Darwin.

Douglass, Frederick. *The Life of Frederick Douglass, An American Slave*. New York: Penguin Classics, 1986.

Edgerton, R. B. *Death of Glory: The Legacy of the Crimean War*. New York: Basic Books, 2000.
▸ The Crimean War and its effects on European politics.

Himmelfarb, Gertrude. *The Idea of Poverty: England in the Early Industrial Age*. London: Faber and Faber, 1984.
▸ A study of industrial England in the nineteenth century.

Janson, H. W. *Nineteenth-century Sculpture*. New York: Abrams, 1985.
▸ A general survey.

McMurtry, Larry. *Crazy Horse*. New York: Viking, 1999.
▸ A short biography, one of a series of biographies by well-known authors.

Marx, Karl, and Friedrich Engels. *The Communist Manifesto*. Atlanta, GA: Pathfinder Press, 1970.
▸ Marx's political treatise on international communism.

Meredith, Roy. *Mr. Lincoln's Camera Man*, 2nd ed. New York: Dover Publications, 1974.
▸ Mathew Brady's Civil War photographic notebooks.

Newhall, Beaumont. *History of Photography: From 1839 to the Present Day*. London: Secker and Warburg, 1982.
▸ A general introduction.

Pflanze, O. *Bismarck and the Development of Germany*, 3 vols. Princeton, NJ: Princeton University Press, 1990.
▸ A biography of Bismarck and the history of Germany.

Robertson, P. *An Experience of Women: Pattern and Change in Nineteenth-century Europe*. Philadelphia: Temple University Press, 1982.
▸ A survey dealing with the lives of women in nineteenth-century Europe.

Zall, Paul M. (ed.). *Lincoln's Legacy: The Emancipation Proclamation and the Gettysburg Address*. San Marino, CA: Huntington Library Press, 1994.
▸ Source documents.

SUGGESTED FILMS

1930 *Abraham Lincoln*, dir. D. W. Griffith

1930 *Tom Sawyer* (based on Mark Twain), dir. John Cromwell

1931 *The Dreyfus Case* (based on Zola), dir. F. W. Kraemer and Milton Rosmer

1933 *Madame Bovary* (based on Flaubert), dir. Jean Renoir

1935 *Crime and Punishment* (based on Doestoevsky), dir. Josef von Sternberg

1936 *The Story of Louis Pasteur*, dir. Milliam Dieterle

1939 *Gone with the Wind*, dir. Victor Fleming, George Cukor, and Sam Wood

1939 *Young Mr. Lincoln*, dir. John Ford

1945 *Le Père Goriot* (based on Balzac), dir. Robert Vernay

1946 *Dance of Death* (*Danse de la Mort*) (based on Strindberg), dir. Marcel Cravenne

1949 *Madame Bovary* (based on Flaubert), dir. Vincente Minnelli

1956 *War and Peace* (based on Tolstoy), dir. King Vidor

1957 *I Accuse* (based on Zola), dir. José Ferrer

1958 *The Brothers Karamazov* (based on Doestoevsky), dir. Richard Brooks

1960 *The Adventures of Huckleberry Finn* (based on Mark Twain), dir. Michael Curtiz

1966 *Le Horla* (based on Maupassant), dir. Jean-Daniel Pollet

1968 *Charge of the Light Brigade*, dir. Tony Richardson

1973 *A Doll's House* (based on Ibsen), dir. Joseph Losey

1978 *Hedda Gabler* (based on Ibsen), dir. Jan Decorte

1982 *Nana* (based on Zola), dir. Dan Wolman

1987 *Uncle Tom's Cabin*, dir. Stan Lathan

1991 *Madame Bovary* (based on Flaubert), dir. Claude Chabrol

1993 *Germinal* (based on Zola), dir. Claude Berri

1997 *Anna Karenina* (based on Tolstoy), dir. Bernard Rose

2002 *Crime and Punishment* (based on Dostoevsky), dir. Menahem Golan

20 "Modern Life": The Late Nineteenth Century

"Take up the White Man's burden."

(RUDYARD KIPLING)

Beginning in the late 1860s the notion of "modern life" was taken up in the visual arts, literature, music, and theater. Modern life as a concept was part of a complex trend called "Modernism," which shared with Realism a desire to challenge conventions of middle-class morality. In contrast to the Realists, the Modernists focused as much, if not more, on formal aesthetics as on social, political, and economic matters. The Modernist styles developed in an age of new technologies and systems of communication, increasing urbanization, and European expansionism around the world.

During the latter decades of the nineteenth century, European businessmen looked overseas for new markets for the manufactured goods of the Industrial Revolution, such as cotton, which was made into finished cloth in Britain. Raw materials could be transported more quickly and efficiently than ever before. From the early sixteenth century European exploration had forged economic ties between Europe and the Far East, Africa, and the Middle East, but by the nineteenth century Europe also dominated the culture and economy in parts of these regions.

Although the terms "imperialism" and "colonialism" are sometimes regarded as interchangeable, there are important distinctions between them. Whereas imperialism refers to European domination of existing cultures, colonialism applies to Europeans founding settlements and taking land in technologically underdeveloped cultures. The results of imperialism and colonialism were positive as well as negative. The West brought democratic ideals and individual rights, advances in science and medicine, and technology to other parts of the world. But in profiting from cheap labor and from the often forced markets created by imperialism and colonization, the West caused social, economic, and political problems that would take generations to resolve.

The notion of the "White Man's burden"—the title of the poem by Rudyard Kipling (1865–1936) cited at the beginning of the chapter—emerged in the nineteenth century. Kipling's poem reflects the view that whites are a superior race, morally obligated to assume the "burden" of ruling inferior races in Africa, India, and elsewhere. Born in Bombay to English parents, Kipling wrote poetry and stories (the Just So Stories*) that are still popular among young readers today. His best-known novel,* Kim *(1901), is about a white boy who grows up in India and is a*

Key Topics

Culture and Empire

Colonialism and imperialism
"Modern life"
Industry

Technology and Art

Electric lights
Typewriters
Telephones
Bicycles
The birth of film

The Unconscious

Freud
Swedenborg
Bergson

Style

Impressionism
Post-Impressionism
Japonisme
Symbolism

Music

Debussy

TIMELINE	LATE-NINETEENTH-CENTURY EUROPE	LATE-NINETEENTH-CENTURY UNITED STATES
HISTORY AND CULTURE 	Imperialism and colonialism Britain rules largest colonial empire in the world One third of European populations live in urban areas, by 1900 Women's movements gather momentum Nobel (1833–1896) establishes Nobel Prize Britain fights Opium Wars in China, 1839–1842, 1856–1860	Free mail delivery voted by Congress, 1863 Increasing urbanization, by 1900
SCIENCE, TECHNOLOGY, AND PSYCHOLOGY	Major improvements in layouts of European cities Modernization of sewage treatment reduces epidemics, Paris London Underground built, 1863 Chain bicycle invented, 1871 Bell invents telephone, 1876 Russia begins construction of Trans-Siberian Railroad, 1891 Freud and Breuer, *Studies on Hysteria*, 1893–1895 Freud, *The Interpretation of Dreams*, 1899 Marconi's wireless replaces transatlantic cable, 1901	Typewriters, electric lights, and bicycles widely used, from 1870s
ART 	Hiroshige, "One Hundred Views of Edo," 1856 Impressionism begins in Paris, 1860s Paris World's Fair, 1862, inspires *japonisme* Manet, *Olympia*, 1865; *Nana*, 1877 Moreau, *The Peri*, *c.* 1870–1875 Monet, *Impression: Sunrise*, 1872; *La Japonaise*, 1875; *Arrival of a Train, Gare Saint-Lazare*, 1877 Degas, *Monsieur Perrot's Dance Class*, *c.* 1875 Renoir, *The Swing*, 1876 Pissarro, *The Outer Boulevards: Snow Effect*, 1879 Rodin, *The Kiss*, 1886 Development of Post-Impressionism, late 1880s Seurat, *A Sunday Afternoon on the Island of La Grande Jatte*, 1884–1886 van Gogh, *The Sower with Setting Sun*, 1888; *Self-Portrait*, 1889 Gauguin, *Ia Orana Maria*, 1891 Toulouse-Lautrec, *Jane Avril at the "Jardin de Paris,"* 1893 Munch, *The Scream*, 1893 Cézanne, *The Great Bathers*, 1898–1905	Whistler, *The Princess from the Land of Porcelain* and *Harmony in Blue and Gold*, 1876–1877 Cassatt, *A Woman and a Girl Driving*, 1881
PHOTOGRAPHY AND FILM 	Muybridge, "Female Figure Hopping," 1887 Lumière brothers invent first motion picture camera, 1894; present first public film screening, Paris, 1895; *Break at the Lumière Factory*, 1895; *The Blacksmiths*, 1895; *The Arrival of a Train at the Station*, 1895; *The Demolition of a Wall*, 1896 Méliès first to approach film as art form; *Cinderella*, 1899; *The Trip to the Moon*, 1902; *The Palace of the Arabian Nights*, 1905	Eastman (1854–1932) manufactures coated light-sensitive paper Edison produces kinetoscope; *Record of a Sneeze*, 1894
LITERATURE AND PHILOSOPHY 	Symbolist poetry Baudelaire, *Les Fleurs du mal*, 1857 Verlaine, *Fêtes galantes*, 1869 Rimbaud, "Vowels," 1871; "Illuminations" Mallarmé, "The Afternoon of a Faun," 1876; *Jadis et naguère*, 1885 Symbolist Movement codified in *XIXe Siècle* manifesto, published by Moréas, 1886 Kipling, *Kim*, 1901	
THEATER	Maeterlinck, *Pelléas et Mélisande*, 1892	
MUSIC	Debussy, *Suite bergamasque*, 1890; *Prelude to "The Afternoon of a Faun,"* 1894; *Pelléas et Mélisande*, 1902; *Pagodes*, 1903; *La Mer*, 1905	

vivid portrayal of that country. During his lifetime Kipling was considered the poet of empire.

In the visual arts, Impressionism, Symbolism, and Post-Impressionism, unlike Realism, were not primarily concerned with social conditions. The Impressionists thought of themselves as "optical" realists, depicting light and color according to the way these elements affect our perceptions. But the Impressionists were also painters of modern life. They recorded the changing character of nineteenth-century society and, as with Realist pictures, Impressionist viewpoints often reflect photographic viewpoints—panoramic, aerial, close-up, and cropped.

Impressionists painted figures belonging to specific classes of society and urban scenes, and they showed the encroachment of industry on landscape. They were also drawn to scenes of leisure and entertainment, representing café life, theater and concerts, opera, ballet, and dance halls. Impressionist music conveys fleeting impressions of nature through fluid movement and tone color. And Symbolist theater creates atmospheric moods, portraying meaning as much through symbolic actions as through dialogue.

The Symbolist Movement strictly began in 1885, but its precursors appeared earlier and included authors as well as painters. Symbolists were concerned with a form of subjective realism, giving sensation, imagination, myth, and dreams precedence over the empirical observation of nature and society. The Post-Impressionists were a group of late-nineteenth-century painters who shared certain interests with both the Impressionists and the Symbolists. At the end of the century, technological advances in photography culminated in the birth of the motion picture, which also reflected the Impressionist interest in time and movement.

THE EMERGENCE OF "MODERN LIFE"

The world shrank in the late nineteenth century, thanks to the Industrial Revolution. Samuel Morse's telegraph was replaced by the wireless, the invention of Guglielmo Marconi (1874–1937), which began operating between Britain and France in 1898 and had replaced the transatlantic cable by 1901. International mail service came into use, and in the United States free mail delivery was voted by Congress in 1863. The Scottish-born American Alexander Graham Bell (1847–1922) invented the telephone in 1876. In 1891, Russia began construction on the Trans-Siberian Railroad from Moscow to Vladivostok, which linked new colonies in the eastern provinces to Moscow.

The invention of refrigeration made transporting perishable goods easier. Oil and electricity, which were more efficient than water and steam, were now widely used to generate energy. In America, typewriters, electric lights, and bicycles were manufactured and widely used from the 1870s. George Eastman (1854–1932), the founder of Kodak, manufactured coated light-sensitive paper, making photographs both clearer and more popular, and in France the Lumière brothers had invented the first motion picture camera by 1894.

Cities continued to grow in the late nineteenth century, and by 1900 a third of the European and American populations lived in urban areas. Despite the enormous advantages brought about by industry, the problems that accompanied urbanization continued. The increasing wealth of the middle and upper classes went hand in hand with worsening conditions for workers, resulting in the abuses discussed in Chapter 19.

Women's movements also gathered momentum in the late nineteenth century, as reformers fought to change laws restricting women's rights to property and divorce. But reform came slowly. Although women in New Zealand gained the right to vote in 1893, American women could not vote until 1920, and French women had to wait until 1945.

Under Napoleon III radical changes in urban design were undertaken to modernize Paris, improve its appearance, and eliminate slums that were considered breeding grounds for rebellion. By 1870 the designs of Baron Georges-Eugène Haussmann (1809–1891) had transformed Paris into a city of radiating boulevards, tree-lined streets (figure **20.1**), and large parks decorated with fountains. Bridges over the Seine improved the flow of traffic, modernized treatment of sewage reduced the incidence of epidemics, and gas lamps illuminated the city at night. Similar renovations took place in other European cities—the ring roads in Vienna, for example, and the London Underground, which was in place by 1863. The invention of the chain bicycle in 1871 also made urban transportation more efficient.

IMPERIALISM AND THE INTERNATIONAL ECONOMY

In the latter decades of the nineteenth century colonialism took on a new cast. Colonial ambition merged with the notion of imperialism as European nations competed to dominate foreign cultures and to control natural resources around the world (map **20.1**). At the time, imperialism was particularly focused on South Africa, with its diamonds, South America, with its minerals, and Asia, with its textiles, tea,

20.1 Camille Pissarro, *The Outer Boulevards: Snow Effect*, 1879. Oil on canvas, $21\frac{1}{4} \times 25\frac{5}{8}$ in. (54×65 cm). Marmottan Museum, Paris.

Camille Pissarro (1830–1903) was born in St. Thomas, in the Caribbean, but studied and lived mainly in France. This painting of a tree-lined Parisian boulevard reflects the Impressionist interest in the ways weather affects light and color. Here, the whiteness of the snow fills the air and absorbs the colors of the street. Human figures and horse-drawn carriages form patterns of dark on light. The expanse of the street seems to extend into the distance as the trees and buildings dissolve into white.

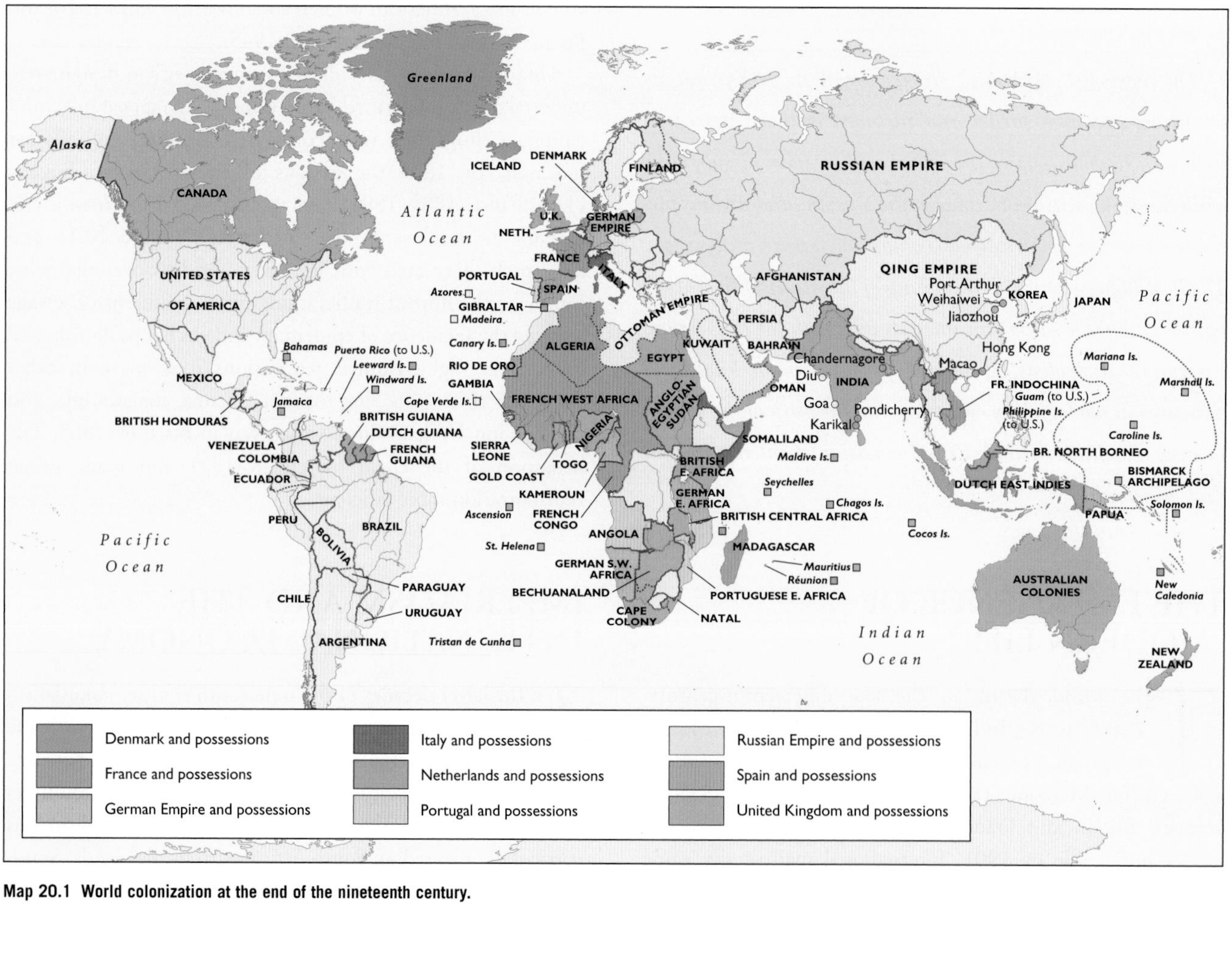

Map 20.1 World colonization at the end of the nineteenth century.

and coffee. During the 1870s in central Asia Russia took control of important sites along the Silk Roads, such as Tashkent, Bokhara, and Samarkand. The French colonized Indochina (modern Laos, Cambodia, and Vietnam) from 1859 to 1893, and the Netherlands continued to control the Dutch East Indies (now Indonesia). In Southeast Asia only Siam (modern Thailand) remained independent. The African nations were divided among France, Spain, Belgium, Portugal, Italy, Germany, and Britain. Only Ethiopia maintained its independence.

The British Empire

Britain ruled the largest colonial empire in the world. Eager for African diamonds, the British colonized South Africa, where Cecil Rhodes (1853–1902) founded the De Beers mining company in 1880. (As of 2004 De Beers still controlled 60 percent of the world diamond market.) Britain had already colonized Australia and New Zealand and now took outright control of parts of Asia. In India the British imposed more efficient systems of administration, established English-style schools, built railroads that helped to industrialize the country, improved commerce, and regulated crops such as coffee, tea, and opium. Britain also banned some Hindu religious practices such as *sati* (suttee)—the expectation that a widow would submit to being burned alive on her husband's funeral pyre.

Despite certain advantages of British imperialism in Africa, Asia, and elsewhere, some effects were devastating. As early as the late eighteenth century Britain was importing fuel from Bengal to benefit its own industry but not to help Bengal. The British over-taxed the Indians, causing famines and widespread starvation. Local Indian textile production was systematically suppressed in order to create markets for British goods. As a result of the mixed effects of British imperialism, historians continue to debate the advantages and disadvantages of colonial rule.

In China the British took advantage of their power to the detriment of the country's population. Britain fought two Opium Wars (1839–1842 and 1856–1860) against China to protect sales of opium to the Chinese. Early in the nineteenth century Britain established a triangular trade policy to block the flow of British silver and gold used to buy goods from China. To achieve this, the British exported opium from India to China, and China exported tea and other products to Britain. As a result, many Chinese became addicted to opium, including the emperor's son, who died of an overdose. Recognizing the seriousness of the drug problem in China, the emperor's diplomats exhorted Queen Victoria to help stem the opium trade, but her government declined to oblige, making war inevitable. When the Chinese tried to block opium imports, the British besieged Canton and occupied Shanghai, establishing a threatening Western presence in China that contributed to longstanding anti-Western nationalism.

IMPRESSIONISM

Impressionist painting began in Paris in the 1860s among a group of artists who regularly gathered to exchange ideas at the Café Guerbois in the Montmartre area of the city. Although the works of Impressionist painters are highly valued today, for a generation or more most people did not understand the style. Compared with the precise edges and smooth surfaces of Neoclassicism, the prominent brushstrokes of Impressionist paintings made them seem rushed and careless. As painters strove for more realism in representing light and color, they tried to capture a moment in time using quick, visible brushstrokes to depict the way the eye sees. Critics objected not only to the rapid effect of the brushstrokes but also to the Impressionist interest in modern life. Like the general public, critics preferred the historical and mythological subjects of earlier styles such as Neoclassical. Struggling to find buyers, the new artists had a kind of outsider status, related to the Romantic notion of *la vie bohème* ("the Bohemian life"). Rejected by the official Parisian exhibition spaces (the Salon), the Impressionists organized eight exhibitions of their own between 1874 and 1886.

Although mainly a French style centered in Paris, Impressionism was influenced by Japanese woodblock prints of the Edo period (1600–1867), which became known in Europe through new global contacts. In 1853 the isolation of Japan was broken when the American commander Matthew Perry forced open the ports of Tokyo (formerly called Edo). Japanese goods—especially screens, craft items, and costumes—poured into the West, and many were exhibited at the Paris World's Fair in 1862. They inspired a new aesthetic, which became known as **japonisme** (see Box, p. 566).

Claude Monet

The leading Impressionist painter was Claude Monet (1840–1926), whose long life and prolific output spanned the entire Impressionist period. Born in Paris, Monet was raised in the northern port city of Le Havre, on the Atlantic Ocean, which may have been responsible for the prevalence of water in his iconography. As an adult, he studied art in Paris, where he lived for most of his career. His painting of 1872 entitled *Impression: Sunrise* (figure **20.4a**) inspired the name given to the style. At first this was a derogatory term denoting a carelessness on the part of the artists, who were accused of hurriedly placing their first "impressions" on the canvas. In fact, however, Monet has accurately conveyed the atmospheric effects of early morning at the port of Le Havre. Formally structuring the picture are distant boats and factories merging into the lavender mist, and the two silhouetted boats in the foreground provide sturdy accents of black. In the detail of *Impression: Sunrise* (figure **20.4b**) we can see how the visible brushstrokes cause the forms to disappear.

Cross-cultural Influences

The Appeal of *Japonisme* and the Japanese Woodblock Print

In the seventeenth century Japanese artists began to produce complex woodblock prints in color. A different block was used for each color, and each had to be printed separately and precisely. The prints that most interested European artists date from the Edo period and belong to the *Ukiyo-e* ("Floating World") school of painting. *Ukiyo-e* prints illustrate aspects of the transient, "floating," world of entertainment, including theater, dance, opera, tea houses, and prostitution, as well as scenes of daily life.

Figure **20.2** shows a view of Mount Fuji from the street Suruga-cho, named for the province in which the famous mountain is located. It is a commercial street, bustling with activity, seen from above like Pissarro's snow-covered boulevard (see figure 20.1) and extending far into the distance. The taste for creating movement with flattened, silhouetted patterns that appears in Pissarro's cityscape can also be seen here.

The portrait of his wife in Japanese costume by Claude Monet reflects the enthusiasm for *japonisme* in late-nineteenth-century France (figure **20.3**). Madame Monet wears a bright red kimono embroidered with birds and foliage. She tilts back slightly, creating a diagonal that is echoed in the patterns of Japanese fans. Counterbalancing her spiral pose is the striking swirl of the Samurai warrior facing in the opposite direction.

20.2 Utagawa Hiroshige, "One Hundred Views of Edo" series, No. 8, *Suruga-cho*, 1856. Woodblock print, 13½ × 8⅝ in. (34.2 × 22 cm). Brooklyn Museum, New York.

20.3 Claude Monet, *La Japonaise*, 1875. Oil on canvas, 7 ft. 7 in. × 4 ft. 8 in. (2.3 × 1.42 m). Museum of Fine Arts, Boston.

Monet's aim in painting was to replicate the way people actually see. He painted landscapes outdoors rather than in a studio—hence the term *plein air* ("open air") painter, which was applied to Monet and other Impressionists. In his later years Monet moved to a country house in Giverny, about 40 miles (65 km) from Paris, where he painted waterlilies and other local landscapes.

In *Interior of St. Lazare Station* (figure **20.5**), Monet's

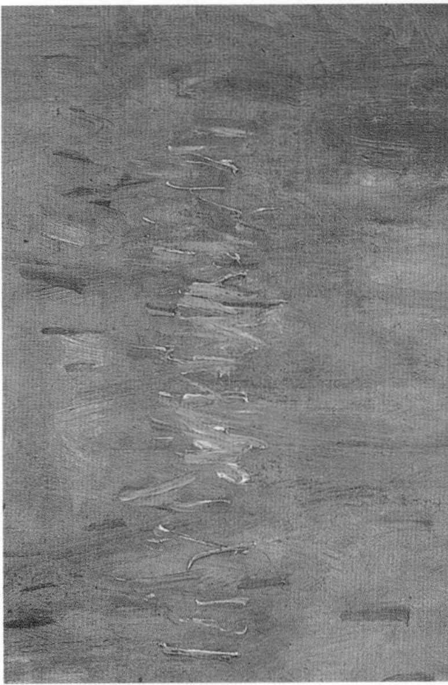

20.4b Detail of *Impression: Sunrise* showing brushstrokes.

20.4a Claude Monet, *Impression: Sunrise*, 1872. Oil on canvas, 19½ × 14½ in. (49.5 × 64.8 cm). Marmottan Museum, Paris. The sun is a crisp orange circle, whereas its reflection in the water is composed of horizontal strokes of orange, red, and white. This Impressionist technique, known as broken color, depicts movement: the sun is a static circle, whereas the horizontal brushstrokes depicting the water indicate that it is flowing sideways. Note also that the paint representing the sun's reflection is dense near the horizon and dissipates as it approaches the picture plane. This creates the impression that we are farther from the sun than we are from the silhouetted boats.

industrial subject is a typical image of modern life in the late nineteenth century. The train in the center steams into the Paris station of St. Lazare, pouring out blue smoke that absorbs the surrounding light. Japanese influence is evident in the patterned verticals at the left and the shadows falling on the tracks, in the silhouetting, and in the cropped viewpoint. The predominant browns contain the blues and rose colors in the atmosphere, while a sharp red can be seen in the car to the right of the black engine. Throughout the picture, industrial smoke envelops form just as industry itself dominated the nineteenth-century cities of Western Europe.

20.5 Claude Monet, *Interior of St. Lazare Station*, 1877. Oil on canvas, 29¾ × 42 in. (75.5 × 104 cm). Musée d'Orsay, Paris.

EDOUARD MANET

Edouard Manet painted in the Realist style in the 1860s (see Chapter 19), but in the 1870s, inspired by the Impressionist interest in light and color, he expanded his palette. Whereas the 1865 *Olympia* (see figure 19.11) was predominantly composed of dark browns and greens, with the reclining nude highlighted in a harsh light, *Nana* of 1877 has richer, more varied colors and textures (figure **20.6**). There is also an increase in the use of broken color to create tactile illusions. As with Olympia, Nana was immediately recognizable as a prostitute. She was a character in Zola's popular novel *L'Assommoir* (1877) about an alcoholic laundress and her daughter Nana. In Manet's picture Nana stands half-dressed before a mirror and pauses in the midst of applying make-up to gaze at the viewer. The two candles by the mirror are traditional *vanitas* symbols, alluding to the passage of time and the inevitability of decay and death. The large Japanese screen in the background shows an elegantly feathered bird—a metaphor for Nana herself—strutting by the shore. Nana's male client, cropped as in a candid photograph, observes her as we do.

20.6 *above* **Edouard Manet, *Nana*, 1877. Oil on canvas, 5 ft. 5/8 in. × 3 ft. 9 3/4 in. (1.54 × 1.15 m). Kunsthalle, Hamburg.**
Rejected for the Salon of 1877, this painting was exhibited in a shop window on one of the Paris boulevards. It attracted a great deal of attention for its subject matter—the model was a well-known actress and the mistress of the Prince of Orange. Her nickname was "Lemon."

EDGAR DEGAS

Hilaire-Germain-Edgar Degas (1834–1917) came from a wealthy family and joined the Impressionists in the 1860s. Among his enormous output are scenes of café life, ballerinas, bathers, circuses, concerts, horse-races, and portraits. Degas was interested in forms moving through space and in the juxtaposition of motion and stasis.

In *Monsieur Perrot's Dance Class* (figure **20.7**) the artist juxtaposes the strong vertical stance of the teacher and his cane with the varied movements and poses of the dancers. The ballet master, together with the green marble columns, structures the painting formally and stabilizes the slanting floor. This tilt is a sign of a progressive flattening of the picture space in nineteenth-century painting. It also conveys the impression of a candid camera view—as if the photographer had not quite centered the scene or aligned the camera with the floor. In the foreground a watering can echoes the pose of the dancer holding the fan, and the small dog gazing past her enhances the candid effect of the scene.

20.7 *right* **Edgar Degas, *Monsieur Perrot's Dance Class*, *c.* 1875. Oil on canvas, 33 1/2 × 29 in. (85 × 74 cm). Musée d'Orsay, Paris.**

PIERRE-AUGUSTE RENOIR

Pierre-Auguste Renoir (1841–1919) painted scenes of everyday life, Paris streets, and later, nudes. His father was a tailor from Limoges, who moved to Paris when Renoir was three years old. Renoir first studied porcelain painting and then fine arts in Paris, where he was a member of the Impressionist

20.8 Pierre-Auguste Renoir, *The Swing*, 1876. Oil on canvas, 36¼ × 28¾ in. (92 × 73 cm). Musée d'Orsay, Paris.

group. Throughout his career he was plagued by serious physical problems. In 1880, after breaking his right arm, he learned to paint with his left hand. Eight years later he was diagnosed with rheumatoid arthritis and by 1910 was partly paralyzed and had to paint from a wheelchair. Eventually, the brush had to be tied to his hand so that he could continue to work.

Renoir shared the Impressionist interest in the appearance of figures and objects in outdoor light and shadow, which he explored in *The Swing* of 1876 (figure **20.8**). The scene takes place outdoors, in a park. The foreground shows a warm, sunny day, with members of a family leisurely watching a woman on a swing. Spots of sunlight filter through the foliage, creating fleeting patterns of shadow. Broken color pervades the canvas, resulting in an impression of all-over movement bathing the figures and the ground. In the distance a second group of figures is nearly engulfed by the prominent brushstrokes.

The little girl at the far left stares fixedly at the scene, whereas the man behind the tree looks out at the viewer. There is also a kind of photographic, positive/negative effect in the dark blue bows on the woman's light dress juxtaposed with the light patches on the man's dark blue jacket. The tilted ground and flattened patterns indicate both Japanese and photographic influence.

MARY CASSATT

Mary Cassatt (1844–1926) was the leading American artist to exhibit regularly with the Impressionists in Paris. Her career benefited from the support of her lifelong friend, Edgar Degas, and Cassatt, in turn, tried to help the Impressionists by encouraging her wealthy American friends and relatives to buy their works. Her own subjects are usually mothers and children, which seems to be the case in *A Woman and a Girl Driving* (figure **20.9**). In reality, however, the woman is the artist's older sister, Lydia, and the girl is Degas's niece, Odile. The horse-and-cart and groom belonged to Cassatt's wealthy Philadelphia family, which had moved to Paris in 1887. The fact that a woman is driving is perhaps an indication of Cassatt's independent spirit.

20.9 *below* Mary Cassatt, *A Woman and a Girl Driving*, 1881. Oil on canvas, 35⁵⁄₁₆ × 51⅜ in. (89.7 × 130.5 cm). Philadelphia Museum of Art.

JAMES MCNEILL WHISTLER

The American Impressionist James McNeill Whistler (1834–1903), who also worked outside the United States, had a flamboyant personality and was a successful portrait painter. He was born in Lowell, Massachusetts, spent part of his childhood in Russia, where his father was the engineer in charge of constructing the Moscow–St. Petersburg Railroad, visited Paris, and finally settled in London. His wealthy British patron, the shipping magnate Frederick Leyland, commissioned him to decorate the dining room of his London house as a setting for *The Princess from the Land of Porcelain.* This painting shows a white woman in Oriental costume standing by a screen. Her robe reflects the Impressionist interest in Far Eastern motifs, while the blurred form and visible brushstrokes are characteristic of Impressionist technique. The room as a whole, entitled *Harmony in Blue and Gold* (figure **20.10**), was a showcase for Leyland's collection of Chinese porcelain, to which Whistler added Japanese motifs. But Whistler went beyond the original commission and decorated the window shutters with blue and gold peacocks and painted turquoise peacock feathers all over the walls. Leyland was not pleased, and, to memorialize his patron's irritation, Whistler painted two fighting peacocks, one representing himself, and the other, perching on gold coins, the wealthy Leyland.

On February 15, 1877, an article on the Peacock Room appeared in London's *Pall Mall Gazette.* Whistler, unbeknownst to his patron, had invited the press to view his work:

> We have lately had the opportunity of inspecting a very remarkable specimen of decorative painting executed by Mr. Whistler for the dining room of Mr. Leyland's house in Prince's Gate. The artist has chosen different tints of blue and gold as the material of his work, and he has taken the plumage of the peacock as the foundation of his design . . .
>
> Peacocks have been painted before, and blue and gold is no new combination of colour; but it is nevertheless true that in Mr. Whistler's hands these familiar materials take an entirely new form and become a thing of original and independent invention . . . The contrasted masses of blue and gold . . . here assume a light and fairy-like character; and we feel no more disposed to reproach the artist for the brilliancy of his colouring or the fantastic freedom of his design than we should be to lecture the peacock itself upon its plumage, or to object to the pride of its movement.

20.10 James McNeill Whistler, *Harmony in Blue and Gold: The Peacock Room*, northeast corner, with *The Princess from the Land of Porcelain* over the fireplace, 1876–1877. Oil paint and gold leaf on canvas, leather, and wood. Room 14 ft. (4.26 m) high. Freer Gallery, Smithsonian Institution, Washington, D.C.

AUGUSTE RODIN

Sculpture is not generally associated with Impressionism, but the rough surface textures of Rodin's work share the Impressionist interest in making the viewer aware of the artist's medium. Although he worked in a Realist style (see figure 19.5), Rodin left many of his sculptures with a rough surface. This creates a sense that the work is not "finished." Rodin's famous sculpture *The Kiss* (figure **20.11**) portrays an intimate moment and also reveals the presence of the artist in a new way. The marble figures merge into a mutual embrace as they emerge from the textured stone on which they sit. The right hip of the woman, for example, belongs both to the polished surface of the body and to the chipped, unpolished stone from which she was formed. As in his *Balzac*, Rodin's *Kiss* retains the sense of the artist's sculptural process, in contrast to the more "finished" surfaces of Renaissance and Baroque sculptures.

20.11 Auguste Rodin, *The Kiss*, 1886. Marble, 6 ft. 2 in. (1.9 m) high. Rodin Museum, Paris.

THE SYMBOLIST MOVEMENT

The Symbolist Movement flourished in the last decades of the nineteenth century. Symbolism was concerned with the unconscious mind, the imagination, and sensation, and it appealed to painters, poets, dramatists, and musicians. Although there is no Symbolist philosophy *per se*, certain philosophical ideas have been related to Symbolism. The Symbolists admired the writings of the eighteenth-century Swedish thinker Emanuel Swedenborg (1688–1772), a naturalist who turned to mysticism. His descriptions of visions from the spirit world influenced Symbolist imagery.

The ideas about time, sensation, and intuition of the French philosopher Henri Bergson (1859–1941) also had affinities with Symbolism. Bergson believed that sensation is more profound and therefore more real than intellect. Sensation, like a dream, can merge time into a single image or feeling state and is thus more fluid and imaginative than rational, logically ordered thought.

Another important force in Symbolism were the early publications of the Austrian physician and psychoanalyst Sigmund Freud (1856–1939). Freud studied hypnosis in Paris and, with his Austrian colleague, Dr. Josef Breuer (1842–1925), discovered the emotional basis of hysterical symptoms. They published the results of their work in *Studies on Hysteria* (1893–1895). Since most recognized nineteenth-century cases of hysteria occurred in women, it can be said that Freud was the first doctor in the history of Western medicine to listen to women and to consider their physical and emotional illnesses with the same seriousness as those of men.

In *The Interpretation of Dreams* (1899) Freud produced the first scientific explanation of the formation of dreams. In that work he also introduced the theory of the Oedipus Complex. Basing his theory on clinical experience as well as on Sophocles' play and Greek myth (see Chapter 6), Freud described the Oedipus Complex as a universal, and biologically determined, fantasy in the life of every child, although at first he focused mainly on the boy's Oedipus Complex. During the course of his career Freud continued to revise and refine his theories. In addition to its impact on Symbolism, Freud's work had an enormous influence on literature, art, psychology, and medical practice in the twentieth century (see Box, p. 572).

READING SELECTION

Freud and Breuer, *1900: a Fin-de-siècle Reader*, on Anna O. and the founding of psychoanalysis, PWC5-240

In the same year that Freud published *The Interpretation of Dreams*, Bergson published *Time and Free Will.* Like Freud, Bergson understood that there is no time in the unconscious, a fact that became an important aspect of Symbolist style.

20.12 Gustave Moreau, *The Peri*, c. 1870–1875. Pen and pencil, 11½ × 7 in. (29 × 18 cm). Musée Moreau, Paris.
In Persian myth, the peri is a graceful sorceress formed from fire and excluded from heaven. She combines beauty and benevolence with evil, and is thus both dangerous and seductive.

In 1886 the Symbolist Movement was codified in the manifesto published by the Greek-born French poet Jean Moréas (1856–1910). Entitled *XIXe Siècle (19th Century)*, the manifesto describes the aims of Symbolism as giving form to ideas, myths, and dreams. Rejecting the Realist interest in social class, the Impressionist painting of modern life, Romantic politics, and Neoclassical historical works, Symbolists depicted the world of the imagination, and their works are often imbued with macabre, perverse, or erotic elements.

The Symbolist Movement was centered mainly in France and Belgium. In France the leading Symbolist painter was Gustave Moreau (1826–1898), whose *The Peri* (figure **20.12**) captures the sense of a slightly unsettling dreamworld. The peri (a Persian sprite) is carried aloft by a winged dragon. Moreau conveys an erotic impression in the peri's languid pose, the phallic forms of the dragon (tail, wings, long neck), and in the open flower buds. At the right, curious domed towers suggest the mysterious East as a rocky landscape fades into the horizon on the left.

Society and Culture

The Interpretation of Dreams and the Oedipus Complex

Sigmund Freud first mentions the Oedipus Complex in his 1899 publication *The Interpretation of Dreams.* Based on early clinical work and his own self-analysis, Freud made two momentous discoveries in the late nineteenth century. He identified the mechanisms of dream formation, and he uncovered the nature of early childhood sexual fantasies.

Freud lists four psychic phenomena that produce dreams: representability, displacement, condensation, and symbolization. Dreams are nearly always images, hence the requirement of representability: in order to construct a dream, its underlying idea must be translated into a picture. **Displacement** is the means by which the mind moves an image from one place or one time to another. We might, for example, think we are in Paris in a dream, but the city we see looks like New York. In that case, we have displaced, or superimposed, Paris onto New York.

The mechanism that makes displacement possible is called **condensation**, for the dreamer has to condense (or merge) the two cities. Finally, **symbolization** is the ability to create symbols; in dreams things are rarely what they seem. If, for example, we dream of the Eiffel Tower, which is both a phallic symbol because of its shape and a symbol of Paris because of its location, we might be expressing a wish for sexual potency, which we associate with the romance of Paris. When he wrote *The Interpretation of Dreams*, therefore, Freud believed that dreams were representations of unfulfilled wishes. However, he later modified this view when studying nightmares of shell-shock victims from World War I (see Chapter 21).

Freud's discovery of the Oedipus Complex, like a great deal of Realist art and literature, challenged conventional thought. Children had generally been assumed to be sexually innocent, but Freud identified a universal fantasy—the Oedipus Complex—in which children create a romance with parents (or parental figures). In the early part of his career Freud focused on the boy's Oedipus Complex. A boy (from about the age of three in Freud's formulation) wants exclusive possession of his mother, which entails eliminating his father. This makes the boy feel guilty and fear his father's retaliation in the form of castration. Gradually, the boy renounces his wish for exclusivity with his mother and identifies with his father (which generally happens between five and six years of age). This leads to the formation of the boy's superego, or conscience, and is the root of his sense of morality.

In the early twentieth century Freud refined his view of the Oedipus Complex. He discussed homosexual and heterosexual outcomes of the Complex as well as various factors that influence these outcomes. The girl's Oedipus Complex, Freud discovered, is more complicated than the boy's, because her first love object is usually a maternal figure. In contrast to the boy, therefore, the girl's heterosexual development requires her to shift her attachment from women to men. Freud did not formulate the nature of the girl's development for many years, and he did not publish a full explanation of it until 1930.

SYMBOLIST POETRY

The most famous Symbolist poets were French, although they were influenced by the poetic rhythms and macabre imagination of Edgar Allan Poe (see Chapter 18). Symbolist imagery, like dreams, can be elusive and enigmatic. Symbolist poets aimed to convey suggestion, implication, and evocation, rather than focusing on empirical observation and detailed descriptions. They evoked unconscious moods by writing incomplete, unfinished lines, which force the reader to supply connecting syntax.

CHARLES BAUDELAIRE Charles Baudelaire (1821–1867), a friend of Gustave Courbet (see Chapter 19), began his career as a Realist art critic. In his review of the 1846 Salon, he agreed with Courbet that artists should paint modern life. But he later abandoned Realism and turned to a kind of proto-Symbolist poetry, in which he celebrated the beauty of evil. Baudelaire's influence on the Symbolist Movement was profound.

Called a poetic "decadent," Baudelaire led a Bohemian life in the Latin Quarter of Paris. His father died when he was very young, and the boy took his mother's remarriage as a personal affront. Later involved in a homosexual scandal, Baudelaire was whisked away from France by his family and taken on a trip to India. He returned to Paris after ten months and began an affair with Jeanne Duval, a Mulatto woman, who inspired his poem "La Vénus noire" ("Black Venus"). His outraged family cut off his inheritance, forcing him to live frugally for the rest of his life.

In 1857 Baudelaire published his famous *Les Fleurs du mal* (*Flowers of Evil*); the second edition of 1861 contained 129 poems. "Dans ce livre atroce," he wrote, "j'ai mis toute ma pensée, tout mon coeur, toute ma réligion (travestie), toute ma haine." ("In this atrocious book, I have put all of my thought, my whole heart, my entire religion (a travesty), and all my hate.")

Baudelaire believed in "correspondences"—that is, in mystical connections between the supernatural and natural worlds—and making these connections possible, in his view, was sensation:

> Nature is a temple whose living pillars
> Sometimes allow confused words to escape:
> Man passes by through forests of symbols
> That observe him with a familiar glance.

In "Hymn to Beauty," Baudelaire conveys his ambivalent view of beauty as both divine and infernal. He queries whether the source of beauty, which inspires evil and contentment, is heaven or hell. The effect of beauty, he says, is similar to that of wine in being unpredictable as well as desirable:

> Do you hail from the sky or the abyss,
> O Beauty? Your appearance, infernal and divine,
> pours dimly benefits and crime,
> and for that it can be compared to wine.

READING SELECTION

Baudelaire, *Les Fleurs du mal*, concerning a swan and a prostitute, PWC5-139

STÉPHANE MALLARMÉ Stéphane Mallarmé (1842–1898), a leader of the Symbolist Movement, dedicated his life to poetry. He studied in Paris, read *Les Fleurs du mal* in 1861, traveled to England, and married in 1863. He taught school to earn a living, first in the South of France, and then in Paris. An ardent admirer of Poe, Mallarmé believed that poetry mediates between the divine and the human and between art and non-art. In his view, poets should use words to suggest impressions, rather than to name them explicitly. They should depict not a thing itself, but rather its effect.

"Brise Marine" ("Sea Breeze") of 1865 expresses his overwhelming sense of *ennui*. He envies the birds who seem intoxicated by their release into an unknown freedom. He is weighed down by a humdrum existence, but birds defy gravity and soar over the sea:

> The flesh is dulled, alas! And I have read all the books.
> Flee, flee over yonder. I sense that the birds are drunk
> on the unknown foam of sea and sky.

Mallarmé's best-known poem, "The Afternoon of a Faun" (1876), is the story of a hybrid mythological creature, the faun (part human and part goat). Caught in the transitional state of reverie, the faun wonders if his recollection of pursuing a nymph is real or only a dream. His daydream satisfies the Symbolist attraction to states of mind that fluctuate between reality and unreality, nature and imagination, and intellect and sensation.

PAUL VERLAINE Paul Verlaine (1844–1896) studied in Paris and worked in city administration. In his spare time he frequented literary café society and came to know Baudelaire, whose influence is reflected in his *Fêtes galantes* (1869). In these poems Verlaine writes of refined sensations, conveying emotional ambivalence just as Baudelaire had done when musing on the nature of beauty. The elegant grace of Verlaine's verse and his poetic landscapes are also reminiscent of Watteau (see Chapter 17). The last stanza describes the soul as a landscape populated by *fêtes galantes*. Figures sing sadly in a minor key by the light of the moon:

> By the calm light of the moon, sad and beautiful
> Which makes the birds in the trees dream
> And the fountains sob in ecstasy
> The delicate fountains among the marbles.

In *Jadis et naguère* (*Formerly and of Late*) of 1885 Verlaine describes the spiritual qualities of love. This collection contains his well-known "L'Art poétique" ("The Art of Poetry"), a celebration of poetry-as-music, which has been considered a manifesto of Symbolist poetry. It begins with the famous line: *De la musique avant toute chose* ("Music above all else").

Music above all else
And for that impair* is preferable
More vague and soluble in the air
Weightless and fluid.

* A type of fluid verse in which the syntax is literary rather than grammatically correct.

(De la musique avant toute chose,
Et pour cela préfère l'impair,
Plus vague et plus soluble dans l'air,
Sans rien en lui qui pese ou qui pose.)

ARTHUR RIMBAUD Arthur Rimbaud (1854–1891) was an adolescent genius and a rebel, who began writing great poetry at the age of sixteen. He resisted bourgeois convention and opposed imperialism and Napoleon III. He was also anti-clerical and strongly disapproved of organized religion. Life on the margins of society appealed to Rimbaud's sense of adventure and to his craving for all forms of love, madness, and suffering.

Rimbaud created an original form of free verse, which he called the "Alchemy of the Verb"—a language of sounds, smells, and colors that combines hallucinatory images with childhood memory. In "Vowels" (1871) he makes the relation between letters and colors explicit: "A black, E white, I red, U green, O blue: vowels."

In "Illuminations" in the sense of an illuminated manuscript page, Rimbaud creates brief word-pictures, or words-as-pictures. For example:

Dawn

I embraced the dawn of summer.
Nothing moved in front of the palace. The water was dead.
The camps of shadows remained on the forest path.
I walked, reviving breaths that were quick [alive] yet lukewarm;
And precious stones watched, and wings rose up in silence.

Rimbaud ceased writing when he was twenty-one and simply traveled until a tumor of the knee took him back to France. His leg was amputated, and he died shortly thereafter.

SYMBOLIST THEATER: MAETERLINCK

Symbolist theater was strongly anti-Realist. Its characters tended to symbolize the playwright's inner life rather than portray contemporary society. Although there are symbolic elements in most plays, they are the central feature in Symbolist theater.

The Belgian author Maurice Maeterlinck (1862–1949) was the leading Symbolist playwright. Influenced by the musical language and atmospheric effects of Mallarmé and Verlaine, Maeterlinck believed theater should evoke mysterious atmospheres and that dialogue should be both elusive and allusive.

Maeterlinck's most famous Symbolist play, *Pelléas et Mélisande* (1892), is the story of the adolescent girl Mélisande and her illicit romance. Although married to the widower prince, Golaud, Mélisande falls in love with his brother, Pelléas. Her infidelity to Golaud is shown symbolically when she drops her wedding ring into a fountain. When Golaud discovers their romance he kills Pelléas, and Mélisande commits suicide.

The tragic quality of Maeterlinck's play is reinforced by the staging, which evokes a sense of foreboding. A gauze curtain separates the audience from the stage, creating mysterious shadows and blurring the action. Backdrops are dark, props are minimal, and costumes are not identifiable as to time or place, in contrast to the here and now of Realist theater.

In 1911, Maeterlinck was awarded the Nobel Prize (see Box) for literature.

Society and Culture

Alfred Nobel and the Nobel Prize

Alfred Bernhard Nobel (1833–1896), a Swedish chemist and industrialist, invented dynamite in 1867. In 1875 he patented the more powerful explosive, gelignite, and produced smokeless gunpowder, balistite (compare the word "ballistic"), in 1887. With the fortune he made manufacturing explosives and drilling for oil in Azerbaijan, near the Caspian Sea, he established the Nobel Prize. His will endowed prizes in physics, chemistry, medicine, literature, and world peace. Recipients are chosen by committees in Norway and Sweden, but only the peace prize is presented in Oslo—the rest are awarded in Stockholm every December 12. The Swedish National Bank endowed an additional prize in economics, which was first awarded in 1969.

MUSIC: DEBUSSY

The French composer Claude Debussy (1862–1918) has been considered both Impressionist and Symbolist. Like the Impressionist artists, he wanted to create moods and impressions by focusing on "colors." He thus used unique and delicate combinations of instruments and extreme ranges of pitch. He also created subtle harmonies that stand on their own as decorative elements rather than serving as functional chords that resolve in traditional ways. However, his friends were authors rather than painters, and he set Symbolist poetry—especially by Verlaine—to music in his songs. In the poems of the Symbolists he found fantasy, freedom, and concentration of feeling which could be paralleled in music.

Debussy's first great success, an orchestral piece based on a poem by Mallarmé, was his *Prelude to "The Afternoon of a Faun"* (1894). A musical equivalent of the poem, it is a dreamy, sensuous work with prominent flute and harp writing. The main theme slides mellifluously down and up a chromatic scale of five notes, typically unsuggestive of any particular tonality. Debussy was searching for a musical style that was precisely imagined yet fluid and unrestrained by rules. He wanted simplicity, space, and sometimes silence.

Another source of Debussy's inspiration was Southeast Asian music, especially the Indonesian **gamelan** (see Box), which he heard in 1889 at the Paris World's Fair. A few of his works have Eastern titles—*Pagodes* (1903) for piano is an example—but many others sound somewhat Oriental because of their use of modes and of melodic decoration.

Poetic images of water and moonlight pervade Debussy's music, as in "Clair de lune," the third movement of the *Suite bergamasque* (1890) for piano solo. Evoking mysteries associated with the moon and its nighttime magic, this piece is arranged in the Listening Selection for full orchestra. Listen for the rhythms, at first vague and hesitant, then flowing smoothly, for rippling effects, for fragmented melody, for poignancy and then a build-up of volume and passion.

MUSIC LISTENING SELECTION

Debussy, *Suite bergamasque*, "Clair de lune." Slovak Radio Orchestra, conductor Keith Clark, CD track 19

It has been said that Debussy took music out of the salon and concert hall into the open air. One such "open-air" work is his orchestral piece *La Mer* (*The Sea*, 1905). The atmosphere of the ocean is evoked in the titles of each of its three movements—"From dawn to noon on the sea," "Play of the waves," and "Dialogue of the wind and the sea." Musically, the form is free, taking its structure from variation in texture and orchestration. Thus the strings may be divided into fifteen parts to create a shimmer of sound, or they may play in unison to draw the music to a climax. In *La Mer* the music flows like the tides and sparkles like the sun's reflections on the surface of the sea.

In 1902, Debussy finished his only complete opera. A rendition of Maeterlinck's *Pelléas et Mélisande*, it is atmospheric, dream-like, and elusive (figure **20.13**). This story of love and death in the kingdom of *Allemonde* (all the world) has little action, which leaves space for Debussy to capture the feelings of the characters. A reticent work, it uses the orchestra to express a concentration of emotion. In a letter of 1911, Debussy wrote: "How much one has first to find and then suppress, to reach the naked flesh of emotion."

Debussy had a profound effect on the music of the twentieth century. His improvisational fluidity, his presentation of several planes of timbre and material simultaneously, his combination of modality and chromaticism, and his breakdown of form are summed up in his assertion: "There is no theory. You have merely to listen."

Society and Culture

The Indonesian Gamelan

At the Paris World's Fair, Debussy attended performances of the gamelan (literally "musical ensemble"), the characteristic orchestra of the islands of Java and Bali. Gamelan music was traditionally performed in courts, but it was also played in Hindu temples in villages in Bali and to accompany dance, drama, and puppet shows.

The gamelan ensemble, which has several regional varieties, consists mostly of metal xylophones and sets of small and large gongs. These can be supplemented by drums, as well as other instruments, and by singing. Compositions are often structured in the form of repeated melodies (**ostinatos**) set to extended metric cycles punctuated by gongs. While Balinese gamelan music has a manic-sounding energy, the characteristic gamelan music of Java is statelier. It is sometimes compared to a moonlit, flowing river, and its dreamy quality inspired late nineteenth-century composers such as Debussy.

20.13 Symbolist atmosphere created by the décor of Debussy's *Pelléas et Mélisande*, after Maeterlinck.
Note that by backlighting the scenery, the director silhouettes both the décor and the actors. As a result, the characters merge into the mysterious setting, which appears to extend far back into an unknown distance.

POST-IMPRESSIONISM

Post-Impressionism, literally "after Impressionism," is something of a catch-all term for the work of a group of late-nineteenth-century painters. They continued and expanded Impressionist interests, and several were also involved in the Symbolist Movement. Post-Impressionist pictures are typically colorful, with distinctive, prominent brushstrokes. In their response to modern life, Post-Impressionist painters chose similar subject matter to that of the Impressionists, although some incorporate Symbolist elements into their iconography. In contrast to the Impressionists, who often created blurred forms, Post-Impressionist painters generally preferred to maintain clear edges. As a result, their paintings appear more structured than those of the Impressionists.

20.14 Henri de Toulouse-Lautrec, *Jane Avril at the "Jardin de Paris,"* 1893. Lithograph poster, $51\frac{1}{8} \times 37\frac{1}{2}$ in. (130×95 cm).
The poster advertises the dancer Jane Avril doing the can-can on the stage of the Jardin de Paris (Garden of Paris), a well-known nightclub. As in Degas's canvases, the floor tilts sharply, and Lautrec shows us a cropped viewpoint. Echoing the diagonal of the dancer's raised leg is the prominent double bass denoting the orchestra pit. The bright orange and yellow of Jane Avril's costume and her red lips attract the viewer's gaze and engage us with the dynamic energy of her dance.

HENRI DE TOULOUSE-LAUTREC

The Post-Impressionist painter Henri de Toulouse-Lautrec (1864–1901) popularized the poster as a form of advertisement (figure **20.14**). Like Degas and Manet, Toulouse-Lautrec came from a wealthy family and did not have to struggle to earn a living. Like the Impressionists, his subjects include the cafés, dance halls, nightclubs, and brothels that were associated with "modern life." Left crippled by two childhood accidents, Lautrec enjoyed watching dancers perform and in his work aimed to capture their movements through space. He considered himself ugly and found beauty in ugliness. "Ugliness," he declared, "always and everywhere has its enchanting side; it is exciting to hit upon it where no one has ever noticed it before." Toulouse-Lautrec died from alcoholism at the age of thirty-seven.

GEORGES SEURAT

Georges Seurat (1859–1891) studied Delacroix's writings on color as a prelude to evolving his own color theories. His interest in contemporary scientific studies of vision led to his theory of Divisionism, which was based on optical mixtures. He subscribed to the Symbolist notion, advanced by Henri Bergson, that juxtaposed colors are read by the viewer's eye as their combined color—that is, a blue next to a yellow is perceived as green, a red next to a yellow as orange, and a blue next to a red as purple. Seurat died at the age of thirty-two, leaving others to test his theories further.

A painstaking worker, Seurat typically applied paint in dots of color. He called himself a Divisionist, though the term "pointillism" is more often used to describe his technique. His scenes of leisure include entertainment and the upper-middle-class promenade (figure **20.15**), but even when he depicts movement, his figures have a curiously static, geometric quality. In this painting Seurat demonstrates an Impressionist discovery about light and shadow—namely, that shadows are not gray or black, as they had been painted for centuries. Instead, Seurat painted the shadows on the grass a dark green, and the reflections in the water are the same colors as the reflected objects.

PAUL CÉZANNE

Like Giotto in the fourteenth century, Paul Cézanne (1839–1906) changed the way of representing space in painting and had an enormous influence on later styles. Cézanne's innovation was to restructure pictorial space so that it resembled the faceted composition of a crystal. As a result, in contrast to previous styles, Cezanne created spatial shifts that obscure the traditional distinction between foreground and background. His brushstrokes are typically rectangular even when depicting a rounded object such as an apple. Cézanne believed that nature was composed of geometric forms—"a cone, a sphere, and a cylinder"—and that painters should render nature geometrically.

20.15 Georges Seurat, *A Sunday Afternoon on the Island of La Grande Jatte*, 1884–1886. Oil on canvas, 6 ft. 9 in. × 10 ft. ³⁄₈ in. (2.07 × 3.08 m). Art Institute of Chicago.

Cézanne came from a financially comfortable, bourgeois family in Provence, in the South of France. Classically educated, he resisted his father's ambition that he become a lawyer or banker and decided to make his mark in Paris as a great painter. His early paintings are dark—he was called the "black painter"—and their subjects are violent or erotic, but later he expanded his palette and reduced his content primarily to portraits, still lifes, landscapes, and bathers (figure **20.16**).

20.16 *right* **Paul Cézanne, *The Great Bathers*, 1898–1905. Oil on canvas, 6 ft. 10 in. × 8 ft. 3 in. (2.08 × 2.52 m). Philadelphia Museum of Art.**
Here Cézanne combines bathers with landscape. The figures and trees form a pyramid that structures the picture plane. The crystalline brushstrokes seem in constant motion. Blues shift in front of, and behind, the trees. The browns comprising the trees and ground are found again in the sky. Cézanne's landscape, like nature itself, is thus in continual flux, making it difficult to identify a particular time or place.

PAUL GAUGUIN

The Post-Impressionist Paul Gauguin (1848–1903) was born in Paris, lived for a time in Peru with his mother's family, joined the French navy, and worked as a stockbroker. He deserted his wife and children in 1871 to devote himself to painting with the Impressionists. He then became influenced by Symbolism, especially when he was painting in Brittany, in the north of France. He also traveled to the Caribbean, Central America, and the South Pacific. Gauguin thought of Tahiti, where he spent the last eight years of his life, as a new Eden. In his best-known style he combines Tahitian myth with Christian narrative and Symbolism with Post-Impressionism (figure **20.17**).

Gauguin considered Europe a ruined, degenerate culture and sought paradise in Oceania. He painted many pictures during the time he spent there, and kept an autobiographical journal, *Noa Noa*, describing his impressions. On the silence of a Tahitian night, he wrote:

> the rays of the moon play through the bamboo reeds, standing equidistant from each other before my hut, and reach even to my bed. And these regular intervals of light suggest a musical instrument to me—the reed-pipe of the ancients, which was familiar to the Maori, and is called *vivo* by them. The moon and the bamboo reeds made it assume an exaggerated form—an instrument that remained silent throughout the day, but at night by the grace of the moon calls forth in the memory of the dreamer well-loved melodies. Under this music I fell asleep.

20.17 Paul Gauguin, *Ia Orana Maria* (*Ave Maria*), 1891. Oil on canvas, $44^{3}/_{4} \times 34^{1}/_{2}$ in. (113.7 × 87.6 cm). The Metropolitan Museum of Art, New York. Gauguin's interest in Tahiti and Polynesian subjects coincided with the European vogue for Oceania, which is sometimes called "Primitivism" and which overlapped with the vogue for *japonisme*. In this painting he merges the Christian Annunciation with a lush Polynesian setting. At the far left, partly hidden by a green tree, is a Tahitian angel Gabriel announcing Christ's birth to a Tahitian version of the Virgin Mary at the right. Her columnar form supports an infant, recalling the totemic structures of the South Pacific, and both she and the infant are haloed. Two worshippers approach in adoration.

VINCENT VAN GOGH

Vincent van Gogh (1853–1890) painted for only the last ten years of his short life, but after his death he became one of the most valued and widely studied artists of the late nineteenth century. Born in the Netherlands to a stern clergyman and a mother depressed over the infant death of an older brother, also named Vincent, van Gogh led a lonely childhood. He studied for the ministry, trying to emulate his father, but failed to become ordained. He worked for a time as a school teacher in England and as an assistant in his uncle's art gallery in Belgium, and then moved to Paris where his brother, Theo, was an art dealer. Vincent lived his entire life in poverty, unable—with one possible exception—to sell a single painting, and was financially dependent on Theo. The two men exchanged letters regularly, and these have become a valuable source for van Gogh's many biographers.

Aside from a brief stint in an art class, van Gogh was a self-taught artist. He read Delacroix's writings on color and studied the Rembrandts on view in Holland. Like Rembrandt, van Gogh produced many self-portraits (figure **20.18**), but in contrast to his Dutch predecessor, van Gogh created form through Post-Impressionist color rather than by Baroque shifts in light and dark. Here he structures his face in yellows and greens and sets it against a purple background enlivened by thick brushstrokes. The whites of his eyes are green, as is the interior of his ear, and the artist's orange beard contrasts sharply with the blue painter's smock, blue being opposite orange on the color wheel.

The entire surface of the canvas is covered with broken color, creating the fluid dynamism for which van Gogh's works are known. He holds a palette, which contains the very colors used in the self-portrait, showing himself specifically as the painter of this picture.

In addition to his revealing self-portraits, van Gogh painted many pictures with autobiographical content. His *Sower with*

20.18 *left* Vincent van Gogh, ***Self-portrait***, 1889. Oil on canvas, 22½ × 17¼ in. (57 × 43.5 cm). National Gallery of Art, Washington, D.C.

Setting Sun (figure **20.19**), for example, is one of several works on the same theme. Stylistically the image is derived from the flattened patterns of Japanese woodblock prints, which van Gogh collected. The thick brushstrokes and dynamic colors are characteristic of his late period. Van Gogh's efforts to identify with his minister-father are suggested by the position of the large, haloesque sun, a frequent motif in his paintings and one that has a traditional association with the light of Jesus. The image of the sower, which van Gogh also repeated, has been read in relation to the broad theme of fertilizing. In that context the sower alludes to van Gogh's unfulfilled wish to marry and have children.

READING SELECTION

van Gogh, *Letters*, a painter on the edge, PWC5-002-B

20.19 Vincent van Gogh, ***The Sower with Setting Sun (After Millet), Arles, November 1888.*** Oil on jute, mounted on canvas, 29 × 36½ in. (73.5 × 93 cm). Foundation E. G. Bührle Collection, Zurich.

EDVARD MUNCH

The style of the Norwegian Edvard Munch (1863–1944) combines the Symbolist expression of moods and emotion with Post-Impressionist color and vibrant brushstrokes (figure **20.20**). Munch's pictures, like van Gogh's, reflect a troubled life. His mother died of tuberculosis when he was five, and his sister died ten years later. In 1880 Munch abandoned his engineering studies to become a painter, traveled to Paris, and came under the influence of Manet. His paintings, which reveal the artist's nervous, depressive disposition, shocked the public.

20.20 Edvard Munch, *The Scream*, 1893. Oil on cardboard, $35^1/_2 \times 28^3/_4$ in. (91×73.5 cm). Stolen from the Munch Museum, Oslo.
Munch's best-known painting, of which he made some 50 versions, depicts a man crossing a bridge in Oslo, when he is seized by anxiety. The entire landscape begins to disintegrate, and a pair of ominous figures in black symbolizes approaching insanity. Munch described the experience that inspired the picture: "Suddenly the sky turned blood-red . . . there was blood and tongues of fire above the blue-black fjord and the city . . . I sensed an endless scream passing through Nature."

THE BIRTH OF FILM

Motion pictures (movies) were the offspring of a fruitful marriage between technology and art. Since the seventeenth century, still images had been projected from so-called magic lanterns and in the eighteenth and nineteenth centuries it became possible to create illusions of motion from still pictures. With the invention of still photography and the ability to fix images, it was only a matter of time before moving pictures developed.

A number of developments converged with the birth of motion pictures. The Realist interest in recording the conditions of society and in scientific accuracy was advanced by film. The medium was also well suited to the Symbolist interest in portraying atmosphere, mood, and the unconscious through juxtaposed and superimposed images. The Impressionist and Post-Impressionist interest in the fleeting impressions of everyday life coincided with the study of photographic techniques and capturing forms as they move through space.

At the end of the nineteenth century the English photographer Eadweard Muybridge (1830–1904), who worked mainly in America, recorded sequences of human and animal locomotion through series of connected stills. His *Female Figure Hopping* (figure **20.21**) creates a sense of lively movement through time and space. In the top row we see the figure in profile, in the center she is in back view, and below she hops forward on a diagonal surface. By a combination of repetition, sequencing, and shifting direction, Muybridge creates the illusion of movement.

THOMAS EDISON

In 1887 Thomas Edison, who was working in New Jersey (see Chapter 19), began to research a visual equivalent of the phonograph. Within two years he had produced the kinetograph. This used Eastman's flexible film and moved it by a shutter. The resulting image was of poor quality, and Edison next developed the kinetoscope, in which film was attached to a rotating belt and viewed through the eye-piece of a wooden box. The popularity of this device, which functioned as a peepshow, was enormous. Kinetoscope parlors opened in New York City in 1894 and soon sprang up in cities across Europe and America. Crowds gathered to watch the films, which included sequences of dancers and other performers, comedy skits, and sports. In 1894 Edison produced the *Record of a Sneeze*, a sequence showing one Fred Ott sneezing (figure **20.22**), which is widely believed to be the earliest motion picture.

Recognizing the future that motion pictures would have, Edison founded a production company, and his film studio, Black Maria, was the first of its kind. The exterior was insulated with strips of tar paper, and the roof could be opened to let in daylight. Daylight was the only source of lighting used in films until around 1907, when new types of artificial lamps were developed.

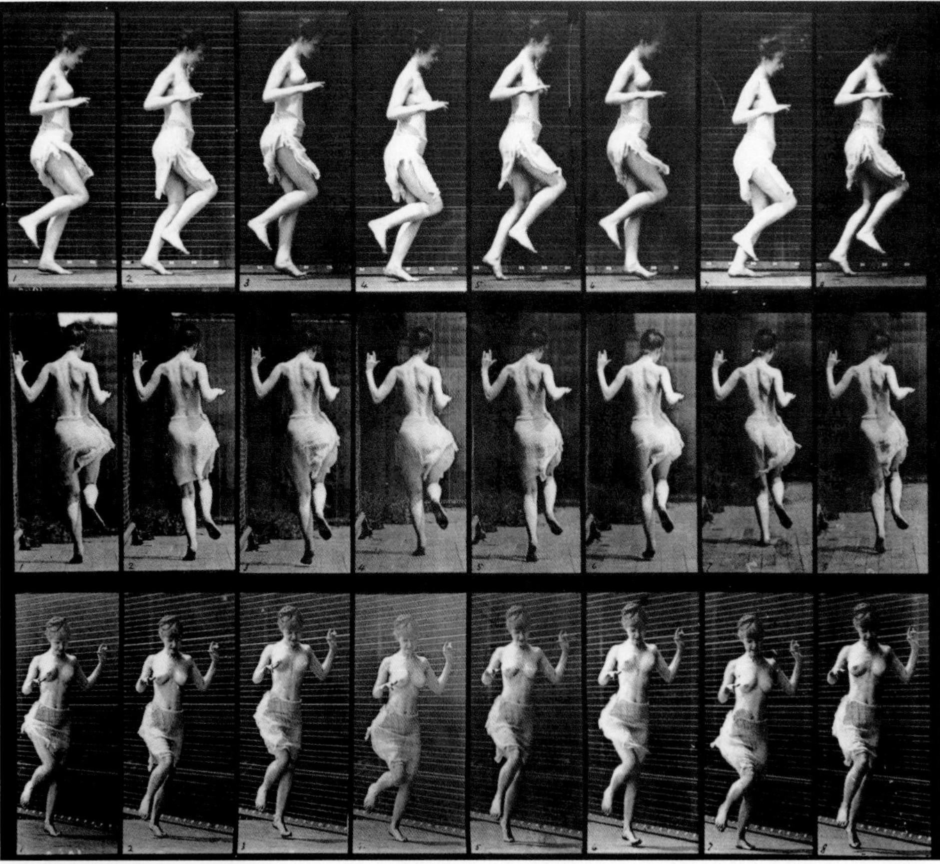

20.21 Eadweard Muybridge, "Female Figure Hopping," plate 185 from *Animal Locomotion*,1887. Sequence photography. National Museum of Design, Cooper-Hewitt Museum, New York.

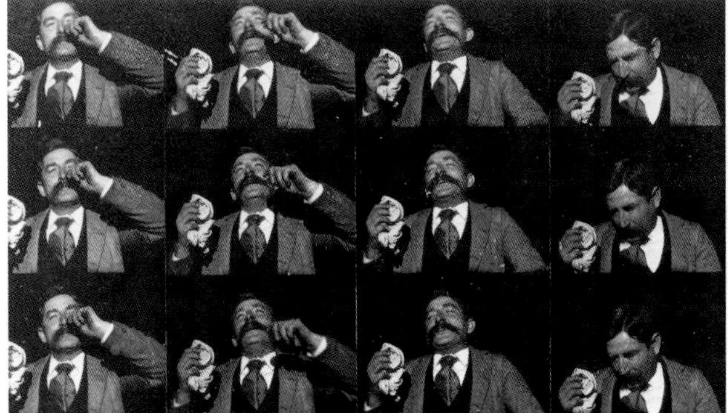

20.22 Thomas Edison, *Record of a Sneeze* (*Fred Ott's Sneeze*).

THE LUMIÈRE BROTHERS

The earliest films were black-and-white and silent. By 1894 two French brothers, Louis (1865–1948) and Auguste (1862–1954) Lumière, had invented the cinematograph, a combination movie camera and projector (see Box, p. 582). This made it possible for films to be projected onto a screen. In contrast to Edison, the Lumières filmed outdoors, and their films included brief sequences, such as comic skits and people at work—in 1895 *Break at the Lumière Factory* and *The Blacksmiths*, and in 1896 *The Demolition of a Wall*. Later the Lumières traveled the world filming exotic locales. Their arrival in New York threatened Edison with serious competition. In response, he filed for a number of patents and launched a series of lawsuits charging copyright violation—an early example of an intellectual property dispute.

GEORGES MÉLIÈS

The French filmmaker Georges Méliès (1861–1938) is considered the first to have approached film as an art form. He made films based on fantasy, such as *Cinderella* in 1899 and *The Trip to the Moon* in 1902 (figure **20.23**). This still, in which the

20.23 Georges Méliès, still from *The Trip to the Moon*, 1902.

Defining Moment

The Invention of the Motion Picture Camera

Many names come to mind when we celebrate the origins of film. Eadweard Muybridge, for example, settled an argument over whether all four of a horse's feet ever left the ground at the same time by developing time-lapsed sequences of galloping horses. George Eastman and Thomas Edison created machines designed to replicate moving images. What was still needed, however, was a way to project these images. That challenge was taken up by Louis and Auguste Lumière, who developed the cinematograph in 1895.

The Lumière brothers are credited with presenting the first public film screening on December 28, 1895, in Paris. They believed there was no future for films because the same images could be seen in everyday life. Their short films included pictures of workers leaving a factory and waves crashing on the shore. One exciting film, *The Arrival of a Train at the Station* (1895; figure **20.24**), showed a mail train coming directly toward the audience. Viewers screamed and ducked for cover, convinced that the train would run them over as it streamed diagonally across the screen. The Lumière brothers pioneered not only certain technical attributes of film but also its aesthetic effects, while concentrating on capturing the factual image. In the words of Louis Lumière:

> *The apparatus devised by Messieurs Lumière will be of considerable assistance to the photographic study of motion. Not only does it enable us to capture movement in its various stages, but we can recompose it at will, since the crank is hand-operated. Motions can be slow, very slow if we wish, so that no detail escapes our attention; and then, subsequently, we can accelerate it, should we so desire, back to normal speed. We shall then possess absolutely perfect reproduction of real movement.*

The Lumière brothers have been credited with making over 1425 different short films and had filmed aerial shots years before the first airplane aerial shots.

Critical Question Louis Lumière said: "The cinema is an invention without a future." Why was he so wrong in his prediction? What film techniques are used to make the film version of an object or incident different from the "real version"?

20.24 Lumière brothers, still from *The Arrival of a Train at the Station*, 1895.

space capsule penetrates the eye of the man in the moon, is an early example of a **special effect**. Méliès was known for his cinematic tricks, artistic backdrops, and elaborate costumes. He pioneered such techniques as the **fade-in**, the **fade-out**, and the **dissolve**. In 1899 his film *The Dreyfus Affair* (see Chapter 19) caused a scandal for its pro-Dreyfus bias, and his *The Palace of the Arabian Nights* (1905) was noteworthy for its lavish sets and costumes inspired by Oriental designs. After 1912, however, overwhelmed by costs and competition from rapidly developing technology, Méliès gave up making films and turned exclusively to the theater.

The possibilities of motion pictures were vast. Film was used by scientists and became a teaching tool for medical students. Once the novelty wore off, serious creative innovators such as Méliès became attracted to the new medium.

In the twentieth century, newsreels would bring images of current events to a wide audience, and the art of film evolved into a multi-billion dollar entertainment industry. Film also became a powerful means of political propaganda, of social documentation, and a new artistic medium with enormous creative potential.

With the close of the nineteenth century, we approach the upheavals of the twentieth—a century of innovation and creativity, but also of the most destructive wars in human history. With the new attention to the media of painting and the prominence of brushstrokes, artists began to search for new ways to depict the world around them. The notion of Modernism and modern life would evolve into the notion of the avant garde—newness for its own sake. Contributing to the avant garde was the influence of non-Western art and culture that had become widespread through international exhibitions in nineteenth-century Europe. The invention of film would also have a global impact on the twentieth century.

KEY TERMS

condensation in psychoanalysis, the representation of different objects or ideas by a single element, especially in dreams, fantasies, and neurotic symptoms.

displacement in psychoanalysis, the relocation of an element from its original or usual setting to another place.

dissolve in cinematography, the superimposition of one picture over another followed by disappearance of the latter, usually to mark a transition or change of scene.

fade-in in cinematography, the emergence of a picture from darkness to full visibility.

fade-out in cinematography, the reduction in visibility of a picture to signal a transition or conclusion.

gamelan a Southeast Asian percussion instrument similar to a xylophone; also an orchestra consisting of such instruments and gongs.

japonisme a trait of style reminiscent of Japanese culture.

ostinato a musical pattern that is persistently repeated while other elements change.

special effect in cinematography, a feature, often artificial or illusory, that is added to a film during its processing.

symbolization in psychoanalysis, the process of making symbols, in which one thing stands for another.

KEY QUESTIONS

1. Historians continue to debate the advantages and disadvantages of colonial rule. Summarize both sides of this issue.
2. What did Impressionists borrow from photographers? What did the Post-Impressionists borrow from the Impressionists?
3. What was the Symbolist movement? What did it include? What single statement might best summarize Symbolism?
4. What are special effects? Who introduced special effects in film? What are their advantages and potential disadvantages?

SUGGESTED READING

Bell, Quentin. *John Ruskin*. New York: George Braziller, 1978.
- A study of the nineteenth-century art critic.

Collins, Bradley, I. *Van Gogh and Gauguin*. Boulder, CO: Westview Press, 2001.
- A psychological study of the styles and relationship of the two artists.

Freud, Sigmund. *The Interpretation of Dreams*, ed. Angela Richards. London: Penguin Books, 1989.
- Freud explains the mechanisms of dream formation.

Geist, Sidney. *Interpreting Cézanne*. Cambridge, MA: Harvard University Press, 1988.
- An original biographical and iconographic approach to meaning in the work of Cézanne.

Gerdts, William H. *American Impressionism*. New York: Abbeville Press, 1984.
- A survey of Impressionism in the United States.

Herbert, Robert L. *Impressionism: Art, Leisure and Parisian Society*. New Haven, CT: Yale University Press, 1988.
- A social view of Impressionism.

Kipling, Rudyard. *Kim*. London: Penguin Books, 1994.
- The story of a white boy growing up in India under British colonial rule during the nineteenth century.

Lane, Richard. *Images from the Floating World: The Japanese Print*. New York: Putnam, 1978.
- A survey of the Edo-period prints that influenced European art.

Rewald, John. *Post-Impressionism from Van Gogh to Gauguin*, 3rd ed. New York: The Museum of Modern Art, 1986.
- A general survey.

Shiff, Richard. *Cézanne and the End of Impressionism*. Chicago and London: University of Chicago Press, 1984.
- Cézanne and the late nineteenth century.

SUGGESTED FILMS

1902 *Trip to the Moon*, dir. Georges Méliès

1905 *The Palace of the Arabian Nights*, dir. Georges Méliès

1943 *The Moon and Sixpence* (based on the life of Gauguin), dir. Albert Lewin

1950 *Kim*, dir. Victor Saville

1952 *Moulin Rouge*, dir. John Huston

1956 *Lust for Life* (based on the life of van Gogh), dir. Vincente Minnelli and George Cukor

1974 *Edvard Munch*, dir. Peter Watkins

1988 *Camille Claudel* (about a pupil and mistress of Auguste Rodin), dir. Bruno Nuytten

1990 *Vincent & Theo*, dir. Robert Altman

2001 *Moulin Rouge*, dir. Baz Luhrmann

21 Turn of the Century to World War I

“*The old Lie:* ‘Dulce et decorum est
Pro patria mori.’
*(‘It is sweet and fitting
to die for one’s country.’)*”

(HORACE, *Ode* III, CITED BY WILFRED OWEN)

By the close of the nineteenth century the most industrialized European countries—Britain, France, Germany, and the north of Italy—had expanded their influence through imperialism and colonization over large areas of the world. Much of Africa was divided among the European powers, and India had long been part of the British Empire. The French controlled Indochina, and the coastal areas of China had been opened up by European commercial interests. But colonization and imperialism contained seeds of future conflict. Competition between the great powers of Europe and their inability to resolve a number of crises led to two great twentieth-century wars, the first of which was World War I (1914–1918), "the war to end all wars."

Literature and art at the turn of the century reflected a sense of unease. The French term fin de siècle *("end of century") became synonymous with the malaise pervading the cultural atmosphere of western Europe. One expression of dissatisfaction was the Art Nouveau movement, which rebelled against industry and produced a style based on natural, organic forms. In straight-laced Vienna, Freud's description of infantile sexuality challenged traditional ideas about childhood innocence and inspired a group of artists—known as the Vienna Secession—who depicted overtly erotic themes. In Britain the author Oscar Wilde and the illustrator Aubrey Beardsley were also drawn to eroticism, and their insistence that art should be free of moral constraints was termed "decadent." Freud's focus on the psychology of children and their fantasy life was consistent with the evolution of children's literature, as well as with music composed for young audiences. The genre of detective fiction also developed around the turn of the century.*

The prevailing unease of the period appeared in fragmentation in the visual arts and atonal, dissonant sounds in music. These developments reflected the late-nineteenth-century notion of Modernism and led to the early-twentieth-century term ***avant garde****, denoting the goal of newness. With the outbreak of World War I a group of avant-garde artists and intellectuals launched the anti-war Dada Movement, which continued into the post-war period.*

World War I was a new kind of war. It marked the beginning of trench warfare and the tactic of firing machine guns along fixed lines. Germany developed the technology to gas and kill troops on an enormous scale. The effects of gas were vividly described by the British poet Wilfred Owen (1893–1918) cited at the beginning of the chapter. Called the poet of the trenches, Owen

Key Topics

"The War to End All Wars"

- Strained alliances
- German militarism
- The *Lusitania* torpedoed

Revolution

- Russians revolt in 1917
- Nicholas II abdicates
- Formation of the Soviet Union

***Fin-de-siècle* Malaise**

- Capitalist expansion
- Archduke assassinated
- Fragmentation in art and literature
- Art Nouveau
- The Dada Movement
- Aestheticism
- Dissonance in music

Signs of Progress

- The League of Nations
- Trans-Siberian railway
- The Wright brothers
- Ford's Model T
- First transatlantic phone call
- Einstein's theory of relativity
- Advances in medicine
- The psychoanalytic movement

TIMELINE	LATE-NINETEENTH AND EARLY-TWENTIETH-CENTURY EUROPE	LATE-NINETEENTH AND EARLY-TWENTIETH-CENTURY UNITED STATES
HISTORY AND CULTURE 	Bismarck ousted by German emperor Wilhelm II (r. 1888–1918) Bloody Sunday massacre in Russia, 1905 Triple Entente between Britain, France, and Austria-Hungary, 1907 Archduke Francis Ferdinand assassinated in Bosnia, 1914 World War I, 1914–1918; 8.5 million men dead German U-boat sinks *Lusitania*, killing 1200, 1915 Russian Revolution, 1917–1919 Treaty of Versailles, 1919 League of Nations, 1920	Capitalism leads to industrial growth and prosperity U.S. enters World War I, 1917
SCIENCE, TECHNOLOGY, AND PSYCHOLOGY	Röntgen discovers X-ray, 1895 Curies discover radium and polonium, 1898 Planck's quantum theory, 1900 Zeppelin makes first flight, 1900 Freud, *Three Essays on Infantile Sexuality*, 1905; *Beyond the Pleasure Principle*, 1920; *The Ego and the Id*, 1923; *Civilization and its Discontents*, 1929–1930 Jung (1875–1961): the collective unconscious; archetypes Bell makes first transatlantic phone call, 1915	Wright brothers fly first airplane, 1903 Einstein formulates special theory of relativity, 1905 Ford introduces Model T, 1908
ART 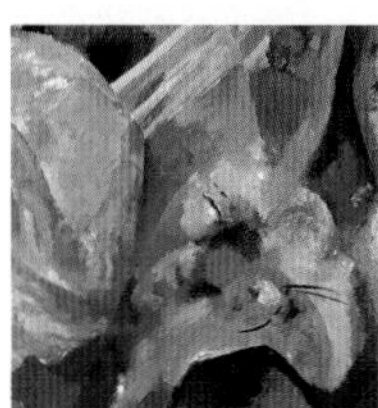	Modernism and the avant garde Art Nouveau; Vienna Secession Expressionism, Dada Movement, Fauvism, Futurism, Cubism Picasso, *The Tragedy*, 1903; *Women of Avignon*, 1906–1907 Matisse, *Woman with the Hat*, 1905 Marinetti publishes "Futurist Manifesto," 1909 Rousseau, *The Dream*, 1910 Kandinsky, *Flood Improvisation*, 1913 Boccioni, *Unique Forms of Continuity in Space*, 1913 Malevich, *Black Square*, 1915 Arp, *Collage Arranged According to the Laws of Chance*, 1916–1917	Stieglitz, *The Steerage*, 1907 Sloan, *McSorley's Bar*, 1912 Duchamp, *Nude Descending a Staircase No. 2*, 1912 Armory Show, 1913 Griffith, *The Birth of a Nation*, 1915 O'Keeffe, *From the Lake No. 21*, 1924
ARCHITECTURE	Guimard, Métro, Paris, 1900 Gaudí, Casa Milá, Barcelona, 1907	
LITERATURE 	Detective fiction; children's literature Wilde and Beardsley champion Aestheticism in Britain Carroll, *Alice's Adventures in Wonderland*, 1865; *Through the Looking-Glass*, 1871; *The Hunting of the Snark*, 1876 Collins, *The Moonstone*, 1868 Stevenson, *Treasure Island*, 1883; *Dr. Jekyll and Mr. Hyde*, 1886 Yeats, "The Lake Isle of Innisfree," 1888 Doyle, *The Adventures of Sherlock Holmes*, 1891 Hardy, *Tess of the d'Urbervilles*, 1891 Wilde, *The Picture of Dorian Grey*, 1891 Potter, *Peter Rabbit*, 1901 Barrie, *Peter Pan*, 1904 Rilke, *The Book of Hours*, 1905; *Letters on Cézanne*, 1907 Chesterton, Father Brown stories, 1911 Proust, *A la recherche du temps perdu*, 1913–1928 Owen (1893–1918): poet of the trenches; "Dulce et decorum est" Kafka, *The Trial*, 1914; "The Metamorphosis," 1915 Joyce, *A Portrait of the Artist as a Young Man*, 1914–1915 Strachey, *Eminent Victorians*, 1918	Alcott, *Little Women*, 1868 Frost, "Mending Wall," 1914 Doolittle, *Sea Garden*, 1916 Pound, "The Garden," 1916
THEATER AND BALLET 	Diaghilev founds Ballets Russes Gilbert and Sullivan, *Patience*, 1881; *The Mikado*, 1885 Wilde, *Salomé*, 1893; *The Importance of Being Ernest*, 1895 Yeats, *The Celtic Twilight*, 1893; *Cathleen Ni Houlihan*, 1902 Rostand, *Cyrano de Bergerac*, 1897 Shaw, *Mrs. Warren's Profession*, 1902; *Pygmalion*, 1913 Gregory, *Spreading the News*, 1904; *Kincora*, 1905 Synge, *Playboy of the Western World*, 1907 Jarry, *Ubu Roi*, 1908 Claudel, *L'Annonce faite à Marie*, 1912	Ragtime and blues Joplin, "Maple Leaf Rag," 1899 Jazz evolves in New Orleans, from 1900 Handy, "Father of the Blues," forms first band, 1902; "St. Louis Blues," 1914 First jazz recordings, Original Dixieland Jazz Band, 1917
MUSIC	Strauss, *Till Eulenspiegel*, 1895; *Salome*, 1905 Schoenberg, *Verklärte Nacht*, 1899; *Pierrot lunaire*, 1912 Ravel, *Spanish Rhapsody*, 1908; *Boléro*, 1928 Mahler, symphonies; *Das Lied von der Erde*, 1909 Stravinsky, *The Firebird*, 1910; *The Rite of Spring*, 1913	

was killed at the age of twenty-five, a week before the war ended. His poem "Dulce et Decorum Est" ("It is Sweet and Fitting")—its title and last line taken from an ode of the Roman poet Horace (see Chapter 7)—is a bitterly ironic indictment of war:

Bent double, like old beggars under sacks,
Knock-kneed, coughing like hags, we cursed through sludge,
Till on the haunting flares we turned our backs
And towards our distant rest began to trudge.
Men marched asleep. Many had lost their boots
But limped on, blood-shod . . .

Gas! GAS! Quick, boys!—An ecstasy of fumbling,
Fitting the clumsy helmets just in time;
But someone still was yelling out and stumbling
And flound'ring like a man in fire or lime . . .
Dim, through the misty panes and thick green light,
As under a green sea, I saw him drowning.

Owen denounces war and cites the Horatian ode to show that people have not learned the lessons of history. His conclusion challenges the persistent lie that romanticizes war:

The old Lie: *Dulce et decorum est*
Pro patria mori.
("It is sweet and fitting
to die for one's country.")

Horace, *Ode* III, ii, 13

SOCIETY AND POLITICS IN THE EARLY TWENTIETH CENTURY

In addition to competition among European nations, there was a great deal of internal unrest. In central and eastern Europe ethnic conflicts erupted between Slavs (Czechs and Slovaks) on the one hand and Austrians and Hungarians on the other. The industrial nations saw worsening urban slums and greater disparity between rich and poor. In the United States and Europe the rich were becoming richer as the poor became poorer. American capitalism led to industrial growth, an expanding economy, and enormous prosperity engendered by big business—often at the expense of workers. In response, factory workers began to organize into political groups advocating trade unions (figure **21.1**).

In France the Third Republic was polarized by clashes between socialists and conservatives and between monarchists and republicans. Britain, in contrast, managed to stem some of the protest with new laws designed to benefit workers and the poor, including state-sponsored education, which gave new hope to the lower echelons of society. Nevertheless, an economic downturn during the 1880s led to the establishment of the British Labour Party in 1900.

21.1 Käthe Kollwitz, *March of the Weavers*, 1897. Etching, 8³/₈ × 11⁵/₈ in. (21 × 29 cm). University of Michigan Museum of Art, Ann Arbor.
The etchings of Käthe Kollwitz (1867–1945) expressed the unrest among German workers. This frieze-like portrayal of a workers' rebellion reflects Kollwitz's identification with the disenfranchised sectors of society, even though she was financially comfortable herself. Men are shown wielding picks and axes, brandishing rocks, and clenching their fists in anger. In the foreground, a woman carries a sleeping child. Kollwitz conveys the dynamic force of workers on the march and the sense of rising power in the mob's determination.

WORLD WAR I

THE PATH TO WAR

After the Franco-Prussian War (1870–1871) the northern and southern German states were unified under the emperor (*Kaiser*) Wilhelm I, and France ceded Alsace and part of Lorraine to Germany. Because of its size and military power, a unified Germany was a threat to its neighbors, especially Austria, France, and the disintegrating Ottoman Empire.

In 1888 a new German emperor, Wilhelm II (ruled 1888–1918), a grandson of Queen Victoria but jealous of Britain's empire and navy, ascended the throne. One of his first actions was to dismiss Bismarck, who had tried to maintain a balance of power by restraining German territorial ambitions (figure **21.2**). The Kaiser then went on to assert Germany's right to be a major player on the world stage. Britain, historically friendly toward Germany and disinclined to involve itself in central European conflicts, entered into a series of new alliances. First, Britain agreed to defend Japan's Far Eastern interests against Russia; second, it formed the Entente Cordiale with France to resolve colonial disputes. The Entente acknowledged British control over Egypt and ceded Morocco to France. In 1907 Britain signed a treaty with Russia to end disagreements over Central Asia. Britain, France, and Russia formed the Triple Entente, opposing Germany, Italy, and Austria-Hungary (the Triple Alliance) and shattering Bismarck's carefully constructed political equilibrium (map **21.1**).

THE ARCHDUKE ASSASSINATED

The Balkans had been a source of unrest since the beginning of the century. In Sarajevo (Bosnia's capital) on June 28, 1914, a Serb nationalist assassinated Archduke Francis Ferdinand (see Box). A month later Austria-Hungary declared war on Serbia; Russia mobilized against Austria-Hungary and went to the aid of Serbia. Germany invaded Luxembourg and Belgium, hoping to surround France before Russia could attack. But the German invasion violated Belgian neutrality, which had been guaranteed by Britain in 1830.

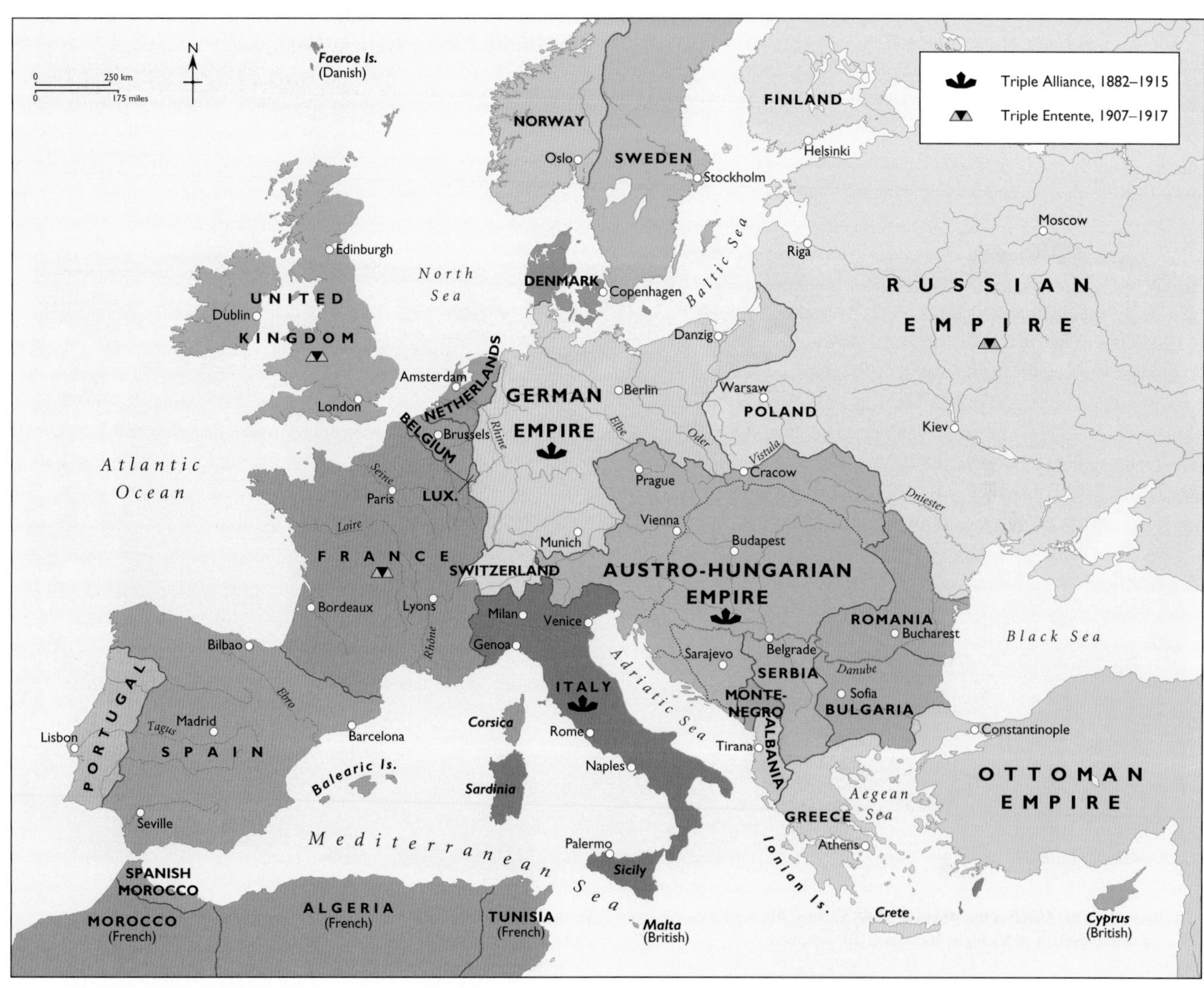

Map 21.1 Europe on the eve of World War I.

Defining Moment

The Assassination of Archduke Francis Ferdinand: The Beginning of the End of an Era

On June 28, 1914, Europe was shocked by the assassination of Archduke Francis Ferdinand, heir to the Austrian throne (figure **21.3**). This event sparked World War I and ended an era. A nineteen-year-old Serb terrorist, Gavrilo Princip (1895–1918), armed with a Browning revolver, and probably aided by members of the Serbian government, organized and carried out the assassination of the archduke and his wife, Sophie, during an official visit to Sarajevo, the capital of the recently annexed Austro-Hungarian dependency of Bosnia. Princip belonged to the Black Hand, a Serbian terrorist group of students, workers, peasants, Croats, Muslims, and intellectuals who wanted to free the Slavic population from Habsburg rule.

The archduke and his wife were not greatly mourned, but the Austro-Hungarian monarchy felt obliged to retaliate against the Serbian government. They had no evidence to justify their allegation of a Serbian conspiracy, but on July 23, 1914, Austria-Hungary issued an ultimatum that would have stripped Serbia of its independence. In spite of Serbia's efforts at conciliation, the Austrian government declared war on July 28, 1914.

Complex international alliances now went into action. The Germans were long-standing allies of Austria, and the Russians, who had recently rebuilt their army, defended their fellow Slavs. The French, who had entered into an alliance with the Russians, also mobilized. The British, who were allied with the French, realized that a German military response to France would violate the neutrality of Belgium, which Britain had guaranteed to defend nearly a century before. Although all of Europe was at peace in the first week of June 1914, by the first week of August the carnage of World War I had begun.

Perhaps war would have been declared even without the assassination. Colonial and imperial policies, German militarism, and various alliances would probably have led to war on one front or another, but this conflict was fought on a new level and on an unprecedented scale.

Critical Question How much should later generations hold past generations responsible for their actions?

21.3 A Serbian fires at the archduke and his wife as they ride through Sarajevo on June 28, 1914.

21.2 *left* **"Dropping the Pilot," cartoon from *Punch*, March 1890.** This famous political cartoon published in *Punch*, a humorous British magazine, shows Bismarck, the ship's pilot, descending the gangway at the command of the captain, Kaiser Wilhelm II.

A NEW TYPE OF WAR

Germany failed to surround the French army, and France counter-attacked, halting the German army at the Battle of the Marne. The two armies dug hundreds of miles of trenches, stretching from the North Sea to the Swiss border, which were protected by barbed wire and machine guns. In 1916 the British introduced tanks, but their effectiveness was not realized at first and they were used sparingly. The Germans gassed millions of Allied soldiers, and the Allies, in turn, also used gas.

Russia suffered heavy casualties on the Eastern Front. Japan honored its treaty with Britain and entered the war. Italy joined Britain and its allies and engaged the Austrian army, but its effect was slight. Nearly every country, no matter what its size, was drawn into hostilities by the major nations. Even Arab states rebelled against Turkey and assisted the British.

The British navy blockaded the North Sea ports of Germany, which used submarines more than other navies and declared all waters around Britain a war zone. In May 1915 a German U-boat torpedoed the British civilian liner *Lusitania*, killing 1200 people (including 118 American passengers). This attack was a factor in drawing the United States into the war.

In December 1916 President Woodrow Wilson (presidency 1913–1921) tried and failed to negotiate a peace. Germany continued submarine warfare, and in 1917 the Russian Revolution erupted, ending the tsarist alliance with Britain and France. Finally, in April 1917, America entered the war on the side of the British and French (the Allies) and helped crush the German offensive. By the end of the war 8.5 million men had been killed and another 21 million wounded.

THE END OF THE WAR AND ITS AFTERMATH

Kaiser Wilhelm II abdicated in November 1918 and a new republican government acknowledged Germany's defeat and signed an armistice. In early 1919 the Allies met at Versailles, near Paris, and dictated the terms of peace. They required Germany to accept responsibility for the war and to return Alsace-Lorraine to France and territory in the east to Poland (see map 22.1). Germany also had to disarm permanently, limit its fleet to coastal defense, and repay the Allies for damage caused by the war. This proposal was not only unworkable but also devastating to the German economy.

In 1920 Woodrow Wilson enthusiastically supported the foundation of the League of Nations, headquartered in Geneva, Switzerland, to keep Europe safe for the future. Germany and the Soviet Union (U.S.S.R.) were not invited to join, the former because of its offensive role in World War I and the latter because it advocated the overthrow of all non-communist governments. Despite some humanitarian successes, the League was generally ineffective because it had no army to back up its decisions, which had to be unanimous, and the United States Senate refused to join, despite Wilson's advocacy. Furthermore, without the participation of Germany and the Soviet Union, the League could not claim to represent all the major European powers.

DEVELOPMENTS IN RUSSIA

Russia, weighed down by a huge bureaucracy and the power of the tsars, did not become industrialized until the 1890s. A huge peasant population suffered from declining grain prices and high taxes. In 1905 Russia was defeated by Japan (the most powerful and most industrialized nation in Asia), leading to greater repression and simmering dissent under Tsar Nicholas II (ruled 1894–1917). In 1905 Russian troops fired on workers demonstrating peacefully in St. Petersburg, killing a hundred of them. The day this happened is known as Bloody Sunday. Workers who survived the incident were exiled to Siberia.

In response to growing unrest, Nicholas II issued the October Manifesto, which promised a constitutional government, but he was weak and unpopular and felt to be under the thumb of his German wife, Alexandra (1872–1918). She, in turn, was dominated by the dissolute, faith-healing monk, Gregory Rasputin (1871–1916), who claimed to be able to cure her son of hemophilia. In 1916 Rasputin was assassinated by a group of nobles, who feared his power over the royal family.

REVOLUTION

Russia fought with the Allies in World War I, but events at home cut short its involvement. By 1917, as the last year of the war began, Russia suffered heavy casualties—nearly 5 million men—and a collapse of military discipline. This, combined with food shortages, strikes, and continued discontent among the peasantry, undermined the tsarist government.

The Russian Revolution erupted in 1917 with demonstrations in Petrograd (St. Petersburg). On March 3 Nicholas II abdicated, and groups with elected officials, known as soviets, began to organize. The Marxist soviet leader, Vladimir Ilyich Ulyanov, who called himself Lenin (1870–1924), had escaped to Switzerland after Bloody Sunday. His return in April 1917 was followed by a three-year civil war between the Red Army (dominated by the Bolsheviks, who wanted to nationalize land and give it to the peasants, put workers in control of the factories, and take over banks and church property) and the White Army, which opposed Bolshevism. The victorious Reds called for a new society based on the precepts of Karl Marx (see Chapter 19).

Russia (now called the Soviet Union) extricated itself from World War I in March 1918, after the communists seized power. Despite the Soviet commitment to the Marxist ideal of a nationalized economy, Lenin realized that practical difficulties remained. In 1921 he eased economic tensions by allowing some private enterprise, but his death in 1924 opened the way for the rise of Stalin (see Chapter 22).

READING SELECTION

Lenin, *The State and Revolution*, on making a revolution, PWC6-009-C

TECHNOLOGY, SCIENCE, AND PSYCHOLOGY

As the new century dawned, science and technology provided both the means of progress and seeds of anxiety. Scientists learned more about time, space, and radioactivity but also realized that total self-destruction was becoming a distinct possibility. The turn of the century was thus a period of ambivalence. On the one hand, there was growing unease about the likelihood of war, and, on the other, a conviction that progress could make the world a better place. The positive view of the period is reflected in the term *belle époque* ("beautiful era"), which was current in late-nineteenth-century Paris. *Fin-de-siècle* malaise notwithstanding, the technological progress that led to more creature comforts and more rapid communication was a source of energy and optimism.

In 1891 construction of the Trans-Siberian Railroad began. Nine years later the Zeppelin made its first flight, and in 1902 a manned balloon crossed the Irish Sea. On December 13, 1903, Orville (1871–1948) and Wilbur (1867–1912) Wright flew the first airplane at Kitty Hawk, North Carolina.

In 1908 the Model T (the "Tin Lizzie") was introduced by Henry Ford (1863–1947), and a year later assembly line production began at the Ford plant. In a letter of 1906 Henry Ford expressed the optimistic view that technology improves the quality of life:

> There are more people in this country who can buy automobiles than in any other country on the face of the globe . . . The greatest need today is a light, low-priced car with an up-to-date engine of ample horsepower, and built of the very best material. One that . . . is in every way an automobile and not a toy; and, most important of all, one that will not be a wrecker of tires and a spoiler of the owner's disposition . . . We are today in a position to build and deliver 10,000 of our four-cylinder runabouts. I am now making arrangements whereby we can build and deliver 20,000 of these runabouts, and all within twelve months.

In 1878 Alexander Graham Bell (1847–1922) had demonstrated his telephone to Queen Victoria, and in 1915 he made the first transatlantic phone call. All these innovations contributed to a sense that the world could become a more connected, peaceful place. In addition, there were significant advances in science and psychology that changed the outlook of the Western world. These reinforced the sense of progress and fuelled the excitement that comes with new discoveries.

RADIOACTIVITY AND ATOMIC RESEARCH

A number of discoveries around the turn of the century opened the way to splitting the atom, which could be a source either of great advancement or of devastating destruction. In 1895 the German physicist Wilhelm Konrad Röntgen (1845–1923) discovered the X-ray, today a staple of medical practice. Building on his discovery, in 1898 the Polish physicist and chemist Marie Sklodowska Curie (1867–1934) and her French husband, Pierre (1859–1906), discovered radium and polonium. In 1911 Marie isolated pure radium metal. She became the first person to win two Nobel Prizes (one for chemistry and one for physics), but she died of radiation poisoning, whose fatal effects were unknown at the time. The discoveries of the Curies were among the major steps in the history of atomic research and eventually in producing nuclear weapons.

In 1900, the German Max Planck (1858–1947) showed that radioactive energy does not flow in smooth waves but in bursts of energy. Planck's **quantum theory** won him the Nobel Prize for physics in 1911, and his research facilitated the work of the Danish physicist Niels Bohr (1885–1962), who applied quantum theory to the atom in the 1930s. Their discoveries eventually made it possible for physicists to split the atom and construct an atom bomb.

The other influential scientist of the early twentieth century was the German-born Albert Einstein (1879–1955), who emigrated to America and taught at Princeton. His discoveries of time-space relationships led him to formulate the **special theory of relativity** in 1905, showing that movement and its position in time and space are relative, the only absolute being the speed of light.

In 1907 Einstein formulated the equation $E = mc^2$ to define mathematically the relationship of mass to energy: energy (E) equals mass (m) times the speed of light in a vacuum (c) squared. The finding that some of the energy stored as mass can be released in nuclear, radioactive reactions was an important step toward creating nuclear weapons.

THE UNIVERSE OF THE UNCONSCIOUS

Another revolution, this one in the realm of the mind rather than the cosmos, had begun in the late nineteenth century with Freud's discovery of the unconscious (see Chapter 20). Just as the Copernican revolution (see Chapter 15) had challenged geocentricism and Einstein altered the traditional view of the universe, so the Freudian revolution toppled the Enlightenment belief in human intellectual control. He showed that consciousness is only a very small part of the mind. The much larger unconscious, the repository of all experience (beginning with birth) that cannot be held in conscious memory, determines much of what we think and do, but usually without our awareness. As with the Copernican revolution and the opposition of the Catholic Church to Galileo (see Chapter 16), Freud's views created heated controversy, which continues today.

Freud established the clinical technique of psychoanalysis as a means of gaining access to the unconscious and of relieving people of inhibitions and other neurotic symptoms that interfere with success. By encouraging his patients to free associate—that is, to say whatever comes into their mind without editing—Freud not only devised a landmark system of psychotherapy but also had an enormous influence on the way we think about creativity. Like Socrates (see Chapter 6), Freud believed that the more we know about ourselves, the more creative and effective our lives can be.

The publication of *The Interpretation of Dreams* (see Chapter 20) in 1899 had an enormous influence on the arts in the twentieth century. Freud showed that dreams provide access to repressed memories and fantasies—he had called dreams the "royal road to the unconscious." In 1910 the French artist Henri Rousseau (1844–1910) painted *The Dream*, illustrating the mechanisms of dreaming described by Freud (figure **21.4**). Rousseau transformed the traditional motif of the reclining nude into a dreamer inside her own erotic dream.

In the first decades of the twentieth century, Freud published a number of works that illustrate the evolution of his theories. His *Psychopathology of Everyday Life* (1901) demonstrates the eruption of unconscious thinking in daily life. Apparently random phenomena such as mistakes, coincidences, forgetting, and slips of the tongue are shown to be explicable if submitted to analysis. In 1905 Freud published the *Three Essays on Infantile Sexuality*, shocking conservative Vienna with the discovery that sexuality is an important part of early childhood. The same year, in *Jokes and their Relation to the Unconscious*, he demonstrated the structural similarity between jokes, puns, and dreams. In 1913 in *Totem and Taboo* (one of Freud's most contested studies) he traced the origins of the Oedipus Complex to prehistory and applied psychoanalytic interpretation to non-Western cultures.

A year after the Treaty of Versailles was signed Freud published *Beyond the Pleasure Principle* (1920). This was a revision of his earlier view that people naturally seek pleasure and avoid pain. But as he studied the gassed, shell-shocked victims of World War I, he changed his mind. Pouring into the hospitals were soldiers who continually relived the traumas of battle through repeated nightmares. These, Freud concluded, were not consistent with the pleasure principle or with his notion that dreams are wish-fulfillments. Recurring nightmares, he decided, were unsuccessful attempts to resolve traumas by repeating them—the repetition compulsion.

Freud continued his revolutionary theoretical writings into the 1930s. In 1923, with *The Ego and the Id*, he described the mind as composed of three agencies: the id, the ego, and the superego. Known as the structural theory of the mind, this formulation was integrated with earlier discussions of the conscious and the unconscious. The id (which comprises instincts and impulses) is unconscious, as are parts of the ego and superego. But the ego and superego also have elements of consciousness. The ego can be thought of as that part of the mind that is in contact with everyday reality, whereas the superego is the moral sense that controls feelings of guilt. In dreams, according to Freud, the wishes and impulses of the id are expressed safely—

21.4 Henri Rousseau, *The Dream*, 1910. Oil on canvas, 6 ft. 8½ in. × 9 ft. 9½ in. (2.05 × 2.99 m). The Museum of Modern Art, New York. Henri Rousseau worked as a customs inspector until his retirement at the age of forty-one, when he became a full-time painter. Because he had no formal training, he is known as a naive or self-taught artist. In this work he shows the four mechanisms of dreaming described by Freud: (1) representability (it is a picture); (2) displacement (the nude and the couch are displaced from a French drawing room to a jungle); (3) condensation (the space and time between France and the jungle has been compressed and the locations superimposed); and (4) symbolization (erotic symbols, such as the open flowers, the snake, the flautist).

since one is asleep and cannot act—and thus relieve pressures built up during the day. Censorship is provided by the superego.

Repressed material, such as can emerge in dreams, is an important aspect of Freud's landmark study of 1929–1930, *Civilization and its Discontents.* The main theme of this book is the persistent conflict between the id's instinctual demands and the ego's rein on instinct that maintains civilization. In order to achieve this, according to Freud, instinct must be **sublimated**—that is channeled into creative or culturally productive activity (such as art, music, theater, sports, science, and so forth). "Civilization," he wrote, "is built up upon a renunciation of instinct." He compares controlling instinctual aggression to setting up a garrison in a conquered city—in other words, it is the superego of a society that maintains law and order, ethics and morality. The problem is always how to negotiate a balance between civilization and the discontent aroused by repressing destructive impulses. With this study, Freud defined the psychic mechanisms accounting for tensions that had erupted in World War I and would erupt again in World War II (see Chapter 22).

The international psychoanalytic movement grew out of Freud's work, generating schisms and new theoretical orientations. An influential alternative theory was developed by the Swiss psychologist Carl Jung (1875–1961), who challenged the sexual basis of the Oedipus Complex. He formulated instead the somewhat mystical theory of the **collective unconscious**, the notion that the unconscious is not an individual phenomenon, but rather occurs "collectively" and transcends different cultures. He advocated the existence of **archetypes**, universal patterns of thought expressed in dreams, myths, and neurotic symptoms. Examples of Jungian archetypes include the image of the father as a God or a devil, of the mother as a saint or a witch, of the hero, of the rescuer and the rescued, and of the trickster. Jung believed that such archetypes are an inborn, inherited aspect of human nature. In popular parlance, we thus speak of something being "archetypal" when we mean that it is the perfect and universal example of what we are referring to. Jung's notion of archetypes also encompasses the view of the duality of the soul, which he saw in terms of the **anima** (the female aspect) and the **animus** (the male aspect). Because of his interest in cultural patterns, Jung's writings had an enormous influence on the study of myth, literary analysis, and anthropology. Also much in use today are Jung's terms "introversion" and "extroversion" to describe personality types.

At first Jung was an associate of Freud, but the two men parted company on theoretical and personal grounds. Freud also disapproved of Jung's clinical methods, in particular his willingness to enter into romantic relationships with patients.

READING SELECTION

Jung, on the collective unconscious, PWC6-060

FIN DE SIÈCLE AND THE ARTS

At the turn of the century Vienna was one of Europe's leading cultural centers, where an entrenched conservatism clashed with Modernism. In art, the innovative painter Gustav Klimt (1862–1918) led the Vienna Secession. This movement began in 1897, rejected the prevailing academic style, and contributed to *fin-de-siècle* malaise.

Influenced by the dream world described by Freud, Klimt's imagery is frankly sexual, somewhat macabre, and deals with psychological themes. In 1902 Klimt created the *Beethoven Frieze* for an exhibition at the Secession House in Vienna. Based on mythological themes, the frieze was a symbolic rendering of Beethoven's Ninth Symphony (see Chapter 18) (figure **21.5**). The frieze was a failure with a public repelled by sinister females and exuberant, unfamiliar flattened forms; viewers were also disturbed by the thinly veiled eroticism of the imagery.

21.5 Gustav Klimt, detail of the *Beethoven Frieze, Hymn to Joy*, 1902. Casein color on stucco with semi-precious inlay and a reed base, total height 7 ft. 2½ in. (2.20 m), total length 78 ft. 8¾ in. (240 m). Österreichische Galerie, Vienna. This detail shows a dark-haired woman fingering what may be a keyboard. Her head and gestures are reminiscent of ancient Egyptian painting. Dynamic gold patterns suggest musical instruments, swords, and helmets. The frontal, abstract face with prominent eyes on the woman's dress alludes to the Gorgoneion, and thus identifies the figure as Athena. A goddess of war, wisdom, and the arts (weaving), Athena personifies the vogue for powerful, deadly women in turn-of-the-century Vienna.

21.6 Antonio Gaudí, Casa Milá, Barcelona, Spain, 1907. Steel frame and hammered stone.

21.7 *left* **Hector Guimard, Métro entrance, Paris, 1900. Pre-fabricated glass and ironwork.**

ART NOUVEAU

The style associated with the Vienna Secession, Art Nouveau (New Art), emphasized organic design patterns, avoiding Realist social observation and allusions to industry. This can be seen in the organic appearance of the buildings designed by the Spanish architect Antonio Gaudí (1852–1926) (figure **21.6**). Constructed around a steel frame, the exterior walls create a series of undulating curves animating the surface. They have been hammered to create the impression of natural weathering and are enlivened by foliate, ironwork balconies.

In Paris the designer Hector Guimard (1867–1942) used Art Nouveau forms for the Métro (subway) entrance in figure **21.7**. At the front, the iron framework fans outward as if in the process of growth. The interior walls are decorated with curvilinear patterns. In addition, the word "Metropolitain" has an irregular, organic quality.

OSCAR WILDE AND AUBREY BEARDSLEY

In Britain the two main exponents of *fin-de-siècle* decadence were the Irish author Oscar Fingal O'Flahertie Wills Wilde (1854–1900) and the British author and illustrator Aubrey Vincent Beardsley (1872–1898). Both championed Aestheticism, a British philosophy that values art not for its moral qualities but for its intrinsic beauty. Conventional morality

21.8 Aubrey Beardsley, "The Dancer's Reward" from *Salomé*, 1894. Pen drawing, 9 × 6½ in. (23 × 16.5 cm). Fogg Art Museum, Cambridge, Massachusetts.
In the Bible Salome dances for King Herod and demands the head of John the Baptist on a plate as a reward. In this illustration, Salomé holds the plate with the severed head and drips of blood echo the strands of John's hair. Salomé's expression suggests that she is erotically attracted to the head, a traditional theme in Western art, but its macabre quality in this illustration is typical of *fin-de-siècle* decadence.

was of little concern to either Beardsley or Wilde, and their art as well as their lifestyle embodied the notion of decadence.

Wilde was born in Dublin, married in 1884, and jailed for homosexuality in 1895 after a notorious public trial. He later moved to Paris, where he died. An amoral cynic, Wilde delighted and shocked the London public with his sharp wit and his unconventional velvet suits decorated with flowers. He contributed to children's literature by writing fairytales for his sons, and he satirized convention in his plays written for adult audiences. In *Lady Windermere's Fan* (1892) Wilde satirizes society through his main character, a divorced woman who engages in blackmail, but sacrifices herself out of maternal love. In 1895 Wilde produced another comedy of manners, *The Importance of Being Earnest.* The title is a pun on the quality of earnestness and the play's fictitious character named Ernest.

Like the French Symbolists, Wilde believed that art is without social or moral value. His most Symbolist work is *Salomé*, written in French in 1893. The play was banned in London by the Lord Chamberlain because its biblical characters engage in immoral behavior. *Salomé* was first produced in Paris in 1896, starring the leading French actress of the day, Sarah Bernhardt. In the British publication of 1894, *Salomé* was illustrated by Beardsley (figure **21.8**).

Wilde's only novel, *The Picture of Dorian Gray* (1891), is one of his most decadent works. Inspired by the Faust theme (see Chapter 18), the main character, Dorian Gray, sells his soul to the devil in the person of Lord Henry Wotton. Dorian kills the virtuous portrait painter Basil Hallward, whose picture of Dorian ages while Dorian himself remains young, handsome, and devoted to a life of pleasure. A portrayal of the conflict between elegant surfaces and underlying evil, the novel is a masterpiece of perverse horror. It concludes with the picture returning to its youthful state and Dorian lying dead, old and withered, with a knife through his heart. Wilde's Preface makes clear his view that art should not be concerned with morality as well as his talent for biting satire (see Box):

> The nineteenth century dislike of realism is the rage of Caliban [Shakespeare's sub-human slave in *The Tempest*] seeing his own face in a glass. The nineteenth century dislike of romanticism is the rage of Caliban not seeing his own face in a glass . . .
>
> No artist has ethical sympathies. An ethical sympathy in an artist is an unpardonable mannerism of style . . .
>
> It is the spectator, and not life, that art really mirrors. Diversity of opinion about a work of art shows that the work is new, complex, and vital. When critics disagree, the artist is in accord with himself.

READING SELECTION

Wilde, "The Happy Prince" and "The Selfish Giant," PWC5-049-B

Gilbert and Sullivan, The "Savoy Operas"

Turn-of-the-century satire characterizes the output of librettist William S. Gilbert (1836–1911) and composer Arthur S. Sullivan (1842–1900). Theirs was one of the most successful collaborations in the history of theater—despite personal incompatibility. Between 1871 and 1896, Gilbert and Sullivan composed fourteen **operettas** (light operas) for the theatrical manager Richard D'Oyly Carte (1844–1901). Most were first produced at the Savoy Theater in London.

Gilbert and Sullivan operettas were light and humorous, making fun of the social conventions and cultural movements of their time. *Patience* (1881), for example, satirized Aestheticism, while *The Mikado* (1885) was a comic treatment of *japonisme* (see Chapter 20). Other works include *H.M.S. Pinafore, Iolanthe, The Pirates of Penzance, Ruddigore,* and *The Yeoman of the Guard.* Enormously popular with audiences at the time, these comic operas are still regularly performed.

EUROPEAN LITERATURE

The late nineteenth and early twentieth centuries produced a wealth of important literature. The period saw the expansion of different genres, such as children's literature and detective fiction, and there was also a proliferation of major writers, poets, and playwrights, particularly in Britain and France. Their themes reflected a number of different contemporary trends, including a taste for decadence, the conscious portrayal of the unconscious, and Symbolism.

CHILDREN'S LITERATURE

The idea that books written for children are a distinct literary genre did not exist before the seventeenth century, but, under the influence first of Rousseau and later of Freud, books for children began to be taken seriously. In Germany in 1823 the Grimm brothers, Jacob Ludwig (1785–1863) and Wilhelm Carl (1786–1859), had published fairytales based on national folklore, and in Denmark the stories of Hans Christian Andersen (1805–1875), published in 1846, were less frightening than those by the Brothers Grimm. In the United States, *Little Women* (1868) by Louisa May Alcott (1832–1888) was inspired by her childhood memories of New England during the Civil War. The hero of the *Jungle Books* (1894–1895) by Rudyard Kipling (see Chapter 20) is a boy reared by wolves and taught the law of the jungle by a bear and a black panther. In 1901 the British author Beatrix Potter (1866–1943) published *Peter Rabbit*, and in 1906 the Swedish Nobel Prize winner Selma Lagerlöf (1858–1940) interwove Scandinavian folklore and legend with realism in *The Wonderful Adventures of Nils*. Some authors wrote exclusively for children, but more and more adult authors were producing what would become classics of children's literature.

LEWIS CARROLL In 1865 Charles Lutwidge Dodgson (1832–1898), an Oxford lecturer in mathematics who is better known as Lewis Carroll, published *Alice's Adventures in Wonderland*. Carroll captures the child's view of the world and the wish to change size in a world of adults. In *Through the Looking-Glass and What Alice Found There* (1871) Carroll explores nonsense as a literary device. His mock epic poem, *The Hunting of the Snark: An Agony in Eight Fits* (1876) seems meaningless but is enormously appealing because of the way Carroll uses language (see Box). He himself claimed not to know what the poem meant. "Fit the First: The Landing" sets the tone:

"Just the place for a Snark!" the Bellman cried,
  As he landed his crew with care;
Supporting each man on the top of the tide
  By a finger entwined in his hair.

The members of the crew include a barrister, a maker of bonnets and hoods, a broker, a billiard-maker, a banker, baker, and butcher. They embark on a futile hunt for the Snark, which concludes with "Fit the Eighth, the Vanishing":

They hunted till darkness came on, but they found
  Not a button, or feather, or mark,
By which they could tell that they stood on the ground
  Where the Baker had met with the Snark.

In the midst of the word he was trying to say,
  In the midst of his laughter and glee,
He had softly and suddenly vanished away—
  For the Snark *was* a Boojum, you see.

READING SELECTION
Carroll, *Alice's Adventures in Wonderland* and *Through the Looking-Glass and What Alice Found There*, a mad tea party, PWC5-019

ROBERT LOUIS STEVENSON The adventurous life of the Scottish author Robert Louis Stevenson (1850–1894) is reflected in his many adult poems and works for children. Stevenson's classic of children's literature, *Treasure Island* (1883), has

Nonsense and the Portmanteau Word

Lewis Carroll invented a new vocabulary of nonsense words in his Alice novels. In such poems as "Jabberwocky" in *Through the Looking-Glass*, Carroll created the **portmanteau word**, a word formed by combining two or more words, such as the modern word smog, which derives from smoke and fog. Carroll, however, was never so ordinary in his portmanteaus. "Jabberwocky" begins:

'Twas brillig, and the slithy toves
Did gyre and gimble in the wabe;
All mimsy were the borogoves,
And the mome raths outgrabe.

When Alice asks Humpty Dumpty to explain the meaning of the poem, he replies that: *brillig* means four p.m., when food is being boiled for dinner, while *slithy* combines lithe and slimy. Humpty Dumpty says that *toves* are like badgers, lizards, and corkscrews: to *gyre* is to rotate like a gyroscope; *gimble* is to make holes like a gimlet; the *wabe* is the grass around a sundial; *borogove* is a ratty bird resembling a mop that's alive; *rath* is a green pig; *mome* means "away from home" or "lost"; *mimsy* is a condensation of flimsy and miserable; and *outgrabe* combines a bellow, a sneezing, and a whistle. Humpty's gloss extends the range of nonsense by making nonsense of the art of interpretation.

enriched the imagination of generations of young readers. Among the memorable characters is the peg-legged pirate, Long John Silver, who befriends the hero, Jim Hawkins, and then tries to steal the treasure. In *The Strange Case of Dr. Jekyll and Mr. Hyde* (1886) Stevenson tackles the shifts between the conscious and unconscious mind through the two main characters. The good Dr. Jekyll discovers a potion that turns him into the evil Mr. Hyde, but eventually Dr. Jekyll loses the ability to control the transformation and his evil side takes over. He resolves the conflict by committing suicide.

Stevenson's attraction to themes of psychological duality—good and evil, conscious and unconscious—appears in his poem "My Shadow," from *A Child's Garden of Verses*. As with Jekyll and Hyde, the poem reflects the universal fascination with one's double, reflection, or alter-ego:

> I have a little shadow that goes in and out with me,
> And what can be the use of him is more than I can see.
> He is very very like me from the heels up to the head,
> And I see him jump before me when I jump into my bed.

J. M. BARRIE The psychological power of the shadow recurs in J. M. Barrie's (1860–1937) *Peter Pan*, which begins with Peter, the boy who refused to grow up, going to great lengths to recover his lost shadow. First performed in London in 1904, *Peter Pan* is the best known of Barrie's many works. It reflects the current interest, seen also in *Dorian Gray*, in achieving eternal youth as well as insights into the psychology of childhood. Barrie juxtaposes the universal wish to remain young, embodied by Peter (*Pan* is the Greek word for "all"), with human destiny to grow up and live in the real world (embodied by the heroine, Wendy Darling).

BRITAIN AND IRELAND

THOMAS HARDY AND JAMES JOYCE Two major authors of the late nineteenth and early twentieth centuries, Thomas Hardy (1840–1928) and James Joyce (1882–1941), had a significant impact on later writers. Both drew on Classical themes but adapted them to their own time. Hardy uses devices drawn from Greek tragedy and superimposes them on local English characters and settings. Joyce's work starts out in relatively conventional, usually Irish, settings but his greatest novels break with tradition. His use of fragmentation echoes the arts of the period and his portrayal of the unconscious mind indicates his familiarity with the latest psychological discoveries.

Hardy has been called both a Realist and a Romantic. He studied architecture and considered becoming a minister before turning to literature. His novels, which herald twentieth-century literary developments, deal with the struggle against the evil inherent in human nature and in the natural environment. Like the ancient Greek playwrights, Hardy portrays characters in conflict with the forces of fate. He introduced the open-ended novel form, often leaving plots unresolved, rather than tying up all the loose ends as Charles Dickens does (see Chapter 19).

Hardy was particularly drawn to the landscape and inhabitants of Wessex, an old name for southwestern England and the setting for his novel *Tess of the d'Urbervilles* (1891), which at the time struck many critics as pessimistic and immoral. The novel deals with social pretense and errors of judgment that are destined to end in tragedy. The heroine, Tess Durbeyfield, comes from a poor family that mistakenly believes itself descended from the noble, ancestral d'Urbervilles. The local family of this name has, however, only assumed the title.

Tess works on the poultry farm of Mrs d'Urberville where she is seduced and abandoned by her son, Alex d'Urberville. Alex and Tess have a child who later dies, and eventually Tess works on a dairy farm. There she meets and marries Angel Clare, the son of a clergyman, but he abandons her when she reveals her past. After suffering further misfortune, Tess murders Alex and is hanged for the crime as Angel and her sister watch her execution from a distance. Hardy's conclusion—that justice is done and "the President of the Immortals" had finished toying with Tess—recalls the Greek tragedies of Aeschylus (see Chapter 6).

The most innovative of all early twentieth-century authors in the English language, James Augustine Aloysius Joyce was born in Dublin. He was the oldest of ten children, attended a Jesuit school, and left Ireland for Paris in 1902. He taught English in Trieste, and in 1915 went to Zurich for the duration of World War I. His entire life was a struggle against poverty. Influenced by an enormous number of authors, Joyce was a gifted linguist with a musical ear that pervades all his work.

Joyce's first publication, *Chamber Music* (1907), conveys the musical character of his language:

> I
>
> Strings in the earth and air
>   Make music sweet;
> Strings by the river where
>   The willows meet.
>
> There's music along the river
>   For Love wanders there,
> Pale flowers on his mantle,
>   Dark leaves on his hair.
>
> All softly playing,
>   With head to the music bent,
> And fingers straying
>   Upon an instrument.

Dubliners (1914) is a collection of fifteen short stories intended as a "moral history" of Ireland. Each paints a vivid picture of Irish life, as Joyce creates mood through images of place. "Araby," for example opens with a street in Dublin and the personification of its houses:

> North Richmond Street, being blind, was a quiet street except at the hour when the Christian Brothers' School set the boys free. An uninhabited house of two storeys stood at the blind end, detached from its neighbours in a square ground. The other houses of the street, conscious of decent lives within them, gazed at one another with brown imperturbable faces.

A Portrait of the Artist as a Young Man (1914–1915) is an autobiographical novel, whose hero, Stephen Dedalus, suffers from guilt and loss of faith. He will reappear in Joyce's later, less conventionally structured works (see Chapter 22). Even here, however, it is possible to discern the germ of later innovations, which include stream of consciousness (related to Freud's free association), word play and punning, and shifting time and space from childhood to the present. The novel opens as follows:

> Once upon a time and a very good time it was there was a moocow coming down along the road and this moocow that was coming down along the road met a nicens little boy named baby Tuckoo . . .
>
> His father told him that story: his father looked at him through a glass: he had a hairy face.

DETECTIVE FICTION Toward the end of the nineteenth century the genre of detective fiction became popular. Although there had been crime novels earlier in the century and Edgar Allan Poe (see Chapter 18) had written prototypical detective stories, the genre came into its own after the publication of *The Moonstone* (1868) by Wilkie Collins (1824–1889), which recounts the theft and recovery of a huge Indian diamond.

In 1887 Sir Arthur Conan Doyle (1859–1930) introduced the pipe-smoking, amateur detective Sherlock Holmes in *A Study in Scarlet*, followed by *The Adventures of Sherlock Holmes* (1891), *The Memoirs of Sherlock Holmes* (1893), and *The Hound of the Baskervilles* (1902). Holmes is a bachelor who lives on Baker Street in London with his housekeeper, Mrs. Hudson. His friend and literary foil, Dr. Watson, serves as a transition between the fictional character and the reader/spectator to whom Holmes explains his brilliant deductions.

The British-style detective story, in which good triumphs over evil, usually has a distinctive hero who solves a crime using the same clues as those given to the reader. A prototype of this genre is the series by the novelist and journalist, G. K. Chesterton (1874–1936). His detective, the Catholic priest Father Brown, made his debut in 1911. This type of detective fiction continued until the middle of the twentieth century, with Agatha Christie (1890–1976) its acknowledged queen. Her detectives—the mustachioed Belgian dandy, Hercule Poirot, and Miss Marple, the deceptively distracted old lady who lives in the English village of St. Mary Meade—invariably use deductive reasoning to identify a culprit. Following this classic style of British detective fiction after World War II (1939–1945) came the American tough-guy crime novel and other approaches to the genre.

THEATER The plays of the Dublin-born George Bernard Shaw (1856–1950) are derived from Realist theater. Most convey the author's interest in social issues, but some, such as *Caesar and Cleopatra* (1899), are drawn from historical events. Shaw believed in free will, and one of his main themes was the conflict between intellect and faith. The majority of his more than fifty plays—comedies with serious social messages—are set in contemporary Britain. *Mrs. Warren's Profession*, which deals with prostitution, was first performed in 1902. *Pygmalion* (1913) transformed the Greek myth about bringing a statue to life in order to create the perfect woman into a satire on social distinctions in nineteenth-century London. In 1925 Shaw received the Nobel Prize for literature, and in 1956 *My Fair Lady*, the enormously successful musical version of *Pygmalion*, was staged in New York.

In 1904 the Abbey, a distinctive and influential theater that early on reflected Ireland's national spirit, opened in Dublin. At the time its three leading authors were the Nobel Prize winning poet and dramatist William Butler Yeats (1865–1939), Lady Augusta Gregory (1852–1932), and John Millington Synge (1871–1909). Yeats studied art, which he abandoned to write plays for the Abbey until around 1910. At first inspired by French Symbolism, Yeats's early play *Cathleen Ni Houlihan* (1902) was an evocation of the Irish spirit. This was embodied in the character of an old but eternally beautiful woman transformed into a young girl. *The Celtic Twilight* (1893) is a collection of short stories dealing with Irish legends. And in his poem "The Lake Isle of Innisfree" (1888) Yeats conveys his sense of oneness with Ireland:

> I will arise and go now, and go to Innisfree,
> And a small cabin build there, of clay and wattles made;
> Nine bean-rows will I have there, a hive for the honey-bee,
> And live alone in the bee-loud glade.
>
> And I shall have some peace there, for peace comes dropping slow,
> Dropping from the veils of the morning to where the cricket sings,
> There midnight's all a glimmer, and noon a purple glow,
> And evening full of the linnet's wings.
>
> I will arise and go now, for always night and day
> I hear lake water lapping with low sounds by the shore;
> While I stand on the roadway, or on the pavements grey,
> I hear it in the deep heart's core.

Lady Gregory was a founding member of the Abbey Theatre, for which she wrote and directed plays. Irish folk traditions are the subject of *Poets and Dreamers* (1903) and *Kincora* (1905). In the peasant comedy *Spreading the News* (1904) Gregory shows how a story changes as it is told from one person to another.

Synge rejected the Realist style of Ibsen in favor of the more colorful, poetic language of Ireland. He recreated the colloquial style of old Irish, evoking the spirit of Gaelic and transposing its linguistic forms into English. Synge created a major controversy with his comedy *The Playboy of the Western World* (1907). It is the story of a man, idolized by a village and irresistible to women, who brags about killing his abusive father. But the hero's popularity suffers when it turns out that his father was only wounded. The play provoked riots when it was first performed, as audiences complained that the author had debased the spirit of Ireland.

FRANCE

As in Britain, literature in France at the turn of the twentieth century reflected the taste for decadence, the conscious portrayal of the unconscious, satire, and Symbolism.

Marcel Proust (1871–1922), for whom art was religion, was associated with decadence. His fourteen-volume autobiographical work, *A la recherche du temps perdu* (*Remembrance of Things Past*), published from 1913 to 1928, chronicles the French aristocracy and upper bourgeois society. In the first volume, *Swann's Way* (*Du côté de chez Swann*), Proust shifts from his inner psychic world to the outside world of everyday reality and portrays his interest in time and memories aroused through sensation. The most famous of these is the evocation of his childhood when, as an adult, he visits his mother. She offers him tea and a *madeleine* (a French biscuit), which he had enjoyed as a child. The instant the *madeleine* touches his palate, he trembles, realizing that something extraordinary is happening inside him:

> A delicate pleasure rushed through me, isolated, without knowing the cause . . . I ceased to think of myself as mediocre . . . as mortal. From whence came this powerful joy? . . . I put down my cup and turned to my soul. That is where the truth resides.

When Proust tasted the *madeleine*, sensation confirmed Freud's discovery that there is no time in the unconscious and gave Proust the illusion of immortality. Inspired by Proust's experience, this evocation of a past feeling is called *déjà vu* (literally, something that has already been seen).

THEATER French theater moved away from late-nineteenth-century Realism and introduced new themes. Romanticism, comedy, and tragedy were combined in the plays of Edmond Rostand (1868–1918), and the farces of Alfred Jarry (1873–1907) showed the absurdity of contemporary life. The staunchly Catholic Paul Claudel (1868–1955) evoked the atmosphere of the Middle Ages and created events imbued with Christian mystery.

Rostand's popular romance *Cyrano de Bergerac* (1897) also contains elements of tragedy. It is the story of an unattractive suitor with an extremely large nose. He is in love with his cousin Roxanne and persuades his handsome friend Christian to woo her with his (Cyrano's) words. When Christian is killed, Roxanne retires to a convent. Cyrano visits her and, just before he dies, his secret is exposed. Roxanne finally realizes that she has always loved Cyrano.

21.9 Alfred Jarry's *Ubu Roi* at the Théâtre Antoine, from *Le Figaro*, February 16, 1908.

The comic farce of Alfred Jarry has affinities with Symbolist brevity and the creation of imagery with words. With lines such as "I want to be rich, and then I will kill everyone and depart," his *Ubu Roi* (*King Ubu*) is considered the beginning of the Theater of the Absurd (see Chapter 23) (figure **21.9**). Jarry shows the world upside-down through Père Ubu (Father Ubu), a fat, amoral character whose propensity for violence is a negative reflection on society. He usurps the throne of Poland and kills his opponents. Eventually ousted from power, Ubu vows to behave elsewhere as he has in Poland.

The prolific Catholic author Paul Claudel combined nostalgia for Christianity with the musical styles and poetic moods of Symbolism. *L'Annonce faite à Marie* (*The Annunciation to Mary*) of 1912 is set in the late Middle Ages and evokes the atmosphere of medieval mystery plays. It is the story of two sisters—the evil, dark-haired Mara, and the virtuous, blonde, blue-eyed Violaine. Both are in love with Jacques Hury, who loves only Violaine. But Mara tricks him into believing that Violaine has been unfaithful and he marries Mara instead. Violaine assumes the suffering of the cathedral-builder, Pierre de Craon, who has contracted leprosy and become blind. When she kisses him, she also becomes a leper. The play reflects Claudel's view that inspiration is a form of divine grace, and poetry an act of faith. It contains his characteristic themes of love and self-sacrifice, jealousy and forgiveness, and family tensions that end in tragedy.

MODERNISM AND THE AVANT GARDE

From the turn of the twentieth century to World War I, several trends in the visual arts can be identified. Expressionism explored bright, exuberant color, and Fauvism used color to create form. Futurism celebrated technological progress and mechanization, and Cubism structured form and space geometrically.

Until World War I broke out the main European centers of the avant garde were Munich, Dresden, Moscow, and Paris. Artists in those cities explored expressive color, fantasy and dreams, and new approaches to form and space. Many artists, like Gauguin (see Chapter 20), were drawn to primitivism—the vogue for non-Western art and its unclassical representations of the human figure (figure **21.10**).

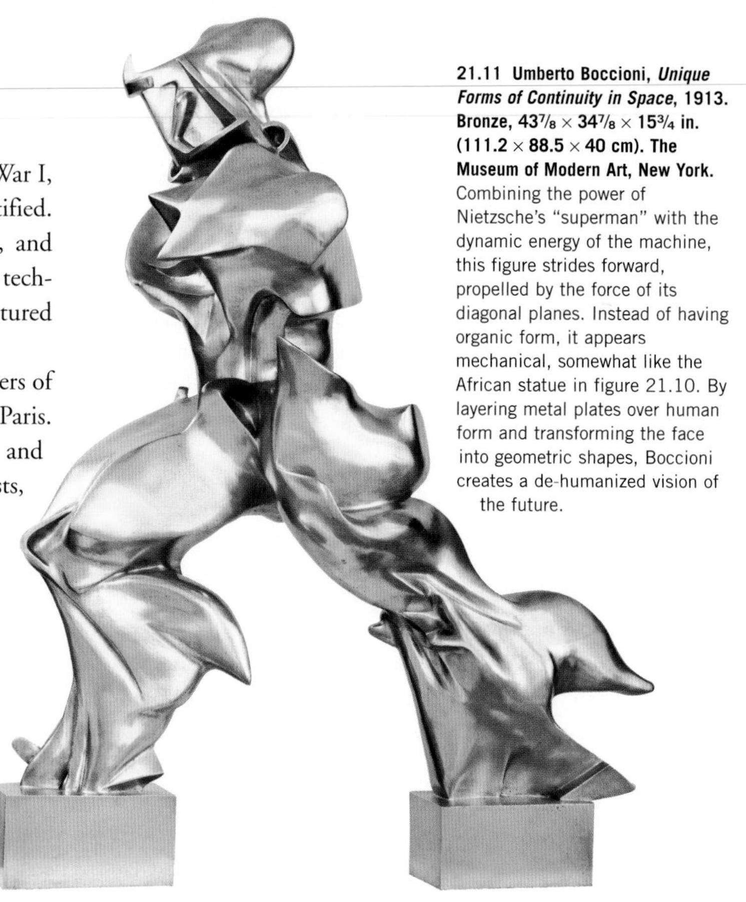

21.11 Umberto Boccioni, *Unique Forms of Continuity in Space*, 1913. Bronze, 43⅞ × 34⅞ × 15¾ in. (111.2 × 88.5 × 40 cm). The Museum of Modern Art, New York.
Combining the power of Nietzsche's "superman" with the dynamic energy of the machine, this figure strides forward, propelled by the force of its diagonal planes. Instead of having organic form, it appears mechanical, somewhat like the African statue in figure 21.10. By layering metal plates over human form and transforming the face into geometric shapes, Boccioni creates a de-humanized vision of the future.

FUTURISM: 1909–1915

The visual arts at the turn of the century evolved more quickly than in previous centuries. Synthetic plastic media, such as acrylic, and new techniques, such as collage, became popular. For the group of Italian artists known as the Futurists, speed and progress were characteristic themes.

On February 20, 1909, the poet Filippo Marinetti (1876–1944) published his "Futurist Manifesto" in the Paris newspaper *Le Figaro*. Angered by the cultural deterioration of Italy, the decadence of its aristocracy, and its political weakness, Marinetti was inspired by Nietzsche's notion of a "superman" or *Übermensch* (see Chapter 19). Marinetti advocated anarchy and violence to promote social change. The ideals of Futurism were later used as Fascist propaganda before World War II (see Chapter 22).

Futurists believed that art should reflect the dynamic energy of a future dominated by machines. They wanted to eradicate the past, including books and libraries, works of art, and museums. Embodying this view is *Unique Forms of Continuity in Space* (figure **21.11**) by Umberto Boccioni (1882–1916).

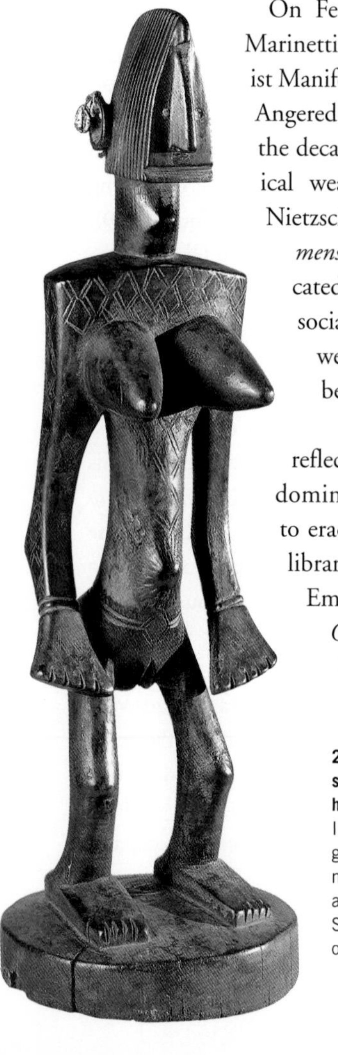

21.10 Female figure, from Bamana, Mali. Wood, string, cowrie shell, and iron, 24 in. (61 cm) high. New Orleans Museum of Art.
In this figure organic form is transformed into geometric structure. The angular limbs appear mechanical and thus interested the European avant garde after the Industrial Revolution. Some Western artists found the unfamiliarity of such works liberating.

EXPRESSIONISM IN ART AND LITERATURE: THE AVANT GARDE IN GERMANY AND RUSSIA, 1904–1915

The prevailing Modernist style in turn-of-the-century Germany was Expressionism. Expressionist painters used formal elements—lines, shapes, and colors—to create spiritual and emotional moods rather than to depict the natural world. Similarly, authors used feeling and emotion to propel a narrative and to define character.

WASSILY KANDINSKY In 1905, artists in Dresden formed a group they called The Bridge (*Die Brücke*), intended to "bridge" or make a transition from the avant garde. In 1911, a group in Munich, called The Blue Rider (*Der blaue Reiter*) after Moscow's city emblem showing St. George and the Dragon ushering in the new millennium, was more drawn to non-figurative abstraction than The Bridge. The founder and most avant-garde member of The Blue Rider was the Russian artist Wassily Kandinsky (1866–1944). In 1911 Kandinsky published his book *Concerning the Spiritual in Art*, which stated his artistic aims. In his view, colors had specific meanings and expressive qualities. Red, he believed, has unlimited warmth and an inner glow; yellow is irresponsible but appealing; blue is the color of heaven and creates a restful mood (figure **21.12**). Kandinsky often used musical titles to convey the abstraction of his works.

21.12 Wassily Kandinsky, *Flood Improvisation*, 1913. Oil on canvas, 37½ in. × 4 ft. 11 in. (95 × 150 cm). Städtische Galerie im Lenbachhaus.
Inspired by the apocalyptic theme of the flood, this is one of Kandinsky's most dynamic pictures. The first artist to paint totally non-figurative works, Kandinsky creates a powerful sense of upheaval and turbulence without figurative imagery. Rich colors shift exuberantly from one to another and seem to swirl like flood waters. Diagonals move our gaze back and forth and up and down throughout the picture plane. A sense of impending doom appears in the blacks that surround and begin to engulf the colors.

KAZIMIR MALEVICH In Russia the most avant-garde style was the Suprematism of Kazimir Malevich (1878–1935), who shared Kandinsky's interest in achieving spirituality through abstraction. Malevich was also inspired by a Cézanne exhibition held in Moscow in 1908. Suprematism, which was Malevich's own creation, was intended to express pure cosmic sensation by avoiding visual and tactile references to reality. The Suprematist "feels," wrote Malevich in his book, *The Non-Objective World* (1926); he does not see or touch. The first known Suprematist painting is Malevich's *Black Square* (figure **21.13**), which was exhibited in St. Petersburg in 1915.

After the communist revolution of 1917 Malevich became commissar in charge of art preservation. Later, however, the totalitarian Soviet regime arrested him for artistic deviation, and he changed his style to figuration.

SERGEI DIAGHILEV Another Russian member of the avant garde, Sergei Diaghilev (1872–1929), founded the Ballets Russes (Russian Ballet), which toured Europe in the early twentieth century. Involved in international cultural exchanges, he worked in Paris in 1909, where he was admired for his innovative choreography, costumes, and set design. Many of his sets were created by artists in Paris, and musicians of various nationalities composed music for his productions. Unlike Malevich, Diaghilev remained in the West after 1917.

FRANZ KAFKA The leading Expressionist author, Franz Kafka (1883–1924), was born in Prague, but spoke and wrote in German. He worked in an insurance claims office and died in a tuberculosis sanatorium near Vienna. Most of his writing was published posthumously.

Kafka's novels and stories reflect his sense of alienation, and they are Expressionist in the superimposition of his own feelings on reality. He conveys despair and paranoia through inexplicable events and uncanny characters. In *The Trial* (written in 1914; published in 1925) the hero, Joseph K., wakes up to find a stranger in his room. The stranger informs K. that he is under arrest but does not identify K.'s crime. K. is convicted by an elusive court and executed by anonymous bureaucrats.

21.13 Kazimir Malevich, *Black Square*, first version 1915, later destroyed and reproduced by the artist. Oil on canvas, 31¼ in. (79.4 cm) square. State Tretiakov Gallery, Moscow.

Assuming that Kafka identified with K., the novel depicts the author engulfed by the oppressive atmosphere of a mechanized, illogical, and inhumane justice system. He knows he is guilty, but not why. He cannot shake the conviction that he must submit to an incomprehensible destiny. Today the term kafka-esque is used to describe the sense of being trapped in a faceless, bureaucratic nightmare from which one cannot escape. In his short story "The Metamorphosis" (1915) Kafka conveys the dehumanization of the period as the main character awakens to find himself changing into a cockroach.

READING SELECTION

Kafka, "The Metamorphosis," a young man wakes up as an insect, PWC6-067-B

RAINER MARIA RILKE The German Rainer Maria Rilke (1875–1926) is considered one of the greatest lyric poets of his generation. His style has Expressionist elements, and two visits to Russia inspired an interest in spirituality, reflected in *The Book of Hours* (*Das Stundenbuch*) of 1905. After a trip to Paris and a period as Rodin's secretary, Rilke developed an interest in avant-garde art, especially the work of Cézanne. In 1907 he wrote *Letters on Cézanne* to translate the essence of the artist into words. Just as Cézanne had broken space into geometric, faceted units (and as scientists were looking for the basic units of matter), so Rilke searched for the smallest linguistic unit. In "The Cadet Picture of My Father," Rilke applies the notion of the image to content as well as to style:

There's absence in the eyes. The brow's in touch
with something far. Now distant boyishness
and seduction shadow his enormous lips,
the slender aristocratic uniform
with its Franz Josef braid; both the hands bulge
like gloves upon the saber's basket hilt.
The hands are quiet, they reach out toward nothing—

I hardly see them now, as if they were
the first to grasp distance and disappear,
and all the rest lies curtained in itself,
and so withdrawn, I cannot understand
my father as he bleaches on this page—

Oh quickly disappearing photograph
in my more slowly disappearing hand!

THE AVANT GARDE IN PARIS

Gertrude Stein (1874–1946), the American art collector and author, famously said: "Paris was where the twentieth century was." She meant that in the early decades of the twentieth century Paris was the hub of artistic and intellectual innovation. The first person to buy the paintings of Matisse and Picasso, Stein presided over a *salon* frequented by leading European and American artists and writers and was a central figure in the cultural life of Paris.

MATISSE AND THE FAUVES In 1905 an exhibition of work by young painters in Paris caused a sensation for the brilliant colors of their canvases. Stunned by the vivid yellows, reds, and oranges, an art critic coined the term *fauve*, meaning "wild beast," because he was reminded of a tropical jungle. The impact of Fauvism was considerable, although the style itself was short-lived.

The leader of the group, Henri Matisse (1869–1954), was influenced by Impressionist and Post-Impressionist color and the atmospheric moods of Symbolism. He traveled in Europe, America, Oceania, and North Africa, where he was inspired by Moorish subjects and colorful patterned designs. After 1914 he lived mainly on the French Riviera.

Matisse used color to build form in *Woman with the Hat* (figure **21.14**), which depicts his wife, seated and turned toward the viewer. The background is identified only by brushstrokes; Madame Matisse and her outfit are entirely composed of color patches. Sharp greens slash across the forehead, nose, and jaw. The neck, lips, hair, and waistband are orange. The whites of the eye and one side of the nose are light blue. Greens, browns, blues, and oranges define the enormous hat that seems too large for the head. The white collar is composed

21.14 Henri Matisse, *Woman with the Hat*, 1905. Oil on canvas, 31¾ × 23½ in. (80.7 × 59.7 cm). San Francisco Museum of Modern Art.

21.15 *right* **Pablo Picasso, *The Tragedy*, 1903. Oil on wood, $41\frac{1}{2} \times 27\frac{1}{8}$ in. (105.4 × 69 cm). National Gallery of Art, Washington, D.C.** Affected by the suicide of his friend Carlos Casagemas, Picasso's Blue Period pictures convey a depressive "blue" mood. The three figures and their setting are blue, which expands the space. Picasso imbues the figures with a sense of loss and isolation, the only physical contact between them being the boy's hand on the man's thigh. They hunch forward and turn in on themselves. The columnar nature of the woman's dress and her strong vertical make her appear the sturdiest of the three. The formal space between her and the male figures denotes their psychological distance from each other.

not only of whites but also of greens, oranges, browns, and yellows, and the hand is green.

Although not a critical success, *Woman with the Hat* was purchased by Michael Stein, Gertrude's brother, which launched Matisse's reputation in Paris. As interest in Fauvism declined, Matisse explored new approaches to color and worked in various media, such as sculpture and collage, and with Picasso, he became one of the most influential artists of the twentieth century.

PABLO PICASSO The Spanish artist Pablo Picasso (1881–1973) is unusual for having worked in many different styles. His first distinct style, called the Blue Period, lasted from 1901 to around 1904. Picasso was living in Spain at the time, and the predominance of mood-creating color reflected a Symbolist aesthetic (figure **21.15**).

The end of the Blue Period coincided with Picasso's move to France, where he lived for most of his long life. In 1906 he painted Gertrude Stein's portrait in the colors of the Rose Period (figure **21.16**). The imposing portrait shows an early stage of Picasso's evolution toward shifting space, as Stein's left arm is flattened whereas the right arm is massive. In contrast to the organically depicted figures of the Blue Period, Stein is shown with a hardened face, which has a wooden quality similar to that of certain African masks. This is accentuated by the flat ear and the sharp edges around the eyes and at the side of the cheek. Picasso shows Stein as a bulky, imposing character, reminiscent of Ingres's M. Bertin (see thumbnail); both Picasso and Ingres were inhibited by the power of their subjects and required many sittings to finish the portraits.

Ingres, *Louis-Francois Bertin*
see figure 18.8

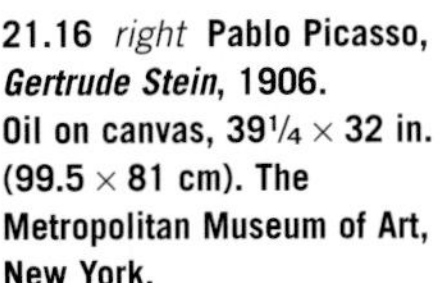

21.16 *right* **Pablo Picasso, *Gertrude Stein*, 1906. Oil on canvas, $39\frac{1}{4} \times 32$ in. (99.5 × 81 cm). The Metropolitan Museum of Art, New York.**

less about the personality of the subject and more about fragmented space. The torso dissolves into the surrounding area through shared, geometric solids, and the head seems to be transforming itself into crystalline structure. Picasso has thus extended Cézanne's spatial revolution to a new level of abstraction.

In 1911 two Cubist exhibitions were held in Paris, bringing the latest artistic innovations before the public. The style had reached its logical conclusion but would exert an enormous influence on future twentieth-century artists. The fragmented character of Cubism soon evolved into the new medium of **collage**. Derived from the French word *coller* ("to glue" or "paste"), collage consists of pasting lightweight materials onto a surface. A good example of collage can be seen in Picasso's *Guitar* of 1913 (figure **21.19**).

21.17 Pablo Picasso, *Women of Avignon*, 1906–1907. Oil on canvas, 8 ft. × 7 ft. 8 in. (2.4 × 2.3 m). The Museum of Modern Art, New York.
The title refers to the Carrer d'Avinyo, a street in Barcelona lined with bordellos. It shows five prostitutes and a still life of fruit. The seated figure at the right (known as the "squatter") is depicted so that her face is frontal but her body is seen from the back. This kind of double, or simultaneous, viewpoint, which in reality would require us to go around the figure, shortens the time it takes us to see and thus speeds our visual perception.

In the groundbreaking *Women of Avignon* of 1906–1907 (figure **21.17**), fragmentation of form is readily apparent. Picasso has disrupted facial symmetry, transformed the nudes into angular, geometric shapes, and altered the natural relation of foreground to background. He has also juxtaposed a number of easily recognizable motifs—the standing figure at the left is inspired by statues of Egyptian kings, the figures with raised arms are based on the traditional reclining nude, and the elongated faces at the left are inspired by African masks. This work caused a sensation because of its original conception. It is considered a precursor of the Analytic Cubist style, in which forms and space are structured geometrically rather than naturally.

Picasso's painting of a Paris art dealer, *Portrait of Ambroise Vollard* (figure **21.18**), brings us closer to pure Analytic Cubism, in which the range of color is reduced to browns, grays, and gray-greens, and the shapes are geometric. Compared with the portrait of Gertrude Stein, Vollard's portrait is

21.18 *right* **Pablo Picasso, *Portrait of Ambroise Vollard*, 1910. Oil on canvas, 36¼ × 25⅝ in. (92 × 65 cm). Pushkin Museum, Moscow.**

21.19 Pablo Picasso, *Guitar*, 1913. Collage, charcoal, pencil, ink, newspaper, colored paper, and wallpaper, $12^{1}/_{8} \times 19^{1}/_{2}$ in. (30.8 × 49.5 cm). The Museum of Modern Art, New York.

In this collage fragments from everyday life are cut up and rearranged to create shifting planes and viewpoints. The sound hole of the guitar, for example, is also a piece of newsprint, and the guitar box is composed of two asymmetrical sides, one white and one of wallpaper. By using newspaper and wallpaper, Picasso merges text with texture; and by using real objects and drawing, he merges reality with fiction.

21.20 Jean (Hans) Arp, *Collage Arranged According to the Laws of Chance*, 1916–1917. Pasted paper, $19^{1}/_{2} \times 13^{5}/_{8}$ in. (49.5 × 34.6 cm). The Museum of Modern Art, New York.

DADA

In the light of the political fragmentation of Europe that culminated in the devastation of World War I, fragmentation in the arts seems prophetic indeed. The artists who belonged to the Dada Movement, which was launched in Switzerland around 1914, expressed the despair of World War I by rejecting convention and tradition. Dada has been called a form of anti-art because of its pessimistic **nihilism** (literally a philosophy of "nothingness"). The Dadaists wished to start over, suggested by the enigmatic term *dada*, which has been variously identified as the child's first spoken syllables, as the French word for "hobby-horse," and as the Russian for "yes-yes." The work that best expresses early Dada is the *Collage Arranged According to the Laws of Chance* (figure **21.20**) by the Swiss artist Jean (Hans) Arp (1887–1966), who wanted to replicate the senselessness of war and modern society. In fact, however, his collage is the product of a creative idea, in which *de*struction is followed by *con*struction. He tore up pieces of paper, subjected them to chance by letting them drop onto a surface, and pasted them where they fell. He thus created a new image out of what had been destroyed (torn up). After World War I the Dada Movement spread to Germany and the United States (see Chapter 22).

MUSIC AND THE AVANT GARDE IN EUROPE

Musical Modernism arose against the backdrop of Wagner's chromaticism (see Chapter 18). Debussy, with his shimmering, Oriental-flavored color, was a primary contemporary influence (see Chapter 20). As in literature, the visual arts, and theater, strands of nationalism came together, but music also grew in internationalism. The increased speed of communication affecting all the arts made cross-cultural diversity—European, American, and non-Western—more available. Avant-garde music was frequently dissonant and atonal, having affinities with the harsh edges of Cubism and the absence of narrative in abstract painting.

MAURICE RAVEL

The French composer Maurice Ravel (1875–1937) is often associated with Debussy, although Ravel's music is more classically oriented. Ravel uses modal melodies and clusters of notes in discords but often retains structures of classicism, as in his String Quartet (1903) and Violin Sonata (1927). Repetition—

of a note or a musical figure—is also a feature of his style, as in his orchestral ballet music *Boléro* (1928), where the same rhythm hypnotically pulses throughout the piece. Ravel is particularly acclaimed for precise orchestral writing, careful craftsmanship, and elegant sensuousness of style.

Like contemporary literature, music of this period reflected a growing interest in the fantasy life of children. Ravel's fairy-tale ballet *Ma mère l'oye* (*Mother Goose*, 1911) combines wistfulness with clarity, while the plot of his second opera, *L'Enfant et les sortilèges* (*The Child and the Spells*, 1925), brings to life household and garden objects, which scold a naughty child until he breaks the spell by being kind. The unreal situation is mirrored in the music, with its bright, quirky orchestration.

GUSTAV MAHLER

Gustav Mahler (1860–1911) was born in Bohemia and studied at the Vienna Conservatory. One of the last composers in the Austro-German tradition that includes Mozart, Beethoven, and Brahms, he worked for most of his career as a conductor, composing principally for the orchestra: nine symphonies, a tenth that remains unfinished, and songs for voice with orchestra.

Mahler's symphonies are conceived on a grand scale, lasting for an hour or more. Following Beethoven's example, Mahler added voices to several, which often include programmatic elements expressing themes such as doubt turning to hope and triumph, the artist as hero, and impending doom.

Mahler's sense of the symphony as narrative journey is reflected in his tonality. His symphonies are tonal, but several depart from convention by starting in one key and ending in another. Mahler brings in elements of folk music, dances like the waltz, marches, and fanfares. There is often parody and irony, as in Symphony No. 4, where *ländler* dances are played on a mistuned violin. Interested in orchestral color, Mahler expanded the orchestra, generating weight through thick textures and drawing out small groups of solo players. He scored for unusual instruments—cowbells, for example, evoke the pastures of the Alps.

Despite its grand scale, much of Mahler's music is introspective and melancholy. *Das Lied von der Erde* (*The Song of the Earth*, 1909), a song cycle with orchestra, ends with an extended farewell that portends his own death. In a way, too, it laments the demise of nineteenth-century European culture and foretells the fate of Europe on the brink of a world war.

RICHARD STRAUSS

The composer and conductor Richard Strauss (1864–1949) was regarded for over sixty years as the foremost German composer. Born only four years after Mahler, Strauss also excelled in orchestral and song writing, but he made an important contribution in opera as well.

Whereas Mahler wrote symphonies, Strauss adopted the tone poem as his preferred orchestral form. Works like *Till Eulenspiegels lustige Streiche* (*Till Eulenspiegel's Merry Pranks*, 1895) narrate a wordless, often heroic, story. Orchestration is huge and sumptuous, with special instrumental combinations creating vivid effects.

Strauss wrote over two hundred songs, most between 1885 and 1906, but from around 1900 he turned his focus onto opera. He wrote fifteen operas, including *Salome* (1905) and *Der Rosenkavalier* (*The Cavalier of the Rose*, 1911). *Salome* is a setting of Wilde's play on the biblical story of the beheading of John the Baptist. A one-act piece focusing on female obsession, it incorporates psychological insights gleaned from Freud and epitomizes decadent *fin-de-siècle* Romanticism. The opera caused great scandal—one that fed success, for it was performed at fifty different opera houses within two years of its composition. The emotional turmoil of the plot is matched by music of harmonic extremity, rich in discord.

Der Rosenkavalier, by contrast, is a look to the past—an erotic comedy set in eighteenth-century Vienna. Its music returns to tonality and is imbued with waltz rhythms. Sometimes sentimental, sometimes farcical, it centers around the love triangle of the Marschallin (the field marshal's wife), Octavian, and Sophie, and the outwitting and humiliation of the lecherous Baron Ochs. One of the most sublime ensemble pieces in all opera is the trio in which the Marschallin ends her affair with Octavian so he and Sophie may enjoy their love for each other. The sweeping themes, rich orchestral underpinning, sensual harmonies, and expressive beauty of these operas signify Strauss's great contributions to turn-of-the-century music.

ARNOLD SCHOENBERG

Born in Vienna and virtually self-educated in composition, Arnold Schoenberg (1874–1951) believed that his music continued the tradition of Mozart, Beethoven, and Mahler. Like other composers of the period, he gradually reduced the large, Romantic orchestra to modest proportions, and over half his output was chamber music. Early works, such as the string **sextet** *Verklärte Nacht* (*Transfigured Night*, 1899), are densely contrapuntal and heavily chromatic, but still tonal.

Although composers had undermined the tonal system for decades, Schoenberg made the break to atonality in 1908, which started a musical revolution. Rejecting the traditional orientation of music progressing toward a home key, he explored dissonance for its own sonorous effect. Previously, dissonances (clashes) were introduced, but were then resolved onto **consonances** (sweet sounds). Now they were left unresolved. The Listening Selection gives a flavor of this in a brief fast movement (*etwas rasch* is German for "somewhat hasty") from Schoenberg's *Six Little Piano Pieces*, Opus 19 (1911). Note how the rhythm, like the tonality, has been set free and fails to articulate an obvious meter.

MUSIC LISTENING SELECTION
Schoenberg, *Six Little Piano Pieces*, Etwas rasch. Peter Hill, piano, CD track 20

In his song cycle *Pierrot lunaire* (*Moonstruck Pierrot*, 1912), Schoenberg set twenty-one short Symbolist poems for singer and chamber ensemble (flute, clarinet, violin, cello, and piano). Based on the *commedia dell'arte* clown, Pierrot is sad, alienated, and verging on madness. The macabre, dreamlike atmosphere contrasts with the "light, ironic, satirical tone" intended by Schoenberg. The cycle incorporates a special vocal technique, **Sprechgesang** ("speech-song"), in which the singer is guided by the pitches indicated in the score but immediately rises or falls away after sounding them. The alienation and uncertainty expressed in *Pierrot lunaire* were characteristic of music before the war.

Schoenberg is closely associated with the development of the **twelve-tone technique**, the compositional method he used for works from the 1920s, such as the Suite for Piano, Op. 25 (1923). With the abandonment of tonality, the harmonic and melodic basis of Western music since the Renaissance, Schoenberg proposed his "method of composing with twelve notes which are related only to one another" as a new structuring principle. In this system a sequence of tones, called a "tone-row," replaced the traditional scale as the fundamental building blocks of a composition. Schoenberg formulated rules for composing with rows to ensure that the musical fabric would avoid suggestion of a tonal center.

A tone-row usually includes all twelve notes of the octave (on a piano, the black and white keys between two notes of the same name). The composer may sound each tone in the row sequentially, transposed (starting on another pitch), backward, inverted (in mirror image, i.e. exchanging going up a semitone for going down a semitone), or simultaneously in a chord. This compositional method left listeners unclear about where the piece was going. However, it offered inner logic and organic unity as its philosophical basis.

In 1933, Schoenberg escaped Nazi persecution (see Chapter 22) and moved to the United States. He continued to explore the twelve-tone technique in his teaching and compositions, including his Piano Concerto (1942) and String Trio (1946). His music and theories were not widely understood in his lifetime, but since his death he has been recognized as a significant and highly influential figure in the history of Western music.

IGOR STRAVINSKY

The Russian composer Igor Stravinsky (1882–1971) set out to find radical new alternatives to the symphonic traditions of the past. His best-known music is characterized by its rhythms—often repeated, pounding, insistent, and breaking with regular metrical patterns.

Stravinsky's international career began in 1910, when the ballet choreographer Sergei Diaghilev (1872–1929) commissioned him to compose a one-act ballet based on the Russian fairytale of the Firebird. First performed by the Russian Ballet in Paris (capital of the international musical world at the time) to great acclaim, it was followed by two further ballets, *Petrushka* (1911) and *The Rite of Spring* (1913). Imbued with Symbolist imagery, *Petrushka* is a circus story about a puppet that comes to life. Mime sequences expressing his opposing inanimate and human natures are musically paralleled by the clash of two simultaneously sounded tonal centers. At the other extreme, the score offers simple Russian peasant dances.

The Rite of Spring is among the most notorious musical compositions of the twentieth century. At its first performance the ballet caused a riot. The story portrays an imaginary pagan spring festival in Russia, culminating in the sacrifice of a virgin. The daring choreography suggested earth-worship, fertility rites, and human sacrifice. Stravinsky's primitivist score was a musical counterpart of Picasso's adoption of African art. Pulsing, primal rhythms dominate, with unprecedented energy and harshness. Melody is virtually absent as drums pound and even stringed instruments are used percussively. Repetition, unresolved discord, and violent changes of dynamic complete the effect of ruthless, elemental power.

MUSIC LISTENING SELECTION
Stravinsky, *The Rite of Spring*, "Dance of Youths and Maidens." Belgian Radio and Television Philharmonic Orchestra, conductor Alexander Rabhari, CD track 21

In the 1920s, Stravinsky turned from the large-scale, overt style of his pre-war ballets toward Neoclassicism, composing spare, contained works, such as the Wind Octet (1923), with its dry sonorities, simpler rhythms, and references to eighteenth-century forms and sounds.

By the time Stravinsky composed his Neoclassical opera, *The Rake's Progress* (1951), he had emigrated to the United States, become a professor at Harvard University, and adopted American citizenship. He commissioned W. H. Auden (see Chapter 23) to write the libretto, with action set in the eighteenth century and based on a set of Hogarth engravings he had seen at the Art Institute of Chicago in 1947 (see Chapter 17). Stravinsky accordingly used Classical-period divisions of ensemble, arias, and recitative with harpsichord accompaniment. His largest composition, *The Rake's Progress* was first performed in Venice—the city he chose as his final resting place.

TURN-OF-THE-CENTURY AMERICA

With the exception of the avant garde, the United States at the turn of the century was relatively removed from cultural developments in Europe. The dichotomy between Modernism and tradition caused the same tensions in America as in Europe, but they evolved in a different cultural environment. Industry and innovation, although not without problems, were highly valued in America. In the arts, on the other hand, America was less attuned to newness than Europe was. Such issues as nationalism versus internationalism, abstraction versus realism, and harmony versus dissonance were only beginning to infiltrate the American consciousness.

POETRY: FROST, POUND, AND H.D.

There were two main threads of poetic style in early twentieth-century America: traditional and lyrical on the one hand, and abstract (or Imagist) on the other. The former is embodied in the poetry of Robert Frost (1874–1963), whose rhythms are regular and whose content is specifically American. Frost was drawn to landscape, particularly that of New England where he lived from the age of eleven, and his poetry is rich in symbolic allusions to man's relationship with nature.

The famous first line of "Mending Wall" (1914)—"Something there is that doesn't love a wall"—conveys the poem's message that fences do *not* necessarily make good neighbors. Implying that wall-building is the result of a primitive, ancestral, and "savage" impulse, Frost refers to psychological as well as to literal fences. His ambivalence is clear as he wonders what purpose the neighbor's wall will serve:

Before I built a wall I'd ask to know
What I was walling in or walling out,
And to whom I was like to give offense . . .
I see him there
Bringing a stone grasped firmly by the top
In each hand, like an old-stone savage armed.
He moves in darkness as it seems to me,
Not of woods only and the shade of trees.
He will not go behind his father's saying,
And he likes having thought of it so well
He says again, "Good fences make good neighbors."

Ezra Pound (1885–1972) was born in Idaho and educated in New England. In his early twenties he moved to Europe, where he became acquainted with Yeats and Joyce. By 1912 he was involved with Imagism, a style characterized by brevity, free verse, linguistic abstraction, and pictorial presentations of language. In "The Garden" (1916), Pound's Imagism creates a picture of decline, ennui, and tension:

Like a skein of loose silk blown against a wall
She walks by the railing of a path in Kensington Gardens,
And she is dying piece-meal
of a sort of emotional-anaemia.

Hilda Doolittle (1886–1961), known as H.D., was also an Imagist, and she was engaged for a short time to Pound. She was born in Pennsylvania, spent World War I in London, then left her English husband to live with another woman, Bryher (Winifred Ellerman). H.D.'s earliest collection of poems, *Sea Garden* (1916), reveals her admiration for ancient Greece, especially the work of Sappho (see Chapter 5). Her short verses generally take an object from nature as a metaphor for a human mood. In "Heat," H.D. makes heat into a solid, resistant form, just as the Cubists made air space into solid geometry:

O wind, rend open the heat,
cut apart the heat,
rend it to tatters.

Fruit cannot drop
through this thick air—
that presses up and blunts
the point of pears
and rounds the grapes.

Cut the heat—
plow through it,
turning it on either side
of your path.

H.D. was a patient of Freud's from 1933 to 1934, an experience about which she wrote in *Tribute to Freud* (1956).

THE VISUAL ARTS

Early-twentieth-century American painting styles were predominantly traditional, but a group of eight painters, calling themselves the Eight, formed in New York City to address modern life. They rejected Realism and sought to capture the immediacy of the city with scenes of everyday life. In contrast to the contemporary avant garde in Europe, however, the Eight retained naturalistic form. Both the critics and the general public found their subject matter vulgar and low-class and applied the name Ashcan School to the group.

The most important of the Eight painters was John Sloan (1871–1951), who moved to New York from Philadelphia in 1904. Originally a newspaper illustrator, Sloan used reportage in his paintings, which capture passing moments of the urban scene (figure **21.21**).

One of the major forces in introducing the European avant garde to the United States was the photographer Alfred Stieglitz (1864–1946). Born in New Jersey, he began taking photographs in Germany, where he was a student in 1883. When he returned to the United States he took impressionistic pictures of New York. He considered *The Steerage* (figure **21.22**) his most important New York picture.

In 1905 Stieglitz founded the Photo-Secession Gallery at 291 Fifth Avenue to exhibit avant-garde artists, and in 1911 he gave Picasso his first one-man show in America. Stieglitz offered Georgia O'Keeffe (1887–1986) her first one-woman show in 1917. O'Keeffe was raised on a Wisconsin farm, moved to Virginia when she was fifteen, and studied art in Chicago. Influenced by Kandinsky's *Concerning the Spiritual in Art*, she painted colors and shapes to reflect feelings rather than to represent recognizable figures or objects (figure **21.23**).

In the course of her long and successful career, O'Keeffe painted, in addition to pure abstractions, cityscapes, architecture, close-ups of flowers, and from 1929 the desert of the American Southwest. She married Stieglitz in 1924 and was for a time one of his most constant photographic subjects.

21.21 John Sloan, *McSorley's Bar*, 1912. Oil on canvas, 26 × 32 in. (66 × 81.3 cm). Detroit Institute of Arts.
McSorley's Bar, located on East 11th Street in Manhattan, was a favorite subject of Sloan's. As with European Impressionism, Sloan's prominent brushstrokes simulate texture. At the center, the light defining the waiter and the bartender anchors the picture, which depicts the bar as a microcosm of the city.

21.22 Alfred Stieglitz, *The Steerage*, 1907. Photograph. Library of Congress, Washington, D.C.
Stieglitz was on the S.S. *Kaiser Wilhelm II* about to sail from New York to Europe, when he caught sight of steerage (the lowest class on a ship) and rushed to get his camera and capture the appearance of immigrants from the Old World. The diagonal plank with its ropes divides the picture as well as the social classes on the ship; the upper classes are above and the lower classes below.

21.23 Georgia O'Keeffe, *From the Lake No. 1*, 1924. Oil on canvas, 37⅛ × 31 in. (94.3 × 78.7 cm). Des Moines Arts Center, Iowa.
This abstract depiction of a lake suggests the flowing motion of water and its merged reflections of sky and landscape. O'Keeffe varies the textures by combining softened, shaded areas of color (mainly grays and blues) with sharp edges and bright yellows and greens. She has captured a dynamic energy that conveys the organic sense of nature's on-going process of change and motion.

21.24 *left* **Marcel Duchamp, *Nude Descending a Staircase, No. 2*, 1912. Oil on canvas, 4 ft. 10 in. × 2 ft. 11 in. (147 × 89 cm). Philadelphia Museum of Art.** Duchamp combines the mechanical speed of Futurism, the solid geometry and small chromatic range of Cubism, and the sequencing of film. Outraged critics called the picture a "heap of broken violins," a "dynamited suit of Japanese armor," and an "explosion in a shingle factory."

The Armory Show: 1913

The full impact of the avant garde reached America in 1913 with the Armory Show, an exhibition of some thirteen hundred works by Modernist European and American artists held at the Sixty-ninth Regiment Armory in New York City. It was the first time that the American public was exposed to new artistic developments in Europe, and, as with many innovations, these were shocking. The work that caught the most attention—much of it negative—was *Nude Descending a Staircase No. 2* (figure **21.24**) by Marcel Duchamp (1887–1968).

Born in France, Duchamp moved to New York in 1915. He retired from art in 1923 to play chess and became an American citizen in 1955. He would be a seminal figure in the avant garde during and immediately following World War I (see Chapter 22).

Film: D. W. Griffith

From the late nineteenth century film technology had steadily advanced. The greatest early American film-maker, D. W. (David Wark) Griffith (1875–1948), was born in the South, a fact reflected in his great epic of the Civil War, *The Birth of a Nation* (1915). Griffith's father had been a colonel in the Confederate Army, and when he died, his son and widow moved to Louisville, Kentucky, where they lived in poverty. Griffith was interested in the power of narrative and pioneered many film techniques, including the use of multiple cameras, flashbacks, close-ups and long shots, and angled views for dramatic effect (figure **21.25**).

21.25 D. W. Griffith, battle scene from *The Birth of a Nation*, 1915, Kobal Collection. In this long shot, Griffith places the spectator at an elevated vantage point and creates a narrative within a single frame. We see the soldiers closest to us at the lower left enter the frame and follow the S-curve down the hill toward the fighting. Denoting the battle itself is the cloud of smoke and the burning stockade. By placing us at a distance, Griffith gives us a panoramic view of the silhouetted soldiers and conveys the brutal anonymity of war.

Griffith's genius as a technician reinforced his genius as a director and story-teller. *The Birth of a Nation* is a silent film, lasting three hours, that emphasizes the virtues of the Old South, its chivalrous lifestyle, and its suffering in such scenes as the burning of Atlanta. Griffith saw the Civil War as the birth of the nation, followed by Lincoln's assassination and Reconstruction, in which the North tried to crush the South by giving power to former slaves.

Made in an era of rising racism in America, *The Birth of a Nation* conveys a negative view of blacks as a threat to the white race. The notion that black men are generic rapists of white women and that the Ku Klux Klan are the

21.26 Poster for *The Birth of a Nation*, 1915.
This poster was designed to suggest that the Ku Klux Klan are heroic Christian soldiers. Masquerading as a crusader defending the faith, the clansman rides a rearing horse and brandishes a burning cross. His portrayal as an equestrian hero recalls the imperial traditions of ancient Rome (see thumbnail).

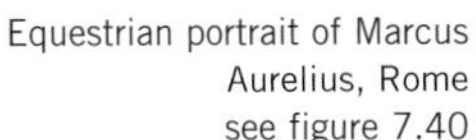
Equestrian portrait of Marcus Aurelius, Rome
see figure 7.40

proverbial knights in shining armor led to the revival of that organization (figure **21.26**).

Griffith's film was a powerful piece of propaganda seen by over 3 million viewers. The recently founded NAACP (National Association for the Advancement of Colored People) tried, and failed, to have the film banned. Technically and dramatically a work of genius, historically biased, and by modern standards outrageously racist, *The Birth of a Nation* laid the groundwork for the future of American cinema.

MUSIC IN THE UNITED STATES

The most distinctive musical styles in America at the turn of the century—**ragtime**, **blues**, and **jazz**—emerged from African-American culture. Ragtime, a fusion of African-American rhythms and European-style harmonies, enjoyed enormous popularity between 1890 and 1915. Its most distinctive feature is its **syncopated** ("ragged") melody, with accents falling on unstressed beats, accompanied by regular, "boom-chuck-boom-chuck" rhythms. Although ragtime was played on different instruments in different styles, it is best known as a piano style. Structured in sixteen-measure strains, each divided into four clear phrases, it has a "square" format that betrays its origins in military marches and the banjo tunes that accompanied minstrel shows. Scott Joplin (1868–1917) is the best-known ragtime composer. During the early-twentieth-century ragtime craze, the sheet music for Joplin's "Maple Leaf Rag" (1899) sold over a million copies.

The "blues" folksong style evolved along with the *field holler* and the *group work song* as African Americans labored. Originally unaccompanied, these forms expressed the hardships of life; the style's name is thought to have arisen because singers performed to chase away "the blues." Typical subject matter might be imprisonment, unrequited love, or loneliness. A distinctive feature of blues—which has since pervaded much American popular music, like rock—is the use of the "blues scale," in which certain scale degrees (especially the third, fifth, and seventh) are treated as "bent notes," being rendered with slides.

Blues flourished in several forms, from the sharecropper singing and strumming his guitar on his porch, to more professional styles played by ensembles and even sold as sheet music. The different kinds of blues generally shared some standard features, such as conventional lyric topics, use of the blues scale, typical chordal accompaniment patterns, and an *AAB* strophic form in which a line of verse would be repeated, followed by a rhyming line. In professional contexts, such as the Chicago-based "classic" blues of the 1920s and other urban styles later flourishing in that city, the "twelve-bar blues" form became standardized, comprising three four-bar units each containing the line of verse and an instrumental, often improvised, "response."

In 1902, W. C. Handy (1873–1958), the "Father of the Blues," formed his first band. In Memphis, Tennessee, he co-owned a music publishing company and disseminated his own compositions, including the best-selling "St. Louis Blues" (1914). This lament for a lost lover became popular in Europe, Africa, and the United States.

MUSIC LISTENING SELECTION

W. C. Handy, "St. Louis Blues." Louis Armstrong Orchestra, Louis Armstrong, cornet, CD track 25

The term "jazz," of uncertain origin, had come into popular usage by 1917, when the first jazz recordings were made by the Original Dixieland Jazz Band. Jazz was a product of the particular social and musical configuration in turn-of-the-century Storyville, the red-light district of New Orleans. The style evolved from the interaction of a "downtown" music culture dominated by formally trained Creoles with an "uptown" African-American music scene based on blues and ragtime.

New Orleans jazz, or "classic" jazz, which flourished in the first two decades of the twentieth century, combined syncopated rhythms of ragtime, harmonies derived from blues and other sources, and new forms of instrumental improvisation, as played by a small combo typically consisting of trumpet, trombone, clarinet, bass (tuba, or later, string bass), perhaps piano and banjo, and the newly evolving drum set. Particularly characteristic of classic jazz was the process of collective improvisation, in which the trumpet, trombone, and clarinet all improvised at once. The somewhat merry cacophony could be varied by devices like the insertion of **breaks**, in which all accompanying instruments stopped for an instant, or perhaps played staccato bursts, in a technique called "stop-time."

The period encompassed by the turn of the twentieth century to World War I exemplifies the theme of Freud's Civilization and its Discontents. *On the one hand, it was a period of enormous creative expansion in all the arts and in the sciences and, on the other, it was fraught with anxiety and tension. Revolution in Russia, atomic research, and fragmentation in art and literature heralded the eruption of destructive impulses that culminated in the war that was termed "the war to end all wars." The end of World War I marks a break with the past and the beginning of what many historians call "the modern world."*

KEY TERMS

anima the female aspect of Jung's archetypal soul.

animus the male aspect of Jung's archetypal soul.

archetypes universal images, such as the good or bad parent, the hero, the wise man, and so forth.

avant garde newness for its own sake.

blues an African-American style of music, existing in folk and urban popular forms, with lyrics typically expressing the hardships of life.

break a short musical passage like a cadenza, played by one or more of the instruments in jazz or blues.

collage a technique of making an image by pasting objects onto a surface.

collective unconscious an idea or belief held collectively and unconsciously by a group rather than an individual.

consonance the sounding together of tones that sound harmonious, the opposite of dissonance.

jazz music improvised by performers in ensembles over a framework of chords, which grew out of African-American experience and developed in New Orleans at the start of the twentieth century.

nihilism the philosophy of nothingness.

operetta a light opera, generally with spoken dialogue, songs, and dances.

portmanteau word a word formed by combining two or more words.

quantum theory Planck's theory that radioactive energy moves in bursts of energy.

ragtime an African-American precursor of jazz that flourished between 1890 and 1915, characterized by syncopated melody and mostly composed for the piano.

sextet a piece of chamber music for six players, or the group that performs such a piece.

special theory of relativity Einstein's theory that movement in time and space is relative; only the speed of light is absolute.

Sprechgesang ("speech-song") a twentieth-century vocal technique in which the performer is guided by the pitches indicated in the score, but immediately rises or falls away after sounding them; used extensively by Schoenberg.

sublimation in psychoanalysis, the transformation of instinct into creative, socially productive activity.

syncopation in music, accents on beats that are not normally stressed.

twelve-tone technique a twentieth-century compositional method in which all twelve notes of the octave are ordered in a "tone-row," which is manipulated in various prescribed ways to shape the musical content; formulated by Schoenberg.

KEY QUESTIONS

1. Would this period be better described as a *belle époque* or one of *fin-de-siècle* malaise?
2. What anxieties accompany an understanding of Freud's and Einstein's theories? Would such anxieties be specific to this period or would they characterize all periods?
3. What newly discovered psychological insights are used by artists in this period? Name two works that illustrate these insights.
4. The fragmentation and devastation of Europe brought about by World War I influenced many art styles and literary themes. How does Dada, for example, reflect the period in its choice of themes, style, and technique?
5. Compare the maps of Europe before and after World War I (maps 21.1 and 22.1). What changes are immediately apparent? How is Europe structured differently?

SUGGESTED READING

Alastair, Duncan. *Art Nouveau*. London: Thames and Hudson, 1994.
▸ A survey of the style.

Barr, Jr., Alfred H. *Cubism and Abstract Art, Photography, Architcture, and Industrial Art, Theater, Films, Posters*. Cambridge, MA: Belknap Press of Harvard University Press, 1986.
▸ The avant garde in art.

Blier, Suzanne. *The Royal Arts of Africa: The Majesty of Form*. New York: Harry N. Abrams, 1998.
▸ An account of African art.

Flam, Jack. *Matisse: The Man and His Art 1869–1918*. Ithaca, NY: Cornell University Press, 1986.
▸ The artist's early career.

——. *Matisse on Art*. London: Phaidon Press, 1973.
▸ Matisse's writings on art.

Hale, O. *The Great Illusion, 1900–1914*. London: HarperCollins, 1971.
▸ A general overview of the period.

Herbert, James D. *Fauve Painting: The Making of Cultural Politics*. New Haven, CT: Yale University Press, 1992.
▸ A contextual approach to Fauvism.

Hulton, Pontus. *Futurism and Futurisms*. New York: Abbeville Press, 1986.
▸ A study of the Futurist Movement in art and society.

Joll, J. *The Origins of the First World War*. London: Longman, 1984.
▸ A short, accessible account.

Keegan, J. *The First World War*. London: Pimlico, 1999.
▸ A narrative account of the war.

Lloyd, Jill. *German Expressionism: Primitivism and Modernity*. New Haven, CT: Yale University Press, 1991.
▸ German Expressionism and the avant garde.

O'Brien, Edna. *James Joyce*. New York: Viking, 1999.
▸ A short biography, part of a series by well-known authors on famous figures.

Parkinson, David. *History of Film*. New York and London: Thames and Hudson, 1995.
▸ A brief general history.

Schorske, C. E. *Fin de Siècle Vienna: Politics and Culture*. New York: Random House, 1980.
▸ Studies on intellectual developments in turn-of-the-century Vienna.

Wilson, Edmund. *To the Finland Station*. London: Penguin Books, 1991.
▸ Lenin returns to Russia to lead the revolution.

SUGGESTED FILMS

1915 *The Birth of a Nation*, dir. D. W. Griffith

1916 *Intolerance*, dir. D. W. Griffith

1925 *Lady Windermere's Fan* (based on Wilde), dir. Ernst Lubitsch

1930 *All Quiet on the Western Front* (based on Remarque), dir. Lewis Milestone

1931 *Dr. Jekyll and Mr. Hyde* (based on Stevenson), dir. Rouben Mamoulian

1939 *The Hound of the Baskervilles* (based on Conan Doyle), dir. Sidney Lanfield

1945 *The Picture of Dorian Gray* (based on Wilde), dir. Albert Lewin

1950 *Treasure Island* (based on Stevenson), dir. Wilfred Jackson, Clyde Geronomi, and Hamilton Luske

1960 *The Trials of Oscar Wilde*, dir. Ken Hughes

1971 *Nicholas and Alexandra*, dir. Franklin Schaffner

1972 *Alice's Adventures in Wonderland*, dir. William Sterling

1979 *Tess* (based on Hardy), dir. Roman Polanski

1981 *Boléro* (*Uns et Les Autres*), dir. Claude Lelouch

1981 *Reds*, dir. Warren Beatty

1987 *Roxanne*, (based on Rostand), dir. Fred Schepsi

1999 *Topsy-Turvy* (about Gilbert and Sullivan), dir. Mike Leigh

22 World War I through World War II

> *"There never was a war more easy to stop than that which has just wrecked what was left of the world from the previous struggle."*
>
> (WINSTON CHURCHILL, *The Gathering Storm*)

The two decades following World War I were a period of recovery and a relentless march toward the cataclysm of World War II (1939–1945). This chapter is framed by these two world wars, which caused the deaths of some 40 to 60 million people and permanently disabled millions more. During World War II, **genocide** *(the deliberate extinction of a race or nation) occurred on a vast, well-organized scale unprecedented in European history.*

Despite the carnage of World War I, the 1920s was a decade of economic prosperity in parts of Europe and the United States, where the increasing availability of household appliances improved daily life. Modernism in art and literature reached its height and mass culture—radios, newspapers, comic strips, popular films, and the Broadway musical—evolved. In 1928 Walt Disney (1901–1966) created the animated character Mickey Mouse, which became an American icon.

The 1920s was also the "jazz age," when jazz began to infiltrate mainstream musical genres. Jazz appealed to Western composers interested in non-Western cultures and fueled the Harlem Renaissance, a movement that inspired creative energy among African Americans. The 1920s came to a disastrous close with the crash of the New York Stock Exchange on October 29, 1929—the event that heralded the world-wide Great Depression of the 1930s.

During the 1930s, brutal totalitarian regimes in Europe and Japan set the stage for World War II. Elements of German society resented the Treaty of Versailles (see Chapter 21) and, under the National Socialists (the Nazis), defied the treaty and rearmed. The League of Nations failed and the United States withdrew into isolationism. **Fascism** *took hold in Italy and Spain, Russia was controlled by a repressive communist regime, and, in the Far East, Japan built up a powerful army in the service of the emperor.*

Among others, including socialist leaders in Europe, the British statesman Winston Churchill (1874–1965) saw war coming and tried to prevent it. By his own account he later told the American president, Franklin D. Roosevelt (presidency 1933–1945), that he considered World War II the "Unnecessary War." Churchill believed, as he stated in the quotation that opens the chapter, that not only could the war have been easily avoided, but also that it had destroyed what remained of civilization.

Key Topics

Destabilizing Factors

- War reparations
- Stock speculation
- Economic depression

Rising Totalitarianism

- Fascism
- National Socialism
- Genocide
- The Holocaust
- Communism

Art in Context

- Dada
- Regionalism
- Harlem Renaissance
- Surrealism
- De Stijl
- Prairie Style
- Modernism

Music

- The Jazz Age
- The American musical

Philosophy

- Logical positivism
- Existentialism

TIMELINE	EARLY-TWENTIETH-CENTURY EUROPE	EARLY-TWENTIETH-CENTURY UNITED STATES
HISTORY AND CULTURE 	Totalitarianism in Russia, Italy, Germany, Spain, and Japan Sinking of the *Titanic*, 1912 Bolsheviks under Lenin take power in Russia, 1918 Stalin controls Communist Party in Russia, 1924 Hitler, *Mein Kampf*, 1924; German chancellor, 1933 Great Purges in Russia, 1934–1939 Spanish Civil War, 1936–1939 World War II, 1939–1945 Churchill becomes British prime minister, 1940 Pétain forms Vichy Government in France, 1940 D-Day Invasion of Normandy by Allies, 1944 Nuremberg Trials in Germany, 1945	Jazz Age, 1920s Harlem Renaissance, 1920s Hoover elected president, 1929 Stock market crash, 1929 Great Depression, 1930s Roosevelt elected president; New Deal policy, 1933 Social Security Act, 1935 National Labor Relations Act, 1935 Japanese bomb Pearl Harbor; U.S. enters war, 1941 U.S. drops atom bombs on Hiroshima and Nagasaki in Japan, 1945
SCIENCE, TECHNOLOGY, AND PSYCHOLOGY	Amundsen first to reach South Pole, 1911 Schweitzer founds hospital in French Equatorial Africa, 1913 Shackleton leads expedition to Antarctic, 1914–1917 Fleming discovers penicillin, 1928 Heyerdahl, *Kon-Tiki* expedition, 1947	Peary first to reach North Pole, 1909 Lindbergh: first solo flight across Atlantic, 1927 Mead, *Coming of Age in Samoa*, 1928 Manhattan Project, 1941 Carrel and Lindbergh invent first artificial heart, 1942
ART 	Dada, Surrealism, and Futurism International Style (*De Stijl*), 1917–1930s Höch, *Cut with the Kitchen Knife*, c. 1919 Ernst, *The Hat Makes the Man*, 1920 Mondrian, *Composition with Large Red Plane . . .* , 1921 Brancusi, *White Negress III*, c. 1923 Breton publishes "Surrealist Manifesto," 1924 Miró, *The Policeman*, 1925 Picasso, *Guernica*, 1937 Matisse, "Jazz," 1947	Regionalism Duchamp, *L.H.O.O.Q.*, 1919 Calder, *Josephine Baker*, 1927–1929 Man Ray, *Tears*, 1932–1933 Benton, *Pioneer Days and Early Settlement*, 1936 Lawrence, "Migration" Series No. 1, 1940–1941 Mexico: Kahlo, *Self-Portrait as a Tehuana*, 1943
ARCHITECTURE	Gropius (1883–1969): Bauhaus, Dresden Le Corbusier, Villa Savoye, France, 1928–1930	Wright, Kaufmann House (Fallingwater), Bear Run, Pennsylvania, 1936
FILM 	Eisenstein, *Battleship Potemkin*, 1925; *Alexander Nevsky*, 1938; *Ivan the Terrible*, 1945 Sound and color in film, by 1928 Riefenstahl, *Triumph of the Will*, 1936; *Olympia*, 1938	Cruze, *The Covered Wagon*, 1923 Disney, *Steamboat Willie*, 1928; *Fantasia*, 1940; *Alice in Wonderland*, 1951; *Mary Poppins*, 1964 Vidor, *Hallelujah!*, 1929 Berkeley, *Footlight Parade*, 1933 Chaplin, *Modern Times*, 1936; *The Great Dictator*, 1940 Fleming, *Gone with the Wind*, 1939 Welles, *Citizen Kane*, 1941
LITERATURE 	Hamsun, *Growth of the Soil*, 1917 Eliot, *The Waste Land*, 1922; "The Hollow Men," 1925 Joyce, *Ulysses*, 1922; *Finnegans Wake*, 1939 Hesse, *Siddhartha*, 1922; *Der Steppenwolf*, 1927 Woolf, *Mrs. Dalloway*, 1925; *A Room of One's Own*, 1929 Sholokhov, *And Quiet Flows the Don*, 1928 Remarque, *All Quiet on the Western Front*, 1929 Huxley, *Brave New World*, 1932 Laxness, *Independent People*, 1934–1935 Sartre, *Being and Nothingness*, 1943 Lägerkvist, *The Dwarf*, 1944	Cather, *My Antonia*, 1918; *One of Ours*, 1922 Cullen (1903–1946), "Heritage" Lewis, *Main Street*, 1920 Cummings, *The Enormous Room*, 1922 Dreiser, *An American Tragedy*, 1925 Fitzgerald, *The Great Gatsby*, 1925 Hemingway, *The Sun Also Rises*, 1926 Johnson, *God's Trombones*, 1927 Hurston, *How it Feels to be Colored Me*, 1928 Faulkner, *The Sound and the Fury*, 1929 Steinbeck, *The Grapes of Wrath*, 1939
THEATER AND BALLET	Pirandello, *Six Characters in Search of an Author*, 1921 O'Casey, *The Plough and the Stars*, 1926 Brecht, *The Three-Penny Opera*, 1928; *Mother Courage*, 1941 Lorca, *Blood Wedding*, 1933; *Yerma*, 1934 Giraudoux, *Tiger at the Gates*, 1935; *Electra*, 1937 Anouilh, *Le Voyageur sans bagage*, 1937; *Antigone*, 1944	Martha Graham designs innovative ballets, 1920s O'Neill, *Anna Christie*, 1921; *Mourning Becomes Electra*, 1931; *Long Day's Journey into Night*, 1957
MUSIC	American jazz popular in Paris, 1920s Baker in *La Revue Nègre*, 1925	Ives, *The Unanswered Question*, 1906 Bessie Smith, "Down Hearted Blues," 1923 Armstrong, "Potato Head Blues," 1927 Kern and Hammerstein, *Show Boat*, 1927 Gershwin, *An American in Paris*, 1928 Duke Ellington, "Mood Indigo," 1930 Still, *Afro-American Symphony*, 1931 Copland, *Billy the Kid*, 1938; *Rodeo*, 1942 Rodgers and Hammerstein, *Oklahoma!*, 1943 Parker (1920–1955), "Anthropology"; "Ornithology"

THE POLITICAL AND ECONOMIC AFTERMATH OF WORLD WAR I

The Treaty of Versailles was unworkable and the United States Senate refused to ratify it. Reeling from the millions of lives lost, Britain distanced itself from the rest of Europe. Although Germany initially suffered from reparations, it became quite prosperous by the late 1920s. In eastern Europe, on the other hand, the provisions of the treaty contributed to economic failure.

One major source of political tension in Europe arose from the "Mandate System," which required colonial powers to encourage their colonies to advance toward independence. Little headway, however, was made in freeing the colonies. The Ottoman Empire was replaced by a small Turkish republic, Britain controlled Iraq and Palestine, and France controlled Syria and Lebanon. Britain, France, and South Africa carved up the German colonies in Africa; in the South Pacific Australia, New Zealand, and Japan acquired German territories.

THE GREAT DEPRESSION IN THE UNITED STATES

Partly because there was no effective financial leadership in Europe after the war and partly because reparations were unrealistic, economic problems worsened worldwide during the later 1920s. European currencies, especially the German mark, which never quite stabilized after the war, grew more inflated and dependent on American money. But from 1928, Americans preferred to invest in the New York stock market, and many withdrew funds from Europe.

Widespread speculation in American stocks led to inflated prices and the practice of buying on margin (with borrowed money). When prices declined and banks called in loans, many investors could not come up with the necessary capital, causing bank failures. Because small deposits were uninsured, people went broke overnight. Homelessness became widespread, and shanty-towns, called Hoovervilles after Herbert Hoover (presidency 1929–1933), were suddenly part of the American landscape. So, too, were breadlines and soup kitchens. By 1932 13 million American workers had lost their jobs.

The Great Depression inspired President Franklin D. Roosevelt's New Deal, a policy of government-sponsored programs designed to relieve the economic crisis. In 1933 the Federal Emergency Relief Administration extended funds to state governments and private charities to help alleviate hunger and homelessness. The same year a new law insured bank accounts up to about $40,000, and the following year regulatory oversight of the stock market was instituted. (Today, bank accounts are federally insured up to $100,000.) In 1935 Congress enacted both the Social Security Act, providing benefits to people unable to work, and the National Labor Relations Act, guaranteeing protection to workers' unions. With funds from the Farm Security Administration (FSA), the federal government hired documentary photographers to record the reality of nation-wide poverty (figure **22.1**).

Some viewed the Great Depression as a natural adjustment in a free-market economy, whereas others saw it as exemplifying the dangers of unrestrained capitalism. In either case, the conflict between government regulation and laissez-faire economics (see Chapter 19) revived. In Europe, where the effects of the Depression were even worse than in the United States, the British economist John Maynard Keynes (1883–1946) concluded that governments should provide jobs. He published his views in *The General Theory of Employment, Interest, and Money* (1935). This became the foundation of **macroeconomics**, the study of economics on a national level, with particular attention to production, employment, inflation, and balancing of budgets.

22.1 Arthur Rothstein, *The Wife and Children of a Sharecropper*, Washington County, Arkansas, August, 1935. Featured in "Sharecropper Children," *Look Magazine*, March 1937.
This photograph, by Arthur Rothstein (born 1915), the first person hired by the FSA, depicts rural poverty in the American South. The wooden house has a ramshackle appearance, accentuated by the old broom and pail at the lower right. The mother looks worried, and her three, shabbily dressed, barefoot children are underfed. Rothstein, like other FSA photographers, captures a moment that encapsulates poverty during the Depression.

COMMUNISM IN RUSSIA

In the view of communist Russia (now called the Soviet Union), the American stock market crash heralded the end of capitalism and the inevitable, international embrace of communism. The three-year civil war was won by the Red Army in 1918 and led to a take-over by the Bolsheviks (meaning "majority") under Lenin. They imposed a harsh totalitarian regime, sustained by a secret police and funded by state seizure of banks, industry, and transportation. A naval rebellion in 1921 resulted in swift retribution, after which Lenin eased the most stringent Bolshevik policies and restored some stability.

With Lenin's death in 1924, two leaders vied for power—Leon Trotsky (1879–1940) and Joseph Stalin (1879–1953). Trotsky encouraged international revolution to reinforce Russian communism. At first he advocated terror to achieve his ends but later he agreed to entertain dialogue. In 1927 the Bolsheviks exiled Trotsky to Siberia and then to Mexico, where he was assassinated by a Stalinist agent.

Stalin, meanwhile, took control of the Communist Party and established a ruthless dictatorship. The son of a Georgian shoemaker, he studied for the priesthood but was expelled for his Marxist views.

From 1928 Soviet industry improved through a series of Five Year Plans. Under Stalin, the state owned the factories and collectivized the farms, but the policy led to widespread starvation. Stalin controlled the press, the police, the school system, family life, the judiciary, science, and the arts (figure **22.2**) in the Soviet Union. His policy of terror culminated in the Great Purges of 1934 to 1939. Over 10 million people were sent to the gulag (forced labor camps in Siberia) or killed for dissenting political views.

Because of its call for international revolution, communism aroused fear in the West, and one response was the rise of Fascism.

22.2 ***Stalin—father of his country*, 1939. Poster.**
This propaganda poster shows Stalin as a colossus towering over the Soviet army, with the walls of the Kremlin visible in the background. The banner proclaims Stalin's spirit as the strength of the army and the country. Stylistically, this exemplifies Socialist Realism, the official art of the Soviet Union.

THE RISE OF FASCISM AND NATIONAL SOCIALISM

Totalitarian militaristic regimes opposing Soviet-style communism were established in Italy, Germany, Spain, and Japan. These regimes were imbued with nationalist ideology and xenophobia (fear of foreigners). In Italy and Germany dictators used the economic downturn to rally people to their cause.

ITALY The Fascist movement led by Benito Mussolini (1883–1945) originated in Milan in 1919. Italians felt that they had been unfairly treated at Versailles and that Italy had been unjustly deprived of territory ceded to Yugoslavia. Civil unrest weakened the government, and gangs of *fascisti* (referring to gangs of hoodlums wearing black shirts) terrorized and murdered liberals, communists, and socialists. The king, Victor Emmanuel III (ruled 1900–1946), did nothing to oppose Fascism and, in order to promote political stability, persuaded parliament to declare Mussolini dictator for a year.

Once in power, Mussolini recognized Catholicism as the official Italian religion and gained the pope's support. He paid the pope for land taken from the Papal States in the nineteenth century and absolved the Church of having to pay taxes. Then, backed by the Black Shirts, he suppressed all opposition to his regime.

22.3 Hubert Lanzinger, *Hitler as a Medieval Knight*, *c.* 1936. Oil on canvas. Reminiscent of the equestrian portraits of Charlemagne and the Roman emperors, Hitler is shown as a medieval knight in shining armor. He sits proudly astride his war horse. His banner bears the swastika, which became the Nazi emblem, just as the medieval crusaders carried images of the Cross.

GERMANY At the end of World War I (map **22.1**) Germany formed a constitution in the city of Weimar—hence the term Weimar Republic—supported by liberals and Social Democrats. This was the first democratic government in German history, but it did not last. During the 1920s, militaristic and nationalistic opponents of the Weimar Republic argued that their country had been humiliated by the Treaty of Versailles. Rampant inflation of the German mark and galloping unemployment fired resentment of foreigners and minorities (especially Jews), who became scapegoats for Germany's problems. In 1923 Adolf Hitler (1889–1945), a failed Austrian artist and veteran of World War I, entered the political stage.

A charismatic orator, Hitler joined the anti-Semitic National Socialist (Nazi) party, whose Storm Troopers (the SA), known as the Brown Shirts, were the equivalent of the Black Shirts in Italy. In 1924, while briefly in jail for an unsuccessful *putsch* (rebellion) in Munich, Hitler wrote *Mein Kampf* (*My Struggle*), describing his political philosophy. He wanted to transform Germany into a new empire, the Third Reich, which would last a thousand years. The First Reich had been the Holy Roman Empire; the Second Reich was the German Empire, which lasted from the end of the Franco-Prussian War until the end of World War I.

As Mussolini appealed to Italian nostalgia for the power and grandeur of the ancient Roman Empire, so Hitler called on Germans to identify with Charlemagne and the Holy Roman Empire (figure **22.3**).

In the late 1920s the German economy began to improve. A series of accords between Germany, France, Britain, and Italy seemed to stabilize Europe. But Germany continued to resent the reparations, and the New York stock market crash spread economic disaster to Europe. Britain's parliamentary system withstood political extremes, but in France the right wing, anti-Semitic *Action Française* gained power. It opposed parliamentary rule and, fearing socialism and communism, backed Fascism and National Socialism.

In Germany the Nazi Party won a majority vote in the 1930 election, and in January 1933 Hitler legally became the German chancellor thanks to a provision in the Weimar Constitution that allowed the president to become temporary dictator in times of crisis. There was little opposition to Hitler's policies or to the terror tactics he used to enforce them. By the end of the year, he commanded over a million Storm Troopers.

SPAIN: CIVIL WAR Spain suffered political and economic unrest during most of the 1920s. In 1931 King Alfonso XIII (ruled 1886–1931) was overthrown and a secular, constitutional republic was established. However, there was turmoil among peasants, workers, landowners, and separatists from the northeast, and when the Popular Front government, representing Spain's entire political spectrum, was elected in 1936, the Spanish Fascists (Falangists) ignored the results and launched a three-year civil war. Their leader, Francisco Franco (1892–1975), supported by Mussolini and Hitler, invaded Spain with an army of Moroccan troops. Thousands of volunteers came from Europe to join the Loyalist fight against the Falangists, and American volunteers formed the Abraham Lincoln Brigade to defend the Popular Front against Fascism.

The war in Spain reinforced the alliance between Germany and Italy, which formed the Rome–Berlin Axis in 1936. Hitler supplied Franco with arms, and in 1937 German war planes bombed the unarmed northern town of Guernica, killing thousands of civilians. The atrocity was memorialized in Picasso's monumental painting created for the 1937 Paris World's Fair (figure **22.4**).

Despite their fierce resistance, the Loyalists were defeated by the Falangists. A Fascist dictatorship was established in Spain and lasted until Franco's death in 1975.

Map 22.1 Europe between the world wars.

22.4 Pablo Picasso, *Guernica*, 1937. Oil on canvas, 11 ft. 5½ in. × 25 ft. 5¼ in. (3.49 × 7.77 m). Centro de Arte Reina Sofia, Madrid.

This huge painting, filled with complex imagery and multiple layers of meaning, is divided into three sections. The central triangle contains a dismembered soldier with a broken sword, a woman running, a dying horse (Picasso's personal symbol of civilization), a woman with a lamp signifying liberty, and (at the top) a combined eye and lightbulb. At the right, a figure screams in a burning building. At the left, a minotaur (an allusion to Franco's tyrannical rule) towers over a mother and her dead infant. Picasso's message: Fascist brutality is destroying civilization and, with it, human dignity.

WORLD WAR II

World War II, even more than World War I, was a global conflict, involving Europe, Asia, and, from 1941, the United States. Hitler used resentment of the Treaty of Versailles to rally support and in 1936 he defied the treaty by rearming and moving troops into the Rhineland. Hitler's military use of speed and surprise over the next few years inspired the term *Blitzkrieg*, meaning "lightning war." Germany also had the most advanced weaponry, including tanks, a well-trained, well-armed infantry, a navy equipped with submarines (U-boats), and an air force. Despite Hitler's aggression and defiance of the Treaty of Versailles, the rest of Europe did nothing to halt his advance.

In 1938, a year after the bombing of Guernica, Hitler marched into Austria and annexed it (the *Anschluss*) to Germany, leaving Czechoslovakia vulnerable. Hoping to avoid war, the British prime minister, Neville Chamberlain (1869–1940), pursued a policy of appeasement. France went along with the British, and the United States, embroiled in its own economic problems, stayed out of European politics. On September 1, 1939, Hitler invaded Poland, and on September 3 Britain and France declared war.

Hitler's political program included virulent anti-Semitism and genocide. He manipulated Germany's centuries-old suspicion of Jews to promote his plans for the purification of the so-called master Aryan race. Throughout the 1930s German

22.6 Image by the French Institute of Jewish Issues under the Vichy Government. The "scientific study" of the effect of Jews on French society concluded that Jews were like a cancer eating away at France. Here the Jew is shown as an octopus, with each arm strangling a French institution—the army, the press, commerce, sports, literature, theater, public education, and finance.

22.5 George Rodger, Bergen-Belsen Concentration Camp, April 1945. The British photographer George Rodger (1908–1995) took this photograph just after the Allies had liberated the Bergen-Belson concentration camp. A row of emaciated bodies, the remains of the camp's inmates, stretches out beside the road. A lone boy averts his head to avoid the gruesome sight of the victims of mass extermination. This photograph reflects Rodger's ability to convey a historical moment in a single image.

Jews were fired from administrative and academic positions, and in 1935 the Nuremberg Laws revoked their German citizenship. In 1938, on *Kristallnacht* ("Crystal Night"—night of broken glass), the Nazis destroyed German synagogues and burned down many businesses belonging to Jews. In 1942 Hitler devised a so-called Final Solution, designed to exterminate all the Jews in Europe. Concentration camps capable of gassing hundreds of people at a time were constructed throughout Poland, Germany, and Austria, and Jews were rounded up in conquered nations, packed into railroad cars, and sent to the camps. By the end of the war, over 6 million Jews had been killed in what is called the **Holocaust** (figure **22.5**) (see Box, p. 622).

In addition to Jews, gypsies, homosexuals, mental patients, and intellectuals were exterminated under Hitler. In the Soviet Union, Hitler's special squads exterminated 30 million Slavs.

By 1940, after Germany invaded Denmark, Norway, Belgium, the Netherlands, and Luxembourg, the Nazis controlled most of Europe. By spring, under the Vichy Government of Maréchal Henri Philippe Pétain (1856–1951), France surrendered to the Germans. A military hero in World War I, Pétain collaborated with the German policy of genocide and enacted even more stringent racial laws than those in Germany (figure **22.6**). In France, anyone with two Jewish grandparents (rather than three as in Germany) was considered a Jew. Pétain forced all Jews to wear a yellow Star of David inscribed *Juif*

Defining Moment

The Holocaust

As Nazi power spread across Europe from 1933 to 1945, millions of people were persecuted and killed in the name of Aryan racial superiority. This systematic, state-sponsored policy of genocide is called the Holocaust. The term itself comes from a Greek word meaning "the burning of the whole"—that is, a total destruction by fire, often with sacrificial overtones. With the purification of the so-called Aryan race as its goal, the Nazis targeted Jews, gypsies, the physically and mentally handicapped, homosexuals, and Slavs, all of whom they considered genetically inferior.

In 1933 over 9 million Jews lived in Europe. By 1945 nearly 6 million Jews had been "exterminated" in the Final Solution, Hitler's policy of ridding Europe of every Jew. Jews were identified—often denounced by non-Jews—and their property was seized or destroyed. They were fired from their jobs, and confined first to urban ghettos and then sent to concentration camps.

Mass genocide began when Hitler's army invaded Poland in 1939 and continued during the invasion of the Soviet Union in 1941. In Operation Barbarossa, special murder squads of the SS (the elite military arm of the Nazi party) shot millions of Russians and disposed of their corpses in mass graves. The SS chief, Heinrich Himmler (1900–1945), demanded a more efficient means of extermination requiring less manpower. Consequently, vans filled with exhaust fumes were used in place of firing squads. In Poland Himmler replaced the vans with permanent buildings, housing gas chambers that used Zyklon B, a pesticide developed by the chemical firm I. G. Farben. It was used to exterminate inmates of concentration camps.

In 1939 Hitler's Nazi government began structuring an extensive network of death. It is estimated that the Nazis established 15,000 camps in the occupied countries, including small camps, which were created for limited killings of resistant local populations. When the Allied army liberated the concentration camps, they found thousands of emaciated survivors, piles of corpses and bones, and hoards of gold extracted from inmates' teeth. Nazi guards raped and tortured inmates before gassing them, and Nazi scientists and doctors performed sadistic experiments on men, women, and children.

The document in figure **22.7** attests the carnage of the Holocaust. It was at the Auschwitz concentration camp in Poland that the greatest number of Jews died—over one million. Only those who were young and healthy enough to work were kept alive. The rest succumbed to hard labor, starvation, and disease, especially typhus and tuberculosis, and the gas chambers.

The bureaucratic efficiency of the Nazis and the organized extermination process account for the lack of effective resistance on the part of the victims, in addition to which resistance by non-Jews was limited. The Swedish diplomat Raoul Wallenberg (1912–*c.* 1947) interceded on behalf of the Hungarian Jews, and the king of Denmark, informed that the Nazis had ordered Danish Jews to wear a yellow star, declared that he and his family would wear the star as a "badge of honor." Collaborationist governments, such as the Vichy Government in France, and occupied nations cooperated with Nazi extermination policies.

Germans who knew of the death camps were convinced by Nazi propaganda that benefits to Germany justified extermination of approximately 11 million people. In 1945 the Nuremberg Trials attempted to bring those responsible for the Holocaust to justice, but most of those who were convicted spent little time in prison. Many Nazi scientists were later hired by the United States as the Cold War began, while others fled to South America.

Critical Question Would it be better to understand the motivations of those who carried out the Holocaust—and more recent attacks of terrorism—or simply to fight against them?

Documenting the Gas Chambers at Auschwitz

I, Dr. Hans Münch hereby attest that, as an SS physician on duty in Auschwitz in 1944, I witnessed the selection process of those who were to live and those who were to die. Other SS physicians on duty in the camps made selections at the platform where the transports arrived. They also made selections in the barracks. I was exempt from performing selections because I had refused to do so.

I further attest that I saw thousands of people gassed here at Auschwitz. Children, old people, the sick and those unable to work were sent to the gas chambers. These were innocent human beings: Jews, Gypsies, homosexuals, Hitler's political opponents -- anyone who did not fit Hitler's idea of a pure Aryan race.

I am signing this paper of my own free will to help document the cruel intolerance of my fellow SS.

I, a former SS physician, witnessed the dropping of Zyklon B into simulated exhaust vents from outside the gas chamber. Zyklon B began to work as soon as it was released from the canisters. The effects of the gas were observed through a peephole by an assigned doctor or the SS officer on duty. After three to five minutes, death could be certified, and the doors were opened as a sign that the corpses were cleared to be burned.

This is the nightmare I continue to live with fifty years later.

I am so sorry that in some way I was part of it. Under the prevailing circumstances I did the best I could to save as many lives as possible. Joining the SS was a mistake. I was young. I was an opportunist. And once I joined, there was no way out.

Dr. Hans Münch
January 27, 1995, Auschwitz

Witness *Witness*
Witness *Witness*
Witness *Witness*

22.7 Münch attestation "Documenting the Gas Chambers at Auschwitz."

(Jew); hundreds of thousands of French citizens were rounded up and sent to concentration camps. (In 1945 Pétain was convicted of treason, and he died in jail six years later.)

Britain now stood alone against Germany. In 1940 Winston Churchill became prime minister, brilliantly leading the country through the German bombing campaign—the Blitz—in and around London. Living in Britain at the time was the French general Charles André Joseph Marie de Gaulle (1890–1970), who had fled France. He organized the Free French to resist the Germans and encouraged occupied France through daily radio broadcasts from London. After the war, de Gaulle retired but was called back to public service and became president from 1958 to 1969.

THE UNITED STATES DECLARES WAR: 1941–1945

Japan, relatively prosperous in the 1920s, was driven more by militarism and colonial ambition than economic depression. The most powerful military force in the Far East, Japan joined the Axis powers and in 1937 invaded mainland China, committing atrocities against the Chinese people. This led to increasing tension with the United States and fueled Japan's resentment of its dependence on America for oil and steel. Finally, in an effort to destroy a large part of the American navy and eliminate American opposition to Japanese expansion, Japan made a surprise bombing raid on the American naval base at Pearl Harbor, in Hawaii, on December 7, 1941. Over two thousand Americans were killed.

The bombing of Pearl Harbor jolted the United States out of its isolationist policies, and the United States and Britain declared war on Japan. In response, Germany and Italy declared war on the United States.

While fighting the Japanese in Asia, the Allies were also fighting Germany for control of North Africa and Europe. The British armies were now assisted by the Americans under the leadership of General Dwight David Eisenhower (1890–1969). During the Battle of Stalingrad, which lasted several months in 1942, millions of Russians were killed. In 1943 Italy surrendered to the Allied forces and Rome was declared an open city. The Allies carried out saturation bombing of Germany and virtually eliminated its air power.

On June 6, 1944, the Allies, under the command of Eisenhower, launched around five thousand ships from the south coast of England to invade Normandy in northern France. This was not only the most massive operation of its kind in Western history, it also heralded the defeat of Germany. The codename for the attack was Operation Overlord and D-Day denoted the day on which it would be launched. Hitler continued fighting until May 1, 1945, when he committed suicide in Berlin. Germany surrendered on May 8.

By 1943 the Americans had recaptured the major Pacific islands, from which they were able to launch attacks on Japan, but mainland Japan continued to fight. Millions of lives had been lost on both sides by the time President Harry S. Truman (1884–1972) made the decision to bring war in the Pacific to a decisive end. On August 6 and 9, 1945, respectively, he ordered American planes to drop atomic bombs on the cities of Hiroshima and Nagasaki. On August 14, Japan surrendered and a peace was signed on September 2.

The Axis powers were in ruins. In Germany the Nuremberg Trials began in 1945 to assign responsibility for the Holocaust and to punish war criminals. France dissolved the Third Republic, ratified a new constitution, and established the Fourth Republic. Europe now had decades of reconstruction to look forward to. Assistance from the United States' Marshall Plan provided an enormous infusion of funds and advisers to war-torn Europe (see map 23.1).

The Allies broke with the Soviet Union over fear of international communism. The two leading world powers emerging from the war were the United States and the Soviet Union. Conflicts between these powers initiated the Cold War, which dominated the twentieth century from 1945 to 1989 (see Chapter 23).

The League of Nations, unable to prevent World War II and unwilling to oppose the aggression of the Axis powers, was superseded in 1945 by the United Nations.

TECHNOLOGY AND EXPANDING HORIZONS

Despite the worsening political situation between the wars, technology continued to advance. This, and the speed of communication, fuelled the development of **mass culture**. The radio, early television, and newsreels improved the flow of information. By 1917 the Trans-Siberian Railroad, begun in 1891, linked Europe with Russia, and in 1923 the Soviet Union founded Aeroflot, then the world's largest airline. Solo flights heralded modern air travel. In 1927 Charles Lindbergh (1902–1974) flew from New York to Paris in 33½ hours in *The Spirit of Saint Louis*—the first, non-stop, solo flight across the Atlantic. Five years later Amelia Earhart (1897–1937) became the first woman to cross the Atlantic alone; she flew from Newfoundland to Ireland in 13½ hours. Despite the sinking of the *Titanic* in 1912, travel by ocean liner across the Atlantic also became popular.

Another development that evolved just before the wars and continued past World War II was a new Western approach to the non-Western world. Moving beyond imperialism and colonial expansion, humanitarian workers and medical researchers, explorers, and anthropologists traveled overseas. In 1913 the German physician and philosopher Albert Schweitzer (1875–1965) founded a hospital at Lambaréné, in French Equatorial Africa (later Gabon), advancing the knowledge of tropical medicine along with his humanitarian medical and

22.8 ***Kon-Tiki*, Kon-Tiki Museum, Oslo.**

missionary work. He was also an accomplished organist and the author of a standard biography of Bach.

Little known parts of the globe attracted explorers in the early decades of the twentieth century. In 1909 the American Robert Edwin Peary (1856–1920) had become the first person to reach the North Pole. Two years later the Norwegian Roald Amundsen (1872–1928) achieved that milestone at the South Pole. Between 1914 and 1917 the British explorer Sir Ernest Henry Shackleton (1874–1922) led an expedition to the Antarctic. He and his men were marooned and their dramatic rescue became the subject of *South* (1919), a classic account of polar exploration.

Studies of isolated civilizations provided new information about other cultures. In 1928 the American anthropologist Margaret Mead (1901–1978) published *Coming of Age in Samoa*, her famous account of adolescent development among tribes in the southwest Pacific. Mead wrote about different cultures, she said, so that Westerners would better understand themselves. In 1947 the Norwegian ethnologist Thor Heyerdahl (1914–2002) set out to prove that the Polynesians could have originated in South America—as he believed they had. He constructed a raft of balsa wood, the *Kon-Tiki* (now on display in Oslo's Kon-Tiki Museum), and with a crew of five sailed it some 5000 miles (8000 km) across the Pacific (figure **22.8**). Heyerdahl's account of the voyage was published in 1950.

Horizons also expanded in science and medicine. In 1928 the Scottish bacteriologist Alexander Fleming (1881–1955) isolated a mold and grew it into a pure culture, which led to the discovery of penicillin, the first antibiotic medication. Sulfa drugs had been used to treat pneumonia, wounds, and other infections since 1935, and penicillin became generally available in 1941. In 1942 the French-born American surgeon Alexis Carrel (1873–1944), together with Charles Lindbergh, invented the first artificial heart. Insulin was first used to control diabetes in 1937, the first electron microscope was demonstrated in 1940, and 1941 marked the beginning of the Manhattan Project (the code name for the development of the atom bomb during World War II). That same year Enrico Fermi (1901–1954), a member of the Manhattan Project, split the atom, and in 1945 the United States exploded the first atom bomb in New Mexico.

In psychology **projective testing**, in which subjects are asked to look at pictures and describe what they see, was developed. The responses are analyzed as a means of contributing to a personality profile. One of the best-known such tests was invented in 1920 by the Swiss psychiatrist Herman Rorschach (1884–1922). Composed of cards with abstract images, it is popularly called the **inkblot**, or Rorschach, test.

In 1927 the Russian physiologist Ivan Petrovich Pavlov (1849–1936) announced his findings on the **conditioned reflex**. He discovered that dogs learn by a system of reward and punishment, known as conditioning. This was an important development in learning theory and influenced behavioral psychology, especially in the United States.

PHILOSOPHY

The pessimism engendered by World War I and the search for creative ways to improve the world emerged in two major philosophical trends: **logical positivism** and **existentialism**. The former emphasized logical reasoning based on empirical facts; the latter addressed human anxiety and responsibility for finding meaning in life, given the inevitability of death.

Logical Positivism

The Austrian-born Ludwig Wittgenstein (1889–1951), who lived in England, blamed poor philosophical methods for the cultural decline of the West. He believed that philosophy should be a scientific discipline based on mathematical reasoning, which he discussed in *Tractatus logico-philosophicus* (1921). In Wittgenstein's view, verifiable truth consists of provable facts and is independent of ethical or moral concerns (which philosophers had traditionally considered fundamental to their discipline). Wittgenstein argued that language is open to misunderstandings but verifiable facts are not. Although he later revised the critique of language, his ideas led to logical positivism, which is best known for the verification principle—that is, only sentences that are verifiable by sense experience are meaningful. For example, "there are mountains in Switzerland" is meaningful because we can verify it. Likewise, the sentence "there are mountains on Jupiter" is meaningful because we know how to verify it. But value judgments, such as "murder is wrong," are meaningless because they cannot be verified.

EXISTENTIALISM

For the two main existential philosophers, Martin Heidegger (1889–1976) and Jean-Paul Sartre (1905–1980), the human condition was anxiety and the defining point of life was death. Existentialists place responsibility on the individual rather than on God, faith, or reason. In their view it is up to the individual to assert his or her existence by meeting the inevitability of death head on, especially through acts of self-realization.

The founder of existentialism, which became a major philosophical and literary movement by the mid-twentieth century, Heidegger was a university professor in Germany. In his most important, though somewhat obscure, work, *Being and Time* (1927), he argues that anxiety is based on the knowledge of death. Rooted in the philosophy of Goethe and Nietzsche (see Chapters 18 and 19), Heidegger defined existence in terms of the decision to face death and to fight it by asserting one's creativity. Immersed in German nationalist sentiment, Heidegger backed National Socialism, which alienated some people from existential philosophy.

Sartre, Heidegger's best-known French follower, was strongly anti-Nazi. He published *Being and Nothingness* (*L'Etre et le néant*) in 1943, four years into World War II. Sartre saw the human struggle as having to accept freedom, despite the reality of death, and he argued that although individuals face nothingness (*le néant*) they must insist on their existence (*l'être*, or "being"). Since there is no God in Sartre's view, each person is responsible for his or her own existence, decisions, and actions. Sartre never abandoned his notion of personal responsibility, thus taking a moral, though atheist, position. After the war, largely as a reaction against Fascism and National Socialism, Sartre became a Marxist.

ART AND ARCHITECTURE BETWEEN THE WARS

Several art movements flourished in Europe and the United States between World War I and World War II. Dada (see Chapter 21) spread from Zurich to Berlin and New York, and Surrealism, influenced by Freud, also became a major style. Fascist Italy admired the mechanized sense of power expressed by the Futurists just before World War I. In Germany and the Soviet Union, however, artistic innovation essentially came to a halt with government censorship of the avant garde. American art, in contrast, was enriched by the influx of avant-garde artists from Europe who emigrated to escape persecution and totalitarianism. At the same time, some artists in the United States worked in a local, Regionalist Style that resisted modern trends.

THE EXPANSION OF THE DADA MOVEMENT AFTER WORLD WAR I

Dada spread to New York primarily through Marcel Duchamp, who had shocked the American public at the 1913 Armory show with his *Nude Descending the Staircase No. 2* (see figure 21.24). Duchamp's work expressed the original Dada intent to destroy the past and create new beginnings, as well as the Freudian interest in wit and punning that is characteristic of dreams. Duchamp invented a new art form, which he called the **ready-made**. This was a manufactured object to which the artist added a title and occasionally a signature, thereby rendering it a work of art. Among Duchamp's ready-mades were a shovel entitled *In Advance of a Broken Arm*, a urinal entitled *Fountain* and signed R. Mutt, and a box of Kleenex entitled *Why Not Sneeze?*

Duchamp also invented the "**ready-made aided**," a ready-made to which he added something besides a title and his signature, thereby "aiding," or touching it up. His graffiti-like *L.H.O.O.Q.* of 1919 (figure **22.9**) was a postcard reproduction

22.9 Marcel Duchamp, *Replica of L.H.O.O.Q., from "Boîte-en-Valise,"* 1919. Color reproduction of the *Mona Lisa* altered with a pencil, 7¾ × 5 in. (19.7 × 12.7 cm). Philadelphia Museum of Art.

22.10 Hannah Höch, *Cut with the Kitchen Knife*, *c.* 1919. Collage, 44⅞ × 35⅜ in. (114 × 90 cm). Preussischer Kulturbesitz, National Gallery, State Museums, Berlin.
This collage juxtaposes fragments of photographs and newspapers. Artists pose with Marx and Lenin. The word "Dada" and the prefix "anti" allude to a rebellion against convention. At the center, a dancing figure frantically tosses its own head in the air.

of the *Mona Lisa* (see figure 14.5), onto which he penciled a beard and mustache. As with graffiti, this image raises the question: when is an intervention a creative act, and when is it destructive?

The Dada work of Hannah Höch (1889–1978) reflects the fragmented, cynical post-war mood in Berlin. In *Cut with the Kitchen Knife* (figure **22.10**), she uses photomontage to criticize contemporary society, depicting Berlin—cut up, frenzied, and mechanized—with fragments of photographs and newspapers.

The Dada Movement lasted in Europe until around 1920 and in New York until 1923. After 1924 the movement came to an end, but the artists continued to work and many turned to Surrealism.

22.11 Max Ernst, *The Hat Makes the Man*, 1920. Collage with gouache, ink, and pencil on cardboard, 14 × 18 in. (35.6 × 45.7 cm). The Museum of Modern Art, New York.
Influenced by Cubism, Ernst has connected a group of hats with colored cylinders. The image puns on the hat as a symbol of repetitive middle-class convention and plays on the expression "the clothes make the man," which suggests that bourgeois life is superficial and mundane.

SURREALISM

In 1924 the French physician André Breton (1896–1966) published a "Surrealist Manifesto," in which he proposed applying Freud's discoveries to art and literature. Breton believed that through free association artists and writers could access their unconscious, which would fire the imagination, inspire creativity, and lead to a higher (*surreal*) reality usually hidden from consciousness. The Dada interest in play, punning, and fantasy thus became aspects of Surrealism.

Each Surrealist artist worked in a distinctive formal style, but most incorporated Freud's observations into their work. The German artist Max Ernst (1891–1976) lived in France after World War I, and then moved to New York and married the American art collector Peggy Guggenheim. Ernst's conscious use of unconscious imagery can be seen in his well-known collage *The Hat Makes the Man* (figure **22.11**).

As a young boy, the Romanian artist Constantin Brancusi (1876–1957) ran away from his abusive peasant family and settled in Paris. He created a Surrealist pun on the avant-garde attraction to non-Western art in his *White Negress III* of 1923 (figure **22.12**). Brancusi placed a white marble cylinder on a cruciform base and perched the head on top. The smooth oval head recalls the elongation of certain African masks, while the emphasis on geometry and the minimal depiction of facial features is Cubist as well as Surrealist. By carving a black African head out of white marble, Brancusi puns on the notion of black and white in race as well as in art.

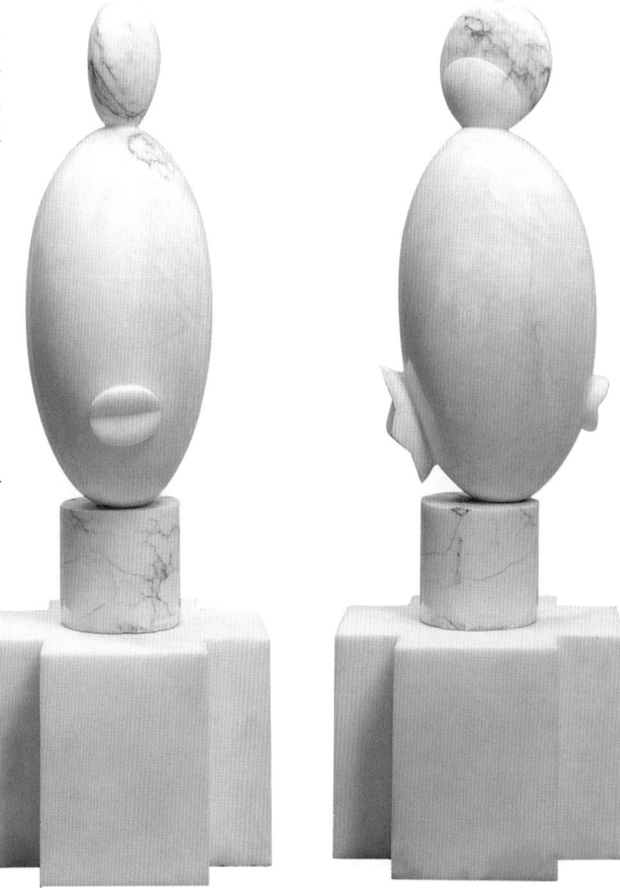

22.12 Constantin Brancusi, *White Negress III* (front and side view), *c.* 1923. Veined white marble, 19 in. (48.3 cm) high, base 6$^3/_8$ in. (16.2 cm) high. Philadelphia Museum of Art.

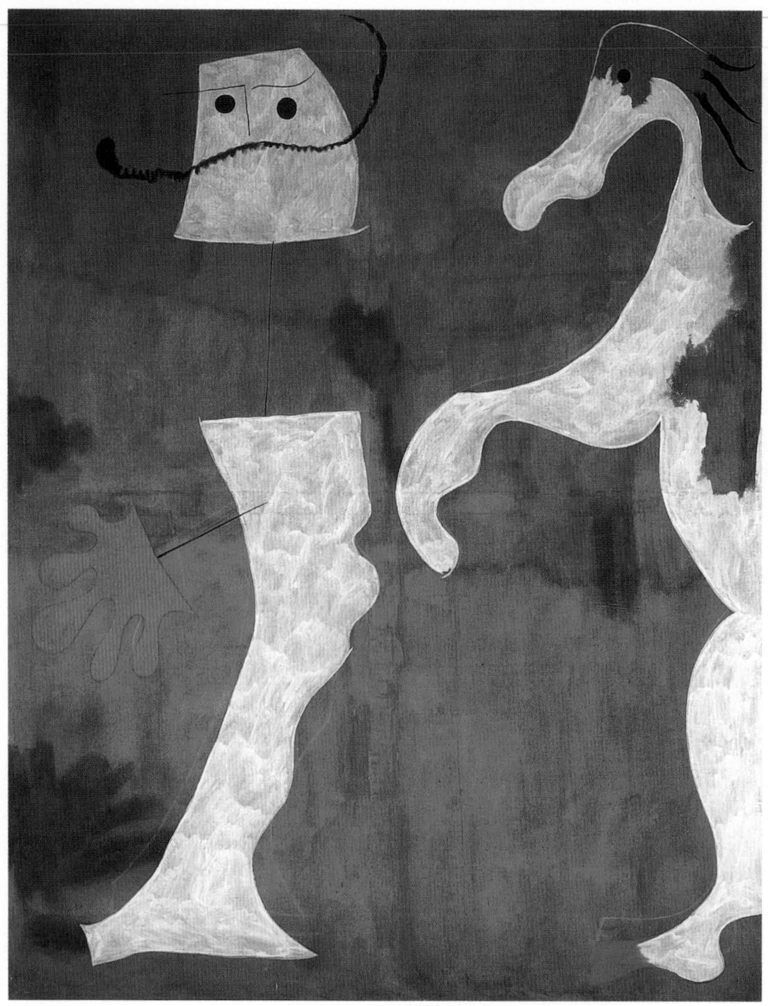

22.13 Joan Miró, *The Policeman (Figure and Horse)*, 1925. Oil on canvas, 8 ft. 1⅝ in. × 6 ft. 4¾ in. (2.48 × 1.95 m). Art Institute of Chicago.

22.14 René Magritte, study for the cover of André Breton's *Qu'est-ce que le Surréalisme?*, 1934.

The Policeman (figure **22.13**) by the Spanish artist Joan Miró (1893–1983) depicts the playful wit of Surrealism. Miró's white, toy-like horse has a blue hoof and a brown mane, which merges into a stark brown background reminiscent of the rugged Spanish landscape. The shape of the policeman's head resembles his hat, the rim of which merges into the eyebrow. The broad mustache exaggerates the French style of the period, and a thin line connects the head and the red hand to the leg. The child-like quality of Miró's work reflects the creative aspect of spontaneous, youthful imagination that appealed to both the Dadaists and the Surrealists.

In 1934 André Breton published a second manifesto of Surrealism entitled *Qu'est-ce que le Surréalisme?* (*What is Surrealism?*). The cover image (figure **22.14**), designed by the Belgian René Magritte (1898–1967), illustrates Freud's discovery of upward and downward displacement, in which a lower part of the body is displaced upward and vice versa. Magritte has made a visual pun out of a sexual pun, mirroring a process that occurs in dreams, in the unconscious, and in jokes.

The American Surrealist Man Ray (1890–1977) went to Paris and became a fashion and portrait photographer. He invented the **Rayogram**—a photograph made without a negative by passing light over objects placed on light-sensitive paper in the darkroom. He also used **solarization**, in which the photographer briefly exposes the print to light before the image is fixed. This results in an eerie reversal of the expected relation of light to dark in the final print. By manipulating the developing process, Man Ray created dream-like imagery to convey the inner world of imagination (figure **22.15**).

The Surrealism of the Mexican Frida Kahlo (1907–1954) is overtly autobiographical. She suffered severe pain her entire life as the result of a tramway crash and was forced to undergo several surgical procedures. Much of her imagery depicts the theme of physical torture from back braces and other primitive medical devices. As a young art student, Kahlo became enamored of, and married, the Mexican muralist Diego Rivera. Despite his psychological abuse of Kahlo, Diego admired and encouraged her work. She, in turn, was unable to leave the relationship, which was also a rich source of her iconography (figure **22.16**).

22.15 Man Ray, *Tears (Larmes)*, 1932–1933. Gelatin silver print, image 9 × 11¾ in. (22.9 × 29.8 cm). The J. Paul Getty Museum, Malibu, California.
The eyes are a favorite Surrealist motif because of their psychological power. Here, the woman's eyes look upward at something we cannot see as five tears (which are actually glass beads) seem to roll down her face. Both the eye and the glass reflect Man Ray's interest in light and the ways in which it can be manipulated in photography.

22.16 Frida Kahlo, *Self-Portrait as a Tehuana (Diego on My Mind)*, 1943. Oil on canvas, 38 × 31⅞ in. (96.5 × 81 cm). Kahlo Museum, Coyoacan, Mexico.
Diego Rivera is literally "on her mind." Kahlo wears the costume of a Tehuana from southwestern Mexico. Its bridal associations, like the repeated black and white strings and the little portrait of Diego Rivera on her forehead, indicate her obsessive connection with him.

THE INTERNATIONAL STYLE: *DE STIJL*

Between 1917 and the 1930s an International Style, influenced by Cubist geometry, originated in the Netherlands, where it was called *De Stijl* (The Style). The leading *De Stijl* painter in the Netherlands was Piet Mondrian (1872–1944), who sought a purity of form that could be universally understood. He hoped to unify the arts with the practical concerns of living, ending the separation of art from society (figure **22.17**).

In Germany the center of the International Style movement was the Bauhaus, a school of art and design in Dessau. Under the leadership of Walter Gropius (1883–1969), the Bauhaus aimed to combine art, architecture, and interior design with the benefits of industry. Although it was closed down by Hitler in 1933, its ideas spread across Europe, and many Bauhaus artists emigrated to America.

The most important International Style architect working in France was the Swiss Charles-Edouard Jeanneret, known as Le Corbusier (1887–1965). He subscribed to the Bauhaus philosophy that architecture should be produced for the masses and that a house should be a "machine for living." His Villa Savoye, located in a suburb of Paris (figure **22.18**), is supported by slim, reinforced concrete pillars and has a three-car garage space at ground level. A central stairway leads to the living area on the second floor, and a ramp continues to the third-floor deck. In its functionality and stark, white, rectilinear design, the Villa Savoye embodied the post-World War I International Style ideal of practicality and comfort.

22.17 Piet Mondrian, *Composition with Large Red Plane, Yellow, Black, Gray, and Blue*, 1921. Oil on canvas, 23⅜ × 23⅜ in. (59.5 × 59.5 cm). Haags Gementemuseum, The Hague. © 2006 Mondrian/Holtzman Trust c/o hcr@hcrinternational.com.
Mondrian believed that the most perfect lines are strict horizontals and verticals and that the purest colors are the primaries—red, yellow, and blue. He believed that such purity conveyed the spirit of a new, ideal society, which would emerge after the destruction of World War I.

22.18 Le Corbusier, Villa Savoye, Poissy-sur-Seine, France, 1928–1930.

The Prairie Style: Frank Lloyd Wright

The American Frank Lloyd Wright (1867–1959) took an entirely different approach to architecture. Inspired by the American landscape, Wright's Prairie Style was organic, rather than industrial. He used local materials so that his houses would blend with the surrounding landscape.

One of his best-known private houses, located in Bear Run, Pennsylvania, was commissioned by the family of Edgar Kaufmann (figure **22.19**). Like the Villa Savoye, this was a weekend retreat, but its character and style are very different. Wright used **cantilevered**, reinforced concrete balconies that project from the house and echo the horizontal rock formations. These, together with the verticals that repeat the trees, make the Kaufmann House seem to emerge naturally from its wooded surroundings. In addition, the predominance of glass walls makes the exterior visible from the interior, so that the landscape is present inside the house.

American Regionalism: Thomas Hart Benton

Despite the migration of the avant garde from Europe to the United States, a great deal of American art between the wars had a regional character. The Regionalist painter Thomas Hart Benton (1889–1975) was born in Iowa and studied in Europe before World War I, but his themes are distinctly American. They reflect both the political isolationism of the United States and the artist's optimistic view of the future despite the Great Depression. Benton is best known for his murals of American Midwestern life. In *Pioneer Days and Early Settlement* (figure **22.20**), Benton juxtaposes scenes from Missouri history, energized by rugged, muscular figures building a nation. Above the doorway, we can see Huckleberry Finn and Jim, who were immortalized by Mark Twain (see Chapter 19). In the background, a riverboat, the *Sam Clemens* (Mark Twain's real name), throws out billows of smoke in the moonlight. Benton's iconography, like the powerful dynamism of his forms, depicts a country on the move, looking forward to a thriving economic future sparked by Roosevelt's New Deal.

22.19 Frank Lloyd Wright, Kaufmann House (Fallingwater), Bear Run, Pennsylvania, 1936.

22.20 Thomas Hart Benton, *Pioneer Days and Early Settlement*, north wall, from *A Social History of the State of Missouri*, 1936. Oil and tempera on linen mounted on panel, 25 ft. × 14 ft. 2 in. (7.6 × 4.3 m). House of Representatives' Lounge, State Capitol Building, Jefferson City, Missouri.

THE JAZZ AGE

The term Roaring Twenties expresses the buoyant spirit of the post-war decade, reflected in the vitality of jazz. Although jazz had emerged before World War I (see Chapter 21), its range and influence expanded enormously when war ended. During the 1920s blues reached a peak of popularity, fed by a dynasty of blues singers. Following the closure of New Orleans' Storyville quarter by order of the U.S. Navy in 1917, Chicago became the main jazz center. "Hot" jazz bands grew in size, and for the first time white musicians took on a significant role. In the 1930s, swing jazz, as played by big bands, became the most popular dance music of the country. The 1940s saw a reversion to smaller ensembles, with prominent use of the rhythm section—a style called "bop" or "bebop" after the nonsense syllables sung to the music of Charlie Parker (see p. 633).

BLUES

In the 1920s, blues came to flourish as an urban professional style of music, especially in Chicago as performed by female singers. The most famous was Bessie Smith (1894–1937), the "Empress of the Blues." Working initially in touring minstrel shows and cabaret, she made her first recording, "Down Hearted Blues," in 1923. It achieved enormous success, and she went on to make almost two hundred records, topping 2 million in sales. Notable among them is her rendition of the "St. Louis Blues" (see Chapter 21) with Louis Armstrong (see below). Smith's expressive voice and blue-note distortions brought the emotional intensity of blues into the jazz arena, and she sometimes engaged in spoken, rhythmic dialogue with an instrumental melody. Smith earned—and squandered—a fortune. She died after a car crash, when the local hospital refused to admit her because she was black.

HOT JAZZ: CHICAGO-BASED JAZZ OF THE 1920S

With the closing of Storyville, many musicians migrated—along with tens of thousands of rural blacks from the South—to Chicago, which became the new center for jazz innovation. In Chicago jazz, two distinct trends were seen, both of which departed from the festive but somewhat chaotic collective improvisation style of classic jazz. One trend was toward larger groups and more ensemble cohesion, especially as represented by the band of pianist, composer, and bandleader Ferdinand Joseph La Menthe, better known as Jelly Roll Morton (1885–1941). A contrasting trend was toward featuring a soloist who improvised melodies over the chord progressions of a popular song. Especially important in this development was the trumpeter, singer, and bandleader Louis "Satchmo"

("Satchelmouth") Armstrong (1900–1971), a leading hot jazz soloist.

Raised among New Orleans jazz musicians, Armstrong went to Chicago in 1922, when cornetist Joe "King" Oliver invited him to join his Creole Jazz Band. From the mid-1920s Armstrong's own Hot Five and Hot Seven bands were highly influential, their recordings establishing his international reputation. In "Potato Head Blues" (1927) Armstrong attacks and sustains notes, controls **vibrato** (rapid slight fluctuation in pitch) for emotional effect, and pushes the range of the trumpet upward. Famous for his gravelly voice, he was one of the earliest **scat singers**, improvising using nonsense syllables.

In 1947 Armstrong formed the All-Stars, a sextet with which he worked until his death. He appeared in several Hollywood movies, notably *Pennies from Heaven* (1936) and *High Society* (1956) with Bing Crosby, Grace Kelly, and Frank Sinatra.

SWING

In the 1930s swing jazz became America's popular dance music, enjoyed by whites, blacks, and urbanites as well as rural people. The standard ensemble was the big band, which could fill a large dance-hall with sound and also offered new opportunities for ensemble writing. Particularly important was the practice of sectional arrangement: contrasting passages were written for distinct "sections" of saxophones, trumpets, trombones, and the "rhythm section" of piano, bass, and drums.

The most innovative and "hot" big bands were those led by the Kansas City-based Count Basie (1904–1984) and by Duke

Cross-cultural Influences

The Cotton Club of Harlem

In 1923 the heavyweight boxer John Johnson sold his defunct Club De Lux on Lenox Avenue in Harlem to Owney Madden, a brewer and gangster. The De Lux was reborn as the Cotton Club, which soon became the hottest nightclub in New York (figures **22.21** and **22.22**). With décor based on Southern plantation styles, the Cotton Club featured lavish shows and the most talented black entertainers of the day wearing extravagant costumes. Ironically, the audiences were nearly all white. Among the celebrity clientele were the singer and actor Bing Crosby, the comedian Jimmy Durante, the song writers Irving Berlin and Cole Porter, the heiress Doris Duke, and the gangster Dutch Schultz. In 1936 the club moved to West 48th Street and in 1978 returned to Harlem.

Duke Ellington got his first major break at the Cotton Club and was in residence there from 1927 to 1932. The atmospheric composition "Mood Indigo" (1930) achieved international success, and his most creative years followed. "Ko-Ko" (1940), a big band piece, presents his distinctive jungle style, suffused with unusual instrumental coloring —blocks of smooth saxophone sound providing a backdrop for raucous "wa-wa" effects on muted trumpets, offset by snarling, syncopated trombones.

African-American performers who rose to fame through the Cotton Club include the bandleader and singer Cab Calloway, Bill "Bojangles" Robinson (who made tap-dancing into an art form), the singer Lena Horne, and actresses Dorothy Dandridge and Ethel Waters.

22.22 *above* **Poster advertising Duke Ellington at the Cotton Club.**

22.21 *left* **The Cotton Club in 1938.**

Ellington (1899–1974). Ellington's band played regularly at the Cotton Club in Harlem (see Box) between 1927 and 1932. One of the most influential jazz composers, Ellington composed most of the works he recorded—possibly as many as six thousand, including instrumental pieces, songs, and over fifty film scores. Ellington's music was remarkable for its stylistic diversity, including programmatic pieces for cabaret shows at the Cotton Club, catchy dance tunes like "Satin Doll," soulful ballads such as "In a Sentimental Mood," art-oriented concert pieces, and even a jazz Mass. Creating jazz with big bands required a mixture of improvisation and composition. Sometimes Ellington would simply provide an idea to his band and then supervise a session of improvisation, until the basics of a piece emerged. More commonly, he composed a piece utilizing the abilities of each player. The "King of Swing," Benny Goodman (1909–1986), was another famous bandleader of the period. A virtuoso clarinetist and composer, Goodman was the first white bandleader to achieve such success.

African-American big-band musicians, like Count Basie's group, who made their living touring the southern U.S.A., acutely experienced the vicissitudes of the "Jim Crow" system of racial discrimination that prevailed in the South until the 1960s. Often they had to play hungry, after arriving at a town in their tour bus in the early evening to find no place to eat, as white restaurants would not serve them and restaurants for blacks were scarce. After playing for several hours for ecstatically appreciative white audiences, they would be told to get out of town if there was no hotel or rooming house that lodged black people. Racially mixed bands were generally not allowed, although Goodman attempted to overcome this effective prohibition.

BOP

In the 1940s, from jam sessions (musicians meeting to play together for enjoyment) at a nightclub in Harlem, a new jazz style emerged. Bop musicians withdrew from playing big-band dance music in order to cultivate the art of complex improvised solos, played by small combos, often for small but discerning audiences. A typical combo consisted of saxophone, trumpet, and the "rhythm section" of piano, bass, and drums.

Among the first bop artists, the trumpeter Dizzy Gillespie (1917–1993) brought harmonic innovation to jazz, often showing virtuosic flair, playing with the trumpet bell bent up forty-five degrees. In 1944 he played alongside saxophonist Charlie Parker (1920–1955) in the Billy Eckstine big band, introducing bop to the nightclubs of 52nd Street, New York. One of the most brilliant of all jazz improvisers, Parker was central to the development of bop, making over thirty recordings with Gillespie in 1945. Parker's most famous recordings include "Anthropology," based on Gershwin's "I Got Rhythm" (see p. 644), and "Ornithology," built on the chord changes of the popular song "How High the Moon."

THE JAZZ AGE IN PARIS

American jazz was especially popular in Paris, where African-American musicians felt more welcome than in the United States. One of the most sensational performers was the dancer and singer Josephine Baker (1906–1975; figure **22.23**). Born in Missouri, she joined a dance troupe at age thirteen and eventually made her way to Paris. In 1925 she appeared in *La Revue Nègre* (*The Negro Revue*) and was an instant success. Famous for her Rainbow Tribe of adopted children of all races, Baker was awarded the French Legion of Honor after World War II for her work against Fascism.

American jazz appealed to European artists, writers, and musicians for much of the twentieth century. In 1947 Matisse (see Chapter 21) created a series of cut-out collages entitled "Jazz," published in book form. The example in figure **22.24** shows two black silhouettes suggesting a mounted cowboy roping a leaping figure. Pasted onto a background of bright colors, the vigorous diagonals and curved edges create the lively, exuberant, dance-like rhythms characteristic of jazz.

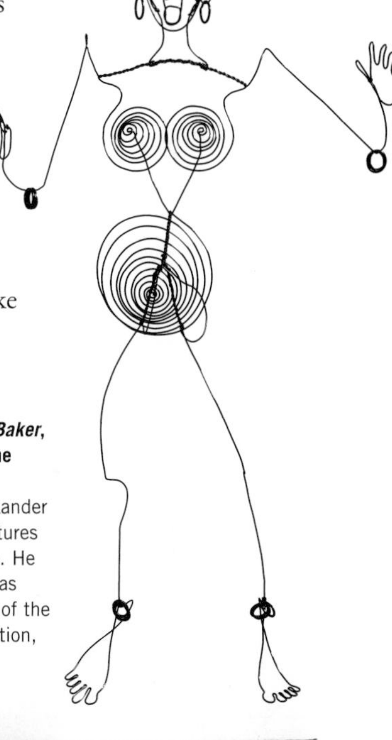

22.23 *right* **Alexander Calder, *Josephine Baker*, 1927–1929. Wire, 39 in. (99 cm) high. The Museum of Modern Art, New York.**
The works of the American sculptor Alexander Calder (1898–1976) include wire sculptures animated by the artist's witty use of line. He shows Josephine Baker swaying slightly as she sings. The shifting circular patterns of the torso indicate a slow, back-and-forth motion, and two ovals below the waist represent Baker's famous banana skirt.

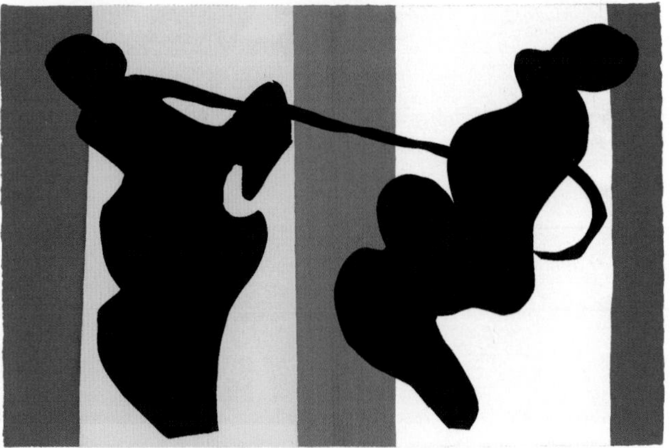

22.24 Henri Matisse, "Jazz" series, *The Cowboy*, 1947. Stencil print on paper, 12¾ × 16¾ in. (32.5 × 42.5 cm). Private collection.
Matisse uses color to create rhythms of blue, yellow, green, and white. Then a blue, followed by a white, picks up the sequence, indicating that the progression continues beyond the space of the page.

THE HARLEM RENAISSANCE

In the 1920s American blacks began to leave the South and move North. Many settled in Harlem, in New York City. With the enthusiasm for jazz and the avant garde's interest in non-Western art forms, a new climate for black intellectuals developed in America, evolving into the cultural movement called the Harlem Renaissance. This included philosophers, such as Alain Locke (1886–1954), who urged black artists to use Africa as an inspiration in their work, as well as politicians, authors, painters, sculptors, photographers, and musicians. The movement of blacks to the North was memorialized in the "Migration" series by Jacob Lawrence (1917–2000) (figure **22.25**).

The Harlem Renaissance also produced a number of black authors, who drew on their African-American roots and on the role of blacks in American society. In music, black composers incorporated African-American genres into traditional Western styles.

JAMES WELDON JOHNSON

James Weldon Johnson (1871–1938) led the NAACP (National Association for the Advancement of Colored People) in the 1920s. He was the first black admitted to the Florida Bar and the first black professor at New York University.

Johnson believed that poetry would bridge the gap between blacks and whites. His most famous collection of poems, *God's Trombones: Seven Negro Sermons in Verse*, was published in 1927, during the heyday of the Harlem Renaissance. His poetry combines a biblical tone with the rhythm of spirituals and gospel songs. In "The Creation," Johnson evokes a sense of limitless, primordial space, juxtaposed with solitude. And like the God of Genesis, he conveys the dramatic appearance of light in a dark universe:

And God stepped out on space,
And he looked around and said:
I'm lonely—
I'll make me a world.

And far as the eye of God could see
Darkness covered everything,
Blacker than a hundred midnights
Down in a cypress swamp.

Then God smiled,
And the light broke,
And the darkness rolled up on one side,
And the light stood shining on the other,
And God said: "That's good!"

22.25 Jacob Lawrence, "Migration" series No. 1, *During the World War there was a great migration North by Southern Negroes*, 1940–1941. Casein tempera on hardboard, 12 × 18 in. (30.5 × 45.7 cm). Phillips Collection, Washington, D.C.

The first picture in the "Migration" series, this shows blacks leaving the South for Chicago, St. Louis, and New York in the hope of escaping discrimination, gaining political recognition, and finding jobs. Lawrence creates a sense of urgency in the packed figures streaming into light, open spaces, which suggest social and intellectual freedom. The diagonals emphasize the forward thrust of the crowd, and the silhouetting makes the crowd anonymous. Flat shapes of color and geometric forms reflect the influence of the avant garde on Lawrence's style.

LANGSTON HUGHES

Langston Hughes (1902–1967), the leading Harlem Renaissance poet of the 1930s, is best known for his jazz poetry, which matched verse to music. He was also a dramatist, instrumental in establishing theater groups and producing plays that dealt with themes of racial prejudice and racial pride. In *I, Too* (1923) he confronts readers with contemporary racial conflict and the striving of blacks for social equality: "I, too, sing America./I am the darker brother."

Hughes's poetry combines blues and jazz rhythms with African-American dialect. This is particularly evident in the slow blues tempo of "The Weary Blues," which appeared in his first volume of poetry (1926):

Droning a drowsy syncopated tune,
Rocking back and forth to a mellow croon,
  I heard a Negro play.
Down on Lenox Avenue the other night
By the pale dull pallor of an old gas light
  He did a lazy sway . . .
  He did a lazy sway . . .
To the tune o' those Weary blues.

COUNTEE CULLEN

The poet Countee Cullen (1903–1946) used his African-American heritage as a powerful source of inspiration and strength. In "Heritage," he combines his African background with contemporary American society and depicts a nostalgic view of Africa as a lush Garden of Eden:

What is Africa to me:
Copper sun or scarlet sea,
Jungle star or jungle track,
Strong bronzed men, or regal black
Women from whose loins I sprang
When the birds of Eden sang?
One three centuries removed
From the scenes his father loved,
Spicy grove, cinnamon tree,
What is Africa to me?

ZORA NEALE HURSTON

Zora Neale Hurston (*c.* 1903–1960) was born in Florida and studied anthropology with Franz Boas (who was also Margaret Mead's professor) at Columbia University. Hurston concentrated on the folklore of Southern blacks and the Caribbean, and in *How It Feels to be Colored Me* (1928) she wrote about being black and female in a predominantly white society. Her style evokes folk tales and replicates the musical rhythms of certain black speech patterns: "'Looka theah, folkses!' cried Elijah Mosley, slapping his leg gleefully. 'Theah they go, big as life an' brassy as tacks'" (from *Spunk*). Hurston's best-known work is the novel *Their Eyes Were Watching God* (1937), which features a black folk heroine. Two years later she wrote a book about Moses from the double vantage point of the Bible and black tradition.

WILLIAM GRANT STILL

The leading Harlem Renaissance musician, William Grant Still (1895–1978), was raised in Arkansas and studied science in Ohio before devoting himself to music. After World War I Still went to New York, where he composed popular and orchestral music. In the *Afro-American Symphony*, Still incorporated blues, spirituals, and jazz and included a tenor banjo in the orchestra. His aims were to show that blues could hold its own in a symphonic setting and that he could merge African-American heritage with mainstream Western music. This work was performed in 1931 by the Rochester Philharmonic Orchestra—the first time a prominent American orchestra played the work of a black composer.

LITERATURE BETWEEN THE WARS

The period between the two world wars inspired an enormous body of literature. Some was directly influenced by war, some by the Great Depression, and some by the discoveries of Freud. Strains of nationalism reverberate through many major novels of the period, and some writers challenged conventional gender roles and sexual mores.

Stylistically, Modernism came to the fore with experimental techniques such as fragmentation, free association, and **stream of consciousness** (a kind of interior dialogue resulting from free association), which also characterized the avant garde in the visual arts. One purpose of this technique was to present the spontaneous, unedited thoughts of a character. Expressing the notion that there is no time in the unconscious, authors using stream of consciousness allow a character's thoughts and emotions to move freely between past and present, and between fantasy and reality. Believing that order and regularity engendered false hope in a hopeless period, some writers rejected narrative unity and traditional literary forms. Their themes included the isolation and alienation caused by World War I, immigration and emigration, urbanization and technology, and the changing political and social landscape. In literature the breakdown of civilization led to anxiety and despair as well as to hope for a better future.

AMERICAN POETS AND NOVELISTS

In the United States literature between the wars tends to fall into two camps: works that deal directly with World War I and its alienating effect on people, and works that focus on American life, regional landscape, and the Great Depression.

EFFECTS OF WAR: HEMINGWAY AND CATHER Ernest Miller Hemingway (1899–1961) was wounded in 1918 while serving in an ambulance unit during World War I. His novels and short stories exemplify the loss of faith and alienation characteristic of the post-World War I period. *The Sun Also Rises* (1926), Hemingway's first major success, explores the "lost generation" (a term coined by Gertrude Stein). He conveys a sense of isolation and frenetic despair through the sexual impotence of the hero, Jake Barnes, and his unfulfilled relationship with Lady Brett Ashley.

Hemingway's anti-Falangist sympathies during the Spanish Civil War inspired *For Whom the Bell Tolls* (1940). Its hero, the American Robert Jordan, joins the Loyalists against Franco. Jordan receives an order from a Russian general to blow up a bridge, and he falls in love with a Spanish girl, Maria, who has been tortured by the Falangists. Filled with intense characterizations of Spanish guerrillas and with conflicts—between peasants and foreigners, bravery and cowardice, love and hate—*For Whom the Bell Tolls* vividly portrays the struggle between Fascism and freedom in Spain during the 1930s.

The themes of Willa Siebert Cather (1873–1947) include the effects of World War I on American life, immigration, and the changing roles of women. She grew up in Red Cloud, Nebraska, and was acutely aware of the difficulty of taming a harsh land. The first sentence of *O Pioneers!* expresses the fragility of civilization in the face of an unforgiving landscape:

> One January day, thirty years ago, the little town of Hanover, anchored on a windy Nebraska tableland, was trying not to be blown away.

Cather's best-known novel, *My Antonia* (1918), deals with the problems of Bohemian immigrants, especially women, in America. It is written in the form of a memoir by Jim Burden about his childhood friend, Antonia Shimerda, in Black Hawk, Nebraska. The suicide of Antonia's father forces her to work first in the fields, and then for a family in town. She quits when the father insists that she stop attending Saturday-night dances. When she finds work with another family, the father makes sexual advances and she leaves. Later she is seduced by a man who deserts her when she becomes pregnant. Returning to her mother's farm, Antonia eventually marries another Bohemian immigrant. Together they expand the farm, giving Antonia a feeling of success in hard work.

In 1922, inspired by World War I, Cather published *One of Ours*, in which a boy from the Plains enlists in the army and is killed fighting in France. As with her other novels, *One of Ours* reflects Cather's attachment to the American landscape. But here it is war rather than nature that is at odds with civilization, and the hero, who has made a bad marriage, is at odds with himself. His fragmented life and early death are metaphors for the state of the Western world at the time.

AMERICAN SOCIETY AND LANDSCAPE: DREISER, LEWIS, DOS PASSOS, FITZGERALD, AND STEINBECK Theodore Herman Albert Dreiser (1871–1945) was the ninth of ten children from a poor, German immigrant family in Indiana. He moved to Chicago when he was fifteen and worked as a journalist. During the Spanish Civil War he supported the Loyalists and embraced Marxism. Dreiser's novels criticize American society, especially its class system. His classic novel *Sister Carrie* (1900) deals with themes of ambition, success and decline, and the failed American Dream of an immigrant working girl.

In 1925 Dreiser published *An American Tragedy*, one of several novels dealing with the illusions dispelled when a hero or heroine leaves home in search of a better life. In this case, Clyde Griffiths leaves his family to become a bell-boy in a Kansas City hotel and then works in a New York State factory. Hoping to marry a wealthy local girl, Clyde drowns his pregnant mistress. He is arrested, convicted of murder, and condemned to death. Through Clyde's adventures, Dreiser conveys the base materialism of American society and the destructive effects of industrialization.

(Harry) Sinclair Lewis (1885–1951), a native of Minnesota, dropped out of Yale to join an experimental socialist colony and soon became one of America's most acclaimed novelists. In *Main Street* (1920), his most famous novel, Lewis describes dull, Midwestern life in Gopher Prairie, Minnesota. He portrays the hypocrisy of this paradigmatic American town through the eyes of Carol Milford, who marries the good-natured but provincial Dr. Kennicott.

Carol sees through the social pretensions of people who thrive on gossip, of church-goers who lack Christian values, and of self-proclaimed intellectuals who are uninterested in literature. She tries in vain to improve the aesthetic quality of architecture in Gopher Prairie but, frustrated by the lack of support, leaves town. Two years later, courted again by her husband, she returns and accepts Gopher Prairie for what it is.

John Roderigo Dos Passos (1896–1970), a native of Chicago, worked for the French and Italian ambulance services during World War I, which inspired his first major novel, *Three Soldiers* (1921). His greatest work, the trilogy *U.S.A.* (1930–1936), draws on American society between the wars and is a severe indictment of capitalism. Using the literary technique known as **newsreels**, Dos Passos intersperses fiction with news headlines, advertisements, song lyrics, political speeches, and historical events from between the wars, thereby creating a literary collage of life in the United States. The unnamed hero is identified as "The Camera's Eye," and the reader sees his thoughts unfolding in cinematic, stream-of-consciousness passages.

The novelist and short-story writer F. (Francis) Scott Key Fitzgerald (1896–1940) was born in Minnesota. He fought in World War I, and after the war he and his wife, Zelda Sayre, came to embody the decadent lifestyle of the Jazz Age. Fitzgerald later worked as a screenwriter in Hollywood but was fired for alcoholism. Both Scott and Zelda were attracted to wealth and glamour and both suffered mental breakdowns.

Fitzgerald's masterpiece, *The Great Gatsby* (1925), is the story of the financier Jay Gatsby (originally Gatz), whose past is mysterious and whose wealth comes from dubious sources. Seeking glamour and social acceptance, Gatsby buys a mansion in West Egg, a *nouveau riche* area on the fashionable North Shore of Long Island. He is obsessed with Daisy Buchanan, who comes from "old money" and lives in the aristocratic town of East Egg. By juxtaposing East and West Egg and delving into the sordid life of New York City, Fitzgerald contrasts traditional American values embodied by the Midwest with the decadence of Eastern snobbery. Representing moral rectitude, the narrator, Nick Carraway, comes from Minnesota and is Gatsby's next-door neighbor in West Egg.

One of the novel's themes is the decaying of the American Dream during the extravagant 1920s. Populated by a generation disillusioned by World War I, *The Great Gatsby* depicts unrestrained financial greed, vain social ambition, and moral corruption. In the end, Gatsby is shot in his swimming pool and Nick returns to the Midwest.

John Ernst Steinbeck (1902–1968) wrote the most dramatic depiction of the Great Depression in *The Grapes of Wrath* (1939). He conveys the abject poverty of the Midwest through the imagery of the American dust bowl:

> The dawn came, but no day. In the gray sky a red sun appeared, a dim red circle that gave a little light, like dusk; and as that day advanced, the dusk slipped back toward darkness, and the wind cried and whimpered over the fallen corn.
>
> Men and women huddled in their houses, and they tied handkerchiefs over their noses when they went out, and wore goggles to protect their eyes.

The novel revolves around an immigrant farm family from Oklahoma—Okies—slowly making its way to California (where Steinbeck himself was born). Steinbeck exposes the irony of the American myth that California is a promised land, which he contrasts with the arid atmosphere of the Midwest during the Depression. The harsh distinctions of class and wealth in American society portrayed in *The Grapes of Wrath* were especially marked in the 1930s.

MODERNIST AUTHORS: CUMMINGS, ELIOT, AND FAULKNER The innovative, Modernist literary approach of E. (Edward) E. (Estlin) Cummings (1894–1962) is evident in his practice of using lower case, his avoidance of punctuation, and his use of original word combinations. Cummings' first novel, *The Enormous Room* (1922), describes his three-month imprisonment in a French detention camp during World War I. His observations of character are enriched by his use of satirical irony.

As a poet, E. E. Cummings was influenced by Romanticism, Dada, Ezra Pound, and jazz. In his poetry the occasional effect of free association is enhanced by minimal punctuation and experimentation with syntax and tense. In "when god decided to invent," Cummings is "at a loss for words" as he confronts the enormity of man's capacity for self-destruction:

> when god decided to invent
> everything he took one
> breath bigger than a circustent
> and everything began
>
> when man determined to destroy
> himself he picked the was
> of shall and finding only why
> smashed it into because

One of the most experimental Modernist American poets, T. (Thomas) S. (Stearns) Eliot (1888–1965), was born in St. Louis, Missouri, but lived in London from 1915. A friend of Ezra Pound (see Chapter 21), Eliot quotes from multiple authors and includes phrases and song fragments from foreign languages in his poetry. "The Love Song of J. Alfred Prufrock" (1917) reflects the era's pessimism, its sense of alienation, and the emotional void of modern life. Prufrock feels anaesthetized and bored as he describes vain efforts to overcome his anxiety:

> Let us go then, you and I,
> When the evening is spread out against the sky
> Like a patient etherized upon a table;
> Let us go, through certain half-deserted streets,
> The muttering retreats
> Of restless nights in one-night cheap hotels
> And sawdust restaurants with oyster-shells:
> Streets that follow like a tedious argument
> Of insidious intent
> To lead you to an overwhelming question . . .
> Oh, do not ask, "What is it?"
> Let us go and make our visit.
>
> In the room the women come and go
> Talking of Michelangelo.

The first four lines of *The Waste Land* (1922) reflect the overwhelming sense of waste that followed World War I. The opening of the poem is derived from Chaucer's *Canterbury Tales* (see Chapter 12). Like Chaucer, Eliot begins with the month of April:

> April is the cruellest month, breeding
> Lilacs out of the dead land, mixing
> Memory and desire, stirring
> Dull roots with spring rain.

"The Hollow Men" (1925) shows the depth of Eliot's despair. Everything has become meaningless, dry, overrun with vermin, and the human race is hollow and lifeless, as if made of straw:

We are the hollow men
We are the stuffed men
Leaning together
Headpiece filled with straw. Alas!
Our dried voices, when
We whisper together
Are quiet and meaningless
As wind in dry grass
Or rats' feet over broken glass
In our dry cellar.

William Cuthbert Faulkner (1897–1962), who explored social themes in the American South after World War I, used a number of Modernist literary devices. He grew up in Oxford, Mississippi, and although he traveled in Europe, he wrote mainly about his native state. Focusing on themes of hidden sexual transgression in Southern families, Faulkner insightfully depicts poor whites and downtrodden blacks. He invented the memorable county of Yoknapatawpha as a metaphor for the tragic decay of the Old South.

In *The Sound and the Fury* (1929), which takes place in Yoknapatawpha County, Faulkner explores the Compson family through the eyes of their thirty-three-year-old mentally retarded son, Benjy. Benjy's main obsession is with his sister Caddy and her sexual development. By using stream of consciousness, Faulkner conveys Benjy's spontaneous, unedited observations of his deteriorating family. The novel opens with Benjy's matter-of-fact description of hitting:

> Through the fence, between the curling flower spaces, I could see them hitting. They were coming toward where the flag was and I went along the fence. Luster was hunting in the grass by the flower tree. They took the flag out, and they were hitting. Then they put the flag back and they went to the table, and he hit and the other hit.

Faulkner's repetition of the words "hitting" and "hit" punctuates both the text and the forcefulness it describes. Benjy's memory shifts from one action to another as image after image flashes through his mind. Because Benjy is mentally retarded, he is a vehicle for spontaneous free association devoid of grammatical logic and syntax. Faulkner thus depicts memory as Proust does, showing through stream of consciousness that there is no time in the unconscious.

MAJOR EUROPEAN NOVELISTS

European authors, like American authors, wrote about alienation, despair, and, in some cases, the hope for a better future. Among the major subjects were rural and urban landscape and social change, often using satire and Modernist techniques.

RUSSIA: MIKHAIL SHOLOKHOV *And Quiet Flows the Don* (1928), the epic novel by Mikhail Sholokhov (1905–1984), is a panorama of Cossack life during the Russian Revolution and World War I. Appalled by the destruction of the war, Sholokhov found hope in communism. He himself had Cossack roots and came from the lower middle class.

Sholokhov describes the rugged existence of the Russian steppe by the River Don, reflecting the national feeling for landscape and the narrow prejudices of the Cossacks. The novel opens in the village of Tatarsk. When livestock begin to die of unknown causes, the villagers blame the Turkish wife of a Cossack because she is a foreigner and they beat her to death.

In addition to vivid character portrayals, Sholokhov describes the intensity of the steppe:

> A sultry, sunny July haze lay over the steppe. The ripe floods of wheat smoked with yellow dust. The metal parts of the reapers were too hot to be touched with the hand. It was painful to look up at the bluish-yellow flaming sky. Where the wheat ended, a saffron sweep of clover began.

When he describes the Don, Sholokhov is more lyrical and his prose flows like the river itself. He compares the motion of the water to the rustling of a woman's skirt:

> From the Don came a flowing whisper, rustle, and crunch, as though a strongly-built, gaily-dressed woman as tall as a poplar were passing by, her great, invisible skirts rustling.

BRITISH MODERNISTS: WOOLF AND JOYCE Literature in Britain between the wars was imbued with a sense of social alienation, satire, and an awareness that a second great war loomed on the political horizon. Several authors produced innovative works of creative fiction that embody the notion of Modernism and reflect the changing social mores of the time.

(Adeline) Virginia Woolf (1882–1941), a leading member of the Bloomsbury Group, wrote literary criticism and, with her husband Leonard, founded the Hogarth Press, which published standard editions of Freud's works. Beset by mental problems for most of her life, she eventually drowned herself. Her novels, which reflect her emotional turmoil, her feminist leanings, and the atmosphere in Europe after World War I, use several important Modernist literary techniques.

The opening line of *Mrs. Dalloway* (1925)—"Mrs. Dalloway said she would buy the flowers herself"—sets the tone for the point of view of a determined character, devoted to her family and her social life. The story, which is told largely in stream of consciousness, takes place on a single day in London as the fifty-one-year-old Clarissa Dalloway, wife of a Member of Parliament, prepares for a party that same evening. Through her interior dialogue we encounter her acquaintances, past and present, and experience the sights and sounds of London. Time is marked by the chimes of Big Ben (the clock that towers over the British Houses of Parliament).

World War I, Mrs. Dalloway observes, is over, but its effects linger and keep running through her mind. She thinks of the deaths of friends and relatives and of shell-shocked Septimus Warren Smith, who committed suicide:

> For it was the middle of June. The War was over, except for some one like Mrs. Foxcroft at the Embassy last night eating her heart out because that nice boy was killed and now the old Manor House must go to a cousin; or Lady Bexborough who opened a bazaar, they said, with the telegram in her hand, John her favourite killed; but it was over; thank Heaven—over. It was June.

Woolf championed the cause of women, in particular their status as intellectuals. In *A Room of One's Own* (1929) she argues for a woman's right to a private space in which to create (write)—and an income that allows her the time to do it.

James Joyce, whose style challenged traditional literary structure (see Chapter 21), was the most innovative author in the English language between the wars (figure **22.26**). In 1922 he published *Ulysses* (in France), which is based on Homer's *Odyssey* (see Chapter 4) but which takes place over twenty-four hours in early-twentieth-century Dublin. Joyce rebelled against his Irish Catholic background, although it provided rich material for his novels. The main characters are Stephen Dedalus (the hero of *A Portrait of the Artist as a Young Man*, see Chapter 21), who represents the author, Leopold Bloom, a Jew who works in advertising, and Bloom's wife, Molly. The men wander through Dublin, with each episode loosely related to the travels of Homer's Odysseus (Ulysses in Latin). Bloom's visit to a brothel (Nighttown) echoes Odysseus's descent into the Underworld. Bloom is thus a modern Odysseus, Stephen a modern Telemachus (Odysseus's son), and Molly a modern Penelope (the faithful wife of Odysseus).

Joyce's attraction to themes of guilt and redemption and his satirical view of religion offended the Roman Catholic Church. In the opening lines of *Ulysses* he compares the morning ritual of shaving to a priest performing Mass:

> Stately plump Buck Mulligan [Stephen's roommate] came from the stairhead, bearing a bowl of lather on which a mirror and a razor lay crossed . . . He held the bowl aloft and intoned:—*Introibo ad altare Dei* ["I shall go unto the altar of God"].

Joyce takes liberties with punctuation, often omitting it entirely to replicate free flowing, associative thought and stream of consciousness. The last forty-five pages, devoted to Molly Bloom's erotic monologue as she drifts into sleep, are unpunctuated. They begin and end with "yes."

Ulysses was placed on the *Index of Forbidden Books* by the Catholic Church, and when five hundred copies of the book arrived at the United States Post Office in 1922, they were burned.

In 1939 Joyce published *Finnegans Wake*, one of the most complex and original works of literature in any language. It is filled with humor and lyricism, using the full range of linguistic possibilities—puns, foreign and portmanteau words, dream language, free association, and musical rhythms. The structure of the book is circular: the unpunctuated last line—"A way a lone a last a loved a long the"—flows into the first line, which begins with a lower case letter—"riverrun, past Eve and Adam's, from swerve of shore to bend of bay, brings us by a commodius vicus of recirculation back to Howth Castle and Environs." Howth Castle is in Dublin and Eve and Adam is a pub. The hero is HCE (for Humphrey Chimpden Earwicker), who runs the pub. HCE also stands for Everyman (Here Comes Everybody), and his wife is Anna Livia Plurabelle. She is celebrated in a poetic montage of the Lord's Prayer and the invocation of Allah:

22.26 Berenice Abbot, James Joyce, 1928. Photograph, 13½ × 10⅜ in. (34.3 × 26.3 cm).
Berenice Abbot (1898–1991) moved from the American Midwest to Paris in 1921 and set up a portrait studio in 1926. There she photographed the leading intellectuals and celebrities of the day. This portrait of James Joyce is typical of her direct, straightforward recording of character. Joyce stands out clearly from a gray background, each texture precisely captured. His slightly downcast expression, slouching pose, creased forehead, and limp hands seem to reflect his continual problems with money, his wife's illness, and his daughter's madness.

> In the name of Annah the Allmaziful, the Everliving, the Bringer of Plurabilities, haloed be her eve, her singtime sung, her rill be run, unhemmed as it is uneven!

The novel, like the Judeo-Christian world, opens with the Fall of Man. Joyce compares this event with the death of Finnegan and with Humpty Dumpty falling off the wall, which he incorporates into a eulogy for Finnegan at his wake:

> The great fall of the offwall entailed at such short notice the pftjschute of Finnegan, erse solid man, that the humptyhillhead of humself prumptly sends an unqiring one well to the west in quest of his tumptytumtoes.

SOCIAL COMMENTARY IN BRITAIN: LAWRENCE AND HUXLEY D. (David) H. (Herbert) Lawrence (1885–1930), the author of fiction and non-fiction, pushed the limits of propriety by using explicit sexual language. The son of a coalminer in the English Midlands, Lawrence dropped out of school, briefly worked as a teacher, and ran off with the wife of a professor. He lived in Italy and France after World War I and died of tuberculosis at the age of forty-four.

Lawrence scandalized readers with his novel of sexual liberation, *Lady Chatterley's Lover* (privately published 1928). It is the story of a woman married to an impotent aristocrat who was wounded in the war and confined to a wheelchair. Lady Chatterley's emotionally satisfying affair with the gamekeeper, Oliver Mellors, offended social convention. The intensity of the affair exemplified Lawrence's wish to recover his feelings after the numbness caused by war. But the novel, with its explicit language, poetic descriptions of love-making, and liberal use of four-letter words, was censored in Britain. The full text was not published until 1960, after a notorious trial in which the publisher was prosecuted under Britain's Obscene Publications Act. The verdict to acquit helped to liberate British publishing from censorship.

READING SELECTION

Lawrence, *Lady Chatterley's Lover*, an aristocrat reflects on the importance of English tradition, PWC6-097

Aldous Leonard Huxley (1894–1963) worked as a journalist and lived for a time in Italy. He published *Brave New World* in 1932. The novel is a satire on totalitarianism, then on the rise in Europe, and is set in the year A.F. 632—the seventh century after Henry Ford. Huxley's Ford was a god of industry who signaled the dawn of a new, mechanized civilization. The New World is run by World Controllers, who maintain social stability through a regulated caste-system: at the top are Alphas and Betas, and the workers are Gammas, Deltas, and Epsilons. There is no pain or resentment, because everyone receives a daily dose of the mood-altering drug Soma.

Huxley's new world is ruled by his Fordship, Mustapha Mond, who disdains the former world for its wars, its suffering, and its economic crises. When the reformers took over, they eliminated religion and traditional marriage and controlled the birth rate. Babies are hatched in the Central London Hatchery and Conditioning Center, which is emblazoned with a shield bearing the motto: COMMUNITY, IDENTITY, STABILITY. Infants are divided into classes, and some are conditioned according to a Neo-Pavlovian system: placed in a room filled with roses and books, they are shocked by alarms so that they will learn to avoid literature and sensation. Others are trained by "infant hypnotism," which teaches ethics through tapes that play moral sayings as they sleep. History, science, and religion are banned, because they are sources of conflict. Human emotions and creative energy are subsumed by the machine, and people who become too individualistic are banished to an island.

GERMANY: HESSE AND REMARQUE German novels of the 1920s and 1930s reflect intense disillusionment following the country's defeat in World War I. Some works deal with the search for renewed creativity and spiritual well-being, while others are direct portrayals of the horrors of war.

Hermann Hesse (1877–1962), who was born in the German town of Calw, opposed World War I, became a pacifist, and moved to Switzerland. His works reveal his interest in psychoanalysis as well as the impact of war on Europe, and among his most prominent themes are nostalgia for the past and a utopian vision of the future.

Hesse's mysticism, which is a traditional strain in German Romanticism, inspired his most popular book, *Siddhartha* (1922). Named for the Buddha's given name, the novel deals with two Hindu friends seeking spirituality. As with the original Siddhartha (whom Hesse's hero encounters), Hesse's Siddhartha seeks understanding from the outside world, only to discover that true knowledge is found within. *Der Steppenwolf* (1927) reflects the influence of Carl Jung (see Chapter 21), who psychoanalyzed Hesse, and German Romanticism in its theme of dual personality (human and wolf).

One of the most powerful indictments of war, *All Quiet on the Western Front* (1929), was written by Erich Maria Remarque (1898–1970), a veteran of World War I. Seen through the eyes of Paul Bäumer, a frightened young German soldier, the war portends hopelessness and death. Paul's message to students at his former school—"When it comes to dying for one's country, it is preferable not to die at all"—was considered unpatriotic. The book was later made into a popular film, which ends with Paul's hand reaching for a butterfly as he dies.

In 1931 Remarque published *The Road Back*, about the ruin of the German army. He was deprived of his German citizenship, his books were burned by the Nazis in 1933, and he moved to Switzerland. He later became an American citizen and married the film actress Paulette Goddard.

SCANDINAVIA: HAMSUN, LAXNESS, AND LAGERKVIST The Norwegian author Knut Hamsun (1859–1952), whose youth was marked by extreme poverty, was impressed by the strain of German Romanticism associated with Heidegger and Nazi ideology. In 1917, a year before the end of World War I, Hamsun published *Growth of the Soil*, written in a powerful but lyrical style. The hero, Isak, embodies Hamsun's ideal of the romantic "first man," an Adamic figure who ventures alone into the world of nature. The theme of the heroic peasant, linked with German nationalism in which the connection with land is a source of strength, was consistent with Hamsun's support of Hitler. In 1946 the Norwegian government fined Hamsun for collaborating with the Nazis.

The Icelandic novelist Halldór Laxness (1902–1998), born near Reykjavik, began writing as an adolescent and published over sixty books. His masterpiece, *Independent People* (1934–1935), is the story of Bjartur of Summerhouses, a sheep farmer determined to become financially independent after eighteen years of indentured servitude. In his single-mindedness he ignores the hardships inflicted on his family, all of whom die or desert him. The exception is Asta Sollilja, the daughter of his deceased wife, whom he raises as his own.

Isolated in the bleak, treeless landscape of Iceland, Bjartur momentarily gives in to his attraction to Asta and lightly touches her bare leg. Horrified by his impulse, he withdraws from his step-daughter, resolving never to repeat the transgression. She does not understand his aloofness, and her decision to become independent of him leads to a silent, intense struggle between two strong-willed people. Throughout the novel, there are vague allusions to a great war taking place somewhere in Europe. Bjartur dismisses this as characteristic of continental madness, but he is pleased that the conflict is inflating the price of wool and mutton.

The major Swedish author of his generation, Par Lägerkvist (1891–1974) began writing while he was still at school and spent World War I in Denmark. Affected by the war, he searched for meaning in a destructive world. He compared the rise of Fascism and Nazism in the 1930s with contemporary gangsterism and medieval torture.

Lägerkvist's novels are often imbued with biblical or Classical themes and infiltrated by a sense of mystery and imagination. *The Dwarf* (1944), an allegory of evil set at a Renaissance court, made his international reputation. The hero is a venomous dwarf who loves death and is mentally perverse as well as physically stunted. As with Faulkner's idiot, Benjy Compson (see p. 638), Lägerkvist's deformed hero is a vehicle for truthful observation. Written in the voice of the dwarf's diary, the novel juxtaposes themes of creativity and destruction that preoccupied European intellectuals from before World War I through World War II.

THEATER BETWEEN THE WARS

Theater between the wars used the boundary between illusion and reality as a dramatic theme. Modernist playwrights rejected naturalism and turned to contemporary political and social issues. In so doing, they used new poetic forms, revived Classical theater, restaged ancient plays in contemporary settings, and broke with traditional dramatic conventions.

Italy: Luigi Pirandello

Luigi Pirandello (1867–1936), the most important Italian playwright in the 1920s, ran the Art Theater of Rome from 1924 to 1928. He was one of the first Europeans to reject naturalism. In his best-known work, *Six Characters in Search of an Author* (1921), six actors arrive on the set to rehearse a play by Pirandello, only to find that the plot has not been resolved. They need an author to finish the play so that they can come alive. The director agrees to fill in the story, but the actors reject his narrative and decide to write their own. At the end a boy shoots himself, and his mother screams and runs him over. The director and the audience are unsure of what is true and what is illusion. Finally, the director announces that the rehearsal—and with it the play—is at an end. Pirandello has thus constructed his play around the very process of playwriting, casting, and directing. In so doing, he makes form into content and transforms the characters into the author.

Germany: Bertolt Brecht

The leading German playwright between the wars, Bertolt Brecht (1898–1956), studied medicine before turning to theater. Like Pirandello, he rejected naturalism but wanted his work to bring about social and political change. He called his plays **epic theater**, which he hoped would alienate his audience, create anxiety, and inspire action. In contrast to the Classical unities of time and place, Brecht's scenes are loosely structured, and dialogue alternates with singing that comments on the action.

Brecht's first successful work, *The Three-Penny Opera* (1928), was set to music by the German composer Kurt Weill (1900–1950). It is based on the eighteenth-century *Beggar's Opera* by the English author John Gay. The gangster hero, Mack the Knife, echoes the Marxist sentiments of Brecht. Set in America during the 1920s, *The Three-Penny Opera* is a satire on capitalism, portraying a decaying society that is politically, financially, and morally corrupt. Weill's new and original song style demonstrated how a serious modern composer could write attractively for the wider public without sacrificing originality

In *Mother Courage* (1941) Brecht uses the Thirty Years War waged in the seventeenth century (see Chapter 16) as a metaphor for modern warfare. The title character, whose name is ironic, is a war profiteer who follows the army from place to place with her canteen wagon. She switches loyalty, betrays her friends and acquaintances, and refuses to help local peasants who need the medicines and bandages she transports for the army. The climax occurs when her daughter realizes that soldiers from the Catholic army (an allusion to the Nazis) are planning to kill innocent townspeople. She climbs to the roof of a house, beats a drum, and is shot by the soldiers. By then, however, she has awakened the town (as Brecht hoped to awaken his audiences), which defends itself with a cannon. Mother Courage pays for her daughter's funeral and returns to work, revealing once again her commitment to profit, rather than to courage or loyalty.

SPAIN: GARCÍA LORCA

Federico García Lorca (1898–1936) was an important poet and the major playwright in Spain during the 1930s. Born near Granada, he earned a law degree and was poet in residence at Columbia University from 1929 to 1930. His experience in New York during the early years of the Depression inspired his *Poeta en Nueva York* (*Poet in New York*, 1940), in which he describes a city demoralized by economic crisis.

Lorca's three most famous plays are notable for their powerful female characters, the use of lyrical language to convey violent passions lurking beneath the repressive conventions of Catholic Spain, and the rugged landscape of his native Andalusia. Primitive suspicions preoccupy his characters, and events seem impelled by natural forces controlled by the moon and the earth. Lorca's themes revolve around contrasts between life and death, fertility and sterility, and fiery passion and rigid control.

Blood Wedding (1933), written in poetic form, takes place in the context of a traditional blood feud between two Andalusian families. When a bride escapes from her arranged marriage and elopes with her lover on her wedding day, she reawakens the feud, which erupts with a powerful, macho intensity. *Yerma* (1934) is the story of a woman married to an infertile husband. Bound by tradition not to leave him, she kills him instead. In *The House of Bernarda Alba* (1936) five daughters are dominated by a tyrannical mother. All seek love but are held captive by Spanish morality until the youngest daughter finds freedom in suicide.

Although not involved in politics himself, Lorca was acquainted with artists and intellectuals distrusted by the Fascist regime of Franco. In 1936 he was executed by the Falangists, buried in an unmarked grave, and his books were burned in a public square in Granada.

FRANCE: GIRAUDOUX AND ANOUILH

French theater following World War I was influenced by the anti-war sentiments of Dada and by international collaborations between directors, choreographers, and musicians. The Ballets Suédois performed in Paris after 1915, and Diaghilev continued to direct the interdisciplinary Ballets Russes, joined by Stravinsky until Diaghilev's death in 1929. He brought several important Russian artists to the West, via Paris, including the dancers Vaslav Nijinsky (1890–1950) and Anna Pavlova (1881–1931) and the avant-garde choreographer George Balanchine (1904–1983). In 1933 Balanchine moved permanently to New York, where he founded the School of American Ballet and became the first director of the New York City Ballet.

The most important French playwright before World War II, Jean Giraudoux (1882–1944), was also a novelist and diplomat. His comedies and tragedies juxtapose themes of war and peace, loyalty and disloyalty, and fate versus free will. Many are inspired by ancient Greek literature. In *Electra* (1937) Giraudoux takes the essentially humanist position that people decide their own fate, even though it is controlled by the gods. *La Guerre de Troie n'aura pas lieu* (literally "The Trojan War won't take place" but given the English title *Tiger at the Gates*), produced in 1935, was related to the contemporary threat of war. As with Greek tragedies, even though we know the outcome, the author keeps us in suspense. At the core of the plot is the relationship between the Trojan prince Hector and his pregnant wife, Andromache. Hector promises that there will be no war and implores his brother Paris to return Helen to the Greeks. Paris refuses, and the Trojan War does, in fact, take place. Europe, too, had failed to prevent World War I, and Giraudoux warns that World War II will soon break out.

Jean Anouilh (1910–1987), the author of forty plays, wrote *Le Voyageur sans bagage* (*Traveler Without Luggage*) in 1937, two years before Hitler's invasion of Poland. The hero is a man who has lost his memory but discovers that he is a nasty character and then discards his former self. Anouilh thus holds out the possibility that people can change and, by implication, avoid a second great war. *Antigone* (1944) was a direct attack on the Nazis and the collaborationist Vichy Government of France. The doomed Antigone is pitted against Fascism, embodied by Creon, her tyrannical uncle, who is king of Thebes.

IRELAND: SEAN O'CASEY

The Abbey Theatre in Dublin continued to be a force in the English-speaking theater between the wars. Its most important playwright was Sean O'Casey (1880–1964), who was born into an impoverished Protestant family.

The political backdrop of his plays is the centuries-old struggle for Irish independence from Britain and the conflict between Catholics and Protestants in Ireland. The minority Catholics in Northern Ireland want union with the Republic of Ireland in the south, whereas the Protestants generally support political union with mainland Britain.

O'Casey wrote for the Abbey while working as a laborer. *The Shadow of a Gunman* (1923) is about an Irish house taken over by the British army in 1920; *Juno and the Paycock* (1924) takes place during the 1922 civil war; and *The Plough and the Stars* (1926) is set in Dublin during the Easter Rising of 1916. All exemplify O'Casey's early interest in realism and contemporary life rather than in traditional Irish legends.

THE UNITED STATES: EUGENE O'NEILL

The major American playwright between the wars, Eugene O'Neill (1888–1953) was born in New York to an acting family. His plays, which are based on many aspects of American life, include *The Emperor Jones* (1921), about the rise and tragic fall of a Caribbean ruler; *Anna Christie* (1921), about a prostitute who frequents the New York waterfront; *Desire Under the Elms* (1924), about vengeance, incest, and infanticide;

and *The Iceman Cometh* (1946), about alcoholics waiting in a bar for an ice salesman (representing their illusions) who never comes.

In *Mourning Becomes Electra* (1931) O'Neill merges the influence of Freud with Greek tragedy. The play is a six-hour trilogy like the *Oresteia* of Aeschylus on which it is based (see Chapter 6), but the cursed family of Atreus has become the house of Mannon. The mother (Christine, for Clytemnestra) kills the father (Ezra Mannon, for Agamemnon), the son (Orin, for Orestes) kills the mother's lover, and the mother kills herself. Instead of Mycenae after the Trojan War, New England following the American Civil War is O'Neill's setting; gods and fates have been replaced by the workings of the human mind. Lavinia, like Electra, is destined to mourn; at the end she locks herself in the house with only her memories of the dead for company. Like Aeschylus, O'Neill deals with themes of incest, murder, and guilt as they continue from one generation to the next.

22.27 Barbara Morgan, Martha Graham in *Letter to the World*, 1944. Detail of photograph.
Barbara Morgan (1900–1992) used speedlamps and flash in artificially illuminated photographs of dancers in motion. This example was staged for the camera, making a painting with light and dark as Graham made "paintings" of her own dances. Morgan wrote that her medium was light and that the partner of dance was action.

O'Neill's second epic play, the autobiographical *A Long Day's Journey into Night* (1957), is the story of a family cursed by alcoholism and drug addiction, religious conflict, and the continuing impact of past events on the present. The communication breakdown is reflected in obsessive, repetitive dialogue, although O'Neill offers a ray of hope in the hero's ability to come to terms with his past. Like Orestes, he gains some measure of self-knowledge as the play draws to a close.

MUSIC AND DANCE IN AMERICA

The **musical** was a prominent genre of the interwar years in America. A comic or romantic story is told in spoken dialogue supported by songs, choruses, dances, and imaginative stage direction. In this period, public recognition began to be accorded to American composers, both of popular songs and of modern art music, such as Ives and Copland. The Modernists found bold ways of combining national folk melodies with the stark musical language of the early twentieth century.

DANCE: MARTHA GRAHAM

Ballet in America was enriched by avant-garde émigrés from Europe, who deviated from Classical tradition and incorporated non-Western elements into their work. A pioneer of American modern dance choreography, Martha Graham (1894–1991) designed innovative ballets beginning in the 1920s (figure **22.27**). Graham wanted dance to convey the inner emotions of the dancers and the subjects they portrayed, and her choreography created a kind of painting in motion. In Morgan's photograph, Graham's horizontal torso flows organically into the broad curves of her long skirt. The folds create varied patterns of light and dark that respond to the dancer's movements. In contrast to Classical dance, Martha Graham, like avant-garde artists and writers, made visible the process of dance. Technique thus became form and content. In the 1930s she founded her own dance company.

THE AMERICAN MUSICAL

The golden age of the American musical began in the 1920s with such famous creators as Jerome Kern (1885–1945), Richard Rodgers (1902–1979), and Oscar Hammerstein II (1895–1960). They are often referred to as "songwriters" rather than composers, as their principal task was to create new numbers for a string of new shows. Although great melodists, many had not received formal musical training and handed their ideas to professional arrangers and orchestrators to flesh out for performance.

The first significant musical, *Show Boat* (1927), with music by Kern and lyrics by Hammerstein, tells of fifty years in the life of Magnolia Hawks and her romance with Gaylord

Ravenal. When Gaylord gambles away his money, the lovers separate. The depth of the story, with its interracial subplot, was unusual for its time. Well-known numbers include "Ol' Man River," "Can't Help Lovin' Dat Man," and "Why Do I Love You?" *Show Boat*'s significance in the history of music theater lies in the way Hammerstein and Kern shaped the production with songs that revealed character and advanced the plot.

By 1943, when *Oklahoma!* reached the New York stage, the musical was well established. Hammerstein teamed up with Richard Rodgers to create a show that integrated song, dance, and drama within a romance dealing with themes of rivalry, rage, and the determination of American territories to gain statehood. A wealth of memorable songs show exuberance ("Oklahoma!"), humor ("I'm Just a Girl who Can't Say No"), and melancholy ("Poor Judd is Dead"), while dramatic dance sequences include a ballet. A masterpiece of American musical theater, *Oklahoma!* won the Pulitzer Prize for drama in 1944.

George Gershwin

One of the most original American composers, George Gershwin (1898–1937) combined a career in songwriting and musicals with serious composition in traditional forms. After growing up in poverty in Manhattan, he taught himself to play the piano and found work performing new songs for a music publisher. His first big success came in 1919 with the song "Swanee." Commissions followed, and he formed a lasting collaboration with his brother Ira (1896–1983) as lyricist. Gershwin wrote many successful songs, composed over twenty musicals in the 1920s, including *Lady, Be Good!* (1924) featuring the singing and tap-dancing of Fred Astaire, and created four film scores in the 1930s.

Gershwin's most famous piece, *Rhapsody in Blue* (1924), was a commission for jazz band and solo piano. Although an arranger completed the orchestration, it represents his unique synthesis of popular song, jazz, and piano rhapsody. The memorable opening clarinet **glissando** (unbroken slide) was introduced after the clarinetist played it as a joke in rehearsal and Gershwin liked the effect. His symphonic poem, *An American in Paris* (1928), celebrates expatriate life in France, using taxi horns to replicate the sounds of modern urban life.

In Gershwin's opera, *Porgy and Bess* (1935), written with his brother, the dialogue and songs are characterized by local speech patterns among poor blacks in Charleston, South Carolina, where the opera is set. When an argument leads to murder, the murderer's girlfriend Bess finds shelter with the crippled beggar Porgy, who falls in love with her. At the end, Bess leaves for New York and Porgy climbs into his cart and sets off after her. Well-known songs from the opera include "Summertime," "I Got Plenty o' Nuttin'," and "Bess, You is My Woman Now."

MUSIC LISTENING SELECTION

Gershwin, *Porgy and Bess*, "Bess, You is My Woman Now." Paul Robeson, bass-baritone, Eva Jessye Choir, Decca Symphony Orchestra, conductor Alexander Smallens, CD track 22

Charles Ives

Charles Ives (1874–1954) led art music into new, distinctively American territory. His father was a Civil War bandmaster, and Ives grew up hearing church hymns and popular band tunes. His father taught him to play melodies in different keys at the same time, to compose using whole-tone scales, and to hear tiny increments of pitch between the semitones of the Western scales. He continued his musical training at Yale University, then went into the insurance business, composing in his spare time.

In his works, Ives frequently quotes church, dance, and military band melodies as a way of connecting local American life with universal ideas and feelings. These musical quotations are often superimposed, so listeners experience polytonality, polyharmony, and polyrhythm—as if two or three sound sources or bands are playing unrelated pieces simultaneously. His works seem to express memories of childhood times and places, infused with the philosophies of New England transcendentalism, particularly the words and ideas of Emerson and Thoreau (see Chapter 18). In *The Unanswered Question* (1906) a trumpet plays a questioning phrase of music several times, the individual questioning society in the form of two ensembles—a flute quartet and offstage strings. Each timbral group has a distinct musical character: cross-rhythms and melodic leaps in the trumpet; fast, chromatic movement in the flutes; and sustained, peaceful chords in the strings.

Ives's output includes four symphonies, choral music, string quartets, violin and piano sonatas, and over 180 songs. He was prolific as well as pioneering, and by layering different textures, tunes, and dissonant flights of fancy, he created a complex musical world inspired by the spiritual American values he so admired.

Aaron Copland

Born to a Russian immigrant family in Brooklyn, New York, Aaron Copland (1900–1990) searched for a truly American style. Like that of Ives, Copland's music is notable for the use of folksong, dance music, and hymn tunes within a modern compositional style. There is a strong American flavor to his ballet scores *Billy the Kid* (1938; figure **22.28**), *Rodeo* (1942), and *Appalachian Spring* (1944). Tuneful and accessible, they have achieved lasting popularity.

22.28 Scene from Aaron Copland's *Billy the Kid*, choreographed by Eugene Loring, 1938. Detail of photograph by George Platt Lynes, gelatin silver print. New York Public Library for the Performing Arts.

Copland experimented with contemporary compositional techniques. His Piano Variations (1930) express a spare, harshly dissonant ultra-Modernism, using a brief musical idea that sounds and in places is manipulated like a five-note row (see Chapter 21). In contrast, his grand Symphony No. 3 (1946) is permeated by transformations of his war theme "Fanfare for the Common Man," which is boldly sounded in the finale in powerful, almost Neoclassical, simplicity. Just a few years later, he experimented in his introspective Piano Quartet (1950) with **serialism** (a post-World War II extension of the twelve-tone technique, in which various parameters in addition to pitch, such as dynamics and rhythm, are ordered and manipulated according to prescribed rules). At the other extreme, he composed eight film scores and a set of simple arrangements of *Old American Songs* (1952). This stylistic dichotomy symbolizes the dilemma of twentieth-century creativity: does innovation necessarily imply that art becomes inaccessible to general audiences?

FILM

Film is a relatively new medium in the history of the creative arts. It offered unprecedented expressive possibilities and immediately caught on during the 1920s. Early films were used as mass entertainment, as well as for propaganda, social commentary, and news. At first films were in black and white and had no audible dialogue, but there could be background music. Written dialogue flashed on the screen following the images. By 1928 both sound and color had been introduced.

GERMANY: LENI RIEFENSTAHL

Hitler commissioned two important films for propaganda purposes, both of which were directed by Leni Riefenstahl (1902–2003). In *Triumph of the Will* (1936) Riefenstahl conveys Nazi power by showing Hitler as a messianic figure, adored by huge crowds at the 1934 rally in Nuremberg. With her use of varied angles, slow-motion, and close-ups, Riefenstahl's films were innovative and effective enough to be prohibited in the United States, Canada, and Britain during World War II.

In 1938 she released her second great propaganda film, *Olympia*, recording the Olympic Games held in Germany in 1936. Here she relates Hitler's Germany to the Greek Olympics by idealizing the athletes and representing them as the Supermen of Nietszche's philosophy (see Chapter 19). In fact, however, her film shows the perversion of ancient Greek ideals by the Nazi government. Although both were warrior cultures, the Greeks halted their wars to provide safe travel for athletes, whereas Germany used the Games to glorify the military build-up of the Third Reich (figure **22.29**).

22.29 Leni Riefenstahl, scene from the diving sequence of *Olympia*, 1936. From this angle, Riefenstahl silhouettes the diver so that he could be seen as both flying and diving. The sense of a figure soaring through the air creates the impression of a Superman, able to defy gravity and control space.

THE SOVIET UNION: SERGEI EISENSTEIN

The Russian Sergei Eisenstein (1898–1948) was a pioneer of early film. The son of a Latvian architect, Eisenstein became a member of the avant-garde Moscow theater in 1920, where Stanislavski (see Chapter 19) regularly lectured on Method acting. Eisenstein was not only an innovative director, he was also one of the greatest Western film theorists. He produced six films in his twenty-five-year career and wrote two classic works on film theory, *The Film Sense* (1942) and *The Film Form* (1948). Eisenstein used the technique of montage to arrange scenes for maximum visual and psychological effect.

In *The Film Sense* he cites the imagistic power of Lewis Carroll's portmanteau words (see Chapter 21), Joyce's linguistic puns in *Finnegans Wake*, and Freud's word combinations—for example, alcoholidays for alcohol and holidays—that have a stronger impact than the component words alone. Eisenstein similarly juxtaposed and sequenced shots that add up to more than the sum of each individual shot. In addition to the images, Eisenstein wanted sight and sound synchronized to maximize the emotional effect of a montage.

Eisenstein's *Battleship Potemkin* (1925) reflects his support for the 1917 revolution. It is the story of a 1905 mutiny aboard the *Potemkin* following riots in Odessa. The most impressive editing comes in the third part of the film, when the Cossacks fire on civilians (figure **22.30**).

22.30 *left* **Eisenstein, Odessa Steps sequence from *The Battleship Potemkin*, 1925. A mother carries her injured child up the stairs toward advancing soldiers.** The mother is shown in back view, carrying her wounded child up a flight of steps strewn with dead bodies. They have been shot by the neatly uniformed, orderly line of Cossacks who, it is evident, will also kill the mother. Eisenstein arranges the scene to evoke sympathy with the collective dead and the individual mother. A bright light falls on the steps just above the mother and child, suggesting their innocence compared with the evil, unrelenting soldiers.

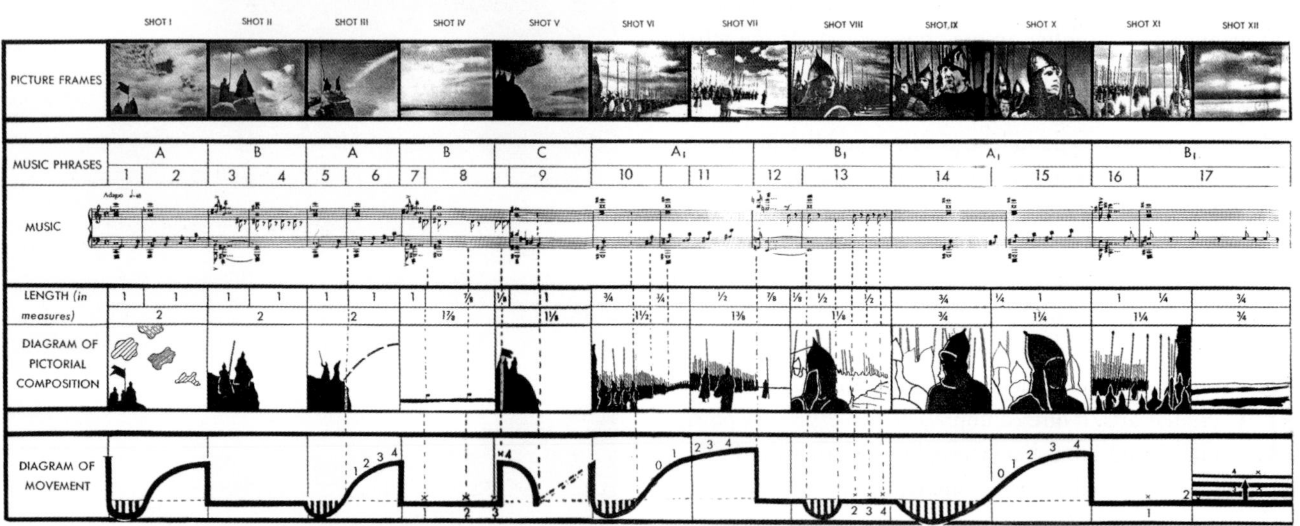

22.31 Sergei Eisenstein, diagram of the first twelve shots of the Battle on the Ice in *Alexander Nevsky*, 1938.
Eisenstein's diagram includes the synchronized music score by Sergei Prokofiev (1891–1953). Prokofiev had left the new Soviet Union in 1918, fearing that the country then had little use for new music, but he remained in touch with developments at home and returned in 1936. His *Peter and the Wolf* (1936), a classic for children, combines traditional melody with the grating dissonance characteristic of the twentieth century.

In 1937, convinced that the Nazis were about to invade Russia, the Soviet government commissioned Eisenstein to make *Alexander Nevsky* (1938), a patriotic film celebrating the thirteenth-century prince of Novgorod, who repelled an invasion of Teutonic (German) knights. Here Eisenstein creates mounting tension and intensity, which he illustrates in *The Film Sense* (figure **22.31**). He demonstrates the correspondence between sight and sound with twelve frames showing the army preparing to attack. The greatest impact occurs between frames 3 and 4, which correspond to measures 5 to 8 in the score. Following the images, the music arches upward and then drops suddenly. In frame 4 the bleak horizon is punctuated only by two distant flags. In frame 5 the army emerges in a close-up, followed by long perspectival views of the soldiers. Eisenstein then shifts abruptly from the anonymous army to close-ups of faces and helmets, evoking our identification with the fighters. As the frames flatten out, so does the music.

Alexander Nevsky was originally made to glorify Russian bravery, but the film was not shown after Russia and Germany signed a non-aggression treaty in 1939. Two years later, when Germany invaded Russia, the film was re-released. In 1945 Eisenstein made the two-part *Ivan the Terrible*, also scored by Prokofiev. The culmination of Eisenstein's career, *Ivan the Terrible* was a majestic epic with one dance sequence. To enhance its wild emotion the scene was shot in Agfacolor, which had been captured from the defeated Germans. Eisenstein used the sixteenth-century unification of Russia to arouse patriotic sentiment in a victorious Soviet Union that had suffered millions of casualties fighting Hitler.

22.32 Poster for James Cruze's film *The Covered Wagon*, 1923.
This shows horse-drawn covered wagons, men on foot, dogs, women huddled in the wagons, traversing a wild, mountainous terrain. The diminishing perspective of the wagon train conveys the impression of a vast distance. The rugged landscape and rifles are signs of the hardships encountered along the way and the need to be ever alert to danger. The orange sun casts a glow over the scene and endows it with a softness that romanticizes the harsh realities of settling the Wild West.

THE UNITED STATES

Despite the economic problems of the Depression, a number of film genres—romance, westerns, comedies, gangsters, war, horror, social commentary, musicals, animated cartoons—became enormously popular in the United States. Between 1907 and 1913 the American film industry was established in Hollywood, a suburb of Los Angeles. The Studio System that developed during the 1930s was dominated by powerful businessmen known as movie moguls.

THE WESTERN: JAMES CRUZE In 1923 James Cruze made one of the earliest epic westerns, *The Covered Wagon* (figure **22.32**), for the Paramount Studio. The western genre offered clear-cut depictions of good and evil, simply portrayed. The heroes were physically attractive and rode white horses, and the bad, unattractive cowboys rode black horses. Major themes included conflicts between Native Americans, cowboys, and settlers, between lawmen and law-abiding citizens and thieves (bank robbers, train robbers, and stage-coach robbers). Generally, good won out over evil. Above all, the Wild West was a place to be explored, tamed, and eventually civilized, and westerns extolled the rugged individualism of the American spirit.

SOCIAL COMMENTARY: CHAPLIN AND WELLES The British-born Charlie Chaplin (1889–1977) became an icon of American movies and eventually opened his own studio. His films contain a wide variety of themes, including the ills of American society, the rise of Fascism in Europe, and romance—in Chaplin's films the underdog wins the girl in the end. In the silent film *The Gold Rush* (1925) Chaplin's signature persona, the little tramp, finds himself starving during the 1898 California gold rush. In the most famous scene, the tramp makes a meal out of a pair of boots, with the shoelaces as spaghetti.

In figure **22.33**, a scene from *Modern Times* (1936), which is about the role of mechanization in modern life, the little tramp is precariously balanced on a metal bar as his boss orders him around. The little tramp is fired and sent to jail, but he triumphs in the end by befriending the heroine, and together they set off to look for new jobs.

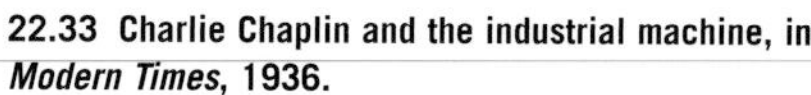

22.33 Charlie Chaplin and the industrial machine, in *Modern Times*, 1936.

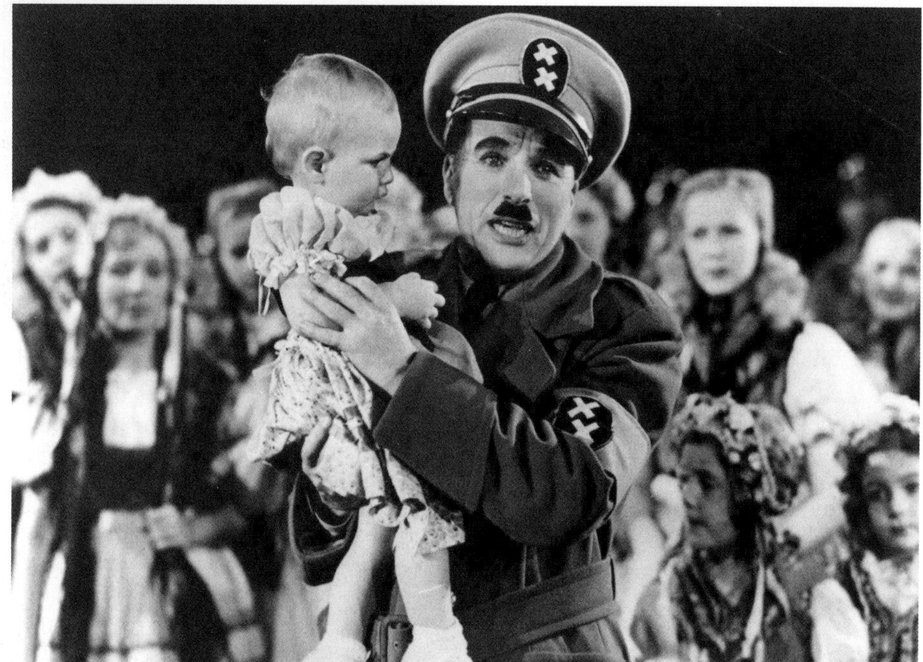

22.34 Charlie Chaplin as Hitler in *The Great Dictator*, 1940.

Chaplin's first sound film was *The Great Dictator* (1940), in which he plays both Hitler and one of Hitler's victims (figure **22.34**). Here, Chaplin as Hitler, wearing a Nazi uniform, a Hitler mustache, and a forced smile, is surrounded by adoring women. Both Chaplin's Hitler and the blond baby, a symbol of the purified Aryan race, appear slightly uncomfortable. Chaplin thus satirizes Hitler as well as the "baby-kissing" practiced by American politicians.

The Great Dictator was banned in Germany, and in 1952 Chaplin was ostracized for his left-wing politics and forced to leave America. He moved to Switzerland, where he married the daughter of Eugene O'Neill.

On October 30, 1938, the actor, film-maker, and director Orson Welles (1915–1985) caused a national panic with his radio broadcast, *The War of the Worlds*. His convincing announcement that the earth had been invaded by Martians sent people running from American cities—and made his reputation. Welles made his first film, *Citizen Kane*, in 1941, when he was twenty-five. It is a story of media power, based on the life of the publishing mogul William Randolph Hearst.

Welles used several new cinematic techniques, including soft focus to create moods, wide-angle lenses to increase depth of field, and overlapping rather than sequential dialogue. Reversing narrative convention, the film opens with Kane's death, which is shown as if in a newsreel. The scene in figure **22.35** was made with a wide-angle lens and shows the young Kane straddling piles of newspapers tied up and ready for delivery. He stands like a colossus, wearing a gangster's fedora, striped jacket, and white silk scarf and handkerchief. Such distortions of scale are used to show aspects of character, in this case, Kane's grandiosity.

The real William Randolph Hearst held up the release of the film because of his unflattering portrayal as a ruthless manipulator of the press.

22.35 Orson Welles straddling piles of newspapers in *Citizen Kane*, 1941.

22.36 The revival scene from King Vidor's *Hallelujah!*, 1929.

MUSICALS: VIDOR AND BERKELEY The musical *Hallelujah!* (1929) by King Vidor (1894–1982) was the earliest all-black film using sound. Vidor was the first American film-maker to use **post-synchronization**—that is, a film shot without sound, which is added later in the studio. In the scene shown in figure **22.36**, Vidor used music, dramatic movement, and contrasts of light and dark to capture the rhythmic energy of the revival spirit. The Dixie Jubilee Singers are in the midst of a religious revival, with emphasis on the movement of their hands. Accents of light in the foreground contrast with the shadowed figures against the back wall of the church and the darkened close-up hats of the foreground figures.

With the choreography of Busby Berkeley (1895–1976), the musical extravaganza was born. Using special effects and unusual angles, Berkeley created designs out of human (usually female) figures. Lightly clad dancers (figure **22.37**) create triangular patterns on a multi-tiered structure that spouts jets of water.

22.37 Busby Berkeley, scene from *Footlight Parade*, 1933.

ANIMATION: WALT DISNEY Walt Disney (1901–1966) studied art in Kansas City, then moved to Los Angeles, where his brother backed his movie venture. Disney hired his fellow art students to animate his stories and, in 1923, founded Disney Studios. Mickey Mouse made his first appearance in *Steamboat Willie* (1928), the earliest animated film to synchronize images with music (figure **22.38**). In this scene, a goat has swallowed a sheet of music, and Minnie Mouse cranks his tail, which causes the goat to sing the swallowed music. Note that Mickey's nose (as well as Minnie's) is somewhat elongated; this more mouse-like appearance was later changed to a rounded, baby-face shape to expand the appeal of the characters.

22.38 Walt Disney Studios, sound/image integration in *Steamboat Willie*, 1928.

Many of Disney's later classic films are based on well-known fairytales, such as *Cinderella* (1950), *Snow White and the Seven Dwarfs* (1937), and *Pinocchio* (1940); and on children's literature, such as *Dumbo* (1941), *Mary Poppins* (1964), and *Alice in Wonderland* (1951). In *Fantasia* (1940), Disney integrated animation with classical music. His animators produced brilliant, metaphorical, and imaginative images; today's animators use computers to aid in their work.

ROMANCE: *GONE WITH THE WIND* *Gone with the Wind* (1936), the epic novel by Margaret Mitchell (1900–1949) about the dying American South, inspired one of the most popular films about the Civil War. The narrative of *Gone with the Wind* (1939) moves dramatically from one impressive scene to another, creating a broad panorama of the period. One of the most spectacular scenes was the first to be shot; the burning of Atlanta (figure **22.39**) was filmed from many different angles by the seven color cameras then available in Hollywood. *Gone with the Wind* was the first to use fine-grained Technicolor film, which added to the depth of field and created subtle color variations reflecting different moods.

Most American movie-goers are familiar with the film's romantic hero, the charming, swashbuckling war profiteer Rhett Butler (Clark Gable), who is in love with the beautiful, unscrupulous Southern belle Scarlett O'Hara (Vivien Leigh) of Tara. She, in turn, is in love with the dreamy, impractical Ashley Wilkes (Leslie Howard), who is married to the virtuous Melanie (Olivia de Havilland). The incomparable role of Mammy (Hattie McDaniel), the O'Hara family's black nanny, has become a classic figure in American cinema. More than just an intense romance, magnificently filmed, and brilliantly acted, *Gone with the Wind* is the story of a conflagration in which an entire civilization dies. It was made, appropriately, on the eve of World War II.

After the war, the film industry became progressively more global. Not only did individual film-makers draw on cross-cultural themes (see Box), but their collaboration with creative people—actors, designers, musicians, and so forth—became international in scope.

22.39 The burning of Atlanta from *Gone with the Wind*, 1939.

Although the period between World War I and World War II was fraught with anxiety, it was also a period of immense creativity in the arts, music, literature, and film. Developments in technology and science offered many new ways of improving the quality of life but also made possible the total destruction of the world. After World War II, especially in the United States, new social movements began to erupt, demanding, among other things, equality between blacks and whites, and more rights for women. The Cold War and actual wars, such as those in Korea and, especially, Vietnam, would lead to massive anti-war protests, which dominated the post-war political landscape.

Cross-cultural Influences

Films in Japan: Akira Kurosawa

Although hard hit by World War II, the Japanese film industry produced notable films in the 1940s. Japan's best-known director, Akira Kurosawa (1910–1998), studied Western painting before turning to film, and although he was influenced by Western imagery, he retained a commitment to Japanese values, style, and history. At the same time, his original approach to editing and montage made him popular in the West after World War II and influenced Western films.

Kurosawa made *Sanshiro Sugata* in 1943, when Japan was still at war. The film, which is about judo, glorified the Japanese warrior tradition and was highly regarded by Japan's ministry of propaganda. Scenes of combat in slow motion, with rapid changes from one angle to another, echo the stylized movements of judo. The following year Kurosawa made *The Most Beautiful* about women in a war munitions plant making lenses for gunsights used in airplanes. This is another view of Japanese war-time culture, but here focused on dramatic events in the lives of individual characters.

During the American occupation following the war, U.S. films poured into Japan, influencing the style and content of Japanese films. Kurosawa soon emerged as a great film-maker, dealing with themes of democracy and the changing roles of women in contemporary society. *Rashomon*, the story of a murder shown from four viewpoints, appeared in 1950, and illustrates the notion that truth is relative.

Later films by Kurosawa are often based on Western literature. In 1951 he produced a film inspired by Dostoevsky's *The Idiot*. His epic *The Seven Samurai* (1954; figure **22.40**), influenced by Eisenstein's *Battleship Potemkin* and by American westerns, was set in sixteenth-century Japan. It was remade in the U.S. as *The Magnificent Seven* (1960). Kurosawa's *Throne of Blood* (1956) is based on *Macbeth*, and *Ran* (1985) is a samurai version of *King Lear*.

22.40 Still from film *The Seven Samurai*, directed by Akira Kurosawa.

KEY TERMS

cantilever a projecting beam or girder, supported at only one end.

conditioned reflex an act or reaction by habit to a repeated stimulus or set of stimuli.

epic theater the name given to his plays by Brecht; his aim was to alienate his audience through his work.

existentialism a post-World War II philosophical system that holds that human beings are totally responsible for their acts and that the universe is godless.

Fascism a set of political principles that tend to be authoritarian, nationalistic, anti-democratic, anti-Marxist, and frequently anti-Semitic.

genocide the extermination of a cultural or racial group; the destruction of the group's culture.

glissando a vocal or instrumental slide up or down, a continuum of pitches filling in the regular notes of the scale.

Holocaust the extermination between 1940 and 1945 by the Nazis of millions of European Jews; also known as the "Final Solution."

inkblot an image resembling a blot of ink, used for psychological testing (as in the Rorschach Test).

logical positivism a philosophical system distinguished by a special emphasis on logic.

macroeconomics the study of the economic system as a whole, with particular attention to the general level of income and production (as opposed to microeconomics).

mass culture popular culture that has wide appeal.

musical a drama in spoken dialogue supported by songs, choruses, dances, and imaginative stage direction; the form originated in the early twentieth century.

newsreel a short motion picture dealing with news or current events; also a literary technique interspersing fiction with news headlines.

post-synchronization a technique of shooting a film without sound and then dubbing it in the studio.

projective testing a psychological testing technique in which an individual's reactions to ambiguous or unstructured material are analyzed.

Rayogram a photograph made without a negative by exposing objects to light on light-sensitive paper.

ready-made a manufactured object given a title by an artist and so turned into an artwork.

ready-made aided a ready-made that has been touched up by the artist.

scat singing a jazz technique in which performers improvise using nonsense syllables.

serialism a term used to describe post-World War II music composed using the twelve-tone technique, in which various parameters in addition to pitch, such as dynamics and rhythm, are ordered and manipulated according to prescribed rules.

solarization the exposure of a photograph to light during the developing process.

stream of consciousness spontaneous, unedited thought.

vibrato rapid, slight fluctuations in pitch, used by musicians for emotional effect.

KEY QUESTIONS

1. Outline three political and economic factors following World War I that contributed to World War II.
2. How was science applied to philosophy? What philosophies developed in the twentieth century reflect science? Discuss in the context of existentialism.
3. How did artists between the wars respond to their time and place? What, for example, were the priorities of the Regionalists and Dadaists?
4. Explain how form became content in the early decades of the twentieth century.
5. Despite the pessimism present in many early-twentieth-century works, hints of optimism also appear. Prove or disprove this statement.

SUGGESTED READING

Bosworth, R. J. *Mussolini*. London: Hodder Arnold, 2002.
▸ A biography of the Italian leader.

Botwinick, R. S. *A History of the Holocaust: From Ideology to Annihilations*, 2nd ed. Englewood Cliffs, NJ: Prentice-Hall, 2002.
▸ The motives, nature, and effects of the Holocaust.

Brown, Milton. *The Story of the Armory Show*. New York: Abbeville Press, 1988.
▸ The impact of the avant garde on American art.

Churchill, Winston. *The Second World War, Volume 1: The Gathering Storm*. London: Cassell, 1950.
▸ Events leading to World War II.

Conquest, R. *The Great Terror: Stalin's Purges of the Thirties.* London: Macmillan, 1968.
▸ A study of Stalin's terrorist politics.

Cooke, Mervyn. *Jazz.* London: Thames and Hudson, 1998.
▸ A brief general survey.

Fitzpatrick, S. *The Russian Revolution, 1917–1932.* Oxford: Oxford University Press, 1994.
▸ A short introduction.

Foucault, Michel. *This is Not a Pipe*, trans. J. Harkness. Berkeley: University of California Press, 1992.
▸ Discussion of a much-discussed work.

Geist, Sidney. *The Kiss.* New York: Harper and Row, 1978.
▸ The iconography of the kiss in the work of Brancusi.

——. *Brancusi: The Sculpture and Drawings.* New York: Harry N. Abrams, 1975.
▸ The definitive catalogue of Brancusi's work.

Heyerdahl, Thor. *Kontiki: Across the Pacific by Raft.* New York: Simon and Schuster, 1995.

Kindleberger, C. *The World in Depression, 1929–1939.* London: Allen Lane/The Penguin Press, 1973.
▸ An analysis of the Great Depression.

Pais, A. *Subtle is the Lord: The Science and Life of Albert Einstein.* Oxford: Oxford University Press, 1983.
▸ A scientific biography accessible to the general reader.

Powell, Richard J. *Black Art and Culture in the 20th Century*, London: Thames and Hudson, 1997.
▸ A survey of black art and culture.

Rubin, William. *Dada and Surrealist Art.* New York: Harry N. Abrams, 1968.
▸ The history and style of Dada and Surrealism.

Schweitzer, Albert. *Out of My Life and Thought*, trans. A. B. Lemke. New York: Henry Holt, 1990.
▸ Schweitzer's philosophical autobiography.

Service, R. *Lenin: A Biography.* London: Macmillan, 2000.
▸ An up-to-date biography using the latest source material.

Shackleton, Ernest. *South: A Memoir of the "Endurance" Voyage*, London: Constable and Robinson, 1998.
▸ Shackleton's account of his journey to the Antarctic.

Thomas, H. *The Spanish Civil War.* London: HarperCollins, 1986.
▸ An authoritative account of the Spanish Civil War.

SUGGESTED FILMS

1923 *The Covered Wagon*, dir. James Cruze

1925 *The Battleship Potemkin*, dir. Sergei Eisenstein

1925 *The Gold Rush*, dir. Charlie Chaplin

1929 *Hallelujah!*, dir. King Vidor

1931 *An American Tragedy* (based on Dreiser), dir. Josef von Sternberg

1931 *Die Dreigroschenoper* (*The Threepenny Opera*), dir. G. W. Pabst

1933 *Footlight Parade*, dir. Lloyd Bacon, choreography Busby Berkeley

1935 *Modern Times*, dir. Charlie Chaplin

1936 *Olympia* (*Olympische Spiele*), dir. Leni Riefenstahl

1936 *Showboat*, dir. James Whale

1937 *Snow White and the Seven Dwarfs* (Walt Disney Studio), dir. David Hand

1938 *Alexander Nevsky*, dir. Sergei Eisenstein

1939 *Gone with the Wind*, dir. Victor Fleming, George Cukor, and Sam Wood

1940 *Fantasia* (Walt Disney Studio), dir. Edward H. Plumb and Ben Sharpsteen

1940 *The Grapes of Wrath* (based on Steinbeck), dir. John Ford

1940 *The Great Dictator*, dir. Charlie Chaplin

1941 *Citizen Kane*, dir. Orson Welles

1941 *Dumbo* (Walt Disney Studio), dir. Ben Sharpsteen

1942 *Casablanca*, dir. Michael Curtiz

1943 *For Whom the Bell Tolls* (based on Hemingway), dir. Sam Wood

1943 *Sanshiro Sugata*, dir. Akira Kurosawa

1944 *The Most Beautiful*, dir. Akira Kurosawa

1945 *Ivan the Terrible*, dir. Sergei Eisenstein

1945 *To Have and Have Not* (based on Hemingway), dir. Howard Hawks

1950 *Rashomon*, dir. Akira Kurosawa

1951 *Alice in Wonderland* (Walt Disney Studio), dir. Clyde Geronimi, Hamilton Luske, and Wilfred Jackson

1951 *An American in Paris*, dir. Vincente Minnelli

1955 *Oklahoma!*, dir. Fred Zinnemann

1956 *High Society*, dir. Charles Walters

1956 *The Seven Samurai*, dir. Akira Kurosawa

1956 *Throne of Blood*, dir. Akira Kurosawa

1957 *The Sun Also Rises* (based on Hemingway), dir. Henry King

1959 *Porgy and Bess*, dir. Otto Preminger

1964 *Mary Poppins* (Walt Disney Studio), dir. Robert Stevenson

1972 *Cabaret*, dir. Bob Fosse

1985 *Ran*, dir. Akira Kurosawa

1993 *Schindler's List*, dir. Steven Spielberg

23 1945 to 1989: The Cold War to Détente

"I know not with what weapons World War III will be fought, but World War IV will be fought with sticks and stones."

(ALBERT EINSTEIN)

The end of World War II was followed by a new kind of war, the Cold War. This was essentially a stand-off between the world's superpowers—the United States and the Soviet Union—and their allies. The United States and Soviet Union competed to develop nuclear weapons and to conquer outer space. They also vied for influence in developing countries, many of which resisted colonial domination and became susceptible to outside influence. The Cold War lasted until 1989, when the ice began to thaw and communism collapsed in eastern Europe.*

Fear of atomic weapons kept the world from engaging in major conflicts during the Cold War. Nevertheless, fierce regional wars were waged between communists and non-communists, notably in Korea in the 1950s and Vietnam in the 1960s and early 1970s. The latter war, in particular, contributed to unrest in Europe and the United States, which was reflected in social changes and in the arts. In the United States civil rights activists challenged traditional racial stereotypes, the feminist movement challenged traditional roles of women, and advances in science and medicine continued to challenge traditional religious attitudes.

Literature, theater, film, and the visual arts were inspired by World War II, by social turmoil, and by post-colonialism. The Theater of the Absurd reflected the irrational quality of human existence through alienated characters and fragmented dialogue. ***Semiotic*** *theoretical systems—from Structuralism to Deconstruction—codified the alienation from humanism and used language to reveal ways in which conventions were breaking down. A wide variety of art styles proliferated, with a new one arising virtually every decade.*

The potential for total self-destruction was expressed in the assertion by Albert Einstein (1879–1955) that is cited at the beginning of the chapter. During World War II, afraid that Germany would build an atom bomb and use it against the Allies, Einstein had advised President Franklin D. Roosevelt to develop one first, but when he saw the devastation caused by nuclear weapons in Hiroshima and Nagasaki (see Chapter 22), he changed his mind and became an advocate of nuclear disarmament. He believed that World War III would propel the human race back into the Stone Age—hence the Fourth World War "fought with sticks and stones."

Key Topics

Cold and Hot Wars

- The Iron Curtain speech
- Communist aggression
- North Korea invades South Korea
- The domino theory
- The Vietnam War
- Conflict in the Middle East

Anxiety and Change

- The Cold War
- Existentialism
- Nuclear proliferation
- The civil rights movement
- The women's movement
- Anti-war protests
- Theater of the Absurd

Art Movements

- Abstract Expressionism
- Pop Art
- Earth art
- Performance art
- Conceptualism
- Super Realism
- Minimalism
- Postmodernism

Philosophy

- Structuralism
- Post-Structuralism
- Deconstruction

Film

- Art film
- New Wave
- Neorealism

TIMELINE	EUROPE	UNITED STATES, CANADA, AND LATIN AMERICA	MIDDLE EAST, ASIA, AND AFRICA
HISTORY AND CULTURE 	Cold War, 1945–1989 Churchill's "Iron Curtain" speech, 1946 Berlin Blockade, 1948; Berlin Airlift, 1949 NATO, 1949; EEC, 1957 Solidarity in Poland, 1978 U.S.S.R. invades Afghanistan, 1979 Gorbachev: perestroika and glasnost, 1980s Berlin Wall dismantled, 1989	Marshall Plan, 1947 HUAC hearings, 1953–1954 Cuban missile crisis, 1962 King's "I Have a Dream" speech, 1963 Kennedy assassinated, 1963 Voting Rights Act, 1965 National Organization for Women, 1966 Watergate scandal; Nixon resigns, 1974	Partition of India, 1947 Creation of Israel, 1948 Korean War, 1950–1953 Vietnam War, 1954–1975 Cultural Revolution in China, 1966 Khomeini seizes power in Iran, 1979 Tiananmen Square, 1989
SCIENCE AND TECHNOLOGY 	ENIAC, first digital computer, 1946 First polaroid camera, 1947 Polio vaccine, 1950s; DNA decoded, 1950s First organ transplant, 1950 Color television, 1951 U.S.S.R. puts first man in space, 1957 World Wide Web developed, 1989	Apollo Space Program, 1961 Armstrong first man on moon, 1969 Microsoft founded, 1975 First test-tube baby produced, 1978 IBM make first individual computers, 1982	
ART 	Beuys, *How to Explain Pictures to a Dead Hare*, 1965 Goldsworthy, *Slab of Snow Carved into Leaving a Translucent Layer*, 1987	Pollock, *Number 27*, 1950 Rothko, *Number 10*, 1950 Johns, *Painted Bronze (Ale Cans)*, 1960 Warhol, *Twenty-Five Colored Marilyns*, 1962 Hesse, *Right After*, 1969 Smithson, *Spiral Jetty*, 1970 Hanson, *Young Shopper*, 1973 Chicago, *The Dinner Party*, 1974–1979 Basquiat, *Horn Players*, 1983 Mapplethorpe, *Ken and Tyler*, 1985 Paik, *Family of Robot, Uncle*, 1986 LeWitt, *Wall Drawing No. 623*, 1989	
ARCHITECTURE	Pei, Louvre Pyramid, Paris, 1988	Moore and Hersey, Piazza d'Italia, New Orleans, 1978–1979 Johnson and Burgee, ATT Building, New York, 1979–1984	
FILM	Fellini, *La Strada*, 1954 Bergman, *The Seventh Seal*, 1957 Rohmer, *Claire's Knee*, 1970	Spielberg, *Jaws*, 1975; *Raiders of the Lost Ark*, 1981; *E.T.*, 1982 Lucas, *Star Wars*, 1977–1983	Ray, Apu trilogy, 1955–1959
LITERATURE AND PHILOSOPHY	Existentialism; Theater of the Absurd Structuralism, Post-Structuralism, and Deconstruction, 1960s Camus, *The Stranger*, 1942; *The Plague*, 1947 Orwell, *Animal Farm*, 1945; *1984*, 1949 Thomas, "Do Not Go Gentle," 1952; *Under Milk Wood*, 1954 Pasternak, *Dr. Zhivago*, 1957 Lévi-Strauss, *Structural Anthropology*, 1958 Wiesel, *Night*, 1958 Solzhenitsyn, *The Gulag Archipelago*, 1973 Barthes, *Camera Lucida*, 1980	Hersey, *A Bell for Adano*, 1944 Auden, *The Age of Anxiety*, 1947 Neruda, *Canto General*, 1950 Salinger, *Catcher in the Rye*, 1951 Baldwin, *Go Tell it on the Mountain*, 1953 Ginsberg, "Howl," 1956; Kerouac, *On the Road*, 1957 Heller, *Catch 22*, 1961 Friedan, *The Feminine Mystique*, 1963 Márquez, *One Hundred Years of Solitude*, 1967 Allende, *The House of the Spirits*, 1985 Morrison, *Beloved*, 1987	Japan: Kawabata, *Snow Country*, 1935–1947 Lessing, *The Children of Violence*, 1952–1969 Achebe, *Things Fall Apart*, 1958; *Anthills of the Savannah*, 1987 Soyinka, *Aké: The Years of Childhood*, 1981
THEATER AND DANCE	Camus, *Caligula*, 1938 Sartre, *No Exit*, 1944 Beckett, *Waiting for Godot*, 1953 Ionesco, *Rhinoceros*, 1959	Miller, *Death of a Salesman*, 1949; *The Crucible*, 1953 Ailey, *Revelations*, 1960 Albee, *Who's Afraid of Virginia Woolf?*, 1962	
MUSIC 	Messiaen, *Quatuor pour la fin du temps*, 1940–1941 Shostakovich, symphonies Britten, *Peter Grimes*, 1945; *War Requiem*, 1961 Boulez, *Le marteau sans maître*, 1953–1955 Stockhausen, *Gesang der Jünglinge*, 1956 Beatles, *Yellow Submarine*, 1968 Webber and Rice, *Jesus Christ Superstar*, 1970	Rodgers and Hammerstein, *South Pacific*, 1949; *The King and I*, 1951 Cage, *4' 33"*, 1952 Bill Haley and the Comets, "Rock Around the Clock," 1954 Lerner and Loewe, *My Fair Lady*, 1956 Presley, "Jailhouse Rock," 1957 Bernstein, *West Side Story*, 1957 Dylan, "Blowin' in the Wind," 1963 McDermott, *Hair*, 1967 Glass, *Einstein on the Beach*, 1976	

THE COLD WAR

Tension between the United States and the Soviet Union mounted as World War II drew to a close. After defeating German forces in Russia in August 1944, the Soviet army continued west, and in 1945 it occupied Berlin. After the war Germany was disarmed, de-Nazified, and divided into four zones—Soviet, American, British, and French. But because Berlin was in the Soviet zone, the Soviet Union tried to block Allied access to the city with the Berlin Blockade in 1948. The Allies overcame the blockade in May of the following year with the Berlin Airlift, flying food and other supplies into the city. By 1949 the four zones had coalesced into East Germany under Soviet control, and West Germany under Allied control.

The Soviets, mindful that Russia had been invaded four times in two hundred years, wanted a buffer zone, and this meant exerting complete control over eastern Europe, to which Britain objected. The United States wanted to bring its soldiers home but also wanted to maintain a free economy in Europe—the so-called Open Door policy. In addition, American alarm at the growth of communism in France, Italy, and elsewhere had been fueled by Churchill's famous "Iron Curtain" speech of 1946 (see Box).

In 1947 the United States put the Marshall Plan into effect. Named for George C. Marshall (1880–1959), Secretary of State under President Truman, the plan encouraged cooperation between nations and gave large amounts of financial aid to Europe for post-war reconstruction. The Soviet Union, wishing to remain independent of the West, refused to accept the aid, not only for itself but also for its eastern satellites (map **23.1**). Truman advocated using economic aid to help free nations help themselves and believed that the United States should take the lead in the United Nations. His views later came to be called the Truman Doctrine.

In 1949 eastern Europe and the Soviet Union formed **Comecon** (Council for Mutual Economic Assistance), which was designed to reinforce economic cooperation between communist nations. The same year, NATO (North Atlantic Treaty Organization) was created for the mutual defense of non-communist countries. NATO included the U.S., Canada, and most west European countries. Later, Greece, Turkey, and West Germany also joined NATO.

In 1955 the communist bloc formed the Warsaw Pact, officially acknowledging the Soviet Union as the leader of eastern Europe and the United States as the leader of NATO. In 1957 western Europe created the European Economic Community (the EEC), or Common Market, to foster tariff-free trade. The effects of the EEC were to encourage workers and capital to move more easily from one country to another and to make salaries and benefits more nearly equal.

West Germany benefited from its post-World War II government and relatively capitalist economy, and by 1969 it was the leading industrial nation of Europe. In contrast East Germany, politically dominated by the Soviet Union, had a weak, stagnant economy. In 1961 the Soviet Union and East Germany constructed the concrete Berlin Wall to prevent East Germans from escaping to the West in search of a better life.

Society and Culture

Churchill's "Iron Curtain Speech"

On March 5, 1946, the year that the United Nations was established with its headquarters in New York City, Winston Churchill (figure **23.1**) delivered his famous "Iron Curtain" speech at Westminster College, in Fulton, Missouri. His message reflected post-war tensions between the United States and its allies and the Soviet Union.

Churchill declared his high regard for the Russian people and praised Stalin's resistance to Germany during World War II. But he also said that "an iron curtain has descended across the [European] continent" separating the free West from the oppressed East. A fifth column—members of the Communist Party and fellow travelers—was, he warned, threatening to infiltrate the West and the Far East. Churchill argued that the Soviet Union admired strength; peace, Churchill said, could be maintained only by a strong and effective United Nations that had the backing of the entire English-speaking world. Under no conditions must another world war be permitted to occur; peace, Churchill said, could best be achieved by adhering to the charter of the United Nations.

23.1 British prime minister Winston Churchill gives the "victory" sign outside No. 10 Downing Street, London, June 1943.

Map 23.1 Europe after World War II, showing Soviet satellites.

In Japan, as in Germany, the Allies imposed a constitution and barred military build-up, making the emperor a figurehead with no real power. Japan then became the leading commercial nation in the Far East. Spain and Portugal, whose Fascist leaders were allowed to remain in power, continued to be ruled by dictators until the 1970s.

The Soviet Union and Eastern Europe

The Soviet Union's policy of expansionism continued under Stalin. In 1947 he helped organize **Cominform** to make communism an international movement. He feared that the Soviet satellites would follow the example of the leader of Yugoslavia, Josip (Broz) Tito (1892–1980), who had remained relatively free of Soviet control. Stalin was also threatened by growing cooperation among Western nations, especially the organization of NATO.

Nikita Khrushchev (1894–1971), who succeeded Stalin in 1953, instituted a few reforms, including decentralizing the Soviet economy and allowing agricultural enterprise. Three years later, Khrushchev gave a speech critical of Stalin's purges of the 1930s (see Chapter 22) and removed the most zealous Stalinists from power. This marked the beginning of a thaw within the Soviet Union, although Khrushchev opposed autonomy in satellite countries. Thus in 1956, in response to uprisings in Hungary and Poland, Khrushchev sent in Soviet troops and installed strongly pro-communist leaders.

In 1964 the repressive Leonid Brezhnev (1906–1982) became president of the Soviet Union, but his policies incited opposition. He expelled dissidents while making it difficult for Jews to leave for Israel. By 1968, when Alexander Dubček (1921–1992) became president of Czechoslovakia, signs of liberalization and freedom of expression began to emerge. Czechoslovakia wanted to be free from total Soviet control and establish an independent government. The Prague Spring, as the movement was known, was ruthlessly crushed by Soviet tanks. As with Hungary and Poland, NATO did nothing.

The election in 1978 of a staunchly anti-communist Polish pope, John Paul II, led the regime in Poland to revive its opposition to the Catholic Church. But the declining economy inspired the trade union leader Lech Walesa (born 1943) to found in 1980 the free trade union Solidarity, which organized a series of strikes, especially among shipyard workers, and lobbied for economic improvement and greater political freedom. Poles won the right to unionize and to practice Catholicism, but this freedom was blocked by the communist government in 1981, and martial law was imposed until 1983.

In 1979 the Soviet Union under Brezhnev invaded Afghanistan. The United States reacted strongly, as did China, and both aided the Afghan rebels (among whom were militant Islamic fundamentalists called the Taliban who were being trained by the CIA). After ten years of fighting a guerrilla war they could not win, the Soviets withdrew.

In 1985 Mikhail Gorbachev (born 1931) came to power in the Soviet Union and began to institute lasting reforms. He considered the Soviet government inefficient and its policies economically and politically weak. He introduced a policy of **perestroika** ("restructuring"), which allowed limited private ownership and increased political participation on the part of Soviet citizens. The term **glasnost** ("openness") refers to Gorbachev's tolerance of public criticism of Soviet and communist history. With these two policies, Gorbachev broke the military control of Soviet politics, decentralized the government, and opened the way to **détente** (the thawing of tensions between the United States and the Soviet Union), which culminated in 1989. Several eastern European nations—Poland, Hungary, Czechoslovakia, Bulgaria, Romania, the Baltic and Slavic states, and East Germany—achieved freedom from Soviet control. The same year, the Berlin Wall was torn down and Germany was reunified.

THE UNITED STATES

At the end of World War II, although the United States was the richest and most powerful country in the world, it was suspicious of the Soviet Union and of communist influence abroad. Communist regimes in Cuba and Latin America brought the ideological conflict between communism and capitalism closer to home.

Partly influenced by Churchill's "Iron Curtain" speech in 1946 (see p. 657), the House of Representatives formed the House UnAmerican Activities Committee (HUAC) to investigate communist infiltration in the United States. Leading the HUAC was Senator Joseph McCarthy (1908–1957) of Wisconsin. A fanatical anti-communist, he held hearings from 1953 to 1954 that amounted to a witch-hunt, persecuting intellectuals suspected of having ties to communism. Whipping up hysterical (and unrealistic) fears of the Soviet Union, McCarthy manipulated Cold War tensions to advance his paranoid agenda. He was finally discredited, but not before he and his committee had destroyed the careers of many academics, authors, intellectuals, actors, and others.

THE KOREAN WAR In the Far East the United States became embroiled in war in Korea (1950–1953). After World War II Japan was expelled from Korea, which was divided into two countries along the 38th parallel. North Korea was supported by China; South Korea was supported by the United States. In 1950 the North invaded the South, and, backed by the United Nations, the United States sent troops to defend the South. China, which had been under communist leadership since 1949, supplied troops to the North. When an armistice was signed in 1953, Korea remained divided at the 38th parallel and American troops remained in the South.

LATIN AMERICA In Latin America the United States claimed to pursue its good neighbor policy, but it was in fact ambivalent toward its neighbors south of the border. Throughout the Cold War a fear of communism led the United States to support a number of dictators, notably Juan Perón (1895–1974) in Argentina and Augusto Pinochet (born 1915) in Chile. Most alarming of all to the United States was the 1959 communist revolution in Cuba. The Cuban dictator Fulgencio Batista (1901–1973) was overthrown by Fidel Castro (born 1927), and the United States broke off diplomatic ties with Cuba. In 1961 President John F. Kennedy (1917–1963) authorized an unsuccessful invasion by United States-backed Cuban exiles at the Bay of Pigs. The Soviet Union had planted nuclear missiles in Cuba, which could easily reach the United States, leading to the so-called Cuban Missile Crisis in October 1962. This was resolved after a week of intense negotiations, and the following year the United States and the Soviet Union signed a treaty banning nuclear testing.

THE VIETNAM WAR The 1960s and early 1970s were dominated by war in Vietnam, which began as a civil conflict between the North and South and became a Cold War struggle, with the United States backing the South, and the Soviet Union and China supporting the North. Vietnam had been partitioned as a result of fighting for its independence from France. The Vietnamese nationalist Ho Chi Minh (1892–1969) founded the Viet Minh Independence League in 1941, and when France refused to renounce its hold on the country, he embraced communism. Ho organized the Viet Minh—guerrillas trained originally to fight the Japanese. Inspired by the American Declaration of Independence, Ho (who had studied for a time at Columbia University) declared Vietnam a democracy and established his capital at Hanoi in the North. France continued to claim control and Ho's followers fought the French in the Indochina War (1946–1954). Hostilities continued until 1954, when the Vietnamese, with the backing of China and the Soviet Union, defeated the French garrison at Dien Bien Phu.

The United States at first favored independence for Vietnam but changed its mind with the onset of the Korean War and supported France. When the French withdrew in 1954, the United States took over the fight against Ho Chi

Minh. The **domino theory**, advanced by Eisenhower (presidency 1953–1961), argued that unless the free world intervened, Southeast Asian countries would fall like dominoes to the communists.

The Geneva Accords of 1954 divided Vietnam into North and South and called for elections to be held in 1956. Fearing a communist victory, the United States backed the corrupt Catholic, anti-Buddhist Ngo Dinh Diem (1901–1963), who wanted to control the South. Diem led the country into war by opposing elections and suppressing freedom of religion.

In 1960 communist insurgents (the Viet Cong) rallied against Diem, the United States withdrew its support, Diem was assassinated in 1963, and the power vacuum was filled by a series of generals. John F. Kennedy (presidency 1961–1963) was assassinated in Dallas, Texas, in 1963—an event that shocked the world—and Lyndon Johnson (presidency 1963–1969) escalated the war. Photographs such as the one in figure **23.2** fueled the growing opposition to the war at home and abroad. Finally, Richard Nixon (presidency 1969–1974) began a policy of Vietnamization (disengagement from the Vietnam War) and, when American troops finally withdrew from Vietnam in 1975, North Vietnam overran the South.

Public opinion in the United States and Europe was sharply divided on the Vietnam War. Many Americans refused to fight on moral grounds and left the country. Peace marches grew in frequency and in numbers, and at the University of California in Berkeley a strong anti-war faction evolved in the Free Speech Movement. Opponents of the war produced a new genre of protest songs, performances, films, paintings, and sculptures (figure **23.3**).

Several years after the United States withdrew from Vietnam, a competition was held for a national Vietnam War memorial. The winner was Maya Ying Lin (born 1960), a twenty-one-year-old architecture student at Yale. Her long, V-shaped wall of polished black granite, on which the names of all the dead and missing in the war are inscribed in the order of their death or disappearance, has become one of the most visited sites in the United States (figure **23.4**). The lasting impact of the monument resides in its formal simplicity and elegant surface, the multiple meanings contained in the very notion of a wall, and the power of a name written in stone.

DÉTENTE Détente with the Soviet Union led to arms reductions and new trade agreements. Nixon also traveled to communist China in the early 1970s, opening up relations with that country for the first time in decades. But when his involvement in the Watergate scandal, which entailed bugging the Democratic Party Headquarters in Washington, D.C., was revealed, he was forced to resign. Nixon's vice president, Gerald Ford (presidency 1974–1977), became president and pursued détente even further. He agreed to the Helsinki Accords, which guaranteed civil rights in the countries of the signatories (most of Europe, the United States, and Canada) and also recognized Soviet control of eastern Europe. Nuclear agreements were less successful, for both the Soviet Union and the United States continued the arms race. By the early 1980s the Soviet military force was about equal to that of the United States.

23.2 Vietnamese children fleeing from Trang Bang, South Vietnam, June 8, 1972. The children were burned by American napalm. Napalm is a form of petroleum in bombs and flame-throwers. It expands in the air when exploded, adhering to, and burning, whatever it touches. The American use of napalm caused extensive injury and death among the civilian population.

23.3 Edward Kienholz, *Portable War Memorial*, 1968. Mixed media, 9 ft. 4 in. × 7 ft. 10 in. × 12 ft. 2 in. (2.85 × 2.4 × 9.5 m). Museum Ludwig, Cologne.
This sculptural installation shows the "portable" nature of justifications for war—that they are a "movable feast." Kienholz (1927–1994) conveys his rage against the war by alluding to the famous World War II photograph of 1945 showing six U.S. marines planting the American flag on the Pacific island of Iwo Jima. The photograph later became the model for a bronze statue at Arlington National Cemetery, D.C. Here the marines are inserted into an everyday street scene, with a garbage can torso/skirt of a sawed-off woman and a diner-style hot-dog stand. The gray tones create the dream-like quality of the past.

The one event that became a metaphor for détente was the dismantling of the Berlin Wall in 1989. The wall came down partly because a new generation of communists recognized the need for change and partly because President Gorbachev agreed not to intervene. This opened up new contacts between east and west Europe and reunited many German families.

DOMESTIC TURMOIL IN THE UNITED STATES In the United States protestors rallied in the 1960s to eliminate the color bar separating blacks and whites. Racial prejudice was more overt in the South, where blacks were legally denied access to restaurants, forced to use separate restrooms, and moved to the back of a bus if a white person wanted their seat, and where the Ku Klux Klan had revived in 1915. Although legal separation was not characteristic of the North, there was prejudice nevertheless. During the 1960s, white and black activists challenged the color bar head on in the civil rights movement, which fought for equal rights for blacks and whites in America. The 1960s also witnessed a surge in the women's movement, which had begun many decades earlier with the drive for women's suffrage.

THE CIVIL RIGHTS MOVEMENT The legacy of slavery has been a persistent problem in American history. In the late nineteenth century the principle of "separate but equal" was established so that there would be no mingling of the black and white races. But in 1954 the Supreme Court ruled in the case of Brown v. Board of Education of Topeka [Kansas] that segregation in public places was unconstitutional, as

23.4 Maya Ying Lin, *Vietnam Veterans Memorial*, Washington, D.C., 1981–1983. Black granite, each wing 246 ft. (79 m) long.

was the notion of "separate but equal" education. The Court ruled that racially segregated schools were by nature unconstitutional.

In 1955 in Montgomery, Alabama, Rosa Parks (born 1913), a forty-two-year-old black woman, refused to give up her seat on a bus to a white passenger as required by Alabama law (see Box). Her arrest sparked protests and a public bus boycott led by the black Baptist minister, Martin Luther King, Jr. (1929–1968). King became a tireless advocate of civil rights (see Box, p. 663), as did Rosa Parks. In 1964 the Civil Rights Act banned segregation in hiring and in public places, and in 1965 the Voting Rights Act guaranteed access to the polls to all citizens, black and white.

Despite victories for racial equality, protests continued. In 1966 another approach to civil rights appeared with the Black Panthers movement, which advocated violence against whites and the formation of an independent black nation. A proponent of these views, Malcolm Little (1925–1965), converted to Islam and changed his last name to X. He became a civil rights activist, arguing that whites were evil and that blacks should have their own nation. After a pilgrimage to Mecca, however, he turned to a vision of world brotherhood. The story of his extraordinary life, *The Autobiography of Malcolm X*, was compiled from a series of interviews and published in 1965. That same year, Malcolm X was assassinated by radical Black Muslims who believed that his views were not sufficiently fundamentalist. Martin Luther King, Jr. was assassinated by a white man in 1968.

THE FEMINIST MOVEMENT Women won the right to vote in the United States in 1920, but between the two world wars women's issues were overshadowed by international politics. With so many men drafted into the armed forces, new jobs opened up for women in Europe and the United States. In the 1960s, however, the feminist movement gathered new momentum and became more widespread. Protest marches and a new genre of feminist literature called for changes in the status of women, who demanded equal pay for equal work and greater access to employment. Many women also wanted reproduction and abortion rights.

Defining Moment

Rosa Parks Keeps her Seat on the Bus

On December 1, 1955, the civil rights movement began in Montgomery, Alabama, with a boycott of public buses. Some have argued that Rosa Parks, a forty-two-year-old black seamstress, sparked this boycott by refusing to give up her seat to a white passenger and move to the back of the bus as required by Alabama law (figure **23.5**). She was later arrested for her action.

Twelve years earlier, in 1943, Rosa Parks became involved in civil rights when, after she had paid her bus fare, the bus drove off without her. She worked with the National Association for the Advancement of Colored People (NAACP). Parks described her early civil rights activity as follows:

> *I worked on numerous cases with the NAACP, but we did not get the publicity. There were cases of flogging, peonage, murder, and rape. We didn't seem to have too many successes. It was more a matter of trying to challenge the powers that be, and to let it be known that we did not wish to continue being second-class citizens.*

After Parks's arrest in 1955 community groups formed the Montgomery Improvement Association (MIA) and elected Martin Luther King, Jr. to be its president. They launched a bus boycott but did not expect it to last. On December 8, the fourth day of the boycott, King and other MIA officials met with lawyers and officials from the bus company and presented a moderate desegregation plan similar to the one already implemented in other Southern cities. The bus company refused to cooperate. While the world watched, court cases against the boycotters began. King was the first defendant. He was ordered to pay $500 in fines plus $500 in court costs or spend 386 days in the state penitentiary. Efforts to break the boycott failed, but on November 13, 1956, the Supreme Court upheld a federal court ruling that segregation on buses was unconstitutional. The boycott was officially over.

In Atlanta, Georgia, ministers from the MIA joined other ministers from around the South. They founded the Southern Christian Leadership Conference and elected Martin Luther King, Jr. its president. In 1957 Rosa Parks and her husband moved to Detroit, where she served on the staff of United States Representative John Conyers. The Southern Christian Leadership Council established an annual Rosa Parks Freedom Award in her honor.

Critical Question Does a change in the law precede or follow a change in people's attitudes about injustice?

23.5 Rosa Parks on the bus, Montgomery, Alabama.

Martin Luther King's "I Have a Dream" Speech

King's famous speech was delivered on the steps of the Lincoln Memorial in August 1963, during the culmination of a civil rights march on Washington, D.C. Using biblical imagery reminiscent of the Emancipation Proclamation (1863), King began:

> *Five score years ago, a great American, in whose symbolic shadow we stand today, signed the Emancipation Proclamation. This momentous decree came as a great beacon of light of hope to millions of Negro slaves who had been seared in the flames of withering injustice. It came as a joyous daybreak to end the long night of captivity. But one hundred years later, the Negro is still not free.*

And later in the same speech:

> *I have a dream that one day this nation will rise up and live out the true meaning of its creed: "We hold these truths to be self-evident: that all men are created equal." . . .*
>
> *I have a dream that my four children will one day live in a nation where they will not be judged by the color of their skin but by the content of their character. I have a dream today.*

The role of women in society has been a literary theme for centuries, but from around the mid-twentieth century, women began writing on this subject with increasing determination. The publication in France in 1949 of *The Second Sex* (*Le Deuxième sexe*) by Simone de Beauvoir (1908–1986) brought to the fore problems in women's lives, such as spousal abuse and preferential treatment for men in family law and in jobs. De Beauvoir dealt with the social effects of being female and the personal and cultural alienation of women, and she argued that women should be accorded social and economic equality with men. De Beauvoir was herself a leading French intellectual and the companion of the existentialist philosopher Jean-Paul Sartre (see Chapter 22). Her insistence that women should control their lives can be related to the existential notion that people are responsible for their own acts in a godless universe. De Beauvoir's writing had a major impact on the feminist movement, and today women in France are accorded greater equality in employment, longer maternity leave, and more reproductive rights than women in the United States.

In 1963 the modern feminist movement was launched in the United States with the publication of *The Feminine Mystique* by Betty Friedan (born 1921). Friedan challenged the American myth (mystique) of what constitutes femininity—being a housewife and a mother exclusively devoted to family and social life. Women, she argued, should not take their identity solely from their husbands and their families. Instead they should function as thinking and working individuals in their own right. In arriving at these views, Friedan used her own experience as an educated woman who gave up a career in journalism when she married.

The Feminine Mystique was enormously successful and influenced generations of American women. In 1966 Friedan founded the National Organization for Women (NOW), which became a prominent voice for change in women's rights, but Friedan herself was never as radical as some feminists later became.

ISRAEL AND CONFLICT IN THE MIDDLE EAST

When the Allies realized the scale of the Holocaust (see Chapter 22), they decided to provide the Jews with a country of their own. The idea of a Jewish state had emerged as early as 1896, when the Hungarian Theodor Herzl (1860–1904), responding to European anti-Semitism and in particular to the Dreyfus Affair (see Chapter 19), founded the World Zionist Organization. In 1917 Britain issued the Balfour Declaration, advocating a Jewish state in Palestine.

In 1947 the United Nations passed a resolution dividing Palestine, which had been under British rule, into two states, one Arab and one Jewish. Britain withdrew from Palestine, and in May 1948 the independent state of Israel was born. The arrival of the Jews displaced Palestinian Arabs already living in the region, and the issue of these refugees, who continue to live in camps in neighboring countries, remains one of the thorniest problems in the Middle East. Lebanon, Syria, Jordan, Iraq, and Egypt declared war on Israel in 1948. The Israeli victory in 1949 gained additional territory for the Jews, but most Palestinians and many Arab countries maintained that Israel had no right to exist.

The Arab and other Middle Eastern nations considered the expansion of Israeli settlers into conquered territory to be a form of terrorism. Wars between Israel and the Arabs continued after 1948, erupting in 1956, 1967, 1973, and 1982. The Palestine Liberation Organization (PLO) was formed in 1964 to advance the Palestinian cause. Beginning in 1987, Palestinians terrorized Israeli civilians with suicide attacks, which prompted Israel to respond militarily.

The rise of Islamic fundamentalism increased tensions in the Middle East as well as around the world. In 1979 Iran overthrew its pro-Western shah, and the radical fundamentalist Ayatolla Ruhollah Khomeini (1902–1989) formed a nationalist, anti-Western, Islamic theocracy. In 1990 Iraq invaded Kuwait to take over its oil supplies. This sparked the First Gulf War, in which the United States and a coalition of allies defeated Iraq.

The Emerging Developing World

Nationalism was on the rise in Africa, Asia, and the Middle East after World War II, as former colonies began to demand independence (map **23.2**; compare map 20.1). For different reasons, the Soviet Union, the United States, and the United Nations all objected to colonialism. In 1949 the Dutch East Indies became Indonesia; in 1960 Belgium granted independence to the Congo; in 1974 Portugal freed Angola and Mozambique; and as of 1979 Rhodesia (present-day Zimbabwe) was no longer ruled solely by whites.

In Africa forty nations became independent between 1945 and 1975. Although Africa is rich in natural resources, few of its citizens are educated in Western-style democracy and its populations are largely illiterate. In addition, tribal religions often conflict with those imposed by colonists, who were usually Christian or Muslim. The result was a series of military coups and a proliferation of dictatorships that made the transition to democracy difficult.

SOUTH AFRICA South Africa, the most industrialized African nation, also had the largest white population. By the 1970s there were 4 million whites (the only group legally able to vote or hold public office), 20 million blacks (who were disenfranchised and restricted to menial occupations), and 2 million "Coloreds" (people of mixed race, whose political rights were limited). The white Afrikaners, descendants of the Dutch settlers who had traded and farmed in South Africa since the mid-seventeenth century, had established a policy of **apartheid** ("separate development") to maintain the separation of the races. Laws were stringently enforced to prevent interracial socializing, public intercourse, and intermarriage.

Protests against apartheid in the 1960s and 1970s were brutally suppressed, but in 1983 Colored and Asian minorities were granted the right to vote. In 1986 the black Anglican bishop Desmond Tutu (born 1939), winner of the 1984 Nobel Peace Prize, called on Western nations to apply sanctions against South Africa until apartheid was ended. In 1990 Nelson Mandela (born 1918), a leader of the banned anti-apartheid African National Congress (ANC), was released after twenty-seven years in jail. The principles of a new democratic constitution, including the end of apartheid, were agreed in 1993, and in the first post-apartheid elections in 1994, the ANC won 62.7 percent of the vote. Nelson Mandela became the first black president of South Africa.

INDIA AND PAKISTAN Britain, the largest colonial power, ceded most of its empire after World War II. The best-known instance of resistance to British rule came in India, under the

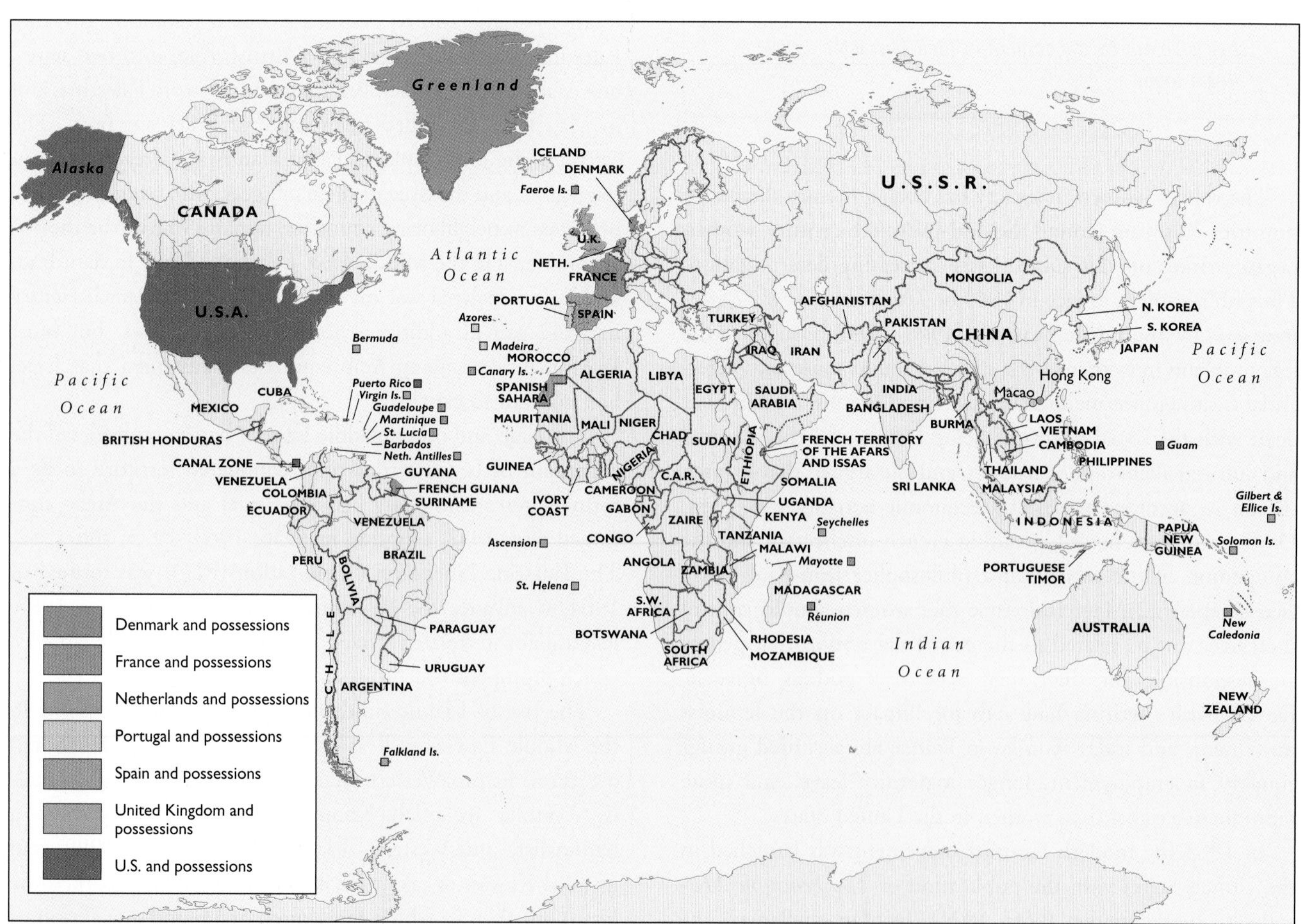

Map 23.2 Colonies worldwide and decolonization, *c.* 1975.

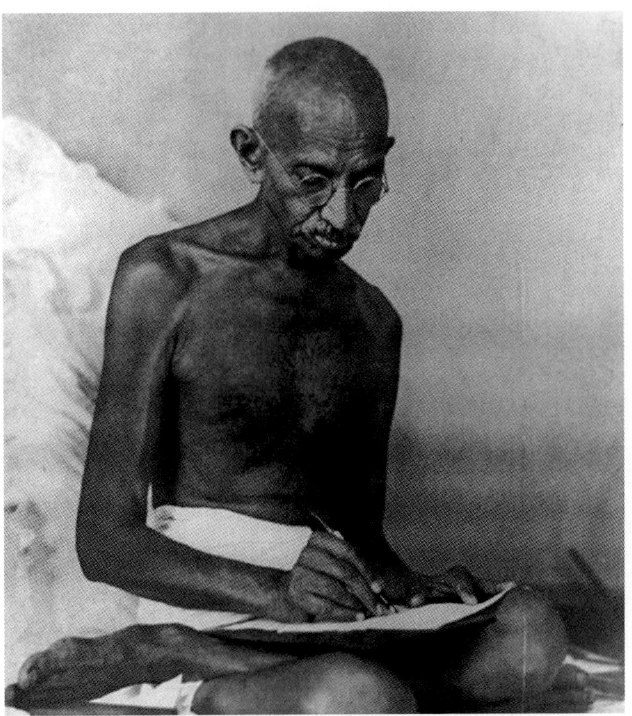

23.6 Mohandas Gandhi, *c.* 1940–1950. Halftone photomechanical print. Library of Congress, Washington, D.C.

leadership of Mohandas Gandhi (1869–1948), known as Mahatma ("great soul") (figure **23.6**). Gandhi had studied law in London and worked for Indians living in South Africa before returning to his native India in 1915. He launched a campaign of resistance to British rule that lasted from 1919 to 1947, when the British departed. Gandhi was a spiritual as well as a political leader, advocating non-violence—unless the alternative was cowardice. Frequently jailed for refusing to pay taxes and for disobeying colonial laws, Gandhi went on long public protest fasts and encouraged Indians to disrupt British control by peaceful means. A champion of human rights, Gandhi denounced the treatment of the lower Hindu castes. He was assassinated in 1948 by a religious fanatic.

Gandhi's vision of a culturally diverse India was rejected by Muslims, who wanted an Islamic state. As a result, when the British departed in 1947, India was partitioned into India (mainly Hindu) and Pakistan (mainly Muslim). Some 12 million people were forced to move and about 200,000 were killed in the process. Today, India and Pakistan, both of which have nuclear arms, maintain an uneasy coexistence, despite periodic clashes over control of Kashmir, a largely Muslim area in northwest India and Pakistan that abuts Afghanistan and China. In 1971 Pakistan itself was split after the eastern province of Bangladesh declared its independence following a violent civil war.

THE FRENCH COLONIES France was confronted with the problem of a large French population that considered Algeria its home, but native Algerians had been primarily Muslim since the Islamic conquests of the eighth century. The activities of the FLN (Front de Libération Nationale, National Liberation Front), founded after World War II, led to civil war in 1954. One side claimed that Algeria was part of France; the other demanded an independent Muslim state. President Charles de Gaulle (see Chapter 22), back in France after the war, pulled French troops from Algeria, a protracted process resisted by the army, and in 1962 Algeria became independent. As a result, the French living in Algeria, who were called *pieds noirs* ("black feet"), returned to France along with thousands of Muslims.

France lost Indochina (Vietnam, Cambodia, and Laos) in 1954. The United States sponsored the formation of SEATO (South East Asian Treaty Organization), and the U.S. interest in Indochina extended the theater of Cold War.

CHINA In 1911 the Manchu Dynasty was overthrown, ending a 2000-year empire. The nationalist Guomindang party (National People's Party) led by Chiang Kai-shek (Jian Jieshi) (1887–1975) was established, and the Communist Party was founded in 1921. The Guomindang opposed the imperial warlords and the communists and by 1927 had suppressed both. In 1934–1935 the Guomindang besieged communist strongholds in the south, forcing them into the retreat known as the Long March. This was a 370-day, 6000-mile (9600-km) strategic relocation of the communists to the northeast under the leadership of the young organizer Mao Zedong (1893–1976). After the march, in which 90 percent of the marchers were killed either by harsh conditions or by Chiang's troops, Mao was elected chairman of the Communist Party. Continued fighting between nationalists and communists amounted to all-out civil war, which persisted until 1937, when Japan became a threat, and then resumed in 1945 after World War II.

The communists took over Manchuria and were strengthened after World War II. In 1949 Chiang and the Guomindang, supported by the United States, were driven from the mainland to Taiwan, which became a non-communist democratic state. This left Mao to rule the communist People's Republic of China on the mainland.

From 1952 the government of China, influenced by Stalin's ideas, collectivized industry, agriculture, and social institutions, and confiscated private property. But, as in the Soviet Union, communist agricultural policies failed and some 10 million peasants died in famines. Massive purges resulted in the execution of millions of Guomindang supporters and of those considered political or class "enemies." People who had flourished before the revolution were arrested and "re-educated" or executed. All religious groups were suppressed, and Mao dominated the press, family life, and education. In 1958–1961 Mao's Great Leap Forward unsuccessfully tried to speed the pace of development by substituting labor for capital investment. In 1961 Chinese peasants were allowed to own small farms and the economy improved somewhat. By the early

23.7 Poster of Mao Zedong and his followers. Mao emerges from, and towers over, an endless crowd of devoted followers as smiling youths read from the *Little Red Book* of his philosophical sayings. The poster is in stark contrast to the reality of Mao's repressive regime.

1960s Mao's revolutionary militancy began to diverge from Soviet revisionist policies under Khrushchev, leading to armed border disputes between China and the Soviet Union.

In 1966 Mao launched the Cultural Revolution, which was intended to impose an egalitarian utopian program domestically and to spread revolution abroad. He formed the Red Guards to carry out his policies in China (figure **23.7**). China's financial and intellectual elite were sent to the countryside for "re-education" and forced to work in the fields.

When Mao died in 1976, pragmatists came to power, and a nationwide purge of orthodox Maoists ensued. The so-called Gang of Four—a propaganda official, a literary critic, a security guard, and Mao's widow Jiang Qing (1914–1991)—was arrested. The Four had been formed during the Cultural Revolution and influenced policy through the 1970s. China's new leaders tried the Gang in 1980; two (including Mao's widow) were given suspended death sentences and two went to prison. Pro-Mao propaganda declined, and more than 100,000 political prisoners were released.

Under Deng Xiaoping (1904–1997) trade and political and cultural ties with Japan and the West expanded, and censorship of the arts declined. China relaxed state control in the interests of attracting foreign investment and trade. Deng also encouraged science and technology, in which China had fallen far behind the West. Nevertheless, China remained essentially a totalitarian nation. In 1989 university students in Beijing staged a protest rally in Tiananmen Square against the repressive government. The demonstrators demanded liberalization and raised a replica of the Statue of Liberty. The government responded with tanks and soldiers, crushing some students and shooting others—the death toll was estimated unofficially at between 500 and 7000 demonstrators. In all, 10,000 dissidents were arrested and thirty-one were tried and executed.

In 1997 the former British colony of Hong Kong reverted to China. China, in turn, agreed to a policy of "one country, two systems," allowing Hong Kong to retain its capitalist economy for fifty years.

SCIENCE AND TECHNOLOGY

While the United States and the Soviet Union competed for influence in the developing world, they were also spending enormous sums of money on the race to conquer outer space. The Soviet Union launched the unmanned Sputnik 1 in 1957 and put a man in space for the first time in 1961. President Kennedy then launched the Apollo Space Program in the same year. In 1969 the American astronaut Neil Armstrong (born 1930) became the first person to walk on the moon, an achievement he called "one small step for man, one giant leap for mankind" (figure **23.8**). The Apollo program ended in 1975 when the United States and the Soviet Union began to cooperate on the Apollo–Soyuz link-up in space. This program put over thirty astronauts in space and twelve on the moon.

Advances in photography, video, and computers also took place after World War II. Polaroid cameras, which could produce instantaneous photographs, came into use in 1947. Color television was developed in 1951, and with the invention of the first digital computer (ENIAC, Electronic Numerical Integrator and Computer) in 1946, the computer age began. The invention of the microchip allowed computers to become smaller, more efficient, and more popular. In 1964 the computer mouse was invented, eleven years later Microsoft was founded, and, in 1982, IBM made the first small-scale individual computers (PCs, Personal Computers). The World Wide Web was developed in 1989, and today it is possible to shop, do research, pay bills, receive instant news reports, and remain in constant contact with people around the globe—all via the Web.

Medicine and genetic technology since World War II have improved the lives of millions of people, but these advances have also raised controversial ethical issues. In the 1950s the combined research of Albert Sabin (1906–1993) and Jonas Salk (1914–1995) produced the polio vaccine, making it possible to eradicate a potentially fatal disease that causes paralysis, especially in children. The first organ transplant was performed in 1950, and chemotherapy and radiation became standard treatments for cancer. The development of an effective birth control pill in 1956 allowed women to make more independent decisions about their reproductive life, although the use of the birth control pill was prohibited by the Catholic Church and some other religious groups. Nevertheless, reproductive experimentation continued and the first "test tube" baby was born in 1978.

The discovery in the 1950s of the double-helix molecular structure of DNA (the genetic blueprint for life) by four biophysicists, the Britons Francis Crick (1916–2004), Rosalind Franklin (1920–1958), and Maurice Wilkins (born 1916) and the American James Watson (born 1928), has been followed by other discoveries in biological science. Geneticists have identified the human genome, composed of some 3 billion units of DNA and organized into forty-six chromosomes, which in turn form twenty-three pairs. Identifying the genome has led to gene replacement therapy (GRT), in which defective genes are replaced or changed to minimize hereditary diseases and alleviate immune deficiency. It is also possible to alter crops and seeds genetically, a controversial discovery that could potentially solve the problem of world hunger. More recently, genetic engineering has led to the cloning of animals (that is, making an exact genetic replica), which has raised ethical issues about whether people have the right to create life using scientific techniques.

23.8 Buzz Aldrin standing by the American flag on the moon, *c.* July 16–24, 1969. Photograph taken by Neil Armstrong.

PHILOSOPHY

Existentialism was the dominant philosophy after World War II until the 1960s, when Structuralism, Post-Structuralism, and Deconstruction came to the fore. All are aspects of the broader theoretical system known as semiotics, which is concerned with the relationship of signs to society and culture. While also applicable to works of art, semiotics had the strongest impact on anthropology, linguistics, and literary theory. The Structuralist emphasis on language was inspired largely by logical positivism (see Chapter 22) and the belief that all cultural products are governed by linguistic systems.

STRUCTURALISM

The Swiss professor of linguistics Ferdinand de Saussure (1857–1913) believed that language was a system of signs for communication. He noted that words do not conform to what they refer to—for example, the letters D-O-G are not naturally related to our mental image of a dog or to what a dog is. The relation between D-O-G and an actual dog is arbitrary.

Saussure argued that there are two main linguistic structures: synchronic and diachronic. The synchronic structure denotes language in a given time and space as expressed by fixed grammatical principles. The term synchronic comes from two Greek words *syn* ("with") and *chronos* ("time"). Synchrony thus refers to linguistic meanings existing "within a given time period."

Diachronic structure denotes the fluidity of language as it evolves. The term comes from the Greek words *dia* ("through") and *chronos* ("time"). Diachrony thus deals with ways in which structures of language (or other entities, such as social conventions) change over time.

Saussure's system of synchrony and diachrony was applied to patterns of culture by the French anthropologist Claude Lévi-Strauss (born 1908). In *Structural Anthropology* (1958) Lévi-Strauss argued that cultural expressions, such as myths, have both synchronic and diachronic significance—that is, they reveal the character of a culture in a particular time and place (synchrony), but they also contain features (for example, the notion that humans are created by gods) that are applicable to all cultures and these are more subject to change (diachrony) as they move from one culture to another. Lévi-Strauss believed that understanding structures would reveal the logic of a culture.

According to the American linguist Noam Chomsky (born 1928), human linguistic structure is universal. Lévi-Strauss discussed the same idea in relation to society in his 1967 study, *The Elementary Structures of Kinship*. Applying Structuralism to psychoanalysis, the French psychoanalyst Jacques Lacan (1908–1981) was influenced by Saussure when he argued that the unconscious is structured like a language. Structuralism has more affinities with Jungian than with Freudian psychoanalysis because of the interest in myth patterns. The focus on patterns appealed to the archetypal view of cultures espoused by Jung, whereas Freud laid greater emphasis on individual development.

Structuralists believe that meaning is arbitrary. They see cultural expression, whether in modes of dress, advertising, works of art and literature, or religion, as a coded system independent of the individual, a notion that led to the expression "the Death of the Author." Later, however, Structuralism evolved into Post-Structuralism and readmitted authorship, especially as regards art and literature.

Post-Structuralism and Deconstruction

The French Post-Structuralist philosopher Roland Barthes (1915–1980) not only reintroduced the Author but also emphasized the role of the spectator. In his study of photography, *Camera Lucida* (1980), Barthes describes the power of the photograph as the impression of "being there" at the moment a picture is taken. He begins with a photograph of Napoleon's youngest brother and declares his amazement at the realization: "I am looking at eyes that looked at the Emperor." The photograph, in Barthes's view, is a record and an expression of a time and place as well as something to which each viewer responds in a personal way (figure **23.9**). As such, photographs have both synchronic and diachronic meaning—that is, they mark a particular time and place—but when spectatorship is considered, the meaning of an image evolves over time as the spectators change.

The leading figure of Post-Structuralism, the French theorist Jacques Derrida (1930–2004), introduced a new approach to Post-Structuralism called Deconstruction. His main interest was the relationship of philosophy to language and literature. Through his own method of questioning Derrida revealed ambivalence, metaphors, and puns inherent in literary texts. He himself was also ambivalent, bringing the spectator into a dialogue with a work by a series of child-like questions. Unlike the Structuralists, Derrida believed that meaning is never fixed or finite; it is always open to question.

23.9 G. W. Wilson, Queen Victoria, 1863. Photograph.
Roland Barthes advanced the notion of the *studium* and the *punctum* in analyzing photographs. The *studium* is the culturally coded aspect of the picture, in this case the figure of the queen on horseback. The *punctum*, on the other hand, is the detail that catches Barthes's attention and causes him to "puncture" the image with his gaze. Here the *punctum* is the Scottish groom, with his cap and kilt, who holds the horse's reins.

ART AND ARCHITECTURE

Increasingly rapid communication, visual as well as verbal, led to the appearance of new art styles in almost every decade after World War II. New York, the post-war center of the international art world, became the gathering place of many avant-garde artists, and from the 1980s travel and the simultaneous transmittal of images over the Internet expanded the global reach of the art world.

Late Modern styles after World War II reflect the anxiety, alienation, and fragmentation of the post-war period. Late Modern art was informed by social and political concerns, such as the fear of nuclear destruction, mass culture, feminism, race and gender issues, and ecology and the environment. New media, such as video art, responded to a growing interest in technology.

The term Postmodern is often applied to the styles, especially architecture, that appeared after 1970. Postmodernism has certain affinities with Structuralism in being attuned to mass culture and being a-historical in the juxtaposition of art forms from diverse times and places.

The American Scene: Edward Hopper

The American painter Edward Hopper (1882–1967) was drawn to the theme of isolation. He studied in Paris, where he was influenced by Impressionist light and color. He used light to reinforce the mysterious sense of inner psychology conveyed by isolated figures and contrasted with the wide open spaces of the American landscape. In *Hotel by a Railroad* (figure **23.10**) the figures are waiting, presumably for a train, and appear alienated from one another. The woman reads introspectively, while the man smokes as he gazes out of the window. The exterior walls restrict the perspective and seem to close in on the hotel room. Tension is created by the absence of contact between the figures and the different ways in which they deal with an enforced waiting that they cannot control.

23.10 Edward Hopper, *Hotel by a Railroad*, 1952. Oil on canvas, 31¼ × 40 in. (79.4 × 101.9 cm). Hirshhorn Museum and Sculpture Garden, Smithsonian Institution, Washington, D.C.
Hopper plays on the theme of looking and being looked at by juxtaposing the open window with the opaque window in the adjacent wall and with the interior mirror, which reflects only patches of color. The red frame of the mirror echoes the pink slip and the red chest, whereas the man's black and white clothing echoes the exterior walls. Interior and exterior are thus subliminally associated with female and male character, the former seated and absorbed in a book, the latter standing and focused on the outside.

Abstract Expressionism

With émigrés fleeing the rise of Fascism, New York became an artistic melting pot from the 1930s. The style that put American art on the international map was Abstract Expressionism, which was influenced by stream-of-consciousness thought, by the Surrealist interest in myths and dreams, and by the Dada notion of chance and spontaneity as a means of accessing the unconscious mind. The Abstract Expressionist artists who congregated in New York City during the 1940s and 1950s are referred to as the New York School.

There were varying degrees of narrative and non-figuration among the Abstract Expressionists. The best-known series of paintings by Robert Motherwell (1915–1991)—"Elegy to the Spanish Republic" (figure **23.11**)—appears to be without recognizable objects, but each commemorates a specific moment in twentieth-century history. Deeply affected by the writings of García Lorca (see Chapter 22), who was executed by Franco's Falangists, Motherwell began the series in 1948 and pursued it throughout his career. The textured edges of the forms and the splattered paint reveal the artist's process, which is a characteristic of Abstract Expressionism.

23.11 Robert Motherwell, "Elegy to the Spanish Republic," series, *No. 78*, 1962. Oil and plastic on canvas, 5 ft. 11 in. × 11 ft.¼ in. (1.8 × 3.36 m). Yale University Art Gallery, New Haven, Connecticut.
The paintings in this series, inspired by García Lorca's poetry, consist of black ovals and a thick black curve. They lament the death of the Spanish Republic and protest Spain's domination by the Fascist regime of Francisco Franco.

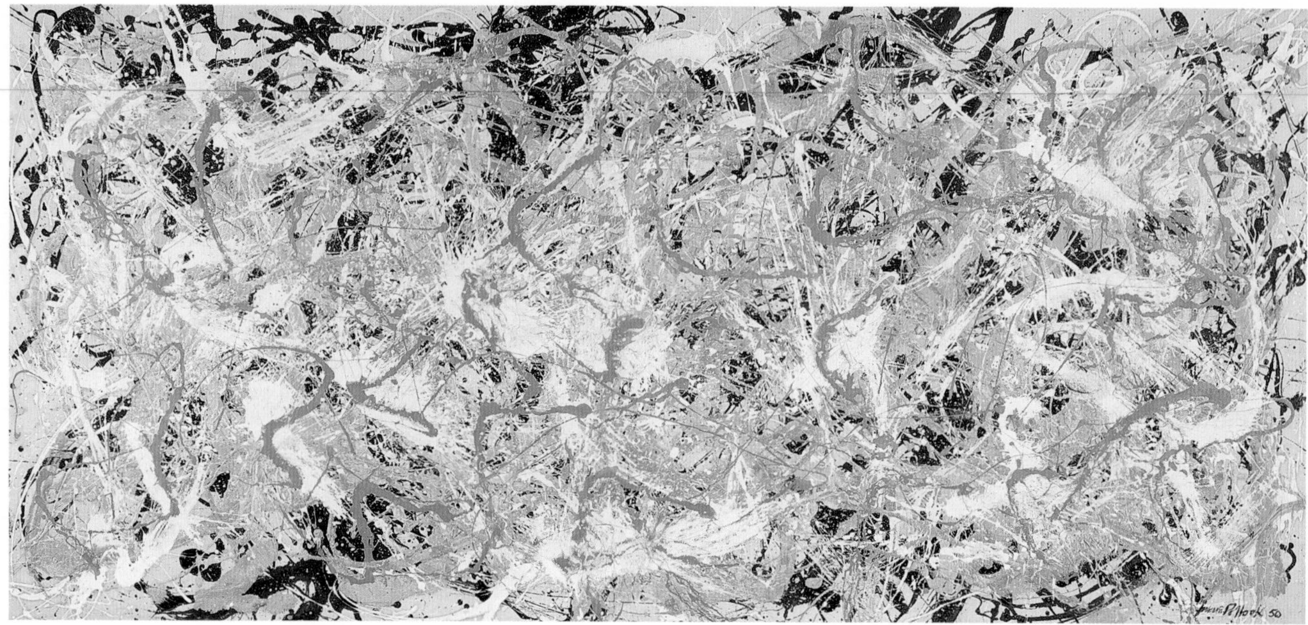

23.12 Jackson Pollock, *Number 27*, 1950. Oil on canvas, 4 ft. 1 in. × 8 ft. 10 in. (1.24 × 2.69 m). Whitney Museum of American Art, New York. The dynamic energy of this picture is typical of Pollock. The all-over drips place the image right where it is, on the surface of the canvas. There is no longer a foreground and background, only a foreground, and the light is contained in the paint itself or in the canvas. Pollock believed that he and his art were one and the same, and that the painting, like the painter, "has a life of its own."

The interest in making visible the process of creating art led to **action painting**, in which the gestures of the artist are reflected in the finished work. The leading gestural action painter was Jackson Pollock (1912–1956). He was born in Cody, Wyoming, and studied art in California and then in New York with the Regionalist Thomas Hart Benton (see Chapter 22). Although Pollock was, at first, a figurative painter like Benton, his works of the late 1940s and early 1950s were devoid of narrative content and recognizable form. With titles such as *Number 27* (figure **23.12**), Pollock forced the viewer to confront his process. He typically placed the canvas on the ground and moved around or even on the canvas as he dripped, splattered, and spread housepainter's paint in energetic, circular motions. Pollock identified with the Navajo sand painters of the Southwest, whose temporary images are created with a view to healing a sick person. Pollock, too, felt that the act of creating an image had a power beyond itself.

The sculptor Isamu Noguchi (1904–1988) was associated with Abstract Expressionism. He combined the cultures of his American mother and Japanese father in his work. He grew up in Japan, was a premed student at Columbia University, and studied sculpture with Brancusi (see Chapter 22). Straddling the two cultures of his heritage, Noguchi's taste for stone was influenced by Japanese rock gardens, and his biomorphic abstraction by the European avant garde. Despite its abstract forms, in *Humpty Dumpty* (figure **23.13**) Noguchi creates the sense of a standing, living figure.

The work of Mark Rothko (1903–1970) is referred to as Color Field and is also considered Abstract Expressionist. His work is not gestural in the sense that Pollock's is, but from 1949 it eliminates the figure entirely. Rothko was born in Latvia, emigrated to the United States at the age of ten, and lived in Oregon until 1923, when he moved to New York and joined the New York School. Like Pollock, Rothko was influenced by Surrealism before renouncing figuration altogether. The painting in figure **23.14** is typical of Rothko's style from 1949 until his death. Rectangles of color seem to float in space, one above the other. The

23.13 Isamu Noguchi, *Humpty Dumpty*, 1946. Ribbon slate, 4 ft. 10¾ in. (1.49 m) high. Whitney Museum of American Art, New York.
Like the Abstract Expressionist painters, Noguchi was interested in myth, dreams, and the mysteries of the unconscious mind. In this work, organic shapes seem to shift between human and animal forms, as if human elements are in the process of evolving from lower forms of life. The repeated ovals (egg shapes) suggest Humpty Dumpty (himself an egg). As in *Finnegans Wake* (see Chapter 21), there is a pun on the notion of the Fall of Man (compare Joyce's "great fall of the offwall"), and thus Noguchi evokes the beginning of human time.

23.14 Mark Rothko, *Number 10*, 1950. Oil on canvas, 7 ft. $6\frac{3}{8}$ in. × 4 ft. $9\frac{1}{2}$ in. (2.29 × 1.46 m). The Museum of Modern Art, New York.

soft edges blur the boundary between foreground and background, creating a continually shifting spatial tension. Rothko's work is silent and often described as spiritual, with light seeming to penetrate the texture of the canvas from behind the fields of color.

POP ART

The 1960s was the decade of Pop Art in the United States. Rejecting non-figurative Abstract Expressionism, Pop Artists returned to the object with a vengeance. Jasper Johns (born 1930) maintained the textural sense of the Abstract Expressionists and used traditional media, while also insisting on the presence of everyday ("popular") objects. In *Painted Bronze (Ale Cans)* (figure **23.15**), he infuses the familiar with new meaning. Cast in bronze, the ale cans announce their presence as a pair and the prominent labels identify (and advertise) their contents. Johns thus merges modern advertising imagery, packaging, and the notion of commodity with the ancient techniques of bronze casting and painting.

23.15 Jasper Johns, *Painted Bronze (Ale Cans)*, 1960. Painted bronze, $5\frac{1}{2} \times 8 \times 4\frac{3}{4}$ in. (14 × 20 × 12 cm). Ludwig Museum, Cologne.

Andy Warhol (1928–1987) epitomized the consumer imagery of Pop Art. He lived and worked in New York City, where he became a cult figure, making sculptures, paintings, prints, and underground films. In *Twenty-Five Colored Marilyns* (figure **23.16**) Warhol creates the impression of a contact

23.16 Andy Warhol, *Twenty-Five Colored Marilyns*, 1962. Acrylic on canvas, 6 ft. 10 in. × 5 ft. $6\frac{1}{4}$ in. (2.08 × 1.68 m). Modern Art Museum of Fort Worth, Texas.

sheet of colorized photographs. Marilyn Monroe, an iconic American movie star, is shown with bright yellow hair, her signature red lips, and blue eyelids against a blue background. The repetition makes her a commodity of Hollywood image-making, just as advertising repeats its messages to consumers.

PERFORMANCE

Performance art became popular in the United States during the 1960s. Partly inspired by the Dada performances of World War I (see Chapter 21), the performances of the 1960s, also called **happenings**, typically made a political or social point. The German artist Joseph Beuys (1921–1986) was a pilot in the German air force during World War II. According to his account, he was shot down over Siberia and rescued by local Tartars, who coated him with animal fat and wrapped him in felt to keep him alive. Taking his rescue as a miracle, Beuys began to see himself as a modern shaman, navigating between the human and animal worlds. In addition, he sought world peace through art by taking his performances to different countries.

In 1965 he performed *How to Explain Pictures to a Dead Hare* (figure **23.17**) in a gallery in Germany. The audience remained outdoors, watching the performance through a window, while Beuys sat with a dead hare on his lap. His head coated with honey and gold leaf, Beuys explained the nature of art to the animal.

23.17 Joseph Beuys, *How to Explain Pictures to a Dead Hare*, 1965. Galerie Schmela, Düsseldorf, Germany.
In the belief that animals have special powers, and distressed by the inability of people to understand art, Beuys intended to show that even a dead hare was a better listener than most humans. People, according to Beuys, are blocked from feeling and seeing freshly by preconceived ideas and socially imposed inhibitions.

MINIMALISM

From the late 1960s and early 1970s, Minimalist artists sought to remove the impression of the artist's presence in a work. They tended to use manufactured media, and their content was pared down to a "minimal" level. This is the case with the sculptures of Donald Judd (1928–1994) (figure **23.18**). In his view, art had no significance beyond the empirical experience of the work. His commercially made objects, here a column of

23.18 Donald Judd, *Untitled*, 1967. Galvanized iron with green lacquer on front and sides, twelve units 9 × 40 × 31 in. (22.9 × 101.6 × 78.7 cm). Helman Collection, New York.

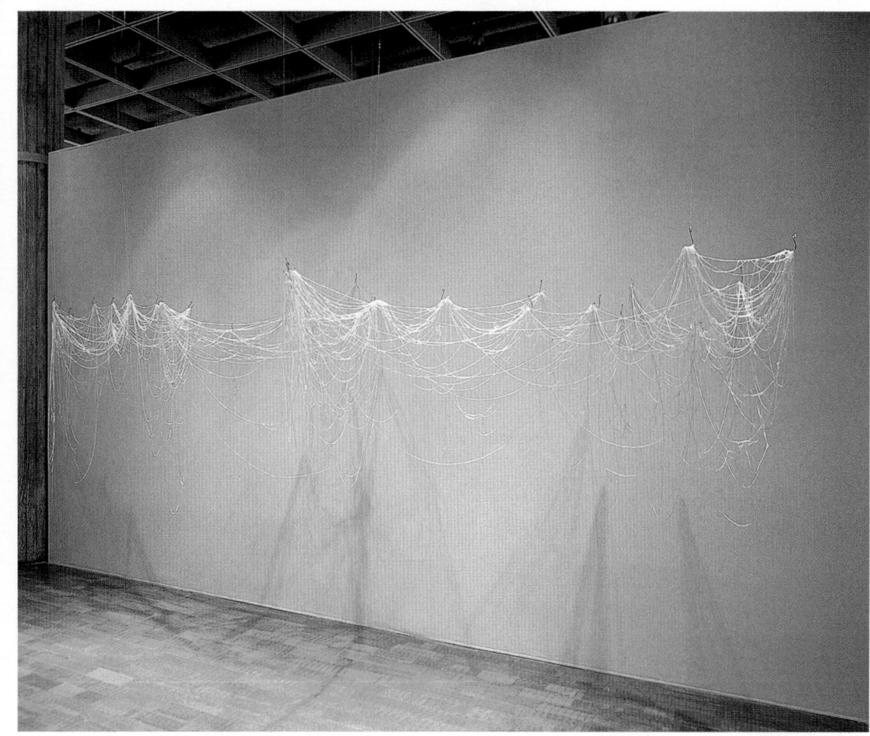

23.19 Eva Hesse, *Right After*, 1969. Fiberglass, 5 × 18 × 4 ft. (1.5 × 5.5 × 1.2 m). Milwaukee Art Museum.

green-lacquered iron boxes attached to a wall, are arranged at regular intervals to create purely geometric patterns.

The German-born sculptor Eva Hesse (1936–1970) is associated with Minimalism because of her spare imagery, although she infused her work with personal meaning. She also used natural materials, such as rope, rather than manufactured materials. A Jew, she escaped the Nazis by fleeing from Germany to the Netherlands and then to New York. She studied at Yale and produced an important body of work before she died at thirty-four. In *Right After* (figure **23.19**), Hesse hung ropes dipped in fiberglass across the space of a room. Rope and string signified for her the connections she had lost in being separated from her country, from her mother who committed suicide, and from her husband from whom she was divorced. These particular ropes are both taut and sagging, reflecting her personal tension between optimistic, dynamic creativity and limp despair.

CONCEPTUAL ART: SOL LEWITT

In Conceptualism, which began in the 1960s, the idea behind the work of art is as important as—or more important than—the work itself. A pioneering Conceptual artist, Sol LeWitt (born 1928) makes small diagrams of an idea, its color arrangement, and instructions on how the work is to be installed on a wall (figure **23.20**). His early designs were exclusively black and white, but after 1975 he began adding color. The result in this case is the appearance of expanding three-dimensional, tent-like pyramids that proceed around the wall.

23.20 Sol LeWitt, *Wall Drawing No. 623, Double asymmetrical pyramids with color ink washes superimposed*, November 14–17, 1989. Color ink wash, 20 ft. 3¼ in. × 38 ft. 8½ in. (6.18 × 11.8 m) (two walls at right angles). National Gallery of Canada, Ottawa.

SUPER REALISM

In the 1970s artists again turned to figuration, not so much to the object *per se* as to illusionism and *trompe l'oeil* (literally making an image so realistic that it fools the eye into perceiving it as real). The leading Super Realist painter is Richard Estes (born 1936), whose paintings resemble color photographs. As with Barthes's astonishment at seeing the picture of Napoleon's brother whose eyes had looked on the emperor, viewers of Estes's paintings have the impression of "being there" when a photograph was taken, even though in this case they are seeing a painting and not a photograph (figure **23.21**).

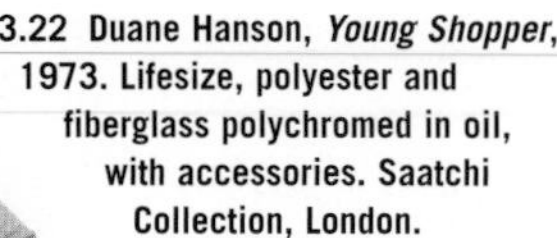

23.22 Duane Hanson, *Young Shopper*, 1973. Lifesize, polyester and fiberglass polychromed in oil, with accessories. Saatchi Collection, London.

The leading Super Realist sculptor, Duane Hanson (1925– 1996), the son of a dairy farmer, was born in Minnesota. He studied art in Seattle, St. Paul, and Michigan, but he later lived mainly in New York and Florida. Just as Estes's paintings are often mistaken for photographs of real places, so Hanson's sculptures are often assumed to be real people. They represent figures that are unmistakably American types. His *Young Shopper* (figure **23.22**), for example, humorously depicts an overweight young woman with disheveled hair, in an outfit that does not quite fit or match. Endowed with poor taste and an inelegant appearance, she is an avid member of the consumer culture, laden down with bags of designer clothing.

23.21 Richard Estes, *Bus Reflections (Ansonia)*, 1972. Oil on canvas, 3 ft. 4 in. × 4 ft. 4 in. (1.02 × 1.3 m). Private collection.
Estes shows the perspective view of an urban scene. In the absence of pedestrians, the observer becomes the person on the street, drawn into the space by its illusionistic perspective. Mirror reflections on chrome and glass surfaces create the illusion of multiple viewpoints. Enhancing the fiction are the precisely delineated edges, the textures of the street, and signs.

EARTH ART

The post-war concern for ecology and preserving the environment influenced Robert Smithson (1938–1973), who used the natural environment as a site, and earth as a medium. When he used earth and rocks as media for indoor works, he called them "non-sites" and "earthworks." In 1973 Smithson died in a plane crash while photographing a new site. His most famous "earthwork" is the monumental *Spiral Jetty* (figure **23.23**), which he made by moving tons of earth and rock from the shore and forming a

23.23 Robert Smithson, *Spiral Jetty*, Great Salt Lake, Utah, 1970. Rock, salt crystals, earth, algae, coil 1500 ft. (457 m) long.

giant spiral on the water's surface. Because algae are trapped inside the spiral, the water is reddest at the center. In this work Smithson unites the land and water, exploring new ways to disrupt traditional boundaries and to express concerns about the environment.

More recently, the British artist Andy Goldsworthy (born 1960) has taken nature as a medium, shaping and photographing temporary works and also creating permanent ones. Like Smithson, Goldsworthy uses the spiral and other natural shapes, which he forms into sculptures and then records them in photographs (figure **23.24**). Here he has carved a slab of snow, leaving a thin, circular layer at the center. Its translucency causes the light to brighten, which is accentuated by the dark stalks attached to the snow. The sculpture melts as the weather changes, dissolving and evolving along with nature.

23.24 Andy Goldsworthy, *Slab of Snow Carved into Leaving a Translucent Layer*, December 27, 1987. Snow and horse chestnut stalks pinned together with thin bamboo. Izumi-Mura, Japan.

FEMINIST ICONOGRAPHY: JUDY CHICAGO

Feminism became a self-conscious iconography during the 1970s as women artists challenged the male canon of art history by insisting on the importance of women artists and of media associated with women. The feminist movement in art is summed up in the large installation, *The Dinner Party* of 1979 (figure **23.25**) by Judy Chicago (born Judy Cohen in 1939). Together with hundreds of female collaborators, Chicago constructed a triangular dinner table set for thirty-nine famous women. The abstract designs of the painted china plates are based on female sexual imagery, and the names of 999 additional women are inscribed on the tile floor under the table. Details alluded to traditional female pursuits such as craft, needlepoint, and embroidery. The triangular shape of the table is itself symbolic. In addition to connoting female sexuality, the triangle is a three-sided figure. As such, it evokes the Christian Trinity and the Last Supper, attended by Jesus and his twelve apostles (a multiple of three), with women conspicuously absent.

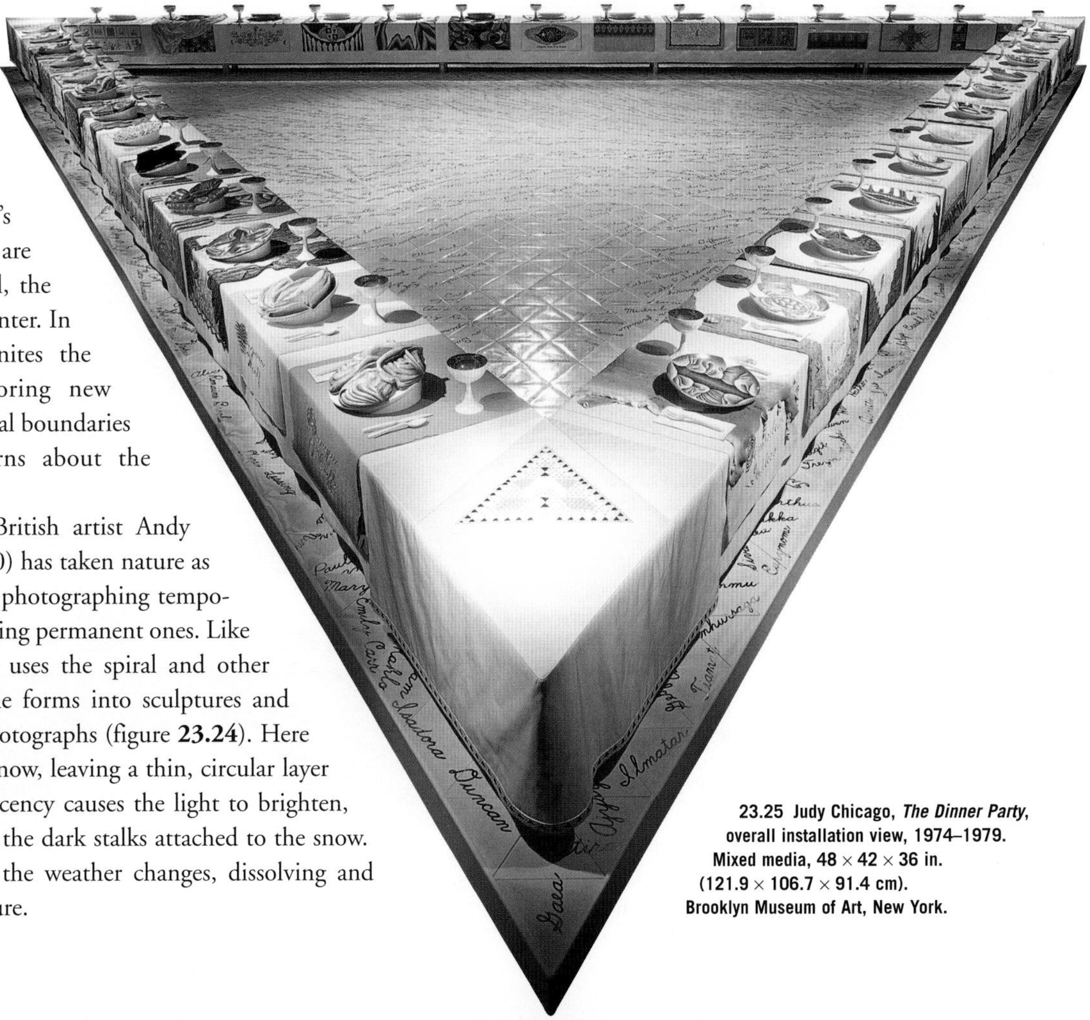

23.25 Judy Chicago, *The Dinner Party*, overall installation view, 1974–1979. Mixed media, 48 × 42 × 36 in. (121.9 × 106.7 × 91.4 cm). Brooklyn Museum of Art, New York.

GENDER: ROBERT MAPPLETHORPE

Related to feminist iconography are issues of gender. One of the most controversial challenges to convention came in the 1980s with exhibitions of photographs by Robert Mapplethorpe (1946–1989). Government funding of his work has been hotly disputed by conservatives, and one exhibition was challenged in court. Mapplethorpe's photographs of children, his homosexual themes, and his provocative images, some of them overtly sado-masochistic, offend many viewers and raise issues of censorship. At the same time, his style is highly original and his printing techniques impeccably elegant. In *Ken and Tyler* (figure **23.26**), Mapplethorpe shows two nude men, one black and one white, with diagonal shadows falling across their flesh. They are engaged in an ambiguous relationship to each other, and they move, like dancers, in unison.

23.26 Robert Mapplethorpe, *Ken and Tyler*, 1985. Platinum print, edition of three, 25½ × 22 in. (64.8 × 55.9 cm). G. H. Dalsheimer Gallery, Baltimore.

23.27 Emanuel Leutze, *Washington Crossing the Delaware*, 1851. Oil on canvas, 12 ft. 5 in. × 21 ft. 3 in. (3.78 × 6.48 m). The Metropolitan Museum of Art, New York.

AFRICAN-AMERICAN APPROPRIATION: ROBERT COLESCOTT

The Postmodernist Robert Colescott (born 1925) appropriates traditional works of Western art and transforms them into witty satires. As feminists challenge the male canon and as Mapplethorpe challenged gender roles, so Colescott makes fun of American racial stereotypes. Colescott revises the painting by Emanuel Leutze, *Washington Crossing the Delaware* (figure **23.27**), in *George Washington Carver Crossing the Delaware: Page from an American History Textbook* (figure **23.28**). George Washington is replaced by George Washington Carver (the agricultural chemist who invented peanut butter products), and the Revolutionary army is replaced by black stock characters: a fisherman, a cook, an Aunt Jemima, a drinker, and a cigar-smoking banjo player. All are having a good time, with the American flag prominently displayed and ice floes bobbing in the foreground. The intentional flatness of the colors is reminiscent of popular "painting by number" pictures. Bright colors correspond to the gaiety of the scene, with the grinning figures both having fun and making fun of the viewer and of social and art historical tradition.

23.28 Robert Colescott, *George Washington Carver Crossing the Delaware: Page from an American History Textbook*, 1975. Oil on canvas, 4 ft. 6 in. × 9 ft. (1.37 × 2.74 m). Phyllis Kind Gallery, New York.

GRAFFITI ART: JEAN-MICHEL BASQUIAT

A generation of graffiti artists posed another challenge to artistic convention in the 1980s, as they raised issues about the propriety of decorating surfaces, such as subway walls and lampposts, with graffiti. By painting on public property, graffiti artists question the borderline between creation and destruction.

The Neo-Expressionist graffiti artist Jean-Michel Basquiat (1960–1988), who came from a Haitian-Hispanic family, frequented the East Village in New York. He used the name SAMO as a conflation of "Sambo" (from "little Black Sambo") and the expression "same old shit" when signing his graffiti pictures. By the time he was twenty-eight, Basquiat had become a wealthy celebrity, but he died the same year of a drug overdose. In *Horn Players* (figure **23.29**) he combines words and images to convey a social message. Portraits of the black musicians Dizzy Gillespie and Charlie Parker, their instruments, and a few red notes are scratched on the canvas. The loose brushwork and paint textures are characteristic of Neo-Expressionism, as is the social-political theme.

VIDEO ART: NAM JUNE PAIK

The leading figure in video art, Nam June Paik (born 1932), was born in Korea and studied philosophy in Tokyo and music in Germany, where he collaborated with Joseph Beuys (see p. 672). For several years he was involved in performance art, which he gave up in favor of sculptures made of television monitors. Such sculptures can be individual figures, such as the *Family of Robot, Uncle* (figure **23.30**), or large-scale installations. They tend to emphasize the international quality of video and the fact that information can now be immediately transmitted around the globe. In the work shown here, Paik combines the monitors with their inner workings, revealing the interior and exterior of a mechanical construction. The upper torso contains the wiring, while from the waist down the screens show moving images. Despite the mechanization of the figure, however, he comes across as a cheerful, living character. His arms are open and welcoming, and his features slant very slightly upwards, as if he is pleased to see us.

23.29 Jean-Michel Basquiat, *Horn Players*, 1983. Acrylic and oil paintstick on three canvas panels, 8 ft. × 6 ft. 3 in. (2.44 × 1.9 m). Broad Art Foundation, Santa Monica, California.

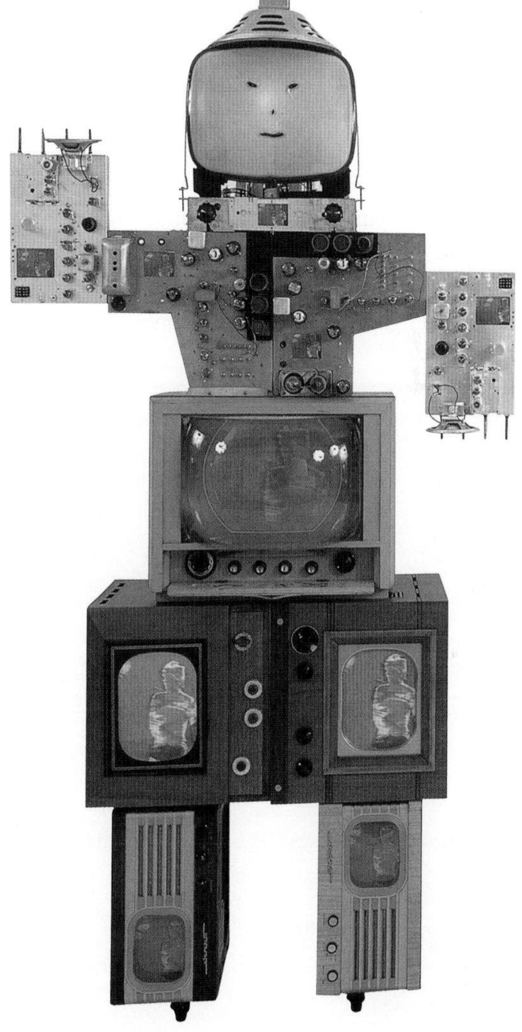

23.30 Nam June Paik, *Family of Robot, Uncle*, 1986. Private collection, Hamburg.

POSTMODERN ARCHITECTURE

Postmodern architecture, like paintings and sculptures of the 1970s and 1980s, incorporates elements of the past and transforms them into new meanings. In contrast to the International Style, Postmodern forms are often independent of their function. They have been considered a-historical because they tend to combine features of different styles and time periods for purely aesthetic reasons.

In New Orleans the Piazza d'Italia designed by Charles Moore (born 1925) was built to honor Italian immigrants to the city (figure **23.31**). The building combines the Classical Greek Orders with the round arches of ancient Rome and the Renaissance, as well as with Baroque curved walls. Color is provided not by the traditional means of paint or variations in stone, but rather by fluorescent lighting reflected in the pool below. Moore and his associates thus merge modern manufactured materials with historical styles.

23.31 Charles W. Moore and William Hersey, Piazza d'Italia, New Orleans, 1978–1979.

The Louvre Pyramid in Paris by I. M. Pei (born 1917) caused controversy when it was completed in 1988 (figure **23.32**). Viewers were divided over the merits of its Postmodernism, consisting of a large pyramid made of diamond-shaped glass panels in the courtyard of the sedate and imposing Louvre Museum. Pei used a modern building material (glass) for a structure traditionally made of stone (the pyramid) and characteristic of Old Kingdom Egyptian burials (see thumbnail). He also

Pyramids of Khufu, Khafre, and Menkaure, Giza
see figure 3.9

23.32 I. M. Pei and Associates, Louvre Pyramid, Paris, 1988.

juxtaposed the notion of Old Masters housed in the Louvre, the national museum of France, with Modernism. Formally, the clear glass, together with pools of water and erupting fountains, creates a strong contrast with the long stone horizontal of the Baroque museum.

The American Telephone and Telegraph building in New York City (figure **23.33**) combines a steel frame with a stone exterior. The pediment-like crown is broken at the center where it forms an open circle reminiscent of furniture design. The architects used Classical elements, such as a columnar vertical with a base, a shaft-like center, and a crowning element with curved and diagonal outlines. But the relationships of these parts to each other and to the whole structure depart from convention. By placing the largest windows on the top story, the architects defy the expectation of greater visual weight at the base.

23.33 Philip C. Johnson and John Burgee, American Telephone and Telegraph Headquarters Building, New York, 1979–1984.

LITERATURE

Like visual artists, many post-World War II authors were strongly affected by the war and its aftermath. Their work is imbued with a new consciousness of the destructive potential of nuclear weapons and the dangers of totalitarianism. Many French authors reacted to post-war anxiety by espousing existentialism and by writing the fragmented dialogue characteristic of the Theater of the Absurd. A few German authors addressed the Holocaust, and in the 1980s Soviet novelists began to write openly about the abuses of communism. In Britain, authors satirized totalitarianism and wrote detailed observations of small-town life. Much American literature dealt with lives of soldiers and the effects of nuclear weapons. The work of the new black, feminist, and "Beat generation" authors reflected post-war social changes. African and South African authors incorporated the legacy of colonialism into their novels, while in Latin America the new genre of **magic realism** evolved.

FRANCE: ALBERT CAMUS

Albert Camus (1913–1960) is associated with existentialism and the Absurd. He was born in Algeria, the setting of most of his novels, and raised in abject poverty. A humanist committed to individual rights, he joined the Communist Party for a brief period and was a member of the French Resistance during World War II.

Camus's famous novel of alienation, *The Stranger* (*L'Étranger*, 1942), is narrated by Mersault, the main character, who acts without apparent motive. Convinced that life is absurd, Mersault kills an Arab on an Algerian beach when struck by sunlight glancing off the Arab's knife. Mersault is tried and convicted, not because of his crime, but because he failed to cry at his mother's funeral, which the court reads as a sign of inhuman cruelty. He does not tell the court why he killed the Arab—nor does Camus tell the reader—though doing so might have reduced his sentence. Mersault is detached both from the events leading to his death and from himself. Although driven by an absurd fatalism, Mersault remains in control of his own will.

In *The Plague* (*La Peste*, 1947) the Algerian port of Oran is struck with plague. Victims are everywhere and the doctors are helpless. The authorities declare a "state of plague"—a metaphor for "state of siege"—and quarantine the city. Some of the citizens become profiteers, some are paralyzed by fear, and others pass the time playing mindless games. Those who are courageous, in Camus's view, face the plague squarely and try to help its victims. Eventually, the epidemic subsides and the city is joyful.

The existential world is godless, Camus believed, and the mark of humanity resides in individual choice. The doctor in *The Plague*, Bernard Rieux, who struggles to deal with the unexpected crisis, embodies Camus's ideal of commitment to action. Camus's conclusion—that "there is more to admire than to disdain in men"—is essentially an optimistic view of the human spirit. Nevertheless, the epidemic in Oran, and the notion that the plague bacillus is never completely eradicated, is a metaphor for the German occupation of France and other evils that overrun society. For Camus, the destructive aspects of nature, especially human nature, are permanently present in germ form and can break out at any time.

In *The Myth of Sisyphus* (1942) Camus takes the Greek myth as a metaphor for the human condition. Punished for hubris against the gods, Sisyphus is condemned to roll a heavy boulder up a mountain in Hades. The boulder rolls down again, and Sisyphus has to repeat his task throughout eternity. Camus imagines Sisyphus happy because he struggles to achieve in an existential world.

READING SELECTION
Camus, "The Myth of Sisyphus," PWC6-076

LITERATURE OF THE HOLOCAUST

In 1947, when *The Diary of Anne Frank* was first published, readers were stunned by a young girl's intimate account of her experiences during World War II. In 1933 Anne Frank (1929–1945) fled the Nazis with her Jewish family from Frankfurt, in Germany, to the Netherlands. But in 1940 the Germans invaded Holland where the Frank family hid for two years (1942–1944) in an attic in Amsterdam. They were eventually denounced and sent to the Bergen-Belsen concentration camp, where Anne died at the age of fifteen. Against a backdrop of fear and anxiety, Anne records the psychological turmoil of early adolescence as she tries to understand both the personal relationships forming under the intense pressure of hiding in cramped quarters and the Nazi crimes against her people.

The most outspoken survivor of the Holocaust has been Elie Wiesel (born 1928), who was born in Romania and survived Auschwitz. His mother, younger sister, and father all died in concentration camps. Wiesel moved to Paris after the war and became a journalist, recording accounts of life in the camps. He took up the cause of the Jews and lectures widely on the Holocaust, which he describes in *Night* (1958). It is an autobiographical memoir of Nazi atrocities, including torture, indiscriminate murder of men, women, and children, and a pervasive sense of having been abandoned by God. Wiesel became an American citizen in 1963, and was named Professor of Humanities at Boston University in 1976. Ten years later, he was awarded the Nobel Peace Prize.

THE SOVIET UNION: PASTERNAK AND SOLZHENITSYN

The two leading post-war authors in the Soviet Union, Boris Pasternak (1890–1960) and Alexander Solzhenitsyn (born 1918), were somewhat freer under Khrushchev than they had been under Stalin. Solzhenitsyn was an officer in the Red Army but was sent to a gulag for criticizing Stalin. Both authors were awarded the Nobel Prize for literature, but Pasternak was forbidden to accept it by the Soviet authorities.

Pasternak's father was a painter, his mother was a pianist, and he himself studied philosophy in Germany. He wrote *Dr. Zhivago*—a panoramic account of Russian history from the Bolshevik Revolution through World War II—in 1957, but it was banned in the Soviet Union until 1987. The hero, Dr. Yuri Zhivago, was orphaned as a child and raised by his uncle. Yuri marries an old friend, but remains emotionally and physically attached to his mistress, Lara. The novel portrays Dr. Zhivago's romantic conflicts as a mirror of Russian history during the first half of the twentieth century.

Solzhenitsyn's *One Day in the Life of Ivan Denisovich* (1962), the story of one man's routine, anonymous existence in a labor camp, was inspired by his own imprisonment. The hero, Ivan Denisovich Shukhov, fights dehumanization in the gulag by making relationships with other inmates, by attaching significance to each material possession, and by small triumphs over the guards. A careful observer of his surroundings, Ivan has a penchant for humor that makes him resilient in a dulled environment.

In 1973 in Paris Solzhenitsyn printed a detailed account of Soviet labor camps—*The Gulag Archipelago*. This, together with his aversion to Marxism, led to his exile from the Soviet Union. He went to live in Vermont, where he became an advocate of Christian fundamentalism but continued to praise the cultural supremacy of the Soviet Union over America and other nations. In 1994, after the fall of communism, Solzhenitsyn returned to Russia.

BRITAIN: ORWELL AND THOMAS

The British writer George Orwell (Eric Arthur Blair, 1903–1950) was born in Bengal but educated in England. Among his essays and novels are prophetic satires denouncing both imperialism, which he experienced at first hand in India, and totalitarianism. Orwell's best-known novels are the political satire *Animal Farm* (1945) and the social satire *1984* (1949).

Animal Farm is a strong indictment of revolution, especially the Russian Revolution. The pigs on Mr. Jones's farm foment a rebellion against their human masters. The leader, modeled on Stalin, is Napoleon, who exiles the idealist pig Snowball (modeled on Trotsky). But no sooner is the rebellion over than Napoleon becomes corrupted and installs a new tyranny, just as the real Napoleon had done in 1804 (see Chapter 18). The loyal and steadfast carthorse, Boxer, represents the positive aspects of human nature.

The opening sentence of *1984*—"It was a bright cold day in April, and the clocks were striking thirteen"—sets the novel out of ordinary time. The hero is Winston Smith, who wishes only for a life based on truth and human decency, but he lives in a society without privacy and in which original ideas are punished by death. Law and order are maintained by the thought police. Society's ideals are embodied in three slogans—WAR IS PEACE, FREEDOM IS SLAVERY, and IGNORANCE IS STRENGTH—which appear outside the Ministry of Truth. Ruling society is the party leader, Big Brother, whose image appears on posters placed at each landing of Winston's house and on the building across the street. His eyes follow Winston wherever he goes, and the caption on the poster reads: "Big Brother is watching you."

READING SELECTION

Orwell, *1984*, a flaw in the pattern, PWC6-121

The musical rhythms and Modernist poetic structure of the Welsh author Dylan Thomas (1914–1953) can seem obscure, but his writing, as in his children's prose classic, *A Child's Christmas in Wales* (1954), is eminently readable. Thomas worked as a journalist in Wales and London, and died of alcohol poisoning while on a lecture tour in New York. His poem "The Hand that Signed the Paper" (1936) conveys the faceless anonymity of political decisions and the fact that rulers are not concerned with the effects of their decisions on individuals:

The hand that signed the paper felled a city;
Five sovereign fingers taxed the breath,
Doubled the globe of dead and halved a country;
These five kings did a king to death . . .

The five kings count the dead but do not soften
The crusted wound nor stroke the brow;
A hand rules pity as a hand rules heaven;
Hands have no tears to flow.

Thomas reacted to post-war alienation with intense creative energy. His best-known poem, "Do Not Go Gentle," written in 1952 after his father's death, reflects his rage to live:

Do not go gentle into that good night,
Old age should burn and rave at close of day;
Rage, rage against the dying of the light.

The radio play *Under Milk Wood* (1954) paints the picture of a small town in Wales:

To begin at the beginning: It is Spring, moonless night in the small town, starless and bible-black, the cobblestreets silent and the hunched courters'-and-rabbits' wood limping invisible down to the sloeblack, blow, black, crowblack fishingboat-bobbing sea.

The town, with its colorful cast of characters, is Llaregub-by-the-Sea. Thomas's affectionate approach to satire reflects his impulse to keep a society and its mores alive by writing about them. The romantic, loose woman, Polly Garter, dreams of men, and Captain Cat, retired and blind (like Thomas's father), dreams of the sea and lost loves. The obsessively neat Mrs. Ogmore-Pritchard polishes potatoes and doesn't want "persons" in her "nice clean rooms breathing all over the chairs," and Organ Morgan's obsession with the organ makes his wife "a martyr to music." Mr. Pugh buys a book on "how to do in Mrs. Pugh," and Nogood Boyo wants to be Good Boyo, but "no one will let him."

THE UNITED STATES

While much important American post-war literature dealt with the effects of war, it also covered the range of social developments in the United States, including feminism, civil rights protests, and the rise of an alienated Beat generation. Adolescence too, which is itself about a period of alienation and the struggle for identity, was an appealing subject for post-war authors.

W. H. AUDEN The poet W. (Wystan) H. (Hugh) Auden (1907–1973) was born in Britain but became an American citizen in 1946, although his poetic voice remained more British than American. His work explores a wide variety of verse forms and reflects a vast range of literary sources. In 1939 he issued the following warning against Fascism:

Exiled Thucydides knew
All that a speech can say
About Democracy,
And what dictators do,
The elderly rubbish they talk
To an apathetic grave.

In his long poem *The Age of Anxiety* (1947) Auden portrays the existential anxiety of the post-war period through a dialogue between four characters in a bar who, hampered by alcoholic delusions, search for identity. Periodically the radio interrupts with news of the war. Through the device of monologue, Auden reveals that each character lives in a symbolic hell. Malin, watching the bubbles rise in his glass, forgets that he is a medical intelligence officer in the Canadian Air Force. Rosetta lights a cigarette and enjoys the fact that she has made money—possible only in America—as a department-store buyer. Emble, who enlisted in the navy during his sophomore year of college, is anxious about his future and the war. Quant talks to himself in a mirror, facing himself but not reality:

My deuce, my double, my dear image,
Is it lively there, that land of glass
Where song is a grimace, sound logic
A suite of gestures? You seem amused.

Auden's "Epitaph for the Unknown Soldier" (October 1953) conveys the futility of war:

> To save your world, you asked this man to die:
> Would this man, could he see you now, ask why?

JOHN HERSEY John Hersey (1914–1993), who wrote novels as well as stories and magazine articles, published two works about World War II. The hero of *A Bell for Adano* (1944) is Joppolo, an Italian-American from the Bronx, who arrives with the Allied forces in the Sicilian town of Adano. The seven-hundred-year-old bell, whose chimes marked the rhythms of the town for centuries, has been melted down by the Fascists for ammunition. Joppolo bonds with the people of Adano as he tries to restore the bell along with order and democracy.

In *Hiroshima* (1946) Hersey dispassionately describes the effects of nuclear radiation through six characters who survive the American atomic bomb. Although Hersey's opinion is fairly clear, he leaves his readers with the moral dilemma still debated today: did the expediency of the bomb justify its use?

JOSEPH HELLER Joseph Heller (1923–1999), a pilot in World War II, used his experiences to write *Catch-22* (1961), about American fliers dehumanized by the war. He uses **black humor** to convey the destructive effects of war and emphasizes life's most absurd aspects. The novel, which is set in an American base off the Italian coast, describes a system the soldiers have devised of flying contraband on the black market. The profit motive has become more important than patriotism, and morality is subordinated to bureaucracy and mass culture. While graphically describing the wounding and killing of men, Heller shifts from humor to satire to horror, to show the adverse effects of war on human character.

J. D. SALINGER J. (Jerome) D. (David) Salinger (born 1919) was born in New York, served in World War II, and afterwards wrote short stories for the *New Yorker* magazine. His novel *Catcher in the Rye* (1951), a cult classic that evolved from several short stories, is about an adolescent boy's search for identity. The hero, Holden Caulfield, aged sixteen, has just been dismissed from his fourth prep-school. He narrates the novel in the first person, using contemporary speech. Holden observes the hypocrisy of adults, as when a teacher calls reality a "game." To achieve success, the teacher advises Holden, one must obey the rules of the game. Holden visits New York City, where for a few days he skims the surface of low-life society, exploring the borderline between childhood innocence and the sordid aspects of adult reality.

SYLVIA PLATH An entirely different mood characterizes the work of Sylvia Plath (1932–1963), a young American poet who committed suicide soon after publishing her only novel, the autobiographical *The Bell Jar* (1963). Plath lived in Britain and America, writing poetry filled with wit as well as with disturbing themes such as mental illness, suffering, and death.

The Bell Jar begins in 1953, the year that Ethel and Julius Rosenberg were executed as Soviet spies during the McCarthy era. Their story is a recurring theme in the novel, which reflects the anti-McCarthy position of the author and her fear of tyranny. The narrative tells of a college girl who works for a women's magazine. She reminisces about her boyfriend in medical school, who represents the sameness of bourgeois life and the notion than men have more career opportunities than women. Like Plath herself, her heroine suffers from the perceived constraints of a woman's place in society and has a mental breakdown (as Plath did when she was in college).

THE BEAT WRITERS In the 1950s the writers of the Beat Generation took the alienation of existentialism to new extremes and set the stage for the hippies of the 1960s. The Beat writers, a group of poets and novelists who first met in New York City, challenged social and literary conventions. The leading Beat poet, Allen Ginsberg (1926–1997), was influenced by Far Eastern philosophy, especially the meditation techniques of Zen Buddhism. He was also an advocate of the drug culture that swept America from the late 1950s. His best-known poem, "Howl" (1956), which criticizes American bourgeois society, praises youthful rebellion, drug use, and sexual experimentation. Ginsberg's strong, explicit language, liberally spiced with four-letter words, sparked a California lawsuit for obscenity.

Jack Kerouac (1922–1969) came from a French-Canadian family that emigrated to Massachusetts. He dropped out of college to join the Merchant Marine before becoming a writer. In New York he associated with the Beat Generation authors and published his novel *On the Road* in 1957. The story of four car trips through America is told by the narrator, the aspiring author Sal Paradise. The novel's message is that the variety and intensity of life "on the road" is superior to a repetitive, bourgeois existence.

Unified by the theme of friendship—between Sal, who is from New Jersey, and Dean, who lives in San Francisco—the book is a panorama of the American landscape. On the road Sal encounters trailer homes, diners, billboards, and truck-stops. He frequents the "dull bars" of New Orleans, the crowds of Mexico City, and Chicago that "glowed red before our eyes." With an ear for local speech patterns—"I got a sister there [in Denver] but I ain't seed her for several years"—Kerouac creates a sense of America as a dynamic, diversified land in the process of change and development.

Chapter 4 opens in the Midwest:

> The greatest ride in my life was about to come up, a truck, with a flatboard at the back, with about six or seven boys sprawled out on it, and the drivers, two young blond farmers from Minnesota, were picking up every single soul they found on that road—the most smiling, cheerful couple of handsome bumpkins you could ever wish to see, both wearing cotton shirts and overalls, nothing else; both thick-wristed and earnest, with broad houareyou smiles for anybody and anything that came across their path.

In downtown Mexico City:

> Thousands of hipsters in floppy straw hats and long-lapeled jackets over bare chests padded along the main drag, some of them selling crucifixes and weed in the alleys, some of them kneeling in beat chapels next to Mexican burlesque shows in sheds . . . You had to jump over a ditch to get your drink, and in the bottom of the ditch was the ancient lake of the Aztec.

AFRICAN-AMERICAN THEMES As America struggled with civil rights, black authors wrote novels describing their experiences. Ralph Ellison (1914–1994) was born in Oklahoma and worked for a time as a journalist. In the 1930s he went to Harlem, where he studied jazz composition and sculpture. His novel *Invisible Man* (1952) conveys the alienation of blacks in urban America and Ellison's own feeling of being "invisible" in white culture. Written in the first person, the novel contains powerful observations on the advantages and disadvantages of being unseen. Ellison describes being bumped into but hardly noticed, to the point where he begins to doubt his own existence. Sensing that he is someone else's dream, the narrator struggles to be seen and recognized. When he is confronted with the hostility of a white man, he becomes enraged and nearly kills him, but when he realizes that the white man has no concept of who a black man is, he ceases to take his hostility personally and lets him go.

James Baldwin (1924–1987), who grew up in a poor family of nine children in Harlem, hoped his writing would have a positive effect on society and improve the lot of the blacks in America. Between 1948 and 1957 Baldwin lived in France, where he became friends with the American expatriates there. Baldwin's first and best novel, *Go Tell it on the Mountain* (1953), reflects his rage at racial discrimination, which he portrays in biblical tones. The main character is Johnny Grimes, raised in Harlem, the son of an abusive deacon. Racial issues, including the self-hatred of blacks, are explored in a religious context during a single day, Johnny's fourteenth birthday. Although there is a sense that New York holds the potential for personal achievement, in Baldwin's Harlem the blacks feel safer at home than on the streets. Racial conflicts are mirrored in the tension between Johnny and his father:

> "Praise the Lord," said his father. He did not move to touch him, did not kiss him, did not smile. They stood before each other in silence, while the saints rejoiced; and John struggled to speak the authoritative, the living word that would conquer the great division between his father and himself. But it did not come, the living word; in the silence something died in John, and something came alive.

The Color Purple (1982) by Alice Walker (born 1944) combines feminist themes with problems of black life. The main character, Celie, lives in the early twentieth century and narrates events through letters written to God and her sister, a missionary in Africa. Celie is victimized both by white society and by abusive black men. When her father rapes her, he warns her not to tell of it except to God, hence her letters to God. Her father's abuse becomes a blueprint for her future relationships with men. She marries Mister (who stands for all abusive men) and takes care of his two children. When Mister's promiscuous mistress, Shug, gets sick and comes to live with them, a friendship forms between the two women. Through this bond Celie begins to gain a sense of self. Eventually she leaves Mister and becomes her own person.

Toni Morrison (born 1931), born in Ohio, worked as an editor and teacher before turning to writing. In 1993 she became the first African-American woman to receive a Nobel Prize for literature. She depicts the physical and psychological violence of racism, especially as it affects women. Her writing style merges African myth and legend with biblical allusions, supernatural elements, and the American vernacular. In *Beloved* (1987), which is based on actual events, the main character, Sethe, is a runaway slave during and after the Civil War. Sethe kills her daughter rather than allow her to return to slavery. The word "Beloved" is inscribed on her daughter's tombstone, but her name is absent for lack of money to pay for a longer inscription.

The novel opens with the emotional violence that is its main theme: "124 WAS SPITEFUL. Full of a baby's venom. The women in the house knew it and so did the children. For years each put up with the spite in his own way." Morrison shows how the alienating effects of slavery, its attack on identity, and its destruction of families can lead to depression and madness. One of her main themes is the way in which language is manipulated to create racial stereotypes. Thus, when the school teacher says that "definitions belong to the definers," she is referring to the notion that "history is written by the victors."

AFRICA: COLONIAL THEMES

As the reins of colonialism loosened after World War II, increasing numbers of writers addressed issues arising from the domination of one culture by another. Doris Lessing (born 1919) was born in Iran, grew up in Southern Rhodesia (modern Zimbabwe), left school at 15, and took several jobs in Africa before moving to Britain in 1949. Throughout her career, her main themes have been race relations, feminism, the nature of creativity, and politics.

Her series of five novels, *The Children of Violence* (1952–1969), chronicles the decline of British and Dutch domination as black Africans struggle for independence. The main character, Martha Quest, is, as her name implies, searching for social and psychological independence beyond family life. This personal quest mirrors the political and cultural independence sought by Africans.

Two authors from Nigeria, Chinua Achebe (born 1930) and Wole Soyinka (born 1934), have also explored colonial and postcolonial themes. Achebe, the son of a clergyman, was educated in Nigeria and London, and his works reflect the African context. He portrays tribal communities and shows that oral traditions of myth-making and storytelling are uniquely human products. His first novel, *Things Fall Apart* (1958), deals with the culture of an Ibo village in the late nineteenth century and the destructive effects of white colonialism. Nearly thirty years later Achebe published *Anthills of the Savannah* (1987), which takes place in the imaginary land of Kangan, somewhere in West Africa. Here, too, Achebe's themes revolve around power and its impact on a traditional community.

Wole Soyinka was born in West Nigeria, where his father worked as a school administrator. Like Achebe, he has studied and worked in Britain as well as in Africa, which has given his writing a cross-cultural perspective. Soyinka has written, produced, and acted in plays, published poems and novels, and in 1981 he published his autobiography, *Aké: The Years of Childhood.* In that work he uses memory, myth, and the child's viewpoint to navigate between the past and the present and between Western Christianity and the traditional Yoruba culture of Nigeria.

LATIN AMERICA: MAGIC REALISM

After World War II literature from around the globe began to receive more international attention, especially in the West. Authors in Latin America are known for their use of magic realism, in which fantasy and magic are interwoven with the mundane details of daily life. The result is often surreal, with time being cyclical, juxtaposed, or superimposed rather than sequential.

The leading Chilean poet, Pablo Neruda (1904–1973), worked as a diplomat and traveled widely. He was involved in politics, identifying with the poor, and impressed by the Spanish republicans fighting against Franco (see Chapter 22). In 1939, stunned by the assassination of Federico García Lorca, Neruda joined the Communist Party and devoted himself to the cause of democracy.

Neruda's *Canto General* (*The General's Song*) (1950), an epic cycle of 320 poems dealing with South American history, combines drama, lyricism, and mysticism. The poems are filled with metaphorical images and striking juxtapositions. In "The Beggars" Neruda identifies with society's outcasts. He compares beggars to the monstrous gargoyle-drainpipes that project from Gothic cathedral walls (see thumbnail). Both, in Neruda's imagery, are "outsiders":

Gargoyle,
Notre Dame, Paris
see figure 11.12

By the cathedrals, clothing
the walls, they deploy
with their bundles, their black looks, their limbs,
ripped tins of provender,
the livid increase of the gargoyles;
beyond, on the obdurate
unction of stone
they nurture a gutter-flower the flower
of legitimized plague, in migrations.

Neruda's aversion to dictatorship is apparent in "The Dictators," in which he conveys the adverse, long-lasting effects of political tyranny. He juxtaposes the eternity of death with renewed life, and the comfortable, uniformed petty ruler (the satrap) with the bones of the dictator's victims "festering" in their graves:

An odor stayed in the cane fields:
carrion, blood, and a nausea
of harrowing petals.
Between coconut palms lay the graves, a stilled
strangulation, a festering surfeit of bones.
A finical satrap conversed
with wineglasses, collars, and piping.

The Colombian author Gabriel García Márquez (born 1928) worked as a journalist in Europe and has written short stories, novels, and memoirs. His *One Hundred Years of Solitude* (1967) takes place in the colorful, decaying fictional town of Macondo, which, like Faulkner's Yoknapatawpha County in Mississippi (see Chapter 22), is destined for ruin. Macondo is a metaphor for the corrupting effects of politics and big business on an idyllic setting. Time travels through generations of the incestuous Buendía family, obsessed by the curse of conceiving a child with a pig's tail. Kept alive by a matriarchal grandmother, the myth persists and eventually becomes reality. Like Oedipus, who tried to avoid his destiny, Márquez's characters meet their fate, embodying the theme that one must know history in order to avoid repeating it.

More recently, the work of the Chilean Isabel Allende (born 1942) combines magic realism with a feminist cast. In her first novel, *The House of the Spirits* (1985), she interweaves history, politics, and religion with the theme of the woman's role in society. The history of Chile is told from a matrilineal viewpoint, juxtaposing the patriarchal rigidity of Chilean men with the intellect and moral fiber of women. Allende, the niece of a Chilean president overthrown in a CIA-assisted coup, is a staunch opponent of dictatorship, which she equates with dominating and abusive husbands.

JAPAN: YASUNARI KAWABATA

The novels of Yasunari Kawabata (1899–1972) have had a great deal of success in the West. *Snow Country* (1935–1947), his best-known novel, is influenced by ***haiku***, traditional Japanese poems of seventeen syllables that create visual images by juxtaposing unlikely terms. Like haiku, *Snow Country* is condensed, austere, and pictorial. It tells the story of a doomed romance between the hero Shimamura and the geisha Komako. Details such as the embroidery on a Japanese kimono are precisely delineated and take on metaphorical meaning. Published shortly after the end of World War II, the novel portrays the isolation of the period and at the same time maintains aspects of traditional Japanese culture.

Describing the reflection of a train's mirror on a girl's face, Kawabata intertwines landscape and humanity so that they become inseparable:

> The light moved across the face, though not to light it up. It was a distant, cold light. As it sent its small ray through the pupil of the girl's eye, as the eye and light were superimposed one on the other, the eye became a weirdly beautiful bit of phosphorescence on the sea of evening mountains.

THEATER

The most significant post-war development in theater was the Theater of the Absurd, which originated in France. Absurdist playwrights sought to show the irrationality of life and the disjunction between human individuality and society's inhumanity. Often, as in Structuralism, words and meanings are arbitrary, and their disconnection is meant to show the absurdity of socially constructed convention. By fragmenting language, the Absurdists, like the Dadaists, convey the fragmentation of modern life. American playwrights, less influenced by the Absurd than the French, tended to illustrate the illusions of contemporary life.

FRANCE

The existentialist Jean-Paul Sartre was an important playwright in the Theater of the Absurd. During World War II Sartre had been imprisoned by the Germans and had experienced at first hand the atrocities committed by Hitler. After escaping, Sartre joined the French Resistance. He demonstrated his disdain for bourgeois values by turning down the Nobel Prize for literature in 1964.

In his one-act play *No Exit* (*Huis clos*, 1944), hell is a metaphor for the doomed lives of three characters who repeat mistakes and make their lives a living hell from which there is no exit. The play is set in a sordid hotel lobby, where the journalist Garcin introduces two women to each other. Estelle talks about pneumonia; Inès talks about gas. The characters gradually reveal their past crimes: Estelle has killed her infant, Inès is a lesbian who secretly enjoys the suffering of others, and Garcin is a cowardly deserter from the army.

Although the three characters try to support each other, their mutual disdain proves to be a torture more devastating than physical punishment. Each is eternally condemned to the disapproving gaze of the other two. Sartre's famous conclusion *"L'enfer, c'est les autres"* ("Hell is other people") reveals the underlying truthfulness of the Absurd.

Albert Camus also conveyed the absurdity of life in his plays. In *Caligula* (1938), the Roman emperor discovers upon the death of his sister that life has no meaning. Modeled on Hitler, Caligula uses his power to visit his perverse insanity on Rome, teaching the world that life is absurd by ordering a series of senseless murders.

Another major Absurd playwright, the Irish Samuel Beckett (1906–1989) lived in France from 1930 and wrote in French. A novelist, poet, and dramatist, Beckett wrote three novels, *Molloy* and *Malone Dies* (both 1951) and *The Unnamable* (1953), which express the fragmentation of modern life. They are written in the form of monologues; the characters live mainly inside their own heads and are isolated from society.

Beckett's famous play *Waiting for Godot* was first performed in 1953. It has become the paradigm of the Theater of the Absurd. Two characters, Vladimir and Estragon, are waiting, which Beckett presents as life's main activity. They pass the time, separate, and then reunite. Each needs the other to confirm his existence and to remind him of his past (his identity). Two other characters, Lucky and Pozzo, imply that fulfillment is possible, even though it is never achieved. The language is terse and to the point, although it is not always clear what the point is. Vladimir and Estragon are waiting for Godot, who is never identified and has been interpreted in many ways. When asked if he meant God, Beckett replied that, if he had meant God, he would have written God.

There is little action, the dialogue is enigmatic, occasionally humorous, and phrases such as "Nothing to be done . . ." are repeated throughout. At the end, the possibility of suicide arises, but the necessary equipment is nowhere to be found:

> VLADIMIR: Everything's dead but the tree.
> ESTRAGON: What is it?
> VLADIMIR: It's the tree.
> ESTRAGON: Yes, but what kind?
> VLADIMIR: I don't know. A willow.
> ESTRAGON: Why don't we hang ourselves?
> VLADIMIR: With what?
> ESTRAGON: You haven't got a bit of rope?
> VLADIMIR: No.
> ESTRAGON: Then we can't.

Eugene Ionesco (1912–1994), whose father was Romanian and whose mother was French, grew up in France, spent his adolescence in Romania, and then settled permanently in France. His plays combine comedy and tragedy and satirize the absurdity of life by deconstructing language, notably in his one-act play *The Bald Soprano* (1950). As the curtain opens, Mr. and Mrs. Smith have finished dinner, which they discuss in the language of an English primer:

MR. SMITH: Well, it is nine p.m. We dined on soup, fish, potatoes cooked in lard, and English salad. The children drank English water. We ate well this evening. Because we live in the suburbs of London and our name is Smith.

Soon the maid announces the arrival of their guests, Mr. and Mrs. Martin. The disconnection between this couple is revealed as they discover that they are the parents of the same children, travel on the same train, and live in the same house. As they are discovering that they are married to each other, the door bell rings. The maid answers but no one is there. Finally Mr. Smith opens the door to the fire chief, who recites a poem in which everything catches fire, destroying property just as Ionesco's language demolishes sense. As the fire chief turns to leave, he asks "Apropos, and the bald soprano?" to which Mrs. Smith absurdly replies, "She still does her hair the same way." At this point, the play dissolves into chaos and ends with the characters chanting "It's this way, it's not that way."

In *Rhinoceros* (1959) Ionesco portrays totalitarianism as a disease that turns people into rhinoceroses. At first, the hero, Berenger, is afraid when he sees rhinoceroses running through the streets, but then he realizes that they are people who have been transformed into rhinoceroses. Every one except himself has changed, and he is distressed to discover that he is different from the others. He despairs that there is no horn growing on his forehead, that his skin has not thickened, and that he cannot roar. He cannot communicate with his former friends and becomes convinced that he is an ugly monster because he has remained human. In the end, however, he resolves to survive until he is the last man alive, and, in true existential fashion, refuses to capitulate.

THE UNITED STATES

The leading post-war American playwright and the author of over thirty plays, Arthur Miller (1915–2005) was not part of the Theater of the Absurd. He was born in New York City, where his father owned a clothing company that he lost during the Depression. Familiar with poverty, Miller worked in a variety of jobs after high school and attended the University of Michigan, where he began writing plays. His themes of alienation and self-delusion, as well as his commitment to social justice, reflect his lifelong engagement with politics.

In *Death of a Salesman* (1949) Miller dramatizes the failure of the American Dream. His hero Willy Loman (compare "Low-man") is actually an anti-hero and the epitome of unsuccess. He works on commission as a salesman and barely makes ends meet. Willy's illusory search for personal dignity and moral principle ruins his life, for he fails to see the reality that he is doomed to fail. He imagines that he and his sons, Hap and Biff, are destined for success, but he is actually dried up, incapable of change or insight, and constantly confused about time. In the end, Willy kills himself so that Biff can claim his life insurance.

In an effort to raise political awareness in his audience, Miller dramatized the outrages of McCarthy's HUAC in *The Crucible* (1953). He had been summoned to testify before the committee and was convicted of being a communist (although the verdict was overturned in 1957). The experience inspired *The Crucible*, which uses the seventeenth-century witch hunts in puritanical Salem, Massachusetts, as a metaphor for McCarthy's persecutions of American left-wing intellectuals during the 1950s.

In Salem in 1692 several people were convicted of witchcraft and hanged, solely on the evidence of hysterical adolescent girls. Miller's hero, who stands for truth, is John Proctor, who is accused of witchcraft and consorting with the devil by a girl with whom he had an affair. Also accused are the innocent slave, Tituba, and two housewives, Goody Good and Goody Osborne. The "proof" ranges from the presence of a mole on their skin to allegations of having stuck pins in dolls. Like the victims of McCarthyism, John Proctor is in the position of having to confess to save himself and also to accuse others, or to "name names," as it was known in the 1950s. The character of the hypocritical minister is modeled on McCarthy, and the suggestible, hysterical girls embody the anti-communist hysteria that swept America during the 1950s. In the end, John Proctor follows his conscience, refuses to confess to a lie, and is hanged.

In contrast to Miller's work, the early plays of Edward Albee (born 1928) were greatly influenced by the Theater of the Absurd. The title of *Who's Afraid of Virginia Woolf?* (1962) plays on the children's rhyme "Who's Afraid of the Big Bad Wolf?" and the feminism of Virginia Woolf (see Chapter 22). As with Ionesco's *Bald Soprano*, Albee's play focuses on two couples, but Albee is psychologically destructive, whereas Ionesco deconstructs language. Albee's characters, George and Martha, and their guests, Nick and Honey, spend the night drinking and systematically tearing away each other's façades and illusions:

GEORGE: Martha's tastes in liquor have come down . . . simplified over the years . . . crystallized. Back when I was courting Martha—well, I don't know if that's exactly the right word for it—but back when I was courting Martha . . .

MARTHA: Screw, sweetie!

GEORGE: At any rate, back when I was courting Martha, she'd order the damndest things! You wouldn't believe it! We'd go into a bar . . . you know, a *bar* . . . a whiskey, beer, and bourbon *bar* . . . and what she'd do would be, she'd screw up her face, think real hard, and come up with . . . brandy Alexanders, crème de cacao frappes, gimlets, flaming punch bowls . . . seven-layer things.

MARTHA: They were good . . . I liked them.

GEORGE: Real lady-like drinkies.

MARTHA: Hey, where's my rubbing alcohol?
GEORGE: But the years have brought to Martha a sense of essentials . . . the knowledge that cream is for coffee, lime juice for pies . . . and alcohol pure and simple . . . here you are, angel . . . for the pure and simple. For the mind's blind eye, the heart's ease, and the liver's craw. Down the hatch all.
MARTHA: Cheers, dears. You have a poetic nature, George . . . A Dylan Thomas-y quality that gets me right where I live.
GEORGE: Vulgar girl! With guests here!

MUSIC

Like literature and theater, music and dance were clearly affected by World War II. European politics and the war itself had caused a marked reduction in musical activity, and many prominent composers and musicians emigrated to Britain and the United States. The musical scene at the end of the war was diverse. Some composers pursued traditional forms such as the symphony and opera in styles based on tonality, while others experimented with atonality, using serial methods to control compositional elements such as pitch and volume. Some introduced untraditional elements, such as chance, as structuring principles for their works, while still others explored ways to produce sounds electronically. Non-Western elements entered the international musical language and, as in art, Minimalism was explored—in this case, using mesmeric repetition of musical motifs.

Musicals, too, showed a new interest in other cultures and in the era's social changes. Popular music developed exponentially as the technologies of recording and television took it to enormous audiences. Emerging from a fusion of folk music, country and western, and jazz, rock music became the music of youth culture. Sometimes it dealt with the political and social concerns of the time, but most often its theme was love.

DMITRY SHOSTAKOVICH: SYMPHONIES

Russian composer Dmitry Shostakovich (1906–1975) lived under dictatorships from the earliest years of his career, subject to the Soviet requirements for music that was inspiring, direct, and avoided "formalism." A leading Soviet composer of the mid-twentieth century, he produced some 150 works, including fifteen symphonies, fifteen string quartets, operas, concertos, and thirty-six film scores. The greatest symphonist of the period, he expressed a range of emotions, from epic grandeur to irony to personal anguish. His style is rooted in tradition and tonality, using dissonance for expressive effect.

When Germany invaded Russia in 1941, Leningrad was held under siege, inspiring Shostakovich to compose his "Leningrad" Symphony (No. 7), a vivid description of war that became an icon of resistance. He originally titled the movements "War," "Evocation," "Native Expanse," and "Victory." In his words, "I saw the struggle of the Russian people and tried to inculcate the pictures of their heroic deeds in my music." Symphony No. 8 (1943) is another war work, a meditation on the horrors of conflict, widely recognized as pessimistic and grieving.

In 1948, a tightening of Soviet artistic controls led to the denunciation of Shostakovich, along with other composers, for "formalistic perversions and anti-democratic tendencies in music," with specific reference to atonality and any dissonance that transformed music into "cacophony." As part of his "rehabilitation," Shostakovich avoided composing symphonies until after Stalin's death in 1953. The state required "Socialist Realism," and that is what he produced in Symphonies No. 11, "The Year 1905" (1957), and No. 12, "The Year 1917" (1961). Both conformist symphonies incorporated songs related to the Revolution. His next symphony, "Babi-Yar," was obliquely critical of the former Stalinist regime and had to be revised after the first performance in 1962. A setting of poems by Evgeny Yevtushenko (born 1933) for baritone soloist, male choir, and orchestra, it satirizes tyrants. The third movement identifies with the deprivation suffered by Russian women and the fourth is an enthusiastic endorsement of outspoken truth.

Despite its twentieth-century musical language, Shostakovich's output may be seen as a continuation of earlier traditions. Meanwhile other composers were taking entirely different musical paths.

THE EMERGENCE OF AN INTERNATIONAL AVANT GARDE

After World War II, young European composers were eager to learn about pre-war compositional developments that had been largely unavailable since the mid-1930s. Their creative minds did not merely build on inherited ideas and techniques, but—as in architecture and the other arts—sought to reformulate them, molding a post-war Modernist aesthetic.

While a prisoner of war, French composer and organist Olivier Messiaen (1908–1992) produced one of the most spiritual and significant works of the period—*Quatuor pour la fin du temps* (*Quartet for the End of Time*, 1940–1941) for violin, cello, clarinet, and piano—and performed it with fellow inmates to a huge audience of prisoners. Following the war, Messiaen turned initially to the symphonic tradition in the vigorous, appealing, ten-movement *Turangalîla-symphonie* (1946–1948) for orchestra, solo piano, and *ondes martinot* (an early electronic instrument). However, he then turned his back on tradition, choosing to explore implications of Schoenberg's twelve-tone technique, which manipulated pitch by organizing the twelve notes of the chromatic scale within a sequence or row (see Chapter 21). In *Mode de valeurs et d'intensités* (*Mode of Values and Intensities*, 1949) for solo piano, Messiaen applied this technique to other compositional parameters, devising twelve-member sets for pitch, rhythm, dynamics, etc.; the sets determined the organization of these elements within the work's atonal landscape. Although Messiaen did not continue on this compositional path in subsequent works, *Mode de valeurs* proved an influential prototype for his students, not least composer and conductor Pierre Boulez (born 1925).

In Paris in the late 1940s, Boulez studied with various teachers, including Messiaen, gaining a thorough understanding of atonality and the twelve-tone technique. But he soon developed an entirely new approach to composition, based on principles derived not from Schoenberg, but from the works of Schoenberg's student, Anton Webern (1883–1945). In the monumental, four-movement Second Piano Sonata (1946–1948), Boulez's explorations paved the way for the sounds and textures of the post-war avant garde; he rethought the function and interaction of musical elements, moving music toward a new, pointillistic soundscape.

In the year following the sonata's completion, Messiaen's *Mode de valeurs* was performed at the summer course in the German city of Darmstadt, an important gathering place for composers after the war. The work pushed composers toward serialism, a compositional method that satisfied their quest for organization and control. Serialism involved systematic manipulation of musical elements organized in series. In *Le marteau sans maître* (*The Hammer without a Master*, 1953–1955) Boulez set texts by René Char (1907–1988) for contralto and an ensemble of alto flute, viola, guitar, vibraphone, xylorimba (a large xylophone), and unpitched percussion. Now considered a keystone of twentieth-century music, this serial work treats timbre and rhythm with individuality, leading to a complex, percussive, yet static, sound world.

Serialism helped to establish the expectation that avant-garde composers would predetermine a compositional language for each work, illustrating the twentieth-century aesthetic that valued individuality as an essential feature of creativity. In parallel with this, musical analysis rose to prominence, providing necessary, if highly technical, keys to unlocking and explaining the foundations of works that were complex and often difficult to fathom. Others significant to the development of serialism include the German composer Karlheinz Stockhausen (born 1928) and the American Milton Babbitt (born 1916). Serialism dominated art music composition until the 1980s.

Electro-acoustic Music

Electro-acoustic music—music generated using electronic equipment—was a phenomenon of the post-war era, though there had been earlier experimentation. Its development was spurred on in the 1950s by the advent of magnetic tape as a recording medium. An early form, *musique concrète*, developed in Paris. Composers manipulated recorded sounds—for example, by splicing tapes together or by altering the speed of playback to raise or lower pitch. Around the same time, a studio for composing with entirely electronically generated sounds was established in Cologne, Germany. Stockhausen worked at this studio, creating *Gesang der Jünglinge* (*Song of the Youths*, 1956) for magnetic tape and five loudspeakers—the first major multi-track work, noted for using spatialization (the placement of sound in space) as a compositional element. The voice of a boy soloist, singing the German version of the Christian canticle "O all ye works of the Lord, bless ye the Lord," merges with electronically generated sounds. Stockhausen reduces the text to individual syllables and sounds, experimenting with sound textures as language fades in and out of comprehensibility.

Aleatory Music and Chance

Aleatory music, like Dada, uses randomness (chance) as a major principle. Developing in the post-war era and closely associated with the American composer John Cage (1912–1992), this approach owes much to his interest in Eastern philosophies—in particular, the Zen Buddhist notion of adapting to the world rather than shaping it. In contrast to serialism and electro-acoustic music, in which composers increased control over their works, aleatory music aimed to reduce composer control. Thus in Cage's *Music of Changes* (1951) a coin is tossed to decide the sequence of notes, their duration, and so on. And *Imaginary Landscape No. 4* (1951) is scored for twelve radio sets, ensuring different collections of sounds at every performance. The concept is taken to an extreme in *4' 33"* (1952), during which the performer makes no sound at all, thus framing sounds of the performance environment. Cage demonstrates that all sounds may be understood as music, even those normally regarded as noise—coughing in the audience, or car horns outside—sensitizing listeners to their surroundings and to the "art" that is the fabric of life.

Opera

In the field of opera, post-war trends were as diverse as in other areas of music composition. The Italian-American Gian Carlo Menotti (born 1911) was influenced by the *verismo* of Puccini (see Chapter 19), writing tuneful, often tragic, works steeped in the experiences and emotions of everyday interactions. His best-known opera was also the first created for television. *Amahl and the Night Visitors* (1951) has become a Christmas classic in the United States, telling of a night during the three Magi's journey to Bethlehem to see the new-born Jesus. In later works, he continued to explore the developing medium of television as a means of disseminating and popularizing opera.

British composer Benjamin Britten (1913–1976) composed in a tonally based, but highly individual, style. His operas are among the most performed by a twentieth-century composer, and he also composed the well-known *Young Person's Guide to the Orchestra* (1946), song cycles, string quartets, and the powerful *War Requiem* (1961). His first major opera, *Peter Grimes* (1945), tells the story of a visionary man condemned by society for his uncontrollable violence. A number of themes —the social outsider, childhood innocence, community trials, and individual justice, themes which may be interpreted in relation to Britten's experiences as a homosexual in an unaccepting society—recur in many of his later operas. These include *Billy Budd* (1951), based on a menacing short story by Herman Melville; *A Midsummer Night's Dream* (1960), after Shakespeare; and *Death in Venice* (1973), based on Thomas Mann's novella about an aging, isolated writer and his obsession with a young boy. To retain control over performances of his works, Britten co-founded a chamber opera company, the English Opera Group, for which he composed the allegorical post-war work *The Rape of Lucretia* (1946); the comic opera *Albert Herring* (1947); and *The Turn of the Screw* (1954), based on the Henry James story of childhood fantasy and the allure of evil.

The eclectic, interdisciplinary works of American producer Robert Wilson (born 1941) combine elements of Surrealism and Minimalism with popular, classical, and non-Western music. He came to New York from Texas in the 1960s and studied painting and design, dance, theater, and opera. Wilson regards each production as both an artistic installation and a dramatic musical event. In 1976 he produced the five-hour-long *Einstein on the Beach*, a non-narrative, four-act opera inspired by Nevil Shute's novel *On the Beach*, about the last two survivors of a nuclear explosion. Invoking stream of consciousness, Wilson projected filmed segments of Einstein's life onto a backdrop. Mathematic signs visible during the final scene (figure **23.34**) allude to Einstein's theories and his opposition to the nuclear arms race.

The opera's music was composed by Philip Glass (born 1937) and choreography was by Lucinda Childs (born 1940). Four actors with speaking roles were accompanied by chamber chorus, synthesizers, saxophones, bass clarinet, piccolo, and flutes. The hypnotic quality of Childs' choreography married well with Glass's repetitive, Minimalist music. Glass had worked with Indian sitar player and composer Ravi Shankar (born 1920), learning Eastern techniques that he applied to his compositions. His conception of Minimalism involved repetition of short, tonally based chordal patterns within insistent rhythms. Minimalism was formulated in the mid-1960s by young American composers seeking to remove barriers that separated music from the other arts and to make simple sounds the focus of music. The key element is repetition, of motif, rhythm, or chord, within unvarying tempo and with minute changes perceptible only over time.

Einstein on the Beach was the first of a trilogy of Glass's operas about men who changed the world in which they lived through the power of their ideas. The second was *Satyagraha* (1980), setting a text adapted from the *Bhagavad Gita*, exploring Gandhi's development of non-violent political protest. The trilogy ends with *Akhnaten* (1984), a series of tableaux describing the rise, reign, and fall of the Egyptian pharaoh. In the Listening Selection, note the haunting, mystical sound created by the fluid texture, with constant movement overlying monotonous chords that supply a regular beat. The essence of this music is its texture; there is little melody, the harmony is static, and the instruments circle repeatedly around one pitch.

MUSIC LISTENING SELECTION

Glass, *Akhnaten*, dance from Act 2, scene 3. Ulster Orchestra, conductor Takuo Yuasa, CD track 24

DANCE

The innovative American dancer and choreographer Alvin Ailey (1931–1989) combined jazz with modern and African dance and the black experience in America. Ailey was born in Texas and raised in South Carolina. He moved to New York in 1954 and studied with Martha Graham. In 1958 he founded the Alvin Ailey American Dance Theater, which he directed from 1958 until his death. His signature work, *Revelations* (1960) (figure **23.35**), exemplifies his original choreography and willingness to experiment with new dance forms. Altogether Ailey created seventy-nine ballets, and after his death, Judith Jamison (born 1943) continued his innovative productions as the artistic director of the company.

23.34 Robert Wilson, Philip Glass, and Lucinda Childs, final scene of *Einstein on the Beach*, 1976.

23.35 Scene from *Revelations* by Alvin Ailey, 1960, "Rocka My Soul in the Bosom of Abraham."

MUSICALS

Musical theater in the 1950s continued the trend set by *Oklahoma!* (see Chapter 22) toward substantial plots and integrated works. Characters and dialogue needed to be credible, and it became increasingly important to have a cooperative team of composer, lyricist, director, choreographer, and orchestrator.

Pre-World-War II plots were generally set in America, but after the war demand for variety led to foreign locations. Rodgers and Hammerstein's *South Pacific* (1949), for example, was about GIs in the Pacific islands, while *The King and I* (1951), inspired by the novel *Anna and the King of Siam*, tells of a nineteenth-century English tutor hired to teach the Siamese king and his children about the West. Lavish post-war musicals included *Brigadoon* (1947) by Alan Jay Lerner and Frederick Loewe, about an idyllic town in the highlands of Scotland, and *My Fair Lady* (1956), based on George Bernard Shaw's *Pygmalion* (see Chapter 21).

In 1957 Leonard Bernstein (1918–1990) pioneered the tragic musical with *West Side Story*, a modern version of *Romeo and Juliet*. Bernstein substituted gang warfare on the New York streets for the rival families of Shakespeare's Verona. The Montagues became the Anglo Jets gang, while the Capulets were the rival Puerto Ricans. An exciting dance scene involving both gangs is featured in the Listening Selection, with music based on the Latin American mambo, a syncopated pair dance that features kicks and twists.

MUSIC LISTENING SELECTION
Bernstein, *West Side Story*, "Mambo." Nashville Symphony Orchestra, conductor Kenneth Schermerhorn, CD track 23

The rock musical (see Rock Music below) developed in the late 1960s. *Hair* (subtitled *American Tribal Love-Rock Musical*) by Galt MacDermot, Gerome Ragni, and James Rado, was first performed in 1967. Its hero, loosely modeled on the Dionysian image of the Greek wine god, embodies an ideal of hippie culture, rejecting convention, ignoring the work ethic, denouncing the Vietnam War, and advocating universal love and the use of hallucinogenic drugs. Songs like "The Age of Aquarius" reflect the appeal of a future without war, free of bourgeois morality and restrictive social conventions.

In 1970 British composer Andrew Lloyd Webber (born 1948) and lyricist Tim Rice (born 1944) staged *Jesus Christ Superstar*, about Jesus' seven last days. Webber challenged traditions of Christian patriarchy by giving Mary Magdalene a prominent role in Christ's life. Judas, the narrator, denounces Jesus, but then realizes that God has tricked him into making Jesus a martyr. Judas hangs himself—and Jesus becomes a superstar.

POPULAR MUSIC

RHYTHM AND BLUES In the 1940s and 1950s, the migration of African-American musicians to northern cities—especially Chicago—led to new styles of urban blues (see Chapter 21). The gritty, urban, electric blues music of Muddy Waters (1915–1983) developed alongside the more commercial **rhythm and blues**. This synthesized blues forms with popular song formats more oriented toward the mass media and was produced by, among others, Ray Charles (1930–2004) and Louis Jordan (1908–1975). Rhythm and blues thrived in the 1940s and 1950s, mostly as performed for urban black audiences, although a few artists, such as Muddy Waters, subsequently developed followings among white youth and helped inspire early rock and roll. Like earlier forms of blues, rhythm and blues featured lyrics about hard times, bad luck, and the pleasures and charms of the hard-drinking, womanizing "hootchie-kootchie man."

The 1960s saw great social ferment in the African-American community, with corresponding changes in music. The civil rights era and the increasing movement of blacks into the middle classes inspired young African Americans to reject the blues and their associated values of fatalism, passivity, and resolute hedonism. A new music, called **soul**, arose. Though commercial rather than political in orientation, it expressed the buoyant optimism of the era, in a manner that also appealed to white teenagers on a mass level. It adopted both specific musical features and an upbeat spirit from the gospel music that had thrived in African-American churches for several decades. Soul music comprised a variety of styles, from the hard-driving, blues-inflected music of "shouters" like James Brown (born 1928) to the softer, more pop-oriented "blue-eyed soul" of the Detroit-based Motown label, as performed by groups like the Four Tops, Temptations, and the Supremes.

ROCK MUSIC **Rock music** has dominated Western popular music since the 1950s. Mixing features of rhythm and blues, gospel music, and jazz with elements of country and western music, it arose as part of the post-war youth culture movement. Heavily dependent on the electric guitar and amplified sound, rock has developed its own harmonic practices, incorporating and elaborating elements of blues and Western functional tonality while using a variety of song formats, including versions of the familiar thirty-two bar *AABA* form prevalent in earlier Tin Pan Alley music.

Rock and roll was the earliest form of rock. It emerged in the early 1950s as the preferred music of a younger baby-boom generation empowered by their purchasing power, the eager attention of the entertainment industry, and a desire to break free from what they perceived as the dull music and sexual inhibitions of their parents. While drawing from country and western music, young rock and rollers found particular inspiration in black rhythm and blues, with its sense of rebellious hedonism (just as black audiences were rejecting this music). Many early rock and roll numbers were essentially cleaned-up versions of songs by Muddy Waters, Howlin' Wolf, and other bluesmen. Nevertheless, rock soon developed its own conventions and aesthetics, and a great variety of sub-styles.

The group Bill Haley and the Comets had the first rock and roll hit with "Rock Around the Clock" (1954). Elvis Presley (1935–1977), with his energy, directness, and sultry voice, dominated the genre as the king of rock and roll with hits such as "Love Me Tender" (1956) and "Jailhouse Rock" (1957) (see Box, p. 695).

Early rock music was mostly an American phenomenon, but in 1964 the Beatles made a famous appearance on American television, heralding the "British Invasion" of rock by bands such as the Rolling Stones and the Who. With the Beatles, rock music became at once artistic, innovative, eclectic, and commercially appealing. The group consisted of Paul McCartney (born 1942), John Lennon (1940–1980), George Harrison (1943–2001), and Ringo Starr (born 1940). The Beatles' engaging personalities made them enormously popular, and their irreverence was poetic enough to be acceptable to most listeners. Their 1967 album *Sgt. Pepper's Lonely Hearts Club Band* illustrated how artistically diverse, sophisticated, and original rock had become. The music of the Beatles was particularly enjoyed for its clever and thematically varied lyrics, memorable melodies, and "art-rock" complexity. The theme song for the animated film *Yellow Submarine* (1968), with music by the Beatles, easily lent itself to being interpreted as drug culture and the wish to escape from reality:

> We all live in a yellow submarine,
> Yellow submarine, yellow submarine
> As we live a life of ease
> Everyone of us has all we need
> Sky of blue and sea of green
> In our yellow submarine.

Their song "Lucy in the Sky with Diamonds" (note the initials LSD) made use of fantasy images associated with psychedelic drugs:

> Picture yourself in a boat on a river,
> with tangerine trees and marmalade skies.
> Somebody calls you, you answer quite slowly,
> A girl with kaleidoscope eyes.

In the 1960s such songs became known as psychedelic rock, centered in San Francisco. Also imbued with the drug culture and anti-war sentiment was the neo-folk-rock protest music of the 1960s. Bob Dylan (born 1941) (figure **23.36**) was one of the most original musicians of the era, and the most popular of the neo-folk "singer-songwriters," who composed their own material, singing incisive, poetic lyrics while accompanying themselves on the guitar. In the 1965 "Mr. Tambourine Man" (a slang term for a drug pusher), the singer craves drug-induced oblivion—"take me disappearin' through the smoke rings of my mind"—while in "Blowin' in the Wind" (1963), Dylan protests against war:

> How many roads must a man walk down
> Before you call him a man?
> Yes, 'n' how many seas must a white dove sail
> Before she sleeps in the sand?
> Yes, 'n' how many times must the cannon balls fly
> Before they're forever banned?
> The answer, my friend, is blowin' in the wind,
> The answer is blowin' in the wind.
>
> (stanza 1)

Other rock styles of the late 1960s included country rock, exemplified by the group Buffalo Springfield; Latin rock, made famous by the band Santana; and hard rock, with its thunderous volume and virtuoso guitar solos.

23.36 Milton Glaser, *Bob Dylan*, 1966. Columbia Records poster. This poster is typical of the innovative graphic designs of Milton Glaser (born 1929). The flat, colorful patterning of Dylan's hair corresponds to the poetic, fluid rhythms of his songs and also reflects the psychedelic aesthetic popular in the 1960s.

In the 1970s, rock and soul lost some of the socio-political fervor associated with 1960s counter-culture, protest music, and the civil rights movement. Yet American popular music continued to diversify and evolve, with audiences often dividing into distinct groups. Young blacks and many working-class urban whites gravitated toward the new styles of African-American popular music—especially disco, which forsook the rough, improvisatory rock ethos in favor of a slick, ostinato-based sound suited to the dance floor. Reaffirming the rebellious spirit of early rock was punk, as performed by groups like the Sex Pistols. It emerged in the latter 1970s as a self-consciously abrasive, amateurish garage-band music, with corresponding styles of attire and demeanor calculated to outrage outsiders. New forms of studied flamboyance, celebrating androgyny and stylized "decadence," marked the stage personae of glam rock performers like David Bowie (born 1947). Some white Americans and British—particularly those alienated by these trends—turned for inspiration to Jamaican reggae, with its distinctively catchy rhythms. Especially as performed by Bob Marley (1945–1981), reggae seemed to revive the 1960s commitment to justice and liberation. It became the first music from the developing world to enjoy popularity in the West, opening the way for other "world beat" musics such as African *soukous* and French Caribbean *zouk*.

Another sub-genre of rock was heavy metal. Inspired by the British band Led Zeppelin and Jimi Hendrix (1942–1970), it cultivated an aesthetic of exuberant (primarily male) power and mastery, especially as personified in the figure of the virtuoso electric guitarist. Heavy metal continued to evolve and flourish through the 1980s alongside less commercial "alternative" rock, played on college radio stations, and various forms more slanted toward the mainstream mass media.

The most distinctive musical development of the years around 1980 was the emergence in New York City's black community of hip-hop, or rap, which was also associated with break-dancing and, to some extent, subway graffiti (including the early art works of Basquiat). Rap emerged from parties in the Bronx at which disc jockeys used turntables as musical instruments, repeating instrumental "break" passages and shouting snippets of verse over them. It soon went on to become phenomenally popular among both white and black American youth, as performed by white as well as black artists, then evolving into an international genre taken up in many different languages.

FILM

The film industry expanded after World War II, and new cinematic techniques began to be used. Science fiction, westerns, horror, crime, fantasy, and Surrealism continued to be popular, and new genres emerged. Neorealism first appeared in Italy and dealt mainly with the poverty of the post-war period. Other genres include the **art film**, in which a particular style of film-making became associated with a particular director. The French word *auteurs* (literally "authors") is often used to describe the **New Wave** (*Nouvelle Vague*) directors of the 1950s and 1960s. Film has remained part of mass culture, often reflecting social and political concerns.

ITALY: FEDERICO FELLINI

A pioneer of Neorealism, Federico Fellini (1920–1993) produced *La Strada* (*The Street*, 1954), a film that went beyond Neorealism to deal with universal themes of love and fidelity, and abandonment and betrayal. Set in post-war Italy, *La Strada* is a visually poetic story about the circus strongman Zampano (played by Anthony Quinn) and Gelsomina (played by Fellini's wife, Giulietta Masina), the child-like woman he buys to be his assistant (figure **23.37**).

23.37 *left* **Federico Fellini, scene from *La Strada*, 1954.** This scene shows the self-satisfied and cocky Zampano. His narcissistic self-confidence is reflected in his pose and expression as he displays his physique. His silk shirt (held by Gelsomina) contrasts with Gelsomina's old, ill-fitting coat. Although made-up to appear cheerful, her whimsical expression and broad gesture suggest that she is uncomfortable with her part, both on stage and off.

SWEDEN: INGMAR BERGMAN

One of the greatest film *auteurs* is the Swedish director Ingmar Bergman (born 1918). The son of a Lutheran clergyman, Bergman directed both comic and tragic films from the 1940s and is still active in film and theater. He often wrote his films in novel form before transposing them into screenplays. Many of his productions draw

23.38 Ingmar Bergman, Death playing chess with a knight, from *The Seventh Seal*, 1957.

23.39 Satyajit Ray, scene from *Pather Panchali*, 1955.

on Swedish history and legend as well as on contemporary society. In *The Seventh Seal* (1957) he addresses universal subjects, such as life, death, and religion. The story revolves around a chess game between Death and a knight (figure **23.38**), a game the knight is destined to lose. Set in the Middle Ages, in an atmosphere of plague, fear of the devil, and religious intolerance, the film conveys the relentless isolation of death, for which the stark, wintry Swedish landscape is an appropriate background. In this scene the contest—"to the death"—between the players is reinforced by their intense gazes and the dramatic sky. The fact that chess is itself a medieval game traditionally played with black and white pieces corresponds to both the context and the medium of the film.

INDIA: SATYAJIT RAY

Like Japan (see Chapter 22), India had a thriving film industry from the 1940s, but it was little known internationally. Then, with the work of Satyajit Ray (1921–1992) in the 1950s, Indian cinema caught the attention of the world.

Ray had studied painting and worked in advertising in Calcutta, where he founded a film society. He met European filmmakers working in India and was influenced by Neorealism. Ray's most famous work is the Apu Trilogy—*Pather Panchali* (1955), *Aparajito* (1956), and *The World of Apu* (1959)—which follows the life of an impoverished Bengali boy from childhood to adulthood (figure **23.39**). Like the European Neorealists, Ray confronts poverty and its effects directly, and his themes include East–West cultural conflicts, greed, the permanence of nature, and the inevitability of death. He worked mainly with amateur actors, and his local settings are enriched by symbolic meanings embedded in everyday scenes.

From the 1970s the Indian film industry has produced more films than any country. Its base is Mumbai—formerly Bombay, hence the term Bollywood.

FRANCE: THE NEW WAVE

The New Wave (*Nouvelle Vague*) films of François Truffaut (1932–1984) and Jean-Luc Godard (born 1930) are products of the protest culture of the 1950s and 1960s and portray characters overcome with a sense of *ennui*. Toward the end of the New Wave movement the director Eric Rohmer (born 1920) made a series of films in which conversation laced with psychological undercurrents, rather than action, dominates.

Rohmer began making films in the 1940s but did not become widely known until 1969 with *My Night with Maud* (*Ma Nuit chez Maud*). It is a story of the middle class, told through characters conversing with each other about topics ranging from emotion to religion. Rohmer's *Claire's Knee* (*Le Genou de Claire*, 1970) is a straightforward, low-key, humorous psychological portrayal of a man's obsession—almost a fetish—with Claire's knee. In the scene shown in figure **23.40**), Jérome's passion for knees is contrasted with Claire's apparent unawareness. Playing on the traditional role of the

23.40 Eric Rohmer, scene from *Claire's Knee*, 1970.

ambivalent adolescent girl whose sexuality is just beginning to emerge, Rohmer shows her looking away from Jérome while also making her knee available to his gaze.

THE UNITED STATES

Among the best-known film-makers working in the United States was the British-born Alfred Hitchcock (1899–1980), who made most of his psychological crime films in Hollywood. Howard Hawks (1896–1977) was a successful director of westerns, comedies, musicals, and dramas.

After America landed the first man on the moon in 1969, films began to reflect the interest in space. One of the first of these was *Star Wars* (1977), directed by George Lucas (born 1944), which launched the inter-galactic morality epic. Other successful movies by Lucas include *American Graffiti* (1973), and the sequels to *Star Wars*: *The Empire Strikes Back* (1980) and *Return of the Jedi* (1983). *Star Wars* is a mythic tale for the space age, summing up the fear of annihilation and confronting audiences with conflicts between good and evil: an evil empire takes control of our galaxy and threatens to destroy the planet earth. Computer animation enhances the special effects, as the characters struggle with good and evil within themselves. This is embodied in the text from the film that has become a household phrase: "May the force be with you."

Figure **23.41** shows the villain, Darth Vader, dueling with the force of good, represented by Obi-Wan Kenobi. Lucas uses conventional visual techniques to portray the figures as they battle with light-swords. The music is synchronized to reflect changes in character and situation. Darth Vader's aggressive, menacing quality is revealed in the films mainly through martial music and low trombones. As he dies while saving Luke Skywalker in the final film of the trilogy, the music becomes softer and slower. Stringed instruments and harps are used to symbolize salvation.

23.42 E.T. created by Carlo Rambaldi for *E.T.*, 1982.

23.41 George Lucas, scene from *Star Wars*, episode 4, in which Darth Vader duels with Ben (Obi-Wan) Kenobi (played by Alec Guinness).

Costumes and physiognomy also identify personality. Darth Vader wears the black leather and steel helmet associated with Hitler's Storm Troopers. Here he is shown in back view, making him simultaneously unseen and sinister. In contrast, the humanity of Obi-Wan Kenobi is shown through his gentle features. The viewer recognizes that his strength comes from inner moral "force" as well as from intelligence and skill. Obi-Wan Kenobi assumes the stance of a Samurai warrior and literally "faces down" his evil opponent.

Another American film-maker, Steven Spielberg (born 1946), made his reputation with the summer-resort horror movie *Jaws* (1975). He collaborated with George Lucas on the archaeological adventure *Raiders of the Lost Ark* (1981) and its sequels. Spielberg's interest in science fiction and his understanding of child psychology is apparent in his enormously successful *E.T.: The Extra-Terrestrial* of 1982 (figure **23.42**).

Thematic Parallels

Heartthrobs of Western History

After World War II the American media created the phenomenon of the "pop star," launching certain singers onto a global stage. But throughout Western history many kinds of performers have captured the public imagination. The so-called "heartthrob" is a male performer whose appeal, usually to a female audience, is so great that he becomes a cultural hero.

In ancient Rome (see Chapter 7) gladiators who fought in the Colosseum fulfilled the role of male icon. Although most were slaves, aristocrats and even emperors staged combats in which they participated, capitalizing on the gladiators' enormous popularity. These fighters catered to the Roman spectators' thirst for violence and displays of physical strength. An inscription in the amphitheater at Pompeii records that one Publius Ostorius was victorious in fifty-one contests and well paid for his efforts. Another wall inscription reports that Celadus was the "sigh" and glory of the girls.

From the mid-seventeenth century, **castrati**—males castrated before their voices changed (usually between the age of six and eight) so they could sing with a soprano or alto voice as adults—were "all the rage" among music lovers in parts of western Europe. Their powerful voices offered a quality with huge appeal, applauded and rewarded by kings and popes.

The Catholic Church was ambivalent toward *castrati*, excommunicating those who performed the castrations but, at the same time, enjoying performances of the singers. *Castrati* performed regularly in church choirs, especially in Italy. Pope Clement VIII (papacy 1592–1605) approved this form of mutilation on the grounds that it helped men sing "for the glory of God," and it was not until 1903 that *castrati* were formally banned from the papal choir.

From the time of Sixtus V (papacy 1585–1590), women were not allowed to perform on stage, and so *castrati* were necessary for female roles in Baroque opera. Composers such as Monteverdi and Handel (see Chapter 16) included in their *opera seria* heroic male roles set for high voices, to exploit the vocal strength and agility of the *castrati*. In France, however, the practice was not endorsed and *castrati* did not appear in performances there.

Like modern pop stars, many of the most successful *castrati* were known for their temperamental behavior, and some commanded enormous salaries. One of the most famous was the Italian Carlo Broschi (1705–1782), called the "Divine Farinelli." He made his public debut at the age of fifteen, singing for the birthday of the Habsburg empress. From 1724 he toured the European courts, adored for his voice's beauty and wide range, his breath control, and the agility of his ornamentation—but not for his stiff acting. At thirty-two he retired from the stage to perform exclusively for King Philip V of Spain.

With the rise of film in the early twentieth century, the "matinée idol" was born. America's first was Rudolph Valentino (1895–1926), admired as a "Latin lover." Born in Castellaneta, Italy, Valentino made his way to New York, where he worked as a dancer and a waiter, and then to Hollywood. He achieved star status with his performance in the silent film *The Four Horsemen of the Apocalypse* (1921). His soft, handsome face, dark eyes, and piercing gaze, combined with a sensual tango performance, created a seductive aura of romance.

Valentino's best-known film today is *The Sheik* (1921), the story of an Arab chief who kidnaps an English socialite. They come to admire each other, resolving in part the conflict between their cultures. When Valentino died at the age of thirty-one, the world went into mourning.

In the United States the 1950s witnessed the rise of the "rock star." In particular, Elvis Presley became one of the world's best-known performers. His energetic rock and roll music and the sexuality of his gyrations drove audiences wild. By the time of his death, he had been in thirty-three films, made numerous appearances on television, and sold over a billion records worldwide. Despite being the biggest-selling artist in history, Elvis died in his early forties from a combination of obesity and drug abuse. His home, the Graceland mansion in Memphis, Tennessee, remains a major tourist attraction, and in 1993 he was commemorated with a U.S. postage stamp that has sold more than any other.

Early death or premature retirement seem occupational hazards of being a "heartthrob" in Western culture. As with the Romantic poets (see Chapter 18), who also died young—or the Homeric hero Achilles, who chose early death and fame over long life and obscurity (see Chapter 4)—there is an element of "romance" in preserving the aura of youth by never growing old. As a result, these popular idols remain eternally youthful in our imaginations.

E.T. reflects the space age from the point of view of a child's fantasy. It is the story of an alien creature, E.T., who has been left behind on earth by his space ship. He spends the movie getting to know a little boy, Elliot, who learns to love and understand him, as he tries to find his way back home. In the scene shown here E.T. gazes into space and raises his finger, which lights up when he receives a communication from his planet. His friendship with Elliot transcends not only cultures, but planets. Despite the differences between E.T. and the human race, he and Elliot form a bond.

The film is shot from the child's low vantage point, accentuating the different ways children and adults perceive the world. The adults do not understand E.T. any more than they believe in a child's imaginary friend. Driven by fear, they try to kill the alien, but Elliot and his companions fight to save him. In the end, good wins out, as Elliot bicycles through the air, returning E.T. to his spaceship.

The end of World War II in 1945, like the end of World War I in 1918, led to a period of recovery and creative expansion. New social awareness led to the civil rights and women's movements, both of which brought about significant cultural changes but also created domestic unrest, particularly in the United States. With the end of the Cold War and the dismantling of the Berlin Wall in 1989, globalization accelerated and, aided by the development of the Internet, affected all aspects of politics, society, and the arts. As the world advanced toward the twenty-first century, new conflicts arose and old conflicts persisted—especially the tension between Islamic fundamentalism and Western culture.

KEY TERMS

action painting a technique of applying paint to canvas that includes dripping, spraying, and throwing.

aleatory music a post-war musical style that uses chance or randomness as a prime principle.

apartheid the policy of racial "separate development" pursued in South Africa from 1948.

art film a term used to describe films that often have greater artistic value and innovation than "commercial" productions.

black humor humor with a macabre quality.

castrato from the late sixteenth through the nineteenth century, a male castrated before his voice changed (usually between the age of six and eight) so he could sing with a soprano or alto voice as an adult.

Comecon (Council for Mutual Economic Assistance) the organization formed in 1949 to improve trade between the Soviet Union and its eastern European satellite countries.

Cominform (Communist Information Bureau) an organization formed in 1947 to coordinate the activity of Communist Parties throughout Europe.

détente a thawing of international tension.

domino theory the notion (originating in the Eisenhower administration) that countries in Southeast Asia would fall to the communists like dominoes if not stopped by the West.

electro-acoustic music music generated using electronic equipment.

glasnost literally "openness" in Russian; the policy introduced in the 1980s of permitting criticism of the Communist Party in the Soviet Union.

happening an improvised theatrical event with an appearance of spontaneity, popular in the 1960s.

magic realism a film-making and literary style in which miraculous and imaginary events are presented as if they are real.

New Wave a term (derived from the French expression *nouvelle vague*) denoting a group of new, non-traditional film-makers.

perestroika literally "restructuring" in Russian; the attempt in the 1980s to reform the Soviet economy.

rhythm and blues an African-American style of urban popular music that flourished in the 1940s and 1950s, synthesizing aspects of blues with popular song format; from the 1970s, the term denotes African-American popular song (as opposed to rap) in general.

rock and roll the earliest form of rock music, which had its classic period from 1954 to 1959.

rock music a style of popular music heavily dependent on the electric guitar and amplified sound that has dominated the West since the 1950s, combining features of rhythm and blues, gospel music, jazz, and country and western music.

semiotics the study of signs and symbols in a range of fields, especially language, which includes Structuralism, Post-Structuralism, and Deconstruction.

soul music a type of African-American commercial popular music that flourished mostly in the 1960s, with elements derived from gospel music.

KEY QUESTIONS

1. Cite examples of works of art, literature, or music that explore the following:
   a. existential anxiety
   b. the Nuclear Age
   c. the Cold War era
   d. the civil rights movement
   e. the feminist movement
2. What social and political visions did Gandhi and Martin Luther King share?
3. What are the goals of performance and Earth art? What media are used in these genres?
4. What elements of Postmodernism characterize the works of Charles Moore, Philip Johnson, and I. M. Pei?
5. Writers concerned about problems of colonialism explored the theme of domination of one culture over another. What other themes did they explore?

SUGGESTED READING

Alloway, Lawrence. *American Pop Art*. New York: Whitney Museum, 1974.
- The style of the 1960s.

——. *Topics in American Art Since 1945*. New York: W.W. Norton, 1975.
- A general survey.

Ansprenger, F. *The Dissolution of Colonial Empires*. London: Routledge, 1989.
- A general survey.

Baker, Kenneth. *Minimalism*. New York: Abbeville Press, 1990.
- A survey of the style.

Brinkley, Douglas. *Rosa Parks*. New York: Viking, 2000.
- A short biography, part of a series by well-known authors on famous figures.

Crow, Thomas. *The Rise of the Sixties: American and European Art in the Era of Dissent*. New York: Harry N. Abrams, 1996.
- The art of the 1960s in its political context.

Darwin, J. *Britain and Decolonization: The Retreat from Empire in the Postwar World*. London: Palgrave Macmillan, 1988.
- An accessible account of the decline of the British Empire.

Ellman, M., and V. Kontorovich. *The Disintegration of the Soviet Economic System*. London: Routledge, 1992.
- A discussion of factors that caused tension in the Soviet Union.

Erikson, Erik. *Gandhi's Truth*. New York: W. W. Norton, 1970.
- A biography of the Indian leader.

Geldzahler, Henry. *New York Painting and Sculpture: 1940–1970*. New York: E. P. Dutton, 1969.
- A discussion of Abstract Expressionism and Pop Art.

Lucie-Smith, Edward. *Art in the Seventies*. Ithaca, NY: Cornell University Press, 1980.
- Art styles in the 1970s.

——. *Movements in Art since 1945*. London: Thames and Hudson, 1984.
- A general survey.

——. *Art in the Eighties*. London: Phaidon Press, 1985.
- Style in the 1980s.

Rubin, William (ed.). *Primitivism in 20th-Century Art*, 2 vols. New York: The Museum of Modern Art, 1984.
- Essays by major scholars on the influence of non-Western art on the Western avant garde.

Sandler, Irving. *American Art of the 1960s*. New York: Harper and Row, 1989.
- A study of American art styles in the 1960s.

Walker, M. *The Cold War and the Making of the Modern World*. London: Vintage Books, 1994.
- A recent study of the effects of the Cold War.

SUGGESTED FILMS

1948 *Arch of Triumph* (based on Remarque), dir. Lewis Milestone
1953 *Gentlemen Prefer Blondes*, dir. Howard Hawks
1954 *Brigadoon*, dir. Vincente Minnelli
1954 *Dial M for Murder*, dir. Alfred Hitchcock
1954 *La Strada*, dir. Federico Fellini
1955 *Pather Panchali*, dir. Satyajit Ray
1956 *Aparajito*, dir. Satyajit Ray
1956 *The King and I*, dir. Walter Lang
1957 *The Seventh Seal*, dir. Ingmar Bergman
1958 *Apur Sansar* (*The World of Apu*), dir. Satyajit Ray
1958 *South Pacific*, dir. Joshua Logan
1960 *Breathless* (*A bout de souffle*), dir. Jean-Luc Godard
1960 *La Dolce Vita*, dir. Federico Fellini
1960 *Shoot the Pianist*, dir. François Truffaut
1961 *West Side Story*, dir. Robert Wise and Jerome Robbins
1962 *Jules et Jim*, dir. François Truffaut
1962 *The Manchurian Candidate*, dir. John Frankenheimer
1964 *My Fair Lady*, dir. George Cukor
1965 *Help!*, dir. Richard Lester
1966 *Who's Afraid of Virginia Woolf?*, dir. Mike Nicholls
1968 *Yellow Submarine*, dir. George Duning
1969 *My Night with Maud*, dir. Eric Rohmer
1969 *Satyricon*, dir. Federico Fellini
1970 *Claire's Knee*, dir. Eric Rohmer
1973 *American Graffiti*, dir. George Lucas
1975 *Jaws*, dir. Steven Spielberg
1977 *Star Wars* (*Star Wars IV: A New Hope*), dir. George Lucas
1979 *Hair*, dir. Milos Forman
1980 *The Empire Strikes Back*, dir. George Lucas
1981 *Raiders of the Lost Ark*, dir. Steven Spielberg
1982 *E.T.: The Extra-Terrestrial*, dir. Steven Spielberg
1982 *Gandhi*, dir. Richard Attenborough
1983 *Return of the Jedi* (*Star Wars VI: Return of the Jedi*), dir. George Lucas
1984 *The Killing Fields*, dir. Roland Joffé
1987 *The Last Emperor*, dir. Bernardo Bertolucci
2001 *Pollock*, dir. Ed Harris
2003 *The Quiet American* (based on Greene), dir. Phillip Noyce

24 After 1989

> "*Where are your monuments, your battles, martyrs? Where is your tribal memory? Sirs, in that gray vault. The sea. The sea has locked them up. The sea is history.*"
>
> (DEREK WALCOTT, "THE SEA IS HISTORY")

After the dissolution of the communist bloc in eastern Europe and the division of the Soviet Union into independent states in 1989–1990, the United States became the world's only superpower. The threat of nuclear war, which had been a defining feature of the Cold War, had begun to subside by the mid-1980s. Nevertheless, the 1990s and early years of the twenty-first century witnessed continuing discord, sometimes erupting into outright war.

The conflicts were of a new kind and posed new challenges to world peace. Ethnic and religious dissent destroyed the stability of the Balkans, the Middle East, and parts of Africa. However, the most alarming problem facing the twenty-first century is global terrorism, as growing Islamic fundamentalism causes conflicts between Muslim and non-Muslim states, as well as within the Muslim states themselves. Acts of terrorism by radical Muslims, motivated in part by a desire to expel American troops from Islamic countries, in part by opposition to the state of Israel, and in part by determination to impose Islamic theocracies and Islamic law on existing states, have polarized the world.

Technology continues to advance in the twenty-first century. Internet and cell-phone use make global communication more rapid and efficient, and space exploration continues, despite serious setbacks.

Health issues are also prominent, as famines ravage parts of the developing world. The AIDS crisis has become a global issue, raising questions of how much financial and medical assistance can and should be provided by the West and how cultural changes in the sexual practices of the developing world might improve the crisis. Medical researchers continue to confront new diseases, as bacteria mutate into new strains: outbreaks of SARS (Severe Acute Respiratory Syndrome) and avian flu in China have killed hundreds of people since 2002 and have had global economic repercussions. Scientists have warned of the possibility of imminent global epidemics. New strains of AIDS, resistant to the drugs developed to help control the disease, have also appeared.

Key Topics

Politics and Society

- AIDS
- Feminism
- Ecology and the environment
- Genetic manipulation
- Globalization
- Global terrorism

Ethnic Conflict

- Europe after the Cold War
- Détente
- Immigration
- Genocide

Postmodernism

- Architecture
- Digital installation
- Environmental alteration

Film

- Social commentary
- Special effects
- Animation

The Spirit of the Humanities

- Seamus Heaney
- Derek Walcott

TIMELINE	EUROPE	UNITED STATES, CANADA, AND LATIN AMERICA	MIDDLE EAST, ASIA, AND AFRICA
HISTORY AND CULTURE 	Lockerbie bombing by Muslim terrorists, Scotland, 1988 Reunification of Germany, 1990 Islamic uprisings in Chechnya, Bosnia, 1990s Walesa president of Poland, 1990 Yeltsin president of Russia, 1991 EC abolishes trade barriers, 1993 Putin president of Russia, 2000 Russia–NATO Council formed, 2002 Terrorism in Moscow, 2003, 2004 Euro adopted as currency by most European nations, 2004 Muslim terrorism: Madrid, 2004; London, 2005	U.S. world's only superpower Negotiations to end arms race concluded, 1991 Muslim terrorists attack World Trade Center in New York, September 11, 2001 Bush launches anti-terrorism policy, 2001 U.S. and U.K. invade Iraq, 2003	AIDS crisis, particularly in Africa Tokyo stock market crash, 1989 First Gulf War, 1991 Taliban in Afghanistan, 1990s–2001 Oslo Accords, 1993 Muslim terrorists attack U.S. embassies in East Africa, 1993, 1998; USS *Cole* in Yemen, 1995; Bali nightclub, 2003 Mandela elected president of South Africa, 1994 Second Gulf War, 2003 Tsunami in Asia, 2004 Congo, Africa, suffers outbreak of Marburg Disease, 2005
SCIENCE AND TECHNOLOGY 	Growth of communication; World Wide Web and cell-phone Ecology and environmental pollution a global concern U.S.S.R. launches Mir Space Station, 1986 Outbreak of BSE ("Mad Cow Disease") in Europe, 1990s Dolly the sheep cloned in Scotland, 1997 Kyoto Protocol on global warming, 2001	Human Genome Project, 1990 U.S. refuses to sign Kyoto Protocol, 2001 Late-term abortion prohibited, 2003	
ART 	Christo and Jeanne-Claude, *Wrapped Reichstag*, 1971–1995 Redl, *Shifting, Very Slowly*, 1998–1999 Eliasson, *Green River*, 2000	Serrano, *Blood Cross*, 1985 Haring, *Ignorance=Fear*, 1989 Holzer, *Untitled*, LED installations, Guggenheim Museum, New York, 1989–1990 Scott, *Women's House*, 1993 Barney, "Cremaster" series No. 4, *The Loughton Candidate*, 1994 Fifield, *Ghost Dancer Ascending*, 1995	Youhan, *Mao Voting*, 1993
ARCHITECTURE	Gehry, Guggenheim Museum, Bilbao, Spain, 1997	Stern, Feature Animation Building, Burbank, California, 1995	Pelli, Petronas Twin Towers, Kuala Lumpur, Malaysia, 1991–1997
FILM 	Boyle, *Trainspotting*, 1996	Jackson, *The Lord of the Rings* trilogy, 2001–2003 Disney, *Finding Nemo*, 2003	Zhang, *Red Sorghum*, 1987; *Jou dou*, 1990; *Raise the Red Lantern*, 1991; *House of Flying Daggers*, 2004 Barmak, *Osama*, 2003
LITERATURE	Grass, *The Tin Drum*, 1959; *Show Your Tongue*, 1988; *My Century*, 1999; *Crabwalk*, 2002 Heaney, "xix," 1991; translation: *Beowulf*, 1999	Atwood, *The Handmaid's Tale*, 1985; *Oryx and Crake*, 2003 Walcott, "The Sea is History," 1979; *Omeros*, 1990	Oe, *A Personal Matter*, 1964; *Hiroshima Notes*, 1965; *The Silent Cry*, 1967; *The Flaming Green Tree* trilogy, 1990s Coetzee, *Waiting for the Barbarians*, 1980; *Disgrace*, 1999 Ishiguro, *A Pale View of Hills*, 1982; *An Artist of the Floating World*, 1986; *The Remains of the Day*, 1989; *When We Were Orphans*, 2000 Roy, *The God of Small Things*, 1997 Jin, *Waiting*, 1999
THEATER	Stoppard, *Rosencrantz and Guildenstern are Dead*, 1966; *Arcadia*, 1993; *Indian Ink*, 1995 Heaney, *The Cure at Troy*, 1990 Churchill, *A Number*, 2002	Mamet, *Glengarry Glen Ross*, 1983; *Oleanna*, 1992 Wilson, *The Piano Lesson*, 1988; *Two Trains Running*, 1990 Kushner, *Angels in America*, 1993	
MUSIC		Zwilich, *Millennium Fantasy*, 1998 Adams, *El Niño*, 2000	

Video and digital art owe their existence to the new technologies. There is now an iconography of genetic mutation in painting and sculpture. In architecture, Postmodernism continues to flourish. Jazz has acquired respectability; rock and protest music have become widespread in the former Soviet Union and in Africa and Asia, while non-Western styles have infiltrated pop around the world. Increasing globalization has also affected classical music. Other issues include the redefinition of music in relation to everyday life. Themes of protest pervade works by leading poets, novelists, and playwrights. In general, as a result of the media, the Internet, and the constant reformulation of perceived canons, there is greater awareness of global literature, music, and film than ever before.

The opening quotation of this chapter is from the poem entitled "The Sea is History" (1979) by the Caribbean author Derek Walcott (born 1930). He alludes to the role of the sea in the history of African Americans, whose ancestors were brought to the United States in slave-ships, but he also means that history, like the sea, is a repository of time. History is recorded and remembered only in fragments, like debris surfacing from the depths of the ocean. And like the sea, history is fluid, dynamic, and continually changing, while at the same time repeating itself as it ebbs and flows to and from the shore. Similarly, the humanities are constantly evolving, as people allow their creativity to emerge from the depths of their imagination. As a mirror of human behavior, history reflects our capacity for creative thinking as well as for self-destruction. But the humanities, which are a tribute to the tradition of humanism, embody advances made by the human race since the dawn of history.

A modern advocate of the Classical tradition, which he integrates seamlessly with his Caribbean heritage, Walcott is the author of many works of poetry. Among these is his epic poem Omeros *(1990), which merges the Homeric epics with his own love of the sea and a cast of local characters named after those found in Homer. The very title* Omeros *implies a historical, poetic, and psychological process of human continuity and creativity. Walcott's final chapter of* Omeros *recalls the opening lines of the* Iliad*:*

I sang of quiet Achilles, Afolabe's son,
who never ascended an elevator,
who had no passport, since the horizon needs none.

EUROPE AND THE COLLAPSE OF COMMUNISM

One of the most remarkable political developments of the last decades of the twentieth century was the fall of communism in Europe. Although President Gorbachev (see Chapter 23) believed in strong, centralized government, he encouraged economic competition within the Soviet Union and renounced the policy of military intervention in satellite nations. As a result, in the late 1980s and 1990s Soviet troops began to withdraw from the communist countries of eastern Europe, opening the way for political reform. Over the course of one extraordinary year, 1989, all six satellite nations rejected their pro-Soviet governments. In Czechoslovakia, Václav Havel (born 1936), a popular dissident author, was elected president. In 1990 the dock-worker Lech Walesa became president of Poland (see Chapter 23). Hungary, which was already an independent republic, negotiated the withdrawal of the Red Army from its territory. Finally, in December 1989, during widespread popular protests backed by the army, the dictator of Romania, Nicolae Ceauşescu (1918–1989), and his wife were captured and executed.

The Soviets did intervene militarily in the Baltic region, but Estonia, Latvia, and Lithuania declared their independence in 1991. The Commonwealth of Independent States, consisting of twelve former republics of the Soviet Union, was created in 1991 and, with the exception of Ukraine, became a free-trade zone in 1993. New problems arose for Gorbachev's successor, Boris Yeltsin (born 1931), who became president of the new Russian Republic in 1991. Faced with uprisings in Chechnya, an Islamic area in the Caucasus demanding independence, Yeltsin despatched troops to quell the fundamentalist separatist movement. Yeltsin also faced internal economic difficulties and resigned in 2000, whereupon the premier, Vladimir Putin (born 1952), became Russia's president.

YUGOSLAVIA

In Yugoslavia long-standing ethnic and religious conflicts re-emerged with the fall of the U.S.S.R. Created as a nation after World War I, Yugoslavia was made up of six main groups that had been at odds for over a hundred years: Bosnian Muslims, Roman Catholic Croats and Slovenes, Eastern Orthodox Serbs, Macedonians, and Montenegrins. Under Tito (see Chapter 23) communist Yugoslavia had remained independent of Stalin, but after Tito's death in 1980 a rise in nationalism provoked violence as each group declared independence between 1991 and 1992, marking the end of Yugoslavia as a single nation. Among the worst offenders in the conflict was the Serbian Slobodan Milošević (born 1941), who launched a campaign of "ethnic cleansing" to eradicate the Bosnian Muslims.

The United Nations failed to control the situation, forcing NATO to intervene with air power. In 1995 a peace was signed in Dayton, Ohio (the Dayton Accords), but fighting revived in 1998, this time with the Serbians committed to eliminating the Muslim Albanians. In 1999 NATO intervened with ground troops as well as air power. Milošević was ousted and put on trial for war crimes at the International Criminal Tribunal for former Yugoslavia (ICTY) in The Hague. The former Yugoslavia was replaced by Croatia, Bosnia-Herzegovina (which includes Kosovo), and Serbia and Montenegro.

EUROPE AFTER THE COLD WAR

When the Berlin Wall was torn down in 1989 by jubilant German citizens, trade and travel opened between East and West Germany, and families that had been separated for decades were reunited. In 1990 the two zones of Germany were officially reunified.

Most European governments since World War II were politically centrist, with occasional eruptions of right-wing nationalism or left-wing liberalism. By 1992, in an effort to unify Europe and reduce trading costs between its partners, the European Community (EC, renamed European Union in 1993) abolished trade barriers. In 1994 the Channel Tunnel, linking Britain with France, was opened to ease travel and trade between Britain and continental Europe. The tunnel was set up in the form of a public company, which, as of 2005, had been unsuccessful financially. The **Euro**, a single currency adopted in 2002, was one of several efforts to maintain unity in the EU, although jostling for political advantage continued. Most, but not all, of the EU's member countries had begun using the Euro by 2004, but Denmark, Sweden, and Britain had yet to adopt it.

Another force for unification lay in NATO's wish to admit former members of the Soviet bloc that are attracted by Western economies. The Russia–NATO Council was formed in 2002 to encourage cooperation between all European nations. At the end of 2004 Turkey was given the go-ahead to apply for NATO membership, although on the understanding that this process could take up to ten years.

Disagreements between European countries over foreign policy and an ambivalent attitude toward American power continued. When NATO bombed Serbia, Europe's dependence on the U.S. military alarmed certain countries. France, in particular, has been wary of "Americanization" in the form of American television programs and U.S. fast-food and clothing chains. The increasing number of English words infiltrating the French language are seen by some as eroding French culture.

Another source of internal conflict in Europe has come from growing immigrant populations from former colonies. New immigrants provide cheap labor, but they also polarize politics. This situation has provoked an increase in nationalist sentiment against immigration in western Europe, and disputes over how to deal with groups—especially Muslims—who either do not want to assimilate or have been discouraged from doing so. Apart from Britain, which grants immediate voting rights to immigrants from Commonwealth countries, the rest of Europe tends to isolate immigrants (even those from former colonies) and make assimilation more difficult. In some countries, notably France and some states in Germany, Islamic religious demands are at odds with the secular character of the political and educational systems and the commitment to separation of Church and State.

THE UNITED STATES AND THE GLOBAL STRUGGLE WITH TERRORISM

Gerald Ford (presidency 1974–1977) had encouraged détente and signed the Helsinki Accords (see Chapter 23), but Ronald Reagan (presidency 1981–1989), who continued to suspect Soviet motives, prolonged Cold War tensions by calling the Soviet Union an "evil empire" and warning of its aggressive ambitions. He increased the military budget and financed the missile system known as "Star Wars," which was designed to block a nuclear attack. In response, the Soviet Union also increased military spending, leading to a new arms race. Negotiations to end the arms race were opened in 1986 and were concluded in 1991 by President George H. W. Bush (presidency 1989–1993).

Even before the Cold War ended, the United States, other Western countries, and the former Soviet Union faced new threats from Islamic fundamentalists. Beginning in the 1920s radical Islamists opposed secularization in Syria and Egypt. As colonial control of Africa and the Middle East declined, some countries, such as Saudi Arabia, Kuwait, and Morocco, fell under the rule of royal families, while others, such as Iraq, Syria, and Libya, were taken over by totalitarian regimes backed by an army. Oil-rich Saudi Arabia, Kuwait, and the Gulf States became enormously prosperous, but some states are plagued by economic problems and have to accommodate large, disenfranchised populations. Each of these countries has to find its own way to deal with Islamic fundamentalism, which holds views totally opposed to those of Western secular states, especially the United States. In Saudi Arabia fundamentalism dominates the educational system. The curriculum, based on Wahabism, teaches a traditional form of Islam, including the submission of women, the rejection of modern technology, and a return to Muslim society as it existed in the seventh century, when Muhammad was alive.

From the 1990s until 2001 the radically conservative Taliban regime in Afghanistan offered protection to training camps run by al-Qaeda, a secretive network of Islamic terrorists. The Taliban governed Afghanistan according to strict Islamic (*Shari'a*) law, which advocates public mutilations, stoning, and beheadings for crimes such as theft and adultery. The Taliban also objected to works of art that were not strictly approved by Islam, and in February 2001 they blew up two ancient colossal statues of the Buddha (figure **24.1**). In so doing, they defied the 1972 UNESCO World Heritage Convention and the Geneva Convention riders of 1977 and 1997 designed to protect cultural property.

The Taliban was partly financed by funds from Saudia Arabia, and was bolstered by the system of education in neighboring Pakistan, where Islamic schools (*madrasas*) teach religious fundamentalism, rejecting secular government, liberal thought, and Western values in general. In particular, the *madrasas* teach hatred of the United States and Israel.

Beginning in the late 1980s a series of terrorist attacks by Islamic militants were launched against the West, particularly the United States and its interests overseas. In 1988 terrorists from Islamic Libya blew up an American plane over Lockerbie, Scotland, killing hundreds of passengers, many of whom were students. Muslims bombed the New York World Trade Center in 1993 and American embassies in East Africa in 1993 and 1998. They attacked the United States army in Saudi Arabia in 1995 and the USS *Cole* (an American ship) in Yemen's port of Aden.

On September 11, 2001, Islamic terrorists trained by al-Qaeda hijacked and crashed four passenger airlines in the United States (see Box, p. 704). More than three thousand civilians died in the biggest act of terrorism in history. In the wake of this outrage, President George W. Bush (presidency from 2000) announced a new policy of preemptive strikes against nations or groups considered to pose a direct danger to U.S. security. The first adversary in the new "war on terror" was Afghanistan, where al-Qaeda and its leader, Osama bin Laden, were based. The United States drove the Taliban from power, but terrorist elements soon regrouped in Afghanistan and elsewhere in the Middle East and parts of Asia. In addition, Afghanistan reverted to being the largest grower of opium poppies, thereby contributing to the drug problem worldwide.

Since 2001, cells of Islamic fundamentalists have pursued a policy of terror throughout the world. A series of terrorist attacks against Russian civilians was launched from Chechnya in the 1990s. In 2003 terrorists occupied a Moscow theater and took hostages; hundreds of people were killed when Russian troops intervened. In February 2004 terrorists bombed a Moscow subway train during rush hour, killing thirty-nine people and wounding many more. Later that same year terrorists seized a school building in Beslan, in Russia, and killed more than three hundred children, parents, and teachers who had arrived for the first day of class. In Bali in 2003 a nightclub filled with Australian civilians was bombed, and in Istanbul bombs aimed at synagogues and British and American interests were set off, killing dozens of people. In 2004 Islamic terrorists bombed commuter trains in Madrid, after which Spain decided to withdraw its troops from Iraq. Coinciding with a meeting of world leaders in Britain to discuss poverty in Africa and global climate change, in July 2005 terrorists set off three bombs on London subway trains and blew up a bus during the morning rush hour. Seven hundred people were injured and over fifty died in the attack.

In 1990 the president of Iraq, Saddam Hussein (born 1937), invaded the small, oil-rich, neighboring country of Kuwait, and sparked the First Gulf War (1991). The Saudi government requested the help of the United States to oust the Iraqis and protect their oil fields. President George H. W. Bush mustered an international coalition and dispatched troops to the region. Iraq was defeated and the United Nations imposed sanctions on the country after the war, but Saddam continued to rule Iraq, presiding over one of the world's most brutal regimes. He also used chemical and biological weapons to massacre thousands of Kurds and other ethnic groups inside Iraq.

After the First Gulf War, United Nations arms inspectors searched Iraq for nuclear and biological weapons that Saddam Hussein was mandated by the United Nations to destroy. But Saddam expelled the inspectors in 1998 and did not readmit them until five years later under international pressure.

On the grounds of Saddam's history of genocide using chemical weapons and George W. Bush's conviction that weapons of mass destruction and nuclear programs were part of his plans, the United States and Britain, with support from certain other countries, invaded Iraq in March 2003. Faced with a veto in the United Nations Security Council by France,

24.1 Colossal Buddha, Bamiyan, Afghanistan, 2nd–5th century A.D., destroyed 2001. Stone, 180 ft. (55 m) high.

Germany, and Russia, the United States and its allies acted without seeking formal UN support. The war thus increased tensions between the United States and Europe and threatened the unity of NATO. In 2004 a CIA report concluded that Saddam no longer had weapons of mass destruction but that he retained the capacity to restart his weapons program and probably planned to do so as soon as UN sanctions were lifted.

Meanwhile, the longstanding conflict between Israel and Palestine continued. In 1993 the former terrorist and chairman of the Palestinian Liberation Organization (PLO) Yasir Arafat (1929–2004) signed the Oslo Accords, which called for Palestinian self-rule in Jericho, the West Bank, and the Gaza Strip in exchange for working out details that would lead to peace with Israel. But this treaty soon collapsed. The moderate Israeli prime minister Yitzhak Rabin (1922–1995) was assassinated in 1995 by an Israeli extremist. In 1999 Ehud Barak (born 1942) was elected prime minister of Israel. The following year, in an effort to build on the positive steps toward peace of the earlier Camp David Accords (1978) and the Oslo Accords (1993), President Clinton (presidency 1993–2001) invited Barak and Arafat to a summit meeting at Camp David (the presidential retreat in Maryland). The summit ended

Defining Moment

September 11, 2001

The terrorist attacks on the United States on September 11, 2001, killed more than three thousand people and destroyed the twin towers of the World Trade Center in New York. The attack launched a global "war on terror," the full effects of which will not be known for many years. But it is clear that the United States was changed forever after 9/11, as it is commonly called.

On that morning, nineteen Islamic terrorists hijacked four commercial airplanes and flew two of them into the World Trade Center towers, where thousands of people had begun their working day. A third plane was flown into the Pentagon—the administrative headquarters of the U.S. military—in Arlington, Virginia, and a fourth airplane, whose destination might have been the Capitol Building or the White House in Washington, crashed into a field in Pennsylvania. The passengers on this flight took action against the hijackers and downed the plane. Several passengers called home on their cellphones, alerting their families to their imminent deaths.

As anxious relatives waited while the dead were identified by DNA, fingerprints, dental records, personal belongings, and physical remains, the United States came to realize the magnitude of this act of terrorism. New York City's Health Department released a preliminary report on April 18, 2002 on the demographics of World Trade Center victims. The report listed 2,617 death certificates filed for the victims through January 25, including those on the planes.

A feeling of national unity followed 9/11, along with disputes about the causes and responsibilities for the attack. Americans became more concerned about national security, President George W. Bush established a department of homeland security, and Congress passed the Patriot Act, making it easier for law enforcement agencies to cooperate on intelligence gathering. The 9/11 Commission was set up to report on the event and called for structural changes, including a National Counter-Intelligence Center, intelligence reform bills, and a new directorate of National Intelligence.

Few artists have so far attempted to portray the 9/11 tragedy (figure **24.2**), but many photographers and videographers captured images of the World Trade Center collapse. When the planes hit the towers, cameras caught scenes of people jumping from windows over ninety stories high to escape the flames. Policemen and firemen who rushed to the rescue were killed. Hospitals were on the alert for survivors who never came.

Critical Question Is it possible to make majestic art out of massive human tragedy? How did Picasso's *Guernica*, Goya's *Disasters of War*, and Maya Lin's *Vietnam Veterans Memorial* depict epic human tragedy?

24.2 Julian La Verdiere and Paul Myoda, *Tribute in Light over the Brooklyn Bridge*, from the portfolio *Tribute in Light: Artists' Renderings*, 2001–2002. Portfolio of 12 c-prints, matted in an archival box, 24 × 20 in. (61 × 51 cm), edition of 500 on behalf of the Tribute in Light Initiative produced by Creative Time.
This memorial commemorates the victims of the terrorist attack on the World Trade Center, including thousands of office workers and hundreds of police and firemen who rushed to the scene. The memorial recalls the buildings in a pair of light beams projected skyward from forty-four 7000-watt search lamps.

without a formal agreement, but the Israeli and Palestinian leaders agreed on a set of principles on which to base further negotiations.

In the face of the continuing development of Jewish settlements in the occupied territories, Palestinians launched terrorist attacks against Israel, mostly in the form of suicide bombings in crowded civilian areas, such as restaurants and bus stops. Until the American invasion of Iraq in 2003 Saddam Hussein (along with some other Middle Eastern countries) rewarded the families of the bombers with cash payments. The Israelis retaliated by blowing up the bombers' homes and refused to hold peace talks until terrorist networks in Palestine were curbed.

ASIA AND THE DEVELOPING WORLD

After the massacre of students in Tiananmen Square (see Chapter 23) China relaxed some of its repressive policies. Today it is more open to tourism and student and cultural exchanges with the West, and has experienced several years of steady commercial and economic development. In 2008 Beijing will host the Olympic Games.

Japan had been the leading financial nation in the Far East until the Tokyo stock market crashed in 1989 and severe problems in its banking system came to light in the 1990s. Since then Japan's economic performance has been sluggish at best, and it has yielded its position as the force behind Southeast Asia's growth to smaller countries such as Taiwan, Singapore, Hong Kong, and South Korea. North Korea remains an impoverished country, run by a communist dictator and determined to pursue a nuclear weapons program. In addition, there is evidence that North Korea sold nuclear materials to terrorists.

In 1997 control of Hong Kong returned to mainland China after 155 years as a British colony. The Beijing government assumed its right to appoint a chief executive in Hong Kong; its stated policy of "one country, two systems," under which Hong Kong would continue to enjoy a high degree of autonomy, was frequently challenged by political demonstrations in Hong Kong. Hindu India and Muslim Pakistan continued to quarrel (and sometimes fight) over Kashmir.

Developing countries are plagued by poverty (map **24.1**) and struggle with over-population, malnutrition, and poor medical services. The sexually transmitted, incurable disease AIDS (Acquired Immune Deficiency Syndrome), which is caused by HIV (Human Immunodeficiency Virus), has

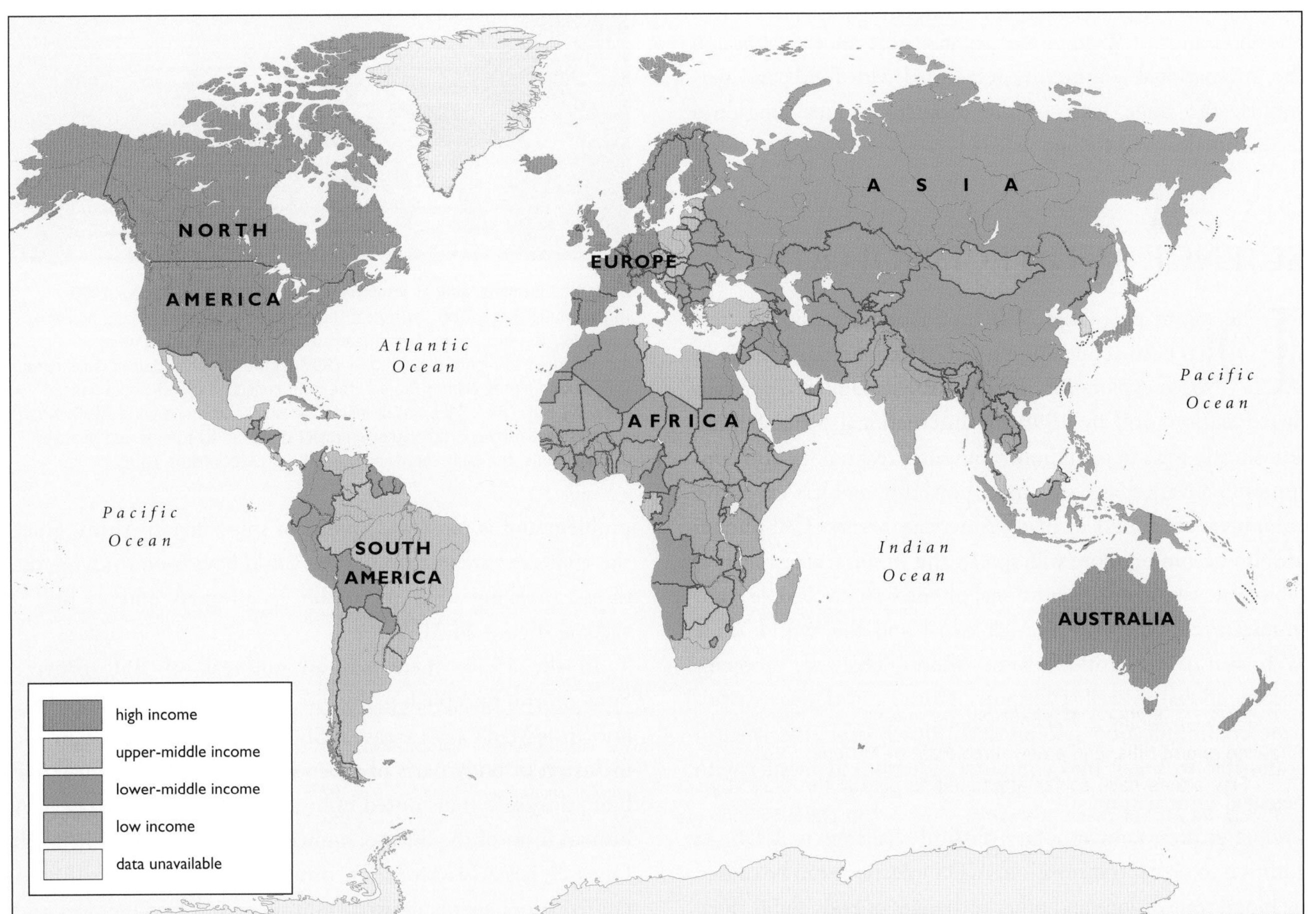

Map 24.1 The world, showing relative wealth, 2005.

ravaged vast areas of Africa, where it has killed millions of adults and orphaned millions more children.

In 2005 the Congo suffered an outbreak of deadly Marburg disease, which kills nine out of ten of its victims. The exploitation of children is rampant in some developing countries, where many are forced to work at a very young age, often as prostitutes. In Islamic Indonesia terrorist groups recruit and train children to fight as soldiers for the cause of radical fundamentalism. The international convention on the rights of the child, sponsored in 1989 by the United Nations, has had little impact.

White rule ended in South Africa, and Nelson Mandela (see Chapter 23) was elected as president of the Republic in 1994. Mandela's efforts to achieve peace and democracy through a ruling coalition of whites and blacks—he appointed the white leader Frederik Willem De Klerk (born 1936) to his government—led to a Nobel Prize for peace shared with de Klerk in 1994. Elsewhere in Africa, however, genocidal conflicts have caused economic and social devastation. In Rwanda in 1994 Hutus massacred over half a million of their fellow Rwandans, members of the Tutsi tribe. In 2004 in Darfur, in the Sudan, millions of black Muslims were displaced, raped, or killed by government-backed Arab Muslim militias.

In 2004, Indonesia and other parts of Asia were inundated by a tsunami (a tidal wave created by seismic activity under the ocean) which destroyed entire villages and killed hundreds of thousands of people. The dead included local populations and also thousands of Western tourists at seaside resorts. Although the international community responded with funds and personnel, the huge scale of the disaster requires long-term reconstruction and foreign aid.

24.3 AIDS memorial quilt as displayed in Washington, D.C., October 1996. In the United States the arts reflect the world's on-going social and political concerns. The thousands of Americans who have died of AIDS were memorialized in a quilt displayed in 1996 on the National Mall in Washington, D.C. Known as the Names Project, the quilt consisted of individual panels each 3 × 6 ft. (91 × 183 cm) in memory of someone who died of AIDS. Not a professional artwork, but rather a project designed by friends and relatives of the victims, the quilt contained over 37,000 sections by 1996.

SCIENCE AND TECHNOLOGY

Despite post-Cold War international tensions, there has been cooperation between nations, particularly in space exploration. In 1986 Russia launched the Mir Space Station, and by 1998 the International Space Station and shuttle were in operation. Computer technology also continues to advance, as faster, more powerful, and less expensive computers are found in many American homes. Cell-phones are also becoming more widespread and in some areas, such as China, are supplanting traditional phone systems. People communicate conveniently through email and the World Wide Web. But as the world becomes more globalized, problems become global as well. Computer viruses can destroy worldwide communication systems and privacy is at risk, since it is possible to break into computer systems and tamper with personal information.

The greatest contemporary medical challenge is AIDS. In addition to sexual transmission, AIDS infections can be caused by blood transfusions and other exchanges of body fluids. First identified in 1983, AIDS has become an international problem and is most widespread in sub-Saharan Africa. Since the 1980s researchers around the world have been studying the disease, seeking ways to inhibit its progress and to find a vaccine (figure **24.3**).

In the 1990s there was an outbreak of BSE (Bovine Spongiform Encephalopathy) in cattle in Britain. Popularly known as Mad Cow Disease, BSE is transmitted to cows by the inclusion of body parts of sheep in cattle feed. The incurable brain disease is transmitted to humans who eat tainted beef. A human form of the disease, known as CJD (Creutzfeldt-Jakob Disease), has existed for some time and can be contracted from tainted supplements derived from sheep or by eating deer and elk. The BSE outbreak led to international bans on British beef, although the disease also cropped up elsewhere in Europe and Japan. At the end of 2003 the United States officially admitted to its first case of BSE, allegedly transmitted through Canadian beef. Having ignored warnings by medical researchers, the United States government (lobbied by beef interests) had not instituted effective testing as was used in Japan and Britain, nor was the practice of including body parts of sheep in cattle feed discontinued.

As is often the case in human history, a number of medical advances since 1989 caused controversy. The subject of abortion and women's reproductive rights reemerged in 1989. After three decades of legal access to abortion, in 2003 the United States Congress passed a bill prohibiting late-term ("partial birth") abortion with no exception for the mother's health or life. Pro-choice advocates argued that this medical procedure was performed rarely and then only to save the mother's life or because the fetus was hopelessly deformed. They believed that reproductive decisions should be left to women and their doctors. Pro-life advocates argued that life begins at conception and that any form of abortion is tantamount to murder.

With the discovery of DNA (see Chapter 23), the next step is to map the genetic make-up of humans and other organisms. Known as the **Human Genome Project**, such research could result in the early detection of genetic predispositions to certain diseases, such as cancer and Alzheimer's disease, and revolutionize the way medicine is practiced.

Genetic research made it possible to clone organisms. In 1997 in Scotland a sheep named Dolly was created by cloning the DNA of one parent, and other clones have followed. The hope is that such research can eventually help prevent cancer cells from multiplying, produce replacement organs, or predict and repair genetic defects. A related issue is the future of stem-cell research, in which scientists study undifferentiated cells that appear naturally in the early phases of embryonic development and try to understand how such cells specialize. Scientists envision that stem-cell therapy could be used to treat Parkinson's, Alzheimer's, diabetes, and serious conditions such as nerve damage and loss of cartilage. Aside from the physical dangers involved in any new medical process, some people worry that couples wanting children will try to determine gender and other attributes by manipulating genes and chromosomes.

In addition to the modification of human and animal genes, crops and seeds can be genetically altered to increase and improve the food supply. But some people, disturbed by the idea of tampering with nature, fear that modifying food might make it unsafe for human consumption and adversely affect the environment. Vigorous opposition to genetic research has come from church groups, worried about people attempting to "play God" and interfering with nature.

Another recent concern that has taken on international proportions is ecology and environmental pollution. People are increasingly worried about preserving natural resources. Dependence on Middle Eastern oil for energy, the effect of acid rain on foliage, industrial waste poisoning water supplies, and nuclear reactors leaking radiation have inspired political activism against polluting the environment.

The issue of global warming has also become international in scope. Industrial gases released into the air have reduced the ozone layer that protects the earth's atmosphere from the sun's natural radiation. In 1988 this inspired the UN to launch a study of global warming. The following year a report recommended the reduction of industrial emissions of chemical substances (especially carbon dioxide) dangerous to the atmosphere. In 1992 an agreement was signed by fourteen countries to limit voluntarily their industrial pollution. In 2001 another treaty—the Kyoto Protocol—called for mandatory rather than voluntary compliance. Most countries signed the agreement, but the United States refused to do so, in part because the administration of George W. Bush disagreed with the findings of the report, and in part because of lobbying by large corporations.

ART AND ARCHITECTURE

The visual arts reflect many of the social and political concerns of the 1990s and the early twenty-first century. Prominent among recent themes in the arts are the AIDS crisis, feminism, the environment, genetic mutation, and globalization. Art media expanded to include the human body itself, as well as new electronic and computer technologies.

Body fluids constitute much of the subject matter of the American photographer Andres Serrano (born 1950). As in the case of Mapplethorpe (see Chapter 23), United States government support of Serrano was criticized by conservative church groups that considered his work indecent and offensive (figure **24.4**).

24.4 Andres Serrano, *Blood Cross*, 1985. Cibachrome, silicone, plexiglas, wood frame, edition of 4, 3 ft. 4 in. × 5 ft. (1.02 × 1.52 m).
Using blood from a butcher's shop poured into a cross of Plexiglass and photographed against a dramatic sky, the artist alludes to the AIDS crisis and associates it with Christ's suffering.

Not only does Serrano's work challenge religious and artistic convention, but it also espouses political agendas, such as improving the treatment of the homeless, whom the artist ennobled in a series of portraits, and attacking racial prejudice, as reflected in his photographs of the Ku Klux Klan.

Keith Haring (1958–1990), a New York graffiti artist (see Chapter 23) who died of AIDS at the age of thirty-two, addressed AIDS as a prominent theme in his work. Haring was noted for paintings on subway walls. His *Ignorance=Fear* of 1989 (figure **24.5**) is composed of graffiti-like, linear figures imitating dancing poses of the three monkeys—See No Evil, Hear No Evil, and Speak No Evil. The accompanying text pleads for tolerance toward victims of AIDS and for confronting the disease openly and honestly. Silence, Haring writes, equals death; and ignorance equals fear. In the lower right corner, he calls for action: *Fight AIDS, Act up*.

24.5 Keith Haring, *Ignorance=Fear*, 1989. Sumi ink on paper, 24 × 43⅛ in. (61 × 109.5 cm). Collection the Estate of Keith Haring.

DIGITAL INSTALLATION

Modern technology makes digital art possible. In 1989 the American Jenny Holzer (born 1950) installed hundreds of LEDs (light emitting diodes) in the Guggenheim Museum in New York to create signs that make various political points (figure **24.6**). Inspired by the use for commercial advertising of the same type of lights, her installation used the circular ramp of the museum to enhance the messages. Below, on the floor, granite benches arranged in a circle were also inscribed with messages. In the view illustrated here, the top message—"Private property created crime"—is a Marxist-inspired indictment of capitalism.

The Austrian artist Erwin Redl (born 1963) also uses LED lights. In *Shifting, Very Slowly* (figure **24.7**), he arranged a curtain of lights that created regular patterns in a specific architectural setting. As the lights slowly changed color, they disrupted the notion of architecture as stable and unchanging. At the same time, however, the lights endowed the space with a sense of solidity, challenging the boundary between solid and void.

24.6 Jenny Holzer, *Untitled* (Selections from *Truisms*, *Inflammatory Essays*, *The Living Series*, *The Survival Series*, *Under a Rock*, *Laments*, and *Child Text*), December 1989–February 1990. Extended helical tricolor LED electronic display signboard, 16 in. × 162 ft. × 6 in. (40.6 cm × 49 m × 15 cm). Solomon R. Guggenheim Museum, New York.

24.7 Erwin Redl, *Shifting, Very Slowly*, 1998–1999. Computer controlled LED light installation exhibition image. Apex Art, New York.

24.8 Christo and Jeanne-Claude, *Wrapped Reichstag*, Berlin, 1971–1995.
The Reichstag, built in 1894, has become a symbol of Berlin. It was set on fire in 1933 to protest Hitler's rise to power and bombed in 1945 by the Allies. Restored in 1990, the Reichstag houses the Bundestag (the Lower Parliament) after the reunification of Germany. It is thus a symbol of German democracy. In 1994 the Bundestag voted to give the Christos permission to wrap the building. The wrapping was carried out by climbers and installation workers, using 1,076,000 sq ft. (99,964 sq m) of material, equipment made by local German companies, and 51,181 ft. (15,600 m) of rope.

ALTERING THE ENVIRONMENT

In recent decades artists have explored new ways to alter the environment, often to send a political message. In 1995, after twenty-four attempts to gain permission for the project, Christo and Jeanne-Claude (both born 1935) wrapped the German Reichstag in Berlin (figure **24.8**). Aesthetically the form of the building is changed by the nature of the material, which reveals underlying structure like folds of clothing in Classical sculpture. The *Wrapped Reichstag*, like the Christos' other projects around the world, was an international happening, recorded in photographs and on film. After two weeks, the project was dismantled and the materials recycled.

Another, more explicitly political, approach to altering the environment can be seen in the ecological iconography of *Green River* (figure **24.9**). The Icelandic artist Olafur Eliasson (born 1967) alarmed local inhabitants by pouring green dye into the Stockholm River. The Swedish authorities offered no explanation for the sudden green color. This was the result desired by Eliasson, who intended to show the elusiveness of politicians when confronted with a potential crisis.

24.9 Olafur Eliasson, *Green River*, Stockholm, Sweden, 2000.

ICONOGRAPHY OF GENETIC MUTATION: MATTHEW BARNEY

The American Matthew Barney (born 1967) uses video, sculpture, and other media to explore boundaries between species. Figure **24.10** is a self-portrait of the artist mutating into a satyr. It is from the series entitled "Cremaster," which consists of videos and an iconography that fuses myth, history, and genetics. Here, the eerie colors—orange hair, red lips, pink skin, and white suit—add to the disturbing character of the figure. Barney shows himself with ram-like ears, precise curls on either side of his parted hair, and stretched, rubbery skin. The shift in the eyes, the slant of the nostrils, and thinness of the lips have an elusive, non-human quality. Barney seems to be in the process of metamorphosing from man to beast.

CROSS-CULTURAL ART IN AMERICA

Cultural history has become a self-conscious feature of art in America since 1989. For example, *Women's House* (figure **24.11**) by John Scott (born 1940) is influenced by the cultural traditions of Western history, African and other non-Western societies, and feminism. Non-Western and feminist themes converge in the notion of a women's house. Its iconography alludes to the social isolation of women and to the men's houses in Melanesia, in the South Pacific, used in initiation rites for boys. The form at the top resembling the arc of a bow refers to the African diddley bow legend that inspired the artist. According to the myth, the bow is turned into a one-stringed fiddle by African hunters and played to appease the spirit of the animal they kill.

24.10 Matthew Barney, still from "Cremaster" series No. 4, *The Loughton Candidate*, 1994. Color photograph in cast plastic frame, edition of 30, $19^{1/2} \times 17^{3/4}$ in. (49.5 × 45.2 cm). Barbara Gladstone Gallery, New York.

24.11 John Scott, *Women's House*, 1993. Painted metal, 29 × 19 × 44 in. (73.7 × 48.3 × 111.8 cm). Galerie Simonne Stern, New Orleans.
Note the influence of Calder's kinetic sculptures and of the brightly colored *Jazz* cut-outs by Matisse (see Chapter 22).

Modern Native American artists often refer to their history, especially the effects of European settlement and the loss of their land. In *Ghost Dancer Ascending* (figure **24.12**), the Iroquois-Oneida Lisa Fifield (born 1957) illustrates a Ghost Dance. She wears the traditional dress of a Ghost Dancer, who believed herself impervious to the white man's weapons and longed for the past. She dreamed of the period before European contact, when buffalo roamed freely and Native American culture was intact.

24.12 Lisa Fifield, *Ghost Dancer Ascending*, 1995. Watercolor on paper, 32 × 22 in. (81.3 × 55.9 cm). Private collection.

24.13 Yu Youhan, *Mao Voting*, 1993. Acrylic on canvas, 3 ft. 10½ in. × 5 ft. 5⅜ in. (1.18 × 1.66 m). Hanart TZ Gallery, Hong Kong.

Modernism in China

Art movements from the West have more and more influenced the Far East and vice versa. With the relaxation of government control in China after Tiananmen Square, freedom of expression in the arts also expanded. Yu Youhan, a lecturer on art in Shanghai, is influenced by Pop Art and Chinese folk traditions in *Mao Voting* (figure **24.13**). The bright, flat colors are drawn from Pop Art, and the juxtaposition of rectangles from quilting patterns. The background stars allude to the Chinese flag, and the floral designs to the "Hundred Flowers" Movement (1956–1957) that took its name from Mao Zedong's speech in which he apparently promoted pluralism—"Let a hundred flowers bloom and a hundred schools of criticism compete"—but that quickly resulted in a government backlash. In Youhan's painting, Mao wears his signature jacket as he ironically places a ballot in a ballot-box, despite having led a regime that prohibited free elections.

Postmodern Architecture after 1989

Postmodernist architects continue to combine traditional forms in new ways. In 1995 Robert Stern (born 1939) designed the Feature Animation Building for The Walt Disney Company (figure **24.14**). The long, industrial-looking building has triple

24.14 Robert A. M. Stern, Feature Animation Building, The Walt Disney Company, Burbank, California, 1995.

24.15 Frank O. Gehry, Guggenheim Museum, Bilbao, Spain, 1997.

round arches drawn from Roman architecture at one end, a series of verticals inspired by punk, Mohawk haircuts, and a giant cone over the side entrance. The cone is decorated with a crescent moon and stars resembling the wizard's hat worn by Mickey Mouse in the film *Fantasia*. Towering over the building, like a Disney version of a Gothic spire, the cone stands behind large, freestanding letters that spell ANIMATION and announce the purpose of the building.

The Canadian architect Frank O. Gehry (born 1929) designed the Guggenheim Museum, Bilbao (figure **24.15**), which was commissioned by the Spanish government as part of an urban renewal project and completed in 1999. The museum is clad in titanium to resist erosion, giving the exterior a shimmering surface that reflects the surrounding light. Set on the bank of the Nervion River, the museum's curved walls and biomorphic shapes seem to expand and contract like a living organism. The complex design was planned with the help of the French computer program, Catia, which was invented for aerospace projects.

In 1998 the Argentine architect Cesar Pelli (born 1926), who studied in the United States and designed buildings around the world, completed the Petronas Twin Towers in Kuala Lumpur, Malaysia (figure **24.16**). In Pelli's view, a building should reflect the character and culture of its site. As of 1998, these towers, with

24.16 Cesar Pelli, Petronas Twin Towers, Kuala Lumpur, Malaysia, 1991–1997. 1483 ft. (453 m) tall.

their antennae seeming to pierce the sky, were the world's tallest buildings. Their façades consist of stainless steel hexagons with strips of windows creating sharply defined patterns. Accentuating the soaring verticals is the diminishing size of the towers, which decrease six times as the buildings rise. At the same time, the viewer's eye is carried around the towers by the alternation between curved and flat walls. The ground-level building between the towers is a concert hall.

MUSIC AT THE TURN OF THE TWENTY-FIRST CENTURY

Jazz, originally a downtown genre rooted in the traditions of African Americans, has taken on the mantle of America's "classical music." Under the leadership of trumpeter Wynton Marsalis (born 1961) at Lincoln Center, New York, jazz has acquired respectability, perhaps at the cost of spontaneity. A new generation of exciting young musicians, such as saxophonist Joshua Redman (born 1969), is flourishing, creating performances that are, in his words, "evocative, infectious, timeless, and uplifting." Jazz is more open to women than before, and academic programs for its study proliferate.

Popular music in America has continued to diversify in the new millennium. Established styles like those of rap, 1960s-style rock, and black rhythm and blues (a generic term for commercial black music, as distinct from rap) still dominate the airwaves. They are joined by new sounds such as reggaeton—a Spanish-language adaptation of Jamaican dance-hall music, which has become popular among Anglo-American and black audiences. Digital sampling techniques have spawned various developments, including a vogue of "remixes" in which existing pop songs are recycled, altered, or combined with other songs. Many westerners have come to cultivate interests in various musics from outside the Western mainstream, including flamenco, Indian classical music, Congolese *soukous*, the Trinidadian *soca*, the Dominican *merengue*, Jamaican reggae, and Hispanic-Caribbean salsa. Also enriching the music scene are various "crossover" combinations, such as a recording by classical cellist Yo-Yo Ma with jazz and pop vocalist Bobby McFerrin.

For the first time in history, listeners have unprecedented access to the international music scene via the Internet, television, radio, and different kinds of recordings. With cassettes, CDs, and home studios, the cost of producing music has decreased and this, too, contributes to its worldwide availability.

In the West, the tastes of those who listen to classical music lie most popularly in the eighteenth and nineteenth century. Early-twentieth-century music, like that of Schoenberg (see Chapter 21), appeals to a small audience. A challenge taken up by some contemporary composers is the creation of a musical language for today. America's John Adams (born 1947) takes Minimalism as a starting point for this, constructing an audience-friendly, direct style that includes elements of rock and jazz but also revisits music of the past. His beautiful, witty pieces show mastery of rhythm, texture, and color, conveying a wide range of ideas and moods—spiritual, erotic, extravagant, severe. *El Niño* (*The Little Boy*, 2000), for example, is an oratorio that retells the story of the Nativity, representing Jesus' birth as an event to be reenacted in every age. Expressing the essence of contemporary America, Adams's Joseph and Mary seek shelter on the freeways, beaches, and parking lots of southern California. The text is based not only on the Gospels, but also on tales from the Apocrypha and on poems by Latin-American women about the miracle of childbirth.

Another American composer seeking aural appeal is Ellen Taaffe Zwilich (born 1939). Her output includes symphonies, concertos, and string quartets, which assimilate the past in a cogent and expressive way. The music has an intensity of purpose; simple motifs are turned into rich overlays of sound, and colorful orchestral effects are set off by the virtuosity of solo instruments. *Millennium Fantasy* (1998) for piano and orchestra is based on an old folksong, projecting an optimistic outlook as the composer envisages the twenty-first century. In *Rituals* (2003) for orchestra and five percussion players, the music takes in tangos and African dances, using non-Western instruments such as Chinese cloud gongs and Balinese cymbals. Zwilich's works reflect the international nature of music in the new millennium.

LITERATURE

Literature at the turn of the twenty-first century became more widely available throughout the world. Current issues, such as abortion and reproductive rights, the environment and ecology, racism, and the effects of new medical technology are among the major literary themes. But the impact of the two world wars, raising issues of tolerance and totalitarianism, also continued to appear in contemporary novels. In Germany themes of guilt and the Holocaust are still being explored, and Japanese authors are still preoccupied with the radical changes in their culture following World War II. These issues, like the aftermath of colonialism in India and South Africa, can now be viewed from the perspective of greater distance. Likewise, Chinese literature is beginning to deal more openly and realistically with life during the Cultural Revolution.

Advances in medicine inspired satirical futuristic novels warning that science and technology might fall into the wrong hands. With the modern ability (and inclination) to save premature and physically challenged infants, the effect of birth defects on individuals and their families has become a literary subject. In this section, we consider a few Eastern and Western authors whose work spans the period from the end of World War II to the turn of the century, as well as a new novel by a young Indian woman.

GÜNTER GRASS: REFLECTIONS OF THE TWENTIETH CENTURY

In 1999 Günter Grass (born 1927), the leading German poet and novelist after World War II, received the Nobel Prize for literature. His enormous output spans the post-war period and continues into the twenty-first century. Through his writing, Grass has become one of the most important witnesses to the twentieth century.

Born in Danzig (present-day Gdansk), which was then part of Germany, Grass joined the Hitler Youth Movement as an adolescent and fought in the German army. After the war he studied art. His best-known work, *The Tin Drum* (1959), is the first novel of his Danzig Trilogy, which deals with post-war Germany. It is the story of Oskar Matzerath, who decides not to grow up. Oskar remains attached to his toy tin drum, which is his primary method of communication and a metaphor for his life. He beats the drum to interrupt Nazi meetings and shrieks to shatter glass. After the war, Oskar decides to grow a few inches but develops into a hunchback. He becomes wealthy working the black market in West Germany but cannot shake off his guilt for Nazi crimes. At times amusing, sadistic, or grotesque, the novel expresses a view of the human condition as infantile, corrupt, guilt-ridden, and helpless in the face of tyranny.

Subsequent novels by Grass deal with Germany after reunification, with German myth and history, and with cross-cultural themes. Grass lived in India for two years in the 1970s, which inspired *Show Your Tongue* (1988). In that work, written in diary form, he examines his ambivalent fascination with the poverty and dynamism of Calcutta. In *My Century* (1999), Grass wrote a hundred short pieces, each reflecting one year of the century. *Crabwalk* (2002) is about German guilt and tells the story of the disastrous sinking in 1945 of the German ship the *Wilhelm Gustloff* by a Soviet submarine. Grass traces the history of a German family through three generations, showing how, with the passage of time, memory fades and history is revised and evolves into cultural myths.

SOUTH AFRICA: J. M. COETZEE

John Michael Coetzee (born 1940) grew up in South Africa and later studied in Texas, eventually teaching in the United States and in South Africa. In most of his novels Coetzee examines universal themes through characters caught up in the political and cultural turmoil of a specific time and place. His novel *Waiting for the Barbarians* (1980) is an allegory of colonial oppression. It is narrated by the Magistrate, an official in an unnamed frontier empire (probably referring to colonial white South Africa) in an unspecified era. The inhabitants of the empire fear and persecute the native barbarians beyond its borders. The Magistrate's character begins to develop when he becomes involved with a captive girl who has been crippled and blinded in one eye by imperial torturers. When the Magistrate's involvement with the girl is discovered, he is publicly shamed and tortured. Eventually the Magistrate betrays the empire he had previously defended.

Coetzee's highly acclaimed *Disgrace* (1999) takes place in contemporary South Africa. It explores themes of guilt and love through the story of a middle-aged academic who loses his job because of an affair with a female student. This exposes him to the ridicule of friends, colleagues, and his former wife. Coetzee's spare, minimalist writing style echoes the novel's harsh atmosphere and accentuates the recurring theme of violent change among blacks and whites, and men and women, in modern South Africa.

CANADA: MARGARET ATWOOD—FUTURISTIC FEMINISM

The Canadian author Margaret Atwood (born 1939), the daughter of an etymologist, was influenced by her father's interest in word origins. Her own writing style is characterized by a precise use of language and an interest in myth and culture. She makes use of **dystopia** (a utopia gone wrong) in two futuristic works, *The Handmaid's Tale* (1985) and *Oryx and Crake* (2003). Both are allegorical satires, written with dark humor and biting wit.

Influenced by Orwell's *1984* (see Chapter 23), *The Handmaid's Tale* satirizes totalitarianism. It takes place in the Republic of Gilead somewhere in the United States, where women of one class, the handmaids, are sent to live with the Commanders and their wives in order to become pregnant by the Commanders. The rulers of Gilead, who are modeled on right-wing dictators, are motivated by their opposition to feminism. They control the reproductive rights of the handmaids, who have remained fertile although most of the human race has been sterilized by pollution. All women, except the wives of the Commanders, are denied the right to read and speak. An Unwoman is one who is unable to have children. Men who might encourage women to think for themselves, and women who do so, are publicly hanged from the city wall as an example to others.

The heroine is Offred, whose ovaries are valued because they have survived the radioactive chemicals of modern industry. She is careful to ration her thoughts to ensure her survival. Whatever disaster has occurred, it is recent enough for Offred still to recognize people she had known in her previous life, "the time before." Through memory fragments, Offred has flashes of walking in the park with her mother, of witnessing book-burning, and of life with her husband and young daughter.

In the futuristic *Oryx and Crake* the planet earth is nearly destroyed. It opens with Snowman, the narrator, sleeping in a tree and starving. He is thinking of his friend Crake and his beloved Oryx. Memory is an important theme, as it is in *The Handmaid's Tale*, for Snowman, like Offred, searches his mind for an explanation of how the world came to its present state. He embarks on a double journey, one to Crake's high-tech bubble dome and another into his past where he tries to figure out what happened to the world.

It seems that the Paradice Project, planned in Crake's bubble dome to achieve physical perfection and eternal youth, was somehow the cause of the world's near extinction. This is reflected in the video game *Extincathon*, which Snowman and Crake played as children. The new world is strictly controlled, and power is in the hands of corporate giants who live in self-contained compounds, whereas the low-class Pleeblands (compare "plebeian") are open and accessible.

JAPAN: KENZABURO OE AND KAZUO ISHIGURO

The career of the Japanese Kenzaburo Oe (born 1935), like that of Günter Grass, spans the period from the end of World War II into the twenty-first century. Oe, however, surveys the century from an Asian vantage point. He grew up in a traditional Japanese village, whose myths and legends he incorporates into his novels, notably *The Silent Cry* (1967). He also studied Western and Zen philosophy as sources of cross-cultural inspiration.

Oe was raised in the militaristic culture of pre-war Japan, when the emperor was regarded as a god. But he read Western books as a child—in his Nobel Prize acceptance speech, he singled out *Huckleberry Finn* (see Chapter 19) and Selma Lagerlöf's *The Wonderful Adventures of Nils* (see Chapter 21) as two books for children that influenced his literary formation. After the war, Japan underwent radical changes, agreeing not to rearm and to become a constitutional democracy. Oe then studied French literature at Tokyo University and began writing in the 1950s.

A defining moment of Oe's life was the birth in 1963 of his severely brain-damaged son, Hikari, who was not expected to live more than a few weeks. The effect of Hikari's survival on Oe and his wife is the subject of his novel *A Personal Matter* (1964). Gradually Oe accepted his son, and they forged a deep bond, which became the theme of several later books. In *Hiroshima Notes* (1965) Oe recorded the recollections of atomic bomb victims. During the early 1990s, he began a trilogy, *The Flaming Green Tree*, which he considers the culmination of his career. He was inspired by a poem by Yeats (see Chapter 21), which he combines with a sense of Japanese locale and the Greek myth of Cybele and Adonis. The main character, Gee, returns to his village after living abroad and founds a Society of the Woods, which evolves into an organized Church. Its aim is to save the environment and create a society co-existing harmoniously with nature.

The novels of Kazuo Ishiguro (born 1954) deal with British and Japanese themes and the role of art and memory in the modern world. Ishiguro was born in Japan, but he and his family moved to London when he was six, forcing him to adapt to two very different cultures. His novel *A Pale View of Hills* (1982) is about a Japanese widow living in England, and in *An Artist of the Floating World* (1986) Ishiguro's main character is a Japanese artist reminiscing about his country after World War II. The narrator is Masuji Ono, who creates "mindscapes" (imagined settings) and wanders through them. As a young man Ono inhabited the "Floating World," the fleeting world of entertainment that inspired the Japanese woodblock prints admired by the Impressionist painters (see Chapter 20). He then devoted his work to imperial propaganda. When the war ends, after the death of Ono's wife and son and the destruction of his house and city, he embarks on a mental tour of his earlier life. His daughters, who survive the war, try to hide his political past while he is hopeful that the next generation will produce a better world. The story of Ono is, for Ishiguro, a metaphor of contrasts—between generations, past and future, teachers and students, and various political ideologies.

In *The Remains of the Day* (1989) Ishiguro again deals with characters who try to hide their past. The novel takes place in Britain after World War II, largely in the mind of Stevens, the perfectly reserved butler in service to the Nazi collaborator Lord Darlington. When his master dies, Stevens drives to the country in search of the housekeeper he loved but let go. Like Ono, Stevens wishes to revise the past by hiding it, but he also travels through it in his mind. Just as Ono identified with the power of the emperor, so Stevens's sense of self comes from his view that Darlington was a great man. In both cases, the hero has deluded himself and must come to terms with his delusion.

Ishiguro's novel *When We Were Orphans* (2000) moves between London and Shanghai. It deals again with themes of memory and the attraction of a familiar place. The first part of the novel takes place in London in the 1930s. Detective Christopher Banks, who works in London, is haunted by his parents' disappearance when he was ten and his family lived in Shanghai. In the second part of the novel, Banks returns to Shanghai to find out why his parents disappeared. His hunt through the winding streets of the city reminds him of the detective games that he played with his childhood friend, Akira. His memory shifts back and forth between his past and the present.

There is a Freudian quality in Ishiguro's depiction of the mind, which is mirrored politically and historically. Like Freud, Ishiguro recognizes the persistence of childhood in the adult and the revisions and distortions of memory created by the interplay between the conscious and the unconscious mind. On a political level, Banks is angry at the behavior of Western colonial powers in Shanghai, who failed to do for China what they could have. Similarly, like a child, he is angry at his parents for deserting him.

INDIA: ARUNDHATI ROY

The Indian author Arundhati Roy (born 1961) studied architecture before writing her first novel, *The God of Small Things* (1997). Roy grew up in India, where she was affected by the remnants of colonialism and became politically committed. The novel, which takes place in Kerala, in southernmost India, is the story of Indian twins (Esthappen and Rahel) and their family. When their young cousin, Sophie Mol, and her mother arrive for a Christmas visit from Britain, Sophie dies and her death becomes a central event. Like India itself, the novel is a study in cultural and religious contrasts, where Christians, Muslims, and Hindus coexist, although not without conflict. The family is seen through the eyes of the children, who observe with insight the isolation of their mother, their blind grandmother who plays the violin, and their lecherous, wealthy, Marxist uncle. Weighing down the atmosphere is an overriding sense of danger and the inexorable power of fate.

Roy's descriptions evoke the rich colors of Indian textiles and the exotic scents of Indian spices. Tropical indolence is conveyed chromatically in the opening lines:

> May in Ayemenem is a hot, brooding month. The days are long and humid. The river shrinks and black crows gorge on bright mangoes in still, dustgreen trees. Red bananas ripen. Jackfruits burst. Dissolute bluebottles hum vacuously in the fruity air. Then they stun themselves against clear windowpanes and die, fatly baffled in the sun.

CHINA: HA JIN

Growing up in a small Chinese village during the Cultural Revolution, Ha Jin (born 1956) joined the army at the age of fourteen. He came to the United States after the Tiananmen Square protests in 1989 and now teaches at Emory University in Atlanta, Georgia. He writes in English and depicts communist China under the Maoist regime.

Ha Jin's first full-length novel, *Waiting* (1999), is the story of Lin Kong, a Chinese army doctor trapped in an arranged marriage with his uneducated peasant wife, Shuyu, and their daughter. Stationed a day's journey from his village, Lin Kong falls in love with an educated nurse, Manna Wu. Each year he asks his wife for a divorce and she finally agrees, but when she comes before the court, she changes her mind and Lin Kong returns to work. According to Chinese law, Lin and Manna are not allowed any physical contact while he is married, but there is a loophole in the law that permits divorce without mutual consent after an eighteen-year waiting period.

Lin Kong lives in suspense under the weight of communist repression and goes about his life with resignation. His wife has been waiting for him to recognize her value and stop asking for a divorce. When Lin Kong is finally free to divorce Shuyu, he does not. In this novel, as in other works, Ha Jin implies that, under Mao Zedong, ordinary people went about their lives with a sense of "waiting out" the Cultural Revolution.

THEATER

In the latter part of the twentieth century and in the early years of the twenty-first, new developments emerged in theater, especially in direction, staging, and set design. Often, as in the works of Robert Wilson, Philip Glass, and John Cage (see Chapter 23), these developments involve new technologies and interdisciplinary media. In addition to drawing inspiration from traditional theater, contemporary playwrights deal with national and international social issues, colonialism, feminism, notions of progress, and the future.

THE UNITED STATES: WILSON, MAMET, AND KUSHNER

August Wilson (1945–2005) was born in Pittsburgh and became disillusioned by racism and life in the ghetto. He dropped out of school and began reading and writing on his own. Inspired by the Harlem Renaissance and the music of Bessie Smith (see Chapter 22), his plays deal realistically with twentieth-century African-American themes. Two of his plays, *The Piano Lesson* (1988) and *Two Trains Running* (1990), confront these themes directly. In *The Piano Lesson* the central issue is whether to sell a piano that has been in the Lymon family for generations. Built by a slave, the piano symbolizes black history. Selling it would make it possible to buy land, but in Wilson's view black history is not for sale. In *Two Trains Running* friends become involved in anti-Vietnam War protests and the civil rights movement.

The playwright David Mamet (born 1947) is a native of Illinois and studied theater in Vermont and New York. He worked as an actor and writes screen and stage plays. His style is minimalist, spare and powerful—his language is sometimes referred to as Mametspeak—and his most effective characters are strong-willed men. Mamet's main theme is the corruption and debasement caused by American materialism and greed. This is the core of his 1983 play *Glengarry Glen Ross*, which is about an unsuccessful real-estate salesman desperate to succeed. It is an updated version of Miller's *Death of a Salesman* (see Chapter 23), with the individual "loser" replaced by the updated notion of "group sales." In Mamet's play salesmen succumb to pathetic delusions as they struggle to sell what no one wants to buy.

In *Oleanna* (1992) Mamet pits a female student, Carol, against a male professor, John, and portrays the effect of sexual harassment on an academic. Carol has failed John's course and comes to his office to discuss her grade. In Mamet's dialogue the student seems to be demolished by the professor's greater grasp of language. John uses words as weapons, with which Carol cannot compete. She can and does, however, bring him up on charges before the Tenure Committee. He, in turn, falls apart when confronted, his command of language breaks down, and he regresses to a point where he attacks the student physically and loses his job. Mamet thus explores both the professor's abuse of power and the student's abuse of political correctness.

Homosexuality and AIDS are the predominant themes of the seven-hour play *Angels in America* (1993) by Tony Kushner (born 1956). The play was written in two parts, *Millennium Approaches* and *Perestroika* (named after Gorbachev's policy of reform), and AIDS is the manifest content. It deals with relationships between men, their dread of contracting AIDS, and their reactions when they become infected. At times humorous and supernatural, the play's subtext concerns American attitudes toward difference.

BRITAIN: STOPPARD AND CHURCHILL

The prolific British playwright Tom Stoppard (born 1937) was born in Czechoslovakia but grew up in Shanghai and India. He moved to England when his widowed mother married a British army officer. Stoppard's first success, *Rosencrantz and Guildenstern are Dead* (1966), was influenced by Beckett. Building on the existential theme of the Absurd, Stoppard uses as his protagonists two minor characters from Shakespeare's *Hamlet* (see Chapter 15) and shows the absurdity of their existence through their obliviousness to the important events taking place at the court of Denmark, which results in their meaningless deaths.

Stoppard's later plays deal with modern science and cross-cultural themes in dialogue that is intellectual in style. In *Arcadia* (1993), set in both the past and the present, the plot revolves around an orderly eighteenth-century English garden being modernized into a nineteenth-century Romantic one. The transformation of the garden is a metaphor for scientific progress, which becomes an object of satire. The dialogue is distinctive for its scientific discussions of thermodynamics, fractals, and chaos theory. Another thread deals with poetry, juxtaposing Isaac Newton with Byron and implying that poets and philosophers are more essential to progress than science.

In *Indian Ink* (1995) Stoppard draws on his recollections of India. Set in 1930, the story follows an English poet who travels to India for her health. She settles in Jummapur to write, and a young artist comes to paint her portrait. In the course of the play, the characters discuss their cultural differences, primarily her independence and his attachment to tradition. Colonial domination and creativity form the basis of their conversations, which are infused with erotic tension.

The feminist playwright Caryl Churchill (born 1938) was born in London, lived for a time in Canada, and then returned to Britain to attend Oxford University. She has experimented with all-female and all-male casts, and her subjects include gender, colonialism, and freedom of expression.

Cloning is the subject of her 2002 play, *A Number*. A father, whose wife died giving birth to a son, decides to have his son cloned. On Christmas Eve three of the clones visit their father, who has to come to terms with his guilt and take responsibility for his actions. Woven into the narrative is the question of whether personality is determined by heredity or the environment. Because the clones have been raised in different contexts but have the same genetic make-up, they provide evidence for debating this controversy. Tension is built up through fragmented dialogue and the Oedipal struggle between father and son. When the play was performed in New York in 2004, the set was designed to resemble an operating theater, emphasizing the clinical aspect of the story.

FILM

Contemporary film, like theater, reflects the social concerns of the period. People are increasingly able to see films from other parts of the world as soon as they are released, and developing countries, such as China, are emerging as important sources of original, modern films. Technology has also expanded the use of special effects. Previews are available on the Internet long before films are released, and the films themselves are often international productions, with actors, directors, and financing coming from different parts of the world.

SOCIAL COMMENTARY FILMS

FILM IN CHINA: ZHANG YIMOU Zhang Yimou (born 1951) is an internationally known Chinese film-maker. He was born in Xi'an and worked on farms and in factories during the Cultural Revolution. He studied in Beijing among a group of new Chinese film directors who came to prominence in the 1980s. They rejected the Socialist Realism of Mao Zedong and pursued themes about Modernism in traditional China.

Zhang's films are best known for painterly techniques, which produce rich color, and close-ups emphasizing female beauty. His trilogy of symbolic films—*Red Sorghum* (1987), *Jou dou* (1990), and *Raise the Red Lantern* (1991)—made his reputation abroad. But the last two were banned in China and in 1994 the authorities banned him from making films for five years. The actress Gong Li starred in all three films.

The trilogy deals with the theme of declining patriarchy, a symbol of the decline of old ways as China modernizes. In *Red Sorghum* the tradition of selling young women as brides to old

24.17 Still from *Jou dou*, directed by Zhang Yimou, 1990, showing the brightly colored cloths.

men results in violence and murder. The heroine, Jiu'er, has a son by her lover, her elderly husband is murdered, and she is killed by the Japanese. Red is the color of both the wedding at the beginning of the film and the destructive fire at the end. In *Jou dou* (figure **24.17**) the heroine's son by her lover kills her husband and her lover, and she kills herself. The story takes place in a dye factory, with the vivid colors—especially reds—of graceful cloths creating remarkable visual effects. They both reinforce and contrast with the intense emotions simmering beneath the surface.

Raise the Red Lantern portrays the social and psychological confinement of women in Chinese society. A wealthy husband with four wives signals which one he will spend the night with by raising a lighted red lantern before her house. The wives compete through sexual favors, physical beauty, and, above all, in producing a son. The heroine, Songlian, the fourth wife, realizes she must resort to subterfuge to survive. When she pretends to be pregnant and the pretense is discovered, her lanterns are permanently extinguished and she goes mad.

Zhang's 2004 film *House of Flying Daggers* is a love story set in the year 859. It uses special effects, evocative color, and also has a feminist quality in the power given to women. It features a number of remarkable scenes in which daggers fly through the air, are able to turn around to find their mark, and can split numerous bamboo stalks in unison.

***TRAINSPOTTING*: THE DRUG CULTURE** The Scottish film *Trainspotting*, which came out in 1996, is a graphic account of drug abuse. Directed by Danny Boyle (born 1956), it depicts the effects of heroin on a group of friends living in Edinburgh. Their lives are so totally absorbed by drugs that work, family, and other relationships become meaningless. Driven by their addiction, they are willing to do whatever is necessary, even commit crimes and cause an infant to die from neglect, for the next fix.

Having originally turned to drugs to escape their alienation from modern life, the characters find that there is no easy road to happiness. The combination of graphic reality and surreal imagery is one of the most powerful features of the film. In one scene the main character, Renton, loses his drug-filled suppository while going to the toilet. He panics at the thought of foregoing the drug's high and dives into the toilet bowl, "the filthiest in Scotland." In a surrealistic shift, the water expands and Renton swims through it in search of his suppository.

OSAMA *Osama* (2003), the first Afghan film shot after the Taliban lost control of Afghanistan, is not about Osama bin Laden. Written and directed on a low budget by Siddiq Barmak, who studied in Moscow, the film depicts the terror dominating the lives of women in Kabul under Taliban rule. It shows the sadism of the Taliban in the name of religion, the willingness to see women starve rather than be free to earn a living, and the brutal view of society and law.

Osama is the story of a twelve-year-old girl who lives with her grandmother and her widowed mother. The women have no rights, not even the right to earn a living. When starvation threatens them, the girl is renamed Osama, her hair is cut short, and she is dressed to look like a boy and sent out to work. As the girl fights to survive, she symbolizes the struggle for human dignity. Her ultimate fate, however, reflects the disastrous and destructive effects of extreme Islamic fundamentalism. When she is revealed to be a girl, she is arrested and forced to become the fourth wife of a local mullah.

Special Effects and Animation

THE LORD OF THE RINGS The trilogy of films (2001–2003) based on the trilogy *The Lord of the Rings* by J. (John) R. (Ronald) R. (Reuel) Tolkien (1892–1973), which was originally published in 1954–1955, exemplifies the global flavor of many contemporary productions. The director, Peter Jackson, and much of the cast came from New Zealand, where the film was made, but technically it is a Hollywood production. A wealth of special effects conveys the fantasy world inspired by the Anglo-Saxon language, Norse mythology, the epic of *Beowulf*, the Finnish poems and ballads known as the *Kalevala*, and the Icelandic *Edda* (see Chapter 10). Tolkien studied philology, fought in World War I, and became professor of Anglo-Saxon literature at Oxford University. *The Lord of the Rings* is a story of an attempt by evil forces and the tyrants Sauron and

Saruman to take over the world. Although Tolkien denied any such connection, his tyrants bear a close resemblance to historical dictators such as Hitler and Stalin.

Reflecting the adverse effects of the Industrial Revolution in nineteenth-century Britain and the modern disregard of the environment by big business, Tolkien's tyrants threaten to destroy nature. The elves, dwarves, and hobbits, along with the good wizard Gandalf, set out to save the world. The story revolves around the ring, which comes into the possession of Frodo, a hobbit, who has the qualities of the traditional epic hero. Because the ring is a source of evil as well as of good, its owner can choose either path. At first, evil is presented as an external threat, but Frodo comes to realize that the only way to defeat evil is through his own spiritual maturity. To achieve this, he has to destroy the ring. Like the traditional epic hero, Frodo descends into a lower world and then ascends into the natural world. When he defeats the evil within himself he enters a supernatural world.

24.18 Disney/Pixar, still from *Finding Nemo*, 2003.

FINDING NEMO New animation techniques at the turn of the century were inspired by digital imaging. In 2004 the Walt Disney Studios decided to abandon the use of cel animation traditionally used to make cartoons. Digital animation techniques devised by Pixar Animation Studios, then a Disney partner, were used to create *Finding Nemo* (2003). It is the story of Nemo (also the name of a fictional sea captain), the only son of the clownfish Marlin, who has lost his wife in a shark attack. Nemo is captured from the Great Barrier Reef by a diver and ends up in the fish tank of a dentist. Marlin and his forgetful fish-friend, Dory, set out to locate Nemo, while Nemo and the other occupants of the tank plot ways to escape.

The still in figure **24.18** illustrates the vivid colors and rich textures achievable with digital animation. In the earlier cel technique each movement of a figure was individually drawn and colored by hand, leaving the forms unshaded. The Pixar technique, in contrast, takes an artist's conception and either sculpts it three-dimensionally by hand and scans it into a computer, or models it directly into a computer using a three-dimensional graphics program. Once the character has been created in the computer, hinges (called "avars") are added, which allow the figure to move. Animation is achieved by manipulating the avars, and transitions between poses and scenes are created by adjusting the models. A separate software program is used to generate the impression of mood and shading through the provision of color, texture, and directional lighting. Once the overall images are completed, music and sound effects are added.

EPILOGUE: THE SPIRIT OF THE HUMANITIES

It is fitting to conclude this text with two contemporary poets—both winners of the Nobel Prize for literature—who embody the creative spirit of the humanities: Seamus Heaney (born 1939) and Derek Walcott (born 1930). Both have enormous respect for the past, which they see as continually evolving in the present. They are committed to a knowledge of history and to the human spirit as foundations of civilization. In addition, both recognize the broad Classical basis of Western culture and gain strength from identifying with their places of origin, Heaney with Ireland and Walcott with the Antilles and the Caribbean Sea. They also take a global approach to all aspects of creative imagination.

The early poems of Seamus Heaney, one of nine children, are inspired by his childhood amid the farms of County Derry, north of Belfast, in Northern Ireland. He became interested in politics, especially Irish politics, and writes essays as well as poems. Heaney's poetic style is packed with imagery as he muses on themes of death, memory, and history. Several of his poems are versions of works by Classical authors, including Aeschylus, Virgil, and Dante. In 1989 Heaney was appointed professor of poetry at Oxford University, a post he held until 1994.

In his play *The Cure at Troy* (1990) Heaney composed a version of Sophocles' *Philoctetes*. According to Greek myth, Philoctetes agreed to light the funeral pyre of Heracles. Suffering from the gift of a poisoned cloak, Heracles rewarded Philoctetes for ending his misery by giving him his bow and arrows. Philoctetes later joined the Greeks in the Trojan War but was bitten on the foot by a snake and the wound would not heal. The wily Odysseus persuaded Agamemnon to abandon Philoctetes on a deserted island, where he remained for ten years. Later Odysseus learned from an oracle that Troy could not be won without the bow and arrows of Heracles and he set out to recover them. To do so, he used his wiles to persuade Philoctetes to return to Troy. Once at Troy, Philoctetes was healed and killed Priam's son Paris with Heracles' arrow.

In the opening lines of the chorus, Heaney recreates the atmosphere of the Greek heroic age, while observing that men willingly repeat their mistakes, making the present a reprise of the past:

> Philoctetes.
>   Hercules [Heracles].
>   Odysseus.
> Heroes. Victims. Gods and human beings.
> All throwing shapes, every one of them
> Convinced he's in the right, all of them glad
> To repeat themselves and their every last mistake,
> No matter what.

In "xix" of 1991, Heaney explores the relationship between memory and the impulse to order history:

> Memory as a building or a city,
> Well lighted, well laid out, appointed with
> *Tableaux vivants* and costumed effigies—
>
> Statues in purple cloaks, or painted red,
> Ones wearing crowns, ones smeared with mud or blood:
> So that the mind's eye could haunt itself
>
> With fixed associations and learn to read
> Its own contents in meaningful order,
> Ancient textbooks recommended that
>
> Familiar places be linked deliberately
> With a code of images. You knew the portent
> In each setting, you blinked and concentrated.

In 1999 Heaney translated the Anglo-Saxon epic *Beowulf.* He saw this task as a way of contacting his linguistic past through the act of transforming (translating) the ancient language into modern English. As a combination of history and poetry, Heaney's translation shows that language evolves over time, but is also a storehouse of history.

Derek Walcott was born in St. Lucia, in the Antilles, and has lived in Trinidad since 1953. The author of poems and plays and a writing instructor at Boston University, Walcott published his epic masterpiece *Omeros* in 1990. Inspired by the epics of Homer, Walcott created a vast poetic panorama set in the Caribbean that draws on world literature, myth, and history. His range of language, humor, and imagery springs from local dialect, stream-of-consciousness thought, and Classical allusions.

Like all epics, *Omeros* is about a journey—as much a journey of the imagination as a geographic journey, which reflects Walcott's extensive travel—but *Omeros* is not a chronological narrative. Instead, ships are followed through time, place, and distant cultures, from ancient Egypt and Greece to the seventeenth-century Dutch merchants, from the Harlem Renaissance to World War II, to the present-day villages of the Caribbean.

Walcott's imagery is constructed from fragments of world literature, from the *Ramayana* to the Bible and the Koran, and from works of art, from Monet's *Water Lilies* to local woven baskets.

In the lecture he gave when he received the Nobel Prize for literature in 1992, Walcott addressed the poet's relation to memory and history. He compared poetry to archaeology, both being processes of "excavation and self-discovery." Poetry, like a broken artifact, he said, is composed of fragments, which are reassembled into a creative whole. In *Omeros* he evokes the heroic past with characters and epithets named for their Homeric counterparts: Achilles (his poetic alter-ego), Helen, Hector, the Cyclops, and the wine-dark sea.

The epic opens with Philoctete, a Caribbean version of Philoctetes:

> "This is how, one sunrise, we cut down them canoes."
> Philoctete smiles for the tourists, who try taking
> his soul with their cameras.

Walcott regards Philoctete's wound as a legacy of his African past, when captives bound for slavery were chained by the ankle and shipped to the New World. Just as one is never free from the past, in Walcott's view, so Philoctete's wound will remain:

> The itch in the sore
> tingles like the tendrils of the anemone,
> and the puffed blister of Portuguese man-o'-war.
>
> He believed the swelling came from the chained ankles
> of his grandfathers. Or else why was there no cure?

Recent history is generally less well fixed in the cultural memory and thus more subject to revision than earlier eras. The recent past seems immediate and looms large in our minds. But our access to the past is limited to the fragments of what has been preserved—recorded documents, works of art and architecture, surviving literary products, and oral tradition. The modern age may be more technologically and scientifically advanced than previous centuries, but whether it is more creative, more ethical, or more moral is a matter of debate.

In the light of Derek Walcott's assertion that "the sea is history," we recognize that our historical survey can only touch on a few remembered highlights of time. History is written from the fragments of texts, artifacts, buildings, myths, and legends. Its authors rely on whatever floats to the surface of the vast sea that Walcott calls history.

KEY TERMS

dystopia a utopia gone wrong.

Euro the single European currency, adopted in 2002 by most, but not all, of the member countries of the EU.

Human Genome Project research to map the genetic make-up of humans and other organisms.

KEY QUESTIONS

1. How are issues of ethnic conflict and efforts toward international cooperation central to the modern age?
2. What work of art would illustrate the following?
   a. the AIDS crisis
   b. feminism
   c. the environment
   d. genetic mutation
   e. globalization
3. Which musical styles have become transnational? What is the difference between transnational styles and "cross-over" musical combinations?
4. How has digital technology influenced art and film? Give examples of each.
5. How is history recorded and remembered? Why can history be thought of as fluid and dynamic like the sea?

SUGGESTED READING

Ambrosius, G., and W. H. Hubbard. *A Social and Economic History of Twentieth-Century Europe*. Cambridge, MA: Harvard University Press, 1989.
▸ A one-volume survey.

Beardsley, Richard. *Earthworks and Beyond: Contemporary Art in the Landscape*. New York: Abbeville Press, 1984.
▸ Art, landscape, and Earth Art.

Bernstein, R. *Out of the Blue: The Story of September 11, 2001*. New York: New York Times Books, 2002.
▸ A study by a leading journalist.

Bin Laden, Carmen. *Inside the Kingdom*. New York: Warner Books, 2004.
▸ A personal account of the dismal life of women in Saudi Arabia and the author's escape from it.

Bramwell, E. *Ecology in the 20th Century*. New Haven, CT: Yale University Press, 1989.
▸ Environmentalism from the late nineteenth century through the 1980s.

Eisenstein, Sergei. *The Film Sense*, trans. Jay Leyda. New York: Harcourt Brace, 1970.
▸ Eisenstein's classic study of film montage.

Goldberg, Rose Lee. *Performance Art from Futurism to the Present*. New York: Harry N. Abrams, 1988.
▸ A survey of performance art in the twentieth century.

Heaney, Seamus. *Seeing Things: Poems*. New York: Farrar, Straus and Giroux, 1991.
▸ Poems by Seamus Heaney.

Maltby, R. (ed.). *Passing Parade: A History of Popular Culture in the Twentieth Century*. Oxford: Oxford University Press, 1989.
▸ Popular culture from a scholarly perspective.

Sandler, Irving. *Art of the Postmodern Era*. New York: HarperCollins, 1996.
▸ Postmodernism in the twentieth century.

Walcott, Derek. *Omeros*. New York: Farrar, Straus and Giroux, 1990.
▸ A Caribbean version of the Homeric epics.

SUGGESTED FILMS

1987 *Red Sorghum*, dir. Zhang Yimou

1990 *The Handmaid's Tale*, dir. Volker Schlöndorff

1990 *Jou dou*, dir. Zhang Yimou

1991 *Raise the Red Lantern*, dir. Zhang Yimou

1992 *Glengarry Glen Ross*, dir. James Foley

1994 *Oleanna*, dir. David Mamet

1996 *Trainspotting*, dir. Danny Boyle

2000 *Crouching Tiger, Hidden Dragon*, dir. Ang Lee

2001 *A.I. Artificial Intelligence*, dir. Steven Spielberg

2001–2003 *The Lord of the Rings* (trilogy), dir. Peter Jackson

2003 *Finding Nemo* (Disney/Pixar)

2003 *Osama*, dir. Siddiq Barmak

2004 *House of Flying Daggers*, dir. Zhang Yimou

GLOSSARY

abacus the square element of the Doric capital.

abolitionist an advocate of the abolition of slavery.

action painting a technique of applying paint to canvas that includes dripping, spraying, and throwing.

agora an open public space in a city.

aleatory music a post-war musical style that uses chance or randomness as a prime principle.

Althing in medieval Iceland, a general assembly governed according to a law code.

ambulatory in a church, the curved passageway that surrounds an apse.

anima the female aspect of Jung's archetypal soul.

animus the male aspect of Jung's archetypal soul.

antechamber a room before, and leading into, another room.

anthropomorphic human in form.

antiphon in music, a liturgical chant with a Latin text sung with a psalm.

antiphonal in music, a style of composition using two or more groups of performers to create effects of echo or contrast.

antipope the name given to a rival pope, often resident in Avignon, but not legitimized by the Roman Church.

apartheid the policy of racial "separate development" pursued in South Africa from 1948.

apse the curved section at the end of a nave.

aqueduct a structure designed to transport water.

archetypes universal images, such as the good or bad parent, the hero, the wise man, and so forth.

architrave the lowest long horizontal part of the entablature, which rests directly on the capital of a column.

archivolts the attached arches around the tympanum.

aria a composition for solo voice with orchestral accompaniment; usually part of an opera or oratorio.

Ark of the Covenant the original container for the Tablets containing the Ten Commandments.

art film a term used to describe films that often have greater artistic value and innovation than "commercial" productions.

art song a composed song (as opposed to a folksong or popular song), often the concert setting of a poem; the term is commonly applied to the German *lied* of the Romantic period.

ashlar rectangular blocks of stone.

aulos (plural **auloi**) a double-reed pipe.

autocracy absolute rule by one person.

avant-garde newness for its own sake.

ballett (balletto) in Italian music, a lilting, dance-like song.

baptistery a building in which baptisms are performed.

barrel vault a vault made by extending a round arch through space.

bay a space in a building defined by piers.

Beghards in medieval northern Europe, a group of lay men dedicated to leading a spiritual life and working for the community.

Beguines in medieval northern Europe, a group of lay women who established spiritual centers.

benefice originally land granted for services, the word later included ecclesiastical offices.

binary the form of a piece of music in two sections, *AB*.

bipedal able to walk upright on two feet.

black humor humor with a macabre quality.

blues an African-American style of music, existing in folk and urban popular forms, with lyrics typically expressing the hardships of life.

bourgeoisie in Marxist theory, the upper-middle classes who own the means of production.

break a short musical passage like a cadenza, played by one or more of the instruments in jazz or blues.

burin a sharp instrument used for incising.

bust a sculpture or picture showing a figure from the head to just below the shoulders.

cadence the close of a musical phrase.

cadenza a solo virtuosic display, sometimes improvised, near the end of an aria or a movement of a concerto.

caliph a Muslim ruler or leader.

canonical authorized; used with reference to a collection of writings or works applying to a particular religion or author.

canopic jar a container for organs removed during mummification.

cantata a composition for one or more voices with instrumental accompaniment; church cantatas are sacred pieces, but there are also secular cantatas.

cantilever a projecting beam or girder, supported at only one end.

cantor in Jewish worship, the singer who chants Bible readings, prayers, or parts of the liturgy.

capital the decorated top of a column.

cartouche a rectangle with curved ends framing the name of a king.

caryatid a supporting column carved to represent a woman; the male equivalent is an *atlantis* (plural *atlantes*).

castrato from the late sixteenth through the nineteenth century, a male castrated before his voice changed (usually between the age of six and eight) so he could sing with a soprano or alto voice as an adult.

catacomb an underground burial place or cemetery, held sacred by the Romans.

catharsis "cleansing"; a term used by Aristotle to describe the emotional effect of a tragic drama on the audience.

centering a means of holding stones in place during the construction of an arch.

ceramics pottery made by firing (heating) clay.

chamber music (literally, "room music") music for a small number of instruments.

chanson (French, "song") a secular polyphonic song in the Middle Ages and Renaissance; the form includes rondeaux, ballades, and virelais.

chivalry a code of values in which knights promised service and loyalty to a lord in return for protection.

chorale a congregational hymn in the German Protestant church.

chorale prelude an organ piece based on a chorale theme.

chordal progression a sequence of chords.

chromatic harmony harmony containing notes that do not belong to the key in which the music is written.

chthonic relating to underground aspects of the earth.

citadel a fortified elevated area or city.

clerestory in a church or temple, an upper story of the nave, above the aisle, that is pierced with windows to admit light.

coda a closing section of a piece of music, added to round it off rather than as a main part of the structure.

coffer a recessed geometric panel in a ceiling.

collage a technique of making an image by pasting objects onto a surface.

collective unconscious an idea or belief held collectively and unconsciously by a group rather than an individual.

colonnade a row of columns.

column cluster a group of attached columns.

Comecon (Council for Mutual Economic Assistance) the organization formed in 1949 to improve trade between the Soviet Union and its eastern European satellite countries.

Cominform (Communist Information Bureau) an organization formed in 1947 to coordinate the activity of Communist Parties throughout Europe.

conceit in literature, a witty and complex turn of phrase.

concerto a musical work for soloist (or soloists) and orchestra, exploiting the contrast between small and large forces.

concerto grosso in the Baroque period, a musical composition for a small group of solo instruments accompanied by an orchestra.

condensation in psychoanalysis, the representation of different objects or ideas by a single element, especially in dreams, fantasies, and neurotic symptoms.

conditioned reflex an act or reaction by habit to a repeated stimulus or set of stimuli.

condottiere in medieval and Renaissance Italy, a soldier of fortune.

consonance the sounding together of tones that sound harmonious, the opposite of dissonance.

consort a set of musical instruments of the same family for playing music composed before about 1700.

continuo a type of accompaniment in Baroque music that uses a keyboard or plucked instrument to play chords, often with a low sustaining instrument playing the bass line of the music.

contrapposto a type of pose characterized by a twist at the waist.

convention an accepted practice.

corbel brick or masonry courses arranged to form an arch or dome.

cornice the topmost horizontal part of an entablature.

counterpoint (adj. **contrapuntal**) performing two or more melodies simultaneously; polyphony.

couplet two consecutive lines in a poem that rhyme or have some other correspondence.

courses layers of stone.

covenant a formal agreement; the conditional promises made between God and his people in the Bible.

creed a formal statement of the beliefs of a particular religion or philosophy.

cromlech a circle of stones, characteristic of the Neolithic period in western Europe.

cross-vault (or **groin vault**) a vault made by the intersection of two barrel vaults.

cuneiform a form of writing used in Mesopotamia and consisting of wedge-shaped characters.

cursive handwriting in flowing strokes with the letters joined together.

curvilinear having curved forms.

cyclopaean masonry huge stone blocks used to construct walls, especially in the Mycenaean citadels.

deductive method a method of reasoning in which the conclusion follows logically from a given premise.

deme a unit of local government.

détente a thawing of international tension.

development in music, (a) a process of expanding, elaborating, and transforming a musical theme; (b) the section of a movement in which development occurs (commonly the middle section of a movement in sonata form).

diptych a two-paneled painting.

discant in medieval music, a style in which the lower, tenor voice sings in a steady rhythm, while one or more higher voices sing slightly faster melodies above.

displacement in psychoanalysis, the relocation of an element from its original or usual setting to another place.

dissolve in cinematography, the superimposition of one picture over another followed by disappearance of the latter, usually to mark a transition or change of scene.

dissonance the effect produced when musical notes that clash with each other are sounded simultaneously.

dithyramb a type of lyric poem sung and accompanied by flute music.

dome a hemispherical roof or ceiling; made by rotating a round arch.

domino theory the notion (originating in the Eisenhower administration) that countries in Southeast Asia would fall to the communists like dominoes if not stopped by the West.

dromos a roadway.

drum the circular support of a dome.

duet a piece of music for two performers, or two soloists plus accompaniment.

dynasty a family of kings.

dystopia a utopia gone wrong.

echinus (Greek, "hedgehog") part of the Greek Orders above the abacus.

edda a type of Icelandic poetry that recounts myths and legends.

electro-acoustic music music generated using electronic equipment.

encaustic a type of paint in which beeswax is mixed with pigment.

engaged column a column that is attached to a wall.

entablature the portion above the capital on a column; it includes the architrave, the frieze, and the cornice.

entasis (Greek, "stretching") the bulge in the shaft of a Greek column.

epic theater the name given to his plays by Brecht; his aim was to alienate his audience through his work.

epistolary a type of novel, which uses letters or diaries to reveal character and to move the plot along.

epithet an identifying adjective or phrase.

equestrian monument a portrait of a ruler on horseback.

étude (French, "study") an instrumental piece written to develop or display playing technique.

Euro the single European currency, adopted in 2002 by most, but not all, of the member countries of the EU.

existentialism a post-World War II philosophical system that holds that human beings are totally responsible for their acts and that the universe is godless.

Exodus the forty-year journey made by the Israelites, led by Moses, out of Egypt to freedom; also, the second book of the Hebrew Bible.

exposition the first section of a piece of music (especially a movement in sonata form), in which the principal themes are stated.

fade-in in cinematography, the emergence of a picture from darkness to full visibility.

fade-out in cinematography, the reduction in visibility of a picture to signal a transition or conclusion.

falling action the means by which a complication in a literary work is unraveled and resolved.

Fascism a set of political principles that tend to be authoritarian, nationalistic, anti-democratic, anti-Marxist, and frequently anti-Semitic.

fealty an oath of allegiance sworn by a vassal to a lord.

feudalism in medieval Europe, a fluid political, military, and social organization based on mutual obligations between lords and their vassals, who swore allegiance to them.

finial a decorative feature at the top of an object or building.

fix in photography, to make an image permanent.

foliate leaf-shaped.

folk music orally transmitted music of unknown origin.

foreshortened shown in perspective.

forum the public center of an ancient Roman city.

freeman a property-owning peasant, who turned the property over to a lord in return for protection and certain economic and legal rights.

fresco a technique of applying water-based paint to a damp plaster surface, usually a wall or ceiling.

friar a member of a mendicant ("begging") Order.

frieze the central section of an entablature, often containing relief sculpture.

frontal facing front.

frottola a lighthearted, generally amorous poem for three or four voices sung to instrumental accompaniment, usually chordal in style.

fugue a type of polyphonic musical composition with a formal structure that uses imitation between voices systematically.

galant describing a light, elegant, tuneful, and relatively simple style of eighteenth-century music.

gallery a row of figures.

gamelan a Southeast Asian percussion instrument similar to a xylophone; also an orchestra consisting of such instruments and gongs.

gene a unit of heredity by which characteristics are transmitted from parents to their offspring.

genocide the extermination of a cultural or racial group; the destruction of the group's culture.

geocentrism the view that the sun orbits the earth.

gesso a white coating of chalk, plaster, and resin that is applied to a surface to make it more receptive to paint.

ghazal a Middle Eastern poem in couplets having strict meter and a double rhyme scheme.

glasnost literally "openness" in Russian; the policy introduced in the 1980s of permitting criticism of the Communist Party in the Soviet Union.

glaze a translucent paint layer that enriches colors.

glissando a vocal or instrumental slide up or down, a continuum of pitches filling in the regular notes of the scale.

gorgoneion the severed head of the Gorgon Medusa.

groundling in Elizabethan theater, a spectator standing in the area (the pit) in front of the stage.

guild an organization of workers within a particular craft.

happening an improvised theatrical event with an appearance of spontaneity, popular in the 1960s.

heliocentrism the notion that the sun is at the center of the solar system.

helot a member of the native population enslaved by the Spartans.

heresy a belief or practice that is contrary to established Church teaching.

hierarchical proportion a convention in ancient art in which size is equated with status.

hieratic a cursive script derived from hieroglyphs.

hieroglyphs a writing system using pictorial representations as characters.

Holocaust the extermination between 1940 and 1945 by the Nazis of millions of European Jews; also known as the "Final Solution."

hoplite a heavily armed ancient Greek foot-soldier who fought in close formation (phalanx).

hoplon a shield carried by a hoplite.

hubris arrogant grandiosity, often characterizing Greek tragic heroes.

Human Genome Project research to map the genetic make-up of humans and other organisms.

humanism an intellectual and artistic trend, beginning in the late thirteenth century and based on a renewed interest in the Classical tradition.

hymn a song praising a god.

hypostyle a hall with a roof supported by rows of columns; the center columns are taller than those at the sides.

icon a sacred image.

iconoclasm the destruction of religious images.

iconography the apparent meaning of an image and its underlying symbolism.

iconophile someone who supports religious imagery.

idée fixe a term used by the composer Berlioz to describe a recurring theme in a large-scale work.

ideogram a pictorial representation of an idea.

idyll a short descriptive poem describing rural life.

illumination the decoration of biblical and other sacred manuscript texts with painted images.

illusionistic a type of representation in which objects appear real.

impost the support of an arch attached to a wall.

incidental music music composed as background or accompaniment to a stage production.

incise to cut designs or letters into wood or metal with a sharp instrument.

inkblot an image resembling a blot of ink, used for psychological testing (as in the Rorschach Test).

Inquisitors officials appointed by the Roman Church to combat heresy.

intaglio a process in which lines or images are incised in a surface.

interval in music, a difference in pitch between two notes.

irony a literary device in which the implication of the words is the opposite of their literal meaning.

isocephaly the horizontal alignment of heads in a painting or sculpture.

isorhythm in fourteenth-century music, the use of a repeated rhythmic scheme, usually applied to a plainsong melody.

japonisme a trait of style reminiscent of Japanese culture.

jazz music improvised by performers in ensembles over a framework of chords, which grew out of African-American experience and developed in New Orleans at the start of the twentieth century.

kennings concrete, compound words used to enrich a narrative.

keystone in a round arch, the top center stone holding the voussoirs in place.

knight in the Middle Ages, a man who carried out military service in return for the right to hold land.

krater an ancient Greek vessel in which wine and water are mixed.

lancet a tall, narrow arched window.

lapis lazuli a semi-precious, light blue stone.

Lares and Penates Roman household gods.

lay a short poem, sung to the accompaniment of a harp.

leitmotif in a dramatic musical work, a recurrent theme that can represent a particular person, object, or more abstract idea; a term used initially by Wagner, and by commentators on his music since.

libation the pouring of a drink as an offering to a god.

libretto the text for an opera or oratorio.

Linear A undeciphered Minoan writing used for record-keeping and religious dedications.

Linear B readable Mycenaean script; an early form of Greek.

lintel a horizontal cross-beam.

litany a type of prayer in which a leader and a congregation speak alternately.

lithography a printing medium using a stone press on which areas are made receptive to ink.

liturgy rites of worship.

logical positivism a philosophical system distinguished by a special emphasis on logic.

lunette a half-moon shaped wall section.

maat the Egyptian concept of cosmic order, truth, and justice; also (when capitalized) the name of the goddess embodying those qualities.

macroeconomics the study of the economic system as a whole, with particular attention to the general level of income and production (as opposed to microeconomics).

madrigal a secular contrapuntal song for several voices, from the Renaissance.

magic realism a film-making and literary style in which miraculous and imaginary events are presented as if they are real.

mandorla an oval of light around the entire body.

manor in the Middle Ages, a group of farms and villages.

manorialism in medieval Europe, a social system organized around a manor in which a landlord allowed peasants to live and work on the land in exchange for a percentage of their produce and other obligations.

maqam in Arabic music, a specific scale having certain phrases and patterns.

martyr a person who dies for his or her beliefs (the meaning of the Greek word is "witness").

martyrium (plural **martyria**) a structure built over the tomb of a martyr.

Marxism the political, economic, and social principles advocated by Marx, Engels, and their followers.

masque a short dramatic composition of allegorical content, usually performed as court entertainment and consisting of mime, music, and dancing.

mass culture popular culture that has wide appeal.

master-builder one who supervises the building of a cathedral.

mausoleum (plural **mausolea**) a large, elaborate round tomb.

mayor of the palace in Merovingian France, the king's major-domo (prime minister) and often the real ruler.

mazurka a Polish country dance in triple meter with off-beat accents.

megalithic a Neolithic structure made of large stones.

megaron the main building in the Mycenaean citadel.

melismatic music in which several notes are sung to one syllable.

mendicant a member of a religious Order who wandered from town to town begging.

menhir a single upright stone.

menorah a candelabrum with seven candlesticks, three on each side and one in the center.

mercantilism the belief that a nation's wealth depends on the possession of precious metals and that, to achieve this, a government must encourage overseas trade and the foundation of colonies.

metaphor a comparison without using "like" or "as" in which one thing stands for another.

metaphysics a type of philosophy that deals with first principles, such as existence and understanding.

meter in music, regular division into set numbers of rhythmic beats.

"method" acting a school of acting, based on the theory of Stanislavsky, in which actors identify with their characters' inner motivations.

metope the square area between the triglyphs of a Doric frieze, often containing relief sculpture.

minaret a thin tower on the exterior of a mosque.

minstrel a wandering performer who sang secular songs in medieval courts.

minuscule a small cursive script.

miracle play a medieval religious play dramatizing miracles.

misogynist someone who dislikes and distrusts women.

mode in ancient music, an arrangement of notes forming a scale; Dorian mode: strong and military; Phrygian mode: passionate; Lydian mode: mournful; Mixolydian mode: elegiac.

modulate in music, change from one key to another.

monody a style of music in which a single voice carries a melody.

monophonic consisting of a single line of music.

monotheism a religion whose adherents believe in a single god.

morality play a medieval religious play that gives dramatic form to the human struggle between good and evil.

Morse code a code (invented by Samuel Morse) in which letters, numerals, and other symbols are represented by dots and dashes.

mosaic an image on a wall, ceiling, or floor created from small pieces of colored tile, glass, or stone.

motet a polyphonic choral work, generally written in Latin for church performance; some early motets were secular and multilingual.

motif in music, a short rhythmic or melodic pattern used recurrently to unify a movement or a whole piece.

muezzin in Islam, a crier who calls the faithful to prayer from a minaret.

mummification in ancient Egypt, a process taking seventy-two days in which bodies were embalmed and organs were removed.

musical a drama in spoken dialogue supported by songs, choruses, dances, and imaginative stage direction; the form originated in the early twentieth century.

mystery (or **mystery cult**) cultish religion, based on ancient myths, of a type that was common in Greece and throughout the Roman Empire.

mystery play a medieval religious play based on a Bible story.

narrative sequence a story that follows chronologically.

narthex a vestibule or porch across the west end of a church.

natural selection a process described by Charles Darwin in which individuals or groups survive only if they can adapt to their environment.

naturalistic representing objects as they actually appear in nature.

nave in basilicas, a wide central aisle separated from the side aisles by rows of columns.

necking the lowest of three elements comprising the capital of a Greek column.

necropolis (plural **necropoleis**) a city of the dead.

neume in plainsong, a diagonal mark indicating a note or group of notes over the word to be sung.

New Wave a term (derived from the French expression *nouvelle vague*) denoting a group of new, non-traditional film-makers.

newsreel a short motion picture dealing with news or current events; also a literary technique interspersing fiction with news headlines.

nihilism the philosophy of nothingness.

nocturne a musical composition that expresses the character of night, often written for the piano.

nominalism in philosophy, the belief that universals (general ideas, abstract concepts) are nothing more than names; the opposite of realism.

obelisk a tall, pointed, square pillar.

obverse the front of a coin.

Ockham's razor the principle of reducing—shaving—an assumption to its simplest form.

octave in music, the interval between two notes of the same name, twelve semitones apart; in poetry, a stanza of eight lines.

oculus a round opening in a wall or ceiling.

ode a lyric poem.

oligarchy a form of government by a few people.

onomatopoeic the use of words that sound like the objects to which they refer.

opera a dramatic performance set to music, for vocal soloists, chorus, and orchestra.

operetta a light opera, generally with spoken dialogue, songs, and dances.

oracle the revelation of a god, the person who utters the revelation, or the place the revelation is spoken.

oratorio an unstaged dramatic religious text set to music, for vocal soloists, chorus, and orchestra.

Order one of the architectural systems—Doric, Ionic, Corinthian—used by the Greeks to build their temples.

organum a form of plainsong in which two or more melodic lines are sung at once; a type of polyphony.

orthogonal consisting of, or relating to, right angles, or a line perpendicular to the plane of a relief or a picture.

ostinato a musical pattern that is persistently repeated while other elements change.

oxymoron a figure of speech using an apparent contradiction.

pagoda in Buddhist architecture, a multi-tiered tower that contains relics.

paradox a statement that seems to contradict common sense.

parchment the treated and dyed skin of a sheep or calf used for manuscripts.

Passion an unstaged musical setting of the story of the events leading up to Jesus' Crucifixion, for vocal soloists, chorus, and orchestra, originally performed within church services.

pastoral a poem dealing with the life and loves of shepherds.

pediment the triangular section at the end of a gable-roof, often decorated with sculpture.

pendentive an architectural feature resembling a curved triangle between the lunettes of a dome.

pentatonic a term used to describe a scale or mode consisting of only five notes.

perestroika literally "restructuring" in Russian; the attempt in the 1980s to reform the Soviet economy.

peristyle the freestanding columns surrounding a building.

personify embody as a person.

phalanx an ancient Greek military formation in which heavily armed soldiers lined up close together in deep ranks, defended by a wall of shields.

pharaoh a king of ancient Egypt.

phonogram an image denoting sounds.

piazza an open square in an urban area.

pictographic based on pictures.

pier a vertical support, usually rectangular.

pigment a substance used to give color to paints, inks, and dyes.

pilaster a square column.

pit the ground-level area in front of a stage.

pitch in music, height or depth of a tone.

plainsong (sometimes called **plainchant** or **Gregorian chant**) unaccompanied monophonic music sung to Latin texts as part of a church service.

plaque a small, decorated slab.

podium (plural **podia**) the masonry forming the base (usually rectangular) of a temple, arch, or other building.

polis (plural **poleis**) a city-state in ancient Greece.

polonaise a stately Polish processional dance in triple meter.

polyphony a form of music in which two or more melodic lines are sung at once.

polytheism belief in many gods.

Poor Clares nuns who belong to the Order of Abbess Clare.

portmanteau word a word formed by combining two or more words.

Positivism a philosophical movement that recognizes only positive facts and observable phenomena.

post-and-lintel an elevation system in which two upright posts support a horizontal lintel; also called a trilithon.

post-synchronization a technique of shooting a film without sound and then dubbing it in the studio.

precinct a sacred area.

prehistory a period of history before the development of writing systems.

profile the side view of a figure or object.

program in art, a series of related images.

program music instrumental music representing a non-musical idea or story.

projective testing a psychological testing technique in which an individual's reactions to ambiguous or unstructured material are analyzed.

proletariat in Marxist theory, the working class, which is hired and exploited by those who own the means of production.

proportion the relation of one part to another and of parts to the whole in terms of scale.

prothesis the lying-in-state of the dead.

psalter a psalm book.

pylon in ancient Egypt, a massive trapezoidal gateway.

pyramid an Egyptian tomb.

Pythagorean theorem a theory developed by Pythagoras: the square of the hypotenuse of a right-angled triangle equals the sum of the squares of the other two sides.

qawwâli a genre of Muslim devotional song, generally with lyrics in Urdu, popular in north India and Pakistan, typically sung by two to four vocalists, with hand-clapping, harmonium, and barrel-drum accompaniment.

quantum theory Planck's theory that radioactive energy moves in bursts of energy.

quatrain a four-line stanza (verse) in a poem.

radiating chapels chapels placed around an ambulatory.

ragtime an African-American precursor of jazz that flourished between 1890 and 1915, characterized by syncopated melody and mostly composed for the piano.

Rayogram a photograph made without a negative by exposing objects to light on light-sensitive paper.

rayonnant a style in Gothic rose windows in which shapes of glass radiate from the small circle at the center.

ready-made a manufactured object given a title by an artist and so turned into an artwork.

ready-made aided a ready-made that has been touched up by the artist.

realism in philosophy, the belief that universals (general ideas, abstract concepts) have an objective existence; the opposite of nominalism.

Realpolitik the belief that the only realistic policies for a state are those that serve that state's interests.

recapitulation in music, the third section of a movement in sonata form, in which the main themes are restated in the home key.

recitative a vocal passage in an opera or oratorio that has the inflections and rhythms of speech, sung by a soloist with light accompaniment.

Reconstruction the period (1867–1877) following the American Civil War during which the seceding states were reestablished in the Union.

relics the physical remains of saints and martyrs or objects associated with them.

relief a sculpture that is not completely carved away from its original material.

relieving triangle in architecture, a space that reduces the weight on the lintel below it.

reliquary a container housing a sacred relic.

resolution the outcome of a literary narrative.

responsorial a style of music in which a soloist alternates with congregational or choral responses.

reverse the back of a coin.

rhetoric the art of eloquent argument.

rhythm and blues an African-American style of urban popular music that flourished in the 1940s and 1950s, synthesizing aspects of blues with popular song format; from the 1970s, the term denotes African-American popular song (as opposed to rap) in general.

rhyton a drinking cup.

rib vault a vault made by the intersection of pointed arches.

ritornello in Baroque music, an orchestral passage that begins a work and is then repeated, in whole or in part, between episodes performed by soloists.

rock and roll the earliest form of rock music, which had its classic period from 1954 to 1959.

rock music a style of popular music heavily dependent on the electric guitar and amplified sound that has dominated the West since the 1950s, combining features of rhythm and blues, gospel music, jazz, and country and western music.

romance a medieval tale in a Romance language depicting heroic deeds.

rondo a musical form based on a recurrent theme with contrasting material presented between the recurrences; often used for the last movements of Classical symphonies, sonatas, and chamber works.

rose window a large, round window in Gothic cathedrals.

round a musical form in which each voice enters in turn with the same music after the previous one has sung several measures.

rule in monasteries, a systematic regimen.

rune-stone a large, upright memorial stone engraved with runic text.

rusticate to give a rustic appearance to masonry blocks by roughening their surface and beveling their edges.

saga an Icelandic story that mixes history, legend, myth, and folk tradition.

scaldic a type of Norse poetry that recounts tales of kings and heroes.

scat singing a jazz technique in which performers improvise using nonsense syllables.

scherzo (Italian, "joke") a lively movement in triple meter that superseded the minuet in symphonies and string quartets in the early nineteenth century.

scholasticism a system of thought developed in the Gothic period that addressed the apparent contradiction of faith and reason.

scop a type of German performer who sang tales of Germanic heroes in the fifth to seventh centuries.

scribe in ancient Egypt, a professional record-keeper, usually a member of the court.

scriptorium (plural **scriptoria**) a room for writing, usually in a monastery.

semiotics the study of signs and symbols in a range of fields, especially language, which includes Structuralism, Post-Structuralism, and Deconstruction.

sequence a pattern of notes repeated at higher or lower pitch than the original.

serf a peasant worker unable to leave the land.

serialism a term used to describe post-World War II music composed using the twelve-tone technique, in which various parameters in addition to pitch, such as dynamics and rhythm, are ordered and manipulated according to prescribed rules.

sextet a piece of chamber music for six players, or the group that performs such a piece.

shaman a religious figure believed to have supernatural powers, including the ability of self-transformation from human to animal.

simile a comparison using "like" or "as."

simony the selling of spiritual benefices.

sistrum a type of rattle.

slave narrative a genre of literature by freed slaves highlighting the abuses of slavery.

solarization the exposure of a photograph to light during the developing process.

sonata a musical composition in several movements for solo instrument, soloist with accompaniment, or ensemble.

sonata form a musical form used from the Classical period onward, particularly for the first movements of works such as symphonies, sonatas, and string quartets; it consists of exposition, development, and recapitulation.

song cycle a set of songs composed as an ordered unit, often using texts by the same author or based on the same theme.

sonnet a fourteen-line poem, typically composed of four-line stanzas with an alternating rhyming scheme and final rhyming couplet.

soul music a type of African-American commercial popular music that flourished mostly in the 1960s, with elements derived from gospel music.

spandrel in architecture, the triangular area between (1) two adjacent arches or (2) the side of an arch and the right angle that encloses it.

special effect in cinematography, a feature, often artificial or illusory, that is added to a film during its processing.

special theory of relativity Einstein's theory that movement in time and space is relative; only the speed of light is absolute.

sphinx a human-headed lion.

split choir a choir in which groups of singers sing against, or in response to, each other.

Sprechgesang (German, "speech-song") a twentieth-century vocal technique in which the performer is guided by the pitches indicated in the score, but immediately rises or falls away after sounding them; used extensively by Schoenberg.

springing the upward thrust of an arch.

stained glass pieces of colored glass held in place in windows by strips of lead.

stele a vertical stone marker or pillar.

stigmata marks resembling Christ's wounds on the Cross.

stream of consciousness spontaneous, unedited thought.

string quartet an ensemble of two violins, viola, and cello, or a piece of music written for those instruments.

stupa in Buddhist architecture, a round structure derived from the Buddha's burial mound.

stylization a technique in art in which forms are rendered as surface patterns rather than naturalistically

stylobate the top step from which a Doric column rises.

sublimation in psychoanalysis, the transformation of instinct into creative, socially productive activity.

suite in Baroque music, an instrumental work in several movements based on different dance meters.

syllogism a logical system of deductive reasoning, in which a conclusion follows from a major and a minor premise.

symbolization in psychoanalysis, the process of making symbols, in which one thing stands for another.

symmetry a type of balance in which two sides of an object or picture are mirror images of each other.

symphony (literally, a "sounding together") an orchestral work, usually consisting of three or four movements.

symposium a type of Greek banquet.

syncopation in music, accents on beats that are not normally stressed.

syncretism a process through which differing belief systems are assimilated.

synoptic referring to three books of the New Testament, the Gospels of Matthew, Mark, and Luke, which are considered to form a group.

Tablets (Tables) of the Law the stones on which were inscribed the laws given to Moses on Mount Sinai.

taqsim in Arabic music, an improvised elaboration of *maqams* in a free-rhythmic style.

template a diagram of an architectural section used by master-builders.

tenebrism a style of painting, associated with Caravaggio and his followers, in which certain features of a scene are dramatically illuminated while the rest are in darkness.

tenor in medieval music, the low voice singing long held notes of plainchant in polyphonic pieces.

ternary the form of a piece of music in three sections, *ABA*.

tetrachord a series of four notes, with the first and last separated by the interval of a perfect fourth.

tetrarchy a form of government by four co-rulers.

thalassocracy rule through the control of the sea.

theocracy rule by priests or other religious leaders.

tholos (plural **tholoi**) a circular tomb of beehive shape.

tonality in music, a system of keys, which gives the feeling of a "home" pitch.

tondo a painting or relief sculpture having a round frame.

tone poem (symphonic poem) a one-movement orchestral composition based on a non-musical idea.

tonic in music, the home key.

tragic flaw in theater, a characteristic of a hero that causes his or her downfall.

transept in a church, the cross-section corresponding to the arms of the Cross.

transi tomb a tomb with an effigy of the deceased in a state of decay.

translate in religion, to transfer or remove to another place.

transubstantiation in the Mass, a process in which bread and wine are believed to be transformed literally into Christ's body and blood.

transverse arch in a church or cathedral, an arch that spans the nave.

travertine a type of pale limestone, used in Roman building, that turns yellow as it ages.

triadic based on the three notes of the "common" chord in Western music, using notes 1, 3, and 5 of the scale.

triglyphs in a Doric frieze, the three verticals between the metopes.

trilithon a single post-and-lintel.

trill a musical ornament consisting of the rapid alternation of two adjacent notes.

trilogy a set of three related works of literature.

trio sonata a Baroque musical genre in several movements, normally written for two melody instruments and continuo.

trireme an ancient Greek warship with an iron-covered prow.

trope a passage, with or without words, inserted in Gregorian chant.

trumeau the central vertical support of a lintel or tympanum above a wide doorway.

tufa soft, easily workable, volcanic rock, used in Etruscan building.

Tuscan column a form of Doric style, used by the Etruscans.

twelve-tone technique a twentieth-century compositional method in which all twelve notes of the octave are ordered in a "tone-row," which is manipulated in various prescribed ways to shape the musical content; formulated by Schoenberg.

tympanum in Christian architecture, the curved triangular area between an arch and the lintel below it.

tyranny a form of rule in which power is concentrated in a single person.

tyrant an illegitimate leader who exercises absolute power, often oppressively.

Underground Railroad the clandestine network in the United States that helped fugitive slaves to reach the North or Canada.

unison voices singing (or instruments playing) the same melody, rather than performing different lines to make harmony.

Utilitarianism a political philosophy that holds that the aim of all action should be the greatest happiness for the greatest number of people.

utopianism a philosophy that proposes ideal (and often impractical) schemes for the perfection of social and political conditions.

vanishing point in linear perspective, the point at which the orthogonals meet.

vassal in the Middle Ages, a man who held land in return for duties of allegiance to a lord.

verismo (Italian, "realism") a term applied to late-nineteenth-century operas with contemporary settings, true-to-life characters, and strongly expressed emotions.

vernacular the language of a particular country or region.

vibrato rapid, slight fluctuations in pitch, used by musicians for emotional effect.

vignette a small section of decoration or a literary sketch.

villa in ancient Rome, a country estate.

virtuoso a performing artist (usually a musician) of outstanding skill.

voussoir a wedge-shaped stone used in round arches.

whirling dervish a Sufi ascetic who seeks divine ecstasy through whirling to music.

woodcut or **woodblock print** an image incised on a block of wood and printed on paper.

word painting in a vocal work, the musical illustration of the meaning of a word.

ziggurat in Mesopotamia, a monumental stepped building signifying a mountain.

LITERARY CREDITS

Laurence King Publishing, the author, and the literary permissions researcher wish to thank the publishers and individuals who have kindly allowed their copyright material to be reproduced in this book, as listed below. Every effort has been made to contact copyright holders, but should there be any errors or omissions, Laurence King Publishing would be pleased to insert the appropriate acknowledgment in any subsequent edition of this publication.

Starter Kit

p. xxix From "Happy Birthday to You" by Mildred J. Hill, © 1935 by Jessica Hill, administered by International Music Publications Ltd., U.K., on behalf of Warner Chappell Music, reprinted by permission of International Music Publications, London. All Rights Reserved.

p. xxx From Derek Walcott, *Omeros* (New York: Farrar, Straus and Giroux, 1990).

Chapter 2

pp. 16, 24, 25, 27 From *Gilgamesh*, translated by John Gardner and John Maier (New York: Alfred A. Knopf, 1984), © 1984 by Estate of John Gardner and John Maier.

Chapter 3

p. 40 From *Ancient Egyptian Literature: An Anthology*, translated by John L. Foster (Austin, TX: University of Texas Press, 2001), © 2001.

p. 46 From *The British Museum Book of Ancient Egypt*, edited by Stephen Quirke and Jeffrey Spencer (London: British Museum Press, 1992).

pp. 46–47, 49, 53–54 *Ancient Egyptian Literature: An Anthology*, op. cit.

p. 55 From T. G. H. James, *An Introduction to Ancient Egypt* (New York: Farrar, Straus and Giroux, 1979).

p. 61 *Ancient Egyptian Literature: An Anthology*, op. cit.

Chapter 4

pp. 74, 75 From Homer, *The Iliad*, translated by Robert Fagles (New York: Viking Penguin, 1990), © 1990 by Robert Fagles.

p. 77 From *Aeschylus: Volume II, LCL 146*, translated by Herbert Weir Smyth, Cambridge, MA: Harvard University Press, © 1926 by the President and Fellows of Harvard College. The Loeb Classical Library ® is a registered trademark of the President and Fellows of Harvard College.

Chapter 5

pp. 102–103 From *Anacreon: Volume II, LCL 143*, translated by David A. Campbell, Cambridge, MA: Harvard University Press, © 1988 by the President and Fellows of Harvard College. The Loeb Classical Library ® is a registered trademark of the President and Fellows of Harvard College.

Chapter 6

pp. 129–130 From *Euripides: Volume III, LCL 11*, translated by A. S. Way, Cambridge, MA: Harvard University Press, 1912. The Loeb Classical Library ® is a registered trademark of the President and Fellows of Harvard College.

p. 130 From *Aristophanes: Volume II, LCL 488*, translated by Jeffrey Henderson, Cambridge, MA: Harvard University Press, © 1998 by the President and Fellows of Harvard College. The Loeb Classical Library ® is a registered trademark of the President and Fellows of Harvard College.

p. 130 From *Thucydides: Volume 1, LCL 108*, translated by C. F. Smith, Cambridge, MA: Harvard University Press, 1919, © 1928 by the President and Fellows of Harvard College. The Loeb Classical Library ® is a registered trademark of the President and Fellows of Harvard College.

p. 131 From *Aristophanes: Volume III, LCL 180*, translated by B. B. Rogers, Cambridge, MA: Harvard University Press, © 1924 by the President and Fellows of Harvard College. The Loeb Classical Library ® is a registered trademark of the President and Fellows of Harvard College.

p. 138 From *Greek Bucolic Poets [Theocritus], LCL 28*, translated by J. M. Edmonds, Cambridge, MA: Harvard University Press, 1912. The Loeb Classical Library ® is a registered trademark of the President and Fellows of Harvard College.

Chapter 7

p. 161 From *Plautus: Four Comedies*, edited by Erich Segal (translator) (Oxford: Oxford University Press, 1996).

p. 162 From *The Poems of Catullus*, edited by Arthur Guy Lee (translator) (Oxford: Oxford University Press, 1990).

pp. 162–163 From *Horace: The Complete Odes and Epodes*, edited by David West (translator) (Oxford: Oxford University Press, 2000).

p. 175 From Suetonius, *The Twelve Caesars*, translated by Robert Graves (London: Penguin Classics, 1957).

p. 176 From Petronius, *The Satyricon*, translated by J. P. Sullivan (London: Penguin, 1965, 1977), © J. P. Sullivan, 1965, 1969, 1974, 1977, 1986.

Chapter 9

p. 233 From *The Arabian Nights: The Thousand and One Nights*, translated by Husain Haddawy (New York: W. W. Norton, 1990), © 1990 by W. W. Norton and Company, Inc.

p. 233 From Coleman Barks and John Mayne, *The Essential Rumi* (New York: HarperCollins, 1997).

p. 234 From *Drunk on the Wine of the Beloved: 100 Poems of Hafiz*, translated by Thomas Rain Crowe (Boston, MA: Shambhala Publications, 2001), © 2001.

Chapter 10

pp. 251, 252 From *Everyman and Medieval Miracle Plays*, edited by A. C. Cawley (London: Phoenix Editions, 1993).

pp. 254, 255 From *Beowulf: A New Verse Translation* by Seamus Heaney (New York: W. W. Norton, 2001), © 2000 by Seamus Heaney.

p. 259 From *The Poetic Edda*, translated by Lee M. Hollander, 2nd edition, revised (Austin, TX: University of Texas Press, 1990), © 1962, renewed 1990.

Chapter 11

p. 276 From BULL *Summis desiderantes*, published by Pope Innocent VIII (December 5, 1484), from *Translations and Reprints from the Original Sources of European History*, published for the Department of History of the University of Pennsylvania, Philadelphia, University of Pennsylvania Press (1897?–1907?), Volume III: 4, pp. 7–10. Fordham University Center for Medieval Studies, Internet History Sourcebooks Project, edited by Paul Halsall. Online at www. fordhamedu/halsall/sources/witches1.html.

p. 279 From *Abbot Suger on the Abbey Church of St.-Denis and Its Treasures* by Erwin Panofsky (Princeton, NJ: Princeton University Press, 1979).

pp. 293–294 From *The Divine Comedy, Volume 1: The Inferno* by Dante Alighieri, translated by Mark Musa (Bloomington: Indiana University Press, 1997).

pp. 295, 296 From *The Divine Comedy* by Dante Alighieri, translated by John Ciardi (New York: W. W. Norton, 1980), © 1954, 1957, 1959, 1960, 1961, 1965, 1967, 1970 by the Ciardi Family Publishing Trust.

Chapter 12

p. 298 From Petrarch, *Canzoniere and Other Writings*, edited by Mark Musa (translator) (New York: Oxford University Press, 1999).

p. 313 From Geoffrey Chaucer, *The Canterbury Tales*, translated by Nevill Coghill (London: Penguin Classics, 1951, fourth revised edition 1977), © 1951 by Nevill Coghill, © the Estate of Nevill Coghill, 1958, 1960, 1975, 1977.

p. 316 *Canzoniere and Other Writings*, op. cit.

p. 316 From *Petrarch's Africa*, translated by Thomas G. Bergin and Alice S. Wilson (New Haven, CT: Yale University Press, 1977).

Chapter 13

p. 359 From *The Cambridge Music Guide*, edited by Stanley Sadie with Alison Latham (New York: Cambridge University Press, 1990).

Chapter 15

p. 394 From Erasmus, *The Praise of Folly*, translated by Clarence H. Miller (New Haven, CT: Yale University Press, 1979).

pp. 398, 403, 409, 410 From *Perspectives on Western Art*, Volume 2, edited by Linnea H. Wren (Boulder, CO: Westview Press, 1993).

Chapter 16

p. 441 From Miguel de Cervantes, *Don Quixote*, translated by Samuel Putnam (New York: The Modern Library/Random House, 1998).

p. 438 From Howard Hibbard, *Caravaggio* (London: Thames and Hudson, 1983).

Chapter 17

p. 469 From Voltaire, *Candide* (New York: The Modern Library/Random House, 2002).

p. 486 From *Perspectives on Western Art*, Volume 2, edited by Linnea H. Wren (Boulder, CO: Westview Press, 1993).

p. 491 From *Memoirs of Madame Vigée-Lebrun*, translated by Lionel Strachey (New York: George Braziller, 1989).

Chapter 18

p. 515 From (J111) "The bee is not afraid of me," (J324) "Some keep the Sabbath going to church," (J449) "I died for beauty, but was scarce," (J585) "I like to see it lap the miles," (J712) "Because I could not stop for death," from *The Poems of Emily Dickinson*, edited by Thomas H. Johnson (Cambridge, MA: The Belknap Press of Harvard University Press, 1955), © 1951, 1955, 1979, 1983 by the President and Fellows of Harvard College.

Chapter 19

p. 552 From Frederick Douglass, *Narrative of the Life of Frederick Douglass, An American Slave* (London: Penguin Classics, 1986).

p. 552 From *Narrative of Sojourner Truth*, edited by Nell Irvin Painter (London: Penguin Classics, 1998).

Chapter 20

p. 560 From Rudyard Kipling, "The White Man's Burden," from *Selected Poems*, edited by Peter Keating (London: Penguin Twentieth-Century Classics, 1993).

p. 570 From *Whistler, A Retrospective*, edited by Robin Spencer (Westport, CT: Hugh Lauter Levin Associates, 1995).

p. 578 From *Noa Noa: The Tahiti Journal of Paul Gauguin*, translated by O. F. Theis (New York: Dover Publications, 1985).

p. 582 From Auguste and Louis Lumière, *Letters*, edited by Jacques Rittaud-Hutinet (London: Faber and Faber, 1995).

Chapter 21

pp. 584, 587 From "Dulce Et Decorum Est," from *The Collected Poems of Wilfred Owen* (London: Chatto and Windus, 1963).

p. 591 From *Perspectives on Western Art*, Volume 2, edited by Linnea H. Wren (Boulder, CO: Westview Press, 1993).

p. 597 From James Joyce, *Chamber Music*, in *Poems and Exiles,* edited by J. C. C. Mays (London: Penguin Twentieth-Century Classics, 1992).

p. 598 From James Joyce, *Dubliners* (New York: Random House, 1993).

p. 598 W. B. Yeats, "The Lake Isle of Innisfree," from *Collected Poems* (London: Picador, 1990).

p. 599 From Marcel Proust, *Remembrance of Things Past. In Search of Lost Love: Way by Swann's. Volume 1*, translated by C. K. Scott Moncrieff (London: Penguin Classics, 1985).

p. 602 Rainer Maria Rilke, "The Cadet Picture of My Father," translated by Robert Lowell, from *Imitations* by Robert Lowell (New York: Farrar, Straus and Giroux, 1995).

p. 608 From "Mending Wall," from *Robert Frost: Selected Poems*, edited by Ian Hamilton (London: The Penguin Poets, 1973).

p. 608 From Ezra Pound, "The Garden," from *Personae* (New York: New Directions Publishing Corporation, 1990), copyright © 1926 by Ezra Pound.

p. 608 H.D. (Hilda Doolittle), "Heat," from *Collected Poems 1912–1944*, edited by Louis L. Martz (New York: New Directions Publishing Corporation, 1983), © 1982 by The Estate of Hilda Doolittle.

Chapter 22

p. 614 From Winston Churchill, *The Second World War, Volume 1: The Gathering Storm* (London: Cassell, 1950).

p. 634 From "The Creation," from *James Weldon Johnson: Complete Poems* (London: Penguin Books, 2000).

p. 635 From *The Collected Poems of Langston Hughes* (New York: Alfred A. Knopf, 1994), © 1994 by The Estate of Langston Hughes.

p. 635 From "Heritage," from *On These I Stand* by Countee Cullen (New York: Harper and Row, 1925).

p. 635 From Zora Neale Hurston, *Spunk: The Selected Stories* (New York: Marlowe and Company, 1997).

p. 636 From Willa Cather, *O Pioneers!* (New York: Dover Publications, 1994).

p. 637 From John Steinbeck, *The Grapes of Wrath* (New York: Viking Press, 1939).

p. 637 "when god decided to invent," copyright 1944, © 1972, 1991 by the Trustees for the E. E. Cummings Trust, from *Complete Poems, 1904–1962* by E. E. Cummings, edited by George J. Firmage (New York: Liveright Books, 1994).

pp. 637, 638 From "The Love Song of J. Alfred Prufrock," "The Waste Land," and "The Hollow Men," copyright 1936 by Harcourt, Inc., copyright © 1964, 1963 by T. S. Eliot, from *Collected Poems 1909–1962* (Orlando, FL: Harcourt Brace International, 1963).

p. 638 From William Faulkner, *The Sound and the Fury* (New York: Random House, 1992).

p. 638 From Mikhail Sholokov, *And Quietly Flows the Don*, translated by Stephen Garry (New York: Vintage Books, 1989).

p. 639 From Virginia Woolf, *Mrs Dalloway* (New York: Vintage Books, 2004).

p. 639 From James Joyce, *Ulysses* (New York: Random House, 1979).

p. 639 From James Joyce, *Finnegan's Wake* (New York: Viking Press, 1976).

Chapter 23

p. 654 Quote by Albert Einstein.

p. 663 From Ed Clayton, *Martin Luther King: The Peaceful Warrior* (New York: Simon and Schuster, 1968).

p. 681 From "The Hand that Signed the Paper" and "Do Not Go Gentle Into That Good Night," from *Collected Poems 1934–1952* by Dylan Thomas (London: J. M. Dent, 1952).

p. 681 From Dylan Thomas, *Under Milk Wood: A Play for Voices* (London: Penguin Modern Classics, 2000).

p. 681 From "September 1, 1939," copyright 1940 and renewed 1968 by W. H. Auden, and from *The Age of Anxiety*, copyright 1947 by W. H. Auden and renewed 1975 by the Estate of W. H. Auden, from *Collected Poems* by W. H. Auden (New York: Random House, 1976).

p. 682 "Epitaph for the Unknown Soldier," copyright 1940 and renewed 1968 by W. H. Auden, from *Collected Poems* by W. H. Auden (New York: Random House, 1976).

pp. 682–683 From Jack Kerouac, *On the Road* (London: Penguin Books, 2002).

p. 683 From James Baldwin, *Go Tell It on the Mountain* (New York: Modern Library/Random House, 1995).

p. 683 From Toni Morrison, *Beloved* (New York: Alfred A. Knopf, 1987).

p. 684 From "The Beggars" and "The Dictators," from *Five Decades; Selected Poems 1925–1970* by Pablo Neruda, translated by Ben Belitt (New York: Grove Press, 1974), © 1961 by Ben Belitt.

p. 685 From Yasunari Kawabata, *Snow Country*, translated by Edward G. Seidensticker (London: Penguin Books, 1971).

p. 685 From *Waiting for Godot* by Samuel Beckett, from *I Can't Go On, I'll Go On: A Samuel Beckett Reader* (New York: Signet Books, 1967).

pp. 686–687 From Edward Albee, *Who's Afraid of Virginia Woolf* (New York: Dramatists Play Service, Inc., 1962).

p. 691 From *The Beatles Lyrics: The Songs of Lennon, McCartney, Harrison, and Starr* (Milwaukee, WI: Hal Leonard Publishing Corporation, 1993).

p. 691 From "Mr Tambourine Man" by Bob Dylan, © 1963 by Warner Bros. Inc., © renewed 1991 by Special Rider Music, from "Blowin' in the Wind" by Bob Dylan, © 1962 by Warner Bros. Inc., © renewed 1990 by Special Rider Music. All rights reserved. International copyright secured.

Chapter 24

p. 698 From "The Sea is History," from *The Star-Apple Kingdom* by Derek Walcott (New York: Farrar, Straus and Giroux, 1979).

pp. 701, 720 From Derek Walcott, *Omeros* (New York: Farrar, Straus and Giroux, 1990).

p. 716 From Arundhati Roy, *The God of Small Things* (New York: Random House, 1997).

p. 720 From *The Cure at Troy: A Version of Sophocles' Philoctetes* (1990), © 1990 by Seamus Heaney, from *Seeing Things* (1991), in *Opened Ground: Selected Poems 1966–1996* by Seamus Heaney (New York: Farrar, Straus and Giroux, 1998), © 1998 by Seamus Heaney.

PICTURE CREDITS

Laurence King Publishing, the author, and the picture researcher wish to thank the institutions and individuals that have kindly provided photographic material for use in this book. Museum, gallery, and library locations are given in the captions; further details and other sources are listed below.

We apologize in advance for any unintentional omissions or errors, and will be pleased to insert the appropriate acknowledgment to any companies or individuals in any subsequent edition of this book.

Abbreviations

AKG: Archiv für Kunst und Geshichte, London
ARS: Artists' Rights Society, New York
BPK: Bildarchiv Preussischer Kulturbesitz, Berlin
DACS: Design and Artists Copyright Society, London
DI: Digital Image, The Museum of Modern Art, New York/Scala, Florence
Josse: © Photo Josse, Paris
Maeyaert: © Paul M. R. Maeyaert, El Tossal, Spain
Mauzy: Craig and Marie Mauzy, Athens. mauzy@otenet.gr
MET: The Metropolitan Museum of Art, New York
MFA: The Museum of Fine Arts, Boston
NGA: The National Gallery of Art, Washington, D.C.
Pirozzi: © Vincenzo Pirozzi, Rome. fotopirozzi@inwind.it
RMN: Réunion des Musées Nationaux, Paris
SMB: Scala, Florence—courtesy of the Ministero Beni e Att. Culturali
VAGA: The Visual Arts and Galleries Association, New York

Chapter 1

Chapter opener (Stonehenge) A. F. Kersting, London
1.1, 1.4 Colorphoto Hans Hinz, Switzerland
1.2a, 1.2b, 1.7 AKG
1.5 Photo Yanik Le Guillou
1.6 Reproduced by permission of Prentice Hall, Inc., from Stokstad, *Art History*, 2nd edition (2001). © Pearson Education
1.8 © English Heritage Photo Library. Photographer Sky Eye Aerial Photography
1.10 © G. Chaloupka, Australia
1.11 Rock Art Research Unit, University of Witwatersrand, South Africa
1.12 Photo Monika Heidermann

Chapter 2

2.2, 2.7, 2.9, 2.17, 2.18, 2.19 © Hirmer Archive, Munich
2.4a, 2.4b RMN/Hervé Lewandowski
2.5 John Hay Library, Brown University, Rhode Island
2.6 © Ashmolean Museum, Oxford
2.8 BPK. Photo Gudrun Stenzel
2.10 © British Museum, London
2.12, 2.13, 2.14 Josse
2.15 Ancient Art and Architecture Collection, Harrow, U.K.
2.16 Robert Harding World Imagery, London
2.20 BPK
2.21 Werner Forman Archive
2.22 Courtesy of the Oriental Institute of the University of Chicago
2.23 © Danny Lehman/CORBIS
2.24 Bridgeman Art Library, London
2.25 Pirozzi
2.26 Photo Jerry L. Thompson
2.27 MA.36.21.62, Musée de l'Homme, Paris

Chapter 3

3.1 SMB
3.2a, 3.2b © Jurgen Liepe, Berlin
3.3, 3.4, 3.6, 3.7, 3.11, 3.12, 3.20 © British Museum, London
3.5a, 3.5b, 3.5c MFA. Gift of the Egypt Exploration Fund. 95.1407a
3.8 Maeyaert
3.9 Werner Forman Archive/Dr. E. Strouhal
3.13 AKG/Andrea Jemolo
3.15, 3.16, 3.22, 3.31 © 1997 Photo Scala, Florence
3.17 Courtesy of the Oriental Institute of the University of Chicago
3.18 Reproduced by permission, from Robins, *Women in Ancient Egypt*, British Museum Press (1993)
3.19 MET. Purchase: Edward S. Harkness Gift 1926. 26.7.1450. Photograph © 1997 The Metropolitan Museum of Art
3.21 MET. Rogers Fund and Edward S. Harkness Gift, 1929
3.24 Brooklyn Museum, New York. Charles Edwin Wilbour Fund 39.602
3.25 © Araldo de Luca, Rome
3.26 Drawing by Philip Winton, from Richard H. Wilkinson, *The Complete Temples of Ancient Egypt*, Thames and Hudson, Inc., New York (2000)
3.27 Robert Harding World Imagery, London
3.28 Klaus-Peter Kuhlmann
3.30a, 3.30b BPK. Photo Margaret Büsing
3.32 AKG/Erich Lessing

Chapter 4

4.1, 4.4, 4.5, 4.6a, 4.6b, 4.8, 4.10, 4.12, 4.13, 4.16, 4.17 Mauzy
4.2 R. A. Higgins, *The Archaeology of Minoan Crete*, Henry Z. Walck (1973). © Random House, Inc.
4.3 Studio Kontos Photography
4.7 Courtesy John G. Younger
4.9 © Thera Foundation
4.14 Fondazione Giorgio Cini, Istituto di Storia dell'Arte, Venice
4.15 Courtesy of Ekdotike Athenon, S.A.

Chapter 5

5.1 Reproduced by permission of Thames and Hudson, Ltd., from Boardman, *Greek Art* (1985)
5.2 Reproduced by permission of Phaidon Press, from Richter, *Handbook of Greek Art* (1959)
5.3 © 1990 Photo Scala, Florence
5.4, 5.15a, 5.15b, 5.20 Mauzy
5.6 MET. Rogers Fund, 1921. Photograph © 1996 The Metropolitan Museum of Art
5.7, 5.23, 5.24, 5.25 Staatliche Antikensammlungen und Glyptothek, Munich
5.8, 5.12, 5.26 © British Museum, London
5.9 Pirozzi
5.11 Photo Devos, Boulogne
5.13a, 5.13b MFA. Henry Lillie Pierce Fund, 99.538. Photo © 2004 Museum of Fine Arts, Boston
5.17, 5.22 Reproduced by permission of Thames and Hudson, Ltd., from Boardman, *Greek Sculpture: The Archaic Period* (1978)
5.18 Reproduced by permission of Thomson Learning, from Cunningham and Reich, *Culture and Values*, 5th edition (2002)
5.27 Robert Harding World Imagery, London

Chapter 6

6.1a, 6.5, 6.8, 6.19, 6.38 Mauzy
6.1b, 6.18 Studio Kontos/Photostock, Athens, Greece
6.2, 6.27, 6.29, 6.32, 6.37 © Fotografica Foglia, Naples
6.3 Pirozzi
6.4 Alinari/Art Resource, New York
6.6, 6.9, 6.24 AKG/Peter Connolly
6.11 By permission of the Royal Ontario Museum. © ROM
6.12 Professor Ernst Berger, Antikenmuseum Basle und Sammlung Ludwig. Drawing by Miriam Cahn
6.13, 6.14, 6.15, 6.16, 6.17, 6.20a, 6.20b, 6.23 © British Museum, London
6.21, 6.34 Staatliche Antikensammlungen und Glyptothek, Munich
6.22, 6.33 © Hirmer Archive, Munich
6.26 Vatican Museums, Rome. Photo M. Sarri
6.28 SMB
6.30, 6.31 Photograph by John C. Huntingdon, Courtesy of the Huntingdon Archive, Ohio State University
6.35 Josse
6.36 © Araldo de Luca, Rome

Chapter 7

7.1 © 2003 Photo Scala, Florence/Fotografica Foglia
7.2 © Quattrone, Florence
7.3, 7.7, 7.8, 7.10, 7.14, 7.24, 7.25, 7.29, 7.30, 7.37, 7.41 Pirozzi
7.4a MET. Rogers Fund, 1909
7.5, 7.32, 7.33, 7.34 SMB
7.6, 7.13, 7.31 © Araldo de Luca, Rome
7.11 Maeyaert
7.12 AKG/Pirozzi
7.16, 7.17a AKG/Peter Connolly
7.18, 7.19, 7.20, 7.27, 7.28 © Fotografica Foglia, Naples
7.21a, 7.21b MFA. Catherine Page Perkins Fund. 00.250
7.22a, 7.22b © British Museum, London
7.23, 7.40 © 1990 Photo Scala, Florence
7.26 Kunsthistorisches Museum, Vienna
7.35 Reproduced by permission of Perseus Books, Inc., from Roth, *Understanding Architecture* (1994)

7.36 John Burge, James Packer, first published in Fred S. Kleiner and Christin J. Mamiya, *Gardner's Art through the Ages*, 12th edition, Belmont, CA: Wadsworth, 2004, p. 275, fig. 10-41
7.39 NGA. Samuel H. Kress Collection, 1939.1.24. Photo Richard Carafelli
7.42 © Foundation for the Advancement of Mesoamerican Studies, Inc., Florida. Drawing by Katherine Reese Taylor
7.43 © BPK
7.44 Reproduced by permission of Cambridge University Press, from Esther Pastzory, *Pre-Columbian Art* (1998), fig. 31

Chapter 8

8.1 © SMB
8.2, 8.14 © Canali Photobank
8.4 Zev Radovan, Jerusalem
8.5 Alinari
8.6, 8.7, 8.12 © 1990 Photo Scala, Florence
8.8, 8.13 Pirozzi
8.9 Alinari Archives-Anderson Archive, Florence
8.16 Josse

Chapter 9

9.1, 9.2b, 9.8, 9.9, 9.15, 9.16 © Cameraphoto Arte, Venice
9.2a, 9.5 © SMB
9.3 Josse
9.4 BPK/Staatliche Museen, Berlin—Preußischer Kulturbesitz, Münzkabinett
9.7, 9.18 © 1990 Photo Scala, Florence
9.10 © Sonia Halliday Photographs. Photo F. H. C. Birch
9.11, 9.26 Werner Forman Archive
9.13 Zev Radovan, Jerusalem
9.20 AKG/Erich Lessing
9.22, 9.25 A. F. Kersting, London
9.23 Archivio Oronoz, Madrid
9.24 George Holton/Photo Researchers, Inc.
9.27 Courtesy of the Trustees of the V&A
9.28 Freer Gallery of Art, Smithsonian Institution, Washington, D.C. Purchase, F1934.20
9.29 The Art Archive/National Museum, Damascus/Dagli Orti

Chapter 10

10.1 RMN/J. G. J. G. Berizzi
10.3 AKG/Hilbich
10.5, 10.20, 10.21 Bridgeman Art Library, London
10.6 Stiftsbibliothek, St. Gall, Switzerland
10.7 British Architectural Library, Royal Institute of British Architects, London
10.8 The Embassy of Japan, London
10.10 The Board of Trinity College, Dublin
10.11 © Archivio Iconografico, S.A./Corbis
10.12, 10.15, 10.17 © British Museum, London
10.13 AKG/Schütze/Rodemann
10.14 Bibliothèque Nationale, Paris
10.16 © Christer Åhlin/The Museum of National Antiquities, Stockholm, Sweden
10.18 DK Images. Reproduced by permission of the Medieval Academy of America
10.22 The Art Archive/Biblioteca Civica Lucca/Dagli Orti
10.23 Reproduced by permission of McGraw-Hill Education, Inc., from Matthews and Platt, *Western Humanities*, 5th edition
10.24 © Arthur Thévenart/CORBIS
10.25, 10.26 Maeyaert
10.27 © 1990 Photo Scala, Florence
10.28, 10.29 By special permission of the city of Bayeux
10.30 AMR NABIL. © Associated Press
10.31 Panos Pictures, London

Chapter 11

11.1 © 1990 Photo Scala, Florence/Fondo Edifici di Culto—Min. dell'Interno
11.2 AKG/Schütze/Rodemann
11.4 Maeyaert
11.5 From *Arts and Ideas*, 9th edition, by Fleming. © 1995. Reprinted with permission of Wadsworth, a division of Thomson Learning
11.6, 11.19 Bridgeman Art Library, London
11.7, 11.24 A. F. Kersting, London
11.8 © Superstock
11.11 © Sonia Halliday and Laura Lushington
11.12 Lauros/Giraudon/Bridgeman Art Library
11.13 © 1990 Photo Scala, Florence
11.14 The Board of Trinity College, Dublin
11.15 Centre des Monuments Nationaux, Paris
11.16, 11.17 © British Library, London
11.18 © John Elk III
11.20 © 1996 Photo Scala, Florence
11.21 © Angelo Hornak, London
11.22 © Sonia Halliday Photographs, Weston Turville, U.K.
11.23 © James Austin
11.25 © Quattrone, Florence

Chapter 12

12.1, 12.2 © British Library, London
12.3 Alinari Archives-Anderson Archive, Florence
12.4a, 12.4b Bildarchiv Foto Marburg, Germany
12.6, 12.10 Bridgeman Art Library, London
12.7 © A. J. Cassaigne/Photononstop, France
12.8 © RMN/Bulloz
12.9 © SMB
12.11, 12.14, 12.15 © 1990 Photo Scala, Florence
12.12, 12.13, 12.16, 12.17, 12.19, 12.20, 12.21 © Quattrone, Florence
12.18 Alinari

Chapter 13

13.3, 13.11, 13.21, 13.32 © National Gallery, London
13.4 © 2004 Her Majesty Queen Elizabeth II
13.5, 13.7, 13.8, 13.14, 13.15, 13,19, 13.20, 13.22, 13.23, 13.24, 13.26, 13.28a, 13.28b, 13.30 © Quattrone, Florence
13.6, 13.16, 13.29, 13.31 © 1990 Photo Scala, Florence
13.9 © Electa Editrice, Milan
13.10 Alinari, Florence
13.17 © Ralph Lieberman/Laurence King Publishing Archives
13.33, 13.34 Maeyaert
13.35 MET. Robert Lehman Collection, 1975. Photograph © 1993 The Metropolitan Museum of Art
13.36 Josse
13.37 © The Cleveland Museum of Art. Dudley P. Allen Fund, 1927.199
13.38 Boston Athenaeum
p. 361, thumbnail of Piazza d'Italia © Norman McGrath, New York

Chapter 14

14.1, 14.6 © 1990 Photo Scala, Florence
14.2 John Bigelow Taylor/Art Resource, New York
14.3 N. J. Saunders/Werner Forman Archive
14.4, 14.22, 14.26, 14.29 © Quattrone, Florence
14.5 © RMN/Lewandowski/LeMage
14.7 NGA. Widener Collection 1942.9.57. © Board of Trustees, National Gallery of Art, Washington
14.8 Pirozzi
14.12 © James Morris, London
14.13, 14.14, 14.16, 14.24 Vatican Museums, Rome
14.17 Vatican Museums, Rome. Photo A. Bracchetti/P. Zigrossi, 1993
14.18 Vatican Museums, Rome. Photo A. Bracchetti/P. Zigrossi, 1995
14.19 © National Gallery, London
14.20, 14.23 Josse
14.21, 14.31 © Cameraphoto Arte, Venice
14.25 © The J. Paul Getty Museum, Los Angeles
14.27 © Fotografica Foglia, Naples
14.30 The Art Archive/Palazzo del Tè, Mantua/Dagli Orti

Chapter 15

15.1 Photo Amsterdam Rijksprentenkabinet
15.2 Josse
15.3 © Bristol City Museum and Art Gallery, U.K./Bridgeman Art Library, London
15.4, 15.18 Pirozzi
15.5, 15.7 Bridgeman Art Library, London
15.6 © President and Fellows of Harvard College. Courtesy of The Fogg Art Museum, Harvard University Art Museums, Bequest of Paul J. Sachs, "A Testimonial to my friend Felix M. Warburg." Photo Photographic Services
15.8, 15.14 © British Museum, London
15.9 Musée d'Unterlinden, Colmar, France
15.10, 15.11 All rights reserved. © Museo Nacional del Prado, Madrid
15.15, 15.16 © Cameraphoto Arte, Venice
15.17 From Laurie Schneider Adams, *Art Across Time*, reproduced by permission of McGraw-Hill Education, Inc.
15.19 © 1995 Photo Scala, Florence
15.20 NGA. © 2004 Board of Trustees, National Gallery of Art, Washington
15.21 By courtesy of the Marquess of Salisbury
15.24 Topham Picturepoint. Photo Fritz Curson, Performing Arts Library

Chapter 16

16.1, 16.25, 16.27, 16.28, 16.34 Josse
16.2, 16.38 The Royal Collection, Windsor. © 2004 Her Majesty Queen Elizabeth II
16.3 © The Frick Collection, New York
16.4, 16.22, 16.44 © Corbis, London
16.5 © Fotomas Index
16.6 Lawrence Wodehouse and Marian Moffett, *A History of Western Architecture*, 1989. Reproduced by permission of Mayfield Publishing, Inc.

16.8, 16.9, 16.10 © Araldo de Luca, Rome
16.11, 16.12 Pirozzi
16.13, 16.14 © Quattrone, Florence
16.15, 16.16 All rights reserved. © Museo Nacional del Prado, Madrid
16.17 © 1981 by The Massachusetts Institute of Technology. Reproduced from Marcus Whiffen and Frederick Koeper, *American Architecture 1607–1976*, Routledge and Kegan Paul
16.18, 16.19 © South American Pictures, Woodbridge, U.K.
16.20 MET. Harris Brisbane Dick Fund, 1930. Photograph, all rights reserved, The Metropolitan Museum of Art
16.21 RMN
16.24 Agence Enguerand. Photo C. I. Bernard
16.26, 16.33 NGA. © 2004 Board of Trustees, National Gallery of Art, Washington
16.30, 16.35 © 1990 Photo Scala, Florence
16.31 MET. Purchase, special contributions and funds given or bequeathed by friends of the Museum, 1961. Photograph © 1993 The Metropolitan Museum of Art
16.36 San Diego Museum of Art. Edwin Binney 3rd Collection
16.37 Photo courtesy Sothebys
16.39 © The Devonshire Collection, Chatsworth. Reproduced by permission of the Chatsworth Settlement Trustees. Photo Courtauld
16.40 © Angelo Hornak, London
16.41 © Corporation of London. Photo Geremy Butler
16.42 Blaser and Hannaford, *Drawings of Great Buildings*, reproduced by permission of Birkhäuser Verlag
16.43 Space Telescope Science Institute/NASA/ Science Photo Library

Chapter 17
17.1 © 1990 Photo Scala, Florence
17.2 Josse
17.3 BPK, Berlin. Photo Jorg P. Anders
17.4 RMN/Arnaudet
17.5 MET. Gift of Julia A. Berwind, 1953. Photograph © 1980 The Metropolitan Museum of Art
17.6 Maeyaert
17.7 © Florian Monheim, Bildarchiv Monheim, Meerbusch, Germany
17.8 © Achim Bednorz, Bildarchiv Monheim, Meersbusch, Germany
17.9 © Huntingdon Library/Superstock
17.10 © English Heritage Photo Library. Photographer Paul Highnam
17.12 Topham Picturepoint, Edenbridge, U.K.
17.13 Private collection
17.14 MET. Wentworth Fund, 1949. Photograph © 1998 The Metropolitan Museum of Art
17.15 Virginia Museum of Fine Arts, Richmond. The Adolph D. and Wilkins C. Williams Fund. Photo Katherine Wetzel. © Virginia Museum of Fine Arts
17.17 Yale University Art Gallery. Gift of the Society of the Cincinnati in Connecticut
17.18 © Lynne Seldon/Danita Delimont, Bellevue, WA
17.19 Bruce Coleman, New York. © Michael Freeman
17.20, 17.21 RMN
17.22 © Photothèque des musées de la ville de Paris/Cliché Toumazet

Chapter 18
18.1, 18.6, 18.7, 18.8, 18.14 Josse
18.2 RMN/Daniel Arnaudet
18.3 Maeyaert
18.4 All rights reserved. © Museo Nacional del Prado, Madrid
18.5, 18.10 MFA. Photo © 2005 Museum of Fine Arts, Boston
18.9 © National Gallery, London
18.11 © Angelo Hornak, London
18.12 © Peter Ashworth, London
18.13 Artothek, Weilheim, Germany
18.15 © Tate London, 2005
18.16 © V&A Picture Library, London
18.17 Fenimore Art Museum, Cooperstown, NY. Photo Richard Walker

Chapter 19
19.1 Museum of the City of New York. The Hardy T. Peters Collection
19.2 © Corporation of London. Photo Geremy Butler
19.3 Maeyaert
19.4 Custom Medical Stock Photo/Science Photo Library
19.5 Rodin Museum, Paris
19.6 RMN/Hervé Lewandowski
19.7, 19.11, 19.12 Josse
19.8 RMN/Gérard Blot
19.9 Private collection
19.13 © Tate London, 2005
19.14 © Société Française de Photographie
19.15 George Eastman House, Rochester, NY
19.16 © The J. Paul Getty Museum, Los Angeles
19.17 © 2004 Photo Smithsonian American Art Museum/Art Resource/Scala, Florence
19.20 MET. Gift of Mrs Frank B. Porter, 1922. Photograph © 1995 The Metropolitan Museum of Art
19.21 The Long Island Museum of American Art, History and Carriages, Stony Brook, NY. Gift of Mr. and Mrs. Ward Melville, 1955
19.22 © Museum of the City of New York
19.24 Missouri Historical Society
19.25 MET. Brisbane Dick Fund, 1929

Chapter 20
20.1 AKG/Erich Lessing
20.2 Brooklyn Museum of Art. Gift of Anna Ferris
20.3 MFA. Photo © 2005 Museum of Fine Arts, Boston
20.4 RMN
20.5 Maeyaert
20.6 Artothek, Weilheim, Germany
20.7, 20.8 Josse
20.9 Philadelphia Museum of Art. Purchased with the W. P. Wilstach Fund, 1921. Photo Graydon Wood
20.10 Freer Gallery of Art, Smithsonian Institution, Washington, D.C. Gift of Charles Lang Freer, F1904.61
20.11 RMN/Bulloz
20.12 RMN/René-Gabriel Ojéda
20.13 Agence Enguerand. Photo C. I. Bernard
20.15 Photograph © 2002 The Art Institute of Chicago. All Rights Reserved
20.16 Philadelphia Museum of Art. Purchased, W. P. Wilstach Collection
20.17 MET. Bequest of Sam A. Lewisohn, 1951. Photograph © 1986 The Metropolitan Museum of Art
20.18 NGA. © 2004 Board of Trustees, National Gallery of Art, Washington
20.19 The Foundation E. G. Bührle Collection, Zurich
20.20 Photo J. Lathion © National Gallery, Norway. © The Munch-Ellingsen Group, BONO, Oslo/DACS, London, 2005
20.21 Smithsonian Institution Libraries, Cooper-Hewitt, National Design Museum Branch, Smithsonian Institution, Washington, D.C.
20.23 D-N Images, London

Chapter 21
21.1 University of Michigan Museum of Art, Ann Arbor. Museum Purchase. 1956/1.21. © DACS, London, 2005
21.2 © Punch, Ltd.
21.3 Three Lions/Getty Images
21.4 © 2005 DI. Gift of Nelson A. Rockefeller
21.5 Österreichische Galerie Belvedere. Photo Fotostudio Otto 1991
21.6 Archivio Oronoz, Madrid
21.7 Maeyaert
21.8 © 2004 President and Fellows of Harvard College. Courtesy of The Fogg Art Museum, Harvard University Art Museums. Bequest of Grenville L. Winthrop. Photo Katya Kallsen
21.10 New Orleans Museum of Art. Bequest of Victor K. Kiam
21.11 © 2005 DI. Acquired through the Lillie P. Bliss Bequest
21.12 © Photo Städtische Galerie im Lenbachhaus, Munich. © ADAGP, Paris and DACS, London, 2005
21.14 San Francisco Museum of Modern Art. Bequest of Elise S. Haas. Photograph Ben Blackwell. © Succession H. Matisse, Paris/DACS, London, 2005
21.15 NGA. © 2004 Board of Trustees, National Gallery of Art, Washington. © Succession Picasso/DACS, London, 2005
21.16 MET. Bequest of Gertrude Stein, 1946. Photograph © 1996 The Metropolitan Museum of Art. © Succession Picasso/DACS, London, 2005
21.17 © 2005 DI. Acquired through the Lillie P. Bliss Bequest. © Succession Picasso/DACS, London, 2005
21.18 © 1990 Photo Scala, Florence. © Succession Picasso/DACS, London, 2005
21.19 © 2005 DI. Nelson A. Rockefeller Bequest
21.20 © 2005 DI. Purchase. © DACS, London, 2005
21.21 Photo © The Detroit Institute of Arts
21.22 Photo © RMN/Jean Schormans. © ADAGP, Paris and DACS, London, 2005
21.23 Purchased with funds from the Coffin Fine Arts Trust; Nathan Emory Coffin Collection of the Des Moines Art Center. © ARS, New York and DACS, London, 2005
21.24 Philadelphia Museum of Art. Louise and Walter Arensberg Collection. © Succession Marcel Duchamp/ADAGP, Paris and DACS, London, 2005
21.25 Kobal Collection, London
21.26 D-N Images, London

Chapter 22

22.2 David King Collection, London
22.3 AKG
22.4 © Succession Picasso/DACS, London, 2005
22.5 Time Life Pictures/Getty Images
22.6 Collection Michel Annet, A.P.R.A. www.apra.asso.fr
22.7 State Museum of Auschwitz-Birkenau
22.9 Philadelphia Museum of Art. Louise and Walter Arensberg Collection. Photo Lynn Rosenthal, 1998. © Succession Marcel Duchamp/ADAGP, Paris and DACS, London, 2005
22.10 BPK
22.11 © 2005 DI. Purchase. © ADAGP, Paris and DACS, London, 2005
22.12 Philadelphia Museum of Art. Louise and Walter Arensberg Collection. Photo Graydon Wood, 1994. © ADAGP, Paris and DACS, London, 2005
22.13 Photograph © 1995 The Art Institute of Chicago, All Rights Reserved. © Succession Miró/DACS, London, 2005
22.14 Courtesy CalmelsCohen, Paris. © ADAGP, Paris and DACS, London, 2005
22.15 © Man Ray Trust. ADAGP/ARS 1996
22.16 Jacques and Natasha Gelman Collection of Modern and Contemporary Mexican Art, MUROS, Mexico
22.17 © 2005 Mondrian/Holtzman Trust c/o hcr@hcrinternational.com
22.18 Anthony Scibilia/Art Resource, New York
22.19 © Scott Frances/Esto
22.20 Photo courtesy Missouri Division of Tourism. © T. H. Benton and R. P. Benton Testamentary Trusts/VAGA, New York/DACS, London, 2005
22.21 Lebrecht Music Library, London
22.22 Pictorial Press, London
22.23 © 2005 DI. Gift of the artist. © ARS, New York and DACS, London, 2005
22.24 © Succession H. Matisse, Paris/DACS, London, 2005
22.25 © ARS, New York and DACS, London, 2005
22.26 © Commerce Graphics, New York
22.27 © Barbara Morgan, The Barbara Morgan Archive. Photo Jerome Robbins Dance Division, The New York Public Library for the Performing Arts, Aston, Lenox and Tilden Foundations
22.28 Jerome Robbins Dance Division, The New York Public Library for the Performing Arts, Astor, Lenox and Tilden Foundations. © Estate of George Platt Lynes
22.29 Olympia-Film/Kobal Collection
22.30, 22.32 Kobal Collection, London
22.33, 22.38, 22.40 BFI, London
22.34 D-N Images, London
22.35 D-N Images, London. © RKO Pictures, Inc. Licensed by Warner Brothers Entertainment, Inc. All rights reserved
22.36, 22.39 Turner Entertainment Company —a Warner Brothers Entertainment Company. All rights reserved
22.37 D-N Images, London. Turner Entertainment Company—a Warner Brothers Entertainment Company. All rights reserved

Chapter 23

23.1 Hulton Archive. Photo Horace Abrahams/Stringer
23.2, 23.5 © Bettmann/CORBIS
23.3, 23.15 Photo Rheinisches Bildarchiv
23.4 © Peter Aaron/Esto
23.7 David King Collection, London
23.8 Digital Image © 1996 CORBIS. Original image courtesy of NASA/Corbis. Photo Neil Armstrong
23.9 The Royal Archives. © 2005 Her Majesty Queen Elizabeth II
23.10 Hirshhorn Museum and Sculpture Garden, Smithsonian Institution, Washington, D.C. Gift of the Joseph H. Hirshhorn Foundation, 1996. Photo Lee Stalsworth
23.11 © Dedalus Foundation, Inc./VAGA, New York/DACS, London, 2005
23.12 © 1998 Whitney Museum of American Art, New York. Photo Geoffrey Clements. © ARS, New York and DACS, London, 2005
23.13 © 1996 Whitney Museum of American Art, New York. Photography Helga Photo Studio. © ARS, New York and DACS, London, 2005
23.14 © 2005 DI. Gift of Philip Johnson. © Kate Rothko Prizel and Christopher Rothko/ARS, New York and DACS, London, 2005
23.15 © Jasper Johns/VAGA, New York and DACS, London, 2005
23.16 Collection of the Modern Art Museum of Fort Worth, Texas. The Benjamin J. Tillar Memorial Trust, acquired from the collection of Vernon Nikkel, Clovis, New Mexico. Acquired in 1983. © 2005 Andy Warhol Foundation for the Visual Arts/ARS, New York and DACS, London, 2005
23.17 Galerie Schmela, Düsseldorf, Germany. © DACS, London, 2005
23.18 © 2005 DI. Helen Achen Bequest (by exchange) and gift of Joseph Helman. Art © Judd Foundation. Licensed by VAGA, New York and DACS, London, 2005
23.19 Milwaukee Art Museum. Gift of Friends of Art. Photo Larry Sanders
23.20 Purchased 1990, National Gallery of Canada. © ARS, New York and DACS, London, 2005
23.21 © Richard Estes, courtesy Marlborough Gallery, New York
23.22 © Estate of Duane Hanson/VAGA, New York and DACS, London, 2005
23.23 Estate of Robert Smithson. Courtesy James Cohan Gallery, New York. © Estate of Robert Smithson/VAGA, New York/DACS, London, 2005
23.24 Collection of the artist
23.25 © Judy Chicago 1979. Photo © Donald Woodman. © ARS, New York and DACS, London, 2005
23.26 Solomon R. Guggenheim Museum, New York. Gift, Robert Mapplethorpe Foundation, 1996. 96.4373. © The Solomon R. Guggenheim Foundation, New York. Photo David Heald
23.27 MET. Gift of John Stewart Kennedy, 1897. Photograph © 1992 The Metropolitan Museum of Art
23.28 Courtesy Phyllis Kind Gallery, New York
23.29 The Broad Art Foundation. Photo Douglas M. Parker Studio. © ADAGP, Paris and DACS, London, 2005
23.30 Private collection, Hamburg. Courtesy the artist and Holly Solomon Gallery, New York. Photo courtesy The Hayward Gallery, London
23.31 © Norman McGrath, New York
23.32 Maeyaert
23.33 © Peter Mauss/Esto
23.34 © Beatriz Schuller. Photo Jerome Robbins Dance Division, The New York Public Library for the Performing Arts, Aston, Lenox and Tilden Foundations
23.35 Alvin Ailey American Dance Theater in Alvin Ailey's *Revelations*. Photo Paul Kolnik
23.36 Studio Milton Glaser
23.37, 23.39 Kobal Collection, London
23.38 *The Seventh Seal.* © 1957 AB Svensk Filmindustri. Still photographer: Louis Huch. Photo D-N Images, London
23.41 Courtesy of Lucasfilm Ltd. *Star Wars Episode IV: A New Hope* © 1977 and 1997 Lucasfilm Ltd.™ All rights reserved. Used under authorization. Unauthorized duplication is a violation of applicable law. Photo Lucasfilm/20th-Century Fox/Kobal Collection
23.43 Photo BFI, London. © Universal Studios

Chapter 24

24.1 Robert Harding World Imagery
24.2 Towers of Light over the Brooklyn Bridge, conceptual rendering by La Verdiere and Myoda. © 2001. On behalf of the Towers of Light memorial initative by Bennett, Bonevardi, La Verdiere, Marantz, Myoda. With support from Creative Time and the Municipal Art Society
24.3 AP/Wideworld, London
24.4 Courtesy of the Paula Cooper Gallery, New York
24.5 © Estate of Keith Haring
24.6 Photograph David Heald © The Solomon R. Guggenheim Foundation, New York. © ARS, New York and DACS, London, 2005
24.7 Image courtesy Erwin Redl
24.8 Redux Pictures. Photo Wolfgang Volz
24.9 Neugerriemschneider, Berlin, and Tanya Bonakdar Gallery, New York
24.10 © 1994 Matthew Barney. Photo Michael James O'Brien. Courtesy Gladstone Gallery
24.11 Collection of the artist
24.12 Courtesy Lisa Fifield
24.14 © Walt Disney Enterprises. Photo Peter Aaron/Esto. All rights reserved. Used by permission from Disney Enterprises, Inc.
24.15 Photograph David Heald © The Solomon R. Guggenheim Foundation, New York
24.16 Powerstock, London
24.17 Tokuma Enterprises/Kobal Collection
24.18 Photo BFI, London. © 2003 Disney Enterprises, Inc./Pixar Animation Studios

INDEX

A la recherche du temps perdu (Proust) 599
Aachen, Germany: Charlemagne's Palace Chapel 245, 360, **10.3**, **10.4**; palace school 245–6
Abbasid dynasty 225, 244
Abbey Theatre, Dublin 598, 642
Abbot, Berenice: *James Joyce* **22.26**
Abelard, Peter 287, 288; and Héloïse 287
Abikhil, statuette of 21, **2.4**
abolitionism 551–2, 553, 557
Aboriginals, Australian 13; rock art 13, **1.10**
Abraham 38, 186, 198, 225
absolutism 425, 444, 456–7, 465, 499
Abstract Expressionism 669–71
Absurd, Theater of the 679, 685, 686
Abu Bakr 225
academies 334; French 445, 543, **17.5**; Plato's 124, 214 (Athens), 337 (Florence); Royal Academy of Arts, London 475, 479
Acedo, Diego de: portrait (Velázquez) 443, **16.16**
Achaemenid dynasty 32–4; map **2.2**
Achebe, Chinua 683–4
Achilles 73, 74–5, 93, 695; *Achilles* (Laschi) 333
Achilles Ambushes Troilus (fresco) 150, **7.5**
Achilles painter: *Muse Playing a Kithara* 122, **6.21**
Acoma, New Mexico: church 443, **16.17**, **16.18**
Acropolis, Athens 115, **6.5**, **6.6**; Dionysos Theater 127, **6.24**; Erechtheum 120–1, **6.7**, **6.19**, **6.20**; Parthenon 116–19, **6.7–6.17**; Propylaia 115, **6.7**; Temple of Athena Nike 120, **6.18**
Act of Supremacy (1534) 401
Act of Uniformity (1559) 416
action painting 670, 696
Actium, battle of (31 B.C.) 155
Acts of the Apostles 192, 196
Adagia (*Adages*) (Erasmus) 397
Adam (and Eve) 193, 225
Adam, Robert 475; Kenwood House Library 475, **17.10**
Adam Bede (G. Eliot) 540, 541
Adams, John, U.S. President 487
Adams, John 713; *El Niño* 713
Aegean cultures 65, 67, 72; map **4.1**
Aegina 85; Temple of Aphaia 99–101, **5.20–5.25**
Aegisthus 77, 78
Aeneas, Ascanius, and Anchises (statue group) **7.1**
Aeneid (Virgil) 142, 145–6, 152, 157, 165, 459, 479
Aeschylus 127, 130; on chamber pots 477; *Oresteia* 76–7, 127–8, **6.11**
Aesop 292
Afghanistan 659, 665, 702–3; film 718
Africa 5, 43–4, 335, 368, 664; beadwork 37; literature 679, 683–4; map **2.3**; rock art 13; sculpture 37, 600; *see also* slaves; South Africa
Africa (Petrarch) 316–17, 387
African Americans: literature 634–5, 683; music 631–3, 635, 690; painting 634, 676
African National Congress (ANC) 664
Afro-American Symphony (Still) 635
"Afternoon of a Faun, The" (Mallarmé) 573
Agamemnon 74, 76–7; *Agamemnon* (Aeschylus) 77, *see Oresteia*; "Agamemnon's mask" 76, **4.13**
Age of Anxiety, The (Auden) 681
Agesander, Athenodorus, and Polydorus of Rhodes: *Laocoön Group* 138–9, **6.36**
agora, Athens 85, 112
Agra, India: Taj Mahal 230–1, **9.25**
agricultural advances 11, 19, 260, 532, **2.6**
Ahmose, Queen 56
Ahmose I, pharaoh 58
Ahura Mazda 34
Aida (Verdi) 525
AIDS 699, 705, 706, 707, 708, 717; quilt **24.3**
Ailey, Alvin 689; *Revelations* 689, **23.35**
Ain't I a Woman? (Truth) 552
aircraft/air travel 591, 623
Ajanta, India: Buddhist *viharas* 249
Ajax 93–4
Akbar 454
Aké: The Years of Childhood (Soyinka) 684
akh 48
Akhenaten (Glass) 689
Akhenaton (Amenhotep IV) 61; "Hymn to the Sun" 61
Akkadian/Akkadians 3, 19, 23, 26, 27, 28
Akroteri *see* Thera
Alaric, of the Visigoths 209
Albee, Edward: *Who's Afraid of Virginia Woolf?* 686–7
Alberti, Leon Battista 342, 377; *Book of the Family* 342–3; *On Architecture* 343; *On Painting* 342; one-point perspective 341, **13.13**; Rucellai Palace 343, **13.16**; Sant' Andrea 344, **13.17**, **13.18**
Albigensians 202, 275, 276
Alceste (Gluck) 482
Alceste (Lully) 445, **16.20**
alchemy 431, 453
Alcott, Louisa May: *Little Women* 596
Alcuin of York 245–6, 247, 248, 285, 315
Aldine Press, Venice 382
Aldobrandino of Siena: *The Books of Health* **11.17**
Aldrin, Buzz **23.8**
aleatory music 688, 696
Alemanni 241
Alexander I, Tsar 532
Alexander VI, Pope 350
Alexander Nevsky (Eisenstein) 647, **22.31**
Alexander the Great 34, 38, 44, 62, 109, 132–3, 134, 137, 155, 188; map of empire **6.1**
Alexandria, Egypt 137, 219; Library 137
al-Farabi 235; *The Ideas of the Inhabitants of the Virtuous City* 235
Alfonso XIII, of Spain 619
algebra 234
Algeria 665
al-Ghazali 235; *Deliverance from Error* 235; *Incoherence of the Philosophers* 235
Alhambra, Granada, Spain 231, **9.26**
al-Hazen 234
Ali, Caliph 225
Alice's Adventures in Wonderland (Carroll) 596
alienation 601, 607, 635, 641, 679
al-Khwarizimi 234
al-Kindi 235
All Quiet on the Western Front (Remarque) 640
Allah 224, 225, 226
Allegory of Bad Government (Lorenzetti) 324, **12.20**
"Allegory of the Cave" (Plato) 124
Allende, Isabel 684
al-Malik, Abd 227
al-Qaeda 702, 703
al-Razi (Rhazes) 234
Altarpiece of the Lamb see Ghent Altarpiece
altarpieces 317–19, 322–3, 340, 356–7, 383–4
Althing 259
Alvin Ailey American Dance Theater 689
Amahl and the Night Visitors (Menotti) 688
Amarna period sculpture 61, **3.30**
Amasis painter: *Perseus Decapitates Medusa* 94, **5.12**
Ambrose, St. 204
Amenemhet III, head of 57, **3.23**
Amenhotep IV *see* Akhenaton
Amenophis III, of Egypt 60
America 335, 428, 430; map **16.2**; *see* United States
American Civil War 480, 488, 552, 553–5, 556, **19.20**, **19.25**
American Express Train (Palmer) **19.1**
American in Paris, An (Gershwin) 644
American Revolution (1776) 467, 485–6
American Telephone and Telegraph Headquarters Building (P. Johnson and Burgee) 679, **23.33**
American Tragedy, An (Dreiser) 636
Amiens Cathedral, France 288, **11.19**; *Vierge dorée* 290, 306, **11.23**
Amon/Amon-Re 45, 56
Amsterdam 428, 451
Amundsen, Roald 624
Anacreon 102–3
anatomy 334, 395, 403, 430, **13.4**, **15.5**
Anatomy Lesson of Dr. Nicolaes Tulp, The (Rembrandt) 450–1, **16.30**
Anavysos Kouros 82, 96–7, 111, **5.15**
Anaximander 102
Anaximenes 102
ancestor worship 11, 156–7
Ancients and Moderns 445, 508
And Quiet Flows the Don (Sholokhov) 638
Andersen, Hans Christian 596
Andrea da Firenze 325; *Triumph of St. Thomas Aquinas* 325, **12.21**
Andromaque (Racine) 448
Angela, St. (Merici) 409
Angelico, Fra 345; *Mocking of Christ . . .* 345, **13.20**
Angels in America (Kushner) 717
Angkor Thom, Cambodia 36, **2.24**
Angles 241, 252
Anglican Church 416, 430
Anglo-Saxons 252; *Beowulf* 254–5; metalwork 254, **10.12**
Anguissola, Sofonisba: *Self-portrait at a Spinet* 389, **14.27**
anima/animus (Jung) 593, 612
Animal Farm (Orwell) 680–1
Anishnabe Drum 13, **1.12**
Anna Christie (O'Neill) 642
Anna Karenina (Tolstoy) 541
"Annabel Lee" (Poe) 516
Annals (Tacitus) 174
Anne of Austria 444
Anne of Cleves 401
Annonce faite à Marie, L' (Claudel) 599
Anouilh, Jean 642; *Antigone* 642; *Le Voyageur sans bagage* 642
Anthemius of Tralles and Isidorus of Miletus: Hagia Sophia 208, 209, 219–21, **9.10–9.12**
Anthills of the Savannah (Achebe) 684
Anthony of Egypt, St. 202–3, 241
anthropology 624, 635
Antigone (Anouilh) 642
Antigone (Sophocles) 128–9
Antigonus 137
Antioch 219
Antiochus IV, Seleucid ruler of Athens 140
antiphon 219
antipopes 303
anti-Semitism 539, 619, 663, **22.6**; *see also* Holocaust, the
Antonine dynasty (Rome) 169
Antoninus, St. (Antonio Pierozzi) 349
Antwerp 336, 368
Anu 20, 25
Anubis 45, 86, **3.3**
apartheid 664, 696
Aphrodite 86, 87, 92, 103; *Aphrodite of Knidos* (Praxiteles) 136, **6.33**; *Aphrodite of Melos* 138, **6.35**
Apocalypse 192
Apocrypha 186
Apollo 87, 88
Apology for Poetry (Sidney) 418
Appian Way, Italy 153, 154, **7.10**
aqueducts, Roman 154, **7.11**
Aquinas, Thomas 287, 288, 295, 303, 325, **12.21**; *Summa theologiae* 287–8, 296
Ara Pacis Augustae, Rome 165–6, **7.24**, **7.25**
Arabian Nights 232–3
Arafat, Yasir 704
Aragon, the 350
Arc de Triomphe, Paris (Chalgrin *et al.*) 361, 498–9, **18.3**
Arcadia (Sidney) 418
Arcadia (Stoppard) 717
arch and vault construction: Gothic 278–9, 280, 281, **11.5**, **11.8**; Roman 152–3, **7.8**, **7.9**; Romanesque 265, 278, 280
Arch of Titus, Rome 170, 361, **7.3**, **8.5**
Archaic period (Greece) 85, 92–104, 112
archetypes, Jungian 593, 612
Archimedes 132
architectural Orders 98–9, 140, 170, 343, **5.18**
architecture: ancient Egyptian 59–61; ancient Greek 88, 98–9, 115–17, 120–1; ancient Roman 152–3, 157, 158, 168–70, 171, 343; Art Nouveau 594; Baroque 434–5, 444, 458–9; Byzantine 208, 209, 211, 219–21, 222; Carolingian 245; and Counter-Reformation 411, 412, 413, 434; early Christian 198, 200–1; Etruscan 147, 148–9; Federal style

488–9; Gothic 268, 273, 278–85, 288–9, 291, 306, 308, 323; Gothic Revival 504, 506; Hellenistic 139–40, 152; Indus Valley 30; and industrial innovation 532–3, 555–6; International Style 629; Japanese (Buddhist) 249; Mannerist 391–2; medieval 301, 309; Mesopotamian 19–21; Minoan 67–8; Mycenaean 75–6, 79; Neoclassical 361, 475, 488–9, 498–9; Palladian 391–2; Postmodern 678–9, 701, 711–13; Prairie Style 630; Renaissance 339, 343–4, 348, 374–5, 377; Rococo 474, 475; Romanesque 239, 260, 264–5, 267
Ardabil carpet 231–2, **9.27**
Arena Chapel, Padua: frescoes (Giotto) 319–22, **12.14**, **12.15**
Areopagitica (Milton) 459
Ares 85, 87, 92
Arianism/Arius 202, 203, 241
arias 440, 455, 461; ternary 455, 461
Ariosto, Lodovico 387, 417; *The Casket* 387; *Orlando furioso* 365, 387
Aristokles: *Stele of Aristion* 86, **5.3**
Aristophanes 130; *The Clouds* 130; *The Frogs* 130; *Lysistrata* 131
Aristotle 135, 225, 234, 235, 236, 285, 287, 288, 333, 403, 430, 431, 447, 548; *Ethics* 135, 377; *Poetics* 135; *Politics* 135
Aristotle with a Bust of Homer (Rembrandt) 451–2, **16.31**
Ark of the Covenant 187, 188
armies: Greek 90, 91, 92, **5.20**; Roman 152, 155
Armory Show (1913) 610, 625
Armstrong, Louis 631–2
Armstrong, Neil 666
Arnolfini Portrait (van Eyck) 355, **13.32**
Arp, Jean (Hans): *Collage Arranged According to the Laws of Chance* 605, **21.20**
Arrival of a Train at the Station, The (A. and L. Lumière) 582, **20.24**
ars nova 311–12, 358
art films 692, 696
Art Nouveau 594
Art of Love, The (Ovid) 167
"Art poétique, L'" (Verlaine) 573–4
art songs 518, 520–1, 526
Artaxerxes of Persia 33
Artemis 85, 87, 99
Arthurian legend 255–6, 292, 293
Artist of the Floating World, An (Ishiguro) 715
Artist's Studio, The (Daguerre) 548, **19.14**
"As Vesta was from Latmos hill descending" (Weelkes) 417
As You Like It (Shakespeare) 419
Ascham, Roger 415; *The Scholemaster* 415
Ashcan School 608
ashlar 68, 152
Ashur-sharrat, Queen 31, **2.19**
Assommoir, L' (Zola) 538, 568
Assumption of the Virgin (Titian) 383–4, **14.21**
Assurbanipal of Assyria 30–2, **2.18**, **2.19**
Assyria/Assyrians 26, 30–2, 38, 188
Astaire, Fred 644
Astralabe 287
astrology 137, 185, 234
Astronomer, The (Vermeer) 453, **16.34**
astronomy 123, 234, 294–5, 395, 403, 430, 431, 432, 433, 460, 548, **16.43**, **16.44**
Astrophel and Stella (Sidney) 417–18
Atala (Chateaubriand) 508
Aten/Aton 45, 61, **3.6**
Athanasius, St. 203
Athena 85, 87, 93, 100, **5.23**; statue (Phidias) 117, **6.11**; Temple of Athena Nike 120, **6.18**
Athenodorus *see* Agesander
Athens, Greece 73, 80, 85, 91, 104–5, 109, 111, 112, 135, 140; Academy 124, 214; coinage 164, **7.21**; grave stele 86, **5.2**; laws 92–3; Lyceum 135, 214; Olympeium 140, **6.39**; under Pericles 114–15, 130, 131; women 93; *see also* Acropolis
Athos, Mount 299; monastery 222
Atlantis 72
atomic bombs *see* nuclear weapons
Atomists 123, 161
atonality (music) 606
Attalos I, of Pergamon 137
Attila, king of the Huns 209
Attis 185
Atum 45, 46
Atwood, Margaret 714; *The Handmaid's Tale* 714, 715; *Oryx and Crake* 714, 715
Auden, W. H. 607, 681–2; *The Age of Anxiety* 681
Augustine of Canterbury 252
Augustine, St., of Hippo 204, 287, 413, 434; *The City of God* 204–5, 235; *Confessions* 204, 235
Augustus, Emperor (Octavian) 143, 155, 157, 158, 163, 164–6, 167, 174–5; *Augustus of Prima Porta* 164, 165, 177, **7.23**; coin 164, **7.22**
auloi (pipes) 71, 92, 160
Aurelius, Emperor Marcus 173; equestrian monument 173, **7.40**; *Meditations* 173–4
Auschwitz concentration camp 622, **22.7**
Austen, Jane 512; *Pride and Prejudice* 512
Australia 565, 617; *see also* Aboriginals
Australopithecus afarensis 5
Austria 467, 498, 587, 588, 589, 621; music 484–5, 606–7; philosophy 624; *see also* Freud, Sigmund; Vienna
autocracies 214
automobiles 591
autos-da-fé 276
avant garde 361, 585, 612
Avare, L' (Molière) 448
Avars 244
Ave Maria (Josquin Desprez) 359
Averroës 235, 377; *The Incoherence of the Incoherence* 235
Avicenna (Ibn Sina) 234; *Canon medicinae* 234, **9.29**
Avignon, papacy in 302–3
Awakening, The (K. Chopin) 558
Awakening Conscience (Hunt) 547, **19.13**
Aztec civilization 369–70, 444

ba 48
Babbitt, Milton 688
Babel, Tower of 191
Babylon/Babylonians 26, 28–9, 32, 152, 185
Babylonian Captivity (586–539 B.C.) 38, 188
"Babylonian Captivity" (1309–77) 302
Bacchae, The (Euripides) 129–30
Bacchus (Caravaggio) 438, **16.13**
Bach, Johann Sebastian 454, 455, 521
Bacon, Francis: *Novum Organum* 431
Baghdad, Iraq 225, 244; House of Wisdom 235
Baker, Josephine 633; sculpture (Calder) **22.23**
Balanchine, George 642
Bald Soprano, The (Ionesco) 685–6
Baldwin, James 683; *Go Tell It on the Mountain* 683
ball games, Mesoamerican 178–9, **7.42**, **7.44**
ballate 316
ballet 446, 519, 525, 601, 607, 642, 643, 644, 689, **16.23**
Ballets Russes (Russian Ballet) 601, 607, 642
balletts 417, 422
Balzac, Honoré de 537; *La Comédie humaine* 537; *Le Père Goriot* 537; Rodin's monument to **19.5**
Bamiyan, Afghanistan: Buddha 703, **24.1**
Ban Po, China: Neolithic settlement 11
Bandits' Roost . . . (Riis) 555, **19.22**
Banjo Lesson (Tanner) 555, **19.23**
banking 260, 303, 336, 355
baptism, Christian 193
baptisteries 201, 317; Florence 294, 339, **11.25**
Barak, Ehud 704
Barberini Ivory 214–15, **9.3**
Barcelona: Casa Milá (Gaudí) 594, **21.6**
Barmak, Siddiq: *Osama* 718
Barney, Matthew 710; "Cremaster" series 710, **24.10**
Baroque style 425, 427; architecture 434–5, 444, 458–9; music and opera 427, 439–41, 454–6, 482, 695; painting 427, 437–9, 442–3, 449–53; sculpture 436; theater 427, 447–8
Barrie, J. M.: *Peter Pan* 597
Barry, Charles 504; Houses of Parliament, London (with Pugin) 506, **18.12**
Barthes, Roland 668, **23.9**
Basawan: *The Virgin and Child* **16.36**
Basie, Count 632, 633
Basil I, Emperor 212
Basil the Great, bishop of Caesarea 203
Basilica Ulpia, Rome 171, **7.35**, **7.36**
basilicas, early Christian 198, 200
Basquiat, Jean-Michel 677, 692; *Horn Players* 677, **23.29**
Battle of San Romano (Uccello) 347, **13.21**
Battleship Potemkin (Eisenstein) 646, **22.30**
Baudelaire, Charles 573; *Les Fleurs du mal* 573; "Hymn to Beauty" 573
Bauhaus 629
Bayeux Tapestry 267, **10.28**, **10.29**
Bear Run, Penn.: Kaufmann House (Fallingwater) (Wright) 630, **22.19**
Bearded Man from Mohenjo-Daro 30, **2.16**
Beardsley, Aubrey 585, 594–5; *Salomé* 595, **21.8**
Beat writers 679, 682–3
Beatles, the 691
Beauvoir, Simone de: *The Second Sex* 663
Becket, Thomas à 262, 313, 402; reliquary of **10.20**
Beckett, Samuel 685, 717; *Waiting for Godot* 685
Bede, Venerable 246; *History* 252
Beethoven, Ludwig van 465, 483, 485, 518–20, **18.19**
Beethoven Frieze (Klimt) 593, **21.5**
"Beggars, The" (Neruda) 684
Beghards 278
Beguines 277–8
Being and Nothingness (Sartre) 625
Being and Time (Heidegger) 625
Belgium 588, 589, 664
Belisarius 214
Bell, Alexander Graham 534, 563, 591
Bell for Adano, A (J. Hersey) 682
Bell Jar, The (Plath) 682
belle époque 591
Bellini, Giovanni 365, 382; *Madonna of the Meadow* 382, **14.19**
Beloved (Morrison) 683
Benedict of Nursia, St. 248, 295
Benedictine Order 248, 261, 278
Beni Hasan, Egypt: tombs 58
Benin, Republic of: Yoruba beadwork crown 37, **2.27**
Bentham, Jeremy 536
Benton, Thomas Hart 630; *Pioneer Days and Early Settlement* 630, **22.20**
Beowulf 254–5
Bergen-Belsen concentration camp 621, 680, **22.5**
Bergers, Les (Watteau) 472, **17.3**
Bergman, Ingmar 692–3; *Seventh Seal* 693, **23.38**
Bergson, Henri 571, 576; *Time and Free Will* 571
Berkeley, Busby 649; *Footlight Parade* **22.37**
Berlin Wall 657, 659, 661, 702
Berlioz, Hector 521–2
Bernard of Clairvaux, St. 262–3, 265, 267, 278, 287, 295–6
Bernini, Gianlorenzo 434, 435, 458; *David* 436, **16.9**; *The Ecstasy of St. Teresa* 436, **16.10**; St. Peter's piazza, Rome 434, **16.5**
Bernstein, Leonard: *West Side Story* 690
Berry, Jean, duc de 308, 311
Bertin, L.-F.: portrait (Ingres) 504, 603, **18.8**
Bes 45
Beuys, Joseph 672, 677; *How to Explain Pictures to a Dead Hare* 672, **23.17**
Beyond the Pleasure Principle (Freud) 592
Bible(s) 3, 4, 26, 38, 183, 186, 204, 397, 456; Ezekiel 191; Isaiah 182, 183; New Testament 192–3, 195, 196; Psalms of David 190, 205, 219; Septuagint 186, 399, 409; Song of Solomon 190–1; women in 196
Bierstadt, Albert 516; *Sunrise at Yosemite* 516, **18.18**
Big Fish Eating the Little Fish, The (Bruegel) 407, **15.12**
Bilbao: Guggenheim Museum (Gehry) 712, **24.15**
Bilbao Monument, Guatemala 179, **7.43**
Billy Budd (Britten) 689
Billy the Kid (Copland) 644, **22.28**
Bin Laden, Osama 703, 718
bipedalism 6
birth control 667
Birth of a Nation (Griffith) 610–11, **21.25**, **21.26**
Birth of Helen (Caivano painter) 136, **6.32**
Birth of Venus (Botticelli) 347–8, **13.23**
Birth of Venus (Bouguereau) 543, **19.6**
Bismarck, Prince Otto von 531, 588, **21.2**
Bison-man, Chauvet cave, France 10, **1.5**
Bizet, Georges: *Carmen* 543

Black Death 303, 304–5, 306, 317, 323, 325, 329, 332; map **12.1**
black-figure vases, Greek 89, 93, **5.7**, **5.11–5.13**
black humor 682, 696
Black Square (Malevich) 601, **21.13**
Blake, William 509; *Satan in his Original Glory* **18.15**
Blombos Cave people, Africa 6
Blood Cross (Serrano) 707, **24.4**
Blood Wedding (Lorca) 642
Blouet, Guillaume-Abel *see* Chalgrin, J.-F.-T.
"Blowin' in the Wind" (Dylan) 691
Blue Boy, The (Gainsborough) 475, **17.9**
Blue Rider, The (*Der blaue Reiter*) 600
blues 611, 612, 631
Boas, Franz 635
Boccaccio, Giovanni 317, 319, 333, 335, 350; *Decameron* 304–5, 317, 319, 402, 419; *Le livre des cleres et nobles femmes* 301, **12.1**
Boccioni, Umberto: *Unique Forms of Continuity in Space* 600, **21.11**
Boethius, Anicius 211; *The Consolation of Philosophy* 211; *De arithmetica* 312, **12.9**; *De institutione musica* 211
Boffrand, Germain: Salon de la Princesse 468, **17.1**
Bogomils 202
Bohème, La (Puccini) 543
Bohr, Niels 591
Boléro (Ravel) 606
Boleyn, Anne 401, 402, 410
Bolívar, Simón 500
Bolsheviks 590, 618
Bonheur, Rosa 544; *Plowing in the Nivernais . . .* 544–5, **19.8**
Boniface VIII, Pope 275, 276, 302
book-keeping, double-entry 335
Book of the City of Ladies (Christine de Pisan) 314
Book of the Dead 48
Book of the Family (Alberti) 342–3
Books of Hours 308, **11.16**, **12.6**
Booth, John Wilkes 554
bop 633
Borghese, Cardinal Scipione 436, 438
Boris Godunov (Mussorgsky) 526
Borromini, Francesco: San Carlo alle Quattro Fontane, Rome 435, **16.7**, **16.8**
Bosch, Hieronymus 404, 406; (attrib.) *The Cure of Folly* 407, **15.11**; *The Garden of Earthly Delights* 406, **15.10**
Boscotrecase, Italy: villa 167, **7.27**
Bossi, Antonio: stucco, Würzburg Residenz **17.7**
Bossuet, Jacques-Bénigne 427, 444; *Politics Drawn from the Holy Scriptures* 424, 427
Boston, Mass. 485, 486; Massachusetts State House (Bulfinch) 361, **13.38**
Boswell, James: *Life of Samuel Johnson* 480
Botticelli, Sandro: *Birth of Venus* 347–8, **13.23**
Boucher, François 472; *Odalisque* 472, **17.4**
Bouguereau, William-Adolphe 543; *The Birth of Venus* **19.6**
Boulez, Pierre 688
Bourgeois Gentilhomme, Le (Molière) 448
bourgeoisie 536, 558
Bourges, France: Jacques Coeur's house 308, **12.7**
Bowie, David 692
Boyle, Danny: *Trainspotting* 718
Boyle, Robert 431, 453
Bracciolini, Poggio 337
Brady, Mathew 554; *Lincoln . . .* **19.19**
Braggart Soldier, The (Plautus) 161
Brahe, Tycho 403, 431
"Brahma" (Emerson) 514
Brahms, Johannes 521, 525
Bramante, Donato 365, 377; St. Peter's, Rome 375, 458, **14.9**; Tempietto, Rome 374, **14.8**
Brancusi, Constantin 627, 670; *White Negress III* 627, **22.12**
Brandenburg Concertos (Bach) 455
brass instruments 482, 518
Brave New World (A. Huxley) 640
Brazil: cannibals 402
breaks (music) 612
Brecht, Bertolt 641; *Mother Courage* 641; *The Three-Penny Opera* 641
Breton, André: Surrealist manifestos 627, 628, **22.14**
Breuer, Dr. Josef 571
Brezhnev, Leonid 658, 659
Bridge, The (*Die Brücke*) 600
Brigadoon (Lerner and Loewe) 690
Brighton, U.K.: Royal Pavilion (Nash) 506, **18.11**
Brigid, St. 252
"Brise Marine" (Mallarmé) 573
Britain 262, 267, 275, 302, 367, 411, 416, 428, 456–7, 467, 498, 500, 501, 532, 587, 615, 702; architecture 506, *see* London; colonialism 565, 585, 664–5; earth art 675; literature 252, 312–13, 417–18, 459, 461, 479–81, 509–13, 532, 539–41, 585, 587, 594–5, 596–7, 598, 638–40, 680–1; music 416–17, 688–9; painting 475, 476–7, 504, 509, 510, 547, **16.2**, **16.38**; philosophy 433, 471, 500–1, 536; photography 548; scientists 431–3; Stonehenge 12, 14; theater 417–22, 480, 595, 717; World War I 588, 589–90; World War II 621, 623; *see also* Anglo-Saxons
Britannicus (Racine) 448
Britten, Benjamin 688–9
Brontë, Anne 513; *The Tenant of Wildfell Hall* 513
Brontë, Charlotte 513; *Jane Eyre* 513
Brontë, Emily 513; *Wuthering Heights* 513
Bronze Age 65, 67, 88
bronzes: Carolingian **10.1**; Etruscan 147, 149, **7.2**, **7.4**; Greek 89, 131, **5.6**, **6.28**; Italian 339, 344–5, 351–2, 390, 600, **13.7**, **13.8**, **13.19**, **13.29**, **14.29**, **21.11**; Roman 173, **7.7**, **7.40**
Broschi, Carlo 695
Brothers Karamazov (Dostoevsky) 541
Brown, James 690
Brown, John 552
Brücke, Die ("The Bridge") 600
Bruegel, Pieter, the Elder 404, 407; *The Big Fish Eating the Little Fish* 407, **15.12**; *Hunters in the Snow* 407, 409, **15.13**
Brunelleschi, Filippo 338; Florence Cathedral dome 339, 358, **13.6**, **13.9**; perspective system 340, 341, **13.12**; *Sacrifice of Isaac* 339, **13.7**
Bruni, Leonardi 336, 337; *History of the Florentine People* 337; *Panegyric of the City of Florence* 337; tomb 337, **13.5**
Brutus, Marcus Junius 155
BSE (Bovine Spongiform Encephalopathy) 706–7
Buddha 134, 202; statues 134, 703, **6.30**, **6.31**, **24.1**
Buddhism 134, 295; monasticism 249, **10.7**, **10.8**; sites 36, **2.24**, map **2.3**; *see also* Buddha
Buffalo Springfield 691
Bulfinch, Charles: Massachusetts State House, Boston 361, **13.38**
Bulgaria 212, 659; prehistoric pot 11–12, **1.7**
Bull, John (musician) 417
bull motifs 26, 27, 30, 68–9
Burgee, John *see* Johnson, Philip
Burgundians 241
Burial at Ornans, The (Courbet) 544, **19.7**
Burial of Count Orgaz, The (Greco) 413–14, **15.19**
Burke, Edmund: *A Philosophical Enquiry into . . . the Sublime and Beautiful* 500–1, 506
Bus Reflections (Ansonia) (Estes) 674, **23.21**
Bush, George W., U.S. President 702, 703, 704, 707
Butler, Samuel 541: *Erewhon* 541
Byrd, William 416–17
Byron, George Gordon, Lord 511; *Don Juan* 511–12
Byzantine Empire 209, 212–13, 224; architecture 208, 209, 211, 219–21, 222; coinage **9.4**; law code 214, 215–16; maps **9.1**, **9.3**; mosaics 211, 216, 220; painting and icons 221, 318; women 213
Byzantium *see* Constantinople

Cabot, John 335
cadences, musical 415, 422
cadenzas 484, 492
"Cadet Picture of My Father, The" (Rilke) 602
Caedmon 252
Caesar, Julius 155, 162, 163, 164, 174, 316; *Gallic War* 155
Cage, John 688, 716
Caivano painter: *Birth of Helen* 136, **6.32**
Calder, Alexander: *Josephine Baker* **22.23**
calendars 43, 155, 191, 225
California News (Mount) 555, **19.21**
Caligula, Emperor 175
Caligula (Camus) 685
Calloway, Cab 632
Calvin, John 397, 399, 409, 416, 434; *The Institutes of the Christian Religion* 399
Calvinism 399, 449, 513
Cambodia 36, 565, 665
Cambrai: League of 382; Treaty of (1529) 367–8
Campion, Thomas 417
Camus, Albert 679–80, 685; *Caligula* 685; *The Myth of Sisyphus* 680; *The Plague* 679–80; *The Stranger* 679
Canada 712, 714–15
Candide (Voltaire) 469
canopic jars, Egyptian 47
cantatas 454, 455, 461
Canterbury Cathedral, England 262
Canterbury Tales, The (Chaucer) 313, 332
"Canticle of the Sun" (St. Francis) 277
cantilevers 630, 652
Canto General (Neruda) 684
cantus firmus 285
canzoni 292
Capet, Hugh 260
Capetian dynasty 260–1
capitalism 399, 471, 536, 537, 587, 617, 618
Capitoline Wolf **7.7**
Caravaggio 438, 439, 451; *Bacchus* 438, **16.13**; *The Conversion of St. Paul* 438, **16.12**
Caravaggisti 438–9
Caricature, La 545
Carmen (Bizet) 543
carnival songs 349
Carolingian dynasty 241, 242–3
Carolingian Renaissance 243, 245–6; manuscripts 247, **10.5**; music 243, 247–8
carpet, Islamic 231–2, **9.27**
Carrara marble 158
Carrel, Alexis 624
Carroll, Lewis 596, 646; *Alice's Adventures in Wonderland* 596; *The Hunting of the Snark* 596; *Through the Looking Glass* 596
cartes-de-visite 549, **19.15**
Carthage 154
Cartier, Jacques 369
cartouches 62, **3.15**
caryatids 121, **6.20**
Casa Milá, Barcelona (Gaudí) 594, **21.6**
Casket, The (Ariosto) 387
Cassatt, Mary 569; *A Woman and a Girl Driving* 569, **20.9**
cassone panel (Giovanni di Ser Giovanni) **13.26**
Castiglione, Baldassare 386; *The Courtier* 365, 386–7, 419; portrait (Raphael) **14.23**
castrati 695, 696
Castro, Fidel 659
catacombs, Rome 195–6, 197, 198, **8.6**, **8.8**
Çatal Hüyük, Turkey 11
Catalogues of Women and Eoiae (?Hesiod) 64, 67
Catch-22 (Heller) 682
Catcher in the Rye (Salinger) 682
Cathars 202, 275
catharsis 135
cathedrals: Baroque 458–9; Gothic 280–4, 288–90, 291; *see also* St. Peter's, Rome
Cather, Willa 636
Catherine II ("the Great"), of Russia 467
Catherine of Aragon 401, 410
Catholic Church 299, 333, 410, 416; and anti-Semitism 539; architecture 264–5, 278–9, 284–5, 348, 391–2, *see also* cathedrals; and birth control 667; and *castrati* 695; and medieval drama 250–2, 292, 311; and medicine 286; music 205, 219, 247–8, 285–6, 311, 333; pilgrimages 262, 269; relics 262; sacraments 193–4, 205, 275; and scholasticism 287–8, 325; and science 427, 430; and Thirty Years War 425, 428–9; *see also* altarpieces; Christianity, early; Counter-Reformation; Inquisition; missionaries; papacy; Reformation
Catlin, George: *Keokuk, Chief of the Tribe* **19.17**
Cato, Marcus Porcius 154
Catullus, Gaius Valerius 172
Cavalleria rusticana (Mascagni) 543
cave paintings 7, 9–10, **1.1**, **1.3–1.5**
Cavour, Camillo 531
Caxton, William 332, 382
"Ce moys de may" (Dufay) 359

Ceauşescu, Nicolae 701
Cecil, Sir William (Lord Burghley) 416
cell-phones 699, 706
Cellini, Benvenuto 390; *Perseus* 390, 391, **14.29**; saltcellar of Francis I 390, **14.28**
Cervantes, Miguel de 441, 481; *Don Quixote* 441
Cerveteri, Italy 149; sarcophagus 150, **7.6**
Cézanne, Paul 576–7, 602, 604; *The Great Bathers* **20.16**; *The Temptation of St. Anthony* 203, **8.16**
chaitya halls, Buddhist 249, **10.7**
Chalgrin, Jean-François-Thérèse, Blouet, Guillaume-Abel, and Gilbert, Emile-Jacques: Arc de Triomphe, Paris 361, 498–9, **18.3**
chamber music 440, 461
Chamber Music (Joyce) 597
chamber pots 477
Chamberlain, Neville 621
Champlain, Samuel de 369
Champollion, Jean-François 49
Channel Tunnel 702
Chanson de Roland see Song of Roland
chansons 358, 359, 385, 415
chansons de geste 256
Chaplin, Charlie 647; *The Gold Rush* 647; *The Great Dictator* 648, **22.34**; *Modern Times* 647, **22.33**
Char, René 688
Chardin, Jean-Baptiste-Siméon 478; *Young Man Blowing Bubbles* 478, **17.14**
"Charge of the Light Brigade, The" (Tennyson) 532
Charivari, Le 545
Charlemagne 238, 239, 243–4, 247, 360; coronation 244, **10.2**; equestrian statuette of **10.1**; map of empire **10.2**; and monasticism 248; and music 247–8; Palace Chapel 245, 360; palace school 245–6
Charles I, of England 425, 456, 457; *Charles I with M. de St. Antoine* (van Dyck) **16.2**; costume design for (Jones) 457, **16.39**
Charles II, of England 457, 458, 459, 479, 480
Charles II, of France ("the Bald") 250, 289
Charles V, of France 309, 314
Charles V, Holy Roman Emperor 367–8, 371, 383, 399, 401, 438; *Charles V Seated* (Titian) **14.1**; map of empire **14.1**
Charles VII, of France 302, 308, 314, **12.7**; portrait (Fouquet) 357, **13.36**
Charles VIII, of France 367, 371
Charles X, of France 499–500, 503
Charles, Ray 690
Charles Martel 242
Charlottesville, Virginia: Rotunda (Jefferson) 488–9, **17.19**
Chartres Cathedral, France 288, 289, **11.18**, **11.21**; *Belle Verrière* 289, **11.22**
Chateaubriand, François-René de 508
Chaucer, Geoffrey 312, 313, 333, 419; *The Canterbury Tales* 313, 332
Chauvet Cave, France 10, **1.5**
Chechnya 701, 703
Chekhov, Anton 542, 543; *The Cherry Orchard* 542
chess 258, **10.17**
Chesterton, G. K. 598
Chiang Kai-shek 665
chiaroscuro 319, 438
Chicago 631; Chicago School (architecture) 555
Chicago, Judy: *The Dinner Party* 675, **23.25**
Chichén Itzá, Mexico: ball game 178, **7.42**, **7.44**
Chigi Vase (Orientalizing period) 90, 92, **5.9**
Childeric III, Merovingian king 243
Children of Violence, The (Lessing) 683
Children's Crusade 265
Childs, Lucinda: *Einstein on the Beach* 689, **23.34**
Chile 659; literature 684
China 557, 623, 659, 660, 665–6, 699, 705, 706; art 711; Cultural Revolution 666, 713, 716; film 717–18; literature 716; Neolithic settlement 11; Opium Wars 565
chinoiserie 477, **17.13**
Chiron Instructs Achilles in Playing the Lyre (fresco) 139, **6.37**
chiton 97, **5.17**
chivalry, code of 239, 256
Chomsky, Noam 668
Chopin, Frédéric 522–3, 525
Chopin, Kate 556, 558
chorale preludes 455, 461
chorales 399, 422
Christ *see* Jesus Christ
Christianity, early 137, 177, 183, 188, 191, 195–6, 225, 242, 295; and architecture 198, 200–1, **8.10–8.15**; and art 195, 196–8, **8.6–8.9**; and heresies 202; language of worship 205; martyrs 195; and paradise 295; symbolism and iconography 196, 197; and typology 193, 281, 289, **10.21**, **10.27**; and women 195, 196, 202; writers 204–5; *see also* Catholic Church; Eastern Orthodox Church; Jesus Christ; monasteries/monasticism; Paul, St.
Christie, Agatha 598
Christina, Queen of Sweden 429
Christina of Markyate 263
Christine de Pisan 302, 314, 333; *Book of the City of Ladies* 314; *Christine de Pisan presenting her poems to Queen Isabel* **12.10**
Christmas Carol, A (Dickens) 540
Christo and Jeanne-Claude: *Wrapped Reichstag* 709, **24.8**
Christus, Petrus 357; *St. Eloy (Eligius) in His Studio* 357, **13.35**
chromatic harmonies 415, 422, 518, 524
Chronos 85
Chrysoloras, Manuel 336
Churchill, Caryl 717
Churchill, Winston 614, 615, 623, 657, 659, **23.1**
Cicero 162, 314, 333; *On Duties* 162
Cid, Le (Corneille) 447, **16.24**
Cimabue (Cenni di Pepe): *Enthroned Madonna and Child* 317, 318, **12.12**
cinema *see* film
Ciompi rebellion (Florence, 1378) 301
Citizen Kane (Welles) 648, **22.35**
City of God, The (Augustine) 204–5, 235
city-states, Greek (*poleis*) 83, 85, 90, 91, 92, 93, 109, 131, 135
"Civil Disobedience" (Thoreau) 494, 497, 514
Civil Rights Movement 661–2
civil wars *see* American, English *and* Spanish Civil War
Civilization and its Discontents (Freud) 593, 612
"Clair de lune" (Debussy) 575
Claire's Knee (Rohmer) 693–4, **23.40**
Clare, St. 277
Clarissa (Richardson) 481
Clark, William 549
Classical period (Greece) 109–36
Classicism 360–1, 478; *see* Neoclassicism
Claude Lorrain 449; *Landscape with Merchants* **16.26**
Claudel, Paul 599; *L'Annonce faite à Marie* 599
Claudius, Emperor 175
Cleisthenes 111
Clement V, Pope 302
Clement VI, Pope 303
Clement VII, Pope 336, 401
Clement VIII, Pope 695
Cleopatra, Queen of Egypt 155
Clinton, Bill, U.S. President 704
clocks 301
clothes: Etruscan 149; Greek 97, **5.17**; Viking 258, **10.15**
Clotilde 242
Clouds, The (Aristophanes) 130
Clovis, Frankish king 242
Cluniac Order 261, 262
Cluny, France: Abbey 261, 262, 287, **10.18**, **10.21**
Clytemnestra 77, 78
Coat of Arms with a Peasant Standing on His Head (Housebook Master) 397, **15.1**
Cochise, Chief 550
codas, musical 483, 492
Cody, William ("Buffalo Bill") 544
Coetzee, John Michael 714; *Disgrace* 714; *Waiting for the Barbarians* 714
Coeur, Jacques: house (Bourges, France) 308, **12.7**
coffers 172
coinage: Byzantine **9.4**; Florentine 335; Greek 164, **7.21**; Roman 164, **7.22**
Colbert, Jean-Baptiste 444, 445
Cold War 623, 651, 655, 657, 659, 665, 702
Cole, Thomas 516; *The Last of the Mohicans* 516, **18.17**
Coleridge, Samuel 511; "Kubla Khan" 511; *Lyrical Ballads* (with Wordsworth) 509, 510; *The Rime of the Ancient Mariner* 510, 511
Colescott, Robert 676; *George Washington Carver Crossing the Delaware* 676, **23.28**
collage 604, 605, 612, 626, 627, 633, **21.19**, **21.20**, **22.10**, **22.11**, **22.24**
Collage Arranged According to the Laws of Chance (Arp) 605, **21.20**
collective unconscious 593, 612
Colleoni (Verrocchio) 351–2, **13.29**
Cologne, Germany 332; Cathedral 291, **11.24**
Colombia: literature 684
colonialism 369–70, 428, 433, 563, 565, 585, 664, 665, 683; maps **20.1**, **23.2**
Color Field Painting 670–1
Color Purple, The (Walker) 683
Colosseum, Rome 169–70, 178, **7.29**, **7.30**
Columba, St. 202, 252
Columbus, Christopher 276, 335
Comecon 657, 696
Comédie Française, La 447
Comédie humaine, La (Balzac) 537
comedy: Greek and Hellenistic 130, 137; medieval 252, 292, 311; Renaissance 333; Restoration 480; Roman 161, 387; Shakespearean 419, 420–1; 20th-century 598, 599
comets 403, 432
Cominform 658, 696
Commodus, Emperor 174, 185
Common Sense (Paine) 464, 467, 486
communications 460, 534, 563, 591, 699, 706
communism 536–7, 618, 657, 659, 660, 665, 701
Communist Manifesto (Marx and Engels) 536–7
Comnena, Anna 213; *Alexiad* 213
Comnenus, Alexius I 213
Comnenus, John II 213
computers 667, 706
Comte, Auguste 536
conceits 459, 461
concentration camps 621, 622, 680, **22.5**, **22.7**
Conceptual Art/Conceptualism 673
Concerning the Spiritual in Art (Kandinsky) 600, 609
concerti grossi 440–1, 455, 461
concertos 440, 455, 461, 518, 521
concerts, public 465
concrete, Roman 158
condensation (psychoanalysis) 572, 583
conditioned reflexes 624, 652
condottieri 347, 351, 352, 353
Coney, John: *St. Paul's Cathedral* **16.41**
Confessions (Augustine) 204, 235
conquistadores 369, 370, 444
Consecration of Napoleon I . . . (David) 497, **18.1**
Consolation of Philosophy, The (Boethius) 211
consonance 606, 612
Constable, John 504; *The Hay Wain* 504, **18.9**
Constance, Council of (1417) 303
Constantine I, Emperor 177, 196, 209, 212, 295; statue 177, **7.41**
Constantine V, Emperor 222
Constantine VI, Emperor 222
Constantinople (Byzantium; Istanbul) 177, 196, 209, 212, 213, 214, 222, 265, 333, 382; Council of (381) 202; Nika Riots (532) 214; plague 304; *see also* Hagia Sophia
continuo 440, 455, 461
contrapposto 111, 122, 136
Conversion of St. Paul (Caravaggio) 438, **16.12**
Cooper, James Fenimore 514; *The Last of the Mohicans* 514, 516
Copernicus, Nicolaus 403, 409, 431, 460; *On the Revolutions of the Heavenly Spheres* 403
Copland, Aaron 643, 644–5
copperwork, prehistoric 11–12, 19, **1.7**
Corante (newspaper) 557
corbeled arches/domes/vaults 75, 79, **4.11**, **4.16**
Córdoba, Spain: Mosque 228, **9.21–9.23**
Corelli, Arcangelo 440, 455
Corinth, Greece 73, 130, 140; League of 132; pottery 90, 92, 93, **5.8**, **5.9**
Corinthian Order 140
Corneille, Pierre 447; *Le Cid* 447, **16.24**
Cornelia, Mother of the Gracchi (Kauffmann) 478, 479, **17.15**

Cortés, Hernando 369, 370
Cos, island of 124
counterpoint 456, 461
Counter-Reformation, Catholic 395, 409; and architecture 411, 412, 413, 434; and music 415, 454; and painting 411–14, 437
couplets 419, 422
Courbet, Gustave 543, 544, 573; *A Burial at Ornans* 544, **19.7**
Courtier, The (Castiglione) 365, 386–7, 419
Covered Wagon, The (Cruze) 647, **22.32**
Cowboy, The (Matisse) 633, **22.24**
Crabwalk (Grass) 714
Cranach, Lucas, the Elder: *Luther* **15.3**
Crane, Stephen: *The Red Badge of Courage* 556
Crazy Horse 550
Creation, The (Haydn) 484
creation myths viii, 1, 3, 179, 259
Creation of Adam (Michelangelo) 377, **14.16**
Creatures of Prometheus, The (Beethoven) 519
"Cremaster" series (Barney) 710, **24.10**
Crete 65; *see* Minoan civilization
Crick, Francis 667
Crime and Punishment (Dostoevsky) 541
crime novels 598
Crimean War 532, 541, 548
Critias (Plato) 72
Critique of Pure Reason (Kant) 470, 501
Crito (Plato) 124
Cro-Magnon Man 6
cromlechs 12
Cromwell (Hugo) 508
Cromwell, Oliver 457, 459, 480
Crosby, Bing 632
Cross of Muriedach, Ireland 253–4, **10.11**
Crotona: school of philosophy 102
Crucible, The (Miller) 686
Crusades, the 265, 267, 275
Cruze, James: *The Covered Wagon* 647, **22.32**
Crystal Palace, London (Paxton) 533, **19.2**
Cuba 659
Cubism 600, 604
Cullen, Countee 635
Cummings, E. E. 637
cuneiform script 22, 28, **2.5**, **2.7**, **2.14**
Cure at Troy, The (Heaney) 719–20
Cure of Folly, The (Bosch) 407, **15.11**
Curie, Marie and Pierre 591
Cussac Cave, France 9, **1.3**
Custer, George Armstrong 550
Cut with the Kitchen Knife (Höch) 626, **22.10**
Cybele, cult of 185
cyclopaean masonry 79, **4.16**
Cyclopes 78, 79, 86
"Cyclops, The" (Theocritus) 138
Cynics 137
Cyrano de Bergerac (Rostand) 599
Cyrus I ("the Great"), of Persia 32–3
Cyrus II, of Persia 38
Czechoslovakia/Czech Republic 403, 525, 658, 659, 701

Dacians 171, **7.34**
Dada 605, 625, 626, 627, 642
"Daffodils, The" (Wordsworth) 511
Daguerre, Louis-Jacques-Mandé 548; *The Artist's Studio* 548, **19.14**
dance 8, 643, 689; *see also* ballet
Dance of Death 303
Dandridge, Dorothy 632
danse macabre 303
Dante Alighieri 292, 313, 333, 335, 382; *Divine Comedy* 292–6, 316, 318
Darfur, Sudan: genocide 706
Darius I, of Persia 33, 34, 104, **2.22**
Darius III, of Persia 132
Darwin, Charles 4, 123, 534–5; *The Descent of Man . . .* 535; *On the Origin of Species* 4, 535
Dash for the Timber, A (Remington) 550, **19.18**
dating systems 5
Daumier, Honoré 545; *Rue Transnonain* 545, **19.9**; *Third-class Carriage* 545–6, 548, **19.10**
David, King 38, 188, 312, **10.21**; Psalms 190, 205
David (Bernini) 436, **16.9**
David (Donatello) 344–5, **13.19**
David (Michelangelo) 371–2, 436, **14.4**
David, Jacques-Louis: *The Consecration of Napoleon I . . .* 497, **18.1**; *Napoleon at St. Bernard Pass* 498, **18.2**; *The Oath of the Tennis Court* 490, **17.20**
David Copperfield (Dickens) 540
Dayton Accords 702
De arithmetica 312, **12.9**
De institutione musica (Boethius) 211
Dead Sea Scrolls 186
Death, iconography of 306
"Death, be not proud" (Donne) 459
Death in Venice (Britten) 689
Death of Pentheus (Roman fresco) **6.27**
Death of a Salesman (Miller) 686
De Beers mining company 565
Debussy, Claude 574–5, 605; *Pelléas et Mélisande* 575, **20.13**
Decameron (Boccaccio) 304–5, 317, 319, 402, 419
Decius, Emperor 195
Declaration of Independence 486, 487, 551
Decline and Fall of the Roman Empire, The History of the (Gibbon) 471, 480
Deconstruction 667, 668
deductive reasoning 431, 461
Deerslayer, The (Cooper) 514
Defence of Poetry (Sidney) 418
Defoe, Daniel 480; *Robinson Crusoe* 480
Degas, (Hilaire-Germain-)Edgar 568, 569; *Monsieur Perrot's Dance Class* 568, **20.7**
Deir-el-Bahri, Egypt 56
Deism 467–8
De Klerk, Frederik 706
Delacroix, Eugène 502–3, 576; *Liberty Leading the People* 503–4, **18.7**
Delian League 111, 114, 130, 131
Deliverance from Error (al-Ghazali) 235
Delphi, Greece: oracle 88; Temple of Apollo 88, **5.4**
Demeter 87, 185
Democritus 123, 161
Deng Xiaoping 666
Denis, St. 278
Denmark 263, 428, 596
dental care, Etruscan 149
Depression, the *see* Great Depression
Derrida, Jacques 668
dervishes, whirling 232, 233
Descartes, René 433, 434; *Discourse on Method* 434; *Treatise on the Passions of the Soul* 434
Descent of Man . . . , The (Darwin) 535
Desert Sand Hills . . . (O'Sullivan) **19.16**
Desiderius, King of the Lombards 244
Desire Under the Elms (O'Neill) 642
De Stijl 629
detective fiction 598
détente 659, 660–1, 696
deus ex machina 127
development, musical 483, 492
Diaghilev, Sergei 601, 607, 642
Diaspora, Jews of the 188
Dickens, Charles 539–40, 597; *A Christmas Carol* 540; *David Copperfield* 540; *Great Expectations* 540; *Hard Times* 528, 529, 540
Dickinson, Emily 515
"Dictators, The" (Neruda) 684
Dictionary of the English Language, A (S. Johnson) 480
Diderot, Denis 468, 469, 470; bust (Houdon) **17.2**; *Encyclopédie* 468, 480; *Le Neveu de Rameau* 469
Diem, Ngo Dinh 660
digital art 701, 708
Dinner Party, The (Chicago) 675, **23.25**
Diocletian, Emperor 176–7, 195, 209
Diogenes 137, 377
Dionysos 87, 103; cult of 125, 126–7, 132, 137, 138, 185; statue (Phidias) 117, **6.13**
Dipylon krater 88, **5.5**
"Disasters of War" (Goya) 501, **18.5**
Discalced Carmelite Order 409
discant 285
Discourse on Method (Descartes) 434
Discus Thrower (*Discobolus*) (Myron) 112–13, 114, **6.3**
Disdéri, Adolphe-Eugène: *cartes-de-visite* **19.15**
diseases 349, 404, 406, 534, 535, 624, 667, 699, 705–7; plague 329, 332, 349
Disgrace (Coetzee) 714
Disney, Walt/Disney Company 540, 615, 650; Feature Animation Building (Stern) 711–12, **24.14**; *Steamboat Willie* 650, **22.38**
displacement (psychoanalysis) 572, 583, 628
dissolves (film) 582, 583
dissonance, musical 415, 422, 524
dithyramb chorus 127
Divine Comedy (Dante) 292–6, 316, 318
divine right of kings 424, 427, 465, 467, 470
Divisionism 576
DNA 667, 707
"Do Not Go Gentle" (Thomas) 681
Dr. Faustus (Marlowe) 418
Dr. Zhivago (Pasternak) 680
Doctrine and Discipline of Divorce, The (Milton) 459
Doll's House, A (Ibsen) 542
dome construction 172, 220, 339, **7.9**, **7.38**, **13.9**
Dome of the Rock, Jerusalem 227, **9.18–9.20**
Dominic (Guzmán), St. 275–6
Dominican Order 275–6, 287, 315, 325, 345, 349, 371, 400, 410
domino theory 660, 696
Domitian, Emperor 170, 195
Don Giovanni (Mozart) 485
Don Juan (Byron) 511–12
Don Quixote (Cervantes) 441
Donatello di Niccolò Bardi 338, 340, 342; *David* 344–5, **13.19**; *John the Evangelist* 340, **13.10**
Donatus, Aelius 246
Donne, John 459
Doolittle, Hilda *see* H.D.
Dorian mode 126
Dorians 80
Doric Order 98, 99, 116, **5.18**
Dos Passos, John Roderigo 636; *Three Soldiers* 636
Dostoevsky, Fyodor 541; *Brothers Karamazov* 541; *Crime and Punishment* 541; *The Gambler* 541; *The Idiot* 541
Douglass, Frederick 552; *Narrative . . .* 552
Dowland, John 417
Doyle, Sir Arthur Conan 598
Draco 92
Drake, Sir Francis 411, 416
drama *see* theater(s)
Dream, The (H. Rousseau) 592, **21.4**
Dreaming, the 13
dreams 24, 56
Dreiser, Theodore 636; *An American Tragedy* 636; *Sister Carrie* 636
dress *see* clothes
Dreyfus, Alfred 538, 539, 582
Dreyfus Affair, The (Méliès) 582
Drunken Old Woman (Hellenistic) 138, **6.34**
Dryden, John 479
Dualism 102
Dubcek, Alexander 658
Du Bellay, Cardinal Jean 402
Dubliners (Joyce) 597–8
Duccio di Buoninsegna 322; *Maestà* 322–3, **12.17**
Duchamp, Marcel 610; *L.H.O.O.Q.* 625–6, **22.9**; *Nude Descending a Staircase No. 2* 610, 625, **21.24**; "ready-mades" 625
Dufay, Guillaume 358–9; "Ce moys de may" 359
"Dulce et Decorum Est" (Owen) 584, 587
Dulcitius (Hroswitha) 252
Duns Scotus 288
Dunstable, John 358
Dura Europos, Syria 188; *Moses and the Crossing of the Red Sea* (fresco) 188, **8.3**
Dürer, Albrecht 404; *The Last Supper* 404–5, **15.8**; *Self-portrait* **15.7**
Dutch East India Company 428, 449, 565
Dutch painting *see* Netherlands
Dvořák, Antonín 525
Dwarf, The (Lägerkvist) 641
Dyck, Anthony van; *Charles I with M. de St. Antoine* **16.2**; *Henrietta Maria* **16.38**
Dying Warrior (pediment sculpture) 101, **5.24**
Dylan, Bob 691, **23.36**
dystopia 714, 721

Ea 21
Eagle Warrior (Aztec terra-cotta) **14.2**
Earhart, Amelia 623
earth art 674–5
Eastern Orthodox Church 196, 212, 219, 222
Eastman, George 563, 580, 582
Ecerinis (Mussato) 316, 333
Eclogues (Virgil) 162

École des femmes, L' (Molière) 448
economics 471, 536, 617, 652, 702
Ecstasy of St. Teresa, The (Bernini) 436, **16.10**
eddaic verse 259
Edison, Thomas Alva 534, 580, 581, 582; *Record of a Sneeze* 580, **20.22**
education 245–6, 275, 285, 315, 333, 350, 360, 470, 488–9, 587; *see also* academies; universities
Edward III, of England 302, 313
Edward VI, of England 401
Effects of Good Government in the City, The (Lorenzetti) 323–4, **12.19**
Ego and the Id, The (Freud) 592–3
Egypt 4, 38, 41, 155, 186–7, 265, 588, 663, 702; burials 47–8, 55, 58; calendar 43; dynasties 44; jewelry 57; language 23; literature 49, 53–4; map **3.1**; medicine 56; music 54–5; painting 45, 48, 55; pharaohs 37, 44, 45, 56–7, 58, 59; pyramids 50–1; religions (gods) 45–7, 61, 85, 86; scarabs 47, 51; scribes 53–4; sculpture 43, 52–3, 56–8, 61; temples 59–61; trade 43–4, 56; women 54, 55–7; writing systems 41, 49
Eiffel Tower, Paris 533, **19.3**
Eight, the 608
Einhard: *Life of Charlemagne* 243–4
Einstein, Albert 591, 654, 655
Einstein on the Beach (Glass/Wilson) 689, **23.34**
Eisenhower, Dwight D., U.S. President 623, 660
Eisenstein, Sergei 646, 647; *Alexander Nevsky* 647, **22.31**; *Battleship Potemkin* 646, **22.30**
Either/Or (Kierkegaard) 537
Eleatic philosophers 113–14, 123
Electra 77
Electra (Giraudoux) 642
electro-acoustic music 688
"Elegy to the Spanish Republic" series (Motherwell) 669, **23.11**
Elephant (Schongauer) 358, **13.37**
Eleusinian Mysteries 137, 185
"Elgin Marbles" **6.12**
Eliasson, Olafur: *Green River* 709, **24.9**
Eliot, George 540; *Adam Bede* 540, 541; *The Mill on the Floss* 540–1
Eliot, T. S. 637; "The Hollow Men" 637–8; "The Love Song of J. Alfred Prufrock" 637; *The Waste Land* 637
Elizabeth I 401, 410, 415–16, 417, 418, 477; portrait (attrib. Hilliard) **15.21**
Ellington, Duke 632–3, **22.22**
Ellison, Ralph 683; *The Invisible Man* 683
Eloy, St. 357; *St. Eloy (Eligius) in His Studio* (Christus) 357, **13.35**
Emerson, Ralph Waldo 513; "Brahma" 514; *Nature* 513; "Walden" 513
Emile (J.-J. Rousseau) 470
Empedocles 123
Emperor Jones, The (O'Neill) 642
encaustic paint 102, **9.14**
Encyclopédie (ed. Diderot) 468, 480
Engels, Friedrich: *Communist Manifesto* (with Marx) 536–7
England *see* Britain
English Civil War 456–7
engravings 358, **13.37**
Enki 20
Enlightenment, the 467, 468, 471, 495, 501, 504
Enlil 20
Enneads (Plotinus) 186, 235, 236, 338
Enthroned Madonna (Giotto) 317, 318–19, **12.13**
Enthroned Madonna and Child (Cimabue) 317, 318, **12.12**
Entombment of Atala, The (Girodet-Trioson) 508, **18.14**
environmental pollution 707
Epic of Gilgamesh 16, 17, 19, 23–6, 27
epic theater 641, 652
Epicurus/Epicureans/Epicureanism 137, 161, 377
Epiphany 222
"Epitaph for the Unknown Soldier" (Auden) 682
equestrian statues: Aurelius 173, **7.40**; Charlemagne **10.1**; Colleoni (Verrocchio) 351–2, **13.29**
Equiano, Olaudah 504
equites 152, 163
Erasmus, Desiderius 395, 397, 399, 400, 402, 404, 407, **15.4**; *Adagia* 397; *Julius Excluded from Heaven* 397–8; portrait (Holbein) **15.2**; *The Praise of Folly* 394, 395, 402
Ercole I, Duke of Ferrara 359
Erechtheum, Acropolis 120–1, **6.7**, **6.19**, **6.20**
Erewhon (Butler) 541
Erik the Red 259
"Erlking, The" (Schubert) 520
Ernst, Max 627; *The Hat Makes the Man* 627, **22.11**
Eros 86, 87, 103
"Essay Concerning Human Understanding" (Locke) 433
Essay on the Principle of Population (Malthus) 471, 535, 536
Essays (Montaigne) 402, 419, 422
Essene sect 186
Este family 350, 359, 384, 387, **13.31**
Estes, Richard 674; *Bus Reflections (Ansonia)* **23.21**
E.T. (Spielberg) 694–5, **23.42**
Et in Arcadia Ego (Poussin) 449, **16.25**
Ethelbert, King of Kent 252
Ethics (Aristotle) 135, 377
Etruscans 23, 143, 147–9, 150, 152; funerary art 149–50, **7.5**, **7.6**; women 149
études 523, 526
Eucharist 193, 194, 196, 205, 275, 303
Euclid 132, 377; *Elements* 132
Eugene Onegin (Tchaikovsky) 525
Eumenes II, of Pergamon 140
Eumenides, The (Aeschylus) 77; *see Oresteia*
Euphrates, River 17, 19
Euripides 129, 130; *The Bacchae* 129–30; *Medea* 129
Europa 64, 67, 167
Europe, maps of **10.2**, **13.1**, **16.1**, **19.1**, **21.1**, **22.1**, **23.1**
European Union 657, 702
Eusebius 196, 253
Evans, Sir Arthur 67, 79
Everyman (morality play) 251–2, 292, 306
evolution, theories of 3–4, 123, 535
Exekias: *Suicide of Ajax* 93–4, **5.11**
existentialism 624, 625, 652, 667, 679
Exodus 187–8, 190
exploration 335, 369, 624
exposition, musical 483, 492
Expressionism 600
Eyck, Jan van 355, 547; *Altarpiece of the Lamb* (Ghent Altarpiece) 356–7, 406, **13.33**, **13.34**; *Arnolfini Portrait* 355, **13.32**; *Man in a Red Turban* (?self-portrait) 334, 355, **13.3**
Ezekiel, Prophet 191, 192

fade-ins/fade-outs (film) 582, 583
Faerie Queene, The (Spenser) 418
Fallingwater *see* Kaufmann House
Falstaff (Verdi) 525
Familiares (Petrarch) 298, 299, 344
Family of Robot, Uncle (Paik) 677, **23.30**
Farm Security Administration 617
farming *see* agricultural advances
Fascism 600, 615, 618, 619, 625, 652, 681
Fatima (Muhammad's daughter) 224, 225
Faulkner, William 638; *The Sound and the Fury* 638
Faust (Goethe) 507
Faust Symphony (Liszt) 522
Fauves/Fauvism 600, 602–3
Feast in the House of Levi, The (Veronese) 411–12, **15.15**
Federal style 488–9
Fellini, Federico 692
Feltre, Vittorino da 350
Female Figure Hopping (Muybridge) 580, **20.21**
Feminine Mystique, The (Friedan) 663
feminism 662–3, 675, 707, 710, 714, 717
Ferdinand V and Isabella, of Spain 276, 367, 401, **14.8**
Fermi, Enrico 624
Ferrara, Italy 350, 359, 387
Fertile Crescent 19
"Feste Burg ist unser Gott, Ein'" (Luther) 399, 455
Fête Champêtre (Giorgione) 382–3, **14.20**
fêtes galantes 472
Fêtes galantes (Verlaine) 573
feudalism 239, 241, 242
Ficino, Marsilio 337–8, 349, 431
Fidelio (Beethoven) 519
Fielding, Henry 480, 481
Fifield, Lisa: *Ghost Dancer Ascending* 710, **24.12**
film 580–2, 610–11, 645–51, 692–5, 717–19
Film Sense, The (Eisenstein) 646, 647
fin de siècle 585, 591, 593, 594
Finding Nemo (film) 719, **24.18**
Finnegans Wake (Joyce) 639, 646
Fire in the Borgo (Raphael) 388–9, **14.24**
First Blast of the Trumpet against the Monstrous Regiment of Women (Knox) 416
Fitzgerald, F. Scott 636–7
"Five, The" 525–6
Flaming Green Tree, The (Oe) 715
Flaubert, Gustave 537, 538; *Madame Bovary* 538; *Temptation of St. Anthony* 203
Flavian dynasty (Rome) 169–70
Fleming, Alexander 624
Flemish painting 449–50
Fleurs du mal, Les (Baudelaire) 573
Flood Improvisation (Kandinsky) 600, **21.12**
Florence, Italy 275, 329, 335–6, 344, 345, 349–50, 365, 371; Baptistery 294, 339, **11.25**; Bardi Chapel (S. Croce) frescoes (Giotto) 322, **12.16**; Brancacci Chapel (S. Maria del Carmine) frescoes (Masaccio) 342, **13.15**; Bruni's tomb 337, **13.5**; *Camerata* 440; Cathedral 339, 358, **13.6**, **13.9**; Medici Palace 344, 345, 347, **13.21**, **13.22**; music 348–9; plague 304–5, 349; Platonic Academy 337; Rucellai Palace (Alberti) 343, **13.16**; San Marco fresco (Fra Angelico) 345, **13.20**; Santa Maria Novella frescoes 325, **12.21** (Andrea da Firenze), 340–2, **13.14** (Masaccio); University 315; wool industry 301, 335, **12.1**
flying buttresses 280, 281, **11.9**
folk music 522, 525, 526
Fontainebleau, Concordat of 498, 508
For Whom the Bell Tolls (Hemingway) 636
Ford, Gerald, U.S. President 660, 702
Ford, Henry 591, 640
foreshortening *see* perspective
Fouquet, Jean 357; *Charles VII* 357, **13.36**
Four Horsemen of the Apocalypse (film) 695
4'33" (Cage) 688
Four Seasons, The (Vivaldi) 441
France 302, 355, 367, 368, 428, 429, 444–6, 465, 467, 491, 495, 497–8, 499–500, 509, 531, 532, 539, 587, 617, 659, 702; academies 445, 543, **17.5**; architecture 288–90, 361, 445–6, 629, *see also* Paris; cave art 9–10; colonialism 430, 565, 585, 665; explorers 369; film 581–2, 693–4; literature 238, 239, 245, 292, 312, 314, 402, 446–7, 469, 507–9, 537–9, 573–4, 599, 679–80; music and opera 415, 445, 521–2, 543, 574–5, 605–6, 687–8; painting 357, 449, 472–3, 478, 490, 498, 501–4, 543–7, 565–9, 572, 576–8, 602–3, 625–6, **16.1**, **18.1**; philosophy 433, 434, 467–70, 536, 625, 668; photography 548; sculpture 571, **17.2**, **19.5**; theater 447–8, 599, 642, 685–6; World War I 588, 589, 590; World War II 621, 623; *see also* French Revolution; Gaul(s)
Francis of Assisi, St. 275, 276–7, 303, **11.1**; "Canticle of the Sun" 277; *St. Francis rejecting his father's wealth* (Giotto) 322, 336, **12.16**
Francis I, of France 367, 368, 373, 402; saltcellar (Cellini) 390, **14.28**
Francis Ferdinand, Archduke 588, 589, **21.3**
Franciscan Order 277, 288, 303, 315
Franco, General Francisco 619, 642
Franco-Prussian War 500, 548, 588
Frank, Anne 680
Frankenstein (M. Shelley) 471, 513
Franklin, Benjamin, U.S. President 467, 485, 486, 551; *Poor Richard's Almanac* 486
Franklin, Rosalind 667
Franks 241, 242–3, 244
Frau Welt (statue) 306, **12.4**
Frederick II, Emperor 265, 276, 317
Frederick II ("the Great"), of Prussia 467
Frederick the Wise, of Saxony 399
Frederick William, Great Elector 429
French Revolution (1789) 467, 485, 489–92, 495
frescoes: Christian (catacomb) 198, **8.8**; Etruscan 150, **7.5**; Gothic 306, **12.3**; Hellenistic 139, **6.37**; Italian 319–22, 323–4, **12.14–12.16**, **12.19**, **12.20** (early Renaissance), 340–2, 345, 347, 352, 354, 376–8, 380, 381, **13.14**, **13.15**, **13.20**, **13.22**, **13.30**, **13.31**, **14.13–14.18** (Renaissance); Jewish 188, **8.3**; Minoan 68, 69–70, **4.3**, **4.5**;

Roman 159, 167, **6.27**, **7.18**, **7.19**, **7.27**, **7.28**; Theran 72–3, **4.9**
Freud, Sigmund 571, 591–2, 593, 598, 599, 608, 625, 627, 628, 635, 638, 646, 668; *Civilization and its Discontents* 593, 612; *Ego and Id* 592–3; *The Interpretation of Dreams* 571, 572, 592; *Jokes . . .* 592
friars 275
Friedan, Betty: *The Feminine Mystique* 663
Friedrich, Caspar David 506; *Moonrise over the Sea* **18.13**
Frogs, The (Aristophanes) 130
From the Lake No. 1 (O'Keeffe) 609, **21.23**
Frost, Robert: "Mending Wall" 608
frottole 349
fugues 454, 461
Futurism 600, 625

Gabriel, archangel 224
Gabrieli, Andrea 385
Gabrieli, Giovanni 386
Gagarin, Yuri 460
Gaia 86
Gainsborough, Thomas: *The Blue Boy* 475, **17.9**
Gaiseric 209
galant music 481, 492
Galen **13.4**
Galilei, Galileo 431, 460; *Two Chief Systems of the World* 431
Gallic War (Caesar) 155
Gama, Vasco da 335
Gambler, The (Dostoevsky) 541
gamelans 575
Gandharan sculpture 134, **6.30**
Gandhi, Mohandas "Mahatma" 665, **23.6**
"Garden, The" (Pound) 608
Garden of Earthly Delights, The (Bosch) 406, **15.10**
Gargantua and Pantagruel, The Histories of (Rabelais) 402
gargoyles 282, **11.12**
Garibaldi, Giuseppe 531
Gaudí, Antonio 594; Casa Milá, Barcelona **21.6**
Gauguin, Paul 578, 600; *Ia Orana Maria* 578, **20.17**
Gaulle, Charles de 623, 665
Gaulli, Giovanni Battista: *The Triumph of the Name of Jesus* 437, **16.11**
Gaul(s) 137, 152, 155, 242
Geb 45
Gehry, Frank O.: Guggenheim Museum, Bilbao 712, **24.15**
Gemma Augustea 166, **7.26**
genes/genetics 534, 558, 667, 707
Genius of Christianity, The (Chateaubriand) 508
genocide 615, 621, 622, 652, 706
Gentileschi, Artemisia 438–9; *Judith Slaying Holofernes* 439, **16.14**
Gentileschi, Orazio 438–9
geocentrism 460
Geoffrey of Monmouth: *History of the Kings of England* 255
Geometric period (Greece) 85, 88–9
geometry 102, 132
George III, of England 485, 487
Georgics (Virgil) 162
Géricault, Théodore 501; *The Raft of the "Medusa"* 501–2, **18.6**
Germ, The (magazine) 547
German Requiem (Brahms) 521
Germanic tribes 23, 177, 209, 241, 242, 244, 252; map of movements **10.1**; *see also* Franks
Germany 332, 355, 428, 429, 531, 585, 615, 617, 619, 621, 623, 657, 659; architecture 245, 291, 360, 474, 629; film 645; *Frau Welt* 306, **12.4**; literature 507, 596, 601–2, 640, 713, 714; music and opera 415, 454–6, 465, 482, 485, 518–21, 523–4, 606, 688; painting, collage, and prints 404–6, 410, 506, 626, 627; performance art 672; philosophy 470–1, 501, 536–7; theater/drama 250–1, 252, 333, 641; World War I 588, 589–90; World War II *see* Nazis; *see also* Charlemagne; Germanic tribes; Luther, Martin; Nazis
Geronimo 550
Gershwin, George 644
Gesamtkunstwerk 523
Gesang der Jünglinge (Stockhausen) 688
gesso 355
Gesù, Il, Rome (Vignola) 412–13, 415, **15.17**, **15.18**; ceiling fresco (Gaulli) 437, **16.11**
Gettysburg Address (Lincoln) 553, 554
ghazals 233–4
Ghent Altarpiece (van Eyck) 356–7, 406, **13.33**, **13.34**
Ghiberti, Lorenzo 338, 339; *Sacrifice of Isaac* 339, **13.8**
Ghirlandaio, Domenico **14.4**
Ghost Dance movement 550
Ghost Dancer Ascending (Fifield) 710, **24.12**
Ghosts (Ibsen) 542
Gibbon, Edward: *The History of the Decline and Fall of the Roman Empire* 471, 480
Gilbert, Emile-Jacques *see* Chalgrin, J.-F.-T.
Gilbert (William S.) and Sullivan (Arthur S.) 595
Gilgamesh 19, 26, 27; *see Epic of Gilgamesh*
Gillespie, Dizzy 633, 677
Ginsberg, Allen 682; "Howl" 682
Giorgione da Castelfranco 365, 382; *Fête Champêtre (Pastoral Concert)* 382–3, **14.20**
Giotto di Bondone 318, 333, 342; Arena Chapel frescoes 319–22, **12.14**, **12.15**; campanile, Florence **13.6**; *Enthroned Madonna* 317, 318–19, **12.13**; *St. Francis rejecting his father's wealth* 322, 336, **12.16**
Giovanni di Ser Giovanni: *cassone* panel **13.26**
Giraudoux, Jean 642; *Electra* 642; *Tiger at the Gates* 642
Girl with a Pearl Earring (Vermeer) 453, **16.35**
Girodet-Trioson, Anne-Louis: *The Entombment of Atala* 508, **18.14**
Giza: pyramid complex 50–1, **3.9**
gladiators, Roman 695
Glaser, Milton: *Bob Dylan* **23.36**
glasnost 659, 696
Glass, Philip 689, 716; *Einstein on the Beach* 689, **23.34**
Glengarry Glen Ross (Mamet) 716
Glenn, John 460
glissando 644, 652
global warming 707
globalization 701
Globe Playhouse, London 419–20, 440, **15.23**
Glorious Revolution (1688) 457
Gluck, Christoph Willibald 482
Gnosticism 202
Go Tell it on the Mountain (Baldwin) 683
God of Small Things, The (Roy) 716
Godard, Jean-Luc 693
gods and goddesses *see* religions
God's Trombones (J. Johnson) 634
Godwin, William 471
Goethe, Johann von 507, 520, 521, 625; *Faust* 507; *The Sorrows of Young Werther* 507
Gogh, Vincent van 578; *Self-portrait* 578, **20.18**; *Sower with Setting Sun* 578–9, **20.19**
Gold Rush, The (Chaplin) 647
Goldsworthy, Andy 675; *Slab of Snow Carved into Leaving a Translucent Layer* 675, **23.24**
goldwork: Anglo-Saxon 254, **10.12**; Dacian 171; funerary mask of Tutankhamon 62, **3.32**
Goncharov, Ivan: *Oblomov* 541
Goncourt, Edmond and Jules 537
Gone with the Wind (Mitchell) 650; film 650, **22.39**
Gonzaga, Lodovico 352
Gonzaga family 350, 352
Good Shepherd (sculpture) 197, **8.7**
Goodman, Benny 633
Gorbachev, Mikhail 659, 661, 701
Gorgon, the 94
Gospel Book of Otto III 250, **10.9**
Gospel of St. Médard of Soissons 247, **10.5**
Gospels: synoptic 192, 253; of Thomas 202; women in 196
Gothic period 273, 275; architecture 268, 273, 278–85, 288–9, 291, 306, 308, 323, **11.2–11.10**, **11.15**, **11.18–11.21**, **11.24**, **12.18**; banquets 310; literature 292; sculpture 282, 289, 290, 306, **11.12**, **11.21**, **11.23**; stained glass 282, 289, **11.11**, **11.22**; theater 292; *see also* International Gothic
Gothic Revival architecture 504, 506
Goths 143, 155, 177, 209, 214, 241
Götterdämmerung (Wagner) 524
Goya, Francisco de 501; "Disasters of War" 501, **18.5**; *The Third of May, 1808* 501, **18.4**
Gozzoli, Benozzo: *Procession of the Magi* 347, **13.22**
graffiti art 677, 708
Graham, Martha 643, 689, **22.27**
Granada, Spain 224, 367; Alhambra 231, **9.26**
Grant, Ulysses S., U.S. President 554
Grapes of Wrath, The (Steinbeck) 637
Grass, Günter 714
gravity, laws of 431, 432, 433
Great Bathers, The (Cézanne) 577, **20.16**
Great Depression 615, 617, 635, 637, 642
Great Dictator, The (Chaplin) 648, **22.34**
Great Dionysia 126–7, 130
Great Exhibition, London (1851) 533
Great Expectations (Dickens) 540
Great Gatsby, The (Fitzgerald) 637
Great Lion Hunt (Assyrian relief) 30, **2.17**
Great Panathenaic Procession (Phidias) 119, **6.16**
Great Schism (1378–1417) 303, 311
"Greatness of the King, The" (Egyptian hymn) 47
Greco, El 413, 415; *The Burial of Count Orgaz* 413–14, **15.19**; *Laocoön* 414, **15.20**
Greece, ancient 73, 83; Archaic period 85, 92–104, 112; architecture 88, 98–9, 115–17, 120–1; army 90, 91, 92; city-states (*poleis*) 83, 85, 90, 91, 92, 93, 109, 131, 135; Classical period 109–36; coinage 164; colonies 83, 154; creation myth 3; "Dark Age" 80; drama *see* theater(s); dress 97; Geometric period 85, 88–9; homosexuality 104, 344–5; lawgivers 92–3; literature 73–5, 76–9, 86–7, 92, 108, 109; lyric poetry 102–4, 114; map **5.1**; medicine 124–5; music 92, 102, 104, 126; oracles 88; Orientalizing period 85, 90–2; philosophers 83, 101–2, 113–14, 123–4, 135; religion (gods) 74, 83, 85–8, 295; sculpture 95–7, 100–1, 111–13, 122, 131, 136, 360; symposia 103, 125; theater(s) 126–30; trade 90, 92; tyrants 83, 92; vases 88–9, 90, 93–4, 103, 121–2, 136, **5.5**, **5.7–5.9**, **5.11–5.13**, **5.26**, **6.21**, **6.26**, **6.32**; women 87–8, 93, 97, 125; *see also* Hellenistic period
Greek Orthodox Church *see* Eastern Orthodox Church
Green River (Eliasson) 709, **24.9**
Gregorian chant 205
Gregory I, Pope 204, 205, 252
Gregory VII, Pope 261
Gregory IX, Pope 276
Gregory XI, Pope 302
Gregory, bishop of Tours: *History of the Franks* 242
Gregory, Lady Augusta 598
Gregory of Nazianus 203
Grieg, Edvard 526
Grien, Hans Baldung: *Witches' Sabbath* 410, **15.14**
Griffith, D. W. 610; *The Birth of a Nation* 610–11, **21.25**, **21.26**
Grimm, Jacob and Wilhelm 596
Gropius, Walter: Bauhaus 629
Grotius, Hugo 433
groundlings 419, 422
Growth of the Soil (Hamsun) 640
Grünewald, Matthias 404, 406; *Isenheim Altarpiece* 406, **15.9**
Guarneri, Giuseppe 483
Gudea of Lagash 28, 35; statue 28, **2.13**
Guernica (Picasso) 619, **22.4**
Guggenheim, Peggy 627
Guggenheim Museum, Bilbao (Gehry) 712, **24.15**
Guide for the Perplexed, The (Maimonides) 234
Guido of Arezzo 261; musical staff 261–2, **10.19**
guilds 260, 283, 301, 336, **11.13**
guillotine, the 491, 492, **17.22**
Guimard, Hector: Métro entrance 594, **21.7**
Guitar (Picasso) 604, **21.19**
Gulag Archipelago, The (Solzhenitsyn) 680
Gulf Wars: first 663; second 703–4
Gulliver's Travels (Swift) 479
Guomindang, the 665
Gustavus II Adolphus, of Sweden 429
Gutenberg, Johann 331, 332, 382, **13.1**

Ha Jin 716
Hades 85–6, 87
Hadith 226
Hadrian, Emperor 172, 173, 174
Hafiz: *ghazals* 233–4
Hagia Sophia, Istanbul 208, 209, 219–21, **9.10–9.12**

Hagia Triada sarcophagus 70–1, **4.6**
haiku 684–5
Hair (MacDermot, Ragni, and Rado) 690
hajj 226, 269
Haley, Bill, and the Comets 691
Hallelujah! (Vidor) 649, **22.36**
Hals, Frans 452; *Officers of the Haarlem Militia Company of St. Adrian* 450, **16.29**
Hamilton, Alexander 486–7
Hamlet (Shakespeare) 422
Hammerstein, Oscar, II 643–4, 690
Hammurabi 28; stele of 22, 28–9, **2.7**, **2.14**
Hamsun, Knut 640; *Growth of the Soil* 640
"Hand that Signed the Paper, The" (Thomas) 681
Handel, George Frideric 454, 455–6, 521, 695; *Messiah* 456
Handmaid's Tale, The (Atwood) 714, 715
Handy, W. C. 611
Hannibal 154, 316
Hanson, Duane 674; *Young Shopper* 674, **23.22**
happenings 672, 696
Hapy 45, 46
Harald Bluetooth 256
Harald Fairhair, King of Norway 259
Hard Times (Dickens) 528, 529, 540
Hardy, Thomas 597; *Tess of the d'Urbervilles* 597
Haring, Keith 708; *Ignorance=Fear* 708, **24.5**
Harlem Renaissance 634–5, 716
Harmony in Blue and Gold: The Peacock Room (Whistler) 570, **20.10**
Harper's Weekly 554, 557
harps 71, **4.7**, **10.21**
harpsichords 440, 454, 455, 482
Harun-al-Rashid, Caliph 244
Harvester Vase (Minoan) 71, **4.8**
Harvey, William 431
Hat Makes the Man (Ernst) 627, **22.11**
Hathor 45, 53, 54
Hatshepsut 56–7, **3.21**
Haussmann, Baron Georges-Eugène 563
Havel, Václav 701
Hawks, Howard 694
Hawthorne, Nathaniel 514; *The Scarlet Letter* 514; *Twice-Told Tales* 516
Hay Wain, The (Constable) 504, **18.9**
Haydn, Franz Joseph 465, 483, 484, 485, 518, 519
H.D. (Hilda Doolittle) 608; "Heat" 608
Head of a Young Man (Holbein) 404, **15.6**
Heaney, Seamus 719–20
Hearst, William Randolph 648
"Heat" (H.D.) 608
heavy metal 692
Hebe 87
Hebrews 38; *see* Bible, Hebrew; Israelites; Jews
Hector 74–5
Hedda Gabler (Ibsen) 542
Hegel, Georg Wilhelm Friedrich 501
Heidegger, Martin 625
heliocentrism 403, 422, 431
Hellenistic period 109, 133, 137; architecture 139–40, 152; mystery cults 137; philosophies 137; poetry 138; sculpture 138–9; wall paintings 139
Heller, Joseph: *Catch-22* 682
helots, Spartan 93
Helsinki Accords 660, 702
Hemingway, Ernest 636; *For Whom the Bell Tolls* 636; *The Sun Also Rises* 636
Hendrix, Jimi 692
Henrietta Maria, Queen 456; portrait (van Dyck) **16.38**
Henry II, of England 262
Henry IV, of France 410; *Henry IV Receiving the Portrait of Marie de' Medici* (Rubens) 450, **16.28**
Henry V, of England 355
Henry VIII, of England 37, 397, 401–2, 410, 477; portrait (Holbein the Younger) 37, **2.25**, **15.4**
Henry the Navigator, Prince 335
Hephaestos 87
Heptameron (Marguerite of Navarre) 402
Hera 87
Hera and Zeus with Iris (Phidias) 119, **6.17**
Heracles 114, 295, **5.13**; sculpture 101, **5.25**
Heraclitus 102, 377
Herculaneum 157; excavations of 475, 478
heresies/heretics 202, 275, 276, 303, 410
"Heritage" (Cullen) 635
Hermes 87
Hernani (Hugo) 508
Herod Agrippa I 262
Herod the Great 188
Herodotus 108, 109, 111, 292
Herrad, Abbess 263; *The Garden of Delights* 263
Hersey, John 682; *A Bell for Adano* 682; *Hiroshima* 682
Hersey, William *see* Moore, Charles
Herzl, Theodor 663
Hesiod: *Catalogues of Women and Eoiae* 64, 67; *Theogony* 86–7, 92
Hesse, Eva 673; *Right After* 673, **23.19**
Hesse, Hermann 640; *Siddhartha* 640; *Der Steppenwolf* 640
Hestia 87
Heyerdahl, Thor 624
Hidalgo, Miguel de 500
hierarchical proportions **2.12**, **3.14**
hieroglyphs, Egyptian 41, 49
Hilda, St. 252
Hildegard of Bingen 263; *Ordo virtutum* 263; *Vision of Divine Love* 263–4, **10.22**
Hilliard, Nicholas: (attrib.) *Elizabeth I* **15.21**
himaton 97, **5.17**
Himmler, Heinrich 622
Hinduism 295; creation myth 3
hip-hop 692
Hippocrates 124–5, 310
Hippolyte et Aricie (Rameau) 445
Hiroshige, Utagawa: *Suruga-cho* 566, **20.2**
Hiroshima (J. Hersey) 682
Hiroshima, bombing of 623, 655
History of Ancient Art, The (Winckelmann) 478
Hitchcock, Alfred 694
Hitler, Adolf 619, 621, 622, 623, 640, 645, 648; *Hitler as a Medieval Knight* (Lanzinger) 619, **22.3**
Hittites 23, 58
Ho Chi Minh 659–60
Hobbes, Thomas 433, 487; *Leviathan* 433
Höch, Hannah: *Cut with the Kitchen Knife* 626, **22.10**
Hogarth, William 476, 481; *Marriage à la Mode* 476–7, **17.11**; *Night* 477, **17.12**
Hogarth Press 638
Hohokam culture: ball game 179
Holbein, Hans, the Younger 401; *Erasmus Writing* **15.2**; *Head of a Young Man* 404, **15.6**; *Henry VIII* 37, **2.25**, **15.4**
Holland *see* Netherlands, the
"Hollow Men, The" (T. S. Eliot) 637–8
Hollywood film industry 647
Holocaust, the 621, 622, 652, 679, 680, 713
Holy Grail 255
Holy Roman Empire 244, 367, 368, 397, 399, 428, 498; map **14.1**
Holy Sonnets (Donne) 459
Holzer, Jenny: installation 708, **24.6**
Homer 701; *Iliad* 73, 74–5, 79; *Odyssey* 73, 77–9; translations 479 (Pope), 512 (Shelley)
Homer, Winslow 554; *Prisoners from the Front* 554–5, **19.20**; *The War for the Union, 1862—A Bayonet Charge* 557, **19.25**
hominids 4–5, 6
Homo erectus 5, 6, 7
Homo habilis 5, 7
Homo sapiens (*sapiens*) 6, 7, 10
homosexuality 56, 104, 149, 344–5, 438, 573, 595, 676, 689, 717
Hong Kong 666, 705
Hoover, Herbert, U.S. President 617
hoplites 91, 92, 147, **5.10**, **7.2**
Hopper, Edward 668; *Hotel by a Railroad* 668–9, **23.10**
Horace 162, 166; *Odes* 162–3, 584, 587; *Secular Hymn* 166–7
Horla, The (Maupassant) 539
Horn Players (Basquiat) 677, **23.29**
Horne, Lena 632
Horse of Selene (Phidias) 117–18, **6.14**
Horus 45, 46, 185, **3.3**; eye of 51, 56, **3.12**
Horyu-ji monastery, Nara, Japan 249, **10.8**
Hotel by a Railroad (Hopper) 668–9, **23.10**
Hotnica, Bulgaria: copper pot 11–12, **1.7**
Houdon, Jean-Antoine: *Diderot* **17.2**
House of Bernarda Alba, The (Lorca) 642
House of Flying Daggers (Zhang) 718
House of the Spirits, The (Allende) 684
House UnAmerican Activities Committee (HUAC) 659
Housebook Master: *Coat of Arms with a Peasant Standing on His Head* 397, **15.1**
Houses of Parliament, London (Barry and Pugin) 506, **18.12**
How It Feels to be Colored Me (Hurston) 635
How to Explain Pictures to a Dead Hare (Beuys) 672, **23.17**
Howard, Catherine 401
"Howl" (Ginsberg) 682
Hroswitha 252; *Dulcitius* 252
Hubble Space-based Telescope 460, **16.43**, **16.44**
hubris 127, 135
Huckleberry Finn (Twain) 556, 630
Hudson River School 516
Hughes, Langston 635; *I, Too* 635; "The Weary Blues" 635
Hugo, Victor 508; *Cromwell* 508; *Hernani* 508; *Les Misérables* 508; *Notre-Dame de Paris* 508
Huguenots 402, 444
Human Genome Project 707
humanism/humanists 299, 314–15, 316, 317, 323, 329, 333, 338, 348, 382, 386, 387, 433; Christian 395, 397, 402; and music 333, 359; and the State 336–7; women 350
Hume, David 471; *A Treatise of Human Nature* 471
Humpty Dumpty (Noguchi) 670, **23.13**
Hundred Years War (1337–1453) 302, 308
Hungarian Rhapsodies (Liszt) 522
Hungary 498, 587, 588, 589, 658, 659; music 522
Hunnenschlacht (Liszt) 522
Huns 209, 241
Hunt, William Holman 547; *Awakening Conscience* 547, **19.13**
hunter-gatherers, prehistoric 10, 11
Hunters in the Snow (Bruegel) 407, 409, **15.13**
Hunting of the Snark (Carroll) 596
Hurston, Zora Neale 635; *How It Feels to be Colored Me* 635; *Their Eyes Were Watching God* 635
Huxley, Aldous 640; *Brave New World* 640
Hyksos, the 44, 58–9
"Hymn to Beauty" (Baudelaire) 573
"Hymn to the Sun" (Akenaton) 61
hymns: Christian 205, 219, 384; Egyptian 40, 43, 46–7, 49
hypostyles 59, 62

"I Hear America Singing" (Whitman) 514–15
I, Too (L. Hughes) 635
Ia Orana Maria (Gauguin) 578, **20.17**
Ibn Sina *see* Avicenna
Ibsen, Henrik 542; *A Doll's House* 542; *Ghosts* 542; *Hedda Gabler* 542
Iceland 259; literature 259–60, 641
Iceman Cometh, The (O'Neill) 643
Iconoclastic Controversy 222
iconography: Christian 196, 197; of Death 306; of Wealth 308
iconophiles 222
icons 221, **9.14**
Ideas of the Inhabitants of the Virtuous City, The (al-Farabi) 235
idée fixe 522, 526
ideograms 49
Idiot, The (Dostoevsky) 541
idylls 138
Ignorance=Fear (Haring) 708, **24.5**
Iktinos and Kallikrates: Parthenon 116–17, **6.7–6.10**
Iliad (Homer) 73, 74–5, 79
"Illuminations" (Rimbaud) 574
Imaginary Landscape No. 4 (Cage) 688
Imagism 608
Imhotep: step pyramid of King Zoser 50, **3.8**
impasto 478
imperialism 563, 565, 585
Impression: Sunrise (Monet) 565, **20.4**
Impressionism: painting 563, 565–70, 580; sculpture 571
Inanna 17, 20
incidental music 526
Incoherence of the Incoherence, The (Averroës) 235
Incoherence of the Philosophers (al-Ghazali) 235
Independent People (Laxness) 641

Index of Forbidden Books 409, 431, 639
India 23, 132, 232, 532, 565, 664–5, 705; Buddhism 134, 249, 295; film 693; Hinduism 295; *Kumbh Mela* 269, **10.31**; literature 713, 716; Mathuran sculpture 134, **6.31**; Taj Mahal 230–1, **9.25**; *see also* Mughal dynasty
Indian Ink (Stoppard) 717
Indiana (Sand) 508–9
Indo-European languages 23
Indochina 565, 665
Indonesia 575, 664, 703, 706
indulgences, sale of 398, 400
Indus Valley civilization 30; sculpture 30, **2.16**; seals 30, **2.15**
Industrial Revolution 495, 501, 529, 532, 539
Ingeborg of Denmark 263
Ingres, Jean-Auguste-Dominique 504; *Louis-François Bertin* 504, 603, **18.8**
Inka civilization 369, 370; Machu Picchu 370, **14.3**
inkblot test 624, 652
Innocent II, Pope 287
Innocent III, Pope 275
Innocent IV, Pope 276
Innocent VIII, Pope: *Summis desiderantes* 276
Inquisition 276, 317, 367, 410, 411–12, 430, 431
installations 675, 708, **23.3**, **23.25**, **24.6**
Institutes of the Christian Religion (Calvin) 399
insulae 157, **7.15**
Interior of St. Lazare Station (Monet) 566–7, **20.5**
International Gothic style: architecture 291, 308, **12.7**; illumination 308, **12.6**
International Style architecture 629
Internet 667, 696, 699, 701, 706, 713
Interpretation of Dreams (Freud) 571, 572, 592
Invisible Man (Ellison) 683
Ionesco, Eugene 685–6; *The Bald Soprano* 685–6; *Rhinoceros* 686
Ionia 83; school of philosophy 102
Ionic Order 98, 99, 116, **5.18**
Iphigenia Carried to her Sacrifice (Roman fresco) 167, **7.28**
Iphigénie (Racine) 448
Iraq 17, 617, 663, 702; invasion of 703–4; *see also* Baghdad; Ur; Uruk
Ireland 202, 252–3; Book of Kells 253, **10.10**; literature 594–5, 598, 608, 715, 720; stone crosses 253–4, **10.11**; theater 595, 598–9, 642, 685, 719–20
Irene, Empress 222
Isaac, Heinrich 348, 349
Isaiah, Prophet 182, 183, 186
Isenheim Altarpiece (Grünewald) 406, **15.9**
Ishiguro, Kazuo 715–16
Ishmael 225
Ishtar 17, 20, 25
Isidorus of Miletus *see* Anthemius of Tralles
Isis 45, **3.6**; cult of 137, 185
Islam/Islamic culture/Muslims 34, 205, 224–5, 242, 244, 245, 250, 295, 701; in Africa 242, 664, 665, 706; art and architecture 205, 209, 222, 226, 227–8, 230–1; calligraphy 226; carpet 231–2; and Crusades 265; Five Pillars 225–6, 269; fundamentalism 662, 663, 699, 702–3; glasswork 232; Hadith 226; *hajj* 226, 269; *jihad* 226; literature 232–4; map **9.3**; medicine 234; music 232; in Pakistan 665, 703, 705; philosophers 235; science 234; Sunnis and Shi'ites 225, 235; *see also* Qur'an; Spain
isorhythms 312
Israel: ancient 38, 188; map **8.1**; modern 663, 704–5
Israelites 186–8; *see* Jews
Issos, battle of (333 B.C.) 132, **6.29**
Istanbul: bombing of 703; *see also* Constantinople
Italy 315, 367, 531, 618, 619, 625; ancient Greek colonies 83, 154; architecture 412–13, 434–5; colonialism 565, 585; film 296; literature 292–6, 298, 299, 304–5, 316–17, 319, 338, 365, 371, 382, 386–7; map **12.2**; music and opera 316, 415, 440–1, 455, 482, 483, 485, 518, 524–5, 543, 688, 695; painting 411–12, 437–9, 474; sculpture 317, 436, 600; theater 641; *see also* humanism; Mannerism; Renaissance; *and* Florence, Milan, Ravenna, Rome, Venice *etc.*
Iturbide, Augustín de 500
Ivan the Terrible (Eisenstein) 647
Ives, Charles 643, 644
ivories 37, 214–15, **2.26**, **9.3**

"J'Accuse" (Zola) 539
Jacob 186
Jahangir 454
James, St. 262
James I, of England (VI, of Scotland) 416, 430, 456; chamber pot 477
James II, of England 457
Jamison, Judith 689
Jane Avril at the "Jardin de Paris" (Toulouse-Lautrec) 576, **20.14**
Jane Eyre (C. Brontë) 513
Jansenist movement 434
Japan 565, 588, 589, 590, 615, 617, 618, 623, 658, 659, 705; film 651; literature 684–5, 713, 715–16; sculpture 670, **23.13**; woodblock prints 565, 566, **20.2**
Japonaise, La (Monet) 566, **20.3**
japonisme 565, 566, 583
Jarry, Alfred 599; *Ubu Roi* 599, **21.9**
"Java Man" 5
Jay, John 487
Jayavarman VII, of Cambodia 36
jazz 611, 612, 615, 631–3, 701, 713
Jefferson, Thomas, U.S. President 361, 392, 485, 486, 487, 488, 557; Declaration of Independence 486, 487; Rotunda, University of Virginia 488–9, **17.19**; State Capitol, Richmond 488, **17.18**
Jenner, Edward 534
Jericho 11
Jerome, St. 204, 434
Jerusalem 262, 263, 265; Dome of the Rock 227, **9.18–9.20**; Solomon's Temples 38, 170, 188, 189–90, 205, **8.4**
"Jerusalem" (Blake) 509
Jesuits 409, 412, 434, 441, 443, 447, 454, 469
Jesus Christ 183, 191–2, 193, 194, 198, 202, 225, **8.10**; icon of 221, **9.14**; Sermon on the Mount 192–3; and women 196
Jesus Christ Superstar (Webber and Rice) 690
Jesus Washing the Feet of Peter 250, **10.9**
jewelry: Egyptian 57, **3.22**; Etruscan 149; Roman 166, **7.26**; Viking 258, **10.16**
Jewish War, The (Josephus) 189
Jews 38, 186–90, 244; persecution of 276, 303, **12.2**, *see* anti-Semitism; *see also* Israel; Judaism
Jiang Qing (Madame Mao) 666
jihad 226
Joan of Arc 302, 314
Johanson, Dr. Donald 5
John, St: Gospel of 192, 198; *John the Evangelist* (Donatello) 340, **13.10**
John the Baptist, St. 192, 193, 247, 267
John the Divine, St. 192, 289, 294
John the Evangelist (Donatello) 340, **13.10**
John XXIII, antipope 303
John, King of England 275
John of the Cross, St. 409
John of Gaunt, duke of Lancaster 303
John Paul II, Pope 658
Johns, Jasper 671; *Painted Bronze (Ale Cans)* 671, **23.15**
Johnson, James Weldon 634; *God's Trombones* 634
Johnson, Lyndon B., U.S. President 660
Johnson, Philip: American Telephone and Telegraph Building (with Burgee) 679, **23.33**
Johnson, Dr. Samuel 480; *Dictionary . . .* 480
Jokes . . . (Freud) 592
Jonah 193
Jones, Inigo: costume design 457, **16.39**
Joplin, Scott 611
Jordan, Louis 690
Joseph 186–7
Joseph II, Emperor 467
Josephus, Flavius 189; *The Jewish War* 189
Josquin Desprez 359, 384, 415; *Ave Maria* 359; "Woodland Nymphs" 359
Jou dou (Zhang) 717, 718, **24.17**
Joyce, James 597, 608; *Chamber Music* 597; *Dubliners* 597–8; *Finnegans Wake* 639, 646; portrait (Abbot) **22.26**; *A Portrait of the Artist as a Young Man* 598, 639; *Ulysses* 639
Judah 38, 188
Judaism 183, 186, 187, 190, 191, 205, 225
Judd, Donald 672; *Untitled* 672–3, **23.18**
Judith Slaying Holofernes (Gentileschi) 439, **16.14**
Julio-Claudian dynasty (Rome) 167–9, 174
Julius II, Pope 374, 376, 377, 380, 395, 397, 398
Julius Caesar (Shakespeare) 421–22
Julius Excluded from Heaven (Erasmus) 397–8
Jung, Carl 593, 612, 640, 668
Jungle Books (Kipling) 596
Juno and the Paycock (O'Casey) 642
Justin I, Emperor 212
Justinian I, Emperor 212, 214, 215, 221, 295; law code 214, 215–16
Jutes 241, 252
Juvenal: *Satires* 176

ka 48
Ka'bah, Mecca 225, 269, **10.30**
Kaffa, Crimea 304
Kafka, Franz 601; "The Metamorphosis" 601; *The Trial* 601–2
Kahlo, Frida 628; *Self-Portrait as a Tehuana* **22.16**
Kallikrates *see* Iktinos
Kamares ware (Minoan) 67, **4.1**
Kandinsky, Wassily 600; *Concerning the Spiritual in Art* 600, 609; *Flood Improvisation* 600, **21.12**
Kant, Immanuel 470–1; *Critique of Pure Reason* 470, 501
Karachi, Pakistan 134
Karlevi, Sweden: rune-stone 256, **10.13**
Karnak, Egypt: Chapel Rouge relief 54, **3.18**
Kashmir 665, 705
Kauffmann, Angelica 478–9; *Cornelia, Mother of the Gracchi* 478, 489, **17.15**
Kaufmann House (Wright) 630, **22.19**
Kawabata, Yasunari 684; *Snow Country* 684–5
Keats, John 511; "Ode on a Grecian Urn" 512
Kells, Book of 253, **10.10**
Ken and Tyler (Mapplethorpe) 676, **23.26**
Kennedy, John F., U.S. President 659, 660, 666
kennings 255, 259
Kenwood House, London: Library (Adam) 475, **17.10**
Keokuk, Chief of the Tribe (Catlin) **19.17**
Kepler, Johannes 431
Kern, Jerome 643
Kerouac, Jack 682; *On the Road* 682–3
keyboard instruments 417, 440, 454, 455, 482; *see also* pianos/piano music
Keynes, John Maynard 617
Khafre: pyramid of 50, **3.9**; statue of 52, 57, **3.13**
Khomeini, Ayatolla Ruhollah 663
Khrushchev, Nikita 658, 666
Khufu, pyramid of 50, **3.9**
Kienholz, Edward: *Portable War Memorial* **23.3**
Kierkegaard, Søren 537; *Either/Or* 537; *The Sickness unto Death* 537
Kim (Kipling) 561
King, Martin Luther, Jr. 662, 663
King and I (Rodgers and Hammerstein) 690
King Lear (Shakespeare) 421
kingship 26, 37, 77; *see also* divine right of kings
Kipling, Rudyard: *Jungle Books* 596; *Kim* 561; "White Man's Burden" 560, 561
Kiss, The (Rodin) 571, **20.11**
Klimt, Gustav 593; *Beethoven Frieze* 593, **21.5**
Kloeber, Carl von: *Beethoven* **18.19**
knights, medieval 239
Knights of Malta 438
Knossos, Crete 67; *Mistress of the Animals* 68, **4.4**; palace 67–8, **4.2**, **4.3**; *Toreador Fresco* 69–70, **4.5**
Knox, John: *First Blast of the Trumpet against the Monstrous Regiment of Women* 416
Kodak 563
Kollwitz, Käthe: *March of the Weavers* 587, **21.1**
Kongo kingdom 37; Yombe cane finial 37, **2.26**
Kon-Tiki expedition 624, **22.8**
korai (sing. *kore*) 95, 97, **5.16**
Koran *see* Qur'an
Korea 705; Korean War 651, 655, 659
kouroi (sing. *kouros*) 82, 95–7, 111, **5.14**, **5.15**
Kramer, Heinrich *see* Sprenger, James
krater, Geometric 88, **5.5**
Kresilas: *Pericles* **6.4**
Kritios Boy 111, **6.1**
Ku Klux Klan 610–11, 661, 708, **21.26**
"Kubla Khan" (Coleridge) 511
Kufic script 226, 230, **9.17**

Kumbh Mela (festival) 269, **10.31**
Kurosawa, Akira 651; *The Seven Samurai* 651, **22.40**
Kushner, Tony: *Angels in America* 717
Kyoto Protocol 707

Labille-Guiard, Adélaide 472; *Self-portrait with Two Pupils* 472–3, **17.5**
Lacan, Jacques 668
Lady, Be Good! (Gershwin) 644
Lady Chatterley's Lover (D. H. Lawrence) 640
Lafayette, Mme Marie-Madeleine de 446–7; *La Princesse de Clèves* 447
Lagash 28
Lägerkvist, Par 641; *The Dwarf* 641
Lagerlöf, Selma: *The Wonderful Adventures of Nils* 596, 715
"Lake Isle of Innisfree" (Yeats) 598
Landini, Francesco 316
Landscape with Merchants (Claude) 449, **16.26**
languages 19, 23; Church 205, 222
Lanzinger, Hubert: *Hitler as a Medieval Knight* 619, **22.3**
Laocoön (Greco) 414, **15.20**
Laocoön Group (Agesander *et al.*) 138–9, **6.36**
Laos 565, 665
Lapith Battling a Centaur (Phidias) 118, **6.15**
Large Red Plane, Yellow, Black, Gray, and Blue (Mondrian) 629, **22.17**
Lascaux caves, Dordogne, France 9, **1.1**, **1.4**
Laschi, Antonio: *Achilles* 333
Lasso, Orlando di 415
Last Judgment (Michelangelo) 381, 411, **14.18**
Last of the Mohicans (Cole) 516, **18.17**
Last of the Mohicans (Cooper) 514, 516
Last Supper (Dürer) 404–5, **15.8**
Last Supper (Leonardo) 354, **13.31**
Last Supper (Tintoretto) 412, **15.16**
Last Supper (Veronese) 411–12, **15.15**
Latin America 428, 563, 659, 679, 684; *see also* Mexico
Latin League 154
La Venta, Mexico: Olmec Head 35–6, **2.23**
La Verdiere, Julian, and Myoda, Paul: *Tribute in Light over the Brooklyn Bridge* 704, **24.2**
law codes/legislation: Draco 92; Hammurabi 28–9, **2.14**; Justinian 214, 215–16; *Magna Carta* 272, 273, 275; Napoleonic 216, 498, 509; Roman 152, 155; Solon 92–3; Ten Commandments 187
Lawrence, D. H. 640; *Lady Chatterley's Lover* 640
Lawrence, Jacob: "Migration" series 634, **22.25**
Laxness, Halldór 641; *Independent People* 641
lays 292
League of Nations 590, 615, 623
Leakey, Louis and Mary 5
Leaves of Grass (Whitman) 514
Lebanon 617, 663
Le Corbusier 629; Villa Savoye, Poissy 629, **22.18**
Led Zeppelin 692
Lee, General Robert E. 554
Leeuwenhoek, Anton van 433
Leibniz, Gottfried Wilhelm 432, 470; *Theodicy* 470
Leif Erikson 259
leitmotifs 524, 525
lekythoi 122, **6.21**
Lélia (Sand) 509
Lenin, Vladimir Ilyich 590, 618
Leo III, Emperor 222
Leo III, Pope 244, **10.2**
Leo IV, Pope 389
Leo V, Emperor 222
Leo X, Pope 336, 375, 388, 399
Leonardo da Vinci 365, 367, 377, 431, 548; *dissection of organs* 334, **13.4**; *flying machine* 373, **14.6**; *Last Supper* 354, **13.31**; *Mona Lisa* 372–3, **14.5**; *Paragone* 365, 373; *Vitruvian Man* 333, 348, **13.2**, **13.27**
Leoncavallo, Ruggiero: *Pagliacci* 543
Léonin 286; *Magnus liber organi* 286
Lepautre, Jean: *Alceste* **16.20**
Lerner, Alan Jay 690; *Brigadoon* (with Loewe) 690
Lessing, Doris 683; *The Children of Violence* 683
Lettres persanes see Persian Letters
Lettres provinciales (Pascal) 434
Leutze, Emanuel: *Washington Crossing the Delaware* 676, **23.27**
Le Vau, Louis: Marble Court, Versailles **16.20**
Lévi-Strauss, Claude 667–8
Leviathan (Hobbes) 433
Lewis, Meriwether 549
Lewis, Sinclair 636; *Main Street* 636
LeWitt, Sol: *Wall Drawing No. 623* 673, **23.20**
Leyland, Frederick 570
Leyster, Judith 452; *Self-portrait* 452–3, **16.33**
L.H.O.O.Q. (Duchamp) 625–6, **22.9**
Libation Bearers, The (Aeschylus) 77, **6.11**; *see Oresteia*
Liberty Leading the People (Delacroix) 503–4, **18.7**
libraries 137, 333
librettos 523, 526
Libya 702, 730
Libyan Sibyl (Michelangelo) 378, 380, **14.17**
Lied von der Erde, Das (Mahler) 606
Lieder 415
Life of Samuel Johnson (Boswell) 480
Lightning Brothers and Lightning Figures (Aboriginal rock art) 13, **1.10**
Limbourg brothers: *Très riches heures . . .* 308, **12.6**
Limoges enamel 262, **10.20**
Lin, Maya Ying: *Vietnam Veterans Memorial*, Washington, D.C. 660, **23.4**
Lincoln, Abraham, U.S. President 515, 553, 554; Gettysburg Address 553, 554; portrait (Brady) **19.19**
Lindbergh, Charles 623, 624
Linear A and B scripts 67
Lion Gate, Mycenae 75, 79, **4.10**
Liszt, Franz 520, 522, 523, 525, **18.20**
literature: ancient Greek 73–5, 76–9, 86–7, 92, 102–4, 108, 109, 114; Anglo-Saxon 254–5; Baroque 441; Canadian 714–15; children's 596–7; Egyptian 49, 53–4; Gothic period 292; Hellenistic 138; 18th-century 469–70, 479–81; Expressionist 601–2; *fin-de-siècle* 585, 594–5; Harlem Renaissance 634–5; Holocaust 680; Icelandic 259–60, 641; interwar 635–41; Islamic 232–4; medieval 238, 239, 245, 255–6, 292–6, 312–14; Naturalist 537, 538–9; Realist 529, 537–41, 556, 558; Renaissance 328, 331, 336–7, 338, 342–3, 365, 371, 386–7; Roman 142, 145–6, 152, 157, 161, 162–3, 166–7, 172, 174–6; Romance 256; Romantic 507–14, 532; 17th-century 459, 461; Sumerian 16, 17, 19, 23–6, 27; Symbolist 573–4; Transcendentalist 513–14; 20th-century (postwar) 679–85, 713–17
lithographs 545, 558, **19.1**, **19.9**, **20.14**
Little Bighorn, battle of (1876) 550
"Little Russian" Symphony (Tchaikovsky) 525
Little Women (Alcott) 596
liturgy 205; Eastern Orthodox 222
Livia 166
Livy 166; *History of Rome* 298, 299, 316, 317
Locke, Alain 634
Locke, John 424, 427, 433, 465, 469, 470, 486, 487
Lockerbie bombing (1988) 703
Loewe, Frederick *see* Lerner, Alan
Lohengrin (Wagner) 523–4
Lombards 242, 243, 244
London: Crystal Palace (Paxton) 533, **19.2**; Globe Playhouse 419–20, 440, **15.23**; Great Exhibition (1851) 533; Houses of Parliament (Barry and Pugin) 506, **18.12**; Kenwood House Library (Adam) 475, **17.10**; St. Paul's (Wren) 458–9, **16.40–16.42**
Long Day's Journey into Night, A (O'Neill) 643
Lorca, Federico García 642, 669, 684; *Blood Wedding* 642; *The House of Bernarda Alba* 642; *Yerma* 642
Lord of the Rings, The (Tolkien) 718–19; film 718
Lorenzetti, Ambrogio 323; *Allegory of Bad Government* 324, **12.20**; *The Effects of Good Government in the City* 323–4, **12.19**
Loring, Eugene: *Billy the Kid* 645
Lorrain, Claude *see* Claude Lorrain
Lothair 250
Louis I ("the Pious"), of France 250
Louis VI, of France 278
Louis VII, of France 265, 278
Louis IX, of France (St. Louis) 265, 284
Louis XII, of France 367
Louis XIII, of France 444, 450
Louis XIV, of France 425, 427, 444, 445, 446, 447, 448, 467, 477; as Apollo 446, **16.23**; portrait (Rigaud) **16.1**
Louis XV, of France 468, 472, 489
Louis XVI, of France 485, 489, 490, 492; execution 491, **17.22**
Louis XVIII, of France 499–500
Louis-Philippe, of France 504, 545
L'Ouverture, Toussaint 490
Louvre Pyramid, Paris (Pei) 678–9, **23.32**
"Love Song of J. Alfred Prufrock" (T. S. Eliot) 637
Loyola, St. Ignatius 409; *Spiritual Exercises* 409
Lucas, George: *Star Wars* 694, **23.41**
Lucius III, Pope 276
Lucretius 161; *On the Nature of Things* 161
"Lucy" (fossil) 5
"Lucy in the Sky with Diamonds" (Beatles) 5, 691
Ludwig II, of Bavaria 523
Luke, St., Gospel of 192
Lully, Jean-Baptiste 445, 447; *Alceste* **16.20**
Lumière, Auguste and Louis 563, 581, 582; *The Arrival of a Train at the Station* 582, **20.24**
Luminists 516
Lusitania 590
lutes 417, 440
Luther, Martin 395, 397, 398–400, 405, 409, 455; portrait (Cranach the Elder) **15.3**
Lutherans 399, 411
Luxor, Egypt: Temple of Ramses II 59–60, **3.27–3.29**
Lycurgus 91, 93
Lycurgus (Plutarch) 91
Lydian mode 126
Lynes, George Platt: *Billy the Kid* **22.28**
lyres 26–7, 71, 102, **2.9–2.11**, **4.7**
lyric poetry, Greek 102–4
Lyrical Ballads (Wordsworth and Coleridge) 509, 510
Lysippos (attrib.): *Socrates* **6.23**
Lysistrata (Aristophanes) 131

Ma, Yo-Yo 713
maat/Maat 43, 45, 62, **3.3**
Mabinogion, The 255–6
Macbeth (Shakespeare) 421
McCarthy, Senator Joseph 659, 682, 686
MacDermot, Galt 690
McFerrin, Bobby 713
Machaut, Guillaume de 311–12
Machiavelli, Niccolò 371; *The Mandrake* 387; *The Prince* 365, 371
Machu Picchu 370, **14.3**
McSorley's Bar (Sloan) 608, **21.21**
"Mad Cow Disease" 706–7
Madame Bovary (Flaubert) 538
Maderno, Carlo: St. Peter's, Rome 434
Madison, James, U.S. President 486–7
Madonna and Child (Raphael) 374, **14.7**
Madonna of the Long Neck (Parmigianino) 389, **14.26**
Madonna of the Meadow (Bellini) 382, **14.19**
Madrid, bombing of (2004) 703
madrigals 385, 415, 416, 417
Maecenas 162, 166
Maestà (Duccio) 322–3, **12.17**
Maeterlinck, Maurice 574; *Pelléas et Mélisande* 574, 575
Magellan, Ferdinand 369
Magic Flute, The (Mozart) 485
magic realism 679, 684
Magna Carta 272, 273, 275
Magna Graecia 83, 151, 154
Magnus liber organi (Léonin) 286
Magritte, René: cover of *Qu'est-ce que le Surréalisme?* 628, **22.14**
Magyars 250
Mahler, Gustav 606; *Das Lied von der Erde* 606
Maids of Honor, The (Velázquez) 442–3, **16.15**
mail services 563
Maimonides (Moses ben Maimon) 234; *The Guide for the Perplexed* 234
Main Street (S. Lewis) 636
Malade Imaginaire, Le (Molière) 448
Malatesta, Carlo 359
Malatesta family, the 350
Malcolm X 662
Malevich, Kazimir 601; *Black Square* 601, **21.13**
Mali: female figure 600, **21.10**
Mallarmé, Stéphane 573; "The Afternoon of a Faun" 573
Malleus Maleficarum (Sprenger and Kramer) 410

Malone Dies (Beckett) 685
Malory, Thomas: *Le morte d'Arthur* 255
Malpighi, Marcello 431
Malthus, Thomas: *Essay on the Principle of Population* 471, 535, 536
Mamet, David 716–17; *Glengarry Glen Ross* 716; *Oleanna* 716–17
mammoths 10; mammoth-bone house 10, **1.6**
Man in a Red Turban (van Eyck) 334, 355, **13.3**
Mandela, Nelson 664, 706
Mander, Karel van: *The Painter's Book* 404, 438
mandorlas 267
Mandrake, The (Machiavelli) 387
Manet, Edouard 546, 568; *Nana* 568, **20.6**; *Olympia* 546, 568, **19.11**; *Zola* 547, **19.12**
Manetho: list of Egyptian kings 44, 45
Manetti, Giannozzo: *On the Dignity of Man* 328, 331
Manhattan Project 624
Mani/Manichaeism 34, 202
"Manifest Destiny" 549, 550
Mann, Thomas 689
Mannerism 361, 365, 367, 427; architecture 391–2, **14.30**, **14.31**; painting 387–9, 412, **14.24–14.27**; sculpture 390, **14.28**, **14.29**
manorialism 239, 241
Mantegna, Andrea 352, 382; Camera Picta, Mantua 352, **13.30**
Mantua, Italy 350, 352; Camera Picta frescoes, Ducal Palace (Mantegna) 352, **13.30**; Gioiosa 350, 386; Palazzo del Tè (Romano) 391, **14.30**; Sant' Andrea (Alberti) 344, **13.17**, **13.18**
manuscript illumination 244, 247, 250, 253, 286, 306, 308, **10.2**, **10.5**, **10.9**, **10.10**, **11.16**, **11.17**, **12.1**, **12.2**, **12.5**, **12.6**, **12.9**, **12.10**
Manutius, Aldus 382
Mao Voting (Yu) 711, **24.13**
Mao Zedong 665–6, 711, 716, 717
Mapplethorpe, Robert 676; *Ken and Tyler* 676, **23.26**
Marathon, battle of (490 B.C.) 104
Marburg disease 706
March of the Weavers (Kollwitz) 587, **21.1**
Marconi, Guglielmo 563
Marenzio, Luca 415
Marguerite, Queen of Navarre 402; *Heptameron* 402
Maria Theresa, Empress 467
Marie-Antoinette, Queen 490, 491, 492; *Marie-Antoinette à la Rose* (Vigée-Lebrun) 490, **17.21**
Marie de France: lays 292; *Ysopet* 292
Marinatos, Spyridon 72
Marinetti, Filippo: "Futurist Manifesto" 600
Mark, St.: Gospel of 192; *St. Mark* (manuscript illumination) 247, **10.5**
Mark Antony 155, 163
Marley, Bob 692
Marlowe, Christopher 417, 418; *Dr. Faustus* 418, 507; *The Passionate Shepherd to his Love* 418; *Tamburlaine* 418
Márquez, Gabriel García 684; *One Hundred Years of Solitude* 684
Marriage à la Mode (Hogarth) 476–7, **17.11**
marriage and divorce 56, 78, 93, 214, 350
Marriage of Figaro, The (Mozart) 484–5
Marsalis, Wynton 713
Marshall Plan 657
Marsy, Balthasar and Gaspard: Latona Fountain 446, **16.22**
Marteau sans Maître, Le (Boulez) 688
Martin V, Pope 303
martyria 201, 374, **14.8**
martyrs 195, 225, 262, 278, 306
Marx, Karl 536; *Communist Manifesto* (with Engels) 536–7
Marxism 536–7, 558, 590, 625
Mary (Virgin) 193; cult of 256, 289–90
Mary I, of England 401, 410, 415, 416
Mary II, of England 457
Mary, Queen of Scots 416
Mary of Guise 416
Masaccio 338, 340, 342; *Tribute Money* 342, **13.15**; *Trinity* 340–2, **13.14**; *Virgin and Child* 340, **13.11**
Mascagni, Pietro 543
masks: Agamemnon's 76, **4.13**; death (Italian) 156; Greek theatrical 127; Tutankhamon's 62, **3.32**
masques, court 457, **16.39**
mass culture 623, 652
Massachusetts Bay Colony 430, 456
Mass(es) 194, 205, 219, 275, 303, 312, 358, 415
Mathematical Principles of Natural Philosophy (Newton) 431, 432, **16.4**
mathematics 102, 123, 234, 431, 432, 434
Mathuran sculpture 134, **6.31**
Matilda of Canossa 263, 294
Matisse, Henri 602; *The Cowboy* 633, **22.24**; *Woman with the Hat* 602–3, **21.14**
Matthew, St., Gospel of 192–3, 203, **8.10**
Maupassant, Guy de 537, 539; *The Horla* 539
mausolea 201, 211, 230–1, **9.1**, **9.24**, **9.25**
Maximilian I, Emperor 348, 367
Maya civilization: creation myth 3; *Popol Vuh* 179
Mayall, J. J. E.: *carte-de-visite* 549, **19.15**
Mazarin, Cardinal Jules 444, 445
mazurkas 523, 526
Mead, Margaret 624, 635
Mecca, Saudi Arabia 224, 225, 226, 269, **10.30**
Medea (Euripides) 129
Medici, Alessandro de' 371
Medici, Cosimo de' 336, 337, 344, 345, 347, 349
Medici, Cosimo I de', Grand Duke 371, 390, 391
Medici, Giovanni di Bicci de' 336
Medici, Giuliano de' 336, 347
Medici, Lorenzo de' ("The Magnificent") 336, 337, 338, 347, 348, 349, **14.4**; carnival song 349
Medici, Lorenzo de', *gonfaloniere* 371
Medici, Marie de' *see* Rubens, Peter
Medici, Piero de' 336, 347
Medici, Piero de' ("the Unfortunate") 336, 371
Medici family 329, 335, 336, 344, 365, 387
medicine 24, 56, 124–5, 234, 286, 334–5, 404, 431, 534, 535, 571, 623, 624, 667, 713, **9.29**, **11.17**; *see also* anatomy
Medina 225
Meditations (Aurelius) 173–4
Medusa 94
megaliths 12
megarons, Mycenaean 76, **4.14**, **4.15**
Méliès, Georges 581, 582; *The Trip to the Moon* 581–2, **20.23**
Melisende, Queen 263
melismatic chant 205, 248, 285
Melville, Herman 514; *Moby Dick* 514; *Typee* 514
Memories of President Lincoln (Whitman) 515
Memphis, Egypt 45, 53
Mendel, Gregor 534
Mendelssohn, Felix 521
mendicant orders 275
"Mending Wall" (Frost) 608
Menes *see* Narmer
menhirs 12
Meninas, Las (Velázquez) 442–3, **16.15**
Menkaure: pyramid of 50, **3.9**; Triad of 52–3, 95, 96, **3.15**
menorahs 187, **8.2**, **8.5**
Menotti, Gian Carlo 688; *Amahl and the Night Visitors* 688
Mer, La (Debussy) 575
Merovingian dynasty 241, 242, 243
Meru, Mount 36
Mesoamerica: ball games 178–9, **7.42**, **7.44**; map **7.5**
Mesolithic era 3, 11
Mesopotamia 17, 19; architecture 19–21; cosmos and religion 20, 21; kings 26; music 26–7; urbanization 22; *see also* Sumer
Messe de Notre Dame (Machaut) 312
Messiaen, Olivier 687–8
Messiah, the 183, 186, 191, 193
Messiah (Handel) 454, 456
metalwork *see* bronzes; copperwork; goldwork
Metamorphoses (Ovid) 167, 404, 446
"Metamorphosis, The" (Kafka) 602
metaphors 7
metaphysics 470, 492
"method" acting 543, 558, 646
Methodius, Patriarch 222
Mexico: Mexico City Cathedral 444, **16.19**; painting 628; Mexican-American War 549; *see also* Olmec culture
Michael II, Emperor 222
Michelangelo Buonarroti 365, 367, 377; *David* 371–2, 436, **14.4**; St. Peter's 375, 458, **14.11**, **14.12**; Sistine Chapel frescoes 377–8, 380, 381, 411, **14.14–14.18**; sonnets 377
Mickey Mouse 615, 650, 712, **22.38**
microscopes 430, 431, 433
Middle Ages 239, 241
Midsummer's Night's Dream, A (Mendelssohn) 521
"Migration" series (J. Lawrence) 634, **22.25**
mihrabs 228, **9.23**
Milan, Italy 275, 336, 353, 367, 532; Edict of (313) 196, 198; *Last Supper* (Leonardo) 354, **13.31**
Mill, John Stuart 536; *The Subjection of Women* 536
Millais, John Everett 547
Millennium Fantasy (Zwilich) 713
Miller, Arthur 686; *The Crucible* 686; *Death of a Salesman* 686
Mill on the Floss, The (G. Eliot) 540–1
Milošević, Slobodan 701, 702
Miltiades 104
Milton, John 459; *Paradise Lost* 459, 461, 509
minarets 228
Minimalism: music 689, 713; sculpture 672–3
Minoan civilization 65, 67; architecture 67–8, **4.2**, **4.3**; frescoes 68, 69–70, **4.3**, **4.5**; music 71, **4.7**; pottery 67, 71, **4.1**, **4.8**; religion 68–9, 70–1
Minos, King 67, 68, **5.20**; palace 67–8, **4.2**, **4.3**
Minotaur, myth of the 68
minstrels 245, 292
"Minstrel's Song of the Swan" 310
minuscule 247, 270
miracle plays 251, 292, 311
Miró, Joan: *The Policeman* 628, **22.13**
mirrors, Etruscan 149, **7.4**
Misanthrope, Le (Molière) 448
Misérables, Les (Hugo) 508
misogynists 87
Miss Julie (Strindberg) 542
missionaries 202, 205, 252, 256, 259, 409, 434
Mistress of the Animals (Minoan faience) 68, **4.4**
Mitchell, Margaret: *Gone with the Wind* 650
Mithraism 34, 185, 188, 193
Mithras Slaying the Sacred Bull 185, **8.1**
Mixolydian mode 126
Moby Dick (Melville) 514
Mocking of Christ . . . (Fra Angelico) 345, **13.20**
Mode de Valeurs (Messiaen) 687–8
Modern Times (Chaplin) 647, **22.33**
Modernism 561
modulation (music) 440
Mohenjo-Daro 30; *Bearded Man* 30, **2.16**; seal 30, **2.15**
Molière 447, 448; *L'Avare* 448; *Le Bourgeois Gentilhomme* 448; *L'École des femmes* 448; *Le Malade imaginaire* 448; *Le Misanthrope* 448; *Tartuffe* 448
Molloy (Beckett) 685
Mona Lisa (Leonardo) 372–3, **14.5**; *see also L.H.O.O.Q.*
monasteries/monasticism 202–3, 221, 222, 239, 241, 248, 249, 252, 261–2, 275–7, **10.6–10.8**, **10.18**; and women 263–4, 277–8
Mondrian, Piet 629; *Large Red Plane . . .* **22.17**
Monet, Claude 565–6; *Impression: Sunrise* 565, **20.4**; *Interior of St. Lazare Station* 566–7, **20.5**; *La Japonaise* 566, **20.3**
Mongols 225, 304
monody 440
Monroe, Marilyn *see* Warhol, Andy
Monsieur Perrot's Dance Class (Degas) 568, **20.7**
montage (film) 646
Montaigne, Michel de 402; *Essays* 402, 419, 422
Montefeltro, Federico da 350, 351, 373, 374; portrait (Piero della Francesca) 351, **13.28**
Montefeltro, Guidobaldo da 373
Montesquieu, Charles de Secondat, Baron de 468, 469; *Persian Letters* 469–70; *The Spirit of Laws* 470, 487
Monteverdi, Claudio 440, 695; *Orfeo* 440, 482
Montezuma II, of the Aztecs 370
Moonrise over the Sea (Friedrich) 506, **18.13**
Moore, Charles: Piazza d'Italia, New Orleans (with W. Hersey) 361, 678, **23.31**
morality plays 251–2, 263, 292, 306
More, Sir Thomas 402; *Utopia* 402
Moréas, Jean: Symbolist manifesto 572
Moreau, Gustave 572; *The Peri* 572, **20.12**
Morgan, Barbara: *Martha Graham* **22.27**
Morley, Thomas 417
Morocco 588

Morrison, Toni 683; *Beloved* 683
Morse, Samuel 534; Morse code 534, 558, 563
Morton, Jelly Roll 631
mosaics: Byzantine 211, 216, 220, **9.2**, **9.8**, **9.9**; Roman 132, 160, **3.1**, **6.29**, **7.20**; 13th-century Italian 294, **11.25**
Moscow, Russia: terrorism 703
Moses 38, 187–8, 192, 193, 221, 225; *Moses and the Crossing of the Red Sea* 188, **8.3**
mosques 228; Córdoba 228, **9.21–9.23**
motets 285, 359, 384, 415
Mother Courage (Brecht) 641
Mother Goose (Ravel) 606
Motherwell, Robert 669; "Elegy to the Spanish Republic" series 669, **23.11**
motifs, musical 518, 526
motion pictures (movies) *see* film
Mount, William Sidney: *California News* 555, **19.21**
Mourning Becomes Electra (O'Neill) 643
Mozart, Wolfgang Amadeus 465, 483, 484–5
Mrs Dalloway (Woolf) 638–9
Mrs. Warren's Profession (Shaw) 598
Mu'awiya, Caliph 225
muezzins 228
Mughal dynasty 452, 454; miniatures 454, **16.36**
Muhammad, Prophet 205, 224–5, 226, 227, **9.18**
mummification, ancient Egyptian 47, **3.5**
Munch, Edvard 580; *The Scream* **20.20**
Muses, the 86, 87, 295
music and instruments: ancient Egyptian 54–5, **3.17–3.20**; ancient Greek 92, 102, 104, 126; ancient Roman 160, **7.20**; Baroque 427, 439–41, 454–6, 482; Boethius on 211; Carolingian 243, 247–8; chamber 440, 461; Church 205, 219, 247–8, 285–6, 311, 333; and Counter-Reformation 415, 454; Elizabethan 416–17; 15th-century 334, 348–9, 358–9; and humanism 333; Impressionist/Symbolist 574–5; Islamic 232; medieval 261–2, 311–12, 316, **12.9**; Mesopotamian 26–7, **2.9–2.11**; Minoan 71, **4.7**; and nationalism 522, 525–6; Native American 13, **1.12**; Realism in 543; Renaissance 384–6; Romantic 485, 518–23, 525–6; 20th-century 605–7, 611–12, 631–3, 635, 687–9, 690–2, 713; *see also* opera
music drama 523
Music of Changes (Cage) 688
musicals 643–4, 649, 652, 687, 690
musique concrète 688
Muslims *see* Islam
Mussato, Albertino: *Ecerinis* 316, 333
Mussolini, Benito 618, 619
Mussorgsky, Modest 525–6
Muybridge, Eadweard 580, 582; *Female Figure Hopping* 580, **20.21**
My Antonia (Cather) 636
My Century (Grass) 714
My Fair Lady 598, 690
My Night with Maud (Rohmer) 693
Mycenaean civilization 65, 73, 77, 80; architecture 75–6, 79, **4.10–4.12**, **4.14–4.16**; mask 76, **4.13**
Myoda, Paul *see* La Verdiere, Julian
Myron: *Discus Thrower* (*Discobolus*) 112–13, 114, **6.3**
mystery cults: Hellenistic 137; Roman 185
mystery plays 251, 292
Myth of Sisyphus, The (Camus) 680
myths/legends 79; Greek 68, 83, 85–8, 93–4, 118, 132, 295, **6.15**, **6.32**, *see also* Homer; Norse viii, 1, 3, 256, 258, 295; *see also* creation myths

Nadar (Gaspard-Félix Tornachon) 548
Nagasaki, bombing of 623, 655
Names Project (AIDS memorial quilt) **24.3**
Nana (Manet) 568, **20.6**
Nanna 20
Nantes, Edict of (1685) 444
Naples, Italy 275, 315, 317, 336, 350, 367
Napoleon Bonaparte 361, 491, 492, 495, 497–8, 501, 504, 508, 518, 519, 541, 549; map **18.1**; *see also* David, Jacques-Louis
Napoleon III 500, 531, 563, 574
Napoleonic Code 216, 498, 509
Nara, Japan: Horyu-ji monastery 249, **10.8**
Naram-Sin 26; Victory Stele 27, **2.12**
Narmer, Palette of 44, **3.2**
narrative sequence 7
Nash, John: Royal Pavilion, Brighton 506, **18.11**
National Organization for Women (NOW) 663
National Socialists *see* Nazis
nationalism 500, 664; in music 522, 525–6
Native Americans 549–50, **19.17**; Anishnabe Drum 13, **1.12**; Hohokam ball game 179; Mohawk Creation myth 3; Navajo sand painters 670; 20th-century art 710, **24.12**
NATO 657, 658, 701, 702
"natural selection" 4, 535, 558
naturalism (in art) 9, 102, 112, 317
Naturalist literature, French 537, 538–9
Naturalists 3, 534–5
Nature (Emerson) 513
Nazis/National Socialists 615, 619, 621, 622, 625, 640, 642, 645, 647, 680
Neanderthal Man 6–7, 8
Nebamum, tomb of (Thebes) 55, **3.20**
Nebuchadnezzar II, of Babylon 32, 188
Nefretiti, bust of 61, **3.30**
Neoclassicism 361, 495, 497, 500; architecture 361, 475, 488–9, 498–9; painting 475, 478–9; sculpture **17.2**
Neolithic era 3, 11–12, 14, 17, 43, 44, 67
Neoplatonism 186, 235, 262, 278, 285, 338
Nephthys 45, **3.6**
Nero, Emperor 167–8, 175, 176, 195; Golden House 168–9
Neruda, Pablo 684; *Canto General* 684
Netherlands 242, 410, 428, 429, 449, 467, 498; colonialism 433, 449, 565; lens makers 430, 433; painting 334, 355–7, 404, 406–7, 409, 450–3, 578–9, 629; philosophy 433; slave trade 430
Neumann, Balthasar: Residenz, Würzburg 474, **17.6**
neumes 261
Neveu de Rameau, Le (Diderot) 469
New England, USA 259, 335
New Harmony, Indiana 536
New Lanark, Scotland 536
New Mexico 624; *see also* Acoma
New Orleans: Piazza d'Italia 361, 678, **23.31**; Storyville 631
New Wave films 693–4, 696
"New World" Symphony (Dvořák) 525
New York 608, 668, 669, 670; Armory Show 610; Cotton Club 632, 633, **22.21**, **22.22**; "9/11" 703, 704; Photo-Secession Gallery 609; School of American Ballet 642; Stock Exchange 615, 617
New York School 669, 670
New Zealand 449, 563, 565, 617
newspapers 557
newsreels 636, 652
Newton, Sir Isaac 431, 432, 433, 468; epitaph (Pope) 479; *Mathematical Principles of Natural Philosophy* 431, 432, **16.4**
Nicaea, Councils of 202 (325), 222 (787)
Nicholas I, Tsar 532
Nicholas II, Tsar 590
Nicholas V, Pope 350
Niepce, Joseph-Nicéphore 548
Nietzsche, Friedrich 537, 600, 625, 645; *Thus Spake Zarathustra* 537
Night (Hogarth) 477, **17.12**
Night (Wiesel) 680
Nightingale, Florence 534
nihilism 605, 612
Nijinsky, Vaslav 642
Nika Riots (532) 214
Nile, River 41, 43, 46, 60, **3.1**
Nîmes, France: Pont du Gard 154, **7.11**
"xix" (Heaney) 720
1984 (Orwell) 681
Nineveh 32
Ningirsu 28
Ninhursag 20
Niño, El (Adams) 713
Nixon, Richard 660
Njal's Saga 259–60
No Exit (Sartre) 685
Nobel, Alfred 574
Nobel Prize winners 574, 591, 596, 598, 664, 680, 683, 685, 706, 715, 719
"noble savage" 470, 501, 513, 514
nocturnes 523, 526
Noguchi, Isamu 670; *Humpty Dumpty* 670, **23.13**
nominalism 287, 296
Norse mythology viii, 1, 3, 256, 258, 295
Norway 526, 542, 640
Notre Dame Cathedral, Paris 280–2, **11.6–11.8**, **11.10–11.12**; School 285–6
Notre-Dame de Paris (Hugo) 508
Novum Organum (Bacon) 431
"Now is the month of maying" (Morley) 417
Nubia 44, 59
nuclear weapons 591, 623, 624, 655, 660, 679
Nude Descending a Staircase No. 2 (Duchamp) 610, 625, **21.24**
Number, A (C. Churchill) 717
Number 10 (Rothko) 670–1, **23.14**
Number 27 (Pollock) 670, **23.12**
numerals, Arabic 234
Nun (primeval ocean) 45, 61
Nuñez da Balboa, Vasco 369
Nut 45

"O Captain! My Captain!" (Whitman) 515
Oath of the Tennis Court, The (David) 490, **17.20**
obelisks 59
Oblomov (Goncharov) 541
O'Casey, Sean 642
Ockeghem, Johannes 359
Ockham, William of 302, 303; Ockham's razor 303
oculus 172
Odalisque (Boucher) 472, **17.4**
"Ode on a Grecian Urn" (Keats) 512
"Ode to Joy" (Schiller) 520
"Ode to the West Wind" (Shelley) 512
odes: Greek 114; Roman 162–3, 584, 587
Odo, bishop of Bayeux 267
Odo of Metz: Aachen Palace Chapel 245, **10.3**, **10.4**
Odoacer 209
Odysseus 73, 77–9, 93
Odyssey (Homer) 73, 77–9
Oe, Kenzaburo 715
Oedipus answering the riddle of the sphinx (vase painting) **6.26**
Oedipus Complex 571, 572, 592, 593
Oedipus the King (Sophocles) 128, 135
Officers of the Haarlem Militia Company of St. Adrian (Hals) 450, **16.29**
oil painting 355, 382
oinochoe 90, **5.9**
O'Keeffe, Georgia 609; *From the Lake No. 1* **21.23**
Oklahoma! (Rodgers and Hammerstein) 644
Oleanna (Mamet) 716–17
Oliver, Joe "King" 632
Olmec culture: Colossal Heads 35–6, **2.23**; map **2.3**
olpe 90, **5.8**
Olympeium, Athens 140, **6.39**
Olympia, Greece 85
Olympia (Manet) 546, 568, **19.11**
Olympia (Riefenstahl) 645, **22.29**
Olympian gods 86–7
Olympian Ode II (Pindar) 114
Olympias 132
Olympic Games 89, 114, **5.7**
Olympos, Mount 295, 299
Omar Khayyam 233; *Rubáiyát* 233
Omeros (Walcott) 701, 720
On Architecture (Alberti) 343
On Duties (Cicero) 162
On Famous Men (Petrarch) 317
On Germany (Mme de Staël) 508
On Painting (Alberti) 342
On the Dignity of Man (Manetti) 328, 331
On the Nature of Things (Lucretius) 161
On the Origin of Species (Darwin) 4, 535
On the Revolutions of the Heavenly Spheres (Copernicus) 403
On the Road (Kerouac) 682–3
One Day in the Life of Ivan Denisovich (Solzhenitsyn) 680
One Hundred Years of Solitude (Márquez) 684
One of Ours (Cather) 636
O'Neill, Eugene 642–3, 648; *A Long Day's Journey into Night* 643; *Mourning Becomes Electra* 643
"Only Breath" (Rumi) 233
onomatopoeia 130
opera 427, 440, 445, 455–6, 482, 484–5, 518, 523–5, 543, 575, 606, 607, 644, 688–9, 695, **16.20**; *opera buffa* 482; *opéra comique* 482
operettas 612; Gilbert and Sullivan 595

Opium Wars 565
Oplontis, Italy: villa fresco 159, **7.18**
opus reticulatum 343
oracles, Greek 88
Oration on the Dignity of Man (Pico della Mirandola) 338
oratorios 454–5, 456, 461, 484, 521
orchestra, Greek 126–7, **6.25**
orchestras, Classical 482, **17.16**
Orders, architectural 98–9, 140, 170, 343, **5.18**
Ordinary of the Mass 205, 312, 358
Oresteia (Aeschylus) 76–7, 127–8, **6.11**
Orestes 77, 78
Orfeo (Monteverdi) 440, 482
Orfeo ed Euridice (Gluck) 482
organ music 454, 455
organum 248, 285, 286
Orientalizing period (Greece) 85, 90–2
Orlando furioso (Ariosto) 365, 387
Orpheus/Orphism 185
Orthodox Church *see* Eastern Orthodox Church
orthogonals 341, 354, **13.13**, **13.31**
Orwell, George 680; *Animal Farm* 680–1; *1984* 681
Oryx and Crake (Atwood) 714, 715
Osama (Barmak) 718
Osiris 43, 45–6, 51, 137, 183, 185
Oslo Accords 704
ostinatos 575, 583
Ostrogoths 209, 211, 241
O'Sullivan, Timothy: *Desert Sand Hills . . .* **19.16**
Othello (Shakespeare) 421
Otto I, Emperor 250
Ottoman Empire/Turks 213, 333, 368, 532
Ottonian Empire 250
Outer Boulevards: Snow Effect (Pissarro) **20.1**
Ovid 167, 418, 419; *The Art of Love* 167; *Metamorphoses* 167, 404, 446
Owen, Robert 536
Owen, Wilfred 585, 587; "Dulce et Decorum Est" 584, 587
Oxford, Edward de Vere, Earl of 418
Oxford University 287, 303
oxymorons 316
"Ozymandias" (Shelley) 512

Pacheco, Francisco 442
Pachomius 203
Padua, Italy: Arena Chapel frescoes (Giotto) 319–22, **12.14**, **12.15**; humanism 314, 315, 316; University 315, 403
Pagliacci (Leoncavallo) 543
Paik, Nam June 677; *Family of Robot, Uncle* 677, **23.30**
Paine, Thomas 467, 485; *Common Sense* 464, 467, 486
Painted Bronze (Ale Cans) (Johns) 671, **23.15**
Painter's Book (van Mander) 404, 438
painting: Abstract Expressionist 669–71; ancient Egyptian 45, 48, 55; ancient Greek *see* vases *under* Greece; Baroque 427, 437–9, 442–3, 449–53; Byzantine 221, 318; Color Field 670–1; and Counter-Reformation 411–14, 437; *De Stijl* 629; early Christian 197; Expressionist 600; Gothic 318–19; Impressionist 563, 565–70, 580; Italian Renaissance 322–3, 333–4, 340, 347–8, 372–4, 382–4; Mannerist 387–9, 412; Neoclassical 475, 478–9; Northern Renaissance 334, 355–7; Post-Impressionist 563, 576–80; and Protestantism 404–7, 409; Realist 543–7; Regionalist 625, 630; Rococo 471, 472–5; Romantic 501–4, 506, 516; Super-Realist 674; Suprematist 601; 20th-century American 668–72, 673, 674, 676, 677; *see also* frescoes; manuscript illumination
Pakistan 23, 134, 225, 232, 665, 703, 705; sculpture 134, **6.30**
Palace of the Arabian Nights, The (Méliès) 582
Palaeologus, Michael VIII 213
Paleolithic era 3, 4–10, 43
Palestine 186, 244, 265, 617, 663, 704–5
Palestrina, Giovanni Pierluigi da 415
Palette of Narmer 44, **3.2**
Pall Mall Gazette 570
Palladio (Andrea di Pietro) 391, 392, 488; San Giorgio Maggiore, Venice 391–2, **14.31**
Palmer, Frances F.: *American Express Train* **19.1**
Pamela (Richardson) 481
Pandora 87–8
Pannini, Giovanni: *Interior of the Pantheon* **7.39**
Pantheon, Rome 172, **7.37–7.39**
papacy 196, 244, 275, 350; "Babylonian Captivity" 302; Great Schism 303, 311
Papyrus of Hunefer 45, **3.3**
paradise, views of 295
Paradise Lost (Milton) 459, 461, 509
paradoxes 114
Paragone (Leonardo) 365, 373
Parallel Lives (Plutarch) 419, 421
Paré, Ambroise: *Ten Books of Surgery* 404
Paris, France 261, 275, 278, 410, 532, 563, 602, 633, **20.1**; Arc de Triomphe (Chalgrin *et al.*) 361, 498–9, **18.3**; Eiffel Tower 533, **19.3**; Louvre Pyramid (Pei) 678–9, **23.32**; Métro entrance (Guimard) 594, **21.7**; Notre Dame Cathedral 280–2, **11.6–11.8**, **11.10–11.12**; Notre Dame Cathedral School 285–6, 287; St. Denis 278–9, **11.2–11.4**; Sainte-Chapelle 284–5, **11.15**; the Salon 543, 565; Salon de la Princesse, Hôtel de Soubise (Boffrand) **17.1**; *salons* 465, 468; University 287, 303, 397, 402; World's Fairs 533, 575, 619
Paris, Matthew: *Building a Cathedral* 283, **11.14**
Parker, Charlie 631, 633, 677
Parks, Rosa 662, **23.5**
Parmenides 113–14
Parmigianino: *Madonna of the Long Neck* 389, **14.26**
Parr, Catherine 401, 415
Parthenon, Athens 116–17, **6.7–6.10**; sculptures 117–19, **6.11–6.17**
Parthians 165
Pascal, Blaise 433, 434; *Lettres provinciales* 434; *Pensées* 434
Passion plays 311
Passionate Shepherd to his Love, The (Marlowe) 418
Passions 454, 455, 461
Pasternak, Boris 680
Pasteur, Louis 534, 535
Pastoral Concert (Giorgione) 382–3, **14.20**
pastorals 138
Pathfinder, The (Cooper) 514
patricians, Roman 152, 156, 163; *Patrician with two portrait heads* 157, **7.13**
Patrick, St. 202, 252
Paul, St. 192, 194–5, 202; map of journeys **8.2**
Paul III, Pope 375, 383, 395, 409
Paul V, Pope 434, 436
Pavlov, Ivan Petrovich 624
Pavlova, Anna 642
Pax romana 163
Paxton, Joseph: Crystal Palace, London 533, **19.2**
Pazzi conspiracy 336
Peary, Robert Edwin 624
Peasants' Revolt (1381) 301, 303
pectoral of Mereret 57, **3.22**
Peer Gynt (Grieg) 526
Pei, I. M.: Louvre Pyramid 678–9, **23.32**
Peisistratus 111
"Peking Man" 5
Pelléas et Mélisande (Debussy) 575, **20.13**
Pelléas et Mélisande (Maeterlinck) 574, 575
Pelli, Cesar 712; Petronas Twin Towers 712–13, **24.16**
Peloponnesian War (431–404 B.C.) 130–1
Pencil of Nature, The (Talbot) 548
pendentives 220
Pensées (Pascal) 434
pentatonic scales 525, 526
Pepin the Short 243
peplos 97, **5.17**
Peplos Kore 97, **5.16**
Père Goriot, Le (Balzac) 537
perestroika 659, 696
performance art 672
Pergamon 137; Great Altar 139–40, **6.38**
Peri, The (Moreau) 572, **20.12**
Pericles 114–15, 116, 117, 130, 131, **6.4**
Perón, Juan 659
Pérotin 286
Perry, Commander Matthew 565
Persephone 185
Persepolis, Iran: Apadana 33–4, **2.20**, **2.21**
Perseus (Cellini) 390, 391, **14.29**
Perseus Decapitates Medusa (Amasis painter) 94, **5.12**
Persia/Persians 26, 32–4, 188; and Greeks 91, 104–5, 111, 132; map **2.2**
Persian Letters (Montesquieu) 469–70
perspective: Brunelleschi's system 340, 341, **13.12**; and foreshortening 132, 198, 347; one-point 341, **13.13**
Perugino, Pietro 374
Pétain, Maréchal Henri Philippe 621, 623
Peter I, Tsar 428, 429–30, 467
Peter, Venerable 287
Peter Grimes (Britten) 689
Peter Pan (Barrie) 597
Peter Rabbit (Potter) 596
Petrarch (Francesco Petrarca) 316, 319, 333, 335, 336, 382, 387, 404, 407; *Africa* 316–17, 387; *Familiares* 298, 299, 344; *On Famous Men* 317; sonnets 316, 417
Petronas Twin Towers (Pelli) 712–13, **24.16**
Petronius Arbiter 176; *The Satyricon* 176
Petrushka (Stravinsky) 607
phalanx, Greek 90, 91, 92, **5.10**
pharaohs *see* Egypt, ancient
Phèdre (Racine) 445, 448
Phidias: Parthenon sculptures 117–19, **6.11–6.17**
Philip II, of Macedon 132, 135, 299
Philip II, of Spain 368, 383, 410, 428, 449, **14.27**
Philip II Augustus, of France 267
Philip IV, of France ("the Fair") 275, 302
Philip IV, of Spain 425, 427, 428, 441, 442, 443, 449; *Philip IV at Fraga* (Velázquez) **16.3**
Philip V, of Spain 467, 695
Philip VI, of France 302
Philip the Good, of Burgundy 355, 358
Philistines 188
philosophers/philosophies: Boethius 211; Cynicism 137; 18th-century 470–1; Epicureanism 137, 161; Greek 83, 101–2, 113–14, 123–4, 135, **6.23**, *see also* Plato; Islamic 235; Italian 15th-century 337–8; Neoplatonism 186, 235, 262, 278, 285, 338; 19th-century 500–1, 536–7; 17th-century 433–4; Skepticism 137; Stoicism 137, 161, 173–4, 175, 314; 20th-century 624–5, 667–8
Philosopher's Stone, the 431
Philosophes 465, 467, 468, 487, 489
Philosophical Enquiry into . . . the Sublime and Beautiful, A (Burke) 500–1, 506
Phoenicians 154
phonograms 49
photography 548–9, 554–5, 563, 580, 617, 628, 666, 668, 676, 707–8
Phrygian mode 126
Piano Lesson, The (A. Wilson) 716
pianos/piano music 454, 482, 483, 518, 519, 522–3, 575
Picasso, Pablo 602, 603, 607, 609; *Guernica* 619, **22.4**; *Guitar* 604, **21.19**; *Gertrude Stein* 603, **21.16**; *The Tragedy* 603, **21.15**; *Ambroise Vollard* 604, **21.18**; *Women of Avignon* 604, **21.17**
Pico della Mirandola, Giovanni 338; *Oration on the Dignity of Man* 338
pictographs, Sumerian 22, **2.6**
Picts 252
Picture of Dorian Gray, The (Wilde) 595, 597
picture stone, Swedish 256, **10.14**
Pienza, Italy 350, **13.27**
Piero della Francesca: *Battista Sforza* and *Federico da Montefeltro* 351, **13.28**
Pierre Pathelin 333
Pierrot lunaire (Schoenberg) 607
pilgrimage roads/sites 262, 269, **10.30**, **10.31**
Pindar 114; *Olympian Ode II* 114
Pinochet, Augusto 659
Pioneer Days and Early Settlement (Benton) 630, **22.20**
Pirandello, Luigi 641
Piranesi, Giovanni: *St. Peter's* **16.5**
Pisano, Nicola: *Adoration of the Magi* (Pisa Baptistery pulpit) 317, **12.11**
Pissarro, Camille: *The Outer Boulevards: Snow Effect* **20.1**
Pius II, Pope 350
Pius IV, Pope **14.27**
Pius V, Pope 371
Pius VII, Pope 498
Pius XI, Pope 618
Pizarro, Francisco 369, 370

plague 349; *see* Black Death
Plague, The (Camus) 679–80
plainsong/plainchant 205, 248, 261–2
Planck, Max 591
Plataea, battle of (479 B.C.) 105, 111
Plath, Sylvia 682; *The Bell Jar* 682
Plato 102, 123, 124, 126, 135, 236, 262, 315, 333, 337, 338, 344–5, 386, 395; *Apology* 124; *Critias* 72; *Crito* 124; *Giorgias* 123; *Phaedra* 123; *Protagoras* 123–4; *The Republic* 123, 124, 235, 402; *The Symposium* 123, 337, 512; *Timaeus* 376–7
Plautus 161, 333, 387, 448; *Braggart Soldier* 161
Play of Adam (mystery play) 251
Playboy of the Western World (Synge) 599
plebeians 152
Plotinus: *Enneads* 186, 235, 236, 338
Plough and the Stars (O'Casey) 642
Plowing in the Nivernais . . . (Bonheur) 544–5, **19.8**
Plutarch: *Lycurgus* 91; *Parallel Lives* 419, 421
Plymouth Bay Colony, Massachusetts 430, 456
Poe, Edgar Allan 516, 573, 598; "Annabel Lee" 516; "The Raven" 516
Poetic Edda (Sturluson) 259
Poetics (Aristotle) 135
"pointillism" 576
Poland 621, 622, 658–9, 701
poleis see city-states, Greek
Policeman, The (Miró) 628, **22.13**
Politics (Aristotle) 135
Politics Drawn from the Holy Scriptures (Bossuet) 424, 427
Pollock, Jackson 670; *Number 27* 670, **23.12**
polonaises 523, 526
Polydorus of Rhodes *see* Agesander
Polykleitos: *Spearbearer* (*Doryphoros*) 122, **6.22**
polyphonic music 248, 285, 311, 312
Pompadour, Mme de 472
Pompeii 157, 475, 478; bakery 158, **7.16**; frescoes 159, 167, **6.27**, **7.19**, **7.27**; house **7.17**; mosaics 132, 160, **6.29**, **7.20**
Pompey 155
Pont du Gard, nr. Nîmes, France 154, **7.11**
Pontormo, Jacopo 389; *Portrait of a Halberdier* 389, **14.25**
Poor Clares 277
Poor Richard's Almanac (Franklin) 486
Pop Art 671, 711
Pope, Alexander 479
Pope Marcellus Mass (Palestrina) 415
Popol Vuh (Mayan creation epic) 179
Porgy and Bess (Gershwin) 644
Porta, Giacomo della: Il Gesù **15.18**
Portable War Memorial (Kienholz) **23.3**
Portinari, Beatrice 292, 294, 295, 317
portmanteau words 596, 646
Portrait of a Halberdier (Pontormo) 389, **14.25**
Portrait of the Artist as a Young Man (Joyce) 598
Portugal 7, 410; colonialism 402, 565; explorers 335, 369; slave trade 368
Poseidon 87
Positivism 536, 558; logical 624, 652
post-and-lintel construction 12
Post-Impressionist painting 563, 576–80
Postmodernism 668; architecture 678–9, 701, 711–13
Post-Structuralism 667, 668
post-synchronization 649, 652
Potter, Beatrix: *Peter Rabbit* 596
Pound, Ezra 608, 637
Poussin, Nicolas 449, 450; *Et in Arcadia Ego* 449, **16.25**
pozzolana 158
Praeneste: Sanctuary of Fortuna mosaic **3.1**
Prairie Style (Wright) 630
Praise of Folly, The (Erasmus) 394, 395, 402
Prato, Italy: S. Maria delle Carceri (Sangallo) 348, **13.24**, **13.25**
Praxiteles: *Aphrodite of Knidos* 136, **6.33**
prehistory 3, 4–7; art 7–10; map **1.1**; *see* Mesolithic, Neolithic, Paleolithic eras
Prelude to "The Afternoon of a Faun" (Debussy) 574–5
Pre-Raphaelite Brotherhood 547
Presenting the Peacock (miniature) 310, **12.8**
Presley, Elvis 691, 695
Pre-Socratic philosophers 101–2
pressure flaking 7
Pride and Prejudice (Austen) 512
primitivism 600
Prince, The (Machiavelli) 365, 371
Princesse de Clèves, La (Mme de Lafayette) 447
Princip, Gavrilo 589, **21.3**
"*Principia*" (Newton) 431, 432, **16.4**
printing 331–3, 365, 382; of music 384
Prisoners from the Front (W. Homer) 554–5, **19.20**
Procession of the Magi (Gozzoli) 347, **13.22**
Procopius of Caesarea 208, 209, 214, 215
program music 441, 462, 521–2
projective testing 624, 652
Prokofiev, Sergei 647, **22.31**
proletariat 536, 558
Prometheus 3, 87
Prophet, the *see* Muhammad, Prophet
prophets, Hebrew 182, 183, 186, 191
Propylaia, Acropolis 115, **6.7**
Prose Lancelot 255
Protagoras 123; *Protagoras* (Plato) 123–4
Protestants 401, 410, 425, 428–9, 457; *see also* Reformation
prothesis **5.5**
Proust, Marcel 599, 638; *Remembrance of Things Past* 599
Prussia 467, 498, 531; *see* Franco-Prussian War
Psalms of David 190, 205, 219
psalters 263, **12.5**
Psellus, Michael 213
psychoanalysis 571, 572, 591–2
Psychopathology of Everyday Life (Freud) 592
Ptolemaic dynasty 137, 155, 186
Puccini, Giacomo 543, 688
Pugin, Augustus W. N. 504; Houses of Parliament, London (with Barry) 506, **18.12**
Punic Wars 154–5, 316
punk 692
Pushkin, Alexander: *Boris Godunov* 526
Putin, Vladimir 701
Pygmalion (Shaw) 598, 690
pylons 59, 63
Pylos, Greece 73
pyramids, Egyptian 50–1, **3.8–3.10**
Pythagoras 102, 126, 349

qawwâli 232
Qin, Emperor 105; terra-cotta warriors 105, **5.27**
quantum theory 591, 612
Quartet for the End of Time (Messiaen) 687
quatrains 419, 422
Qu'est-ce que le Surréalisme? (Magritte) 628, **22.14**
Qumran community 186
Qur'an (Koran) 225, 226, 232, 295, **9.17**

Rabelais, François 402; *The Histories of Gargantua and Pantagruel* 402
Rabin, Yitzhak 704
Racine, Jean 447; *Andromaque* 448; *Britannicus* 448; *Iphigénie* 448; *Phèdre* 445, 448
racism: in America 610–11, 631, 633, 661–2, 683, 708; *see also* anti-Semitism; apartheid
Rado, James 690
Raft of the "Medusa," The (Géricault) 501–2, **18.6**
Ragni, Gerome 690
ragtime 611, 612
railroads 532, 563, 565, 570, 591
Raise the Red Lantern (Zhang) 717, 718
Rake's Progress, The (Stravinsky) 607
Rambaldi, Carlo: *E.T.* **23.42**
Rameau, Jean-Philippe 445; *Hippolyte et Aricie* 445
Ramirez, Fray Juan 443
rap 692, 713
Rape of the Lock, The (Pope) 479
Raphael 365, 373–4, 377, 391; *Castiglione* **14.23**; *Fire in the Borgo* 388–9, **14.24**; *Madonna and Child* (*The Small Cowper Madonna*) 374, **14.7**; St. Peter's 458; *School of Athens* 376–7, **14.13**
Rasputin, Gregory 590
Ravel, Maurice 605, 606
"Raven, The" (Poe) 516
Ravenna, Italy 209, 211, 216; Mausoleum of Theodoric 211, **9.1**; Sant' Apollinare Nuovo 211, 216, 219, **9.2**, **9.5**; San Vitale 216, 219, 245, **9.6–9.9**
Ray, Man 628; *Tears* 628, **22.15**
Ray, Satyajit 693: Apu Trilogy 693, **23.39**
Rayograms 628, 652
Re 45, 46
ready-mades/ready-made aided 625, 652
Reagan, Ronald 702
realism (of scholastics) 287
Realism, 19th century 529, 536, 558; architecture 555–6; literature 529, 537–41, 556, 558; music 543; painting 543–7; photography 554–5, 580; theater 542–3
Realpolitik 531, 558
recapitulation, musical 483, 492, 520
recitative 440, 482
Reconstruction policy, U.S. 554, 558
Record of a Sneeze (Edison) 580, **20.22**
Red Badge of Courage, The (Crane) 556
red-figure vases, Greek 94, 103, **5.13**, **5.26**
Red Sorghum (Zhang) 717–18
Redl, Erwin: *Shifting, Very Slowly* 708, **24.7**
Redman, Joshua 713
Reformation 395, 397–400, 404, 406
refrigeration 563
reggae 692, 713
Regionalist Style (U.S.) 625, 630
Reims Cathedral, France 288, 311, **11.20**
relativity, theory of 591, 612
relief sculpture: Akkadian 27; Assyrian 30–1; Gothic 289; Greek 118–19; Italian 317; Mesoamerican 179; Persian 33–4; Roman 165–6, 171, 198
religions: Egyptian 45–8; Greek 74, 83, 85–8, 295; Manichaeism 34, 202; Minoan 68–9, 70–1; Mithraism 34, 185, 188, 193; Roman 156, 157, 185–6, 188; Zoroastrianism 34, 137, 202, 377; *see also* Anglican Church; Buddhism; Catholic Church; Christianity, early; Islam; Judaism; Protestantism
reliquaries 262, **10.20**
Remains of the Day (Ishiguro) 715
Remarque, Erich Maria 640; *All Quiet on the Western Front* 640
Rembrandt van Rijn 451, 452; *The Anatomy Lesson of Dr. Nicolaes Tulp* 450–1, **16.30**; *Aristotle with a Bust of Homer* 451–2, **16.31**; *Self-portrait with Saskia* 452, **16.32**; *Shah Jajan* 454, **16.37**
Remembrance of Things Past (Proust) 599
Remington, Frederic: *A Dash for the Timber* 550, **19.18**
Renaissance, the 299, 333–4, 335, 367; architecture 339, 343–4, 348; Italian painting and frescoes 340–2, 345, 347–8, 351, 352, 354, 372–4, 376–8, 380, 381, 382–4; literature 328, 331, 336–7, 338, 342–3, 365, 371, 386–7; music 384–6; Northern painting 334, 355–7; sculpture 337, 340, 344–5, 351–2, 371–2; theater 333, 387; women 343, 350; *see also* humanism
Renoir, Pierre-Auguste 568–9; *The Swing* 569, **20.8**
Republic, The (Plato) 123, 124, 235, 402
Restoration, the 457, 459, 479, 480
Revelation 192
Revelations (Ailey) 689, **23.35**
revolutions *see* American, French, Glorious *and* Russian Revolution
Reynolds, Sir Joshua 475
Rhapsody in Blue (Gershwin) 644
Rhazes *see* al-Razi
Rhea 86
Rheingold, Das (Wagner) 524
rhetoric 123, 162
Rhinoceros (Ionesco) 686
Rhodes, Cecil 565
rhythm and blues 690, 696
rhyton, Minoan 71, **4.8**
Rice, Tim 690
Rich, Lady Penelope 418
Richard I, of England 267
Richard III (Shakespeare) 421
Richardson, Samuel 480; *Clarissa* 481; *Pamela* 481
Richelieu, Cardinal 444, 445, 447
Richmond, Virginia: State Capitol (Jefferson) 488, **17.18**
Riefenstahl, Leni: *Olympia* 645, **22.29**; *Triumph of the Will* 645
Rigaud, Hyacinthe: *Louis XIV* **16.1**
Right After (E. Hesse) 673, **23.19**
Rigoletto (Verdi) 525
Riis, Jacob 555; *Bandits' Roost, Mulberry Street, New York* **19.22**

Rilke, Rainer Maria 602; "The Cadet Picture of My Father" 602
Rimbaud, Arthur 574; "Illuminations" 574; "Vowels" 574
Rime of the Ancient Mariner (Coleridge) 510, 511
Rimini, Italy 350
Ring des Nibelungen, Der (Wagner) 524
Risorgimento 525, 531
Rite of Spring, The (Stravinsky) 607
ritornello 440, 462
Rituals (Zwilich) 713
Rivals, The (Sheridan) 480
Rivero, Diego 628
roads 153, 301, **7.10**
Robert the Wise 317
Robespierre, Maximilien 491
Robinson, Bill "Bojangles" 632
Robinson Crusoe (Defoe) 480
rock art, prehistoric 13, **1.10**, **1.11**
rock music 690, 691–2, 696, 701
Rococo 465, 471, 477; architecture 474, 475, **17.1**; painting 471, 472–5
Rodger, George: *Bergen-Belsen* **22.5**
Rodgers, Richard 643, 644, 690
Rodin, Auguste 571; *The Kiss* 571, **20.11**; *Monument to Balzac* **19.5**
Rohmer, Eric 683; *Claire's Knee* 693–4, **23.40**
Roland *see Song of Roland*
Rolling Stones 691
Roman Empire 143, 163–4, 176–7, 209; emperors 169; map **7.4**; *see* Romans; Rome, ancient
Roman Republic 143, 152, 163; *see* Rome, ancient
Romanesque 260; architecture 239, 260, 264–5, 267; manuscripts 262, 263–4; sculpture 262, 267
Romania 659, 701
Romano, Giulio 391; Palazzo del Tè 391, **14.30**
Romans 140, 360; aqueducts 154; architecture 152–3, 157, 158, 343, *see also* Rome, ancient; army 152, 155; and Christianity 177, 183, 188, 191, 195–6; coinage 164; concrete 158; *equites* 152, 163; Etruscan influences 149, 150; *Gemma Augustea* 166; and Judaism 188, 189–90; laws 152, 155; literature 142, 145–6, 152, 157, 161, 162–3, 166–7, 172, 174–6; mosaics 132, 160, **3.1**, **6.29**, **7.20**; music 160; paintings 159, 167; patricians 152, 156, 163, **7.13**; philosophies 161, 173, 175; Punic Wars 154–5; religions 156–7, 185–6, 188; rhetoric 162; roads 153; sarcophagi 156, 198; sculpture 157, 164–5, 170, *see also* Rome, ancient; senate 152; theater 160, 161; trade 151, 153, **7.3** (map); women 170
Romantic Movement/Romanticism 471, 495, 500; architecture 506; literature 507–14, 532; music 485, 518–23, 525–6; painting 501–4, 506, 516
Rome, ancient 143, 150, 151, 152, 155, 204, 209; *Ara Pacis Augustae* 165–6, **7.24**, **7.25**; Arch of Titus 170, 361, **7.32**, **8.5**; bakeries 158, **7.16**; Basilica Ulpia 171, **7.35**, **7.36**; Colosseum 169–70, 178, **7.29**, **7.30**; Constantine's statue 177, **7.41**; equestrian portrait of Marcus Aurelius 173, **7.40**; fire 167–8; forum 152; founding of 145–7, 152, **7.7**; *insulae* 157, 158, **7.15**; map **7.1**; Pantheon 172, **7.37–7.39**; Santa Maria di Falleri gate 152, **7.28**; Seven Hills 146; Temple of Portunus 157, **7.14**; Trajan's Column 171, **7.33**, **7.34**
Rome, "modern" 195, 262, 315, 350, 434, 531; catacombs 195–6, 197, 198, **8.6**, **8.8**; Il Gesù (Vignola) 412–13, 415, **15.17**, **15.18**; Old St. Peter's 198, 200, **8.10**, **8.11**; San Carlo alle Quattro Fontane (Borromini) 435, **16.7**, **16.8**; St. Peter's 374–5, 395, 398, 434, **14.9–14.12**, **16.5**, **16.6**; Santa Costanza 201, **8.13–8.15**; Santa Maria Maggiore 200–1, **8.12**; Sistine Chapel 377–8, 380, 381, 411, **14.14–14.18**; Tempietto (Bramante) 374, **14.8**; Vatican frescoes (Raphael) 376–7, 388–9, **14.13**, **14.24**
Romeo and Juliet (Shakespeare) 420, **15.24**
Romulus and Remus 146, 146–7
Roncesvalles, battle of (778) 245
rondo 483, 492
Röntgen, Wilhelm Konrad 591
Room of One's Own, A (Woolf) 639
Roosevelt, Franklin D., U.S. President 615, 655; New Deal 617, 630
Rorschach, Herman: inkblot test 624
rose windows, Gothic 281, 282, **11.11**
Rosenberg, Ethel and Julius 682
Rosencrantz and Guildenstern are Dead (Stoppard) 717
Rosenkavalier, Der (Strauss) 606
Rosetta Stone 49, **3.7**
Rossellino, Bernardo: Bruni's tomb 337, **13.5**; Pienza 350, **13.27**; Rucellai Palace 343, **13.16**
Rossetti, Dante Gabriel 547
Rostand, Edmond 599; *Cyrano de Bergerac* 599
Rothko, Mark 670; *Number 10* 670–1, **23.14**
Rothstein, Arthur: *A Sharecropper's Wife and Children* 617, **22.1**
Rotunda, Charlottesville, Virginia (Jefferson) 488–9, **17.19**
Rougon-Macquart, Les (Zola) 538
rounds, musical 311
Rousseau, Henry: *The Dream* 592, **21.4**
Rousseau, Jean-Jacques 468, 470, 501, 513, 514; *Emile* 470; *The Social Contract* 470
Roy, Arundhati 716
Royal Academy of Arts, London 475, 479
Rubáiyát (Omar Khayyam) 233
Rubens, Peter Paul 449, 450; *Marie de' Medici cycle* 450, **16.27**, **16.28**
Rue Transnonain (Daumier) 545, **19.9**
Rumi, Jalal al-Din 233; "Only Breath" 233
rune-stones 256, **10.13**
Russia/Soviet Union 212, 224, 428, 429–30, 467, 498, 532, 618, 658–9, 660, 706; ballet 601; colonialism 565, 664, 666; film 646–7; literature 541, 638, 680; music 525–6, 607, 687; painting 600–1; railroads 563, 570; theater 542; and World War I 588, 589, 590; and World War II 622, 623; *see also* Cold War
Russian Revolution 590, 646
rustication (of masonry) 391
Rwanda: Hutu massacres 706

Sabin, Albert 667
Sacrifice of Isaac 198, **8.8** (catacomb fresco), 339, **13.7** (Brunelleschi), **13.8** (Ghiberti)
Saddam Hussein 703–4, 705
St. Albans Psalter 263
St. Denis, Paris 278–9, **11.2–11.4**
Sainte-Chapelle, Paris 284–5, **11.15**
St. Gall, Switzerland: monastery 248, **10.6**
St. Louis, Missouri: Wainwright Building (Sullivan) 555–6, **19.24**
St. Mark's, Venice 222, 384, 385, 386, **9.15**, **9.16**
St. Matthew's Passion (Bach) 455, 521
St. Paul's, London (Wren) 458–9, **16.40–16.42**
St. Peter's, Rome 374–5, 395, 398, 434, **14.9–14.12**, **16.5**, **16.6**; "Old" St. Peter's 198, 200, **8.10**, **8.11**
St. Petersburg 467, 590
Saint-Simon, Claude Rouvroy, Comte de 536
Saladin, Sultan 234
Salinger, J. D. 682; *Catcher in the Rye* 682
Salk, Jonas 667
Salomé (Beardsley) 595, **21.8**
Salomé (Strauss) 606
Salomé (Wilde) 595
saltcellar of Francis I (Cellini) 390, **14.28**
Salutati, Coluccio 336
Samarkand, Uzbekistan: Mausoleum of Timur Leng 230, **9.24**
San Carlo alle Quattro Fontane, Rome (Borromini) 435, **16.7**, **16.8**
San Vitale, Ravenna 216, 219, 245, **9.6–9.9**
Sand, George 508–9, 523
Sangallo, Antonio da, the Younger: St. Peter's, Rome 375, **14.10**
Sangallo, Giuliano da 348; Santa Maria delle Carceri, Prato 348, **13.24**, **13.25**
Sanshiro Sugata (Kurosawa) 651
Sanson, Charles-Henri 492
Sant' Apollinare Nuovo, Ravenna 211, 216, 219, **9.2**, **9.5**
Santa Costanza, Rome 201, **8.13–8.15**
Santa Maria di Falleri gate, Rome 152, **7.28**
Santa Maria Maggiore, Rome 200–1, **8.12**
Santana 691
Santi, Giovanni 373–4
Santiago de Compostela, Spain 262
Sappho 104
Saqqara, Egypt: step pyramid of King Zoser (Imhotep) 50, **3.8**
sarcophagi: Etruscan 150, **7.6**; Hagia Triada 70–1, **4.6**; Renaissance 337, **13.5**; Roman 156, 198, **7.12**, **8.9**
Sargon I, of Akkad 26
SARS (Severe Acute Respiratory Syndrome) 699
Sartre, Jean-Paul 625, 663, 685; *Being and Nothingness* 625; *No Exit* 685
Satan in his Original Glory (Blake) 509, **18.15**
satire 127, 176, 397, 465, 476, 539, 541, 679, 680–1, **15.1**
Satires (Juvenal) 176
Satyagraha (Glass) 689
satyr plays 127
Satyricon, The (Petronius) 176
Saudi Arabia 702, 703
Saul, King 38, 188
Saussure, Ferdinand de 667
Savonarola, Girolamo 349–50, 371
"Savoy Operas" (Gilbert & Sullivan) 595
Saxons 241, 244, 252
scaldic verse 259
scarabs, Egyptian 47, 51, **3.11**
Scarlet Letter, The (Hawthorne) 514
scat singers 632, 652
scherzo 518, 527
Schiller, Friedrich von 520
Schliemann, Heinrich 73, 76, 79, **4.13**
Schoenberg, Arnold 606–7, 687, 713
Scholastica, St. 248
scholasticism 287–8, 325, 333
Scholemaster, The (Ascham) 415
Schöne Müllerin, Die (Schubert) 520, 521
Schongauer, Martin 358; *Elephant* 358, **13.37**
School of Athens (Raphael) 376–7, **14.13**
Schubert, Franz 518, 520–1
Schumann, Clara (*née* Wieck) 521
Schumann, Robert 521
Schweitzer, Albert 623–4
science and technology 132, 234, 260, 331–3, 334–5, 373, 430–3, 453, 534–5, 591, 666–7, 699, 706–7; and religion 395, 427, 430, 433, 468; *see also* medicine
Scipio Africanus the Elder 316
scop theatrical tradition 250–1
Scotland 202, 252; chess 258, **10.17**
Scott, Dred 551–2
Scott, John: *Women's House* 710, **24.11**
Scream, The (Munch) 580, **20.20**
Scrovegni, Enrico 319, **12.15**
sculpture: Abstract Expressionist 670; African 37, 600; Amarna period 61; ancient Egyptian 43, 52–3, 56–8, 61; ancient Greek 95–7, 100–1, 111–13, 122, 136, 360; Baroque 436; early Christian 197–8; Futurist 600; Gandharan 134; Gothic 282, 289, 290, 306; Hellenistic 138–9; Impressionist 571; Indus Valley 30; Mannerist 390; Mathuran 134; Minimalist 672–3; Neoclassical **17.2**; Neo-Sumerian 28; Olmec 35–6; prehistoric 8; Renaissance 337, 340, 344–5, 351–2, 371–2; Roman 156, 157, 164–5, 170, 177; Romanesque 262, 267; Sumerian 21; Super-Realist 674; Surrealist 627; *see also* bronzes; ivories; relief sculpture
"Sea is History, The" (Walcott) 698, 701
seals: Indus Valley 30, **2.15**; Sumerian 22–3, **2.8**
Secession, Vienna 593, 594
Second Sex, The (de Beauvoir) 663
Second Shepherds' Play, The (Wakefield Master) 311
Secular Hymn (Horace) 166–7
Segovia aqueduct, Spain 154
Seleucids, the 137, 140
Self-portrait as a Tehuana (Kahlo) 628, **22.16**
Self-portrait at a Spinet (Anguissola) 389, **14.27**
Self-portrait with Saskia (Rembrandt) 452, **16.32**
Self-portrait with Two Pupils (Labille-Guiard) 472–3, **17.5**
self-portraits: Dürer **15.7**; van Eyck(?) 334, 335, **13.3**; van Gogh 578, **20.18**; Leyster 452–3, **16.33**; *and see above*
semiotics 655, 696
Senbi, coffin of 58, **3.25**
Seneca 175–6, 314, 333, 387, 402, 419
Senwosret-senebefny and wife, statue of 58, **3.24**
sequences 456, 462
Serbia 588, 589, 701–2
serialism (music) 645, 652, 688

serpentinata 387
Serrano, Andres 707–8; *Blood Cross* **24.4**
Set 45, 51, 185
Seurat, Georges 576; *A Sunday Afternoon on the Island of La Grande Jatte* 576, **20.15**
Seven Samurai, The (Kurosawa) 651, **22.40**
Seven Years War 467, 485, 489
Seventh Seal, The (Bergman) 693, **23.38**
Severan dynasty 169, 174, 176
Sévigné, Madame Marie de 446; *Letters* 446
Sex Pistols 692
sextets 606, 612, 632
Seymour, Jane 401
Sforza, Battista 351, 373; portrait (Piero della Francesca) 351, **13.28**
Sforza, Francesco 353
Sforza, Lodovico ("The Moor") 353, 373, **13.31**
Sgt. Pepper's Lonely Hearts Club Band (Beatles) 691
Shackleton, Sir Ernest Henry 624
Shadow of a Gunman, The (O'Casey) 642
Shah Jahan 230, 454, **16.37**
Shakespeare, William 175, 387, 417, 418, 419, 420, **15.22**; *As You Like It* 419; *Hamlet* 422; *Julius Caesar* 155, 421–2; *King Lear* 421; *Macbeth* 421; *Othello* 421; *Richard III* 421; *Romeo and Juliet* 420, **15.24**; sonnets 418, 419; *The Tempest* 422; *Twelfth Night* 420–1
shamanism 10, 13
Shamash 20, 25, 28, 29
Shankar, Ravi 689
Sharecropper's Wife and Children (Rothstein) 617, **22.1**
Shaw, George Bernard 598; *Pygmalion* 598, 690
Sheik, The (Melford) 695
Shelley, Mary 471, 513; *Frankenstein* 471, 513
Shelley, Percy Bysshe 511, 512; "Ode to the West Wind" 512; "Ozymandias" 512; *Posthumous Poems* 513
Shepherd, Alan 460
Sheridan, Richard Brinsley 480; *The Rivals* 480
Shifting, Very Slowly (Redl) 708, **24.7**
Shi'ites 225, 235
Ship Fresco (Theran) 73, **4.9**
Sholokhov, Mikhail: *And Quiet Flows the Don* 638
Shostakovich, Dmitry 687
Show Boat (Kern and Hammerstein) 643–4
Show Your Tongue (Grass) 714
Sibelius, Jean 526
Sickness unto Death, The (Kierkegaard) 537
Siddhartha (Hesse) 640
Siddhartha Gautama *see* Buddha
Sidney, Sir Philip 417; *Apology for Poetry* 418; *Arcadia* 417; *Astrophel and Stella* 417–18
Siegfried (Wagner) 524
Siena, Italy 315–16, 322; Palazzo Pubblico 322, 323, **12.18** (Lorenzetti frescoes 323–4, **12.19**, **12.20**)
Sigismund, Emperor 303
silk market, Byzantine 214, 215
similes 74
Sinai, Mount 187; St. Catherine 221, **9.13**, **9.14**
Singspiel 484, 485
Sistine Chapel, Rome 377; frescoes (Michelangelo) 377–8, 380, 381, 411, **14.14–14.18**
sistrum 54, **3.19**
Sitting Bull, Chief 550
Six Characters in Search of an Author (Pirandello) 641
Sixtus IV, Pope 350, 377
Sixtus V, Pope 695
Skeptics 137
skyscrapers 555–6
Slab of Snow Carved into Leaving a Translucent Layer (Goldsworthy) 675, **23.24**
Slave Ship, The (Turner) 504, **18.10**
slaves 368, 430, 467, 485, 488, 492; abolition 465, 504, 551–2, 553; narratives 552, 558
Slavonic Dances (Dvořák) 525
Sloan, John 608; *McSorley's Bar* 608, **21.21**
Smith, Adam 471; *The Wealth of Nations* 471, 536
Smith, Bessie 631, 716
Smithson, Robert 674; *Spiral Jetty* 674–5, **23.23**
Snow Country (Kawabata) 684–5
Sobek 45, 46
"social contract" 433
Social Contract, The (J.-J. Rousseau) 470
socialism 536
Socrates 101, 102, 123–4, 234, 315, **6.23**
Soderini, Piero 371, 372
Sofonisba (Trissino) 387
solarization 628, 652
Solomon, King 38, 188; Song of Solomon 190–1
Solomon's Temples, Jerusalem 38, 170, 188, 189–90, 205, **8.4**
Solon 92–3
Solzhenitsyn, Alexander 680; *The Gulag Archipelago* 680; *One Day in the Life of Ivan Denisovich* 680
sonata form 483, 492
sonatas 483, 492
"Song" (Donne) 459
song cycles 518, 527
Song of Roland 238, 239, 245, 250
Song of Solomon (Song of Songs) 190–1
sonnets 316, 377, 417, 418–19, 423, 459
Sophists 123, 149
Sophocles 128; *Antigone* 128–9; *Oedipus the King* 128, 135
Sorrows of Young Werther (Goethe) 507
soul music 690, 692, 696
Sound and the Fury, The (Faulkner) 638
Sounion Kouros 95–6, **5.14**
South Africa 563, 565, 617, 664, 706; literature 679, 713, 714
South America *see* Latin America
South Pacific (Rodgers and Hammerstein) 690
Soviet Union *see* Russia
Sower with Setting Sun (van Gogh) 578–9, **20.19**
Soyinka, Wole 683, 684; *Aké: The Years of Childhood* 684
space exploration 460, 666, 706, **23.8**
Spain 335, 367, 410–11, 416, 428, 434, 467; architecture 443–4, 594; cave paintings 7; colonialism 369, 370, 429, 430, 443–4, 449, 565; explorers 335, 369; Inquisition 276, 367; literature 441, 642; Muslims 224, 225, 228, 265, 292, 367, **9.21–9.23**; painting 442–3, 501, 603–4, 619, 628, **16.3**; theater 642
Spanish Civil War 619, 636, 642
Sparta/Spartans 91, 93, 97, 104–5, 130–1
Spearbearer (*Doryphoros*) (Polykleitos) 122, **6.22**
special effects (film) 582, 583
spectrum, the 431
Spenser, Edmund 417, 418; *The Faerie Queen* 418
sphinxes 59
Spielberg, Steven 694; *E.T.* 694–5, **23.42**
spinets 482, **14.27**
Spiral Jetty (Smithson) 674–5, **23.23**
Spirit of Laws, The (Montesquieu) 470, 487
Spiritual Exercises (Loyola) 409
Sprechgesang 607, 612
Sprenger, James, and Kramer, Heinrich: *The Witches' Hammer* 410
Staël, Mme de 507–8
stained glass windows 282, 289, **11.11**, **11.22**
Stalin, Joseph 590, 618, 657, 658, 687, 701, **22.2**
Stanislavski, Constantin 543, 646
Stanton, Elizabeth Cady 487
Star Wars (Lucas) 694, **23.41**
steam engines 501
Steamboat Willie (Disney) 650, **22.38**
Steerage, The (Stieglitz) 608, **21.22**
Steichen, Edward: *Rodin's Monument to Balzac Seen at Night at Meudon* **19.5**
Stein, Gertrude 602, 636; portrait (Picasso) 603, **21.16**
Stein, Michael 603
Steinbeck, John: *Grapes of Wrath* 637
stelae: Greek grave 86, **5.2**, **5.3**; of Hammurabi 22, 28–9, **2.7**, **2.14**; of Naram-Sin 27, **2.12**
Stephen, St. 413
Steppenwolf, Der (Hesse) 640
Stern, Robert: Disney Feature Animation Building 711–12, **24.14**
Stevenson, Robert L. 596; *A Child's Garden of Verses* 597; *Treasure Island* 596–7; *The Strange Case of Dr. Jekyll and Mr. Hyde* 597
Stieglitz, Alfred 608–9; *The Steerage* 608, **21.22**
stigmata 277
Still, William Grant 635
Stockhausen, Karlheinz 688
Stoics/Stoicism 137, 161, 173–4, 175, 314
Stone Ages *see* Paleolithic era
Stonehenge, England 12, 14, **1.8**, **1.9**
Stoppard, Tom 717; *Arcadia* 717; *Indian Ink* 717; *Rosencrantz and Guildenstern are Dead* 717
Stowe, Harriet Beecher: *Uncle Tom's Cabin* 552–3
Strada, La (Fellini) 692, **23.37**
Stradivarius, Antonio 483
Strange Case of Dr. Jekyll and Mr. Hyde, The (Stevenson) 597
Stranger, The (Camus) 679
Strauss, Richard 606
Stravinsky, Igor 607, 642
stream of consciousness 598, 635, 638, 652
Street Musicians (Roman mosaic) 160, **7.20**
Strindberg, August 542
string quartets 483, 492
stringed instruments 71, 417, 440, 518; *see also* violins
Structuralism 667–8
Structure of the Human Body (Vesalius) 403, **15.5**
stupas 249
Sturluson, Snorri 259; *Poetic Edda* 259
Sturm und Drang movement 507
Subjection of Women, The (Mill) 536
sublimination (psychoanalysis) 593, 612
Suetonius 174; *The Twelve Caesars* 174–5
Suez Canal 532
Sufis/Sufism 225, 232; poetry 233
Suger, Abbot 278, 279, 280, 285, 287, 296
Suicide of Ajax (Exekias) 93–4, **5.11**
suites (music) 455, 462
Sullivan, Louis 555; Wainwright Building, St. Louis 555–6, **19.24**
Sumer/Sumerians 3, 19, 26, 27, 28; gods 20; kings 26; language 23; literature 16, 17, 19, 23–6, 27; lyres 27, **2.10**, **2.11**; sculpture 21, **2.4**; writing 21, 22, **2.5**, **2.6**
"Sumer is icumen in" 311, 313
Summa theologiae (Aquinas) 287–8, 296
Sun Also Rises, The (Hemingway) 636
Sun Tzu: *The Art of War* 105
Sunday Afternoon on the Island of La Grande Jatte, A (Seurat) 576, **20.15**
Sunnis 225, 235
Sunrise at Yosemite (Bierstadt) 516, **18.18**
Superman (*Übermensch*) 537, 600, 645
Super-Realism 674
Suprematism 601
"Surprise" Symphony (Haydn) 484
Surrealism 625, 626, 627–8
Suruga-cho (Hiroshige) 566, **20.2**
Sutton Hoo purse cover 254, **10.12**
Sweden 428, 429, 574; literature 641; picture stone 256, **10.14**; rune-stone 256, **10.13**; theater 542
Swedenborg, Emanuel 571
Swift, Jonathan 479, 481; *Gulliver's Travels* 479
Swing, The (Renoir) 569, **20.8**
swing bands 632–3
Symbolism 563, 571–2; music 574–5; painting 572, 576, 580; poetry 573–4; theater 563, 574, 595
symbolization (psychoanalysis) 572, 583
symphonic poems 518, 527
symphonies 483, 484, 492, 518, 519–20, 521–2, 525, 526, 606, 635, 645, 687
symposia, Greek 103, 125
Symposium, The (Plato) 123, 337, 512
synagogues 190, 205
syncopation 611, 612
syncretism 156
Synge, John Millington 598, 599; *The Playboy of the Western World* 599
Syria 58, 132, 188, 195, 617, 663, 702; bottle 232, **9.27**

Tacitus 174; *Annals* 174
Taiwan 665, 705
Taj Mahal, Agra, India 230–1, **9.25**
Talbot, Henry Fox 548; *The Pencil of Nature* 548
"Tale of Sinuhe" (Egyptian poetry) 49
Taliban, the 659, 702–3, 718
Tamburlaine (Marlowe) 418
Tamerlane *see* Timur Leng
Tanner, Henry Ossawa 555; *Banjo Lesson* 555, **19.23**
Tarquinia, Italy 149; Tomb of the Bulls 150, **7.5**
Tartuffe (Molière) 448
Tasman, Abel 449
Tchaikovksy, Pyotr 525
Tears (Man Ray) 628, **22.15**
technology *see* science and technology
telephones 534, 591

telescopes 430, 460, **16.43**, **16.44**
television 623, 667
Tempest, The (Shakespeare) 422
Tempietto, Rome (Bramante) 374, **14.8**
temples: Egyptian 59–61, **3.26–3.29**; Etruscan 148–9, **7.3**; Greek 88, 98–9, **5.4**, **5.18–5.22**, *see also* Acropolis; Roman 157, **7.14**
Temptation of St. Anthony, The (Cézanne) 203, **8.16**
Ten Commandments, the 187
tenebrism 438, 451, 462
Tennyson, Alfred, Lord: "The Charge of the Light Brigade" 532; *The Idylls of the King* 255
Tenochtitlán, Mexico 369, 370, 444
tenors 248
Terence 161, 387, 448
Teresa of Avila, St. 409, 436, **16.10**
terrorism 702–3, 704, 705
Tertullian 288
Tess of the d'Urbervilles (Hardy) 597
tetrarchy (Roman emperors) 177, 195
Tetzel, Johann 398, 400
thalassocracies 65
Thales of Miletus 102
theater(s)/drama: of the Absurd 679, 685, 686; Baroque 427, 447–8; Elizabethan 417–22; Gothic period 292; Greek and Hellenistic 126–30, 137, **6.24**, **6.25**; medieval 250–2, 311, 316; Realist 542–3; Renaissance 333, 387; Restoration 480; Roman 160, 161; Symbolist 563, 574, 595; 20th-century 598–9, 641–3, 679, 685–7, 716–17, 719–20
Thebes, Egypt 30, 45, 61; tomb of Nebamun 55, **3.20**
Their Eyes Were Watching God (Hurston) 635
theocracies 38, 188, 399
Theocritus 138, 162; "The Cyclops" 138; *Pastoral* I 138
Theodicy (Leibniz) 470
Theodora, Empress 212, 214; Mosaic of 216, **9.9**
Theodoric, Ostrogoth ruler 209, 211
Theodosius, Emperor 89, 202
Theogony (Hesiod) 86–7, 92
Theophilus, Emperor 222
Theopompus of Chios 149
Theososius I, Emperor 196
Thera, island of 65, 72; frescoes 72–3, **4.9**
Thermopylae, battle of (480 B.C.) 104–5
Theron of Acragas 114
Theseus 68
Thespis 127
Things Fall Apart (Achebe) 684
Third-class Carriage (Daumier) 545–6, 548, **19.10**
Third of May, 1808, The (Goya) 501, **18.4**
Thirty Years War 425, 428–9
"This Month of May" (Dufay) 359
"This sweet and merry month of May" (Byrd) 417
tholoi (tombs) 75–6, 79, **4.11**, **4.12**
Thomas, Gnostic Gospel of 202
Thomas, Dylan 681; "Do Not Go Gentle" 681; "The Hand that Signed the Paper" 681; *Under Milk Wood* 681
Thoreau, Henry David 497, 513; "Civil Disobedience" 494, 497, 514; *Walden* . . . 514
"Thorn, The" (Wordsworth) 510
Thousand and One Nights, The 232–3, 477
Three-Penny Opera, The (Brecht) 641
Three Quick and the Three Dead, The 306, **12.5**
Three Soldiers (Dos Passos) 636
Through the Looking Glass (Carroll) 596
Thucydides 130; *History* 130
Thus Spake Zarathustra (Nietzsche) 537
Tiananmen Square, Beijing: massacre 666, 705
Tiberius, Emperor 166, **7.26**
Tiepolo, Giovanni Battista: Würzburg Residenz frescoes 474, **17.8**
Tiger at the Gates (Giraudoux) 642
Tigris, River 17, 19
Till Eulenspiegel (Strauss) 606
Timaeus (Plato) 376–7
Time and Free Will (Bergson) 571
Timur Leng, Mausoleum of (Samarkand) 230, **9.24**
Tin Drum, The (Grass) 714
"Tintern Abbey" (Wordsworth) 509
Tintoretto 412, 413; *The Last Supper* 412, **15.16**
Tiryns, Greece 73; citadel 79, **4.16**
Titans 85–6
Titian 365, 383, 413; *Assumption of the Virgin* 383–4, **14.21**; *Charles V Seated* **14.1**; *Venus of Urbino* 383, 384, 546, **14.22**
Tito, Josip (Broz) 658, 701
Titus, Emperor 170, 189; Arch of 170, **7.3**, **8.5**
toilets 477
Token of St. Agnes 197, **8.6**
Tolentino, Niccolò da 347, 351
Tolkien, J. R. R. 718; *The Lord of the Rings* 718–19
Tolstoy, Leo 541; *Anna Karenina* 541; *War and Peace* 541
Tom Jones (Fielding) 481
tonality (music) 439–40, 462, 518
tone poems 518, 527
tonic (music) 483
tool-making, prehistoric 5, 6
Toreador Fresco (Minoan) 69–70, **4.5**
Tornabuoni, Lucrezia 336, 343
Tosca (Puccini) 543
totalitarianism 679, 680–1, 686
Totem and Taboo (Freud) 592
Toulouse-Lautrec, Henri de 576; *Jane Avril at the "Jardin de Paris"* 576, **20.14**
Toumai (prehistoric skull) 5
trade 19, 43–4, 56, 90, 92, 151, 153, 212, 260, 275, 301, 308, 309, 355, 702; maps **2.1**, **9.2**, **13.1**
trade unions 587
tragedy: Greek 76–7, 127–30, 135, 137; Roman 175
Tragedy, The (Picasso) 603, **21.15**
Traini, Francesco: *Triumph of Death* 306, **12.3**
Trainspotting (Boyle) 718
Trajan, Emperor 171, 195; Trajan's Column, Rome 171, **7.33**, **7.34**
Transcendentalism 470–1, 497, 513–14
transi tombs 306
transplants, organ 667
Trans-Siberian Railroad 563, 591, 623
transubstantiation 194, 275, 303
travertine 158
Traviata, La (Verdi) 525
Treasure Island (Stevenson) 596–7
"Treasury of Atreus," Mycenae 75, **4.12**
Treatise of Human Nature, A (Hume) 471
Treatise on Government (Locke) 433
Treatise on the Passions of the Soul (Descartes) 434
Trebonianus 216
tremolo 518
Trent, Council of (1545–63) 395, 409, 410, 411, 412, 414, 434
Très riches heures du duc de Berry (Limbourg brothers) 308, **12.6**
Triad of Menkaure 52–3, **3.15**
Trial, The (Kafka) 601–2
Tribute in Light over the Brooklyn Bridge (La Verdiere and Myoda) 704, **24.2**
Tribute Money (Masaccio) 342, **13.15**
trilithons 12
trills (music) 417, 423
Trinitarian Order 435
Trinity, the 194, 202
Trinity (Masaccio) 340–2, **13.14**
trio sonatas 440, 462
Trip to the Moon, The (Méliès) 581–2, **20.23**
Trissino, Giangiorgio: *Sofonisba* 387
Tristan and Isolde (Wagner) 523
Triumph of Death (Traini) 306, **12.3**
Triumph of St. Thomas Aquinas (Andrea da Firenze) 325, **12.21**
Triumph of the Name of Jesus (Gaulli) 437, **16.11**
Triumph of the Will (Riefenstahl) 645
Triumphes of Oriana, The (Morley) 417
Trojan War 73–5, 76, 78, 139, 145, 150, **7.5**
tropes 251, 285
Trotsky, Leon 618, 680
troubadours 292
Troyes, Chrétien de 255
Truffaut, François 693
Truman, Harry S., U.S. President 623, 657
Trumbull, John: *General George Washington at Trenton* 488, **17.17**
Truth, Sojourner 552; *Ain't I a Woman?* 552
Tubman, Harriet 552
tufa 148, 152, 158, **7.8**
Turkey 11, 589, 617; *see* Ottoman Empire
Turn of the Screw, The (Britten) 689
Turner, Joseph Mallord William 504; *Interior of Tintern Abbey* 510, **18.16**; *The Slave Ship* 504, **18.10**
Turner, Nat 552
Tuscan Doric Order 170
Tussaud, Madame Marie (*née* Grosholz) 492
Tutankhamon 61; funerary mask 62, **3.32**; thrones 62, **3.31**; tomb 61
Tutmose III, of Egypt 56
Tutu, Archbishop Desmond 664
Twain, Mark 556; *Huckleberry Finn* 556, 630
Twelfth Night (Shakespeare) 420–1
Twelve Caesars, The (Suetonius) 174–5
twelve-tone technique (music) 607, 612, 687
Twenty-Five Colored Marilyns (Warhol) 671–2, **23.16**
Twice-Told Tales (Hawthorne) 516
Twilight of the Gods (Wagner) 524
Two Trains Running (A. Wilson) 716
tympana 267, **10.26**
Typee (Melville) 514
Tyrannicides 112, **6.2**
tyrants, Greek 83, 92

Ubu Roi (Jarry) 599, **21.9**
Uccello, Paolo: *Battle of San Romano* 347, **13.21**
ukiyo-e prints 566
Ulysses (Joyce) 639
Umar 225
Umayyad dynasty 225
Unanswered Question, The (Ives) 644
Uncle Tom's Cabin (Stowe) 552–3
Under Milk Wood (Thomas) 681
Underground Railroad 552, 558
Unique Forms of Continuity in Space (Boccioni) 600, **21.11**
Unitarians 513
United Nations 623, 663, 664, 701, 703
United States of America 486–8, 549, 551, 557, 587, 665, 702, 704; architecture 361, 488–9, 555–6, 630, 679, 711–12; Civil Rights 661–2; earth art 674–5; film 610–11, 647–50, 694–5, 719; graffiti art 677, 708; installations 675, 708, **23.3**; literature 513–16, 552–3, 556, 558, 608, 635–8, 681–3; map **19.2**; music and dance 611–12, 631–3, 643–5, 688, 689–92; painting 516, 550, 554–5, 557, 569–70, 608, 609, 630, 668–72, 673, 674; photography 554, 555, 608–9, 628, 676, 707–8, 713, **19.16**, **19.22**; railroads 532, **19.1**; sculpture 672–3, 674; theater 642–3, 686–7, 716–17; World War I 590; World War II 623; *see also* African Americans; Cold War; Great Depression; Gulf Wars; Korean War; Native Americans; New York; Vietnam War
universities 275, 286–7, 301, 303, 315, 402, 403
Unnamable, The (Beckett) 685
Untitled (Judd) 672–3, **23.18**
uomo universale 387
Ur, Iraq 38; lyres 27, **2.10**, **2.11**; plaque 27, **2.9**
Uranos 86
Urban II, Pope 265, 267
Urban VI, Pope 302–3
Urban VIII, Pope 431
urbanization 14, 22, 301, 563
Urbino, Italy 350, 373, 374, 386
Ursuline Order 409
Uruk (Warka), Iraq 16, 17, 19, 22, 27; ziggurat 19–21, **2.2**, **2.3**
Uthman 225, 226
utilitarianism 536, 558
Utopia (More) 402
utopianism 536, 558
Utrecht, Treaty of (1713) 467
Utu 20

vaccinations 534, 535, 667
Valentino, Rudolf 695
Valerian, Emperor 195
Valhalla 256, 295, **10.14**
Valkyries, The (Wagner) 524
Valtorta Gorge, Spain: cave paintings 7
van Dyck, Anthony *see* Dyck, Anthony van
van Eyck, Jan *see* Eyck, Jan van
van Gogh, Vincent *see* Gogh, Vincent van
Vandals 209, 241
vanishing point 341, 354, **13.13**

Vasari, Giorgio: *Lives . . .* 364, 367, 372, 380, 389, 404, **14.4**
vassals 239, 241
Vatican *see* Rome, "modern"
vaults *see* arch and vault construction
Veii, Italy: Temple of Apollo 148–9, **7.3**
Velázquez, Diego de 442, 449; *Diego de Acedo . . .* 443, **16.16**; *Maids of Honor* (*Las Meninas*) 442–3, **16.15**; *Philip IV at Fraga* **16.3**
Venice, Italy 265, 275, 336, 365, 382; Aldine Press 382; brothels 301; *Colleoni* (Verrocchio) 351–2, **13.29**; music 384–6; painting 382–4; San Giorgio Maggiore (Palladio) 391–2, **14.31**; St. Mark's Cathedral 222, 384, 385, 386, **9.15**, **9.16**
Ventoux, Mount 299
Venus of Urbino (Titian) 383, 384, 546, **14.22**
Venus of Willendorf 8, **1.2**
Verdi, Giuseppe 518, 524–5
verismo 529, 543, 558
Verlaine, Paul 573, 574; "L'Art poétique" 573–4; *Fêtes galantes* 573
Vermeer, Jan 453; *The Astronomer* 453, **16.34**; *Girl with a Pearl Earring* 453, **16.35**
Veronese, Paolo 411; *The Feast in the House of Levi* (*The Last Supper*) 411–12, **15.15**
Verrocchio, Andrea del: *Colleoni* 351–2, **13.29**
Versailles, Palace of 445–6, **16.20**, **16.21**; Latona Fountain (B. and G. Marsy) 446, **16.22**
Versailles, Treaty of 615, 617, 618, 619, 621
Vesalius, Andreas 403; *The Structure of the Human Body* 403, **15.5**
Vespasian, Emperor 169
Vesuvius, Mount 157
Vézelay, France: Ste Marie Madeleine 264–5, 267, **10.23–10.27**
vibrato 632, 652
Victor Emmanuel II, of Italy 531
Victor Emmanuel III, of Italy 618
Victoria, Queen 532, 533, 544, 565, 588, 591, **23.9**; *carte-de-visite* (Mayall) 549, **19.15**
Victoria, Tomás Luis de 415
video art 677, 701
Vidor, King: *Hallelujah!* 649, **22.36**
Vienna 532, 563, 592, 593; Congress of 498; Secession 593, 594
Vietnam 565, 665
Vietnam Veterans Memorial, Washington, D.C. (Lin) 660, **23.4**
Vietnam War 651, 655, 659–60, **23.2**
Vigée-Lebrun, Elisabeth 491; *Marie-Antoinette à la Rose* 490, **17.21**
vignettes, Egyptian 48, **3.6**
Vignola, Giacomo: Il Gesù, Rome 412–13, 415, **15.17**, **15.18**
Vikings 250, 253, 256, 258, 259, 267; map **10.3**
Villa Savoye, Poissy (Le Corbusier) 629, **22.18**
Villanovan period 149
Vindication of the Rights of Woman, A (Wollstonecraft) 471
Vinland Sagas 259
violins 384, 440, 482, 483; concertos 521, 525
Virgil 293, 294, 296, 316, 419; *Aeneid* 142, 145–6, 152, 157, 165, 459, 479; *Eclogues* 162; *Georgics* 162
Virgin and Child (Basawan) **16.36**
Virgin and Child (Masaccio) 340, **13.11**
virginals 482
Virginia, USA 430; *see also* Charlottesville; Richmond
virtuosi 440
Visconti, Filippo Maria 336
Visconti, Giangaleazzo 336
Visconti family 336, 353
Visigoths 177, 204, 209, 241
Vision of Divine Love (Hildegard) 263–4, **10.22**
Vitruvian Man (Leonardo) 333, 348, **13.2**, **13.27**
Vitruvius: *On Architecture* 333, **7.3**
Vitry, Philippe de 311
Vivaldi, Antonio 441, 455
Vollard, Ambroise: portrait (Picasso) 604, **21.18**
Voltaire 468, 469; *Candide* 469
"Vowels" (Rimbaud) 574
Voyageur sans bagage, Le (Anouilh) 642

Wagner, Richard 518, 523–4
Wainwright Building, St. Louis (Sullivan) 555–6, **19.24**
Waiting (Ha Jin) 716
Waiting for Godot (Beckett) 685
Waiting for the Barbarians (Coetzee) 714
Wakefield Master: *The Second Shepherds' Play* 311
Walcott, Derek 719, 720: *Omeros* 701, 720; "The Sea is History" 698, 701
"Walden" (Emerson) 513
Walden, or Life in the Woods (Thoreau) 514
Waldensians 275
Walesa, Lech 659, 701
Walker, Alice: *The Color Purple* 683
Walküre, Die (Wagner) 524
Wall Drawing No. 623 (LeWitt) 673, **23.20**
Wall-painting in a Jewish Catacomb **8.2**
wall paintings *see* frescoes
Wallace, Alfred Russel 4
Walsingham, Sir Francis 416
War and Peace (Tolstoy) 541
War for the Union, 1862—A Bayonet Charge (W. Homer) 557, **19.25**
War of the Austrian Succession 467
War of the Spanish Succession 467
War of the Worlds, The (Welles) 648
Warhol, Andy 671; *Twenty-Five Colored Marilyns* 671–2, **23.16**
Warrior (from Riace) 131, **6.28**
Warrior Vase (Mycenaean) 80, 90, **4.17**
Washington, George, U.S. President 486, 488, 557; *see also* Trumbull, John; Leutze, Emanuel
Waste Land, The (T. S. Eliot) 637
Watergate scandal 660
Waterloo, battle of (1815) 498
Waters, Ethel 632
Waters, Muddy 690, 691
Watson, James 667
Watt, James 501
Watteau, Jean-Antoine 472; *Les Bergers* 472, **17.3**
Way of Perfection, The (St. Teresa of Avila) 409
Wealth, iconography of 308
Wealth of Nations, The (Smith) 471, 536
"Weary Blues, The" (L. Hughes) 635
Webber, Andrew Lloyd 690
Webern, Anton 688
Weelkes, Thomas 415, 417
Weill, Kurt 641
Weimar Republic 619
Well-Tempered Keyboard, The (Bach) 454
Welles, Orson: *Citizen Kane* 648, **22.35**; *The War of the Worlds* 648
Wellington, Arthur Wellesley, Duke of 498
Werther/Wertherism *see Sorrows of Young Werther*
West Side Story (Bernstein) 690
Westphalia, Treaty of (1648) 428, 429; map **16.1**
When We Were Orphans (Ishiguro) 715–16
Whistler, James McNeill 570; *Harmony in Blue and Gold: The Peacock Room* 570, **20.10**
White, T. H.: *The Once and Future King* 255
"White Man's Burden" (Kipling) 560, 561
White Negress III (Brancusi) 627, **22.12**
Whitman, Walt 514–15
Who, The 691
Who's Afraid of Virginia Woolf? (Albee) 686–7
Wiesel, Elie 680
Wilde, Oscar 585, 594–5; *The Picture of Dorian Gray* 595, 597; *Salome* 595, **21.8**
Wilhelm II, Kaiser 588, 590
Wilkins, Maurice 667
Willaert, Adrian 384–5, 415
William I, of England ("the Conqueror") 267, **10.28**, **10.29**
William I, Prince of Orange 449
William III, of Orange 457
William of Champeaux 287
Wilson, Angus 716
Wilson, G. W.: *Queen Victoria* **23.9**
Wilson, Robert 689, 716; *Einstein on the Beach* 689, **23.34**
Wilson, Woodrow, U.S. President 590
Winckelmann, Johann Joachim: *The History of Ancient Art* 478
wind instruments 482, 518
wine 103, 310
witch-hunts 410, 427
Witches' Hammer (Sprenger and Kramer) 410
Witches' Sabbath (Grien) 410, **15.14**
Wittenberg, Germany 398, 400
Wittgenstein, Ludwig 624
Wollstonecraft, Mary 471, 513; *A Vindication of the Rights of Woman* 471
Woman and a Girl Driving, A (Cassatt) 569, **20.9**
Woman with the Hat (Matisse) 602–3, **21.14**
Women of Avignon (Picasso) 604, **21.17**
Women's House (J. Scott) 710, **24.11**
women's rights and issues 471, 487, 492, 536, 552, 563, 662–3, 667, 702, 707; *see also* feminism
Wonderful Adventures of Nils, The (Lagerlöf) 596, 715
woodcuts/woodblock prints 332, 355, 358
"Woodland Nymphs" (Josquin Desprez) 359
wool industry, Florentine 301, 335, **12.1**
Woolf, Leonard 638
Woolf, Virginia 638, 686; *Mrs. Dalloway* 638–9; *A Room of One's Own* 639
word painting 385
Wordsworth, William 509; "The Daffodils" 511; *Lyrical Ballads* (with Coleridge) 509, 510; "The Thorn" 510; "Tintern Abbey" 509
World Wars: First 585, 588, 589, 590, 592, 593, 605, 612, 640; Second 593, 615, 621, 623, 657
Worms, Germany: Concordat of (1122) 250; Edict of (1521) 400; *Frau Welt* 306, **12.4**
Wounded Knee, massacre at 550
Wrapped Reichstag (Christo and Jeanne-Claude) 709, **24.8**
Wren, Christopher 458; St. Paul's Cathedral, London 458–9, **16.40–16.42**
Wright, Frank Lloyd 630; Kaufmann House 630, **22.19**
Wright, Orville and Wilbur 591
writing 4; cuneiform 22, 28, **2.5**, **2.7**, **2.14**; hieratic 41; hieroglyphs 41, 49; Kufic 226, 230, **9.17**; Minoan 67; pictographs 22, **2.6**
Würzburg, Germany: Residenz (Neumann) 474, **17.6**; frescoes (Tiepolo) 474, **17.8**; stucco (Bossi) **17.7**
Wuthering Heights (E. Brontë) 513
Wycliffe, John 302, 303

Xanthippe 123
Xavier, Francis 409
Xerxes I, of Persia 33, 104–5
X-rays 591

Yahweh 186, 187
Yeats, William Butler 598, 608, 715; "The Lake Isle of Innisfree" 598
Yellow Submarine (Beatles) 691
Yeltsin, Boris 701
Yerma (Lorca) 642
Yevtushenko, Evgeny 687
Yombe cane finial 37, **2.26**
Yoruba kingdom: beadwork crown 37, **2.27**
Young Man Blowing Bubbles (Chardin) 478, **17.14**
Young Shopper (Hanson) 674, **23.22**
Ysopet (Marie de France) 292
Yu Youhan: *Mao Voting* 711, **24.13**
Yugoslavia 658, 701–2

Zarathustra *see* Zoroaster
Zealots 189
Zeno 114, 377
Zeppelins 591
Zeus 64, 67, 78, 85, 86, 87, 89, 114, 167
Zeuxis **6.21**
Zhang Yimou 717; *House of Flying Daggers* 718; *Jou dou* 717, 718, **24.17**; *Raise the Red Lantern* 717, 718; *Red Sorghum* 717–18
ziggurats 19–21, 32, **2.1–2.3**
Zimbabwe 664
Zinj (fossil) 5
Zola, Emile 537, 538, 539, 546–7; *L'Assommoir* 538, 568; "J'Accuse" 539; portrait (Manet) 547, **19.12**; *Les Rougon-Macquart* 538
Zoroaster/Zoroastrianism 34, 137, 202, 377
Zoser, King: step pyramid (Imhotep) 50, **3.8**
Zwilich, Ellen Taaffe 713; *Millennium Fantasy* 713; *Rituals* 713